THE
CRIMINAL PRISONS
OF LONDON

University of Chester
Chester

CHESTER CAMPUS
LIBRARY
01244 513301

This book is to be returned on or before the last date stamped below. Overdue charges will be incurred by the late return of books.

THE
CRIMINAL PRISONS
OF LONDON

AND

SCENES OF PRISON LIFE

BY

HENRY MAYHEW

and

JOHN BINNY

With Numerous Illustrations from Photographs

FRANK CASS & CO. LTD.
1971

Published by

FRANK CASS AND COMPANY LIMITED

67 Great Russell Street, London WC1B 3BT

First edition	1862
Second impression	1968
New impression	1971

ISBN 0 7146 1411 4

Printed in Great Britain by
Thomas Nelson (Printers) Ltd., London and Edinburgh

CONTENTS.

INTRODUCTION.

THE ADMINISTRATION OF THE CRIMINAL LAW. 80

THE CONVICT PRISONS OF LONDON 112

CONTENTS.

X CONTENTS.

THE CORRECTIONAL PRISONS OF LONDON—*(continued)* :

∗ *All after page 498 is written by Mr. John Binny.*

LIST OF ILLUSTRATIONS.

———

THE PORT OF LONDON.

THE GREAT WORLD OF LONDON.

INTRODUCTION.

§ 1.

LONDON CONSIDERED AS A GREAT WORLD.

"*Londres n'est plus une ville: c'est une province couverte de maisons,*" says **M. Horace Say**, the celebrated French economist.

The remark, however, like most French *mots*, is more sparkling than lucid; for, if the term "province" be used—and so it often is by the inconsiderate—as if it were synonymous with the Anglo-Saxon "shire," then assuredly there is no county in England nor "*departement*" in France, which, in the extent of its population, is comparable to the British Metropolis. Not only does London contain nearly twice as many souls as the most extensive division of the French Empire, but it houses upwards of a quarter of a million more individuals than any one county in Great Britain.*

How idle, therefore, to speak of London as a mere province, when it comprises within its boundaries a greater number of people than many a kingdom! the population of the British Metropolis exceeding—by some five hundred thousand persons—that of the whole of Hanover, or Saxony, or Wurtemburg; whilst the abstract portion of its people congregated on the Middlesex side of the Thames only, out-numbers the entire body of individuals included within the Grand Duchy of Baden.†

* The population of the *departement du Nord* is, in round numbers, 1,130,000; and that of the Seine 1,365,000. The population of Lancaster, on the other hand, is 2,031,236.

† The population of the above-mentioned countries is, according to the returns of 1850, as follows:—
Saxony, 1,836,433; Hanover, 1,758,856; Wurtemburg, 1,743,827; Baden, 1,349,930.—*M'Culloch's Geographical Dictionary.*

Nay, more: towards the close of the 14th century, there were not nearly so many men, women, and children scattered throughout *all* England as there are now crowded within the Capital alone.[*]

Further: assuming the population of the entire world, according to the calculations of Balbi (as given in the *Balance Politique du Globe*), to be 1075 millions, that of the Great Metropolis constitutes no less than 1-450th part of the whole; so that, in every thousand of the aggregate composing the immense human family, two at least are Londoners.

In short, London may be safely asserted to be the most densely-populated city in all the world—containing one-fourth more people than Pekin, and two-thirds more than Paris; more than twice as many as Constantinople; four times as many as St. Petersburg; five times as many as Vienna, or New York, or Madrid; nearly seven times as many as Berlin; eight times as many as Amsterdam; nine times as many as Rome; fifteen times as many as Copenhagen; and seventeen times as many as Stockholm.[†]

Surely then London, being, as we have shown, more numerously peopled than any single province—and, indeed, than many an entire State—may be regarded as a distinct WORLD; and, in accordance with this view, Addison has spoken of the British Metropolis as composed of different races like a world, instead of being made up of one cognate family like a town.

"When I consider this great city," he says,[‡] "in its several quarters or divisions, I look upon it as an aggregate of *various nations*, distinguished from each other by their respective customs, manners, and interests. The courts of two countries do not so much differ from one another as the Court and City of London in their peculiar ways of life and conversation. In short, the inhabitants of St. James's, notwithstanding they live under the same laws and speak the same language, are a distinct people from those of Cheapside, by several climates and degrees, in their ways of thinking and conversing together."

Viewing the Great Metropolis, therefore, as an absolute world, Belgravia and Bethnal Green become the opposite poles of the London sphere—the frigid zones, as it were, of the Capital; the one icy cold from its exceeding fashion, form, and ceremony; and the other wrapt in a perpetual winter of withering poverty. Of such a world, Temple Bar is the unmistakable equator, dividing the City hemisphere from that of the West End, and with a line of Banks, representative of the Gold Coast, in its immediate neighbourhood. What Greenwich, too, is to the merchant seamen of England, Charing Cross is to the London cabmen—the zero from which all the longitudes of the Metropolitan world are measured.

Then has not the so-called World of London its vast continents, like the veritable world of which it forms a part? What else are the enormous trans-Thamesian territories of South-wark and Lambeth? Moreover, the localities of St. Benetfink, and St. Benetsherehog, or even Bevis Marks, in the heart of the City, are as much *terra incognita*, to the great body of Londoners themselves, as is Lake Tchad in the centre of Africa to all but the Landers or Dr. Barths of our race.

Again, as regards the metropolitan people, the polite Parisian is not more widely different from the barbarous Botecudo, than is the lack-a-daisical dandy at Almack's from the Billingsgate "rough." Ethnologists have reduced the several varieties of mankind into five distinct types; but surely the judges who preside at the courts in Westminster are as morally distinct from the Jew "fences" of Petticoat Lane as the Caucasian from the Malayan race. Is not the "pet parson," too, of some West End Puseyite Chapel as ethically

---

[*] The population of England in the year 1377 was 2,092,978.

[†] The figures from which the above deductions are made are as follows:—Pekin (*reputed population*) 2,000,000; Paris, 1,650,000; Constantinople, 950,000; St. Petersburg, 600,000; Vienna, 500,000; New York, 500,000; Madrid, 450,000; Berlin, 380,000; Amsterdam, 300,000; Rome, 275,000; Copenhagen, 160,000; Stockholm, 150,000.—*Haydyn's Dictionary of Dates. Sixth Edition.*

[‡] *Spectator*, No. 340.

no bigger than summer insects on the water. The largest meadows were about the size of green-baize table covers; and across these we could just trace the line of the South-Western Railway, with the little whiff of white steam issuing from some passing engine, and no greater in volume than the jet of vapour from an ordinary tea-kettle.

Then, as the dusk of evening approached, and the gas-lights along the different lines of road started into light, one after another, the ground seemed to be covered with little illumination lamps, such as are hung on Christmas-trees, and reminding one of those that are occasionally placed, at intervals, along the grass at the edge of the gravel-walks in suburban tea-gardens; whilst the clusters of little lights at the spots where the hamlets were scattered over the scene, appeared like a knot of fire-flies in the air; and in the midst of these the eye could, here and there, distinguish the tiny crimson speck of some railway signal.

In the opposite direction to that in which the wind was insensibly wafting the balloon, lay the leviathan Metropolis, with a dense canopy of smoke hanging over it, and reminding one of the fog of vapour that is often seen steaming up from the fields at early morning. It was impossible to tell where the monster city began or ended, for the buildings stretched not only to the horizon on either side, but far away into the distance, where, owing to the coming shades of evening and the dense fumes from the million chimneys, the town seemed to blend into the sky, so that there was no distinguishing earth from heaven. The multitude of roofs that extended back from the foreground was positively like a dingy red sea, heaving in bricken billows, and the seeming waves rising up one after the other till the eye grew wearied with following them. Here and there we could distinguish little bare green patches of parks, and occasionally make out the tiny circular enclosures of the principal squares, though, from the height, these appeared scarcely bigger than wafers. Further, the fog of smoke that over-shadowed the giant town was pierced with a thousand steeples and pin-like factory-chimneys.

That little building, no bigger than one of the small china houses that are used for burning pastilles in, is Buckingham Palace—with St. James's Park, dwindled to the size of a card-table, stretched out before it. Yonder is Bethlehem Hospital, with its dome, now of about the same dimensions as a bell.

Then the little mites of men, crossing the bridges, seemed to have no more motion in them than the animalcules in cheese; while the streets appeared more like cracks in the soil than highways, and the tiny steamers on the river were only to be distinguished by the thin black thread of smoke trailing after them.

Indeed, it was a most wonderful sight to behold that vast bricken mass of churches and hospitals, banks and prisons, palaces and workhouses, docks and refuges for the destitute, parks and squares, and courts and alleys, which make up London—all blent into one immense black spot—to look down upon the whole as the birds of the air look down upon it, and see it dwindled into a mere rubbish heap—to contemplate from afar that strange conglomeration of vice, avarice, and low cunning, of noble aspirations and humble heroism, and to grasp it in the eye, in all its incongruous integrity, at one single glance—to take, as it were, an angel's view of that huge town where, perhaps, there is more virtue and more iniquity, more wealth and more want, brought together into one dense focus than in any other part of the earth—to hear the hubbub of the restless sea of life and emotion below, and hear it, like the ocean in a shell, whispering of the incessant strugglings and chafings of the distant tide—to swing in the air high above all the petty jealousies and heart-burnings, small ambitions and vain parade of "polite" society, and feel, for once, tranquil as a babe in a cot, and that you are hardly of the earth earthy, as, Jacob-like, you mount the aerial ladder, and half lose sight of the "great commercial world" beneath, where men are regarded as mere counters to play with, and where to *do* your neighbour as your neighbour would *do* you constitutes the first principle in the religion of trade—to feel yourself floating through the endless realms of space, and drinking in the pure thin air of the skies, as you go sailing along almost among the stars, free as "the lark at heaven's gate," and enjoying, for a brief half hour, at least, a foretaste of that Elysian destiny which is the ultimate hope of all.

Such is the scene we behold, and such the thoughts that stir the brain on contemplating London from the car of a balloon.*

* There are some peculiar effects in connection with balloon travelling that are worthy of further mention. The first is the utter absence of all sense of motion in the vehicle. Motion, indeed, at all times is only made known to us by those abrupt changes in our direction which consist of what are termed joltings; for the body, from its "*vis inertiæ*," partaking of the movement of the conveyance in which it is travelling, is, of course, thrown forcibly forwards or sideways, directly the course of the machine is violently arrested or altered. In a balloon, moreover, we are not even made conscious of our motion by the ordinary feeling of the air blowing against the face as we rush through it, for as the vessel travels *with* the wind, no such effect is produced; and it is most striking to find the clouds, from the same cause, apparently as motionless as rocks; for as they too are travelling *with* the balloon, and at precisely the same rate, they naturally cannot but appear to be absolutely still. Hence, under such circumstances, we have no means of telling whether we are ascending or descending, except by pieces of paper thrown out from the car, and which are of course left below if the machine be rising, and above if it be falling; indeed, when the balloon in which Albert Smith ascended from Vauxhall burst, and he and his aerial companions were being precipitated to the earth with the velocity of a stone, the only indication they got of the rate of their descent was by resorting to the little paper "logs," before mentioned. And Mr. Green assured me that though he has travelled in the air during a gale of wind at the rate of ninety-five miles in the hour, he was utterly unconscious not only of the velocity with which he had been projected, as it were, through the atmosphere, but also of the fury of the hurricane itself—feeling as perfectly tranquil all the while as if he had been seated in his easy chair by his own fireside; nor was it until he reached the earth, and the balloon became fixed to the ground by means of the grapnel, that he was sensible of the violence of the wind (and it was the same with us during *our* trip); for *then*, as the machine offered a considerable obstruction to the passage of the air, the power of the gale was rendered apparent—since, strange to say, *without resistance there is no force*. Hence there is but little danger in aeronautic excursions while the balloon remains in the air—and so indeed there is with a ship, as long as it has plenty of sea room; whereas, directly the aerial machine is fixed to the ground, it is like a stranded vessel, and becomes the sport of the wind, as the ship, similarly circumstanced, is of the waves. Another curious effect of the aerial ascent was, that the earth, when we were at our greatest altitude, positively appeared *concave*, looking like a huge dark bowl rather than the convex sphere, such as we naturally expect to see it. This, however, was a mere effect of perspective, for it is a law of vision that the horizon or boundary line of the sight always appears on a level with the eye—the fore-ground being, in all ordinary views, directly at the feet of the spectator, and the extreme back-ground some five feet and a half above it, while the relative *distances* of the intermediate objects are represented pictorially to the eye by their relative *heights* above the lowest, and therefore the nearest object in the scene—so that pictorial distance is really at right angles to tangible distance, the former being a line *parallel* with the body, and the latter one *perpendicular* to it. Hence, as the horizon always appears to be on a level with our eye (which is literally the centre of a hollow sphere rather than of a flat circle during vision), it naturally seems to rise as we rise, until at length the elevation of the circular boundary line of the sight becomes so marked, owing to our own elevation, that the earth assumes the anomalous appearance, as we have said, of a *concave* rather than a *convex* body. This optical illusion has, according to the best of our recollection, never been noticed or explained before, so that it becomes worthy of record. Another curious effect, but upon another sense, was the extraordinary, and indeed painful, pressure upon the ears which occurred at our greatest altitude. This was precisely the same sensation as is produced during a descent in a diving-bell, and it at first seemed strange that such a result, which, in the case of the diving-bell, obviously arises from the extreme *condensation* of the air within the submerged vessel, and its consequent greater pressure on the tympanum—should be brought about in a balloon immediately it enters a stratum of air where the *rarefaction* is greater than usual. Here were two directly opposite causes producing the same effect. A moment's reflection, however, taught us that the sensation experienced in the diving-bell arises from the drum of the ear being unduly strained by the pressure of the *external* air; whereas the sensation experienced in the balloon was produced by the air *inside* the ear acting in the same manner.

———————————

§ 3.

SOME IDEA OF THE SIZE AND POPULATION OF LONDON.

It is strange how hard it is for the mind to arrive at any definite notion as to aggregate numbers or dimensions in space. The savage who can count only up to ten, points to the hairs of his head, in order to convey the complex idea of some score or two of objects; and although educated people can generally form a concrete conception of hundreds, without losing all sense of the individual units composing the sum, it is certain, nevertheless, that when the aggregate reaches thousands and millions, even the best disciplined intellects have a very hazy notion of the distinct numerical elements making up the gross idea— the same as they have of the particular stars that go to form some unresolved nebulæ, or of the several atoms in the forty thousand millions of siliceous shells of insects that Ehrenberg assures us are contained in every cubic inch of the polishing slate of Bilin.

Is it not, then, the mere pedantry of statistics to inform the reader, while professing to describe the size and population of the Great Metropolis, that, according to the returns of the last census, it is 78,029 statute acres, or 122 square miles, in extent; that it contains 327,391 houses; and that it numbers 2,362,236 souls within its boundaries!

Surely the mind is no more enabled to realize the immensity of the largest city in the world by such information as this, than we are helped to comprehend the vastness of the sea by being told that the total area of all the oceans amounts to 145 millions of square miles, and that it contains altogether 6,441 billions of tons of common salt.*

We will, however, endeavour to conjure up a more vivid picture of the giant city in the brain, not only of those who have never visited the spot, but of those who, though living in it all their lives, have hardly any clearer ideas of the town, in its vast integrity, than the fishes have of the Atlantic in which they swim.

We must premise, then, that it is as difficult to tell where the Metropolis begins, and where it ends, as it is to point out the particular line of demarcation between the several colours of the rainbow; for the suburban villages blend so insensibly into the city, that one might as well attempt to define the precise point where the water begins to be salt at the mouth of some estuary.

Hence, it has been found necessary to pass special Acts of Parliament in order to let Londoners know how far London really extends into the country, and to define the size of the Great Metropolis according to law.†

This is, however, very much of a piece with the renowned stroke of legislation performed

---

* See *Ansted's Geology*, page 28.

† The following are the terms of the Burial Act (15 and 16 Vict., cap. 85):—"For the purposes of this Act, the expression 'the Metropolis' shall be construed to mean and include the Cities and Liberties of London and Westminster, the Borough of Southwark, and the Parishes, Precincts, Townships, and Places mentioned in the Schedule (A.) to this Act."

SCHEDULE A.

The City of London and the Liberties thereof, the Inner Temple, and Middle Temple, and all other Places and Parts of Places contained within the exterior Boundaries of the Liberties of the City of London.

In Middlesex.

The City and Liberties of Westminster.

The Parishes of St. Margaret and St. John the Evangelist.

The Parish of St. Martin in the Fields.

The Parish of St. George, Hanover Square.

The Parish of St. James.

The Parish of St. Mary-le-Strand, as well within the Liberty of Westminster as within the Duchy Liberty.

The Parish of St. Clement Danes, as well within the Liberty of Westminster as within the Duchy Liberty.

by the progress-hating King Canute, since it is quite as absurd for rulers to say, " Thus far shalt thou go, and no farther," to the bricks and mortar of London, as to the waves of the ocean.

In the year 1603, for instance, we find that the legal limits of London, " within and without the walls," were but little better than *fifteen hundred* statute acres; whereas in the next century the Metropolis, " according to law," had swollen to upwards of *twenty thousand* acres. Then at the beginning of the present century the area was farther extended to *thirty thousand* acres; and in 1837, it was again increased to *forty-six thousand;* whilst now it is allowed by Act of Parliament to cover a surface of no less than *seventy-eight thousand* acres in extent.

The Parish of St. Paul, Covent Garden.

The Parish of St. Anne, Soho.

Whitehall Gardens (whether the same be parochial or extra-parochial).

Whitehall (whether the same be parochial or extra-parochial).

Richmond Terrace (whether the same be parochial or extra-parochial).

The Close of the Collegiate Church of St. Peter.

———

The Parishes of St. Giles in the Fields and St. George, Bloomsbury.

The Parishes of St. Andrew, Holborn, and St. George the Martyr.

The Liberty of Hatton Garden, Saffron Hill, and Ely Rents.

The Liberty of the Rolls.

The Parish of St. Pancras.

The Parish of St. John, Hampstead.

The Parish of St. Marylebone.

The Parish of Paddington.

The Precinct of the Savoy.

The Parish of St. Luke.

The Liberty of Glasshouse Yard.

The Parish of St. Sepulchre.

The Parish of St. James, Clerkenwell, including both Districts of St. James and St. John.

The Parish of St. Mary, Islington.

The Parish of St. Mary, Stoke Newington.

The Charterhouse.

The Parish of St. Mary, Whitechapel.

The Parish of Christchurch, Spitalfields.

The Parish of St. Leonard, Shoreditch.

The Liberty of Norton Folgate.

The Parish of St. John, Hackney.

The Parish of St. Matthew, Bethnal Green.

The Hamlet of Mile-end Old Town.

The Hamlet of Mile-end New Town.

The Parish of St. Mary, Stratford, Bow.

The Parish of Bromley, St. Leonard.

The Parish of All Saints, Poplar.

The Parish of St. Anne, Limehouse.

The Hamlet of Ratcliffe.

The Parish of St. Paul, Shadwell.

The Parish of St. George in the East.

The Parish of St. John, Wapping.

The Liberty of East Smithfield.

The Precinct of St. Catherine.

The Liberty of Her Majesty's Tower of London, consisting of—

The Liberty of the Old Artillery Ground.

The Parish of Trinity, Minories.

The Old Tower Precinct.

The Precinct of the Tower Within.

The Precinct of Wellclose.

The Parish of Kensington.

The Parish of St. Luke, Chelsea.

The Parish of Fulham.

The Parish of Hammersmith.

Lincoln's Inn.

New Inn.

Gray's Inn.

Staple Inn.

That Part of Furnival's Inn, in the County of Middlesex.

Ely Place.

The Parish of Willesden.

In Kent.

The Parish of St. Paul, Deptford.

The Parish of St. Nicholas, Deptford.

The Parish of Greenwich.

The Parish of Woolwich.

The Parish of Charlton.

The Parish of Plumstead.

In Surrey.

The Borough of Southwark.

The Parish of St. George the Martyr.

The Parish of St. Saviour.

The Parish of St. John, Horsleydown.

The Parish of St. Olave.

The Parish of St. Thomas.

The Parish of Battersea (except the Hamlet of Penge).

The Parish of Bermondsey.

The Parish of Camberwell.

The Parish of Clapham.

The Parish of Lambeth.

The Parish of Newington.

The Parish of Putney.

The Parish of Rotherhithe.

The Parish of Streatham.

The Parish of Tooting.

The Parish of Wandsworth.

The Parish of Christchurch.

The Clink Liberty.

The Hamlet of Hatcham in the Parish of Deptford.

Indeed, the increase of the metropolitan population within the last ten years, tells us that further house-room has to be provided in London every twelvemonth for upwards of forty thousand new comers. Of these about half are strangers; for, as the annual excess of births over deaths in the Metropolis amounts to but little better than half the yearly increase in the number of the people, it is manifest that nearly twenty thousand individuals must come and settle in the town every year, from other parts—a rate of immigration as great as if the entire population of Guernsey had left their native island for the " little village."*

No wonder, then, that the returns show that there are continually 4,000 new houses in the course of erection; for it may be truly said our Metropolis increases annually by the addition of a town of considerable size.

Hence, even though, as Maitland says, London had a century ago absorbed into its body one city, one borough, and forty-three villages, it still continues daily devouring suburbs, and swallowing up green field after green field, and the builders go on raising houses where the market-gardeners a short time ago raised cabbages instead—the Metropolis throwing out its many fibres of streets like the thousand roots of an old tree stretching far into the soil; so that it is evident that though the late Burial Acts pretended to mark out the limits of the Capital in 1852, still, in another decenniad another Act will have to be passed, incorporating other hamlets with the town; even as the Old Bills of Mortality, which were issued by the Company of Parish Clerks in 1603, were forced in a few years after the date to add St. Giles in the Fields and Clerkenwell to the metropolitan circle, and at the end of the century to include also the villages of Hackney, and Islington, and Newington, and Rotherhithe; whilst the New Bills have since encompassed the hamlets of Kensington, and Paddington, and Hammersmith, and Fulham, and Camberwell, and Wandsworth, and Deptford, and Greenwich, and Plumstead, and Lewisham, and Hampstead; until at length the Capital has been made to consist, not only of some score of Wicks, and Townships, and Precincts, and Liberties, but to comprise the two great boroughs of Southwark and Greenwich, as well as the Episcopal Cities of Westminster and London proper. Indeed, the monster Metropolis now comprehends, within its parliamentary boundaries, what once constituted the territories of four Saxon Commonwealths—the kingdom of the Middle Saxons, East Saxons, the South Rick, and the Kentwaras.

Now as regards the actual size of this enormous city, it may be said that its area is considerably more than twice the dimensions of the island of St. Helena, and very nearly double that of Jersey—being not quite so large as Elba, but nearly one-half the superficial extent of Madeira. Not only does it stretch into the three counties of Middlesex, Surrey, and Kent, but the length of that portion of the Thames which traverses the Metropolis—and divides the river, as it winds along, into two great metropolitan provinces as it were—measures no less than twenty miles from Hammersmith to Woolwich; whilst in its course the river receives the waters of the navigable Roding and Lea on the one side, and the Ravensbourne and Wandle on the other, together with many other minor streams that are now buried under the houses, and made to do the duty of sewers, though they were, at one time, of sufficient capacity to be the scenes of naval battles.†

---

* The above statement is proved thus:—

2,362,236	= Population of London in 1851.	
1,948,417	= ,, ,, 1841.	

413,819 = Increase of Population in 10 years.

41,381·9 = Annual increase.

84,944 = Births in London, in 1855.
61,506 = Deaths   ,,   ,,

23,438 = Annual excess of Births over Deaths.
17,943 = Annual Immigration.

41,385· = Annual Increase.

† " Anciently," says Stowe, " until the Conqueror's time, and two hundred years afterwards, the city of London was watered—besides the famous river of Thames, on the south—with the river of Wells, as it was

From east to west, London stretches from Plumstead to Hammersmith on the Middlesex side of the river, and from Woolwich to Wandsworth on the Surrey side, and there is nearly one continuous street of houses joining these extreme points, and measuring about fourteen miles in length; whilst the line of buildings running north and south, and reaching from Holloway to Camberwell, is said to be upwards of twelve miles long.

If, however, we estimate only the solid mass of houses in the centre, where the tenements are packed almost back to back, and nearly as close as the bales of cotton in the hold of a merchant ship, the area so occupied is found to be larger, even, than the Island of Guernsey.*

Again, an enumeration of the gross amount of buildings which make up the dense crowd of houses in London is quite as useless, for all imaginative purposes, as is the specification of the number of statute acres comprised within its area, for helping us to conceive its size. A statement, on the contrary, of the mere length of the line that the buildings would form if joined all together in one continuous row, will give us a far better idea of the gross extent of the whole. This is easily arrived at by assuming each of the tenements to have an average frontage of fifteen feet in width; and thus we find that the entire length of the buildings throughout London amounts to near upon one thousand miles, so that if they were all ranged in a line, they would form one continuous street, long enough to reach across the whole of England and France, from York to the Pyrenees!

If, then, such be the mere length of the aggregate houses in London, it may be readily conceived that the streets of the Metropolis—which, on looking at the map, seem to be a perfect maze of bricks and mortar—should be some thousands in number; and, accordingly, it appears that there are upwards of 10,500 distinct streets, squares, circuses, crescents, terraces, villas, rows, buildings, places, lanes, courts, alleys, mews, yards, rents, &c., particularized in that huge civic encyclopædia, the London Post-Office Directory.

Many of these thoroughfares, too, are of no inconsiderable dimensions. Oxford Street alone is more than one mile and a third long, and Regent Street, from Langham Church to Carlton Terrace, measures nearly one mile in length; whilst the two great lines of thoroughfare parallel to the river, the one extending along Oxford Street, Holborn, Cheapside, Cornhill, and Whitechapel to Mile-end, and which is really but one street with different names, and the other stretching from Knightsbridge along Piccadilly, the Haymarket, Pall Mall East, the Strand, Fleet Street, Cannon Street, Tower Street, and so on by Ratcliffe Highway to the West India Docks—are each above six miles from one end to the other.

then called (but Fleete dike afterwards —"because it runneth past the Fleete," he adds in another place) on the west; with the water called Wallbrooke running through the midst of the city into the river of Thames, serving the heart thereof; and with a fourth water or bourne, which ran within the city through Langbourne ward, watering that part in the east. In the west suburbs was also another great water called Oldborne, which had its fall into the river of Wells." * * * * Moreover, "in a fair book of Parliament records now lately restored to the Tower," he adds, "it appears that a Parliament being holden at Carlisle in the year 1307 (the 35th of Edward I.), Henry Lacy, Earl of Lincoln, complained that whereas in times past the course of water running at London under Oldborne bridge and Fleete bridge into the Thames, had been of such breadth and depth that *ten or twelve ships navies at once, with merchandise, were wont to come to the aforesaid bridge of Fleete and some of them to Oldborne bridge;* now the same course, by filth of the tanners and such others, is sore decayed; also by raising of wharfs; but especially by a diversion of water made by them of the new Temple, in the first year of King John, for their mills, standing without Baynard's Castle, and divers other impediments, so that the said ships cannot enter as they were wont, and as they ought." * * * * Further, we are told by the same historian, that "in the year 1502, the seventh of Henry VII., the whole course of the Fleete dike (then so called) was scowered down to the Thames, so that boats with fish and fuel were rowed to the Fleete bridge and to Oldborne bridge, as they of old time had been accustomed, which was a great commodity to all the inhabitants in that part of the city."—Stowe's *Survey* (Thoms' Edition), pp. 5, 6.

* The comparative density of the buildings in the different parts of London may be indicated by the fact, that in the heart of the city there are upwards of 30 houses to the acre; whereas in the outlying localities of

But "if you wish," said Dr. Johnson, "to have a just notion of the magnitude of this city, you must not be satisfied with seeing its streets and squares, but must survey the little lanes and courts. It is not," he added, "in the showy evolution of buildings, but in the multiplicity of human habitations, which are crowded together, that the wonderful immensity of London consists."

Indeed, the gross extent of the London streets, small as well as great, is almost incredible; for a return by the Police, in 1850, makes the aggregate length of the metropolitan thoroughfares amount to no less that 1750 miles—so that, according to this, the highways and byeways of the Capital must be even longer than the lines of the five principal London railways—the North Western, Great Western, South Western, Great Northern, and Eastern Counties—all added on one to another; or considerably more than three times the length of the railway from London, *via* Calais and Ghent, to Cologne. The cost of forming this astounding length of paved roadway, I have elsewhere shown to amount to no less than £14,000,000; and that not only have these same roadways to be entirely relaid every five years, but the mere repairs upon them cost upwards of £1,800,000 per annum.

Kensington and Camberwell, there are but little more than two houses; and in Hampstead not quite one house to the same extent of ground—as may be seen by the following

TABLE SHOWING THE AREA, NUMBER OF HOUSES, AND PROPORTION OF HOUSES TO EACH ACRE IN LONDON, 1851.

DISTRICTS.	Area in Statute Acres.	Total Number of Houses.	Number of Houses to the Acre.	DISTRICTS.	Area in Statute Acres.	Total Number of Houses.	Number of Houses to the Acre.
WEST DISTRICTS.				**EAST DISTRICTS.**			
Kensington	7374	19,082	2·7	Shoreditch	646	16,182	25·0
Chelsea	865	7,953	9·1	Bethnal Green	760	13,819	18·1
St. George, Hanover Square	1161	9,404	8·0	Whitechapel	406	9,161	22·5
Westminster	917	6,978	7·6	St. George-in-the-East	243	6,351	26·1
St. Martin-in-the-Fields	305	2,465	8·0	Stepney	1,257	17,348	13·8
St. James, Westminster	164	3,533	21·0	Poplar	2,918	7,283	2·4
Total West Districts	10,786	49,505	4·5	Total, East Districts	6,230	70,144	11·2
NORTH DISTRICTS.				**SOUTH DISTRICTS.**			
Marylebone	1,509	16,448	10·9	St. Saviour, Southwark.	250	4,856	19·4
Hampstead	2,252	1,822	0·8	St. Olave „	169	2,436	14·4
Pancras	2,716	19,688	7·2	Bermondsey „	688	7,466	10·8
Islington	3,127	14,736	4·7	St. George, Southwark	282	7,513	26·6
Hackney	3,929	10,517	2·6	Newington	624	11,205	17·9
Total North Districts	13,533	63,221	4·6	Lambeth	4,015	21,659	5·3
CENTRAL DISTRICTS.				Wandsworth	11,695	9,163	0·7
				Camberwell	4,342	10,072	2·3
St. Giles	245	4,996	20·0	Rotherhithe	886	3,058	3·4
Strand	174	4,110	23·6	Greenwich	5,367	1,580	2·9
Holborn	196	4,519	23·0	Lewisham	17,224	6,624	0·3
Clerkenwell	380	7,549	19·8				
St. Luke	220	6,616	30·0	Total, South Districts	45,542	100,453	2·4
East London	153	4,945	32·3				
West London	136	2,850	21·6				
London City	434	8,373	19·2				
Total, Central Districts	1,938	44,058	22·7	Total for all London	78,029	327,451	4·1

Of the enormous mass of human beings comprised in the London population, it is even more difficult to have an adequate conception, than to realize to our minds the gross number of its houses and length of its streets. One way, however, in which we may arrive at a vague idea of the dense human multitude is, by comparing the number of people resident in the Metropolis with those that lined the thoroughfares on the day of the Duke of Wellington's funeral; and judging by the extent of the crowd collected on that occasion, as to the probable dimensions of the mob that would be formed were the people of London to be all gathered together into one body.

It was calculated on that occasion that there were a million and a half of people in the streets to witness the procession, and that these covered the pathways all along the line of route for a distance of three miles. Hence it follows, that were the whole of the metropolitan population ever to be congregated in the streets at one and the same time, they would form a dense mass of human beings near upon five miles long.

Or, to put the matter still more forcibly before the mind, we may say, that if the entire people of the capital were to be drawn up in marching order, two and two, the length of the great army of Londoners would be no less than 670 miles; and, supposing them to move at the rate of three miles an hour, it would require more than nine days and nights for the aggregate population to pass by!*

* The distribution and relative density of the population throughout London is numerically as follows:—

TABLE SHOWING THE DISTRIBUTION AND DENSITY OF THE POPULATION OF LONDON IN 1851.

DISTRICTS.	Area in Statute Acres.	Males.	Females.	Total of Persons.	Number of Persons to Acre.	DISTRICTS.	Area in Statute Acres.	Males.	Females.	Total of Persons.	Number of Persons to Acre.
WEST DISTICTS.						**EAST DISTRICTS.**					
Kensington	7,374	49,949	70,055	120,004	16·2	Shoreditch	646	52,087	57,170	109,257	169·1
Chelsea	865	25,475	31,063	565,38	65·4	Bethnal Green	760	44,081	46,112	90,193	118·6
St. George, Hanover Square	1,161	31,920	41,310	73,230	63·0	Whitechapel	406	40,271	39,488	79,759	196·4
Westminster	917	32,494	33,125	65,609	71·5	St. George-in-the-East	243	23,496	24,880	48,376	199·0
St. Martin-in-the-Fields	305	11,918	12,722	24,640	80·8	Stepney	1,257	52,342	58,433	110,777	88·1
St. James, Westminster	164	17,377	19,029	36,406	213·9	Poplar	2,928	23,902	23,260	47,162	16·1
Total, West Districts	10,786	169,133	207,294	376,427	34·9	Total, East Districts	6,230	236,179	249,343	485,522	77·9
NORTH DISTRICTS.						**SOUTH DISTRICTS.**					
						St. Saviour, Southwark	250	17,432	18,299	35,731	142·9
Marylebone	1,509	69,115	88,581	157,696	104·5	St. Olave, ditto	169	9,660	9,715	19,375	114·6
Hampstead	2,252	4,960	7,026	11,986	5·3	Bermondsey	688	23,511	24,617	48,128	69·9
Pancras	2,716	76,144	90,812	166,956	61·4	St. George, Southwark	282	25,374	26,450	58,824	208·5
Islington	3,127	42,760	52,567	95,329	30·4	Newington	624	30,255	34,561	64,816	103·8
Hackney	3,929	25,083	33,346	58,429	14·8	Lambeth	4,015	63,673	75,652	139,325	34·7
Total, North Districts	13,533	218,064	272,332	490,396	36·2	Wandsworth	11,695	23,011	27,753	50,764	4·6
						Camberwell	4,342	23,574	31,093	54,667	12·5
CENTRAL DISTRICTS.						Rotherhithe	886	9,127	8,678	17,805	20·0
						Greenwich	5,367	50,639	48,726	99,365	6·4
St. Giles	245	25,832	28,382	54,214	221·2	Lewisham	17,224	15,708	19,127	34,835	2·0
Strand	171	21,570	22,890	44,460	255·5	Total, South Districts	45,542	291,964	324,672	616,635	11·3
Holborn	196	22,860	23,761	46,621	237·8						
Clerkenwell	380	31,489	33,289	64,778	170·4						
St. Luke	220	26,178	27,877	54,055	245·7						
East London	153	28,536	22,870	44,406	290·2						
West London	136	14,604	14,186	28,790	211·6						
London City	434	27,149	28,783	55,932	128·8						
Total, Central Districts	1,938	191,218	202,038	393,256	77·9	Total, for all London	78,029	1,106,558	1,258,678	2,362,236	3·0

But a better idea of the comparative density of the population in the several districts of London, will be obtained by reference to the subjoined engraving.

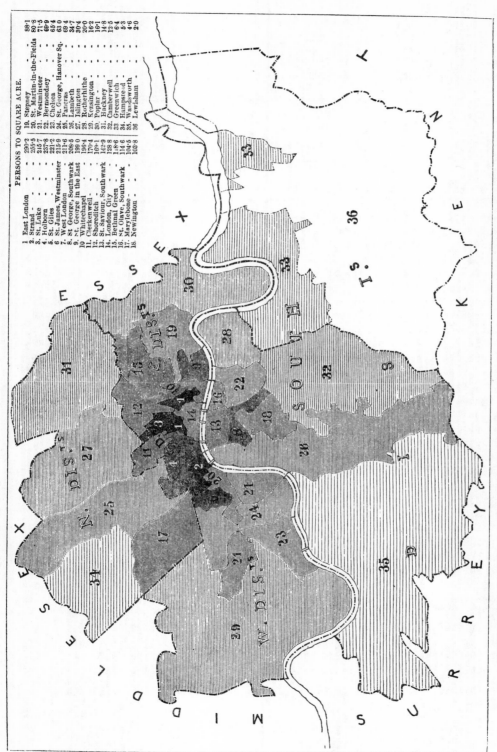

MAP ILLUSTRATIVE OF THE DISTRIBUTION AND DENSITY OF THE POPULATION OF LONDON IN 1851.

The blackest portions indicate the quarters which are the most thickly peopled; and, on the contrary, the lightest portions those in which the population is the thinnest.

Further, to put the matter even more lucidly before the mind, we may say that no less than 169 people die each day in the metropolis, and that a babe is born within its boundaries nearly every five minutes throughout the year !*

---

§ 4.

LONDON FROM DIFFERENT POINTS OF VIEW.

" Considered in connection with the insular position of England in that great highway of nations, the Atlantic," says Sir John Herschel, " it is a fact not a little explanatory of the commercial eminence of our country, that LONDON *occupies very nearly the centre of the terrestrial hemisphere.*"

But whether the merchant fame of Great Britain be due to its geographical good luck, or to that curious commingling of races, which has filled an Englishman's veins with the blood of the noblest tribes belonging to the multiform family of mankind—the Celtic, the Roman, the Saxon, the Scandinavian, and Norman—so that an Englishman is, as it were, an ethnological compound of a Welshman, an Italian, a German, Dane, and Frenchman—to whichever cause the result be due, it is certain that all people regard the British Capital as the largest and busiest human hive in the world.

The mere name, indeed, of London calls up in the mind—not only of Londoners, but of country folk and foreigners as well—a thousand varied trains of thought. Perhaps the first idea that rises in association with it is, that it is at once the biggest bazaar and the richest bank throughout the globe.

Some persons, turning to the west, regard London as a city of palatial thoroughfares, and princely club-houses and mansions, and adorned with parks, and bristling with countless steeples, and crowded with stately asylums for the indigent and afflicted.

Others, mindful but of the City, see, principally, narrow lanes and musty counting-houses, and tall factory chimnies, darkening (till lately) the air with their black clouds of smoke; and huge blocks of warehouses, with doors and cranes at every floor; and docks crowded with shipping, and choked with goods; and streets whose traffic is positively deafening in the stranger's ear; and bridges and broad thoroughfares blocked with the dense mass of passing vehicles.

Others, again, looking to the east, and to the purlieus of the town, are struck with the appalling wretchedness of the people, taking special notice of the half-naked, shoeless children that are usually seen gambling up our courts, and the capless, shaggy-headed women that loll about the alleys or lanes, with their bruised, discoloured features, telling of some recent violence; or else they are impressed with the sight of the drunken, half-starved mobs collected round the glittering bar of some palatial gin-shop, with the foul-mouthed mothers there drugging their infants with the drink.

In fine, this same London is a strange, incongruous chaos of the most astounding riches and prodigious poverty—of feverish ambition and apathetic despair—of the brightest charity and the darkest crime; the great focus of human emotion—the scene, as we have said, of countless daily struggles, failures, and successes; where the very best and the very worst

---

* The returns of the Registrar-General as to the number of births and deaths occurring in London during the year 1855, are as follows :—

1855.—Births, Males	.	.	.	.	43,352	} Total, 84,944.
Females	.	.	.	.	41,592	
1855.—Deaths, Males .	.	.	.	.	37,203	} Total, 61,506.
Females	.	.	.	.	30,303	

types of civilized society are found to prevail—where there are more houses and more house-less—more feasting and more starvation—more philanthropy and more bitter stony-hearted-ness, than on any other spot in the world—and *all* grouped around the one giant centre, whose huge dark dome, with its glittering ball of gold, is seen in every direction, looming through the smoke, and marking out the Capital, no matter from what quarter the traveller may come.

"I have often amused myself," says Dr. Johnson, "with thinking how different a place London is to different people. They whose narrow minds are contracted to the considera-tion of some one particular pursuit, view it only through that medium. A politician thinks of it only as the seat of government in its different departments; a grazier, as a vast market for cattle; a mercantile man, as a place where a prodigious deal of business is done upon 'Change; a dramatic enthusiast, as the grand scene of theatrical entertainments; a man of pleasure, as an assemblage of taverns. * * * * But the intellectual man is struck with it as comprehending the whole of human life in its variety, the contemplation of which is inexhaustible."

Of the first impressions of London, those who drew their infant breath within its smoky atmosphere are, of course, utterly unconscious; and, perhaps, there is no class of people who have so dull a sense of the peculiarities of the great town in which they live, and none who have so little attachment to their native place as Londoners themselves.

The Swiss, it is well known, have almost a woman's love for the mountains amid which they were reared; indeed so fervent is the affection of the Helvetian for his native hills, that it was found necessary to prohibit the playing of the "*Ranz des Vaches*," in the Swiss regiments of the French army, owing to the number of desertions it occasioned. The German, too, in other lands, soon becomes afflicted with, what in the language of the country is termed, "*Heimweh*"—that peculiar settled melancholy and bodily as well as mental depression which results from a continual craving to return to his "fatherland."

Indeed, though the people of almost every other place throughout the globe have, more or less, a strong attachment for the land of their birth, your old-established Londoner is so little remarkable for the quality, that it becomes positively absurd to think of one born within the sound of Bow-bells displaying the least regard for his native paving-stones. For whilst the scion of other parts yearns to get back to the haunts of his childhood, the Londoner is beset with an incessant desire to be off from those of *his*. All the year through he looks forward to his week's or month's autumnal holiday abroad, or down at one of the fashionable English watering-places; and even when he has amassed sufficient means to render him independent of the Metropolis, he seldom or never can bring himself to end his days in some suburban "Paradise Place," or "Prospect Row," that is "within half an hour's ride of the Bank," and (as inviting landladies love to add) "with omnibuses passing the door every five minutes." But he retires, on the contrary, to one of the pleasant and secluded nooks of England, or else to some economical little foreign town, where he can realize the pleasures of cheap claret or hock, and avoid the income-tax. Hence it has come to be a saying among metropolitan genealogists, that London families seldom continue settled in the Capital for three generations together—there being but few persons born and bred in the Metropolis whose great-grandfather was native to the place.

Formerly, in the old coaching days, the entrance into London was a sight that no country in the world could parallel, and one of which the first impression was well calculated to astound the foreigner, who had been accustomed in his own country to travel along roads that were about as loose in the soil and as furrowed with ruts as ploughed fields, and in mails, too, that were a kind of cross between a fly-wagon and an omnibus, and not nearly so rapid as hearses when returning from a funeral, and with the horses harnessed to the unsightly vehicle with traces of rope, and a huge-booted driver continually shouting and swearing at the team.

The entry into the Metropolis, on the contrary, was over a roadway that was positively as hard as steel and as level as water, and upon which the patter of the horses hoofs rang with an almost metallic sound. Then the coachman was often an English gentleman, and even in some cases a person of rank,* whilst the vehicle itself was a very model of lightness and elegance. The horses, too, were such thorough-bred animals as England alone could produce, and their entire leathern trappings as brightly polished as a dandy's boots.

In those days, even London people themselves were so delighted with the sight of the mails and fast coaches leaving the Metropolis at night, that there was a large crowd invariably congregated around the Angel at Islington, the White Horse Cellar, Piccadilly, and the Elephant and Castle across the water, at eight every evening, to see the royal stages start into the country by their different routes. On the King's birthday, too, the scene at those inns was assuredly as picturesque as it was entirely national. The exterior of the taverns was studded over with lights of many colours, arranged in tasty luminous lines, the sleek-coated blood horses were all newly harnessed, and the bright brass ornaments on their trappings glittered again in the glare of the illumination. The coachmen and guards were in unsullied scarlet coats worn for the first time that day; and there were gay rosettes of ribbon and bunches of flowers at each of the horse's heads as well as in each coachman's button-hole; while the freshly painted mails were packed so thickly in front of the tavern-door, that the teams were all of a heap there; and the air kept on continually resounding with the tinny twang of the post horns of the newly arriving or departing vehicles.

¶ i. *The Entry into London by "Rail."*

We are not among those who regret the change in the mode of travelling, and we allude to the old mail-coaches here simply as having been especially characteristic of the country and the Capital. Now that all the world, however, travels by rail, there is but little peculiar in the style by which the entry into London is made, to impress the mind of strangers. Nevertheless, as the trains dart through the different suburbs, the eye must be dull indeed that is not struck with the strange sights seen by the way, even though the journey be performed among the house-tops of the metropolitan outskirts.

What an odd notion the stranger must acquire of the Metropolis, as he enters it by the South-Western Railway! How curious is the flash of the passing Vauxhall Gardens, dreary with their big black trees, and the huge theatrical-looking summer-house, built for the orchestra and half-tumbling to decay; and the momentary glimpse of the Tartarus-like gas-works, with their tall minaret chimneys, and the red mouth of some open retort there glowing like the crater of a burning volcano; and the sudden whisking by of the Lambeth potteries, with their show of sample chimney-pots, and earthen pans, and tubing, ranged along the walls; and, the minute afterwards, the glance at the black rack-like sheds, spotted all over with the snowy ends of lumps of whiting, thrust at intervals through the apertures; and then the sickening stench of the bone-boilers, leaking in through every crevice of the carriage; and the dreary-looking attics of the houses as the roofs fly past; and, lastly,

---

* Aristocracy patronized the coach-box as drivers of stages. Sir Vincent Cotton drove the "Age," Brighton coach; Mr. Willan, the "Magnet;" Sir Thomas Tyrwhitt Jones, the "Pearl;" Mr. Bliss, the "Mazeppa;" and Captain Probin, the "Reading;" all being renowned for their whips and fast coaches, and doing their 10½ and 11 miles per hour. There were also the "Hirondelle," which ran between Cheltenham and Liverpool, 133 miles in 12½ hours; the "Owen Glendower," between Birmingham and Aberystwith, a very hilly country, at the rate of 10½ miles per hour; two coaches, the "Phenomenon" and the "Blue," ran between London and Norwich at a rate of 12 miles per hour, doing 112 miles in 9¼ hours; the "Quicksilver" and the "Shrewsbury Wonder" were likewise famous fast coaches; and the "Manchester Telegraph" ran 13 miles per hour, including stoppages. *Public Carriages of Great Britain.* By J. E. Bradfield.

while the train stops for the collection of the tickets on the high viaduct over the Westminster Bridge Road, the protracted peep down into the broad street above which the carriages rest, and the odd bird's-eye view of the huge linendrapers' shop there, with the diminutive-looking people, and cabs, and carts, hurrying along deep down in the roadway under the train !

Or, if the visitor enter London by the South-Eastern line, coming from Dover, or Brighton, the scene is equally distinctive. No sooner does the train near London than the huge glass temple of the Crystal Palace appears glittering in the light, like so much ice-work. Then stations rush rapidly by, tabletted all over with showy advertising boards and bills announcing cheap clothing, or cheap tea, or bedding, or stationery, or razors, and the huge letters seeming to be smudged one into the other by the speed. Then as the knot of neighbouring lines draw together like so many converging radii, distant trains are seen at all kinds of levels, flitting across the marshes without the least apparent effort, and with a cloud of white steam puffing fitfully from the chimney of the engine at the head, while the little wheels of the carriages are observed to twinkle again with their rapid twirling. In a minute or two the train turns the angle of the line, and then through what a bricken wilderness of roofs it seems to be ploughing its way, and how odd the people look, as they slide swiftly by, in their wretched garrets ! Next, a smell of tan pervades the air; and there are glimpses of brown hides hanging in sheds below. Now, the church of St. John, Horsleydown, shoots by with the strange stone pillar stuck on the top of it, in lieu of a steeple; and immediately afterwards the tangle of railway lines becomes more and more intricate, the closer the train draws to the terminus, till at length the earth appears to be ribbed over with the iron bars in every direction, and the lines to be in such confusion that it seems a miracle how the engine can find its way among the many fibres of the iron web.

Nor, if the visitor come by the London and North Western line from Liverpool or the great manufacturing districts, are the sights less striking; for here the train plunges with a loud shriek into the long, dark perforation under Primrose Hill, and when it shoots into the light again, the green banks are seen studded with little villas, ranged two and two beside the road. Then, as the carriages stop outside the engine-house for the collection of the tickets, what a hurry-skurry and riot there appears to be among the passing locomotives ! Here one engine pants and gasps, as it begins to move, as if it were positively overcome with the exertion, and when the wheels refuse to bite upon the rail, it seems to chuckle again half-savagely at its own failure, as they slip round and round. Another goes tearing by, its shrill whistle screeching like a mad human thing the while, and men shoot out of little sentry-boxes, and shoulder, with a military air, furled-up flags. In a minute or two afterwards the train moves on once more, and the carriages go rattling along the bed, as it were, of some dried-up canal, with little cottage mansions perched on the top of the slanting railway wall, and great iron girders over-head, stretching across the bricken channel like the rafters of a loft.

But the most peculiar and distinctive of all the entries to the Great Metropolis is the one by the river; for, assuredly, there is no scene that impresses the mind with so lively a sense of the wealth and commercial energy of the British Capital as the view of the far-famed Port of London.

¶ ii. *The Port of London.*

Seen from the Custom House, this is indeed a characteristic sight; and some time since we were permitted, by the courtesy of the authorities, to witness the view from the "long room" there.

The broad highway of the river—which at this part is near upon 300 yards in width— was almost blocked with the tiers of shipping; for there was merely a narrow pathway of grey, glittering water left open in the middle; and, on either side, the river was black with the dense mass of hulls collected alongside the quays; while the masts of the craft were as thick as the pine stems in their native forests.

The sun shone bright upon the water, and as its broken beams played upon the surface it sparkled and twinkled in the light, like a crumpled plate of golden foil; and down the "silent highway," barges, tide-borne, floated sideways, with their long slim oars projecting from their sides like the fins of a flying fish; whilst others went along, with their masts slanting down and their windlass clicking as men laboured to raise the "warm-brown" sail that they had lowered to pass under the bridge. Then came a raft of timber, towed by a small boat, and the boatman leaning far back in it as he tugged at the sculls; and presently a rapid river steamer flitted past, the deck crowded so densely with passengers that it reminded one of a cushion stuck all over with black pins; and as it hurried past we caught a whiff, as it were, of music from the little band on board.

The large square blocks of warehouses on the opposite shore were almost hidden in the shadow which came slanting down far into the river, and covering, as with a thick veil of haze, the confused knot of sloops and schooners and "bilanders" that lay there in the dusk, in front of the wharves. Over the tops of the warehouses we could see the trail of white steam, from the railway engines at the neighbouring terminus, darting from among the roofs as they hurried to and fro.

A little way down the river, stood a clump of Irish vessels, with the light peeping through the thicket, as it were, of their masts—some with their sails hanging all loose and limp, and others with them looped in rude festoons to the yards. Beside these lay barges stowed full of barrels of beer and sacks of flour; and a few yards farther on, a huge foreign steamer appeared, with short thick black funnel and blue paddle-boxes. Then came hoys laden with straw and coasting goods, and sunk so deep in the water that, as the steamers dashed by, the white spray was seen to beat against the dark tarpaulins that covered their heaped-up cargoes. Next to these the black, surly-looking colliers were noted, huddled in a dense mass together, with the bare backs of the coalwhippers flashing among the rigging as, in hoisting the "Wallsend" from the hold, they leaped at intervals down upon the deck.

Behind, and through the tangled skeins of the rigging, the eye rested upon the old Suffrance wharves, with their peaked roofs and unwieldy cranes; and far at the back we caught sight of one solitary tree; whilst in the fog of the extreme distance the steeple of St. Mary's, Rotherhithe, loomed over the mast-heads—grey, dim, and spectral-like.

Then, as we turned round and looked towards the bridge, we caught glimpses of barges and boats moving in the broad arcs of light showing through the arches; while above the bridge-parapet were seen just the tops of moving carts, and omnibuses, and high-loaded railway wagons, hurrying along in opposite directions.

Glancing thence to the bridge-wharves on the same side of the river as ourselves, we beheld bales of goods dangling in the air from the cranes that projected from the top of "Nicholson's." Here alongside the quay lay Spanish schooners and brigs, laden with fruits; and as we cast our eye below, we saw puppet-like figures of men with cases of oranges on their backs, bending beneath the load, on their way across the dumb-lighter to the wharf.

Next came Billingsgate, and here we could see the white bellies of the fish showing in the market beneath, and streams of men passing backwards and forwards to the river side, where lay a small crowd of Dutch eel boats, with their gutta-percha-like hulls, and unwieldy, green-tipped rudders. Immediately beneath us was the brown, gravelled walk of the Custom House quay, where trim children strolled with their nursemaids, and hatless and yellow-legged Blue-coat Boys, and there were youths fresh from school, who had come either to have a peep at the shipping, or to skip and play among the barges.

From the neighbouring stairs boats pushed off continually, while men standing in the stern wriggled themselves along by working a scull behind, after the fashion of a fish's tail.

Here, near the front of the quay, lay a tier of huge steamers with gilt sterns and mahogany wheels, and their bright brass binnacles shining as if on fire in the sun. At the foremast head of one of these the "blue Peter" was flying as a summons to the hands on shore to come aboard, while the dense clouds of smoke that poured from the thick red funnel told that the boiler fires were ready lighted for starting.

Further on, might be seen the old "Perseus," the receiving-ship of the navy, with her topmasts down, her black sides towering high, like immense rampart-walls, out of the water, and her long white ventilating sacks hanging over the hatchways. Immediately beyond this, the eye could trace the Tower wharves, with their gravelled walks, and the high-capped and red-coated sentry pacing up and down them, and the square old grey lump of the Tower, with a turret at each of its four corners, peering over the water. In front of this lay another dense crowd of foreign vessels, and with huge lighters beside the wharf, while bales of hemp and crates of hardware swung from the cranes as they were lowered into the craft below.

In the distance, towered the huge massive warehouses of St. Katherine's Dock, with, their big signet letters on their sides, their many prison-like windows, and their cranes and doors to every floor. Beyond this, the view was barred out by the dense grove of masts that rose up from the water, thick as giant reeds beside the shore, and filmed over with the gray mist of vapour rising from the river so that their softened outlines melted gently into the dusk.

As we stood looking down upon the river, the hundred clocks of the hundred churches at our back, with the golden figures on their black dials shining in the sun, chimed the hour of noon, and in a hundred different tones; while solemnly above all boomed forth the deep metallic moan of St. Paul's; and scarcely had the great bell ceased humming in the air, before there rose the sharp tinkling of eight bells from the decks of the multitude of sailing vessels and steamers packed below.

Indeed, there was an exquisite charm in the many different sounds that smote the ear from the busy Port of London. Now we could hear the ringing of the "purlman's" bell, as, in his little boat, he flitted in and out among the several tiers of colliers to serve the grimy and half-naked coalwhippers with drink. Then would come the rattle of some heavy chain suddenly let go, and after this the chorus of many seamen heaving at the ropes; whilst, high above all roared the hoarse voice of some one on the shore, bawling through his hands to a mate aboard the craft. Presently came the clicking of the capstan-palls, telling of the heaving of a neighbouring anchor; and mingling with all this might be heard the rumbling of the wagons and carts in the streets behind, and the panting and throbbing of the passing river steamers in front, together with the shrill scream of the railway whistle from the terminus on the opposite shore.

In fine, look or listen in whatever direction we might, the many sights and sounds that filled the eye and ear told each its different tale of busy trade, bold enterprise, and bound-less capital. In the many bright-coloured flags that fluttered from the mastheads of the vessels crowding the port, we could read how all the corners of the earth had been ransacked each for its peculiar produce. The massive warehouses at the water-side looked *really* like the storehouses of the world's infinite products, and the tall mast-like factory chimneys behind us, with their black plumes of smoke streaming from them, told us how all around that port were hard at work fashioning the products into cunning fabrics.

Then, as we beheld the white clouds of steam from some passing railway engine puffed out once more from among the opposite roofs, and heard the clatter of the thousand vehicles in the streets hard by, and watched the dark tide of carts and wagons pouring over the bridge, and looked down the apparently endless vista of masts that crowded either side of the river—we could not help feeling how every power known to man was here used to bring and diffuse the riches of all parts of the world over our own, and indeed every other country.

¶ iii. *London from the Top of St. Paul's.*

There is, however, one other grand point of view from which the Metropolis may be contemplated, and which is not only extremely characteristic of the Capital, but so popular among strangers, that each new comer generally hastens, as soon as possible after his arrival in London, to the Golden Gallery to see the giant city spread out at his feet. Hence, this introduction to the Great World of London would be imcomplete if we omitted from our general survey to describe the peculiarities of the scene from that point.

It was an exquisitely bright and clear winter's morning on the day we mounted the five hundred and odd steps that lead to the gallery below the ball and cross crowning the cathedral—and yet the view was all smudgy and smeared with smoke. Still the haze, which hung like a thick curtain of shadow before and over everything, increased rather than diminished the monster sublimity of the city stretched out beneath us. It was utterly unlike London as seen below in its every-day bricken and hard-featured reality, seeming to be the spectral illusion of the Great Metropolis—such as one might imagine it in a dream—or the view of some fanciful cloud-land, rather than the most matter-of-fact and prosaic city in the world.

In the extreme distance the faint colourless hills, " picked out" with little bright patches of sunshine, appeared like some far-off shore—or rather as a *mirage* seen in the sky—for they were cut off from the nearer objects by the thick ring of fog that bathed the more distant buildings in impenetrable dusk. Clumps of houses and snatches of parks loomed here and there through the vapour, like distant islands rising out of a sea of smoke ; and isolated patches of palatial ·hospitals, or public buildings, shone in the accidental lights, as if they were miniature models sculptured out of white marble.

And yet dim and unsatisfactory as at first the view appeared, one would hardly on reflection have had it otherwise; since, to behold the Metropolis without its characteristic canopy of smoke, but with its thousand steeples standing out against the clear blue sky, sharp and definite in their outlines, as "cut pieces" in some theatrical scene, is to see London unlike itself—London without its native element. Assuredly, as the vast Capital lay beneath us, half hidden in mist, and with only a glimpse of its greatness visible, it had a much more sublime effect from the very inability of the mind to grasp the whole in all its literal details.

Still, there was quite enough visible to teach one that there was no such other city in the world. Immediately at our feet were the busy streets, like deep fissures in the earth, or as if the great bricken mass had split and cracked in all directions; and these were positively black at the bottom with the tiny-looking living crowd of vehicles and people pouring along the thoroughfares. What a dense dark flood of restless enterprise and competition it seemed ! And there rose to the ear the same roar from it, as rises from the sea at a distance.

The pavements, directly underneath us, were darkened on either side of the roadway with dense streams of busy little men, that looked almost like ants, hurrying along in opposite directions; whilst what with the closely-packed throng of carts, cabs, and omnibuses, the earth seemed all alive with tiny creeping things, as when one looks into the grass on a warm summer's day.

To peep down into the trough of Ludgate Hill was a sight that London alone could show ; for the tops of the vehicles looked so compact below that they reminded one of the illustrations of the " *testudo*," or tortoise-like floor, formed by the up-raised shields of the Roman soldiers, and on which, we are told, people might walk. Here were long lines of omnibuses, no bigger than children's tin toys, and crowded with pigmies on the roof—and tiny Hansom cabs, with doll-like drivers perched at the back—and the flat black and shiny roofs of miniature-like Broughams and private carriages—and brewers' drays, with the round backs of the stalwart team, looking like plump mice, and with their load of beer butts appearing

THE PENITENTIARY, MILLBANK.

no bigger than oyster-barrels—and black looking coal-wagons, that, as you gazed down into them, seemed more like coal-*boxes*—and top-heavy-like railway vans, with their little bales of cotton piled high in the air—and the wholesale linen-drapers' ugly attempts at phætons—and the butchers' carts, with little blue-smocked men in them—indeed every kind of London conveyance was there, all jammed into one dense throng, and so compactly, too, that one might easily have run along the tops of the various vehicles.

Then how strange it was to watch the line of conveyances move on, altogether, for a few paces, as if they were each part of one long railway train; and then suddenly come, every one, to a dead halt, as the counter stream of conveyances at the bottom of the hill was seen to force its way across the road.

As we turned now to note the other points of the surrounding scene, what a forest of church-steeples was seen to bristle around the huge dome on the top of which we were standing! The sight reminded one of the fact, that before the Great Fire there was a church to every three acres of ground within the City walls; for there were the spires still ranged close as nine-pins, and impressing one with a sense that every new street or public building must knock a number of them down, as if they *really* were so many stone skittles; for, as we peered into the fog of smoke, we could make out others in the misty back-ground, whose towers seemed suspended, like Mahomet's coffin, midway between heaven and earth, as if poised in the thick grey air; whilst, amid the steeple crowd, we could distinguish the tall column of the Monument, with its golden crown of flames at the top, and surrounded by a host of factory-chimneys that reminded one of the remaining pillars of the ruined temple of Serapis; so that it would have puzzled a simple foreigner to tell whether the City of London were more remarkable for its manufactures or its piety.

Then what a charm the mind experienced in recognizing the different places and objects that it knew under a wholly different aspect!

Yonder flows the Thames, circling half round the vast bricken mass that we call Lambeth and Southwark. It is a perfect arc of water; and the many bridges spanning it, like girders, seem to link the opposite shores of London into one Metropolis, like the mysterious ligament that joined the two Siamese into one life. Then *there* stands the Exchange, hardly bigger than a twelfth-cake ornament, and with the equestrian statue of Wellington, in front of it, smaller than the bronze horse surmounting some library time-piece; and *there* the Post-office, dwindled down to the dimensions of an architectural model. *That* low, square, flat-roofed building is the dumpy little Bank of England; and *that* ring of houses is Finsbury Circus; it looks from the elevation like the bricken mouth of a well.

This, we mentally exclaim, as we continue our walk round the gallery, is the Old Bailey, with the big cowl to its roof; and close beside it are the high and spiked walls of Newgate prison; we can see half down into the exercising wards of the felons from where we stand. And *this* open space is Smithfield. How desolate it looks now, stript of its market, and with its empty sheep-pens, that seem from the height to cover the ground like a grating! The dingy domed, solitary building beyond it, that appears, up here, like a "round-house," is the Sessions House, Clerkenwell; and *there*, amidst the haze, we can just distinguish another dome, almost the fellow of the one we are standing upon; it's the London University.

Next, glancing towards the river once more, we see, where the mist has cleared a bit, the shadowy form of the Houses of Parliament, with their half-finished towers; from the distance it has the appearance of some tiny Parian toy. But the Nelson and the York Columns are lost to us in the haze; so, too, is the Palace; and yet we can see the Hills of Highgate and Surrey; ay, and even the Crystal Palace, shimmering yonder like a bubble in the light.

So dense, however, is the pall of smoke about the City, that beyond London Bridge nothing is to be traced—neither the Tower, nor the Docks, nor the India House—and the outlines even of the neighbouring streets and turrets are blurred with the thick haze of the fumes, into half-spectral indistinctness. Though, were it otherwise, it would not, we repeat, be a true picture of London.

---

§ 5.

THE CONTRASTS OF LONDON.

It will, doubtlessly, have been noticed that, in speaking of London generally, it has been our wont here to use certain antithetical phrases, such as " wealth and want," " charity and crime," " palaces and workhouses," &c. It must not, however, be supposed that we have done this as a mere rhetorical flourish, for none can object to such piebald painting more than we. The mind's eye must be dim, indeed, that requires things to be put in the strong contrast of black and white before it can distinguish their peculiarities; and as the educated organ of the artist gets to prefer the sober browns and delicate neutral tints to the glare of positive colour, so long literary culture teaches one to despise those mere verbal trickeries which are termed " flowers of speech," and in which a showy arrangement of phrases is used as a cloak for a beggarly array of ideas.

But London is essentially a city of antithesis—a city where life itself is painted in pure black and white, and where the very extremes of society are seen in greater force than any-where else. This constitutes, as it were, the topographical essence of the Great Metropolis— the salient point of its character as a Capital—the distinctive mark which isolates it from all other towns and cities in the world; for though the middle class and the medium forms of civilized life prevail in the Metropolis to an unparalleled extent, this does not constitute its civic idiosyncracy; but it is simply the immensity of the commerce which springs from this same *unparalleled* prevalence of merchant people in London, and the consequent vastness of its wealth, as well as the unprecedented multitude of individuals attracted by such wealth to the spot, that forms the most prominent feature in every one's ideal picture of the town.

Then, again, it is owing partly to the excessive riches of London that its poverty appears to be in excess also—not that there *really* is, perhaps, a greater proportion of misery to be found within the metropolitan boundaries than within other large cities; but as London is the *largest* of all cities, there is naturally the *greatest* amount of human wretchedness to be seen concentrated within it; wretchedness, too, that is made to look still more wretched simply from the fact of its being associated with the most abundant comfort in the world.

Moreover, from the immense mass of houses, the mind is positively startled at the idea of there being any *houseless* in the Capital; and so, too, from the enormous consumption of food by the aggregate population, as well as the sumptuousness of the civic banquets, the anomaly of there being any *famishing* within it, becomes deeply impressed upon the mind; while the exceeding charity of the Metropolis, where many of the asylums, for the humblest even rival in architectural grandeur the dwelling-places of the proudest in the land, naturally, gives a deeper dye, from the mere contrast, to the criminality of the London people—whose pickpockets, it must be confessed, are among the most expert, and whose " dangerous classes" are certainly the most brutally ignorant in all Christendom.

For these reasons, therefore, we shall now proceed to set forth some of the principal social and moral contrasts to be noted in London town.

¶ 1. *Of the Riches and Poverty of London.*

Country people have a saying that the streets of London are paved with gold, and certainly, when we come to consider the aggregate wealth of the Metropolis, it amounts to so enormous a sum as to admit almost of the bullion being spread over the entire surface of the 1,750 miles of paving that make up the London thoroughfares.

In the first place, it has been already stated that the paving of the streets themselves costs no less than £14,000,000 ; so that when we come to learn that the expense of constructing the Metropolitan roadways amounts, upon an average, to £8,000 a mile, the very stones of the streets seem almost to be nuggets of gold.

Again, the treasures buried beneath the soil are equally inconceivable; for there are no less than 1,900 miles of gas-pipes laid under these same London stones, and about the same length of water-pipes as well; so that these, at only a shilling a foot each, would cost nearly half a million of money. Further, there are the subterranean tunnels of the sewers—the bricken bowels, as it were, of the Capital—of which there are also some hundreds of miles stretching through London beneath the pavement.

Hence we find that there is a vast amount of wealth sunk both *in* and *under* the London roadways, and that upon every square yard of earth, trodden under the feet of the people, there has been an enormous sum expended.

The amount of money spent, and the vastness of apparatus employed, simply in lighting London and the suburbs with gas, would seem to dispel all thoughts of poverty; for, according to the account of Mr. Barlow, the capital employed in the pipes, tanks, gas-holders, and apparatus of the aggregate London gas-works, amounts to between £3,000,000 and £4,000,000 ; and the cost of lighting averages more than half a million of money per annum —there being no less than 360,000 gas-lights fringing the streets, and consuming as much as 13,000,000 cubic feet of gas every night.

Those who have seen London only in the day-time, with its flood of life pouring through the arteries to its restless heart, know it not in *all* its grandeur. They have still, in order to comprehend the multiform sublimity of the great city, to contemplate it by night, afar off from an eminence. As noble a prospect as any in the world, it has been well said, is London viewed from the suburbs on a clear winter's evening. Though the stars be shining in the heavens, there is another firmament spread out below with its millions of bright lights glittering at the feet. Line after line sparkles like the trails left by meteors, and cutting and crossing one another till they are lost in the haze of distance. Over the whole, too, there hangs a lurid cloud, bright as if the monster city were in flames, and looking from afar like the sea at dusk, made phosphorescent by the million creatures dwelling within it.

Again, at night it is, that the strange anomalies of London life are best seen. As the hum of life ceases, and the shops darken, and the gaudy gin palaces thrust out their ragged and squalid crowds to pace the streets, London puts on its most solemn look of all. On the benches of the parks, in the niches of the bridges, and in the litter of the markets, are huddled together the homeless and the destitute. The only living things that haunt the streets are the poor wretched Magdalens, who stand shivering in their finery, waiting to catch the drunkard as he goes shouting homewards. There, on a door-step, crouches some shoeless child, whose day's begging has not brought it enough to purchase even the penny night's lodging that his young companions in beggary have gone to. Where the stones are taken up and piled high in the road, while the mains are being mended, and the gas streams from a tall pipe, in a flag of flame, a ragged crowd are grouped round the glowing coke fire —some smoking, and others dozing beside it.

Then, as the streets grow blue with the coming light, and the church spires and roof-tops stand out against the clear sky with a sharpness of outline that is seen only in London before its million chimneys cover the town with their smoke—then come sauntering forth the unwashed poor ; some with greasy wallets on their backs to hunt over each dust-heap, and eke out life by seeking refuse bones, or stray rags and pieces of old iron; others, whilst on their way to their work, are gathered at the corner of some street round the early breakfast-stall, and blowing saucers of steaming coffee, drawn from tall tin cans that have the red-hot charcoal shining crimson through the holes in the fire-pan beneath them ; whilst already the little slattern girl, with her basket slung before her, screams, " Water-*creases !*" through the sleeping streets.

But let us pass to a more cheering subject—let us, in the exceeding wealth of our city, forget for the moment its exceeding misery. We have already shown what a vast amount of treasure is buried, as we said before, not only *in*, but *under* the ground of London; and now we will proceed to portray the immense value of the buildings raised upon it. The gross rental, or yearly income from the houses in the metropolis, as assessed to the property and income tax, amounts to *twelve and a half millions of pounds*, so that at ten years' purchase, the aggregate value of the buildings throughout London, will amount to no less than the prodigious sum of *one hundred and twenty-five millions sterling.**

Nor is this all: this sum, enormous as it is, expresses the value of the houses only; and in order to understand the worth also of the furniture that they contain, we must consult the returns of the Assurance Companies, and thus we shall find that the gross property insured is valued at more than *one hundred and sixty-six million pounds.*†

* TABLE SHEWING THE ASSESSMENT OF PROPERTY TO THE INCOME TAX AND POOR RATES IN THE SEVERAL DISTRICTS THROUGHOUT LONDON.

Districts.	Number of Inhabited Houses.	Assessment. Income Tax for the year 1843.	Assessment. Poor Rate for the year 1849.	Average Income Tax per House.	Average Poor Rate per House.	Districts.	Number of Inhabited Houses.	Assessment. Income Tax for the year 1843.	Assessment. Poor Rate for the year 1849.	Average Income Tax per House.	Average Poor Rate per House.
WEST DISTRICTS.		£	£	£	£	**EAST DISTRICTS.**		£	£	£	£
Kensington	17,151	876,854	650,115	51·1	37·7	Shoreditch	15,337	325,846	215,694	21·2	14·0
Chelsea	7,591	167,897	166,998	22·1	21·9	Bethnal Green	13,298	110,072	130,159	8·2	8·4
St. George, Hanover Square	8,792	1,009,572	675,440	114·7	76·8	Whitechapel	8,812	209,192	177,719	23·7	20·1
Westminster	6,642	272,790	223,200	41·0	33·6	St. George in the East	6,146	184,543	151,343	30·0	21·3
St. Martin in the Fields	2,307	226,852	249,555	98·3	108·0	Stepney	16,259	289,093	279,461	18·3	17·1
St. James, Westminster	3,399	416,843	412,823	122·6	121·4	Poplar	6,881	258,979	193,940	37·9	28·3
Total	45,882	2,970,808	3,378,131	64·7	73·6	Total	66,683	1,386,725	1,148,316	20·7	17·2
NORTH DISTRICTS.						**SOUTH DISTRICTS.**					
Marylebone	15,826	1,132,324	836,372	72·1	52·8	St. Saviour, Southwark	4,600	71,282	122,156	15·4	26·5
Hampstead	1,719	66,656	69,357	38·7	40·3	St. Olave, ditto	2,360	94,231	86,140	39·9	36·5
Pancras‡	18,584	1,251,737	572,731	67·3	30·8	Bermondsey	7,007	107,225	127,667	15·3	18·2
Islington	13,528	309,629	329,781	22·8	23·9	St. George, Southwark	6,992	153,830	113,999	22·0	16·3
Hackney	9,818	170,347	196,073	17·3	14·8	Newington	10,458	207,877	165,900	19·8	15·8
Total	59,475	2,930,693	2,004,314	33·6	33·7	Lambeth	20,447	534,372	458,861	26·1	22·4
						Wandsworth	8,276	368,526	231,476	44·5	27·9
CENTRAL DISTRICTS						Camberwell	9,412	208,338	209,337	22·1	22·2
St. Giles	4,700	305,880	232,129	65·0	49·3	Rotherhithe	2,792	59,677	58,909	21·3	21·0
Strand	3,962	353,786	220,872	89·2	59·8	Greenwich	14,383	290,534	261,987	20·1	18·2
Holborn	4,311	261,665	51,206	60·6	11·9	Lewisham	5,927	150,359	159,283	25·3	26·8
Clerkenwell	7,224	300,928	188,372	41·6	26·0	Total	92,654	2,246,251	1,995,715	24·2	21·5
St. Luke	6,349	193,443	141,658	30·4	22·3						
East London	4,739	202,598	139,767	42·7	29·2						
West London	2,657	256,278	124,540	96·4	46·8						
London City	7,297	1,279,148	1,562,428	175·2	214·2						
Total	41,239	3,153,726	2,760,972	76·4	93·6	Total for all London	305,933	12,688,203	12287448	41·1	40·1

† The revenue derived from the duty paid on Insurances, amounts in round numbers to £250,000 for the London offices only; and this, at 3s. per £100, gives upwards of £166,000,000 for the aggregate value of the London Assurances, though only *two-fifths* of the houses are said to be insured.

‡ The reason of their being so great a difference between the assessments for the income tax and poor's rates in this district, is because the Inns of Court are estimated in the one and not in the other.

If, then, the value of the house property throughout the Metropolis amounts to so incomprehensible a sum, it is almost impossible to believe that any man among us should want a roof to shelter his head at night.

The scenes, however, that are to be witnessed in the winter time at the Refuge for the Destitute, in Playhouse Yard, tell a very different tale; for those who pay a visit to the spot, as we did some few winters back, will find a large crowd of houseless poor gathered about the asylum at dusk, waiting for the first opening of the doors, and with their blue, shoeless feet, ulcerous with the cold, from long exposure to the snow and ice in the street, and the bleak, stinging wind blowing through their rags. To hear the cries of the hungry, shivering children, and the wrangling of the greedy men assembled there to obtain shelter for the night, and a pound of dry bread, is a thing to haunt one for life. At the time of our visit there were four hundred and odd creatures, utterly destitute, collected outside the door. Mothers with infants at their breast—fathers with boys clinging to their side—the friendless—the penniless—the shirtless—the shoeless—breadless—homeless; in a word, the very poorest of this the very richest city in the world.

The records of this extraordinary institution, too, tell a fearful history. There is a world of wisdom and misery to be read in them. The poor who are compelled to avail themselves of its eleemosynary shelter, warmth, and food, come from *all* nations. Here are destitute Frenchmen, Germans, Italians, Scotchmen, Irishmen, Africans, Americans, Spaniards, Portuguese, Poles—besides the destitute of our own country; and there are artisans belonging to all trades as well—compositors, carpenters, tailors, shoemakers, smiths, seamen, sweeps, engineers, watchmakers, artists, clerks and shopmen, milliners and gentlemen's servants, and navvies, and surveyors—indeed the beggared man of every craft and calling whatsoever.

The misery of many that are driven to seek the hospitality of such asylums is assuredly of their own making, and there are many there, too, who pursue mendicancy as a profession, preferring the precarious gains of begging to the regular income of industry. Many who trade upon the sympathy of those who desire to ease the sufferings of the deserving poor.

But with these there also are mixed not a few whose callings yield a subsistence only in the summer time—brickmakers, agricultural labourers, garden women, and the like—whose means of subsistence fails them at the very season when the elements conspire to render their necessities more urgent.

The poverty indicated by the journals of the refuge for the houseless, is quite as startling to all generous natures as are the returns of the house property of London. For we found—making allowance, too, for those who had remained more than one night in the establishment—that, since the opening of the asylum in 1820, as many as 1,141,588 homeless individuals had received shelter within the walls; and that upwards of $2\frac{3}{4}$ millions of pounds, or nearly 10,025 tons, of bread had been distributed among the poor wretches.

If, then, we are proud of our prodigious riches, surely we cannot but feel humbled at our prodigious poverty also.

Again, we turn to the brighter side of the London picture, and once more we ourselves are startled with the army of figures, marshalling the wondrous wealth of this Great Metropolis.

The late Mr. Rothschild called the English Metropolis, in 1832, the bank of the whole world: "I mean," said he, "that all transactions in India and China, in Germany and Russia, are guided and settled here." And no wonder that the statement should be made; for we learn that the amount of capital at the command of the entire London bankers may be estimated at *sixty-four millions of pounds;** and that the deposits or sums ready to be

* See table of the bill currency of the United Kingdom in Banfield's "Statistical Companion" for 1854.

invested by the insurance companies may be taken at ten million pounds, whilst the amount employed in discounts, in the Metropolis alone, equals the inconceivable sum of *seventy-eight million pounds*.

Indeed, it is asserted upon good authority, that the loans of one London house only, exceeded, in the year 1841, thirty millions sterling, which is upon an average nearly three millions of money per month; such loans occasionally amounting to as much as seven hundred thousand pounds in a single day.

But this is not all. In London there exists an establishment called the "clearing-house," whither are taken the checks and bills, on the authority of which a great part of the money paid and received by bankers is made, and where the checks and bills drawn on one banking-house are cancelled by those which it holds on others. In the appendix to the Second Report of the Parliamentary Committee on Banks there is a return of the payments made through the clearing-house for the year 1839, and though all the sums under £100 were omitted in the statement, the total was upwards of 954 million pounds! whilst the annual payments, through *three* bankers only, exceeded 100 millions sterling.

Such an extent of commerce is not only unparalelled, but requires as great faith as a miracle to enable us to credit it. Nevertheless, a walk to the several docks of London—those vast emporia of the riches of the entire world—will enable even the most sceptical to arrive at some sense of the magnitude of our metropolitan trade.

These docks, indeed, are the very focus of the wealth of our merchant princes. The cranes creak again with the mass of riches. In the warehouses are stored heaps of indigo and dye stuffs, that are, as it were, so many ingots of untold gold. Above and below ground you see piles upon piles of treasure that the eye cannot compass. The wealth appears as boundless as the very sea it has traversed, and the brain aches in an attempt to comprehend the amount of riches before, above, and beneath it. There are acres upon acres of treasures —more than enough, one would fancy, to enrich the people of the whole globe.

As you pass along *this* quay, the air is pungent with the vast stores of tobacco. At *that* it overpowers you with the fumes of rum. Then you are nearly sickened with the stench of hides and huge bins of horns; and shortly afterwards, the atmosphere is fragrant with coffee and spice. Nearly everywhere you see stacks of cork, or else yellow bins of sulphur, or lead-coloured copper ore. As you enter one warehouse, the flooring is sticky, as if it had been newly tarred, with the sugar that has leaked through the tiers of casks; and as you descend into the dark vaults, you see long lines of lights hanging from the black arches, and lamps flitting about midway in the air. Here you sniff the fumes of the wine—and there are acres of hogsheads of it—together with the peculiar fungous smell of dry-rot.

Along the quay you see, among the crowd, men with their faces blue with indigo, and gaugers with their long brass tipped rules dripping with spirit fresh from the casks they have been probing. Then will come a group of flaxen-haired sailors, chattering German; and next a black seaman, with a red-cotton handkerchief twisted turban-like round his head. Presently, a blue-smocked butcher pushes through the throng, with fresh meat and a bunch of cabbage in the tray on his shoulder; and shortly afterwards comes a broad straw-hatted mate, carrying green parroquets in a wooden cage. Here, too, you will see sitting on a bench a sorrowful-looking woman, with new bright cooking-tins at her feet, telling you she is some emigrant preparing for her voyage.

Then the jumble of sounds as you pass along the dock blends in anything but sweet concord. The sailors are singing boisterous nigger-songs from the Yankee ship just entering the dock; the cooper is hammering at the casks on the quay; the chains of the cranes, loosed of their weight, rattle as they fly up again; the ropes splash in the water; some captain shouts his orders through his hands; a goat bleats from a ship in the basin; and empty casks roll along the stones with a hollow drum-like sound. Here the heavy-laden ships have their gunwales down in the water, far below the quay, and you descend to them by ladders,

TICKET-OF-LEAVE MEN.

(From a Photograph by Herbert Watkins, of Regent Street.)

whilst in another basin the craft stand high up out of the dock, so that their green copper-sheeting is almost level with the eye of the passenger, and above his head a long line of bowsprits stretch far over the quay, with spars and planks hanging from them as a temporary gangway to each vessel.

"It is impossible," says Mr. M'Culloch, "to form any accurate estimate of the amount of the trade of the Port of London. But if we include the produce conveyed into and from the Port, as well as the home and foreign markets, it will not," he tells us, "be overrated at the prodigious sum of *sixty-five millions sterling* per annum."

Of this enormous extent of commerce the Docks are the headquarters.

But if the incomprehensibility of this wealth rises to sublimity, assuredly the want that co-exists with it is equally incomprehensible and equally sublime.

Pass from the quay and warehouses to the courts and alleys that surround them, and the mind is as bewildered with the destitution of the one place as it is with the superabundance of the other. Many come to see the riches, but few the poverty abounding in absolute masses round the far-famed Port of London.

He, therefore, who wishes to behold one of the most extraordinary and least known scenes of the Metropolis, should wend his way to the London Dock gates at half-past seven in the morning. There he will see congregated, within the principal entrance, masses of men of all ranks, looks, and natures. Decayed and bankrupt master butchers are there, and broken-down master bakers, publicans, and grocers, and old soldiers, sailors, Polish refugees, *quondam* gentlemen, discharged lawyers' clerks, "suspended" government officials, almsmen, pensioners, servants, thieves—indeed every one (for the work requires no training) who wants a loaf, and who is willing to work for it. The London Dock is one of the few places in the Metropolis where men can get employment without character or recommendation.

As the hour approaches eight, you know by the stream pouring through the gates, and the rush towards particular spots, that the " calling foremen" have made their appearance, and that the " casual men" are about to be taken on for the day.

Then begins the scuffling and scrambling, and stretching forth of countless hands high in the air, to catch the eye of him whose nod can give them work. As the foreman calls from a book the names, some men jump up on the back of others, so as to lift themselves high above the rest and attract his notice. All are shouting; some cry aloud his surname, and some his christian name; and some call out their own names to remind him that they are there. Now the appeal is made in Irish blarney; and now in broken English.

Indeed, it is a sight to sadden the most callous to see thousands of men struggling there for only one day's hire, the scuffle being made the fiercer by the knowledge that hundreds out of the assembled throng must be left to idle the day out in want. To look in the faces of that hungry crowd is to see a sight that is to be ever remembered. Some are smiling to the foreman to coax him into remembrance of them; others, with their protruding eyes, are terribly eager to snatch at the hoped-for pass for work. Many, too, have gone there and gone through the same struggle, the same cries, and have left after all without the work they had screamed for.

Until we saw with our own eyes this scene of greedy despair, we could not have believed that there was so mad an anxiety to work, and so bitter a want of it among so vast a body of men. No wonder that the calling foreman should be often carried many yards away by the struggle and rush of the multitude around him, seeking employment at his hands! One of the officials assured us that he had more than once been taken off his feet, and hurried to a distance of a quarter of a mile by the eagerness of the impatient crowd clamouring for work.

If, however, the men fail in getting taken on at the commencement of the day, they then retire to the waiting-yard, at the back of the Docks, there to remain hour after hour in hope that the wind may blow them some stray ship, so that other gangs may be wanted, and the calling foreman come to seek fresh hands there.

It is a sad sight, too, to see the poor fellows waiting in these yards to be hired at fourpence per hour—for such are the terms given in the after-part of the day. There, seated on long benches ranged against the wall, they remain, some telling their miseries, and some their crimes, to one another, while others doze away their time. Rain or sunshine, there are always plenty of them ready to catch the stray shilling or eightpence for the two or three hours' labour. By the size of the shed you can judge how many men sometimes stay there, in the pouring rain, rather than run the chance of losing the stray hour's job. Some loiter on the bridge close by, and directly that their practised eye or ear tells them the calling foreman is in want of another gang, they rush forward in a stream towards the gate— though only six or eight at most can be hired out of the hundred or more that are waiting. Then the same mad fight takes place again as in the morning; the same jumping on benches; the same raising of hands; the same entreaties; ay! and the same failure as before.

It is strange to mark the change that takes place in the manner of the men when the foreman has left. Those that have been engaged go smiling to their labour, while those who are left behind give vent to their disappointment in abuse of him before whom they had been supplicating and smiling but a few minutes previously.

There are not less than 20,000 souls living by Dock labour in the Metropolis. The London Docks are worked by between 1,000 to 3,000 hands, according as the business is brisk or slack—that is, according as the wind is, fair or foul, for the entry of the ships into the Port of London.

Hence there are some thousands of stomachs deprived of food by the mere chopping of the breeze. "It's an ill wind," says the proverb, "that blows nobody any good;" and until we came to investigate the condition of the Dock labourer, we could not have believed it possible that near upon 2,000 souls in one place alone lived, chameleon-like, upon the very air; or that an easterly wind could deprive so many of bread. It is, indeed, "a nipping and an eager air."

That the sustenance of thousands of families should be as fickle as the very breeze itself, that the weather-cock should be the index of daily want or daily ease to such a vast body of men, women, and children, is a climax of misery and wretchedness that could hardly have been imagined to exist in the very heart of our greatest wealth.

Nor is it less wonderful, when we come to consider the immense amount of food consumed in London, that there should be such a thing as *want* known among us.

The returns of the cattle-market, for instance, tell us that the population of London consume some 277,000 bullocks, 30,000 calves, 1,480,000 sheep, and 34,000 pigs; and these, it is estimated by Mr. Hicks, are worth between seven and eight millions sterling.

In the way of bread, the Londoners are said to eat up no less than 1,600,000 quarters of wheat.

Then the list of vegetables supplied by the aggregate London "green markets"—including Covent-garden, Farringdon, Portman, the Borough, and Spitalfields—is as follows:—

310,464,000	pounds	. . . . .	potatoes
89,672,000	plants	. . . . .	cabbages
14,326,000	heads	. . . . .	broccoli and cauliflowers
32,648,000	roots	. . . . .	turnips
1,850,000	junks	. . . . .	ditto, tops
16,817,000	roots	. . . . .	carrots
438,000	bushels	. . . .	peas
133,400	,,	. . . . .	beans
221,100	,,	. . . . .	French beans

19,872	dozen	. . . . .	vegetable marrows
19,560	dozen bundles	. . .	asparagus
34,800	,, ,,	. . .	celery
91,200	,, ,,	. . . .	rhubarb
4,492,800	plants	. . . . .	lettuces
132,912	dozen hands	. . .	radishes
1,489,600	bushels	. . . . .	onions
94,000	dozen bundles	. . .	ditto (spring)
87,360	bushels	. . . . .	cucumbers
32,900	dozen bundles	. . .	herbs*

Again, the list of the gross quantity of fish that is eaten at the London dinners or suppers is equally enormous :—

WET FISH.

3,480,000	pounds of	salmon and salmon trout	29,000 boxes, 14 fish per box
4,000,000	,,	live cod	averaging 10 lbs. each
26,880,000	,,	soles	averaging $\frac{1}{4}$ lb. each
6,752,000	,,	whiting	averaging 6 ounces
5,040,000	,,	haddock	averaging 2 lbs. each
33,600,000	,,	plaice	averaging 1 lb. each
23,250,000	,,	mackerel	averaging 1 lb. each
42,000,000	,,	fresh herrings	250,000 barrels, 700 fish per barrel
252,000,000	,,	,, ,, . . .	in bulk
4,000,000	,,	sprats	
1,505,280	,,	eels from Holland . . . }	6 fish per 1 lb.
127,680	,,	,, England and Ireland }	

DRY FISH.

4,200,000	. . .	barrelled cod	15,000 barrels, 50 fish per barrel
8,000,000	. . .	dried salt cod . . .	5 lbs. each
10,920,000	. . .	smoked haddock . .	25,000 barrels, 300 fish per barrel
10,600,000	. . .	bloaters	265,000 baskets, 150 fish per basket
14,000,000	. . .	red herrings	100,000 barrels, 500 fish per barrel
96,000	. . .	dried sprats	9,600 large bundles, 30 fish per bundle

SHELL FISH.

	. . .	oysters	309,935 barrels, 1,600 fish per barrel
1,200,000	. . .	lobsters	averaging 1 lb. each fish
600,000	. . .	crabs	averaging 1 lb. each fish
192,295 gallons	.	shrimps	324 to the pint
24,300½ bushels	.	whelks	224 to the $\frac{1}{2}$ bushel
50,400	,, .	mussels	1,000 to the $\frac{1}{2}$ bushel
32,400	,, .	cockles	2,000 to the $\frac{1}{2}$ bushel
76,000	,, .	periwinkles	4,000 to the $\frac{1}{2}$ bushel

* These returns, and those of the fish, cattle, and poultry markets, were originally collected by the author, for the first time in London, from the several salesmen at the markets, and cost both much time and money ; though the gentlemen who fabricate books on London, from Mr. M'Culloch downwards, do not hesitate to dig their scissors into the results, taking care to do with them the same as is done with the stolen handkerchiefs in Petticoat Lane—viz., pick out the name of the owner.

Further, in the matter of game poultry, the metropolitan consumption from one market alone (Leadenhall) amounts to the following :—

TAME BIRDS AND DOMESTIC FOWLS.

1,266,000	fowls
188,000	geese
235,000	ducks
60,000	turkeys
284,500	pigeons

Total, 2,033,500

WILD BIRDS, OR ANIMALS, OR GAME.

45,000	grouse
84,500	partridges
43,500	pheasants
10,000	teal
30,000	widgeons
60,000	snipes
28,000	plovers
213,000	larks
39,500	wild birds
48,000	hares
680,000	rabbits

Total, 1,281,500

By way of dessert to this enormous banquet, the supply of fruit furnished by all the London markets is equally inconceivable :—

686,000	bushels of .	apples
353,000	,, .	pears
173,200	dozen lbs. of	cherries
176,500	bushels of .	plums
5,333	,, .	greengages
16,450	,, .	damsons
4,900	,, .	bullace
276,700	,, .	gooseberries
171,000	sieves . .	currants (red)
108,000	,, . .	currants (black)
24,000	,, . .	currants (white)
1,527,500	pottles . .	strawberries
35,250	,, . .	raspberries
127,940	,, . .	mulberries
9,018	bushels of .	hazel nuts
518,400	lbs. of . .	filberts

Then, as a fitting companion to this immense amount of solid food, the quantity of liquids consumed is as follows :—

65,000 pipes of wines
2,000,000 gallons of spirits
43,200,000 gallons of porter and ale
19,215,000,000 gallons of water, supplied by the several companies to the houses.

And lastly, for the purposes of heating and lighting, the Metropolis burns no less than 3,000,000 tons of coal.

But if the great meat and vegetable and poultry markets of the Metropolis are indications of the good living indulged in by a large proportion of the people, there are at the same time other markets which may be cited as proofs of the privation undergone by large numbers also. The wretched man who lives by picking up bits of rag in the street—and there is a considerable army of them—cannot be said to add much to the gross consumption of the Capital; still he even attends *his* market, and has his exchange, even though he deals in *coupons* of linen, and traffics in old iron rather than the precious metals.

Let us, then, by way of contrast to the luxury indicated by the preceding details, follow the bone-grubber to his mart—the exchange for old clothes and rags.

The traffic here consists not of ship-loads of valuables brought from the four quarters of the globe, but simply of wallets of refuse gathered from the areas, mews, and alleys of every part of London; for that which is bought and sold in this locality is not made up of the choicest riches of the world, but simply of what others have cast aside as worthless. Indeed, the wealth in which the merchants of Rag Fair deal, so far from being of any value to ordinary minds, is merely the offal of the well-to-do—the skins sloughed by gentility—the *debris*, as it were, of the fashionable world.

The merchandize of this quarter consists not of gold-dust and ivory, but literally of old metal and bones; not of bales of cotton and pieces of rich silk, but of bits of dirty rag, swept from shop doors and picked up and washed by the needy finders; not of dye-stuffs, nor indigo, nor hides, but of old soleless shoes, to be converted by the alchemy of science into Prussian blue wherewith to tint, perhaps, some nobles' robes, and bits of old iron to be made into new.

Some dozen years ago, one of the Hebrew merchant dealers in old clothes purchased the houses at the back of Phil's Buildings—a court leading out of Houndsditch, immediately facing St. Mary Axe, and formed the present market, now styled the "Old Clothes Exchange," and where Rag Fair may be said to be at present centralized. Prior to this, the market was held in the streets.

About three or four o'clock in winter, and four or five in summer, are the busiest periods at the "Old Clothes Exchange;" and then the passage leading to the Mart from Houndsditch will be seen to be literally black with the mob of old-clothes men congregated outside the gates. Almost all have bags on their backs, and not a few three or four old hats in their hands, while here and there faces with grizzly beards will be seen through the vista of hook noses.

Immediately outside the gateway, at the end of the crowded court, stands the celebrated Barney Aaron, the janitor, with out-stretched hand waiting to receive the halfpenny toll, demanded of each of the buyers and sellers who enter; and with his son by his side, with a leathern pouch filled with half a hundred weight of coppers he has already received, and ready to give change for any silver that may be tendered.

As the stranger passes through the gate, the odour of the collocated old clothes and old rags, and old shoes, together with, in the season, half-putrid hare skins, is almost overpowering. The atmosphere of the place has a peculiar sour smell blended with the mildewy or fungous odour of what is termed "mother;" indeed the stench is a compound of mouldiness, mustiness, and fustiness—a kind of "*bouquet de mille sewers,*" that is far from pleasant to christian nostrils.

The hucksters of tatters as they pour in with their bundles at their backs, one after another, are surrounded by some half-dozen of the more eager Jews, some in greasy gaberdines extending to the heels and clinging almost as tight to the frame as ladies' wet bathing-gowns. Two or three of them seize the hucksters by the arm, and feel the contents of the bundle at his back; and a few tap them on the shoulder as they all clamour for the first sight of the contents of their wallets.

"Ha' you cot any preaking (broken pieces)?" cries one who buys old coats, to cut into cloth caps.

"Cot any fustian, old cordsh, or old poots?" "Yer know me," says another, in a wheedling tone. "I'm little Ikey, the pest of puyers, and always gives a coot prishe."

Such, indeed, is the anxiety and eagerness of the Israelitish buyers to get the first chance of the bargains, that it is as much as the visitor can do to force his way through the greedy and greasy mob.

Once past the entrance, however, the stranger is able to obtain a tolerable view of the place.

The "Exchange" consists of a large square plot of ground, about an acre in extent, and surrounded by a low hoarding, with a narrow sloping roof, hardly wider indeed than the old eaves to farm-houses, and projecting far enough forward to shelter one person from the rain. Across this ground are placed four double rows of benches, ranged back to back, and here sit the sellers of old clothes, with their unsightly and unsavoury store of garments strewn or piled on the ground at their feet, whilst between the rows of petty dealers pass the merchant buyers on the look-out for "bargains."

The first thing that strikes the mind is, that a greater bustle and eagerness appear to rage among the buyers of the refuse of London, than among the traders in the more valuable commodities. Every lot exposed for sale seems to have fulfilled to the utmost the office for which it was designed, and now that its uses are ended, and it seems to be utterly worthless, the novice to such scenes cannot refrain from marvelling what remaining quality can possibly give the least value to the rubbish.

Here a "crockman" (a seller of crockery ware), in a bright-red plush waistcoat and knee-breeches, and with legs like balustrades, sits beside his half-emptied basket of china and earthen-ware, while at his feet is strewn the apparently worthless collection of paletots, and cracked Wellingtons, and greasy napless hats, for which he has exchanged his jugs, basins, and spar ornaments. A few yards from him is a woman, enveloped in a coachman's drab and many-caped box-coat, with a pair of men's cloth boots on her feet, and her limp-looking straw bonnet flattened down on her head, from repeated loads; the ground before her, too, is littered with old tea-coloured stays, and bundles of wooden busks, and little bits of whalebone, whilst beside her, on the seat, lies a small bundle of old parasols tied together, and looking like a quiver full of arrows. In the winter you may see the same woman surrounded with hare skins; some so old and stiff that they seem frozen, and the fresher ones looking shiny and crimson as red tinsel.

Now you come, as you push your way along the narrow passage between the seats, to a man with a small mound of old boots, some of which have the soles torn off, and the broken threads showing underneath like the stump of teeth; others are so brown from long want of blacking, that they seem almost to be pieces of rusty metal, and others again are speckled all over with small white spots of mildew. Beside another huckster is piled a little hillock of washed-out light waistcoats, and old cotton drawers, and straw-bonnets half in shreds. Then you see a Jew boy holding up the remains of a theatrical dress, consisting of a black velvet body stuck all over with bed furniture ornaments, and evidently reminding the young Israelite of some "soul-stirring" melo-drama that he has seen on the Saturday evening at the Pavilion Theatre.

A few steps farther on, you find one of the merchants blowing into the fur of some old imitation-sable muff, that has gone as foxy as a Scotchman's whiskers. Next, your attention is fixed upon a black-chinned and lanthorn-jawed bone-grubber, clad in dirty greasy rags, with his wallet emptied on the stones, and the bones from it, as well as bits of old iron and horse-shoes, and pieces of rags, all sorted into different lots before him; and as he sits there, anxiously waiting for a purchaser, he munches a hunk of mouldy pie crust that he has had given to him on his rounds.

In one part of the Exchange you recognize the swarthy features of some well-known travelling tinker, with a complexion the colour of curry powder, and hands brown, as if recently tarred; while in front of *him* is reared a pyramid of old battered britannia-metal teapots and saucepans; and next to him sits an umbrella mender, before whom is strewn a store of whalebone ribs, and ferruled sticks fitted with sharp pointed bone handles.

Then the buyers, too, are almost as picturesque and motley a group as the sellers, for the purchasers are of all nations, and habited in every description of costume. Some are Greeks, others Swiss, others again Germans; some have come there to buy up the rough old charity clothing and the army great coats for the Irish "market." One man with a long flowing beard and tattered gaberdine, that shines like a tarpaulin with the grease, and who is said to be worth thousands, is there again, as indeed he is day after day, to see if he cannot add another sixpence to his hoard, by dabbling in the rags and refuse with which the ground is covered. Mark how he is wheedling, and whining, and shrugging up his shoulders to that poor wretch, in the hope of inducing him to part with the silver pencil-case he has "found" on his rounds, for a few pence less than its real value.

As the purchasers go pacing up and down the narrow pathways, threading their way, now along the old bottles, bonnets, and rags, and now among the bones, the old metal and stays, the gowns, the hats, and coats, a thick-lipped Jew boy shouts from his high stage in the centre of the market, "Shinsher peer, an aypenny a glarsh!—an aypenny a glarsh, shinsher peer!" Between the seats women worm along carrying baskets of trotters, and screaming as they go, "Legs of mutton, two for a penny! Who'll give me a hansel." And after them comes a man with a large tray of "fatty cakes."

In the middle of the market, too, stands another dealer in street luxuries, with a display of pickled whelks, like huge snails floating in saucers of brine; and next to him is a sweet-meat stall, with a crowd of young Israelites gathered round the keeper eagerly gambling with marbles for "Albert rock" and "Boneyparte's ribs."

At one end of the Exchange stands a coffee and beer shop, inside of which you find Jews playing at draughts, or wrangling as they settle for the articles which they have bought or sold; while, even as you leave by the gate that leads towards Petticoat Lane, there is a girl stationed outside with a horse-pail full of ice, and dispensing halfpenny egg-cupsful of what appears to be very much like frozen soap-suds, and shouting, as she shakes the bucket, and makes the ice in it rattle like broken glass, "Now, boys! here's your coolers, only an aypenny a glass!—an aypenny a glass!"

In fine, it may truly be said that in no other part of the entire world is such a scene of riot, rags, filth, and feasting to be witnessed, as at the Old Clothes Exchange in Houndsditch.

¶ ii. *The Charity and the Crime of London.*

The broad line of demarcation separating our own time from that of all others, is to found in the fuller and more general development of the human sympathies.

Our princes and nobles are no longer the patrons of prize-fights, but the presidents of benevolent institutions. Instead of the bear-gardens and cock-pits that formerly flourished in every quarter of the town, our Capital bristles and glitters with its thousand palaces for the indigent and suffering poor. If we are distinguished among nations for our exceeding wealth, assuredly we are equally illustrious for our abundant charity. Almost every want or ill that can distress human nature has some palatial institution for the mitigation of it. We have rich societies for every conceivable form of benevolence—for the visitation of the sick; for the cure of the maimed, and the crippled; for the alleviation of the pangs of child-birth; for giving shelter to the houseless, support to the aged and the infirm, homes to the orphan and the foundling; for the reformation of juvenile offenders and prostitutes, the reception of the children of convicts, the liberation of debtors, the suppression of vice; for educating the ragged, teaching the blind, the deaf and the dumb; for guarding and soothing the mad; protecting the idiotic, clothing the naked, and feeding the hungry. Nor does our charity cease with our own countrymen; for the very ship-of-war which we build to destroy the people of other lands, we ultimately convert into a floating hospital to save and comfort them in the hour of their affliction among us.

Of the sums devoted to the maintenance of these various institutions, the excellent little work of Mr. Sampson Low, jun., on the "Charities of London in 1852-3," enables us to come to a ready and very accurate conclusion.

Accordingly we find, upon reference to this work, that there are altogether in the Metropolis 530 charitable institutions, viz.:—

Ninety-two Medical Charities, having an aggregate income during the year of £266,925.

Twelve Societies for the Preservation of Life, Health, and Public Morals, whose yearly incomes equal altogether, £35,717.

Seventeen for Reclaiming the Fallen, or Penitentiary and Reformatory Asylums = £39,486.

Thirteen for the Relief of Street Destitution and Distress = £18,326.

Fourteen for the Relief of Specific Distress = £27,387.

One hundred and twenty-six Asylums for the Reception of the Aged = £87,630.

Nine for the Benefit of the Blind, Deaf and Dumb = £25,050.

Thirteen Asylums for the Maintenance of Orphans = £45,464.

Fifteen for the Maintenance of other Children (exclusive of Parochial Schools) = £88,228.

Twenty-one Societies for the Promotion of Schools and their efficiency = £72,247.

Twenty-five Jewish Miscellaneous Charities = £10,000.

Nineteen for the Benefit of the Industrious = £9,124.

Twelve Benevolent Pension Societies = £23,667.

Fifteen Clergy Aid Funds = £35,301.

Thirty-two other Professional and Trade Benevolent Funds = £53,467.

Thirty Trade Provident = £25,000.

Forty-three Home Mission Societies (several combining extensive operations abroad) = £319,705.

Fourteen Foreign Mission Societies = £459,668.*

To this list must be added five unclassed Societies = £3,252.

Also an amount of £160,000, raised during the year for special funds, including the proposed Wellington College, the new Medical College, the Wellington Benevolent Fund, &c. —making altogether, as the subject of our "Report,"—

Five hundred and thirty Charitable Societies in London, with an aggregate amount disbursed during the year of £1,805,635.†

But the above aggregate amount of the metropolitan charitable donations, large as the sum is, refers only to the moneys entrusted to public *societies* to distribute. Of the amount disbursed by *private* individuals in charity to their poorer neighbours, of course no accurate estimate can be formed. But if we assume that as much money is given in private as in public charity (and from our inquiries among the London beggars, and especially the "screeving" or begging-letter writing class, we have reason to believe that there is much more), we shall have, in round numbers, a gross total of *three and a half millions* of money annually distributed by the rich among the poor.

Now, as a set-off against this noble indication of the benevolence of our people, we will

---

* The sales of Bibles and other religious publications, realising above £100,000, is not included in either of the last-mentioned amounts.

† These figures have been compiled from the various statements of the year during 1852-3, for the which they are respectively made up to—averaging March 31, 1853. Grammar Schools and Educational Establishments, as Merchant Taylors' and St. Paul's, are not included—neither Parochial and other Local Schools—or Miscellaneous Endowments in the gift of City Companies and Parishes.

ble the Londoner's pride by giving him a faint notion of the criminality of a large
.ondon folk.

Reports of the Poor-Law Commissioners we find that between the years 1848 and
.e were no less than 143,064 vagrants, or tramps, admitted into the casual wards of
.khouses throughout the metropolitan districts.*

There are, then, no less than 143,000 admissions of vagrants to the casual wards of the
Metropolis in the course of the year; and granting that many of these temporary inmates
appear more than once in the calculation (for it is the habit of the class to go from one
eleemosynary asylum to another), still we shall have a large number distributed throughout
the Metropolis. The conclusion we have come to, after consulting with the best authorities
on the subject, is, that there are just upon 4,000 habitual vagabonds distributed about
London, and the cost of their support annually amounts to very nearly £50,000.†

"One of the worst concomitants of vagrant mendicancy," says the Poor-Law Report, "is
the fever of a dangerous typhoid character which has universally marked the path of the
mendicant. There is scarcely a workhouse in which this pestilence does not prevail in a
greater or less degree; and numerous Union officers have fallen victims to it." Those who
are acquainted with the exceeding filth of the persons frequenting the casual wards, will not
wonder at the fever which follows in the wake of the vagrants. "Many have the itch. I
have seen," says Mr. Boase, "a party of twenty all scratching themselves at once, before
settling into their rest in the straw. Lice exist in great numbers upon them."

That vagrancy is the nursery of crime, and that the habitual tramps are first beggars
then thieves, and finally the convicts of the country, the evidence of all parties goes to prove.

But we cannot give the reader a better general idea of the character and habits of this
class than by detailing the particulars of a meeting of that curious body of people which we
once held, and when as many as 150 were present. Never was witnessed a more distressing

---

* The items making up the above total—that is to say, the number of vagrants admitted into the several
Metropolitan Workhouses—may be given as follows :—Pancras, 19,859; Chelsea, 15,199; Stepney, 12,869;
West London, 9,777; Fulham, 9,017; Holborn, 7,947; St. Margaret, Westminster, 7,410; St. George,
Southwark, 6,918; London City, 6,825; Newington, 9,575; Shoreditch, 5,921; Paddington, 5,378; East
London, 4,912; Islington, 4,561; Kensington, 3,917; Wandsworth, 3,848; St. Luke's, 3,409; Whitechapel,
3,304; Rotherhithe, 2,627; Lambeth, 2,516; Camberwell, 2,104; St. Martin's in the Fields, 1,823; Poplar,
1,737; Bethnal Green, 1,620; Greenwich, 1,404; Hackney, 833; St. Giles, 581; St. James, Westminster,
371; Clerkenwell, 88; Strand, 68; St. George in the East, 31; St. Saviour, 15; Lewisham, 12; St. Olave,
Southwark, 0; Bermondsey, 0; St. George, Hanover Square, 0; Marylebone, 0; Hampstead, 0.

† The above conclusion has been arrived at from the following data :—

Average number of Vagrants relieved each night in the Metropolitan Unions . .		849
Average number of Vagrants resident in the Mendicants' Lodging-houses of London .		2,431
Average number of individuals relieved at the Metropolitan Asylums for the houseless poor		750
Total		4,030

Now, as five per cent. of this amount is said to consist of characters really destitute and deserving, we
arrive at the conclusion that there are 3,829 vagrants in London, living either by mendicancy or theft.

The cost of the vagrants in London in the year 1848, may be estimated as follows :—

	£	s.	d.
310,058 vagrants relieved at the Metropolitan Unions, at the cost of 2d. per head	£2,584	13	0
67,500 nights' lodgings afforded to the houseless poor at the Metropolitan Asylums, including the West End Asylum, Market Street, Edgeware Road	3,134	1	4½
2,431 inmates of the Mendicants' Lodging-houses in London, gaining by "cadging" upon an average. 1s. per day, or altogether, per year .	44,365	15	0
	£50,084	9	4½
Deduct 5 per cent. for the cost of relief for the truly deserving . .	2,504	4	5
The total will then be	£47,580	4	11½

spectacle of squalor, rags, and wretchedness. Some were young men, and some were children. One, who styled himself a "cadger," was six years of age, and several who confessed themselves as "prigs" were only ten. The countenances of the boys were of various character. Many were not only good-looking, but had a frank ingenuous expression, that seemed in no way connected with innate roguery. Many, on the other hand, had the deep-sunk and half-averted eye, which is so characteristic of natural dishonesty and cunning. Some had the regular features of lads born of parents in easy circumstances. The hair of most of the lads was cut very close to the head, showing their recent liberation from prison; indeed, one might tell, by the comparative length of the crop, the time that each boy had been out of gaol. All but a few of the elder lads were remarkable, amidst the rags, filth, and wretchedness of their external appearance, for the mirth and carelessness impressed upon the countenance.

At first their behaviour was very noisy and disorderly, coarse and ribald jokes were freely cracked, exciting general bursts of laughter; while howls, cat-calls, and all manner of unearthly and indescribable yells threatened for a time to render all attempts at order utterly abortive. At one moment, a lad would imitate the bray of the jackass, and immediately the whole hundred and fifty would fall to braying like him. Then some ragged urchin would crow like a cock; whereupon the place would echo with a hundred and fifty cock-crows! Next, as a negro-boy entered the room, one of the young vagabonds would shout out swe-ee-p; this would be received with peals of laughter, and followed by a general repetition of the same cry. Presently a hundred and fifty cat-calls, of the shrillest possible description, would almost split the ears. These would be succeeded by cries of, "Strike up, catgut scrapers!" "Go on with your barrow!" "Flare up, my never-sweats!" and a variety of other street sayings.

Indeed, the uproar which went on before the commencement of the meeting will be best understood, if we compare it to the scene presented by a public menagerie at feeding time. The greatest difficulty, as might be expected, was experienced in collecting the subjoined statistics as to the character and condition of those present on the occasion. By a persevering mode of inquiry, however, the following facts were elicited :—

With respect to age, the youngest boy present was six years old; he styled himself a cadger, and said that his mother, who was a widow, and suffering from ill health, sent him into the streets to beg. There were 7 of ten years of age, 3 of twelve, and 3 of thirteen, 10 of fourteen, 26 of fifteen, 11 of sixteen, 20 of seventeen, 26 of eighteen, and 45 of nineteen.

Then 19 had fathers and mothers still living, 39 had only one parent, and 80 were orphans, in the fullest sense of the word, having neither father nor mother alive.

Of professed beggars, there were 50; whilst 66 acknowledged themselves to be habitual "prigs;" the anouncement that the greater number present were thieves pleased them exceedingly, and was received with three rounds of applause.

Next it was ascertained that 12 of them had been in prison once (2 of these were but ten years of age), 5 had been in prison twice, 3 thrice, 4 four times, 7 five times, 8 six times, 5 seven times, 4 eight times, 2 nine times (and 1 of these thirteen years of age), 5 ten times, 5 twelve times, 2 thirteen times, 3 fourteen times, 2 sixteen times, 3 seventeen times, 2 eighteen times, 5 twenty times, 6 twenty-four times, 1 twenty-five times, 1 twenty-six times, and 1 twenty-nine times.

The announcements in reply to the question as to the number of times that any of them had been in gaol, were received with great applause, which became more and more boisterous as the number of imprisonments increased. When it was announced that one, though only nineteen years of age, had been incarcerated as many as twenty-nine times, the clapping of hands, the cat-calls, and shouts of "bray-vo!" lasted for several minutes, whilst the whole of the boys rose to look at the distinguished individual. Some chalked on their hats the figures which designated the sum of the several times they had been in gaol.

As to the cause of their vagabondism, it was found that 22 had run away from their homes, owing to the ill-treatment of their parents; 18 confessed to having been ruined ~~~ their parents allowing them to run wild in the streets, and to be led astray by bad ~~~~ ; and 15 acknowledged that they had been first taught thieving in a lodging-house.

Concerning the vagrant habits of the youths, the following facts were elicited:—78 regularly roam through the country every year; 65 sleep regularly in the casual-wards of the unions; and 52 occasionally slept in trampers' lodging-houses throughout the country.

Respecting their education, according to the popular meaning of the term, 63 of the 150 were able to read and write, and they were principally thieves. 50 of this number said they had read "Jack Sheppard," and the lives of "Dick Turpin," and "Claude du Val," and all the other popular thieves' novels, as well as the Newgate Calendar, and lives of the robbers and pirates. Those who could not read themselves, said that "Jack Sheppard" was read out to them at the lodging-houses. Numbers avowed that they had been induced to resort to an abandoned course of life from reading the lives of notorious thieves, and novels about highway robbers. When asked what they thought of Jack Sheppard, several bawled out—"He's a regular brick!"—a sentiment which was almost universally concurred in by the deafening shouts and plaudits which followed. When questioned as to whether they would like to have been Jack Sheppard, the answer was, "Yes, if the times were the same now as they were then!" 13 confessed that they had taken to thieving in order to go to the low theatres; and one lad said he had lost a good situation on the Birmingham railway through his love of the play. 20 stated that they had been flogged in prison, many of them having been so punished two, three, and four different times.

A policeman in plain clothes was present, but their acute eyes were not long before they detected his real character, notwithstanding his disguise. Several demanded that he should be turned out. The officer was accordingly given to understand that the meeting was a private one, and requested to withdraw. Having apologized for intruding, he proceeded to leave the room; and no sooner did the boys see the "Peeler" move towards the door than they gave vent to several rounds of very hearty applause, accompanied with hisses, groans, and cries of "Throw him over!"

Now, we have paid some little attention to such strange members of the human family as these, and others at war with all social institutions. We have thought the peculiarities of their nature as worthy of study in an ethnological point of view, as those of the people of other countries, and we have learnt to look upon them as a distinct race of individuals, as distinct as the Malay is from the Caucasian tribe. We have sought, moreover, to reduce their several varieties into something like system, believing it quite as requisite that we should have an attempt at a scientific classification of the criminal classes, as of the Infusoriæ or the Cryptogamia. An enumeration of the several natural orders and species of criminals will let the reader see that the class is as multifarious, and surely, in a scientific point of view, as worthy of being studied as the varieties of animalcules.

In the first place, then, the criminal classes are divisible into three distinct families, i.e., the beggars, the cheats, and the thieves.

Of the beggars there are many distinct species. (1.) The naval and the military beggars; as turnpike sailors and "raw" veterans. (2.) Distressed operative beggars; as pretended starved-out manufacturers, or sham frozen-out gardeners, or tricky hand-loom weavers, &c. (3.) Respectable beggars; as sham broken-down tradesmen, poor ushers or distressed authors, clean family beggars, with children in very white pinafores and their faces cleanly washed, and the ashamed beggars, who pretend to hide their faces with a written petition. (4.) Disaster beggars; as shipwrecked mariners, or blown-up miners, or burnt-out tradesmen, and lucifer droppers. (5.) Bodily afflicted beggars; such as those having real or pretended sores or swollen legs, or being crippled or deformed, maimed, or paralyzed, or else being blind, or deaf, or dumb, or subject to fits, or in a decline and appearing with bandages round the head, or playing the "shallow cove," *i. e.*, appearing half-clad in the streets. (6.) Famished beggars; as those who chalk on the pavement, "I am starving," or else remain stationary, and hold up a piece of paper before their face similarly inscribed. (7.) Foreign beggars, who stop you in the street, and request to know if you can speak French; or destitute Poles, Indians, or Lascars, or Negroes. (8.) Petty trading beggars; as tract sellers, lucifer match sellers, boot lace venders, &c. (9.) Musical beggars; or those who play on some musical instrument, as a cloak for begging—as scraping fiddlers, hurdy-gurdy and clarionet players. (10.) Dependents of beggars; as screevers or the writers of "slums" (letters) and "fakements" (petitions), and referees, or those who give characters to professional beggars.

The second criminal class consists of cheats, and these are subdivisible into—(1.) Government defrauders; as "jiggers" (defrauding the excise by working illicit stills), and smugglers who defraud the customs. (2.) Those who cheat the public; as swindlers, who cheat those of whom they buy; and duffers and horse-chanters, who cheat those to whom they sell; and "charley pitchers," or low gamblers, cheating those with whom they play; and "bouncers and besters," who cheat by laying wagers; and "flat catchers," or ring-droppers, who cheat by pretending to find valuables in the street; and bubble-men, who institute sham annuity offices or assurance companies; and douceur-men, who cheat by pretending to get government situations, or provide servants with places, or to tell persons of something to their advantage. (3.) The dependents of cheats; as "jollies" and "magsmen," or the confederates of other cheats; and "bonnets," or those who attend gaming tables; and referees, who give false characters to servants.

The last of the criminal classes are the thieves, who admit of being classified as follows :—(1.) Those who plunder with *violence;* as "cracksmen," who break into houses; "rampsmen," who stop people on the highway; "bludgers" or "stick slingers," who rob in company with low women. (2.) Those who hocus or plunder persons by *stupefying;* as "drummers," who drug liquor; and "bug-hunters," who plunder drunken men. (3.) Those who plunder by *stealth*, as (i.) "mobsmen," or those who plunder by manual dexterity, like "buzzers," who pick gentlemen's pockets; "wires," who pick ladies' pockets; "prop-nailers," who steal pins or brooches; and "thumble screwers," who wrench off watches; and shoplifters, who purloin goods from shops; (ii.) "sneaksmen," or petty cowardly thieves, and of these there are two distinct varieties, according as they sneak off with either goods or animals. Belonging to the first variety, or those who sneak off with goods, are "drag-sneaks," who make off with goods from carts or coaches; "snoozers," who sleep at railway hotels, and make off with either apparel or luggage in the morning; "sawney-hunters," who purloin cheese or bacon from cheesemongers' doors; "noisy racket men," who make off with china or crockery-ware from earthenware shops; "snow-gatherers," who make off with clean clothes from hedges; "cat and kitten hunters," who make off with quart or pint pots from area railings; "area sneaks," who steal from the area; "dead-lurkers," who steal from the passages of houses; "till friskers," who make off with the contents of tills; "bluey-hunters," who take lead from the tops of houses; "toshers," who purloin copper from ships and along shore; "star-glazers," who cut the panes of glass from windows; "skinners," or women and boys who strip children of their clothes; and mudlarks, who steal pieces of rope, coal, and wood from the barges at the wharves.

Those sneaks-men, on the other hand, who purloin animals, are either horse-stealers or "woolly bird" (sheep) stealers, or deer-stealers, or dog-stealers, or poachers, or "lady and gentlemen racket-men," who steal cocks and hens, or cat-stealers or body snatchers.

Then there is still another class of plunderers, who are neither sneaks-men nor mobs-men, but simply breach-of-trust-men, taking those articles only which have been confided to them; these are either embezzlers, who rob their employers; or illegal pawners, who pledge the blankets, &c., at their lodgings, or the work of their employers; dishonest servants, who go off with the plate, or let robbers into their master's houses, bill stealers, and letter stealers.

Beside these there are (4) the " *shoful-men*," or those who plunder by counterfeits; as coiners and forgers of checks, and notes, and wills; and, lastly, we have (5) the dependents of thieves; as "fences," or receivers of stolen goods; and "smashers," or the utterers of base coin.

Now, as regards the number of this extensive family of criminals, the return published by the Constabulary Commissioners is still the best authority; and, according to this, there were in the Metropolis at the time of making the report, 107 burglars; 110 house-breakers; 38 highway robbers; 773 pickpockets; 3,657 sneaks-men, or common thieves; 11 horse-stealers, and 141 dog-stealers; 3 forgers; 28 coiners, and 317 utterers of base coin; 141 swindlers or obtainers of goods under false pretences, and 182 cheats; 343 receivers of stolen goods; 2,768 habitual rioters; 1,205 vagrants; 50 begging letter writers; 86 bearers of begging letters, and 6,371 prostitutes; besides 470 not otherwise described: making altogether a total of 16,900 criminals known to the police; so that it would appear that one in every hundred and forty of the London population belongs to the criminal class.

Further, the police returns tell us the total value of the property which this large section of metropolitan society are known to make away with, amounts to very nearly £42,000 per annum.

Thus, in the course of the year 1853, property to the amount of £2,854 was stolen by burglary; £135 by breaking into dwelling-houses; and £143 by breaking into shops, &c.; £1,158 by embezzlement; £579 by forgery; £1,615 by fraud; £46 by robbery on the highway; £250 by horse stealing; and £104 by cattle stealing; £78 by dog stealing; £1,249 by stealing goods exposed for sale; £413 stealing lead, &c., from unfurnished houses; £1597 by stealing from carts and carriages; £122 by stealing linen exposed to dry; £421 by stealing poultry from an outhouse; £1,888 stolen from dwelling-houses by means of false keys; £2,936 by lodgers; £8,866 by servants; £4,500 by doors being left open; £2,175 by false messages; £2,848 by lifting the window or breaking the glass; £559 by entry through the attic windows from an empty house; £795 by means unknown; £3,018 by picking pockets; £729 was taken from drunken persons; £48 from children; £2024 by prostitutes; £418 by larceny on the river—amounting altogether to £41,988; and this only in those robberies which became known to the police.

Now, as there is a market even for the rags gathered by the bone-grubber, so is there an "exchange" for the articles collected by the thieves. This is the celebrated Petticoat Lane, or Middlesex Street, as it is now styled, where the Jew fences most do congregate, and where all manner of things are bought and no questions asked. Our picture of the contrasts of London—of the extreme forms of metropolitan life—would be incomplete without the following sketch of the place.

The antipodes to the fashionable world is Petticoat Lane,, which is, as it were, the capital of the *un*fashionable empire—the metropolis of the *bas-ton*. It is to the East End what Regent Street is to the West.

Proceeding up the Lane from Aldgate, the locality seems to be hardly different from other byeways in the same district; indeed it has much the character of the entry to Leather Lane out of Holborn, being narrow and dark, and flanked by shops which evidently depend little upon display for their trade. The small strip of roadway as you turn into the Lane is generally blocked up by some costermonger's barrow, with its flat projecting tray on the top, littered with little hard knubbly-looking pears, scarcely bigger than turnip-radishes, and which is brought to a dead halt every dozen paces, while the corduroyed proprietor pauses to turn round, and roar, "Sixteen a penny, lumping pears!"

As you worm your way along, you pass little slits of blind alleys, with old sheets and patchwork counterpanes, like large fancy chess-boards, stretched to dry across the court, and hanging so still and straight that you see at a glance how stagnant the air is in these dismal quarters. The gutters are all grey, and bubbling with soap-suds, and on the door-steps sit crouching fluffy-haired women; whilst at the entrance are clusters of sharp-featured boys, some in men's coats, with the cuffs turned half-way up the sleeves, and the tails trailing on the stones, and others with the end of their trousers rolled up, and the waist-bands braced with string high across their chests.

As you move by them, you see the pennies spin from the midst of them into the air, and the eager young group suddenly draw back and peer intently on the ground, as the coins are heard to jingle on the stones.

Up another alley you catch sight of some women engaged in scrubbing an old French bedstead that stretches half across the court, while others are busy beating the coffee-coloured mattress that leans against the wall, previous to making its appearance at the furniture-stall above. In the opposite court may be seen a newly-opened barrel of pickled herrings, with the slimy, metallic-looking fish ranged like a cockade within; and here against the wall dangle the split bodies of drying fish—hard-looking "finny-haddies" (Finnan haddocks), brown and tarry-like as a sailor's "sou'-wester," and seeming as if they were bats asleep, as they hang spread open in the dusky corners of the place.

A little higher up, the Lane appears to be devoted chiefly to the preparation and sale of such eatables as the Israelites generally delight in. Almost every other shop is an "establish-ment" for the cooking and distribution of fried fish, the air around being redolent of the vapours of hot oil; and, as you pass on your way, you hear the flounders and soles frizzing in the back parlours, whilst hot-looking hook-nosed women rush out with smoking frying-pans in their hands, their aprons stained with grease almost as if they were water-proofed with it, and their cheeks red and shiny as tinsel-foil with the fire. The sloping shop-boards here are covered with the dishes filled with the fresh-cooked fish, looking brown as the bottom of a newly-sanded bird-cage; by the side of these are ranged oyster-tubs filled with pickled cucum-bers, the soft, swollen vegetables floating in the vinegar like huge fat caterpillars.

Mingled with these are strange-looking butchers' shops, with small pieces of pale, blood-less meat dangling from the hooks, and each having a curious tin ticket, like a metallic cap-sule, fastened to it. This is the seal of the Rabbi, certifying that the animal was slaughtered according to the Jewish rites; and here are seen odd-looking Hebrew butchers and butcher-boys, with their black, curly hair, greasier even than the locks of the Whitechapel Israelites on a Saturday, and speckled with bits of suet. Their faces, too, appear, to eyes unused to the sight, so unnaturally grim above their blue smocks, that they have very much the appear-ance of a small family of O. Smiths costumed for the part in a piece of Adelphi *diablerie*.

Nor are the bakers' shops in this locality of a less peculiar or striking cast; for here the heads and eyebrows of the Hebrew master bakers are unnaturally white with the flour, and give them the same grotesque look as would characterize a powdered Jew footman in the upper circles; while among the loaves and bags of flour in the shop, you often catch sight of dusty, thin, passover biscuits, nearly as big as targets.

As you proceed up the Lane, the trade of the place assumes a totally different character; *there* the emporia of fried fish, and butcher's meat, and pickled cucumbers pass into petty marts for old furniture and repositories of second-hand tools. Now, in front of one shop, you see nothing but old foot-rules and long carpenters' planes, all ranged in straight lines and shiny and yellow with recent bees-wax. Behind the trellis of tools, too, you occasionally catch sight of the figure of a man engaged in polishing-up the handle of an old centre-bit, or scouring away at the rusty blade of some second-hand saw.

The pavement in front of the furniture-shops is littered with old deal chairs and tables; and imitation chests of drawers with the fronts removed, and showing the coarse brown-paper-like sacking of the doubled-up bed within; and huge unwieldy sofas are there with a kind of canvas tank sunk under the seat, and reminding one of those odd-looking carts in

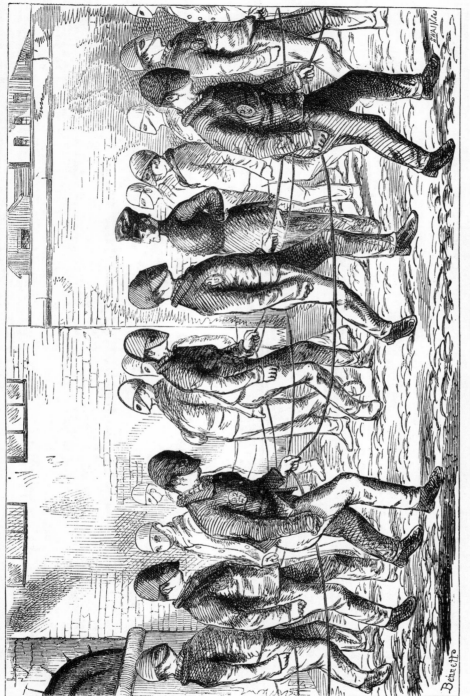

CONVICTS EXERCISING IN PENTONVILLE PRISON.

which the load is placed below the axle of the wheels. As you pass along the line of lumbered-up shops, you discover vistas of curious triangular cupboards; bulky, square-looking arm-chairs in their canvas undress; narrow brown tables, with semicircular flaps hanging at their sides, and quaint oval looking-glasses; and yellow-painted bamboo chairs, with the rushes showing underneath, as ragged as an old fish-basket; while the floor is encumbered with feather beds, doubled up, and looking like lumps of dirty dough.

Adjoining the old furniture-shops are second-hand clothes marts, with the entire fronts of the shops covered outside with rows of old fustian trousers, washed as white as the inside of a fresh hide, and with tripey corduroys, and fluffy carpenters' flannel jackets; the door-posts, moreover, are decked with faded gaudy waistcoats, ornamented with fancy buttons, that have much the appearance of small brandy-balls.

A few paces further on, you come to a hatter's, with the men at work in the shop, their irons, heavy as the sole of a club-boot, standing on the counter by their side, and the place filled with varnished brown paper hat-shapes, that seem as if they had been modelled in hard-bake.

Nor are the Jewesses of Petticoat Lane the least remarkable of the characters appertaining to the place. In front of almost every doorway is seated some fat Hebrew woman, with gold ear-rings dangling by her neck, as big as a chandelier drop, and her fingers hooped with thick gold rings. Some of the ladies are rubbing up old brass candlesticks, and some scouring old tarnished tea-kettles, their hands and faces, amidst all their finery, begrimed with dirt. In one part of the Lane, you behold one of the women with a bunch of bright blue artificial flowers in her cap, as big as the nosegays with which coachmen delight to decorate their horses' heads on the 1st of May, busy extracting the grease from the collar of a threadbare surtout; in another part you may perceive an Israelite maiden, almost as grubby and tawdry as My Lady on May Day, engaged in the act of blacking a pair of high-lows; while at the door of some rag and bottle warehouse, where, from the poverty-stricken aspect of the place, you would imagine that the people could hardly be one week's remove from the workhouse, you see some grand lady with a lace-edged parasol in her white-kidded hand, and a bright green and red cashmere shawl spread out over her back, taking leave of her greasy-looking daughters, previous to emerging into all the elegancies of Aldgate.

Were it not for such curious sights as the above, it would be difficult to account for that strange medley of want and luxury—that incongruous association of the sale of jewellery and artificial flowers, with that of old clothes, rags, and old metal, which constitutes, perhaps, one of the most startling features of Petticoat Lane.

"How is it," the mind naturally inquires, "that, in a place where the people who come to sell or buy are among the very poorest in the land, there can be the least demand for such trumpery as rings, brooches, and artificial roses? Does the bone-grubber who rummages the muck-heaps for some bit of rag, or metal, that will help to bring him a few pence at the day's end—does *he* feast on fried fish and pickled cucumbers? Is *he*, poor wretch! who cannot even get bread enough to stay his cravings, the purchaser of the halfpenny ices? Are the fatty cakes made for them who come here to sell the shirt off their backs for a meal?"

Verily, the luxuries and the finery are not for such as these; but for those who live, and trade, and fatten upon the misery of the poor and the vice of the criminal.

If all the old rags and clothes, and tools and beds in Petticoat Lane, had tongues, what stories of unknown sufferings or infatuate vice would they not tell! In those old tool shops alone what volumes of silent misery are there not contained! They who know what a mechanic will suffer before he parts with the implements of his trade—who know how he will pawn or sell every valuable, however useful, make away with every relic, however much prized, before he is driven to dispose of those implements which are another pair of hands to him, and without which it is impossible for him to get either work or bread—those who know this, and know further how a long illness, a fever, laying prostrate a working man's whole family, and brought on, most probably, by living in some cheap, close, pent-up court, will compel a poor fellow to part, bit by bit, with each little piece of property that he has accumulated out of his earnings when in health and strength—how his watch, as well as the humble trinkets of his wife, will go first to get the necessary food or physic for them all—how the extra suit of Sunday clothes, and the one silk gown, and the thick warm shawl are parted with next—how, after this, the blankets and under-clothing of the wife and children disappear, one by one, for though they shiver in the streets, at least no one *sees* how thinly they are clad, or *knows* how cold they lie at night—how then the bedding is sold from under them to keep them a few days longer from the dreaded poor-house—and how, last of all, when wife and children are stripped nearly naked, when the man has sold the shirt from his back to stay the cravings of his little ones, when they have nothing but the boards to lie upon—how *then*, and not *till* then, the planes and saws and centre-bits are disposed of, and each with the same pang too, as if the right hand of the man was being cut from him—those, we say, who know the sufferings which have preceded the sale of many of these implements —who know, too, the despair which fills the mind of a working man as he sees his only means of independence wrested from him, will not pass the old tool shops in Petticoat Lane idly by, but rather read in each wretched article some sad tale of humble misery.

Still *all* the tools are not there from such a cause ; no ! nor half of them ; perhaps the greater part would be found, if the matter were opened up, to have been disposed of for drink—by fatuous sots, who first swilled themselves out of work, and then guzzled away now a plane and now a saw, raising first a glass on this to stay the trembling of the hand in the morning, and then a drop on that to keep down the " horrors"—until at length nothing remained but " the house," or street-cadging and lying, as the broken-down mechanic.

But are we all so immaculate that we have no sympathy but for the *deserving* poor. Is our pity limited merely to those only who suffer the least, because they suffer with an unaccusing conscience ; and must we *entirely* shut out from our commiseration the wretch who is tormented not only with hunger, but with the self-reproaches of his own bosom. Granting that this cast-iron philosophy is right and good for society, shall not the thought of the suffering wife and children, even of the drunkard and the trickster, move us to the least tenderness ?

"How long," the thoughtful traveller will wonder to himself, as he continues his journey mournfully up the Lane, " did the family go without food before that bed was brought here for sale ? Those fustian and flannel jackets, what sad privations were experienced by their former owners, ere they were forced to take them off their backs to raise a meal ? What is the wretched history of those foot-rules and chisels ? How long did the little ones starve before that pair of baby's boots were stripped from the tiny feet and sold for a bite and a sup—ay, or if you will, Mr. Puritan, for another glass of gin ? Did the parting with those wedding rings cost more or less agony of body ? Where is the owner of the little boots *now* ? In a workhouse, or walking the streets with gayer boots than ever ?

" That silk pocket handkerchief, too—the one in which we can just see where the mark has been picked from the corner—what is the story in connection with it ? Is the lad who stole it, and who sold it to the Jew there for not one-fourth the sum that it is now ticketed at —is he at the hulks *yet* ? Was *he* one out of the many families that have been turned into the streets, on the breaking up of the hundred homes to which these piles of old furniture belonged ? Or was he wilfully bad—one of those that Mr. Carlyle would have shot, and swept into the dust bin."

Yonder, at the corner of one of the courts higher up the Lane, is a group of eager lads peeping over the shoulders of one another, while one shows some silver spoons.

The Jew who buys them is a regular attendant at synagogue, and wears the laws of Moses next his skin. But he asks no questions, and has a crucible always ready on the fire.

His daughters are like Indian idols—all gold and dirt now, but next Saturday you shall see them parading Aldgate in the highest style of fashion. The old man has no end of money to leave Ruth and Rachel, when he dies and is gathered—as he *hopes* to be—to the bosom of Abraham.

Now, sapient reader, you can guess, perhaps, who it is that buys the artificial flowers, and the fried fish, and the jewellery that you see exposed among the old tools and clothes and furniture in Petticoat Lane.

---

§ 6.

OF THE LONDON STREETS, THEIR TRAFFIC, NAMES, AND CHARACTER.

The thoroughfares of London constitute, assuredly, the finest and most remarkable of all the sights that London contains. Not that this is due to their architectural display, even though at the West End there are streets which are long lines of palaces—such as Pall Mall, with its stately array of club-houses—and Regent Street, where the fronts of each distinct block of buildings are united so as to form one imposing façade, and where every façade is different, so that, as we walk along, a kind of architectural panorama glides before the eye— and Belgravia and Tyburnia, where the squares and terraces are vast palatial colonies. Nor yet is it due to the magnificence of its shops—those crystal storehouses of which the sheets of glass are like sheets of the clearest lake ice, both in their dimensions and transparency, and gorgeous with the display of the richest products in the world. Nor yet, again, is it owing to the capacious Docks at the East End of the Metropolis, where the surrounding streets have all the nautical oddness of an amphibious Dutch town, from the mingling of the many mast-heads with the chimney-pots, and where the sense of the immensity of the aggregate merchant-wealth is positively overpowering to contemplate. Neither is it owing to the broad green parks, that are so many bright snatches of the country scattered round the smoke-dried city, and where the verdure of the fields is rendered doubly grateful, not only from their contrast with the dense rusty-red mass of bricks and mortar with which they are encompassed, but from being vast aerial reservoirs—great sylvan tanks, as it were, of oxygen—for the supply of health and spirits to the walled-in multitude. But these same London thoroughfares *are*, simply, the finest of all sights—in the world, we may say—on account of the never-ending and infinite variety of life to be seen in them.

Beyond doubt, the enormous multitudes ever pouring through the principal metropolitan thoroughfares strike the first deep impression upon the stranger's mind; and we ourselves never contemplate the tumultuous scene without feeling that here lies the true grandeur of the Capital—the one distinctive mark that gives a special sublimity to the spot.

Travellers speak of the awful magnificence of the great torrent of Niagara, where thousands upon thousands of tons of liquid are ever pouring over the rocks in one immense, terrific flood. But what is this in grandeur to the vast human tide—the stupendous living torrent of thousands upon thousands of restless souls, each quickened with some different purpose, and for ever rushing along the great leading thoroughfares of the Metropolis? what the aggregate power of the greatest cataract in the world to the united might of the several emotions and wills stirring each of the homuncular atoms composing that dense human stream. And if the roar of the precipitated waters bewilders and affrights the mind, assuredly the riot and tumult of the traffic of London at once stun and terrify the brain of those who hear it for the first time.

There is no scene in the wide world, indeed, equal in grandeur to the contemplation of the immensity of this same London traffic. Can the masses of the pyramids impress the mind with such an overwhelming sense of labour and everlastingness as is inspired by the apparently never-ending and never-tiring industry of the masses of people in our streets? If the desert be the very intensity of the sublime from the feeling of tragic loneliness—of terrible isolation that it induces—from the awful solemnity of the great ocean of desolation encompassing the traveller; surely this monster Metropolis is equally sublime, though from the opposite cause—from the sense of the infinite multitude of people with which we are surrounded, and yet of our comparative, if not absolute, friendlessness and isolation in the very midst of *such* an infinite multitude.

Is there any other sight in the Metropolis, moreover, so thoroughly *Londonesque* as this is in its character? Will our Law Courts, though justice be dispensed there with a fairness and even mercy to the accused, that is utterly unknown in other lands, give the foreigner as lively an idea of the genius of our people? Will our Houses of Parliament, where the policy of every new law is discussed by the national representatives with an honesty and freedom impossible to be met with in the Chambers of other States, show him so much of our character? Will the stranger be so astounded even at the internal economy of our great newspaper printing-offices, where the intelligence of the entire world is focussed, as it were, into one enormous daily sheet, that is filled with finer essays than any to be found in "the British Classics," and printed far more elegantly than library books on the Continent, —even though the greater portion of the matter has been written, and the million bits of type composing it have been picked up, in the course of the preceding night? Or will our leviathan breweries, or our races, or our cattle-shows, or cricket matches, or, indeed, any of the institutions, or customs, or enterprises peculiar to the land, sink so deeply into the stranger's mind as the contemplation of the several miles of crowd—the long and dense commercial train of men and vehicles each day flooding the leading thoroughfares of this giant city!

Let the visitor from some quiet country or foreign town behold the city at five in the day, and see the people crowding the great lines of streets like a flock of sheep in a narrow lane; and the conveyances, too, packed full of human beings, and jammed as compactly together as the stones on the paving beneath, and find, moreover—go which way he will—the same black multitude pervading the thoroughfares almost as far as he can travel before nightfall— behold every one of the civic arteries leading to the mighty heart of London, charged with its thousands of human globules, all busy, as they circulate through them, sustaining the life and energy and well-being of the land; and assuredly he will allow that the world has no wonder—amongst the whole of its far-famed seven—in the least comparable to this.

Let us now, however, descend to particulars, and endeavour to set forth the actual amount of traffic going on through the leading London thoroughfares.

By a return which was kindly furnished to us by Mr. Haywood, the City Surveyor, we are enabled to come at this point with greater accuracy than might be imagined. The return of which we speak was of a very elaborate character, and specified not only the total number of vehicles drawn by one horse, as well as two, three, or more horses, that passed over 24 of the principal City thoroughfares in the course of twelve hours, but also set forth the number of each kind of conveyance traversing the city for every hour throughout the day.

By means of this table, then, we find there are two tides, as it were, in the daily stream of locomotion flowing through the city—the one coming to its highest point at eleven in the forenoon, up to which time the number of vehicles gradually increases, and so rapidly, too, that there are very nearly twice as many conveyances in the streets at eleven, as there are at nine o'clock in the morning. After eleven o'clock the tide of the traffic, however, begins to ebb—the number of carriages gradually decreasing, till two in the afternoon, when there is one-sixth less vehicles in the leading thoroughfares than at eleven. After two, again, another change occurs, and the crowd of conveyances continues to increase in number till five o'clock, when there are a few hundreds more collected within the city boundaries than there were at eleven. After five, the locomotive current ebbs once more, and does not attain its next flood until eleven the next day.

Now, by this return it is shown, that the gross number of vehicles passing along the City thoroughfares, in the course of twelve hours, ordinarily amounts to one-eighth of a million, or upwards of 125,000.* But many of these, it should be added, are reckoned more than once in the statement; if, however, we sum up only the number appearing in the distinct lines of thoroughfares—like Holborn, Fleet Street, Leadenhall Street, Blackfriars Bridge, Bishopsgate Street, Finsbury Pavement, &c.—the amount of city traffic, will even then reach nearly 60,000 vehicles, passing and re-passing through the streets every day.

Now, that this estimate is not very wide of the truth, is proven by the fact, that there are no less than 3000 cabs plying in London streets; nearly 1000 omnibuses; and more than 10,000 private and job carriages and carts, belonging to various individuals throughout the Metropolis (as is shown by the returns of the Stamp and Tax Office). Moreover, it is calculated, that some 3000 conveyances enter the Metropolis daily from the surrounding country; whilst the amount of mileage duty paid by the Metropolitan Stage Carriages, in the year 1853, prove that the united London omnibuses and short stages must have travelled over not less than 21,800,000 miles of ground in the course of that year—a distance which is very nearly equal to one-fourth that of the earth from the sun!

Hence, it will appear that the above estimate, as to the number of vehicles passing and repassing through the City streets every day, does not exceed the bounds of reason.

But the thoroughfares within the City boundaries are not one-thirtieth of the length of those without them; and as there are two distinct lines of streets, traversing London from east to west, each six miles long, and at least four distinct highways, stretching north and south, each four miles in length at least; whilst along each and all of these a dense stream of foot passengers and conveyances is maintained throughout the day; it will therefore be found, by calculation, that at five o'clock, when almost every one of these thoroughfares may be said to be positively crowded with the traffic, that there is a dense stream of omnibuses, cabs, carts, and carriages, as well as foot passengers, flowing through London at one and the same time, that is near upon 30 miles long altogether!

We have before spoken of the prodigious length of the aggregate streets and lanes of the Metropolis, and a peep at the balloon map of London† will convince the stranger what a tangled knot of highways and byeways is the town. A plexus of nerves or capillary vessels is

---

* The following are the data for the above statement:—

RETURN, SHOWING THE TOTAL NUMBER OF VEHICLES PASSING IN THE COURSE OF TWELVE HOURS (FROM NINE A.M. TO NINE P.M.) THROUGH THE PRINCIPAL STREETS OF THE CITY OF LONDON.

Lower Thames Street, by Botolph Lane	1,380	Gracechurch Street, by St. Peter's Alley	4,887
Threadneedle Street	2,150	Cornhill, by the Royal Exchange	4,916
Lombard Street, by Birchin Lane	2,228	Blackfriars Bridge	5,262
Upper Thames Street (in rear of Queen Street)	2,331	Leadenhall Street, in rear of the East India	
Aldersgate Street, by Fann Street	2,590	House	5,930
Tower Street, by Mark Lane	2,890	Newgate Street, by Old Bailey	6,375
Smithfield Bars	3,108	Ludgate Hill, by Pilgrim Street	6,829
Fenchurch Street	3,642	Holborn Hill, by St. Andrew's Church	6,906
Eastcheap, by Philpot Lane	4,102	Temple Bar Gate	7,741
Bishopsgate Street Without, by City boundary	4,110	Poultry, by the Mansion House	10,274
Finsbury Pavement, by South Place	4,460	Cheapside, by Foster Lane	11,053
Aldgate High Street, by City boundary	4,754	London Bridge	13,099
Bishopsgate Street Within, by Great St. Helen's	4,842	Total	125,859

† An excellent map of the kind above specified is published by Appleyard and Hetling of Farringdon Street, and it will be found to be more easily comprehensible to strangers than the ordinary ground-plans of the London streets.

not more intricate than they. As well might we seek to find order and systematic arrangement among a ball of worms as in that conglomeration of thoroughfares constituting the British Metropolis.

"I began to study the Map of London," says Southey, in his Espriella's Letters, "though dismayed at the sight of its prodigious extent. The river is of no assistance to a stranger in finding his way; there is no street along its banks; nor is there any eminence whence you can look around and take your bearings."

But the nomenclature of the London streets is about as unsystematic as is the general plan of the thoroughfares, and cannot but be extremely puzzling to the stranger. Every one knows how the Frenchman was perplexed with the hundred significations given to the English term "box"—such as band-box, Christmas-box, coach-box, box on the ears, shooting-box, box-tree, private box, the wrong box, boxing the compass, and a boxing match. And, assuredly, he must be equally bothered on finding the same name applied to some score or two of different thoroughfares, that are often so far apart, that, if he happen to be the bearer of a letter of introduction with the address of "*King Street, London*," the unhappy wight would probably be driven about from district to district—from King Street, Golden Square, maybe, to King street, Cheapside, and then back again to King Street, Covent Garden—and so on until he had tried the whole of the forty-two King Streets that are now set down in the Post-office Directory.

¶ i. *Of the Nomenclature of the London Streets.*

A painstaking friend of ours has, at our request, been at the trouble of classifying the various thoroughfares of London, and he finds that of the streets, squares, terraces, &c., bearing a *loyal* title, there are no less than seventy-three christened King, seventy-eight Queen, forty-two called Prince's, and four Princess's; twenty-six styled Duke, one Duchess, and twenty-eight having the title of Regent; while there are thirty-one Crown Streets, or Courts, and one Regina Villa.

Then many thoroughfares are named after the titles of *nobles*. Thus there are no less than eighty-nine localities called York, after the Duke of ditto; fifty-eight entitled Gloucester; forty-four Brunswick, in honour of that "house;" thirty-nine Bedford, thirty-five Devonshire, thirty-six Portland, thirty-four Cambridge, twenty-eight Lansdowne, twenty-seven Montague, twenty-six Cumberland, twenty-two Claremont and Clarence, twenty Clarendon, twenty-three Russell, twenty-one Norfolk—besides many other highways or byeways styled Cavendish, or Cecil, or Buckingham, or Northumberland, or Stanhope.

Next, in illustration of the principle of *hero-worship*, there are fifty-two thoroughfares called after Wellington, twenty-nine after Marlborough, and eleven after Nelson; there are, moreover, twenty styled Waterloo, and fifteen Trafalgar, thirteen Blenheim, one Boyne, and three Navarino; whilst, in honour of Prime Ministers, there are six localities called after Pitt, two after Fox, and three after Canning; in celebration of Lord Chancellors, five are named Eldon; for Politicians, one Place is styled Cobden, and two streets Burdett; and to commemorate the name of great poets and philosophers, there is one Shakespeare's Walk (at Shadwell), one Ben Jonson's Fields, eight Milton Streets, and seven thoroughfares bearing the name of Addison, and one that of Cato.

Of the number of thoroughfares called by simple *Christian* names, the following are the principal examples:—There are fifty-eight localities known as George, forty christened Victoria, forty-three Albert, and eight Adelaide. Then there are forty-seven Johns, forty-nine Charleses, thirty-five Jameses, thirty-three Edwards, thirty Alfreds, twenty Charlottes, and the same number of Elizabeths and Fredericks, together with a small number of Roberts, and Anns, and Peters, and Pauls, and Adams, and Amelias, and Marys, beside eight King Edwards, two King Williams, one King John, and one King Henry.

Many streets, on the other hand, bear the *surnames* of their builders or landlords; and, accordingly, we have several thoroughfares rejoicing in the illustrious names of Smith or Baker, or Newman, or Perry, or Nicholas, or Milman, or Warren, or Leigh, or Beaufoy, and indeed one locality bearing the euphonious title of Bugsby's Reach.

Religious titles, again, are not uncommon. Not only have we the celebrated Paternoster Row, and Ave-Maria Lane, and Amen Corner, and Adam and Eve Court, but there are All Hallows Chambers, and a number of Providence Rows and Streets. Moreover, there is a large family called either Church or Chapel, besides a Bishop's Walk, a Dean's Yard, and a Mitre Court, together with not a few christened College or Abbey; whilst there is a Tabernacle Row, Square, and Walk, as well as a well-known Worship Street, and no less than twenty distinct places bearing the name of Trinity, as well as two large districts styled Whitefriars and Blackfriars, and a bevy of streets called after the entire calendar of Saints, together with a posse of Angel Courts and Lanes.

Other places, on the contrary, delight in *Pagan* titles; for in the suburbs we find two Neptune Streets, four Minerva Terraces, two Apollo Buildings, one Diana Place, a Hermes Street, and a Hercules Passage; besides several streets dedicated to England's mythological patroness, Britannia, and some half-dozen roads, or cottages, or places, glorying in the title of the imaginary Scotch goddess, Caledonia. The same patriotic spirit seems to make the name of Albion very popular among the godfathers or godmothers of thoroughfares, for there are no less than some fifty buildings, chambers, cottages, groves, mews, squares, &c., rejoicing in the national cognomen.

Further, there is a large number of *astronomically-named* highways, such as those called Sun Street or Sols' Row, or Half-Moon Street, or Star Alley, or Corner. And, again, we have many of an *aquatic* turn, as witness the Thames Streets and River Terraces, and Brook Streets, and Wells Streets, and Water Lanes—ay, and one Ocean Row.

Others delight in *zoological* titles, such as Fish Street, Elephant Gardens, or Stairs, Cow Lane, Lamb Alley, and Bear Street, as well as Duck Lane, and Drake Street, and Raven Row, and Dove Court, with many Swan Streets and Lanes and Alleys, and Eagle Streets, and Swallow Streets, and one Sparrow Corner. In the same category, too, we must class the thoroughfares christened after fabulous monsters, such as the Red Lion and White Lion Streets, the Mermaid Courts, and Phœnix Places and Wharves.

In addition to these must be mentioned the *gastronomical* localities, such as Milk Street, Beer Street, Bread Street, Pine-Apple Place, Sugar-Loaf Court, and Vinegar Yard; and the old Pie Lane, and Pudding Corner; besides Orange Street, and Lemon Street, and the horticultural Pear-Tree Court, Fig-Tree ditto, Cherry-Tree Lane, and Walnut-Tree Walk.

Others, again, have *botanical* names given to them : thus, there are ten Rose Villas, Terraces, Lanes, or Courts; nine Holly ditto; seven Ivy Cottages or Places; one Lily Terrace; two Woodbine Villas; the same number of Fir Groves; a Lavender Hill and Place; twelve Willow Walks and Cottages, besides three Acacia and Avenue Roads or Gardens; one Coppice Row; and no less than fifty-four Cottages, or Crescents, or Parks styled Grove— though mostly all are as leafless as boot-trees.

A large number of thoroughfares, on the other hand, are called after their *size* or *shape*: Thus there are twenty-three Streets, Courts, Pavements, Walls, and Ways styled Broad; but only three Streets called Narrow. There are, however, six Acres, Alleys, or Lanes called Long; and an equal number of Buildings denominated Short. Then we have as many as thirty-five styled High, four called Back, and the same number bearing the opposite title of Fore; whilst there are no less than ten Rows denominated Middle, and twenty Courts, Lanes, &c. christened Cross, as well as one dubbed Turnagain. In addition to these there are three Ovals, four Triangles, two Polygons, and one Quadrant; besides an innumerable quantity of Squares, Circuses, and Crescents.

Some places, on the other hand, appear to have *chromatic* names, though this arises from the pigmentary patronymics of their original landlords. Hence there are sixteen thorough-fares called Green, two White, and one Grey.

Further, we have a considerable quantity named after the *cardinal points* of the compass, there being as many as forty-eight denominated North, not a few of which lie in a wholly different direction, and forty-four bearing the title of South; whilst there are twenty-nine nicknamed East, and an equal number West; but only one styled North-East .

In the suburbs the topographical titles are often of a *laudatory* character, and generally eulogistic of the view that was (originally, perhaps,) to be obtained from the Buildings, or Crescent, or Cottages, or Row, to which the inviting title has been applied. Accordingly we find that there are twenty-four Prospect Cottages and Places; four Belle-Vues, and a like number of Belvideres; whilst there is one Fair-View Place; besides nearly a score of Pleasant Places, four Mount Pleasants, sixteen Paradise Terraces or Cottages, and six Paragon Villas or Rows.

Others, still, are christened after particular *trades*. Thus, the Butchers have two Rows called after them; the Fishmongers two Alleys; the Dyers, three Courts or Buildings; the Barbers, one Yard; the Sadlers, three Buildings or Places; the Stonecutters, one Street; the Potters, a few Fields; the Weavers, two Streets; the Ironmongers, one Lane; and the Ropemakers, one Walk; whilst there are no less than thirty-three thoroughfares having the general title of Commercial. Further, in honour of the Bootmakers, there is one Place styled Crispin, one Lane called Shoe, and one Street bearing the name of Boot—besides a Petticoat Lane in honour of the ladies, and, for the poorer classes, a Rag Fair.

Then, of thoroughfares named after *materials*, there are eight Wood Streets, one Stone Buildings, one Iron and one Golden Square, seven Silver Streets, and two Diamond Rows.

Lastly, there is a large class of streets called after some *public place* near which they are situate. For instance, there are just upon one hundred localities having the prefix Park, and thirty-seven entitled Bridge, nineteen are called Market, twelve styled Palace, fourteen Castle, nine Tower, two Parliament, two Asylum, three Spital (the short for Hospital), one Museum, four Custom House, and a like number Charter House; but as yet there exist only two Railway Places, and one Tunnel Square.

Nor would the catalogue be complete if we omitted to enumerate the London *Hills*, such as Snow, Corn, Ludgate, Holborn, Primrose, Saffron, and Mutton; or the streets named after the ancient *Gates*, as Newgate, Ludgate, Aldgate, Aldersgate, Bishopsgate, and Moorgate; or those *cosmopolitan* thoroughfares dubbed Portugal Street, Spanish Place, America Square, Greek Street, Turk's Row, Denmark Hill, and Copenhagen Fields, not forgetting the ancient Petty France and the modern Little Britain.

¶ ii. *Character of the London Streets.*

The physiognomy of the metropolitan thoroughfares is well worthy of the study of some civic Lavater. The finely-chiselled features of an English aristocrat, are not more distinct from the common countenance of a Common Councilman, than is the stately Belgravian square from its vulgar brother in Barbican; and as there exists in society a medium class of people, between the noble and the citizen, who may be regarded as the patterns of ostensible respectability among us, such as bankers, lawyers, and physicians; so have we in London a class of respectable localities, whose architecture is not only as prim as the silver hair, or as cold-looking as the bald head, which is so distinctive of the "genteel" types above specified; but it is as different from the ornate and stately character of the buildings about the parks as they, on the other hand, differ from the heavy and ruddy look of the City squares; for what the Belgravian districts are in their "build" to the Bedfordian, and the Bedfordian again to the Towerian, so is there the same ratio in social rank and character among nobles, professional gentry, and citizens.

Again, the very east-end of the town, such as Bethnal green, is as marked in the cut of its bricks and mortar—in the "long lights" of the weavers' houses about Spitalfields, and the latticed pigeon-house, surmounting almost every roof—as is May Fair from Rag Fair; and so striking is this physiognomical expression—the different cast of countenance, as it were—in the houses of the several localities inhabited by the various grades of society, that to him who knows London well, a walk through its divers districts is as peculiar as a geographical excursion through the multiform regions of the globe.

Stroll through the streets, for instance, that constitute the environs of Fitzroy Square, and surely it needs not brass cards upon the doors to say that this is the artistic quarter of London. Notice the high window in the middle of the first floor, the shutters closed in the day time at all but the upper part of the casement, so as to give a "top light." See, too, the cobwebby window panes and the flat sticks of the old-fashioned parlour blinds leaning different ways— all betokening the residence of one who hardly belongs to the well-to-do classes. Observe, as you continue your walk, the group of artists' colour-men's shops, with the boxes of moist colours in the windows, and some large brown photographs, or water-colour drawings exposed for sale; and mark, in another street hard by, the warehouses of plaster casts, where you see bits of arms, or isolated hands, modelled in whiting; and chalk figures of horses, with all the muscles showing. After this, the mind's eye that cannot, at a glance, detect that hereabouts dwell the gentry who indulge in odd beards and hats, and delight in a picturesque "make-up," must need some intellectual spectacles to aid its perception.

Travel then across Regent Street to Saville Row, and, if you be there about noon, it will not be necessary to read the small brass tablets graven with "NIGHT-BELL," to learn that here some renowned physician or surgeon dwells in every other house; for you will see a seedy carriage, with fagged-looking horses, waiting at nearly all the thresholds, and pale people, with black patches of respirators over their mouths, in the act of leaving or entering the premises; so that you will readily discover that the gentry frequenting *this* locality are about to hurry round the Metropolis, and feel some score of pulses, and look at some score of tongues, at the rate of ten guineas per hour.

Next wend your way to Chancery Lane, and give heed to the black-coated gentry, with bundles of papers tied with red-tape in their hands, the door-posts striped with a small catalogue of names, the street-doors set wide open, and individuals in black clerical-looking gowns and powdered coachmen-like wigs, tripping along the pavement towards the Courts; and stationers' shops, in which hang legal almanacs, and skins of parchment, as greasy-looking as tracing-paper, with "this indenture" flourished in the corner, and law lists bound in bright red leather, and law books in sleek yellow calf. Note, too, the furniture shops, with leathern-topped writing-tables and pigeon-holes, and what-nots for papers, and square piles of drawers, and huge iron safes and japanned tin boxes, that seem as if they had had a coat of raspberry jam by way of paint, against which the boys had been dabbing their fingers— all which, of course, will apprise you that you are in the legal quarter of the town.

Then, how different the squares in the different parts of London—the squares which are so purely national—so utterly unlike your foreign "place," or "*platz*," that bare paved or gravelled space, with nothing but a fountain, a statue, or column, in the centre of it. True, the trees may grow as black in London as human beings at the tropics; but still there is the broad carpet of green sward in the centre, and occasionally the patches of bright-coloured flowers that speak of the English love of gardening—the Londoner's craving for country life.

What a distinctive air, we repeat, have the fashionable West End squares; how different from the "genteel" affairs in the northern districts of the Metropolis, as well as from the odd and desolate places in the City, or the obsolete and antiquated spots on the south side of Holborn and Oxford Street—like Leicester and Soho.

How spacious are the handsome old mansions around Grosvenor Square, with their quoins, windows, and door-cases of stone, bordering the sombre "rubbed" brick fronts. In France or Germany such enormous buildings would have a different noble family lodging on every "flat." The inclosure, too, is a small park, or palace garden, rather than the paved court-yard of foreign places.

Then there is Grosvenor's twin brother, Portman Square, where the houses are all but as imposing in appearance—and St. James's Square—and Berkeley—and Cavendish—and Hanover—and Manchester—with the still more stately and gorgeous Belgrave and Eaton Squares.

Next to these rank the respectable and genteel squares, such as Montague, and Bryanstone, and Connaught, and Cadogan, at the West End, and Fitzroy, and Russell, and Bedford, and Bloomsbury, and Tavistock, and Torrington, and Gordon, and Euston, and Mecklenburg, and Brunswick, and Queen's, and Finsbury—all lying in that district east of Tottenham Court Road which was the celebrated *terra incognita* of John Wilson Croker.

After these come the City squares—those intensely quiet places immured in the very centre of London, which seem as still and desolate as cloisters; and where the desire for peace is so strong upon the inhabitants, that there is generally a liveried street-keeper or beadle maintained to cane off the boys, as well as dispel the flock of organ-grinders and Punch-and-Judy men, and acrobats, who would look upon the tranquillity of the place as a mine of wealth to them. To this class belong Devonshire Square, Bishopsgate; Bridgewater Square, Barbican; America Square, Minories; Wellclose Square, London Docks; Trinity Square, Tower; Nelson Square, Blackfriars; Warwick Square, Newgate Street; and Gough and Salisbury Squares, Fleet Street; though many of these are but the mere bald "places" of the continent.

Further, we have the obsolete, or "used up" old squares, that lie south of Oxford Street and Holborn, and east of Regent Street, and which have mostly passed from fashionable residences into mere quadrangles, full of shops, or hotels, or exhibitions, or chambers; such are the squares of Soho, Leicester, Golden, Lincoln's-Inn-Fields, and even Covent Garden.

And, lastly, we have the pretentious *parvenu*-like suburban squares, such as Thurlow and Trevor, by Brompton; and Sloane, by Chelsea; and Edwardes, by Kensington; and Oakley, by Camden Town; and Holford and Claremont Squares, by Pentonville; and Islington Square; and Green Arbour Square, by Stepney; and Surrey Square, by the Old Kent Road; and the Oval, by Kennington.

In fine, there are now upwards of one hundred squares distributed throughout London, and these are generally in such extreme favour among the surrounding inhabitants, that they are each regarded as the headquarters of the *élite* of the district by all aspirants for fashionable distinction; so that the pretentious traders of Gower Street and the like, instead of writing down their address as Gower Street, Tottenham Court Road, love to exaggerate it into Gower Street, Bedford Square.

Of streets, again, we find the same distinctive classes as of the squares. There are, first, the fashionable streets, such as Arlington Street St. James's, and Park Lane, and Portland Place, and Richmond and Carlton Terraces, and Privy Gardens.

Then come the respectable or "genteel" thoroughfares of Clarges Street, and Harley Street, and Gloucester Place, and Woburn Place, and Keppel Street, &c.

After these we have the lodging-house localities, comprised in the several streets running out of the Strand.

Moreover, mention must be made of the distinctive streets, and narrow commercial lanes, crowding about the bank, where the houses are as full of merchants and clerks as a low lodging-house is full of tramps.

Further, there are the streets and districts for particular trades, as Long Acre, where the carriage-makers abound ; and Lombard Street, where the bankers love to congregate ; and Clerkenwell, the district for the watch-makers ; and Hatton Garden for the Italian glass-blowers; and the Borough for the hatters; Bermondsey for the tanners; Lambeth for the potters; and Spitalfields for weavers ; and Catherine Street for the newsvendors ; and Paternoster Row for the booksellers ; and the New Road for the zinc-workers : and Lower Thames Street for the merchants in oranges and foreign fruits ; and Mincing Lane for the wholesale grocers ; and Holywell Street and Rosemary Lane for old clothes ; and so on.

Again, one of the most distinctive quarters about London is in the neighbourhood of the Docks. The streets themselves in this locality have all, more or less, a maritime character; every other store is either stocked with gear for the ship or the sailor ; and the front of many a shop is filled with quadrants and bright brass sextants, chronometers, and ships' binnacles, with their compass cards trembling with the motion of the cabs and waggons passing in the street, whilst over the doorway is fixed a huge figure of a naval officer in a cocked hat, taking a perpetual sight at the people in the first-floor on the opposite side of the way. Then come the sailors' cheap shoe marts, rejoicing in the attractive sign of "Jack and his Mother;" every public house, too, is a "Jolly Jack Tar," or something equally taking, and there are "Free Concerts" at the back of every bar. Here, also, the sailmakers' shops abound, with their windows stowed with ropes, and smelling of tar as you pass them. All the neighbouring grocers are provision agents, and exhibit in their windows tin cases of meat and biscuits, and every article is "warranted to keep in any climate." The corners of the streets, moreover, are mostly monopolized by slopsellers, their windows parti-coloured with the bright red and blue flannel shirts, and the doors nearly blocked up with hammocks and well-oiled nor'-westers; whilst the front of the house itself is half covered with canvas trousers, rough pilot-coats, and shinny black dread-noughts. The foot-passengers alone would tell you that you were in the maritime district of London, for you pass now a satin waistcoated mate, and now a black sailor with a large fur cap on his head, and then a custom-house officer in his brass-buttoned jacket.

Nor would this account of the peculiarities of the London streets be complete if we omitted to mention the large body of people who derive their living from exercising some art or craft, or of carrying on some trade in them. This portion of people are generally to be seen in the greatest numbers at the London Street Markets of a Saturday night, and a more peculiar sight is not to be witnessed in any other capital of the world.

It is at these street markets that many of the working classes purchase their Sunday's dinner, and after pay-time on a Saturday night, the crowd in some parts is almost impassable. Indeed, the scene at such places has more the character of a fair than a market. There are hundreds of stalls, and every stall has its one or two lights; either it is illuminated by the intense white light of the new self-generating gas lamp, or else it is brightened up by the red smoky flame of the old-fashioned grease lamp. One man shows off his yellow haddocks with a candle stuck in a bundle of firewood ; his neighbours make a candlestick of a huge turnip, and the tallow gutters over its sides; whilst the boy shouting, "Eight a penny, stunning pears!" has surrounded his "dip" with a thick roll of brown paper that flares away in the wind. Some stalls are crimsom, with the fire shining through the holes beneath the baked chestnut stove; others have handsome octohedral lamps; while a few have a candle shining through a sieve; these, with the sparkling ground-glass globes of the tea-dealers' shops, and the butchers' gas-lights streaming and fluttering in the wind like flags of flame, pour forth such a flood of light, that at a distance the atmosphere immediately above the spot is as lurid as if the street were on fire.

The pavement and the road are crowded with purchasers and street sellers. The house-wife in a thick shawl, with the market-basket on her arm, walks slowly on, stopping now to look at the stall of caps, and now to cheapen a bunch of greens. Little boys holding three or four onions in their hand, creep between the people, wriggling their way through every interstice in the crowd, and asking for custom in whining tones as if seeking charity.

Then the tumult of the thousand cries of the eager dealers, all shouting at the top of their voices at one and the same time, is almost bewildering. "So-old again!" roars one. "Chesnuts, all ott!—A penny a score!" bawls another. "An aypenny a skin, blacking!" shrieks a boy. "Buy, buy, buy, buy, buy,—bu-u-wy!" jabbers the butcher. "Half-a-quire of paper for a penny!" bellows the street stationer. "An aypenny a lot, inguns!" "Tuppence a pound, grapes!" "Three-a-penny, Yarmouth bloaters!" "Who'll buy a bonnet for fourpence?" "Pick 'em out cheap, here! three pair for an aypenny, boot-laces." "Now's your time! beautiful whelks, a penny a lot!" "Here's ha-p-orths!" shouts the perambulating confectioner. "Come and look at e'm!—prime toasters!" bellows one with a Yarmouth bloater stuck on a toasting fork. "Penny a lot, fine russets—penny a lot!" calls the apple woman. And so the Babel goes on.

One man stands with his red-edged mats hanging over his back and chest like a herald's coat; and the girl, with her basket of walnuts, lifts her brown-stained fingers to her mouth, as she screams, "Fine warnuts! sixteen a penny, fine war-r-nuts!" At one of the neigh-bouring shops, a boot-maker, to attract custom, has illuminated his shop-front with a line of gas, and in its full glare stands a blind beggar, his eyes turned up so as to show only the whites, and mumbling some begging rhymes, that are drowned in the shrill notes of the player on the bamboo-flute, next to him. The boys' sharp shoutings; the women's cracked voices; the gruff hoarse roar of the men—are all mingled together. Sometimes an Irishman is heard, with his cry of "Fine 'ating apples!" or else the jingling music of an unseen organ breaks out as the trio of street singers rest between the verses.

Then the sights, as you elbow your way through the crowd, are equally multifarious. Here is a stall glittering with new tin saucepans; there another, bright with its blue and yellow crockery and sparkling white glass. Now you come to a row of old shoes, arranged along the pavement; now to a stand of gaudy tea-trays; then to a shop, with red hand-kerchiefs and blue checked shirts, fluttering backwards and forwards, and a temporary counter built up on the kerb, behind which shop-boys are beseeching custom. At the door of a tea-shop, with its hundreds of white globes of light, stands a man delivering bills, "thanking the public for past favours and defying competition." Here, alongside the road, are some half-dozen headless tailors' dummies, dressed in Chesterfields and fustian jackets, each labelled, "LOOK AT THE PRICES," or "OBSERVE THE QUALITY." Next, we pass a butcher's shop, crimson and white, with the meat piled up to the first-floor; in front of which, the butcher himself, in his blue coat, walks up and down sharpening his knife on the steel that hangs to his waist, saying to each woman as she passes, "What can I do for you, my dear?" A little further on, stands the clean family begging; the father, with his head down, as if ashamed to be seen, and a box of lucifers held forth in his hand; the boys, in newly-worked pinafores, and the tidily got-up mother, with a child at her breast.

One stall is green and white with bunches of turnips—another red with apples; the next yellow with onions; and the one after that purple with pickling cabbages. One minute you pass a man with an umbrella turned inside upwards, and full of prints. The next moment you hear a fellow with a peep-show of Mazeppa, and Paul Jones the pirate, describing the pictures to the crowd of boys as some of them spy in at the little round windows. Then you are startled by the sharp snap of percussion caps from the crowd of lads, firing at the target for nuts, at the corner of the street; and the minute afterwards you see a black man clad in thin white garments, and shivering in the cold, with tracts in his hand, or else you hear the sounds of music from "Frazier's Circus," on the other side of the road, and the man outside the door of the penny concert beseeching the passers-by to "be in time! be in time!" as Mr. Somebody is just about to sing his favourite song of "The Knife-grinder."

Such, indeed, is the riot, the struggle, and the scramble for a living, that the confusion and uproar of the London Street Market on Saturday night have a bewildering and half-saddening effect upon the thoughtful mind.

Each salesman tries his utmost to sell his wares, tempting the passers-by with his bargains. The boy with his stock of herbs, offers a "double 'andful of fine parsley for a penny." The man with the donkey-cart filled with turnips, has three lads to shout for him to their utmost, with their " Ho ! ho ! hi-i-i ! What do you think of this here ? A penny a bunch ! —-a penny a bunch ! Hurrah for free trade ! Here's your turnips !"

Until the scene and tumult are witnessed and heard, it is impossible to have a sense of the scramble that is going on throughout London for a living—the shouting and the struggling of hundreds to get the penny profit out of the poor man's Sunday's dinner.

𝔅𝔬𝔬𝔨 𝔱𝔥𝔢 𝔉𝔦𝔯𝔰𝔱.

—◆—

PROFESSIONAL LONDON.

WE now pass from our general survey of the Metropolis, to consider its several parts in detail. For as geographers usually prefix to their Atlases a map of the northern and southern hemispheres of the globe, so have we, in this our literary Atlas of the World of London, first laid down a chart of the two opposite spheres of metropolitan society—the very rich and the very poor—a kind of Mercator's plan, as it were, wherein the antipodes of London life are brought under one view.

This done, however, we now proceed, in due geographical order, to deal *seriatim* with each of the quarters of the Metropolitan World.

And first of Professional London.

Professional London, we consider to include that portion of metropolitan society of which the members follow some intellectual calling—living by mental, rather than manual dexterity; that is to say, deriving their income from the exercise of *talent* rather than *skill*. For the members of every profession must be more or less talented, even as every handicraftsman must be more or less skilful; and as the working engineer acquires, by practice, a certain expertness in the use of his fingers, so the member of a profession learns, by education, a certain quickness of perception and soundness of judgment in connection with the matters to which he attends; and thus people, lacking the faculty which he possesses, are glad to avail themselves of his services in that respect.

According to the above definition, the members of the professions are not limited merely to lawyers, doctors, and clergymen, but include also professors, teachers, scientific men, authors, artists, musicians, actors—indeed all who live " by their wits," as the opprobrious phrase runs, as if it were a dishonour for a person to gain a livelihood by the exercise of his intellect; and the judge did not depend upon his mental faculties for his subsistence, as much as the *chevalier d'industrie* whom he tries.

The professional or intellectual class is not a large one, even when thus extended beyond its usual limited signification; for in all Great Britain there are, in round numbers, only 230,000 people gaining a subsistence by their talents, out of a population of very nearly 21 millions; and this is barely a ninetieth part of the whole.

Altogether, there are throughout England, Wales, and Scotland, 30,047 clergymen and ministers, 18,422 lawyers, and 22,383 medical men. Indeed, the Commissioners of the Census tell us, that the three professions, even with their allied and subordinate members, amount to only 112,193, and " though their importance cannot be overrated," they add, " yet, in numbers, they would be out-voted by the tailors of the United Kingdom."

Of the *unrecognized* professions, the authors in Great Britain are 2,981 in number; the artists, 9,148; the professors of science (returned as such), only 491; while the teachers amount to 106,344;—making a total of 118,964 individuals

Now, let us see what proportion of the body of professional people existing throughout Great Britain, is found located in the Metropolis.

According to the returns of the last census, the gross number of persons living by the exercise of their talents in London (including the same classes as were before mentioned), amounts to 47,746; and this out of a population of 2,362,236—so that the proportion is just upon one-fiftieth of the whole. Hence we find that whereas there are eleven people in every thousand belonging to the intellectual classes throughout Great Britain, or rather more than one per cent. of the gross population,* the ratio in the Capital is a fraction beyond twenty to the thousand, or about two per cent. of the entire metropolitan people.

* The distribution of the Professional Classes throughout the country, and the ratio they bear to the rest of the adult population is as follows :—

TABLE SHOWING THE DISTRIBUTION OF THE PROFESSIONAL CLASSES (MALES AND FEMALES ABOVE 20 YEARS) THROUGHOUT ENGLAND AND WALES, A.D. 1851.

DIVISIONS.	Clergymen, Prot. Ministers, Priests, &c.	Barristers, Solicitors, and others.	Physicians, Surgeons, and others	Authors, Editors, and others.	Artists, Architects, and others.	Scientific Persons.	Music, School, and other Masters.	Total.	Population above Twenty years.	Number to every 1000.
DIVISION I.—LONDON . .	2,388	5,703	5,100	1,160	3,666	146	14,570	32,733	1,394,963	23·4
DIVISION II. — SOUTHERN-EASTERN COUNTIES.										
Surrey (ex-Metro.) . . .	372	360	247	23	82	3	1,444	2,531	111,025	22·7
Kent (ex-Metro.)	779	332	502	45	145	6	2,678	4,487	263,292	17·0
Sussex	659	345	412	53	99	8	2,316	3,892	182,164	21·3
Hampshire	744	292	372	43	138	8	2,260	3,857	222,633	17·3
Berkshire	417	147	194	20	45	..	1,165	1,988	108,017	18·4
Total . . .	2,971	1,476	1,727	184	509	25	9,863	16,755	887,131	18·9
DIVISION III.—SOUTH MIDLAND COUNTIES.										
Middlesex (ex-Metro.) . .	251	270	243	33	91	4	1,255	2,147	84,190	25·5
Hertfordshire	315	115	231	6	26	2	904	1,599	92,152	17·3
Buckinghamshire	301	79	99	18	18	..	668	1,183	76,570	15·4
Oxfordshire	479	104	145	101	35	3	915	1,782	92,252	19·3
Northamptonshire . . .	453	105	155	5	30	1	1,022	1,771	115,735	15·3
Huntingdonshire	128	32	37	2	2	..	305	506	31,260	16·1
Bedfordshire	228	45	92	4	16	1	453	839	67,029	12·5
Cambridgeshire	393	113	131	123	27	8	934	1,729	101,587	17·0
Total . . .	2,548	863	1,133	292	245	19	6,456	11,556	660,775	17·4
DIVISION IV.—EASTERN COUNTIES.										
Essex	624	194	282	29	53	5	1,834	3,021	183,845	16·4
Suffolk	686	172	248	24	54	4	1,672	2,860	180,371	15·8
Norfolk	860	292	294	25	72	5	2,192	3,740	239,504	15·6
Total . . .	2,170	658	824	78	179	14	5,698	9,621	603,720	15·9
DIVISION V.—SOUTH-WESTERN COUNTIES.										
Wiltshire	484	142	172	22	25	5	1,213	2,063	129,245	15·9
Dorsetshire	375	121	139	16	35	..	960	1,646	95,612	17·2
Devonshire	1064	497	625	52	174	9	3,110	5,531	318,707	17·3
Cornwall	450	162	230	17	33	5	1,401	2,298	184,879	12·3
Somersetshire	979	403	473	38	131	10	2,635	4,669	249,581	18·7
Total . . .	3,352	1,325	1,639	145	398	29	9,319	16,207	978,024	16·5

For continuation of Table see next page.

When, therefore, we come to consider that the above estimate includes the whole of the "learned professions" (as they are invidiously styled), as well as all those whose lives are

DIVISIONS.	Clergymen, Prot. Ministers, Priests, &c.	Barristers, Solicitors, and others.	Physicians, Surgeons, and others.	Authors, Editors, and others.	Painters, Architects, and others.	Scientific Persons.	Music, School, and other Masters.	Total.	Population above Twenty years.	Number to every 1000.
DIVISION VI.—WEST MIDLAND COUNTIES.										
Gloucestershire	837	478	517	67	201	19	2,478	4,597	236,002	19·4
Herefordshire	217	100	83	20	15	1	447	883	56,320	15·6
Shropshire	466	187	229	18	36	3	1,100	2,039	134,691	15·1
Staffordshire	623	278	361	29	147	10	2,209	3,657	329,602	11·0
Worcestershire. . . .	421	257	214	22	93	2	1,314	2,323	140,867	16·4
Warwickshire	656	234	459	57	245	5	2,226	3,882	262,905	14·7
Total . . .	3,220	1,534	1,863	213	737	40	9,774	17,381	1,160,387	14·9
DIVISION VII.—NORTH MIDLAND COUNTIES.										
Leicestershire . . . ,	422	100	167	17	61	5	1,159	1,931	127,425	15·1
Rutlandshire	74	8	16	1	1	..	131	231	13,260	17·4
Lincolnshire	729	207	325	19	61	7	2,060	3,408	213,229	15·9
Nottinghamshire . . .	366	118	184	20	69	5	1,348	2,110	160,197	13·1
Derbyshire	320	126	185	14	43	4	1,030	1,722	140,568	12·2
Total . . .	1,911	559	877	71	235	21	5,728	9,402	654,679	14·3
DIVISION VIII.—NORTH-WESTERN COUNTIES.										
Cheshire	489	307	312	36	106	8	1,819	3,077	229,013	13·4
Lancashire	1,567	1025	1338	120	633	52	6,488	11,223	1,122,817	10·0
Total . . .	2,056	1,332	1,650	156	739	60	8,307	14,300	1,351,830	10·6
DIVISION IX.—YORKSHIRE.										
West Riding	1256	611	857	71	284	28	4,726	7,833	712,114	11·0
East Riding.	401	232	282	30	115	3	1,430	2,493	142,672	17·4
North Riding	349	121	183	9	28	2	1,018	1,710	107,159	15·9
Total . . .	2,006	964	1,322	110	427	33	7,174	12,036	961,945	12·5
DIVISION X.—NORTHERN COUNTIES.										
Durham	382	175	311	31	68	13	1,496	2,476	216,638	11·4
Northumberland . . .	335	169	277	34	80	6	1,058	1,959	166,152	11·8
Cumberland	274	102	142	12	24	5	845	1,404	106,908	13·1
Westmoreland	128	31	54	7	16	1	283	520	31,762	16·0
Total . . .	1,119	477	784	84	188	25	3,682	6,359	521,460	12·2
DIVISION XI.—MONMOUTHSHIRE AND WALES.										
Monmouthshire	309	82	126	1	21	4	513	1,056	96,821	11·0
South Wales	1160	246	300	37	80	2	1,493	3,318	326,367	10·2
North Wales	762	158	224	16	29	..	884	2,073	278,492	7·4
Total . . .	2,231	486	650	54	130	6	2,890	6,447	701,680	9·2
Total for England and Wales	25,975	15,377	16,969	2,547	7,453	418	83,461	152,797	9,876,594	15·0

By the above table, it will be seen that the professional or highly-educated classes range from about 7·5 to

devoted to the equally learned pursuits of literature, art, science, and education; that is to say, not only those versed in divinity, law, and physic, but the historian, the poet, the critic, the painter, the sculptor, the architect, the natural philosopher, and the musician, together with the teachers of youth and professors of science—in fine, not only the modern Butlers and Paleys, the Blackstones and Bacons, the Harveys and Hunters, but, in the words of the Census Commissioners, the living "Shakespeares, Humes, Handels, Raphaels, Michael Angelos, Wrens, and Newtons"—when we consider this, we repeat, it must be confessed that the proportion of one, or even two, per cent. of such folk to the entire population, appears but little complimentary to the taste or culture of our race. Otherwise, surely every hundred persons in Great Britain would think it requisite to maintain *more than one* person for the joint cure of their bodies and souls, as well as the redress of their wrongs and the enlightenment or refinement of their minds.

Still, another view must, in prudence, be taken of the matter. However much the intellectual classes may contribute to the honour and glory of a nation, nevertheless, we must admit, they add—*directly*—but little, if any, to its material wealth. Religion, health, justice, literature, art, science, education—admirable as they all be—are mental and spiritual riches, instead of commodities having an *exchangeable* value—being metaphysical luxuries, rather than physical necessities: for wisdom, taste, and piety do not tend to appease those grosser wants of our nature, which the grosser riches of a country go to satisfy; nor will the possession of them fill the stomach, or clothe the limbs, or shelter the head; so that those who give up their lives to such pursuits cannot possibly be ranked as self-supporting individuals, since they must be provided for out of the stock of such as serve directly, by their capital or their labour, to increase the products of the nation.

Accordingly, the maintenance of even *one* such unproductive person to every hundred individuals (especially when we bear in mind that three-fourths in every such hundred must, naturally, be incapacitated from the severer labours of life, by either sex or age, as women and the very old and very young) reflects no little credit on our countrymen; since, in order to uphold that ratio, every twenty-five producers (*i.e.*, one-fourth of each century of people) throughout the kingdom, must, in addition to the support of their own families (which may be taken at three-fourths in every such century), voluntarily part with a considerable portion of their creature comforts, in order to enjoy the benefit of the teachings, the advice, or the aspirations of their "professional" brethren.*

It is, however, hardly fair to rank professional men among the non-producers of a country; for though your doctors in divinity, law, and physic, as well as poets, philosophers, and pedagogues, till not, "neither do they spin," it is certain that they contribute, *indirectly*, to the wealth of a nation, as much—if not more, perhaps—than any other class.

Newton, for instance, by the invention of the sextant, as well as by that vast opening-up of our astronomical knowledge which served to render navigation simpler and safer, did more to extend our maritime commerce than any merchant enterprise could ever have effected. Again, all must allow that the steam-labourer created by Watt has tended to

---

25·5 individuals to every 1000 of the adult population throughout England and Wales; and that whilst the highest ratio of professional people is found in Middlesex, London, Surrey, and Sussex, the lowest proportion obtains in Northumberland, Durham, Stafford, the West Riding of York, Lancaster, Monmouth, and South and North Wales. This result coincides nearly with the returns of the relative amount of education prevailing throughout the several counties of England and Wales, as indicated by the number of persons who sign the marriage register with marks; and by which returns it appears that there is the least number of educated persons in Monmouth, South Wales, and North Wales, and the greatest number in Surrey and Middlesex. Thus we perceive that the proportion of professional classes is an indication of the educated state of the people in the various counties.

* The average number of persons to a family in England and Wales is 4·827.—*Census Report for* 1851.

increase our manufactures more than many million pairs of hands; whilst the steam-carriage of Stephenson has helped to distribute the products of particular districts over the entire country, far beyond the powers of an infinite number of carriers. How many working men would it have taken to have enriched the nation to the same amount as Arkwright, the penny barber, did by his single invention of the spinning-jenny? What number of weavers would be required to make as much cloth as he, who devised the power-loom, produced by the mere effort of his brain? Surely, too, Lee, the university scholar, has given more stockings to the poor, by the invention of his "frame," than all the knitters that ever lived. Farther, have not the manures discovered by our chemists increased our crops to a greater extent than the whole of the agricultural labourers throughout the kingdom, and the reasonings of our geologists and metallurgists added to our mineral wealth more than the entire body of our miners and smelters?

Still, these are merely the "economical" results springing from science and education; those results, on the other hand, which are due to the practice of the "learned" professions, though perhaps less brilliant, are equally indisputable. The medical skill which restores the disabled workman to health and strength surely cannot be regarded as *valueless* in the State; nor can we justly consider the knowledge which has prolonged the term of life, and consequently of industry, in this country, as yielding nothing to the wealth-fund of the nation. Moreover, that honourable vocation which has for its object the prevention and redress of wrong, and the recovery of every man's due, serves not only to give a greater security to capital, and so to induce the wealthy to *employ* rather than hoard their gains, but also to protect the poor against the greed and power of the avaricious rich—this, too, cannot but be acknowledged to be intimately concerned in promoting the industry and increasing the riches of the community; whilst that still higher calling, which seeks to make all men charitable and kind, rather than sternly just, to their less favoured brethren, which teaches that there are higher things in life than the "rights of capital" and political economy, and which, by inculcating special respect and duties to the poor, has been mainly instrumental in emancipating the labourer from the thraldom of villanage, and consequently in giving a tenfold return to his industry as a free workman—such a calling may also be said to have a positive commercial *value* among us.

Surely, then, professions which yield products like these cannot be regarded as altogether unproductive in the land.

The professional classes constitute what, in the cant language of literature, is styled "the aristocracy of intellect;" and it must be admitted, even by those who object to the introduction of the title *aristos* into the republic of letters, that the body of professional men form by themselves a great intellectual clan—the tribe which is specially distinguished from all others by the learning, wisdom, or taste of its members, and the one, moreover, which in all philosophic minds cannot but occupy the *foremost* position in society. For, without any disposition to disparage those classes who owe their social pre-eminence either to their birth or their wealth, we should be untrue to our own class and vocation if we did not, without arrogance, claim for it—despite the "order of precedence" prevalent at Court—a position second to none in the community; and, surely, even those who feel an honourable pride in the deeds and glory of their ancestors, and they too, who, on the other hand, find a special virtue in the possession of inordinate riches or estates, must themselves allow that high intellectual endowments have an *intrinsic* nobility belonging to them, compared with which the *extrinsic* nobility of "blood" or "lands" is a mere assumption and pretence.

Now it must not be inferred, from the tenor of the above remarks, that we are adverse to the aristocratic institutions of this country. Far from it; we believe in no equality on this side of the grave: for as Nature has made one man wiser, or better, or braver, or more

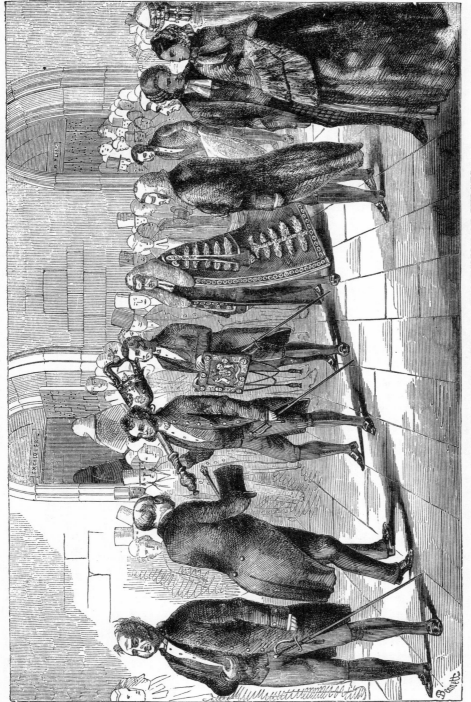

OPENING OF COURTS, WESTMINSTER.—PROCESSION OF JUDGES.

prudent than another, it is our creed that society must always own a "superior class" of some sort—superior in intellect, goodness, heroism, or worldly possessions, according as the nation chooses to measure by one or more of those standards. The Stanleys, the Howards, the Russells, &c., are, to all unprejudiced minds, unquestionably more worthy of social respect, as nature's own gentlemen, than the descendants of Greenacre, Burke, and Rush—nature's own ruffians; and so, again, we cannot but regard the Barings and the Jones-Lloyds as more dignified and useful members of the community than your able-bodied pauper or sturdy vagrant.

But, while making these admissions, we must at the same time acknowledge that we hold the Shakespeares, the Newtons, the Watts, the Blackstones, the Harveys, the Fullers, the Reynolds, the Purcells, and indeed all who have distinguished themselves either in law, divinity, medicine, literature, art, science, or education, not only as being among the very worthiest of England's worthies, but as constituting the class which lends the chief dignity to a nation in the eyes of all foreign countries—the untitled nobility of the world, rather than of any mere isolated empire.

Nor would it be just to ourselves, and our own order, if we did not here assert that the literary vocation—truthfully, righteously, and perfectly carried out—claims kindred, not only with all philosophy as the ground-work of each particular science, and ethics as the basis of all law, and humanism which enters so largely into medical knowledge, and æsthetics as the foundation of all arts connected with the beautiful, but also with religion itself, in its inculcation of the Christian principles—its use of the parabular* form of instruction—as well as its denunciation of wrong, and its encouragement of good-will and charity among all men.

Moreover, it is our pride to add, that, of all pursuits and ranks in the world, there is none which depends so thoroughly on public acclaim, and so little on sovereign caprice, for the honour and glory of its members; and none, therefore, in which honours and glories cast so high and sterling a dignity upon its chiefs.

Well, it is with the professional, or rather let us say the intellectual, portion of metropolitan society that we purpose first dealing here.

The professionals resident in London number, as we have said, 47,000 and odd individuals in the aggregate; and, therefore, constitute nearly one-fifth of the entire intellectual class distributed throughout Great Britain.

Included in the gross number of metropolitan professionals are, 5,863 lawyers, 5,631 doctors, 2,393 clergymen and ministers, and 11,210 "subordinates"—making altogether 25,097 persons belonging to the so-called "learned" professions; whilst to these must be added the sum of 22,649 persons connected with the "unrecognized" professions; and including 1,195 literary men, 17,241 teachers, 156 professors of science, and 4,057 artists and architects.†

Of each and all of these varieties of Professional London it is our intention to treat, seriatim, under the several divisions of Legal London—Medical London—Religious London—Literary London—Artistic London—Scholastic London, and so on, dealing with each of those phases of Metropolitan life as if it were a distinct Metropolis—estimating its population—marking out its boundaries and districts—and treating of the manners and customs of the people belonging to it, from the highest to the lowest; indeed, attempting for the first time to write and photograph the history of our multifarious Capital, in the nineteenth cen-

---

* This word is hardly formed upon correct etymological principles, the Latin adjectival affix, "ular" —as in tabular, from "table"—cannot strictly be applied to a Greek substantive. The use, however, of the true græco-adjective "parabolic" in a wholly different sense is, perhaps, sufficient apology for the formation of the mongrel term.

† The distribution of the professional classes throughout the several districts of London is as follows:—

tury; and we shall now begin to set forth the several details in connection with the first of those divisions.

TABLE SHOWING THE DISTRIBUTION OF THE PROFESSIONAL CLASSES (MALES AND FEMALES, 20 YEARS AND UPWARDS) THROUGHOUT LONDON.

DISTRICTS.	Clergymen, Prot. Ministers, Priests, &c.	Barristers, Solicitors, and others.	Physicians, Surgeons, and others.	Authors, Editors, and others.	Painters, Architects, and others.	Scientific Persons.	Music, School, and other Masters.	Total.	Population, above Twenty years.	Number to every 1000.
WEST DISTRICTS.										
Kensington	219	722	394	89	337	8	1,334	3,103	73,205	42·4
Chelsea	80	130	119	29	122	3	470	953	33,619	28·3
St. George (Hanover Sq.)	121	329	380	52	153	7	589	1,631	48,969	33·3
Westminster	59	130	74	32	90	..	366	751	39,722	18·9
St. Martin in the Fields	35	90	107	31	67	..	141	471	16,154	29·1
St. James, Westminster	41	159	192	41	91	4	199	727	24,023	30·2
Total West Districts	555	1,560	1,266	274	860	22	3,099	7,636	235,692	32·4
NORTH DISTRICTS.										
Marylebone	195	477	558	79	429	23	1,344	3,105	99,445	31·2
Hampstead	36	101	41	9	32	1	165	385	7,110	54·1
Pancras	209	661	515	149	710	13	1,450	3,707	99,809	37·1
Islington	146	255	192	57	167	9	888	1,714	55,446	30·9
Hackney	103	126	111	26	60	1	584	1,021	33,268	30·7
Total North Districts	689	1,620	1,417	330	1,398	47	4,431	9,932	295,078	33·6
CENTRAL DISTRICTS.										
St. Giles	67	381	206	41	147	6	297	1,145	34,469	32·2
Strand	33	267	141	82	124	10	232	889	27,317	32·5
Holborn	47	403	101	40	80	3	203	885	28,104	31·5
Clerkenwell	47	121	127	35	87	3	383	803	37,749	21·2
St. Luke	29	35	93	5	24	..	194	380	31,231	12·1
East London	26	25	84	8	13	2	186	344	26,194	13·1
West London	18	138	70	19	23	..	87	355	17,890	19·8
London City	74	120	146	22	42	4	242	650	34,656	18·7
Total Central Districts	341	1,490	968	252	540	28	1,824	5,451	237,610	22·9
EAST DISTRICTS.										
Shoreditch	52	37	100	28	72	3	487	779	61,150	12·7
Bethnal Green	61	17	51	10	25	9	262	435	47,636	9·1
Whitechapel	36	12	83	5	19	5	221	381	45,988	8·3
St. George in the East	24	7	47	5	13	6	169	271	27,894	9·7
Stepney	77	32	114	13	56	4	564	860	62,661	13·7
Poplar	23	12	43	1	19	..	180	278	26,398	10·5
Total East Districts	273	117	438	62	204	27	1,883	3,004	271,727	11·0
SOUTH DISTRICTS.										
St. Saviour (Southwark)	13	15	65	7	41	..	130	271	21,040	12·8
St. Olave (Southwark)	13	4	79	2	3	..	72	173	12,342	14·0
Bermondsey	23	5	35	4	21	..	214	302	26,587	11·3
St. George (Southwark)	41	45	79	13	50	1	264	493	29,924	16·5
Newington	47	82	112	44	97	2	365	749	37,298	20·0
Lambeth	114	284	253	90	223	4	1,084	2,052	80,322	25·5
Wandsworth	84	159	83	20	46	3	543	938	29,236	32·1
Camberwell	57	130	109	30	94	2	521	943	31,699	29·7
Rotherhithe	9	3	13	1	6	..	80	112	10,026	11·1
Greenwich	68	92	132	18	56	8	616	990	58,033	17·0
Lewisham	61	97	51	14	27	2	336	588	19,303	30·4
Total South Districts	530	916	1,011	243	664	22	4,225	7,611	355,810	21·4
Total for all London	2,388	5,703	5,100	1,161	3,667	146	15,462	33,634	1,395,917	24·0

DIVISION I.

LEGAL LONDON.

THERE is a legal district of London as unmistakably as there is a Jews' quarter in Frankfort; for the *Juden-gasse* of the German free town is hardly more distinct from the *Zeil*, than Chancery Lane and its environs from the City or West End of our Metropolis.

And as there are several foreign colonies scattered throughout the British Capital—as Hatton Garden and its purlieus, swarming with glass-blowers and organ-grinders, is the Metropolitan ITALIA; the neighbourhood of Leicester Square, with its congregation of beards and soft hats, the Cockney GALLIA ULTERIOR; and the parish of St. Giles, where the courts and cellars teem with hod-men and market-women, the London HIBERNIA; so is there a peculiar race of people grouped around the Courts of Law and Inns of Court—Westminster and Lincoln's Inn being the two great legal provinces of London, even as York and Canterbury are the two great ecclesiastical provinces of England.

A reference to the annexed maps will show that Legal London is composed not only of lawyers' residences and chambers, but of Inns of Court and Law Courts—Civil as well as Criminal, "Superior" as well as Petty—and County Courts, and Police Courts, and Prisons; and that whilst the Criminal, the County, and Police Courts, as well as the Prisons, are dotted, at intervals, all over the Metropolis, the Superior Law Courts are focussed at Westminster and Guildhall; the Inns of Court being grouped round Chancery Lane, and the legal residences, or rather "chambers" (for lawyers, like merchants, now-a-days live mostly away from their place of business), concentrated into a dense mass about the same classic spot, but thinning gradually off towards Guildhall and Westminster, as if they were the connecting links between the legal courts and the legal inns.

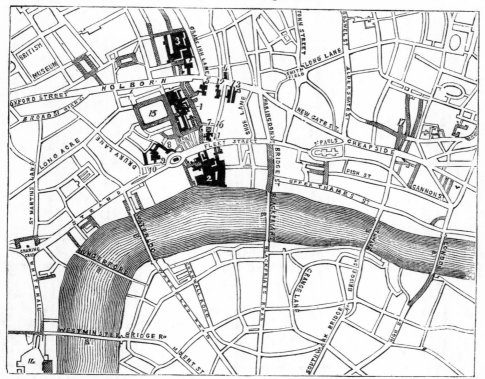

MAP OF THE INNS OF COURTS AND DISTRICTS INHABITED BY LAWYERS.
(*The Tinted Thoroughfares show the Streets inhabited by Lawyers.*)

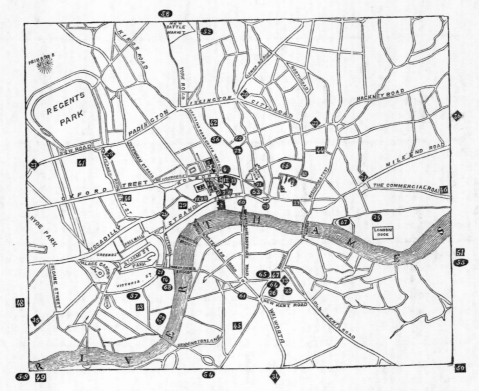

MAP OF THE SUPERIOR LAW COURTS, COUNTY COURTS, SESSIONS HOUSES, POLICE COURTS, AND PRISONS THROUGHOUT LONDON.

The Circles represent Inns of Court and Law Courts; the Diamonds, County Courts; the Squares, Police Courts; and the Ovals, Prisons.

INNS OF COURT.
1. Lincoln's Inn.
2. Temple.
3. Gray's Inn.
4. Furnival's Inn.
5. Staple Inn
6. Sergeant's Inn.
7. Clifford's Inn.
8. Clement's Inn.
9. New Inn.
10. Lyon's Inn.
11. Symond's Inn.
12. Barnard's Inn.
13. Thavies' Inn.

LAW COURTS.
14. Westminster Hall.

15. Lincoln's Inn.
16. Rolls Court.
17. Guildhall
18. Bankruptcy.
19. Insolvent Debtors'.
20. Ecclesiastical and Admiralty.
21. Central Criminal Court.
22. Middlesex Sessions House
23. Surrey Sessions House.
24. Westminster Sessions Ho.
25. Tower Liberty Sessions House,
26. Southwark Sessions Ho.

COUNTY COURTS.
27. Marylebone.

28. Bloomsbury.
29. Westminster.
30. Clerkenwell.
31. Whitechapel.
32. Shoreditch.
33. Southwark.
34. Lambeth.
35. Brompton.
36. Bow.

POLICE COURTS.
37. Mansion House.
38. Guildhall.
39. Bow Street.
40. Marlborough Street.
41. Marylebone.
42. Clerkenwell.

43. Westminster.
44. Worship Street.
45. Lambeth.
46. Thames.
47. Southwark
48. Hammersmith.
49. Wandsworth.
50. Greenwich.
51. Woolwich.

PRISONS.
52. Pentonville.
53. Millbank.
54. Female Convict, Brixton
55. Hulks, Woolwich.
56. House of Correction.
57. Middlesex House of Correction.

58. City House of Correction Holloway.
59. Surrey House of Correction.
60. Bridewell Hospital.
61. Bridewell House of Occupation, Saint George's Fields.
62. Middlesex House of Detention.
63. Newgate.
64. Surrey County Gaol.
65. Queen's Bench.
66. Whitecross Street.
67. Tower.
68. Strong Room, House o Commons.

The Inns of Court are themselves sufficiently peculiar to give a strong distinctive mark to the locality in which they exist; for here are seen broad open squares like huge court-yards, paved and treeless, and flanked with grubby mansions—as big and cheerless-looking as barracks—every one of them being destitute of doors, and having a string of names painted in stripes upon the door-posts, that reminds one of the lists displayed at an estate-agent's office and there is generally a chapel-like edifice called the "hall," that is devoted to feeding rather than praying, and where the lawyerlings " qualify" for the bar by eating so many dinners,; and become at length—gastronomically—" learned in the law." Then how peculiar are the tidy legal gardens attached to the principal Inns, with their close-shaven grass-plots looking as sleek and bright as so much green plush, and the clean-swept gravel walks thronged with children, and nursemaids, and law-students. How odd, too, are the desolate-looking legal alleys or courts adjoining these Inns, with nothing but a pump or a cane-bearing street-keeper to be seen in the midst of them, and occasionally at one corner, beside a crypt-like passage, stray dark and dingy barber's shop, with its seedy display of powdered horsehair wigs of the same dirty-white hue as London snow. Who, moreover, has not noted the windows of the legal fruiterers and law stationers hereabouts, stuck over with small announcements of clerkships wanted, each penned in the well-known formidable straight-up-and-down three-and-fourpenny hand, and beginning—with a "𝔗𝔥𝔦𝔰-𝔦𝔫𝔡𝔢𝔫𝔱𝔲𝔯𝔢"-like flourish of German text—"𝔗𝔥𝔢 𝔚𝔯𝔦𝔱𝔢𝔯 𝔥𝔢𝔯𝔢𝔬𝔣," &c. Who, too, while threading his way through the monastic-like byways of such places, has not been startled to find himself suddenly light upon a small enclosure, comprising a tree or two, and a little circular pool, hardly bigger than a lawyer's inkstand, with a so-called fountain in the centre, squirting up the water in one long thick thread, as if it were the nozzle of a fire-engine.

But such are the features only of the more important Inns of Court, as Lincoln's and Gray's, and the Temple; but, in addition to these, there exists a large series of legal blind alleys, or yards, which are entitled "Inns of Chancery," and among which may be classed the lugubrious localities of Lyon's Inn and Barnard's ditto, and Clement's, and Clifford's, and Sergeants', and Staple, and the like. In some of these, one solitary, lanky-looking lamp-post is the only ornament in the centre of the backyard-like square, and the grass is seen struggling up between the interstices of the pavement, as if each paving-stone were trimmed with green *chenille*. In another you find the statue of a kneeling negro, holding a platter-like sun-dial over his head, and seeming, while doomed to tell the time, to be continually inquiring of the surrounding gentlemen in black, whether he is not "a man and a brother?" In another you observe crowds of lawyers' clerks, with their hands full of red-tape-tied papers, assembled outside the doors of new clubhouse-like buildings. Moreover, to nearly every one of these legal nooks and corners the entrance is through some archway or iron gate that has a high bar left standing in the middle, so as to obstruct the passage of any porter's load into the chancery sanctuary; and there is generally a little porter's lodge, not unlike a French *conciergerie*, adjoining the gate, about which loiter liveried street-keepers to awe off little boys, who would otherwise be sure to dedicate the tranquil spots to the more innocent pursuit of marbles or leap-frog.

The various classes of Law Courts too have, one and all, some picturesque characteristics about them. For example, is not the atmosphere of Westminster Hall essentially distinct from that of the Old Bailey? During term time the Hall at Westminster (which is not unlike an empty railway terminus, with the exception that the rib-like rafters are of carved oak rather than iron) is thronged with suitors and witnesses waiting for their cases to be heard, and pacing the Hall pavement the while, in rows of three or four, and with barristers here and there walking up and down in close communion with attorneys; and there are sprucely-dressed strangers from the country, either bobbing in and out of the various courts, or else standing still, with their necks bent back and their mouths open, as they stare at the wooden angels at the corners of the oaken timbers overhead.

The Courts here are, as it were, a series of ante-chambers ranged along one side of the spacious Hall; and as you enter some of them, you have to bob your head beneath a heavy red cloth curtain. The judge, or judges, are seated on a long, soft-looking, crimson-covered bench, and costumed in wigs that fall on either side their face, like enormous spaniel's ears, and with periwigged barristers piled up in rows before them, as if they were so many mediæval medical students attending the lectures at some antiquated hospital. Then there is the legal fruit-stall, in one of the neighbouring passages, for the distribution of " apples, oranges, biscuits, ginger-beer"—and sandwiches—to the famished attendants at Court; and the quiet, old-fashioned hotels, for the accommodation of witnesses from the country, ranged along the opposite side of Palace Yard.

How different is all this from the Central Criminal Court at the Old Bailey! There we find a large boiled-beef establishment, with red, steaming rounds in the window, side by side with the temple of justice, and a mob of greasy, petty larceny-like friends of the "prisoner at the bar," and prim-looking policemen, gathered round the Court doors and beside the gateway leading to the sheriffs' entrance at the back, waiting the issue of that day's trials. Then, within the Court, upon the bench, there are the aldermen, reading the daily papers or writing letters, attired in their purple silk gowns trimmed with fur, and with heavy gold S collars about their neck; and the under-sheriffs in their court suits, with their lace frills and ruffles—the latter encircling the hand like the cut paper round bouquets— with their black rapiers at their side, and all on the same seat with the full-wigged judges; and the barristers below crowded round a huge loo-table, that is littered with bags and briefs; and the jury packed in their box at one side of the little court—which, by the by, seems hardly bigger than a back parlour—with a long "day-reflector" suspended over their heads, and throwing an unnatural light upon their faces; whilst in the capacious square dock, facing the bench, stands the prisoner at the bar awaiting his doom, with the Governor of Newgate seated at one corner of the compartment, and a turnkey at the other.

This, again, is all very different from the shabby-genteel crowd, with its melange of "tip-staffs" and sham-attorneys, gathered about the Insolvent Court, and the neighbouring public-houses, in Portugal Street; that, too, utterly unlike the quaint, old-fashioned tribunals in Doctor's Commons; these, moreover, the very opposite to the petty County Courts, that have little to distinguish them from private houses, except the crowd of excited debtors, and creditors, and pettifoggers grouped outside the doors; and those, on the other hand, entirely distinct from the still more insignificant Police Courts, with their group of policemen on the door-step, and where, at certain hours, may be seen the sombre-looking prison-van, that is like a cross between a hearse and an omnibus, with the turnkey conductor seated in a kind of japan-leather basket beside the door at the end of the vehicle.

Farther, there are the several prisons scattered throughout the Metropolis, and forming an essential part of the Legal Capital: the gloomy, and yet handsome prison pile of Newgate, with its bunch of fetters over each doorway—the odd polygon-shaped and rampart-like Penitentiary, perched on the river bank by Vauxhall—the new prison at Pentonville, with its noble, portcullis-like gateway—the City Prison at Holloway, half castle half madhouse, with its tall central tower, reminding one of some ancient stronghold—besides the less picturesque and bare-walled Coldbath Fields, and Tothill Fields, and Horsemonger Lane, and the House of Detention, and Whitecross Street, and the Queen's Bench—not forgetting the mastless Hulks, with their grim-looking barred port-holes.

These, however, constitute rather the legal institutions of London than the legal localities; and that there are certain districts that are chiefly occupied by lawyers, and which have a peculiarly lugubrious legal air about them, a half-hour's stroll along the purlieus of the Inns of Court is sufficient to convince us.

Of this Legal London, Chancery Lane may be considered the capital; and here, as we have before said, everything smacks of the law. The brokers deal only in legal furniture— the publishers only in "FEARNE ON REMAINDERS" and "IMPEY'S PRACTICE," and such like dry legal books—and the stationers in skins of parchment and forms of wills, and law-lists and almanacs, and other legal appliances. Then the dining-rooms and "larders," so plentiful in this quarter, are adapted to the taste and pockets of lawyers' clerks; and there are fruiterers, and oyster-rooms, and "café-restaurant" bakers, and "COCKS," and "RAINBOWS," for barristers and attorneys to lunch at; and "sponging-houses," barred like small lunatic asylums, and with an exercising yard at the back like a bird-cage; and patent-offices; and public-houses, frequented by bailiffs' followers and managing clerks; and quiet-looking taverns, which serve occasionally as courts for commissions "de lunatico."

Then stretching in all directions from the legal capital, with its adjacent attorney byways of Cook's Court, and Quality Court, and Boswell Court, and Southampton Buildings, we have what may be termed the legal suburbs, such as Bedford Row, with its annexed James and John Streets, and the doleful Red Lion and Bloomsbury Squares, and Southampton Street, Holborn. In the opposite direction, we find the equally legal Essex Street, and Lancaster

Place, and Somerset Place, and Adam Street (Adelphi), and Buckingham Street, and White-hall Place, and Parliament Street, and Great George Street, all connecting, by a series cf legal links, Chancery Lane to Westminster. Again, along Holborn we have the out-of-the-way legal nooks of Bartlett's Buildings and Ely Place. Whilst, in the neighbourhood of the City Courts of Guildhall, there are the like legal localities of King Street, Cheapside, and Bucklersbury, and Basinghall Street, and Old Jewry Chambers, and Coleman Street, and Tokenhouse Yard, and Copthall Buildings, and Crosby Chambers, and New Broad Street, with even a portion of the legal Metropolis stretching across the water to Wellington Street in the Borough.*

* The subjoined is a list of the legal localities throughout London, as indicated by the Post-office Directory—a legal locality being considered to be one in which the number of resident lawyers is equal to at least one-fourth of the number of residences :—

	No. of Resident Barristers and Attorneys.	No. of Houses		No. of Resident Barristers and Attorneys.	No of Houses.		No. of Resident Barristers and Attorneys.	No. of Houses.
Lincoln's Inn New Square	266	14	Verulam Buildings, Gray's Inn	19	5	Symond's Inn, Chancery Lane	8	10
„ Old Square	217	62	Churchyard Ct., Temple	19	3	Bartlett's Buildings, Holborn	8	31
„ Fields	198	60	Sergeants' Inn, Chancery Lane	18	3	Ironmonger Lane, City	8	31
Chancery Lane	150	125	King's Street, Cheapside	17	30	Fenchurch Buildings	7	18
King's Bench Walk, Temple	129	13	Tokenhouse Yard, Lothbury	15	27	Field Court, Gray's Inn	6	4
Stone Buildings, Lincoln's Inn	128	7	Mitre Court Buildings, Temple	15	2	Buckingham St., Strand	6	28
Paper Buildings, Temple	82	5	Bloomsbury Square	15	43	Angel Court, Throgmorton Street, City	6	16
Pump Court „	73	6	Devereux Court, Strand	15	23	Lyon's Inn, Fleet Street.	5	8
Bedford Row	99	51	Lancaster Place, Strand	15	10	Adam Street, Adelphi	5	20
Furnival's Inn	64	16	Austin Friars, City	15	30	Barge Yard, Bucklersbury	5	5
Inner Temple Lane, Temple	57	9	Whitehall Place, Westmr.	14	22	Copthall Buildings, City	5	5
Brick Court, „	56	5	Barnard's Inn	14	9	Church Court, Clement's Lane, City	5	5
Elm Court	58	5	Walbrook, City	14	38	Tanfield Chambers	5	2
South Square, Gray's Inn	55	14	New Bridge St., Blackfriars	13	42	Wellington St., Borough	4	16
Essex Court, Temple	43	5	John Street, Bedford Row	13	38	Temple Chambers, Falcon Court, Fleet Street	4	2
Plowden Buildings	40	5	Great George Street, Westminster	13	37	Trafalgar Square, Charing Cross	4	4
Figtree Court „	39	8	Gresham Street, City	12	48	Somerset Place, Somerset House	4	9
Hare Court „	37	5	Southampton St., Holborn	12	23	Cook's Ct., Lincoln's Inn	4	15
Sergeants' Inn, Fleet Street	37	16	New Court, Temple	12	1	Old Palace Yard, Westminster	3	7
Southampton Buildings, Chancery Lane	37	47	Temple Garden Court	12	4	Arthur Street, City	3	11
Essex Street, Strand	35	49	New Broad Street, City	11	38	Temple Church Porch Chambers	3	1
Old Jewry Street, City	35	37	Quality Court, Chancery Lane	11	9	Walbrook Buildings	3	3
New Inn, Wych Street, Strand }	34	13	Sise Lane, Bucklersbury	11	18	Whitehall Chambers	3	5
Harcourt Buildings	34	4	Farrar's Buildings, Temple	11	10	Twisden Buildings, Temple	2	1
Basinghall Street, City	34	84	John Street, Adelphi	11	22		2417	2069
Great James Street, Bedford Row	32	42	King's Arms Yard, Coleman Street, City	11	20			
Tanfield Court, Temple	31	3	King's Road, Bedford Row	11	22	*Doctor's Commons.*		
Carey Street, Lincoln's Inn	30	68	Gray's Inn Place	10	11		No. of Advocates and Proctors.	No. of Houses
Coleman Street, City	29	81	Clement's Inn, Strand—New Inn	10	18	Great Knight Rider St.	31	22
Bucklersbury, Cheapside	28	38	Clement's Lane, Lombard Street	10	30	College, Doctor's Commons	18	17
Serle Street, Lincoln's Inn	28	16	Temple Cloisters, Inner Temple Lane	10	2	Great Carter Lane	15	34
Mitre Court, Temple	27	12	Inner Temple Hall Staircase	9	1	Godliman Street	23	15
Middle Temple Lane	27	6	Lamb Buildings	9	4	Dean's Court	8	
Staple Inn, Holborn	27	12	Red Lion Sq., Holborn	8	38	Bell Yard	4	10
Crown Office Row, Temple	27	11	Nicholas Lane, Lombard Street, City	8	39	Paul's Bakehouse Court	4	
Raymond's Buildings, Gray's Inn	35	6	Great Knight Rider Street	8	22	Pope's Head Alley, Cornhill	3	7
New Boswell Court, Carey Street	25	17	Bell Yard, Doctor's Commons	8	10		106	115
Parliament Street, Westminster	25	55						
Ely Place, Holborn	23	42						
Clifford's Inn, Fleet St.	21	17						

The following, on the other hand, is the distribution of the lawyers and the lawyers' clerks and law-

Now, the people inhabiting the legal localities of the Metropolis are a distinct tribe, impressed with views of life and theories of human nature widely different from the more simple portion of humanity. With the legal gentry all is doubt and suspicion. No man is worthy of being trusted by word of mouth, and none fit to be believed but on his oath. Your true lawyer opines, with the arch-diplomatist Talleyrand, that speech was given to man not to express but to conceal his thoughts; and, we may add, it is the legal creed that the faculty of reason was conferred on us merely to enable human beings to "special plead," *i.e.*, to split logical hairs, and to demonstrate to dunderhead jurymen that black is white.

What beauty is to a quaker, and philanthropy to a political economist, honour is to your gentleman of the long robe—a moral will-o'-the-wisp, that is almost sure to mislead those who trust to it. The only safe social guide, cries the legal philosopher, is to consider every one a rogue till you find him honest, and to take the blackest view of all men's natures in your dealings with your friends and associates; believing that there is no bright side, as has been well said, even to the new moon, until experience shows that it is not entirely dark. In legal eyes, the idea of any one's word being as good as his bond is stark folly; and though, say the lawyers, our chief aim in life should be to get others to reduce their thoughts to writing towards *us*, yet *we* should abstain from pen, ink, and paper as long as possible, so as to avoid "committing ourselves" towards *them*. Or if, in the frank communion of friendship, we are ever incautious enough to be betrayed into professions that might hereafter interfere with our pecuniary interests, we should never fail, before concluding our letter, to have sufficient worldly prudence to change the subscription of "Yours, sincerely," into "Yours, *without prejudice*."

That lawyers see many examples in life to afford grounds for such social opinions, all must admit; but as well might surgeons believe, because generally dealing with sores and ulcers, that *none* are healthy; and physicians advise us to abstain from all close communion with our fellows, so as to avoid the chance of contagion, because *some* are diseased. Nor would it be fair to assert that *every* lawyer adopts so unchristian and Hobbesian a creed. There are many gentlemen on the rolls, at the bar, and on the bench, who lean rather to the chivalrous and trusting than the cynic and sceptical view of life; and many who, though naturally

court officers, above twenty years of age, throughout the several districts of London, according to the returns of the Census Commissioners, by which it will be seen that the greatest number of lawyers are resident in the western districts by Kensington, whereas the greatest number of clerks are found located in the northern districts by St. Pancras and Islington; whilst at the east end of the town, such as Whitechapel and Poplar, on the Middesex side, and Rotherhithe, and St. Olave, Southwark, on the Surrey side of the water, but few lawyers or clerks are to be found :—

	Lawyers.	Clerks, &c.	Total.	No. to 1000.		Lawyers.	Clerks, &c.	Total.	No. to 1000.		Lawyers.	Clerks, &c.	Total.	No. to 1000.
Kensington .	722	118	840	29·5	Holborn .	403	295	698	51·3	Bermondsey .	5	45	50	3·9
Chelsea . .	130	95	225	15·7	Clerkenwell .	121	291	412	22·9	St. George,				
St. George, Ha-					St. Luke's .	35	77	112	7·5	Southwark	45	88	133	9·2
nover Sq. .	329	99	428	20·7	East London .	25	34	59	4·7	Newington .	82	221	303	1·8
Westminster .	130	130	260	13·4	West London .	138	160	298	33·1	Lambeth .	284	421	705	20·1
St. Martin's .	90	39	129	16·5	London City .	120	104	224	13·7	Wandsworth	159	72	231	18·5
St. James .	159	25	184	15·9	Total					Camberwell .	130	160	£90	22·7
Total					Central Dists.	1498	1391	2810	25·4	Rotherhithe .	3	13	16	3·1
W. Districts	1560	506	2066	20·2						Greenwich .	92	58	150	5·0
										Lewisham .	97	38	135	16·2
					Shoreditch .	37	311	348	12·3	Total				
					Bethnal Green	17	64	81	3·5	S. Districts	916	1215	2131	13·0
Marylebone .	477	181	658	16·0	Whitechapel .	12	33	45	1·9					
Hampstead .	101	21	122	44·5	St. George in									
St. Pancras .	661	680	1341	30·7	the East .	7	30	37	2·7	West Districts	1560	506	2066	20·2
Islington .	255	664	919	38·6	Stepney .	32	127	159	5·5	North ,,	1620	1712	3332	18·7
Hackney .	126	166	292	2·2	Poplar . .	12	20	32	2·4	Central ,,	1490	1391	2881	25·4
Total					Total					East ,,	117	585	702	5·4
N. Districts	1620	1712	3332	18·7	E. Districts	117	585	702	5·4	South ,,	916	1215	2131	13·0
										Total				
St. Giles .	381	129	510	31·7	St. Saviour .	15	84	99	9·8	all London	5703	5409	11,112	17·5
Strand . .	267	301	568	43·4	St. Olave .	4	15	19	2·9					

inclining towards the Brutus philosophy, and preferring stoical justice to Christian generosity, are still sufficiently poetic to see a glimpse of " good in all things."

Moreover, it is our duty and our pride to add, that if among the body of legal gentry there are to be found such enormities as " sharp practitioners " and " pettifoggers "— scoundrels who seek to render law a matter of *in*justice, and who use that which was intended to prevent injury and robbery as the means of plunder and oppression—who regard it as their interest to retard, rather than advance justice, and who love equity and its long delays simply on account of the iniquity of its costs—if there be such miscreants as these included among the legal profession, there are, on the other hand, the most noble judges of the land comprised among its members; and granting we should estimate the true dignity of a vocation by those who are at once the most honourable and honoured types of it, we must candidly admit that there is no office which sheds so pure and brilliant a glory upon our nation, as that filled by the righteous and reproachless band of English gentlemen who occupy the judgment-seats of this country. For whilst in every other kingdom the judge is but little better than a quibbling and one-sided advocate—a government hireling, trying his hardest to convict the prisoner—the British arbiter weighs, with an exquisitely even hand, the conflicting testimony in favour of and against those who are arraigned at his tribunal, and with a gracious mercy casts into the trembling scale—in cases of indecision—the lingering doubt, so as to make the evidence on behalf of the accused outweigh that of his accusers. Nor can even the most sceptical believe that it is possible for governments or private individuals to tempt our judges to swerve from the strictest justice between man and man, by any bribe, however precious, or by any worldly honours, however dazzling. Indeed, if there be one class in whose iron integrity every Englishman has the most steadfast faith—of whose Pilate-like righteousness he has the profoundest respect, and in the immaculateness of whose honour he feels a national pride—it is the class to whom the high privilege of dispensing justice among us has been intrusted, and who constitute at once the chiefs and the ornaments of the profession of which we are about to treat.

Concerning the population of this same Legal London, it may be said to comprise the following numbers and classes of persons above 20 years of age:—

Barristers	1,513
Solicitors	3,418
Other lawyers (as advocates, proctors, &c.)	772
	5,703
Law clerks	4,340
Law court officers (including 8 females) and law stationers	1,069
	5,409
	11,112*

Hence, if we include the families of the above individuals (and, according to the returns of the Census Commissioners, there are, upon an average, 4·827 persons to each family throughout England and Wales), we arrive at the conclusion that Legal London comprises an aggregate population of 53,638 souls, which is exactly one forty-fourth part of the entire metropolitan population.

Now, the next question that presents itself to our consideration concerns the order and method to be adopted in our treatment of each of the several classes of people and institutions connected with the administration of the laws in the Metropolis.

In our previous specification of the various details comprised under the term Legal

* According to the census returns, there are—in addition to the above—160 lawyers and 1,530 clerks &c.—or, altogether, 1,690 persons—connected with the law in London who are under twenty years of age; so that, adding these to the total above given, the aggregate of lawyers and their " subordinates " resident in

London, we have spoken of it as comprehending the Inns of Court and the people in connection therewith—the Superior Courts of Law, Civil, as well as Criminal, and their various legal functionaries, as judges, solicitors, law clerks, and law-court officers—the County Courts, and Police Courts, together with their attendant judges, magistrates, clerks, and practitioners—and, lastly, the Prisons, with the governors, turnkeys, and teachers attached to them.

Such a list, however, has but little logical distinctness among the parts or congruous unity in the whole; hence, we must seek for some more systematic arrangement and classification, under which to generalize the various particulars.

The most simple and natural mode of dividing the subject appears to be into two principal heads, namely :—

The Metropolitan Institutions and People connected with the Administration of the *Civil* Law.

And the Metropolitan Institutions, and People connected with the Administration of the *Criminal* Law.

Under the first of these general heads is comprised the following particulars :—

The Courts of Equity, and the persons connected therewith.

The Courts of Common Law, Superior as well as Petty and Local, and the several functionaries and practitioners appertaining to them.

The Courts of Bankruptcy and Insolvency, with the professional gentry attached to the same.

The Debtors' Prisons, and their associate officers.

the Metropolis would amount to 12,802. The distribution of the lawyers and their subordinates throughout the several counties of England and Wales, is as follows :—

TABLE SHOWING THE DISTRIBUTION OF LAWYERS AND THEIR CLERKS (ABOVE 20 YEARS OF AGE) THROUGHOUT ENGLAND AND WALES.

DIVISION I.—METROPOLIS.

	Lawyers.	Clerks, &c.	Total.	No. to 1000.
London	5703	5401	11,104	17·5

DIVISION II.—SOUTH EASTERN COUNTIES.

	Lawyers.	Clerks, &c.	Total.	No. to 1000.
Surrey (ex-Metro.)	360	86	446	8·2
Kent (ex-Metro.)	332	208	540	4·1
Sussex	345	112	457	5·2
Hampshire	292	146	438	4·0
Berkshire	147	84	231	4·3
Total	1476	636	2112	4·8

DIVISION III.—SOUTH MIDLAND COUNTIES.

	Lawyers.	Clerks, &c.	Total.	No. to 1000.
Middlesex (ex-Metro.)	270	80	350	8·9
Hertfordshire	115	51	166	3·6
Buckinghamshire	79	60	139	3·8
Oxfordshire	104	54	158	3·4
Northamptonshire	105	59	164	2·8
Huntingdonshire	32	31	63	4·1
Bedfordshire	45	24	69	2·2
Cambridgeshire	113	94	207	4·1
Total	863	453	1316	4·1

DIVISION V.—EASTERN COUNTIES.

	Lawyers.	Clerks, &c.	Total.	No. to 1000.
Essex	194	131	325	3·5
Suffolk	172	115	287	3·4
Norfolk	292	194	486	4·2
Total	658	440	1098	3·7

DIVISION V.—SOUTH WESTERN COUNTIES.

	Lawyers.	Clerks, &c.	Total.	No. to 1000.
Wiltshire	142	98	240	3·8
Dorsetshire	121	84	205	4·5
Devonshire	497	275	772	5·3
Cornwall	162	123	285	3·3
Somersetshire	403	226	629	5·5
Total	1325	806	2131	4·7

DIVISION VI.—WEST MIDLAND COUNTIES.

	Lawyers.	Clerks, &c.	Total.	No. to 1000.
Glo'stershire	478	243	721	6·6
Herefordshire	100	58	158	5·6
Shropshire	187	150	337	5·0
Staffordshire	278	234	512	3·0
Worcestershire	257	147	404	5·9
Warwickshire	234	233	467	3·6
Total	1534	1065	2599	5·6

DIVISION VII.—NORTH MIDLAND COUNTIES.

	Lawyers.	Clerks, &c.	Total.	No. to 1000.
Leicestershire	100	84	184	3·0
Rutlandshire	8	5	13	1·9
Lincolnshire	207	183	390	3·6
Nottinghamshire	118	106	224	2·9
Derbyshire	126	64	190	2·7
Total	559	442	1001	3·2

DIVISION VIII.—NORTH WESTERN COUNTIES.

	Lawyers.	Clerks, &c.	Total.	No. to 1000.
Cheshire	307	244	551	2·4
Lancashire	1025	777	1802	3·3
Total	1332	1021	2353	3·3

DIVISION IX.—YORKSHIRE.

	Lawyers.	Clerks, &c.	Total.	No. to 1000.
West Riding	611	467	1078	3·1
East Riding	232	186	418	6·1
North Riding	121	64	185	3·5
Total	964	717	1681	3·5

DIVISION X.—NORTHERN COUNTIES.

	Lawyers.	Clerks, &c.	Total.	No. to 1000.
Durham	175	138	313	2·9
Northumberland	169	111	280	3·5
Cumberland	102	73	175	3·4
Westmoreland	31	21	52	3·3
Total	477	343	820	3·2

DIVISION XI.—MONMOUTHSHIRE AND WALES.

	Lawyers.	Clerks, &c.	Total.	No. to 1000.
Monmouthshire	82	55	137	2·6
South Wales	246	223	469	2·9
North Wales	158	137	295	2·8
Total	486	415	901	5·7
Total for all England and Wales	15,377	11,739	27,116	5·7

The Ecclesiastical and Admiralty Courts, with their attendant judges, advocates, proctors, &c.

Whereas, under the second head of the Metropolitan Institutions and people in connection with the *Criminal* Law, we have the following sub-heads :—

The Criminal Courts and Sessions Houses, with their several officers and practitioners.

The Police Courts and the magistrates, their clerks and others attached thereto.

The Coroners' Courts, and the several people connected with them.

The Criminal Prisons, and their associate governors, turnkeys, &c.

Such an arrangement appears to exhaust the subject, especially when certain minor points come to be filled in—as, for example, the Patent Offices and Lunacy Commissions in connection with the jurisdiction of the Lord Chancellor, and the granting of licenses at the various Sessions Houses by the justices of the peace—which latter function, though hardly connected with the Criminal Law, must still (for the sake of avoiding an over-complicity of details) be treated of under that head.

There are, of course, two ways of dealing with the above particulars—either we may commence with the beginning, and so work *down* to the end; or we may reverse the process, and beginning at the bottom, proceed gradually *up* to the top. The first method is the one generally adopted by systematic writers. On the present occasion, however, we purpose taking the opposite course; and we do so, not from mere caprice, but because there happen to be such things as "terms and returns" in Law, which give a periodical rather than a continuous character to legal proceedings, and so prevent attention to such matters at *all* times. Accordingly, as neither perspicuity nor interest is lost by pursuing the latter plan, we shall here begin our exposition of the character, scenes, and doings of Legal London, by dealing first with the Criminal Prisons of the Metropolis.

Sub-division A.—The Metropolitan Institutions, and People connected with the Administration of the Criminal Law.

§ 1.

THE CRIMINAL PRISONS AND PRISON-POPULATION OF LONDON.

There is a long and multifarious list of prisons distributed throughout London, if we include all the places of confinement, from the state or political stronghold down to the common jail for the county—from the debtor's prison to the sponging-house—from the penitentiary to the district "lock-up." Thus we have the Tower and the Hulks; and Whitecross Street prison, and the Houses of Correction and Detention; and the Queen's Bench, and the Penitentiary at Millbank; as well as the Female Convict Prison at Brixton, and the common jail, Horsemonger Lane; besides the "Model" at Pentonville, the New City Prison at Holloway, and the well-known quarters at Newgate; together with the cells at the several station-houses of the Metropolitan and City Police, and the sponging-houses in the neighbourhood of Chancery Lane—all of which come under the denomination of places of safe custody, if not of punishment and reform.

We shall find, however, amid the apparent confusion of details, that there are in London only three distinct kinds of places of safe custody, viz. :—

POLITICAL or STATE PRISONS—such as the Tower and the Strong-room of the House of Commons;

CIVIL or DEBTORS' PRISONS—as the Queen's Bench and the one in Whitecross Street, together with a portion of Horsemonger Lane Jail; and

CRIMINAL PRISONS; of which we are about to treat.

Of these same Criminal Prisons there are just upon a dozen scattered through London; and it is essential to a proper understanding of the subject that we should first discriminate accurately between the several members of the family. As yet no one has attempted to group the places of confinement for criminals into distinct classes; and we have, therefore, only so many vague terms—as "Convict" Prisons (though, strictly, every offender—the misdemeanant as well as the transport—is *after conviction* a convict) and "Houses of Correction," "Houses of Detention," "Bridewells," &c., to prevent us confounding one species of Criminal Prison with another.

Formerly every class of criminals and graduate in vice—from the simple novice to the artful adept—the debtor, the pickpocket, the burglar, the coiner, the poacher, the highwayman, the vagrant, the murderer, the prostitute—were all of them huddled together in one and the same place of durance, called the "Common Jail" (for even "Houses of Correction"—for vagrants and thieves *only*—are comparatively modern inventions); and it was not until the year 1823 that any systematic legal steps were taken to enforce a separation of the great body of prisoners into *classes*, much more into *individuals*—the latter being a regulation of very recent date.

Of late years, however, we have made rapid advances towards the establishment of a kind of criminal quarantine, in order to stay the spread of that vicious infection which is found to accompany the association of the morally disordered with the comparatively uncontaminated; for assuredly there is a criminal epidemic—a very plague, as it were, of profligacy—that diffuses itself among the people with as much fatality to society as even the putrid fever or black vomit.

Consequently it becomes necessary, whilst seeking here to arrange our present prisons into something like system, to classify them according to the grades of offenders they are designed to keep in safe custody; for it is one of the marked features of our times that the old Common Jail is becoming as obsolete among us as bull-baiting, and that the one indiscriminate stronghold has been divided and parcelled out into many distinct places of durance, where the reformation of the offender obtains more consideration, perhaps, than even his punishment.

Now the first main division of the criminal prisons of London is into—

Prisons for offenders *before* conviction; and

Prisons for offenders *after* conviction.

This is not only the natural but *just* division of the subject, since it is now admitted that society has no right to treat a man *as* a criminal until he has been proven to be one by the laws of his country; and hence we have prisons for the *untried*—distinct from those for the convict, or rather convicted.

The prisons for offenders *after* conviction are again divisible into places of confinement for such as are condemned to *longer* or *shorter* terms of imprisonment. To the latter class of institutions belong the Houses of Correction, to which a person may be sentenced for not more than two years; and Bridewells, to which a person may be condemned for not more than three months.*

The prisons, on the other hand, for the reception of those condemned to *longer* terms, such

---

* " There is a species of jail," says the new edition of Blackstone, "which does not fall under the sheriff's charge, but is governed by a keeper wholly independent of that officer. It is termed, by way of distinction from the common jail, a House of Correction, or (in the City of London) a Bridewell. These houses of correction (which were first established, as it would seem, in the reign of Elizabeth) were originally designed for the penal confinement, after conviction, of paupers refusing to work, and other persons falling under the legal description of *vagrant*. And this was at first their only application, for in other cases the common jail of the county, city, or town in which the offender was triable was (generally speaking) the only legal place of commitment. The practice, however, in this respect was, to a certain extent, altered in the reign of George I., when 'vagrants and other persons charged with small offences' were, for the first time, allowed to be committed to the house of correction for safe custody, before conviction; and at a subsequent period it was provided that, as to vagrants, the house of correction should be the *only* legal place of commitment. The uses, however, of a jail of this description have been lately carried much farther; for by 5 and 6 William IV., c. 38, s. 34, reciting that great inconvenience and expense had been found to result from the committing to the common jail, where it happens to be remote from the place of trial, it is enacted that a justice of the peace or coroner may commit, for safe custody, to any house of correction situate near the place where the assizes or sessions are to be held, and that offenders sentenced in those courts to death, transportation, or imprisonment, may be committed in execution of such sentence to any house of correction for the county."— *Stephens' Blackstone*, 3rd ed., vol. iii., p. 209.

The City Bridewell (Bridge Street, Blackfriars) has been closed for the last two years. The prison here was originally a place of penal confinement for unruly apprentices, sturdy beggars, and disorderly persons committed to jail for three months and less. Where the City Bridewell now stands there is said to have been anciently a holy well of medicinal water, called St. Bride's Well, upon which was founded an hospital for the poor. (Stowe, however, says nothing of this, speaking only of a *palace* standing there.) After the Reformation, Edward VI. chartered this to the City, and whilst Christchurch was dedicated to the education of the young, and St. Thomas's Hospital, in the Borough, for the cure of the sick, Bridewell Hospital was converted into a place of confinement and "penitentiary amendment" for unruly London apprentices and disorderly persons, as well as sturdy beggars and vagrants. "Here," says Mr. Timbs, in his curious and learned work on the Curiosities of London, "was a portrait of Edward VI. with these lines—

' This *Edward* of fair memory the Sixt,
In whom with Great Goodness was commixt,
Gave this *Bridewell*, a palace in olden times,
For a Chastening House of vagrant crimes.' "

After this, the houses of correction in various parts of the country got to be called "bridewells"—the particular name coming, in course of time, to be used as a general term for a place of penitentiary amendment. A "house of correction" is now understood to be a place of safe custody, punishment, and reformation, to which criminals are committed when sentenced to imprisonment for terms varying from seven days up to two years.

as transportation and "penal service," are those at Pentonville, Millbank, and Brixton, as well as the Hulks at Woolwich.

The prisons, moreover, which are for the reception of criminals *before* conviction, are either—

Prisons in which offenders are confined while awaiting their trial *after* having been committed by a magistrate—such as the prisons of Newgate and Horsemonger Lane, as well as the House of Detention; or "Lock-ups," in which offenders are confined *previous* to being brought up before, and committed by, the sitting magistrate—such as the cells at the various station-houses.

According, then, to the above classification, the Criminal Prisons admit of being arranged into the following groups :—

I. PRISONS FOR OFFENDERS *AFTER* CONVICTION.

    A. *"Convict" Prisons* *—for transports and "penal service" men.
        1. Pentonville Prison.
        2. Millbank Prison.
        3. Female Convict Prison, Brixton.
        4. Hulks, Woolwich.

    B. *"Correctional" Prisons*—for persons sentenced to short terms of punishment.
        1. City House of Correction (Holloway).
        2. Middlesex Houses of Correction.
            a. Coldbath Fields Prison, for adult males.
            b. Tothill Fields Prison, for boys and adult females.
        3. Surrey House of Correction (Wandsworth Common).

II. PRISONS FOR OFFENDERS *BEFORE* CONVICTION.

    A. *Detentional Prisons*—for persons *after* committal by a magistrate.
        1. Middlesex House of Detention (Clerkenwell).
        2. Newgate.
        3. Horsemonger Lane Jail.†

    B. *Lock-ups*—for persons *previous* to committal by a magistrate.
        1. Metropolitan Police Cells.
        2. City   do   do.‡

** *Of the Prison Population of London.*—The number of offenders said to pass annually through the metropolitan prisons is stated at about 36,000. These statistics, however, are of rather ancient date, and proceed from no very reliable source. We will therefore endeavour to sum up, with as much precision as possible, the great army of criminals that pass through the several jails of London in the course of the year :—

   * This is the Government term ;—the law distinguishing between a "convict" (or, literally, a *convicted felon*) and a "convicted misdemeanant."

   † This is the only existing Common Jail in London, *i. e.*, the only place where debtors are still confined under the same roof as felons.

   ‡ The cant or thieves' names for the several London prisons or "sturbons" (Ger. *ge-storben*, dead, and hence a place of execution), is as follows :—

Pentonville Prison	*The Model.*
Millbank Prison	„ *'Tench* (abbreviated from Penitentiary).
The Hulks, or any Public Works . .	„ *Boat.*
House of Correction, Coldbath Fields . .	„ *Steel.*
House of Correction, Tothill Fields . .	„ *Downs.*
City Bridewell, Bridge Street, Blackfriars .	„ *Old Horse.*
Newgate	„ *Start.*
Horsemonger Lane Jail . . .	„ *Lane.*

NUMBER OF PRISONERS "PASSING THROUGH" THE LONDON PRISONS DURING THE YEAR.

Pentonville Prison (A.D. 1854-5)		925
Millbank ,, ,,		2,461
Brixton ,, ,,		664
Hulks ,, ,,		1,513
Total Population of the London Convict Prisons		5,563
City House of Correction (A.D. 1854-5)		1,978
Coldbath-fields ,, ,,		7,743
Tothill Fields ,, ,,		7,268
Surrey ,, ,,		5,170
Total Population of the Correctional Prisons		22,159
House of Detention		11,262
Newgate		1,840
Horsemonger Lane Jail		3,010
Total Population of the Detentional Prisons		16,112
Grand Total of the Population of the London Prisons		43,834
Metropolitan Police Stations (1854)		76,614
City Police Stations ,,		4,487
Total Population of the London Police Stations		81,101
Total Population of all London Prisons and Lock-ups		124,935*

But a considerable proportion of this large number of prisoners appear more than once in the returns, as they pass from the police-stations, after *committal* by the magistrates, to the detentional prisons, there to await their trial, and are thence transferred, after *conviction*, either to correctional or "convict" prisons, according as they are condemned to longer or shorter terms of imprisonment. Moreover, even of those condemned to three, or indeed to six, months' imprisonment, many appear *repeatedly* in the aggregate of the correctional prisons for the *entire year;* so that it becomes extremely difficult to state, with any exactitude, what may be the number of *different* offenders who enter the London prisons in the course of twelve months. The sum-total may, however, be roughly estimated at about 20,000 individuals; for this is a little less than the aggregate of the convict and correctional prisons of the Metropolis, and of course includes those passing first through the detentional prisons and lock-ups, the difference between that aggregate and the sum of the convict and correctional prisons being a set-off against those who appear more than once in the year at the houses of correction.

This, however, is the *successive* prison population for the whole year; the *simultaneous* prison population, on the other hand, for any *particular* period of the year, may be cited at somewhere about 6,000 individuals; for, according to the Government returns, there were at the time of taking the last Census rather more than that number of criminals confined within

* The returns above given rest upon the following authority:—The number of criminals in the convict prisons is quoted from the Reports of those prisons. The numbers of the correctional and detentional prisons have been kindly and expressly furnished by the Governors of those institutions respectively; whilst those of the Metropolitan Police are copied from the last report on the subject, and those of the City Police supplied by the Commissioner.

The number of debtors confined in the Metropolitan prisons in the summer of 1855 was as follows:—

Whitecross Street Prison (on the 18th August, 1855)		233
Queen's Bench ,,		134
Horsemonger Lane Jail (on the 20th August, 1855)		46
		413

the metropolitan jails—and this is very nearly the population of the entire town of Folke-stone.*

Further, the gross annual expense of these same criminal prisons of London is about £170,000, or very nearly one-third of all the prisons in England and Wales, which, according to the Government returns, cost, in round numbers, £385,000 per annum.†

₊ *Of the Character of the London Criminals.*—In the Report of the Constabulary Commissioners, published in 1837, and which remains the most trustworthy and practical treatise on the criminal classes that has yet been published—the information having been derived from the most eminent and experienced prison and police authorities—there is a definition of predatory crime, which expresses no theoretical view of the subject, but the bare fact—referring habitual dishonesty neither to ignorance nor to drunkenness, nor to poverty, nor to over-crowding in towns, nor to temptation from surrounding wealth, nor, indeed, to any one of the many indirect causes to which it is sometimes referred, but simply declaring it to "proceed from a disposition to acquire property with a less degree of labour than ordinary industry." Hence the predatory class are the non-working class—that is to say, those who

---

* The gross number of prisoners passing through the prisons of England and Wales, in the course of the year 1849, was as under :—

Criminals of both sexes	. . . . .	157,273
Debtors	. . . . . .	9,669
Total	. . . . .	166,942

Hence it follows that the criminals passing annually through the London prisons (43,834) form more than one-third of the entire number passing, in the same period, through all the prisons of England and Wales; for out of every 1000 offenders entering the jails throughout the whole country during the twelvemonth, 284 appear in the jails of London alone.

Such is the *successive* ratio between the prisoners confined in the London prisons, and those of all England and Wales. The *simultaneous* ratio on the other hand is as follows :—

The number of prisoners (debtors inclusive) confined in the prisons of England and Wales on the day of taking the last Census was 23,768
The number of prisoners confined in the London prisons on the same day . . . 6,188

Thus it appears that in every 1000 prisoners confined in the prisons of England and Wales at one and the same time, 280 belong to London.

† The total yearly expense of the several London prisons (exclusive of repairs, alterations, and additions), and the average cost per head, is as follows :—

	TOTAL EXPENSE.			EXPENSE PER HEAD.		
	£	s.	d.	£	s.	d.
Convict Prisons—						
Pentonville (A.D. 1854-55)	14,912	18	9	26	11	8
Millbank "	33,175	0	6	25	10	4
Brixton "	12,218	0	0	17	9	1
Hulks at Woolwich "	26,297	9	10	27	13	0
Correctional Prisons—						
Coldbath Fields "	30,067	18	1	21	13	3
Tothill Fields (A.D. 1849)	14,798	16	0	19	9	10½
City House of Correction, Holloway (A.D. 1854-55)	4,599	3	3½	25	7	10⅕
Surrey House of Correction, Wandsworth "	12,158	4	4	18	8	7½
Detentional Prisons—						
House of Detention (A.D. 1854-55)	7,141	9	1	55	4	2
Newgate "	5,800	6	2	37	8	2
Horsemonger Lane Jail (inclusive of debtors) "	4,693	1	9	30	0	8¾

Now, by the above list, the items of which have been mostly supplied expressly for this work by the officials, it will be found that the total expense of all the London prisons for one year amounts to £158,733 1s. 1d.; whilst, according to the Fifteenth Report of the Prison Inspectors, the total expense of *all* the prisons in England and Wales is £385,704 18s. 4½d., so that the cost of the London prisons is nearly *one-half* of those throughout the whole of the country.

CONVICTS.

(From Photographs by Herbert Watkins, 179, Regent Street.)

MALE CONVICT AT PENTONVILLE PRISON. | FEMALE CONVICT AT MILLBANK PRISON.

love to " shake a free leg," and lead a roving life, as they term it, rather than settle down to any continuous employment.

To inquire, therefore, into the mode and means of living peculiar to the criminal classes, involves an investigation into the character and causes of crime. Crime, vice, and sin are three terms used for the infraction of three different kinds of laws—social, moral, and religious. Crime, for instance, is the transgression of some social law, even as vice is the breach of some moral law, and sin the violation of some religious one. These laws often differ only in emanating from different authorities, the infraction of them being simply an offence against a different power. To thieve, however, is to offend, at once socially, morally, and religiously; for not only does the social, but the moral and religious law, one and all, enjoin that we should respect the property of others.

But there are offences against the social powers other than those committed by such as object to labour for their livelihood; for the crimes perpetrated by the professional criminals are, so to speak, *habitual* ones, whereas those perpetrated occasionally by the other classes of society are *accidental* crimes, arising from the pressure or concomitance of a variety of circumstances.

Here, then, we have a most important and fundamental distinction. All crimes, and consequently all criminals, are divisible into two different classes, *the habitual and the casual* —that is to say, there are two distinct orders of people continually offending against the laws of society, viz. (1) those who indulge in dishonest practices as a regular means of living; (2) those who are dishonest from some accidental cause.

Now, it is impossible to arrive at any accurate knowledge of the subject of crime and criminals generally, without first making this analysis of the several species of offences according to their causes; or, in other words, without arranging them into distinct groups or classes, according as they arise, either from an habitual indisposition to labour on the part of some of the offenders, or from the temporary pressure of circumstances upon others.

The official returns on this subject are as unphilosophic as the generality of such documents, and consist of a crude mass of incongruous facts, being a statistical illustration of the "*rudis indigestaque moles*" in connection with a criminal chaos, and where a murderer is classed in the same category with the bigamist, a sheep-stealer with the embezzler, and the Irish rebel or traitor grouped with the keeper of a disorderly house, and he, again, with the poacher and perjurer.

Thus the several crimes committed throughout the country are officially arranged under four heads :—

1. *Offences against the person*—including murder, rape, bigamy, attempts to procure miscarriage, and common assaults.
2. *Offences against property*. (a) With violence—as burglary, robbery, piracy, and sending menacing letters. (b) Without violence—including cattle-stealing, larceny by servants, embezzling, and cheating. (c) Malicious offences against property—as arson, incendiarism, maiming cattle, &c.
3. *Forgery, and offences against the currency*—under which head are comprised the forging of wills, bank notes, and coining.
4. *Other offences*—including high treason, poaching, working illicit stills, perjury, brothel-keeping, &c.

M. Guerry, the eminent French statist, adopts a far more philosophic arrangement, and divides the several crimes into—

1. *Crimes against the State*—as high treason, &c.
2. *Crimes against personal safety*—as murder, assault, &c.
3. *Crimes against morals* (with or without violence)—as rape, bigamy, &c.
4. *Crimes against property* (proceeding from cupidity, or malice)—as larceny, embezzlement, incendiarism, and the like.

The same fundamental error, however, which renders the legal and official classification comparatively worthless, deprives that of the French philosopher of all practical value. It gives us no knowledge of the people committing the crimes, since the offences are classified according to the objects against which they are committed, rather than the causes and passions giving rise to them; and such an arrangement consequently sinks into a mere system of criminal mnemonics, or easy method of remembering the several crimes. The classes in both systems are but so many mental pigeon-holes for the arbitrary separation of the various infractions of the law, and farther than this they cannot serve us.

Whatever other information the inquirer may desire, he must obtain for himself. If he wish to learn something as to the causes of the crimes, and consequently as to the character and passions of the criminals themselves, he must begin *de novo*; and using the official facts, but rejecting the official system of classification, proceed to arrange all the several offences into two classes, according as they are of a professional or casual character, committed by habitual or occasional offenders.

Adopting this principle, it will be found that the crimes committed by the casual offenders consist mainly of murder, assaults, incendiarism, ravishment, bigamy, embezzlement, high treason, and the like; for it is evident that none can make a trade or profession of the commission of these crimes, or resort to them as a regular means of subsistence.

The habitual crimes, on the other hand, will be generally found to include burglary, robbery, poaching, coining, smuggling, working of illicit stills, larceny from the person, simple larceny, &c., because each and all of these are regular crafts, requiring almost the same apprenticeships as any other mode of life—house-breaking, and picking pockets, and working illicit stills, being crafts to which no man without some previous training can adapt himself.

Hence, to ascertain whether the number of these dishonest handicrafts—for such they really are—be annually on the increase or not, is to solve the most important portion of the criminal problem. It is to learn whether crime pursued as a special profession or business is being augmented among us—to discover whether the criminal class, as a distinct body of people, is or is not on the advance.

The casual or accidental crimes, on the other hand, will furnish us with equally curious results, showing a yearly impress of the character of the times; for these, being only occasional offences, the number of such offenders in different years will of course give us a knowledge of the intensity of the several occasions inducing the crimes of such years.

The *accidental* crimes, classified according to their causes, may be said to consist of

1. *Crimes of Brutality and Malice*, exercised either against the person or property of the object—as murder, intents to maim or do bodily harm, manslaughter, assaults, killing and maiming cattle, ill-treating animals, malicious destruction of property, setting fire to crops, arson, &c.
2. *Crimes of Lust, Perverted Appetites, and Indecency*—as rape, carnally abusing girls, unnatural crimes, indecently exposing the person, bigamy, abduction, &c.
3. *Crimes of Shame*—as concealing the birth of infants, attempts to procure miscarriage, &c.
4. *Crimes of Temptation, or Cupidity*, with or without breach of trust—as embezzlement, larceny by servants, illegal pawning, forgery, &c.
5. *Crimes of Evil Speaking*—as perjury, slander, libel, sending menacing letters, &c.
6. *Crimes of Political Prejudices*—as high treason, sedition, &c.

Those who resort to crime as a means of subsistence when in extreme want, cannot be said to belong to those who prefer idleness to labouring for their living, since many such would willingly work to increase their sustenance, if that end were attainable by these means; but the poor shirt-makers, slop-tailors, and the like, have not the power of earning more

COURT, NEWGATE.

than the barest subsistence by their labour, so that the pawning of the work intrusted to them by their employers becomes an act to which they are immediately impelled for "dear life," on the occurrence of the least illness or mishap among them. Such *offenders*, therefore, belong more properly to those who cannot work for their living, or rather, cannot live by their working; and though they offend against the laws in the same manner as those who object to work, they certainly cannot be said to belong to the same class.

The *habitual* criminals, on the other hand, are a distinct body of people. Such classes appertain to even the rudest nations, they being, as it were, the human parasites of every civilized and barbarous community. The Hottentots have their "*Sonquas*," and the Kaffirs their "*Fingoes*," as we have our "prigs" and "cadgers." Those who object to labour for the food they consume appear to be part and parcel of every State—an essential element of the social fabric. Go where you will—to what corner of the earth you please—search out or propound what new-fangled or obsolete form of society you may—you will be sure to find some members of it more apathetic than the rest, who will object to work; even as there will be some more infirm than others, who are unable, though willing, to earn their own living; and some, again, more thrifty, who, from their prudence and their savings, will have no need to labour for their subsistence.

These several forms are but the necessary consequences of specific differences in the constitution of different beings. Circumstances may tend to give an unnatural development to either one or the other of the classes. The criminal class, the pauper class, or the wealthy class may be in excess in one form of society as compared with another, or they may be repressed by certain social arrangements—nevertheless, to a greater or less degree, there they *will*, and, we believe, *must* ever be.

Since, then, there is an essentially distinct class of persons who have an innate aversion to any settled industry, and since work is a necessary condition of the human organization, the question becomes, "How do such people live?" There is but one answer—If they will not labour to procure their own food, of course they must live on the food procured by the labour of others.

The means by which the criminal classes obtain their living constitute the essential points of difference among them, and form, indeed, the methods of distinction among themselves. The "Rampsmen," the "Drummers," the "Mobsmen," the "Sneaksmen," and the "Shofulmen," which are the terms by which the thieves themselves designate the several branches of the "profession," are but so many expressions indicating the several modes of obtaining the property of which they become possessed.

The "*Rampsman*," or "*Cracksman*," plunders by force—as the burglar, footpad, &c.

The "*Drummer*" plunders by stupefaction—as the "hocusser."

The "*Mobsman*" plunders by manual dexterity—as the pickpocket.

The "*Sneaksman*" plunders by stealth—as the petty-larceny boy. And

The "*Shofulman*" plunders by counterfeits—as the coiner.

Now, each and all of these are a distinct species of the criminal genus, having little or no connection with the others. The "cracksman," or housebreaker, would no more think of associating with the "sneaksman," than a barrister would dream of sitting down to dinner with an attorney. The perils braved by the housebreaker or the footpad, make the cowardice of the sneaksman contemptible to him; and the one is distinguished by a kind of bull-dog insensibility to danger, while the other is marked by a low, cat-like cunning.

The "Mobsman," on the other hand, is more of a handicraftsman than either, and is comparatively refined, by the society he is obliged to keep. He usually dresses in the same elaborate style of fashion as a Jew on a Saturday (in which case he is more particularly described by the prefix "swell"), and "mixes" generally in the "best of company," frequenting, for the purposes of business, all the places of public entertainment, and often being a regular attendant at church, and the more elegant chapels—especially during charity sermons. The mobsman takes his name from the gregarious habits of the class to which he belongs, it being necessary for the successful picking of pockets that the work be done in small gangs or mobs, so as to "cover" the operator.

Among the sneaksmen, again, the purloiners of animals (such as the horse-stealers, the sheep-stealers, &c.) all—with the exception of the dog-stealers—belong to a particular tribe; these are agricultural thieves; whereas the mobsmen are generally of a more civic character.

The shofulmen, or coiners, moreover, constitute another species; and upon them, like the others, is impressed the stamp of the peculiar line of roguery they may chance to follow as a means of subsistence.

Such are the more salient features of that portion of the habitually dishonest classes, who live by *taking* what they want from others. The other moiety of the same class, who live by getting what they want *given* to them, is equally peculiar. These consist of the "Flat-catchers," the "Hunters," and "Charley* Pitchers," the "Bouncers," and "Besters," the "Cadgers," and the "Vagrants."

The "*Flat-catchers*" obtain their means by false pretences—as swindlers, duffers, ring-droppers, and cheats of all kinds.

The "*Hunters*" and "*Charley Pitchers*" live by low gaming—as thimblerig-men.

The "*Bouncers*" and "*Besters*" by betting, intimidating, or talking people out of their property.

The "*Cadgers*," by begging and exciting false sympathy.

The "*Vagrants*," by declaring on the casual ward of the parish workhouse.

Each of these, again, are unmistakably distinguished from the rest. The "Flat-catchers" are generally remarkable for great shrewdness, especially in the knowledge of human character, and ingenuity in designing and carrying out their several schemes. The "Charley Pitchers" appertain more to the conjuring or sleight-of-hand and black-leg class. The "Cadgers," on the other hand, are to the class of cheats what the "Sneaksman" is to the thieves—the lowest of all—being the least distinguished for those characteristics which mark the other members of the same body. As the "Sneaksman" is the least daring and expert of all the "prigs," so is the "Cadger" the least intellectual and cunning of all the cheats. A "Shallow cove"—that is to say, one who exhibits himself half-naked in the streets, as a means of obtaining his living—is looked upon as the most despicable of all creatures, since the act requires neither courage, intellect, nor dexterity for the execution of it. Lastly, the "Vagrants" are the wanderers—the English Bedouins—those who, in their own words, "love to shake a free leg"—the thoughtless and the careless vagabonds of our race.

Such, then, are the characters of the habitual criminals, or professionally dishonest classes—the vagrants, beggars, cheats, and thieves—each order expressing some different mode of existence adopted by those who hate working for their living. The vagrants, who love a roving life, exist principally by declaring on the parish funds for the time being; the beggars, as deficient in courage and intellect as in pride, prefer to live by soliciting alms from the public; the cheats, possessed of considerable cunning and ingenuity, choose rather to subsist by fraud and deception; the thieves, distinguished generally by a hardihood and comparative disregard of danger, find greater delight in risking their liberty and taking what they want, instead of waiting to have it given to them.

In prisons, the criminals are usually divided into first, second, and third class prisoners, according to the amount of education they have received. Among the first, or well-educated class, are generally to be found the casual criminals, as forgers, embezzlers, &c.; the second, or imperfectly educated class, contains a large proportion of the town criminals—as pickpockets, smashers, thimblerig-men, &c.; whilst the third, or comparatively uneducated class, is mostly

* A "*Charley* Pitcher" seems to be one who pitches to the *Ceorla* (A. S. for countryman), and hence is equivalent to the term *Yokel-hunter*.

made up of the lower kind of city thieves, as well as the agricultural labourers who have turned sheep-stealers, and the like. Of these three classes, the first and the last furnish the greater number of cases of reformation, whilst the middle class is exceedingly difficult of real improvement, though the most ready of all to *feign* conversion.

As regards the criminal period of life, we shall find, upon calculating the ratio between the criminals of different ages, that by far the largest proportion of such people is to be found between the ages of 15 and 25. This period of life is known to physiologists to be that at which the character or ruling principle is developed. Up to fifteen, the will or volition of an individual is almost in abeyance, and the youth consequently remains, in the greater number of cases, under the control of his parents, acting according to their directions. After fifteen, however, the parental dominion begins to be shaken off, and the being to act for himself, having acquired, as the phrase runs, " a will of his own." This is the most dangerous time of life to all characters; whilst to those who fall among bad companions, or whose natures are marked by vicious impulses, it is a term of great trouble and degradation. The ratio between the population of 15 and 25 years of age and that of all ages, throughout England and Wales, is but 19·0 per cent.; whereas the ratio between prisoners from 15 to 25 years old and those of all ages is, for England and Wales, as high as 48·7; and for the Metropolis, 49·6 per cent.; so that whilst the young men and women form hardly *one-fifth* of *all* classes, they constitute very nearly *one-half* of the *criminal* class. The boys in prison are found to be the most difficult to deal with, for among these occur the greater number of refractory cases.*

---

§ 1—a.

THE LONDON CONVICT PRISONS AND THE CONVICT POPULATION.

The Convict Prisons of the Metropolis, as we have shown, consist of four distinct establishments—distinct, not only in their localities, but also in the character of their construction, as well as in the discipline to which the inmates are submitted. At Pentonville Prison, for instance, the convicts are treated under a modified form of the " separate system "—at Millbank the "mixed system" is in force; and, at the Hulks, on the other hand, the prisoners, though arranged in wards, have but little restraint imposed upon their intercommunication;

* The following tables, copied from the Census of 1851, furnish the data for the above statements:—

AGES OF PRISONERS IN ENGLAND AND WALES.

From 5 to 10 years old	20	From 40 to 45 years old	1,278	From 75 to 80 years old	23
„ 10 „ 15 „	875	„ 45 „ 50 „	826	„ 80 „ 85 „	13
„ 15 „ 20 „	5,081	„ 50 „ 55 „	684	„ 85 „ 90 „	3
„ 20 „ 25 „	6,496	„ 55 „ 60 „	333	„ 90 „ 95 „	1
„ 25 „ 30 „	3,693	„ 60 „ 65 ,	267		
„ 30 „ 35 „	2,402	„ 65 „ 70 „	132	Total of ages	23,768
„ 35 „ 40 „	1,568	„ 70 „ 75 „	73		

Per centage of prisoners between 15 and 25 to those of all ages, 48·7

Total population of all ages in England and Wales 17,927,609
Ditto between 15 and 25 years in ditto . . · 3,423,769
Per centage of persons between 15 and 25 years to persons of all ages, 19·0

AGES OF PRISONERS IN LONDON PRISONS.

From 5 to 10 years old	1	From 35 to 40 years old	362	From 65 to 70 years old	25
„ 10 „ 15 „	299	„ 40 „ 45 „	325	„ 70 „ 75 „	4
„ 15 „ 20 „	1,413	„ 45 „ 50 „	223	„ 75 „ 80 „	1
„ 20 „ 25 „	1,659	„ 50 „ 55 „	191	„ 80 „ 85 „	1
„ 25 „ 30 „	863	„ 55 „ 60 „	81		
„ 30 „ 35 „	596	„ 60 „ 65 „	39	Total of all ages	6,188

Per centage of London prisoners between 15 and 25 to those of all ages, 49·6.

whilst at Brixton, which is an establishment for female convicts only, a different course of treatment, again, is adopted.

The convict prisons, with the exception of the Hulks, were formerly merely the receiving-houses for those who had been sentenced by law to be banished, or rather transported, from the kingdom.

The system of transportation is generally dated as far back as the statute for the banishment of dangerous rogues and vagabonds, which was passed in the 39th year of Elizabeth's reign; and James I. was the first to have felons transported to America, for in a letter he commanded the authorities "to send a hundred dissolute persons to Virginia, that the Knight-Marshal was to deliver for that purpose."

Transportation, however, is not spoken of in any Act of Parliament until the 18th Charles II., c. 3, which empowers the judges either to sentence the moss-troopers of Cumberland and Northumberland to be executed or transported to America for life. Nevertheless, this mode of punishment was not commonly resorted to prior to the year 1718 (4th George I., c. 2); for, by an Act passed in that year, a discretionary power was given to judges to order felons, who were entitled to the benefit of clergy, to be transported to the American plantations; and, under this and other Acts, transportation to America continued from the year 1718 till the commencement of the War of Independence, 1775. During that period, England was repeatedly reproached by foreign nations for banishing, as felons, persons whose offences were comparatively venial—one John Eyre, Esq., a gentleman of fortune, having, among others, been sentenced to transportation for stealing a few quires of paper (November 1st, 1771); and, even as recently as the year 1818, the Rev. Dr. Halloran having been transported for forging a frank to cover a tenpenny postage.

After the outbreak of the American War, a plan for the establishment of penitentiaries was taken into consideration by Parliament, but not carried out with any vigour; for in the year 1784, transportation was resumed, and an Act passed, empowering the King in council to transport offenders to any place beyond the seas, either within or without the British dominions, as his Majesty might appoint; and two years afterwards an order in council was published, fixing upon the eastern coast of Australia, and the adjacent islands, as the future penal colonies. In the month of May, 1787, the first band of transports left this country for Botany Bay, and in the succeeding year, founded the colony of New South Wales.

This system of transporting felons to Australia continued in such force that, in fifty years from the date of its introduction (1787—1836), 100,000 convicts (including 13,000 women) had been shipped off from this country to the Australian penal colonies. This is at the rate of 2,000 per annum; and according to the returns published up to the time that the practice was modified by Parliament, such would appear to have been the average number of felons annually sent out of the country: thus—

	In 1851.	1852.
The number of prisoners remaining in the Convict Prisons throughout the Kingdom at the beginning of the year was	6,130	6,572
The number received during the year	2,903	2,953
The total convict population during the year	9,033	9,525
The number embarked for penal settlements, and otherwise disposed of	2,548	2,658*
The number remaining in convict prisons at the end of the year	6,485	6,867

* The numbers embarked in these years for the penal colonies were 2,224 in 1851, and 2,345 in 1852. There were, moreover, 37 convicts in 1851, and 43 in 1852 removed to other institutions; and 147 pardoned in the first year, and 125 in the second. Besides these, 9 escaped, and 111 died in the one year, and 14 and 137 in the other year.

THE "DEFENCE" HULK AND THE "UNITE" CONVICT HOSPITAL SHIP, OFF WOOLWICH.

In the month of August, 1853, an Act (16 and 17 Vict., c. 99) was passed, " to substitute, in certain cases, other punishment in lieu of transportation ;" and by this it was ordained, that " whereas, by reason of the difficulty of transporting offenders beyond the seas, it has become expedient to substitute some other punishment ;" therefore, "no person shall be sentenced to transportation for any term less than fourteen years, and only those conveyed beyond the seas who have been sentenced to transportation for life, or for fourteen years and upwards ;" so that transportation for the term of seven or ten years was then and there abolished, a term of four years' penal servitude being substituted in lieu of the former, and six years' penal servitude instead of the latter.

This Act was passed, we repeat, in August 1853, and accordingly we find a great difference in the number of convicts embarked in that and the following years, the Government returns being as follows :—

	In 1853.	1854.	1855.
The number of convicts remaining in the convict prisons throughout the kingdom, at the beginning of the year, was	6,873	7,718	7,744
The number received during the year	2,354	2,378	2,799
The total convict population	9,227	10,096	10,543

Disposed of during the year—

	In 1853.	1854.	1855.			
Embarked for Western Australia, and Gibraltar	700	280	1,312			
Removed to other institutions	45	29	66			
Pardoned	560	1,826	2,491			
Escaped	4	8	17			
Expiration of sentence	0	6	6			
Died	158	173	114			
Total disposed of				1,467	2,322	4,006
The number remaining in the convict prisons at the end of the year				7,760	7,774	6,537

Hence we perceive that, though the Act for abolishing the shorter terms of transportation was passed only at the end of the summer of 1853, the number of transports embarked in the course of the year, had decreased from 2,224 in 1851, and 2,345 in 1852, to 700 in 1853, 280 in 1854, and 1,312 in 1855; whilst the number of pardons, which was only 147 in 1851, and 125 in 1852, had risen as high as 560 in 1853, and 1,826 in 1854, and 2,491 in 1855—no less than 276 convicts having been liberated in the course of 1853, and 1,801 in 1854, and 2,459 in 1855, under "an order of license," or ticket-of-leave, as it is sometimes called, an item which, till lately, had not made its appearance in the home convict returns.

Now, it forms no part of our present object to weigh the advantages and disadvantages of the altered mode of dealing with our convicts. We have only to set forth the history and statistics of the matter, for we purpose, in this section, merely estimating the convict population of the Metropolis, and comparing it with that of the country in general.

Well, by the preceding returns we have shown that the convict population of Great Britain averages rather more than 9,000 individuals, whilst the convict population of the Metropolis may be stated at upwards of 3,000, so that London would appear to contain about one-third of the whole, or as many convicts as there are people in the town of Epsom.

We have shown, moreover, that this same convict population is annually increased by an influx of between 2,000 and 3,000 fresh prisoners, so that in a few years the band of convicted felons would amount to a considerable army among us if retained at home. Nor do we say this with any view to alarm society as to the dangers of abolishing transportation, for, in our opinion, it is unworthy of a great and wise nation to make a moral dust-bin of its colonies, and, by thrusting the refuse of its population from under its nose, to believe that it is best consulting the social health of its people at home. Our present purpose is simply to draw attention to the fact that—despite our array of schools, and prison-chaplains, and refined systems of penal discipline, and large army of police, besides the vast increase of churches and chapels—our felon population increases among us as fast as fungi in a rank and fœtid atmosphere.

Now the gross cost of maintaining our immense body of convicted felons is not very far short of a quarter of a million of money, the returns of 1854-5 showing that the maintenance and guardianship of 8,359 convicts cost, within a fraction, £219,000, which is at the rate of about £26 per head.

The cost of the four London establishments would appear to be altogether £86,600 a-year, which is, upon an average, £24 13s. 2d. for the food and care of each man.*

* The following table is abridged from the returns of the Surveyor-General of Prisons :—

COMPARATIVE ABSTRACT OF THE ESTIMATES FOR THE MAINTENANCE OF THE CONVICT PRISONS FOR THE YEAR 1854-5, SHOWING THE AMOUNT UNDER EACH HEAD OF SERVICE, THE NUMBER OF PRISONERS, AND THE COST PER HEAD.

HEADS OF SERVICE.	PENTONVILLE. 561 Prisoners.		MILLBANK. 1,300 Prisoners.		BRIXTON. 700 Prisoners.		WOOLWICH HULKS. 951 Prisoners.		SUMMARY OF GOVERNMENT PRISONS. 8,359 Prisoners.	
	Gross Cost.	Cost per prisoner	Gross Cost.	Cost per prisoner	Gross Cost.	Cost per prisoner	Gross Cost.	Cost per prisoner	Gross Cost.	Cost per prisoner
	£ s. d.	£ s. d.	£ s. d.	£ s. d.	£ s. d.	£ s. d.	£ s. d.	£ s. d.	£ s. d.	£ s. d.
Salaries of Principal Officers and Clerks, and Wages of Inferior Officers and Servants, and of Manufacturing or Labour Department . . .	5,971 6 6	10 12 10	13,371 0 6	10 5 8	3,373 10 0	4 16 2	8,214 5 7	8 12 9	72,014 3 6	8 12 4
Cost of Rations and Uniforms for Officers and Servants .	730 0 0	1 6 0	2,244 0 0	1 14 6	530 0 0	0 15 2	1,782 11 10	1 17 5	13,920 0 0	1 13 3
Victualling Prisoners .	5,105 2 0	9 2 0	9,750 0 0	7 10 0	4,900 0 0	7 0 0	9,034 10 0	9 10 0	74,816 2 0	8 19 0
Clothing Prisoners .	1,262 5 0	2 5 0	2,600 0 0	2 0 0	1,225 0 0	1 15 0	2,853 0 0	3 0 0	24,841 5 0	2 19 5
Bedding Prisoners .	147 5 3	0 5 3	325 0 0	0 5 0	175 0 0	0 5 0	475 10 0	0 10 0	2,773 5 3	0 6 8
Clothing and Travelling Expenses of Prisoners on Liberation .	50 0 0	0 1 9	30 0 0	0 0 0	250 0 0	0 7 1	1,066 2 10	1 2 5	6,380 0 0	0 15 3
Fuel and Light for General Purposes .	700 0 0	1 4 10	3,000 0 0	2 6 2	800 0 0	1 2 10	675 4 5	0 14 2	10,450 0 0	1 5 0
Other Expenses . .	947 0 0	1 13 1	1,855 0 0	1 8 6	964 10 0	1 7 10	2,196 5 2	2 6 3	13,767 0 0	1 12 11
Gross Total	14,912 18 9	26 11 8	33,175 0 6	25 10 4	12,218 0 0	17 9 1	26,297 9 10	27 13 0	218,961 15 9	26 3 10

The following is an estimate of the cost of transporting and taking care of 100,000 convicts in the penal colonies, from the year 1786 to March 1837—about fifty years :—

Cost of Transport	£2,729,790
Disbursement for General Convict and Colonial Services .	4,091,581
Military Expenditure	1,632,302
Ordnance	29,846
Total	£8,483,519
Deduct for Premium on Bills	507,195
	£7,976,324

The average cost of transport for each convict was £28 per head, and the various expenses of residence and

Appendix.—§ 1—a.

OF PRISON DISCIPLINE.

We have said that at each of the different prisons of the Metropolis a different mode of treatment, or discipline, is adopted towards the prisoners. Hence it becomes expedient, in order that the general reader may be in a position to judge as to the character of the London prisons, that we should give a brief account of the several kinds of prison discipline at present in force.

₊ *Condition of the Prisons in the Olden Time.*—The history of prison improvements in this country begins with the labours of Howard. In the year 1775 he published his work entitled, "The State of the Prisons in England and Wales;" and in the first section of this he gave a summary of the abuses which then existed in the management of criminals. These abuses were principally of a physical and moral kind. Under the one head were comprised—bad food, bad ventilation, and bad drainage; and under the other— want of classification, or separation among the inmates, so that each prison was not only a scene of riot and lawless revelry, and filth and fever, but it was also a college for young criminals, where the juvenile offender could be duly educated in vice by the more experienced professors of iniquity.*

Formerly, we are told, the prisons were farmed out to individuals, willing to take charge of the inmates

---

punishment £54; or, altogether, £82 per head. The average *annual* expense entailed upon this country by the penal colonies, since the commencement of transportation to 1837, amounted to £160,000.

Since the latter period, however, the cost of transportation and maintenance of convicts abroad has considerably increased, the Government estimate for the Convict Service for 1852-3 having been as follows :—

Transport to Australian Colonies	£95,000
Transport to Bermuda and Gibraltar	6,041
Convict Service at Australian Colonies	188,744
Convict Service at Bermuda and Gibraltar	48,842
	£338,627

In 1853 there were 6,212 convicts in Australia, and 2,650 in Bermuda and Gibraltar.

The gross annual expense for the convict service in 1852-3, inclusive of the convict prisons at home, was estimated by the Surveyor-General at £587,294; whereas the estimates for the modification of the system, in substituting imprisonment at home for a proportion of the sentences of transportation abroad, are £337,336.

RETURN SHEWING THE NUMBER OF CONVICTS WHO ARRIVED AT VAN DIEMEN'S LAND IN EACH YEAR FOR 20 YEARS, FROM THE 1ST OF JANUARY, 1831 TO 31ST OF DECEMBER, 1850.

Years.	Number of Arrivals.	Years.	Number of Arrivals.	Years.	Number of Arrivals.	Years.	Number of Arrivals.
1831	2,241	1836	2,565	1841	3,488	1846	2,444
1832	1,401	1837	1,547	1842	5,520	1847	1,186
1833	2,672	1838	2,224	1843	3,727	1848	1,158
1834	1,531	1839	1,441	1844	4,966	1849	1,729
1845	2,493	1840	1,365	1845	3,357	1850	2,894

Total in each
5 years   10,338   9,142   21,058   9,411

Total in each 10 years..19,480.. 30,469
Total in 20 years............. 49,949
Average per annum........................... 2,497

---

* It appears, by parliamentary returns, says the Fifth Report of the Prison Discipline Society, that, in the year 1818, out of 518 prisons in the United Kingdom (to which upwards of 107,000 persons were committed in the course of that year) in 23 of such prisons only the inmates were separated or divided according to law; in 59 of the number, there was no division whatever—not even separation of males from females; in 136 there was only one division of the inmates into separate classes, though the 24th George III., cap. 54, had enjoined that eleven such divisions should be made; in 68 there were but two divisions, and so on; whilst in only 23 were the prisoners separated according to the statute. Again, in 445 of the 518 prisons no work of any description had been introduced. And in the remaining 73, the employment carried on was of the slightest possible description. Farther, in 100 jails, which had been built to contain only 8,545 prisoners, there were at one time as many as 13,057 persons confined. The classification enjoined by the Act above mentioned was as follows :—(1) Prisoners convicted of felony; (2) Prisoners committed on charge or suspicion of felony; (3) Prisoners committed for, or adjudged to be guilty of, misdemeanours only; (4) Debtors; (5) The males of each class to be separated from the females; (6) A separate place of confinement to be provided for such prisoners as are intended to be examined as witnesses on behalf of any prosecution of any indictment for felony; (7) Separate infirmaries, or sick wards, for the men and the women.

at the allowance of threepence or fourpence per day for each; the profit from which, together with fees made compulsory on the prisoners when discharged, constituted the keeper's salary. The debtor—the prisoner discharged, by the expiration of his term of sentence, by acquittal, or pardon from the Crown—had alike to pay those fees, or to languish in confinement. A committal to prison, moreover, was equivalent, in many cases, to a sentence of death by some frightful disease; and in all, to suffering by the utmost extremes of hunger and cold. One disease, generated by the want of proper ventilation, warmth, cleanliness, and food, became known as the jail fever. It swept away hundreds every year, and sent out others on their liberation miserably enfeebled. So rife was this disorder, that prisoners arraigned in the dock brought with them on one occasion such a pestilential halo, as caused many in the court-house to sicken and die. In some jails men and women were together in the day-room; in all, idleness, obscenity, and blasphemy reigned undisturbed. The keeper cared for none of these things. His highest duty was to keep his prisoner safe, and his highest aspiration the fees squeezed out of their miserable relatives.—(v. *Chapters on Prisons and Prisoners*).

This system of prison libertinism continued down to so recent a period, that even in the year 1829 Captain Chesterton found, on entering upon the office of Governor of Coldbath Fields Prison, the internal economy of that institution to be as follows :—

"The best acquainted with the prison," says the Captain, in his Autobiography (vol. ii., p. 247), "were utterly ignorant of the frightful extent of its demoralization. . . . . The procurement of dishonest gains was the only rule—from the late governor downwards—and with the exception of one or two officers, too recently appointed to have learned the villainous arcana of the place, all were engaged in a race of frightful enormity. . . . . It is impossible for the mind to conceive a spectacle more gross and revolting than the internal economy of this polluted spot. . . . . The great majority of the officers were a cunning and extortionate crew, practising every species of duplicity and chicanery. . . . . From one end of the prison to the other a vast illicit commerce prevailed, at a rate of profit so exorbitant as none but the most elastic consciences could have devised and sustained. The law forbade every species of indulgence, and yet there was not one that was not easily purchasable. The first question asked of a prisoner was—'Had he any money, or anything that could be turned into money? or would any friend, if written to, advance him some?' and if the answer were affirmative, then the game of spoliation commenced. In some instances, as much as seven or eight shillings in the pound went to the turnkey, with a couple of shillings to the 'yards-man,' who was himself a prisoner, and had purchased his appointment from the turnkey, at a cost of never less than five pounds, and frequently more. Then a fellow called the 'passage-man' would put in a claim also, and thus the prison novice would soon discover that he was in a place where fees were exorbitant and charges multiplied. . . . . If a sense of injustice led him to complain, he was called 'a nose,' and had to run the gauntlet of the whole yard, by passing through a double file of scoundrels, who, facing inwards, assailed him with short ropes or well-knotted handkerchiefs. . . . . The poor and friendless prisoner was a wretchedly oppressed man; he was kicked and buffeted, made to do any revolting work, and dared not complain. . . . . If a magistrate casually visited the prison, rapid signals communicated the fact, and he would walk through something like outward order. . . . . Little, however, was the unsuspecting justice aware that almost every cell was hollowed out to constitute a hidden store, where tobacco and pipes, tea and coffee, butter and cheese, reposed safe from inquisitive observation; and frequently, besides, bottles of wine and spirits, fish-sauce, and various strange luxuries. In the evening, when farther intrusion was unlooked-for, smoking, and drinking, and singing, the recital of thievish exploits, and every species of demoralizing conversation prevailed. The prisoners slept three in a cell, or in crowded rooms; and no one, whose mind was previously undefiled, could sustain one pure and honest sentiment under a system so frightfully corrupting. . . . . Upon one occasion, during my nightly rounds," continues the late governor, "I overheard a young man of really honest principles arguing with two hardened scoundrels. He was in prison for theft, but declared that, had it not been for a severe illness, which had utterly reduced him, he would never have stolen. His companions laughed at his scruples, and advocated general spoliation. In a tone of indignant remonstrance, the young man said, 'Surely you would not rob a poor countryman, who had arrived in town with only a few shillings in his pocket!' Whereupon, one of his companions, turning lazily in his crib, and yawning as he did so, exclaimed in answer, 'By God Almighty, I would rob my own father, if I could get a shilling out of him.'" *

Further, Mr. Hepworth Dixon, writing on the London prisons—even so lately as the year 1850—says, "The mind must be lost to all sense of shame which can witness the abominations of Horsemonger Lane or Giltspur Street Compter" (the latter has since been removed), "without feelings of scorn and indignation. In Giltspur Street Compter, the prisoners sleep in small cells, little more than half the size of those at Pentonville, though the latter are calculated to be only just large enough for *one* inmate, even when ventilated upon the best plan that science can suggest. But the cell in Giltspur Street Compter is either not ventilated at all, or ventilated very imperfectly; and though little more than half the dimensions of the 'model cells' constructed for *one* prisoner, I have seen *five* persons locked up at four o'clock in the day, to be there confined

* *Peace, War, and Adventure, an Autobiography*, by Charles Laval Chesterton.

till the next morning in darkness and idleness, to do all the offices of nature, not merely in each other's presence, but crushed by the narrowness of their den, into a state of filthy contact, which brute beasts would have resisted to the last gasp of life. . . . . Could five of the purest men in the world live together in such a manner, without losing every attribute of good which had once belonged to them?"

At Newgate, on the other hand, continues the same authority, "in any of the female wards may be seen a week before the sessions, a collection of persons of every shade of guilt and some who are innocent. I remember one case particularly. A servant girl of about sixteen, a fresh-looking healthy creature, recently up from the country, was charged by her mistress with stealing a brooch. She was in the same room—lived all day, slept all night, with the most abandoned of her sex. They were left alone; they had no work to do, no books—except a few tracts, for which they had no taste—to read. The whole day was spent, as is usual in such prisons, in telling stories—the gross and guilty stories of their own lives. There is no form of wickedness, no aspect of vice, with which the poor creature's mind would not be compelled to grow familiar in the few weeks which she passed in Newgate awaiting trial. When the day came the evidence against her was found to be utterly lame and weak, and she was at once acquitted. That she entered Newgate innocent, I have no doubt; but who shall answer for the state in which she left it?"*

₊ *Of the Several Kinds of Prison Discipline.*—The above statements will give the reader a faint notion of the condition of some of the metropolitan prisons, even in our own time. As a remedy for such defective prison-economy, no less than five different systems have been proposed and tried. These are as follows:— (1.) The classification of prisoners; (2.) The silent associated system; (3.) The separate system; (4.) The mixed system; (5.) The mark system; to which must be added that original system which allows the indiscriminate association and communion of prisoners as above described, and which is generally styled the "city system," or no system at all—"the chief *negative* features" of which, according to Mr. Dixon, are "no work, no instruction, no superintendence;" while its "*positive* features" are "idleness, illicit gambling, filthiness, unnatural crowding, unlimited licence (broken at times by severities at which the sense of justice revolts), and universal corruption of each prisoner by his fellows."†

₊ *The Classification of Prisoners.*—As regards that system of prison discipline which seeks to prevent the further demoralization of the criminal, by the separation of prisoners into classes, according to the offences with which they are charged or convicted, it has been said, by the Inspectors of Prisons for the Home District :‡—"A prison would soon lose its terrors as a place of punishment, if its depraved occupants were suffered to indulge in the kind of society within the jail which they had always preferred when at large; and, instead of a place of reformation, the jail would become the best institution that could be devised for instructing its inmates in all the mysteries of vice and crime, if the professors of guilt confined there were suffered to make disciples of such as might be comparatively innocent. To remedy this evil, therefore," the Prison Inspectors add, "we must resort to *classification*. The young," they say, "must be separated from the old; then we must make a division between the novice and practised offenders. Again, subdivisions will be indispensable, in proportion as in each of the classes there are found individuals of different degrees of depravity, and among whom must be numbered, not only the corrupters, but those who are ready to receive their lessons."

But though it would seem to be a consequence of this mode of discipline, as Colonel Jebb well observes, in his work on "Modern Prisons," that "if each jail class respectively be composed of burglars, or assault and battery men, or sturdy beggars, they will acquire under it increased proficiency only in picking locks, fighting, or imposing on the tender mercies of mankind;" nevertheless, it was found, immediately the classification of prisoners was brought into operation, that "a very difficult and unforeseen condition had to be dealt with. The burglar was occasionally sent to prison for trying his hand at begging—a professed sheep-stealer for doing a little business as a thimblerig man—and a London thief for showing fight at a country fair." Hence, by the classification of prisoners according to the offences of which they were convicted, such people were brought into fellowship, during their imprisonment, with a class wholly different from their own, and "often came to be associated for some months in jail with the simple clown who had been detected, perhaps, in his first petty offence."

"Classification of prisoners," says Mr. Kingsmill, too, "allows no approach, seemingly, towards separating the very bad from the better sort. They are continually changing places; those in for felony at one sessions being in for larceny or assault the next, and *vice versâ*."

"Farther," observe the Home Inspectors, "grades in moral guilt are not the immediate subject of human observation, nor, if discovered, are they capable of being so nicely discriminated as to enable us to assign to each individual criminal his precise place in the comparative scale of vice, whilst, if they *could* be accurately perceived by us, it would appear that no two individuals were contaminated in exactly the same

---

* *London Prisons,* by Hepworth Dixon, pp. 7—10.　　　† Ibid.　　　‡ *Vide* 3rd Report, pp. 59, 60.

degree. Moreover, even if these difficulties could be surmounted, and a class formed of criminals who had advanced just to the same point, not only of offence, but of moral depravity, still their association in prison would be sure to produce a farther progress in both."

When, therefore, public attention was called to the defective construction, as well as to the demoralizing and neglected discipline of the prisons of this country, some twenty or thirty years ago, "it was most unfortunate for all the interests concerned," writes the Surveyor-General of Prisons, "that a step was made in the wrong direction; for it was considered that if prisoners could be classified, everything would be effected that could be desired in the way of punishment and reformation.* . . . . Accordingly, vast sums of money were expended in the erection of prisons calculated to facilitate the classification of prisoners. New prisons for carrying out this discipline were constructed on a radiating principle—a central tower was supposed to contain an Argus (or point of universal inspection), and from four to six or eight detached blocks of cells radiated (spoke-fashion) from it—the intervals between the buildings forming the exercising yards for the different classes. Each of the detached blocks contained a certain number of small cells (generally about 8 feet × 5); and there were day-rooms in them, where the prisoners of the class would sit over the fire, and while away time by instructing each other in the mysteries of their respective avocations; for it was not intended by this mode of discipline to check the recognized right of each class to amuse themselves as they pleased. In fact," adds the Colonel, "had it been an object to make provision for compulsory education in crime, no better plan could have been devised."

* *The Silent Associated System.*—Next as to the "*silent*," or, as it is sometimes called, the "silent associated," system, the following is a brief review of its characteristics and results. Whilst the classification of offenders continues to this day to be the discipline carried out in many prisons, the prevention of contamination is sought to be attained in others, where hardly any such classification exists, by the prohibition of all intercourse by word of mouth among the prisoners. "If the members of each class of prisoners," says an eminent authority, "instead of being left, as they are in most prisons, to unrestricted social intercourse, were compelled to work, under the immediate superintendence of an officer whose duty it would be to punish any man who, by word of mouth, look, or sign, attempted to communicate with his fellow-prisoner, we should have the silent system in operation." But as minute classification is not, under the silent system, so absolutely necessary as when intercourse is permitted, the usual practice is to associate such classes as can be properly brought together, in order to economise superintendence; and hence its name of the Silent Associated System, in contradistinction to the Classified System, under which intercommunication is permitted.

---

* The Act of Parliament enjoining the classification of prisoners was the 4th of George IV. (A.D. 1823), cap. 64, and had the following preamble:—"Whereas the laws now existing relative to the building, repairing, and regulating of jails and houses of correction in England and Wales are complicated, and have in many cases been found ineffectual: And whereas it is expedient that such measures should be adopted and such arrangements made as shall not only provide for the safe custody, but shall also tend more effectually to preserve the health and improve the morals of the prisoners confined therein, as well as ensure the proper measure of punishment to convicted offenders: And whereas due classification, inspection, regular labour, and employment, and religious and moral instruction, are essential to the discipline of a prison, and to the reformation of offenders," &c., &c.; therefore the following rules and regulations (among others are ordained to be observed in all jails:—

"The male and female prisoners shall be confined," says this statute, "in separate buildings or parts of the prison, so as to prevent them from seeing, conversing, or holding any intercourse with each other.

"The prisoners of each sex shall be divided into distinct classes, care being taken that prisoners of the following classes do not intermix with each other:—

In Jails.	*In Houses of Correction.*
1st. Debtors and persons confined for contempt of court or civil process.	1st. Prisoners convicted of felony.
2nd. Prisoners convicted of felony.	2nd. Prisoners convicted of misdemeanors.
3rd. Prisoners convicted of misdemeanors.	3rd. Prisoners committed on charge or suspicion of felony.
4th. Prisoners convicted on charge or suspicion of felony.	4th Prisoners committed on charge or suspicion of misdemeanors.
5th. Prisoners convicted on charge or suspicion of misdemeanors, or for want of sureties.	5th. Vagrants.

"Such prisoners," adds the Act, "as are intended to be examined as witnesses in behalf of the Crown in any prosecution shall also be kept separate in all jails and houses of correction."

Again, by the 2nd and 3rd of Victoria (A.D. 1839), cap. 56, it is enacted, "that the prisoners of each sex in every jail, house of correction, bridewell, or penitentiary, in England and Wales, which, before the passing of this Act, did not come within the provisions of the 4th of George IV., and in which a more minute classification or individual separation shall not be in force, shall be at least divided into the following classes (that is to say):—

1st. Debtors in those prisons in which debtors can be lawfully confined.
2nd. Prisoners committed for trial.
3rd. Prisoners convicted and sentenced to hard labour.
4th. Prisoners convicted and sentenced to hard labour.
5th. Prisoners not included in the foregoing classes.

"And that in every prison in England and Wales separate rules and regulations shall be made for each distinct class of prisoners in that prison."

The silent system originated in a deep conviction of the great and manifold evils of jail *association*, the advocates of that system naturally supposing that the demoralization of criminals would be checked if all communication among them were cut off; and the greater number of prisons, in which any fundamental change of discipline has been effected during the last twenty years, are now conducted on the silent plan. At Coldbath Fields Prison this system has been carried to its utmost. It was introduced there on the 29th December, 1834. "On which day," says Captain Chesterton, in his Autobiography, "the number of 914 prisoners were suddenly apprised that all intercommunication by word, gesture, or sign was prohibited; and without any approach to overt opposition, the silent system thenceforth became the rule of the prison. . . . . . Those who had watched and deplored the former system," adds the late Governor, "could not but regard the change with heartfelt satisfaction. There was now a real protection to morals, and it no longer became the reproach of authority, that the comparatively innocent were consigned to certain demoralization and ruin. For eighteen years has this system been maintained in this prison with unswerving strictness. . . . I unhesitatingly avow my conviction, that the silent system, properly administered, is calculated to effect as much good as, by any penal process, we can hope to realize."

The objections to the system, however, appear to be manifold and cogent. First, the silent system seems to require an inordinate number of officers to prevent that intercommunication among prisoners "by word, sign, or gesture," which constitutes its essence. At Coldbath Fields Prison, for instance, no less than 272 persons (54 warders $+$ 218 prisoners, appointed to act as monitors over their fellow-criminals) were employed to superintend 682 inmates, which is in the ratio of 10 officers to every 25 prisoners. Nevertheless, even this large body of overseers was found insufficient to prevent all communication among the criminals—the rule of silence being repeatedly infracted, and the prison punishments increasing considerably after the silent system had been introduced. "Punishments," says the late Governor, "are more frequent now than when we began the system." Indeed, "in one year," we are told, "no less than 6,794 punishments were inflicted for talking, &c."*

But if it be difficult to prevent prisoners from audibly talking with each other, it is next to impossible, even by the most extensive *surveillance*, to check the interchange of significant *signs* among them. "Although there is a turnkey stationed in each tread-wheel yard," says the Second Report of Inspectors of Prisons for the Home District, "and two monitors, or wardsmen, selected from the prisoners, stand constantly by, the men on the wheel can, and do, speak to each other. They ask one another how long they are sentenced for, and when they are going out; and answers are given by laying two or three fingers on the wheel to signify so many months, or by pointing to some of the many inscriptions carved on the tread-wheel as to the terms of imprisonment suffered by former prisoners, or else they turn their hands to express unlockings or days."

Again: "The posture of stooping, in which the prisoners work at picking oakum or cotton (we are told in the Rev. Mr. Kingsmill's "Chapters on Prisons and Prisoners"), gives ample opportunity of carrying on a lengthened conversation without much chance of discovery; so that the rule of silence is a dead letter to many. At meals, also, in spite of the strictness with which the prisoners are watched, the order is constantly infringed. The time of exercise again affords an almost unlimited power of communicating with each other; for the closeness of the prisoners' position, and the noise of their feet render intercommunication at such times a very easy matter. . . . . Farther, the prisoners, attend chapel daily, and this may be termed the golden period of the day to most of them; for it is here, by holding their books to their faces and pretending to read with the chaplain, that they can carry on the most uninterrupted conversation."

Not only, however, is the silent system open to grave objections, because it fails in its attempt to prevent intercourse among prisoners promiscuously associated, but it has even more serious evils connected with it. "The mind of the prisoner," it has been well said, "is kept perpetually on the fret by the prohibition of speech, and it is drawn from the contemplation of his own conduct and degraded position, to the invention of devices for defeating his overseers, or for carrying on a clandestine communication with his fellow-prisoners, deriving no benefit meanwhile from the offices of religion, but rather converting such offices into an opportunity for eluding the vigilance of the warders, and being still farther depraved by frequent punishment for offences of a purely arbitrary character; for surely to place a number of social beings in association, and then not only interdict all intercourse between them, but to punish such as yield to that most powerful

---

* The number of punishments which were inflicted under the silent system, in three London prisons, in the course of one year, was as follows:—

	Number of Prisoners (Male and Female) in the course of one year.	Number of Punishments for Offences within the Prison in the course of one year.
Brixton House of Correction	3,285	1,171
Westminster Bridewell (Tothill Fields)	5,524	4,848
Coldbath Fields House of Correction	9,750	13,812

(*Second Report of Inspectors of Prisons for Home District.*)

The average expense of each convict kept in a house of correction, under the silent system, is about £14 per annum, or between £55 and £56 for four years.

of human impulses—the desire of communing with those with whom we are thrown into connection—is an act of refined tyranny, that is at once unjust and impossible of being thoroughly carried out.

** The Separate System.—It is almost self-evident that every system of prison discipline must be associative, separative, or mixed. 1. The prisoners may be either allowed to associate indiscriminately, and to indulge in unrestrained intercourse; or else, in order to prevent the evils of unrestricted communion, among the older and younger criminals, as well as the more expert and the less artful, when associated together, the prisoners may be made to labour as well as take their exercise and meals in perfect silence. 2. We may put a stop to such association, either *partially* or *entirely*, by separating the prisoners into *classes*, according to their crimes, ages, or characters, or else by separating them *individually*, each from the other, and thus endeavour to check the injurious effect of indiscriminate intercourse among the depraved, by positive isolation rather than classification. 3. We may permit them to associate in silence during the day, and isolate them at night—the latter method constituting what is termed the mixed system of prison discipline.

The separate system is defined by the Surveyor-General of Prisons as that mode of penal discipline " in which each individual prisoner is confined in a cell, which becomes his workshop by day and his bed-room by night, so as to be effectually prevented from holding communication with, or even being seen sufficiently to be recognized by a fellow-prisoner."

The object of this discipline is stated to be twofold. It is enforced, not only to prevent the prisoner having intercourse with his fellow-prisoners, but to compel him to hold communion with himself. He is excluded from the society of the other criminal inmates of the prison, because experience has shown that such society is injurious, and he is urged to make his conduct the subject of his own reflections, because it is almost universally found that such self-communion is the precursor of moral amendment.

No other system of prison discipline, say the advocates of the separate system—neither the classified nor the silent system—has any tendency to incline the prisoner to turn his thoughts back upon himself—to cause him to reconsider his life and prospects, or to estimate the wickedness and unprofitableness of crime. The silent system, we are told, can call forth no new resolves, nor any settled determinations of amendment, whilst it fails in *wholly* securing the prisoner from contamination, and sets the mind upon the rack to devise means for evading the irritating restrictions imposed upon it.

The advantages of individual separation, therefore, say those who believe this system to be superior to all others, are not merely of a preventive character—preventive of the inevitable evils of association—preventive of the contamination which the comparatively innocent cannot escape from, when brought into contact with the polluted; but separation at once renders corrupt intercourse impracticable, and affords to the prisoner direct facilities for reflection and self-improvement.

"Under this discipline," says the Rev. Mr. Kingsmill, chaplain of Pentonville Prison, "the propagation of crime is impossible—the continuity of vicious habits is broken off—the mind is driven to reflection, and conscience resumes her sway."

The convicted criminal, under this system, is confined day and night in a cell that is fitted with every convenience essential to ensure ventilation, warmth, cleanliness, and personal exercise. Whatever is necessary to the preservation of the prisoner's well-being, moral as well as physical, is strictly attended to. So far from being consigned to the gloomy terrors of solitary confinement, he is visited by the governor as well as by the chaplain, and other prison officers daily; he is provided with work which furnishes employment for his mind—has access to profitable books—is allowed to take exercise once in every twenty-four hours in the open air—is required to attend every day in the chapel, and, if uneducated, at the school; and, in case of illness or sudden emergency, he has the means of making his wants known to the officers of the prison.

" On reviewing our opinions" (with respect to the moral effect of the discipline of separate confinement), says the Fifth Report of the Board of Commissioners appointed to superintend the working of Pentonville Prison, "and taking advantage of the experience of another year, we feel warranted in expressing our firm conviction, that the moral results of the system have been most encouraging, and attended with a success which we believe is *without parallel in the history of prison discipline.*" Farther, the Commissioners add " the result of our entire experience is the conclusion, that the separation of one prisoner from another is *the only sound basis* on which a reformatory can be established with any reasonable hope of success."

Again, the Governor of Pentonville Prison (who has watched the operation of the system from its introduction in 1842) says, in his Sixth Report, " If I may express an abstract opinion on the subject, not supported by facts and reasons, it shall be to this effect—that having at the first felt confidence in the powers and capabilities of the system for the accomplishment of its objects, and that no valid objection could be raised against it, if rightly administered, on the ground of its being injurious to physical or mental health; a period of more than five years of close personal experience of its working has left that sentiment not only unimpaired, but confirmed and strengthened."

Such are the eminent eulogiums uttered by the advocates of the separate system of penal discipline; and let us now in fairness give a summary of the objections raised against it. It is alleged, in the first place, that the discipline is unwarrantably severe. It is represented as abandoning its victim to despair, by consigning a vacant or guilty mind to all the terrible depression of unbroken solitude. Indeed, it is often condemned as being another form of solitary confinement, the idea of which is so closely connected in the public mind with the dark dungeons and oppressive cruelty of the Middle Ages, as to be sufficient to excite the strongest emotions of abhorrence in every English bosom.

Colonel Jebb tells us, that there is a wide difference between *separate* and *solitary* confinement. He says, that in the Act (2nd and 3rd Victoria, cap. 56) which rendered separate confinement legal, it was specially enjoined that "no cell should be used for that purpose which is not of such a size, and lighted, and warm, ventilated and fitted up in such a manner as may be required by a due regard to health, and furnished with the means of enabling the prisoner to communicate at any time with an officer of the prison." It was further provided, too, by the same Act, that each prisoner should have the means of taking exercise when required; that he should be supplied with the means of moral and religious instruction—with books, and also with labour and employment. "Whereas, a prisoner under *solitary* confinement," says the Surveyor-General of Prisons, "may be not only placed in any kind of cell, but is generally locked up and fed on bread and water only, no farther trouble being taken about him. A mode of discipline so severe," he adds, "that it cannot be legally enforced for more than a month at a time, nor for more than three months in any one year."

"Under *solitary* confinement," another prison authority observes, "the prisoner is deprived of intercourse with all other human beings. Under *separate* confinement, he is kept rigidly apart only from other *criminals*, but is allowed as much intercourse with instructors and officers, as is compatible with judicious economy."—Burt's *Results of Separate Confinement.*

A second objection to the separate or cellular system is, that it breaks down the mental and bodily health of the prisoners—that it forces the mind to be continually brooding over its own guilt—constantly urging the prisoner to contemplate the degradation of his position, and seeking to impress upon him that his crimes have caused him to be excluded from all society; and that with the better class of criminals, especially those with whom the ties of kindred are strong, it produces not only such a continued sorrow at being cut off from all relatives, and indeed every one but prison officers, but such a long insatiate yearning to get back to all that is held dear, that the punishment becomes more than natures which are not utterly callous are able to withstand; so that, instead of reforming, it utterly overwhelms and destroys. With more vacant intellects and hardened hearts, however, it serves to make the prisoners even more unfeeling and unthinking; for sympathy alone develops sympathy, and thought in others is required to call forth thought in us. In a word, it is urged that this mode of penal discipline cages a man up as if he were some dangerous beast, allowing his den to be entered only by his "keeper," and that it ends in his becoming as irrational and furious *as* a beast; in fine, say the opponents of the system, "it violates the great social law instituted by the Almighty, and so working contrary to nature, it is idle to expect any good of it."

Now, let us see whether there is truth in such strictures, or whether they be mere empty rhodomontade. Fortunately, we possess ample means, and those of a most trustworthy character, for testing the validity of these objections. Let us see, then, what is the proportionate number of criminal lunatics to the total prison population in England and Wales; and in order to guard against the errors of generalizing upon a small number of particulars, let us draw our conclusions from as large a series of phenomena as possible.

The tables given in the Fifteenth Report of the Inspectors of Prisons for the Home District, extend over eight years (1842-1849, both inclusive), and show that in the course of that period there were altogether 680 cases of lunacy (or an average of 85 cases per annum) occurring in all the prisons of England and Wales, among an aggregate of 1,156,166 prisoners (or an average yearly prison population of 144,520 individuals). This is at the rate of 5·8 criminal lunatics in every 10,000 prisoners, and such may, therefore, be taken as the *normal* proportion of lunatic cases in a given number of criminal offenders.[*] If, therefore, any mode of prison discipline be found to yield a greater ratio of lunatics to the number of offenders brought under that discipline, we may safely conclude that it is unduly severe; and *vice versâ* (assuming crime itself to be

[*] The following are the returns from which the above conclusions are drawn:—

Years.	Total Prison Population in England and Wales.	No. of Criminal Lunatics.	No. of Criminal Lunatics to 10,000 Criminals.
1842	153,136	76	4·9
1843	152,445	64	4·1
1844	143,979	96	6·6
1845	124,110	99	7·9
1846	123,236	92	7·4
1847	131,949	96	7·2
1848	160,369	89	5·6
1849	166,942	68	4·0
Total . . .	1,156,166	680	5·8
Annual Mean	144,520	85	5·8

Fifteenth Report of Prison Inspectors, p. xxxiv.

closely connected with mental aberration), if it yield a less proportion than the above, then it is exerting a beneficial agency on the criminal temperament.

The returns of Pentonville prison are for a period of eight years also (from the 22nd of December, 1842, to the 31st of December, 1850), and these show that in an aggregate of 3,546 prisoners (or an annual mean of 443 individuals), there were no less than 22 attacked with insanity, which is at the rate of 62·0, instead of 5·8, cases of lunacy in every 10,000 prisoners; so that the discipline pursued at this prison yields *upwards of ten times more lunatics* than should be the case according to the normal rate.*

According to these returns, therefore, we find that had the prisoners confined at Pentonville prison been treated in the same manner as at the other jails throughout the country, there would, in all probability, have been only 2 instead of 22 cases of lunacy in the eight years, among the 3,546 prisoners (for 1,156,166 : 680 :: 3,546 : 2); and, on the other hand, had the million and odd criminals confined in the whole of the prisons of England and Wales been submitted to the same stringent discipline as those at Pentonville, the gross number of lunatics among them would, as far as we can judge, have been increased from 680 to 7,173 (for 3,546 : 22 :: 1,156,166 : 7,173).

These figures, it must be confessed, tell awful tales of long suffering and deep mental affliction; for the breaking down of the weaker minds is merely evidence of the intense moral agony that must be suffered by all except the absolutely insensible. Nor can we ourselves, after such overwhelming proofs, see one Christian reason to justify the discipline—especially when we add, that in addition to there being upwards of tenfold more madmen turned out of Pentonville prison than any other jail in England and Wales, no less than 26 cases of "*slight* mental affections" or delusions, and 8 suicides also having occurred there within the eight years above alluded to! Nor is this an isolated case: Dr. Baly, the Visiting Physician of Millbank, in his Report on Separate Confinement, published in the year 1852, gives a table which shows that in a period of 8 years (1844-51, both inclusive) there were 65 cases of insanity there, among an aggregate of 7,393 prisoners; this is at the rate of 87·5 cases (instead of the normal proportion of 5·8) to every 10,000 individuals. Moreover, in America, in pursuance of a law passed in 1821, 80 convicts were selected, and, as a matter of experiment, placed in *solitary* cells, which had been prepared for the purpose, under the direction of the Inspectors of the State Prison, at Auburn. In 1823, however, about eighteen months after the commencement of the experiment, it was found that the most disastrous results had followed, *especially as regarded insanity*—the greater number of the convicts being attacked with mental disease.

Now, to show that separate confinement—"the seclusion of the separate cell"—is allowed, even by the advocates of the system, to "have *some* tendency to produce insanity, by withdrawing those vicious alleviations to the mind which are supplied by the intercourse of prisoners in association" (these are the words of the late assistant chaplain), we may add that the Rev. Mr. Burt says, in his "Results of Separate Confinement" (page 136), that "It is one of the few known laws of mental disease, that periods of transition from

* The subjoined is the Table given by the Rev. Mr. Burt, in his "Results of Separate Confinement at Pentonville:"—

TABLE, *showing the Criminal Character and Sentences of Twenty-two Prisoners attacked with Insanity, from the Opening of the Prison to the 31st December,* 1850; *also the Proportions between the Number admitted and the Number attacked in each Class; also the Numbers of Single and Married Men admitted and attacked.*

Classes of Prisoners.	No. of Prisoners attacked with Insanity.	No. of Prisoners admitted since the opening of Prison.	No. attacked with Insanity in every 1,000 of each class.	Classes of Prisoners.	No. of Prisoners attacked with Insanity	No. of Prisoners admitted since the opening of Prison.	No. attacked with Insanity in every 1,000 of each class.
Sentenced to seven years and under ten	10	1,777	5·62	Not included in the above classes	0	382	0
„ ten years	8	1,263	6·33	Not known to have been previously convicted	10	1,835	5·4
„ above ten years	4	506	7·90	Previously convicted	12	1,711	7·6
Stealing, larceny, and felony undefined	9	1,744	5·2				
House-breaking and robbery	6	876	6·9				
Horse, sheep, and cattle stealing	3	306	9·8	Married	4	964	4·1
Forgery and uttering	1	98	10·02	Single and widowers	18	2,582	6·9
Rape, and assault with intent, &c. (including unnatural crimes)	1	69	14·5				
Stabbing and shooting with intent, &c. (cases of manslaughter and cutting and wounding being included)	2	71	28·2	Totals of all classes	22	3,546	6·2

The above returns are very useful, in another point of view, as showing in what classes of criminals there is the greatest tendency to madness. Thus we perceive that those who have a tendency to commit bodily injuries are the nearest to insanity—those whose offences are of a libidinous character are the next in the scale of proximate aberration—the forgers and "smashers" next—the cattle-stealers the next—the burglars the next—whereas, of all criminals, the common thieves have the least disposition to madness. It shows, moreover, that the longest sentences produce the greatest number of cases of mental derangement; those who have been convicted more than once being more frequently diseased in mind than those undergoing their first conviction.

one extreme feeling to its opposite, are marked as critical to reason. Men inured to suffering will bear misery without much danger. It is the *sudden* inroad of misfortune which either overwhelms the mind, or calls forth too violent an effort of resistance. That excessive effort will be followed by a prostration of mental energies, and *derangement will, in some cases, ensue,* or the mind will be left in the power of slight disturbing causes until it is rallied under new and invigorating influences." "Upon the mind of the criminal in separation, especially upon the convict under sentence of transportation," Mr. Burt tells us, "there are three classes of adverse influences in operation—(1.) The heavy blow of punishment. (2.) Excessive demoralization of character. (3.) The *withdrawal of those associations which in ordinary life divert and sustain the mind.* But," he adds, "the disturbing influence of each one of these causes is greatest during the *early* period of imprisonment"—in plain language, if the poor wretch do not go mad under the treatment in the first twelvemonths, then he will bear being caged up as long as we please.*

The prison authorities, however, speak far more cautiously, and, we must add, considerately, as to the working of the separate system, than the late Assistant-Chaplain at the Model Prison; indeed, the very fact of the period of confinement there having been changed from eighteen to nine months is a tacit acknowledgment that the original term of separation was more than ordinary natures could bear without derangement.

"Beyond twelve months," says Colonel Jebb, the thoughtful and kind-hearted Surveyor-General of Prisons, in his Report for 1853, "I think the system of separate confinement requires greater care and watchfulness than would perhaps be ensured under ordinary circumstances. And there are grounds for believing that it is neither necessary nor desirable so to extend it."

Again, Mr. Kingsmill, the Chaplain of Pentonville, says, "There seems to be no sufficient reason for wishing for any extension of separation beyond eighteen months, *but the reverse ;*" for the experiment appears to him, he tells us, *not* to have succeeded, as regards the advantages of separate confinement for longer periods than fifteen or eighteen months. "Where the ties of kindred are strong," he adds, "the galling feeling at the loss of liberty and society is increased, and though the mass are still patient and cheerful to the last, it may well be questioned whether it be safe to keep them longer separated, when the mind has ceased to be active in acquiring knowledge." To this Colonel Jebb subjoins, "it is not the *use* but the *abuse* of *separate* confinement that is to be guarded against—that is, pressing it beyond the limits under which advantage is derived from placing a prisoner, under favourable circumstances, for reflection and receiving instruction." Further, the Surveyor-General assures us, that the statistics of the medical officer "afford convincing proof that diminishing the extent of the imprisonment from what it had originally been—increasing the daily exercise—substituting rapid exercise for that which was taken in the separate yards—improving the ventilation by admitting the outer air direct to the cells, and at once relaxing the discipline when any injury to health was apprehended—have been found to have a favourable influence.

*** *Of the "Mixed" System of Prison Discipline.*—This is the system pursued at Millbank Prison. It consists of a combination of the silent and separate modes of criminal treatment—that is to say, the men work together in *silence* by day, and sleep in *separate* cells by night. It has all the faults of the silent system, and but little, if any, of the good derivable from the self-communion and worldly retirement of the separate system.

*** *Of the "Mark" System of Prison Discipline.*—As this system, so far as our knowledge goes, forms part of the discipline at no penal establishment in this country at present, it requires but little explanation here. The great feature of the mark system, according to Mr. Hepworth Dixon, who styles it "the most comprehensive and philosophical of all schemes of criminal treatment in this country," is, that "it substitutes labour sentences for time sentences." Instead of condemning a man to fourteen years' imprisonment, Captain Maconochie, the author of this peculiar mode of discipline, would have him sentenced to perform a certain

---

* Mr. Burt, who is a staunch advocate for the separate system, and that carried out to its full extreme, cites the following table, in order to show that the majority of the cases of insanity occur within the first twelvemonths of the term of imprisonment. How strange it is a gentleman of his generous nature should never have asked himself the question whether, as there *were* such a large number of cases of insanity occurring within the earlier period of the discipline, the separate system were really justifiable in the eyes of God or man.

TABLE *showing the Periods at which all Cases of Mental Affection have occurred at Pentonville during Eight Years, from the opening of the Prison, on the 22nd of December, 1842, to the 31st of December, 1850.*

Description of Mental Affection.	Six Months, and under.	From Six to Twelve Months.	From Twelve to Eighteen Months.	From Eighteen Months to Two Years.	Total.
Insanity . . .	14	5	3	0	22
Delusions . . .	13	9	2	2	26
Suicides . . .	2	1	0	0	3
Total .	29	15	5	2	51

quantity of labour—the labour being represented by "marks" instead of money—whence the name of the system. The whole of this labour, we are told, the convict would be bound to perform before he could regain his freedom, whether he chose to occupy one year or twenty years about it.

The advantages of this mode of prison discipline, its advocates aver, are, that it places the criminal's fate, to some extent, in his own power. Labour punishment, they say, gives a convict the feeling of personal responsibility, which the present mode of punishment robs him of. The man serving a fixed period has no object but to kill the time. An absolute disregard of the value of time is thus begotten in the mind of the convict—time becoming associated with the idea of suffering and restraint. The time sentence puts the offender under restraint for a term, but does not force him to do anything to make any active reparation to society for the crime, and it takes away all stimulus to exertion on the part of the criminal, who knows that, "idle or industrious, dissolute or orderly, he must still serve out an inexorable number of weeks and years. The labour sentence, on the other hand, induces a habit of hard work, and the habit which is thus made to earn for the man his liberty will afterwards become the means of preserving it."

As yet this system has been tried only in Norfolk Island—where, it is alleged, no conceivable system would or could work well—amongst transported transports, the most self-abandoned human beings, perhaps, on the earth's surface. But "even there," adds Mr. Dixon, "it did not fail."

*** *Conclusion.*—Such, then, are the several modes of discipline that at present make up the science of what is termed "*penology.*"

Now the objects of all penal inflictions and treatment are, of course, twofold—punishment and reformation; the one instituted not only as a penance for a particular offence, but as the means of deterring future offenders; and the other sought after with the view of correcting the habits of the present offenders.

Hence we are enabled to put the several forms of criminal treatment pursued in this country to a practical test; for if our methods of penal discipline are *really* deterring future offenders and reforming present ones, we ought to be able to show the result in figures, and to point to the criminal statistics as a proof that we are reducing crime among us by the regimen of our jails. The subjoined table will enable us to see if such be the case :—

NUMBER OF CRIMINALS IN ENGLAND AND WALES DURING THE FOLLOWING YEARS :—

1834	. .	22,451	1844	. .	26,542
1835	. .	20,731	1845	. .	24,303
1836	. .	20,984	1846	. .	25,107
1837	. .	23,612	1847	. .	28,833
1838	. .	23,094	1848	. .	30,349
		110,872			135,134
1839	. .	24,443	1849	. :	27,816
1840	. .	27,187	1850	. .	26,813
1841	. .	27,760	1851	. .	27,960
1842	. .	31,309	1852	. .	27,510
1843	. .	29,591	1853	. .	27,057
		140,290			137,156
		251,162			272,290

Increase in crime between first and last year . . . . . 20·5 per cent.

Increase between the first and last ten years . . . . 8·0 ,,

Increase in population of England and Wales from 1841—51 . . 12·6 ,,

Absolutely considered, then, we find that, despite the spread of education among us, and increase of churches and chapels, together with the greater activity of the ministry of all denominations, and the rapid development of benevolent and religious societies, including "Home Missions" and "Reformatories"—despite all these appliances, we say, the crime of the country has increased no less than *twenty* per cent. within the last twenty years; whilst considered relatively to the increase of the population, we find that it has decreased only to the extent of *four* per cent. in ten years. Hence, if we take into consideration the vast *external* machinery for improving the morals and instructing the minds of the people in the present day, we shall see good reason to conclude that the *internal* economy of our prisons has made but small impression upon the great body of criminals.

Nevertheless this is hardly a precise mode of testing the value of the several forms of penal discipline at present in vogue, as the greater proportion of the offenders included in the totals above specified may be regarded as being, so to speak, young in crime, and as never having been in prison before, so that the treatment pursued within the jails could not directly have affected them.

The number of the *recommittals*, however, may be cited as positive proof upon the matter ; and hence the following table, copied from the Fifth Report of the Inspectors of Prisons for the Home District, becomes the most condemnatory evidence as regards the inefficacy of our treatment of criminal offenders :—

ENGLAND AND WALES.

Years.	Total of Criminal Committals.	Total of Recommittals.	Per Centage of Recommittals to Committals.
1842	112,927	53,862	29·9
1843	112,752	34,383	30·5
1844	107,243	34,731	32·4
1845	99,049	33,113	33·4
1846	98,984	32,458	32·8
1847	105,041	32,925	31·3
1848	124,342	37,225	29·9
1849	129,697	39,826	30·7

Increase of recommittals between first and last year . . . 0·8 per cent.

Thus we discover how utterly abortive are all our modes of penal discipline, since the old "jail-birds," so far from being either reformed or deterred from future offences, are here shown continually to return to the prisons throughout the country. Moreover, of the number of criminals who are recommitted in the course of the year, many have appeared more than once before in the jails ; and the Report from which the above table has been extracted has another table whereby we find that—though in 1842 there was no less than 6 per cent. of criminal offenders who had been *recommitted* four times and more—nevertheless the per centage of that class of inveterate criminals had risen as high as 7·7 in 1849.

There must, then, be some grave and serious errors in our present penal system, since it is plain from the above facts that our treatment of criminals neither deters nor reforms.

Let us endeavour, therefore, to detect where the errors lie.

Now, it appears to us—and we speak with all humility upon the subject—that the first substantial objection against the prison discipline of the present day is, that our silent systems and separate systems are as much *in extremis* as was the old plan of allowing indiscriminate intercourse to take place among all classes of prisoners. Society, some years ago, opened its eyes and discovered that to permit the young offender to associate and commune with the old, and the comparatively innocent with the inveterately depraved, was to convert the jail into an academy for inexperienced criminals, where they might receive the best possible tuition in vice. Therefore, in the suddenness of our indignation at the short-comings of such a method of dealing with the inmates of our jails, we rushed to the opposite extreme, and declared that because the liberty of speech among such people was found to be fraught with evil, they should henceforth not speak at all ; and because it was dangerous to allow them to associate, they should for the future be cut off from all society, and caged, like animals in a menagerie, each in separate dens.

A love of extremes, however, belongs to the fanatical rather than the rational mind, and perhaps the worst form of all bigotry is that of disciplinarians who invariably sacrifice common sense to some love of super-strictness.

Surely all that is necessary, in order to check the evils of unrestricted intercourse among criminals, is to prevent them talking upon *vicious* subjects one to the other. To go farther than this, and stop all communion among them, is not only absurd as overreaching the end in view, but positively wicked as ignoring the highest gift of the Almighty to man—that wondrous faculty of speech, which some philosophers have held to be more distinctive of human nature than even reason itself.

Moreover, by overstepping what Shakspeare beautifully terms "the *modesty* of nature," we force the poor wretches, whose tongues we figuratively cut out, into all kinds of cheats and low cunning, in order to gratify what, if rightly used, is not only a harmless but a noble impulse. It seems, therefore, that the entire object which the silent system has in view would be attained by placing an intelligent officer to watch over a certain number of prisoners, and whose duty it should be not only to restrain them from conversing upon vicious subjects, but to read to them, while they were at work, from interesting and high-minded books, as well as to lead the discourse at other times into innocent and elevated channels. Nor should this officer be one who would be likely to "*bore*" the people with prosy views and explanations upon matters of philosophy or religion. We have sufficient faith in goodness to believe that he is but a poor disciple of the Great Teacher, who cannot make that which possesses the highest beauty a matter of the highest attraction, even to the lowest minds—who cannot speak of the wonders of creation or of the loving-kindness of Christ without being as dull as a religious tract, or as dry as a lecturer at a mechanic's institution. We would have it received as a rule, that inattention on the part of the prisoners was a sign of inability on the part of the officer, or the authors selected by him, to discourse pleasantly—to clothe interesting subjects in an interesting form ; and, indeed, that it arose from a fault in the teacher (or the books) rather than the scholars, so that instead of blaming the latter, the former should be dismissed from his office—even as the dramatist is hissed as an incapable from the stage, when he is found to lack the power to rivet the attention of his audience.

By such an arrangement, it is obvious that all necessity for imprisoning the criminals in separate cells would be at end. Hence all dangers of insanity would cease, and the mind and conscience rather be brought to their proper mastery over the passions and desires, than deprived of all power by long-continued depression.

But one of the main evils of the present systems of penal discipline is, that they one and all make labour a *punishment* to the criminal. This, in fact, is the great stumbling-block to reformation among the class. The only true definition of crime, so far as regards the predatory phase of it, that we have seen, is that laid down in the Report of the Constabulary Commissioners, and which involves neither an educational nor a teetotal view, but simply a matter-of-fact consideration of the subject, asserting that such crime is "*simply the desire to acquire property with a less degree of labour than by ordinary industry;*" in a word, that it arises from an indisposition to work for a livelihood.

Now that this expresses the bare truth, and is the only plain practical explanation to be given of the subject, none can doubt who have paid the least attention to the criminal character; for not only is the greater proportion of those who are of predatory habits likewise of a vagabond disposition (out of 16,000 such characters known to the police, upwards of 10,000 were returned in the same Report as being of migratory habits), but this same wandering nature appertains to their minds as well as their bodies; for so erratic are criminals both in thought and action, that it is extremely difficult to fix their attention for any length of time to one subject, or to get them to pursue any *settled* occupation in life. Hence labour becomes extremely irksome to them, and (as the mind *must* busy itself about something) amusement grows as attractive as regular work is repulsive to their natures. Legislators seem to have taken this view of the question, and to have sentenced such people to imprisonment with hard labour, simply because they believed that work was the severest punishment they could inflict upon them. But punishments, especially those which are begotten in the fury of our indignation for certain offences, are not always remarkable for their wisdom; since to sentence a criminal to a term of hard labour because he has an aversion to work, is about as rational as it would be to punish a child who objected to jalap, by condemning it to a six months' course of it.

So far, indeed, from such a sentence serving to eradicate the antipathy of the criminal to industrious pursuits, it tends rather to confirm him in his prejudice against regular labour. "Well," says the pickpocket to himself, on leaving prison, "I always thought working for one's living was by no means pleasant; and after the dose I have just had, I'm blest if I a'n't *convinced* of it."

The defect of such penal discipline becomes obvious to all minds when thus plainly set before them; for is it not manifest that, if we wish to inculcate habits of industry in criminals, we should strive to make labour a delight rather than use it as a scourge to them?

Now the great Author of our natures has ordained, that, though labour be a curse, there should be certain modes by which it may be rendered agreeable to us, and these are—(1) by variety or change of occupation; (2) by the inculcation of industrial habits; (3) by association with some purpose or object.

The first of these modes by which work is made pleasant is the natural or primitive one. Every person is aware how the mere transition from one employment to another seems to inspire him with fresh energy, for monotony of all kinds fatigues and distresses the mind; and as active attention to any matter requires a continuous mental effort in order to sustain it, therefore those natures which are more erratic and volatile than others become the sooner tired, and consequently less able to support the sameness of a *settled* occupation.

The second mode of rendering labour agreeable consists in the wonderful educational power of that mysterious principle of habit by which any mental or muscular operation, however irksome at first, comes, by regular and frequent repetition, to be not only pleasant to perform, but after a time positively unpleasant for us to abstain from.

The third and last method of making industry delightful to us is, however, by far the most efficacious, for we have but to inspire a person with some special purpose, to make his muscles move nimbly, and agreeably too. It is the presence of some such purpose that sets the more honest portion of the world working for the food of themselves and their families; and it is precisely because your true predatory and migratory criminal is *purposeless* and *objectless*, that he wanders through the country without any settled aim or end, now turning this way, now that, according to the mere impulse of the moment. Nor is it possible that he should be other than a criminal, the slave of his brute passions and propensities, loving liberty and hating control, and pursuing a roving rather than a settled life, until some honourable motive can be excited in his bosom.

If therefore, we conclude, society seeks, by any system of penal discipline, to change criminals into honest men, it can do so *only* and *securely* by working in conformity, rather than in opposition, to those laws which the Almighty has impressed upon all men's being; and consequently it must abandon all systems of silence and isolation as utterly incompatible with the very foundation of social economy. It must

SEPARATE CELL IN PENTONVILLE PRISON.

WITH HAMMOCK SLUNG FOR SLEEPING, AND LOOM FOR DAY-WORK.

also give up every notion of making labour a punishment, and seek to render it a pleasure to one who is merely a criminal because he has an inordinate aversion to work. The "mark" system attains the latter object, by making labour the means of liberation to the prisoner; but this motive lasts only so long as the term of imprisonment, for there is no reason to believe that when the liberty is attained the prisoner will continue labouring *beyond* that period. What is wanted is to excite in the mind of the prisoner some object to work for, which will endure through life. No man labours for nothing, nor can we expect criminals to do so. Industry is pursued by all, either for the love of what it brings—money, honour, or power—or else for the love of the work itself; and if we desire to make criminal offenders exert themselves like the rest of the world, we must convince them that they can obtain as good a living, and a far more honourable and pleasant one, by honest than dishonest pursuits.

Still, some good people will doubtlessly urge against the above strictures on penal discipline, that no mention is made of that religious element from which all true changes of nature must spring. The Rev. Mr. Kingsmill has put this part of the subject so simply and forcibly before the mind, that it would be unfair to such as profess the same opinions not to cite the remarks here.

"No human punishment," says the Chaplain of Pentonville Prison, "has ever reformed a man from habits of theft to a life of honesty—of vice to virtue; nor can any mode of treating prisoners, as yet thought of, however specious, accomplish anything of the kind. Good principle and good motives are the sad wants of criminals. God alone can give these by his Spirit; and the appointed means for this, primarily, is the teaching of his word. 'Wherewithal shall a young man cleanse his way, even by taking heed thereto according to thy word.'" Now in answer to this, we say that it is admitted by every one that these same conversions are *miracles* wrought by the grace of God; and we do not hesitate to declare our opinion that it is not wise, nor is it even religious (betraying as it does an utter infidelity in those natural laws which are as much institutions of the Almighty as even the scriptural commandments themselves), to frame schemes for the reformation of criminals which depend upon miraculous interferences for their success. Almost as rational, indeed, would it be to return to the superstition of the dark ages; and, because divine goodness has *occasionally* healed the sick in a marvellous and supernatural manner, therefore to go forth with the priest, in case of any bodily affliction, and pray at some holy shrine, rather than seek the aid of the physician who, by continual study of God's sanitary laws, is enabled to restore to us the health we have lost through some blind breach of His Will in that respect. To put faith in the supernatural, and to trust to that for our guide in *natural* things, is simply what is termed "*superstition;*" and surely the enlightened philosophy of the present day should teach us that, in acting conformably with natural laws, we are following out God's decrees far more reverently than by reasoning upon supernatural phenomena; since what is beyond nature is beyond reason also, and has no more right to enter into the social matter of prison discipline, than the feeding of people with manna in the wilderness should form (instead of the ordinary laws of ploughing, manuring, and sowing) a part of agricultural economy.

Moreover, we deny that the majority of individuals who abstain from thieving are led to prefer honest to dishonest practices from purely *religious* motives. Can it be said that the merchant in the city honours his bills for the love of God? Is it not rather to uphold his worldly credit? Do *you*, gentle reader, when you pay your accounts, hand the money over to your tradesman because the Almighty has cleansed your heart from original sin? and would even the jail chaplain himself continue to labour in his vocation, if there were no salary in connection with the office?

If, then, nine hundred and ninety-nine in every thousand of ordinary men abstain from picking pockets, not because the Holy Ghost has entered their bosoms, but from prudential, or, if you will, honourable motives —if it be true that the great mass of people are induced to work for their living mainly, if not solely, to get money rather than serve God—then it is worse than foolish to strive to give any such canting motives to criminals, and certainly *not* true, when it is asserted that people cannot be made honest by any other means than by special interpositions of Providence. If the man who lives by "twisting," as it is called—that is to say, by passing pewter half-crowns in lieu of silver ones—can make his five pounds a week, and be quit of bodily labour, when he could not earn, perhaps, a pound a week by honest industry—if the London "buzman" (swell mobsman) can keep his pony by abstracting "skins" (purses) from gentlemen's pockets, when, perhaps, he could hardly get a pair of decent shoes to his feet as a lawyer's clerk—do you believe that any preaching from the pulpit will be likely to induce such as these to adopt a form of life which has far more labour and far less gains connected with it?

We do not intend to deny that supernatural conversions of men from wickedness to righteousness *occasionally* take place; but, say we, these are the exceptions rather than the rule of life, and the great mass of mankind is led to pursue an upright course, simply because they find that there is associated with it a greater amount of happiness and comfort, both to themselves and those who are near and dear to them, than with the opposite practice. To turn the criminal, therefore, to the righteous path, we must be prepared to show him that an honest life is calculated to yield to himself and his relatives more real pleasure than a dishonest one; and so long as we seek by our present mode of prison discipline to make saints of thieves, just so long shall we continue to produce a thousand canting hypocrites to one *real* convert.

PORTCULLIS GATEWAY OF PENTONVILLE PRISON.
(*Designed by Sir Charles Barry.*)

¶ i.

PENTONVILLE PRISON.

Half-way along that extreme northern thoroughfare which runs almost parallel with the Thames, and which, under the name of the New Road, stretches from the "YORKSHIRE STINGO," by Paddington, to that great metropolitan anomaly the city turnpike, there stands an obeliskine lamp-post in the centre of the roadway. This spot is now known as "King's Cross," in commemoration of a rude stucco statue of George the Fourth, that was once erected here by an artistic bricklayer, and had a small police station in its pedestal, but which has long since been broken up and used to mend the highway that it formerly encumbered.

Here is seen the terminus of the Great Northern Railway, with its brace of huge glass archways, looking like a crystal imitation of the Thames Tunnel; here, too, are found giant public-houses, with "double frontage," or doors before and behind; and would-be grand architectural depôts for quack medicines; and enormous "crystal-palace" slop-shops, with the front walls converted into one broad and high window, where the "Oxonian coats," and "Talma capes," and "Sydenham trousers," and "Fancy vests," are piled up several storeys high, while the doorway is set round with sprucely-dressed "dummies" of young gentlemen that have their gloved fingers spread out like bunches of radishes, and images of grinning countrymen in "wide-awakes," and red plush waistcoats.

This same King's Cross is the Seven Dials of the New Road, whence a series of streets diverge like spokes from the nave of a wheel; and there is almost always the same crowd of "cads" and "do-nothings" loitering about the public-houses in this quarter, and waiting either for a job or a share of a gratuitous "quartern and three outs."

Proceeding hence by the roadway that radiates in a north-easterly direction, we cross the vault-like bridge that spans the Regent's Canal, whose banks here bristle with a crowd of tall factory chimneys; and then, after passing a series of newly-built "genteel" suburban "terraces," the houses of which have each a little strip of garden, or rather grass-plot, in front of them, we see the viaduct of the railway stretching across the road, high above the pavement, and the tall signal posts, with their telegraphic arms, piercing the air. Immediately beyond this we behold a large new building walled all round, with a long series of mad-house-like windows, showing above the tall bricken boundary. In front of this, upon the raised bank beside the roadway, stands a remarkable portcullis-like gateway, jutting, like a huge square porch or palatial archway, from the main entrance of the building, and with a little square clock-tower just peeping up behind it.

This is Pentonville Prison, vulgarly known as "the Model," and situate in the Caledonian Road, that stretches from Bagnigge Wells to Holloway.

¶ i—a.

The History and Architectural Details of the Prison.

Before entering the prison, let us gather all we can concerning the history and character of the building.

It is a somewhat curious coincidence, that the system of separate confinement which the Model Prison at Pentonville was built to carry out, was originally commenced at the House of Correction, at Gloucester, under the auspices of (among others) Sir George Onesiphorus Paul, the relative of one who is at present suffering imprisonment within its walls.

This system of penal discipline was originally advocated by Sir William Blackstone and the great prison reformer, Howard; and though it was made the subject of an Act of Parliament in 1778, it was not put in practice till some few years afterwards, and even then the experiment at Gloucester "was not prosecuted," says the Government Reports, "so as to lead to any definite result."

The subject of separate confinement, however, was afterwards warmly taken up at Philadelphia; "and the late Mr. Crawford," we are told, "was sent to America, in 1834, to examine into and report his opinion upon the mode of penal discipline as there established."

On the presentation to Parliament of the very able papers drawn up by Mr. Crawford and Mr. Whitworth Russell, the Inspectors of the Prisons for the Home District, the subject came to be much discussed; and, in 1837, Lord John Russell, then Secretary of State for the Home Department, issued a circular to the magistracy, recommending the separate system of penal discipline to their consideration.

Shortly after this it was determined to erect Pentonville Prison, as a preliminary step, for the purpose of practically testing this "separate" method of penal treatment, and the name originally applied to it was "the Model Prison, on the separate system," it being proposed to apply the plan, if successful, to the several jails throughout the kingdom.

The building was commenced on the 10th of April, 1840, and completed in 1842, at a cost of about £85,000, after plans furnished by Lieut.-Col. Jebb, R.E. It was first occupied in December of the latter year, and was appropriated, by direction of Sir James Graham, the Home Secretary at that period, to the reception of a *selected* body of convicts, who were there to undergo a term of probationary discipline previous to their transportation to the colonies. Indeed, the letter which Sir James Graham addressed to the Commissioners who had been appointed to superintend the penal experiment, is so admirably illustrative of the objects aimed at in the institution of the prison at Pentonville, that we cannot do better than repeat it here.

"Considering the excessive supply of labour in this country," says Sir James, "its consequent depreciation, and the fastidious rejection of all those whose character is tainted, I wish to admit no prisoner into Pentonville who is not sentenced to transportation, and who is not doomed to be transported; for the convict on whom such discipline might produce the most salutary effect would, when liberated and thrown back on society in this country, be still branded as a criminal, and have but an indifferent chance of a livelihood from the profitable exercise of honest industry. . . . . . I propose, therefore, that no prisoner shall be admitted into Pentonville without the knowledge that it is the portal to the penal colony, and without the certainty that he bids adieu to his connections in England, and that he must henceforth look forward to a life of labour in another hemisphere.

"But from the day of his entrance into prison, while I extinguish the hope of return to his family and friends, I would open to him, fully and distinctly, the fate which awaits him, and the degree of influence which his own conduct will infallibly have over his future fortunes.

"He should be made to feel that from that day he enters on a new career. He should be told that his imprisonment is a period of probation; that it will not be prolonged above eighteen months; that an opportunity of learning those arts which will enable him to earn his bread will be afforded under the best instructors; that moral and religious knowledge will be imparted to him as a guide to his future life; that at the end of eighteen months, when a just estimate can be formed of the effect produced by the discipline on his character, he will be sent to Van Diemen's Land; there, if he behave well, at once to receive a ticket-of-leave, which is equivalent to freedom, with a certainty of abundant maintenance—the fruit of industry.

"If, however, he behave indifferently, he will, on being transported to Van Diemen's Land, receive a probationary pass, which will secure to him only a limited portion of his earnings, and impose certain galling restraints on his personal liberty.

"If, on the other hand, he behave ill, and the discipline of the prison be ineffectual, he will be transported to Tasman's Peninsula, there to work in a probationary gang, without wages, and deprived of liberty—an abject convict."

Now, for the due carrying out of these objects, a Board of Commissioners was appointed, among whom were two medical gentlemen of the highest reputation in their profession, and whose duty it was to watch narrowly the effect of the system upon the health of the prisoners.

"Eighteen months of the discipline," said Sir James Graham, in his letter to these gentlemen, "appear to me to be ample for its full application. In that time the real character will be developed, instruction will be imparted, new habits will be formed, a better frame of mind will have been moulded, or else the heart will have been hardened, and the case be desperate. The period of imprisonment at Pentonville, therefore," he adds, "will be strictly limited to eighteen months."

Thus we perceive that the Model Prison was intended to be a place of instruction and probation, rather than one of oppressive discipline, and was originally limited to adults only, between the ages of eighteen and thirty-five.

From the year 1843 to 1848, with a slight exception on the opening of the establishment, the prisoners admitted into Pentonville were most carefully selected from the whole body of convicts. A change, however, in the class of prisoners was the cause of some adverse results in the year 1848, and in their Report for that year the Commissioners say—"We are sorry that, as to the health and mental condition of the prisoners, we have to make a much less satisfactory report than in any of the former years since the prison was established. . . . . . It may be difficult," they add, " to offer a certain explanation of the great number of cases of death and of insanity that have occurred within the last year. We have, however, reason to believe that in the earlier years of this institution, the convicts sent here were selected from a large number, and the selection was made with a more exclusive regard to their physical capacity for undergoing this species of punishment."

Experience, then, appearing to indicate the necessity of some modification of the discipline at Pentonville, which, without any sacrifice of its efficiency, would render it more safe and more generally available to all classes of convicts, " Sir George Grey," we are told, " concurred in the opinion of Sir Benjamin Brodie and Dr. Ferguson, that the utmost watchfulness and discretion on the part of the governor, chaplain, and medical attendants would be requisite, in order to administer, with safety, the system established there."

It being no longer necessary to continue the experiment upon prison discipline, which had been in full operation from 1843 to 1849, it was brought to a close, and the accommodation in Pentonville prison was thus rendered available for the general purposes of the convict service.

Accordingly, the period of confinement in Pentonville Prison was first reduced from eighteen to twelve months, and subsequently to nine months. Nevertheless, at the commencement of 1852, says an official document, " there occurred an *unusually large* number of cases of mental affection among the prisoners, and it was therefore deemed necessary to increase the amount of exercise in the open air, and to introduce the plan of brisk walking, as pursued at Wakefield." The change, we are told, produced a most marked and beneficial effect upon the general health of the inmates. Indeed, so much so, that " in the course of the year following, there was," say the reports, "not one removal to Bedlam."*

* The number of removals from Pentonville to Bedlam, on the ground of insanity, as compared with the preceding years, was, in the year 1851, found to be—

27 in 10,000 from 1842-49
32 ,, ,, ,, 1850
16 ,, ,, ,, 1851
16 ,, ,, ,, 1852
0 ,, ,, ,, 1853
10 ,, ,, ,, 1854
20 ,, ,, ,, 1854

The above ratio, however, expresses only the proportion per 10,000 prisoners removed to Bedlam as insane, but the following table, which has been kindly furnished us by Mr. Bradley, the eminent medical officer of Pentonville prison, gives the proportion of cases of mental disease occurring annually, after first 10 years :—

In 10 years, from 1843 to 1852 . . . . 120 per 10,000 prisoners.
,, ,, 1853 . . . . 60 ,, ,,
,, ,; 1854 . . . . 38 ,, ,,
,, ,, 1855 . . . . 59 ,, ,,

Hence it would appear that the improved treatment of shortened term of separation, rapid exercise, and superior ventilation, has decreased the rate of insane cases to less than one-half what it was in the first 10 years. Still, much has to be done to bring the proportion down to the *normal standard of all other prisons*, which is only 5·8 per 10,000 prisoners. *Vide* p. 103 of GREAT WORLD OF LONDON.

It is but just to state here that the Reports of the Commissioners, one and all, evince a marked consideration and anxiety for the health of the convicts placed under their care ; and we are happy to have it in our power to add, that our own personal experience teaches us that none could possibly show a greater interest, sympathy, and kindness, for all "prisoners and captives," than the Surveyor-General of Prisons. It is a high satisfaction to find, when one comes to deal with prisons and prisoners, that almost every gentleman placed in authority over the convicts appears to be actuated by the most humane and kindly motives towards them. Nor do we, in saying thus much, judge merely from manner and external appearances. Our peculiar investigations throw us into communication with many a liberated convict, who has served his probationary term at the Model, and we can conscientiously aver, that we have never heard any speak but in the very highest terms, both of the Governor of Pentonville, the Chaplain, and the Surveyor-General himself.

The ventilation was also improved by admitting the outer air direct to the cells, and the discipline was at once relaxed when any injury to health was apprehended. Farther, whenever there was reason to believe that a prisoner was likely to be injuriously affected by the discipline, he was, in conformity with the instructions of the directors, removed from strict separate confinement, and put to work in association with other prisoners.*

Such, then, is the history of the institution, and the reasons for the changes connected with the discipline, of Pentonville Prison.

As regards the details of the building itself, the following are the technical particulars :—
The prison occupies an area of 6¾ acres. It has "a curtain wall with massive posterns in front," where, as we have said, stands a large entrance gateway, the latter designed by Barry, whose arches are filled with portcullis work; whilst from the main building rises an "Italian" clock-tower. From the central corridor within radiate four wings, constructed after the fashion of spokes to a half-wheel, and one long entrance hall, leading to the central point. The interior of each of the four wings or "corridors" is fitted with 130 cells, arranged in three "galleries" or storeys, one above the other, and each floor contains some forty-odd apartments for separate confinement.

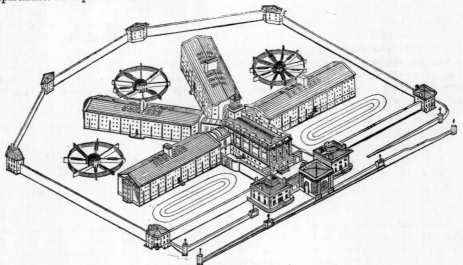

BIRD'S-EYE VIEW OF PENTONVILLE PRISON.
(From a Drawing in the Report of the Surveyor-General of Prisons.)

Every cell is 13½ feet long by 7½ feet broad, and 9 feet high, and contains an earthenware water-closet, and copper wash-basin, supplied with water; a three-legged stool, table, and shaded gas-burner—besides a hammock for slinging at night, furnished with mattress and

---

* The total number withdrawn from separation in the year 1854 was 66, and 23 of these were put to work in association on mental grounds, consisting of cases in which men of low intellect began under separate confinement to exhibit mental excitement, depression, or irritability, whilst 12 more were removed to public works before the expiration of their term of separate confinement, because they were, in the words of the medical officer, "likely to be injuriously affected by the discipline of the prison." By a summary of a list of the cases requiring medical treatment—as given in the Medical Officer's Report for 1855—we find, that of the diseases, 35·9 per cent. consist of constipation, and 16·5 per cent. of dyspepsia—the other affections being "catarrhs," of which the proportion is 20·7 per cent., and diarrhœa 10·0 per cent., whilst the remaining 16·9 per cent. was made up of a variety of trivial and anomalous cases.

blankets. In the door of every cell is an eyelet-hole, through which the officer on duty may observe what is going on within from without. Each of the cells is said to have cost, on an average, upwards of £150.

The building is heated by hot water on the basement, and the ventilation is maintained by an immense shaft in the roof of each wing. The prison has also a chapel on the separate system, fitted with some four hundred distinct stalls or sittings, for the prisoners, and so arranged that the officers on duty, during divine service, may have each man under their *surveillance*. There are also exercising yards for single prisoners, between each of the radiating wings, and two larger yards—one on either side of the entrance-hall—for exercising large bodies of the prisoners collectively.

Moreover, there are artesian wells for supplying the prison with water, and a gas-factory for lighting the building. Indeed, the prison is constructed and fitted according to all the refinements of modern science, and complete in all its appliances.*

¶ i—β.

The Interior of Pentonville Prison.

Artists and Poets clamour loudly about "ideals," but these same artistic and poetic idealities are, in most cases, utterly unlike the realities of life, being usually images begotten by narrow sentiments rather than the abstract results of large observation; for idealization

---

* On March the 13th, 1856, there were 368 prisoners confined here; and these were thus distributed over the building :—

Corridor A $\left\{\begin{array}{l}\text{No. 1 Ward 24 prisoners}\\ \text{,, 2 ,, 27 ,,}\\ \text{,, 3 ,, 42a ,,}\end{array}\right\}$ 93   Corridor C $\left\{\begin{array}{l}\text{No. 1 Ward 26 prisoners}\\ \text{,, 2 ,, 21 ,,}\\ \text{,, 3 ,, 38 ,,}\end{array}\right\}$ 85

Corridor B $\left\{\begin{array}{l}\text{No. 1 Ward 26a prisoners}\\ \text{,, 2 ,, 22 ,,}\\ \text{,, 3 ,, 32 ,,}\end{array}\right\}$ 80   Corridor D $\left\{\begin{array}{l}\text{No. 1 Ward 20b prisoners}\\ \text{,, 2 ,, 40a ,,}\\ \text{,, 3 ,, 21aa ,,}\\ \text{,, 4 ,, 29 ,,}\end{array}\right\}$ 110

368

The letter *a* affixed to some of the numbers above given, signifies that one man, and *aa*, two men, out of that ward were confined in the refractory cells; and *b* that there was one from that part of the building sick in the infirmary-ward. D 4 is the associated ward, and at the basement of the southern part of the building.

The following table gives a statement of the number of prisoners received and sent away in the course of a year :—

NUMBER AND DISPOSAL OF PRISONERS AT PENTONVILLE PRISON DURING THE YEAR 1854.

Remaining 31st December, 1853 . . 489	Pardoned free 1
Admitted during the year 1854 . . 436	,, conditional . . . 3
— 925	,, on medical grounds . . 1
These 925 prisoners were disposed of as follows :—	,, on licence . . . 37
	Died 8
Transferred to Portland Prison . . 193	Suicide 1
,, Portsmouth . . . 120	— 387
,, Dartmoor . . . 20	
,, "Stirling Castle" Hulk . 2	Remaining 31st December, 1854 . . 538
,, Bethlehem Hospital (insane) 1	— 925

Of the 436 prisoners admitted during 1854, the following is a statement of the ages :—

3 were under the age of 17 years.

243 were between ,, 17 and 25 years.
79 ,, ,, 25 ,, 30 ,,
51 ,, ,, 30 ,, 35 ,,
28 ,, ,, 35 ,, 40 ,,
11 ,, ,, 40 ,, 45 ,,

13 were between the age of 45 and 50 years.
6 ,, ,, 50 ,, 55 ,,
2 ,, ,, 55 ,, 60 ,,

436

Proportion of prisoners between 17 and 25 years, 55·7

is—or at least should be—in matters of art what generalization is in science, since a pictorial "type" is but the æsthetic equivalent of a natural "order;" and as the "genus" in philosophy should express merely the point of agreement among a number of diverse phenomena, even so that graphic essence which is termed "character" should represent the peculiar form common to a variety of visible things.

We remember once seeing an engraving that was intended for an *ideal* portrait of the common hangman, in which the hair was of the approved convict cut, with a small villainous valance left dangling in front—the forehead as low as an ape's—the brow repulsively beetled and overhanging as eaves, whilst the sunken eyes were like miniature embrasures pregnant with their black artillery. And yet, when we made the acquaintance of Calcraft, we found him bearing the impress of no such monster, but rather so "respectable" in his appearance, that on first beholding a gentleman in a broad brimmed hat and bushy iron gray hair, seated at the little table in the lobby of Newgate, with his hands, too, resting on the knob of his Malacca cane, we mistook him for some dissenting minister, who had come to offer consolation to one of the wretched inmates. Nor could we help mentally contrasting the loathsome artistic ideality with the almost humane-looking reality before us.

The same violence, too, is done to our preconceived notions by the first sight of the jailer of the present day. The ideal leads us to picture such a functionary in our minds as a kind of human Cerberus—a creature that looks as surly and sullen as an officer of the Inquisition, and with a bunch of huge keys fastened to his waist, whose jangle, as he moves, reminds one of the clink of fetters. The reality, however, proves on acquaintance to be generally a gentleman with a half military air, who, so far from being characterized by any of the vulgar notions of the stern and cruel-minded prison-keeper, is usually marked by an almost tender consideration for those placed under his charge, and who is certainly prompted by the same desire that distinguishes all better-class people now-a-days, to ameliorate the condition of their unfortunate fellows.

At Pentonville, the same mental conflict between vulgar preconceptions and strange matter of fact ensues; for the prison there is utterly unlike all our imaginary pictures of prisons—the governor a kind-hearted gentleman, rather than approaching to the fanciful type of the unfeeling jailer—and the turnkeys a kind of mixture between policemen and military officers in undress, instead of the ferocious-looking prison-officials ordinarily represented on the stage.

No sooner is the prison door opened in answer to our summons at the bell, than we might believe we were inside some little park lodge, so tidy and cozy and unjail-like is the place; and here is the same capacious hooded chair, like the head of a gigantic cradle, that is usually found in the hall of large mansions.

The officer, as he holds back the portal, and listens to our inquiry as to whether the Governor be visible, raises his hand to his glazed military cap, and salutes us soldier-fashion, as he replies briskly, "Yessir."

Having produced our Government order, to allow us to inspect the prison, we are ushered across a small paved court-yard, and then up a broad flight of stone steps to the large glass door that admits us to the passage leading to the prison itself. The officer who accompanies us is habited in a single-breasted, policeman-like, frock coat, with a bright brass crown bulging from its stiff, stand-up collar, and round his waist he wears a broad leathern strap, with a shiny cartouche-box behind, in which he carries his keys. These keys are now withdrawn, and the semi-glass door—that is so utterly unlike the gloomy and ponderous prison portal of olden times—is thrown back for us to pass through.

We are then at the end of a long and broad passage, which is more like the lengthy hall to some Government office, than the entrance to an old-fashioned jail, and at the opposite extremity we can just see, through the windows of the other door there, figures flitting backwards and forwards in the bright light of what we afterwards learn is the "centre corridor" of the building.

The first thing that strikes the mind on entering the prison passage, is the wondrous and perfectly Dutch-like cleanliness pervading the place. The floor, which is of asphalte, has been polished, by continual sweeping, so bright that we can hardly believe it has not been black-leaded, and so utterly free from dust are all the mouldings of the trim stucco walls, that we would defy the sharpest housewife to get as much off upon her fingers as she could brush even from a butterfly's wing.

In no private house is it possible to see the like of this dainty cleanliness, and as we walk along the passage we cannot help wondering why it is that we should find the perfection of the domestic virtue in such an abiding-place.

We are shown into a small waiting-room on one side of the passage, while the officer goes to apprise the governor of our presence; and here we have to enter our name in a book, and specify the date, as well as by whose permission we have come. Here, too, we find the same scrupulous tidiness, and utter freedom from dirt—the stove being as lustrous, from its frequent coats of "black-lead," as if it had been newly carved out of solid plumbago.

A few minutes afterwards, we are handed over to a warder, who receives instructions to accompany us round the prison; and then, being conducted through the glass door at the other end of the passage, we stand, for the first time, in the "centre corridor" of the "Model Prison."

CORRIDOR AT PENTONVILLE PRISON.
(From a Drawing in the Report of the Surveyor-General of Prisons.)

To conceive the peculiar character of this building, the reader must imagine four long "wings," or "corridors," as they are officially styled, radiating from a centre, like the spokes in a half-wheel; or, what is better, a series of light and lofty tunnels, all diverging from one point, after the manner of the prongs in an open fan. Indeed, when we first entered the inner part of the prison, the lengthy and high corridors, with their sky-light roofs, seemed to us like a bunch of Burlington Arcades, that had been fitted up in the style of the opera-box lobbies, with an infinity of little doors—these same doors being ranged, not only one *after* another, but one *above* another, three storeys high, till the walls of the arcades were pierced as thick with them as the tall and lengthy sides of a man-of-war with its hundred port-holes.

Then there are narrow iron galleries stretching along in front of each of the upper floors, after the manner of lengthy balconies, and reaching from one end of the arcades to the other, whilst these are so light in their construction, that in the extreme length of the several wings they look almost like ledges jutting from the walls.

Half-way down each corridor, too, there is seen, high in the air, a light bridge, similar to the one joining the paddle-boxes on board a steamer, connecting the galleries on either side of every floor.

Nevertheless, it is not the long, arcade-like corridors, nor the opera-lobby-like series of doors, nor the lengthy balconies stretching along each gallery, nor the paddle-box-like bridges connecting the opposite sides of the arcade, that constitute the peculiar character of Pentonville prison. Its distinctive feature, on the contrary—the one that renders it utterly dissimilar from all other jails—is the extremely bright, and cheerful, and airy quality of the building; so that, with its long, light corridors, it strikes the mind, on first entering it, as a bit of the Crystal Palace, stripped of all its contents. There is none of the gloom, nor dungeon-like character of a jail appertaining to it; nor are there bolts and heavy locks to grate upon the ear at every turn; whilst even the windows are destitute of the proverbial prison-bars— the frames of these being made of iron, and the panes so small that they serve at once as safeguards and sashes.

Moreover, so admirably is the ventilation of the building contrived and kept up, that there is not the least sense of closeness pervading it, for we feel, immediately we set foot in the place, how fresh and pure is the atmosphere there; and that, at least, in *that* prison, no wretched captive can sigh to breathe the "free air of Heaven," since in the open country itself it could not be less stagnant than in the "model" jail—even though there be, as at the time of our visit, upwards of 400 men confined day and night—sleeping, breathing, and performing all the functions of nature in their 400 separate cells throughout the place.

The cells distributed throughout this magnificent building are about the size of the interior of a large and roomy omnibus, but some feet higher, and they seem to those who are not doomed to dwell in them—apart from all the world without—really comfortable apartments. In such, however, as contain a loom (and a large number of the cells on the ground-floor are fitted with those instruments), there is not a superabundance of spare room. Nevertheless, there is sufficient capacity, as well as light, in each, to make the place seem to a free man a light, airy, and cheerful abode. Against the wall, on one side, is set the bright, copper hand-basin —not unlike a big funnel—with a tap of water immediately above it; at the extreme end of the cell is the small closet, well supplied with water-pipes; and in another part you see the shaded gas-jet, whilst in one of the corners by the door are some two or three triangular shelves, where the prisoner's spoon, platter, mug, and soap-box, &c., are stowed. On the upper of these shelves, the rolled-up hammock, with its bedding, stands on end, like a huge muff, and let into the wall on either side, some three feet from the ground, are two large bright eyelet holes, to which the hammock is slung at night, as shown in the engraving. Then there is a little table and stool, and occasionally on the former may be found some brown paper-covered book or periodical, with which the prisoner has been supplied from the prison library. In one cell which we entered, while the men were at exercise in the yard, we found a copy of " Old Humphrey's Thoughts," and in another, a recent number of " Chambers's Edinburgh Journal" left open on the table. Moreover, hanging against the wall is a pasteboard bill, headed, " Notice to Convicts," and the " Rules and Regulations" of the prison, as well as the little card inscribed with the prisoner's " registered number" (for in Pentonville prison all names cease), and citing not only his previous occupation, but term of sentence, date of conviction, &c. Further, there is, in the corner near the cupboard, a button, which, on being turned, causes a small gong to be struck in the corridor without, and at the same moment makes a metal plate or "index" outside the door start out at right angles to the wall, so that the warder, when summoned by the bell, may know which prisoner has rung.

On this index is painted the number of the cell, and as you walk along the corridors you observe, not only a large black letter painted at the entrance of each arcade, but a series of these same indices, each inscribed with a different number, and (except where the gong has been recently sounded) flat against the wall beside the door. Now these letters on the corridors, as well as the indices beside the doors, are used not only to express the position of the cell, but, strange to say, the name of the prisoner confined within it; for here, as we said, men have no longer Christian and surnames to distinguish them one from the other, but are called merely after the position of cell they occupy. Hence, no matter what the appella-. tion of a man may have been—or even whether he bore a noble title before entering the prison—immediately he comes as a convict within its precincts, he is from that time known as D 3, 4, or B 2, 10, as the case may be, and wears at his breast a charity-boy-like brass badge so inscribed, to mark him from the rest. Thus he is no longer James This, or Mr. That, or even Sir John So-and-so, but simply the prisoner confined in corridor D, gallery 3, and cell 4, or else the one in corridor B, gallery 2, and cell 10; so that instead of addressing prisoners here as Brown, Jones, and Robinson, the warder in whose gallery and corridor those convicts may happen to be calls them, for brevity sake, simply and individually by the number of the cells they occupy in his part of the building. Accordingly the officer on duty may occasionally be heard to cry to some one of the prisoners under his charge, "Now step out there 4, will you?" or, "Turn out here, Number 6."*

* The following is a list of the several officers of Pentonville Prison in the year 1856 :—

Name.	Rank.	Name.	Rank.
Robert Hosking	Governor	John Donegan	Assistant Warder
Rev. Joseph Kingsmill	Chaplain	James Hampton	,,
Ambrose Sherwin	Assistant do.		
Charles L. Bradley	Medical Officer	Joseph Matthews	Warder Instructor
		John Baptie	,,
William H. Foster	Steward & Manufacturer	Thomas Hirst	,,
Alfred P. Nantes	Governor's Clerk	John Armstrong	,,
Angus Macpherson	Accountant Clerk	John Fitzgerald	,,
Edward Tottenham	Steward's Clerk	Martin Burke	,,
Robert Yellsly	Assistant do.	Amos Driver	,,
Thomas Carr	Manufacturer's Clerk	William Callway	Assist. Warder Instructor
James Maya	Assistant do.	John White	,,
		Edward Bevan	,,
John Wilson	Schoolmaster	Thomas Charlesworth	,,
Charles Gregg	Assistant do.	Samuel Whitley	,,
Edward J. Hoare	Do. and Organist		
Terence Nulty	Chief Warder	Arthur Keenan	Infirmary Warder
John Jenkins	Principal Warder	William Matthis	Gate Porter
David Adamson	Ditto	George Larkin	Inner Gate Porter
		Thomas R. Yeates	Messenger
John Smart	Warder		
William Wood	,,	Thomas Rogers	Foreman of Works
Adam Corrie	,,	Stephen Oatley	Plumber
William Keating	,,	Robert Lyon	Gasmaker
Senthil Lindsay	,,	Charles Poole	Assistant ditto
David Darling	,,	John Pride	Engine-man
Michael Laffan	,,	Edward Gannon	Stoker
Robert Green	,,		
John Snellgrove	,,	Matthew Yates	Steward's Porter
Edward Edwards	,,	William Butler	Manufacturers' Porter
		Griffin Crannis	Carter
James Snowball	Assistant Warder		
Richard Wilcocks	,,	John Beckley	Cook
Peter Cameron	,,	John Cladingbowl	Baker
John Whitehurst	,,		

¶ i — γ.

A Work-Day at Pentonville.

To understand the "routine" of Pentonville Prison, it is necessary to spend one entire long day in the establishment, from the very opening to the closing of the prison; and if there be any convicts leaving for the public works, as on the day we chose for our visit, the stranger must be prepared to stay at least eighteen hours within the walls. Nor, to our mind, can time be more interestingly passed.

The stars were still shining coldly in the silver gray sky on the morning when we left our home to witness the departure of some thirty-odd prisoners from Pentonville for Portsmouth. We were anxious to discover with what feelings the poor wretches, who had spent their nine months at the Model, excluded from all intercourse but that of prison officers, would look forward to their liberation from separate confinement; and though we had been informed over-night that the "batch" was to leave as early as a quarter past 5 a.m., we did not regret having to turn out into the streets, with the cold March morning winds blowing so sharp in the face as to fill the eyes with tears.

As we slammed our door after us, the deserted street seemed to tremble as it echoed again with the noise. On the opposite side of the way, the policeman, in his long great coat, was busy throwing the light of his bull's-eye upon the doors and parlour windows, and down into the areas, as he passed on his rounds, making the dark walls flicker with the glare as if a Jack-a-Dandy had been cast upon them, and, startled by the sound, he turned suddenly round to direct his lantern towards us as if he really took us for one of the burglarious characters we were about to visit.

The cabmen at the nearest stand were asleep inside their rickety old broughams, and as we turned into Tottenham Court Road we encountered the early street coffee-stall keeper with his large coffee-cans dangling from either end of a yoke across his shoulders, and the red fire shining through the holes of the fire-pan beneath like spots of crimson foil.

Then, as we hurried on, we passed here and there a butcher's light "chay-cart" with the name painted on the side, hurrying off to the early meat-markets, and the men huddled in the bottom of the vehicle, behind the driver with their coat-collars turned up, and dozing as they went. Next came some tall and stalwart brewer's drayman (they are always the first in the streets), in his dirty drab flushing jacket, and leathern leggings, hastening towards the brewery; and, at some long distance after him, we met an old ragged crone, tottering on her way to the Farringdon water-cress market with her "shallow" under her arm, and her old rusty frayed shawl drawn tight round her; whilst here and there we should see a stray bone-grubber, or "pure" finder, in his shiny grimy tatters, "routing" among the precious muck-heaps for rich rags and valuable refuse.

Strange and almost fearful was the silence of the streets, at that hour! So still, indeed, were they that we could hear the heavy single knock, followed by the shrill cry of the chimney-sweep, echoing through the desolate thoroughfares, as he waited at some door hard by and shrieked, "Swe—e—eep!" to rouse the sleeping cook-maid. Then every foot-fall seemed to tell upon the pavement like the tramp of the night-police, and we could hear the early workmen trudging away, long before we saw them coming towards us, some with their basin of food for the day done up in a handkerchief, and dangling from their hand—and others like the smoky and unwashed smiths with an old nut-basket full of tools slung over their shoulder upon the head of a hammer—the bricklayer with his large wooden level and coarse nailbag full of trowels hanging at his back—and the carpenter on his way to some new suburban building in his flannel jacket and rolled-up apron, and with the end of his saw and jack-plane peeping from his tool-basket behind; while here and there, as we got into the neighbourhood of King's Cross, we should pass some railway guard or porter on his way to the terminus for the early trains.

While jogging along in the darkness—for still there was not a gleam of daybreak visible—we could not help thinking, what would the wretched creatures we were about to visit not give to be allowed one half-hour's walk through those cold and gloomy streets, and how beautiful one such stroll in the London thoroughfares would appear to them—beautiful as quitting the house, after a long sickness, is to us.

Nor could we help, at the same time, speculating as to the perversity of the natures that, despite all the long privations of jail, and the severe trial of separate confinement, would, nevertheless, many of them, as we knew, return to their former practices immediately they were liberated. Granted, said we to ourselves (forgetting, in our reveries, to continue our observations of the passing objects), that some would be honest if society would but cease to persecute them for their former crimes. Still many, we were aware, were utterly incapable of reformation, for figures prove to us that there is a certain per centage among the criminal class who are absolutely incorrigible. Nevertheless, the very fact of there *being* such a per centage, and this same perversity of nature being reducible to a law, seemed to us to rank it like lunacy, among the inscrutable decrees of the All-Wise, and thus to temper our indignation with pity. Then we could not help thinking of the tearful homes that these wretched people had left outside their prison walls, for, hardened as we may fancy them, they and theirs are marked by the same love of kindred as ourselves—such love, indeed, being often the only channel left open to their heart; and, moreover, how sorely, in punishing the guilty, we are compelled to punish the innocent also.*

We were suddenly aroused from our reverie by the scream of the early goods' train, and presently the long line of railway wagons came rattling and rumbling across the viaduct over the street, the clouds of steam from the engine seeming almost an iron gray colour in the darkness.

The next minute we were at the Model Prison, Pentonville; but as the warders were not yet assembled outside the gate, and we saw bright lines of light shining through the cracks over and under the door of one of the neighbouring shops, we made bold to knock and claim a short shelter there.

* As a proof that no "morbid sentimentality" gave rise to the above remarks, we will quote the following letter as one among many that it is our lot to receive :—

"March 24th, 1856.

"SIR,—An anxious mother, who has an unfortunate son now about to be liberated from the convict prison, Portsmouth, is very desirous of obtaining an interview with you on his behalf, and would feel truly grateful for such a favour.—From your most obedient and humble servant,

"A. S."

Here is another illustration of the fact, that one guilty man's misery involves that of many innocent people :—

"March 19th, 1845.

"SIR,—I am a poor, unfortunate, characterless man, who have returned from jail, with a desire to earn an honest living for the future, and I make bold to write to you, begging your kind assistance in my present distress.

"I left the House of Correction on Wednesday last, 12th inst., after an incarceration of six calendar months, to which I was sentenced for obtaining money by means of representing myself as a solicitor, and to which offence I pleaded guilty. My prosecutors, finding that I was induced to commit myself through poverty, would gladly have withdrawn from the case, but could not, being bound over.

"Coming home, I found a wife and five children depending upon me for support—the parish having at once stopped the relief, and the army work (at which they earned a few shillings) having fallen off altogether; therefore I am in a most distressed position, not having clothes out of pledge to go after employment in, or I doubt not but that I could get employment, as I have a friend who would become surety for me in a situation.

"If, therefore, you can render me any assistance, you will indeed confer a favour on, Sir, your very obedient servant,

"J. B."

It happened to be a coffee-shop. We found the little room in a thick fog of smoke from the newly-lighted fire, and the proprietor busy making the morning's supply of the "best Mocha"—possible, at a penny a cup.

We had not long to wait, for presently the shopkeeper apprised us that the warders were beginning to assemble; and truly, on reaching the gateway once more, we found a group of some two dozen officers waiting to be admitted to the prison.

Presently the outer door was opened, when the warders passed into the court-yard and stood upon the broad flight of steps, in a group round the glass door leading to the entrance-hall. Here they reckoned among themselves as to whether they were all assembled, and finding that one or two were wanting, the rest looked up at the clock and said, "Oh, it wants five minutes to the quarter yet."

"They are safe to be here," said one to us, privately; "for there's a heavy fine if a man isn't true to his time." Sure enough, the next moment the two missing warders entered the yard, and the glass door being opened, we all proceeded, in company with one of the principal warders—marked by the gold lace band round his cap—into a small room on the left-hand side of the passage.

"The chief warder sleeps here, sir," said the officer whom the governor had kindly directed to attend us through the day, and to instruct us upon all the details of the prison.

There was no sign of bed in the room, and the only indication we had that the chief officer had passed the night in the building was, that he was in the act of slipping on his coat as we entered the apartment.

A large iron safe, let into the wall of this room, was now unlocked, and a covered tray, or drawer, that was not unlike an immense wooden portable desk, was withdrawn and carried into the lobby, while the contents jangled so loudly with the motion, that it was not difficult to surmise that in it the officers' keys were kept. Here it was placed upon a chair, and, when opened, revealed some twenty-eight bunches of large keys hanging upon as many different hooks.

These were distributed by one of the principal warders to the several officers throughout the building, and this done, we were once more conducted into the interior of the prison, where we found the gas still burning in the corridors and the lights shining on the polished asphalte floors, in long luminous lines, like the lamps in the streets reflected upon the pavement on a wet night.

The blue light of early dawn was now just beginning to show through the skylights of the long arcades, but hardly had we noticed the cold azure look of the coming day, contrasting, as it did, with the warm yellow light of the gas within, than the corridors began to hum again with the booming of the clock-tower bell, ringing, as usual, at half-past five, to call the officials.

We walked with the warder down the several corridors, and, as we did so, the officers on duty proceeded to carry the bread and cocoa round to the prisoners who were about to leave that morning for the public works at Portsmouth. And then the halls rang, now with the rattling of the trucks on which the breakfast was being wheeled from cell to cell, and now with the opening and shutting of the little trap in each cell-door, through which the food was given to the prisoner within; the rapid succession of the noises telling you how briskly and dexterously the work was done.

"You see those clothes, and tables, and chairs outside the cell-doors, there?" said the warder, as he led us along the corridors; "they belong to men who have attempted to break out of other prisons, so we leave them nothing but their bed and bare walls for the night. Now there, at that door, you perceive, are merely the clothes, and shoes, and tools of the prisoner within; he's one of the bricklayers who has worked out in the grounds, so we trust such as him with nothing but the flannel drawers they sleep in from nine at night till six in the morning. Oh, yes, sir! we are obliged to be very particular here, for the men have tools given them to work with, and therefore we make them put all such articles outside their cell-doors just before they go to bed; but when a man is a notoriously desperate prison-breaker, we don't even allow him so much as a tin can for his soup, for we know that, if we did so, he would probably convert the wire round the rim into a pick-lock, to open his door. Yes, sir, convicts are mostly very ingenious at such things."

By this time we had reached the end of the ward, where stood a small counting-house-like desk, partitioned off from the other part of the corridor.

"This is the warders' office," our informant continued, "and the clock you see there, in front of it, is the 'tell-tale.' There is one such in each ward. It has, you observe, a number of pegs, one at every quarter of an hour, projecting like cogs from round the edge of the dial-plate, which is here made to revolve instead of the hands. At the side, you perceive, there's a string for pulling down the small metal tongue that stands just over the top peg, and the consequence is, that unless the officer who is on duty in the night comes here on his rounds *precisely* at the moment when that top peg should be pushed down, it will have passed from under the tongue, and stand up as a register of neglect of duty against him. There are a number of these clocks throughout the prison, and the warders have to pull some of the pegs at the quarters, some at the half-hours, and others at the hours. They are all set by the large time-piece in the centre, and so as just to allow the officer to go from one ward to the other."

"If a man's bell rings in the night?" asked we.

"Why," was the ready answer, "the trap of his cell-door is let down, and the officer on duty thrusts in a bull's-eye lantern so as to see what is the matter; the prisoner makes his complaint, and, if sick, the chief warder is called, who orders, if he thinks it necessary, the infirmary warder to come to him. There are four warders on duty every night, from ten till six the next morning, and each of the four has to keep two hours' watch."

** Departure of Convicts.—Scarcely had our attendant finished his account of the night duties, when a large town-crier's bell clattered through the building. This was the quarter-to-six summons to wake the prisoners; and, five minutes afterwards, the bell was rung again, to call the officers a second time.

The chief warder now took up his station in the centre corridor, and saying to the officer near him, "Turn down!" the big brass bell once more rattled in the ears, whereupon a stream of brown-clad convicts came pouring from out their cells, and marched at a rapid pace along the northern corridor (A) towards the centre of the building. These were some of the prisoners who were about to leave for the public works at Portsmouth. The smiles upon their faces said as much.

"Fall in!" cried the chief warder, and in a moment the whole of the men drew themselves up, like soldiers, in a line across the centre corridor, each holding his registry-card close up at his breast; but now the deep cloth peaks to their prison caps were bent up, and no longer served as a mask to the face.

Hardly was this over before another brown gang of prisoners hastened from the southern corridor (D), and drew themselves briskly up in the rear of the others.

Then the chief warder proceeded to call over the registered number and name of each convict, whilst one of the principals stood by to check the card as the name was cried out; and directly this was finished, the gang was made to "face" and march, through the glass doors, into the entrance hall.

Here they were drawn up on one side of the passage; then an officer cried, in a military tone, "Turn up your right-hand cuffs, all of you!" and thereupon the warders proceeded to fasten round each of their wrists one of the bright steel handcuffs that were ranged upon a little table in the lobby. This done, a stout steel chain was reaved through each of the eyelet holes attached to the cuffs, and some ten or a dozen of the prisoners thus strung together. When the first detachment was chained to each other, another half-score went through the same operation, whilst the previous string of prisoners moved down towards the end of the passage, each pulling a different way, like coupled hounds, and the chain grating as they dragged one another along.

We followed the wretched fellows to the door, to watch the expression of their faces when they beheld the three omnibuses waiting in the court-yard to carry them to the Terminus of the South-Western Railway. As the men stood ranged along the passage beside the doorway, many of them craned their necks forward to get a peep at the vehicles without, smiling again as they beheld them.

"Yes, sir, they like it well enough," said our attendant, who was still at our elbow; "it's a great change for them—a great change—after being nine months in one place."

"Are you pleased to go away, my man?" said we, to the one nearest the door.

"Oh, yes!" replied he, in a country accent. He had been convicted of sheep-stealing, and the agricultural class of convicts, the prison authorities all agree, is the best disposed of the men who come under their charge. As the prisoner spake the words, we could see his very eyes twinkle again at the prospect of another peep at the fields.

"What have you got there?" cried an officer, in a commanding tone, to one of the gang, who had a bundle of something tied in a handkerchief.

"They're books, sir; hymn-books and tracts that the chaplain has allowed me to have," replied the prisoner in a meek tone.

"That man yonder," whispered a warder to us, "two off from the one with the books, has passed thirty-eight years of his life in prison, and he's only forty-seven years old."

"Remember, men," said the chief warder, addressing the prisoners before they passed into the court-yard, "the officer who goes with you has power to speak well of you; and the first thing that will be asked of him at Portsmouth will be, 'How have the men behaved on the way down?' So do you all take care and have a good character from him, for it will serve you where you're going."

"Now, warder Corrie!" the chief officer adds to the warder on duty; and instantly the doors are unlocked, and the three strings of prisoners are let out into the court-yard, one after the other—the foremost man of each dragging at the chain to pull the others after him, and those in the rear holding back so as to prevent their wrists being suddenly jerked forwards, while the iron links almost crackle again as they reave to and fro.

The omnibuses waiting in the court-yard were the ordinary public vehicles, such as one sees, every day, streaming through the streets to the Bank; and perched high on the little coach-box sat the usual seedy and would-be "fast"-looking driver, whilst beside the door, instead of the customary placard of "6d. all the way," was pasted on each carriage a large sheet of paper, inscribed either 1, 2, or 3, for the occasion.

The prisoners went scrambling up the steps of the vehicles, dragging at the chain as before, while the officers in attendance cried to those who hung back to keep off the strain— "Come, move on there behind—will you?"

When the omnibuses were filled with their ten or twelve prisoners, an officer entered each, and seated himself near the doorway, whereupon the chief warder proceeded to the steps of the vehicles one after another, and asked—"Now, warder, how many men have you got?" "Ten!" was shouted, in reply, from the interior of one carriage, and "Twelve!" from another. After which one of the principal warders—distinguished by the gold-lace band round his cap—mounted the box of the first, and sat down beside the driver.

"He goes with them, sir, to clear the bridges," whispered our attendant; and scarcely had he spoken the words before there was a cry of "All right!—go on!" and instantly the huge, massive gates that open out upon the stately porch in front of the prison were thrown back, and we could see the light of early morning glittering through the squares of the portcullis without.   Then the stones clattered with the patter of the iron hoofs and rumble of the wheels; and one could observe the heads of the prisoners all in motion within the vehicle —some looking through the doorway back upon the prison, and others peeping through the windows at the comparatively new scene outside the walls.

And, it must be confessed, there was not one tearful eye to be noted among that unfortunate convict troop; on the contrary, every cheek was puckered with smiles at the sense that they were bidding adieu to the place of their long isolation from the world.

We would cheerfully, had it been possible, have travelled with the prisoners to their destination at Portsmouth; for, to the student of human nature, it would have been a high lesson to have seen the sudden delight beam in every face as the omnibus passed by some familiar scene, or, may-be, the dwellings of their friends or kindred, by the way; and, as the railway train darted with them through the country, to have watched the various emotions play in their countenances as they beheld once more the green fields, and river, and the hills and woods, and envied, perhaps, the very sheep and cattle grazing at liberty upon the plains.

"Still," said we to ourselves, as we mused mournfully after the departure of the convict vehicles, "the reality doubtlessly would be wholly unlike our preconceptions of the scene;" for with such men as those we had watched away there is often a mere vacuity of mind—a kind of waking dreaminess—a mental and moral anæsthesia, as it were, that renders them insensible to the more delicate impressions of human nature, so that the beauties of the outer, and indeed inner, world are almost wasted upon them, and it becomes half sentimentalism to imagine that their duller brains would be moved in the same manner as our own.   Nevertheless, we must not, on the other hand, believe this class of people to be utterly callous to every tender tie, or indeed the ruder physical pleasures of external life.   We ourselves have seen a body of such beings melted to tears as the chaplain touched feelingly upon their separation from their families; and they would be little removed from polypes—mere living stomachs—if after nine long months' entombment, as it were, in separate cells, they did not feel, upon going back into the world of light and colour, almost the same strange thrill tingling through their veins as moved Lazarus himself when summoned by the trumpet-tongue of Christ from out his very grave.

Some there are, however, who think and speak of these wretched men as very dogs— creatures fit only, as one of our modern philosophers has preached, to be shot down and swept into the dust-bin.   But surely even he who has seen a dog, after it has been chained night and day close to its kennel, and rendered dangerously furious by the continual chafing of its collar, burst off with a spasmodic energy in every limb directly it was let loose, and go bounding along and springing into the air, as it wheeled round and round, gasping and panting the while, as if it could not sufficiently feel and taste the exquisite delight of its freedom—he who, we say, has watched such a scene, must have possessed a nature as callous even as the wretched convicts themselves, could he have witnessed them pass out of those prison gates into the outward world without feeling the hot tears stinging his eyes, and without uttering in his heart a faint " God speed you."

How is it possible for you, or ourselves, reader, to make out to our imaginations the terrors of separate confinement?   How can we, whose lives are blessed with continual liberty, and upon whose will there is scarcely any restraint—we, who can live among those we love, and move where we list—we, to whom the wide world, with its infinite beauties of sunshine and tint, and form, and air, and odour, and even sound, are a perpetual fountain of health and joy; how, we say, can *we* possibly comprehend what intense misery it is to be cut off from all such enjoyments—to have our lives hemmed in by four white blank walls—to see no faces but those of task-masters—to hear no voice but that of *commanding* officers—to be denied all exercise of will whatever—and to be converted into mere living automata, forced to do the bidding of others?

If you have ever lain on a sick-bed, day after day and week after week, till you knew every speck and tiny crack of the walls that surrounded you—if you have seen the golden lustre of the spring sun shining without, and heard the voices of the birds telling their love of liberty in a very spasm, as it were, of melody, and then felt the unquenchable thirst that comes upon the soul to be out in the open air; and if you remember the grateful joy you have experienced at such times to have friends and relations near you to comfort and relieve your sufferings, not only by their love and care, but by reading to you the thoughts or fancies of the wisest and kindest minds, then you *may* perhaps be able to appreciate the subtle agony that must be endured by men in separate confinement—men, too, who are perhaps the most self-willed of all God's creatures, and consequently likely to feel any restraint tenfold more irksome than we; and men whose untutored minds are incapable of knowing the charms of intellectual culture or occupation; and who, therefore, can only fret and chafe under their terrible imprisonment, even as the tameless hyæna may be seen at the beast-garden for ever fretting and chafing in its cage.

*** *Cleaning the Prison.*—It was now only six o'clock, and as we returned from the court-yard to the corridors, we heard the chief warder cry, "Unlock!" and instantly the officers attached to the different wards proceeded to pass rapidly from cell-door to cell-door, with their keys in their hands, turning the locks as they went, and the noise resounding throughout the long and echoing corridors like the click of so many musket-triggers. Then the doors began to bang, and the metal pail-handles to jangle, till the very prison seemed suddenly roused out of its silent sleep into busy life.

As we passed up and down the wards, we saw the prisoners in their flannel drawers come to the door to take in their clothes, and the tub to wash their cell; and, on glancing in at the doorway, we caught sight of the long, narrow hammock slung across the cell, just above the ground, and the dark frame of the loom showing at the back.

The next moment a stream of some dozen or two prisoners poured from the cells, carrying their coats on their arms, and drew themselves up in two files across the centre corridor. Then we heard the warder cry, "Cleaners, face!—Cooks, face!—Bakers, face!" whereupon the men wheeled round with almost military precision, and retired, some to wash the entrance passages and offices, others to help in the kitchen, and others in the bakehouse.

By this time (ten minutes past six), the prison was all alive, and humming like a hive with the activity of its inmates. Some of the convicts, clad in their suits of mud-brown cloth, were out in the long corridors sweeping the black asphalte pavement till it glistened again as if polished with black-lead. Others, in the narrow galleries above, were on their knees washing the flags of slate that now grew blue-black around them with the water; others, again, in the centre corridor, were hearthstoning the steps, and making them as white as slabs of biscuit-china; and others, too, in their cells, cleaning the floors and furniture there. A warder stood watching the work on each of the little mid-air bridges that connect the opposite storeys of every corridor, whilst other officers were distributed throughout the building, so as to command the best points for observing the movements of the prisoners.

Our attendant led us to an elevated part of the building, so that we might have a bird's-eye view of the scene; and assuredly it was a strange sight to look down upon the long arcade-like corridors, that were now half-fogged with the cloud of dust rising from the sweepers' brooms, and witness the bustle and life of that place, which on our entrance seemed as still as so many cloisters; while the commingling of the many different sounds—the rattling of pails, the banging of doors, the scouring of the stones, the rumbling of trucks, the tramping of feet up the metal stairs, all echoing through the long tunnels—added greatly to the peculiarity of the scene.

"Ah, sir," said our attendant warder, "everything is done with great precision here;

there's just so many minutes allowed for each part of the work. You will notice, sir, that it will take from twelve minutes to a quarter of an hour to wash either side of the building; and directly the clock comes to twenty-five minutes past six, we shall begin to unlock the opposite side of the corridors to that where the men are now at work—when a new set of cleaners will come out, and the present ones retire into their cells. This is done to prevent communication, which would be almost sure to take place if the men worked on opposite sides of the galleries at the same time. For the cleaning," continued our communicative friend, " each gallery contributes five men to each side, or ten in all, and each ward gives one man to the centre corridor, and each corridor four men for sweeping below."

The officer now drew our attention to the fact that the hands of the clock were pointing to the time he had mentioned, and that the men who had been at work along one side of the galleries had all finished, and withdrawn. Then began the same succession of noises— like the clicking, as we have said, of so many musket-triggers—indicating the unlocking of the opposite cells; and we could see, whence we stood, the officers hastening along the corridors, unfastening each door, as they went, with greater rapidity than even lamplighters travel from lamp to lamp along a street; and immediately afterwards we beheld a fresh batch of cleaners come out into each gallery, and the sweepers below cross over and begin working under them, whilst the same noises resounded through the building as before.

A few moments after this the big brass hand-bell clattered once more through the building. This was the half-past six o'clock summons for the prisoners to commence work in their cells, and soon afterwards we saw the " trade instructors " going round the several wards, to see that the men had sufficient materials for their labour; whilst, in a few minutes, the lower wards echoed with the rattling of the looms, and we could hear the prolonged tapping of the shoemakers up above, hammering away at the leather, so that now the building assumed the busy aspect of a large factory, giving forth the same half-bewildering noise of work and machinery.

The next part of the cleansing operations was the gathering the dust from the cells, and this was performed as rapidly and dexterously as the other processes. A convict, carrying a large wicker basket lined with tin (such as is ordinarily used for dinner plates), went before one of the officers, who held a dust-pan in his hand, and as the warder unlocked each cell-door on his round, and thrust his pan within, the prisoner in the cell emptied the dust, which he had ready collected, into the officer's pan, closing the door immediately afterwards, whilst the convict bearing the basket stood a few paces in advance of the warder, so as to receive the contents of his pan when filled. This process was performed more rapidly than it can be told, and so quickly, indeed, that though we walked by the side of the officer, we had hardly to halt by the way, and as we went the corridor rang again with the twanging of the prisoners' dust-pans, thrown, as they were emptied, one after another, out of their cells.

On our return from watching the last-mentioned operation, we found the corridors almost empty again—the cleaners having finished their work, and retired to their cells, and the building being comparatively quiet. It was, however, but a temporary lull; for a few moments after, the seven o'clock bell rang, and this was the signal for " double-locking," whereupon the same trigger-like noise pervaded every part of the building.

"Each cell-door, you see, sir, is always on the single lock," said our guide; "but before the warders go to breakfast (and the last bell was the signal for their doing so), the prisoners' doors and every outlet to the building is ' double-shotted' for the sake of security."

Scarcely had our attendant communicated the intelligence to us before the work was done, and the warders came thronging to the spiral staircase, and went twisting round and round, one after another, as they descended to their breakfast in the mess-room below.

₊ *The Prison Breakfast.*—From seven to half-past the corridors of Pentonville Prison

are as deserted as Burlington Arcade on a Sunday, and nothing is heard the while but the clacking of the prisoners' looms, and the tapping of the convict-shoemakers' hammers, and occasionally the sharp "ting-ng-ng!" of the gong in connection with the cells, for summoning the solitary warder left in attendance.

"If you like, sir, we will now go below to the kitchen and bakehouse," said the officer, who still remained at our side, "and see them preparing the breakfast for the prisoners."

Accordingly, we descended the spiral staircase into the basement; and after traversing sundry passages, we knew, by the peculiar smell of bread pervading the place, that we had entered the bakery. There was but little distinctive about this part of the prison; for we found the same heap of dusty white-looking sacks, and the same lot of men, with the flour, like hair-powder, clinging to their eyebrows and whiskers (four of these were prisoners, and the other a free man—"the master baker" placed over them), as usually characterises such a place. It was, however, infinitely cleaner than all ordinary bakehouses; neither were the men slip-shod and without stockings, nor had they the appearance of walking plaster-casts, like the generality of journeymen bakers when at work. Here we learnt that the bread of the prison was unfermented, owing to the impossibility of working "the sponge" there during the night; and of course we were invited to taste a bit. It was really what would have been considered "cake" in some continental states; indeed, a German servant, to whom we gave a piece of the prison loaf, was absolutely amazed at the English prodigality, and crying, "*Wunder-schön!*" assured us that the "*König von Preussen*" himself hardly ate better stuff.

From the bakery we passed to the kitchen, where the floor was like a newly-cleaned bird-cage, with its layer of fresh sand that crunched, as garden walks are wont to do, beneath the feet. Here was a strong odour of the steaming cocoa that one of the assistant cooks (a prisoner) was busy serving, out of huge bright coppers, into large tin pails, like milk-cans. The master cook was in the ordinary white jacket and cap, and the assistants had white aprons over their brown convict trowsers, so that it would have been hard to have told that any were prisoners there.

The allowance for breakfast "is ten ounces of bread," said the master cook to us, "and three-quarters of a pint of cocoa, made with three-quarters of an ounce of the solid flake, and flavoured with two ounces of pure milk and six drachms of molasses. Please to taste a little of the cocoa, sir. It's such as you'd find it difficult to get outside, I can assure you; for the berries are ground on the premises by the steam-engine, and so we can vouch for its being perfectly pure."

It struck us as strange evidence of the "civilization" of our time, that a person must—in these days of "lie-tea," and chicory-mocha, and alumed bread, and brain-thickened milk, and watered butter—really go to prison to live upon unadulterated food. The best porter we ever drank was at a parish union—for the British pauper alone can enjoy the decoction of veritable malt and hops; and certainly the most genuine cocoa we ever sipped was at this same Model Prison, for not only was it made of the unsophisticated berries, but with the very purest water, too—water, not of the slushy Thames, but which had been raised from an artesian well several hundred feet below the surface, expressly for the use of these same convicts.

"For dinner," continued the cook, "the rations are—half a pint of good soup, four ounces of meat every day—beef and mutton alternately—without bone, and which is equal to about half a pound of uncooked meat with an ordinary quantity of bone; besides this there are five ounces of bread and one pound of potatoes for each man, except those working in association, who have two pounds. For supper every prisoner gets a pint of gruel, made with an ounce and a half of meal, and sweetened with six drachms of molasses, together with five more ounces of bread, so that each convict has twenty ounces of bread throughout the day.

"Yonder are some of the ten-ounce loaves, that are just going to be served out for break-fast," added the cook; and, as he said the words, he pointed to a slab of miniature half-quarterns, that looked not unlike a block of small paving-stones cemented together. "Any-thing additional," continued the cook, "is ordered by the medical officer. There you see, sir, that free man yonder has just brought in some extras; they're for a prisoner in the infirmary. It's two ounces of butter, you observe, and an egg.

"Yes, sir, that's my slate," added the man, as he saw us looking up at a long black board that was nailed against the wall in the serving-room, and inscribed with the letters and figures of the several wards of the prison, together with various hieroglyphics that needed the cook himself to interpret. "On that board I chalk up," he proceeded, "the number of prisoners in each ward, so as to know what rations I have to serve. The letter K there, underneath the figures, signifies that one man out of that particular ward is at work in the kitchen, and B, that one prisoner is employed in the bakehouse. That mark up there stands for an extra loaf to be sent up to the ward it's placed under, and these dots here for two extra meats; whilst yonder sign is to tell me that there is one man out of that part of the building gone into the infirmary. Yes, sir, we let the infirmary prisoners have just whatever the medical officer pleases to order—jelly, or fish, or indeed chicken if required."

We then inquired what was the diet for men under punishment.

"Why, sir," answered the cook, "the punishment allowance is sixteen ounces of bread per diem, and nothing else except water. You see I am just going to cut up the rations for the three prisoners in the refractory wards to-day; and so I take one of these twenty-ounce loaves, and cut it into three, and let the prisoner have the benefit of the trifling excess, for six ounces for breakfast, five for dinner, and five for supper, is all he's entitled to."

"How much," said we, "will a prisoner lose in weight upon such diet?"

"Why, I have known men to come out as much as four or five pounds lighter after three days of it," replied the cook; "but there's a register book upstairs that will tell you exactly, sir.* When a man is under long punishment," continued the cook, "for instance, when he has got twenty-eight days, he has full rations every fourth day, and is then found to gain flesh upon the food."

"I have known some prisoners come out as much as three pounds lighter than when they were first locked up," chimed in the warder; "though it depends mainly upon the temper

* We were afterwards favoured with a sight of the above-named register, from which we made the following extracts as to the weights of the men before being placed upon punishment diet, and at the expira-tion of the sentence :—

Registered Number of Prisoners placed in dark cell on Punishment Diet.	Weight of Prisoner. on going in.	Weight of Prisoner. on coming out.	Number of Days under Punishment.	Average Loss of Weight per Diem.
6,216	9 st. 2 lbs.	8 st. 13 lbs.	3 days.	1 lb.
6,257	9 st. 2 lbs.	8 st. 11 lbs.	2 ,,	2½ lbs.
6,419	12 st.	11 st. 11 lbs.	1 ,,	3 lbs.
6,257	9 st.	Not yet out of dark cell.	6 ,,	

The above table indicates that the main loss of weight occurs upon the first day—the severity of the punishment doubtlessly affecting the body through the mind less intensely after the first twenty-four hours. We, at the same time, were allowed to inspect the sick report for the day of our visit, appended to which were the following recommendations of the medical officer :—

"6,144, A I, 15, to have one pint of arrowroot and five ounces of bread for dinner per diem, and to keep cell.

"6,277, D I, 23, to have cocoa for supper instead of gruel.

"6,076, A III, 27, to go to the infirmary."

Others were to be off trade, others to keep their cell. "If the doctor suspects a man to be scheming," whispered the warder to us, as we glanced over the sick report, "he puts him on low diet; and that soon brings him to, especially when he's kept off his meat and potatoes."

of the men, for if they fret much over their punishment they lose the more in weight; and we know by *that* whether the punishment has worked upon them or not."

"Yes, sir," said the cook, "there are few persons that can hold out against short commons; the belly can tame every man. Now there's that man in A 3, he declared that no mortal thing should pass his lips, and that he meant to starve himself to death; that was the day before yesterday, but last night he was forced to give in, and take his gruel. Ah, sir, it takes stronger-minded men than they are to hold out against the cravings of the stomach. Just dock a prisoner's food, and it hurts him more than any 'cat' that could be laid across his back."

It was nearly half-past seven, and the warders were beginning to ascend the spiral stair-case from below, and the corridors to rumble with the rolling of the trucks along the pavement, and that of the "food-carriages" along the tops of the gallery railings, in preparation for the serving of the prisoners' breakfast.

At the time of our visit there were nearly three hundred and seventy convicts in the prison, and the warder had told us that the rations were distributed to the whole of these men in about eight minutes. We had seen sufficient of the admirable regulations of this prison to satisfy us that if the enormous building could be cleansed from end to end, and that in a manner surpassing all private establishments, in little more than half an hour, it was quite possible to accomplish the distribution of nearly four hundred breakfasts in less than ten minutes. Still we could not help wondering by what division of labour the task was to be achieved, especially when it is remembered that each of the four corridors is as long as an arcade, and as high as the nave of a large church, having double galleries one above the other.

While we were speculating as to the process, the brass hand-bell was rung once more, to announce that the prisoners' breakfast hour (half-past seven) had arrived; and the bell had scarcely ceased pealing before the two oaken flaps let into the black asphalte pavement at the corners of the central hall, so that each stood between two of the four corridors, raised themselves as if by magic, and there ascended from below, through either flap, a tray laden with four large cans of cocoa, and two baskets of bread. These trays were raised by means of a "lifting machine," the bright iron rods of which stretched from the bottom to the top of the building, and served as guides for the friction-rollers of the trays. No sooner were the cans and bread-baskets brought up from below, than a couple of warders and trade instructors, two to either of the adjoining corridors, seized each half the quantity, and placing it on the trucks that stood ready by the flaps, away the warder and instructor went, the one wheeling the barrow of cocoa along the side of the corridor, and the other hastening to open the small trap in each cell-door as he served the men with the bread.

This is done almost as rapidly as walking, for no sooner does the trade-instructor apply his key to the cell-door than the little trap falls down and forms a kind of ledge, on which the officer may place the loaf, and the prisoner at the same time deposit his mug for the cocoa. This mug the warder who wheels the cocoa truck fills with the beverage, ladling it out as milkmen do the contents of their pails, and, when full, he thrusts the mug back through the aperture in the cell-door, and closes the trap with a slam.

The process goes on in each ground-floor of the four corridors at one and the same time and scarcely has it commenced before the bell of the lifting apparatus tinkles, and the emptied tray descends and brings up another load of steaming cans and bread. But these are now carried up to the galleries of the first floor, and there being received by the warders as before. the contents are placed upon the food-carriages, which are not unlike the small vehicles on tram-roads, and reach from side to side of each arcade, the top of the iron balcony to the galleries serving as rails for the carriage wheels to travel along.

The distribution here goes on in the same rapid manner as below, and while this is taking place the lifting bell tinkles again, and the trays having descended once more, up they

THE CHAPEL, ON THE "SEPARATE SYSTEM," IN PENTONVILLE PRISON, DURING DIVINE SERVICE.

come a third time laden with a fresh supply of food, which now mounts to the upper floor, and being there received in the same manner as previously, is immediately distributed by means of the same kind of food-carriages throughout the upper ward.

The sound of the rumbling of the trucks and food-carriages as the wheels travel along the pavement and the rails, the tinkling of the bell of the lifting apparatus, and the rapid succession of reports made by the slamming of the traps of the 360 cell-doors, are all necessary in order to give the reader a vivid sense of the rapidity of the distribution—which is assuredly about as curious and busy a process as one can well witness, every portion of the duty being conducted with such ease, and yet with such marvellous despatch, that there is hardly a finer instance of the feats that can be accomplished by the division of labour than this same serving of nearly 400 breakfasts in less than ten minutes.

*** *The Refractory Wards and Prison Punishments.*—A few moments after the above busy scene has come to an end, the prison is as still and quiet as the City on the Sabbath. The warders have nearly all gone below to "clean themselves," the looms have ceased clacking, and the shoemakers tapping, and even the gong in connection with the cells is no longer heard to sound in the corridors. For a time one would fancy the whole prison was asleep again.

Presently, however, the glass doors at the end of the passage are thrown open, and the governor enters with his keys in his hand. Then one of the warders who remains on duty hurries on before him, crying, "Governor-r-r! Governor-r-r! Governor-r-r!" as he opens each of the cell-doors. The chief prison authority walks past the several cells, saying, as he goes, "All right!—all right!" to each prisoner, who stands ready drawn up at the door, as stiff as a soldier in his sentry-box, with his hand raised, by way of salute, to the side of his cap; whilst no sooner have the words been spoken than the door is closed again, and the building echoes with the concussion.

This done, the governor proceeds to visit the refractory cells; but before accompanying him thither, let us prepare the reader with an idea of the nature of such places.

The refractory, or, as they are sometimes called, "dark cells," are situate in the basement of corridor C. It was mid-day when we first visited these apartments at Pentonville.

"Light a lantern, Wood," said the chief warder to one of the subordinate officers, "so that this gentleman may look at the dark cells."

The lamp lighted at noon gave us a notion of what we were to expect, and yet it was a poor conception of what we saw.

Descending a small flight of stairs, we came to a narrow passage, hardly as wide as the area before second-rate houses; and here was a line of black doors, not unlike the entrances to the front cellars of such houses. These were the refractory cells.

The officer who accompanied us threw back one of the doors, which turned as heavily on its hinges, and gave forth the same hollow sound, as the massive door of an iron safe. The interior which it revealed was absolutely and literally "*pitch* dark." Not a thing was visible in the cell; and so utterly black did it look within, that we could not believe but that there was another door between us and the interior. The officer, however, introduced his lantern, and then we could see the rays diverging from the bull's-eye, and streaking the darkness with a bright, luminous mist, as we have all seen a sunbeam stripe the dusky atmosphere of some cathedral. The light from the lantern fell in a bright, Jack-a-dandy-like patch upon the white walls, and we then discovered, as the warder flickered the rays into the several corners of the chamber, that the refractory cell was about the size of the other cells in which the men lived, but that it was utterly bare of all furniture, excepting, in one corner, a small raised bench, with a sloping head-piece, that was like a wooden mattress, placed upon the ground. This, we were told, was, with a rug for covering, the only bed allowed.

"Would you like to step inside," asked the warder, "and see how dark it is when the door is closed?"

We entered the terrible place with a shudder, for there is something intensely horrible in absolute darkness to all minds, confess it or not as they may; and as the warder shut the door upon us—and we felt the cell walls shake and moan again, like a tomb, as he did so —the utter darkness was, as Milton sublimely says—"*visible.*" The eyes not only saw, but *felt* the absolute negation of their sense in such a place. Let them strain their utmost, not one luminous chink or crack could the sight detect. Indeed, the very air seemed as impervious to vision as so much black marble, and the body seemed to be positively encompassed with the blackness, as if it were buried alive, deep down in the earth itself. Though we remained several minutes in the hope that we should shortly gain the use of our eyes, and begin to make out, in the thick dusk, bit after bit of the apartment, the darkness was at the end of the time quite as impenetrable as at first, so that the continual straining of the eyeballs, and taxing of the brains, in order to get them to do their wonted duty, soon produced a sense of mental fatigue, that we could readily understand would end in conjuring up all kinds of terrible apparitions to the mind.

"Have you had enough, sir?" inquired the warder to us, as he re-opened the door, and whisked the light of his lantern in our eyes.

An owl, suddenly roused from its sleep in the daylight, could not have been more dazzled and bewildered with the glitter of the rays than we. The light was now as blinding to us as had been the darkness itself, and such was the dilatation of the pupils that we had to rub our eyes, like one newly waked from sleep, before we could distinguish anything on leaving the place; and when we mounted the steps and entered the corridor once more, the air had the same blue tint to us as that of early morning.

"Well, sir, I think," said the warder, in answer to our question as to how many intractables the prison contained, "we have altogether about three or four per cent. of refractory people here, and they are mostly the boys and second probation men, as we call them. Separate confinement in Pentonville Prison for nine months now constitutes the first or probationary stage to the convict; and then he is transferred to the public works, either at Woolwich, or Portsmouth, or Portland, as the case may be, which forms the second stage. But if the man won't conform to discipline at the public works, why then he is sent back to us again, and such people constitute what we call 'second probation men.' Some of them are very difficult to deal with, I can assure you, sir. The Glasgow boys in the prison are perhaps the worst class of all. I can hardly say what is the reason of *their* being so bad. I don't think it is the lax discipline of the Glasgow prison; but the race, you see, is half Scotch and half Irish, and that is a very bad mixture, to my mind. On the other hand, the sheep-stealers and the convicts who have been farm-labourers are about the easiest managed of all the prisoners here. Then, what we call the first-class men, such as those who have been well educated, like the clerks, and forgers, and embezzlers, and so forth, give us little or no trouble; and, generally speaking, the old jail-birds fall into the discipline very well, for they know it is no use knocking their head against the wall. The boys, however, who come here for the first time, are sad, troublesome fellows, and will stand an awful deal of punishment surely before their temper is broke."

We had visited the dark cells at six o'clock in the morning of the day which we spent within the prison. At that time there were four prisoners confined in the refractory ward, and we found a boy, with an officer in attendance, turned out into the passage to wash himself at the sink, and to fold up the rug he had to cover himself with during the night. He had been sentenced to one day's confinement in the dark cell, we were told, for communicating in chapel.

"Any complaint?" said the warder. "None," was the brief reply. Then the bull's-eye was thrust into the cell, and the light flirted through every part of the chamber so as to show whether or not any depredations had been committed. The boy gave us a sullen look as we passed by him, and the warder told us, while we mounted the steps, that when the lad had finished washing, another prisoner would be let out to perform the same operation.

Some hour and a half after this, during the governor's morning visit, we went once more to the same place. The officer, who preceded the governor, threw open the doors one by one, crying, "Governor-r-r!" as before, and the prisoners stood drawn up at the cell-doors as the others had done.

"Please to release me, sir," said the first under punishment, "and I'll promise you I won't do so again."

"We never remit any punishment here," was the governor's brief answer; and immediately the door of the dark cell was closed upon the prisoner once more.

The second man had a less dogged and surly expression, and the governor exclaimed, as his quick eye detected the signs of yielding temper in his face, "Oh! you're coming to your senses are you? Well, I am glad to hear it; and you'll be more careful for the future."

The last but one under confinement was "a bad fellow," the governor told us, and was in for six days; whilst the last of all had been sent back from the works at Portland as incorrigible. These two were merely inspected, and asked whether all was right; but not a word was spoken in return by the men, who looked the very picture of bitter sullenness. So the heavy doors closed upon them, and the wretched creatures were again shut up in their living tombs.

"Ah! sir," said one of the warders to us, at a later part of the day, "some of the convicts are *very* difficult to deal with. I remember once we had forty of the worst fellows sent to us here—the forty thieves we used to call them. They were men who had gone the round of the public prisons and the "hulks," and some of them had been sent back, before their sentences expired, from the public works at Gibraltar. When they came in, the governor was told that one of the men, who was in chains, was so dangerous that it wouldn't be safe to allow him anything but a wooden spoon to eat with. Well, sir, the governor spoke to them all, and said if they would only obey orders they should be treated like other men; but if they would not conform to discipline, why he was prepared to compel them. So he made no more ado but ordered the irons to be took off the most dangerous of them; and sure enough that man became quite an altered character. However, we didn't like having such people here, I can tell you; for we always expected an attempt would be made to break prison by the lot of them all at once; and whenever many of them were brought together (as in the chapel, for instance), a sufficient number of officers was kept under arms, within call, ready to act in case of need. But, thank goodness, all went well, and the greater part of those very men not only left here with good characters, but merely a few of them had to be punished. But another prisoner, not of the same gang, but a returned convict who had been in Norfolk Island, was much more difficult to manage than even these; and I remember, after he had been confined in the refractory cell, he swore, on being let out, that he would murder any man who attempted to come down to him there. He had made a spring at the officer near him, and would assuredly have bitten his nose off had the warder not retreated up the stairs, so that the man was down below all alone, vowing and declaring he would have the life of the first person that tried to get him up. Well, you see, we knew we could master him directly we had him in the corridor; but as we couldn't take *his* life, and he could *ours*, he was more than a match for us down in the refractory ward. Accordingly the governor had to devise some means by which to get him up stairs without hurting him—and how d'ye think he did it, sir? Why, he got some cayenne pepper and burnt it in a fumigating bellows, and then blew the smoke down into the ward where the fellow was. The man stood it for some time; but, bless you, he was soon glad to surrender, for, as we sent in puff after puff, it set him coughing and sneezing, and rubbing his eyes, and stamping with the pain, as the fumes got not only into his throat and up his nose, but under his eyelids, and made them smart, till the tears ran down his cheeks as if he had been a little child. Then immediately afterwards we threw ourselves upon him, and effectually secured him against doing any further harm. Oh! no, sir," added the officer, with a smile and a knowing shake of the head, "he never tried the same game on after that; one dose of cayenne pepper smoke was quite enough for him, I can assure you.

"When we first came here," continued our informant, "we used to have some weapons to prevent a prisoner from injuring any of us in his cell; for, you see, we are obliged to allow the convicts knives and hammers when they are employed as shoemakers, so that they may do their work in their cells. Well, some one or other of the prisoners used occasionally to get furious, and swear that they would stick us with their knives or knock our brains out with their hammers if we dared to come near them, and we could see by their expressions that they meant it too. But how do you think we used to do in such cases? Why, one of us used to put on a large shield that was made of basket-work, well stuffed and covered with leather, and almost big enough to screen a person's whole body behind it; and when the officer saw a good opportunity, he would suddenly rush into the cell, thrusting the shield right in front of the prisoner, and whilst the fellow was taken aback with this, another officer would dart in, holding a long pole with a large padded crutch like an enormous pitch-fork at the end of it; and thrusting this at the upper part of the prisoner's body, he would pinion him right up against the wall. No sooner, too, would this be done than another officer, bearing a similar crutch, but somewhat smaller, would make a drive at the fellow's legs, and pin these in a like manner; whilst immediately that was accomplished, the other warders would pour in and overpower the man. We have, however, now done away with all such things, for we find that if a convict is rebellious he is much sooner brought to himself by putting him on low diet than by all the fetters in the world. Only stop his meat and potatoes, as the cook said to you this morning, sir, and he'll soon give in, I warrant."

Later in the day we were present when two prisoners, who had been reported for refractory conduct, were brought in for examination before the governor in his office. The report-book lay upon the table, and the governor pointed out to us that the offence of the one was refusal to wash the slates and go to chapel, and that of the other wilful disturbance of the congregation in the chapel by clapping his hands.

The former of these had been liberated from the dark cell only that morning. He was, comparatively speaking, a mere boy, and entered the governor's office in a determined manner. But seeing us there he became frightened, mistaking us, we were told, for some awful government authority. So when the governor asked him what he had to say, and whether he admitted the charge, he nodded his head sullenly in assent, and was immediately marched off to the dark cell once more.

The next offender was the church-disturber. He was one of the Glasgow boys of whom we have before spoken, and had been sent back to Pentonville from Parkhurst. He had already been punished four times before. His face, which was almost flat and broad, was remarkable for the extreme self-will depicted in him, and he had that peculiar thick bull-neck which is so characteristic of stubbornness of temper.

On being asked what he had to say, he stoutly denied the charge, declaring that it was all false, and that the officer had a spite against him. "Then," said the governor, "let the officer state his case." The warder stepped forward and declared that, during prayers that morning, the boy had clapped his hands loudly at the end of the service. The officer said he was sure it was the prisoner, because the lad stood upon a stool in the chapel, being short, and he had his eyes fixed upon him while he committed the offence.

"Well," said the governor, "what have you to say now?"

"I say it aint true," muttered the boy, shaking his head, and frowning with a deter-mined air.

"Take him away to the dark cell," said the governor; and he proceeded to write in the book that his punishment was to be three days' confinement in the refractory ward upon punishment diet, with loss of stripe and removal from the A division, which is the part of the prison occupied by the convicts who are permitted to work in partial association after having passed nine months in separation.

"You see," said the governor, turning to us when the boy had left, "I am obliged to support my officers."*

But if there be punishments at Pentonville, there are, on the other hand, rewards; and many of the penal inflictions for breaches of discipline and riotous conduct consist merely in the withdrawal of the premiums given for good behaviour. "Do you find," said we, some time back to one of the turnkeys of another prison (Newgate), as he walked with us through the ancient "press-yard"—where formerly prisoners who had refused to plead at the bar, in order to save their property, suffered the "*peine forte et dure*," or, in other words, were "pressed to death"—"Do you find," we asked, "that you have the inmates of the jail under the same control now as in the days of 'thumb-screws,' and 'gags,' and brandings?"

"I think we have greater power over them, sir," was the answer; "for at present, you see, we cut off the right of receiving and sending letters, as well as stop the visits of their friends; and a man feels those things much more than any torture that he could be put to."

The prison authorities now-a-days, therefore, have learnt that *negative* punishments are far more effective than *positive* ones. But as these same negative punishments consist merely of the deprivation of certain privileges or enjoyments, rather than the infliction of actual cruelties, it is essential that the granting of such privileges, as rewards for good conduct, should form part of the modern prison discipline.

Accordingly, in Pentonville Prison, as we have already seen, one part of the punishment consists in the reduction of the ordinary diet to bread and water; whilst another form of punishment, to which we have before alluded, is the loss of the red stripe or stripes decorating

* The following is an epitome of the punishments in this prison for one entire year:—

LIST OF PUNISHMENTS IN PENTONVILLE PRISON DURING 1854.

No. of Prisoners Punished.	No. of Times Punished.	No. of Punishments.	No. of Prisoners Punished.	No. of Times Punished.	No. of Punishments.
158	Once	158	1	11 times	11
43	Twice	86	2	12 ,,	24
24	Thrice	72	1	14 ,,	14
13	4 times	52	1	16 ,,	16
7	5 ,,	35	1	17 ,,	17
4	6 ,,	24	1	23 ,,	23
4	7 ,,	28	1	24 ,,	24
1	8 ,,	8			
1	9 ,,	9	263		601

The *offences* for which the prisoners were punished were as under :—

149 were for disobedience (such as refusing to work or attend school or exercise); 83 for disturbing prison by shouting, whistling, or singing obscene and other songs; 102 for misconduct in school, such as talking, whistling, &c.; 33 for obscene communications or drawings (on books and chapel-stalls); 33 for misconduct in chapel during service; 171 for communicating with fellow-prisoners (either by writing, talking at exercise, or by knocking on cell-walls or through water-pipes); 2 for trying to send letters out of prison; 64 for wilfully destroying prison property; 25 for boring holes in cell-window, &c.; 9 for assaulting officers; 29 for using bad language to officers, &c.; 5 for false charges against officers; 30 for fighting and wrangling with fellow-prisoners in association; 9 for attempting to escape; 3 for proposing to other prisoners to escape; 4 for feigning suicide; 3 for threatening to commit ditto; 4 for dirty cells; 22 for purloining bread, meat, &c.; 14 for having tobacco, &c., in possession.

The nature of the *punishments* for the above offences was as follows :—

534 were confined to the dark cell (292 of these with punishment diet, and 244 with ordinary diet, 18 with loss of stripes, and 10 with loss of one stripe); 40 of these 534 were so confined for one day, 236 for two days, 249 for three days, 4 between five and ten days, and 4 between ten and twenty-one days. 11 were confined to the light cell (9 with punishment diet, and 2 with ordinary diet). 26 were confined to their own cell (19 with ordinary diet, and 7 with their secular books withdrawn). 18 were withdrawn from working in association, and 7 from school. 1 suffered corporal punishment (36 lashes); and 4 were removed from the working party in A division.

the arm of those who have conducted themselves well during the first six months of their incarceration.*

Nor is this badge of good conduct a mere honorary distinction, for those who have obtained it become entitled to receive a certain gratuity for their labour, according to the quantity of work done; and only the best behaved among these are removed from separate confinement in the day, and allowed to work in association—a privilege, moreover, which entitles them to an extra pound of potatoes at dinner.

At the time of our visit, there was about 8 per cent. of the prisoners (or 29 in 368) working together; and so highly is this indulgence prized, that it becomes one of the severest inflictions to send an associated man back to separate confinement.

Again, only well-conducted prisoners are allowed to receive a visit from their friends.†

* The following are the official rules and regulations concerning good and bad conduct, a copy of which is suspended in each cell :—

"NOTICE TO CONVICTS UNDER SENTENCE OF TRANSPORTATION AND PENAL SERVITUDE.

"Transportation for certain offences having been abolished by Act of Parliament, and certain periods of imprisonment of much shorter duration, under the term "penal servitude," having been substituted in place of the sentences of seven and ten years' transportation, which had been usually awarded, no remission, as a general rule, of any part of the term of penal servitude will be granted; the period of detention, in place of a longer sentence of transportation, having been settled by law. The Secretary of State will, however, be prepared to consider any case of any convict whose conduct may be the subject of special recommendation. The Secretary of State is also desirous, as a general rule, of holding out encouragement to good conduct by establishing successive stages of discipline, to each of which some special privileges will be attached. Convicts of good conduct, maintaining a character for willing industry, will by this rule be enabled, after certain fixed periods, to obtain the higher stages, and gain the privileges attached to them.

"For the present, and until further orders, the following rules will be observed :—

"All convicts under sentence of penal servitude will be subjected to a period of separate confinement, followed by labour on public works.

"Convicts under sentence of transportation will be subject to the same discipline so long as they are imprisoned in this country.

"SEPARATE CONFINEMENT.

"1. Convicts, as a general rule, will be detained in separate confinement for a period of nine months from the date of their reception in a government prison.

"2. Every convict who, during a detention of six months in the prison, may have conducted himself in a satisfactory manner, will be allowed to wear a badge, which will entitle him to receive a visit from his friends. A second badge, with the privilege of a second visit, will be granted at the end of three additional months, provided his conduct has continued to be satisfactory.

"3. Convicts wearing badges will be recommended for gratuities to be placed to their credit, according to the scale approved by the Secretary of State.

"4. In the event of a convict being deprived of a badge through misconduct, he will, at the same time, forfeit all advantages he had derived from it, including the gratuity already credited to him (if so ordered). He may, however, regain the forfeited badge after an interval of two months if specially recommended by the Governor and Chaplain.

"5. On removal of convicts from separate confinement to public works, they will be placed in the first, second, or third class, according to their conduct, attention to instruction, and industry. This classification will affect their position in the following stages of their servitude.

"6. Convicts deemed to be incorrigible, will be specially dealt with."

† The subjoined are the regulations respecting such visits :—

"The prisoner has leave to receive one visit from his friends, provided—

"1st. If the visit is made within one month.

"2nd. If the prisoner is well behaved in the mean time ;—badly behaved prisoners are not allowed to see friends when they come.

"3rd. The visit to last only fifteen minutes.

"4th. Visitors admitted only between the hours of 2 and 4 o'clock in the afternoon.

"5th. No visit allowed on Sundays.

"6th. Such of the above-named friends as wish to visit, must all attend at the same time, and produce this order.'

Farther, another curious privilege granted to well-conducted prisoners in Pentonville, is the liberty of labouring; for so terrible is separate confinement found to be, without occupation, that one of the forms of punishment peculiar to this prison is the stoppage of a man's work, and forcing him to remain in his own cell in a state of idleness throughout the day.

What high penal refinement is here shown, in making the feelings of monotony and vacuity of mind so keen a pain to the erratic natures of criminals (ever bent as they are upon change and amusement) that, though the convicts be remarkable for their innate aversion to labour outside the prison walls, the deprivation of work within them becomes a means of discipline to such characters!

₊ *Exercising and Health of the Prisoners.*—At eight o'clock in the morning the "Model Prison" is noisier and fuller of life and bustle than ever, and the transition from the silence during breakfast-time to the sudden outpouring of the convicts is a strongly-marked feature of the place.

No sooner does the clock point to the hour above mentioned, than the bell for morning prayers in the chapel is heard booming and humming overhead throughout the resonant arcades, and instantly the cell-doors are successively thrown open, and the brown-clad prisoners stream forth from every part of the building; above, below, on this side, and on that, lines of convicts come hurrying along the corridors and galleries at a rapid pace, one after the other, and each at the distance of some four or five yards apart, while the warders, who stand by, watching their movements, keep crying to the men as they pass, " Now, step out there, will you—step out!"

This is accompanied with a noise and clatter that is as bewildering as the sight—the tramping of the feet, the rattling of the iron staircases by the bridges as the prisoners pass up and down them, the slamming of the cell-doors, and the tolling of the bell overhead—all keep up such an incessant commotion in the brain that the mind becomes half-distracted with what it sees and hears. Nor does the tumult cease in a second or two, for as it takes some seven or eight minutes to empty the prison when full, the lines of convicts streaming along from all parts of the building seem to be endless, and impress you with the idea of the number being positively infinite.

Moreover, each of the prisoners is not only clad alike—and brown as so many bees pouring from the countless cells of a hive—but every one wears a peculiar brown cloth cap, and the peak of this (which is also of cloth) hangs so low down as to cover the face like a mask, the eyes alone of the individual appearing through the two holes cut in the front, and seeming almost like phosphoric lights shining through the sockets of a skull. This gives to the prisoners a half-spectral look, and though they have hardly the same hideous appearance as the diver at the Polytechnic, with his big hydrocephalous head and glass-window eyes, nevertheless the costume of the men seems like the outward vestment to some wandering soul rather than that of a human being; for the eyes, glistening through the apertures in the mask, give one the notion of a spirit peeping out behind it, so that there is something positively terrible in the idea that these are men whose crimes have caused their very features to be hidden from the world. It is strange, too, how different the convicts look under such circumstances from the ordinary coarse-featured men seen in the chapel; for at Pentonville the screening of the faces gives a kind of tragic solemnity to the figures, and thus there appears to be nothing vulgar nor brutal about them.

We are here speaking of first impressions only, for after a time, when the spectral sentiment has worn off, the imposition of these same masks—though originally designed, it must be confessed, with every kindness and consideration to the prisoners, in order that their faces might not be seen in their shame—cannot but be regarded as a piece of wretched frippery, and as idle in use as they are theatrical in character; for the men at "the Model" being all destined either for transportation abroad, or for labour at the public works at home, where no such masquerading is indulged in, it becomes positively silly to impose such a costume on the prisoners as a means of preventing recognition in after life, since all such restraints are removed during the latter part of their punishment.*

At the same hour as that for morning service, exercise begins in the " rope-walk," as it is called, and two divisions of the men, who then come pouring forth from their cells, are led off for airing into a spacious yard, while the other two divisions are sent into the chapel— the prisoners from B and D corridors being at exercise while those from A and C are at prayers, so that the prison at this hour is emptied of all but such as may be invalided at the time.

Let us follow the men to their exercise now, and reserve the scene in the chapel for future description.

At Pentonville there are five exercising yards, and it will be seen, on reference to the bird's-eye view of the prison given at page 116, that the two larger yards, which are for exercising in common, and called the " rope-yards," are situate on either side of the long entrance hall leading from the portcullis porch, and marked by a series of concentric rings, whilst the three others (which are for exercising apart) lie between the several corridors, and are wheel-shaped, the several radii, or spokes, consisting of walls or partitions, to separate the men walking there one from the other, and the centre serving as a small " argus," or station, for a warder, whence to survey the whole of the prisoners at one glance. These exercising yards are numbered in rotation, that on the left-hand side of the entrance hall being called No. 1, and that on the right-hand side No. 5, and the smaller private yards styled No. 2, 3, and 4, respectively.

The men who were put to exercise at the hour above mentioned, turned out into yard No. 1 ; and as they descended a small flight of steps a warder standing there cried out, " Left !" " Right !" according to the appointed station of the convicts. The concentric rings here consisted of a narrow line of bricken paving let into the soil, and on this lay a long rope knotted at distances of fifteen feet apart. Here the prisoners took up their station, one at every knot, all with masks down, and with a warder to watch over each of the circles of men at exercise, so as to prevent all communication between them individually.

When the whole of the men were assembled in the yard, and each at their different stations, holding the rope in their hands, the principal warder cried in a loud voice, " Forwar-r-r-d !" and instantly the whole of the 130 convicts there began to wheel round and round, and to move along at the same rapid pace as if they were so many circles of lamp-lighters.

There was a sharp easterly wind blowing on the morning of our visit that stung the skin and flooded the eyes, as it swept by, and made one really envy the brisk movements of the prisoners. "Now, move on, will you—come, move on !" one warder would cry to the flagging ones. " Step out there, men, step out !" another would exclaim, as the convicts filed rapidly by them.

Presently the principal warder roared, " Ha-a-a-lt !" and instantaneously the whole of the brown rings that before were circling round and round, like some cavalcade at a circus, came to a sudden stop with almost military precision ; and immediately afterwards the warder shouted, " Face about !" whereupon they one and all turned on their heels and

---

* It is but right to add, that this bit of prison foppery is to be abolished. Colonel Jebb, in a letter addressed to the Under-Secretary of State, quotes the following resolution come to by a Board of Inquiry in favour of its discontinuance :—"That the mask or peak does not prevent prisoners from recognising each other in the prison ; moreover, that as prisoners see each other before they are brought to the prison, come in considerable bodies, and are assembled together when they leave the prison, it would be desirable to discontinue it, since the use of it appears calculated to depress the spirits of the men, without obtaining any corresponding advantage."—*Report on the Discipline and Management of Convict Prisons for the Year* 1853.

commenced pacing in an opposite direction, the officers crying as before, " Step out, men," and " Move on there," as they one after another went striding past them.

At first one is astonished at the rapid rate at which the prisoners keep moving, but a reference to the Government reports tells us that this mode of exercise has been adopted after the plan pursued at Wakefield, where we are informed the prisoners are made to walk briskly round paved paths, forming three concentric rings; and which plan has been introduced at Pentonville, because, as Colonel Jebb says, " experience has shown the necessity of the greatest precautions in the administration of the discipline of strict separation, in order to guard against its tendency to depress and otherwise affect the mental energies of the prisoners."

The rapid exercise, therefore, at Pentonville Prison partakes more of the character of a shaking to a drowsy man, than an airing to a wakeful one; and as medical instructions enjoin us to drag, pinch, kick, or indeed to resort to any forcible means to induce muscular exercise in a person who is suffering from an opiate, so the " brisk walking " at " the Model" is intended to rouse and stir the men out of the depression induced by separate confinement—to shake up their half-thickened blood, as one does a doctor's draught before it can be made to do its duty.

Indeed, we find in the report of the medical officer of the prison (given at page 116), that the diseases prevalent at Pentonville are precisely those which are known to arise from undue confinement—no less than 52 per cent. of the entire disorders consisting of dyspepsia and constipation—so that out of a total of 1732 cases requiring medical treatment, no less than 1103 were affections of the organs of digestion.

Nevertheless, it must be confessed that the men whom we saw previous to their departure for Portsmouth appeared to be perfectly healthy, and to be in no way subject to any depression of spirits.*

* Since the publication of the previous part of THE GREAT WORLD OF LONDON, we have received a letter from a gentleman, who is at once a strenuous and well-meaning advocate of the separate system, remonstrating against the conclusions we have drawn as to the operation of this mode of prison discipline ; and as we ourselves have no other object than the truth, we readily append his remarks—which are worthy of every consideration, as well from the character as position of the writer—so that the public may decide fairly upon the subject. (1.) He writes, " At pages 103 and 104, you attempt to show that the discipline of Pentonville produced, in a given time, upwards of ten times more than the average proportion of lunacy in all other prisons throughout England and Wales ; whereas it is impossible to institute any fair comparison in such a case. For what parallel is there between Pentonville, in which, under the separate system, the term was 18 months, and upwards, and 'all other prisons,' &c., in which, under short sentences and summary convictions, it averaged *so very much less ?*

(2.) " Again, your rate of 5·8 of criminal lunatics in every 10,000 of an average annual population in 'all prisons,' &c.—(which, although not so stated, was probably derived from the number found to have been insane on *trial*)—must fall very far short of the cases of insanity which actually occurred in every such 10,000 *in the year.* For, as shown by Mr. Burt, at p. 99 of his book, the proportion of lunatics was ascertained to have been 13 (persons acquitted as insane) in every 10,000 of the prison population (tried) ; but it being impossible to discover the average period that elapsed between the attack (of insanity) and the prisoners' trial, the interval was assumed, for example, to have been 6 or 4 months—and thus the cases of insanity occurring *during the entire year* must have been, according to that rate, in the proportion of 26 or 39 in 10,000. And it did not appear that the highest of such proportions was too high.

(3.) " Mr. Burt further showed, from another table, that the annual mean number of cases of lunacy throughout the prisons of England and Wales reported for each year between 1843 and 1847 was 89·4—the average daily population being 14,689—giving a proportion of 63 cases of insanity in every 10,000, which is a far larger proportion than occurred under the separate system, when carried out in its integrity, for the longest terms, with the greatest strictness, and co-extensively with that same period of time, at Pentonville.

(4.) " Again, at the pages referred to, and at page 115, you ascribe to the separate system, *properly so called*, results which it utterly repudiates. That system, commencing in 1843, and ending in 1847, or at latest in February, 1848, lasted 5 years and 2 months, and *no longer.* Within that period, when its *own* conditions and requirements were fulfilled—and *not beyond* that period, when they were violated and distorted,

At a later hour of the day—for from eight to half-past twelve the prisoners are continually going to and returning from exercise—we were led towards the private exercising yards, and,

and when innovations, against which it protests, were introduced—you must therefore look for its legitimate results; and these, whatever may be said, and by whomsoever, to the contrary, are the very reverse of the hideous dimensions you describe. But instead of drawing a broad line after the termination of these five years (the duration of the system), so as unmistakably to distinguish it from that other system—for which I know no name—which succeeded it, and which in the three following years of 1848, 1849, 1850, was attended with the most disastrous results, viz., with at least a four-fold larger proportion of insanity than occurred under the separate system altogether; results which, as compared with the last four *consecutive* years of it, were greater, by eight times and upwards, than under the original system—(instead of distinguishing between these different systems) you have confounded the results of the *two* under a *common* name; not, I believe, intentionally, but probably because others whose writings you may have consulted had done so before."

Now, against the first of the above remarks, we would urge that it is asserted by the advocates of the separate system, as "carried out in its integrity" at Pentonville, that the greatest number of cases of insanity occur during the *early part* of the imprisonment; and Mr. Burt, in his "Results of Separate Confinement" (page 132), cites a table, in which he shows that, out of 51 cases of mental affection, no less than 29 occurred within the first six months *and under*; and 15 between six and twelve months; whereas only 5 occurred between twelve and eighteen months; and not more than 2 between eighteen months and two years; or, in other words, that whereas 44 cases of mental disorder occurred within the first year, there were but 7 within the second. Hence, in opposition to the first of the above objections, we say—with all deference—that there *is* some parallel between Pentonville, "where the term of imprisonment used to be eighteen months and upwards," and all other prisons where "the term averages so much less."

Against the second observation we can only adduce the fact that, in the Government tables from which the normal rate of lunacy was deduced, it is *not* stated that the number of lunatics there given refers to the persons acquitted as insane "*upon trial*," and that no reason appears for making such an assumption. But even assuming such to be the case, and increasing the ratio to the same extent as Mr. Burt for *the entire year*, we raise the proportion of lunacy merely to 11·6 or 17·4 in the 10,000 prisoners, which is still widely different from 62·0 to the 10,000 which is the proportion at Pentonville.

In opposition to the third remark, in which it is shown that the proportion of cases of insanity to the *average daily population* of the whole prisons of England and Wales, is 63 in every 10,000 prisoners, we answer, that there *is assuredly no* parallel here, since the Pentonville returns are made out according to the gross number of convicts entering the prison, and *not according to the daily average* number of prisoners (see Burt's "Results," page 122), whilst those from which the normal rate of lunacy was deduced refer, also, *not to the daily average* of prisoners, but to the *gross prison population* of England and Wales.

With reference to the fourth remark, we can but quote the following table given by Mr. Bradley, the medical officer of the prison, in his report for the year 1853, and which is arranged to show the proportion of lunacy in every thousand prisoners *seriatim* as they entered "the Model," but which we have here increased to ten thousand, by the addition of a cypher to the ratio, in order to reduce the whole of the statistics to one uniform standard, and so facilitate the comparison :—

	No. of Cases of Insanity.	No. of Cases of Delusion.	No. of Suicides.	Total.
Amongst the 1st (ten) thousand prisoners	60	100	0	160
„ 2nd „	100	50	10	160
„ 3rd „	40	90	20	150
„ 4th „	90	70	0	160
„ 5th „	20	0	0	20
„ 6th „	10	0	10	20

For the first and second items the term of imprisonment in Pentonville, says Mr. Bradley (a gentleman, be it observed, who is often commended by the Surveyor-General of Prisons for the accuracy and lucidity of his statistical tables), was eighteen months, whereas with the third and fourth it was only twelve months, so that if calculated for an *uniform period*, he says, there would be an increase of one-third in the ratio of lunacy for the third and fourth items over that of the first and second. This increase Mr. Bradley attributes to the fact that the earlier prisoners were picked men, whereas the later ones were the ordinary convicts of a low intellectual standard. The diminution in the ratio of insanity in the fifth item the medical officer ascribes to the following causes :—(1) The shortening of the term of imprisonment in Pentonville. (2) Increased quantity of out-door exercise, and the substitution of exercise in common for exercise in separate yards. (3) Better ventilation of the cells. (4) Relaxation of the discipline in all cases of danger. (5) Awakening the prisoner's interest in the pursuit of his trade. (6) Increased amount of school instruction given to the most ignorant.

The same officer, moreover, adds that though much has been gained by the measures adopted during

as we went, we passed a detachment of " associated" convicts at work with barrows and spades in the prison grounds, and with an officer attending in their rear.

These private yards consist, as we have said, each of a series of eight compartments, or deep narrow dens, as it were, that seem, with their partitions, not unlike the elongated stalls of a stable, all radiating from a small octagonal house in the centre, where sits a warder watching the prisoners. Here the invalids and refractory or dangerous prisoners are put to exercise.

As we neared yard No. 4, the warder whispered in our ear that the short man with red hair, whom we should see exercising in one of the compartments, was in for a murder committed at Carlisle; and, indeed, had had so narrow an escape from the gallows, that his respite had arrived only on the Saturday before his appointed execution on the Monday.

As we passed, we could not help fixing our gaze upon the blood-shedder, who was pacing the yard moodily, with his hands buried in his pockets; and as the men, in this part of the prison, exercise with their cap-peaks up, we saw sufficient of the features of the felon—for he returned our glance with a savage stare and scowl—to teach us, or rather to make us believe (and it is astonishing what physiognomical foresight we obtain *after* such traits of character), that he was thoroughly capable of the act for which he was suffering. He had been a pitman in the north, and had the peculiar freckled, iron-mouldy, Scotch complexion, whilst his cheek bones were high, his face broad and flat, and his neck short and thick as a bull-terrier's, to which animal, indeed, he appeared to be a kind of human counterpart. As we saw him prowling there, round and round within his deep, narrow yard, he reminded us of a man-beast caged up in some anthropo-zoological gardens.

Scarcely had we passed this one, before our eye fell upon another prisoner, whose more "respectable" features and figure, as well as silver hair, told that he did not belong to the ordinary convict class; and though we could not but consider his sentence an honour and glory to the unswerving justice of the country, as proving the falsity of there being one law for the rich and another for the poor, nevertheless, we could not, at the same time, refrain from sympathising with the misery and shame of those innocent relatives and friends whom the crime of this wretched man has involved in utter social ruin.

It forms no part of our office to pander to the idle curiosity of the public as to how a titled criminal may bear himself in prison, and as we knew that every word we penned on the subject would be gall and wormwood to the bruised hearts of those belonging to, or connected with the family, we closed our note-book before reaching the private yard where the individual was exercising, and turned our head away, so that even he might not fancy that we had come to exult over, and make still more public, his degradation.

₂ *Arrival of Convicts.*—At a little before nine, A.M., the men return from their morning's exercise and prayer, and the corridors, which have remained for nearly an hour drained of all their inmates, begin to swarm again with prisoners, as the men come pouring back from the yards and chapel; and then the arcades, and galleries, and staircases are once more lined with the masked convict troops filing along, one after another, as rapidly as they can stride towards their separate cells.

At nine o'clock the parade of the prison officers takes place.

recent years as regards the reduction of the cases of mental disorder, *the limits of safety have scarcely yet been reached*.

To Mr. Bradley, again, the merit seems to be due of recommending that the daily amount of out-door exercise should be increased, and that such exercise should be of a healthy and exhilarating character rather than the monotonous and listless walk of separate yards, as formerly practised at the prison.

Now such statements and figures, it will be observed, are at variance with the strictures of our correspondent; and we can but add that, when authorities disagree, it is our duty to state the two cases as fairly as possible, and leave the public to decide.

"Fall in!" cries the chief warder as the hour is striking, and instantly the twenty and odd officers draw themselves up in a double line across the centre corridor. They are habited in their glazed caps and short work-day jackets, that are not unlike a policeman's coat shorn of its tails, and ornamented with a small brass crown on the stand-up collar, whilst each wears a broad black leathern belt round the waist, with a shiny cartouche-box for his prison keys projecting from the hip.

No sooner are the men arranged in military lines than the head warder shouts—"Stand at ease!—Eyes front!—Rear rank fall back!" and instantly the officers behind step a pace backwards, their feet moving as one man. The chief warder passes between the ranks, and when he has finished his inspection of the warders, cries again—"Rear rank, forward!" whereupon the men behind draw close up to the rank in front, and then the head officer proceeds to read over the regulations and duties for the next day; after which he shouts "Break!" and immediately the warders disperse to their several quarters—the regulations just read over being placed on the desk in the centre corridor for the inspection of the officers throughout the day.

Presently a man appears carrying a letter-box, with a padlock at its side and a slit at the top. The one we saw was marked B, for it was the receiving-box for the corridor so inscribed, and contained the convicts' letters to their friends, which had been just collected from that division of the prison.

"That box, sir," said the warder who acted as our guide, "is taken to the chaplain, who reads the letters in it, and after that to the governor, who does the same; and if they are found to contain nothing improper or contrary to the prison rules, they are despatched to the prisoners' friends. The schoolmaster supplies the men with the paper," continued our informant, "and the prisoner writing to his friends says, over night, to the officer on duty, 'I shall have a letter to send to-morrow morning.'" *

* The following are the official regulations respecting the sending and receiving of letters by convicts, and which are usually printed on the first page of the letter-paper supplied to them:—

"*Convicts are permitted to write one letter on reception, and another at the end of three months. They may also receive one letter (prepaid) every three months during their stay. Matters of private importance to a convict may be communicated at any time by letter (prepaid) to the Governor or Chaplain, who will inform the convict thereof, if expedient.*

"*In case of misconduct, the privilege of receiving or writing a letter may be forfeited for the time.*

"*All letters of an improper or idle tendency, either to or from convicts, or containing slang or other objectionable expressions, will be suppressed. The permission to write and receive letters is given to the convicts for the purpose of enabling them to keep up a connection with their respectable friends, and not that they may hear the news of the day.*

"*All letters are read by the Governor or Chaplain, and must be legibly written, and not crossed.*

"*Neither clothes, money, nor any other articles are allowed to be received at the prison for the use of convicts, except through the Governor. Persons attempting otherwise to introduce any article to or for a convict, are liable to fine or imprisonment, and the convict concerned is liable to be severely punished.*"

By way of showing the kind of letters written by convicts of the better class, we here append one from a youth who had been imprisoned for defrauding his employer. It is headed by the subjoined official instructions:—"The convict's writing to be confined to the two inner pages. In writing to the convict, direct to No.— C—— J——." The letter itself is as follows:—

"MY DEAR MOTHER

"I am sorry that you should have been kept waiting so long to hear from me but the reason is because I wanted to let you know what Mr. D—— said and I did not hear from him until last Monday and he did not answer my letter sooner because he had been waiting to see if he could hear of anything that would suit me and he says he was sorry that he had not at that time he seems to think that it would be advisable not to return to L —— and he also says that he should have no objections to employ me as far as he himself is concerned but that is business concerns other people so much that they might not think it advisable he wishes me well and hopes you may be able to meet with something to suit me I was recommended for my liberty last Saturday but cannot say to a month when I shall come home when called upon by the Chaplain I could

By a curious coincidence, it so happened that we were able to witness the arrival as well as the departure of a batch of convicts in the course of the same day; and early on the morning of our visit we had seen placed in the corridor bundles of clothes, which we were told had been sorted ready for the coming prisoners from Millbank.

Pentonville Prison, it should here be observed, is a kind of probationary asylum, where convicts are qualified, either for transportation abroad, or for duty at the public works at home, such as Woolwich, Portsmouth, Portland, &c.; indeed, it is a kind of penal purgatory, where men are submitted to the chastisement of separate confinement, so as to fit them for the after state. Originally, the Model Prison was designed as a convict academy for transports, where the inmates were not only to be taught a trade that would be a means of subsistence to them in the colonies, but where a certain moral, if not religious, impression was to be made upon them, in order to render them good members of the new society they were about to enter upon; and, in the first years of the working of this institution, the prisoners used to be fitted out in a kind of sailors' costume, and assembled in the central corridor, in their straw hats, and with their "kits" at their side, previous to their departure for the convict ship.

Since the comparative abolition of the transport system, however, the convicts *leaving* Pentonville are sent either to Portsmouth (as we have seen), or else to Woolwich or to Portland, according as men are wanted at one or other of those establishments. On the other hand, convicts *arriving* at Pentonville come from Millbank, which prison now serves as a kind of *depôt* for the reception of convicts generally, and whither they are sent from the several detentional prisons after they have been found guilty, and sentenced for the offences with which they were charged.

Early in the forenoon of the day that we passed at Pentonville, we were informed that the expected new batch of convicts was outside the gates; and that, if we would step towards the court-yard, we could see them received at the doors.

We found the governor, with the chief warder and other officers, assembled on the steps at the end of the prison hall. As soon as we reached the spot a whistle was given, and, the outer gates being thrown back, we saw some omnibuses drawn up in the large portcullis porch without. Then the doors of the several vehicles were opened, and out came a string of some ten convicts from each of the carriages.

The miserable wretches were chained together by the wrists in lines, after the same fashion as we have already described. Some were habited in the ordinary light snuff-brown convict suits, and others wore gray jackets, all having Scotch caps, and small bundles of Bibles and hymn-books, tied in handkerchiefs, under their arm; whilst all the articles they wore—jacket, trousers, cap, and even their gray stockings—were marked by the red stripe which is characteristic of all convict apparel; for not only are the clothes, but even the sheets and flannels of the Government prisons so distinguished.

On descending from the omnibus, the new prisoners were drawn up in five rows on one side of the court-yard. They were of all ages—from mere boys to old men of between fifty and sixty. Nor were their expressions of features less various; some looked, as a physiognomist would say, "really bad fellows," whilst others appeared to have even a "respectable" cast of

only give yourself as a reference and the Governor told me on Saturday that I had a good one come I shall be here to write another letter and think to be at home the beginning of April but perhaps can tell more about it in my next

"Wishing you all well I conclude with my kindest love to my dear brothers sisters relations and friends and accept the same dear Mother yourself

"I remain,

"Your affectionate and loving Son,

"Please to write soon God bless you " "Cs. J————.

The writer of the above letter has since been liberated on "license," and been provided with a situation, through the kindness of one of our own friends. He seems likely to go on well.

countenance, the features being well formed rather than coarse, and the expression marked by frankness rather than cunning, so that one could not help wondering what hard pressure of circumstances had brought *them* there. It did not require much skill in detecting character to pick out the habitual offender from the casual criminal, or to distinguish the simple, broad brown face of the agricultural convict from the knowing, sharp, pale features of the town thief.

"That's the youngest boy I ever saw in this prison," said one of the warders, as he pointed to a convict-lad among the troop, who seemed scarcely fourteen years of age.

"No wonder we get them here so young," exclaimed the chief warder, "for late last evening I saw three boys stuffed in a hole under the railway, just where the man has a fire in the day-time to roast his nuts and apples, so that the place is a little warm at night for the poor things."

Here an officer, with a gold-lace band round his cap, marking him as the principal warder who had come with the convict batch, stepped forward and delivered his papers to the Pentonville authorities.

"You see," said the governor to us, "the officer from Millbank brings us the caption-papers, with the sentence and order of Court, as well as the certificates of conduct in connection with each man during his imprisonment, so that we may know all the antecedents of those we receive. Then we give a receipt for the bodies on the warrant of the Secretary of State, a duplicate of which has been lodged with us some days previously."

"Please to unlock them," said the Pentonville chief warder to the Millbank officer; and instantly the official with the gold-lace band proceeded to do as requested, whilst the other Millbank officers drew the stout curb-chain through the holes of the handcuffs, and so detached the prisoners one from the other.

Then the governor's clerk called over the names of the men contained in the Secretary of State's warrant; and as the convicts cried, "Here, sir!" they passed over, one after another, to the other side of the yard.

After this the medical officer inspected the new prisoners, even though he had been furnished with a certificate that the convicts sent were "free from infectious or contagious disease, and fit to be removed."

"Are you in good health?" the doctor asks of each man, as he walks along the line with a note-book in his hand, and ready to enter any answer to the contrary—"Are you in good health?" and if the reply be in the affirmative, the man is dismissed to the reception wards below, there to pass through the other preliminary examinations.

On the day on which we were present there were but one or two men among the fresh arrivals who complained of being sickly, and one of these was a ghastly, featureless spectacle from syphilis.

"What can we do with *such* a man here?" said the doctor, turning to us.

"Can you read, my man?" he asked of another prisoner, the "facial angle" of whose head showed him to be a man of low intellect. "No, sir," was the answer, "but I know my letters." "And he will never know anything more," added the medical officer in an under-tone, when he had dismissed the prisoner, "for he is one of the men we often get here that no teaching on earth could instruct."

"Do you find the convicts generally persons of inferior understanding?" asked we.

"*Generally* speaking, I should say certainly," was the cautious reply. "There are exceptions, of course; but as a body, I consider them to be *badly developed* people. Yonder, however, is one of the contradictions we occasionally meet with," whispered the medical officer to us.

The man the doctor alluded to was a person of a highly intellectual cast of countenance, and, what struck us as being more peculiar, his forehead was not only broad and high, but the head bald—for it is rather an extraordinary circumstance, that when the convicts at a Government prison are mustered altogether, as in chapel, we seldom or never see one bald or gray head among the 400 or 500 individuals that may be there assembled.

On inquiry, the new prisoner proved to be a German "physician," or natural philosopher (for in Germany the term physician is used in a different sense from what it is in England), belonging to Berlin. He had been sentenced for stealing a portmanteau at a railway station, and not only tried under a false name, but refused to give any information as to his friends.

The medical officer then informed us that they were often awkwardly situated with the foreigners sent to the prison. A little while ago there had been two Chinamen there, and among the "batch" that we saw arrive, there were, besides the German physician above alluded to, no less than three Frenchmen; there was, moreover, a Spaniard already in the prison, who called himself a physician, and who, being unable to speak English, communicated with the doctor in a kind of Spanish dog-Latin.*

When the medical officer has finished his examination of the fresh prisoners, the governor proceeds below to say a few words to the men, as to the rules and regulations of the prison.

We accompanied the governor down to the reception ward for this purpose, and there found the convicts drawn up partly in a narrow passage, and partly in a small room at the side. The address was at once dignified and kindly. The governor told the men that he hoped they would conform to the distressing circumstances in which they had placed themselves, and save him the pain of punishing them for a breach of the prison rules. It was his duty, he said, to see those rules strictly carried out, and he made a point of never swerving from it. At that prison, all intercommunication among prisoners was strictly forbidden, and though some might think an infringement of this rule a trivial offence, nevertheless the authorities could not look upon it in such a light, and therefore an attempt on the part of any man to hold communion with his fellow-prisoners would be immediately punished. But if there were punishments, the men would find that there were rewards also; and these rewards were open to any prisoner to gain by good conduct, without the least favour. They would find, too, that exemplary behaviour would serve them, not only in that prison, but in the one to which they might be sent hereafter; so he trusted they would spare him the exercise of the painful duty of punishing, and allow him the more pleasant office of rewarding them there, so that he might give them each a first-class character when they left, and thus render their imprisonment as light as it possibly could be made consistently with public duty.

When the governor had finished his oration, the chaplain came and spoke to them also. His address was of a more *touching* character; for the clergyman said he was well aware what a sad trial it was for them to be parted from all their friends, and it was the most painful part of his office to be visited by the relatives of prisoners—to witness the heavy affliction that convicts brought upon their families by their disgrace and punishment. He begged of them, therefore, to conduct themselves well, and to turn their thoughts to the one Great Being who was still ready to receive and welcome them to a share of His love; and to remember that though all the world might shun them in their shame, and that though they

---

* The medical officer of Pentonville obliged us with the last letter he had received from this Spanish convict. It ran as follows:—

"Abitavid in est domo non manducavid sine panis et potatorum, caro non posum masticare, et debilitacio apod eravid ore et enfirmetas aumentaverum, ego volo si posum sine manducare ad expensas meas, abeo domus et terras cui sua productione dad suficiens rentam; enfirmetas meas sunt anticuarum, ego abeo metodum (almor) in iniectionem aquarum malv: calida (reumats) Lac cum decoctum Sarsparill calidum et multarum rerum."

We append as literal a translation as is possible of the above jargon:—

"I have lived in this house, not eating anything except bread and potatoes—flesh I cannot chew, and my debility and infirmities augment. I wish, if I can, to eat at my own expense. I have houses and lands, the produce (or income) of which gives a sufficient rent. My infirmities are ancient; I have a method—or system of cure—(*almor*) in an injection of water of mallows hot (*rheum*), milk with a decoction of sarsaparilla hot, and many things."

had hardly one friend left to say a kindly word for them, there was One who had suffered on earth for their sakes, and who was ever ready to plead for mercy—where mercy was most needed—in their behalf. He hoped that they would all do this, so that when their friends came or wrote to him, to learn some tidings of them, he might be able to soothe their anguish with the assurance that they had become better men, and might still live to be a comfort and a joy to those upon whose heads they had, as yet, only brought down shame and sorrow.

We watched the men intently while the tender exhortation was being delivered to them, and when the chaplain spoke of their friends and relatives, they one and all hung their heads, whilst some, we could see, bit their lip to stay the rising tear; and when the speech was finished, there was many a moistened eye, and many a cry of "Bless you, sir!" as the minister took his leave.

After the new-comers had been spoken to as above by the governor and chaplain, they were ordered into two small rooms in the same part of the building as that in which they had been addressed; and on our returning to the "reception-room" a few moments after-wards, we heard the buzz of many voices, and found the men chattering away as hard as school boys in play-time, for they knew it was the last talk they would be able to indulge in for the next three-quarters of a year; whilst outside the door was an officer giving notice to the men that they would not be allowed to take anything into the prison but their Bibles and Prayer-books.

"Have any of you got any letters, or locks of hair, or anything else to give up?" cried the officer, as he put his head into the room; "for if they're found on you in the prison they'll be destroyed."

"I've got a letter," exclaimed one, holding out a piece of paper, and as he handed over the article, the officer proceeded to write on the back the owner's name, and to deposit it in a tray by his side. The warder then told us that the various packets collected would be put under the care of the steward, who kept a book of all that was entrusted to him, and on the convicts' leaving, the articles would be either restored or transferred to the prison to which they might be sent. He added, that the prisoners set great store upon such things, and that numbers of them entered the prison with locks of hair hung round their neck. "There are several locks there, you see, sir, that I have collected already," said the warder, pointing to some small packets done up after the fashion of "kisses" at a confectioner's.

By this time the usual preliminary bath was ready, whilst the other end of the passage was filled with a white fog of steam as thick as that pervading a laundry.

Then began the examination of the prisoners previous to bathing. For this purpose they were had out into the passage one by one, as soon as they had stripped themselves of their clothes, and made to stand before the officer in a perfect state of nudity, while he examined every part of their person.

"There now, place your feet on the mat. What's the use of you're going on the cold stones when there's a rug put for you?" exclaimed the officer in an authoritative tone. "Now, open your mouth," he continued, when the prisoner had stationed himself as directed, "and lift up your tongue. Did I say *put out* your tongue, man? Lift it up, don't you hear?" whereupon the officer proceeded to spy into the open jaws of the convict, as closely as a magpie does down a bone; and when he had satisfied himself that there was no money nor anything else secreted within it, he moved to the back of the man and cried, "Bend your head down!" and then commenced examining the roots of the prisoner's hair, as well as behind his ears. This done, the next order was, "Hold up your arms!" and then the naked man raised his hands high above his head, one after the other, while the officer assured himself that he had nothing hidden there.

After this, the convict was commanded to place himself on all fours, so as to rest on his hands and feet, and then to raise his legs one at a time, so that the warder might see whether anything were concealed under his toes.

"There, that'll do. Clap this rug over your shoulders and run away to the bath," added the official, when the examination was concluded.

"We can't be too careful, sir," said the warder, turning to us, as he held up the man's Bible by the covers, and proceeded to shake the pendent leaves backwards and forwards, in order to satisfy himself that nothing had been inserted between the pages. "Sometimes a piece of silver has been found stowed away in a man's mouth, and some convicts have been known to bring in keys and pick-locks hidden about their bodies in the most inconceivable places."

The next process was the bathing, and as we entered the bath-room we found the floor strewn with bundles of clothes, and a prisoner, with his hair wet and clinging in matted "pencils" about his face, busy dressing himself in the Pentonville flannels, shirt, and stockings, and with a couple of warders in large aprons standing by. In the adjoining bath-room was another convict splashing about in the warm-bath, and evidently enjoying the luxury of the brief immersion in the hot water.

"There, go outside into the passage and get your coat and trousers," said the warder to the man who was half-dressed; whilst to the naked one, who came running along with a rug over his shoulders, he cried, "In you go, and look sharp!" as he beckoned him towards the bath and ordered the other to come out.

On the opposite side of the passage to the bath-room the governor's clerk and another were busy making out the register-number for each of the new-comers, and examining the men and their papers previous to entering their names on the prison books, as well as assigning to them their several trades.

On entering this room we found the boy that the chief warder had before drawn our attention to, as being the youngest lad that had ever been confined within the walls of that prison, undergoing his examination. In his caption-papers he was marked sixteen years of age, but certainly did not look fourteen. He had been imprisoned twelve times for one month, two months, and so on up to twelve months, and was now sentenced to four years' penal servitude for stealing a handkerchief value one shilling. He had all the sharp, cunning appearance of the habitual London thief, and as he spoke he feigned a simplicity that you could see, by the curl and quivering at the corners of his mouth, required but the least frivolous word to make him break through and burst into laughter.

The next convict who entered belonged to the agricultural class, and he had been sentenced to four years' penal service also, for stealing a broom and a pair of leathern mittens. "What have you been?" inquired one of the clerks of the man. "A gardener," was the brief and timid reply. "Ever worked at anything else?" was the next question. "Always at that kind of work," the man answered. "Been in prison before?" "Yes, sir." "Learn anything there?" "I learnt mat-making, if you please, sir." "Can you make a mat?" "Well, I'll try, sir." Whereupon the man was dismissed.

The trades carried on in Pentonville Prison, we were told, consisted of weaving, mat-making, tailoring, and shoemaking; and, in the distribution of these employments, the officers look principally to the physical and mental capabilities of the convicts. Strong, broad-shouldered men are put to weaving and to mat-making, whilst the more feeble class of prisoners are set to work as tailors.

At Pentonville the authorities make four distinct classes of prisoners. (1) The dangerous men, or those that are notorious prison-breakers, and convicts of known desperate characters; (2) Second probation men, or those unruly prisoners who have been sent back from the public works to undergo another term of separate confinement; (3) Ordinary "separate men," or those who are working out their first probation of nine months; and (4) The associated men, or those who, having conducted themselves well while in separation, are allowed to work in company with other well-conducted convicts.

There are, moreover, prisoners of first, second, and third class characters, according to their behaviour during their term of incarceration. The first class constitutes by far the largest proportion, and consists generally of the well-educated embezzlers and forgers, as well as the more ignorant agricultural prisoners, together with the first-offence men, and the old jail-birds. The second class characters mostly belong to the more thoughtless and careless of the convicts, who are carried away by temptation or temper; whilst the third class characters usually appertain to the self-willed and refractory boys, who are from 15 to 25 years of age.*

Again, as regards the mental qualifications of the convicts, they are divided into first, second, and third class men. The first class consists of prisoners who have no necessity to go to school, being able, not only to read and write well, but acquainted with arithmetic as far as the rule of proportion. The second class comprises men who can read and write, and work sums as far as the compound rules; whereas the third class men are those who are imperfectly educated, and whose arithmetical knowledge extends no farther than the simple rules. This third class again is sub-divided into three sub-classes; the first of which includes those who can read and write, and do the simple rules in arithmetic, whilst to the second belong such as are learning the simple rules, and the third comprises all who can read, write, and cypher only imperfectly, or not at all.

Of the well-educated class of prisoners the proportion is about 14 per cent. of the whole; of the moderately-educated class there is not quite 8 per cent.; whilst the imperfectly-educated prisoners average very nearly 80 per cent.†

---

* We were present on another occasion, when some 24 prisoners, who were going away to Portland on the following morning, were had into the governor's room, so that he might say a few words to them previous to their departure. Of these, 21 were about to leave with first class characters, whilst only two had second class ones, and the remaining prisoner a third class. Among the first-class prisoners, there were 4 who had been sentenced for 6 years, one for 5, one for 8, one for 21, and one for life, whilst the majority had been condemned to 4 years' penal service. Among the number, too, one had been in prison six times before, and another seven; but few had been punished while at Pentonville, and of these only two had been punished more than once; one of these two, however, had been seven times in the dark cell. The first class men were told that their good conduct would serve them where they were going to, and that they would find it to their welfare to strive and keep the good character they had earned. The two with the second class characters were mere boys, and they were had in separately, and exhorted to behave better for the future; whilst the other, having the third class character, was likewise spoken to alone, and entreated to try and be a good lad at the place he was going to; whereupon he said that he had made up his mind to turn over a new leaf. This boy was far from ill-looking, and his expression betokened no depraved nature. He had come to Pentonville, however, with a bad character from Birmingham; still the governor told us that he did not believe the lad to be utterly vicious, but weak and wayward in character. "If [he falls in with boys, he will most likely turn out badly, but if he gets among sensible men, he may do well enough," were the governor's observations to us on the lad's leaving.

† Mr. Wilson, the schoolmaster of Pentonville Prison, was kind enough to prepare the following return for us in connection with this part of the subject:—

RETURN SHOWING THE PER CENTAGE OF PRISONERS BELONGING TO EACH OF THE SCHOOL CLASSES IN
PENTONVILLE PRISON.

	No. of Scholars in every 100.
Belonging to the first class (or those who can read and write well and cypher as far as the rule of proportion)	. 14
Belonging to the second class (or those who can read and write well, and cypher as far as the compound rules)	. 6·75
Belonging to the third class (or those whose arithmetical knowledge extends no farther than the simple rules)—	
Belonging to the first sub-class (or those who can work the simple rules of arithmetic)	17·75
Belonging to the second sub-class (or those who are learning the simple rules of arithmetic)	. 41·75
Belonging to the third sub-class (or those who can read, write, and cypher only imperfectly, or not at all)	. 19·75
	——— 79·25

N.B.—The above average is deduced from four hundred examples.   100·00

∗ *Prison Work and Gratuities.*—We have already spoken incidentally of the work done by the Pentonville prisoners, and we shall now proceed to set forth the details in connection with that part of our subject.

As early as half-past six, A.M., the prison labour begins, and continues throughout the day—with the intervals of meal time, and the chapel service, as well as the period set apart for exercise—up to seven o'clock, P.M.

The trades carried on within the "Model Prison," consist of weaving and mat-making, occupations which are pursued principally in the lower wards; tailoring, at which the prisoners on the first tier are set to work; and shoemaking, in which trade the men on the upper tier are generally engaged. In addition to these, there are a few convicts employed as carpenters and blacksmiths, and to them the "shops" in the basement of C division are devoted, whilst there are still some others working as cooks, bakers, and cleaners, besides a few bricklayers employed in the grounds.*

The labour at Pentonville, owing to the monotony of separate confinement is, as we said before, so far from being looked upon as a punishment, regarded rather as an indulgence by the generality of prisoners, so that one of the penal inflictions in that institution is to stop a man's work.

"There are *some* men, however," said the warder to us, as we walked through the various work-shops, "who are so naturally averse to all kinds of employment, that they would rather lie down like pigs than be put to any labour. 'If you don't do your work quicker and better,' perhaps an officer may say to such men, 'I shall report you.' '*Do!*' they'll answer, 'that's just what I want, for then I shall have a little rest.'

"With the greater part of the men, however," continued our attendant, "an occupation attracts a man's mind, and he gets to feel a bit proud of his abilities when he finds he's able to do something for himself, even though it's only to make a pair of shoes, or to turn out a few yards of cloth. He seems to think himself more of a man directly he knows he's got some trade at his fingers' ends at which he can earn a living, if he likes, when his time's up.†

The sentences of the prisoners confined at Pentonville in the year 1854 were as follows, out of a total of 387 prisoners :—

210 men, or 54·2 per cent. of the whole, were sentenced to 7 years' transportation.

94	,,	24·3	,,	,,	10	,,
33	,,	8·5	,,	,,	15	,,
15	,,	3·9	,,	,,	14	,,
14	,,	3·6	,,	,,	transportation for life.
1	,,	0·3	,,	,,	12 years' transportation.
1	·,	0·3	,,	,,	20	,,
1	,,	0·3	,,	,,	21	,,
15	,,	3·9	,,	,,	4 years' penal servitude.
3	,,	0·7	,,	,,	5	,,

387   100·0

* In the year 1854, the distribution of trades among the Pentonville prisoners was as follows :—

Out of a gross average of 523 convicts employed throughout the year, there were 181, or 34 per cent., occupied as tailors ; 108, or 21 per cent., working as shoemakers ; 107, or 20 per cent., as weavers ; 81, or 16 per cent., as matmakers ; 30, or 6 per cent., as bricklayers, carpenters, smiths, &c. ; whilst the remaining 16, or 3 per cent., were sick, and put to no employment whatever.

Moreover, of the gross average of 523 prisoners, about 456, or 87 per cent., were at work in a state of separation from the others, and the remaining 67, or 13 per cent., placed in association ; whilst of the 67 "associated men," 4 were tailors, 4 shoemakers, 7 weavers, 5 mat-makers, 4 carpenters, 5 cooks, 4 bakers, 13 were at work at other trades on medical grounds ; 7 were sick in the infirmary, and 11 were other prisoners working in the cleaning department.

† The great defect of the industrial training at Pentonville is, that it leads to no definite end. The "Model Prison" was originally designed, as we have seen, as a kind of moral and industrial school for con-

At half-past six, as we said, the trade-instructors go round the several wards to see whether the men have sufficient work, though enough is usually given out by them on the preceding day to last the prisoners till eight or ten o'clock the next morning; and early in the forenoon, as we went our rounds with the warder, we found, lying on the asphalte pavement in one of the corridors, two large bright-coloured mats, like hearth-rugs; these were the work, we were told, of the man in the neighbouring cell.

"He's only been four months at mat-making, sir," said the trade-warder to us; "and yet he's very clever at it now—isn't he?"

victs intended for transportation to the colonies; and yet the trades which the men were taught there were precisely those that were the least of all needed in young countries, since the products of the weavers', tailors', and shoemakers' crafts admit of being imported from other parts, so that there is necessarily but little demand in those countries for such forms of labour; and, notwithstanding farming and agricultural work are naturally the most desirable and valuable of all occupations in primitive states, these were exactly the employments that were *not* taught at the Model, even though at the time of its erection there was no deficiency of land in the neighbourhood.

But if the forms of labour taught at Pentonville were ill-adapted to the requirements of the convicts in the first instance, they are worse than useless as a means of benefiting them at present; for now that the transportation of offenders has been comparatively abolished, and our convicts are mostly sent to the public works at home, either to labour in the quarries, or to do mere manual work in the arsenal and dockyards, where on earth can be the good of giving prisoners a nine months' course in tailoring, shoemaking, or weaving, previous to going to such places? The main object, we fancy, of teaching men trades in prison is (apart from making them contribute to their own support), to furnish them with a means of subsistence on their leaving jail. This should, under a high system of prison discipline, always constitute one of the principal ends in view, viz., to convert a member of the community, who is not only valueless, but positively an incumbrance to the state, into a productive agent, and so make him individually contribute some little to, rather than abstracting a considerable quantity from, the general stock of wealth. Such an end, however, can only be attained by long-continued industrial training and teaching, and certainly not by putting men to school for nine months at handicrafts which require several years' hard practice before any proficiency can be attained in them, and afterwards setting these incipient tailors, shoemakers, and weavers to dig, drag, break stones, or quarry, according to the exigencies of the public works. What amount of skill, for instance, can possibly be acquired in the arts of tailoring, shoemaking, or weaving, after working for only three-quarters of a year at the craft? The instruction in such trades, so far from elevating a man into the dignity of a skilled labourer, degrades him to the level of the slop-worker; and we have known many such who, on leaving jail, served only to swell the ranks of those rude and inexperienced work-people, who become the prey of the cheap Jew manufacturers, and who, consequently, are made the means of dragging down the earnings of the better-class workman, while they themselves do not get even scavengers' wages at the labour. Again, some convicts learn in prison only just sufficient of carpenters' or smiths' work to render them adepts in the art of housebreaking, though mere bunglers in the fashioning of wood or metal into useful forms; and we know one "cracksman" who learnt his *trade* as a burglar at the Government works at Bermuda. Surely, however, when convicts are sentenced to *several years'* penal servitude, the time might be profitably employed in *perfecting* them in some *one* handicraft, rather than putting them for a few months to an art, and then keeping them for several years afterwards at the ruder forms of manual labour. If it be thought expedient to employ convicts at the dockyards and the arsenal, assuredly in the ten years' penal servitude that many of the men have to undergo, there would be time enough to render them experienced and skillful ship-wrights, or anchor-smiths, or cannon-founders, or sail-makers; so that not only might they be made to take part in the building or fitting of our ships, but at the expiration of their sentence they would be proficients in a trade that would at once yield them a considerable income, and be an attractive and honourable art for them to pursue; whilst to those convicts who had conducted themselves well during their servitude, the Government might offer, on their liberation, to continue their employment at the wages of free men.

Indeed, until some such industrial schools be established for *perfecting* dexterous prisoners in the higher forms of labour, in which Government itself has the means of finding employment for them when liberated, there can be but little hope of reducing the criminal population of the country, or of preventing those who have been once or twice in prison continually returning to it. The experience of Pentonville is so far satisfactory that it shows a strong desire on the part of the convicts to be made acquainted with the skilled forms of labour, as well as great aptitude for learning such matters, for all the prison authorities there agree, that the majority of the convicts get to think more highly of themselves, and to have a greater sense of self-reliance, when they find that they are able to produce the smallest article of utility; so that it is really lamentable to see such experience wasted as it is at the present day.

"It's astonishing," rejoined our guide, "the quickness that some men display at learning their trades."

The trade-instructor proceeded to spread the rugs out upon the pavement, so that we might see them to better advantage. They were both of a kind of rude velvet pile-work, and the one had a blue ground, with a red and white pattern tastefully worked upon it, while the ground of the other was a chocolate-brown, with red and blue figures. They had been made by the same man, and the trade-instructor, we could see, was not a little proud of his pupil.

After this we were led by our guide to the shoemakers' little shop, at the corner of one of the corridors. Here, of course, there was a strong smell of leather, and the place was littered with lasts, and boots, and small stacks of soles, like cakes of gutta-percha. The officer who had charge of the shop showed us a pair of high-lows that had been made in the prison by an agricultural labourer. "He had never put stitch to leather, sir, before coming into the prison," said the official, as he twisted the boots over and over for our inspection. Then he produced a pair of convict boots with upper leathers as stiff as mill-board, and heavy soles the hob-nails upon which reminded one of a prison-door. These had been made by a farm servant who is a convict, and were worth, said the officer, "at least twelve shillings." Some men, he informed us, would do a pair of such boots in the course of a day's work at Pentonville, which was not like a day outside, he continued, on account of the many interruptions.

"It's strange," repeated our attendant warder, "how some men pick up a trade. We always find farm servants learn the quickest, and that simply because they aint above doing as they are told, like the well-educated clerks and others that we get here." The trade-instructor then produced a pair of cloth boots, with patent leather at the toes and sides; these had been made, he told us, by one who was not a very good hand when he came to the prison, but had so far improved as to turn out a pair of boots like those, which would pass muster in many a shop."

Next we were shown a pair with elastic sides. "A farm-labouring lad closed that pair," he went on, "and a regular shoemaker (who is in the prison) finished them."

After this we descended to the steward's stores in the basement of the building. Here we found immense rolls of the peculiar gingerbread-coloured convict cloth, with a red stripe in it; and there was the usual woollen-drapery smell clinging to the place.

"We supply all the Government prisons, sir, with the convict cloth," said the store-keeper; "and in some years we weave upwards of 50,000 yards here. But we not only weave the cloth, sir—we make up the clothes as well; and in the year 1853 the tailors here turned out more than 5,000 jackets, 4,000 vests, and nearly 7,000 trousers, besides repairing 4,500 old ones; and that isn't such a very bad allowance of work, seeing that we had only 150 tailors in the prison.

"Perhaps you've seen some of the shoes we make here, sir?" continued the store-keeper, as he grew proud of the prison labour.

"That's what I call a good, strong, useful article," exclaimed the clerk, as he produced a pair of the heavy convict boots before described; "and it's quite a credit to the men how readily they take to the work. A year or two ago, sir, we manufactured very nearly 5,000 pairs of boots and shoes for the Government prisons."

Then the attendant drew our attention to some really handsome mats and rugs, the surface of which was almost like Utrecht velvet. "Some of those, sir, I call uncommon tasty things," continued the official, "and such as no regular factory might be ashamed of. Our average manufacture here is about 4,000 of those bordered mats and rugs, and about 2,000 of those 'double-thrumb' there," he added, as he directed our attention to a commoner sort. "Yes, sir, a man gets to see his value when he begins to do such things as those. Besides this, we make up all the hammocks for the men at the Hulks and at Chatham."

"Have you got a hammock you can let the gentleman see?" asked the guide of the storekeeper.

"Oh, yes! certainly," was the willing reply, as the man hurried off to produce one of the convict beds.

"There, now, that's a really good, strong, serviceable hammock, sir, as good a one as could be bought in the shops. It's for Chatham, I believe; for I know we've got an order for that place. Last year we made up more than 500 hammocks here, and fitted the heads and supplied double the number of straps and girths. Our shoemakers make the one, and the tailors the others. Then, again, we manufacture all the check-lining, and all the twill for the convicts' handkerchiefs, besides about 10,000 yards of shirting for the prisoners, and some 5,000 yards of sheeting and towelling as well. Yes, sir, everything made for the convicts has a red stripe in it—sheets, stockings, towels, flannels, and all. We make those bed-rugs, too, sir," added the officer, pointing up to a roll of yellowish-brown counterpanes, that were packed above the large presses. "We supply all the convict prisons with those rugs. We make, indeed, almost every bit of clothing that the convicts require. The work makes a man think more of himself than if he could do nothing."

We inquired as to the time it took for the convicts to learn the different trades.

"Now that twill, sir, is beautifully done; and a man will do such an one after two months teaching," was the reply. "I don't think that the prisoner who made that has been quite so long here. In three months we reckon that a man ought to be able to sew all prison garments, or, if he's been put to shoemaking, to make the prison boots and shoes. Some do it in less time, and some never do it at all. In each ward, you see, sir," continued the storekeeper, "there is a discipline officer that we call the trade-instructor, or trade-warder, and he has to take part in the prison discipline as well as to teach the men their work; and for that purpose he has to see his prisoner in his cell as often as he can, and to show him how to do the work, as well as to observe how he gets on. We've got twelve such instructors here, sir, and they take their turn at watching every sixth night, as well as the regular warders—they're on duty from six in the morning until six at night, just the same as the other officers."

In answer to a question of ours as to whether the prisoners received any reward for their labour, and whether they had a certain task or quantity of work given out to them, the official informed us that after a man had been six months in the prison, and he had obtained a badge for good conduct, he was entitled to receive a certain gratuity, which varied from fourpence to eightpence a week, according to the work done.* "This gratuity," he added,

---

* We subjoin the official regulations concerning the remuneration given to the prisoners for their work :—
"The following Rules and Scale for Regulating Gratuities to Convicts in Separate Confinement for work performed will be for the present in force :—

"1. Prisoners who have passed six months in the prison, and whose good conduct entitles them to a badge, will be credited with gratuities according to the following scale, viz. :—

Trade or Occupation.	4d. per Week.	6d. per Week.	8d. per Week.
Shoemakers (work equal to) .	2½ pairs of Shoes	3 pairs	4 pairs
Tailors ,, .	2 suits of Prison Garments	3 suits	4 suits
Mat-workers ,, .	36 square feet (red bordered)	45 square feet	54 square feet
Cloth-weavers ,, .	33 yards of Prison Cloth, in-cluding winding bobbins	36 yards	42 yards
Cotton weavers ,, .	24 yards	30 yards	36 yards
Cotton Handkerchiefs .	2 dozen Handkerchiefs	2½ dozen	3 dozen

Carpenters .⎫
Smiths . . ⎬ according to industry and superior workmanship.
Other Trades ⎭
Cooks . . .⎫ 8d. per week.
Bakers . . ⎭
Washers . . 6d.   ,,

"is placed to the convict's account in the prison books, and transferred to the public works when he leaves here, so that it goes to form a fund for him on the expiration of his term of imprisonment. Some long-sentence men have as much as £20 to receive on getting their liberty, and then they have a good suit of clothes given to them as well—according to their station—in order that they may have a fair start in the world again."

"Would you like to see some of the 'liberty clothing,' sir?" inquired the storekeeper, as he pulled down a bundle of new clothes. "There, sir," he continued, "that's as genteel a paletôt as a man could wish to put on, and one in which no one could be taken for a person just fresh from a convict prison. We give such as these to men who have been clerks or better-class mechanics. We buy them, I should tell you, and they stand us in about fifteen shillings the suit. The clothing for the prisoners who have been farm servants and agricultural labourers, we mostly make ourselves. That bale of moleskin you see there," he added, pointing to a roll of mouse-coloured fustian, "is intended for those who have been labouring men, and who may be released upon ticket-of-leave."

"I know a man," chimed in our attendant warder, "who was a forger, and had seven years of it, but he got off with a ticket-of-leave, and is now earning his three pounds a week regular, at a respectable trade. It's quite wonderful what a few ticket-of-leave men come back, sir, whatever people may say."

From the store-rooms, we passed into the shops and wards for the associated prisoners.

We have before said that the A, B, and C divisions of Pentonville Prison have only three wards in connection with them, whilst the D division has four, viz.: one under-ground, or in the basement of the building, where some thirty associated prisoners have their cells. This is somewhat like a crypt, and was formerly the old refractory-ward; but since the modification of the separate system at Pentonville, and the admission of a small number of the best-conducted prisoners to associated labour, the lower part of the prison has been devoted to this purpose.

"It's only the very well-behaved men that we put into association, sir," said the warder who still accompanied us on our rounds; "we very rarely allow prisoners to associate who have been even so much as once reported; and it's merely on medical grounds if we *do* occasionally break through the rules. The cleaners you saw this morning, sir," continued the officer, "and the prisoners working out in the grounds, and the carpenters and blacksmiths put to labour in the shops, under C divison, as well as the men in the bakehouse and kitchen, are all chosen from the best class of prisoners; for the liberty to labour in common, with the cap-peak up, is one of the highest rewards we have here for good conduct.

"This is the tailors' shop, or cutting-room," said our guide, as he led us down a passage out of the associated ward towards a largish room, that had a kind of dresser or shop-board along one side of it. Here we found the place littered with bales of cloth, and three prisoners at work; one seated on the board cross-legged like an Indian idol, and without shoes or braces, in true tailor fashion, whilst he stitched away at a "bespoke" waistcoat; and the other two cutting out the brown convict cloth with huge shears, the blades of which gnashed at every snip. Here, too, there was the same unpleasant smell of scorched wool, or hair, so peculiar to Sartorian establishments, and which seems to be a kind of odoriferous mixture of a washerwoman's ironing-room and a barber's shop. One of the convicts at work in this shop,

"2. No gratuity will be allowed unless the work be done to the satisfaction of the manufacturer.

"3. No prisoner on the sick list will be allowed any gratuity while unable to work.

"4. No fraction of a week can be allowed.

"5. No prisoner under punishment shall be allowed any gratuity for the week in which he may be punished.

"6. Any prisoner forfeiting his badge will cease to be credited with a gratuity until he has regained his badge; and in the event of the prisoner committing a serious offence, he may, at the discretion of the directors, be liable to forfeit all former gratuity to which he would otherwise have had a claim."

and who had formerly been employed as cutter at a large outfitting warehouse, showed us the American sewing-machine that was occasionally employed at Pentonville for stitching the seams of the prison trousers.

Hence we passed to the shop where the warps are arranged for the convict weavers, and the floor of this place was littered with baskets full of red and brown thread, whilst there were large hanks or skeins of blue and white yarn lying about. Here were four men engaged in preparing the warp for a piece of prison handkerchiefs, two were winding the threads, whilst the others were busy holding the large comb through the teeth of which the threads passed.

One of these men was of "noble family," and had been convicted for forgery in a merchant's office.

From this we went to the shop for the associated mat-makers, where the mats that are made in the cells are cut to a uniform length of pile, by means of a shearing-machine that stands in the centre of the room. The three prisoners engaged at this work were, when we entered, busy setting the spiral knives that extend from end to end along the narrow cylinder; and when the cutters were sharp enough a mat was put through and through the machine, whilst one turned the wheel and the others helped to pass the mat in and out the instrument, the air being charged with a cloud of fibres by the time the operation was finished. Here, too, were bundles of coir, and large sheep-shears for clipping the coarser kind of mats.

After this we were led back to the A division of the building, where, it was explained to us, convicts who had been nine months and more in separate confinement were placed, and allowed to work with their cell-doors open from nine till one, and from two till five every day except Sundays.* Finally, we learnt that the estimated amount of the earnings of the gross number of prisoners in Pentonville, in 1854, was, in round numbers, £2,850; whilst the gross expense of the prison was nearly £17,000;—so that the convicts at the establishment contribute not quite one-sixth to the annual cost of the establishment—indeed,

---

* We append the official rules concerning the association of those convicts who have been upwards of nine months on separate confinement :—

"Prisoners who shall have been nine months and upwards in this, or any other separate prison, since conviction, are to occupy the cells in A division, and undergo the discipline presently described.

"As a general rule they must be qualified with one or more good conduct badges; nevertheless, prisoners who shall not have been in this prison long enough to have obtained a badge—but whose good conduct, in this and other separate prisons, since conviction, would entitle them thereto, had the whole time been passed in this prison—will be eligible for the privilege.

"The loss of, or misconduct which would incur the loss of badges, if possessed, will be a disqualification.

"The cell-doors (circumstances permitting) are always, except on Sundays, to be open from 9 till 1, and from 2 till 5 o'clock. The prisoners may sit close thereto, and work with cap-peaks turned up, but not pass out of their cells or other places assigned to them, as presently mentioned; or intercommunicate, or in any way violate good order.

"Should the qualified prisoners exceed the number of cells in A division, the excess are to be brought, during the hours aforesaid, from the other divisions into the corridor of that division, and kept together according to their trades, and the divisions whence they came, but each apart at least —— feet from the others.

"These are to bring with them their necessary work-seats, tools, and implements for labour, and remove them back again on return to their cells.

"Medical prisoners (so far as circumstances permit) are to be subject to the same form of discipline, but to be kept together, and, as a body, as far apart as possible from the others.

"The manufacturer is to arrange that the prisoners generally are properly attended to and instructed in trades. Besides the proper discipline officers of A division, and the trade-warders, who impart instruction, at least two will be appointed specially to exercise supervision, to be selected alternately from the different divisions and wards, with regard to a strict equalization of time and labour.

"The prisoners are to be exercised with cap-peaks turned up, two hours, and one hour on alternate days."

the estimated value of their labour is but one-half that of their food, so that the convicts there are still far from being a self-supporting body.*

⁎ *Closing the Prison for the Night.*—The remainder of the routine at Pentonville consists merely of repetitions of processes that have been already described.

At one o'clock the prisoners dine (the principals, as usual, having taken their meal previously), and the distribution of the dinner is effected in the same manner as that of the breakfast, with the exception that it is served up from the kitchen (where each portion is regularly weighed) in wooden trays, each containing sixteen tins—not unlike the vessels in which bill-stickers carry their paste—having a division in the middle, on one side of which the potatoes are placed, and on the other the meat and soup.

This soup we were invited to try, of course, and found it far superior to the thickened trash sold at the pastry-cooks', and *really* tasting of meat instead of flour. We discovered at the same time, too, that the convicts in the infirmary were allowed their mug of porter in addition to the mutton-chop or bit of codfish that may have been ordered for their dinner.

Then at half-past five the prisoners have their supper of gruel and bread, and the work is given out by the trade-instructor for the next day. A little before six o'clock two warders go round each ward—one a-head turning the tops of the gas-pipes, whilst the other lets down the trap of each cell-door, and introduces a small lantern for the prisoner to light the jet in his cell. After this the officers assemble in the centre corridor previous to going off duty—each with his great-coat on and his keys in his hand ready to be delivered up to his principal. Then the chief warder cries, "Fall in!" and "'Tention!" as at the morning parade; whereupon, the warders being arranged in rank and file, the head officer reads over the list of prisoners who have been received that day, as well as the register-number of those who are to be specially watched on account of their having attempted to escape from other prisons.

Then the keys are collected from the discipline officers (those of the non-discipline officers—such as the cook, baker, plumber, engineer, &c.—having been given up at the gate some five minutes before), and this is done in the entrance passage, the same as during the giving of them out in the morning—the key-box being placed upon a chair, and each man proceeding to hang up his bunch on the hook assigned to him, while one of the principal warders standing by sees that the number tallies with the list on the back of the box. At this hour all but eight sets of keys are delivered in, four of which remain to be collected at the final closing of the prison at ten at night. And when the principal has satisfied himself that all the keys which should be delivered in at six are there, the box is removed to the iron-safe in the chief warder's room by way of security.

At seven o'clock in the evening, the prisoners' work is suspended, and then there is

* The annexed are the official returns in connection with this part of the subject:—

STATEMENT OF THE AVERAGE NUMBER OF PRISONERS EMPLOYED IN EACH TRADE, AND THE ESTIMATED AMOUNT OF EARNINGS PER PRISONER.

Average Number of Prisoners employed.	Trades.	Total Earnings.			Average Earnings per Prisoner.		
		£	s.	d.	£	s.	d.
181	Tailors	708	5	3½	3	18	2¾
107	Weavers	1,096	13	2	10	4	11½
108	Shoemakers	567	13	2	5	5	1¼
81	Matmakers	365	5	6¼	4	10	2⅖
30	Bricklayers, carpenters, and smiths	116	1	5	3	14	0½
16	Sick	Nil.			Nil.		
523		£2,853	18	6¾			

scarcely a sound, except that of the occasional stroke of the gong, to be heard in the corridors. From this time till nine o'clock, the prisoners are allowed to read such books as they may have obtained from the library. To show us that the men were generally so occupied, the officer who had attended us throughout the day led us now from cell to cell, and drew aside the small metal screen that hung down before the little peep-hole in each door, when, on looking through it, we found almost every prisoner whom we peeped in upon seated close to the gas-light, and busily engaged in perusing either some book or periodical that was spread out before him.

Eight o'clock is the hour for the table, tools, tub, &c., to be placed outside the cell-door of those convicts who have attempted to break out of prison; the tools and brooms of all other convicts confined within the walls are also put out at the same hour. The prison now once more resounds with the successive slamming of some hundred doors, and scarcely has this ceased before the noise is heard of the warder double-locking each prisoner's cell, while the officers are seen flitting along in the dusk of the corridors as they pass rapidly from door to door.

This done, the night-duty roll is placed upon the desk in the centre corridor, inscribed with the number of prisoners contained in each of the wards of the four divisions of the prison, together with the name of the officer attached to each of those divisions for the night.

At a quarter to nine, the last bell rings for the prisoners to prepare for bed, as well as for the dangerous or suspicious men to put out their clothes, so that in case of their breaking prison in the night they may have nothing to go away in; after this the cell-lights are extinguished, the sailor-like cutlasses that are worn by the warders during the night are brought out, and placed ready in the corner of the central corridor, whilst the warders on duty pass rapidly along, turning the tap of each gas-jet outside every cell as they go. Then the corridor lights are lowered, and the officers put on their felt overshoes, so that by the time the hour of nine sounds through the galleries, all is as still as a catacomb—the few remaining gas-lights shining in the black pavement in long, yellow, luminous lines, and the only sound heard there being the faint jangling of the warder's keys, as he moves from place to place. Nor is there any other living creature seen moving about, excepting the solitary "convict-cat" that is attached to the prison.

Now begins the inspection of every part of the building, and the trial of every outlet, in order to be assured that all is safe for the night.

We followed the principal warder on his rounds to ascertain the security of the place, and first mounted to the warders' sleeping-room, where the officers who are on duty for the night retire to rest, until the time for their watch comes on. Here in one corner was an alarum fastened to the wall; this was to rouse the warders, and had a series of pendulums marked A, B, C, D, to indicate the division of the prison whence the signal might come. The alarum was set by the principal for the night, so that the officer on duty might ring it in case of danger.

Thence we were led into the chapel with merely a bull's-eye lantern to light us by the way, and we went scrambling up the dark stairs, one after another, as hard as we could go, for there are upwards of sixty doors to see secured, and every part of the enormous building but the cells—within and without—above and below—to be visited within the hour. The chapel was pitch dark, but the warder's lantern was flickered into every corner, so that the officers might satisfy themselves that no one was hidden there.

After this we hurried away, up the clock-tower, to the chapel roof, and when we had thoroughly examined this, we hastened down again, the warders telling strange stories by the way of ingenious escapes; as to how one Hackett had cut a passage for his body through the floor of his chapel-stall during divine service, and escaped through a small hole in the wall made for the purposes of ventilation; and how, too, another convict had cast a key to fit his door out of a piece of the water-pipe in his cell, but had been detected, after opening his door, owing to the metal of the key being so soft that it bent in the lock, and rendered it impossible to be withdrawn.

Then we passed along the corridors, to try the gates and side-doors leading to the exercising grounds, and, finding these all fast, we hastened down the spiral stairs to the associated ward below; and here the warder and the principal proceeded to lock the passage doors one after another—the noise of the bolts flying, sounding in the silence under ground with a double intensity.

This done, we returned once more to the corridors, and looked to the other outlets to the exercising yards, the tramp of the feet as we went being echoed through the building, till it seemed like the march of many troops heard in the night.

Now we hastened below into the basement of corridor C, where we saw that the carpenters' and blacksmiths' shops were all safe, and examined as to whether the ladders were duly chained up for the night; whereupon, on ascending the steps again, one of the warders proceeded to fasten down the trap at the top of the stairs.

The next part of the duty was to inspect the refractory ward, and here the door of one of the dark cells was opened, so as to see whether the prisoner was safe.

"All right, boy, eh?" cried the officer, as he whisked the light of his bull's-eye full into the face of the wretched lad, who lay huddled up in his rug on the rude wooden couch, but who gave no answer in return.

"He'll be up in the morning," said the other warder, as he suddenly closed the door, and made the building ring again with the deep metallic sound. "He's the only one we've got in to-night."

On this being completed, we hastened back to the centre corridor, and passing through the glass doors, commenced inspecting the several offices on either side of the passage, whilst the warders raked out the expiring fires in those rooms that had been used up till a late hour.

Hence we hurried, all of us, up the stairs to the infirmary wards, where we found the two invalids asleep, and the infirmary warder there seated by their side; and thence we descended to the reception wards below, and inspected every hole and corner of them.

From this part of the building we stepped out into the grounds—the sound of the feet, grating on the gravel as we paced along, seeming almost to startle the intense stillness of the place; and thus we passed first into the steward's offices to see that the fires, &c., were safe, and afterwards across the yard into the stores, the tramp of the many boots along the wooden passage now filling the building with a hollow noise.

Here, dark as the place was, we could still tell by the smell—now of cloth, then of leather, and then of the yarn for warping—the character of the stores we were passing by the way; whilst, on entering the kitchen, the pent-up heat and odour of cooking, and the scrunching of the sanded floor under the sole of the foot, were sufficient, without the light of the lantern, to tell us whereabouts we were.

Next we entered the bakehouse, where there was a peculiar smell of bread and flour, and after that we went into the steward's provision store, and here was a characteristic perfume of cocoa, oatmeal, and treacle all blent together.

From the latter part of the building we passed for a moment or two into the exercising ground. The bleak March air rushed in as soon as the side-door was opened, and the moon-light sky without looked as uninviting and cold as steel, so that it set one shivering to step into the air after the stifling heat of the kitchen.

On our return thence the warders entered their own mess-room; and, having put on their great-coats, they sallied forth to the prison grounds once more, but now leaving their lamps behind. This was done to see whether there were any lights in the cells, for the prisoners, they said, occasionally made candles out of their meat-fat and pieces of the thread supplied them for their work. By examining the building from without they were enabled to detect any improper lights burning within it. Accordingly, the officers retired far back to the grass-plots, and there turned round to gaze up at the several wings of the prison. The walls and windows, however, were pitch-black in the darkness, with the exception of the long streaks of yellow light shining through the casements of the corridors. When the officers had satisfied themselves that all was right here, they proceeded to try the several entrances to the building from the outside, as they passed round within the walls.

At length we returned to the warders' mess again, where we found another officer raking out the remains of the mess-room fire for the night. And thus ended the inspection of the prison, the search having occupied near upon an hour, although it was executed at a most rapid pace; for there were some scores of rooms and shops to examine and "secure," besides no end of doors to fasten, and many a flight of stairs to ascend, in addition to making the entire circuit of the grounds.

Still the last office of all had to be performed—the four of the eight sets of keys that were retained at the six o'clock muster had now to be delivered up. These were handed over by the warders going off duty at ten o'clock, to the principal on special duty for the night, and by him carried to the chief warder's room, where they were placed with the rest in the iron-safe, and the metal door securely locked for the night.

Then the fire annihilators that stood in the corner of the apartment were duly looked to, and the prison finally reported to the governor as "all secure."

¶ i—δ.

A Sunday Morning at Pentonville.

Strange and interesting as are the scenes witnessed at the Model Prison on a week day, nevertheless the strangest and most interesting of all the sights is the performance of divine service on the Sabbath. Nor do we say this after one solitary visit, for being anxious to watch the effect of prayers on the convicts at this institution, we made a point of attending service in the chapel on several occasions, so that we might speak from no *single* observation of the ceremony.

The chapel itself reminds one of a moderately-sized music-hall, for it is merely a spacious room without either naves or aisles, or pillars, or galleries to give it a church-like character; and at the end facing the pulpit there is a series of seats rising one above the other, after the fashion of a lecture-room at an hospital or philosophical institution. These seats are divided off in the same manner as the pit-stalls at a theatre, but in appearance they resemble a small box or pew rather than the imitation arm-chair peculiar to the orchestral "reserved seats." Indeed, the reader has but to imagine the ordinary pews of a church to be arranged on an inclined plane, one above the other, rather than on a level floor, and to be each divided into a series of compartments just large enough to hold one person, to have a tolerably definite notion of the sittings in the chapel under the "separate system" at Pentonville.

Of the separate sittings or individual pews there are altogether some 270 in the Pentonville convict chapel, and the prisoner who sits nearest the wall in each row of seats has to enter first, and he, on the other hand, whose place is nearest the middle, last; for the partitions between each of the sittings serve also as doors, so that when they are turned back a passage is formed to the farthest unoccupied seat from the middle or general entrance.

Another peculiarity of the Pentonville chapel consists in the raised and detached sittings appropriated to the warders, for as it is the duty of the officers attending service there to see that no attempts at intercommunication are made by the prisoners, it becomes necessary that they should be placed in such exalted positions throughout the chapel as to be able to look down into each separate stall near them. Accordingly, it will be observed, on reference to the engraving, that two warders are placed on elevated seats immediately in front of the separate pews, and one at the end of each of the narrow galleries that stretch half along either side of the chapel (the farther extremity only of these being shown in the accompanying illustration), whilst two more warders occupy similarly raised stations immediately under the organ, so as to be able to survey the prisoners in the upper stalls.*

We have already described the swarming of the convicts from every part of the building for daily prayers, and the long lines of men—each prisoner being some twelve or fifteen feet behind the other—that then come streaming along the galleries as the chapel bell is heard booming fitfully overhead. The scene is in no way different on the Sunday, and it is astonishing, on entering the chapel, to find how silently it is filled with the prisoners. Every man, as he enters, knows the precise row and seat that he has to occupy, and though some few pass in

---

* The chapel is the great place of communication among prisoners under separate confinement. Such communication is carried on either by the convict who occupies (say) stall No. 10 leaving a letter in stall No. 9 as he passes towards his own seat, or else by pushing a letter during divine service under the partition-door of the stall; or, if the prisoner be very daring, by passing it over his stall. Sometimes those who are short men put their mouth to the stall-door, and say what they wish to communicate, whilst pretending to pray; or, if they be of the usual height, they speak to their next door neighbour while the singing is going on.

There is not, however, much communication carried on among the prisoners in school, and very little during the operation of cleaning the prison. The authorities, however, expect that a large amount of intercourse takes place among the men while they are out in the exercising grounds, and we are assured that double the inspection could not prevent it there. Other convicts, moreover, fling letters into the cells as they go by from chapel, "though this," adds our informant, "should not occur under vigilant inspection."

The means of communication adopted by the prisoners are often curious. Some men scratch what they want to say on the tin dinner-cans; others talk from cell to cell by means of the water-taps; others, again, use a short and abrupt cough in the chapel with the view of directing another convict's attention to some communication they wish to make. Under the silent system, moreover, it is usual for the prisoners to speak while on the tread-wheel, either by their fingers or pointing to certain figures and numbers that have been carved by previous prisoners about the place; and others, again, accustom themselves to talk without moving the lips, so that they can look a warder full in the face while conversing with their neighbour, and yet the warder detect no signs of any communication going on.

Under the separate system the prisoners have an ingenious method of communicating by means of knocking on the cell-walls. "The following description," says Mr. Burt, in his "Results of Separate Confinement," from which book the account is copied, "is printed precisely as it was given me by a prisoner deserving of credit. 'The plan is this (as taught me by a youth who desired, in case we might be neighbours, to hold a regular communication) to write upon a piece of paper the letters of the alphabet, and under each letter to place a number, commencing at one, thus: $\frac{A.\ B.\ C.\ D.}{1.\ 2.\ 3.\ 4.}$, &c. &c. A person wishing to communicate with his neighbour would then rap with his knuckle or nail on the wall, spelling the words with numbers instead of letters. Thus, to propose the question, 'How do you get on?' I should knock thus:— $\frac{h\ o\ w\ \ d\ o\ g\ e\ t\ \ o\ n}{8\ 15\ 23\ \ 4\ 15\ \ 7\ 5\ 20\ \ 15\ 14}$; and between each word give three rapid knocks, to imply the word was complete. This system of corresponding, although at first sight it may appear tedious, is much less so than one would imagine; for regular practitioners are so thoroughly acquainted with the numbers of each letter, that a conversation is carried on with the same facility as by talking with the fingers; besides, in this system there are many abbreviations for yes, no, &c., and a sort of freemasonry, or certain signs, both rapid and convincing, and perfectly intelligible to each other. Many may doubt this statement, as I did myself when I was first initiated; but I can positively assert, that I have *myself*, with my limited knowledge of this curious system, learnt a great portion of the history of a party who never opened his lips to me, nor would I desire that he ever should. From this individual I learnt his name, place of birth, offence, sentence, the date of his coming into the prison, and many other circumstances, which he contrived to make me acquainted with before I had ever seen him, or had been in my cell four-and-twenty hours.'

"The truth of this statement," adds Mr. Burt, "was verified by the fact that the name, birth-place, crime, and sentence of the prisoner in the adjoining cell were correctly stated by my informant, although they had no previous knowledge whatever of each other. It may be added, that the prisoner who communicated the information was convicted in a wrong name, while no officer of the prison knew that he had another name until it was discovered in this manner. Other prisoners have given me a similar description of this method of communication, which may be termed the *prisoners' electric telegraph*."—(P. 271).

together at the same moment, these go to opposite quarters of the gallery—either to the one side or the other of the upper or lower stalls, as the case may be—so that, owing to the intervals between the men in the several lines of prisoners pouring into the edifice from different parts of the prison at one and the same time, each convict is able to get to his seat, and to close the partition-door of his stall after him, before the one following his steps has time to enter the same row. The consequence is, that neither riot nor confusion prevails, and the quarter of a thousand and more convicts, who are distributed throughout the chapel gallery, are stowed away, every one in his proper place—and that in some few minutes, too —with as little noise and disorder as occurs at a Quakers' meeting.

When the chapel is filled, it is a most peculiar sight to behold near upon three hundred heads of convicts—and the heads *only*, the whole of the prisoner's body being hidden by the front of the stalls—ranged, as it were, in so many pigeon-holes (for the partitions on either side produce somewhat of this appearance), and each with the round, brass, charity-boy-like badge of his register number hung up, just above him, on the ledge of the stall at his back.

Nor are the heads there assembled such as physiognomical or phrenological prejudice would lead one to anticipate, for now that the mask-caps are off we see features and crania of every possible form and expression—almost from the best type down to the very lowest. True, as we have said, there is scarcely one bald head to be observed, and only two remarkable men with gray, or rather silver, hair—the latter, however, being extraordinary exceptions to the rule, and coming from a very different class from the ordinary convict stock. Neverthe- less, the general run of the countenances and skulls assembled in Pentonville Chapel are far from being of that brutal or semi-idiotic character, such as caricaturists love to picture as connected with the criminal race. Some of the convicts, indeed, have a frank and positively ingenuous look, whilst a few are certainly remarkable for the coarse and rudely-moulded features—the high cheek-bones and prognathous mouths—that are often associated with the *hard-bred* portion of our people. Still it has been noticed by others, who have had far better opportunities of judging than ourselves, that the old convict head of the last century has disappeared from our prisons and hulks; and certainly, out of the 270 odd faces that one sees assembled at Pentonville chapel, there is hardly one that bears the least resemblance to the vulgar baboon-like types that unobservant artists still depict as representative of the con- vict character.

There are few countenances, be it remarked, that will bear framing in the Old Bailey dock, and few to which the convict garb—despite our study of Lavater and Gall—does not lend what we cannot but imagine, from the irresistible force of association, to be an *unmis- takably* criminal expression. At Pentonville chapel, however, as we have said, we see only the heads, without any of the convict costume to mislead the mind in its observations, and assuredly, if one were to assemble a like number of individuals from the same ranks of society as those from which most of our criminals come—such as farm-labourers, costermongers, sweeps, cabmen, porters, mechanics, and even clerks—we should find that their cast of countenances differed so little from those seen at the Model Prison, that even the keenest eye for character would be unable to distinguish a photograph of the criminal from the non- criminal congregation.*

* The only criminal trait we ourselves have been able to detect among the ordinary convict class, is a certain kind of dogged and half-sullen expression, denoting stubbornness and waywardness of temper, whilst many of the young men who are habitual thieves certainly appear to us to have a peculiar cunning and side- long look, together with an odd turn at the corners of the mouth, as if they were ready to burst into laughter at the least frivolity, thus denoting that it is almost impossible to excite in their minds any deep or lasting impression. Nor, so far as our experience goes, have even the "brutal-violence" men in general their charac- ters stamped upon their faces. We heard, only recently, a "rough" declare that Calcraft's situation was just the thing to suit him, as there was good pay and little to do connected with the berth; and yet, to have judged by the fellow's countenance, one might have mistaken him, had he been clad in a suit of black, for a city

There is something, even to the lightest minds, inexpressibly grand in the simultaneous outpouring of many prayers, so that the confessions of transgression, and the supplications for mercy, as well as the thanksgivings, the invocation of blessings upon all those who are in sickness or want, and the hymns of praise, uttered by some hundreds of voices, become one of the most sublime and solemn ceremonies the mind can contemplate. Go into what assembly or what country we will—let us differ from the adopted creed as much as we may—we cannot but respect the divine aspirations of every multitude gathered together for the worship of the Most High; for though the form of such worship may not be the precise ceremony to which our notions have been squared, and though we may believe, clinging to some human theory of election and salvation, that there is another and a shorter way to Heaven, nevertheless we cannot but reverence the outpouring of several souls as the one common yearning after goodness, the universal veneration of all that is deemed to be just and true.

But if this be the mental and moral effect of every religious assembly, composed of righteous men, how much more touching do such aspirations and supplications become when the wretched beings confessing their sins and imploring mercy, are those whom the world has been compelled to cut off from all society, on account of the wrongs done by them to their fellow-creatures; and we are not ashamed to confess that when we heard the convict multitude at Pentonville, cry aloud to their Almighty and most merciful Father, that they had " erred and strayed from his ways like lost sheep," saying with one voice, " we have followed too much the devices and desires of our own hearts," and then entreating one and all for mercy as " miserable offenders," and begging that they might " hereafter live a godly, righteous, and sober life"—the prayer of these same wretched outcasts, we are not ashamed to confess, so far touched our heart that the tears filled our eyes, and choked the most devout " *Amen*" we ever uttered in all our life.

And such a prayer, too, in such a place, repeated by felon lips, is not without its Christian lesson on the soul; for though the first feeling is naturally to consider the above confession as specially fit for that same convict congregration, and to fancy, when we acknowledge with the rest " *we* have left undone those things which we ought to have done, and done those things which we ought not to have done," that the " we" has particular reference to the wretched beings before us rather than to ourselves.

The next moment, however, the mind, stripped of all social prejudice at such a time, gets to despise the petty worldly pride that prompted the vain distinction, and to ask itself, as it calls up its many shortcomings—its petty social cheats and tricks—as well as its infinite selfish delinquencies, what vast difference in the eyes of the All-wise and Just can there be between us and these same " miserable offenders," whom we, in the earthly arrogance of our hearts, have learnt to loathe.

And as the lesson of Christian charity and brotherhood steals across the soul, we get to inquire of ourselves, what did we ever do to better the lot of any like those before us? Have we not then really left undone the things that we ought to have done, towards such as they, whispers the obtrusive conscience? If we are a little bit better than they, is it

missionary, or even a philanthropist. Nevertheless, the generality of the "brutal-violence" class of criminals are characterized by a peculiar lascivious look—a trait which is as much developed in the attention paid to the arrangement of the hair, as it is in the look of the eye or play of the mouth. They are, however, mostly remarkable for that short and thick kind of neck which is termed "bull," and which is generally characteristic of strong animal passions. As a body, moreover, the habitual criminals of London are said to be, in nine cases out of ten, " Irish Cockneys," *i. e.*, persons born of Irish parents in the Metropolis; and this is doubtlessly owing to the extreme poverty of the parents on their coming over to this country, and the consequent neglect experienced by the class in their youth, as well as the natural quickness of the Hibernian race for good or evil, together with that extreme excitability of temperament which leads, under circumstances of want and destitution, to savage outrages—even as, in better social conditions, it conduces to high generosity if not heroism.

not simply because we have been a great deal more favoured than they? Did we make our own fate in life? Did you or I, by any merit on our own part, win our way into a rank of society where we were not only trained from early childhood to honest courses, as regularly as those less lucky (though equally deserving) wretches were schooled in dishonest ones? and where *we* were as much removed from temptation by the comforts and blessings with which we were surrounded, as *they* were steeped to the very lips in it, by the want and misery which always encompassed them? Have we ever devoted the least portion of the gifts and endowments we have received, and of which assuredly we are but the stewards rather than the *rightful* possessors, to the rendering of the lot of the wretched a whit less wretched in this world? Did we ever do a thing or give a fraction to make them better, or wiser, or happier? Or, if we have done or given some little, could we not have done and given *more?* Honestly, truthfully, we must answer; for there is no shirking the question at such an hour and in such a place, with those hundreds of convict eyes turned towards us, and those hundreds of felon lips crying aloud, " There is none other that fighteth for us but Thou, O God !"

Nor can we then and there stifle our conscience with the paltry excuse that the men are unworthy of such feelings being displayed towards them; for, as we hear them repeat the responses, we cannot but fancy there is a profundity of grief and repentance, as well as devout supplication, expressed in the very tones of their voices, when they cry, after the solemn passages of the litany, " O God, the Father of Heaven, have mercy upon us, miserable sinners !" " O God the Son, Redeemer of the World, have mercy upon us, miserable sinners !" Or else, in answer to the prayer of the minister, " that it may please thee to show thy pity upon all prisoners and captives !" say one and all, " We beseech thee to hear us, good Lord !"

Indeed, the attention of the men is so marked, that during the reading of the lessons the leaves of the Bibles are turned over by the prisoners at one and the same time, so that the noise sounds positively like the sudden rustling of a forest.

One convict we noted with his hands raised high above his head, and clasped continually in prayer, while others seldom or never raised their eyes from their book; and it struck us as not a little extraordinary to hear so many scores of felons, and even some one or two manslayers, that were congregated under that chapel roof, say, with apparently unfeigned devotion—as the minister read from the communion table the Commandments, " Thou shalt do no murder !" and " Thou shalt not steal !"—" Lord have mercy upon us, and incline our hearts to keep this law !"

Nor is the attention of the convicts to the clergyman's discourse less decorous and marked, than their conduct during the prayers; and on one of our visits, the assistant-chaplain related an anecdote at the conclusion of his sermon which showed how easily these men are moved by any appeal to family ties. The minister told them how it had once been his sad duty to be present at the funeral of a young woman and her infant, by torchlight, saying that the reason of the ceremony being delayed until so late an hour, was in order that the father might see the last melancholy office performed over the body of his child; and he had had to travel on foot for many miles, from the town in which he resided.

It was curious to watch, as the humble history grew in interest, how every prisoner's head was stretched forward from his little stall, and their eyes became more and more intently rivetted on the clergyman.

When the old man saw the coffin of his girl and her babe lowered into the grave, proceeded the minister, his tears streamed down the furrows of his cheeks; and when the service was over, and the sexton was about to begin shovelling the earth into the grave, and hide, for ever the remains of his children, from his view, he bade the man desist while he took a last look at all that once bound him to the world. As he did so, the old father cried through his sobs that he would rather see her and her little one dead in their grave, than have beheld her living with it in her shame.

When the tale was told, there was hardly one dry eye to be noticed among those so-called hardened convicts; some buried their faces in their handkerchiefs, in very grief at the misery they too had heaped on some parent's head; and others sobbed aloud from a like cause, so that we could hear their gasps and sighs, telling of the homes that they had made wretched by their shame.

** Quitting the Chapel.—For the order of leaving the chapel, an instrument is employed as a means of signalling to the prisoners the letters of the rows and numbers of the stalls in the succession that the men in them are to retire to their cells.

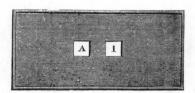

This instrument consists of an oblong board, raised upon a high shaft, and has two apertures in front, so as to show a small portion of the edge of two wooden discs that are placed at the back of the board. One disc is inscribed with letters, and the other with figures round the rim, and arranged in such a manner, that, by causing one or other to revolve behind the board by means of a string passed over the centre, as shown in the annexed drawing, a fresh letter or number is made to appear at either aperture, according as the right or left hand wheel is worked—the letter and the number appearing to the prisoners, as represented in the upper diagram, giving the front of the board, and the wheels being arranged as pictured in the lower or back view of the apparatus.

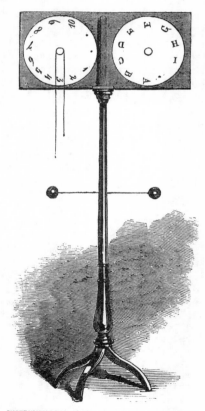

When the service is over, the instrument is moved to the space in front of the communion table, and a warder proceeds to work the wheels from behind, so as to shift either the letters or the numbers, as may be required.

Each row of seats on either side of the entrance passage in the middle of the chapel gallery is similarly lettered, and corresponds with the characters on one of the wheels, whilst the several stalls or pews in those rows are numbered alike on either side of such entrance-passage, and correspond with the figures on the other wheel; so that when the warder turns the one wheel round, and lets the letter A appear at the aperture, the convicts in that row put on their caps and prepare to move; whilst immediately the figure 1 is brought to the other aperture, then the first stall on either side of the central passage pull down their cap-peaks, and throwing back the partition-door, hasten from the chapel; and when the numbered wheel is turned a little farther round, so as to bring the figure 2 in the

INSTRUMENT FOR SIGNALLING TO THE PRISONERS AT PENTONVILLE THE ORDER OF LEAVING THE CHAPEL.

aperture, then the convicts, on either side the passage occupying the stall next to the one just vacated, likewise turn down their cap-peaks, and throwing back the division of their stall, pass in a similar manner out of the chapel. Then number 3 stalls are signalled away in like manner, each prisoner, as before, making a passage for those who are to come after him, by pushing back the division-door of his stall, and so on up to number 10; after which the letter-wheel is revolved a little more, so as to present another character to the prisoners' view. Then another row prepares to leave, as before; and thus the chapel is entirely emptied, not only with considerable rapidity, but without any disturbance or confusion.*

¶ i—ε.

Of the Moral Effects of the Discipline at Pentonville.

We have already spoken of the mental effects of the separate system as carried out at Pentonville Prison, and shown that, whereas the proportion of lunacy is not quite 0·6 in every thousand of the prison population throughout England and Wales, the ratio of insanity at Pentonville was more than ten times that amount, or 6·0 in the first thousand convicts that entered the Model Prison; whereas it was 10 in the second thousand, 4 in the third, and 9 in the fourth; so that, had the prisoners throughout England and Wales been treated according to the same system, there would have been, instead of an average of 85 lunatics per year in the entire prison population of the country, upwards of 850 madmen produced.

Great credit is due, however, to the authorities for relaxing the discipline immediately they became impressed with the conviction of its danger to the intellects of the prisoners; for, as driving a man mad formed no part of the original sentence of a convict, it is clear that the prison authorities had no earthly right to submit a criminal to a course of penal treatment which had the effect of depriving him of his reason. Since the alteration, however, in the working of the separate system, and the introduction of the present method of brisk walking, together with an increased quantity of out-door exercise, and a more perfect system of ventilation, as well as shortening the term of imprisonment to one-half its original duration, the ratio of insanity has been reduced from 6·0 to 1·0 per thousand prisoners (see page 144). Nevertheless, as the medical officer says, "though much has been gained, *the limits of safety have scarcely yet been reached,*" the ratio of lunacy at Pentonville being still almost as high again as the normal rate deduced from the average of all other prisons.

Were it not for this terrible drawback, it must be admitted that the separate system is the best of all the existing modes of penal discipline—better than the "silent system," which has, to recommend it, only the *negative* benefit of preventing intercourse among the criminals—and better than the "mark system," which would have convicts sentenced to do

---

* The arrangement of the chapel into stalls is not generally approved, even by the advocates of the separate system; and surely, if such an arrangement be not *indispensably* necessary for the carrying out of that system, they should be immediately condemned as bearing a most offensive aspect, and one that hardly consorts with a Christian edifice, where the minister speaks of even the convicts as "brethren."

"As regards the division of the chapel into separate stalls," says Colonel Jebb, in his Report for the year, 1852, "Mr. Reynolds, the chaplain at Wakefield, who is a warm advocate of the separate system, thus expresses his opinion :—'I am of opinion that the plan of the chapel is very objectionable. I object to it, in the first place, because I think it is calculated to produce disagreeable associations in the minds of the prisoners regarding a place of public worship. I object to it, in the second place, because I believe it to produce a chilling feeling of isolation opposed to the proper social character of public worship. I object to it, in the third place, because, instead of preventing communication between different prisoners, it affords increased facilities for communication; in the fourth, because it affords an opportunity to the ill-disposed to employ their time in chapel in writing on the wood-work of the stalls instead of attending to the service, and opportunities, also, of disturbing the worship of the other prisoners, by making noises, which it is very difficult to trace to any particular prisoner.'" In these opinions Mr Shepherd, the governor of Wakefield Prison, expresses his concurrence; whilst Colonel Jebb himself adds :—"Much of the inconvenience pointed out by the governor and chaplain at Wakefield has been experienced at Pentonville. Writing of the most objectionable character appears on the wood-work in many places, and punishments for attempts to communicate have been frequent."

a certain task of work, rather than to suffer a definite term of imprisonment; but task-work was never yet known to make labour a pleasure to a man, though this is the main point claimed by the advocates of that system as rendering it superior to all others.

The separate system, however, not only prevents the communion of criminals far more effectually than the silent system can possibly hope to do, and makes labour so agreeable a relief to the monotony of solitude, that it positively becomes a punishment to withhold it, and thus, by rendering idleness absolutely irksome to the prisoner, causes him to find a pleasure in industry—a feat that the "mark," or, more properly speaking, "task" system, can never hope to accomplish; but, by cutting the prisoner off from all society, the separate system of prison discipline compels him to hold communion with himself—to turn his thoughts inward—to reflect on the wickedness of his past career with the view of his forming new resolves for the future, and so gives to his punishment the true enlightened character of a penance and a chastisement (or chastening) rather than a mere vindictive infliction of so much pain.

That the separate system has really produced such effects as the above, the records of Pentonville Prison thoroughly attest. It is urged, however, by those who object to that mode of prison discipline, that the reformations it assumes to work are mere temporary depressions of spirits produced by physical causes, rather than being conversions of nature wrought by the power of religion.

It should, however, be borne in mind that it is impossible for any one to repent of his past misdeeds—to be overcome with remorse for an ill-spent life—and yet be lively and happy over the matter. Grief necessarily has a tendency to depress the mind and body, and so, too, mental or physical depression has a tendency to induce grief; consequently, there being here a state of action and reaction, it is but natural that the dejection or lowness of spirits resulting from separate confinement should induce sorrow for the past, and that this same sorrow again should serve to increase such dejection. Whoever became a better man without lamenting over his former transgressions? If, therefore, we really wish to excite in the mind that state of contrition which must infallibly precede all reformation, if not positive conversion of character, we must place the individual in precisely those circumstances which will serve to *depress* his haughty nature and to humble his proud spirit; and this is just the effect which, according to the medical evidence, the system of separate confinement is calculated to produce.

But it is said that these reformations, so far from being real permanent changes of nature, are mere temporary impressions, caused by the long confinement to which the assumed converts have been subjected, and that they owe their momentary results to that derangement of the organs of digestion which arises from the want not only of proper air and exercise, but the stimulus of agreeable society; so that men get to mistake a fit of the "megrims" for a religious frame of mind, or, in the words of Thomas Hood—

"Think they're pious when they're only bilious."

Others urge, again, that these same professed conversions are mere hypocritical assumptions on the part of the prisoners for the sake of cajoling the chaplain out of a "ticket-of-leave" long before the expiration of their sentence; for as it has been found that many of these same converted convicts soon relapse, after regaining their liberty, to their former course of life, people immediately conclude that the religious turn of mind, previous to their being set free, was merely simulated for the particular purpose. Moreover, we are well aware that the other convicts generally believe these displays of religion on the part of their fellow-prisoners to be mere shams, calling those who indulge in them by the nickname of "Joeys." We have been assured, too, by the warders, that the prisoners know the very footsteps of the chaplain, and that many of them fall down on their knees as they hear him coming, so that he may find them engaged in prayer on visiting their cell; whereas, immediately he has left, they put their tongue in their cheek, and laugh at his gullibility.

Nevertheless, we are inclined to believe that there is a greater desire for religious consolation among prisoners than is usually supposed. Indeed, it is our creed that men oftener deceive themselves in this world, than they do others. Again, it should be borne in mind, that criminals are essentially creatures of impulse, and though liable to be deeply affected for the moment, are seldom subject to steady and permanent impressions. This very unsettledness of purpose or object, is the distinctive point of the criminal character, so that such people become incapable of all continuity of action as well as thought. Hence, it is quite in keeping with the nature of criminals, that when subjected to the depressing influence of separate confinement, they should exhibit not only deep sorrow for their past career, but also make earnest resolves to lead a new life for the future, as well as offer up devout prayers for strength to carry out their intentions—even though in a few days or months afterwards, they themselves should be found scoffing at their own weakness, and pursuing, without the least remorse, the very same course for which a little while ago they had expressed such intense contrition—contrition that was as fervent and truthful as a child's at the time, but unfortunately quite as evanescent.

Still, amid all this fickleness of purpose and its consequent semblance of hypocrisy, and amid, too, a large amount of positive religious trickery and deceit, there are undoubted cases of lasting changes having been produced by the discipline of separate confinement. As an illustration of this fact, the following letter may be cited, for though written by a mere boy prisoner, previous to his leaving for Australia, we have the best assurances that the after character of the man fully bore out the mature professions of his youth, and that he has since returned to this country, not only honest, but a highly prosperous person, having amassed a considerable fortune in the colonies, and still continuing to lead the godly, righteous, and sober life that he had so often prayed to have strength to pursue, in the very chapel where we had but lately heard the other convicts supplicating—and apparently as devoutly—for the same power :—

COPY OF A LETTER WRITTEN BY J——— D——— BEFORE LEAVING PENTONVILLE PRISON.
(The orthography as in the original.)

"I, J——— D———, came to this prison on Sepr. 28th 1843 in a most pitiful condition. Destitute of true religion, of any morality, of any sound or useful knowledge, or of any desire to acquire the same, with a hard, wicked, and perverse heart fully bent to, and set on, all manner of mischief, altogether ignorant of my spiritual condition, a child of the Devil, a lover of the World, a slave to Sin, under a most miserable condemnation, having no hope and without God in the World. This is somewhat the condition I was in on coming to this prison, until by degrees the grace of God began to change and new modle me, by showing to me my sins and then leading me to repentance, by giving me desires to love and fear God my Saviour, by enabling me rightly to understand the word and way of Salvation; and savingly, with faith to receive the same. I can say now, what I could not then ; that I love those commands which were so grievous to me in my unregenerate state. I delight to read, study, hear and obey the blessed, pure and holy precepts of God's Word, and I hope I may ever continue to do the same to my life's end ; they shall be my guide, my teacher, and director through the dark passage of this world. I can say with sincerity I have enjoyed my Sabbaths of affliction and solitude far more than the days spent in sinful pursuits, and I have been always as comfortable here as I could desire to be. I have been taught most Godly, truly, savingly, and soundly, the truths and doctrines of God's Word, in which is contained all my hopes, comfort, and Salvation, by my faithful Pastors; and I have most haply had given me a heart to receive and understand the same to my great comfort. I do truly intend to follow the faith that my ministers have taught me, and to live according to it, God's grace preserving me. I am simply and only trusting on my Saviour for Pardon, Righteousness, Sanctification, and Redemption, or in other words a Joyful Salvation. And

CHIEF WARDER AT THE PENTONVILLE
PRISON.

PRINCIPAL MATRON AT THE FEMALE CONVICT
PRISON, BRIXTON.

(From Photographs by Herbert Watkins, 179, Regent Street.

I do think it my bounden duty, after receiving these manifold blessings and priveleges, at all times, and at every period of my life to keep God's commandments by loving him Supremely with all my heart, and by doing to all men as I would they should do unto me—the sum of all the Commands. The breaking of these has been the cause of all my trouble and misfortune, but the keeping of them will be my future hapiness and prosperity in this short life, and in the world to come through the merit of my Gracious Saviour, Whom I hope to know better, to love more and to worship in his fear evermore, Amen. I have always found my officers very kind to me especially my warder and Extra Warder, with whom I have had most to do. My schoolmasters have taught me a great deal of useful knowledge, and have taken every pains to instruct me in what was good. * * * * * I have learnt Grammar so far as to parse a sentence well. Arithmetic I have made great progress in. I could not do on coming here Simple Proportion, but I have gone through my arithmetic, and began to study Algebra so far as fractions. I have also acquired a little knowledge of Geography and Astronomy, with other useful subjects. * * * *

"And in this condition I leave this Prison a changed and altered person to what I was on coming to it. But by the Grace of God I am what I am. And so I go my way to a distant land, steadfastly purposing to lead an upright life, and to dwell in love and charity with all men, thanking God for this affliction which hath confered so many blessings upon me.

"J——— D————, Aged 21, June 29th, 1845."

In addition to the above we may farther quote some verses that were written by one of the Pentonville convicts, upon the subject of the anecdote of the burial of a young woman and her child by torchlight, which has been already mentioned in our description of the service in the Pentonville chapel; for these verses will go far to illustrate the point we have been insisting upon, namely, the susceptibility of prisoners in separate confinement to religious and other grave impressions for the time being :—

VERSES WRITTEN BY ONE OF THE PRISONERS IN PENTONVILLE UPON A SERMON DELIVERED BY THE ASSISTANT-CHAPLAIN, MARCH, 1856.

And were those joyful tears the old man shed?
Could he unfeigned rejoice? his daughter dead,
When by the lantern's gleam, in darkest night,
The grave received her once lov'd form from sight.
He'd travelled far that day that he might gaze
Upon this scene; this caused delay; her face
He could not see again : upon her breast,
Her little babe in death's embrace did rest :
His hoary head was bare, with grief his voice
Exclaimed, "My God, I do indeed rejoice,
That thou my child hast taken in her prime,
And saved from farther guilt, and shame, and crime!"

The minister of God, one Sabbath morn,
The fact affirmed, to many prisoners; torn
From evil ways, and friends : and for their good
Confined with best intent to solitude.
But how describe the workings of the mind?
Of all, some felt, and wept, and some were blind,
With hardened hearts, and steeped in guilt, the most
Could glory in their shame, their crimes their boast

Some fathers, too, were there, with daughters left
In the wide world, of fostering care bereft :
Their anguish great, the tears fall down their face,
They almost felt inclined to curse their race.

But better feelings ruled, as one they heard,
The minister explain the written Word ;
With studious zeal, his love for souls was great,
He felt commiseration for their state ;
His text the miracle that Jesus wrought,
When unto Nain's city He, unsought,
Brought joy for mourning, dried the widow's eyes,
And gracious spoke—"Young man, I say, arise !"
His glorious theme, the Saviour's wondrous love,
Caused many hearts to pity, melt, and move,
And earnest pray that God the Spirit's voice
Might now be heard—"Young man, I say, arise !"
That some poor souls, immersed in guilt and sin,
Might feel the power of love, new life begin
To find ; forsake their guilty paths ; repent,
The ways of heaven pursue with pure intent,
Might hunger after righteousness divine,
And let their future conversation shine ;
Might have a blessed hope beyond the skies,
When the last trump shall sound, "Arise ! Arise !"

¶ ii.

THE FEMALE CONVICT PRISON AT BRIXTON.

The Female Convict Prison at Brixton lies in a diametrically opposite direction to the "Model Prison" at Pentonville—the former bearing south, and the latter north, of the heart of London ; and the one being some six miles removed from the other.

It is a pleasant enough drive down to the old House of Correction, on Brixton Hill, especially if the journey be made, as ours was, early one spring morning, without a cloud to dim the clear silver-gray sky, and before the fires had darkened and thickened the atmosphere of the Metropolis.

It is curious, by the by, to note the signs of spring-time that come to the Londoner's ear. Not only does the woman's shrill cry of "Two bunches a-penny—sweet wa-a-ll-flowers !" resound through the streets, telling of the waking earth and the bursting buds, and wafting the mind far away to fields and gardens ; but there are long trucks in the thoroughfares, the tops of which are a bright canary-yellow, with their hundred roots of blooming primroses, and others a pale delicate green, with the mass of trailing musk-plants, while the hoarse-voiced barrow-men are shouting, "All a-blowing ! all a-growing !" as they halt by the way. Then there are tiny boys and girls either crying their bunches of exquisitely odorous sweetbriar, or thrusting little bouquets of violets almost under your nose, and following you half-down the street as you go ; whilst many of the omnibus-drivers have a small sprig of downy-looking palm stuck out at one corner of their mouth. Farther, there are the hawkers balancing their loads of spring vegetables on their heads, the baskets laden with bundles of bright flesh-coloured rhubarb, and with small white wicker platters, as it were, in their hands, some filled with pale waxen-looking sea-kale, and others bright green, with an early dishful of spring salad.

Moreover, the streets echo throughout the day with women's cries of "Any o-ornaments for your fire stove!" pleasantly reminding one of the coming warmth; and presently you see these same women flit by your window, carrying a number of light and bright-hued cut papers that are not unlike so many well-be-flounced ladies' muslin aprons, and bearing on their arm a basket filled with tinted shavings, that remind one of a quantity of parti-coloured soapsuds, or, better still, the top of a confectioner's trifle.

On the morning of our visit to Brixton, as we passed along the streets towards West-minster Bridge, we met hawkers coming from the early market at Covent Garden, with their trucks and baskets laden with the pretty and welcome treasures of the spring; and the tank-like watering-carts were out in the thoroughfares, playing their hundred threads of water upon the dusty roadways for the first time, that we had noted, in the course of the present year. Then it was peculiar to be able to see right down to the end of the long thorough-fares, and to find the view of the distant houses no longer filmed with mist, but the gables of the buildings, and the steeples of the churches, and the unfinished towers of the Houses of Parliament standing out sharp and definite against the blue back-ground of the morning sky; whilst, as we crossed the crazy old Westminster Bridge—where the masons seem destined to be for ever at work—the pathways were crowded with lines of workmen (though it was not yet six o'clock) streaming along to their labour, and each with his little bundle of food for the day, dangling from his hand.

Then, shortly after our "Hansom" had dived beneath the railway viaduct that spans the Westminster Road, we came suddenly into the region of palatial hospitals and philan-thropic institutions, as well as Catholic cathedrals and St. Paul's-like lunatic asylums, and handsome gothic schools for the blind, together with obeliskine lamp-posts built in the centre of the many converging roads, and gigantic coaching taverns, too—that one and all serve to make up the "West End," as it were, of the large and distinct Metropolis over the water.

The atmosphere was still so clear and fresh, that though we turned off by the Orphan Asylum we could see far down the bifid thoroughfares, and behold the dome of Bethlem Hospital, as well as the cathedral tower of Saint George's, soaring into the air high above the neighbouring roofs.

In a few minutes afterwards we were in the peculiar suburban regions of London, where the houses are excruciatingly genteel, and each is prefaced by a small grass-plat hardly bigger than a Turkey carpet; and where, in the longer garden at the back, an insane attempt is usually being made to grow cabbages and cucumbers at something under a crown a-piece—the realm of Cockney terraces, and crescents, and ovals, and commons, and greens, and Horns Taverns, and donkey stands, as well as those unpleasant hints, in the shape of lodge-like turnpikes, that one is approaching the outskirts of London.

Then, as we turn off by St. Mary's Church, the thoroughfare begins to assume a still more suburban look; for now the houses get to be semi-detached, the two small residences clubbing together so as to make each other appear twice as big as it really is; while every couple of villas is struggling to look like a small mansion in a tiny park, with a joint-stock carriage-drive in front, that is devoted to the use of *the* fly that is occasionally hired to take the ladies out to tea and scandal, with the female president, may-be, of the Blanket, Coal, and Baby-linen Society, in the neighbourhood. Here the residents are mostly of a commercial and evan-gelical character; the gentlemen all go up to town in the "Paragons" every morning to attend at the Stock Exchange; and the young ladies set forth on their rounds in connection with the district visiting societies—their only dissipation being the novelty of a sermon from some black missionary preacher who may come down to the neighbouring chapel.

Here are seen gloomy-looking shops, inscribed "Tract Depôts;" and as we pass the church at the angle of the road, with the showy tomb standing at the extreme point of the burying-ground, and begin to mount the hill, we see houses with a kind of summer-house built on the roof for enjoying the extensive view of the cloud of London smoke for ever hanging over the adjacent Metropolis.

Here, again, are large half-rustic half-cockney taverns, where the City and West End omnibuses start from, and here, at the end of a rural "blind alley" hard by—a narrowish lane, known as the Prison Road, to which there is no outlet at the other extremity—stands what was once the Surrey House of Correction, and is now the Female Convict Prison.

¶ ii—a.

The History, Plan, and Discipline of the Prison.

The Brixton, or rather Surrey House of Correction, is situate in one of the most open and salubrious spots in the southern surburbs of London. "Like all the jails erected about forty or sixty years ago," says Mr. Dixon, in his work on the "London Prisons," "it was built in the form of a rude crescent, the governor's house being in the common centre, and his drawing-room window commanding a view of all the yards. It was, *par excellence*," he adds, "a hard-labour prison." Indeed, the treadmill, which now generally forms a part of the machinery of correctional prisons, was first set up at Brixton. This was in the year 1817, the apparatus having been invented by Mr. Cubitt, of Ipswich.

This prison was originally built and adapted for 175 prisoners, having been fitted with 149 separate cells, and 12 double ones. The separate cells were each $8 \times 7\frac{1}{2} \times 6$ feet, and almost unventilated, so that they were considerably more than half as small again as the "Model cells" at Pentonville, the latter having a capacity of 911 cubic feet, whilst the capacity of those at Brixton was only 360 cubic feet; and yet, though from their defective ventilation they were unfitted for the confinement of *one* prisoner, and because the law did not allow two persons to be placed in one cell, it was the practice, in order to evade the statute by a legal quibble, to cram as many as three into each of the "dog-holes"—as the Germans term their ancient dungeons—while bedding was supplied only for two. The consequence was, that though the prison was built for the accommodation of only 175 prisoners, the usual number confined within it was more than double that amount, or upwards of 400. Hence it is not to be wondered at, that, despite its standing in the healthiest situation, the old Surrey House of Correction was one of the unhealthiest of all the London prisons; and that out of 4,043 persons passing through it in the course of the year, there should have been not less than 1,085 sick cases reported, 249 of which were fevers, caused, in the surgeon's opinion, by the over-crowded state of the jail.

On the removal of the Surrey House of Correction to the New Prison at Wandsworth, the Brixton Jail was ordered to be pulled down; but, owing to sentences of penal servitude at home having been substituted for transportation abroad (16 and 17 Vic.), it became necessary to establish a prison for female convicts. With this view the Surveyor-General was authorized to treat for the Brixton House of Correction. It was ultimately purchased of the county for the sum of £13,000; and immediately afterwards certain additions and alterations were commenced, so as to render it capable of accommodating from 700 to 800 female convicts.

These additions consisted principally of the erection of two wings—one at either end or horn of the old crescent-shaped range of buildings—as well as a new chapel, laundry, and houses for the superintendent and chaplain. The wings were adapted for the accommodation of 212 prisoners in each, so that the prison accommodation, when these were finished, consisted of 158 separate cells, 12 punishment cells, 424 separate sleeping cells, besides two sets of four association rooms—one at the south-eastern and the other at the south-western angle of the building, and each capable of containing some 60 prisoners (15 in each room), or 120 in all; so that altogether the present accommodation afforded by the new prison cells and the old ones is sufficient for about 700 prisoners, whilst the altered building has now the general appearance and arrangement shown on page 176.*

" In the course of the autumn of 1853," say the Government Reports, " steps were taken to organize the staff for the new establishment. It was then decided that the efficient female officers at Millbank should be removed to Brixton, and that the female establishment at the former prison should be gradually broken up, all articles that could be used being made available for the latter.

" Towards the end of November in the above-mentioned year, there were 75 cells completed and fit for occupation, and as the numbers of female convicts in the several prisons—

* At the time of our visit, the following were the number and distribution of the female convicts confined within this prison :—

DISTRIBUTION OF PRISONERS AT BRIXTON PRISON, 18TH APRIL, 1856.

Division.	Wards.	In Wards.	In Infirmary.	Under Punishment.	Total Prisoners.	Grand Total.	Division.	Wards.	In Wards.	In Infirmary.	Under Punishment.	Total Prisoners.	Grand Total.
Old Prison Cells (for probationary prisoners.)	A	16	0	0	16		West Wing . (for 1st class prisoners.)	A	50	5	..	55	
	B	20	4	0	24			B	51	2	..	53	
	C	8	7	0	15			C	51	2	..	53	
	D	17	0	1	18			D	51	3	..	54	
	E	20	2	1	23								
	F	14	1	0	15		Total .		203	12	..		215
Total . .		95	14	2		111							
Ditto, ditto, Associated Rooms	1	19	4	0	23		East Wing (for 2nd and 3rd class prisoners.)	A	49	7	..	56	
	2	16	4	0	20			B	49	4	..	53	
	3	15	1	0	16			C	51	2	..	53	
	4	16	1	0	17			D	50	4	..	54	
Total . .		66	10	0		76	Total .		199	17			216

Total in the Prison 618

Number of prisoners in each class :—

First Class 367
Second Class 194
Third Class, and Probation 57
——— 618

On the other hand, the subjoined table shows on one side the number of prisoners received at Brixton in the course of the year 1854, and on the other side how some of these were disposed of :—

ANNUAL STATEMENT OF THE REMOVAL OF CONVICTS TO AND FROM BRIXTON PRISON, BETWEEN 1ST AND 31ST DECEMBER, 1854.

On the 1st January, 1854 :—		Disposed of during the Year, by—	
The Number of Convicts in Brixton Prison .	75	Discharged by License	9
Received during the Year from Millbank Prison	178	Ditto, on Medical Grounds	4
From County and Borough Jails . .	410	Pardons . . { Free	1
Lunatic Asylum	1	{ Conditional	1
	——— 411	Removed to Lunatic Asylum	2
		Died	4
		Number remaining 31st December, 1854 .	643
Total :	664	Total	664

augmented by the cessation of transportation—had increased to an inconvenient extent, it was thought desirable to relieve them by making use of even this limited amount of accommodation. Accordingly that number of females was removed from Millbank to Brixton on

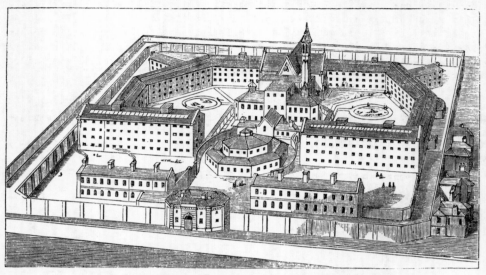

BIRD'S-EYE VIEW OF THE FEMALE CONVICT PRISON AT BRIXTON.

the 24th of November, 1853—those selected for removal being chosen in consequence of their previous good behaviour and their acquaintance with prison discipline."

As regards the discipline enforced at Brixton prison, it may be said to consist of a preliminary stage of separation as a period of probation, and afterwards of advancement into successive stages of discipline, each having superior privileges to those which preceded it; so that whilst the preliminary stage consists of a state of comparative isolation from the world, the female prisoners in the latter stages of the treatment are subject to less and less stringent regulations, and thus pass gradually through states first of what are termed "silent association," under which they are allowed to work in common without speaking, and afterwards advance to a state of association and intercommunication during the day, though still sleeping apart at night.

The following are the reasons assigned for this mode of treatment :—

"Until very lately female convicts," the authorities tell us, "were taught to regard expatriation as the inevitable consequence of their sentence ; and when detained in Millbank —usually for some months, waiting embarkation—they were reconciled to the discipline, however strict, by the knowledge that it would soon cease, and that it was only a necessary step towards all but absolute freedom in a colony. Now, however, the circumstances being materially altered, and discharge from prison in this country becoming the rule, it is essential that a corresponding change in the treatment of female prisoners should take place, with the view to preparing them to re-enter the world. Hence the necessity for establishing a system commencing with penal coercion, followed by appreciable advantages for continued good behaviour.

"As therefore a systematized classification, denoted by badges, and the placing of small gratuities for industry to the credit of the deserving, have been found by experience in all the convict prisons to produce the most satisfactory results, the same principle has been extended to Brixton."

With this view the prisoners there are divided into the following classes:—(1) First Class—(2) Second Class—(3) Third Class—(4) Probation Class.

All prisoners on reception are placed in the probation class, and confined in the cells of the old prison—in ordinary cases for a period of four months, and in special cases for a longer term, according to their conduct; and no prisoner in the probation class is allowed to receive a visit.

On leaving the probation class the prisoner is promoted to the third class, and when she has conducted herself well in that class for the space of two months, she is allowed to receive a visit. Then, if her conduct continue good for a period of six months after promotion to the third class, she is transferred to the second class, and is not only allowed to wear a badge marked 2, as indicative of her promotion, but becomes entitled to a gratuity of from sixpence to eightpence a week for her labour, such gratuity going to form a fund for her on her liberation.

If after this she still continue to behave herself well, while in the second class, for another period of six months, she then is raised into the first class, and allowed to wear a badge marked 1, as well as becoming entitled to a gratuity of eightpence to a shilling a week for her work.

No prisoner is recommended for removal or discharge on license (or ticket-of-leave) until she has proved herself worthy of being intrusted with her liberty previous to the expiration of her sentence.

Old or invalid prisoners, or those who have infants, or who, from any other cause, may be unable to work, have their case specially considered (after having gained their promotion to the first or second class), with a view to their being credited with some small weekly gratuity.

Prisoners may be degraded (with the sanction of a director) from a higher to a lower class through misconduct, but their former position may be regained by good conduct, and that without passing the full time in each class over again. All privileges, moreover, for good behaviour, such as gratuities for work, and the permission to receive visits, may be forfeited by bad behaviour.

"The means at our command," add the directors, "for improving, if not actually reforming, female convicts in prison, though carefully designed and faithfully executed, will be insufficient in many instances unless some asylum be found to receive them on their discharge from prison. The difficulties in the way of such women, as the majority of these prisoners, returning to respectability are too notorious to require description or enumeration. They beset them in every direction the moment they are discharged, and drive them back to their former evil ways and bad associates, if they be not rescued through the medium of a refuge from whence they may obtain service."

¶ ii—β.

Interior of the Brixton Prison.

It was not much after six o'clock when we began our day's rounds at the above institution. The gateway here looks as ordinary and ugly as that of Pentonville appears picturesque and stately, the Brixton portal being merely the old-fashioned arched gateway, with a series of "dabbed" stones projecting round the edge, and the door itself studded with huge nails.

On the gate being opened, we were saluted in military style by the ordinary prison gate-keeper, and shown into the little lodge, or old-fashioned porter's office at the side, where we were soon joined by the principal matron (whom the superintendent had kindly directed to accompany us for the entire day), and requested to follow her to the interior of the building.

The matron was habited in what we afterwards learnt was the official costume or uniform belonging to her station; there was, however, so little peculiar about her dress that it was not until we saw the other principal matrons in the same coloured ribbons and gowns that we had the slightest notion that such a costume partook in any way of a *uniform* character. She wore a dove-coloured, fine woollen dress, with a black-cloth mantle, and straw bonnet, trimmed with white ribbons, such being the official costume of the principal matrons. The uniform of the matrons, on the other hand, consists of the same coloured gown, but the bonnet is trimmed with deep blue, and when in the exercising grounds, the cloak they wear is a large, deep-caped affair, that reaches nearly to the feet, and is made of green woollen plaid.

While treating of this part of the subject, we may add that one of the main peculiarities of Brixton Prison is, that the great body of officials there belong to the softer sex, so that the discipline and order maintained at that institution become the more interesting as being the work of those whom the world generally considers to be ill-adapted for government. So much are we the creatures of prejudice, however, that it sounds almost ludicrous at first to hear Miss So-and-so spoken of as an experienced officer, or Mrs. Such-a-one described as having been many years in the service, as well as to learn that it is some young lady's turn to be on duty that night, or else that another fair one is to act as the night-patrol. It will be seen, too, by the subjoined list of officers at Brixton Prison,* that even the posts of superin-

* The following is a list of the several officers of the Female Convict Prison, Brixton, in the year 1856:—

LIST OF PRINCIPAL OFFICERS AND CLERKS.

Emma M. Martin	Superintendent	(Vacant)	Steward's clerk
Melhuish	Deputy ditto	W. F. Ralph	Foreman of Works
Rev. J. H. Moran	Chaplain	Julia Sims	Scripture Reader
Jas. D. Rendle	Surgeon	Sarah Smith	Schoolmistress
Fred. S. Parkyn	Steward	Caroline Hassall	„
John Face	Superintendent's clerk	Augusta Maclesh	„
Edwin Mills	Steward's ditto	Eleanor Millington	„

LIST OF OFFICERS IN THE MANUFACTURING OR LABOUR DEPARTMENT.

John Wildman	Steward's clerk	Chas. Purnell	Engineer
Sarah Mott	Workmistress	Fredk. King	Steward's porter
Margaret Hall	Cutter	Geo. Aylward	„ „

LIST OF SUBORDINATE OFFICERS AND SERVANTS.

Catherine Hewitt	Principal Matron	Jane Alderson	Assistant Matron
Mary Ann Donnelly	„ „	Caroline Tucker	„
Susannah White	„ „	Elizabeth White	„
Elizabeth Jones	Do. acting as clerk to Superintendent.	Martha A. Dickson	„
		Margaret Foley	„
Maria Hill	Do. do. to Chaplain.	Eliza Leatherdale	„
		Margaret Hughes	„
Mary Jane Bennett	Matron	Maria Hutchinson	„
Sarah Rogers	„	Lavinia Macpherson	„
Ellen Jones	„	Emma Melhuish	„
Ann Rediough	„	Maria Palmer	„
Ellen Cordwent	„	Louisa Face	„
Emma Fox	„	Elizabeth A. Baber	„
Harriet White	„	Merrion Halliday	„
Mary F. Mackins	„	Mary Smith	Head Nurse
Merrion Stewart	„	George Luckett	Gatekeeper
Mary Deaville	„	William Mant	Baker
Agnes J. Mayne	„	Mary Mant	Cook
Susan Edwards	„	William Allan	Messenger
Catherine Reeves	„	Thomas Roberts	Watchman
Constance Crosling	Assistant do.		
Marianne Fry	„	John Simmance	Carpenter
Elizabeth Harrison	„	Thos. Hawkins	Plumber
Ann Stevenson	„	Stephen Pankhurst	Labourer
Mary A. Hall	„		

THE CONVICT NURSERY AT BRIXTON.

tendent's and chaplain's clerks are women; but those who are inclined to smile at such matters should pay a visit to the Female Convict Prison at Brixton, and see how admirably the ladies really manage such affairs.

There is but little architectural or engineering skill to be noticed in the building at Brixton, after the eye has been accustomed to the comparative elegance and scientific refinement visible in the arrangements of Pentonville.

At the end of a large court-yard, as we enter, stands a clumsy-looking octagonal house, that was originally the governor's residence, or " argus," as such places were formerly styled, whence he was supposed to inspect the various exercising yards and sides of the jail itself. This argus, however, is now devoted to the several stores and principal offices required for the management of the prison.

The most remarkable parts of the jail are the two new wings built at the corners, or horns, as we have said, of the old crescent-shaped building. These consist each of one long corridor, the character of which is somewhat like the interior of a tall and narrow terminus to some railway station; for the corridors here are neither so spacious nor yet so desolate-looking as those at Pentonville, since at Brixton there are stoves and tables arranged down the centre of the arcades, and the cell-doors are as close as those of the cabins in a ship, to which, indeed, the cells themselves, ranged along the galleries, one after another, bear a considerable resemblance.

But though there are many more doors visible here than at the largest railway hotel, and though the galleries or balconies above, with their long range of sleeping apartments stretching round the building, call to mind the arrangements at the yards of the old coaching inns, nevertheless there is nothing of the ordinary prison character or gloomy look about this part of the building; and though the corridors are built somewhat on the same plan as the arcades at Pentonville, they have a considerably more cheerful look than the apparently tenantless tunnels at that prison.

The old parts of Brixton Prison are the very opposite to the newer portions of it, for in them we see the type of a gloomy and pent-up jail. There the passages are intensely long and narrow—like flattened tubes, as it were—and extend from one point of the crescent to the other, at the back of every floor; the doors of the cells too are heavy cumbrous affairs, with a large perforated circular plate in each, such as is seen at the top of stoves, for admitting or shutting-off the heated air—which clumsy arrangement was originally intended as a means of peeping into the cells from without.

These passages of the old prison are as white as snow with their coats of lime, and seem, from the monotony of their colour and arrangement, to be positively endless, as you pass by door after door, fitted with the same big metal wheel for spying through, and the huge ugly lock of the old prison kind.

The cells in this part of the building are not unlike so many cleanly cellars, with the exception that their roofs are not vaulted, and there is a small " long-light " of a window near the ceiling.

These cells are each provided with a gas-jet and chimney, and triangular shelves, as well as a small stool and table, and a little deal box for keeping cloths in, and which can also be used as a rest for the feet. Then there is a hammock, to be slung from wall to wall, as at Pentonville, and the rugs and blankets of which are usually folded up and stacked against the side, as shown in the annexed engraving.

The cells here are all whitewashed, and as white as Alpine snow, with their coat of lime, so that they try the sight sorely after a time; indeed, we were told that a gipsy woman (one of the Coopers) who was imprisoned here, suffered severely in her eyes from the dazzling whiteness of the walls that continually surrounded her; and if it be true that perpetually gazing at snow has a tendency to produce " *gutta serena* " in some people, we can readily understand the acute pain that must be experienced by those whose sight is unable to bear such intense glare, and from which it is impossible to transfer the eye even up to the blue of the sky by way of a relief. We were informed that the gipsy woman was very violent during her incarceration, and it does not require a great stretch of fancy to conceive the extreme mental and physical agony that must have been inflicted upon such a person, unaccustomed as she had been all her life even to the confinement of a house, and whose eye had been looking upon the green fields ever since her infancy; so that it is not difficult to understand how the four blank white walls for ever hemming in this wretched creature, must have seemed

SEPARATE CELL IN THE OLD PART OF THE PRISON AT BRIXTON.

not only to have half-stifled her with their closeness, but almost have maddened her with the intensity of their snow-like glare.

The cells in the east and west wings, though smaller than those in the old part of the prison, have not nearly so jail-like a look about them; for the sides of these are built of corrugated iron, and though fitted with precisely the same furniture as the cells before described, they greatly resemble, as we have said, the cabin of a ship (see engraving on next page), whilst the arrangements made for the ventilation of each chamber are as perfect as they well can be under the circumstances.

Respecting the character of the inmates of this prison, the Government reports furnish us with some curious information. "The prisoners," say the Directors of her Majesty's Convict Prisons, "may generally be classed, as regards their conduct, in two divisions, viz., the many who are good, and the few who are bad. In one or other extreme these unfortunate females have been usually found. It also by no means uncommonly occurs that a woman who has conducted herself for several months outrageously, and been to all appearance insensible to shame, to kindness, to punishment, will suddenly alter and continue without even a reprimand to the end of her imprisonment; whereas, on the other hand, one who has behaved so well as to be put into the first class, and on whom apparently every dependence may be placed, will suddenly break out, give way to uncontrollable passion, and in utter desperation commit a succession of offences, as if it were her object to revenge herself upon herself.

"Among the worst prisoners were women who had been sentenced to transportation just

SEPARATE SLEEPING-CELL IN ONE OF THE NEW WINGS OF THE FEMALE
CONVICT PRISON AT BRIXTON.

previously to the passing of the Act which practically substituted imprisonment in this country for expatriation. A few of these had, according to their own statement, even pleaded guilty for the purpose of being sent abroad; but when they became aware that they were to be eventually discharged in this country after a protracted penal detention, disappointment rendered them thoroughly reckless; hope died within them; they actually courted punishment; and their delight and occupation consisted in doing as much mischief as they could. They constantly destroyed their clothes, tore up their bedding, and smashed their windows. They frequently threatened the officers with violence, though it must be stated, at the same time, they seldom proceeded to put their threats in force; and when they did so, some among them—and generally those who were most obnoxious to discipline—invariably took the officers' part to protect them from personal injury.

"Of these a few are not at all improved, notwithstanding the kindness they have met with, or the punishments they have undergone, or the moral and religious instruction they have received; and they will probably remain so until their sentences have expired. Some, however, are doing very well, and give promise of real amendment."

Farther, the medical officer, in his report for the year 1854, says, "I may, perhaps, be here allowed to state that my experience of the past year has convinced me that the female prisoners, *as a body*, do not bear imprisonment so well as the male prisoners; they get anxious, restless, more irritable in temper, and are more readily excited, and they look forward to the future with much less hope of regaining their former position in life.

"Neither can I refrain from saying that there are circumstances which help to reconcile the male prisoner to his sentence, but which are altogether wanting in the case of the female. The male prisoner not only gets a change from one prison to another—and though small as this change be, yet it is a something which, for the time, breaks the sameness inseparable from his imprisonment—but, what is of far greater moment, he looks forward to the time when he will be employed *in the open air* on public works.

"The length of the imprisonment of the woman, however, combined with the present uncertainty as to the duration of that portion of her sentence which is to be passed in prison, as well as the more sedentary character of her employment, allowing the mind, as it does, to be continually dwelling on 'her time'—all tend to make a sentence more severe to the woman, than a sentence of the same duration to the man."

Farther, the chaplain gives us the following curious statistics as to the education and causes of the degradation of the several women who have been imprisoned at Brixton:—

"Of the 664 prisoners admitted into this prison from November 24th, 1853, to December 31st, 1854, there were the following proportions of educated and uneducated people:—

Number that could not read at all		104
,, ,, could read a few syllables		53
,, ,, could read imperfectly		192
Total imperfectly-educated		349
Number that could read tolerably, but most of whom had learned in prison or revived what they had learned in youth		315
Moderately-educated		None
Total		664

"Hence it appears," adds the chaplain, "that among 664 prisoners admitted into this prison, there is not one who has received even a moderate amount of education. Among the same number of male prisoners, judging by my past experience, I feel persuaded that there would be many who had received a fair amount of education. This confirms me in the opinion which I expressed last year, 'that the beneficial effects of education are more apparent among females than men.'

"Of the same 664 prisoners, the minister tells us—

453 trace their ruin to drunkenness or bad company, or both united.

97 ran away from home, or from service.

84 assigned various causes of their fall.

6 appear to have been suddenly tempted into crime.

8 state that they were in want.

16 say they are innocent.

664."

¶ ii—γ.

A Day at Brixton.*

On our way across the gravelled court-yard, we had our first peep at the female convicts imprisoned at Brixton, and so simple and picturesque was their convict costume, that they had none of the repulsive and spectral appearance of the brown masked men at Pentonville, nor had they even the unpleasant, gray, pauper look of the male prisoners at Millbank.

Their dress consisted of a loose, dark, claret-brown robe or gown, with a blue check apron and neckerchief, while the cap they wore was a small, close, white muslin one, made after the fashion of a French *bonne's*. The colour of the gown was at once rich and artistically appropriate, and gave great value to the tints of the apron, and even the whiteness of the cap itself. On their arms the prisoners carried some bright brass figures, representing their register number; while some bore, above these, badges in black and white, inscribed one or two, according as they belonged to the first or second class of convicts.

Occasionally there flitted across the yard some female convict, clad in a light-blue kind of over-dress. These, we were informed, were principally at work in the laundry, and the garb, though partaking too much of the butcher-tint to be either pleasing or picturesque, was still both neat and clean.

The first place we visited was the bakery, and on our way thither we passed women carrying large black baskets of coal, and engaged in what is termed the "coal service" in the yard.

The bakery was a pleasant and large light building, adjoining the kitchen, and here we found more females, in light blue gowns, at work on the large dresser, with an immense heap of dough that lay before them like a huge drab-coloured feather-bed, and with the master baker in his flannel jacket standing beside the oven watching the work. Some of the female prisoners were working the dough, that yielded to their pressure like an air-cushion; and some were cutting off pieces and weighing them in the scales before them, and then tossing them over to others, who moulded them into the form of dumplings, or small loaves.

At the end of the bakery was the large prison kitchen, where stood kind of beer-trays—such as the London pot-boys use for the conveyance of the mid-day and nocturnal porter to the houses in the neighbourhood. These trays at Brixton, however, served for the conveyance of the dinner-cans to the several parts of the prison, whilst the huge, bright, spouted tin beer-cans that stood beside them were used for the dispensation of the cocoa that was now steaming in the adjoining coppers, and being served out by more prisoners, ready against the breakfast-hour, at half-past seven.†

---

* We may add here, that the Brixton County House of Correction, according to Brayley's *History of Surrey*, was erected in 1819-20, for the reception and imprisonment of offenders sentenced to hard labour, either at the county assizes or sessions, or summarily convicted before a magistrate. "The boundary-wall," says the county historian, "is about twenty feet in height, the upper part being of open brick-work, and encloses about two and a half acres of ground. This prison is chiefly formed by a semi-octagonal building, having a chapel in the centre, in front of which, but separated by a yard, is the tread-mill, which was formerly more than sufficiently notorious from the severity of its application."

The total cost of the building, together with the sum paid for the purchase of the land and erection of the treadmill, was, we are informed by Mr. Woronzow Greig, the obliging clerk of the peace for Surrey, £51,780 17s. 7d., whilst the sum paid for the construction of the mill itself was £6,913 3s. 6d.

† For breakfast the ordinary prison diet consists of 6 ounces of bread, and ¾ pint of cocoa to each prisoner, whilst those engaged in the labour of the laundry, bakehouse, &c., are severally allowed 8 ounces of bread and one pint of cocoa.

For dinner the prison allowance is 4 ounces of cooked meat, ½ pint of soup, with ½ pound of potatoes and 6 ounces of bread, whilst the labourers get each 5 ounces of meat, and 1 pint of soup, with 1 pound of pota-

⁎ *The Serving of the Dinners at Brixton.*—We were present at the serving of the dinners in this establishment, which were dispensed after the following manner :—

At a few minutes before one o'clock the "breads" are counted out into large wicker baskets, in the shape of those used for dinner-plates, while the tin cans—which, like those at Pentonville, have a partition in the middle, similar to the ones carried by bill-stickers—being filled with soup and meat on one side, and potatoes on the other, are ranged in large potboy-like trays, which are inscribed with the letters of the several wards to which they appertain.

Precisely at one o'clock a bell is heard to ring, and then the matrons of the old prison enter in rotation, each accompanied with four prisoners, one of whom seizes one tray, while two more of the gang go off with another that is heavier laden, and the last hurries off with the basket of bread, with an officer at her heels.

After this, large trucks are brought in, and when stowed with the trays and bread-baskets for the "wings," they are wheeled off by the attendant prisoners, one woman dragging in front, and the others pushing behind.

We followed the two trucks that went to the east wing of the prison, and here we found a small crowd of women waiting, with the matrons at the door, ready to receive the trays as the vehicles were unladen. "That's ours!" cried one of the female officers in attendance ; and immediately the prisoners beside her seized the tray with the basket of bread, and went off with it, as if they were so many pot-girls carrying round the beer.

Then a large bell clattered through the building, and one of the warders screamed at the top of her voice, "O Lord, bless this food to our use, and us to thy service, through Jesus Christ our Lord. Amen!"

No sooner was the grace ended, than the officers of the several wards went along the galleries, opening each cell-door by the way, with three or four prisoners in their wake, carrying the trays. The cell being opened, the matron handed in the bread from the basket which one of the prisoners carried, and then a can of soup from the tray, the door being closed again immediately afterwards, so that the arcade rang with the unlocking and slamming of the doors in the several galleries. When the dinners were all served, the cell-doors were double locked, and then another bell rang for silence ; after which, any prisoner talking, we were told, would be reported to the superintendent for breach of rules.

The distribution of the dinners was at once rapid and orderly, and reflected no slight credit upon the several ladies who are engaged in the conduct of the prison for the almost military precision with which the duty was carried out.

A curious part of the process consisted in the distribution of the knives before dinner, and collection of them afterwards. For the latter purpose, one of the best-conducted prisoners goes round with a box, a matron following in her steps, and then the knives, ready cleaned, are put out under the door. These are all counted, and locked up in store for the next day. But if one of the number be short, the prisoners are not let out of their cells till the missing knife be found, each convict and cell being separately searched, with a view to its discovery.

During the dinner hour we went over to the infirmary kitchen, to see how the sick pri-

---

toes and 6 ounces of bread—the convalescents having the same as the labourers, with the exception of being served with mutton instead of beef.

For supper, on the other hand, the labourers and convalescents have each 8 ounces of bread and 1 pint of tea, whilst the laundry-women have all 1½ ounce of cheese in addition—the ordinary prison diet for the same meal consisting of a pint of gruel and 8 ounces of bread for the No. 3 women, as they are called (*i.e.*, the third-class prisoners) ; whilst the No. 2 women get the same allowance of gruel and bread four times in the week, and a pint of tea instead of gruel three times in the week ; and the No. 1 women a pint of tea every night.

This dietary scale is very nearly the same as that at Pentonville, with the exception that the prisoners there get 1 lb. of potatoes instead of ½ lb., as at Brixton.

soners fared in Brixton.   Here we found the cook busily serving out a small piece of boiled cod for some who had been ordered to be placed on fish diet, and dishing up some mutton chops for others.   Then there were poached eggs for a few, and a batter-pudding and some rice-milk for some of the other invalids; so that it was plain the majority of the poor creatures fared more sumptuously under their punishment than they possibly could have done outside the prison walls.

⁎ *Exercising at Brixton.*—The airing yards at this prison have little of the bare gravel school play-ground character, so common with those at the other jails, for here there are grass-plots and flower-beds, so that, were it not for the series of mad-house-like windows piercing the prison walls, a walk in the exercising grounds of Brixton would be pleasant and unprison-like enough.

The prisoners exercise principally for one hour—from eight till nine; the laundry-women, however, whose work is laborious, walk for only half the usual time.

It is a somewhat curious and interesting sight to see near upon two hundred female convicts pacing in couples round and round the Brixton exercising yards, and chattering as they go like a large school, so that the yard positively rings as if it were a market-place with the gabbling of the many tongues; indeed, the sight of the convicts, filing along in couples, reminds one of the charity children parading through the streets, for the prisoners are dressed in the same plain straw bonnets, and not only have a like cleanly and neat look, but are equally remarkable for the tidiness of their shoes and stockings.   (*See engraving.*)

As we stood, with the principal matron still attending us, watching the prisoners pace round and round, like a cavalcade at a circus, while the warders on duty cried, " Hasten on there, women—hasten on !" our intelligent and communicative guide ran over to us the peculiarities of the several convicts as they passed.

"Those you see exercising there, in the inner ring, sir," she said, "are the invalids, and we let them walk at a slower pace.   This one coming towards us," she whispered, "is in for life, for the murder of her child.   You wouldn't think it, would you, sir, to look at her ?" and assuredly there was no trace of brutal ferocity in her countenance.   " Her conduct here has been always excellent—she's as gentle as a lamb; I really think she's sincerely penitent."

" That one now approaching us," she added, "is one of the worst tempered girls in the whole prison.   By her smile, you would take her to be the very opposite to what she is."

" Yonder woman," continued the matron, "is one of the best we have here, and yet she's in for biting off a man's ear; but the man had been trying to injure her very much before she was roused to it.   They are mostly all in for thieving, and, generally speaking, they have led the most abandoned lives."

The truth of the last remark was evident in the smiles and shamelessness of many; for, as they paraded past us, not a few stared in our face with all the brazen look of the streets, and yet many of their countenances were almost beautiful, so that it was difficult to believe that there was any deep-rooted evil in their hearts.

" It is curious, sir, the vanity of many of these women," whispered our intelligent guide. " Those straw bonnets none of them can bear, and it is as much as ever we can do to make them put them on when they are going to see the doctor.   They think they look much better in their caps.   One woman, I give you my word, took the ropes off her hammock and put them round the bottom of her dress so as to make the skirt seem fuller.   Another we had filled her gown with coals round the bottom for the same object; and others, again, have taken the wire from round the dinner cans and used it as stiffners to their stays. One actually took the tinfoil from under the buttons, and made it into a ring.   You would hardly believe it, perhaps, but I have known women scrape the walls of their cells and use the powder of the whitewash to whiten their complexion.   Indeed, there is hardly any trick they would not be at if we did not keep a sharp eye upon them."

** *The Chapel at Brixton Prison.*—The little church for the female convicts is at once simple and handsome in its internal decorations. The roof, which is of oak, bears a rude resemblance to that of Westminster Hall, ornamented as it is with its brown "hammer-beams" and "collar-beams;" and when the sittings are filled with the convict-congregation, habited in their dark claret gowns and clean white caps, we hardly know a prettier or a more touching sight in the world; for the suspicion of hypocrisy that lurks in the mind, despite the apparent fervour of the prisoners at Pentonville, serves greatly to lessen our sympathy with the contrition of the criminals there. We all know, however, that women are naturally not only less skilled in simulation and cunning, but of a more religious and ardent tempera-ment than men, so that we no sooner hear the confessions of sin and supplications for mercy uttered in the general responses of these wretched unfortunates, than it becomes impossible to withhold our commiseration, or to refrain from adding our own prayer for their forgive-ness to the one common cry.

Moreover, never did we see a congregation more zealous and apparently truthful in their devotions, for though we ourselves were, with the exception of the gate-keeper and the minister, the only male among the number there assembled, and a stranger to the place, nevertheless our presence served in no way to take the attention of the women from their books; and we could tell, by the fixedness of their gaze upon the chaplain during his dis-course, how intent they all were upon his precepts and teachings.

Nor was it any wonder, to those who had previously witnessed the feeling which existed between the minister and the prisoners at Brixton, that the convicts should hang upon his every word as children listen, in purest faith, to all that falls from a father's lips.

We had gone over the prison in company with the chaplain himself, and noted, long before the service commenced, that he was esteemed as a kind and dear friend by every one of the wretched inmates there. The smile in each countenance as he passed, the sparkle in every eye, and the confiding look of all into his face, told us that the wretched women clung, in their sins, to him who was their protector against the fury of the world without—even as the adulterous woman sought shelter from the wrath of her assailants in the loving-kindness of Christ himself.

As the chaplain accompanied us on our rounds, we soon saw that his was no mere *pro-fession* of Christian duty, and that those he had undertaken to watch over and lead into new and happier paths he took no common interest in—being acquainted with almost all the mem-bers of their family, and speaking first to this one of her mother, and then to another of her son, while to a third he told how some old fellow-prisoner whose time had recently expired, was doing well, and in a comfortable situation at last.

Nor was it only the chaplain himself who was thus friendly with the inmates of the jail, for every member of his youthful family was equally well known, and, one could see at a glance, equally beloved by them all; the young people had evidently made them-selves acquainted with the history of each wretched woman under their father's care, and while the sons displayed no little interest in the chaplain's duty, the daughter spoke of the poor fallen women with exquisite tenderness, and delighted to recount to us how some of the convicts had been reclaimed, and how little the world really knew of the trials and temptations of such characters. Indeed, we never met with a finer and nobler instance of Christian charity than we here found practised daily by this most righteous and unassuming family.

** *"Reports," Punishments, and Refractory Cells at Brixton.*—We requested permission of Mrs. Martin, the superintendent, to be present during her examination of the prisoners who had been reported for misconduct. The superintendent sat at her desk, in the principal office of the argus or octagonal house, in the centre of the prison yard, and gave directions to the matron in attendance to bring in the first prisoner who had been reported.

THE CHAPEL AT BRIXTON.

"This," said the superintendent to us, awaiting the return of the matron with the woman, "is a case of quarreling and fighting between two of the prisoners—a charge that, I am sorry to say, is by no means unusual here."

Presently the door opened, and the matron brought in a prisoner whose features and complexion were those of a creole, and who was habited in the blue dress of the laundry-women.

"How is it, prisoner," inquired the lady governor, "that you are brought here again?"

"Well, mum," replied the woman, as she shook her head with considerable emotion, and drew near to the table of the superintendent, "I couldn't stand it no longer! She offered to strike me three times afore ever I touched a hair of her head—that she did, mum; and as my liberty hadn't come, you know, mum—" and the half-caste was about to enter into a long explanation on the latter part of the subject, when she was stopped by the lady saying, "Yes, I know; and I make great allowance for you."

"I was sure you would, mum," briskly replied the woman; "she called me a ——."

"Oh, dear me!—there, I don't want to hear what was said," again interrupted the superintendent. "Well, I shall not punish you until I have looked into the affair; so you may go back to your work."

"Thank you, mum," and the prisoner curtseyed, as she left the room with the matron; whereupon, immediately afterwards, another convict was ushered in.

"You have been behaving very ill, I hear," said the superintendent.

"I'm very sorry," was the prisoner's reply; "but I'm a woman as doesn't like quarreling."

"There, don't say that; for I have your name down here rather often!" returned the superintendent; "besides, my officer tells me that you were at fault, so I shall punish you by stopping your dinner."

"These are all the refractory cases," said the female officer, as the prisoner curtseyed and left the room; "but there are three women who wish to speak with you, ma'am."

"Very well, bring them in," said the superintendent.

The first of these was a young Scotch girl, who said that she came about her letters, and that she hadn't got her letters, though her mother had written her several letters, but that all her letters had been kept back. Whereupon the superintendent explained to her that she was only allowed to receive and write one every two months; and on the female clerk being consulted as to the number the girl had received, the answer returned was that she had been permitted to have three within the stated time; so the prisoner left the room muttering that the letters were from her mother, and that she wanted her letters, and no one had a right to keep back her letters.

"That girl," said the superintendent, "has got ten years, and is very irritable under it; indeed, I often think the women make up the cases for the sake of coming here and getting a little variety to their life."

The second prisoner seeking an interview with the superintendent, was likewise a Scotch woman, and she also came to speak about her letters. "You gave me permission, mum, to write to my son," said the convict; "he's come home from Balaklava, and gone to Bombay since." "Well," was the answer, "if I did, you must leave the letter here and I will see about sending it for you." "Bless you, mum!" said the old woman, as she hobbled, with repeated curtseys, out of the room.

The last woman seeking an interview was one who came to know about being recommended for her ticket-of-leave. "The women that got their badges at the same time as me has had their liberty already, please mum," urged the prisoner. Whereupon the superintendent asked the woman whom she had got to receive her when she was let out. "My sister," was the answer. "And how do you mean to support yourself?" "Oh, please mum, my sister says she'll get me into service," replied the prisoner, curtseying. "I hope you will do well," was the kind-hearted exclamation of the superintendent; "and your recommendation shall be sent up next time."

"Is that all, Miss Donnelly?" the lady-governor asked, as the prisoner retired thanking her; and being informed that she had seen all the applicants, the female officer was dismissed.

"We have sent away altogether upwards of 200 women on ticket-of-leave, and only 4 have come back," said the lady, in answer to a question from us, "and even with those four we can hardly believe them to be guilty; the police are so sharp with the poor things. When they are brought back to me here, the women feel dreadfully ashamed of themselves, and one was the very picture of despair. She's the mother of twins, and has attempted her life several times since. The police are very severe with them, I think; and I can't help feeling an interest in the wretched creatures, just as if they were children of my own. Last night I was obliged to order handcuffs to be put on the ticket-of-leave woman who has just been sent back to us; she had commenced breaking her windows, and threatened to assault her officer. This re-commitment has made her quite different, and I think the state of her mind is very doubtful now. When I first came here," continued the lady, "I'm sure it was like living in another planet. As a clergyman's wife, I used to see all kinds of people of course, but never any like these. Oh, they are most peculiar! There are many of them subject to fits of the most ungovernable fury; very often there is no cause at all for their passion except their own morbid spirits; perhaps their friends haven't written, so they'll sit and work themselves up into a state of almost frenzy, and when the officer comes they will give way. Sometimes they know when the fit is coming on, and will themselves ask to be locked up in the refractory wards.

"When they are in these fits they're terribly violent indeed," the superintendent went on; "they tear up and break everything they can lay their hands on. The other day one of the prisoners not only broke all the windows in her cell, but tore all her bed-clothes into ribbons, and pulled open her bed and tossed all the coir in a heap on the floor; and then she wrenched off the gas-jet, and so managed to pull down the triangular iron shelf that is fixed into the wall at one corner of the cell. When the prisoners work themselves up to such a state as that, we're generally obliged to call the male officers to them. The younger they are the worse they behave. The most violent age, I think, is from seventeen to two or three and twenty—indeed, they are like fiends at that age very often. But, really, I can hardly speak with certainty on the matter, the life is so new to me. Often, when the prisoners have behaved very badly in one prison, they'll be quite different on going to another; a fresh place gives them an opportunity of turning over a new leaf, I fancy. Oh, yes! I find them very sensitive to family ties, and I'm often touched myself to think such wicked creatures should have such tender feelings. The son of that old Scotch woman you saw here writes her the most beautiful letters, and sends her all the money he can scrape together. Generally speaking, they have most of them been previously convicted, and more than once; often, too, the very worst outside are the best behaved in the prison—that makes it so difficult to get situations for them.'

Afterwards, in the course of an interview with the medical officer, we sought to ascertain whether any physical cause could be assigned for these sudden and violent outbursts among the women. The surgeon informed us that he knew of no bodily or organic reason to account for them; four per cent. of the whole of the prisoners, or 20 in 600 were subject to such fits of violent passion, and these were almost invariably from fifteen to twenty-five years of age. The elder women were equally bad in nature—perhaps worse—but they did not break the prison rules like the younger ones. "Women, even in their most furious moments," he told us, "seldom injure themselves or those around them, though they will break their windows, and even occasionally tear their own clothing to ribbons."

On a subsequent occasion we spoke of these ungovernable bursts of violence to a lady friend of ours—one who was really of an exceeding gentle nature; and she frankly confessed that she could understand the luxury of smashing things in an overwhelming fit of temper. "You men," she said, as she saw us smile at her candour, "are stronger than we, and therefore you vent your passions upon the people about you; but women cannot do this from their very weakness, and so those poor ignorant things who have never learnt self-control expend their fury upon the tables, chairs, and glasses, that are unable to turn upon them—even as some husbands vent their passion on their wives, who are incapable of defending themselves against them.

"Temper," she added, "is always cowardly, and wreaks itself only upon such things as it fancies it can master."

At another part of the day we inspected the refractory cells, which are situate in the old prison. These are six in number, and not quite dark, the screen before the windows being pierced with holes; for on entering one, and requesting that the double doors might be closed upon us, we found we could see to write after a few moments, when the eye had grown accustomed to the darkness; and it was curious to watch how each part of the cell that was invisible at first started into sight after a few minutes. Then we could see that there was the same rude wooden couch, with the sloping head-piece, on the floor as in others, and a large air-hole, from the passage near the ceiling, for the ventilation of the cell.

There were also the "hoppered cells," where those women are put who are accustomed to break the windows, or to speak or look out of them—the hopper being a slanting iron screen in front of the casement, so called from its resemblance to that wedge-shaped trough in a mill into which the corn is put to be ground. Six of these cells were without glass and six with, whilst one was constructed upon a new plan, and had a perforated zinc screen to prevent the women smashing the windows.

"The punishments," says the Brixton chaplain, in his report for 1854, "are apparently numerous; but a careful inspection of the misconduct-book will prove that *most of them* have been inflicted upon the *same* persons, and that the great body of the prisoners has not been subjected to any punishment at all. Violence of temper is one great evil with female prisoners: they are so easily excited, and so subject to sudden impulses, that it is very painful to consider what misery they bring upon themselves, owing to the influence of bad temper."*

** *The Convict Nursery at Brixton.*—The most touching portion of the female convict prison, and what distinguishes it essentially from all the penal institutions appropriated to male prisoners, is that which forms the heading of the present portion of our description of the internal economy of the Brixton establishment.

To those who know the early life and education of the habitual criminal—who know how, in many cases, he was born among thieves, reared and schooled among thieves, and thieves only—how he was begotten, perhaps, by a convict father, and nursed by a felon mother, and

* The following list is extracted from the last published Report of the Directors of Convict Prisons :—

RETURN OF PUNISHMENTS AT THE FEMALE CONVICT PRISON, 1854.

In Handcuffs - - - - - - 31	Confined to Cell - - - - 34
Straight Waistcoat - - - - - 1	Withdrawn from Association - - - 70
Refractory Cell { Full Rations - - - 141	Reprimanded - - - - - 257
{ Bread and Water - - 147	Admonished - - - - - 171
On Bread and Water Diet - - - - 92	Not punished on Special Grounds - - 19
Deprived of One Meal or Part of a Meal - 246	Total - - 1209

By the above table it will be seen that the most frequent punishment resorted to was confinement in the refractory cell, of which there were 288 cases in the course of the year. That the next puuishment in the order of frequency was a simple reprimand, of which there were 257 cases, whilst the chastisement, of which the number of cases stood next in the list, was the deprivation of a meal, or part of a meal, and of which there were 246 instances. The more serious impositions, such as handcuffs and straight waistcoat, were comparatively limited.

trained, too, at the earliest age to dishonest practices by light-fingered tutors, as regularly as our children are disciplined into virtuous courses—how he was taught by his companions in crime to look upon the greatest ruffian as the greatest hero; and how with the vagabond and wayward class, from whom his paradoxical morals have been derived, the plundering of the industrious portion of society is regarded as a part of virtue, if not religion—(for the gipsy says to her child, "And now, having said your prayers, go out and steal," even as the Thug offers up his worship to Kalee, before starting to ensnare and murder his victim)— and how, moreover, your true hereditary criminal has learnt from his earliest childhood to admire and approve of only feats of low cunning, and that brute courage, which his class terms "pluck;" and to believe that to "*do* your neighbour, as your neighbour would *do* you," constitutes the real *summum bonum* of life; he, we repeat, who knows this, and who knows, moreover, that there are distinct races of outcasts and wanderers, moved by the very opposite philosophy and principles to that which we and our children have, as Christians, been taught to revere, must surely feel, that had it been his lot to have been born and bred among such tribes, his own conscience would, most probably, have been as warped and tainted as that of those he has learnt to condemn, if not to loathe; and feeling this, the first great lesson of toleration, viz., that even his own individual exemption from jail is due rather to the accident of his birth and parentage, than to any special merit on his part, he cannot but in his heart get to pity the poor wretches who have been less lucky in the lottery of life than he.

But this is mere sentimentality, the sterner reader will perhaps exclaim—maudling philanthropy, that comes of the prevailing morbid desire to cuddle and caress creatures whom we, in our honest indignation, should shun and despise. Those who think thus, we answer, should visit Brixton prison, and see the little babes there, clinging to their convict mothers' skirts, or playing with their rag-dolls in the convict nursery; and then ask themselves what fate they think can await the wretched little things that have made so bad a start in the great race of life. Will not the goal they are destined probably to reach have the vowels transposed, and be written *gaol* instead?—for even though *now* they be, as the Great Teacher said, "types of the kingdom of heaven," and with an almost angel-innocence beaming in their pretty little cherub faces, is it not most likely that, in after life, those who drew their first breath inside the prison walls will come to breathe their last gasp there also? Is this so-called Christian country sufficiently enlightened and charitable yet, think you, to allow such as they the same chance of success in the world as honest men's children? Will they meet with no gibes in years to come, for their felon extraction? Would *you*, reader, like to take them into your household and your family, when they grow up, to tend your own little ones? And if all the arrogant prejudices of society be at war with their advancement, think you they will live at peace with the rest of mankind; or that they can possibly find in after life that honesty is the best policy, when almost every one is prepared to deny them the privilege of labouring for their livelihood—or, in other words, the very means of practising the virtue?

"This," said our attendant, as we entered the pathetic place, while the matron led the first babe she met towards us, "is little Eliza; she was born in the jail at York, and is rather better than two years old."

The tiny creature hung its head, and struggled to get back to its mother, as we stooped down and held our hand out towards it; but the little thing had long been accustomed to see no man's face but that of the chaplain and the surgeon, so it screamed to get farther from us, the nearer we drew towards it. She was a pretty gray-eyed child, and dressed the same as the other infants in the room, in a spotted blue frock—*the convict baby-clothes*. The mother of this one was the wife of a labouring man, and condemned to five years' imprisonment.

With the tears stinging our eyes, we passed on to the next little innocent—innocent for how long? *She* was called Jeanie, and was nearly two years and a half old; she had been

FEMALE CONVICTS EXERCISING IN THE AIRING YARD AT BRIXTON PRISON.

(From a Photograph by Herbert Watkins, 179, Regent Street.)

born in Glasgow prison; the mother was unmarried, and sentenced to four years' penal servitude.

Little Sarah, the next we turned to, was a poor, white-faced infant, that had been born in Brixton prison itself seven months ago, and was sickly with its teething. The mother had to suffer four years' penal servitude, and was married to a private in the Fusilier Guards, but had not heard from him since her conviction.

The next babe was younger still, having been born in Brixton on the 7th of February last. This was a boy, and named Thomas. The mother was unmarried, and had four years' penal servitude to undergo.

Martha was the name of the next convict child; and she was a fair-haired, fresh-cheeked, pretty little thing, rather more than two years old, and asleep in the prison bed.

"That is the most timid child I ever met with," said the kind-hearted matron, who accompanied us throughout the day. "She was born in Lincoln Castle, and the mother—("She's unmarried, sir," whispered the officer, apart, to us, as we jotted down the facts in our note-book)—has ten years' transportation, and more than seven years still to serve."

"Ah! *she's* a sad romp," said our attendant, as we passed on to another child—Annie, she was called. She was tottering along, as she held her mother's finger. "She's two years and three months on the 21st of May, sir," said the mother, in answer to our question, "and was born in Lewes jail. I've got six years' penal servitude." Poor Annie! we inwardly exclaimed; for she was a clean, flaxen-haired, laughing little thing, that smiled as she looked up into our face. "Not married!" added the wretched mother, timidly.

At this moment the chaplain entered, when several of the little things toddled off towards the good man, and he raised them in his arms, and kissed them one after another. "Oh! I saw Tommy's mother, the other day," said he to one of the women, in reference to an old prisoner who had obtained her liberty. "She's been doing very nicely. Tommy's been rather poorly, though. I hope I shall be able to get her another situation."

"There, you see," said the minister, turning to us, and pointing to the tins on an adjacent table, "is the nursery breakfast. There's a pint of milk for each child, and tea for the mothers."

As we left, the matron whispered to us that the pictures for the children, hanging up against the wall, were given by the clergyman. And when we returned to the nursery, later in the day, we found the mothers at work at some new frocks that the chaplain's daughter had presented to the poor little things.

"There's one apiece all round, baby and all," said the matron, as she held up a tiny frock that was finished, by the little short sleeves. It was a neat chintz pattern, that was at once serviceable and pretty. "They'd only those white-spotted blue things before, sir."

At another part of the day we spoke with the chaplain himself concerning the prison regulations upon such matters, and then he told us that at one time there had been as many as thirty children in that establishment; but lately the Secretary of State had issued an order forbidding them to receive children from other prisons. "If the child be born here it is to stay with the mother—how long I cannot say," added the minister, "but if born in jail before the mother comes here, it is to be sent to the Union immediately she is ordered to be removed to this prison. We never had a child older than four years, but at Millbank one little thing had been kept so long incarcerated, that on going out of the prison it called a horse a cat. The little girl that we had here of four years of age, my children used to take to the Sunday school, so that she might mix a little with the world, for she used to exclaim, when she was taken out into the road and saw a horse go by, 'look at that great big doggie.'"

There is, indeed, no place in which there is so much toleration, and true wisdom, if not goodness, to be learnt, as in the convict nursery at Brixton!

WASH-HOUSE AT THE BRIXTON PRISON.

*** *The Delivery of the Prison Letters.*—A letter, at all times, is more highly prized by women than men. The reason is obvious. The letters addressed to males are more frequently upon purely business matters, so that after a time the sight of such documents conjures up no pleasant association in men's minds; whereas the letters of females are, generally, so intimately connected with matters of pleasure, and so often with the outpourings of affection from friends or relations, that the very sight of an envelope bearing their name and address is sufficient to excite in them not only the most lively emotions, but the most intense curiosity.

Towards the evening of the day of our visit to Brixton prison, the chaplain's clerk (who, be it observed, was no serious-looking gentleman in dingy black, but an intelligent and pleasant-looking young woman, who, in the female prison, combines with the clerk's duty the equally male office of general postman) came towards us with a bundle of letters, and asked us whether we would like to accompany her on her rounds. "It's one of the pleasantest duties, sir, that we have to perform here," said the considerate post-woman; "and no one knows but ourselves how the poor prisoners look forward to the arrival of their letters. Day after day they'll ask me to be sure and bring them one soon, as if I could make them quicker."

We told the clerk, as we walked along with her towards one of the wings, that we had that morning had evidence as to the anxiety the prisoners felt about receiving letters from their friends. "Ah, *that* they do," she returned; "and if the letter doesn't come just when the time is due for getting it, they'll sit and mope over it day after day, and work themselves up at last into such a violent fury, that they'll break and tear up everything about them."

IRONING-ROOM AT THE BRIXTON PRISON.

By this time we had reached the cell in the west wing, to which the first letter was addressed. The women were locked up in their cells during tea-time, and the clerk, placing her mouth close against the door, called the name of the prisoner located within.

"Yes, mum," was the answer that came from the cell.

"Here's a letter for you," added the clerk, as she stooped down and threw the document under the door. In a moment after there was a positive scream of delight within, followed by a cry of "Oh! how glad I am." Then we could hear the poor creature tear open the sheet, and begin mumbling the contents to herself in half hysteric tones.

The clerk had hurried on her rounds, while we stood listening by the door, and she remained waiting for us outside the cell of the next prisoner on her list. "Sheridan," she whispered. "Yes, mum," was the rapid reply, as if the inmate of the cell recognized the welcome voice, and anticipated what was coming. Then the letter was slid under the doorway, as before, and this was followed by a simple exclamation of "Oh! thank you, mum!"

"The last prisoner," said the clerk, as she now hastened off towards the laundry, "has more friends in the world than the other, and that is why she received her letter so differently." In the laundry, the prisoner to whom the letter was given smiled gratefully in the clerk's face, as she thrust it into her bosom. "Can you read it?" inquired the letter-carrier, who seemed almost as delighted as the prisoner herself. "Oh, yes, mum, thank you," replied the woman; and she hurried to the other end of the wash-house, to enjoy its contents quietly by herself.

Then three more letters were delivered, one to a prisoner in the kitchen, and the others to women in the east wing. After that, we followed the clerk across the yard to the infirmary, where the last letter was given to the head-nurse.

"I never deliver the letters myself here," added the thoughtful and tender-hearted clerk, " because I don't know the state of health the prisoners may be in, and I'm afraid of exciting them too much."

As a further example of the store set by the female prisoners upon the letters they receive from their relatives and friends, we may mention that there is hardly a cell that is not furnished with some fancy letter-bag, worked by the prisoner, in the form of a large watch-pocket; and we were assured that the documents treasured in such bags are prized as highly as if they were so much bank-paper, and that in the moments of sadness which overcome prisoners, they were invariably withdrawn and read—perhaps for the hundredth time—as the only consolation left them in their friendlessness and affliction.

₊ *Female Convict Labour at Brixton.*—The work done by the women prisoners is, of course, of a different character to that performed either at Pentonville or the hulks. The tailoring at the former establishment gives place to the more appropriate shirt-making, hemming flannels, and stitching stays, &c.; while the hard labour of the prisoners working in the arsenal and dockyard is here replaced by the more feminine occupation of the laundry.*

The laundry at the Brixton prison is no mean establishment. Here the majority of the women whom we have before met in our rounds, habited in their light-blue checked over-dresses, are found, standing on wooden gratings, washing away at the wooden troughs ranged round the spacious wash-house which forms the lower part of the building. Here some, with their bare red arms, are working the soddened flannels against a wooden grooved board that is used to save the rubbing of the clothes, while the tops of the troughs are white and iridescent with the clouds of suds within them. Two women in the centre are turning the handles of the wringing machine that, as the box in which the wet clothes are placed spins round and round, drains the newly-washed linen of its moisture by the mere action of the centrifugal force. In one part is a large wooden boiler heated by steam, and scattered about the place are tubs full of brown wet sheets, large baskets of blankets, and piles of tripey-looking flannels; whilst a dense white mist of steam pervades the entire atmosphere, and the floors are as wet and sloppy as the streets of a Dutch town on a Friday.

From the wash-house we ascended to the drying-rooms over-head, and here one of the doors of what seemed to be a huge press was thrown open, and an immense clothes'-horse drawn out, with rows of unbleached towels and blankets across its rails, while the blast of hot air that rushed forth was even more unpleasant than the dampness of the atmosphere below. Hence we passed into the ironing-room, and as we approached the place, we knew

---

* It is at Brixton that all the clothes are washed for the 350 and odd prisoners confined at Pentonville, and the 820 in Millbank, as well as the linen of the 688 convicts in Brixton prison itself; so that altogether the women in the laundry have to supply clean clothing every week for some 1800 persons. Hence, we are barely surprised, when we read in the return of the work done, that there were more than half a million pieces washed at Brixton in the course of the year 1854. Besides this, we find the prisoners made up during the same time more than 20,000 shirts, and nearly 10,000 flannel drawers and waistcoats, 1,200 shifts, 3,500 petticoats, 5,700 sheets, 2,000 caps, 3,700 pocket-handkerchiefs, 2,800 aprons, 2,300 neckerchiefs, 1,200 jackets, and just upon 3,400 towels; so that the gross value of their united labour was estimated at very nearly £1,800. The scale of gratuities paid to convicts at Brixton is nearly the same as that of other prisons —those in the second class receiving from 6*d*. to 8*d*. per week, and those in the first from 8*d*. to 1*s*. per week, according to their industry.

The expenses of the prison, on the other hand, were upwards of £15,700—the cost of the officers, clerks, and servants being very nearly £3,900; that of victualling the prisoners amounting to £3,000 and odd, while their clothing and bedding came to very nearly £3,000, and the fuel and light for the prison to upwards of £1,200.

FEMALE CONVICTS AT WORK, DURING THE SILENT HOUR, IN BRIXTON PRISON.

(From a Photograph by Herbert Watkins, 179, Regent Street.)

by the smell of burnt flannel the nature of the occupation carried on within. Here were gas-stoves for heating the irons, the ordinary grates being found too hot for the summer, and there was a large blanketed dresser, at which a crowd of clean-looking women were at work, in very white aprons, while the place resounded with the continued click of the irons returned every now and then to their metal stands. On the floor stood baskets of newly-ironed clothes, and plaited, and looking positively like so much moulded snow; whilst, over-head, might be heard the rumbling of the mangles at work on the upper floor.

From eleven till twelve, the women located in the wings pursue their needlework in silence, and seated at their doors; and then it is a most peculiar sight to see the two hundred female convicts ranged along the sides of the arcade, and in each of the three long balconies that run one above the other round the entire building, so that, look which way you will, on this side or on that, you behold nothing but long lines of convict women, each dressed alike, in their clean white caps, and dark, claret-brown gowns, and all with their work upon their knees, stitching away in the most startling silence, as if they were so many automata— the only noise, indeed, that is heard at such a time being the occasional tapping of one of the matrons' hammers upon the metal stove, as she cries, " Silence there ! Keep silence, women !" to some prisoners she detects whispering at the other end of the ward. (*See engraving.*)

As we passed down the different wards, examining the work as we went, each woman rose from her little stool, and curtseyed, while those on the other side stared, with no little wonder at the object of our visit. Some were making flannels, and some shirts. " We make all the shirts for Portland, Pentonville, and Millbank," said the matron, who still accom-panied us; " but those blue-checked shirts are for Moses and Son; we have had many scores of pounds from them !" (No wonder, thought we, that honest women cannot live by the labour of shirt-making, when such as these, who have neither rent, nor food, nor clothing to find, are their competitors.) One of the convicts was engaged upon some open embroidery-work. " She's in for life," whispered the matron, as we passed on—another was busy at a beautiful crotchet collar, that was pronounced to be a rare specimen of such handiwork, the flowers being raised, so that the pattern had more the appearance of being carved in ivory than wrought in cotton. At the upper end of the long arcade stood one (who had evidently belonged to a better class than her fellow-prisoners), cutting out a dress for one of the matrons. We mounted the steps leading to the paddle-box-like bridges that connect the opposite galleries, and, as we walked along, the matron still drew our attention to the various articles made by the women. " That one is engaged in knitting the prison hose; the other is making up the caps for the female convicts. This woman is considered to work very beautifully," added our guide, as she drew our attention to a sleeve in crotchet work, that looked rich and light as point lace. " It's taken me nearly three weeks to do," said the prisoner, in answer to the matron, " but then I have a room to clean, and to go to chapel twice a day, besides." One was ill, and seated inside her cell-door reading the " Leisure Hour," and on looking at the article that engaged her attention we found it to be headed, " An inci-dent in the life of a French prisoner !"

From seven till eight in the evening the same silence and work go on ; but at this period the women sit within their cells on their stools. The chaplain accompanied us round the building at this hour, and, as we passed along, the prisoners in the lower cells rose one by one and curtseyed to the minister, while those in the galleries above stretched their heads from out their cell-doors to see who were pacing the corridor below. After this we passed into the passages of the old prison, and gently turning the " inspection plate " of some of the cells of the women in separate confinement, peeped in unobserved upon the inmates, and found some working, and others reading, but none, strange to say, idling. Then we looked down into the " convalescent ward," and saw the women seated round the fire-places on either side ; and after a time we returned to the west wing, as quietly as possible, so as to avoid being heard by the prisoners; for the matron was anxious we should witness the passage from silence to conversation that occurs precisely at eight here.

The corridor seemed to be entirely deserted, no form being visible but those of the matrons on the cross-bridges above; while the place was so still that, as our attendant said, "No one would believe there were a hundred and ninety-nine women at work within it."

As we waited the arrival of the hour, we saw heads continually stretched out to look at the clock at the end of the corridor; and when the first stroke of the time-piece was heard, the prisoners, one and all, poured out of their cells with their stools in their hands, and seated themselves in couples between their doors, while they placed their lamps on the pavement at their feet, and commenced talking rapidly one to the other. This movement was so simultaneous that it seemed more like a pantomime-trick than a piece of prison discipline; while the change from utter silence to the babbling of some two hundred tongues was so immediate as to tell us, by the noise that pervaded every part of the building, how severe a restraint had been imposed upon the prisoners.

Shortly after this the collection of the scissors began, amidst the continual tapping of the official hammer against the stove, and the cry of the matrons, "You are talking too loud, women! Make less noise, there!" The scissors, when collected, are strung one by one upon a large circular wire, like herrings upon a rush, and then carried to the store-cell, and locked up by the warder for the night.

In the west wing there is no further silence previously to retiring to rest. In the east wing, however, prisoners are ordered to abstain from talking for a quarter of an hour before the bell rings for bed.

We re-entered the latter wing precisely at half-past eight—just as the bell was ringing; the arcade was filled with the noise of shifting the stools, for during this term of silence the women no longer sit in couples between their cells; so they retired with their little wooden seats, and placed themselves just within their doors, where they began reading.

The silence now was even more perfect than ever, and remained so till the bell commenced ringing at the prison-gate, announcing the time to retire to rest. Then instantaneously the prisoners, one and all, rose from their seats, and, seizing the stools, withdrew to their cells; and then putting out their brooms, they closed the doors after them, till the whole corridor rang from end to end with the concussions.

This, again, was but the work of an instant, the act being performed with military precision, and in a minute or two afterwards the principal matron was seen travelling along from cell to cell, and double locking every door herself.

In the other wing the same operations had gone on at the same time, and though it was but five minutes after the quarter when we returned to it, we found all still and close for the night.

It would not be right to close our account of the internal economy of this prison without commending, more directly than we have yet done, the excellent manner in which the government and discipline of the institution is carried out by all the lady-officers connected with it—from the thoughtful and kind-hearted superintendent, down even to the considerate little postwoman. Indeed, we left the establishment with a high sense of the kindness and care that the female authorities exhibited towards the poor creatures under their charge, and it is our duty to add, that we noted that all at Brixton was done more gently and feelingly, and yet not less effectually, than at other prisons—the feminine qualities shining as eminently in the character of warders as in that of nurses.

¶ iii.

THE HULKS AT WOOLWICH.

Half an hour's journey along the North Kent Railway, past the rising meadows near Blackheath, and the bright toy villas, planted in the centre of the greenest conceivable lawns, which make the neighbourhood of Charlton—then through a long dark tunnel—will deposit the traveller within five minutes' walk of the Dockyard gates of Woolwich.

The sign of the public-house, "THE WARRIOR," which shows a gaudy front close to the station, suggests at once the proximity of the hulks. The lazy men, in cotton-velvet-fronted waistcoats, leaning against the door-posts; strong musters of very dingy children; remarkably low shops, exhibiting all kinds of goods at wonderfully cheap prices; and street after street of little houses, where the wives of the regularly employed dock labourers advertise the nature of their industry in their parlour windows—indicate the neighbourhood of a great industrial establishment.

Turning from the entrance of the Dockyard—opposite which is a flourishing public-house, rejoicing in the suggestive sign of "THE OLD SHEER HULK," which probably reminds some of its customers of peculiarly "good old times"—and keeping the high, dark walls of the yard on the left, the way lies past little shops and beer establishments on the right, towards the arsenal. From the elevated churchyard, crowded with graves, the sharp outlines of which are rounded by the waving of the uncut grass, the first view of the river, with the flat Essex marshes beyond, is obtained. Here, immediately opposite the yard, rises the bulky form of the great "WARRIOR" hulk, which, the authorities declare, can hardly hold together. Painted black and white, and with her naked and puny-looking spars degraded to the rank of clothes-props for the convicts, she stands in curious contrast to the light steamers that dance by her, and to the little sloops laden with war stores, and bound for Sheerness or Portsmouth, that glide like summer flies upon the surface of the stream, almost under her stern.

From the churchyard, veering to the right along the busy little High Street, the way lies past a long line of shop windows, displaying capacious tea-pots, flanked by wondrously variegated tea-cups, and offering tempting advantages to the lovers of "a comfortable tea." A dead wall still further suggests the neighbourhood of the hulks; for there the posting-bill of the Woolwich theatre offers to the aspiring youth of the locality the lessons of "THE CHAIN OF CRIME; *or, The Inn on Hounslow Heath!*" Then, before the arsenal gates, which are protected by three or four stern policemen, a broad avenue is seen at noon, marked by a double row of women, standing with their arms a-kimbo, and with baskets of the freshest and reddest-looking radishes upon the ground before them, waiting for the coming of the labourers, who are about to leave the arsenal for dinner.

As we pass through the arsenal gate, noticing a long gun pointed right through the portal, we are asked where we are going.

"To the 'DEFENCE' Hulk," we answer.

Forthwith we are ushered into one of the lodges at the side of the gate, where our name, address, and profession are inscribed in a police book. We are then told to pass on to the water's edge, where we shall find a policeman who will hail the hulk. Through groves of tumbled wheels and masses of timber, past great square buildings, from the roofs of which white feathers of steam, graceful as the "marabout," dart into the clear air, and through the doors of which the glow of fires and the dusky figures of men are seen, we go forward to the flag-staff near the water's edge, and close to the bright little arsenal pier, with its red lamps, and that long iron tube under it, through which the shells are sent to the sloops moored alongside. A heavy mist lies upon the marshes on the opposite bank of the river; yet, in the distance, to the right of the "DEFENCE," Barking Church is visible.

The "DEFENCE" and "UNITÉ," moored head to head, with the bulky hammock-houses reared upon their decks, their barred port-holes, and their rows of convicts' linen swinging from between the stunted poles which now serve them as masts, have a sombre look. From this point we can just see, nearly a mile farther down the river, the heavy form of the "WARRIOR" moored close alongside the Dockyard, with the little, ugly "SULPHUR" (the washing-ship) lying in the offing.

Meantime, the policeman, placing himself in a prominent position upon the pier, has hailed the officer in the gangway of the "DEFENCE ;" and in a few minutes afterwards a long "gig," pulled by four convicts, in their brown dresses and glazed hats, parts from the hulk ; and showing in the stem the stiff, dark form of an officer, steering directly for the landing-place, upon which we are standing.

As the boat touches the shore, one of the convicts places a little mat upon the cushioned seats, upon which we tread as we jump into the craft, telling the officer that we bear an order for the governor. With wonderful precision the convict boatmen obey the orders of the officer, and point the boat's bows back again to the gangway of the hulk.

In a few minutes we are aboard; and, as we pass up the gangway steps, we hear one officer repeat to the other—"For the governor!" And then a warder, with a bright bunch of keys attached by a chain to his waist, conducts us to the governor's drawing-room—a pretty apartment, where, from the stern-windows of the hulk, there is a very picturesque view of the river.

¶ iii—a.

The History of the Hulks.

The idea of converting old ships into prisons arose when, on the breaking out of the American War of Independence, the transportation of our convicts to our transatlantic possessions became an impossibility. For the moment a good was effected, for the crowded prisons were relieved; but from the time when the pressure upon the prisons ceased, down to the present, when the hulks may be said to be doomed, all writers on penology have agreed in condemning the use of old ships for the purposes of penal discipline.

If, however, we follow the wording of the 19th Geo. III., cap. 74, in which the use of ships for prisons is referred to, we shall perceive that an idea of turning convict labour to account, for cleansing the Thames and other navigable rivers, had probably directed the attention of government to the possibility of arranging ships for their crowds of convicts.*

The "JUSTITIA," an old Indiaman, and the "CENSOR," a frigate, were the first floating prisons established in England. This system, though condemned by such men as Howard and Sir William Blackstone,† was not only persevered in, but extended ; till, on the 1st

---

* The section of the act referred to runs thus :—

"And, for the more severe and effectual punishment of atrocious and daring offenders, be it further enacted, That, from and after the First Day of July, one thousand seven hundred and seventy-nine, where any Male Person . . . shall be lawfully convicted of Grand Larceny, or any other Crime, except Petty Larceny, for which he shall be liable by Law to be transported to any Parts beyond the Seas, it shall and may be lawful for the Court . . . to order and adjudge that such Person . . . shall be punished by being kept on Board Ships or Vessels properly accommodated for the Security, Employment, and Health of the Persons to be confined therein, and by being employed in Hard Labour in the raising Sand, Soil, and Gravel from, and cleansing, the River Thames, or any other River Navigable for Ships of Burthen," &c., &c.

† "London Prisons," by Hepworth Dixon, page 124.

of January, 1841, there were 3,552 convicts on board the various hulks in England.*   In 1854 the numbers so confined had been reduced to 1298.

Some idea of the sanitary condition of these establishments, even so recently as 1841, may be gathered from the report of Mr. Peter Bossy, surgeon of the " WARRIOR" hulk, off Woolwich, which shows that in that year, among 638 convicts on board, there were no less than 400 cases of admission to the hospital, and 38 deaths!   At this period there were no less than 11 ships (including those stationed at Bermuda, and the "Euryalus," for juvenile convicts) used by the British government for the purposes of penal discipline—if discipline the then state of things could possibly be called.

There are still officers in the Woolwich hulks who remember a time when the "Justitia" (a second "Justitia," brought from Chatham in 1829) contained no less than 700 convicts; and when, at night, these men were fastened in their dens—a single warder being left on board ship, in charge of them!   The state of morality under such circumstances may be easily conceived—crimes impossible to be mentioned being commonly perpetrated.†   Indeed we

* In 1841, the gross number of convicts received on board the hulks in England during the year was 3,625, and these were natives of the following countries, in the following proportion:—

3,108 were born in England.
80   ,,   Wales.
229   ,,   Scotland.
180   ,,   Ireland.
13   ,,   British Colonies.
15   ,,   Foreign States.

Their occupations had been as follows:—

304 had been Agriculturists.
1,176   ,,   Mechanics and persons instructed in manufactures.
1,986   ,,   Labourers and persons not instructed in manufactures.
82   ,,   Domestic servants.
69   ,,   Clerks, shopmen, and persons employed confidentially.
8   ,,   Superior class, or men of education.

As regards the religion of these same 3,625 convicts, the subjoined are the statistics:—

2,934 belonged to the Established Church.
269   ,,   Roman Catholic ditto.
167   ,,   Scotch ditto.
245   were   Dissenters.
9   ,,   Jews.
1   ,,   Of " another denomination."

Concerning their prison "antecedents"—

1,451 were first-offence men.
487 had been in prison before.
1,625   ,,   convicted before.
10   ,,   in penitentiary.
52   ,,   transported before.

Their ages were as follows:—

3 were under 10 years old.
213 were from 10 to 15 years old.
958   ,,   15 to 20   ,,
1,612   ,,   20 to 30   ,,
839 were above 30 years old.

Lastly:—

1,103 were married.
2,522 were single.

† Even so late as 1849, we find the "Unité," hospital ship at Woolwich, described in the following terms:—
" In the hospital ship, the ' Unité,' the great majority of the patients were infested with vermin; and their persons, in many instances, particularly their feet, begrimed with dirt.   No regular supply of body-linen had been issued; so much so, that many men had been five weeks without a change; and all record had been lost of the time when the blankets had been washed; and the number of sheets was so insufficient, that the

were assured by one of the warders, who had served under the old hulk "*regime*," that he well remembers seeing the shirts of the prisoners, when hung out upon the rigging, so black with vermin that the linen positively appeared to have been sprinkled over with pepper; and that when the cholera broke out on board the convict vessels for the first time, the chaplain refused to bury the dead until there were several corpses aboard, so that the coffins were taken to the marshes by half a dozen at a time, and there interred at a given signal from the clergyman; his reverence remaining behind on the poop of the vessel, afraid to accompany the bodies, reading the burial-service at the distance of a mile from the grave, and letting fall a handkerchief, when he came to "ashes to ashes and dust to dust," as a sign that they were to lower the bodies.

It was impossible that a state of things so scandalous could last; and the successive reports of the directors of convict prisons are evidence of the anxiety with which they urged upon the government the reform—if not the abandonment of the hulk system altogether; for, to the disadvantages inseparable from the conduct of prison discipline on board ship, the governors of hulks were forced to add the rottenness of the vessels intrusted to them. They were expected to govern five hundred convicts in a ship, the same as in a convenient building, and to keep them healthy—in a rotten leaky tub!

The completion of the Portsmouth Convict Prison, in 1852, at length effected an import-ant reduction in the hulk establishments. The "YORK" was given over to the Admiralty to be broken up. In 1851 the "DEFENCE" had been moved to Woolwich to replace two un-serviceable hulks, and the "WARRIOR," which lies off Woolwich Dockyard, and is still called the model hulk, had been reported as unsound. It will be seen, by the accompanying extract from the directors' report for 1852, that they again drew attention to the "WARRIOR;" while in their last report (1854) they have, once more, ventured into a few details.

"The 'WARRIOR,'" say they, "is patched up as well as her unsoundness will permit, but there is no knowing how soon she may become quite unfit for further use, and it will be advisable to take the earliest opportunity that offers of transferring the prisoners to some more suitable place of confinement, as any serious repairs would be quite thrown away on so decayed a hulk, if indeed they would be practicable." To this remonstrance of the directors the governor added his own, in these emphatic words—"It is well known that the hulk is in a most dilapidated condition, and scarcely able to hold together. Recent repairs, sup-porting the lower deck, &c., have rendered her safe from any immediate danger; but the remedy is merely temporary. She is rotten and unsound from stem to stern."

Still the "WARRIOR" remains, in spite of such remonstrances as these, with canvas drawn over her leakages, to keep the damp from the wards, moored off the Woolwich dock-yard, with 436 convicts between her crumbling ribs.

Before passing from this brief history of the hulks, to paint their actual condition, the labour performed by their inmates, and the regulations under which they are conducted, we will quote a paragraph from the general remarks of the directors, addressed to the govern-ment at the beginning of last year on this subject:—"Our opinion on the disadvantages of the hulks, as places of confinement for prisoners, has been so strongly expressed in previous annual reports, that we feel it unnecessary here to say more than that we consider these dis-advantages radical and irremediable, and to urge the necessity of adopting every opportunity that may offer of substituting for them prisons on shore, constructed, as at Portland and Portsmouth, with sleeping cells for all the prisoners. Now that the transportation of crimi-nals can only be carried on to a small extent, it appears of very great importance that every

expedient had been resorted to of only a single sheet at a time, to save appearances. Neither towels nor combs were provided for the prisoners' use, and the unwholesome odour from the imperfect and neglected state of the water-closets was almost insupportable. On the admission of new cases into the hospital, patients were directed to leave their beds and go into hammocks, and the new cases were turned into the vacated beds, without changing the sheets."

defect in connection with their imprisonment which might lessen the prospect of its being effectual as a punishment, and also as a means of their reformation, should be got rid of as speedily as possible, and *of such defects we know none at all approaching in magnitude to the association of the convicts in the prison hulks.*"

It should be remembered, let us add, by the opponents of the ticket-of-leave system, that although it is from these condemned hulks, where the men are herded together and are pretty well free to plot and plan as they please, that they are turned upon society, nevertheless, according to the directors' report just quoted, of five hundred and forty-four convicts discharged in 1854 from the Woolwich hulks only, and one hundred and six discharged before that period—in all six hundred and fifty convicts—there have been but six received back with licenses revoked for misconduct.

As we have already remarked, however, the hulks are doomed. At the present time the "Warrior," lying off Woolwich Dockyard; the little "Sulphur," a floating wash-tub for the convicts, lying opposite the "Warrior;" the "Defence," lying off Woolwich Arsenal; and the "Unité," made fast to the "Defence," and used as the hulk hospital (together with the "Stirling Castle," the invalid depot, and the "Briton" convict hospital at Portsmouth), are the only "floating prisons" in England—though, by the by, the "Warrior," floats only once a fortnight.*

The expense to the country of the hulk establishment (including the "Stirling Castle" and "Briton" at Portsmouth), in 1854, the date of the last returns, was £43,545 9s. 7d. Of this sum the cost of management (including the salaries, rations, and uniforms of officers) was nearly £14,000, and that of victualling and clothing the prisoners about £20,000; while the remainder was made up principally of gratuities to convicts (about £3,000), clothing, and travelling expenses of liberated prisoners (upwards of £1,500), medicine, and medical comforts for the sick (£1,850 odd), fuel and light (£1,500), &c.

The hulk system, condemned, as we have already observed, from the date of its origin to the present time, has been the despair of all penal reformers. *Originally adopted as a make-shift under pressing circumstances,* these old men-of-war have *remained during nearly half a century* the receptacles of the worst class of prisoners from all the jails of the United Kingdom

---

* Statement of the Number of Prisoners received on board the Convict Establishments at Woolwich, and also of the Disposal of such Prisoners, between the 1st January, 1854, and December, 1854.

Number on board.	"Warrior."	"Defence."	Total.
Remaining on board January 1st, 1854	421	521	942
Admitted during the year . .	273	298	571
Total	694	819	1513
How disposed of.			
Discharged to Colonies . . .	25	29	54
Sent to other Prisons . . .	21	22	43
Pardoned	190	216	406
Sent to Lunatic Asylums . . .	0	1	1
Invalided to "Stirling Castle" . .	5	8	13
Escaped	1	1	2
Died	11	16	27 †
Total	253	293	546
Remaining December 31, 1854 . .	441	526	967
Grand Total . . .	694	819	1,513
Average daily number of prisoners .	436	515	951

† 1,270, J. S., on the 20th July, drowned accidentally in canal. 1,240, J. M., on the 20th June, died suddenly from apoplexy on board the "Defence."

—a striking instance of the inertness of government, as well as of its utter callousness as to the fate or reformation of the criminal.

Convicts who have undergone the reformatory discipline of Millbank and Pentonville, are at the hulks suddenly brought into contact with offenders who have undergone no reformatory discipline whatever. All the care which has been taken at Pentonville and at Millbank to prevent the men talking together, and associating with one another, is thrown away, since the first freedom granted to the convict undergoing penal servitude is given when he reaches the hulks, and finds himself in a "mess," where he will probably meet with *one* old companion in crime at least. The authorities declare that in these messes only "rational" conversation is permitted, but it is very clear that forty or fifty men cannot be crammed into one side of a ship's deck, put together upon works, and swung elbow to elbow in hammocks at night without finding ample opportunity for free conversation.

Whatever good is effected, therefore, by the systems of Millbank and Pentonville is effectually destroyed at Woolwich. The reformed convict from Pentonville is at the hulk establishments cast among companions from whom the separate system sought to wean him, while he is put to labour of the hardest and least interesting character. He was, perhaps, a shoemaker, or a tailor, or weaver at Pentonville; at Woolwich, however, he has to lay aside the craft that he has only just learnt, and is set to scrape the rust from shells, or else stack timber. Here he is not only thrown amongst brutal companions, whom it was before considered perdition to allow him to associate with, and even to *see*, but put to do the lowest description of labour—in some instances at the muzzle of a guard's carbine—and impressed with the idea that it is the very *repulsiveness* of this labour which is his punishment, so that it is strange, indeed, if the lessons of Pentonville have not been utterly erased from his memory, granting that the imposed dumbness of the "silent system," or the physical and mental depression induced by the separate system, to have worked some permanent salutary effect on his heart.

¶ iii—β.

Convict Labour and Discipline at Woolwich.

"The hulk system was continued," says Mr. Dixon, "notwithstanding its disastrous consequences soon became patent to all the world; and it still flourishes—if that which only stagnates, debases, and corrupts, can be said to flourish—though condemned by every impartial person who is at all competent to give an opinion on the matter, and this because the labour of the convicts is found useful and valuable to the government—a very good reason for still employing convict labour upon useful public works, but no reason at all for continuing the hulks in their present wretched condition."

As we have already remarked, this labour is of the description called "hard;" that is to say, it is the exercise of irksome brute force, rather than the application of self-gratifying skill; still those persons who are familiar with the working of a dockyard or an arsenal, know that this "hard" work is valuable in both establishments; for in the general report of the directors on the results of 1854, under the head of "Earnings and Expenses," we find that the labour of the convicts confined in the hulks alone was valued at £19,736 5s. 9d. These earnings, however, it should be observed, were exclusive of the estimated value of the labour of the convicts employed as cooks, bakers, washers, shoemakers, tailors, and others engaged in work merely for prison purposes.

The directors tell us that the kind of work performed by the convicts is chiefly labourers' work, such as loading and unloading vessels, moving timber and other materials, and stores, cleaning out ships, &c., at the dockyard; whilst at the royal arsenal the prisoners are employed at jobs of a similar description, with the addition of cleaning guns and shot, and excavating ground for the engineer department—329 prisoners, out of a daily average of 515 on board the "DEFENCE," having been so employed. "*The only artificer's work*," add the directors, "*that the convicts have had an opportunity of performing has been, to a very small extent, in executing repairs and other jobs for the service of the hulks in which they have been confined.*" *

As regards the industry of the prisoners, the directors say "the men generally have worked *willingly* and with good effect, considering the disadvantage inseparable from their being occasionally mixed with, or in the neighbourhood of, numbers of free labourers and others—a circumstance which requires, for the sake of security, considerable restraint to be placed on their freedom of action. Punishments for idleness, though always inflicted where the offence is proved, have been by no means of frequent occurrence." †

The "willingness" here spoken of, however, is of a very negative kind, and might be better described as resignation, or a desire to escape punishment. Nevertheless it should in fairness be added, that the governor of the "WARRIOR" hulk reported to the directors of convict prisons in 1854, that "the value of the convicts' labour might be favourably compared with that of an equal number of free workmen."

* *Value of Labour at the Hulks.*—Let us turn now to the value set upon the labour of the prisoners at the hulks by the directors of convict prisons.

The report for 1854 returns the value of convict dockyard labour at 2s. 5½d. and a fraction daily, per man; while arsenal convict labour, according to the same authority, is worth 2s. 4d. per diem; that of the convict carpenters, blacksmiths, painters, plumbers, and coopers is valued at 2s. 6d. a day, and that of shoemakers, tailors, washers, and cooks at 1s. 6d., whilst the general prison labour, working of boats, &c., is set down at only 1s. 3d. a day.

Now, by this scale we find that the following were the earnings of the convicts at

* RETURN OF EMPLOYMENT OF PRISONERS IN THE "DEFENCE" HULK FOR THE WEEK ENDING 16TH DECEMBER, 1854.

General Occupation.	Average Daily No. employed.	General Occupation.	Average Daily No. employed.	Description of Work.	Average Daily No. employed.	Description of Work.	Average Daily No. employed.
ORDNANCE (A) Working Parties (*as detailed in* col. 3)	329	SICK (C) and unfit for labour (*as detailed in* col. 4)	22	(A) ORDNANCE WORKING PARTIES.		(B) PRISON WORK.	
PRISON WORK (B) (*as detailed in* col. 4)	63	SCHOOL	60	Removing and stacking timber	114	Boarders cleaning ship generally, and attending on sick at hospital	42
Carpenters	4	SEPARATE FOR PUNISHMENT (or other reasons)	3	Discharging mud	14	Boatmen	16
Smith	1			Shipping and unshipping stores	40	Whitewashers	2
Tinker	1		85	Cleaning out sheds	10	Bed-pickers	2
Painter	1			Cleaning shot and shell	27	Net-maker	1
Sawyer	1	Average daily number	515	Carting sundries	14		
Cooper	1			Digging gravel	8		63
Ropemakers	2			Odd jobs not measurable	1		
Bookbinder	1			Making and repairing grummetts and wads	24	(C) SICK.	
Shoemakers	4			Repairing butt and roads	36	Sick at Hospital	16
Tailors	6			Assisting tradesmen	27	Ditto, complaining	6
Washers	12			Cleaning out drains	14		
Cooks	4						22
	101			Total	329		

† *Report of the Directors of the Convict Prisons on the Discipline and Management of the Hulk Establishment,* 1854.

Woolwich, "as calculated according to reasonable wages, for the different descriptions of work performed, per day of 10 hours," during the year 1854 :—

Name of Hulk.	Average daily No. of Prisoners.	Number and Value of Day's Labour performed.				Total estimated Value.	Annual Average per Head.
		By Inferior Workmen.		By Superior Workmen.			
		No. of Days, 10 hrs. each.	Estimated Value	No. of Days, 10 hrs. each.	Estimated Value.		
			£ s. d.		£ s. d.	£ s. d.	
"Defence" . . .	515	96,018	10,067 6 9	2,889,,9	342 2 7	10,409 9 4	20 4 3
"Warrior" . . .	436	68,655,,2	8,453 15 5	11,691,,3	873 1 0	9,326 16 5	21 7 10
Total . .	951	164,673,,2	18,521 2 2	14,581,,2	1,215 3 7	19,736 5 9	20 15 0¾

Here then, we perceive that 951 convicts on board the two Woolwich hulks, performed altogether very nearly 180,000 days' labour in the course of the year, and earned collectively, in round numbers, £20,000, or almost 20 guineas per head.*

* The subjoined is a more detailed account of the quantity and the kind of work done by the convicts in the dockyard and arsenal at Woolwich :—

STATEMENT OF THE VALUE OF LABOUR PERFORMED IN THE ROYAL DOCKYARD, WOOLWICH, BY CONVICTS, IN THE YEAR 1854.

Removing and stacking, &c., cubic timber, 2,825,073 cubic feet, at 12s. per 1,000 feet . . £1,695 0 10½
Removing and stacking superficial timber, 1,726,555 superficial feet, at 4d. per 1,000 feet 388 9 5¼
Removing iron, ballast, stores, &c., 23,916 tons, at 6d. per ton 597 18 0
Weighing and stacking ditto, 25,654 tons, at 4d. per ton 427 11 4
Removing coals, 46,406 tons, at 7d. per ton 1,353 10 2
Weighing and stacking ditto, 33,586 tons, at 5d. per ton 699 14 2
Carting sundries, 3,362 loads, at 6d. per load 84 1 0
Spinning and balling oakum, 228 cwt., at 2s. per cwt. 22 16 0
Cutting up old rope, 193 tons, at 2s. per ton 19 6 0
Picking oakum, 119 lbs., at 5½d. per lb. 2 14 6½
Removing, stacking, and weighing old rope, &c., 1,932 tons, at 6d. per ton . . 48 6 0
Odd jobs not measurable :—Assisting shipwrights and riggers, cleaning out sawmills, steamers, docks, and yard, testing chain cables, &c., docking and undocking vessels, cutting up old iron, staging, pitch scraping, cross-cutting timber, removing boats, &c. &c., 266,948 hours, at 10 hours per day, equal to 26,694 days 8 hours, at 2s. 4d. per day . . 3,414 7 10¼

Total value of dockyard labour £8,453 15 5

STATEMENT OF THE VALUE OF LABOUR PERFORMED FOR THE ORDNANCE DEPARTMENT, ROYAL ARSENAL, BY THE CONVICTS, DURING THE YEAR ENDING 31ST DECEMBER, 1854.

Removing and stacking timber, 2,222,350 cubic feet, at 12s. per 1,000 feet . . £1,333 8 3
Ditto ditto 6,095,636 superficial feet, at 4s. 6d. per 1,000 feet . 1,371 10 4
Making mortar, 329 cube yards, at 11d. per yard 15 1 7
Breaking stones, 3,525 bushels, at 5d. per bushel 73 8 9
Facing stones, 839 superficial feet, at 5d. per foot 17 9 7
Weeding, 59,787 superficial yards, at 1s. 6d. per 100 yards . . . 44 16 9
Raising and removing mud, 13,070 tons, at 5½d. per ton . . . 299 10 5
Removing and shipping stores, &c., 53,037 tons, at 6d. per ton . . . 1,325 18 6
Cleaning shot and shell, 247,370 No., 1s. per 24 shot 515 7 1
Carting sundries, 44,550 loads, at 6d. per load 1,113 15 0
Digging and removing gravel, 8,547 cube yards, at 5d. per yard . . . 178 1 3
Making concrete, 96 cube yards, at 1s. per yard 4 16 0
Odd jobs not measurable :—Cleaning saw-mills, sheds, drains, tanks, and cadets' barracks, making and repairing grummetts, wads, &c., repairing butt and roads, assisting tradesmen, filling hollow shot, whitewashing, cutting sods, mowing, making and stacking hay, spreading mud, clearing away snow, &c. &c., 19,550 days, at 2s. 4d. per day . . 2,280 16 8

Total value of arsenal labour £8,574 0 2

N.B.—The totals above given, though incorrect, are copied literally from the Directors' Report.

∗ *Convicts' Gratuities.*—The gratuities which the convicts, labouring on the public works or in the hulks, are entitled to, are divided into "conduct gratuities" and "industry gratuities," both of which vary according to the class to which the convict belongs. Each prisoner is entitled to his conduct gratuity irrespective of his gratuity for industry, whilst his industry gratuities are measured by the zeal with which he labours. The conduct gratuities, as arranged in the books of the governor of the "DEFENCE," stand thus :—

CONDUCT GRATUITIES.

1st Class Prisoners (receive) .	9*d.*	Weekly.
2nd Class Prisoners ,, ,, .	6*d.*	,,
3rd Class Prisoners ,, ,, .	4*d.*	,,

The industry gratuities, or sums placed to the credit of the convicts according to the amount of work done, vary from 3*d.* for a "good" quantity of labour performed, to 6*d.* for a "very good" quantity.*

We took the trouble to inspect the books of the "DEFENCE," and can testify to the marvellous neatness and accuracy with which they are kept. When a prisoner is reported to the governor, the latter can tell, by a glance at the character-book, the conduct of the former during every week he has spent at the hulk. At the expiration of the convict's term the character-book is summed up, the advantages resulting from the prisoner's class and industry are added together, and he has a bill made out of the sum due to him, in the following form, which we copied from the governor's book :—

J. C., CLASS I.   CONDUCT.

90 weeks, V. G., at 9*d.* per week . .	£3	7	6
13 weeks, G., at 6*d.* per week . .	0	6	6
1 week (infirmary accident) 6*d.* . .	0	0	6

INDUSTRY.

99 weeks, V. G., at 6*d.* per week . .	2	9	6
4 weeks, G., at 3*d.* per week . .	0	1	0
1 week infirmary, 3*d.* per week . .	0	0	3
53 weeks (ticket-of-leave class, at 6*d.* per week)†	1	6	6
	7	11	9
Had in private cash	0	0	4
Total	7	12	1

* The subjoined is extracted from the governor's books :—

INDUSTRY GRATUITIES.

1. ⎫
2. ⎬ As per authorised scale.
3. ⎭

V. G. (very good). If the number of the V. G.'s is under one-third of the total number of weeks that the prisoner has been in the prison, he may receive 4*d.* for every V. G.; if over one-third and under two-thirds of the total number, he may receive 5*d.*; if over two-thirds, he may receive 6*d.* for every V. G.

G. (good). The prisoner may receive 3*d.* for every G. (unless the whole of the gratuities become forfeited by misconduct).

O. Nil.

V. B. (very bad). ⎫
P. (punishment). ⎬ Nil. Being forfeited for misconduct.
B. (bad). ⎭

I. (infirmary). Nil. The infirmary cases are liable for special considerations with reference to class and conduct, but not for extra gratuity.

I. A. (infirmary accident). Discretionary—being governed by the circumstances; but, as a rule, a gratuity is allowed according to the prisoner's previous conduct and industry.

L. (light labour). According to class (as above), but no extra gratuity.

The above scale does not apply where a special scale is authorised for invalids.

† This payment of 6*d.* per week was the compensation made to prisoners who, after the suspension of

This man received on leaving five shillings in cash, £3 15s. in a Post-office order, payable at his declared destination.   Thus a balance of £3 12s. 1d. in his favour remained in the governor's hands, to which he would become entitled when a letter, of which he was furnished with a printed form on leaving the hulks, was received from him, signed by the clergyman, or some other responsible person in his neighbourhood, as a proof that he was leading an honest life.*

The rule is, that if a prisoner's account when he is discharged be under £8, he may receive half on leaving, and the balance two months subsequently; whereas, if his balance exceeds £8 and be under £12, he must wait three months for the balance.   In addition to the money due to him, every prisoner discharged from the hulks is provided with a new suit of clothes and a change of linen.

The gross sum paid in gratuities to the convicts at the hulks amounted to upwards of £2,950 in the course of the year 1854, while the cost of the clothes and travelling expenses for the prisoners, on obtaining their liberation, was £1,650 odd.

*** *Badges, &c.*—A distinctive portion of the discipline carried on at Woolwich consists in the badges worn by the prisoners on the left arm, and the rings worn on the right. These badges are made of black leather, with an edge of red cloth, with white and black letters and figures upon it.   We advanced towards some convicts who were hauling up linen to the mast to dry, and who wore both rings and badges.   The first badge we examined was marked thus :—

```
┌───────────┐
│     7     │
│   V.  G.  │
│     8     │
└───────────┘
```

The 7 meant that the prisoner had been sentenced to *seven* years' transportation; the 8 that he had been in the hulk that number of months, and the V. G., that his conduct had

transportation for short terms, remained in the hulks during the passing of the ticket-of-leave bill.   The weekly allowance was paid to them from the date at which they would have obtained tickets had they proceeded to Australia, till they were set free from the hulks.   Thus J. C. was a prisoner 53 weeks longer than he would have been confined had he been sent to the colonies.

* MEMORANDUM TO BE GIVEN TO A PRISONER ON DISCHARGE, IN CASE ANY BALANCE OF GRATUITY MAY BE DUE TO HIM.

"In the event of your conduct being satisfactory when at liberty, and that you faithfully perform the conditions printed at the back of the License, your claim to the balance of your Gratuity will be admitted on your returning this paper to me at the expiration of three months from your release, backed by the certificate of the Magistrate or Clergyman of the Parish, or other competent and known authority, that you are earning your livelihood by honest means, and have proved yourself deserving of the clemency which has been extended to you by Her Majesty.

"The following particulars must be carefully stated in returning this paper:—

Christian and Surname at length, and Prison Number   .   .   _____

Your Occupation or Calling, or in what manner you are earning ⎞
    your livelihood   .   .   .   .   ⎠ _____

The name of the Post-office at which the order should be made ⎞
    payable   .   .   .   .   ⎠ _____

_____*Prison,*

_____*Governor.*

_____185   .''

been *very good* all the time he had been there.   Another man wore a badge marked thus :—

```
┌─────────────┐
│      4      │
│             │
│  G.    6    │
│             │
│      8      │
└─────────────┘
```

This denoted that the prisoner was suffering *four* years' penal servitude ; that his conduct had been good during *six* months ; and that he had been on board the hulk *eight* months.

These badges are collected once in every month, and conveyed to the governor's office. The character-book, as filled up from the weekly reports of the warders, is gone over in each case, and, at the same time, if the prisoner have behaved badly, his badge is altered, and he loses some of the advantages of his previous good conduct.* Three months' good report in the character-book constitutes a **V.G.**, or *very good,* and advances the wearer three months towards the second stage of penal servitude. Accordingly the man's class is not marked upon his badge.

But the first man whose badge we noticed upon his left arm, had also upon his right arm a blue and two red rings. The blue ring denotes the second stage of penal servitude, and the red rings that he is a first-class convict. One red ring upon the right arm makes a second-class convict ; and the third-class prisoner is known by the absence of all rings from his arm. By this system we are assured that it is almost impossible that a prisoner can be unjustly dealt with.

* " The badges which are given as a record to the prisoner of his actual position with reference to character, have proved to be a great encouragement ; and that they are prized is evidenced by the efforts made to obtain them, and to regain them by good conduct in such cases as they may have been forfeited.

" The Governor of Portland Prison observes :—

" ' The system of wearing conduct-badges on the dress, by which the monthly progress of each convict towards the attainment of his ticket-of-leave is publicly marked, works very satisfactorily, as is evinced by the anxiety of even the ill-conducted prisoners to regain a lost good-conduct mark, and the efforts to keep subsequently clear of the misconduct book.'

" As a means of promoting good conduct, a system of classification has also been adopted, the object of which will be best understood from the rules established with reference to it, which are as follows :—

" ' The prisoners shall be divided into three classes, to be called the first, second, and third classes. The classification shall depend, in the first instance, on the report of character and general conduct since conviction that may be received with a prisoner ; and subsequently, on his actual conduct, industry, and observed character under the discipline of the establishment.

" ' 6. Prisoners in either the first or second classes shall be liable to removal to a lower class for misconduct. The prisoners in the different classes shall be distinguished by badges, indicating the particular class to which each prisoner may belong.

" ' 7. Prisoners who habitually misconduct themselves will be liable to be sent back to separate confinement, or to be removed to some penal establishment under more severe discipline.

" ' 8. The object of the classification is not only to encourage regularity of conduct and a submission to discipline in the prison, by the distinctions that will be maintained in the different classes, but to produce on the mind of the prisoners a practical and habitual conviction of the effect which their own good conduct and industry will have on their welfare and future prospects.

" ' 9. Such distinctions shall be made between the classes, and such privileges granted, as shall promote the object of giving encouragement to those whose good conduct may deserve it, provided such distinctions do not interfere with discipline nor with the execution of a proper amount of labour on public works.' "— *Report on the Discipline and Construction of Portland Prison, and its Connection with the System of Convict Discipline now in operation, by* Lieut.-Col. Jebb, C.B., 1850.

¶ iii—γ.

A Day on Board the "Defence" Hulk.

The cold, gray light of early morning gave to everything its most chilly aspect, when at five A.M. we stepped aboard the "DEFENCE," the old 74-gun ship, with the determination of spending an entire day with her 500 and odd inmates. But before we describe the various duties by which every day in a convict-ship is marked, let us here acknowledge how much we owe to the courtesy and to the lucid explanations of the governor, Mr. S. Byrne. As we run up the gangway of the silent hull, and survey the broad decks, and massive "galleys," and hammock-houses, in the misty light, the only sounds heard are the gurgling of the tide streaming past the sides of the black-looking vessel, and the pacing of the solitary warder-guard—the silence and the stillness of the scene in no way realizing the preconceived idea of a convict hulk. Yet as we pass to the ship's galley, at the fore-part of the vessel, and see the copper sheathing glistening on the floor round the cook's fire, with the large black boiler above it, and the sparkling yellow fire shining through the broad bars, the sight reminds us that there are hundreds of mouths to feed below. The cook sharply rakes the burning coals; and the copper frets, and spurts, and steams, with its unquiet boiling volume of the reddish-brown cocoa.

This cook is the first convict with whom we have come in contact: he is preparing the breakfasts of his fellow-prisoners, who are still sleeping under the hatches. Close at hand is the bread-room, piled with baskets and boxes; while opposite is the officers' galley, with another stove, standing on its plate of glistening copper sheathing. Above, on the forecastle, are the hammock-houses—divided off into large, black, deep cupboards—bulging over the gunwale of the ship. Then we pass the drying-houses for linen (used in wet weather), and the little cabins at the gunwale waist, where the mechanic-convicts employed on board ply their respective handicrafts. Glancing over-head, we observe the shirts and stockings of the prisoners below dangling from the scanty rigging between the masts, and fluttering in the wind—as we had remarked them from the shore in broad daylight on another occasion.

We are now near the top deck hatchway by the forecastle; it is still barred and padlocked. Here the bayonet of the sentry on duty, glistening in the light, attracts our attention. Then we notice the heavy bright bell, swung in front of the hatchway. All is quiet yet. We can hear the water splashing amid the boats at the broad gangway, or along the shelving sides of the ship, under her barred port-holes. The warder who accompanies us, ourselves, and the sentry are still the only people on the spacious decks of the old seventy-four. The poop, given up to the governor's rooms, and to those of his deputy and officers, is railed round; while a series of chimney funnels, projecting here and there, break the regularity of the outline.

The warder proceeds to open the hatchways; and we descend, in company with him, the top deck, in order to see the men in their hammocks, before rising for their day's duties.

** *The "Turning-out" of the Convicts.*—On reaching the top deck we found it divided, by strong iron rails (very like those in the zoological gardens, which protect visitors from the fury of the wild beasts) from one end to the other, into two long cages as it were, with a passage between them. In this passage a warder was pacing to and fro, commanding a view of the men, who were slung up in hammocks, fastened in two rows, in each cage or compartment of the ship. There was also a little transverse passage at the end of each ward, that allowed the officer on duty to take a side view of the sleepers, and to cast the light of his bull's-eye under the hammocks, to assure himself that the men were quiet in their beds.

The glimmering little lanterns attached to the railings, so that the warder on duty could trim them without entering the wards, were still alight. The glazed hats of the men hung up overhead, reflecting the pale beams; and the men themselves were still snoring in their dingy hammocks.

In these two compartments or wards were 105 convicts, parted off into sections, D 1, D 2, and A 1 and A 2. (*See plan*, p. 211.) And a curious sight it was to look upon the great sleeping mass of beings within them! The hammocks were slung so close to one another that they formed a perfect floor of beds on either side of the vessel, seeming like rows of canvas-boats. But one or two of the prisoners turned on their sides as we passed along the deck, and we could not help speculating, as we went, upon the nature of the felon-dreams of those we heard snoring and half-moaning about us. How many, thought we, are with their friends once more, enjoying an ideal liberty!—how many are enacting or planning some brutal robbery!—how many suffering, in imagination, the last penalty of their crimes!—how many weeping on their mother's breast, and promising to abandon their evil courses for ever!—and to how many was sleep an utter blank—a blessed annihilation for a while to their life-long miseries!

The convicts here arranged were first-class men—there being manifest advantages in the top deck over the middle and lower ones, as shown by Mr. Bossy, in his report on the "WARRIOR" hulk, in 1841*. We followed the warder towards the stern of the ship; and, at the extremity of this deck, we crossed a grating, and reached the hatchway leading to the middle deck.

The middle deck was arranged on the same plan as that of the top one; excepting that the passage between the swinging hammocks was wider. Here 129 men were sleeping in the divisions or wards called E 1, E 2; B 1, B 2. (*See plan*, p. 211.) Here, too, the officer was parading between the wards or cages, and splashing about chloride of lime that stood in buckets between the wards. It was still very dark; and the groaning, coughing, and yawning of the sleeping and waking prisoners, had anything but a cheerful effect on the mind. The

* "A STATEMENT of the Number of Prisoners sent to the Hospital, from the 1st of October, 1840, to the 10th May, 1841, inclusive; showing the Deck to which they belonged, and the mortality from each: —

Decks.	Daily average Number of Men.	Total Number sent to the Hospital.	Rate per Cent.	Total Number of Deaths.	Rate per Cent.
Top . .	132	48	36	5	3·7
Middle .	192	134	70	15	7·8
Lower .	284	172	60½	12	4·2
Total .	608	354	58	32	5·2

"The smaller proportion of illness among the prisoners on the upper deck is readily explained by their exemption from depressing causes.

"According to the present system of classification, all prisoners newly arrived who are still smarting under the pain of disgrace and separation from their homes, and have not yet recovered from the anxiety, severe discipline, and spare diet endured in jail; all whose transportation is for a long term of years or for life, and all whose character and conduct are bad, remain the tenants of the lower deck; but if the prisoner's sentence be short, and his character and conduct good, he may in three months be raised to the middle deck, and in twelve months to the upper deck, where if he once arrives, there is a strong expectation he will not leave the country; he feels he has the confidence of the officers; and a cheerful hope of regaining his home sustains and restores a healthy vigour to body and mind.

"If a long-sentenced prisoner is the subject of scrofula, of ulcer, of scurvy, of general infirmity, or of any cause unfitting him for the voyage, he will become by good conduct an inmate of the middle deck, and will remain there for several years; so that we gradually acquire an accumulation of invalids on this deck, and this is one reason of the frequent deaths of its inhabitants.

"The upper deck is much drier, being farther removed from the surface of the river; and, being more fully exposed to the sun, is hotter than the rest. The large size of its ports also affords better ventilation."—*Medical Report, by P. Bossy, surgeon to "The Warrior," for* 1841.

air was close and unpleasant, but not remarkably so, considering that it had been exhausted by the breath of so many men since nine o'clock on the previous night, when they turned in.

We had still another deck to visit; so we followed our warder and descended the hatchway to the lower deck, which was higher, and had a broader passage than the two upper ones through which we had just passed. This deck was arranged to accommodate only 240 men; but, at the time of our visit, it contained only a 190 sleepers, arranged in sections thus,

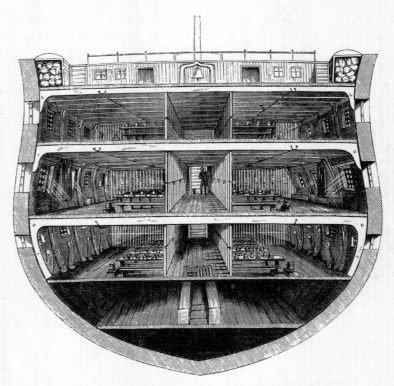

SECTIONAL VIEW OF THE INTERIOR OF THE "DEFENCE" HULK.

F 1, F 2, and F 3, on one side, and C 1, C 2, and C 3 on the other. (*See plan*, p. 211.) This spacious deck stretches right under the fore-part of the poop, the barred port-holes admitting but little light; still the air is fresher than in the decks above, which receive the ascending heat from the 190 sleepers; for, by means of broad openings in the stern and bows of the ship, a constant stream of fresh air is carried through the vessel. Altogether there were, at the time of our visit, 424 convicts stowed between the decks.

The men seem to be comfortably covered, having two blankets and a rug each. The tables used for meals are unshipped, and lean against the bars of the passage; the men's boots are under their hammocks, and their clothes lie upon the benches.

Having passed through this gloomy scene we reach a narrow white-washed passage, at the head of the lower deck, and entering by a side door, we come to the solitary cells. We follow the bull's-eye carried by the warder. Presently he stops, and placing his lantern against a rude opening in the bulkhead, throws its light upon a man in one of the cells within, who is sentenced to "forty-eight hours." Having inspected the sleeper, who is lying huddled in his brown rug upon the ground, for there are no hammocks allowed in this cell, he darkens the place once more and proceeds to the second.

In solitary cell No. 2, the man is sleeping in his hammock, and the scuttle is not darkened. As the light from the bull's-eye falls upon his face, the prisoner blinks his eyes, and calls, "All right!" as he rolls in his bed.

We now pass on to a cell in the bows of the ship. Here the hammock hides the man's face

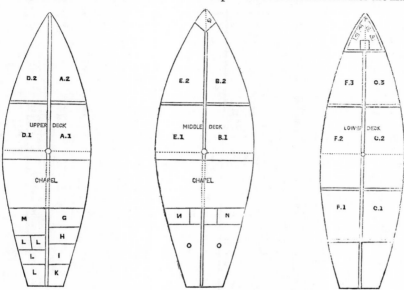

PLANS OF THE DECKS OF THE "DEFENCE" HULK.

(The letters and figures A 1, A 2, D 1, D 2, &c. refer to the several wards on the different decks; G indicates the Schoolmaster, H Chief Warder, I Clerk, K Steward, L L L L Deputy Governor, M Chaplain, N N Principal Warder, O O Warders' Mess-room.)

from our view, so we advance across immense white-washed timbers or "knees," that stand up as solid as milestones, and so on to the opposite cell in the bows. This one is empty; but the next contains a prisoner who is in for three days, on bread and water, for refusing to work in the boats. We then return to the lower deck, through a door at the opposite side to that at which we entered the solitary cell-passage. There are five such cells in all—two on either side, and one in the bows.

As we re-entered the lower deck, we found the lamp-man (a convict), in a gray Scotch cap, blowing out the lamps. He, together with the cooks' and officers' servants, are let out a little before the general call-time; their services being necessary before the prisoners are roused at half-past five o'clock, and the day's business begins.*

The deep-toned bell against the forecastle now sounded three bells. The men had been expecting the unwelcome sound; for, a few minutes before, as we traversed the lower deck to examine the air-passages and ventilators, we saw heads popped up here and there from the dingy hammocks to have a peep at us as we passed. The usual hour for rising was evidently at hand. The effect of the bell, however, was astonishing. In a minute scores and scores of men tumbled out of their beds, and were wriggling and stretching themselves in their blue shirts.

"All up! Turn out, men!" cries the officer; and the convicts are in their trousers in an inconceivably short time.

* We here publish a table citing the distribution of time on board the hulk, extracted from the Report of the Directors of Convict Prisons. This table, however, can give no definite idea of the work really per-

"Let us go to the top deck, and we shall see how the hammocks are lashed," suggests our warder; and on ascending to the upper decks we find many of the men already dressed, and with their hammocks lashed up like huge sausages.

Presently the gates were opened, and the men turned out one after another, carrying their bolster-like beds on their shoulders.

"Now men, go on there! steady—steady!" exclaims the officer. "Come on, men! Come on, the rest of you!" he shouts as we reach the forecastle. The men appear in single file, some carrying one hammock and others two. Those who carry two have, in addition to their own bed, that of a fellow-prisoner, who remains below to forward other work. Some of the men are fully dressed in their brown striped convict's suit; while others are in their blue shirt sleeves. The officers continue shouting to the men, and hastening their movements. "Come on with that hammock! Come on now!"

Long lines of men, with their hammocks upon their shoulders, wind along the decks. The sides of the black hammock-houses are open, discovering lettered compartments, as A 1, A 2, B 1, &c.; and the warders on duty go into the houses, and see the hammocks stowed, as the prisoners deliver them, under their proper letters, varying the work by directions, as

formed, nor of the regularity with which five hundred men are made to conform to certain hours, in the minutest particular.

THE DAILY DISTRIBUTION OF TIME ON BOARD THE "DEFENCE" HULK.

Occupation.	In Summer (longest day). (In intermediate seasons, the hours vary according to light).			In Winter (shortest day).		
	A.M.	A.M.	Hrs. Min.	A.M.	A.M.	Hrs. Min.
Prisoners rise, wash, and roll up hammocks	5 30	6 0	= 0 30	5 30	6 0	= 0 30
Breakfast (officers and servants)	6 0	6 30	= 0 30	6 0	6 30	= 0 30
Cleaning classes	6 30	7 15	= 0 45	6 30	7 15	= 0 45
In readiness to turn out to work (preparing the boats, &c.)	7 15	7 30	= 0 15	7 15	7 30	= 0 15
Labour, including landing and marching to and from working ground	7 30	12 noon	= 4 30	7 30	12 noon	= 4 30
Dinner for officers and prisoners	12 noon	1 P.M.	= 1 0	12 noon	1 P.M.	= 1 0
Labour, including mustering and marching to and from working ground	1 P.M.	5 30	= 4 30	1 P.M.	4 0	= 3 0
Prisoners are mustered, wash, and prepare for supper	5 30	6 0	= 0 30	4 0	4 45	= 0 45
Supper, washing-up, &c.	6 0	6 45	= 0 45	4 45	5 30	= 0 45
Evening prayers, school, and those not at school repairing clothing, &c., mustered intermediately	6 45	8 30	= 1 45	5 30	7 30	= 2 0
Sling hammocks	8 30	9 0	= 0 30	7 30	8 0	= 0 30
All in bed	9 0			8 0		
	Total from 5.30 A.M. to 8.0 P.M.		15 30	Total from 5.30 A.M. to 8.0 P.M.		14 30

ABSTRACT OF THE ABOVE.

Meals		2 15			2 15
Labour, including mustering, and moving to and from		9 0			7 30
In-door occupation, evening instruction, &c., &c.		4 15			4 45
	In Summer	15 30		In Winter	14 30

" Shove that a bit forward there. Now then, stow away there, my lads—stow away! Do you belong here? How came you so late?"

" Any more C 1? Is that the last of C 1? Now then, come on, lads! Move up!"

" We get the whole ship up and stowed in half an hour," said our warder. "The bell went at half-past five, and you'll see, sir, we'll have all the hammocks up by six."

Still the brown line of men moved forward to the hammock-houses, each hammock bearing the prisoner's registered number stitched upon it, and with the word " DEFENCE " printed on the canvas.

The prisoners continue to pour out as we descend again between the decks, and find that many have got the tables shipped against the bars, and the benches ranged beside them. Now some of the men are washing in buckets, placed ready over night; and others arranging their hair by the reflection of the window-pane; and others, again, scrubbing the tables ready for breakfast. Everything and everybody seem to be undergoing a cleansing process more or less searching.

We next proceeded once more to the deck below, following our guide. The scene was a busy one. Some of the prisoners were still combing their hair; others were washing the deck boards, which were shining under the plentiful supply of water; others, again, were covering the white deal tables (which are scrubbed also every morning) with painted canvas table-cloths; then there were groups of men, down on one knee, brushing their boots, while the messmen were busy at the preparations for breakfast. The tables, ranged in a row along the wards, accommodate eight prisoners each. Each man takes his turn as messman, while the service of the ward is divided.

All the breakfast things are in block-tin, and they glisten as though they had never been used. Some of the men have polished theirs over-night, and tied them up in handkerchiefs, to give themselves a little extra time in the morning. " Where's your plates? Where's your plates?" cry the messmen. For water, one prisoner at a time is let out of each ward, and as soon as he returns another is allowed to go on deck.

The various processes, collectively called getting-up, may now be said to be complete, and the prisoners are all fairly padlocked in their wards, under the eye of a single warder. After six o'clock in the morning, however, there are two officers upon the lower deck till nine o'clock in the evening, when the men turn in. The costume of the prisoners, as we now see them completely dressed, is the same as that worn at Pentonville, viz., rusty brown, with red stripes upon it.

The chief warder enters and inquires whether all are up. " All up!" is the answer, as the men give the military salute. " There you see, sir," said our attendant, as four bells (six o'clock) rang, " all the hammocks are on deck, and the men are locked up, as I said they would be."

The first business of the morning being over, the men break into groups or read. Many a one, to our astonishment, took his Bible and began reading it with no little earnestness. Here an altercation ensued between two prisoners about the tins, which one of them was still cleaning. This was promptly suppressed by a cry of " Halloa! What are you about there, losing your temper?"

At this time, too, the doctor's mate appeared, carrying a wooden tray covered with physic bottles and boxes of salve, and followed by an officer holding a paper containing the " invalid list." This officer checks the distribution of the medicine.

*** *Officers' Duties.*—The ship now begins to wear an animated appearance; for at six o'clock the officers, chief warders, and cooks come on board, all those we had seen previously having been on duty throughout the night. The officers at the hulk are arranged into divisions, the first mustering 20 men, and the second 19 men. In answer to our inquiries on this subject, our attendant said—

"There's twenty in first division, and nineteen in second division, and, in addition to these, the chief warder and two principal warders. Twenty officers sleep on board one night, nineteen the next. To the first division there is one principal and the deputy-governor, while the second division is commanded by the chief warder, and one of the principal warders. Well, the first division came on duty yesterday at seven A.M., and will go off duty about six o'clock to-night. It's a very long stretch. The officers came on duty at half-past six this morning, and will remain on duty till six o'clock this evening. They will be on their legs all the time. They will not have more than twenty to twenty-five minutes to get their dinner. It's not only one day, but every day the same thing. They're on their legs all day long, for they are not allowed to sit down. The first night-watch comes on at eight P.M., and remains on duty till half-past ten. The second watch comes on, and remains till one. Then he is relieved by the third watch, who remains till half-past three—the fourth watch doing duty till six o'clock. Now the watch that's just relieved will have a quarter of an hour to wash and shave, for the officers muster at a quarter-past six. So you see there's not much time lost. The breakfast is served down at half-past six. This occupies till a quarter to seven. From a quarter to seven till a quarter past, the warders are at liberty ; but during this time they must breakfast, clean themselves, brush their buttons and the crowns upon their collars, and be on deck to parade at the quarter-past seven. Then they turn to the labour. They're just going to muster the prisoners. Perhaps you'll like to see them."

₊ *Muster and Breakfast, Diet, &c.*—We went down once more between decks. The muster of the prisoners had just commenced. Two officers were occupied in the wards. The prisoners were all ranged behind the tables—" Silence ! keep silence there !" shouted an officer ; and then, while one officer called the names of the prisoners, the other marked down the absentees upon a slate. As each name was called, the man owning it responded, " Yessir," accompanying his reply with a military salute. The replies of " Yessir," in every variety of voice, ran along the wards.

This ceremony over, the registering officers retired, and the warder on duty padlocked the men in once more. We then went to see the muster of the absentees—as the cooks, bakers, and the like—which was carried on in the same way as with the prisoners in the wards, only each absentee, as he cried, " Yessir," and saluted, passed out, to return to the duty from which he had been for the moment withdrawn.

" There you see, now," said our attendant, " every man in the ship has answered to his name."

" All correct, sir !" said the registering warder to the chief.

" Now, then, A ward !" was shouted down the hatchway.

" This is A ward, sir," said our attendant, " coming up for breakfast."

Instantly four of the convicts appeared, following one another. " That's for A ward." " B ward !" was next shouted down. " Now, then, B ward here !" And in this way the messmen of the various wards were summoned from their decks, to fetch the breakfasts of their comrades, the messmen of each deck appearing at different hatchways; for it may be here observed that there is a separate hatchway for each floor of the vessel.

The messmen were now seen moving along in file towards the ship's galley, and presently they re-appeared, each man carrying a large beer-can full of cocoa, the bread being taken down in baskets, and served out by the officers at the ward-doors.

At half-past six the doctor comes on board, when an officer goes round shouting in the wards, " Any men to see the doctor ?" Six men appear in answer, and are formed in line near the galley-door. They are ushered one by one into the little surgery, and here, if the case is considered at all serious, a trap-door is opened, and they are passed at once down into a little separate room underneath, prepared with " bath and other convenience."

THE CONVICT CHAPEL ON BOARD THE "DEFENCE" HULK AT WOOLWICH.

A WARD ON BOARD THE "DEFENCE" HULK ARRANGED FOR THE RETURN OF THE CONVICTS TO DINNER.

Nine-tenths of the calls for medical assistance, however, are dismissed as frivolous, such call being looked upon with great suspicion, as generally evincing a desire to avoid a day's labour in the arsenal.

While remarking the six applicants for medical assistance, we also noticed four men drawn up in a line at the end of the main deck, attended by an officer. These were "reported" men, about to answer for some infraction of prison rules.

We now followed the chief warder below, to see the men at breakfast. "Are the messes all right?" he called out as he reached the wards.

"Keep silence there! keep silence!" shouted the officer on duty.

The men were all ranged at their tables with a tin can full of cocoa before them, and a piece of dry bread beside them, the messmen having just poured out the cocoa from the huge tin vessel in which he received it from the cooks; and the men then proceed to eat their breakfast in silence, the munching of the dry bread by the hundreds of jaws being the only sound heard.*

After this we returned to where the reported prisoners were drawn up, facing the governor's house, upon the quarter-deck. They were called into the office one by one; and as the second man was called, the first re-appeared, and was marched off between two officers to a solitary cell.

"This is my report for yesterday; I give one in every morning," said the officer attending us, as he went to hand the document in, together with a "cell report," stating the number of prisoners under punishment, the days they had done, &c.

Next our attention was directed to the convict boatmen, who were preparing to take the ship's messenger ashore.

"They have already been on shore this morning," continued our persevering informant, to bring off the cook and chief warder. "That's the hospital cutter, sir," and our friend pointed to a little boat, rowed by two prisoners in their brown suits, and carrying three or four warders in the stern.

"Now, sir, our boat's just going aboard the 'Uneet'" (for such is the general pronunciation of the French name). "Here is our sick report, sir, for the day," he continued, showing us the document. "It is delivered in every morning. There are only two men on it now. One, you see, requires light labour, and the other 'low diet.'"

At this moment a dashing little boat, with her stern seats cushioned, and rowed by four men, pulling long oars, appeared at the gangway.

"This is the gig, sir, to take the doctor away."

The officers now begin to exhibit great activity, while the men below are cleaning their tables and tins—having finished their morning's meal.

"That boat won't be back in time unless she's hailed," said one officer, looking towards the shore. "It only wants a few minutes to seven, now."

---

* The following is the Scale of Diet on board the "DEFENCE" Hulk.

BREAKFAST (PER MAN).

12 Ounces of Bread.
1 Pint of Cocoa.

DINNER (PER MAN).

6 Ounces of Meat.
1 Pound of Potatoes.
9 Ounces of Bread.

SUPPER

1 Pint of Gruel.
6 Ounces of Bread.

SOUP DAYS:—Wednesdays, Mondays, and Fridays, when the dinner stands thus:—1 pint of soup, 5 ounces of meat, 1 pound of potatoes, and 9 ounces of bread.

The bread, potatoes, &c., are served by contract.

GRUEL DIET.

1 pint of gruel and 9 ounces of bread for breakfast, dinner, and supper—served when men are on the sick list, in the hulk.

PUNISHMENT DIET.

1 pound of bread per day, and water.

Another boat now pulled towards the ship, rowed by men wearing guernseys, marked " Defence," and glazed hats that had numbers stamped upon them.

"Be as quick as you can, Matthews," shouted one of the officers—"it's only five minutes. Look sharp."

The boat, as directed, went off to the long brown boats, and brought them alongside the gangway, to take the prisoners off to their "hard labour" in the arsenal.

"They're going to take the officers first," said our attendant. "The second division's just coming on duty now, sir." And glancing to the shore, by the side of the bright little arsenal pier, we could perceive a dark group of officers, standing near the landing steps— carrying bundles in handkerchiefs—their glazed caps and bright buttons sparkling in the sunlight as they moved about. "The boats are rather behindhand, for the prisoners should be all in them at the first stroke of seven."

Nine bells (seven o'clock) sounded, as we went once more below, and found that the men had just finished cleaning their tin mugs, and were gathering up the bits of chalk into bags, and arranging these same mugs on top of the inverted plates, round their tables ready for dinner. Some, too, were washing the tables again, to get beforehand with their work; while others were covering their bright tin plates and mugs with the coarse table cloths, to keep the dirt from them; and others, again, were reading their Bibles, or lounging lazily about.

"They know to a minute the time they have, sir; and the officers are as severely taught to obey the progress of the clock, for if they are not at the landing steps at seven precisely, the boat pushes off without them, and will not return to fetch them."

The boat that had gone to bring the warders aboard was soon on its way back to the ship, crowded with the glazed caps and dark uniforms of the officers, relieved by the fresh white guernseys of the convict rowers.

Seven o'clock is the hour for the officers' parade upon the quarter-deck; the object being to see that they are all sober and fit for duty. The parade over, the guard appears on deck. It consists of four men, armed with carbines, and with their cartouche boxes slung behind them by a broad black belt. This guard stands near the gangway; the men having their carbines loaded, and held ready to fire, while the prisoners pass to the boats.

Looking overboard, we now perceive the convict boatmen, in their guernseys and glazed hats, bringing the two long-boats to their proper position opposite the gangway, ready for the debarcation of the prisoners on their way to their work at the arsenal.

At a quarter-past seven the officers for duty ashore are called over by the chief warder, in the presence of the deputy-governor, while a principal checks them. Twelve extra guards, composed chiefly of soldiers from the Crimea, and some wearing clasps upon their warder's uniform (an uniform, by the way, exactly resembling that of the Pentonville officers), now file down the steps, to be ready to receive the prisoners, who begin to appear above the hatchways, marching in single file towards the gangway, with a heavy and rapid tread; and it is an exciting sight to see the never-ending line of convicts stream across the deck, and down the gangway, the steps rattling, as they descend one after another into the capacious boat, amid the cries of the officer at the ship's side—"Come, look sharp there, men! Look sharp!"

₂ *Debarcation of Prisoners for Work in the Arsenal.*—The rowers hold their oars raised in the air, as the brown line of men flows rapidly into the cutter below, some seat themselves in the stern, but the large majority stand in a dense mass in the bottom of the long low craft, dotted here and there by the dark dress of the officers planted in the midst of them. In fine weather no less than 110 convicts are landed in each of these boats or cutters.

It is pretty to watch these long boats glide slowly to the pier, their dense human freight painted brown on the stream. And scarcely has one boat landed its felon crew, before another is filled, and making for the arsenal pier and the shore. (*See engraving.*) Nor is it less picturesque to see the prisoners clamber up to the parade ground; fall in line there with military precision; separate according to the chief officer's directions into working parties (each working party being in charge of a warder); and move off to the scene of their day's labour, in long brown strings. This is a very curious scene, and one that it will be impossible to witness some few years hence.

A third or surplus small cutter puts off with the few remaining prisoners, and more guards. These guards, we observe, wear cutlasses; such cutlasses being carried as a special protection, for the officers wearing them have charge of working parties employed beyond the bounds of the arsenal; as, for instance, upon a mortar battery in the marshes. The men are now off to work. Those prisoners who remain in the ship are in the deck cabins, plying their handicraft for the use of the hulk.

We now left the hulk in the deputy-governor's gig, in company with that officer, who acted himself as steersman.

"Now then, shove off! Altogether! Lay on your oars! Sharp as you can!" were the brisk orders; and as we neared the shore, the directions to the men ran, "Hold water, all of you! Pull all! Hard a-starboard! Port, there! Ship oars!"

The men obeyed these nautical directions with admirable precision, and soon landed us at the arsenal stairs, amid huge stone heaps, piles of cannon tumbled about, and all bounded by long storehouses and workshops that seemed to cross each other in every direction.

We accompanied the deputy-governor in his inspection of the gangs, as the convict crew stood drawn up in lines, headed by their respective officers. It is necessary to change and equalize the gangs daily, we were told, according to the work each has to perform. Here the officers proceeded to search under the men's waistcoats, and to examine their neckcloths, so as to prevent the secretion of clothes about their persons, which would enable them to disguise themselves, and to escape among the free labourers. No less than seventeen such attempts to escape had taken place among the "DEFENCE" convicts in one year, though out of these only three got off. In 1854 there were five attempts at escape, of which but one was successful.

The searching and arrangement of the working parties or gangs being effected, the officer gives the word of command, "Cover!" then, "Face—forward!" and each gang wheels off to the direction of its work, the men walking two abreast, and the rear being brought up by the officer in charge.

As the several gangs leave the parade-ground, the officer in charge gives the number of his party, and that of his men. The parties, or gangs, are numbered from 1 to 30. Thus, as one party passes, the officer calls, "Two—eight;" that is, party No. 2, containing 8 men.

"Close up! close up your party, Matthews—they're all straggling!" cries the deputy-governor to one of the guards, who is taking off his men somewhat carelessly.

The arsenal is now in full activity. The tall chimneys vomit dense clouds of black smoke; steam spurts up here and there; the sharp click of hammers falling upon metal can be heard on all sides; the men are beginning to roll the shells along the miniature railways laid along the ground for the purpose. All the gangs of prisoners are off, leaving a dense cloud of dust behind them.

There are 299 in the arsenal to-day, the deputy-governor informs us. This number is added, he says, to the ascertained number remaining on board the hulk; and then, if the whole tally with the number registered upon the governor's books, all is right.

We then turned our attention to the hulk once more, and re-entered the deputy-governor's gig. As we were jerked through the water by the regular strokes of the men, and the measured working of the rullocks, we noticed the heavy cranes planted along the quay—their wheels covered with small roofs like parasols, but bearing, nevertheless, some evidences of exposure to the weather. "With one of those cranes," said the officer to us, "I have seen a single man lift a cannon on board a ship. They are worked by hydraulic pressure."

No sooner did we reach the gangway of the "DEFENCE" once more, than the principal warder on board cried, as he met the deputy-governor, "Two hundred and ninety-nine, sir!" alluding to the number of prisoners who had left the ship for labour in the arsenal. "All right!" was the laconic reply.

*** *The Library and School at the Hulks.*—"Would you like to come and see the meat, sir?" we were asked by our attendant officer. "I have to go." The steward sees to the proper weight, while the deputy-governor examines the quality of the meat. The piece we saw was an enormous leg of beef, against which prodigious weights were necessary to ascertain its precise value.

The prisoners left aboard the hulk were now busy washing the deck and the gangway. Some dashed buckets of water on the boards, while others were vigorously plying flat scrubbing-brushes, fixed at the extremity of long handles. Below, in a boat, alongside the hulk, were more brown prisoners, pumping at a small engine, and forcing the water, taken from the Artesian-well in the arsenal, into the capacious tanks of the hulk. There is, in fact, one continued splashing of liquid everywhere—on the decks, and in the long-boats, or cutters, which have now returned from the shore. The "DEFENCE," we may add, has twenty tanks, holding two tons each of water.

We next adjourned to the governor's comfortable breakfast-room, with its pretty stern-windows, and its light blue and white walls. The military salute of the convict-servant who entered from time to time, with his white apron about his loins, was the only reminiscence of the hulk as we sat at the morning meal.

After this we visited the chapel and school-room.* The chapel is a square apartment,

* TABULAR STATEMENT OF SCHOOL PROGRESS AT THE "DEFENCE" HULK, DURING THE YEAR 1854.

Date of Reception.	Could not read.	Since learned to read imperfectly.	Read only.	Since learned to read and write imperfectly.	Read and write imperfectly.	Since learned to read and write well.	Made considerable progress in arithmetic.	Read and write well.	Well educated.	Total.
February 11, 1854	—	—	—	—	12	5	4	4	—	16
„ 24 „	—	—	—	—	5	2	1	1	—	6
March 13 „	—	—	4	4	14	5	4	5	1	24
„ 24 „	1	—	2	2	7	3	5	2	2	14
April 20 „	2	—	3	3	16	7	10	5	4	30
May 2 „	6	5	1	1	16	5	7	5	—	28
„ 4 „	3	3	—	—	3	1	6	3	2	11
July 1 „	7	5	6	6	7	3	8	25	—	45
August 11 „	2	2	1	1	3	—	4	4	—	10
„ 14 „	2	1	2	1	2	—	4	3	1	10
October 9 „	2	—	—	—	—	—	—	—	—	2
„ 11 „	13	—	3	—	18	—	5	13	—	47
November 2 „	7	—	—	—	13	—	3	8	—	28
December 19 „	6	—	—	—	5	—	4	7	—	18
„ 23 „	1	—	—	—	4	—	2	4	—	9
Totals	52	16	22	18	125	31	67	89†	10†	298

† The prisoners who could "read and write" well, and those who were "well educated" on reception, have since made considerable advancement in arithmetic and the lower branches of the mathematics.

CONVICTS FORMING A MORTAR BATTERY IN THE WOOLWICH MARSHES.

admirably arranged for its purpose, the part on the level with the top deck forming the galleries, to which the prisoners on that deck pass direct from their wards, while the body of the little church is even with the middle deck, and accommodates the rest of the prisoners.

The pulpit is erected at the stern end of the chapel, between the two decks, and has a bright brass reading lamp to it; its cushions being covered with canvas. Four more lamps are suspended from the ceiling, the whole of the wood-work being painted to imitate oak. It is in the body of this chapel that the black, slanting desks, with inkstand holes (the very models of those which all boys remember with horror), are ranged for the daily school.

At the side of the pulpit is the prison library. The selection of books is suggestive. Let us run over a few titles culled from the backs of the volumes—" Marcet's Conversations on Natural Philosophy," " Paley's works," " The Pursuit of Knowledge under Difficulties," Sturm's " Reflections on the Works of God," " Persian Stories," " Recreations in Physical Geography," " The Rites and Worship of the Jews," " The Penny London Reader," " First Sundays at Church," " Stories from the History of Rome," " Short Stories from the History of Spain," " Swiss Stories," " Scenes from English History," "Rodwell's First Steps to Scottish History," " Stories for Summer Days and Winter Evenings," " Easy Lessons in Mechanics." There are in all 1099 volumes upon the shelves.

In reply to our questions as to the books that are the most popular among the convicts, and the rules on which they were issued, we were informed that each prisoner had a right to have a book, and to keep it ten days. If he wanted it longer, he could generally renew the time. The books most in demand were Chambers' publications, and all kinds of histories and stories. Very few asked for Paley's " Moral Philosophy."

" I think," continued our attendant warder, " that ' Chambers' Miscellany,' ' The Leisure Hour,' and ' Papers for the People,' are generally preferred beyond other publications. There is a great demand for them. We haven't got ' Dickens' Household Words,' or I dare say it would be in request. The chaplain objects to it being in the library."

All friends of education have scouted the idea long since, of leading uneducated men to a love of books by such works as Paley's " Theology" or Sturm's " Reflections." These are now generally regarded as the unread books of Literary institutes—because difficult to understand, and in no way appealing to the minds of the great majority of readers. Let us, therefore, imagine a convict who has been rubbing the rust from cannon-balls all day long, with a copy of Paley for his hour's amusement before he turns in. If he reads he most probably will not understand. A distaste rather than a taste for reading is hereby engendered. Yet books teaching kindly lessons, in the homely accidents of life, and which all may read and comprehend, are hardly to be found upon the chaplain's library shelf.

The school is divided into nine divisions. The first division, subdivided into sections A and B, musters 110 men. The second division musters 55 men, and so on. The divisions, as they attend the school, are generally so managed as to average 55 in number. Some convicts, we were told, cannot read, and no teaching will make them. The teaching includes reading, writing, and arithmetic, as far as " practice." In reply to our inquiry as to the interval that elapsed between the convict's school-days, we were informed that the turn to remain on board for lessons came round once in every nine or ten days.

The prisoners told-off for school now appeared on the ground-floor of the chapel, at the black desks. They were well-washed and brushed, and wore blue and white neckerchiefs, and gray stockings barred with red stripes. The third division is in to-day. The school begins with two psalms and a prayer.

" Now, attention for prayers !" is called out before they begin. Then the clerk reads a chapter of St. Luke; next the schoolmaster cites a verse from a psalm, and the men go stammering after him. It is a melancholy sight. Some of the scholars are old bald-headed men, evidently agricultural labourers. There, amid sharp-featured men, are dogged-looking youths, whom it is pitiful to behold so far astray, and so young. And now the clerk who read the prayers may be seen teaching the men; but it is evidently hard work, and few, it is to be feared, care for the school, further than for the physical repose it secures them.

We now passed to the little rooms off the wards, where a few prisoners were tailoring, while others were making the solid shoes such as the working gangs in the arsenal wear.

We then advanced to the cabins ranged along the sides of the weather-deck. In one a bookbinder was binding the rugged library volumes in black leather. "Take off your cap, sir!" cried our attendant to the prisoner, as we appeared, "and go on with your work!"

Next we passed to the lamp-man's cabin, and found him trimming the night lamps for

CONVICTS SCRAPING SHOT.

the wards. Then we reached the carpenter's shop; and there a gray-headed old prisoner who was planing a deal-board, turned a melancholy face towards us as we entered.

Then we visited the linen-house, where two or three prisoners were arranging the linen of the various wards in little tight rolls. We inquired how often the men had a change. "They change their linen every week, and their flannels every fortnight," was the reply. How gratifying to men who can remember the horrible filth in which, only a few years since, the hulk convicts were allowed to remain.

There was not an idle man on board. Festoons of clothes were drying above our heads, swung from the two stunted masts; while across the main deck, lines of dark-brown string were being twisted by a convict rope-maker, to be turned to account for the hammocks that two other prisoners were mending in a little cabin hard by. Everywhere officers were standing over the men at their labours, each warder being provided with his book, in which he enters the men's industry, or want of energy. Their tone to the men was firm, but not hard or harsh; still they kept them to their task. Every prisoner we approached saluted us, military fashion, then stood still till the officer said, "Go on with your work, sir!—Go on with your work!" when the men turned to their labour again.

₊ *The Working Parties in the Arsenal.*—The governor now called his gig to the gangway to carry us ashore to inspect the labourers in the arsenal. It was a smart little boat, and the rowers were trimly dressed in white, with the word "DEFENCE" printed round the legs of their trousers. The men, with their glazed hats and ruddy faces, looked unlike convicts. Their position is the reward of good conduct. They sit in a little deck-house close to the

THE ESCAPE SIGNAL.

gangway, all day long, ready to be called out at any moment. The men volunteer for boat service. First, they are put into the water-boat, which conveys the well-water to and from the shore; from this service they are promoted to the provision cutter, which also takes off the subordinate officers; and then they reach a seat in the governor's gig. The men like this service, and are sent for misconduct—as when they use bad language—to labour on the public works. We started for the arsenal once more, at a rapid pace; the governor himself steering the pretty gig with its white tiller ropes.

On landing, after passing by the heavy cranes, we came up with the first gang of prisoners, who were loading a bark alongside the quay. "These are the sloops that convey war-stores to Sheerness," we were told. "And yonder black hull is a floating powder-magazine, near which no ship anchors." We remarked the absence of military sentries, and were told that they had been withdrawn from the convicts working in the arsenal, although they still mounted guard. Then the place is pointed out to us where the "DEFENCE" once had a washing-house, which has been taken away by the government; together with a vegetable garden, where the convicts formerly cultivated vegetables for the hulk. "Now we wash on board the little 'SULPHUR' hulk," continued our informant, "and dry on board our own ship."

We walked into the grounds of the arsenal, and soon came up with a second party of prisoners at work digging out shot. As we approached, the officer in charge gave the governor a military salute, saying—

"All right, sir—10-8." The 10 being, as we have already noticed, the number of the gang, and 8 the strength of it. The governor, who knows what the strength of each gang is, can thus assure himself of the presence of all the men. We next turned into the stone-yard, the chosen ground of hard, dull, mechanical labour. Here there was a strong gang of men breaking granite.

"All right! how many?" calls the governor.

"All right, sir—8-9," answers the officer in charge. Then, seeing a free workman at hand, the officer is told to keep him off. Here each man is doing task-work. Every convict must break so many bushels, according to the size to which he is required to reduce them, the size being measured by a wooden machine, through which they are passed. Thus, a man breaking up the stones small, for a garden walk, must break two bushels daily, whereas a man breaking them up less, must fill four or six bushel measures.

We then passed on to huge stacks of valuable timber. "All this," said our companion, "has been piled by convict labour." Through fields of cannon lying in rows—here black as charcoal, there red with rust—past stacks of wheels and wheelless waggons, by sheds where the air was impregnated with turpentine from the freshly-worked timber, under heavy cranes, through mud, and sawdust, and shavings—here hailing a gang turning a wheel, and there a gang clearing rubbish—deep down a grove of conical heaps of rusty shells, where the men were filing and polishing them, we made our round of the convict working parties. All of them were busy. The officer takes care of that; for he is fined one shilling every time one of his men is caught idling, while the escape of one entails his dismissal.

Suddenly we came upon a guard whose duty it was to go the round of the gangs and collect the men who wished to satisfy a call of nature. Then we came upon an angle of the arsenal wall against the Plumstead high-road, where we saw an armed guard with his carbine, marching rapidly backward and forward.

"Now I shall know directly whether all is right," said the governor, as he raised his hand. The sentinel instantly halted, presented arms, then raised his right hand.

"Had there been an escape," continued the governor, "he would have grasped his carbine by the barrel, and held it aloft horizontally. That is the escape signal, and this man is stationed here because escape would be easy over the wall to the high road. Only the other day I caused a drain to be stopped up that led from the arsenal to the marshes; for we once had a hunt, that lasted all day long, after two prisoners who got into that drain. We caught them at its mouth by the Plumstead road.

It is exceedingly difficult to prevent attempts at escape, especially while there are so many free men in the arsenal. Last year there were no less than 14,000 free labourers employed there, and these men taken on without reference to character.

Here the attempts at escape, which prisoners had made from time to time, formed for some time the subject of our conversation.

"The convicts," we were told, "were generally assisted by the free labourers," who deposited clothes for them in some convenient spot. The convict slipped for a moment from his gang, put the clothes on, and passed out of the arsenal gates with the crowds of free men. Or else he made a dash for it, bolted past the sentinels, swam the canal, reached the marshes, and made off to the wood at hand. These attempts sometimes defied the utmost vigilance of the officers. It was the duty of a guard, from whose gang a man escaped, to hasten

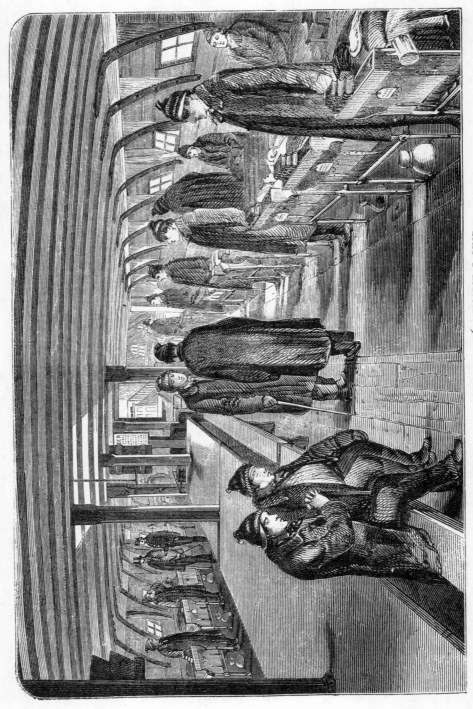

TOP DECK OF THE "UNITÉ" HOSPITAL SHIP,

ATTACHED TO THE HULKS AT WOOLWICH.

on board with the rest of his men (unless he can find an officer to undertake this duty while he runs after the lost man), and report the escape. We then signal to the police authorities by telegraph, to Bow Street, Erith, Guildford, Ilford, Bexley Heath, and Shooter's Hill, so as to surround him with a band of vigilant policemen, and prevent his getting clear. It was impossible to guard entirely against these attempts under this mixed system. They could not prevent the men from talking by night. But how much worse was it under the old system, when some six hundred or seven hundred prisoners were crammed into a hulk smaller than the "DEFENCE," and with only one officer all night to watch them.

We inquired whether the men were very severely punished when they were lazy, and were answered in the affirmative.

"They are sent here to labour," said the governor. "Here, officer, give me your labour-book." This book contained on one side a description of the nature and quantity of the work performed, and on the other the conduct of the men during the work. We were assured, however, that the men have very seldom to be punished for idleness. "They do twice as much as free men," added the governor. "They work excellently."

We now turned from the busy arsenal, crossed the canal bridge, and approached the little black wooden lodge of the policeman who guards the gate leading to the marshes. He salutes us as we pass out to the marshes.

The scene, close by the gate, is singularly English. To the right lies the rising ground of Plumstead, with its red square church-tower peeping from among the dense green cluster of the trees. Below is a cluster of village houses, and beyond swells Abbey Wood up the shelving ground; while beyond this, again, and serving as background, rises Shooter's Hill, capped by two or three surburban villas.

Right before us is a vast earth-work, all, as we are told, raised by convict labour! It is a 5-mortar battery. We approached it (crossing the range where the ordnance authorities try their rifles at the butt, while that solitary man, far over the marshes, comes out of the shed by the side of the mark, after every shot, and with a long pole marks the point hit) and found the prisoners, with their brown jackets thrown off, and some with their legs buried in water-boots, reaching to their thighs, digging the heavy, black, clayey soil, and carrying it away in barrows, under the eyes of two guards, with their cutlasses at their sides and two non-commissioned officers of the sappers and miners, who were directing the works. (See engraving.)

"That's a nice circular cut, sir," said one of the non-commissioned officers, pointing to the earth-work thrown up.

The governor then challenged the guards, who told off their numbers, and gave the usual "All right!" The bright red shell-jackets, and the caps with gay gold bands, stood out in painful contrast with the dingy crew of unfortunate men they were directing. As we looked on at the work going bravely forward, our attention was specially directed to the healthy appearance of the men.

"See," said the governor, evidently not a little proud of their ruddy cheeks, "they are not ill-looking men. I have to punish them very seldom. One or two of the men in the stone-yard were old offenders, and they're the best behaved. There's a fine young chap there, stript to the buff, and working away hard!"

₊ *The Convicts' Burial Ground.*—We turned away, and went farther over the marshes, the ground giving way under our feet; and presently we passed behind the butt, while the Minié balls were whistling through the air, and that solitary man was marking the hits. We approached a low piece of ground—in no way marked off from the rest of the marsh—in no way distinguishable from any section of the dreary expanse, save that the long rank grass had been turned, in one place lately, and that there was an upset barrow lying not far off. Heavy, leaden clouds were rolling over head, and some heavy drops of rain pattered

upon our faces as we stood there. We thought it was one of the dreariest spots we had ever seen.

"This," said the governor, "is the Convicts' Burial Ground!"

We could just trace the rough outline of disturbed ground at our feet. Beyond this was a shed, where cattle found shelter in bad weather; and to the right the land shelved up between the marsh and the river. There was not even a number over the graves; the last, and it was only a month old, was disappearing. In a few months, the rank grass will have closed over it, as over the story of its inmate. And it is, perhaps, well to leave the names of the unfortunate men, whose bones lie in the clay of this dreary marsh, unregistered and unknown. But the feeling with which we look upon its desolation is irrepressible.

THE CONVICTS' BURIAL-GROUND.

We followed the governor up the ridge that separates the marsh from the river, and walked on, back towards the arsenal. As we walked along we were told, that under our feet dead men's bones lay closely packed; the ridge could no longer contain a body, and that was the reason why, during the last five or six years, the lower ground had been taken.

Then there is a legend—an old, old legend, that has passed down to the present time—about a little pale-blue flower, with its purple leaves—the "*rubrum lamium*"—which, it is said, grows only over the convict's grave—a flower, tender and unobtrusive as the kindness for which the legend gives it credit. Botanists, however, will of course ruthlessly destroy the local faith that has given this flower value; for they will tell you it is only a stunted form of the "red dead nettle."

We pass from the graves—meet a perambulating guard, who signals "All right!" by saluting and raising his hand—and then, recrossing the canal-bridge, where the convicts are stacking wood, and the click and ring of bricklayers' trowels are heard, relieved now and then by the reports of the ordnance rifle-practice, we make our way towards the boat saluted by the "All rights" and salutes of the officers of other working parties that we pass by the way.

There are many objects to arrest our attention, as we go, from the exploded wrecks of barrels, &c., lying for sale near the butt bank, where men are digging shot out of the ground. We meet another patrolling guard, who gives the "All right" salute; and whose duty it is, as soon as he hears of an escape, to dash through the enclosure about the arsenal, and, waving his carbine horizontally in the air, communicate the fact to the sentries in the marshes.

Our way lies then by the rocket-sheds, rather celebrated for accidents.

"Occasionally you see the men at work there," said the governor, "rush out with their clothes all in flames, and dive into the canal. Only a month or so ago, two or three sheds blew up, and the rockets were flying about all amongst my men." As we passed, a workman, black as gunpowder, appeared at the door of one of the sheds with a sieve.

Close at hand to the rocket-sheds, were little powder boats, like miniature Lord Mayor's barges, with the windows blocked up and the gilding taken off.

"There are the cartridge-sheds, too; and there the fire-engines are always kept at the water's edge, in case of accident, and with the hose ready in the water, as you see. All right, Mr. Watson?"

"All right, sir! No. 3—10."

Here, opposite the gang of convicts just hailed, and

THE CONVICT'S FLOWER.

who were hard at work stacking planks, were some few idlers upon the top of a barge. "Contrast the conduct of those fellows with my men," was the governor's observation. "Their language is dreadful, as you can hear. You see, too, that new building, with the tall, minaret chimneys, flanked by low stacks, and with crimson tongues of flame at top—that's a shell factory." There are shoots of white steam, and plumes of black smoke issuing from it; and as we advance past endless stacks of heavy timber arranged by the convicts, we hear the rattle of machinery and the noise of wheels. Then as we go by the large new building where mortars are to be cast, the governor approaches a gang, and asks again—

"All right, Mr. Jenning?"

"All right, sir! 10—10," replies the officer.

We now pass through sheds—large as railway stations—under which numerous piles of timber are stacked, together with endless rows of wheelless carts, with their wheels stacked opposite, and here we find the prisoners beginning to march in gangs towards the parade-ground. "It is half-past eleven o'clock, and they must be on board the hulk to dinner at noon precisely," says the governor to us. As we draw nearer and nearer to the parade-ground, we can see them filing along from different directions. There is no confusion on reaching the spot, for each man knows his exact place. Then a strict search of the men is made by the warders, to see that they have not secreted anything while at work—the men opening their waistcoats, and pulling off their cravats, as before, to facilitate the operation.

The searching over, the men descend the stairs, in parties, to the cutters, and return to the hulk in the order in which they left her in the morning. Having made the tour of the arsenal (which, including the section of the marshes turned to use, measures 150 square acres in extent), we also returned on board the hulk with the governor.

"Weigh all!" is the word of command. And in a few minutes we are at the "DEFENCE" gangway. The officers are hurrying the convicts on board.

"Now, Mr. B——, bring your men up!" A long-boat approaches, crammed with men and warders.

"Hoist your oars!" cries an officer as the cutter touches the hulk. The warders land first, and then they hurry the men up the gangway steps. As soon as they reach the deck they advance, in single file, to their respective hatchways, and descend at once to their wards.

The tread of these two hundred men sounds below almost like thunder rolling under the decks! They are at once locked up in their wards, where their tin mug and plate are turned upside down, one upon the other, around each mess-table, previous to dinner.

₊ *The Convicts at Dinner and Leaving for Work.*—Now men appear at the end of the wards with large clothes-baskets full of bread.

"3—7; 4—8; and 5—8!" cries the warder, as he dispenses the loaves to each mess.

The mess-men of these parties advance to the gate of the ward, and receive their proper quantities for their respective messes. Some messes have a loaf and a quarter, others two whole loaves, according to their numerical strength—the men dividing these quantities themselves. There is also upon the mess-tables a deal-board to cut up the meat upon. A man now comes below carrying knife-bags, and distributes them according to the number of men in each compartment. After dinner they are cleaned, put back into the bags, and returned to the proper officer. The men who have been on board all day were in their wards, pacing to and fro, before their companions came pouring down from their arsenal work.

"To your table, men!" cries the chief warder; and accordingly the men range themselves in their proper seats.

"Now A ward!" is shouted down the hatchway. "Come on here—one, two, and three!" A man from each mess answers the call. Presently these messmen are seen returning, each carrying a small tub full of meat, and a net full of potatoes, together with the supper bread. One man at each mess may now be seen serving out the potatoes into tin plates. Then there is a cry of—"All up!"

The men rise, and grace is said. When the men are re-seated, a man proceeds at once to cut up the meat upon the mess-board. The dinner is now portioned out, and we are informed that the men very rarely quarrel over the division of the allowed quantities. When the meat is cut into eight or nine portions, as the case may be, the meat-board is pushed into the middle of the table, and each man takes the piece nearest to him. Then the peeling of potatoes goes actively forward, and the men are soon fairly engaged upon their meal, talking the while in a low, rumbling tone.

"Not too much talking there! Silence—silence here!" cries the warder.

Since the morning, the top deck and the others have undergone a complete change. The windows have been removed, and the atmosphere is fresh and pleasant.

The governor now went his rounds, and was saluted on all sides.

At length one o'clock sounded. At five minutes past we saw the guard go down the gangway with fixed bayonets, followed by one of the principal warders.

"Now, then, turn the hands out, Mr. Webb, and man the gig!" was shouted.

In a few minutes the convicts began to stream up the deck from the hatchways, and to move down the gangway in single file, to the cutters, as in the morning.

"Oars up, here! Oars up!" shouts the guard in the cutter to the rowers, as the first prisoners reach the water's edge. The boat carrying the guards—their bayonets sparkling in the sun—and some officers too, is already off to receive the men on shore.

THE "WARRIOR" HULK WITH THE "SULPHUR" WASHING-SHIP IN THE DISTANCE.

In a few minutes the two hundred men are on their way to the parade-ground; while on board the officers are occupied in mustering the "boarders" and schoolmen.

Once more we push off in the governor's gig, as the sharp crack of the rifles in the marshes reminds us that the ordnance men are still practising at the butt

During the men's absence in the afternoon, the boarders carry the hammocks back from the houses; and while we were watching this operation, our informant related to us the story of a convict who, being employed in the chaplain's room, managed to cut up his black gown, and manufacture it into a pair of black trousers. With only this garment upon him, he contrived, one very dark and gusty night, to drop overboard. He swam clear off, and reached a swamp, where he got entangled in a bed of rushes. Here he got frightened, and cried for help. Some men in a barge, who were passing, picked him up, and suspecting that he was a convict, delivered him up to the prison officers.

The convicts leave their afternoon's work at a quarter-past five, so as to be all collected by half-past, and before the free men leave. It was a pretty sight to see them re-embark for the night; for the slanting rays of the sun threw long shadows from the cutters over the water, and the evening light sparkled warmly upon the tide, and danced as it caught every polished point of the dense mass, while the boats advanced towards the hulk.

As we watched the cutters approach, we inquired into the regulations concerning the receiving visits and letters from their friends by the convicts. In reply we were told that they see their relatives once in three months, and that they are allowed to write every three months. These meetings of the prisoners with their friends are held under the poop—three meetings taking place at a time. There are, however, no regular days for visits; if a friend calls while a man is away at labour, the authorities send for him. The regulations, we should add, appear to be carried out with great consideration.

On the cutters reaching the hulk, the prisoners stream up the gangway in single file as before—then pour down the hatchways, into their respective wards, where gruel is at once served out to them, and they are allowed to rest till chapel-time, at half-past six o'clock.

After chapel, at eight o'clock, the men are mustered in their wards—and the gates of the wards locked for the night. When the officer cries, "The muster's over!" the men jump up, the tables disappear, the forms are ranged along the sides of the ward, and each man gets his hammock from the corner in which they were piled in the afternoon by the boarders. In a few minutes all the hammocks are slung, and the men talking together. "The 4 division is for school to-morrow," cries an officer.

Shortly after this each man is beside his hammock, preparing for bed, and then they are allowed to talk until nine o'clock; but directly the clock strikes, not another word is heard. At nine o'clock the two officers to each deck are relieved by the night officer, and the men are in bed. There are also four guards who relieve one another through the night, at the gangway.

At nine o'clock the countersign is given out by the governor to the chief warder, the chief warder giving it to the officers on the watch, so that after this hour nobody can move about the ship without it.

All is quiet. We hear once more the gurgling of the water about the hulk. Over towards the arsenal, the warm red lights of the little white pier stand out prettily against the dark shore, and there are bright lights shining over the crumpled water, in little golden paths. The shore, too, is studded with lights as with jewels.

We are informed that the countersign for the night is "Smyrna." Then we hear the loud metallic ring of two bells. "Nine o'clock!" cries the warder. Now there is not a sound heard below, but the occasional tramp of footsteps over-head. The men, as they lie in their hammocks, look like huge cocoons. The principal warder tries all the locks of the wards, and at ten o'clock the hatches are padlocked for the night, and the day's duties are ended.

¶ iii—δ.

The " Unité" Hospital Ship.

While the men were performing their afternoon labours in the arsenal, we found time to go, in the captain's gig, on board the convicts' hospital ship, the "UNITÉ"—or "Uneet, according to the local pronunciation.

The "UNITÉ" hospital ship, moored to the "DEFENCE," is an old 36-gun frigate, taken from the French. The officers who steered us on board bade us examine the beauty of her build.

This ship is excellently arranged, and has large airy decks, along which iron bedsteads are placed, at sufficient distances, for the reception of the sick men from the "DEFENCE" and "WARRIOR" labour hulks. The vessel is cleaned by a few healthy convicts; while some of the convalescents, in their blue-gray dresses and odd comical night-caps, are employed as nurses. The top deck is a fine spacious room, covered with matting, and lighted by wide, barred port-holes.

The invalid bedsteads were ranged on either side of the deck from one end to the other, and at the head of them there were small places for books. "Here the temperature in the winter months," said the master, "is kept up to sixty."

We passed one man in bed, who was coughing. It was a case of phthisis. He had chloride of lime hanging all round him, to destroy the odour of the expectoration. Then there was another poor fellow, with his head lying upon a pillow, placed upon a chair at the side of the bed, who had a disease of the heart, and had been spitting blood. The convalescents, in their queer, blue-gray gowns, draw up at the end of their beds as we move along, and salute us. Another man lies in bed, wearing a night-cap, marked "Hospital;" he has a broken leg.

Another, of whom we asked the nature of his illness, replied, "Asthmatical, sir!"

"Two healthy prisoners are employed on each deck," said the master, " to act as nurses. One of the convalescents acts as barber. That's he, with his belt round his waist filled with sheaths and razors."

Then we visited the place where the convalescents assemble for prayers, morning and evening. "We have twenty-four in hospital to-day," the master added; "five were discharged this morning. There is plenty of ventilation, you perceive. A perfect draught is kept up, by means of tubes, right through the ship. We were told that a Bible and Testament were placed at the head of each bed; and we saw one convict reading "Recreations in Astronomy."

We inquired about the scale of diet. In reply the master said, "The man so bad, up-stairs, has 2 eggs, 2 pints of arrowroot and milk, 12 ounces of bread, 1 ounce of butter, 6 ounces of wine, 1 ounce of brandy, 2 oranges, and a sago pudding daily. Another man here is on half a sheep's head, 1 pint of arrowroot and milk, 4 ounces of bread, 1 ounce of butter, 1 pint extra of tea, and 2 ounces of wine daily. Here is the scale of full diet for convalescents :—

BREAKFAST.
4 ounces of bread.
¼ pint of milk.
2 ounces of oatmeal gruel.

SUPPER.
4 ounces of bread.
One-sixth of an ounce of tea.
½ ounce of sugar.
¼ pint of milk.

DINNER.
8 ounces of bread.
8 ounces of mutton (uncooked).
1 pound of potatoes.
½ ounce of salt.
½ pint of porter.
1 pint of soup."

THE CONVICTS RETURNING TO THE HULKS FROM THEIR LABOUR IN THE ARSENAL.

The healthy men employed on board the "UNITÉ" muster twenty strong, including the boatmen, cooks, and washermen.   There are nine warders, an infirmary warder, and principal. The night-watches begin at half-past five, at which hour half the officers leave the ship, and return at seven o'clock on the following morning.   The principal, however, lives on board, and there is also a resident surgeon.

From the directors' report in 1854, we learn that there were on board, on the 1st of January in that year, 58 patients; that in the course of that year 675 patients were admitted; that in the course of the same year 658 patients were discharged; that two patients were pardoned on medical grounds; that 25 died; that two patients were invalided to the "Stirling Castle;" and that on the 31st of December, 1854, there were 36 patients left in the hospital.

¶ iii—ε.

The " Sulphur " Washing Hulk.

From the "UNITÉ" we proceeded, in the gig of the governor of the "DEFENCE," past old steamers, low wharves, flaunting little river-side public-houses, towards the great bulging hulk of the "WARRIOR."   But before being landed at the dockyard steps, to go on board the model hulk, we pulled aside to a little, low, dingy ship, which serves as a floating wash-tub to the Woolwich hulks.

This old sloop of war, once carrying thirty guns, has now fifteen convicts on board, under the orders of a master, whose business it is to wash the clothes of the men in the "WARRIOR" and "DEFENCE" hulks.   There are three washermen, one blacksmith, and two stocking-menders here employed.   On deck there was a solitary soldier keeping guard.   The maindeck was very wet.   Forward there were large square black water-tanks, and beside these a corrugated iron blacksmith's shop, with an old convict filing away inside.   Bundles of convicts' stockings lie waiting to be mended near the poop, while lines, ornamented with linen, dangle over-head.   Below, between the low decks, we groped our way, in the deep gloom, amid damp clothes—past men mending stockings, others folding convict clothes, and tying them up into rolls ready to be worn—in the steam and smell of clothes drying by heat, past capacious vats and boilers, all half-hidden, and looking terrible, because dark and spectral-like.

The warder in charge of the old sloop showed us over his dingy kingdom with great courtesy, and answered our many questions with excellent good-humour.   He told us that all the convicts employed with him throughout the day slept on board the "WARRIOR" opposite.   He alone remained on board all night.

We pushed off from the "SULPHUR," thanking the warder for his courtesy, and pulled for the dockyard steps alongside the "WARRIOR."

¶ iii—ζ.

The " Warrior" Hulk.

This great hulk—an old 74-gun ship, upwards of sixty years of age, which has been the subject of annual remonstrances from the prison directors to the government for some time past and the ribs of which, it is said, hardly hold together—is moored alongside the dockyard, with her head towards London, and serves to house the convicts who work in the dock-yard.

We have so fully described the hulk system on board the "DEFENCE," which differs in no important particular from that pursued on board the "WARRIOR," that it will be unnecessary to do more than glance at the general arrangements of this ship. Even the employment of the prisoners in the dockyard differs little in character from that performed by the convicts who work in the arsenal.

The distribution of the prisoners' time closely resembles that on board the "DEFENCE," there being 2 hours given to meals; 9 hours and 5 minutes to work; and 4 hours and 25 minutes to in-door occupation throughout the summer; while in the winter the meals occupy 2 hours and 5 minutes; work, 7 hours and 55 minutes; and the in-door occu-pation, 5 hours.

The "WARRIOR" is reached, from the dockyard, by a gallery projecting from the quay to the gangway. At the end of the compartment under the forecastle is a large iron palisading, with two gates, which are securely padlocked at night.

"The ship," our attendant-warder informs us, "is lighted by gas—the only one in the world, perhaps, that is so." This is owing to the close contiguity of the vessel to the shore.

The top deck has a fine long wide passage. The wards are divided into two messes, and contain two tables each. The other arrangements are the same as in the "DEFENCE." Here, however, each ward has its little library; and every man has a Bible, a prayer-book, a hymn-book, and a library-book; the last he gets from the schoolmaster. Each ward, too, has a solid bulkhead, which prevent the authorities having too large a body of prisoners together. There is a gas-light at the bulkhead between each ward, so arranged as to light two wards at once, while the passage is darkened, so that the officer on duty can see the men, while they cannot see him.

The middle deck is very fine and spacious, the passage being about five feet in width. There are eight wards on the top deck, ten in the middle deck, and fourteen on the lower deck.

The ship can accommodate four hundred and fifty men. There are now four hundred and forty-nine men in her, and out of this number only ten in the hospital. At the head end of the middle deck is a shoemaker's shop, where we found the convicts mending prisoners' shoes; while opposite them is the tailor's shop, and here the workers were repairing shirts and flannels.

The lower deck is also a fine long deck, reaching right from the head to the stern. There is a current of air right through it. It is, however, very low. At the fore-part of this deck, on one side, is the carpenter's shop; while the seven refractory cells occupy the opposite side.

A black label hangs at each door of the dark cells, and upon this is chalked the name and punishment of the inmate. One runs thus :—" In for 4 days; B and W (bread and water); in 19th, out 23rd." The next man is in for seven days, with bread and water, for having attempted to escape; and a third prisoner is also in for seven days, for extreme insolence to the governor and warders. We now passed on to the chapel, the surgery, &c., and entered the schoolmaster's cabin, where we saw the same class of books as we noted down on board the "DEFENCE."

The school classes are divided into eleven divisions, arranged according to the ability of the men. All the men have half a day's schooling each per week. All take three lessons, viz., one hour's reading, one hour's writing, and one hour's arithmetic. Here we found some trying in vain to write, while one was engaged upon a letter beginning, "Dear brother."

The copies the men were making were generally better than one could expect.* We noticed also the chapel clerks, who were convicts with silver-gray hair, and appeared to belong to a better class. They write letters or petitions, we were told, for the prisoners who are unable to do so themselves. One of these clerks had been a medical man, in practice for himself during twenty-five years, while the other had been a clerk in the Post-office. The clerk had been transported for fourteen years; and the medical man had been sentenced to four years' penal servitude.

The working parties here are arranged as in the arsenal, only the strongest men are selected for the coal-gang, invalids being put to stone-breaking. In the dockyard there are still military sentries attached to each gang of prisoners. We glanced at the parties working, amid the confusion of the dockyard, carrying coals, near the gigantic ribs of a skeleton ship, stacking timber, or drawing carts, like beasts of burden. Now we came upon a labouring party, near a freshly pitched gun-boat, deserted by the free labourers, who had struck for wages, and saw the well-known prison brown of the men carrying timber from the saw-mills. Here the officer called—as at the arsenal—"All right, sir! 27—10." Then there were parties testing chain cables, amid the most deafening hammering. It is hard, very hard, labour the men are performing.

* STATEMENT SHOWING THE PRISONERS' PROGRESS AT SCHOOL ON BOARD THE "WARRIOR" HULK DURING THE YEAR 1854.

Date of Reception.	Could not read when received.	Since learned to read imperfectly.	Could read only when received.	Since learned to read and write imperfectly.	Could read and write imperfectly when received.	Since learned to read and write well.	Have made progress in arithmetic.	Could read and write well when received.	Were well educated when received.	Total.
January 4, 1854 . .	2	1	8	6	6	6	3	—	—	16
February 24 ,, . .	9	5	6	5	12	11	5	12	—	39
March 14 ,, . .	1	1	2	1	1	1	1	—	—	4
,, 24 ,, . .	—	—	2	2	5	5	2	3	—	10
April 20 ,, . .	3	1	5	5	5	5	3	2	—	15
,, 27 ,, . .	5	4	1	1	3	3	2	—	1	10
May 1 ,, . .	2	2	1	1	2	2	1	—	—	5
,, 3 ,, . .	3	2	3	3	1	1	2	3	—	10
June 7 ,, . .	7	4	12	9	10	8	6	5	—	34
,, 15 ,, . .	3	3	2	2	—	—	2	7	—	12
August 14 ,, . .	6	6	5	5	7	7	4	2	—	20
,, 28 ,, . .	1	1	1	1	3	3	2	4	—	9
October 11 ,, . .	1	1	2	2	10	9	3	7	1	21
,, 20 ,, . .	2	1	4	4	5	4	—	9	—	20
,, 27 ,, . .	1	—	—	—	—	—	—	—	—	1
November 2 ,, . .	4	1	3	3	3	3	—	8	—	18
,, 3 ,, . .	1	—	—	—	—	—	—	—	—	1
December 19 ,, . .	2	—	6	—	13	—	—	7	—	28
Totals . .	53	33	63	50	86	68	36	69†	2†	273

† Those who could "read and write well" when received, or were "well educated," have since made considerable progress in arithmetic and other subjects.

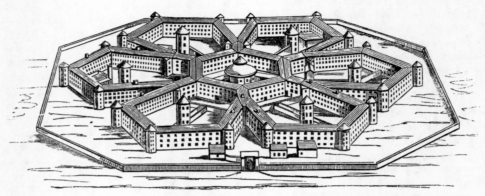

BIRD'S-EYE VIEW OF MILLBANK PRISON.
(Copied from a Model by the Clerk of the Works.)

¶ iv.

MILLBANK PRISON—THE CONVICT DEPOT.

Millbank Prison is only approached by land, in the case of the unfortunate convicts who are taken there.   The visitor instinctively avoids the uninteresting *route* down Parliament Street, Abingdon Street, and the dreary Horseferry Road, and proceeds to the prison by water.

We will suppose him to do as we did, take the boat at Hungerford Stairs, with which view, he must pass through the market of the same name, which is celebrated for its penny ices ("the best in England"), and its twopenny omnibuses (direct to the towns styled Camden and Kentish Town), and also known as the great West-end emporium for fish (including periwinkles and shrimps), flesh, and fowl.   This classic spot was formerly remarkable for its periwinkle market, the glory of which, however, has now altogether departed.

The "SPACIOUS HALL," in which the periwinkle traffic was once carried on, is now, as a very prominent placard informs us, once more "TO BE LET."   When the Cockney taste for periwinkles appeared to be dying out, the hall in question was made the receptacle for various models, which possessed no sort of interest to the sight-seer; after which it was converted into a "Mesmeric Saloon," which took an equally slight hold on the public mind.   Then it was the site of various other failures, and recently it became a Registration and Advertisement Agency, but, as it was imposible to descend any lower in the scale of inutility, it was, on this scheme being abandoned, finally closed, and there is now some probability of its exterior being turned to advantage as a hoarding for the exhibition of external rather than internal placards.

Passing along the arcade, with its massive granite pillars, we notice the "Epping House," celebrated for Epping and other provincial butters so skilfully manufactured in London.   Then suddenly our eyes and noses are attracted by the "HOT MEAT AND FRUIT PIES," exposed on a kind of fishmonger's board, in front of an open window, which also exhibits an announcement to the effect that there is a "*Genteel* Dining-Room Up-stairs."

Then come the poulterers' shops, with the live cocks and hens in coops, and the scarlet combs and black plumage of the birds peeping through the wicker-baskets at the door, while dead geese, with their limp fluffy necks, are hanging over the shelves of the open shop.

At the corner is the grand penny ice shop, the "Tortoni's," of Hungerford. Boys are feasting within, and scooping the frozen syrup in spoonfuls out of the diminutive glasses, while black-chinned and dark-eyed Italians are moulding their "*gaufres*," in large flat curling irons, above a portable stove.

Before reaching the bridge we notice a row of enterprising fishmongers who are speculating in the silvery salmon, the white-bellied turbot, the scarlet lobster, the dun-coloured crab, and the mackerel with its metallic green back, and who salute the passers-by, as they hurry to catch the boat, with subdued cries of " Wink, winks !" or "Any fine serrimps to-day!"

The subterranean music-hall at the southern extremity of the market, promises unheard-of attractions for the evening. The Dolphin and Swan Taverns, on either side, used to be rivals, in the days when holiday-makers, in the absence of steam-boat accommodation, used to drink and smoke, and pick periwinkles, on the roofs " commanding a fine view (of the mud) of the river," and fancy the stench was invigorating and refreshing, as they sparingly threw their halfpence to the mud-larks, who disported themselves so joyously in the filth beneath.

Carefully avoiding the toll-gate, we proceed along a narrow passage by the side, formed for the benefit of steam-boat passengers. The line of placards beside the bridge-house celebrates the merits of " DOWN'S HATS," and " COOPER'S MAGIC PORTRAITS," or teach us how Gordon Cumming (in Scotch attire) saves his fellow-creatures from the jaws of roaring lions by means of a flaming firebrand.

We hurry along the bridge, with its pagoda-like piers, which serve to support the iron chains suspending the platform, and turn down a flight of winding steps, bearing a considerable resemblance to the entrance of a vault or cellar.

On the covered coal barges, that are dignified by the name of the floating pier, are officials in uniform, with bands round their hats, bearing mysterious inscriptions, such as L. and W. S. B. C., the meaning of which is in vain guessed at by persons who have only enough time to enable them to get off by the next boat, and who have had no previous acquaintance with the London and Westminster Steam Boat Company. The words " PAY HERE " are inscribed over little wooden houses, that remind one of the retreats generally found at the end of suburban gardens; and there are men within to receive the money and dispense the " checks," who have so theatrical an air, that they appear like money-takers who have been removed in their boxes to Hungerford Stairs from some temple of the legitimate drama that has recently become insolvent.

We take our ticket amid cries of " Now then, mum, this way for *Cree*morne !" " Oo's for Ungerford ?" " Any one for Lambeth or Chelsea ?" and have just time to set foot on the boat before it shoots through the bridge, leaving behind the usual proportion of persons who have just taken their tickets in time to miss it.

Barges, black with coal, are moored in the roads in long parallel lines beside the bridge on one side the river, and on the other there are timber-yards at the water's edge, crowded with yellow stacks of deal. On the right bank, as we go, are seen the shabby-looking lawns at the back of Privy Gardens and Richmond Terrace, which run down to the river, and which might be let out at exorbitant rents if the dignity of the proprietors would only allow them to convert their strips of sooty grass into " eligible " coal wharves.

Westminster Bridge is latticed over with pile-work; the red signal-boards above the arches point out the few of which the passage is not closed. The parapets are removed, and replaced by a dingy hoarding, above which the tops of carts, and occasionally the driver of a Hansom cab may be seen passing along.

After a slight squeak, and a corresponding jerk, and amid the cries from a distracted boy of " Ease her !" " Stop her !" " Back her !" as if the poor boat were suffering some sudden pain, the steamer is brought to a temporary halt at Westminster pier.

Then, as the boat dashes with a loud noise through one of the least unsound of the arches of the bridge, we come in front of the New Houses of Parliament, with their architecture and decorations of Gothic biscuit-ware. Here are the tall clock-tower, with its huge empty sockets for the reception of the clocks and its scaffolding of bird-cage work at the top, and the lofty massive square tower, like that of Cologne Cathedral, surmounted with its cranes.

Behind is the white-looking Abbey, with its long, straight, black roof, and its pinnacled towers; and a little farther on, behind the grimy coal wharves, is seen a bit of St. John's Church, with its four stone turrets standing up in the air, and justifying the popular comparison which likens it to an inverted table.

On the Lambeth side we note the many boat-builders' yards, and then "Bishop's Walk," as the embanked esplanade, with its shady plantation, adjoining the Archbishop's palace, is called. The palace itself derives more picturesqueness than harmony from the differences existing in the style and colour of its architecture, the towers at the one end being gray and worm-eaten, the centre reminding us somewhat of the Lincolns' Inn dining-hall, while the motley character of the edifice is rendered more thorough by the square, massive, and dark ruby-coloured old bricken tower, which forms the eastern extremity.

The yellow-gray stone turret of Lambeth church, close beside the Archbishop's palace, warns us that we are approaching the stenches which have made Lambeth more celebrated than the very dirtiest of German towns. During six days in the week the effluvium from the bone-crushing establishments is truly nauseating; but on Fridays, when the operation of glazing is performed at the potteries, the united exhalation from the south bank produces suffocation, in addition to sickness—the combined odours resembling what might be expected to arise from the putrefaction of an entire Isle of Dogs. The banks at the side of the river here are lined with distilleries, gas works, and all sorts of factories requiring chimneys of preternatural dimensions. Potteries, with kilns showing just above the roofs, are succeeded by whiting-racks, with the white lumps shining through the long, pitchy, black bars; and huge tubs of gasometers lie at the feet of the lofty gas-works. Everything is, in fact, on a gigantic scale, even to the newly-whitewashed factory inscribed "Ford's Waterproofing Company," which, with a rude attempt at inverted commas, is declared to be "limited."

On the opposite shore we see Chadwick's paving-yard, which is represented in the river by several lines of barges, heavily laden with macadamized granite; the banks being covered with paving stones, which are heaped one upon the other like loaves of bread.

Ahead is Vauxhall bridge, with its open iron work at the sides of the arches, and at its foot, at the back of the dismal Horseferry Road, lies the Millbank prison.

This immense yellow-brown mass of brick-work is surrounded by a low wall of the same material, above which is seen a multitude of small squarish windows, and a series of diminutive roofs of slate, like low retreating foreheads. There is a systematic irregularity about the in-and-out aspect of the building, which gives it the appearance of a gigantic puzzle; and altogether the Millbank prison may be said to be one of the most successful realizations, on a large scale, of the ugly in architecture, being an ungainly combination of the mad-house with the fortress style of building, for it has a series of martello-like towers, one at each of its many angles, and was originally surrounded by a moat, whilst its long lines of embrasure-like windows are barred, after the fashion of Bedlam and St. Luke's.

At night the prison is nothing but a dark, shapeless structure, the hugeness of which is made more apparent by the bright yellow specks which shine from the casements. The Thames then rolls by like a flood of ink, spangled with the reflections from the lights of Vauxhall bridge, and the deep red lamps from those of the Millbank pier, which dart downwards into the stream, like the luminous trails of a rocket reversed. The tall obeliskine chimneys of the southern bank, which give Lambeth so Egyptian an aspect, look more colossal than ever in the darkness; while the river taverns on either side, at which amateurs congregate to enjoy the prospect and fragrance of the Thamesian mud, exhibit clusters of light which

attract the eye from one point to another, along the banks, until it rests at last upon Westminster bridge, where each of the few arches which remain "practicable" for steam-boats
and barges is indicated by a red lamp, which glares from the summit of the vault like a
blood-shot eye.

¶ iv—a.

Plan, History, and Discipline of the Prison.

Millbank prison was formerly guarded, as we said, like a fortress, by a wide moat,
which completely surrounded the exterior wall. This moat has been filled up, and the earth
has yielded a tolerably large crop of long, rank grass, of the kind peculiar to graveyards,
bearing ample testimony to the damp and marshy nature of the soil. The narrow circle of
meadow, which marks where the moat formerly ran, seems to afford very satisfactory grazing
to the solitary cow that may be occasionally seen within its precincts.

The ground-plan of the prison itself resembles a wheel, of which the governor's house
in the centre forms the nave, while each two of the spokes constitute the sides of six long
pentagons with triangular bases, and divergent sides of equal length, at the end of each of
which stands a turret or tower, with a conical slate roof, and a number of vertical slits for
windows. From the two towers the lateral lines converge at equal inclinations towards the
apex, so that each of the pentagonal figures presents a triangular front. (*See Ground-plan,*
p. 237.)

Millbank Prison is a modification of Jeremy Bentham's "Panoptikon, or Inspection
House." The ground on which it stands was purchased from the Marquis of Salisbury, in
1799, for £12,000; and the building itself, which was commenced in 1812, cost half a
million. It is now the general depôt for persons under sentence of transportation, or
waiting to be drafted to government jails, and is the largest of the London prisons.

The entire ground occupied by the establishment is sixteen acres in extent, seven of
which are taken up by the prison itself, and the buildings and yards attached to it, while
the remainder is laid out in gardens, which are cultivated by the convicts.

It was originally built for the confinement of 1,200 prisoners in separate cells, but since
the separate system has been partially abandoned, larger numbers have been admitted, and it
is at present adapted for the reception of about 1,300.

When Jeremy Bentham first proposed the establishment of the penitentiary, his plan
was announced as one "for a new and less expensive mode of employing and reforming
convicts." Although the prison was of course to remain a place of penal detention, it was
at the same time to be made a kind of convict workshop, in which the prisoners were to be
employed in various trades and manufactures, and to be allowed to apply a portion of their
earnings to their own use.

Part of Bentham's system consisted in placing the prisoners under constant surveillance.
From a room in the centre of the building, the governor, and any one else who was admitted
into the interior, were to see into all parts of the building at all periods of the day, while
a reflecting apparatus was even to enable them to watch the prisoners in their cells at
night. There was a contrivance also for putting the visitor into immediate oral communication with any of the prisoners. This, from the beginning, proved a failure, considered
only as a piece of mechanism.

Bentham's plan of constant and general inspection—his "panopticon principle of supervision," as it was called, "was referred to a Parliamentary Committee, in 1810, and, after
some discussion, finally rejected."

In 1812, two years after the abandonment of Bentham's scheme, which provided for the accommodation of 600 convicts, it was determined to erect a penitentiary for the reception of 1,200 convicts on the ground which the panopticon was to have occupied, and to allow each convict a separate cell. This prison, or collection of prisons—for it consisted of several departments, each of which was entirely distinct—was commenced in 1813, and finished in 1821. According to the discipline adopted in the new prison, "each convict's time of imprisoment was divided into two portions; during the former of these he was confined in a separate cell, in which he worked and slept." The separation, however, even under the strictest seclusion, was not complete; the prisoners congregated, from time to time, during the period allotted for working at the mills or water-machines, or while taking exercise in the airing-ground, and on these occasions it was found utterly impossible to prevent intercourse among them. After remaining in the separate class for eighteen months or two years, the prisoners were removed to the second class, in which they laboured in common. The evil tendency of this regulation soon became apparent, and, as in the case at Gloucester, the governer and chaplain remonstrated against it, alleging that the good effects produced by the operation of the discipline enforced in the first class, were speedily and utterly done away with on the prisoner's transfer to the second. The evil was so strongly represented in the superintendent's committee, that in March, 1832, the second class was abolished, and new regulations were made in order to render the separation between the prisoners more complete and effectual.

In time of the "penitentiary" system, the governor of the prison was a reverend gentleman, who placed an undue reliance on the efficacy of religious forms. The prisoners, independently of their frequent attendance in the chapel, were supplied, more than plentifully, with tracts and religious books, and, in fact, taught to do nothing but pray. Even the warders were put to read prayers to them in their cells, and the convicts taking their cue from the reverend governor, with the readiness which always distinguishes them, were not long in assuming a contrite and devout aspect, which, however, found no parallel in their conduct. As the most successful simulator of holiness became the most favoured prisoner, sanctified looks were, as a matter of course, the order of the day, and the most desperate convicts in the prison found it advantageous to complete their criminal character by the addition of hypocrisy.

This irrational and demoralizing system ceased with the reign of the reverend governor.

By the Act 6 and 7 Vict. c. 26, it was provided that the General Penitentiary at Millbank should be called the Millbank Prison, and used as a receptacle for such convicts under sentence or order of transportation as the Secretary of State might direct to be removed there. "They are to continue there," adds the First Report of the Millbank Prison (July 31, 1844), in which an abstract of the act is given, "until transported according to law or conditionally pardoned, or until they become entitled to their freedom, or are directed by the Secretary of State to be removed to any other prison or place of confinement in which they may be lawfully imprisoned;" thus appropriating this extensive penal institution as a *depôt* for the reception of all convicts under sentence or order of transportation in Great Britain, in lieu of their being sent directly, as heretofore, to the hulks.

Although many of the prisoners here are now allowed to work together, or "placed in association," as would be said in prison phraseology, the majority of them are kept in separate confinement. Every prisoner is supplied with moral or religious instruction. Prisoners, not of the Established Church, may obtain leave to be absent from the chapel, and Catholics hear service regularly performed by a minister of their own religion.

Each prisoner is employed, unless prevented by sickness, in such work as the governor may appoint, every day except Sundays, Christmas Day, Good Friday, and every day appointed for a general fast, or thanksgiving; the hours of work in each day being limited to twelve, exclusive of the time allowed for meals. Prisoners attend to the cleaning of the

* Report of Parliamentary Committee on Penitentiary House, 1811.

prison, under the superintendence of the warders, and some also assist in the kitchen and bakehouse under the direction of the bakers and cooks.

The conduct of each prisoner is carefully watched and noted, and the most deserving receive a good-conduct badge to wear on their dress after they have been a certain time in the prison.

Millbank prison, as we have before said, consists of six pentagons which converge towards the centre. On entering the outer gate, pentagon 1 is the first on the right, pentagon 2 the

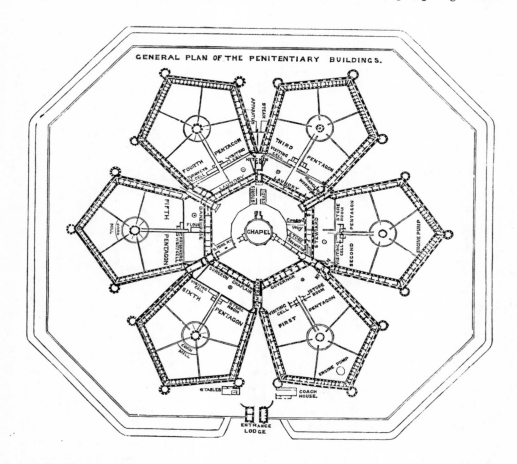

GENERAL PLAN OF THE PENITENTIARY BUILDINGS.

second, and so on until we reach pentagon 6, the last of the radii of the circle, and which is immediately on the left of the entrance.

Pentagon 1 contains the reception-ward, in which the prisoners are all confined separately.

In pentagon 2 the prisoners work at various trades in separate cells.

Pentagon 3 is devoted to the women, who are for the most part in separation.

In pentagon 4 both the separate and associated systems are pursued. This pentagon contains the infirmary.

Pentagon 5, besides its cells for separate confinement, contains the general ward, which consists of four cells knocked into one. This ward is looked upon with a favourable eye by the "old hands," who are well acquainted with the prison habits, and endeavour to gain admission to it for the sake of the conversation which takes place there, and which, in spite of the "silent system," can never be altogether put a stop to.

There are three floors in each of these pentagons, and four wards on each floor.*

* We give, as usual, the following—

STATEMENT OF THE NUMBER AND DISPOSAL OF THE CONVICTS RECEIVED INTO MILLBANK PRISON THROUGHOUT THE YEAR 1854.

Male Prisoners.

The number of male prisoners remaining, on the 1st January, 1854, was . . . 948	These prisoners had been disposed of as follows, viz. :—		
The number received during the year :—	To Parkhurst prison . . . 19		
From Dartmoor convict prison was . 4	„ Pentonville „ . . . 196		
„ Portsmouth „ . 4	„ Philanthropic asylum . . 6		251
„ Brixton „ . 25			
„ Dorchester barracks . 392	To public works :—		
„ "Warrior" convict hulk . 2	Portland prison . . . 92		
„ "Defence" „ . 2	Portsmouth „ . . . 185		
„ Stirling Castle „ . 68	Brixton „ . . . 1		
In contract :—	"Warrior" hulk . . . 20		
Leicester county . . . 2	"Defence" „ . . . 97		
From county and borough jails . . 971	Dorchester barracks . . . 700		1,095
„ Lunatic asylum . 2			
Soldiers under sentence of transportation by courts-martial . . . 41	Deceased 51		
	Transferred to a lunatic asylum . 10		
	Pardoned, free . . . 3		
Total . . 2,461	Licensed 73		
	Conditional pardon . . . 1		138
	As invalids :—		
	To the "Stirling Castle" hulk 112		
	„ Dartmoor prison . . 168		280
	Number remaining, 31st Dec., 1854 . . 697		
			2461

Female Prisoners.

Remaining in prison on 1st Jan., 1854 198	Disposed of as follows :—		
	Transferred to Female Prison at Brixton 178		
	Discharged and licensed . . 19		
	Died 1		198

The greatest number of male prisoners in confinement at any one time was—
On 10th August 1,125
Daily average throughout the year :—
Males . . . . . . 702·8

" It will be remembered," says the report, "that, in the above tables, 700 convicts were removed to Dorchester barracks ; and this took place between the 13th and 17th August, the cholera having broken out on the 3rd of that month.

" The cholera having ceased in this prison, such convicts as remained at Dorchester, amounting to 392, were brought back to Millbank in the months of November and December, and, on the 28th December, Dorchester barracks were finally given over to the Ordnance authorities."

The 700 convicts removed to Dorchester were disposed of as follows :—

Died		1
Removed to Pentonville . . .		8
„ Parkhurst . . .		70
„ Portsmouth . . .		99
„ Portland . . .		130
„ Millbank . . .		392
		700

There is an officer to every two wards, and each ward contains thirty cells, one of which is a store cell.

Every floor has its instructing officer, but the instructing officers appointed by the prison authorities teach nothing but tailoring, and prisoners who are anxious to learn some other trade, must obtain permission to enter a ward in which there is some prisoner capable of giving them the desired instruction.

All the cells are well ventilated, and the prison generally is kept scrupulously clean, but the site of the building is low and marshy, and although enormous sums have been spent in draining and improving the soil, its dampness still renders it very unhealthy—as may be seen by the following comparison of the number of cases of illness occurring in the several convict prisons throughout the Metropolis :—

TABLE SHOWING THE PER CENTAGE OF CASES OF ILLNESS TO THE NUMBER OF PRISONERS PASSING THROUGH EACH OF THE METROPOLITAN CONVICT PRISONS IN THE YEAR 1854.

	Number of Convicts passing through the Prison during the year.	Number of Cases of Illness during the year.	Per Centage of Illness to the Number of Prisoners.
PENTONVILLE	925	1,732	187·2
BRIXTON	664	155	23·3
HULKS ("Defence" and "Warrior")	1,513	723	47·7
MILLBANK (including females) . .	2,659	11,890	447·1
TOTAL	5,761	14,500	251·7

At Millbank, therefore, more than twice as many cases of illness, in proportion to the prison population, occur among the convicts as at Pentonville in the course of the year; ten times as many as at the Hulks; and no less than nineteen times as many as at Brixton, which is the healthiest of all the metropolitan government-prisons.

The per centages of removals and pardons on medical grounds, as well as deaths, with regard to the daily average number of prisoners, exhibit similar marked differences in the relative healthiness of the several convict prisons of London; thus:—

	Per Centage of Removals on Medical Grounds.	Per Centage of Pardons on Medical Grounds.	Per Centage of Deaths.
PENTONVILLE	0·19	0·96	1·10
BRIXTON	0·00	1·00	1·00
HULKS	0·21	0·21	2·4
MILLBANK	2·12	0·00	6·91*

Accordingly, we perceive that at Millbank there are nearly seven times as many deaths in the year as at Brixton, and more than three times as many as at the Hulks.

The greater portion of the convicts confined at Millbank are employed in making soldiers' clothing, biscuit-bags, hammocks, and miscellaneous articles for the army and navy, and other prisons, as well as the shirts, handkerchiefs, and cloth coats and trousers worn by the prisoners themselves.† Others are occupied, and receive instruction, in gardening.

* It is much to be regretted that there is no uniform statistical method of registering the medical returns of the several prisons, both in London and the country. Some of the medical officers, as those of Millbank and Pentonville, favour us with elaborate per centages of the cases of illness, deaths, &c., whereas, the medical statistics of the Hulks and Brixton are given in the crudest possible manner, and not only almost useless to the inquirer as they stand, but signally defective in their arrangement in these scientific days.

† OCCUPATIONS CARRIED ON IN THE SEVERAL PENTAGONS AND WARDS OF MILLBANK PRISON.

Ward.	Pentagon 1.	Pentagon 2.	Pentagon 3.	Pentagon 4.	Pentagon 5.	Pentagon 6.
A	Pickers	Shoemakers	Women	Tailors	Weavers	Pickers
B	Reception Ward	Shoemakers	Women	Tailors	Weavers	Pickers
C	Tailors	Artificers	Women	Infirmary	Tailors	Tailors
D	Tailors	Tailors	Women	Tailors	Tailors	Tailors
E	Tailors	Tailors	Women	Infirmary	Tailors	Tailors
F	Tailors	Tailors	Women	Tailors	Pickers	Tailors

At the time of our visit there were altogether 828 prisoners (*i.e.*, 472 less than the complement) confined within the walls; of these 655 were males, and 173 females, and they were distributed throughout the prison in the following manner:—

DISTRIBUTION AND NUMBER OF CONVICTS IN MILLBANK PRISON, MAY 24, 1856.

Pentagon 1.			Pentagon 2.			Pentagon 3.			Pentagon 4.			Pentagon 5.			Pentagon 6.			General Ward.		
Ward.	No. of Cells.	No. in Cells.	Ward.	No. of Cells.	No. in Cells.	Ward.	No. of Cells.	No. in Cells.	Ward.	No. of Cells.	No. in Cells.	Ward.	No. of Cells.	No. in Cells.	Ward.	No. of Cells.	No. in Cells.	Bay.	No. of Bays.	No. in Bays.
A	29	32	A	28	21	A	29	30	A	29	22	A	15	23	A	29	26	A	28	—
B	0		B	30	29	B	29	31	B	28	22	B	15	30	B	28	24	B	32	—
C	30		C	30	18	C	31	32	D	30	14	C	30	21	C	30	21	C	32	—
D	30		D	30	23	D	16	15	F	60	55	D	30	26	D	30	20	D	28	—
E	30		E	29	21	Penal D Asso.	15	14	G	60	50	E	30	17	E	29	22			
F	30		F	29	25	E Asso.	18	19	H	60	47	F	29	25	F	30	21			
						F	19	32												
Total.	149	32	Total.	176	137	Total.	157	173	Total.	267	210	Total.	149	142	Total.	176	134	Total.	120	

TOTAL NUMBER OF PRISONERS:—

In Pentagon 1 = 32	In Pentagon 5 = 142
Pentagon 2 = 137	Pentagon 6 = 134
Pentagon 3 = 173	General Ward 0
Pentagon 4 = 210	In the whole prison . . . 828

¶ iv—β.

The Present Use and Regulations of the Prison.

The only entrance to the prison at Millbank is facing the Thames.

The door of the "outer gate," on the day of our first visit, was opened in answer to our summons by the usual official, in the same half-police-half-coast-guard kind of uniform, and we were ushered into a small triangular hall, with a staircase, leading to the gate-keeper's rooms above, crammed into one corner, and a table facing it, on which were ranged a series of portable letter-boxes not unlike the poor-boxes to be seen at hospitals and churches. On one of these was written, "*Male Officers' Letter-box*," and on another, "*Female Officers' Letter-box;*" a third was labelled, "*Prisoners' Letter-box*," and a fourth, "*Clerk of the Works.*" A few letters were on the table itself, and over its edge hung a long strip of paper inscribed with a list of the officers on leave for the night. This we learnt was for the guidance of the gate-keeper, so that he might know what officers went off duty that evening; in which case—our informant told us—they were allowed to leave the prison at a quarter-past six P.M., and expected to return at a quarter-past six the next morning to resume their duties—each warder passing one night in, and one night out of, the prison.

Hence we were directed across the long wedge-shaped "outer yard" of the prison—a mere triangular slip, or "tongue," as it is called, of bare, gravelled ground, between the diverging sides of the first and last pentagons; and so we reached the barred "inner gate," set, within a narrow archway at the apex, as it were, of the yard. Here the duty of the gate-keeper is to keep a list of all persons entering and quitting the prison, and to allow no inferior officer to pass without an order from the governor.*

* RULES EXHIBITED AT THE INNER GATE.

"Every officer or servant of the establishment who shall bring or carry out, or endeavour to bring or carry out, or knowingly allow to be brought or carried out, to or for any convict, any money, clothing, provisions, tobacco, letters, papers, or other articles whatsoever not allowed by the rules of the prison, shall be

We were then conducted through a succession of corridors to the governor's room, which is situate in the range of buildings at the base of pentagon 1, forming one side of the hexagonal court surrounding the chapel that constitutes the centre of the prison. This was an ordinary, but neat, apartment, the furniture of which consisted principally of a large official writing-table; and the end window of which, facing the principal entrance, was strongly barred, probably with no view to prevent either egress or ingress, but merely for the sake of being in keeping with the other windows of the establishment. This window is flanked by two doors, through which the prisoners are admitted on their reception into the prison, or whenever, from misconduct or any other cause, they are summoned into the governor's presence. On such occasions a rope is thrown across the room, and forms a species of bar, at which the convicts take their positions.

The governor, on learning the object of our visit, directed one of the principal warders to conduct us through the several wards, and explain to us the various details of the prison.

"Millbank," he said, in answer to a question we put to him, "*is the receptacle for all the convicts of England, Wales, and Scotland, but not for those of Ireland, which has a convict establishment of its own.*"

Males and females of all ages are received here, the prison being the depôt for "*convicts*" of every description. When a man is convicted, and sentenced either to transportation or penal servitude, he remains in the prison in which he was confined previous to his trial, until such time as the order of the Secretary of State is forwarded for his removal; and he is then transferred to us, his "caption papers" (in which are stated the nature of his offence, the date of his conviction, and the length of his sentence) being sent with him. From this prison he is, after a time, removed to some "*probationary*" prison (to undergo a certain term of separate confinement) such as that at Pentonville, or to some such establishment in the country; and thence he goes to the public works either at Portland, Portsmouth, or the Hulks, or else he is transported to Gibraltar, Bermuda, or Western Australia, where he remains till the completion of his sentence.

On the arrival of the prisoners at Millbank, the governor informed us, they are examined by the surgeon, when, if pronounced free from contagious disease, they are placed in the reception ward, and afterwards distributed throughout the prison according to circumstances, having been previously bathed and examined, naked, as at Pentonville.

"If a prisoner be ordered to be placed in association on medical grounds," added the governor, "the order is entered in the book in red ink, otherwise he is located in one of the various pentagons for six months, to undergo confinement in separate cell."

On entering his cell, each prisoner's hair is cut, and the rules of the prison are read over to him, the latter process being repeated every week, and the hair cut as often as required.

When the convict is young he is sent as soon as possible to Parkhurst, provided he be a fit subject, and not convicted of any heinous offence. In the case of a very hardened offender, when there is a probability of his doing considerable mischief, it is for the director of Parkhurst to decide whether or not he will accept him.

When the young convict is of extremely tender years, application is immediately made, by the Millbank authorities, for his removal to the "Philanthropic," at Reigate, her Majesty's pardon being granted conditionally on his being received there.

"One boy," said the governor, "went away on Tuesday; he was not twelve, and had been sentenced for stealing some lead, after a previous conviction. We have one here," he

forthwith suspended from his office by the governor of the prison, who shall report the offence to a director, who, upon proof of the offence, may cause the offender to be apprehended and carried before a justice of the peace, who shall be empowered to hear and determine any such offence in a summary way; and every such officer or servant, upon conviction of such offence before a justice of the peace, shall be liable to pay a penalty not exceeding fifty pounds, or, in the discretion of the justice, to be imprisoned in the common jail or house of correction, there to be kept, with or without hard labour, for any term not exceeding six calendar months."

continued, "at this moment, a child of between twelve and thirteen, who had been employed as a clerk, and had robbed his employer of between ten and twelve thousand pounds." The child, however, we afterwards learnt, had become frightened, and taken the money back; but one of his relations had proceeded against him for the theft, with the view of getting him admitted into a reformatory institution.

"We consider prisoners of tender years," the governor went on, "up to about thirteen. I remember a child," he added, "of not more than nine years of age, who had been twelve times in prison—I do, indeed. That's some years ago now. There's the receipt for the child who left us the other day," he added, as he handed us the following certificate:—

"CERTIFICATE OF DISCHARGE.

"A——— W———.

"This is to certify, that I have this day received, from the custody of the governor of Millbank prison, A——— W———, according to the terms of the conditional pardon granted to him. Dated the 16th day of May, 1856.

"Philanthropic Farm School, Redhill, May 22, 1856.

"For the Rev. SIDNEY TURNER, Secretary."

There have not been any young girls at Millbank lately he told us; some had been sent to Manor Hall, but very few girls of tender years have been received at the Penitentiary.

"I cannot say what would be done with very young girls," said the governor; "I should have to refer for orders. There were two of fifteen here, but *they* were the youngest."

"The females," he continued, "go to the convict prison at Brixton, after they have been with me nine or twelve months, according to the vacancies there. The males go to Pentonville; in fact, we keep Pentonville up. Those that remain here go to the public works, either to Portland, Portsmouth, or the Hulks, according to circumstances. Occasionally we send some to Gibraltar or Bermuda, and to Western Australia. Of course those we send to Western Australia can only be transports; they can't be penal-service men. This prison contains young prisoners, old prisoners, female prisoners, and invalids. Old prisoners, who are able to perform light labour, are sent to Dartmoor. Those incapable of light labour, or of any labour at all, are sent to the 'Stirling Castle,' invalid hulk at Portsmouth."

"If the prisoners are of very tender years," the governor went on, "I generally put them in large rooms, which you will see. We have six distinct prisons here—one in each pentagon," he added, "and, with the general ward, I may say we have seven, for it is quite distinct from the others. Pentagon 3, which contains the female convicts, is quite shut off from the others, and opened with a separate key."

"We have two distinct forms of discipline here," continued the governor. "We pursue the separate system for the first six months, unless the medical officer certifies that the prisoner cannot bear it, in which case we remove him immediately into association. When the men are put together, the silent system is enforced—that is to say, we endeavour to enforce it; for I need not tell you, that when seventy or eighty men are in the same place they are sure to talk, do what we may to prevent them.

The governor here drew up a curtain, and showed us a large ground-plan of the prison, hanging on the wall. We expressed some surprise at its being covered, and inquired what purpose the curtain served.

"The prisoners' eyes are so sharp," was the reply, "that they would understand the entire arrangement of the prison at once. They would discover the weak points of the building, and attempt to escape. We had one man here," he proceeded, "named Ralph (a regular Jack Sheppard), who tried to get out. He made false keys in his cell. The cocoa-mugs used at that time to be made of pewter—we have them of tin now—and he actually melted the metal over his gas-light, and then moulded it into keys. I will show you them;" and accordingly opening his desk, he took from it several rudely-made keys.

"With these," said the governor, as he presented them to us in a bunch, "he could have opened every door in the prison."

This man, we learnt, was a most daring and desperate character, and the terror of every one he came near, when at liberty. We inquired how he behaved in the prison.

"He was as quiet as could be," was the governor's answer; "always well-behaved, and never abused any one."

"You would have thought butter would not have melted in his mouth," said the warder, when referred to for his corroborative testimony. "He was quite an uneducated man," the officer went on to say; "indeed, he got what little education he had from having been transported."

The prisoners are sometimes very violent, but not often. "Look at this hammock-ring," said the governor, as he produced a heavy iron ring, with a rope attached to it; "you've heard of one of our men being nearly murdered? Well, this is what it was done with," he said, giving it a gentle swing. "Luckily, our man was very near to him, so he was not so much hurt as he might have been."

"Here's another instrument for opening a bolt," and he then called our attention to an iron rod, formed out of two pieces, which were joined together with a hinge, like the handle of a lady's parasol, and could be doubled up together somewhat in the same manner.

"They push this through the keyhole," he said, as he extended it before us, "and let the further end drop. Then they move it about until they feel the bolt, and push it back."

"I have been a number of years connected with prisons," pursued our informant, "and yet I find there's something fresh to be learnt every day. How they get the impressions of the locks must appear to strangers not a little wonderful. They do that with a piece of soap."

The conversation then took another turn. "We don't profess to teach anything here but tailoring," the governor went on; "but if they're shoemakers by trade they go to shoemaking, or, if they don't know any trade, perhaps we put them to pick coir. When a man attempts to commit suicide I always put him to pick coir, so that he may have neither tools, nor knives, nor needles to do any harm with."

"It's a great thing," added the governor, "to make a prisoner feel that he is employed on some useful work. Nothing disgusts a man, and makes him feel so querulous, as to let him know that he is labouring and yet doing nothing—like when working at the tread-wheel. I am of opinion that to employ men on work which they know and see is useful has the best possible effect upon men's characters, and much increases their chances of reformation. Every other kind of labour irritates and hardens them. After twenty thousand prisoners have passed through one's hands, one must have had some little experience on such matters. There was a tread-wheel on the premises here, for the use of penal or second-probation men, and those only; but its use has been discontinued for some months."

All men of long sentences, or who are known to be of desperate disposition, are put in the middle floor of each pentagon, which is considered to be the strongest part of the prison, and badges are given to prisoners who conduct themselves well.

"On the first of every month," said the governor, "the conduct-book is brought to me; and in this is kept a list of all the men who have been six months in the prison. Here it is, you see, and in the first column is the register-number of each prisoner, in the second his name, in the third his location in the prison, in the fourth his number of reports, and in the last column the folio of the book which contains those reports. Now, here's one man, you see, who has been reported six times, so he wouldn't get a badge; and here, at the end of the book, is a list of those men who have been nine months in the prison, and who are to get a second badge. It's a great thing to a man," he added, "to get his badge, for if he goes from here without one, and in the third class, *that* entails six months' additional time before his name can be submitted for a ticket-of-leave."

" Oh, yes, it's a great thing," chimed in the warder, " to have a badge. The men think a great deal of it, and feel the loss of it greatly."

" We have first, second, and third class prisoners, according to their conduct," said the governor, " and these classifications are made before the men go to the public works. The fact of a prisoner's being badged always shows him to be a well-behaved man; but even when a man has behaved very badly, if he reforms at last, I give him a first-class character, or else he would become desperate on going down to the public works, and the governor would have a very hard time of it. Every man is also classed according to education when he goes away, but in that matter the first class represents the least educated."

We were anxious to ascertain which class of criminals gave most trouble to the prison authorities. " Sometimes," said the governor, in answer to our inquiries, " the most desperate characters outside the prison are the best conducted inside the walls. It's the little, petty London pickpocket, who has been all his life at bad courses, that turns out the most difficult fellow of all to deal with. These characters are most troublesome. They are up to all sorts of roguery and mischief; and we find the same thing when they come from the manufacturing districts. Your men who have committed heavy offences, and who are sentenced to some long punishment, are very amenable to discipline and most easy to deal with. Give me long-sentence men—I say it as the governor of a prison—they won't try to escape. Most of them have never committed another offence in the course of their lives; but the London pickpockets have been at it all their lives, from their earliest childhood."

" There are not many cases of escape from prison now," said the governor, " but I remember two which occurred at Dartmoor, in which some men succeeded in getting off. One of them got into a bog, and remained sunk in it up to his neck, while the officers were walking about close by, on the look out for him."

¶ iv—γ.

The Interior of the Prison.

** The Reception Ward.—After unlocking a " double-shotted " door, the warder, under whose charge we had been placed, conducted us into a long, lofty passage, like that of a narrow cloister, or rude whitewashed box-lobby to a theatre. On the right, higher than we could conveniently see, were the exterior windows of the pentagon; on the left, the doors of the apparently infinite series of cells.

These doors are double, the inner one being of wood and the outer one of iron lattice-work or " cross-bars."

Every ward consists of two passages or sides of the several pentagons, and ranged along each passage are fifteen cells. The passages are fifty yards long, about ten feet high, and about seven wide, and all of equal size. They are paved and coloured white. The admixture, however, of a very slight bluish tint with the lime diminishes the glare of the whitewash.

Along the wall over the cells runs a long gas-pipe, with branches which carry the gas into the cells themselves. Each cell is about twelve feet long by seven broad, and slightly vaulted.

The inner door is left open in the day time from nine till five, so that all semblance of a communication with the world may not be taken away from the inmate. At night, however, or upon any misconduct on the part of the prisoner, the inner door is closed or " bolted up," as it is termed; nevertheless, he can be seen by the jailer through a small vertical slit in the wall—like that of a perpendicular letter-box. Each cell is provided with a signal-wand, painted black at one end and red at the other, and the prisoner pushes one end of the wand through the slit, in order to communicate his wants to the warder—the black having a special, and the red a general, signification.

At the top of each cell is a ventilating aperture for the exit of the foul air, and in the centre of the passage is a ventilating fire, and an apparatus for introducing hot air. Attached to the wall of the passage is a species of open rack, somewhat like a "press" without a door. We questioned the warder as to the use of this.

"Oh, that's one of the arms' racks," he replied. "You remember the 10th of April, '48, and the Chartist riots. Well, we had to give up the whole of pentagon 1 to the soldiers; we had the Guards here, and that rack is where their arms stood. We had some of them here, too, for the Duke of Wellington's funeral; but those racks were put here during the Chartist riots, and have never been moved since."

At the end of the reception ward is the surgeon's room. This is merely a double cell, paved with flag-stones, and with a small door in the middle of the partition. After bathing, the new-coming prisoners are brought in here, naked, and examined. They are then asked if they, or any of their family, have been insane.

If the examination be satisfactory, a description of the prisoner, with a specification of any private marks which may be found on his body, is entered in a book.

"Most persons of bad repute," said the warder, "have private marks stamped on them—mermaids, naked men and women, and the most extraordinary things you ever saw; they are marked like savages, whilst many of the regular thieves have five dots between their thumb and forefinger, as a sign that they belong to 'the forty thieves,' as they call it."

PRISONER AT WORK MAKING SHOES IN SEPARATE CELL.

The general description entered in the surgeon's book states the height, the colour of the hair, the hue of the complexion, and colour of the eyes, in the style of a foreign passport—the "*marques particulières*" being, for the most part, rather more numerous than is the case with ordinary travellers.

At the end of the passage we come to the bath-room, which is situate in the centre of the reception wards, and at the base of the tower. The bath-room is circular, and contains four baths, the baths being in the pentagon tower. To each pentagon there are three such towers (one at each of the front angles), the foremost, or one in the middle, being called the "general centre tower" of the ward. There is also another tower, in the centre of the exercising yards within each pentagon, and this is styled "the warder's tower."

Pentagons 1 and 2 are alike, and throughout of the strongest construction.

Pentagons 3 and 4, however, were originally built for women, and are of slighter construction; though this is a compliment to the sex which unfortunately they have failed to justify, as the female convicts throughout the prison are pronounced "fifty times more troublesome than the men." The cells here, too, are not vaulted like those of pentagons 1 and 2, and the grated iron gates are less massive.*

*** *The Chain-room.*—"Here," said the warder, as he opened the grating of one of the cells, in the lower ward of pentagon 1, and threw back the wooden door with a bang, "here is our chain-room, or armoury, as we call it."

It was one of the ordinary cells, but literally hung in chains, which were arranged against the walls in festoons and other linear devices. In front of the window there was set out a fancy pattern of leg-irons, apparently in imitation of the ornamental fetter-work over the door of Newgate. The walls glittered with their bright swivel hand-cuffs, like stout horses'-bits, and their closely-linked chains like curbs, reminding one somewhat of the interior of a saddler's shop. But the brilliancy and lightness of some of the articles were in places contrasted with a far more massive style of ironmongery, which appeared to have been originally invented for the Cornwall giants. A few of the manacles of the latter class were literally as large as the handle of a navigator's spade; and there were two massive ankle-cuffs, with chains, such as highwaymen are supposed, by Victoria dramatists, to have danced in, but which would have effectually prevented all attempts at hornpipes on the part of any light-footed as well as light-fingered gentlemen—weighing, as they did, something more than twenty-eight pounds. There were neck-pieces, too, heavy enough to break an ordinary collar-bone; whilst everything was on so gigantic a scale, that we were struck by the absurdity even more than by the cruelty of such monstrous contrivances—even as the horrors of an utterly extravagant melo-drama inspire us with mirth rather than fear. Still, there was something too real about the scene before us to induce any but the grimmest smiles, for by the side of the colossal swivel-cuffs, figure-of-eight-cuffs, and iron waistbands which would have formed appropriate girths for the bronze horse, there were little baby handcuffs, as small in compass as a girl's bracelet, and about twenty times as heavy—objects which impressed the beholder with a notion, that in the days of torture either the juvenile offenders must have been very strong or the jailers very weak otherwise, where the necessity for manacling infants?

"They did not show much mercy to prisoners *then*," said the warder, to whom we communicated our reflections; "and I can remember in my time, too, when the prison authorities weren't much better. I've seen a little boy six years and a half old sentenced to transportation; and the sentence carried into effect, too, though the poor child couldn't speak plain."

The handcuffs with bars attached, and ingeniously fashioned to represent the letter P—the chains as heavy as iron cables, and which were used for fastening together entire gangs—the ankle-cuffs, which seemed adapted only for the ankles of elephants, were all shown to us, and we reflected with a sigh that this museum of fetters—this *dépôt* of criminal harness—this immense collection of stupidities and atrocities in short—was not only a vestige of the sanguinary criminal legislation of the last century, but also a reminder of the discipline of our lunatic asylums as they existed at no very distant period. If it showed us what Newgate was until long after the days of Howard, it also suggested what Bedlam must have been previous to the accomplishment of Pinel's beneficent mission.

"We never use anything here," said the warder, "but a single cuff and chain. With one cuff," he continued, "I'd take the most desperate criminal all over England."

We could not help expressing our satisfaction at the abandonment of so inhuman and useless a practice as that of loading prisoners with fetters which, independently of the mere weight, inflicted severe torture on them whenever they moved.

* Pentagon 3 is at present alone set apart for female prisoners.

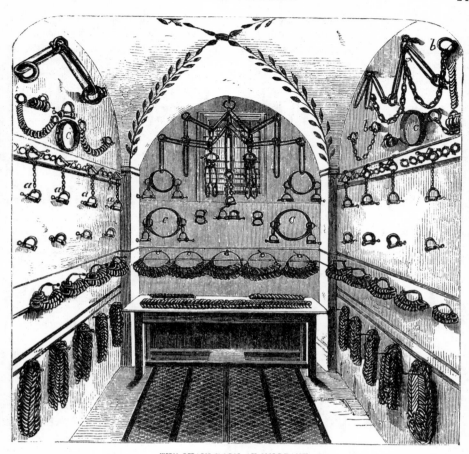

THE CHAIN-ROOM AT MILLBANK.

a, Handcuffs; *b*, Shackles for the legs, fastened round the ankle, and secured to *c*, an Iron Ring or the waist.

"Yes, it's given up everywhere now," was the reply, "*except Scotland; and there they do it still*. The prisoners who come up to us from Scotland have leg-irons and ankle-cuffs; and the cuffs are fastened on to them so tightly, that the people here have to knock away at them for some time with a heavy hammer before they can drive the rivets out. Occasionally the hammer misses the rivet which fastens the cuff, and hits the man's ankle. Any how, he must suffer severe pain, as the cuffs are very tight and the rivets are always hammered in pretty hard."

The most desperate and intractable prisoners, the warder informed us in the course of this conversation, used formerly to be sent to Norfolk Island; but none had been transported there now for some years. The last who was consigned to that settlement was Mark Jeffrey, the most daring ruffian they had ever had in Millbank prison, and who ultimately attempted to murder the chief-mate of the hulk at Woolwich, whereupon he was shipped off to Norfolk Island.

"One man made an attempt to break prison here," continued the warder, "some years since, and with great success. It was not the man spoken of with the false keys, but a fellow named William Howard, who was known to all his companions as 'Punch' Howard. He **was** in the infirmary for venereal at the time, and got through a window about nine feet from the ground. With a knife he cut through the pivot which held the window, and fastened it up so as to remain there until night. He then forced back the iron frame, which was not more than six and a half inches square, and made it serve as a sort of rest, like the things used by painters for window-cleaning. This done, he got upon it, tied his bed-clothes to it, and let himself down by them; after which he scaled the outer walls and went straight off to his mother's, at Uxbridge. I took him there in a brick-field. Of course, I didn't go into the brick-field where he had all his friends, but I got his employer to call him out on some pretext, and then slipped a handcuff on him and brought him back."

*** *The Cells at Millbank.*—Passing through a grated gate we came to the corridor, next to the general centre, and styled passage No. 1, that which we had just quitted being passage No. 2. The two passages are similar; at the end of passage No. 1, a brass bell is seen close to a door which leads to the warder's tower, and which is rung by the officers when the principal is wanted. In the next passage that we entered were located the prisoners who were waiting for their tickets-of-leave, having just returned from Gibraltar— the "Gib" prisoners as they are called.

On the grated gates of the cells here were the register-tickets of the men, with the name of each written on the back.

Two of the men in the first cell rose and saluted us as we passed. Like the rest of the prisoners, they were dressed in gray jackets, brown trousers with a thin red stripe—the same as is introduced into most of the convict fabrics—blue cravats (also crossed with narrow brick-coloured threads), and gray Scotch-like caps.

These prisoners were allowed to converse during the day, and to sit, two or three together, in each cell; but they were separated at night.

"You can take them away now," said the principal warder. "Stand to your gates!" the deputy exclaimed; upon which the officer in the centre of the ward gave two knocks, when all the men turned out at the same time, closed their gates, and, in obedience to the warder's commands to "face about," and "quick march," went out into the yard to exercise, an officer being there ready to receive them.

When the prisoners had left, we entered one of the cells. The colour of the walls we found of a light neutral tint. Beneath the solitary window, which, like all the cell windows, looked towards the "warder's tower," in the centre of the pentagon, was a little square table of plain wood, on which stood a small pyramid of books, consisting of a Bible, a Prayer-book, a hymn-book, an arithmetic-book, a work entitled "Home and Common Things," and other similar publications of the Society for the Promotion of Christian Knowledge, together with a slate and pencil, a wooden platter, two tin pints for cocoa and gruel, a salt-cellar, a wooden spoon, and the signal-stick before alluded to. Underneath the table was a broom for sweeping out the cell, resembling a sweep's brush, two combs, a hair-brush a piece of soap, and a utensil like a pudding-basin.

Affixed to the wall was a card with texts, known in the prison as the "Scripture Card," and a "Notice to Convicts" also; whilst on one side of the table stood a washing-tub and wooden stool, and on the other the hammock and bedding, neatly folded up. The mattress, blankets, and sheets, we were told, have to be arranged in five folds, the coloured night-cap being placed on the centre of the middle fold; and considerable attention is required to be paid to the precise folding of the bed-clothes, so as to form five layers of equal dimensions. The day-cap is placed on the top of the neat square parcel of bedding, which looks scarcely larger than a soldier's knapsack.

"Up above, we have a penal-class prisoner in one of the refractory cells," said our attendant warder; "the cell is not exactly what we call a dark one, but an ordinary cell, with the windows nearly closed up. The penal class prisoners are those who have been sent back from public works for committing some violent assault, or for mutinous or insubordinate conduct. They are returned to us, by order of the directors, to undergo what is called a 'second probation.' When they belong to the penal class, they are bolted up in their cells all day, and treated with greater rigour than men under the ordinary prison discipline."

On reaching one of these cells, we found the hammocks were replaced by iron bedsteads, or rather by iron gratings resting on stone supports at either end, and the table and all the furniture placed in the corridor outside.

"We put the furniture there," said the warder, "to prevent the ceiling being beaten down by the prisoner. We always take the furniture out of the refractory cells, and we like to have those cells situate on the top floor, because the roofs there are much stronger."

These refractory cells resembled the ordinary ones, except in two particulars; the wooden door was outside, and was kept firmly closed over the iron door or grating, while the windows were blocked up so as to admit only the smallest possible number of rays. The warder threw open the door of one of the refractory cells, and asked the prisoner within how he was getting on. The man was under confinement for making use of abusive language to his officer.

"He knew it was his temper," he said, as he spoke behind the grating, "but they took him up so short; he meant, however, to become better if he could."

This prisoner was allowed half a pound of bread in the morning, and half a pound at night; he had nothing to drink but cold water.

. *The School-room.*—"This ward," continued our guide, as we passed through another grated door, "leads to the governor's room, where you sat this morning, and here prisoners are placed who are brought up for report and have to be taken before him. The penal class are searched here before they are taken in to the governor, in order to prevent their having anything secreted about them intended to injure the governor. The governor adjudicates upon reports every morning."

PRISONER IN REFRACTORY CELL.
(The outer door being supposed to be thrown back.)

During the old penitentiary system, we may add, the prisoners used to remain at Millbank for three and four years—they were never sent away; and when they had done the whole of their probationary time, they used to get their freedom as being thoroughly reformed characters, though many of them have since returned and been transported. The officers in those days used to designate the extraordinary religious convicts as "pantilers." The prisoners used to labour as now, and, from being a long time in the one prison, became expert, and used to turn out a great deal of work. The officers in those days used to have to stand and read the Bible in the passages of the wards, while the prisoners were blackguarding them in their cells. The men turned out hypocrites. The reverend governor had the management of the place up to August 1, 1843, when it became a convict prison. When it was a penitentiary, or the "tench," as the thieves called it, if convicts behaved with deception and pretended to be sorry for their offences, they got their discharge after a few years. Harry King, at Pentonville, was one of this kind; he actually had a pair of green spectacles purchased for him, because he read his Bible so hard that his sight became injured by it. He pretended to be thoroughly reformed, but directly he got down to Portland he showed himself in his true character; for he, with others, assaulted the officers and endangered their lives.

Attached to every two pentagons there is a school-room. The schools are divided into four classes, the fourth class being the highest. At one end of the school-room there are maps against the wall of the four quarters of the globe, and a table of Bible chronology; at the other is a tableau, representing the principal animals of creation, in which a very large whale (contrasted with a very small man) occupies a prominent position.

The prisoners, at the time of our visit, were seated in rows on either side of the middle passage, arranged on forms with one long continuous desk or sloping shelf before them. On a huge black board the following arithmetical proposition was chalked :—

"What is the interest of £2726 1s. 4d. at 4½ per cent. per annum, for 3 years 154 days ?"

Here, too, a man of thirty was staring idiotically at the schoolmaster, as he endeavoured to teach him the painful truth, "that nine from nought you can't."

₄ *Working in Separate Cells.*—We now passed to the top floor of pentagon 2, where the prisoners were employed in tailoring. In the first cell, a boy was seated on his board making a soldier's coat. The gratings were closed, but the wooden doors were open.

"In the cells that you saw in pentagon 1," observed the warder, "the prisoners had hammocks. In some of the wards, instead of hammocks they have an iron framework, resting at the head and foot on two large stone supports. Here, you see, we give them one of those boards, instead of the ironwork, so that they have a bedstead and a shopboard at the same time."

The cells here had all the appearance of small tailors' workshops, and at the end of the passage there was a furnace for heating the irons which are used for going over the seams of the garments made by the prisoners.

In one of the cells here a convict was receiving religious instruction. The reverend instructor was reading to the prisoner, whom we heard, as we passed the cell, uttering his responses, in a solemn manner, from time to time.

In this part of the prison we noted an old man, who appeared to have lost all capacity for taking an interest in work, or anything else, and who had, therefore, been put to pick coir. He was sitting down with his jacket off, and a heap of the brown fibre lying loose before him, and reaching nearly up to his knees.

"This old man," said the warder "can't work much. When prisoners have no capacity for tailoring, have bad sight, or such like, we give them coir to pick."

In a cell, where the instructing officer was presiding, several prisoners were engaged cutting out coats, stitching, and fitting in linings.

"That boy, you see there, handles his needle well. How long have you been here, my man ?" inquired the warder.

"Four months, sir !"

"Ah, and you can make a coat now, eh ?"

"I think I can, sir," replied the boy.

In another of the tailoring wards we noticed a cell with the wooden door closed.

"There, you see, that man's been 'bolted up.' He's been talking with the other prisoners, most likely, and so he has been deprived of the privilege of having his door open."

At the top of the martello-like tower, where the pails and tubs of each pentagon are kept, is an immense circular tank. "That's filled with water from Trafalgar Square," said the warder. "We used formerly to pump it up from a large reservoir, which was supplied from the Thames. Now it comes rushing in without any pumping at all."

On the middle floor of pentagon 2 are the mechanics' wards. The prisoners were all at work there, either in the work-room, or in other parts of the prison, where repairs had to be effected. In this ward were painters, glaziers, coopers, blacksmiths, carpenters, masons, bricklayers.

The pavement was striped with the light which came streaming through the grated doors of the cells; but the windows in the passages were all darkened, to prevent the men seeing into pentagon 3, which contains the female convicts.

"All the prisoners out of this ward," said our guide, as we entered another passage, "are at school now; you saw them up stairs. This ward is for tailors."

"Here, now, are more good coats," he continued. "These are for the officers of Dartmoor prison, and those for the navy."

"How long has this man been at his work?" we inquired, in reference to one who appeared to be finishing off his button-holes in a sufficiently artistic manner.

"About ten months," was the reply; "but we can soon see by looking at his register number."

The warder, at the same time, turned up the small slip of card which was tied outside the grating of the cell, and read, "J——— J———, penal class," the inscription on the back.

"Ah, you see he is one of the penal class, who has reformed. He is not treated like the others, because, when one of the officers here was attacked, he went to the warder's assistance, and helped to save his life." The warder afterwards informed us, "the officer was attacked by four convict men as they came off the tread-wheel, and this prisoner stepped in and rescued him from their hands. That's why he's taken out of the penal class."

"We've got C——— here, he who murdered his wife in the Minories, while he was drunk, on Christmas day last," the warder went on to say; "he's a fine scholar—knows several languages—French, German, and Latin—and is a most quiet and respectable man. He had a capital situation in the India House, and was in the receipt of £150 a year. His father was Irish. He tells me he remembers nothing about the murder; he was dead drunk at the time. 'I know I must have done it, because everybody says so,' are the words he uses when he speaks of the affair; 'but it's all like a dream to me!' He was cast for death, and says he thanks the Sheriffs, and Ordinary, and East India Company greatly, for it was through their intercession that he got off. I think he's sincerely repentant." (At a later part of the day we saw this man in his cell; he was a dull, dark, bilious-looking fellow, and had anything but an intelligent cast of head). "I tell you, as the governor told you," went on the warder, "that the men who have the longest sentences are always the best behaved. We have several men who have never been in prison before, and who, if liberated, would behave very well. It's your regular Whitechapel thief—your professional pickpocket—who is all the trouble to us. Those old offenders are only in perhaps for a short time, but they ought never to be let go at all. Directly one of them gets out he meets some of his 'pals,' and the first thing he hears is, 'I say, I'm going to have a crack to-night; there'll be five or ten pounds for you out of it, if you like to come;' and of course he goes. No! those habitual professional thieves are no good either in or out of prison; but they're safest in."

"The first-offence men are sometimes very much to be pitied," continued the warder, "and I feel for some of the soldiers we have here about as much as any of them. May-be a soldier has got drunk and struck his sergeant, and then he gets sentenced to fourteen years for it; when very likely the morning after he'd done it, he knew nothing at all about the matter."

"This," said the officer, coming to a halt, as we reached the centre of the ward, at the angle formed by the two passages, "is the spot where poor Hall, one of the officers of the prison, had his brains knocked out. The man who did it is in Bedlam now. He was a Jew named Francis, a regular Whitechapel thief, and no more mad than you or me—at least he didn't seem to be when I saw him. He told me he meant to murder some one. Well, one day he put the black end of his signal-stick out of the cell, to tell the officer that he wanted to go to the closet. The officer let him out, and he came along here with his utensil in his hand. The officer was leaning over the trough, and the man came behind and knocked him over the head with it, and, when he was on the ground, regularly beat his brains out—there, just where we're standing. Those utensils are very dangerous things; some of them weigh nearly ten pounds. I've weighed them myself, so I'm certain of it."

The smell of leather and the sound of tapping informed us that we were entering the shoemakers' ward.

"How long have you been at shoemaking, my boy?" inquired the warder of a lad who appeared to be hard at work in one of the cells we were then passing.

"Four years," replied the lad, speaking through the iron grating.

"How old are you?"

"Sixteen."

"And how long have you been here, my man?"

"Only came in yesterday," replied the prisoner, starting and touching his cap.

"This ward," we were told, "had earned more than £4 during the previous week." The instructing warder was present, with a long black apron over his uniform. In one of the cells, where the tapping was most vigorous, there were rows of new shoes on the floor; a shoe-closer was in the corner, with bundles of black leather lying on the stones at his feet, and a small shoemaker's tray by his side. Another prisoner was twisting twine over the gas-pipe. Several of the men had all the appearance of regular shoemakers, and many wore leathern aprons, like blacksmiths.

This ward and the next, that is to say, wards A and B of pentagon 2, are the only two wards where shoemaking is carried on in separation.

"How do you do, Mr. Tickel?" said our attendant warder, as he passed the instructing officer.

In the clickers' department we found a collection of boot-fronts, rolls of upper-leather soles, and heaps of shoes, and in the cell next to it a man was rubbing away at a Wellington boot on a last.

"You've got some good Wellington boots here, Mr. Tickel, haven't you?" said the warder.

"Yes," said Mr. Tickel, and leaving the grated gate he went into the cell, and came out with his hand thrust into a boot, which he offered to our inspection.

"That's as good a boot," said he, with no little pride in the work, "as could be found in London. The leather looks a little rough now, but when it's been rubbed up it will be a first-rate article. The man who made it used to work at one of the West-end houses."

"Now, here's a cell," remarked our guide, as he jingled his keys, "in which four or five of the men are at work together."

He opened the door, and we found five prisoners inside.

"They are all good men," observed the officer, "and well-conducted, so we let them talk a little so long as they are together."

"But we have to work very hard," rejoined one of the prisoners as we left the cell.

Having visited all the cells in pentagons 1 and 2, we were conducted into the artisans' shop, where coopering, polishing, &c., are carried on. The workshop is spacious, airy, and light, with a roof supported by iron rods, like that of a railway terminus.

Many of the artisans were away, in different parts of the prison, working in parties under the superintendence of officers. Some dozen men, however, were filling the place with the sound of their hammers, and evidences of their labours were to be seen in all directions.

"These buckets," said the officer, "are for Chatham. Those are for shipboard."

Ascending a flight of wooden steps we reached the carpenters' shop over-head, and this as usual, was pervaded by a strong turpentiny smell of deal. On the walls were hanging tools, planes, &c. In the centre of the room were some half-dozen benches; and at the end was the wooden skeleton of a sofa. A few prison tables were lying about, and one of the prisoners was employed in polishing a table of mahogany, which was intended for the residence of one of the superior officers. There were also several cart-wheels against the wall.

At a later part of the day we passed over pentagons 5 and 6, in many wards of which we found the men busy tailoring in single cells. In some of these (as pentagon 5, E 2) were "light-offence men," we were told—"all under ten years' transportation," said our informant. In other parts (as in pentagon 6, A 1) the men were hammock-making, and bag-making as well; whilst in others, again, there are a few older men coir-picking; "those that have no capacity for tailoring, and are dull men, we set to picking coir, for they're not capable of doing anything else." Again, in pentagon 5, A ward, we found two men in the larger cells busy weaving biscuit-bagging; whilst another was seated on a board on the ground making a pilot-coat; and a fourth prisoner winding bobbins for the two who were weaving.

The cells in this ward were all devoted to "bagging," and there were generally three prisoners in each cell. Here the passage rattled again with the noise of the loom, like the pulsation of paddle-wheels. And so again in B ward of the same pentagon, a similar rattle of looms prevailed, with the whirr of wheels winding bobbins and ringing through the passages, till the din reminded one faintly of Manchester. Here, too, in one large cell, was a calendar machine, where all the sacking was smoothed after being made, and three prisoners engaged in passing a newly-wove piece through the polished metal rollers.

The quantity of work done at this prison far exceeds that at Pentonville, as may be seen by the subjoined returns.*

On another occasion we were shown over the manufacturing department, and found the spacious warerooms there littered with bales of blue cloth for the officers' clothing. ("We're going to make all the prison officers' uniforms for the first time," said the warder in attendance.) There were also rolls of shirting, sheeting, and hammock-stuff and straps, stowed away in square compartments round the room, and shoemakers' lasts hanging from the ceiling over-head. Up stairs here was the cutting-room, with small stacks of the brown convict cloth, at the ends of the room; and beside the door, were square piles of fustian, ready cut up for "liberty clothing," for the prisoners.

"What coats are you cutting now, Mr. Armstrong?" asked Warder Power of the manufacturer. "Greatcoats for the 'Warrior Hulk,' and Chatham and Dartmoor prisons; they're for the officers of each of those establishments."

The clothing for almost all the public works, we were told—Dartmoor, Pentonville, Chatham, Portland, Portsmouth, and the Hulks—is cut and made at Millbank.

---

* STATEMENT OF SUNDRY GARMENTS, STORES, &c., MADE IN THE MANUFACTORY OF MILLBANK PRISON, FOR NINE MONTHS, FROM 1ST APRIL, 1854, TO 31ST DECEMBER, 1854.

Military greatcoats	Nos. 24,145	Belts	No. 254	Beds	No. 332
Jackets	„ 3,275	Pouches	„ 511	Pillows	„ 332
Waistcoats	„ 1,378	Shirts	„ 186	Hammocks	„ 804
Trousers	„ 3,442	Navy flushing jackets	„ 3,245	Miscellaneous articles	„ 10,198
Flannel garments	„ 2,894	Shoes	Pairs 1,920	Cloth woven	Yards 2,712
Jackets (Militia)	„ 816	Shoes repaired	„ 4,047	Handkerchiefs woven	„ 967
Trousers (ditto)	„ 1,542	Biscuit bags for Navy,	No. 414,206	Bagging woven	„ 103,720

"These are flannels, to be cut and made up for public works, too. Some hundreds of thousands of yards of flannel are cut up here annually. Every convict has two sets of flannels given to him directly he comes in here. The female prisoners here work for the large slop-shops in the city."

In the centre of the warehouse below stood square bales of fuzzy coir, for making beds, and bright tins hanging against the wall.

"What orders have you got in now, Mr. Armstrong?" our attendant asked, anxious to glean all the information he could for us.

"Five hundred pairs of shoes for Chatham," was the reply.

"What have you here?" inquired the other, as he placed his hand on several bales of goods.

"They're five hundred suits of clothing, packed up ready, to go down to the new prison at Chatham the moment they're wanted. Everything connected with Chatham—clothing and bedding—is supplied here."

"How many biscuit-bags are you making now weekly for Deptford?" was the next question.

"Only 3,000 now; but in the time of the war we made 20,000 a week, and wove the stuff too. Those are all the hammocks for Chatham, ready to be sent down as well."

Here the manufacturer led us to a large stock of shoes, stored in bins, as it were, in one corner of the room.

"These with the hobnails are for Chatham, and these for 'Establishment'—that's our term for Millbank. Yonder's a roll of blue and white yarn, you see, ready for shirting and handkerchiefs. Yes, sir, our female prisoners do a great deal of work for slop-shops. We work for Jackson in Leadenhall Street; Early and Smith, Houndsditch; Stephens and Clark, Paul's Wharf, Thames Street; Favell and Bousfield, St. Mary Axe; both shirts and coats we do for them. We do a great deal of Moses' soldiers' coats, and Dolan's marine coats, too. We take about £3,000 a year altogether from the slop-shops. We have had as many as 1,000 soldiers' coats in a week to do for Stephens. Those, sir, are some of Favell's shirts," he added, pointing to a bundle near the door. "They're what are called rowing-shirts. It's only a mere trifle they give for making them—fourpence a-piece—and just see what work's in them. We made soldiers' trousers for Moses at twopence-halfpenny a-piece; but that didn't pay."

From the manufacturers' department we passed to the steward's department next door.

"This is the steward, sir," Warder Power said, as he introduced us to that officer.

"I pay all moneys for the prison," the steward replied, in answer to our question, as soon as we entered the office, "and take account of clothing, provisions, necessaries of every sort, and pay all the warders, too, every week. Everything the warders require they must come to me for. They get an order signed by the governor, and I execute it. If the manufacturer wants any materials I issue them; and when he has made anything he sends it in to me, and I issue it to the officers according as it is required. This I do only of course upon authorized demands signed by the governor. Here is an example, you see, sir :—

"*Pentagon* 2·   "Millbank Prison, 24*th June*, 1856.
"*Demand. No.*
          "*Mr. Geddes,*
     "Supply the undermentioned articles :—
          "2794, R————— A————, *to have spectacles, by order of the surgeon.*
                    "*A. W. Sutherland, Principal Warder.*

                    (Signed)   "*John Gambier*" (*Gov.*)

THE WORKSHOP UNDER THE "SILENT SYSTEM," AT MILLBANK PRISON.

"I pay about £1,200 a month," the steward went on, "more or less. Sometimes I have known it to be £1,600 and £1,800, but it's generally about £1,200. A great part of the tradesmen's bills is paid direct by the paymaster-general. The authorities in Parliament Street make demands on that office for such amounts. It's likewise part of my department to take charge of any money or property the prisoners may have on coming in, and also to make up accounts of the money the prisoners have earned while in prison, in case of their going away; not that any money passes here, for it's merely a nominal transaction, and placed to their credit against their time being up, when it is paid to them. Each prisoner before leaving here signs his account with me in acknowledgment of its being correct; and then that account passes on to the place where he goes. Here, you see, is such an account :—

"2670, J———— H————. Amount of private cash—6d. Gratuity—none. Property belonging to the prisoner—1 *hair-brush*, 1 *tooth-brush*, 2 *combs*."

"This man is leaving for Pentonville to-morrow. Some men come and claim their property years afterwards," said our attendant.

We glanced over the account. One man in the list of the convicts going to Pentonville on the morrow was down, under the head of property belonging to him, for a watch and chain, and many had a comb and brush, but few any money. Among the whole fifty there was only 4s. 10d. appertaining to them, and nearly the half of that was the property of one man. Against the name of the man who had recently been condemned to death for the murder of his wife, while in a fit of intoxication, on Christmas day (and who had been respited only the day before that appointed for his execution), there were seven books down as his property.

The steward then showed us round the stores. "These drawers," said he, approaching a large square chest in the centre of the room adjoining the office, "are full of a little of everything. These are our knives, you see," he said, pulling out a drawer, full of tin handleless blades. "Those are the best things ever introduced here," the warder at our side exclaimed with no little enthusiasm. "It's impossible to stab a man with those, for they double up directly they're thrust at anything, and yet they'll cut up a piece of meat well enough."

"Here's the wine for the sick," the steward continued, as he drew out another drawer that was filled with a dozen or so of black bottles, with dabs of white on the upper side. "These gutta-percha mugs are for the penal-class men; but they're no good for cocoa, for they double up with anything hot, so the tins in which the breakfast is served to the penal men are collected immediately afterwards."

"Here, you see, are the prison groceries," said the steward's assistant, opening a cupboard, and showing a row of green-tea canisters. "Here, too, in the outer office, the meat is inspected by the steward, and weighed in his presence every morning."

"These haricot beans," added the man, taking up a handful out of a neighbouring sack, "are what we serve out to the men now instead of potatoes; they have them every other day."

"Here are bins of cocoa, flour, oatmeal, rice; and above, on the shelves, there are new cocoa cans.* In that cask we keep molasses to sweeten the cocoa;" and, as the man removed the deep-rimmed wooden lid from the barrel, the place was immediately filled with

---

* The following is the authorized dietary for this prison :—

DIET TABLE.

	Breakfast.	Dinner.	Supper.
Monday . . Tuesday . . Wednesday . . Thursday . . Friday . . Saturday . . Sunday . .	¾ pint of cocoa, made with ½ oz. of cocoa nibs, ½ oz. molasses, 2 oz. milk, and 8 oz. bread.	5 oz. meat (without bone, and after boiling), 1 lb. potatoes, and 6 oz. bread.	1 pint of gruel, made with 2 oz. of oatmeal or wheaten flour, sweetened with ½ oz. molasses, and 8 oz. bread.

Punishment Diet :—1 lb. of bread per day.

the peculiar smell of treacle. "This store, sir, is devoted to the general line," the assistant went on, as we passed into another room. "Here are hearthstones and candles, Bath-bricks, and brushes, and starch, and blacklead," he added, opening the drawers, one after another, and pointing to the racks at the side of the store-room. "There, you see, are our wooden salt-cellars, and those are black coal-scuttles, hanging over-head; indeed, we keep every-thing, I may say."

"But cradles!" added our guide, with a smile—"though some years ago we *did* have a nursery attached to the female ward."

** *Peculiar Wards.*—In Millbank there are a number of peculiar wards, such, for instance, as "the penal-class ward" (*i.e.*, the men under punishment), which is situate in D ward of pentagon 4, and where there are always two officers on duty, and the cells are continually bolted up.

"There are very few of them here now," said the warder, as we passed along the passage, and found the greater part of the doors unclosed. "The prisoners in this ward are supplied with gutta-percha utensils (for the others are too dangerous for such men as we put here), but, with that exception, the cells and furniture are the same."

At one door that we came to, there was the register number attached, whilst on the back of the card was written the name, " J—— L——, Penal Class." We peeped through the inspection slit, and saw a young man, with his coat off, pacing the cell, and reminding one of the restlessness of the polar bear at the Zoological Gardens. Then we came to another cell, which was occupied. Here the officer looked through the slit, and said to the inmate, "What! are *you* here? Why, you were one of the best-conducted lads I had in the prison. What did you do?"

"It was my own temper," was the reply.

"What was it for, then?"

"Oh, I was mutinous, and insulted an officer."

"Did you strike him?" asked the warder.

"Why, yes, sir; I'll tell you the truth—I kicked him."

"Ah! I thought so, or you would not have come here."

"Well, I don't want to come here any more, that's all."

"All the penal class," said our guide, "are between twenty and thirty. It's seldom or never that old men get among them. They're all able-bodied fellows."

"Did you get your rations to-day, my man?" inquired our warder of another under punishment.

"Yes, sir; and on Tuesday I come out, don't I?"

"Ay," answers the officer, and closes the door. "He's one of the penal class," he adds to us.

"But he seems civil enough," said we.

"Yes," was the reply, "so he is to me; but to others he's quite the reverse."

Before quitting this part of the prison we peeped at another cell, and found another man, with his coat off and arms folded, pacing his cell in a furious manner.

DIETARY FOR FEMALE PRISONERS, MAY, 1847.

Breakfast.—¾ pint of cocoa, made with ½ oz. cocoa nibs, ½ oz. molasses, 2 oz. milk, and 6 oz. bread.

Dinner.—(Sunday, Monday, Tuesday, Wednesday, Thursday, Friday, and Saturday).—4 oz. meat (without bone and after boiling), ½ lb. potatoes, and 6 oz. bread.

Supper.—1 pint of gruel, made with 2 oz. of oatmeal or wheaten flour, sweetened with ½ oz. of molasses, and 8 oz. of bread.

Diet for Prisoners under Punishment for Prison Offences for terms not exceeding three days.—1 lb. of bread daily.

The foregoing dietary for the Millbank Prison I hereby certify as proper to be adopted.

G. GREY.

There are also many Catholic wards in Millbank prison. These are mostly situate in pentagon 4 (D ward) and pentagon 5 (D and F wards).

"There's nothing particular in this ward," says our guide, as we reach the middle floor of pentagon D 4; "only it's a Catholic ward, and tailoring is carried on in it."

The warder lifts up the register number at the cell-door and shows us the name of the inmate, with R C, meaning Roman Catholic, appended to it.

"Please, sir," says a little Irish boy, crying, as we reach the end cell, "will I go away from here before I've served all my time?"

The warder tells him that if he's a good lad he'll go to the Isle of Wight, and learn a trade, and come out a better fellow than if he was with his father or mother.

The boy smiles through his tears, and says, "Oh, thank you, sir."

"Those in D ward here," says the warder to us as we go, "are the worst class of prisoners. The Roman Catholic prisoners are generally the very dregs of society, and the most ignorant of all the convicts we get; they keep for ever tramping through the country when they're out. Many of these boys will maintain five and six people outside the prison. Some of them tell me they get as much as forty pounds a week, regularly, by picking pockets of first-rate people, and being covered by men who go out as 'stalls' with them to receive the property as soon as they've stolen it."

The Catholic prisoners go to school on Wednesday and Saturday, and receive instruction from their priest on Sunday and Wednesday. They're supplied with all Catholic books that the priest allows.

Adjoining the school-room to pentagons 5 and 6 there is a small room for the Catholic clergyman, where the prisoners of that faith confess. The priest also addresses the prisoners in the school-room for about an hour before school begins at three o'clock. The place of worship for the Protestant prisoners, we may add here, is a polygonal building, situate in the very centre of the prison itself. It is entered by three raised passages or arcades, that stretch like rays from the central edifice to the surrounding pentagons.

"The passage on the right," said the warder, "leads to pentagons 1 and 2; the one on the left communicates with pentagons 5 and 6. The prisoners from those two pentagons fill the floor of the chapel, and the other passage is for the prisoners of pentagons 3 and 4, who occupy the gallery." We attended Divine service here, and found the prisoners both attentive and well-conducted.

"This is the convalescent ward," said our warder, as we entered the place; "it's a portion of the infirmary, where men are located when they get better, or if their disease is in any way contagious."

Outside the doors of the cells here were tin tablets for the names of the inmates to be inserted, with the date of their admission.

In one cell that we peeped into, through the inspection slit, we saw a man in bed and others sitting beside him, while some were lying dressed on the other beds, of which there were six in all.

The other cells were similar to the large or treble cells that we had already seen. In one such cell that we peeped into, we saw the wretched little deformed dwarf that murdered the solicitor in Bedford Row. He was by his bedside, on his knees, apparently in the act of prayer. On the tablet outside was written—

"2525, C—— W———,
Admitted 7th May, '56.
Pentagon 6."

The warder told us that this was a favourite attitude with the wretched humpback, and that he told him he knelt down to ease his head.

"My opinion is," added the warder, "he's insane. He's not one of the riotous lunatics, but one of the quiet, sullen kind."

We were about to peep into another cell in the next passage, when the warder pulled us back, saying "Be careful, sir! that's a blackguard fellow in there. He's broken all his cell repeatedly, and is one of the most desperate men on the face of God's earth. You'd better mind, or he'll throw something out upon you if he sees you looking." The man was lying down when we first peeped through the inspection slit, but hearing voices he jumped up, and commenced pacing to and fro in his cell. "He's a young fellow, too—isn't he, sir? He's one of those uncultivated brutes we get here occasionally, that doesn't know B from a bull's-foot, as the saying is, and wants only hoofs and horns to make a beast of him. You had better come away, or he's sure to job something out through the inspection slit, and perhaps blind you for life; nothing would please him better."

₌ *Refractory and Dark Cells.*—At Millbank there is one refractory cell to each pentagon, and this is always on the top floor. These have a little light admitted to them. The dark cells, however, occupy the basement of pentagon 5, and are nine in number. There are also nine dark cells in pentagon 6; but these are not considered healthy, and therefore not used.

"Would you like to see the dark cells?" inquires our attendant, after he has shown us into the kitchen of pentagons 5 and 6, where the sand on the flagstones is worked in curious devices.

Immediately the light is obtained, we sally into the entrance of pentagon 5, and then, turning sharply round, our guide says before we descend—"You must mind your hat coming down here, sir." The officer leads the way, with the flaming candle in his hand.

On reaching the bottom of the low and narrow staircase, the way lies along a close passage, so close that we are almost obliged to proceed sideways. Then we come to a small door. "Now stoop, sir," says the warder; and, as we do so, we enter a narrow, oblong cell, somewhat like a wine-cellar, and having the same fungusy smell as belongs to any underground place.

"What is that noise over-head?" we ask. "It sounds like the quivering of a legion of water-wheels."

"Oh, that's the weavers' looms," is the answer.

The place is intensely dark—the candle throws a faint yellow glare on the walls for a few paces round; but it is impossible to see clearly to the end even of the cell we are in.

"There's a fellow in the cell who pretends to be mad," says the warder. "He declares that they put something in his soup, and that there's a dreadful smell in his cell."

We inquire whether the cell in which he is confined is completely dark? "Dark!" is the answer. "It's impossible to describe the darkness—it's pitch black: no dungeon was ever so dark as it is."

"A week in such a place," we add, "must bring the most stubborn temper down." "Not a bit of it," returns our guide. "The men say they could do a month of it on their head—that's a common expression of their's. We had a lot of women down here for disorderly conduct once. We couldn't keep them up stairs. But our punishment is now nothing to what I've seen here formerly. Our governor is so lenient and kind a man to prisoners, and even officers, that there's a great change indeed."

The men are visited in the dark cells every hour, we were told, "for a man might hang himself up, or be sick," said our informant. "Those round air-holes are for ventilation, sir."

The bed is the same as at Pentonville; a bare wooden couch just a foot above the ground, the cell boarded, and not damp.

The preceding conversation took place in a kind of dark lobby, or ante-chamber, outside the cell itself. Presently the warder proceeded to unbar the massive outer door, and, throwing this back, to talk with the wretched man, through the grated gate, imprisoned within.

"Now, my man," said the warder in a kindly voice, "why don't you try and be a better fellow? You know I begged you off six days last time, and then you gave me your word you would go on differently for the future."

"Well, I know I did," was the reply, "and I kept my word, too, for three weeks; but now I am with men I can't do with any way." And, having delivered himself of this speech, the wretched man proceeded to pace the cell in the darkness, with his hands in his pockets.

"They tried to kill me at Dartmoor," he muttered, "and now they're going to finish it."

"Oh, nonsense!" said the warder, aside; "you behaved well enough under me when you were here before, and why can't you do so now?" The door was closed upon the wretched convict, and we ascended the body of the prison once more.*

₊ *Guarding of the Prison by Night, Opening the Gates, and Cleaning the Cells and Passages in the Morning.*—The official staff at Millbank is composed of 2 chief warders, 9 principal warders, 30 warders, and 62 assistant warders, in all 103 officers, so that as the full complement of prisoners at this jail consists of 1,100 males, there is upon an average 1 officer to nearly every 11 men, whilst at Pentonville the proportion of officers to men is but 1 to 18. One-half of the warders remain in the prison one night, and the other half the next. One officer is deputed by the principal warder to remain in charge of the "Pentagon (or warder's) Tower," and he holds the keys to answer the alarm-bell in case of fire or outbreak. The other officers, who remain in to form a guard, sleep in the main guard-room—a place with broad sloping benches, similar to those seen in the guard-room of barracks. There is a bell from all the pentagons leading to the principal guard-room, so that the officers can be immediately summoned in case of alarm. There are nine night officers on duty in pentagon 4, on account of its containing several large "associated rooms," but in the other pentagons, there are only two, and in some instances but one, on night duty—in addition to the officer stationed in the tower. Besides these there is another officer under arms in the exercising yards of each pentagon, and two sentries stationed in the garden surrounding the prison.

The outer guard-room, which is a kind of rude porter's lodge, on the opposite side to the gate-keeper's room at the principal entrance, is furnished with a stand of carbines, ranged in racks along one side of the wall, and a string of cutlasses on a padlocked chain, hanging down like a fringe below. Here the sergeant of the outer guard remains all night. ("This is Mr. Lenox," said our guide, as he introduced us to the officer in question—"he has been an old soldier himself, sir"). A rude square wooden arm-chair drawn up before the fire seemed to point out the veteran's resting-place. "He visits," our attendant went on, "the sentries in the garden at stated hours throughout the night, nor does he take his sentries off till it is reported to him that all the prisoners are present in their cells in the morning. The reporting is done in this way, sir:—At a quarter before six all the warders who have slept out of the prison are admitted at the gates, and then the officers in

* RETURN OF PUNISHMENTS OF MALE CONVICTS IN MILLBANK PRISON, FOR THE YEAR 1854.

		Adults.	Juveniles.	Total.
Whipped	{ with a Cat	2	0	2
	{ with a Birch	0	4	4
In Handcuffs		3	0	3
Dark Cell	{ with Rations	8	0	8
	{ on Bread and Water.	33	11	44
Refractory Cell	{ with Rations	28	6	34
	{ on Bread and Water	59	11	70
On Bread and Water Diet		315	228	543
Deprived of one Meal		239	105	344
Admonished		314	82	396
		1,001	447	1,448

charge of the several warders' towers let them into the wards of their respective pentagons, when they one and all go round and knock at the different cells, as a notice for the prisoners to put out their signal-sticks—(this is expected to be done immediately after the first bell rings at five minutes to six). The warder then counts the signal-sticks, and if he finds all the prisoners under his charge are present in their cells, he reports his ward as all correct to the principal warder of the pentagon, whose duty it is to be in his tower at six o'clock. The principals then proceed to the sergeant of the main guard, and report 'all correct,' or the contrary, to him; whereupon he communicates as much to the sergeant of the outer guard, who at six waits at the inner gate for orders, and then the garden sentries are dismissed."

In addition to the outer guard-room, with its stand of arms, there is also an arm-room at the inner gate. This is curiously enough placed in a kind of loft above the bed-room of the inner gate-keeper, so as to be of difficult access to the prisoners, in case of an outbreak; this gate-keeper's bed-room is on one side of the archway opposite to the lodge in which he rests by day, and where there is likewise a stand of three or four blunderbusses kept in a rack, ready loaded, to be given out to each warder passing this gate with a party of men.

In the little triangular bed-room of the porter we found a tall slender ladder resting against the wall, near the tidy white counterpaned bed, that was turned down ready for the night, and a small trap-door let into the ceiling. The ladder was placed at the edge of the trap, so that we might inspect the apartment above. The hole was not large enough to allow our body to pass, so, standing on the top rungs, we thrust our head and shoulders into the room, and found the walls covered with rows of dumpy thick-barrelled blunderbusses, and bright steel bayonets and horse-pistols, with a bunch or two of black-handled cutlasses at the top. Beside the window were a vice and a few tools for the repairing and cleaning of the weapons, and in the ceiling above another trap was visible, leading, we were told, to a similarly-stocked apartment on the upper floor.

At six o'clock the second bell begins, and this is the signal for unlocking; whereupon the prisoners are turned out of their cells, and the cleansing operations for the morning begin. For this purpose the men are turned out three at a time to empty their slops, and then to sweep their cells into the adjoining passage.

The process of cleaning the prison at Millbank differs but slightly from that of Pentonville. It forms, of course, the first portion of the day's work, and is executed by the prisoners, each man having to clean out his own cell, and some few being "told off" for the sweeping of the passages as well as the court-yards.

One of our visits to Millbank prison began as early as half-past six in the morning, at which time we found the court-yards and passages alive with cleaners. In the outer court-yard was a gang of men and a warder, the latter armed with a carbine, the brass barrel of which flashed in the light as he moved to and fro; for it is the custom at Millbank as we have said, to allow no prisoner outside the inner gate, unless attended by an officer under arms. Here the men were engaged in tidying the gravelled area; one was rolling the ground—the heavy metal cylinder that he dragged after him emitting a loud, metallic crushing noise as he went; another was drawing along behind him a couple of brooms, ranged side by side, and so lining the earth almost as regularly as the sky of a wood-engraving, till it showed the marks of the comb, as it were, as distinctly as the hair of a newly-washed charity boy.

"Those men you see there," whispered our guide as we passed, "are short-sentence men; for *they* have, of course, the least disposition to escape. Some are *in* only for four or five years—anything under ten years we consider a short sentence, and such men only are put to clean in the yards. Again, they are all men in association, and who have therefore gone through their probation in separate confinement, so that we have some knowledge of their character and conduct before they are let out even thus far."

Then, as we passed the inner gate, we came upon more men sweeping, and rolling, and *combing* the other court-yards, whilst in the passages we encountered prisoner after prisoner, each down on his knees, and, with his jacket off, scouring away at the flags with sand and holystone. On entering the warders' tower, too—the martello-like building that stands in the centre of the exercising yards within each pentagon—the boards of the circular apartment were a dark-brown, with their recent washing. "Here," said our informant, "the officers of this pentagon dine. The tower is in charge of an acting principal warder, and he is responsible that all doors leading to it are 'double-shotted.' No person can go in and out without his permission, excepting a superior officer, who has similar keys."

Against the walls, here, was a fanciful placard, drawn in red and blue ink, which, we were told, was a general roll of all prisoners located in the pentagon; and here, too, was affixed, near the door, another written document, headed "GOVERNOR'S ORDER—*Scale for Cleaning Wards.*"* We went up-stairs to the principal warder's room, and found the officer in his shirt-sleeves busy writing out some official papers for the morning.

⁎⁎ *Breakfast, &c.*—The cleaning of the prison lasts up to twenty minutes past seven, and at twenty-five minutes the bell rings to prepare for the serving of breakfast.

There is a cook-house to every two pentagons, situate on the ground-floor, at the point where the sides of the neighbouring pentagons join. The principal warder who accompanied us on our rounds, knocked with his keys against the door as we approached one of the kitchens. We entered, and found it a sufficiently spacious apartment, the floor of which was brown as the top of a custard, with its fresh coating of sand. The warder-cook was habited in the approved white jacket and apron, and had five prisoners under him, who were dressed in the prison gray trousers and tick-like check shirts, and had each a leathern "stall," or pad, about their knees. Here were large black boilers, with bright-red copper lids, at the end of

---

* GOVERNOR'S ORDER.—SCALE FOR CLEANING WARDS.

9th January, 1856.

Monday Morning.—The officers of the wards will commence their duties at 5·55, by seeing (between first and second bells) that all prisoners put out signal-sticks; and they will report to the principal or tower warder at 6 A.M. (when second bell rings) if all is correct or otherwise. They will then lock the gates at the end of their wards, and the centre gate, leading to No. 2 passage. They will next commence unlocking the gates and unbolting the cells themselves in No. 1 passage, calling out prisoners three at a time, to empty slops, taking care that only one at a time enters the closet. When all the prisoners have emptied their utensils, and swept out their cells into the passage, they will then direct the prisoners to place their dirty linen on their cell-gates, and to show each article separately. Then they will take a prisoner with them, who will carry the linen bag, and place each man's kit in the same bag, as it is counted by the officer, after which they will lock and bolt all gates and doors in No. 1 passage, proceed to No. 2 passage, and perform the same duties. They will then take out eight prisoners, placing one in the centre of the ward, to clean the closet, &c., six others, with their tables and buckets, to clean the windows. The eight prisoners they will cause to sweep the passages and dust the walls. After completing the above duties, they will lock and bolt up their prisoners, when the bell rings, at 7·25, for breakfast. They will then take two prisoners to the kitchen, fetch breakfast, and serve the same in the following manner:—By unbolting and bolting the doors themselves; at the same time they will hand to each convict his bread, and measure his cocoa from the can. After having served all their prisoners, they will proceed with one prisoner to the kitchen, with the can and basket, take the prisoner back to his cell, lock and bolt him up; also examine all their gates and doors before going to their rooms, to prepare for their own breakfast, at 8·20 A.M.

Tuesday.—Passages to be stoned; the men to work backwards, and facing the centre of ward. Four cells are to be cleaned every morning, and one passage stoned (beginning on Tuesday, and going on to Friday—four days—so that passages may be stoned twice a week).

Saturday.—All wards to be washed with brush and cloth.

Sunday.—Nothing required to be done, only the wards swept out and dusted. On this day the men rise an hour later than on week days.

For sweeping the yards, we were informed that the officer of the ward appoints any one he pleases for such duty, each exercising-yard being cleaned by the first ward coming down in the morning. There are three yards to each pentagon, but the centre yard is not used at all for exercising—only those on each side—so that, as there are six wards to each pentagon, each exercising yard belongs to three wards.

the kitchen, steaming and humming with their boiling contents, under the capacious, hood-like chimney and long dressers at the side, and large high-rimmed tables in the centre, that seemed like monster wooden trays.

"They are now preparing for breakfast," said our guide. "There, you see, are the cans for the cocoa," pointing to a goodly muster of bright tin vessels, in size and shape like watering-pots, and each marked with the letters of the wards from A to H. On the table were rows of breads, like penny loaves, arranged in rank and file, as it were.

"This is the female compartment. Here, you see," said the officer, pointing to the farther side of a wooden partition that stood at the end of the kitchen, "is the place where the women enter from pentagon 3, whilst this side is for the men coming from pentagon 4." Presently the door was opened and files of male prisoners were seen, with warders, without.

"Now, they're coming down to have breakfast served," said the cook. "F ward!" cries an officer, and immediately two prisoners enter and run away with a tin can each, while another holds a conical basket and counts bread into it—saying, 6, 12, 18, and so on.

When the males had been all served, and the kitchen was quiet again, the cook said to us, "Now you'll see the females, sir. Are all the cooks out?" he cried in a loud voice; and when he was assured that the prisoners serving in the kitchen had retired, the principal matron came in at the door on the other side of the partition. Presently she cried out, "Now, Miss Gardiner, if you please!" Whereupon the matron so named entered, costumed in a gray straw-bonnet and fawn-coloured merino dress, with a jacket of the same material over it, and attended by some two or three female prisoners habited in their loose, dark-brown gowns, check aprons, and close white cap.

The matron then proceeded to serve and count the bread into a basket, and afterwards handed the basket to one of the females near her. "I wish you people would move quick out of the way there," says the principal female officer to some of the women who betray a disposition to stare. While this is going on, another convict enters and goes off with the tin can full of cocoa.

Then comes another matron with other prisoners, and so on, till all are served, when the cook says, "Good morning, Miss Crosswell," and away the principal matron trips, leaving the kitchen all quiet again—so quiet, indeed, that we hear the sand crunching under the feet.

*** *Exercising.*—In the space enclosed within each pentagon there are two large "airing yards," one of which contains a circular pump, with a long horizontal and bent handle stretching from it on either side. Here one ward of each pentagon is generally put to exercise at a time, though sometimes there *are* two wards out together. Exercising usually commences directly after chapel in the morning (quarter past nine). Each pentagon has six wards to be exercised every day, and the practice is generally to put three to exercise before dinner and three after. Those wards which are for school in the afternoon exercise in the morning, and those which are for morning school exercise in the afternoon. The exercise lasts one hour. The men walk round the large gravelled court, with the walls of the pentagon surrounding them on all sides.

The turn at the pump lasts fifteen minutes, and generally sixteen men are put on—four at each large crank-shaped handle. The others walk round at distances of five or six yards between each man. They go along at an ordinary pace. They may walk as they like—slowly or quickly, only they must keep the fixed distance apart. At the pump the men take off their jackets, and stand generally two on one side of the handle and two on the other. At a given signal they commence working.

In the yards of some pentagons there are no pumps, and there the men walk round merely. The lame are generally placed in the centre, and the attending warders stand on one side. In the warder's tower, which occupies the centre of these airing-grounds, we

BURIAL-GROUND AT MILLBANK PRISON.

(From a Photograph by Herbert Watkins, 179, Regent Street.)

could see the men exercising all round us—some in gray, and some in brown suits, circling along, one after another, till it made one giddy to watch them.

In the airing yards of the general ward belonging to pentagon 5, we, at a later period of the day, found the bakers exercising, walking round and round, each man being about fifteen or twenty feet apart from the next—the least distance allowed is six feet. The clothes of these men were stained with the flour into a kind of whitey-brown, and the master baker, in his white jacket, stood on one side watching them the while.

*** *Large Associated Rooms.*—These large rooms constitute one of the peculiarities of Millbank prison. There are four such associated rooms, all on one floor, and each room of the size of fifteen cells and the passage, thrown into one chamber. They are all in pentagon 4; three of them are workshops—where the men work, as shown in the engraving—and the other is the infirmary. Men are put into these associated rooms after having been six months in separation.

The term for separate confinement in Millbank, it should be remarked, is one-third less than at Pentonville. The governor limits the separation to half a year, we were told, because such was the practice at the prison before the order came out, and he therefore continues to restrict it to that number of months, by a discretionary power from the prison directors.

"Now we'll go into one of the large rooms, and see them all at breakfast, if you please," said Warder Power to us, as we were leaving the kitchen.

Accordingly we mounted the narrow stone staircase, the steps of which were white and sanded. Here we found a warder at the door.

"Stand on one side! Stand on one side!" cried our companion, as we entered.

It was a finely-ventilated apartment, and the air swept freshly by the cheek; nor was the slightest effluvium perceptible, though there was half a hundred people confined in it.

The men sleep here, work here, take their meals here. They roll their beds up into the shape of big muffs, and place them above on the shelf. The tables are "unshipped" at night, and the hammocks are slung to the hooks along the rails on either side of the gangway down the centre.

Our informant explained that these large rooms are exactly the length of a passage, and five yards wide. "They'll hold eighty-three," he said; "but there's not more than fifty-six allowed now."

The roof is lined with sheet-iron, the first or upper roof being boarded; the lower one arched, and of corrugated iron-plate, with small iron rafters below.

These large rooms are severally divided in the centre by a hot-air shaft, which is somewhat like a square kiln whitewashed, and with a huge black letter inscribed in a circle upon it. By this shaft sits the warder, so as to have one entire half of the room under his eye. The men as we entered were sitting upon forms, two at each table, and so silent was the ward, that the warder's voice, speaking to us, sounded distressingly loud, and we could hear the munching of the men at breakfast. Each man was newly washed, and had his hair lined with marks of the comb as regularly as the newly-swept gravel in the court-yards, whilst all had a bright tin mug, full of cocoa, and a small loaf of bread before them. There are seven tables on either side of each half of the large room, and two men at each table. In the centre, by the hot-air shaft, is a small desk with physic bottles on it, each labelled, "—— table-spoonfuls to be taken —— times a day," and the bottle divided into "I, II, III, IV" parts.

Against the walls, on either side, were rolls of hammocks on the top shelves; and on the shelves below were small pyramids of Bibles and Prayer-books, surmounted with a comb and brush, while in the centre of the ward hung a thermometer. "This is the instructing officer of the ward," our attendant whispered, as the officer passed by. "They'll commence their work at 8 o'clock."

Presently, when the breakfast was finished, the instructing warder, at the end of the large room, cried "Attention! Stand up!" Whereupon a prisoner repeated as follows:— "Bless, O Lord, these, Thy good creatures, to our use, and us to Thy service, through Jesus Christ. Amen."

All the prisoners exclaimed, "Amen!" in response, and immediately proceeded to sweep up the crumbs, and put their tins on the shelves above, while some wiped their cocoa cans with cloths, and others swept clean the stones under the tables.

After this they unshipped the tables, and proceeded to work.

"These men," said our warder, "are shoemaking and tailoring. One division is occupied with one trade, and the other with the other."

From H large room we passed into that marked G, where we found the men all tailoring. The place was intensely silent—as silent, indeed, as a quakers' meeting. And thence we passed into F room, where we found them engaged partly in tailoring and partly in biscuit-bag making.

"We have made as many as 20,000 biscuit-bags for the navy in a week here, and wove a greater portion of the cloth, too," the warder said to us, with no little pride in the industry of his men.

We found some of the prisoners here engaged in reading, while waiting till the officers returned from their breakfast. One was perusing a treatise on "Infidelity; its Aspects, Causes, and Agencies;" another, the "Home Friend—a weekly miscellany;" a third, the "Saturday Magazine;" a fourth, the "History of Redemption;" and a fifth, the "Family Quarrel—an humble story."

Suddenly the warder cried, "Attention!" and (these having said grace before we came in) immediately up started the whole of the men; some seized their table, and, unshipping it, ranged it against the wall; others placed the forms in their proper places.

"Sit down to your work, now! Come, sit down to your work quickly!" was then the order. Accordingly, some of the prisoners seated themselves on tables, and commenced working at convict clothes; others, on benches, began stitching at the coarse bags—the bags being fastened to the hammock-hooks. At the end of the ward was a huge pile of new brown bags, ready to be conveyed to the manufacturer's department.

"Let's see, my lad, whether you belong to the 'forty,'" said our guide to one of the workers.

The boy, smiling, put out his hand, and sure enough, there were the five blue dots between the finger and thumb indicative of his being a professional thief.

"If they're not closely watched," added our informant, "they scrape on their cans the cant name that they go by outside, as well as their sentences, so that their 'pals' may know they're in here, and for how long."

*** *The Infirmary.*—The next place we visited was the large room devoted to the sick. Here, outside the door we noted big baths, like huge tin highlows; and on entering we found the room of the same extent, and fitted with the same kind of roofing as the rooms we had just left, but down each side here were ranged small iron bedsteads (seven on either side of the ward), and fitted with the ordinary yellow-brown rugs and blue check curtains. Some of the men were in bed and sitting up reading, and others lying down, looking very ill. The flag-stones were intensely white, and set with small brown cocoa-fibre mats next to every bed. Near these was a small stand, covered with medicine bottles and books.

Here the first man we saw had a large black caustic-made ring round his cheek. He was suffering from erysipelas, and the black circle was to keep it from spreading any farther. Presently a prisoner brought a linseed-meal poultice to one of the invalids. "He's an Italian," the warder whispered in our ear (the dark, raisin-coloured eyes, and the blue mould of the sprouting beard said as much). "He's got an abscess in the groin. It's venereal, I dare say."

The men who are upon the other side of the ward place themselves at the head of their beds, and, as we pass, stand straight up in the attitude of attention.

Now we come to another prisoner, in bed with a bad knee, and he is sitting up and binding a bandage on the joint. Beside him is a convict, who acts as the attendant in the infirmary, and habited in a loose light blue dress, similar to that worn by the convalescents in the "Unité" hospital ship, at Woolwich. Now there is the sound of a bell. "That's the doctor's bell," we are told.

On the other side of the ward is a little brown-faced negro boy, with his tar-coloured cheeks and short-cropt woolly head, just showing above the white sheets. He has a poultice on one side of his face. "What's the matter with you?" says the warder. "Got a breaking out in my cheek, sir," he answers, pointing to the bandage.

"No bad cases, have you?" asks our attendant. "No, sir," is the reply. "*That* man at the end of the room is the worst—him with the erysipelas. The other man's recovering fast."

"What's the matter with you?" says Warder Power, to an old man in a flannel jacket, and in bed. "I've had a very bad throat, please, sir." Then we pass more men, who are up and dressed, and standing at the head of their beds, saluting us as we go by; and presently we reach one bed where the clothes are hooped up in a grave-like mound. "What are *you* suffering from?" our attendant again inquires.

"Case of white swelling, sir," is the answer of the infirmary warder, who walks at our side; and so saying, he turns back the bed-clothes, and reveals a knee as big at the joint as a foot-ball, and the white parchment skin scarred with the still red wounds of old leech-bites. The poor lad is a pasty-white in the face, and has his shoulders swathed in flannel.

Next we noted another bed, with a prisoner half concealed in it. "What's *he* got?" our warder asked. "Inflammation of the lungs," we were told; and the man, as we went, coughed sharp and dry. "Bad case," whispered the infirmary officer.

"*That* man, there," says our guide, pointing to another who sits beside the bed, with his head hanging down on his chest, "was paralyzed here for a long time and on the water-bed. We thought he'd never recover; and now he's quite an idiot."

At the end of the infirmary is a man huddled in bed. "Bronchitis, sir," says the infirmary warder, as he sees us look at the poor fellow.

The man never stirs nor raises his eye, and seems as if unwilling to be noticed.

On our leaving the sad place, the warder stops in the passage immediately outside the door and says to us, "He's in for embezzling a large amount. He was collector of inland revenue in the county of York, and made away with the money he received—several thousands, I've heard."

** The General Ward.—The only other large room is the "general ward," as it is called. This is a separate apartment, built out in the open space or court within pentagon 5. It was originally constructed for juvenile prisoners under eighteen years of age; and, at that time, a system of tailoring, shoemaking, &c., was carried out by the lads located in it. They worked, ate, and slept, in common, in this one room. But when the class of convict boys was found to be diminishing, and the system of transportation was discontinued, excepting for long sentences, the juvenile ward was then converted into the "general ward," for the purpose of receiving prisoners in association; for at that time the associated wards were not large enough to accommodate all the prisoners—the system at Millbank being to place every man in silent association, after having been six months in separate confinement.

"Mr. Hall," said our attendant to a warder near at hand, "just fetch me the key of the general ward." And when the warder returned, we were ushered into the apartment. We found it a large square room, as spacious as a law-court, but under repair—in the course of being whitewashed. In its desolate condition, it struck us as being not unlike a small market-place on a Sunday. The skylighted roof was of light iron-work, like a railway terminus; and there was a kind of a large square counter fixed in the centre of the ward, having a desk within. All round the sides was ranged a series of large compartments, called "bays," and each separated by a light partition from the next. In each of these bays six men, we were told, worked, dined, and slept: three in hammocks below, and three above. These bays were like the boxes at "dining-rooms." The table to each of the compartments had a kind of leg, that "flapped up," and the table itself admitted of being hooked into the wall at the end of the bay. "When the prisoners have finished their meals," our informant said, "they turn over the leaves of the upper part of the table, and draw out supports from the side of the bay, for the leaves to rest upon; and so, by covering over the entire bay, the table forms a shop-board for the prisoners to work upon as tailors. Nothing but tailoring is carried on in the general ward." The flooring is of asphalte, blacked and polished as at Pentonville.

Round the platform, in the centre, were four counters; and here, we were informed, the instructors stand and give out the work to the prisoners in the bays. An instructor is told off for each division, besides discipline officers; and the instructor goes round to the bays and looks after work. All the men—and there are 216 located here when the place is full —work with the greatest precision, and in perfect silence, so that, as the warder assured us, one might hear a pin fall on the floor. The principal warder sits at the central desk on a raised platform, and there are benches ranged on one side of the ward for the school. Each bay has its gaslight, and in summer the skylights can be raised by a simple contrivance. On Sunday the general ward is used as the Catholic chapel, and such prisoners as belong to the Church of Rome attend worship there.

₊ *The Prison Garden and Churchyard.*—At Millbank, owing to the large extent of ground surrounding the prison, like a broad moat within the walls, there is what is termed a garden class of prisoners. This consists principally of convicts labouring under scrofula or falling away in flesh, and it is sometimes termed the "convalescent class" also. Prisoners belonging to it are allowed extra food. They have a pint of new milk in the morning for breakfast, one and a half pound of bread a day, nine ounces of mutton in broth, a small quantity of beer, and a pint of milk again in the evening; they are also permitted to walk in the outer garden for two hours every day. These prisoners are lodged in B ward of pentagon 4. It was here that we met three "privileged men," in light-blue clothes, with two red stripes on the arm. Such men can be kept here instead of being sent to the Hulks or the other public works, we were told. They are always the best-behaved and most trusty of the prisoners. The last of the privileged men that passed us had so different a look from that of the ordinary convict, that we could not help noticing him particularly, and then we recognized the once eminent City merchant, who was sentenced to transportation for fraud some months ago. He saw by our look that we detected him even in his convict garb, and hurried past us

"Yes, sir," said the warder, "the life here must be a great change, for such as him especially. Some of the prisoners are better off than ever they were; but a person like that one, who thought nothing of dealing to the extent of a quarter of a million a day, must feel it sorely."

This person, we were told, found special consolation in the study of languages, and on the table of his cell was a high pyramid of books, consisting of French and German exercises, with others of a religious character.

At another part of the day we visited the garden. Passing through a small door in the large wooden gate, by the side of the main entrance, we found ourselves in a spacious yard in front of pentagon 6, and with the high boundary wall shutting it off from the public way without. Here, in the centre, was an immense oval tank or reservoir (like that formerly in the Green Park, but much smaller), and with a whitewashed bricken rim, standing above the ground. This was divided into three compartments, and was supplied with water from the Thames, originally for the use of the prisoners. The centre compartment was intended to act as a filter for the water passing from one end of the reservoir to the other; but this was found a failure, and so it certainly appeared, for the colour of the liquid on the filtered side was the light-green opaque tint of diluted "absinthe," and but a shade clearer than the unfiltered pool which partook strongly of the horse-pond character—a weak slush. This reservoir is no longer used to supply the prison with water, for after the outbreak of the

CONVICTS WORKING IN THE GARDEN GROUND, ATTENDED BY AN ARMED WARDER.

cholera in '54, the several pentagons were provided with water pumped up from the artesian wells in Trafalgar Square.

Hence we passed through small palisaded gates into the prison kitchen-garden, where there was a broad gravelled walk between trimly-kept beds on either side.

"The garden next the prison," said the warder, who still accompanied us, "belongs to the governor, and that next the boundary wall to the chaplain. The deputy-governor's garden adjoins the chaplain's, a little farther on. There is a gardener, with three prisoners, to manage the whole." Here we found fruit-trees, and currant and other bushes, as well as carefully-tended beds of fresh-looking vegetables.

At the entrance to the tongue or V-shaped strip of land, lying between pentagons 5 and 6, stood a warder, with the barrel of a blunderbuss resting across his arm.

This told us that the prisoners employed in the garden were at work at that part. We went across to see the kind of labour performed, and here, among the convict gang, we noted one whose estate had recently sold for £25,000, dressed in the prison garb and busy hoeing between the rows of beans that were planted there.

Thence our path lay past the deputy-governor's long strip of garden, and so through another low gate in the palisading that divided the kitchen-garden from the ground devoted to the general purposes of the prison. Here on one side of the central pathway the ground was planted with mangold-wurzel, and on the other with white carrots. There are six prisoners at work here all the year round, watched over by an armed officer, either cultivating the ground or rolling the paths.

At the edge of the pathway stood a desolate-looking black sentry-box, erected for the officer who is on duty in the garden at night. The next tongue of land between pentagons 4 and 5 was covered with a crop of rank grass, so thick and tall that it positively undulated in the breeze like a field of green corn. "Nothing else will grow in those places, unless in the very best aspect," our attendant told us. He thought there were altogether about four acres of garden ground round about the prison.

Then as we turned the corner by the general centre tower, at the apex of pentagon 4, we discovered, on the side of the path next the boundary-wall, an oblong piece of land, enclosed within a low black iron rail, and with a solitary elder-tree growing in a round green tuft close beside the fence. This was exactly opposite to the tongue of ground between the pentagons 3 and 4, so that it occupied very nearly the same position at the back of the jail as the outer gate does in front of it.

"That," said Warder Power, "is the churchyard of the prison. It's no longer used as a burying-place for the convicts now. In the cholera of 1848, so many corpses were interred there that the authorities thought it unhealthy. The bodies of convicts dying in the prison are buried at the Victoria Cemetery, Mile End, now. After a *post-mortem* examination has taken place, an officer of the prison goes with the coffin, and is generally the only person present at the ceremony."

We entered the sad spot, and found the earth arranged in mounds, and planted all over with marigolds, the bright orange flowers of which studded the place, and seemed in the sunshine almost to spangle the surface. At one part were three tombstones, raised to the memory of some departed prison officers; but of the remains of the wretched convicts that lay buried there, not a single record was to be found. It was well that no stone chronicled their wretched fate, and yet it was most sad that men should leave the world in such a way.*

* THE FOLLOWING ARE THE INSCRIPTIONS ON THE TOMB-STONES :—

SACRED

To the Memory of

EDMUND JAGO PALMER,

Eldest Son of
The Matron of the General Penitentiary,

Who died of Consumption

The 13th August, 1828,

In his 17th year.

He is gone before.

SACRED

To the Memory of

WILLIAM JAQUES,

Late an Officer in the
General Penitentiary,

Who Departed this Life

19th January, 1838,

Aged 58 Years.

He was much beloved and
lamented by his Wife and
Friends, and highly respected
by his Brother Officers.

HERE LIES THE BODY OF

ELIZA WILKINSON,

LATE MATRON IN THE
GENERAL PENITENTIARY
AT MILLBANK,
WHO DIED AT WOOLWICH,
ON BOARD THE HEROINE,
THEN USED
AS AN HOSPITAL SHIP
FOR FEMALE PRISONERS
BELONGING TO THIS PRISON.
HER DEATH,
WHICH HAPPENED
ON THE 24TH MAY, 1824,
DEPRIVED THE PRISONERS
OF A KIND FRIEND,
AND THIS ESTABLISHMENT
OF AN EXCELLENT OFFICER.

¶ iv.—ϵ.

The Female Convict Prison at Millbank.

The female prison, though forming part of the same building as that devoted to the male prisoners, may still be regarded as a distinct establishment, for it occupies one entire pentagon (pentagon 3), and has not only a set of officers peculiarly its own, but is entered by different keys.

The female prison here is to Brixton what the male prison is to Pentonville—a kind of depôt to which the convicts are forwarded as vacancies occur.

At the time of our visit there were 173 female prisoners located in this establishment, throughout the several wards; a portion of whom were in separate confinement, and the remainder working in association.

"This is Miss Cosgrove, the principal matron, sir," said the warder, as we entered the gate and were introduced to a good-looking young " officer."

"The female uniform, you see," the warder added, " is the same as at Brixton, with the exception of the bonnets—their's is white straw, and our's is gray.

"This yard," said Miss Cosgrove, opening a door at the side of the passage into a long narrow airing ground, where a fat-looking prisoner, in her dark claret-brown gown and check apron, was walking to and fro by herself, " is for such convicts as are too bad to be put to exercise with others. That is one of the women who has been acting in the most obscene and impudent manner at Brixton. When they're bad, they're bad indeed!" said the young matron, as we turned away.

"The female officers," replied the warder, " carry out better discipline here than even at Brixton; a great deal of determination and energy is required by female officers to do the duty.

The matron now opened a heavy door that moaned on its hinges. "This is A ward, and has thirty cells in it, exactly the same as those in the male pentagon."

The cells had register numbers outside, but the grated gate was considerably lighter, though equally as strong as those in the other pentagons.

As we peeped into one of the little cells, we saw a good-looking girl with a skein of thread round her neck, seated and busy making a shirt. The mattress and blankets were rolled up into a square bundle, as in the male cells. There was a small wooden stool and little square table with a gas jet just over it; the bright tins, wooden platter, and salt-box, a few books, and a slate, and signal-stick shaped like a harlequin's wand, were all neatly arranged upon the table and shelf in the corner. The costume of the convicts here is the same as at Brixton.

"The women are mostly in for common larcenies," said the matron, as we walked down the long narrow passage between the cells; "and many of them have been servants; some have been gentlemen's servants, and a good number have been farm servants; but the fewest number are, strange to say, of the unfortunate class in the streets."

"Yes," chimes in the warder, "not a great many of *them* come here."

"Generally speaking," said the matron, as she conducted us through the pentagon, "those who have been very bad outside are found the best in prison both for work and behaviour; and the longest-sentenced females are usually the best behaved."

"The long sentences are, mostly, for murder—child-murder," she added; " and this is usually the first and only offence; but the others are continually in and out, and become at last regular jail people."

"The farm servants," continued Miss Cosgrove, " are, ordinarily, a better class of people; but some are very stubborn. Yes! one we had in here was *very* bad."

The convicts pick coir for the first two months, and, if well-behaved for that time, they are then put to needlework. Their door is bolted up for the first four months of their incarceration.*

We now entered the laundry, which reminded us somewhat of a fish-market, with its wet-looking, black, shiny asphalte floor. The place was empty—work being finished on the Friday. On Saturday mornings, the convicts who are usually employed to do the washing, go to school, and in the afternoon they clean the laundry, so as to have it ready for work on Monday morning. Long dressers stretch round the building; there is a heavy mangle at one side, and cloths'-horses, done up in quires, rest against the wall.

We are next led through the drying and getting-up room, and so into the wash-house. Here we find rows of troughs, with brass taps, for hot and cold water, jutting over them. There is a large bricken boiler at one end of the apartment, pails and tubs stand about, and a few limp-wet clothes are still on the lines. "There are only ten women washing every week now," observed the matron; "we *have* had thirty-six or forty—quite as many as that. We used to do for the whole service, but at present we wash only for the female prisoners and their officers.

* NOTICE TO FEMALE CONVICTS.

Prisoners of good conduct, and maintaining a character for willing industry, will, by this rule, be enabled, after certain fixed periods, to obtain the higher stages, and gain the privileges attached to them.

For the present, and until further orders, the following Rules will be observed :—

The first stage of penal discipline will be carried out at Millbank prison, where two classes will be established, viz., The Probation Class, and the Third Class.

The second stage of discipline will be carried out at Brixton, where the prisoners will be divided into the First, Second, and Third Classes.

The third stage of discipline and industrial training prior to discharge will be carried out at Burlington House, Fulham, for those prisoners who, by their exemplary conduct in the first and second stages, appear deserving of being removed to that establishment.

Millbank Probation Class.

1. All prisoners, on reception, will be placed in the probation class, in ordinary cases, for a period of four months, and, in special cases, for a longer period, according to their conduct. During this time their cell-doors will be bolted up.

2. The strictest silence will be enforced with prisoners in this class on all occasions, and they will be occupied in picking coir, until, by their industry and good conduct, they may appear deserving of other employment.

3. No prisoner in the probation class will be allowed to receive a visit.

4. Every prisoner having passed through the probation class is liable to be sent back thereto, and recommence the period of probation, upon the recommendation of the governor, and with the sanction of a director.

5. On leaving the probation class, the prisoners will be received into the third class.

Discipline of the Third Class.

6. No prisoner will be allowed to receive a visit until she has been well-conducted for the space of two months in the third class.

7. The strictest silence will be enforced with prisoners in this class on all occasions.

8. Prisoners, whose conduct has been exemplary in the third class for a period of four months, will be eligible for removal to Brixton when vacancies occur.

RULES FOR THE PENAL CLASS OF FEMALE CONVICTS AT MILLBANK PRISON.

1. To have their cells bolted up, and be kept in strict separation.

2. To be employed in picking coir or oakum, or in some such occupation, for the first three months after reception.

3. Not to be allowed to receive visits or letters, or to write letters.

4. Not to attend school for the first three months after their reception, and not then unless their conduct may warrant the indulgence. In the event, however, of the governor and chaplain agreeing that any individual female convict in the penal class may be permitted to attend school at an earlier period than three months, she may attend accordingly.

5. In the event of a female convict in the penal class committing any offence against the prison rules, the governor shall have the power of punishing such a prisoner, as laid down in rule 13, page 11, of the rules applicable to the governor, for any term not exceeding seven days.

"We've five matrons, ten assistant-matrons, one infirmary cook, and one principal matron," said Miss Cosgrove, in answer to our inquiry as to the official staff for the female portion of the prison.

"This is B ward—the first probation ward," says the matron, as we enter another passage. Here we find the inner wooden doors thrown back. "These women have all been here less than three months," adds the principal matron. "Such as you have already seen at needlework have been here over two months, and those that have coir to pick have been in less than two months."

"Oh, yes; the brooms and scissors are all taken out every night, the same as at Brixton," said the matron to us.

As we pass, the convicts all jump up and curtsey—some of them bobbing two or three times. All wear the close white prison cap. Some are pretty, and others coarse-featured women; many of them are impudent-looking, and curl their lip, and stare at us as we go by.

"We've got many Mary MacWilliamses (a model incorrigible) here," said the warder to us. "Ah, she's a nice creature! I brought her from Brixton."

"She's going back again," interposed the matron.

"Is she, by George!" rejoined the warder. Then they'll have a nice one to look after. I went to get the incorrigibles from Brixton, and brought them here. We went on very nicely till we got them, and they've done our business. Some of them have softened down wonderfully well though; we'd hard battles at first, but we conquered them at last. I *do* think those who were brought down here were the very worst women in existence. I don't fancy their equal could be found anywhere.

FEMALE CONVICT IN CANVAS DRESS
(UNDER PUNISHMENT FOR TEARING HER CLOTHES).

"*There's* one of our punishment cells," says the dark-eyed young matron, as we quit B ward, passage No. 2. The cell was not quite dark; there was a bed in the corner of it.

"What can the women do there?" asked we. "*Do!*" cried the matron; "why, they can sing and dance, and whistle, and make use, as they do, of the most profane language conceivable."

We now proceeded up stairs to the punishment cell on the landing. This one was intensely dark, with a kind of grating in the walls for ventilation, but no light-hole; and there was a small raised wooden bed in the corner. The cell was shut in first by a grated gate, then a wooden door, lined with iron, with another door outside that; and then a kind of mattress, or large straw-pad, arranged on a slide before the outer door, to deaden the sound from within. "Those are the best dark cells in all England," said our guide, as he closed the many doors. "They're clean, warm, and well ventilated." There were five such cells in a line, and each with the same apparatus outside for deadening the sound within, as we have before described.

"That's one of the women under punishment who's singing now," said the matron, as we stood still to listen. "They generally sing. Oh! *that's* nothing—that's very quiet for them. Their language to the minister is sometimes so horrible, that I am obliged to run away with disgust."

"Some that we've had," went on the matron, "have torn up their beds. They make up songs themselves all about the officers of the prison. Oh! they'll have every one in their verses—the directors, the governor, and all of us." She then repeated the following doggerel from one of the prison songs :—' "If you go to Millbank, and you want to see Miss Cosgrove, you must inquire at the round house;—and they'll add something I can't tell you of."

We went down stairs and listened to the woman in the dark cell, who was singing "Buffalo Gals," but we could not make out a word—we could only catch the tune.

In F ward is the padded cell. "We've not had a woman in here for many months," said the matron, as we entered the place. The apartment was about six feet high; a wainscot of mattresses was ranged all round the walls, and large beds were placed on the ground in one corner, and were big enough to cover the whole cell. "This is for persons subject to fits," says the matron; "but very few suffer from them."

The matron now led us into a double cell, containing an iron bed and tressel. Here the windows were all broken, and many of the sashes shattered as well. This had been done by one of the women with a tin pot, we were informed.

"What is this, Miss Cosgrove?" asked the warder, pointing to a bundle of sticks like firewood in the corner.

"Oh, that's the remains of her table! And if we hadn't come in time, she would have broken up her bedstead as well, I dare say." We now reached the school-room, where we found four women, with a lady in black teaching them.

"They get on very well while in separate confinement," says the teacher to us, "but rather slow when in association."

"*That's* where we weigh the women when they come in," said the matron, as we passed along. "The men are not weighed; it has been discontinued since Major Groves' time. We find some go out the same weight, but very often they are heavier than when they came in, and we seldom find that they have lost flesh."

We next entered C ward, on the middle floor. Here we noted some good-looking women; though the convicts are not generally remarkable for good looks, being often coarse-featured people.

"Some of our best-looking are among the worst behaved of all the prisoners in the female ward," says the matron.

One woman was at work picking coir, with her back turned towards us. We looked at her register number above the door, and read on the back of the card the name of *Alice Grey*.

We now reach D ward, passage No. 2 ; this is the penal ward.

Here the windows were wired inside, and had rude kinds of Venetian blinds fixed on the outside; the cells were comparatively dark, and the prisoners younger and much prettier than any we had yet seen. Many of them smiled impudently as we passed. Here the bedding was ranged in square bundles all along the passage, because the prisoners had been found to wear them for bustles.

"Those bells," points out the matron, "are to call male officers in case of alarm."

Presently we saw, inside one of the cells we passed, a girl in a coarse canvas dress, strapped over her claret-brown convict clothes. This dress was fastened by a belt and straps of the same stuff, and, instead of an ordinary buckle, it was held tight by means of a key acting on a screw attached to the back. The girl had been tearing her clothes, and the coarse canvas dress was put on to prevent her repeating the act.

"These two girls are reformed since I brought them over from Brixton," says the warder to us. "Those three also are quite reformed; it's nine months since I brought them over. They're well-conducted now, or they wouldn't be together." The girl in the canvas dress was now heard laughing as we passed down the ward.

The matron had a canvas dress brought out for our inspection; and while we were examining it a noise of singing was heard once more, whereupon the warder informed us that it proceeded from the lady in the dark cell, who was getting up a key or two higher. The canvas dress we found to be like a coarse sack, with sleeves, and straps at the waist—the latter made to fasten, as we have said before, with small screws. With it we were shown the prison strait-waistcoat, which consisted of a canvas jacket, with black leathern sleeves, like boots closed at the end, and with straps up the arm.

The canvas dress has sometimes been cut up by the women with bits of broken glass. Formerly the women used to break the glass window in the penal ward, by taking the bones out of their stays and pushing them through the wires in front."

"Oh, yes, they'd sooner lose their lives than their hair!" said the warder, in answer to our question as to whether the females were cropped upon entering the prison. "We do not allow them to send locks of the hair cut off to their sweethearts; locks, however, are generally sent to their children, or sisters, or mother, or father, and leave is given to them to do as much; they are allowed, too, to have a lock sent in return, and to keep it with their letters. All books sent here by the prisoners' friends, if passed by the chaplain, the convicts are permitted to retain."

"The locks of hair sent out," adds the officer, "must be stitched to the letters, so as not to come off in the offices."

Our conversation, as we stood at the gate, about to take our departure, was broken off by the cries of "You're a liar!" from one of the females in the cells of the neighbouring wards; whereupon the amiable young matron, scarcely staying to wish us good morning, hastened back to the prison.*

* As regards the ages, sentences, and education of the male convicts at Millbank prison, the following are the official returns for 1854 :—

ADULTS.		JUVENILES.	
Ages.		*Ages.*	
17 years and under 21	383	Under 12 years	6
21 ,, ,, 30	453	12 years and under 14	22
		14 ,, ,, 17	195
Total under 30 years	836		
30 years and upwards	455		222
	1,291		
Sentences.		*Sentences.*	
For 3 years	1	For 4 years	168
,, 4 ,,	745	,, 5 ,,	3
,, 5 ,,	44	,, 6 ,,	26
,, 6 ,,	166	,, 7 ,,	8
,, 7 ,,	92	,, 8 ,,	1
,, 8 ,,	27	,, 10 ,,	4
,, 9 ,,	1	,, 14 ,,	2
,, 10 ,,	97	,, 15 ,,	6
,, 14 ,,	35	,, 21 ,,	3
,, 15 ,,	45	,, Life	1
,, 20 ,,	8		
,, 21 ,,	2		222
,, Life	28		
	1,291		
Education.		*Education.*	
Neither read nor write	233	Neither read nor write	68
Can read only	216	Can read only	42
Both imperfectly	720	Both imperfectly	108
Both well	122	Both well	4
	1,291		222

§ 1—b.

"THE CORRECTIONAL PRISONS OF LONDON.

The Correctional Prisons of the Metropolis are essentially distinct from those of which we have lately been treating. Their main points of difference from the convict prisons may be enumerated as follows :—

1. The *Convict Prisons* are for criminals who have been sentenced either to penal servitude or transportation.

The *Correctional Prisons*, on the other hand, are for criminals sentenced to short terms of imprisonment, extending from seven days up to two years.

2. The *Convict Prisons* are Government institutions, under the management of Her Majesty's Directors of Prisons, and supported by payments out of the "civil list."

The *Correctional Prisons*, however, are county institutions under the management of the magistrates of the shire to which they belong, and supported by payments out of the county rates.

3. At the *Convict Prisons*, criminals are put to labour partly with the view of making them contribute, more or less, to their own support, and partly with the design of keeping them occupied at some industrial pursuit.

At the *Correctional Prisons*, on the contrary, the criminals are condemned to labour, not with any view to profit (either to themselves morally or to the state pecuniarily), but simply as a *punishment ;* and for this purpose such prisons are generally fitted with an apparatus designed to carry out the sentence of hard labour by rendering the work as irksome as possible.

The history of these houses of correction explains to us the reason why such institutions were originally made places of hard labour.

"Houses of correction," says an eminent legal authority, "were first established, as it would seem, in the reign of Elizabeth, and were originally designed for the penal confinement, after conviction, of paupers *refusing to work*, and other persons falling under the legal description of vagrant."—*Stephens' Blackstone*, vol. iii., p. 209.

The Committee of the House of Commons appointed in the year 1597 to determine the best means of decreasing the mendicancy and vagabondage so prevalent at that period, and which committee was composed of Sir Francis Bacon and the most eminent legislators of the time, came to the conclusion that, while it was necessary to provide means for relieving the deserving poor, it was also requisite to institute measures for the punishment of the idle and dissolute. They therefore prepared the statute 39 Eliz. c. 3, which, for the first time, organized the machinery for the relief of the poor in this country by recommending steps to be taken for encouraging the building of "hospitals or abiding and working houses" for the indigent; and, at the same time, introduced an enactment for the suppression of fraudulent vagrancy by establishing *houses of correction*, fitted with stocks and materials for the compulsory employment of such as objected to work ; so that, while granting assistance to the industrious, they enacted, as we are told, severe penalties against the idle.

Houses of Correction, therefore, were originally founded to carry out a discipline that the legislators of the period believed would *correct* the indisposition to labour on the part of rogues and vagabonds. They were, in fact, designed as penal institutions, in which the sturdy beggar's aversion to work was to be taken advantage of, and the very toil that he was endeavouring to fly from to be used as the means of severe punishment to him. But though the committee which originated these measures contained some of the most eminent statesmen of the time, it surely does not require much sagacity now-a-days to perceive that the principle upon which it acted was about as irrational as if a parent, as we have before said, with the view of curing his child's aversion to medicine, were to inflict upon it a six months' course of jalap. Such a mode of treatment, it is manifest, so far from *correcting* an antipathy, could only serve to strengthen it; and even so the rogue, hating labour, can hardly be made to like it by having it rendered more than ordinarily repulsive to him.

Yet such was the reasoning that emanated from the wisdom of our ancestors.

" Well, I always thought labouring for one's living was deuced unpleasant!" exclaims the confirmed rogue to himself, on leaving the House of Correction, "and now, after the dose I've just had, I'm *convinced* of it. Catch me ever doing a stroke of work again, if I can help it!"

One would almost fancy that the common sense of the country would long ago have seen that, instead of such institutions serving to *correct* an indisposition to labour, they really and truly did their best to foster and *confirm* it. But, no! to the present century belongs rather the high philosophic honour of having contrived an apparatus like the tread-wheel, which combines the double moral absurdity of rendering prison labour not only more than usually irksome, but also more than usually profitless. If our forefathers were foolish enough to expect to cure idleness by rendering work a punishment (instead of endeavouring by industrial training to make it a pleasure), it remained for the sages of our own time to seek to impress lazy men with a sense of the beauty and value of industry, by the invention of an instrument which is especially adapted to render labour inordinately repulsive, by making it inordinately useless

" I am a man who don't like work," candidly said an habitual vagabond to the late governor of Coldbath Fields prison; " and, what's more (with an oath), I will not work except when I'm in prison, and then I can't help it!"

The correctional prisons of the metropolis are four in number—two belonging to the county of Middlesex, one to Surrey, and another to the City of London, viz.:—

I. MIDDLESEX HOUSES OF CORRECTION—
    1. Coldbath Fields Prison (for adult males.)
    2. Tothill Fields Prison (for females and juvenile offenders).
II. CITY HOUSE OF CORRECTION—
    Holloway Prison (for all classes of offenders).
III. SURREY HOUSE OF CORRECTION—
    Wandsworth Prison (for all classes).

As regards the number of prisoners passing through these institutions in the course of the year, they would appear to amount to no less than 21,860 odd individuals, and to yield an average daily congregation of about 3,000, while their gross expense to the householders of the neighbouring counties is upwards of £60,000 per annum.

The classes of prisoners confined within these establishments differ, in many respects, from those found at the London convict prisons. At the latter institutions we meet with two distinct kinds of offenders, viz., the long-sentence men, who, in most instances, were once reputable people, and are suffering for their first offence; and the habitual criminal, who, after having gone the round of the correctional prisons for a series of petty larcenies, has at length been condemned either to seven years' transportation, or the more modern four years' penal servitude.

In the correctional prisons, however, there are three distinct kinds of offenders. (1.) Felons, *i.e.*, those who have been convicted of some offence to which is attached the for-feiture of all property belonging to the offender. (2.) Misdemeanants, or those imprisoned for offences of a lower degree than felony. (3.) Vagrants, or those who have been committed either as rogues and vagabonds or reputed thieves.

Each of these classes will afford peculiar examples—ranging from the more desperate housebreaker to the cunning "magsman," and even down to the abject "shallow cove."

"I have never been able to comprehend," says Mr. Chesterton, the late governor of Coldbath Fields, while treating of the peculiarities of vagrants in his work upon "Prison Life," "the preference given by hale, able-bodied men, who, rather than face creditable industry, will stand shivering in the cold, with garments barely sufficient to cloak their nakedness—purposely rent and tattered—in order to provoke a sympathy but rarely excited. Their vocation entails upon them endless imprisonments, and the entire life appears to me to be one of so much privation and discomfort, that it is marvellous how any rational being can voluntarily embrace it.

"The tramps or ubiquitary wanderers," adds the late governor, "display a taste far superior to that of the London 'cadgers.'"

One such tramp assured Mr. Chesterton, that the life he led suited him; he enjoyed the country, he said, realized a pleasing variety, and managed, in one way or another, to get his wants adequately supplied.

Finally, the localities of the various houses of correction, as well as the distribution of the other kinds of prisons throughout the Metropolis, will be best explained by the following map :—

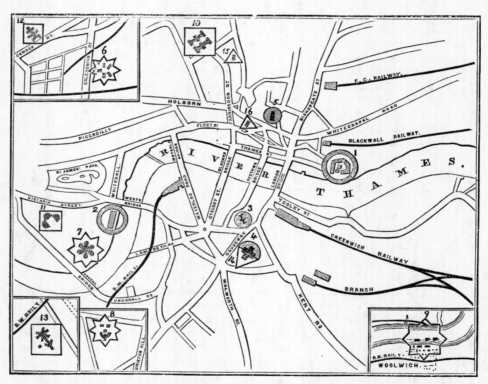

MAP ILLUSTRATIVE OF THE LOCALITY OF THE SEVERAL PRISONS OF THE METROPOLIS.

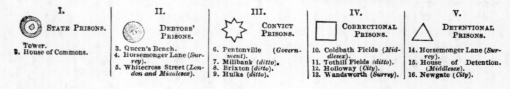

I. STATE PRISONS.	II. DEBTORS' PRISONS.	III. CONVICT PRISONS.	IV. CORRECTIONAL PRISONS.	V. DETENTION PRISONS.
Tower. B. House of Commons.	3. Queen's Bench. 4. Horsemonger Lane (*Surrey*). 5. Whitecross Street (*London and Middlesex*).	6. Pentonville (*Government*). 7. Millbank (*ditto*). 8. Brixton (*ditto*). 9. Hulks (*ditto*).	10. Coldbath Fields (*Middlesex*). 11. Tothill Fields (*ditto*). 12. Holloway (*City*). 13. Wandsworth (*Surrey*).	14. Horsemonger Lane (*Surrey*). 15. House of Detention (*Middlesex*). 16. Newgate (*City*).

GATEWAY OF THE HOUSE OF CORRECTION, COLDBATH FIELDS.

¶ i.

THE MIDDLESEX HOUSE OF CORRECTION, COLDBATH FIELDS,

(FOR ADULT MALE OFFENDERS).

On a dull summer's morning, when the sky was lead-coloured with an impending storm, and the air was hot as though the thick roof of clouds impeded the ventilation of the City, we left our home to make our visit to this prison. A slight shower had fallen, spotting the pavement with large, round drops.

The cocks shut up in the cellars of the green-grocers' and barbers' shops, situated in the streets through which we passed, were crowing as if the light that shone down the iron gratings into the dusty area beneath had aroused them, and they were screeching to be released from their confinement. Over a seedman's shop a lark, whose cage faced the east, was welcoming the streak of early dawn with jerks of melody, whilst the little creature stood fluttering on the small piece of turf placed in the bow of its cage. At one of the cheap hair-dressers, too, where a long pole stretched above the pathway like a bowsprit, we could hear the almost screaming din of birds, all singing at the same time—the sound seeming to pour out from the round holes in the shutter tops in positive gusts of noise.

The whole Metropolis was as yet asleep.

The dull morning appeared to have made the inhabitants stop in their beds longer than usual; for, as we gazed down the now clear perspective of the different streets, we could see but few persons about. The only chimneys that were sending out their smoke were those at the bakers, but even here the curling streams of soot were gradually diminishing in blackness, as though the night's work was over and the fires dying out. As we hurried along, the town put on a different aspect in the bright, early light; the trees of the squares and gardens, and flowers in the balconies, as well as the countless windows, sparkled again, as the black clouds changed into white ones, edged with the many tints of the morning's sun, the panes at length being lighted up by the golden beams, till they shone like plates of burnished metal.

As we gazed around, a newspaper express cart dashed past, taking the direction of the Euston Square Railway. Policemen, with their capes rolled up like black quivers under their arms, were making their way to the different police stations. On one of the doorsteps in Gower Street was seated a milk-maid, with the bright drum-shaped cans before her, waiting until the servant-maid rose to take in the customary "ha'porth."

Then the butchers' carts came rattling past, the wheels trembling as they spun over the stones; and the horse, with freshly-greased hoofs, going at a pace which, as the animal turned the corner, threw the vehicle round sideways, and almost jerked the driver from one end of the seat to the other.

Near to the Foundling we noted, down the stable-yards, a quantity of Hansom cabs ranged in rows, and still dirty with the night's work; and then, a few paces after crossing the Gray's Inn Road, we caught sight of the dull brick wall that encircles the House of Correction, and in a minute or two more had reached our destination.

As few persons in easy worldly circumstances care to reside in the neighbourhood of a prison, it may account for the dingy and distressed appearance of the buildings that surround the jail in Coldbath Fields. The red brick dwellings facing the main entrance have all the appearance of having been at one time "capital town mansions," but the daily sight of the prison van driving up, and the dreary look-out from the front windows upon the tall boundary wall and heavily-spiked roofs, has degraded the dwellings down to the rank of old furniture stores, or lodging-houses for single men, who care not where they obtain house-shelter provided the rent be low. Some of the houses hereabouts are sufficiently antiquated—as, for instance, those in Baynes Row—with the words cut in quaint, long spider letters, in the red brick tablet between the drawing-room windows. Again, in Cobham Row, the heavy white sashes to the casements, the curious iron-work, and the peculiar style of brick-work, strongly indicate the old-fashioned character of the buildings.

Clerkenwell is notoriously the hardest-working quarter of London; and as soon as the immediate vicinity of the prison is passed, the industry begins to show itself. In Dorrington Street, a small colony of brass-founders have established themselves, and the grocers' canister-makers have also permanently settled on the spot.

Turning down Phœnix Place, we see the yards converted into saw-mills, and jets of steam bursting out from the midst of tiled sheds; and we hear, too, the grating, hissing sound of the machinery. One board, over the door of a dingy cottage, tells us that the inmates are "Fancy Brush-board Makers;" and on a closed-up door, the deep-bordered posters of a cheap undertaker caters for patronage for his "Genteel Funerals," at £1 1s.

At the back, or northern side of the prison wall, lie the enormous yards of Mr. Cubitt, the contractor—some of them filled with paving and flag-stones—others bristling with scaffold poles and tapering ladders—and some again occupied by sheds, under and about which are rusting cog-wheels and old machinery, or stone balustrades and pieces of broken sculpture. Here, too, in the waste unpaved ground about the walls, the boys have established their play-ground, and amuse themselves with pitch-in-the-hole, tossing for buttons, and games at marbles, or else they perform their gymnastic exercises on the thick rails and posts, placed across the broad rude pathway to obstruct the passage of cabs and cattle.

Whether the jail has ruined the neighbourhood or not, we cannot say, but the surrounding locality wears a degraded look, as if it also had put on the prison uniform of dirty gray.

We had risen so early, that we reached our destination before the official hour for opening the gates, the warders not being admitted until half-past six, when the night watch is relieved, and the business of the day begins.

One of the main features of the Coldbath Fields prison is the tall brick wall, which surrounds the entire of the nine acres upon which the building stands, and gives to the place the idea of a strong fortress. To the foot-passenger, this high wall hides out every view of the enclosed buildings, and, but for a bell heard now and then ringing within, he might almost imagine the interior to be a burial-ground. It is only at the moment of turning the corner of Phœnix Place, and entering into Dorrington Street, that the first evidence is obtained of the spot being inhabited; for there, at rapidly-recurring intervals, may be seen a black beam darting by, close to the coping-stone of the brick-work, the mystery of which none can fathom but those who have visited the interior of the prison, it being the wings of the fan, or governing machine, which regulates the rapidity of the tread-wheel.

On one side of the public road, passing along the front of the prison, is an unoccupied piece of ground, about half an acre in extent, which fronts the remaining portion of the wall; here the grass has grown so luxuriantly that it may almost be termed a field, especially as half a dozen sheep are feeding, within the palings, on the long herbage.

Looking out upon this grass-plot may be seen the back of the governor's house, a narrow, two-storeyed dwelling, of an ancient style of structure, with heavy iron gratings before each window, which are closed on the basement story, but are thrown back like French blinds at the upper casements.

The huge prison doorway itself has a curious George the Third air about it, with its inscription of black letters cut into the painted stone, telling one that it is

THE HOUSE OF

CORRECTION

FOR THE

COUNTY OF MIDDLESEX

1794

—the writing being similar to that which is seen in old books, and by no means comparable to the well-shaped characters on the sign-boards at the neighbouring public-house. A pair of gigantic knockers, large as pantomime masks, hang low down on the dark-green panels of the folding gates, and under them are the letter-box and the iron-grated wicket, not larger than a gridiron; whilst, arranged in tassels at the top of each side pillar, are enormous black fetters, big enough to frighten any sinful passer-by back into the paths of rectitude. A *chevaux de frise*, like some giant hundred-bladed penknife, is placed on either side of the doorway, where it towers above the wall, and within reading height are placed black boards, with notices painted white upon them. From these we learn where "*Information respecting the Terms of Imprisonment, and the Fines to be paid, may be obtained,*" and are also told that "*No provisions, clothing, or other articles for the use of the prisoners,*" will be permitted to pass the gates; whilst, in another place, the regulations respecting the visits to the prisoners are exposed to view. The county of Middlesex, as if to show its right of ownership, has also placed its crest immediately above the green-painted doors, and the three sabres hang threateningly over the heads of all who enter. This and the large gas-lamp jutting out from the wall form the only ornaments to this peculiarly quaint old prison-entrance. (*See Engraving*, p. 277.)

Before conducting the reader within the walls of the prison, let us set forth, as briefly as possible, the "antecedents," as well as the character of the building.

¶ i—a.

The History and Construction of the Prison.

The term Coldbath Fields, which now stands for a portion of the district lying between Clerkenwell and Pentonville, is said to have been derived from a celebrated well of water that was formerly situate in the fields hereabouts, but which is now covered over, the site being at present occupied by the tread-wheel of the prison.

The original House of Correction, Mr. Hepworth Dixon tells us, was built in the reign of the first James. "The increase of vagabondage," he says, "had become so great about that time, that the City Bridewell no longer served to contain the number of offenders; the judges therefore built this prison, the City authorities giving £500 towards it, for keeping their poor employed."

The oldest portion, however, of the present prison (which stands between the Church of St. James's, Clerkenwell, and the Gray's Inn Road) dates only from the end of the last century.

"The House of Correction, at Coldbath Fields," says Mr. Chesterton, the late governor of the prison, in his entertaining new work, entitled "REVELATIONS OF PRISON LIFE," "was erected in the year 1794. Its site at that epoch well entitled it to the third term in its designation, which it has ever since retained; but the magistrates of that day missed an opportunity of purchasing and enclosing, at a comparatively small cost, a much larger tract of land; so that the prison is now overlooked from buildings abutting upon it—an inconvenience which might have been obviated by timely foresight."

The prison covers a space of nine acres, and "the ground," Mr. Chesterton informs us, "which was purchased for the purpose by the county magistrates, cost £4,350. The original building was constructed at an outlay of £65,656. Comformably with the notions of that period, the building was massive, overloaded with ponderous iron gates, window-frames, and fastenings; while narrow entrances and passages were designed to render a sudden outburst of prisoners impracticable.

"Certain it is," adds the late governor, "that the large outlay of £65,656, at that distant period, merely to produce a structure containing 232 cells, the precise number erected, does appear to be a prodigal expenditure, and quite disproportioned to the accommodation secured."*

Large additions, however, have been made from time to time, since the date of its original construction. In the year 1832, the unlooked-for increase of numbers had, in the words of the late governor, "necessitated a corresponding extension of the buildings, and soon after the completion (in 1830) of a 'vagrants' ward,' calculated to accommodate 150 prisoners, there was added a 'female ward' (now the misdemeanants' prison), designed to contain 300. These buildings were erected on a radiating system, but they were designed ere the new lights on prison structure, derived from the United States of America, had penetrated into this kingdom. Consequently our new buildings were very defective, and much expense was subsequently incurred to amend and enlarge them."

There are at present two houses of correction for the county of Middlesex—one at Coldbath Fields, which is devoted to the reception of such *adult male* prisoners as have not been sentenced to transportation or penal servitude; and the other at Tothill Fields, appropriated to the *female* and *juvenile* portion of the same class.

---

* Pentonville prison, built in 1840-42, and fitted with 130 cells, cost £85,000. Brixton prison, built in 1819-20, and fitted with 161 cells, cost (including the purchase of the land) £51,780; and Millbank prison, built in 1812, and fitted with 550 cells, cost £500,000, exclusive of land.

Coldbath Fields prison has now proper accommodation for about 1,450 prisoners* (919 in separate cells, and 534 in cells capable of containing more than one prisoner), though many more are sometimes thrust into it, causing great confusion of system. The daily average number of prisoners throughout the year 1854-55 was 1,388. Mr. Chesterton tells us that "the prison of Coldbath Fields is one of such surpassing magnitude as to have numbered within its walls, during the year 1854, at one time, no less than 1,495 inmates."†

The prison is in the jurisdiction of fourteen magistrates, appointed at each Quarter Sessions, of whom four go out quarterly by rotation.

The official staff for the management of Coldbath Fields House of Correction consists of the governor, 2 chaplains, 1 surgeon, 1 chief warder, 34 warders, 66 sub-warders, 4 clerks, 1 engineer, and 1 store-keeper; in all, 112 officers. Hence, as there are altogether 100 warders, and the daily average number of prisoners throughout the year 1854 amounted

* The following return as to the accommodation afforded has been kindly supplied us by the present governor :—

NUMBER OF BERTHS AND CELLS CONTAINED IN COLDBATH FIELDS PRISON :—

OLD PRISON.			MISDEMEANOUR PRISON.		VAGRANT PRISON.	
Yards.	Berths in Dormitories.	Cells.	Yards.	Cells.	Yards.	Cells.
First and second . .	99	66	First 87		First and second 88	
Third and fourth . .	101	71	Second 96		Third and fourth 87	
Fifth and sixth . .	99	76	Third 100		Refractory 2	
Seventh and eighth .	98	72	Fourth 96			177
Lower gallery . . .		29	Refractory 7			
Upper gallery . . .		29		386		
Refractory		14				
	397	357				
Cells and Berths . . 754						

Old Prison 357	
Misdemeanour Prison . . . 386	
Vagrant Prison 177	
	920
Berths in the Dormitories . . 397	
	1,317

† NUMBER OF MALE PRISONERS CONFINED IN THE HOUSE OF CORRECTION, COLDBATH FIELDS, IN THE COURSE OF THE YEAR 1854.

1.	2.	3.	4.
In custody at the commencement of the year.	*Received under commitments, and who have not been in custody of other Governors.*	*Received from the custody of other Governors, and enumerated in their returns.*	*Charges, i.e., prisoners committed to the prison for examination, but afterwards discharged, not being fully committed.*
Prisoners for trial . . —	Prisoners for trial . . —	Prisoners for trial . . —	
Convicted at assizes and sessions . . . 874	Prisoners transferred to other Governors for trial . . . . —	Convicted at assizes and sessions . . .1,620	
Convicts under contract with Government . —	Rendered in court for trial . . . . —	Convicts under contract with Government . —	
Summary convictions . 563	Summary convictions .6,123	Summary convictions . —	
For re-examination . —	Ditto transferred to other Governors . —		7,743
	1,437		6,123		

Total in the course of the year 9,180	
Greatest number of Prisoners at any one time in the course of the year 1,495	
The daily average number of Prisoners throughout the year 1,388	

to 1,388, we find that there is one such officer to about every 13 persons confined within the walls.*

The discipline enforced at this prison is that which is termed the "silent associated system," the prisoners working in bodies by day, and being forbidden to hold any communication with each other, either by word or gesture; whilst many of them—some 920—sleep in separate cells at night. "If the system on which the prison is ostensibly conducted," says an author before quoted, "were rigorously carried out, all the prisoners would be separated at night; but the number of separate cells is insufficient. The surplus is, therefore, to be provided for in general dormitories, in which officers are obliged to remain all night, to prevent intercourse or disorder."

Coldbath Fields is one of those prisons at which labour is used as a *punishment*, rather than a means of industrial training or of self-support among the prisoners themselves—the criminals sent here being often condemned to "hard labour," in addition to a certain term of imprisonment. These hard-labour sentences are worked out either upon the tread-wheel, or else in picking oakum or coir, unless the services of the prisoner be required for some work in connection with the jail. For the due carrying out of the hard-labour sentence, there are at Coldbath Fields no less than six distinct tread-wheel yards, and two of these have each four separate wheels working on one long axis, whilst the four remaining yards have each three wheels fixed upon one axle.

This prison bears the reputation of being one of the most salubrious in all London. "The ample space, the full supply of light and air afforded to the prisoners, as well as the general system of the prison," says Mr. Dixon, "causes Coldbath Fields to be one of the healthiest places of confinement in the Metropolis. Though it has an average of from 1,200 to 1,400 occupants the year round, more than three or four persons are seldom found in the infirmary at once—a state of the health-calendar very different from that of Newgate or Millbank, or even that of Pentonville."

Indeed it will be seen, by the returns before given (p. 239), that Coldbath Fields is not only considerably healthier than either Millbank or Pentonville, but the proportion of sick (22·3 per cent.) to the gross number of prisoners confined within it throughout the year is even 1 per cent. lower than that of Brixton.†

"The House of Correction at Coldbath Fields," says the author of "London Prisons," "has the thorough aspect of the old English jail."

The prison is surrounded by a high wall, varying from eighteen to twenty-three feet, and the prison buildings are in three distinct divisions:—

1. The principal, or old building, erected in 1794.
2. The new vagrants' ward, completed in 1830.
3. The female prison, now "the misdemeanants' ward," completed in 1832.

The old or "main" prison stands at a little distance behind the principal entrance, and is of a quadrangular form (with two wings attached), divided by a central passage, which is intersected at right angles by the various "yards"—four on either side of the passage, and

---

* At Pentonville there are 30 warders to a daily average of 519 prisoners, which is in proportion of 1 officer to about every 17 inmates of the jail. At Millbank, on the other hand, there are 101 warders to a daily average of 702 male prisoners, which is almost at the rate of 1 officer to every 7 men.

† In the course of the year 1854-55 there were at Coldbath Fields altogether 131 infirmary cases, and 1,916 cases of slight indisposition, making altogether 2,047 cases of sickness in the course of that year: and as the gross number of prisoners confined within the jail during the same year amounted to 9,180, this gives a proportion of 22·3 cases of sickness to every one hundred prisoners. The per centage of pardons on medical grounds to the daily average number of prisoners at the same prison was 1·0, whilst the per centage of deaths to the daily average number of prisoners was 1·3, which, it will be seen by reference to the previous table (see p. 239), is still considerably lower than at either the Hulks or Millbank, but, on the other hand, higher than either Pentonville or Brixton.

each having the cells ranged along one side, and with the tread-wheels, in some cases, facing them.

The vagrants' ward is on the left of the main entrance, and consists of five radiating wings, proceeding from a semi-circular building, upon the half-wheel principle; and these five wings, with the four intermediate airing courts, constitute four "yards" or divisions.

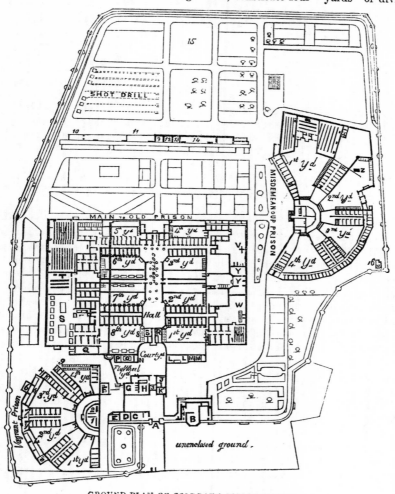

GROUND-PLAN OF COLDBATH FIELDS PRISON.
(References to the Letters and Numbers in the Engraving.)

A. Entrance Gate.
B. Governor's House.
C. Gate Warder's House.
D. Engineer's Office.
E. Blacksmith's Shop.
F. Cocoa Mill and Shed.
G. Governor's House.
H. Gate Warder's Lodge.
J. Clerk's Office.

K. Cashier's Office.
L. Warder's Lodge and Bed-room.
M. Coach-house and Stable.
N. Chaplain's Clerk's Room.
O. Sub-Warder's Rooms.
P. Engineer's Stores.

Q. Plumber's Shop.
R. Governor's Report Offices.
S. Mat Room.
T. School Room.
U. Oakum Room.
V. Cook's House & Larder.
W. Reception Room and Yard.

X. Clothing Room.
Y. Store Rooms.
Z. Laundry.
1 Gardener's Room.
2. Lampman's Room.
3. Visiting Places.
4. Tread-wheels.
5. Dead-house.
6. Lime Shed.

7. Refractory Cells.
8. Slate Washing-boxes.
9. Water Closets.
10. Van Sheds.
11. Coal Shed.
12. Wood Shed.
13. Dresser Shed.
14. Oakum Shed.
15. Dust & Rubbish Heap.

The misdemeanants' ward, formerly appropriated to the female prisoners, stands at a little distance from the north-eastern corner of the old prison, and constitutes a distinct building, but does not differ much in its plan from the vagrants' ward.

There are two chapels, one for males and the other formerly for females, in which there is service every morning.

The main or old prison is principally devoted to the reception of felons, whilst the vagrant ward is set aside for those committed as rogues or vagabonds, including reputed thieves; and that which was formerly the female ward is now appropriated to persons convicted of misdemeanours. At the date (18th October, 1855,) of the last report of the visiting justices, the gross number in custody was 1,325 adult males; and these were composed of the following classes in the following proportion, viz. :—

	Number.	Per Cent.
Felons	697 =	52·6
Misdemeanants	496 =	37·5
Vagrants	132 =	9·9
Total	1,325 =	100·0

In the same report the prison is said to be capable of containing 919 prisoners in separate sleeping cells, and 534 where more than one prisoner sleeps in one cell. Rooms and workshops, not intended as sleeping apartments for prisoners, are used, we are told, as dormitories when a greater extent of accommodation is required.*

₊ *History of the Discipline of Coldbath Fields Prison.*—From the history, construction, and present capacity of the building itself, we pass to the history of that system of management which preceded and led to the one at present in force.

It has been our object to chronicle the origin of the discipline pursued at the various penal institutions of which we have already treated. We have traced the commencement and modifications of the separate system, as carried out at Pentonville Prison—we have given a brief account of the establishment of the Female Convict Prison at Brixton—we have endeavoured to impress the reader with a sense of the utter want of system, and indeed decency, in the management of the Hulks in former times, as well as to give him a notion of the defective arrangements at present existing in those places—we have sought, moreover, to show him how Bentham's crude scheme for a Panopticon merged into the old Penitentiary, where criminals were trained in hypocrisy, and the warders were converted into "Scripture readers," while the governor himself was a gentleman in orders—as well as how this same penitential system was ultimately converted into the present "mixed system" of penal discipline; and now we proceed, in due order, to explain how the promiscuous association of the prisoners at Coldbath Fields, as well as the iniquities practised by the warders there, and even the governors themselves, at length gave way to the more righteous sentiments of the age, and finally settled into "the silent associated system," of which that prison is not only now regarded as the type, but the metropolitan originator.

Luckily for the proper execution of this portion of our task, we have the best possible materials supplied us in the recently-published "Revelations of Prison Life," by Mr. Chesterton, the late governor of the jail in question, and the gentleman to whom the public,

* GENERAL WEEKLY REPORT, FROM FRIDAY, 20TH JUNE, 1856.

	Prisoners.		Prisoners.		Prisoners.
Number in custody last week	1,393	Infirmary Patients	2	Foreigners in prison, viz. :	
		Convalescent Patients	29	Germans	8
Number unlocked this morning	1,375	Number of Irish in prison	100	Poles	1
		Foreigners in prison	38	Portuguese	2
		viz: Americans	2	Spaniards	3
Admitted during the week	134	Swedes	2	Italians	7
Discharged during the week	152	Danes	—	Greeks	—
Died during the same week	—	Russians	1	Mussulmans	—
Increase	—	Dutch	5	Africans	1
Decrease	18	Belgians	1	Hindoos	—
		French	4	West Indians	1

as well as the prisoners themselves, are indebted for the correction of abuses that were a scandal to our country, and who was the first to introduce into it that system of non-intercourse among prisoners, which, at least, if it works no positive change in the criminal character, must be acknowledged to prevent effectually that extended education in crime which arose formerly from the indiscriminate communion of the inmates of our jails.

This gentleman we have long known in private life, and known only to esteem for the kindness of his heart and the soundness of his views, as well as the fine integrity of his principles—points, indeed, of which his recent volumes afford many happy illustrations.

Mr. Chesterton, speaking of the prisons of the early part of the present century, says— "Cleanliness scarcely seemed to be a necessary requirement; all care to insure the space indispensable to common decency was deemed superfluous, and shameless profligacy unblushingly prevailed. The lowest order of men only aspired to dispense the functions of a jail, while the common allusion to 'jail fevers,' attested the foul contagion inseparable from the fœtid hold of the vicious outcast.

"At that period, there did not exist a more neglected or outraged class than the criminals in our numerous jails. The philanthropy of the great Howard appeared to have become extinct, and to have died with him; while the after exertions of Sir George Paul were circumscribed, and seemed to produce no lasting effect. As far as the county of Middlesex was concerned, no care whatever was bestowed upon the prisons, and consequently vicious administrators were left to perpetrate their corrupt devices."

It was the custom in those days, he tells us, for country justices to administer their functions in their own houses, and many so unblushingly received fees, that their residences were known by the by-word of "justice-shops." A magisterial friend of his named one justice then living, who had been distinguished by such discreditable traffic; and in dilating upon the prevailing corruption of the period, Mr. Chesterton's friend expressed his conviction that some magistrates had pocketed gains from the funds allotted for the erection of Coldbath Fields prison.

"The late Mr. Robert Sibley, well known and much respected as the Middlesex surveyor, has frequently," our author adds, "described to me the scenes he witnessed when he first became acquainted with the county. Men and women, boys and girls, were indiscriminately herded together, in this chief county prison, without employment or wholesome control; while smoking, gaming, singing, and every species of brutalizing conversation and demeanour tended to the unlimited advancement of crime and pollution.

"Meanwhile, the governor of that day walked about bearing in his hand a knotted rope, and ever and anon he would seize some unlucky wight by the collar or arm, and rope's-end him severely; thus exhibiting a warning example of summary corporeal chastisement calculated to overawe refractory beholders."

Sir Francis Burdett, at the early period of his career, condemned the monstrosities of Coldbath Fields so vehemently, as to secure for that prison, says Mr. Chesterton, "the name of the 'Bastile.' Governor Aris (who had formerly been a baker in Clerkenwell) was denounced, and became notorious as a reputed tyrant and torturer. He was ultimately ejected from his office, and died in poverty. Many years subsequently to his leaving the prison, Aris and his sons would come and importune me for assistance, and the former never failed to aver that he was unjustly sacrificed to popular clamour.

"I do not know," continues our friend, "that the Middlesex governor was at that epoch a worse specimen of his craft than others of his brother functionaries throughout the country, for all our penal establishments were such sinks of iniquity, that Aris might possibly have been not a whit more guilty than his compeers. However, his accusers prevailed, and he was discarded without provision.

"During the agitation that existed upon the subject, crowds used to assemble without the walls of the prison, and the incarcerated—fully acquainted with public occurrences—would shriek and shout in order to keep alive popular sympathy, until stories of cruelty perpetrated within aroused indignation and invoked redress.

"The thieves of the present day still retain in the cant name of the prison at Coldbath Fields, a portion of the appellation which by-gone agitation had conferred upon it. As an omnibus is familiarly styled a 'bus,' so is the word Bastile abbreviated into 'stile,' pronounced ' *steel*.'

"There could be no doubt whatever of the infamous management which had long disgraced the jails (in those days), for I have seen a *brochure* of such times written expressly to demonstrate the iniquity then prevalent within the walls of Coldbath Fields. This *brochure* is sufficiently intelligible as to the character of that penitentiary, and the scenes enacted therein, to stamp the place as a focus of abomination and impurity.

"After Aris, the prison became successively entrusted to the management of Governors Adkins and Vickery—both of them having previously been distinguished as expert police officers; for a notion prevailed in that day that none but police magistrates and their satellites were competent to cope with public plunderers.

"There is no earthly doubt that these privileged functionaries, the thief-taking governors, held that their primary obligation consisted in feathering their own nests, and at the same time enriching their subordinates. Indeed all their arrangements seemed designed to promote personal privileges and to amass unlimited gains."

On the 27th of July, 1829, Mr. Chesterton made his debut in the prison, and received from the visiting justices the charge of it. He found it "a sink of abomination and pollution; and so close was the combination amongst its corrupt functionaries, that it was difficult to acquire any definite notion of the wide-spread defilement that polluted every hole and corner of the Augean stable. There was scarcely one redeeming feature in the prison administration," he says, "but the whole machinery tended to promote shameless gains by the furtherance of all that was lawless and execrable.

"Each 'turnkey' had a fixed locality, and was the supervisor of a 'yard' containing from 70 to 100 prisoners, while every yard contained a 'yardsman,' *i.e.*, a prisoner who could afford to bid the highest price for acting as deputy-turnkey, and, under his superior, to trade with the prisoners at a stupendous rate of profit to his principal and to himself. Prisoners also occupied the lucrative posts of 'nurses' in the infirmary, while those of 'passage-men,' and other still more subordinate capacities, procurable by money, all tended to enrich the officers and the chosen prisoners at one and the same time.

"From one end of the prison to the other, there existed a vast illicit commerce at an exorbitant rate of profit. The basement of all the cells was hollowed out and made the depositories of numerous interdicted articles. Layers of lime-white, frequently renewed, hid beneath the surface an inlet to such hidden treasures; and thus wine and spirits, tea and coffee, tobacco and pipes, were unsuspectedly stowed away, and even pickles, preserves, and fish sauce, might also be found secreted within those occult receptacles. The walls, too, separating one cell from another, were adapted to like clandestine uses, the key to such deposits being merely a brick or two easily dislodged by any one acquainted with the secret.

"In vain might a magistrate penetrate into the interior of the prison, and cast his inquisitive glances around him. Telegraphic signals would announce the presence of an unwelcome visitor, and all be promptly arranged to defeat suspicion. The prisoners would assume an aspect and demeanour at once subdued and respectful; the doors of cells would fly open to disclose clean basements, edged with thick layers of lime-white (deliberately used to conceal the secrets beneath), pipes would be extinguished and safely stowed away, the tread-wheels fully manned, and other industrial arts set in motion.

"The first question addressed to a prisoner on his arrival was, 'had he money, or anything convertible into money, or would any friend supply him with money.' If the reply were affirmative, the turnkey, or some agent of his, would convey a letter for the requisite contribution, which became subject to the unconscionable deduction of seven or eight shillings, out of every pound sterling transmitted, besides a couple of shillings to the ' yardsman,' and, in many instances, an additional shilling to the ' passage-man.'

"The poor and friendless prisoner was a man wretchedly maltreated and oppressed. Every species of degrading employment was thrust upon him, and daily inflictions rendered his existence hardly supportable. If he presumed to complain, the most inhuman retaliation awaited him. He was called ' a nose,' and was made to run the gauntlet through a double file of scoundrels armed with short ropes or knotted handkerchiefs.

"Here, also," adds the late governor, "I discovered another ample source of profit to those voracious turnkeys. The correspondence of prisoners with their friends was properly defined by an existing regulation, but in this, as in every other particular, rules were nugatory. If, therefore, a prisoner were too poor to pay one shilling or eighteen-pence for a letter, either written to go out, or for one received in, such letter was invariably destroyed. In short, there was no end to the expedients of such corrupt minds, in order to realize unhallowed gains."

It was not until five years after Mr. Chesterton had entered upon the arduous task of governing and reforming such an institution, that he introduced the silent system as part of the discipline of the prison. The following is that gentleman's version of the circumstances which led to so important a change :—

"Mr. Crawford having concluded his report upon the prisons of the United States, travelled into the North of England and to Scotland, and, during his excursion, visited certain of the prisons there. He returned to London much impressed with the condition of two, viz., that of Wakefield in Yorkshire, and the Bridewell of Glasgow.

"At the former, the associated silent system had been recently introduced under the auspices of a zealous magistrate, who was ably seconded by Mr. Shepherd, the governor.

"The practical eye of Mr. Crawford soon discerned the value of these improvements, and he suggested to Mr. Hoare (one of the Middlesex magistrates, and the brother-in-law of Mrs. Fry), that I should be sent down, first to Wakefield, and thence to Glasgow, to witness these two systems in operation, and report upon the practicability of applying either to Coldbath Fields. The suggestion was communicated to the visiting justices by Mr. Hoare, who strongly advised its adoption ; and, consequently, in the month of December, 1834, I set off thus commissioned.

"Properly accredited to the authorities of both localities, I experienced every desirable attention, and was allowed the facility to make the closest observations. I soon perceived that the paucity of cells at Coldbath Fields presented an irremediable obstacle to the adoption of the separate system, even if that mode of discipline should be preferred, but that some practical alterations would enable us to embrace the silent system.*

"On my return, I presented a minute report, which was laid before the court and subsequently published *in extenso* in some of the daily journals. At length the requisite authority was conceded, and all preliminary arrangements perfected; *and on the 29th December, 1834, a population of 914 prisoners was suddenly apprised that all intercommuni-*

* "Hitherto room had been found, in order to compensate for the deficiency of cells, by sleeping three convicts in each cell ; but under the newly-imported discipline this arrangement could no longer be tolerated. We adopted, therefore, the expedient of enclosing in every yard the space under each set of tread-wheels, which were erected on elevated platforms. The previous day-rooms, and every spare room throughout the great building, were then adapted to sleeping, by the construction of berths in three tiers, as in use in the cabins of passenger-vessels ; and opposite to these the monitor slept on an iron bedstead. A mode of inspection from without was open to the night watchman."—*Note by Mr. Chesterton.*

cation by word, gesture, or sign was prohibited ; and, without a murmur, or the least symptom of overt opposition, the silent system became the established rule of the prison.

" In the outset, it was effected by the employment of monitors, selected by their conduct and intelligence from amongst the prisoners. That practice is now prohibited by law, and the interdiction is undoubtedly both just and politic.

" In short, all (except the irreclaimably debased) who had watched and deplored the system, now happily superseded, saw cause to rejoice in the change. There was at length a real protection to morals, and it no longer became the reproach that the comparatively innocent should be consigned to inevitable demoralization and ruin."

Another important change in the discipline in this prison occurred in the introduction of the tread-wheel, though this took place several years prior to the introduction of the silent system. This apparatus, we have before said (p. 174), was first set up in Brixton prison in 1817; and Mr. Chesterton cites the following curious anecdote as to the origin of the contrivance itself:—

" It was the invention of Mr. Cubitt, the engineer of Lowestoft, in Suffolk, a gentleman of science, of extensive professional connections, and of gentle and pleasing deportment. The notion of such a piece of machinery owed its conception in his mind to a singular casualty. I received the following narration from his own lips :—

" All who may be acquainted with the county jail of Suffolk, at Bury St. Edmonds, or rather as it was twenty years and upwards ago, must be aware of the unsightly feature then existing (after passing through the main entrance), of mere open iron fences separating yards occupied by prisoners from the passage trodden by incoming visitors. The inmates, in repulsive groups, were seen lounging idly about, and the whole aspect indicated a demoralizing waste of strength and time.

" Under such dispositions, and some years before Mr. Cubitt's relation to me, that gentleman was in professional communication with the magistrates at the jail of Bury, and there he and a magistrate, the one going out, and the other entering, met in the described passage, from which, as they stood to converse, the prisoners, as usual, were seen idly loitering about.

" ' I wish to God, Mr. Cubitt,' said the justice, ' you could suggest to us some mode of employing those fellows ! Could nothing like a wheel become available ?' An instantaneous idea flashed through the mind of Mr. Cubitt, who whispered to himself, ' the wheel elongated!' and merely saying to his interrogator—' Something has struck me which may prove worthy of further consideration, and perhaps you may hear from me upon the subject,' he took his leave.

" After reflection enabled Mr. Cubitt to fashion all the mechanical requirements into a practical form ; and by such a casual incident did the tread-wheel start into existence, and soon came into general adoption in the prisons of the country as the type of hard labour."

At first, the labour on the tread-wheel was excessive. In utter ignorance of the mischief which such an excess of exertion produced, the authorities at Coldbath Fields apportioned to each male individual 12,000 feet of ascent upon it per diem. That ratio, we are told, proved seriously injurious to health, especially under the circumstances of a diet restricted to the minimum of what was deemed adequate requirement.

" The most robust frames," adds the prison historian, " would become attenuated by it; and a prolonged indulgence in a daily allowance of beer, increased diet, and, in many instances, other prescribed stimulants, hardly sufficed to arrest the mischief. So debilitating were the results of the undue amount of such dispiriting labour, that (before the erection of military prisons) the Royal Artillery abstained from committing their offending men to Coldbath Fields, owing to the injurious effects observable, on their return to their regiment, from the mischievous excess of tread-wheel occupation."

The present amount of ascent is limited to 1,200 feet per diem.

¶ i.—β.

Interior of the Prison.

As the hour advanced at which the gates were to be opened, the warders began to assemble. We could see them hurrying down the streets on all sides, and soon the road in front of the jail was filled with a crowd of men in dark-blue uniform, each with a belt of shining leather over one shoulder, supporting, just above the hip, a pouch, something similar to a soldier's cartouche-box, on which was the brass number that distinguished the official. Some of these warders had fastened on to their stand-up collars, in the same place where a policeman's number is placed, a gilt metal plate, and others a silver one, on which were stamped the Middlesex Arms of the three sabres, this being the distinguishing mark between the warders and the sub-warders.

Many of the men seemed but half awake. They leant against the railings, some smoking, others chatting, until, at twenty-five minutes past six, the sudden report of a gun was heard, making the silent air ring again, and causing a peacock in the vicinity to begin screaming. Instantly down were dashed the pipes of the warders, and up jumped the men, hurrying along the carriage-way to the gates, which now opened to receive them.

We entered a stone-paved yard, on one side of which stood the gate-warder's lodge, and on the other stretched out a gravelled court. A canopy of glass, like the roof of a greenhouse, was suspended in the air like an awning, and covered in the path leading to an iron double gate, which lay some twenty feet off in front; the little yard was hemmed round with thick railings and massive gates, through which we could distinguish the governor's house and the protruding sides of the main prison itself, with its small heavily-barred windows. The detached clump of buildings between us and the main prison seemed more like a private residence than part of a prison; and on inquiry it was explained to us, that the erection was that in which the clerk's and governor's offices, the visiting magistrates' committee-rooms, as well as the armoury and the record office, were situated.

The gate-warder stood by with the bright key inserted in the lock, as the officers entered, ready to turn the bolt at the first order.

We were not long before we made the acquaintance of the deputy-governor, who, in full uniform, with a crimson shield and gold sabre on his collar, and gold band round his cap, came out to review the warders before they began the duties of the day.

"Half-past six," said that gentleman to us, pointing to the time-piece, large as a target, over the double-grating, "is the time to close the gates, but we do not shut them until three minutes past the half-hour, to give the men a little time in case the clocks outside should differ from our own."

At two minutes past the half-hour the men came hurrying through the gates, for there is a fine attached to being late on duty.*

The gate-warder's office was a room full of wainscotted cupboards, and with heavy ledgers in a rack over the desk on one side; and as we stood here looking at a long row of pigeon-holes, alphabetically arranged, with a few letters in them, the warder told us that the letters had been sent by the prisoners' friends, but that as only one epistle was allowed in three months, those we saw had been kept back until the permitted period arrived. There were barely a dozen such epistles.

When the order to close the gates had been given, the warders fell into three lines, as if for a review. As some of them carried umbrellas, and others bundles, the spectacle had not a very military appearance.

---

* For every five minutes that an officer is behind time, he is fined 6*d.*, until the sum of 2*s.* 6*d.* has been forfeited.

"Attention!" cried the deputy-governor, and then the warders became stiff and erect. The superior officer passed down the first line, and examined their dress, observing whether their boots and clothing were cleanly and in proper order, and then giving the command of "Two steps forward—march!" he walked down the alley thus formed between the first and second rows, and inspected the second file.

This examination over, the double iron-gratings were unlocked, and passing through the passage in the centre clump of buildings, we entered the flag-stoned yard facing the main or felons' prison.

There was no doubt now as to the nature of the edifice before us. The squat front of the whitewashed two-storeyed building was so devoid of any attempt at ornament, that even the small windows with the heavy black gratings before them seemed reliefs to its monotonous aspect. A few stone steps led to a low wicket with a row of spikes on its thick swing-door, the spikes being so arranged that they reached within two inches of the thick cross-bars fixed in the circular fan-light over it.

An officer, with a pale, tired face and disordered hair, and who, armed with a cutlass, had been watching through the night, here met the deputy-governor. "All right," reported the man, and moved on.

A gang of prisoners, dressed in their suit of dusty gray, now issued from the main building and crossed the yard, with a warder following them. On the back of each criminal was a square canvas tablet stitched to the jacket, and on the bosom was a long badge worn something like that of a cabman. Each of the wretched men, as he descended the stone steps, and caught sight of the deputy-governor, held up his hand to his worsted cap and gave a half military salute.

"They are vagrants and reputed thieves," explained the officer; "but for want of room in the vagrants' ward they have been sleeping in the felons' cells. We are now waiting," continued the officer, "until the different cells are unlocked, and then it is my duty to make the rounds and count the prisoners."

₊ *The Interior of the "Main" Prison and Counting the Prisoners.*—All confined within the main prison have, as we have said, been convicted as felons. Ascending the stone steps we passed down a few paces of passage, when a second wicket, similar to the first, was unlocked to admit us. We now stood in a kind of hall about forty feet square, in the centre of which were four stout iron pillars, "to support," as we were told, "the chapel above." This vestibule was so bright with whitewash, that the light reflected was almost painful to the eyes. On the walls were large paper placards printed in bold type, with religious texts. One was as follows:—"CONSIDER YOUR WAYS, FOR YE SHALL ALL STAND BEFORE THE JUDGMENT SEAT OF CHRIST." Another ran—"SWEAR NOT AT ALL," which, in a prison conducted on the silent system, struck us as being somewhat out of place. Whilst a third contained the curiously inappropriate quotation—"BEHOLD HOW GOOD AND HOW PLEASANT IT IS FOR BRETHREN TO DWELL TOGETHER IN UNITY." At each corner of this hall there was a gate of thick iron bars leading to the prisoners' cells.

Before us lay a long corridor, down which ran a double row of thick columns, supporting a groined roof. These pillars were stout and dumpy, being more than two feet in diameter, and measuring scarcely six feet from the ground to the overhanging capital whence the arches spring. Yet, although the width of the centre passage was but a few feet, still, from the corridor being nearly one hundred feet in length, the effect was picturesque and agreeable, owing to the pleasing perspective of the columns.

This main building contains eight yards, each one holding from a hundred to a hundred and fifteen prisoners, all felons. The deputy-governor, unlocking one of the strong iron gates in the corner, led us into what is called the first yard. It was an oblong open space, about the size of a racket-ground, lying parallel with the outer wall, or front, of the building, and at right angles with the passage. On one side was what appeared two low wooden sheds built one above the other, and each with long glazed lights running the entire length of the buildings; the under one being the meal-room, and the upper a spare dormitory, at present out of use. As in the other portions of the building we had passed through, here the walls and wood-work were scrupulously clean and fresh with whitewash and paint. Facing these sheds was a row of doors leading, as we found, to the sleeping cells. The doors, with the black bolts drawn back, and the cross-bars slanting upwards, were half opened, showing the inmates had left the cells. Over each door was a massive half-circular grating let into the stone wall, and by means of which the light entered when the men were locked up for the night; whilst at the further end, ranged on one side of the doorway leading to the galleries above, were six slate washing-stands for the use of the prisoners.

Those of the prisoners who slept in the dormitories and cells, in the upper part of the prison, were entering by the last-mentioned door, in a long file, each carrying a wooden tub, which, as he passed a sink in the centre of the yard, he emptied, and then added the vessel to a pile that kept rapidly increasing in height as one after another went by. Then, still continuing in line, the prisoners entered the wooden shed. These men carried also a bundle composed of a towel, a comb, and Bible, Prayer, and reading book. Soon the under shed was filled with the culprits; whereupon the officers mounting on their tall stools, so situated that from them they could overlook the crowd, kept a strict watch that none of them conversed together.

The place, as we entered, was silent as a deserted building. The long rows of wretched men in their dusky pauper gray suits, without one particle of white to relieve the monotony of their prison costume, looked like so many rats in a cage. Their faces seemed pale and careworn, and they turned their eyes towards us with a half idiotic expression, in which there was neither surprise at seeing a stranger amongst them at so early an hour, nor even shame at being seen by a visitor in their degraded position. Amongst the prisoners we noticed one, a lad not more than fifteen years old, and three or four old men, who all seemed equally out of place in such an assembly—the one from his youth, the others from their age. A few of the men were already reading, and never raised their eyes.

The deputy-governor having counted the prisoners, called out the number, and the sub-warders having answered "Right," an entry was made in a book, and the felon's morning toilet commenced. The men took off their coats and opened their blue shirts. Directly the sombre gray clothes were removed, it was strange how altered the appearance of the prisoners became. The colour of the flesh gave them once more a human look.

Twelve at a time they rose and entered the yard. Then, some at the slate lavatories, others at tubs placed on the paved ground, began to soap their neck and faces, and rub them with their wet hands until they were white with the lather. But a few minutes were allowed to each gang, and at the expiration of the time they returned to the shed, there to adjust their shirts, comb their hair, and put on their jackets.

Whilst these operations were going on the iron-barred door of the yard opened, and a prisoner, bearing a tin can entered, accompanied by the infirmary warder. This can contained poultices, and the man called out aloud, " Any want dressings ?" A lad, with sores in his neck, had a soda-water bottle given to him, filled with a gray-coloured wash, and he entered a cell to apply the medicine.

Before leaving the yard the deputy-governor went to a tell-tale clock (similar in construction to those seen at Pentonville, and which, we were assured, were the invention of Mr. Fillary, the engineer to this prison), to see if the night warder had regularly marked the half-hours, and so discover whether he had attended to his duties.

In all the yards that we visited the same counting and cleansing processes were being gone through.

In one of the yards we noticed a negro, a tall, bony fellow, with blood-shot eyes ; in another, an old man of eighty, with hair as white as the prison walls themselves, and which was especially striking from the generality of the prisoners being mere youths. He no sooner saw us enter, than hastily putting on his spectacles, he commenced reading, bending his face down as if to hide it in shame. The deputy-governor told us that he had given a false name, but that it was known he once held a high command in the army. He was there for a nameless offence.

The counting ended, our guide returned to the jail office to consult the locking-up slate, upon which had been marked the number of prisoners within the walls when the doors were fastened the night before. The amount agreeing with the morning's examination, a paper form was filled up to await the governor's signature.

₊ *The Prisoners' Own-Clothes Store.*—As we had a few moments to spare, it was proposed to visit the loft where the clothes, taken from the prisoners on their arrival at the jail, were stowed away.

"Mind you do not knock your head," said the officer, warning us that a beam, as thick as a mast, stuck out in the narrow staircase leading up to the felons' wardrobe. No sooner had we entered the loft, than the disagreeable, gluey odour which attaches itself to moleskin and corduroy, informed us of the materials of which most of the suits were composed.

The first sight of the dirty bundles, piled on the shelves, reminded us of Rag Fair, where the itinerant flower and crockery vendors expose for sale the results of their day's barterings. Each bundle, tied up as tightly as a boiling pudding, had a wooden label, so as to indicate to whom the ragged contents belonged. Here were a pair of trousers, with the linings dirtier than the once black cloth from which they were made. There a stuff waistcoat, made of stuff that was slowly unravelling itself with wear, and becoming as thready and fibrous as the very oakum its owner would have that day to pick.

"That's a countryman's bundle, I should say," said the officer, pointing to a pair of heavily nailed and ironed boots, the iron of which had become red with rust, from being so long unworn.

Some of the hats were "shockingly bad" ones, being as limp as night-caps, and as rusty as if made from cocoa-nut fibre. Others were carefully tied up in handkerchiefs, and some of these had clean showy linings, and a greasy gloss. Our guide told us that occasionally they had some very dandy suits to pack up, taken from the swell-mobsmen, whose fashionable attire often included jewellery.

Smock-frocks and straw hats denoted culprits from the agricultural districts, corduroy waistcoats, with brass buttons, were evidently some costermonger's property. Soldiers' uniforms, with the coarse canvas linings and big brass hooks and eyes showing, were rather plentiful. "Have you remarked," asked our companion, "that nearly all the pocket-handkerchiefs have a red pattern?" And so it was, with so few exceptions, that red may assuredly be written down as the felon's favourite colour.

Before this clothing is stored away, each suit is well fumigated with sulphur, to destroy any vermin that it may contain. At a later period of the day we had an opportunity of witnessing this process. In a large oven, with a fire burning beneath it, the suits, wrapped tightly in a roll, are placed on bars, one above another. The oven will contain 150 suits. A pan, filled with brimstone, is lighted and placed in this chamber, and the doors being closed, the temperature is carefully watched, that the heat should not exceed 212°, for fear that the bakings should be literally done to rags, or burnt to a cinder. The garments retain, on coming out, rather a powerful smell of lucifer matches, but, when compared with their previous odour, the change is not disagreeable.

FUMIGATING PRISONERS' CLOTHES AT COLDBATH FIELDS PRISON.

₊ *Liberation of Prisoners.*—The House of Correction being what may be called a short-term prison, men are discharged from confinement nearly every day; indeed, the usual number of discharges for the week amounts to about 150 prisoners.

We were informed that a gang of twenty prisoners would that morning quit the jail, and asked if we should like to witness their departure. Following the deputy-governor, we hastened to the spot where the men were ranged.

The deputy-governor, looking at a paper which he held in his hand, said to the gang, "Now, my men, stand forward, one at a time, and call out your names." "W——— B———," instantly cried out one of them, quitting the rank. "Go on," was the command then given. "J——— T———," shouted another. "Move on," was the rejoinder; and in this way the whole twenty passed their final examination.

The utter absence of anything like joy or excitement on the part of the men, at the prospect of their approaching liberation, was most remarkable. They stood staring stupidly about them, and answered calmly, precisely in the same manner as, a day or two since, they had replied to any question put to them by the warders.

Whilst the liberation list was being checked in the office, the men exchanged the prison uniform for their own clothes. By the time the papers were prepared, the wretched creatures were also ready. Then the governor himself went up to them, and after kindly congratulating them upon regaining their freedom, added, "Now that you are going to have your liberty, I hope I shall not see you again. Seek the kingdom of God and his righteousness, and, depend upon it, you will prosper."

The men once habited in their own clothes, ragged as they were, had a more human look about them, than when, a quarter of an hour since, they wore the prison gray.

Now began the begging scene, which, we were told, always precedes the departure of prisoners from the jail.

One—a tall fellow, with his bare feet showing through the holes in his burst and mouldy high-lows—begged for an old pair of prison shoes. "Got a long way to go," pleaded the man. "Where are you going?" asked the governor. "To Edmonton, sir; I'm a brick-layer, and got a wife and family," was the answer. "A bad way to help them, coming here," remonstrated the governor, as he gave the necessary order to the storekeeper.

Another man, whose clothes, full of slits and holes, held together in so marvellous a manner that they seemed like a dirty ragged mass of cobwebs, such as are seen in wine-merchants' windows clinging to bottles of "fine old crusted port," had also got a long way to go, and begged for a pair of socks and a trifle of money. He, too, obtained what he wanted.

Another and another came up in his turn, and asked to be assisted. "It was curious," as the governor shrewdly remarked, "the long journeys they all had to perform."

We were standing at the big gate, to enjoy the sight of the men regaining their liberty, when somebody knocked, and, on the warder opening the door, a respectably-dressed person inquired if a man of the name of P——— would not be discharged that day?

"Are you from the parish?" asked the warder; and, from the subsequent conversation, we learnt that during the husband's imprisonment (he had had seven days for drunkenness), his wife and child had been thrown on the parish, and the authorities were now anxious to comply with the forms of law, and hand her back to the husband. Accordingly, when P——— left the jail, the parish officer stepped up to him, and gave him a young girl with an infant in her arms. P——— quietly said, "All right!" and walked off, leaving the woman to follow.

Another such case followed, but with this one there were three little children, whom the parish, having brought down in a cab, handed back to the father the moment he crossed the prison threshold.

We had expected to see, among the crowd gathered about the outer railings, a vast num-ber of the friends of the liberated, and to witness their joy at seeing the long-absent one restored to them. But we were doomed to be disappointed. The "pals" of one or two had certainly come to meet them; but the welcome was given in a calm, unconcerned, nay, almost business-like, manner. Others walked off from the crowd, with women following them, never even looking back at the females at their heels. One youth, a tall strip of a lad, in a Holland coat that fluttered about his pole of a body, had scarcely shown his face at the gate, before a voice in the crowd shouted out—"Now, Jim, can't you come on!" and we saw a thick-chinned man, with a tall, narrow-brimmed hat, motioning angrily to the late prisoner to make haste.

₊ *Arrival of Prisoners.*—When the prison-van is seen driving in the direction of the House of Correction, a crowd begins to form outside, in the hope of catching a glimpse of the prisoners alighting. Butchers with joints "wanted in a hurry," fishmongers' lads with fish "to be sent round directly," nursery-maids with perambulators, coster-women with their shallow baskets—all push for a good place at the railings to have a peep at the sight. On the day that we were at the prison, the spectators on the pavement were doomed to be disappointed, for the big outer gates were opened, and the huge hearse-like omnibus was driven into the yard, the horses sputtering about as they tugged at the heavy vehicle.

"As full as we can cram!" said the conductor, getting down from his small hall-chair-like seat, outside the extreme end of the vehicle. When he unlocked the door, sure enough, even the passage between the two rows of closet-fashioned cells, ranged along the inside of the carriage, was filled with men standing there; they were all felons from Newgate, where the sessions had just terminated.

One by one the men stept out, with a half bound, as if glad to have ended their cramped ride. They stared about them for a second, to see what kind of place they had arrived at, and then, obeying the warder's commanding voice, they passed the double iron gate, where the visits take place, and entered the inner court. There they stood with their backs turned to the main prison, waiting for their names to be called over, and their sentences and offences entered in the prison books.

There were nineteen of them altogether, all of them with unshorn beards, dirty linen, tumbled clothes, and presenting the appearance of having been up all night. One was in a soldier's uniform; another was a respectable-looking man, of stout build and tall stature, and with silver spectacles, who, despite the dullness of his boots and the dusty condition of his clothes, might be styled the gentleman of the gang. Another, a youth, with eyes and skin as dark as a Spaniard's, whose delicate moustache, loose paletôt, and sporting trousers, were after the casino style of fashion, ranked next in gentility of appearance. A lad with a peculiarly-shaped conical head, and who kept nervously buttoning and unbuttoning his surtout, was the next who had anything singular in his look, for all the others had more or less of the thieves' character about them, and wore bright-coloured handkerchiefs loosely tied round their neck, or had rows of brass buttons down their corduroy jackets, and boots made to lace up in front. One was lame and used a crutch, another carried a paper parcel, another a bundle tied up in a handkerchief, whilst the bulgy condition of some of the coat pockets showed that the scanty wardrobe had been stuffed into them.

Whilst the new-comers were thus standing, a file of prisoners, in their prison suits, passed through the yard. Each of the men, in dingy gray, looked hard at those in their "liberty" suits, and the newly-arrived, in their turn, stared curiously at their future companions on the tread-wheel.

Presently the voice of the chief warder was heard ordering the first man to enter the office, where the clerk was to make the necessary entries. The tall, stout man, with the silver spectacles, walked up to the desk, and the examinations commenced in a business-like manner, the questions and answers being equally short.

"Name?" asked the chief warder. "J—— C——," answered the prisoner. "Age?" continued the officer. "Thirty-nine," replied the man. And then the following questions and responses followed in quick succession:—"Read and write?" "Yes." "Ever here before?" "Oh, no!" "Trade?" "Clerk." "What were you tried for?" "Embezzlement." "That will do, you can go back," said the officer; and then turning to the entering clerk, he added, "with hard labour." As the prisoner heard this addition, he stopped at the door and remarked, "I thought it was without labour;" but the officer dispelled his hopes by repeating, "with hard labour."

All the prisoners had to answer to similar questions, all equally short, but often the replies were long, and a kind of cross-examination was required before a decisive answer could be elicited.

A nattily dressed lad, who had a groom's look about him, said that he had been committed "on suspicion." "That won't do," exclaimed the officer, "try and remember." "That's what it was, sir," the man maintained. "Didn't you steal some tools?" "Yes, sir, but ——" "There, no 'buts' about it," answered the chief warder, who directed the clerk to write down "stealing tools."

We felt sorry for one of the lads, a modest, well-spoken boy, who kept his eyes on the ground, and replied in a low voice, as if ashamed. He gave the name of "Smith," and, as the officer remarked when the youth had left the office, "it was evidently not his proper name;" and then he added, knowingly, "All 'Smiths' are doubtful."

One youth, with closely cut hair, and protruding ears, when asked whether he had ever been in prison before, without the least hesitation replied, "Never, s'elp me!" "I know better, replied the warder, looking earnestly at him. "I'm sure I haven't," continued the lad, with an innocent expression of face. "We'll see whether some of the officers will recognize you," said the examiner. "But it wasn't for felony, sir," muttered the lad, who plainly saw that further concealment was of no avail.

The lame man with the crutch was there for highway robbery. A cripple footpad seemed strange enough. "What did you steal?" asked the warder. "Three pound, I think, *she* said I took off her," was the reply that explained the mystery of his success. This fellow was nervous when he gave his replies, so that when asked, "What religion?" he answered, "Carpenter."

The soldier, and two others, were sent to prison for stealing a watch in a skittle-alley. He forgot his age, and made himself a year older than when at Newgate. A man in a brown Holland smock had stolen a sheep, and the one with the conical head had purloined photographic lenses. This boy answered so sharply to the questions, that when he had gone all the clerks exclaimed that they had never seen anybody "so cool." The youth with the dark Spanish complexion had been indicted, together with his brothers, for perjury.

When the examinations were finished, the governor came to look over the list, and then addressing the wretched band, he said, "Now, my men, we shall be some time together, and I hope you will attend to the rules of the prison. You'll find it more comfortable to yourselves to obey the officers!" And, the harangue concluded, a warder led the poor wretches off to the dressing-room, where, after bathing, they would have to exchange the clothes they wore for the prison costume.

₊ *Visits of Prisoners' Friends.*—Presently we had an opportunity of being present during the visits paid to the prisoners by their friends. "Two relations or respectable friends," say the prison rules, "may visit a prisoner, in the presence of an officer, at the end of every three months, between the hours of ten and twelve."

All prisoners, on entering Coldbath Fields, cease to be called by their names, but are christened with a number instead. When a relation or friend calls at the jail on the day appointed for visiting, the criminal is asked for by the number he bears. The officer, to find out which is the man's yard, goes to a huge tablet, almost as large as the top of a kitchen table, and this is a kind of ledger or stock-book of the men in custody. It is ingeniously contrived in this manner:—The numbers from 1 to 1,500 are engraved on the zinc plate forming the tablet, and against each number is a small moveable slip of brass, as big as a key-label, on which is marked the yard and prison in which the man who has received that number is located. For instance, against No. 1,230, was a moveable label with 2 V 60 stamped on it; this meant that the culprit stood 60th in the 2nd yard of the vagrant prison; whilst No. 1,231 had marked on the brass label 5 F 24, implying that this man was the 24th prisoner in the 5th yard of the felon prison.

There are two arrangements in Coldbath Fields by which the prisoners are permitted to see their friends. The one is at the double gate before the building, situate between the entrance doors and the main prison, and the other is at a place built for the purpose in the first yard of the vagrant jail. At the latter a series of niches have been built in the side wall, each one just large enough for a man to enter. Through gratings the prisoners can converse with their visitors, who stand in almost similar niches, separated by a long passage, where a warder patrols. The gratings before the visitors are almost as close as net-work, in order to prevent anything being passed to the inmates of the jail. Only fifteen minutes are permitted for each interview, and, for the correct measurement of the length of the visit, hour-glasses are fastened up over the niches appropriated to the prisoners' friends, as shown in the annexed engraving. The moment the friends and the prisoner enter, this time-keeper

COMPARTMENT ON THE SIDE FOR VISITORS.　　　COMPARTMENT ON THE SIDE FOR PRISONERS.

FRIENDS VISITING PRISONERS.

is turned, and as soon as the sand has run down, all conversation must cease and the strangers depart. An officer keeps watch the while by patroling, as we said, up and down the passage.

A man in the felon's gray was, at the time of our inspecting this part of the prison, chatting with his wife and daughter, both of whom were respectably dressed, with gold brooches to fasten their shawls, and other evidences of being well-to-do in the world. This man, together with his son, was in prison for abduction; a young lady of property having been carried off by the father, and forcibly married to the youth.

" Be sure and let Alfred and Arthur go to school and learn spelling—that's most essential," said the husband to his wife, who, by this time, seemed quite resigned to the family " misfortune."

" Frank's at work in a good situation," answered the woman. And so they continued chatting over the family matters for the permitted quarter of an hour, all of them evidently much calmed and comforted by the meeting.

The other prisoner was one belonging to the poorer class. His wife wore an old straw bonnet that had turned brown as pie-crust with wear, and she frequently raised to her eyes a pocket-handkerchief rolled up as small as an orange, with which she dabbed up her tears.

" Good-bye, love !" said the man, when his time was up; " good-bye, dear, and get some stuff for your rheumatiz."

The handkerchief went up to the poor creature's red eyes as she muttered her good-bye.

She stopped to see him look round once more as he entered the small wicket-gate of the prison, and then turned round and crept off homewards.

In the afternoon we witnessed a scene of a more painful and less frequent occurrence than that of visiting. A poor lady came to inquire after her boy, and to entreat the governor not to permit him to leave the prison until she herself came to fetch him, lest his evil companions should once more entice him into wickedness.

Her dress and manner were those of a wealthy and educated person. Her features were distorted with grief, which every now and then, as she looked up at the small grated windows in the prison walls, seized her suddenly, like a fit. When she began to speak, her throat swelled and choked the words, whilst her arms trembled till her loosely-hanging bracelets clinked with the motion.

From the careless manner in which her shawl and bonnet were put on, she had evidently come out in a hurry. We could not help imagining to ourselves that perhaps the father had sworn that the boy, who had disgraced his family, should never enter his house again, and forbidden the mother from visiting him, so that the poor, kind soul had to creep out on the sly whenever she wished to make inquiries after her erring child.

"I am his mother," sobbed the lady, when the governor had come to her; "I am his mother, I am sorry to say."

"He will be liberated next Tuesday morning at half-past nine," said Captain Colville; "but I will manage to detain him here until the others have left."

"Has anybody been to see him, sir?" asked the mother, with evident anxiety.

The answer of "Two of his companions have been here," seemed to cut her to the heart.

"I'll be here by ten, sir," she added after a time, "and pray don't let him go before that time. I know he will let me take him, if there is no one to tempt him away."

The governor, who was evidently much interested in the case, accompanied the poor lady to the gate, and by his gentleness of manner, more than by his words, showed his sympathy for her sufferings. When he closed the prison-door, he drew in his breath as if he felt the relief of having accomplished the most distressing of all his duties.

This lad, we learnt, was of highly respectable parents, and had fallen into evil ways through the temptations held out to him by the companions he had met with.

₊ *Prisoners' Letters.*—All letters sent by the prisoners to their friends are opened by the governor before they leave the jail, to see that they contain nothing but matters relating to the family or personal business of the writer.* Some of the men, knowing that their epistles are sure to be perused by the governor, endeavour, as is usual at other prisons, to win his good opinion, by giving to their compositions a religious and repentant air, in the hope of easing their labours and bettering their position. For instance, one man whom

---

* Every letter sent by a prisoner to his friends has the following printed heading :—

From No.* _____   House of Correction,
Admitted on the _____   Cold Bath Fields.
and who will be discharged (probably at 9 A.M.) on
the_____   _____185

This No. to be written on letters directed to the prisoner, and to be stated when making inquiries about him.

Prisoners are not permitted to send or to receive more than one letter in every three months, but events of importance to prisoners may be communicated by letter (prepaid) to the GOVERNOR. Letters to or from prisoners are read before delivery; they should not exceed a sheet of letter paper, legibly written, and not crossed. They must contain nothing improper, and no detailed news of the day. Two relations or respectable friends may visit a prisoner, in the presence of an officer, at the end of every three months, between the hours of ten and twelve (Sundays excepted). The visit lasts a quarter of an hour.

These privileges may be forfeited by misconduct.

No clothes, books, or other articles, are admitted for the use of prisoners—except postage stamps or money.

we saw in the prison had been a cab driver; we had an opportunity of listening to a conversation between him and the chief authority. He had a fawning manner of obsequious respect that at first made us fancy he was some felonious footman. When we learnt his former occupation, his mode of speaking seemed such as "cabbies" are wont to use to a generous fare; but there was nothing, either in his bearing or talk, calculated to impress us with the notion that he repented his transgression and was seeking the right path. From a letter written by this man we extract the following passages :—

"Send me word what Richard is doing, and whethear Farthear sends him to school, for i hope they do not let him Run the streets, for there is no good to be found there. * * * * This is a finishing school for me for i hope this will be a good warning to me for the future please God spare me to come home again i shall be a altard man please God i can get some employment and have my Sunday to myself, please God i hope i shall never neglect my going to church for i am sorry to say that as been a great folly on my part."

     *   *   *   *   *   *

Another epistle contained the following piece of poetry :—

<blockquote>
"Aunt cousins and friends for a short time adieu
Once more I bid adieu to all of you
I will own liberty is a jewl
While I myself *have* been a fool
My tale myself I will unfold
I think you will say in sin I am old
</blockquote>

     *   *   *   *   *   *

<blockquote>
O that I ad the wings of a dove
I would begone with liberty and the birds above."
</blockquote>

A third letter, evidently from an old offender, contained a confession of repentance which seemed to be in a measure true, the reasons assigned for it being sufficient and convincing, though hardly to be received as signs of an inward change of character :—

"I assure you for the four months which I am sentenced to at this prison is a deal more severe than it was at holloway for I had to work no treadwell there, which I find is the hardest thing that I have to do, it has I can assure you learnt me a lesson I never shall forget, and will never again do anything that is likely to get me here again."

¶ i.—γ.

Of " Hard" and " Prison Labour."

At the correctional prisons, labour, especially of the kind called "*hard*," forms part of the punishment to which the prisoners are condemned. Out of the 7,743 persons passing through Coldbath Fields in the course of last year, 4,511, or rather more than 58 per cent., were, according to the official returns, employed at "hard labour;" and the remaining 3,232, or not quite 42 per cent., at work *not* being hard labour. We have already given our opinion as to the folly of endeavouring to reform a habit of idleness by making industry a penal infliction, and it now only remains for us to show the nature of the different kinds of labour to which prisoners are subject, when condemned to the *hard* form of it.

Men sentenced to hard labour at Coldbath Fields are employed at :—

Tread-wheel work.	Picking Oakum (3½ lbs. daily).	Cleaning.
Crank Work.	Mat Making.	Tailoring.
Shot Drill.	Washing.	Shoemaking.

There are likewise other handicrafts, to which the men are put after they have been in the prison for some time, provided their behaviour has been good.*

The first three of the above forms of hard labour come under the denomination of useless or profitless work—being work for mere work's sake, applied to no earthly purpose or object whatever—the very worst form of idleness, viz., idleness with all the physical fatigue of industry, without any of industry's rewards; and it is with these forms of work more especially that we intend dealing here. We wish it, however, to be distinctly understood, that in the remarks it will be our duty to make upon this form of "correctional" discipline, it is far from being our intention to impute the least blame to the authorities of Coldbath Fields prison. It is the *system* of useless labour generally that appears to us objectionable, and not the mode in which that system is carried out by the officials at any *one* prison; for the subjoined strictures are as applicable to *all* correctional prisons (with the exception of the Westminster House of Correction) as they are to Coldbath Fields, where we are happy to acknowledge that the labour-punishment is enforced by the governor with every regard to his duty at once to the public and the prisoners.

We are well aware of the difficulty with which the subject of prison labour in general, and that of houses of correction in particular, is beset; and we do not hesitate to allow that it would be wrong and unbecoming in the prison authorities to permit prisoners to pass their time louting about in idleness, as was the case previous to the invention of the tread-wheel. We are well aware, too, that in a "short-term prison," where some of the men are confined for only a few days, it is almost futile to attempt to make labour profitable, owing to the impossibility of teaching the majority of the prisoners any handicraft in so short a space of time.

We are well aware, moreover, how difficult it is to give any pecuniary value to mere physical exertion, especially in towns where field or garden work, on account of the great value and scarcity of land, cannot be adopted on any large scale; nevertheless, if it come to a choice of two evils, we boldly confess we prefer idleness itself to making industry *idle* (because useless), and, therefore, hateful in every prisoner's eyes. Besides, what *necessity* is there for correctional prisons being situate in towns, where they are as much out of place as churchyards, and where prisoners *must* be put to "grind the wind" simply because they cannot be put to till the land.

The late governor of Millbank prison (and he is a gentleman whose prison experience extends over nearly a quarter of a century), speaking of prison labour, told us that "it is a *great* thing to make a prisoner feel that he is employed on some *useful* work. Nothing

---

* The following is the list of the offences which are usually punished with hard labour:—

Abduction.
Assaults, unnatural.
Assaults on women and children, with intent.
Assaults on police constables.
Attempt at burglary.
Bestiality.
Concealing birth of child.
Conspiracies to defraud.
Cruelty to animals (either with or without hard labour).
Cutting and maiming.
Dog stealing.
Disorderly apprentices (either with or without hard labour).
Excise offences (either with or without hard labour).
Embezzlement.
Felonies.
False characters.
Frauds, tried at Sessions.

Frauds, summarily disposed of (either with or without hard labour).
Furious driving, insolence to fares, &c. (either with or without hard labour).
Illegally pawning (either with or without hard labour).
Keeping brothels.
Keeping gaming-house (either with or without hard labour).
Misdemeanours, contempt of court (either with or without hard labour).
Misbehaviour in workhouse.
Riots and assaults (either with or without hard labour).
Receiving embezzled property.
Selling or exposing obscene prints.
Simple larceny.

Stealing fruit, &c.
Threats to deter workmen.
Trespassing, fishing, poaching, &c.
Possession of base coin.
Unlawful possession of property (with or without hard labour).
Unlawful collection of dust.
Wilful and corrupt perjury.
Wilful damage (with or without hard labour).
Begging or sleeping in open air.
Disorderly prostitutes.
Fortune-telling.
Gaming.
Indecent exposure of person.
Incorrigible rogues.
Leaving families chargeable.
Obtaining by false pretences.
Reputed thieves and suspected rogues.

LARGE OAKUM-ROOM (UNDER THE SILENT SYSTEM) AT THE MIDDLESEX HOUSE OF CORRECTION, COLDBATH FIELDS.

disgusts a man and makes him so querulous, as to let him know that he is labouring and yet doing nothing—as when at the tread-wheel. I am of opinion," he said, "that to employ men on work which they know and see is useful, has the best possible effect upon their characters, and much increases their chances of reformation. Every other kind of labour irritates and hardens them. After twenty thousand prisoners have passed through one's hands, one *must have had* some little experience on such matters. There was a tread-wheel on the premises here for the use of 'penal' or 'second-probation men,' and those only; but its use has been discontinued for some months;" and principally, we should add, owing to this gentleman's remonstrances.

Every man's own experience, indeed, can tell him how irksome it is to see the work he has done prove of no avail.

All human beings, we are bold to confess, even the most honest and industrious, have a natural aversion to labour; indeed, Scripture tells us that the necessity for it as a means of mere existence was made a *curse*—"In the sweat of thy face shalt thou eat bread." If labour were naturally pleasant, men would pay wages to be allowed to work, instead of giving money to others to work for them. There are many instances, however, where physical exertion *is* agreeable, and *then* we do not hesitate to part with a considerable sum of money to be permitted to indulge in it, as in dancing, rowing, cricketing, and other muscular exercises, which, because they are pleasing to mankind in general, have been called "*amusements*" and "*sports*."

It is, therefore, in almost every case, the object or utility of the labour which makes it agreeable to us. Some doubt whether the mere labourer takes any delight in his work, though we fancy that even the bricklayer's hodman would be annoyed at having the bricks thrown down from the scaffold as fast as he carried them up. But men generally work, not for any delight they feel in the work, but simply to obtain food, to educate their children, to provide shelter for their family, and to supply the various necessities and luxuries of life. In but a very few instances is work done for mere work's sake, as in gardening, amateur carpentering, turning, literature, painting, &c., &c.; but even in these cases, men undertake the task, not so much for the sake of the labour as from a delight in its products as works of art or utility, and from the pleasure and pride they feel in being able to create such things. None but children ever build up walls for the mere pleasure of knocking them down again, and there is hardly any form of punishment so irritating as being condemned to work hard at doing something which leads to nothing. Hence, we cannot but regard tread-wheels, which are intended to grind nothing, and to do nothing; and cranks, which are made to scoop up sand and pitch it down again; and shot-drill, which consists in transferring cannon-balls from one place to another, for no earthly use whatever—but as inventions based upon the same barbarous principle as that which instituted the tortures of the Inquisition, rather than as enlightened and "*chastening*" punishments.

Now the evil of this *useless* hard labour springs from two sources. In the first place, as we have said, the labour is obliged to be made useless, not only because houses of correction are short-term prisons, but because they are built in cities; for if they were erected in the suburbs, a large portion of land might be attached to them, and the prisoners profitably employed upon market-gardening or field labour—occupations alike healthful and inspiriting, and requiring, moreover, no previous apprenticeship. In the second place, the labour, not only in correctional prisons, but even in all others, can hardly be otherwise than profitless to the workman, because the laws which regulate the world *outside* the prison walls are essentially altered, if not wholly reversed, *inside of them*. In society, every man, unless possessing sufficient means to live in ease, is obliged to labour for his subsistence, and the great cares of life among the poor consist chiefly in providing for the morrow's dinner, or the Saturday's rent, or purchasing clothes. *But no sooner has a man set foot within a prison than all such anxieties cease.* There the rule of human existence is no longer that if any will not work neither shall he eat, as Paul says; for in a jail he soon becomes aware that his daily sustenance is in no way dependent upon his daily labour. Immediately he gets within the gates, he has a good warm suit of clothing given to him; at the appointed hour his dinner is duly served; at nightfall a comfortable bed is provided for him; and all, as he well knows, without being contingent upon the least exertion on his part; for it needs no one to tell him that the tread-wheel work, and crank-work, and shot-drill have nothing at all to do with the procuring of his food, and that really none of these are sufficiently valuable even to furnish the salt he consumes. If the Almighty ordained that labour should be a curse, at least He attached the eating of our bread as a blessing to it. But in prison the sweat of the brow brings no food as its reward; and, therefore, the labour naturally becomes most intolerably irksome to the prisoner, so that his whole nature rebels at it; and when the period arrives for his liberation, he has not only learnt to *expect* his food to be supplied to him *without labouring for it,* but he has also learnt to look upon *industry as a punishment* that he is bound to avoid as much as possible, so that he may taste the sweets of liberty. Instead, therefore, of having increased his self-reliance, of having taught him the very lesson which of all others he required most to learn, viz., to have faith in his own exertions—instead of having inculcated in him a deep and abiding sense that he possesses in himself the means of contributing to his own comfort and enjoyment more than anybody else, we have only demonstrated to him, during his incarceration, that it is *possible* by crime rather than industry to procure a month or two of good wholesome food for his stomach, warm clothing for his body, as well as shelter for his head.

"Crime," said the constabulary commissioners, "proceeds from a desire to acquire the good things of this world with a less degree of industry than ordinary labour." In prison, therefore, the culprit has his criminal propensities doubly strengthened. He learns there not only that he can acquire sufficient to satisfy his wants without any industry at all, but also that the labour which he wishes to avoid is even more irksome and useless than he had fancied it to be.

"But, sir," said the governor of Coldbath Fields to us, "you *must* deter these idle fellows somehow."

Our forefathers thought so too, and accordingly enacted, in the year 1536 (27 Henry VIII., c. 25), that a "sturdy beggar" was to be whipped the first time he was detected begging, to have his right ear cropped for the second offence, and, if again caught begging, to be indicted for "wandering, loitering, and idleness," when, if convicted, he was "to suffer execution of death as a felon and an enemy to the commonwealth." And yet, in spite of such "deterrents," mendicity and vagabondage not only continued, but increased.

"Deter!" exclaimed the chief warder of the prison some time afterwards, as we conversed with him upon the efficacy of punishments in general; "if you were to go out into the streets with a gallows following you, sir, and hung up every thief and rogue you met by the way, you wouldn't deter *one* out of his evil courses."

But surely the number of re-commitments every year (and at Coldbath Fields they amount to $32\frac{1}{2}$ per cent. of the entire number of prisoners) is sufficient to show that the present mode of reforming idleness, by rendering labour more than ordinarily repulsive and utterly useless, has been found positively unavailing, and *that* after more than two and a half centuries' trial of the plan.

There is but one way that we see of doing away with the folly and wickedness of useless labour; and that is, by returning to those natural laws which the Almighty has laid down for the regulation of human life, and making a man's food and enjoyments, whilst in prison, depend upon the amount of work he does, as is the case with the rest of the world *out* of prison.

No man can accuse us of a want of consideration for the feelings and rights of prisoners in general, and it is because we are anxious to win criminals to a sense of the utility and dignity of labour, that we would have every man placed, on his entering a jail, upon the punishment diet, *i.e.*, his eleemosynary allowance of food should be only a pound of bread and water *per diem*. We would *begin* at this point, and make all creature comforts beyond it purchasable, as it were, by the amount of labour done, instead of first leading the prisoner, as now, to believe that he is entitled to receive such creature comforts without work, and being *afterwards* obliged to resort to the punishment diet as a means of enforcing a certain amount of work from him.

Thus, the enjoyments obtained by the labour would make such labour desirable rather than hateful to the prisoner, and so teach him the value of it.

This appears to us to be the *natural and self-supporting plan* of prison discipline; and until prison authorities have the courage, and, we will add, the humanity, to adopt it, in the teeth of mistaken sentimentality, so long must the barbarism of grinding the wind, and crank-work, and shot-drill continue, and continue, too, without avail.

∗ *The Tread-wheel.*—We have before (p. 288) given an account of the origin of the tread-wheel, stating that it was used merely to employ the prisoners, and keep them from louting about the jail. This invention was introduced at most of the prisons more than forty years ago, but the machine, with but few exceptions, has never been applied, even to this day, to any useful purpose. The prisoners style the occupation "grinding the wind," and that is really the only denomination applicable to it—the sole object of the labour of some 150 men, employed for eight hours a day, being simply to put in motion a big fan, or regulator, as it is called, which, impinging on the air as it revolves, serves to add to the severity of the work by increasing the resistance.

There are six tread-wheels at Coldbath Fields, four in the felons' and two in the vagrants' prison. Each of these is so constructed, that, if necessary, twenty-four men can be employed on it; but the present system is for only twelve men to work at one time. At the end of a quarter of an hour these twelve men are relieved by twelve others, each dozen hands being allowed fifteen minutes' rest between their labours. During this interval the prisoners off work may read their books, or do anything they like, except speak with one another.

Each wheel contains twenty-four steps, which are eight inches apart, so that the circumference of the cylinder is sixteen feet. These wheels revolve twice in a minute, and the mechanism is arranged to ring a bell at the end of every thirtieth revolution, and so to announce that the appointed *spell* of work is finished. Every man put to labour at the wheel has to work for fifteen quarters of an hour every day.*

Those who have never visited a correctional prison can have but a vague notion of a tread-wheel. The one we first inspected at Coldbath Fields was erected on the roof of the large, cuddy-like room where the men take their meals. The entire length of the apparatus was divided into twenty-four compartments, each something less than two feet wide, and separated from one another by high wooden partitions, which gave them somewhat

---

* The following official statement as to the size of the tread-wheel, and the number of revolutions made by it, as well as the gross height of the ascent performed by each prisoner working at it, has been furnished to us by the authorities:—

There are	24 steps in the wheel.
The steps are	8 inches distant from each other.
This gives	192 inches ⎫
or	16 feet ⎬ as the circumference of the wheel.
The wheel performs . . .	30 revolutions in each ¼ of an hour.
And therefore each man on it ascends	480 feet in ¼ of an hour.
Each man works altogether . .	15 quarters of an hour a day.
And so ascends in all . . .	7200 feet or 2400 yards = very nearly 1 mile 3 furlongs per diem.

of the appearance of the stalls at a public urinal. The boards at the back of these compartments reach to within four feet of the bottom, and through the unboarded space protrudes the barrel of the wheel, striped with the steps, which are like narrow "floats" to a long paddle-wheel.

When the prisoner has mounted to his place on the topmost step of the wheel, he has the same appearance as if he were standing on the upper side of a huge garden-roller, and somewhat resembles the acrobat we have seen at a circus, perched on the cask that he causes to revolve under his feet.

All the men work with their backs toward the warder, supporting themselves by a hand-rail fixed to the boards at the back of each compartment, and they move their legs as if they were mounting a flight of stairs; but with this difference, that instead of their *ascending*, the steps pass from under them, and, as one of the officers remarked, it is this peculiarity which causes the labour to be so tiring, owing to the want of a firm tread. The sight of the prisoners on the wheel suggested to us the idea of a number of squirrels working outside rather than inside the barrels of their cages.

Only every other man, out of the twenty-four composing the gang on the wheel, work at the same time, each alternate prisoner resting himself while the others labour. When we were at the prison, some of those off work, for the time being, were seated at the bottom of their compartments reading, with the book upon their knees; others, from their high place, were looking listlessly down upon some of their fellow-prisoners, and who were at exercise in the yard beneath, going through a kind of "follow my leader" there. In the meantime, those labouring in the boxes on the wheel were lifting up their legs slowly as a horse in a ploughed field, while the thick iron shaft of the machinery, showing at the end of the yard, was revolving so leisurely, that we expected every moment to see it come to a stand-still. We soon learnt that "grinding the wind" was such hard labour, that speed could not be given to the motion of the machine.

Whilst we were looking on, the bell rang, marking the thirtieth revolution, and instantly the wheel was stopped, and the hands were changed. Those whose turn it was to rest came down from the steps with their faces wet with perspiration and flushed with exercise; while the others shut up their books, and, pulling off their coats, jumped up to their posts. There they stood until, at the word of command, all the men pressed down together, and the long barrel once more began to turn slowly round.

Those who left the wheel sat down, and, taking out their handkerchiefs, commenced wiping the perspiration from their necks and foreheads. One man unbuttoned his shirt-collar, but in a moment the eye of the warder was upon him.

"Fasten up your collar, you there," he shouted, "and throw your coat over your shoulders." Then turning to us, he added, "They are liable to catch cold, sir, if they sit with their bosoms exposed."

We inquired if the work was very laborious, and received the following explanation. "You see the men can get no firm tread like, from the steps always sinking away from under their feet, and *that* makes it very tiring. Again, the compartments are small, and the air becomes very hot, so that the heat at the end of the quarter of an hour renders it difficult to breathe."

We were also assured that the only force required to move the tread-wheel itself is that necessary to start the machine, and that when once the regulator, or fan, begins to revolve, scarcely any exertion is necessary to keep it in motion. Nevertheless, the power that has to be continually exercised, in order that the prisoners may avoid sinking with the wheel, is equal to that of ascending or lifting a man's own weight, or 140 lbs.; and certainly the appearance of the men proved that a quarter of an hour at such work is sufficient to exhaust the strongest for the time being.

Another proof of the severity of the tread-wheel labour is shown by the numerous subterfuges resorted to by the men as a means of getting quit of the work; either they feign illness or else maim the body, in order to escape the task. In the course of last year, according to the surgeon's printed report, there were no less than 3,972 such cases of "feigned complaints."

"We were compelled," writes Mr. Chesterton, the late governor, "to limit the quantity of water, otherwise many would drink it to excess, purposely to disorder the system. In like manner did we narrowly watch the salt, else inordinate saline potations would be swallowed, expressly to derange the stomach. Soap would be 'pinched' (i.e., a piece would be pinched out), and rolled into pills, in order to found the plaint of diarrhœa. Lime white would be applied to the tongue, and any available rubbish bolted to force on a momentary sickness. Daring youths, who winced not at pain, were constantly in the habit of making 'foxes' (artificial sores), and then, by an adroit fall, or an intentional contact with the revolving tread-wheel, would writhe and gesticulate to give colour to their deception. The term 'fox' signifies wilful abrasion of the skin, or laceration of the flesh, and the wounds sometimes inflicted led us to marvel how any rational being could voluntarily court so much torture, rather than heartily perform a practical task and continue sound and active."

Surely, when we read of such self-tormenting deceptions as the above, we need no better proof of the inefficacy of these degrading penal instruments, which have been disguised under the name of *industrial* machines. How is it possible that a youth should, on being liberated, seek to earn his living by toil, when his prison experience has filled him with such a dread of it, that he will prefer no slight amount of self-imposed pain to the performance of his daily task at "grinding the wind." Is it not evident that to such persons a forced sickness or a voluntary wound must have caused them less suffering than that of the " wheel," else why have preferred bodily laceration to muscular exercise? Surely, all but the fatuous-minded must agree with the remark in the Government Report of the Home Inspectors of Prisons, for 1838, which, speaking of the correctional treatment of the criminal, says—" The prison either leaves him to all the baneful effects of utter idleness, or else its discipline consists in teaching him to *tread the wheel*, an *employment which is enough to make him avoid all labour to the end of his days*."

That the labour of the tread-wheel is excessive, is proved by the fact that the gross amount of exertion required for the day's work of four hours and three-quarters, at Coldbath Fields prison, consists in a man having to raise himself (*i.e.*, a weight of 140 lbs.) to a height of 7,200 feet, or through a perpendicular space of one mile and three furlongs in length; and it will be seen below that a bricklayer's hodman, even at his hardest work, when carrying bricks to the top of an ordinary scaffold, does not ascend altogether to a height beyond that of the workers at the tread-wheel.* True, he has his load to carry up in addition to his own

---

* The subjoined statement will enable the reader to compare the labour of the tread-wheel with that of some of the severer forms of work performed by ordinary labourers.

A ten-roomed house is, measuring from the pavement to the coping-stone, about 36 feet high, and the bricklayer's labourer will, when busy, ascend to this elevation on the average twenty times an hour, or 200 times in a day's work of ten hours. The weight of an ordinary hod is 14 lbs., and the bricks with which it is filled, about 72 lbs.; thus a bricklayer's labourer will, in the course of the day's work, ascend to a height of 7,200 feet, or very nearly 1 mile 3 furlongs, carrying with him a weight, in addition to that of his own body (which may be taken on an average at 140 lbs.), equal to 86 lbs., or about that of a nine-gallon cask of beer, and will descend the same distance, carrying with him 14 lbs. weight.

The men suffer from a pain in the chest from the stooping position they are obliged to adopt in order to keep the load on the shoulder whilst mounting. A master informed us that a hodman is not fit for the ladder after he is forty years of age.

The *coalwhippers* generally work in gangs of nine. During their labour of whipping the coals from the hold of the colliers in the river, they raise during the day 1½ cwt. (or 18⅔ lbs. for each man) very nearly eight miles high, or four times as high as a balloon ordinarily mounts in the air; and, in addition to this

weight, but then few of these men are able to continue at the occupation when past forty years of age; and we ourselves know one or two liberated prisoners who have been laid up with fever, owing to excessive labour at the wheel. The very fact, indeed, of the prison rules forbidding men to unfasten their shirt-collars, after their work at the wheel, shows that the authorities themselves are well aware that the labour *has at least a tendency* to induce severe illness; and yet this is considered by some wiseacres to be the best means of teaching men the beauty and utility of industry.

Assuredly there is no place so remarkable as a prison for its utter ignorance of human nature, as well as its gross violation of all those laws which Omniscience has instituted as

the coalwhippers themselves, in running up the steps of an apparatus which they call a "way," ascend rather more than 1½ mile perpendicularly in the course of the day's work. On some days, when there is a stress of business, they perform double this labour.

Dr. Carpenter (following the details given by the author of this work while writing for the *Morning Chronicle*) cites the labour performed by the "*coalbackers*" in raising the coal from the hold of a ship as the most violent that can be performed by man.

These men are engaged in carrying coals on their *back* from the ships and craft moored outside the wharves, and placing them in the waggons. The sack and the coals together usually weigh 238 lbs., and the depth of the hold of the vessels whence they are raised, average from 16 to 20 feet. The burthen is carried this height up a ladder from the hold to the deck, and the ship is usually from 60 to 80 feet removed from the waggon. Each man ascends this height and travels this distance about ninety times a day; hence he will lift himself, with 2 cwt. of coals and a sack weighing 14 lbs. on his back, 1,440 feet at the lowest calculation, or upwards of a quarter of a mile high (*i. e.*, three and a half times the height of St. Paul's), in twelve hours; and, besides this, he will travel 6,300 feet, or more than 1¼ mile, carrying the same weight as he goes, and returning and descending through the same space after getting rid of his burthen. The labour is very hard, and there are few men who can continue at it. Many of the heartiest of the men are knocked up by the bursting of blood-vessels and other casualties, and even the strongest cannot keep at the labour for three days together.

The following is a summary of the above facts, showing the power of an average man, as well as the intensity of the labour performed by each of the working men above-mentioned, in comparison with tread-wheel work. Thus:—

	lbs.	In.	Sec.			Ft.	Hrs.	Min.	Sec.
An ordinary man can support on his shoulders	330								
An ordinary man can lift with both hands	236								
An ordinary man can lift	100	12 high in	1 of time.						
Therefore—									
A bricklayer's labourer can raise himself, and 86 lbs. besides, or altogether	226	5⅓ ,, ,,	1	,, which is at the rate of		7200 in	4	31	42
A coalwhipper can raise himself, or	140	8½ ,, ,,	1	,,	,,	7200 ,,	2	49	25
A prisoner on the tread-wheel can raise himself, or	140	8½ ,, ,,	1	,,	,,	7200 ,,	2	49	25
A coalbacker can raise himself and 238 lbs. besides, or altogether	378	3⅕ ,, ,,	1	,,	,,	1440 ,,	1	30	0

Hence it will be seen, that were the *same power* exerted by all of the above labourers alike, the ascent of the bricklayer's hodman would require about *thrice*, and that of the coalwhipper, as well as the prisoner on the tread-wheel, about *twice*, as long a period for the work as that of the coalbacker; but as the tasks are one and all completed in the *same space of time*, *i. e.*, in one day's labour, it follows that the hodman, though carrying a lighter weight than the backer, but ascending to a greater height, performs, while rising, a task which requires the exercise of *thrice* as much power as that of the coalbacker, in order to be accomplished in the same period; whilst the coalwhipper and tread-wheel worker, for a similar reason, exercise *twice* as much power as the backer, so that the ascending labour of the hodman is *thrice* as great, and that of the whipper and man on the tread-wheel *twice* as great, as that of the coalbacker.

It should be remembered, however, that ascending with such a load forms only one portion of the coal-backer's labour; for, in addition, he has to carry his burthen more than 1¼ mile.

PRISONERS WORKING AT THE TREAD-WHEEL, AND OTHERS EXERCISING, IN THE 3RD YARD OF THE VAGRANTS' PRISON, COLDBATH FIELDS.

(From a Photograph by Herbert Watkins, 179, Regent Street.)

5

motives to mankind—no place where there is so *little* wisdom displayed, and yet none where so *much* is required.

∗ *The Tread-wheel Fan.*—As we were leaving the gate we caught sight, for the first time, of an immense machine situated in the paved court, which leads from the main or felons' prison to that of the vagrants'. In the centre of a mound, shaped like a pyramid, and whose slate covering and lead-bound edges resemble a roof placed on the ground, stands a strong iron shaft, on the top of which is a horizontal beam some twenty feet long, and with three Venetian-blind-like fans standing up at either end, and which was revolving at such a rapid pace that the current of air created by it blew the hair from the temples each time it whizzed past.

This is what is called the regulator of the tread-wheel. By this apparatus the resistance

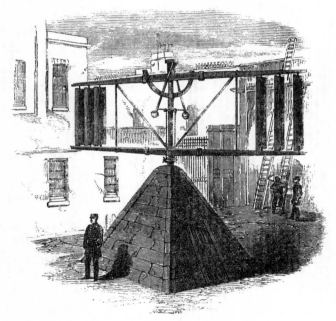

THE TREAD-WHEEL FAN.

necessary for rendering the tread-wheel *hard* labour is obtained. Without it no opposition would be offered to the revolutions of the wheel; for, as that power is applied to no useful purpose,* the only thing which it is made to grind is, as the prisoners themselves say, "the wind." Another method of increasing the resistance of this "regulator" consists in applying to it the apparatus termed by engineers a "governor." If the regulator revolves too quickly, the governor, similar in action and principle to that of a steam-engine, flies open from the increased centrifugal force, and by means of cog-wheels and levers closes the fans at the end of the beams, thus offering a greater resistance to the air, and, consequently, increasing the labour of the prisoners working at the wheel.

∗ *Crank-labour.*—Sometimes a prisoner, tired of working at the tread-wheel, or fatigued

* We were assured that advertisements have often been inserted in the journals, offering to lease the tread-mill power, but without any result.

with the monotony of working at his trade as a tailor or cobbler, will complain of some ailment, such as pains in the back or chest, thereby hoping to obtain a change of labour. In such instances the man is sent to the surgeon to be examined. If he be really ill, he is ordered rest; but if, as often happens, he is "merely shamming," then he is sent back to his former occupation. Should he still continue to complain, he is set to crank-labour, and it is said that after a couple of days at this employment, the most stubborn usually ask to return to their previous occupation.

Crank-labour consists in making 10,000 revolutions of a machine, resembling in appearance a "Kent's Patent Knife-cleaner," for it is a narrow iron drum, placed on legs, with a long handle on one side, which, on being turned, causes a series of cups or scoops in the interior to revolve. At the lower part of the interior of the machine is a thick layer of sand, which the cups, as they come round, scoop up, and carry to the top of the wheel, where they throw it out and empty themselves, after the principle of a dredging-machine. A dial-plate, fixed in front of the iron drum, shows how many revolutions the machine has made.

It is usual to shut up in a cell the man sent to crank-labour, so that the exercise is rendered doubly disagreeable by the solitude. Sometimes a man has been known to smash the glass in front of the dial-plate and alter the hands; but such cases are of rare occurrence.

As may be easily conceived, this labour is very distressing and severe; but it is seldom used, excepting as a punishment, or, rather, as a test of feigned sickness. A man can make, if he work with ordinary speed, about twenty revolutions a minute, and this, at 1,200 the hour, would make his task of 10,000 turns last eight hours and twenty minutes.

*** *Shot-drill.*—This most peculiar exercise takes place in the vacant ground at the back of the prison, where an open space, some thirty feet square and about as large as a racket-court, has been set apart for the purpose, on one side of the plantations of cabbages and peas. There is no object in this exercise beyond that of fatiguing the men and rendering their sojourn in the prison as unpleasant as possible.

We first saw this drill-ground whilst making the round of the prison gardens. The ground had been strewn with cinders, which gave it the loose, black appearance of bog earth; and surrounded as it was by the light-brown mould of the cabbage rows, it seemed like a patch of different material let into the soil, as though the land had been pieced and repaired like a beggar's coat. Along three sides of this square were as many rows of large cannon balls, placed at regular distances, and at the two ends were piled up pyramids of shot, those at the base being prevented from rolling out of their places by a frame of wood. It was difficult to tell whether the cannon balls so spaced out had been left after some game at bowls, or whether the spot had been cleared for action like the deck of a man-of-war, with the shot ready for the guns. We took up one of these balls to examine it, and were surprised at its weight; for, although not larger than a cocoa-nut, it required a considerable effort to lift it.

The shot-drill takes place every day at a quarter-past three, and continues until half-past four. All prisoners sentenced to hard labour, and not specially excused by the surgeon, attend it; those in the prison who are exempted by the medical officer wear a yellow mark on the sleeve of their coat. Prisoners above forty-five years of age are generally excused, for the exercise is of the severest nature, and none but the strongest can endure it. The number of prisoners drilled at one time is fifty-seven, and they generally consist of the young and hale.

The men are ranged so as to form three sides of a square, and stand three deep, each prisoner being three yards distant from his fellow. This equidistance gives them the appearance of chess-men set out on a board. All the faces are turned towards the warder, who occupies a stand in the centre of the open side of the square. The exercise consists in passing the shot, composing the pyramids at one end of the line, down the entire length of the ranks, one after another, until they have all been handed along the file of men, and piled up into similar pyramids at the other end of the line; and when that is done, the operation is reversed and the cannon balls passed back again. But what constitutes the chief labour of the drill is, that every prisoner, at the word of command, has to bend down and carefully deposit the heavy shot in a particular place, and then, on another signal, to stoop a second time and raise it up. It is impossible to imagine anything more *ingeniously useless* than this form of hard labour.

The men, some with their coats and waistcoats off, and others with their sleeves tucked up to the shoulders, were hard at work when we got to the drill-ground. Before we reached the spot, we could hear the warder shouting like a serjeant to raw recruits, constantly repeating, " *One*, TWO—*three*, FOUR!'" at the top of his voice; and each command was either followed by the tramping of many feet, or the dull, plump sound of some heavy weight falling to the ground.

The men did their "work" with the regularity of old soldiers, moving to and fro with great precision, and bending down with simultaneous suddenness.

" *One!*" shouted the officer on duty, and instantly all the men, stooping, took up their heavy shot. "Two!" was scarcely uttered when the entire column advanced sideways, three yards, until each man had taken the place where his neighbour stood before. On hearing " *Three!*" they every one bent down and placed the iron ball on the earth, and at "FOUR!" they shifted back empty-handed to their original stations. Thus, a continual see-saw movement was kept up, the men now advancing sideways, and then returning to their former places, whilst the shot was carried from one spot to another, until it had travelled round the three sides of the square.

"Stand upright, and use both hands to put the shot down!" shouted the warder, staying for a moment his monotonous numerals. "Pay attention to the word of command," he added. "Now, then, 'three!'" and down ducked all the bodies; whereupon there came a succession of thumps from the falling shot, as if fifty paviors' rammers had descended at the same moment.

After a while the prisoners began to move more slowly, and pay less attention to the time, as if all the amusement of the performance had ceased, and it began to be irksome. One, a boy of seventeen, became more and more pink in the face, while his ears grew red. The warder was constantly shouting out, "Move a little quicker, you boy, there!" The shot is about as heavy as a pail of water, and it struck us that so young a boy was no more fitted for such excessive labour than prisoners above the age of forty-five, who are excused.

The men grew hot, and breathed hard. Some, who at the beginning had been yellow as goose-skin, had bright spots appear, almost like dabs of rouge, on their prominent cheek-bones. Now the warder had to keep on calling out either, "Wait for the time, you men at the back," or else, "A little quicker, you in the second row." Many began to drop their shot instead of putting it down carefully; but they were quickly discovered, and a reprimand of "Stoop, and put the shot down, do you hear!" was the consequence.

When all were evidently very tired, a rest of a few seconds was allowed. Then the men pulled out their handkerchiefs and wiped their faces, others who had kept their waistcoats on, took them off, and passed their fingers round their shirt collars, as if the linen were clinging to the flesh, whilst the youth of seventeen rubbed his shirt sleeve over his wet hair as a cat uses its paw when cleaning itself.

Before re-commencing, the warder harangued the troop. "Mind, men, when I say ONE! every man stoop and carry his shot to the right. Now, *One!* Two! Heels close together every time you take up and put down." And the prisoners were off again, see-sawing backwards and forwards.

A warder near to us, with whom we conversed, said, "It tries them worse taking up, because there's nothing to lay hold of, and the hands get hot and slippery with the perspiration, so that the ball is greasy like. The work makes the shoulders very stiff too."

This exercise continues for an hour and a quarter. We counted the distance that each man walked over in the course of a minute, and found that he traversed the three yards' space fourteen times. According to this, he would have to walk altogether about one mile and three-quarters, picking up and putting down, at every alternate three yards, a weight of twenty-four pounds. It is not difficult to understand how exhausting and depressing such useless work must be.

** Oakum Picking.—There are three distinct rooms where the prisoners pick oakum, one in the misdemeanour prison, and the two others in the felons' prison. We shall choose for our illustration and description the larger one in the felons' prison. It has lately been built on so vast a plan that it has seats for nearly 500 men. This immense room is situated to the west of the main or old prison, close to the school-room. It is almost as long as one of the sheds seen at a railway terminus where spare carriages are kept, and seems to have been built after the same style of architecture, for it has a corrugated iron roof, stayed with thin rods, spanning the entire erection. We were told that the extreme length is 90 feet, but that does not convey so good a notion of distance to the mind as the fact of the wall being pierced with eight large chapel windows, and the roof with six skylights. Again, an attendant informed us that there were eleven rows of forms, but all that we could see was a closely-packed mass of heads and pink faces, moving to and fro in every variety of motion, as though the wind was blowing them about, and they were set on stalks instead of necks.

On the side fitted with windows the dark forms of the warders are seen, each perched up on a raised stool. The bright light shines on the faces of the criminals, and the officer keeps his eye rapidly moving in all directions, almost as if it went by clock-work, so as to see that no talking takes place. If a man rest over his work for a moment and raise his head, he sees, hung up on the white walls before him, placards on which texts are printed. One is to the effect that "It is good for a Man that he bear the Yoke in his Youth;" another tells the prisoners that "Godliness with Contentment is a great gain;" whilst a third counsels each of them to "Go to the Ant, thou Sluggard, consider her ways, and be wise."*

---

* One of the peculiarities of Coldbath Fields is the frequent display of Scripture texts, printed in a large bold type, and hung up on every conspicuous part of the prison walls. We believe that this idea originated with the present kind-hearted governor himself—a gentleman whose endeavours to improve the religious feelings of the prisoners under his charge are, from the evidences so plentifully distributed about the prison, unceasing and most enthusiastic. But we doubt very much whether a criminal is to be affected by a printed display of Bible quotations. On the contrary, we rather believe that the constant sight of such placards tends so to accustom him to the religious warnings, that at last he ceases to notice them altogether, and pays no more attention to them than we do to the pattern of the paper on our walls. The obtruded texts become, as it were, part of the furniture, and the felon at last passes them by, giving no more heed to the principles inculcated by them than we do to a notice-board, which, having once read, we do not stop each time we go by to re-peruse. Over the report-office, in the entrance hall of the prison, is placarded, "Swear not at all," which we before noticed, remarking that in a prison conducted on the silent system such a command appeared to us somewhat superfluous. In explanation, the governor tells us that the men, when reported and brought before him, often accompanied their expostulations of innocence with oaths such as "Strike me dead!" "Upon my soul!" &c., and that it was on that account he had the text placed over the entrance door. It would appear, however, that the language of the prisoners has not been much improved by the placard, for the same form of vehement asseverations is said to be still indulged in, nor is it *likely* that a line or two of print should change men, who pay no regard to the laws of society, into persons of gentle speech. Besides, the experiment of these silent warnings has been often tried and failed. The Mohammedan has the very cornice of his ceiling, and the arabesques on his walls, decorated with quotations from the Koran, and

We went to the wall where the warders were, and looked up the sloping floor at the dirty gray mass of life; the faces of the men seemed like the flesh showing through a tattered garment.

The building was full of men, and as silent as if it merely contained so many automata, for the only sound heard was like that of the rustling of a thicket, or, better, the ticking of clock-work—something resembling that heard in a Dutch clockmaker's shop, where hundreds of time-pieces are going together.

The utter absence of noise struck us as being absolutely terrible. The silence seemed, after a time, almost intense enough to hear a flake of snow fall. Perfect stillness is at all times more or less awful, and hence arises a great part of the solemnity of night as well as of death. To behold those whom we have seen full of life and emotion—some wondrous piece of breathing and speaking organism, reduced to the inanimateness of the statue, is assuredly the most appalling and depressing sight we can look upon. The stillness of the silent system, however, has, to our minds, even a more tragic cast about it; for not only is the silence as intense and impressive as that of death itself, but the movements of the workers seem as noiseless, and therefore unearthly, as spectres. Nor does the sense of our being surrounded by some five hundred criminals—men of the wildest passions, and almost brute instincts, all toiling in dumb show and without a single syllable escaping from their lips—in any way detract from the *goblin* character of the sight.

The work-room at the dumb asylum is not half so grim or affecting a scene as the five centuries of silent oakum-pickers at Coldbath Fields; for, at the latter place, we are conscious that the wretched mutes before us *would* speak if they dare, so that we cannot help thinking of the struggling emotions pent up in the several hundred crushed spirits before us. Either the men must have been cowed by discipline into the insensibility of mere automata, or else what gall and bitterness, and suppressed fury, must be rankling in every bosom there, at the sense of having their tongues thus *virtually cut out*. Nor can we help thinking that the excision of the organ of speech itself (after the manner that barbarous nations deal with offending slaves) would be less inhuman as a punishment; for to leave the tongue in a man's mouth, and yet to deny him the liberty of using it (when every little event in life, every act we witness, every feeling we experience, as well as every thought that passes through the brain, suggests some form of speech from the mere force of association; and when, therefore, the restraint imposed upon a man's lips for the whole of his imprisonment must be one long round of irritation upon irritation—a continual series of checkings and curbings of natural impulses, sufficient to infuriate even the best regulated and least irritable natures)—this is surely a piece of refined tyranny, worthy of the enlightenment, if not the humanity, of the nineteenth century. We are well aware of the evil consequences that ensue when unrestricted intercourse is permitted among criminals; but because thieves and

---

yet he cannot order a cup of coffee, or converse on the most ordinary topic, without swearing, "By Allah!" or 'By the Prophet!" at every dozen words. The Pharisees, again, are known to have had their phylacteries covered with short passages from the Bible hung about their necks. The old Puritans, too, were accustomed to interlard their conversation with oaths, such as "By God's wounds!" "By God's blood!" "By the agony of Christ!" and yet, although these phrases were intended to carry with them a scriptural sound, everybody of the present day would certainly denounce them as improper and revolting. Again, the same fanatics loved to put up religious signs even at their drinking booths, as "GOD ENCOMPASSES" (now corrupted into the "GOAT AND COMPASSES"), or, in Saxon English, "GOD IMBUTES" (literally, God surrounds—God is *about*, but now transmogrified into the "GOAT AND BOOTS"). The Bible texts on the walls of Coldbath Fields seem to us of the same *blasphemous* character. To our minds—we confess it boldly—they appear very much like using the most solemn phrases "*in vain*," i.e., idly, or when the mind is not fitted to appreciate them; and surely the plastering the walls of a prison with these religious posting-bills only teaches thieves to adopt the *cant*, rather than feel the *spirit*, of true piety. Suppose every hoarding in the public thoroughfares was to be covered with texts, would the public be a bit better for it, think you? or, rather, would not men be rendered worse, and taught to use Scripture as a slang—to chatter it, as Catholic beggars do, their Latin prayers without thinking of what they themselves are saying, and merely as a means of imposition upon others.

vagabonds become more corrupt by speaking together on bad subjects, surely that affords no sound reason why we should deny such people the right of speech altogether, and so cut off from them the only means that all persons have of improvement, viz., by moral and intellectual communion with other minds.

The quantity of oakum each man has to pick varies according to whether he be condemned to hard labour or not.　In the former case the weight is never less than three, and sometimes as much as six, pounds; for the quantity given out depends upon the quality of the old rope or junk, *i. e.*, according as it is more or less tightly twisted.　The men *not at hard labour* have only two pounds' weight of junk served out to them.

Each picker has by his side his weighed quantity of old rope, cut into lengths about equal to that of a hoop-stick.　Some of the pieces are white and sodden-looking as a washer-woman's hands, whilst others are hard and black with the tar upon them.　The prisoner takes up a length of junk and untwists it, and when he has separated it into so many cork-screw strands, he further unrolls them by sliding them backwards and forwards on his knee with the palm of his hand, until the meshes are loosened.

Then the strand is further unraveled by placing it in the bend of a hook fastened to the knees, and sawing it smartly to and fro, which soon removes the tar and grates the fibres apart.　In this condition, all that remains to be done is to loosen the hemp by pulling it out like cotton wool, when the process is completed.

By the rays of sun-light shining through the window, you can see that the place is full of dust; for the bright rays are sharply defined as those streaming through a cathedral window.　The shoulders of the men, too, are covered with the brown dust almost as thickly as the shirt-front of a snuff-taker.　A prisoner with a bright tin water-can is going the round, handing up drink to the workers, who gulp it down as if choked.

"You're getting too close together on that back seat," presently a warder shouts to some men on a form against the wall, and who instantly separate, till they are spaced out like tumblers on a shelf.

We left the building for a time, and when we returned, we found a man lying on the stone floor with a bundle of picked oakum supporting his head, and a warder unbuttoning his shirt and loosening his waistcoat; he was in an epileptic fit.　His face had turned a bright crimson with the blood flown to the head, so that the clenched teeth between his parted lips seemed as white as a sweep's.　The other prisoners went on working as though it were no business of their's.　After a few minutes a thrill ran down the limbs of the prostrate man, he began to draw in his extended arms, his tightly closed hands opened, and the eyelids quivered.　"How do you feel now, my man?" asked the warder; but the only answer was a deep-drawn breath, like that of a person going into cold water.

"We often have such cases," said the officer to us.　"After letting them lie down for half an hour they are all right again, and go back to their oakum as well as ever."

As the day advanced, the pieces of old rope by the prisoners' sides disappeared bit by bit, and in their place the mound of treacle-brown oakum at their feet grew from the size of a scratch wig to that of a large pumpkin.　At length the men had all completed their tasks, and sat each holding on his knees his immense tar-coloured ball, waiting to take his turn to go to the scales and have his pickings weighed.　Then the silence of the room, which has all along been like that of a sick chamber, is suddenly broken by the warder calling out, "The first three men!"　The voice seems so loud, that it startles one like a scream in the night-time.　Three gray forms rise up obediently as shepherds' dogs, and, carrying their bundles before them, advance to the weighing-machine.　Now the stillness is broken by the shuffling of feet, and the pushing of forms, as prisoner after prisoner obeys the command to give in his oakum.

Two officers stand beside the weighing-machine, and a third, with a big basket before him, receives the roll as soon as it has been passed as correct.　If a prisoner's oakum be found to be light, he is reported and punished; many, we were told, are wont to get rid of their junk, and so ease their labour by perhaps a pound.

"This won't do," says the warder, pointing to the puffy hemp in the scales; "it's half a pound short."

"It's all I had, sir," answers the man. "Ask them as was next me if I haven't picked every bit."

"Report him!" is the warder's answer; and his brother officer writes down the number of the culprit in a book.

When the men had fallen into line, and been marched off to their different yards, we inquired of one of the warders if oakum-picking was a laborious task. "*Not to the old hands*," was the answer. "We've men here that will have done their three or four pounds a couple of hours before some of the fresh prisoners will have done a pound. They learn the knack of it, and make haste to finish, so as to be able to read; but to the new arrivals it's hard work enough; for *most thieves' hands are soft*, and the hard rope cuts and blisters their fingers, so that until the skin hardens, it's very painful."

The quantity of rope picked into oakum at Coldbath Fields prison would average, says the governor, *three and a half tons per week*, which, at the present price of £5 the ton, would produce the sum of £17 10s.

*** *The Tailors' and Shoemakers' Room.*—When a prisoner is brought to the House of Correction, he has the option given him—provided he was not sentenced to hard labour—of picking oakum or working at a trade. Through this arrangement the establishment boasts

THE TAILORS' AND SHOEMAKERS' ROOM AT COLDBATH FIELDS PRISON.

of a numerous staff of tailors and shoemakers, who have a large room, as big as a factory-floor, given up to them, where, under the inspection of three officers, 160 of them pass the day, making and repairing clothing and boots and shoes. After the depressing sight of the tread-wheel yards and the shot-drill, it is quite refreshing to enter this immense workshop, and see the men employing their time at an occupation that is useful, and (judging from the countenances of the men) neither over-fatiguing nor degrading.

One entire side of this workshop is occupied by a raised platform, on which are seated a crowd of tailors, all with their shoes off, and cross-legged, like so many Turks. Tall rows of gas-lights stand up amongst them, most of which are, now that it is summer-time, serving as convenient places for hanging thick skeins of thread upon, or as pegs to support some unfinished work. The men have a certain grade in their work, beginning with repairing the clothes of their fellow-prisoners, then passing to the making of new suits of gray and blue for the future arrivals, and at length reaching the proud climax of working upon the cloth uniforms of the officers. When there is a lack of employment, some of the younger hands are set to work at shirt-making.

The earnings of the prison tailors are estimated at from 3d. to 5s. (!) the day, according to their proficiency, the lads who are just learning to use their needle being put down at a merely nominal sum—the value of everything made in the prison being estimated at what it would cost if the work had been paid for outside the prison. A great quantity of the clothes, boots, and shoes, sent to Hanwell Lunatic Asylum and the House of Detention, are manufactured at Coldbath Fields. A considerable portion of the "estimated profit of work or labour done by the prisoners,"* given in the annual returns, is earned in this large chamber.

After the saddening spectacles of the other forms of labour at this prison, the eye is greatly relieved by the busy sight of these tailors and cobblers engaged at their trades. The prisoners here appear to work as though they found a relief in the employment from the silent monotony of their jail life, and certainly have a less dejected and more human expression of countenance than those to be seen in the other portions of the building.

As we entered the room the tailors' arms were rapidly flying up in the air, and the sound of the clicking of shears told us that, despite the silence, a good amount of work was being rapidly executed. In the centre passage was a stove stuck all over with big irons, almost like half-hundred weights, which the continual roasting had oxidated into a fine squirrel-red. A prisoner, after stuffing his bat-shaped sleeve-board down one of the arms of

---

* The following is the account that has been furnished us of the extent and value of the labour performed by the prisoners of different trades at Coldbath Fields prison, for the year ending 30th September 1855:—

Amount of Work done in the Shoemaking Department.

333 pairs of male officers' boots.	2,500 pairs of prisoners' boots and shoes.
172　　,,　　female officers' boots.	About 12,500 pairs of boots and shoes repaired.

The aggregate estimated value of the shoemakers' labour, £800.

Tailoring Department.

522 uniform coats.	1,008 prisoners' jackets.
199　　,,　　waistcoats.	1,068　　,,　　trousers.
320　　,,　　trousers.	1,104　　,,　　shirts.
23 gambroon coats.	Miscellaneous repairs to officers' uniforms
223 uniform caps.	and prisoners' clothing.
153　　,,　　stocks.	

The aggregate estimated value of the tailors' labour, £850.

The value of the labour executed by other trades, such as bricklayers, plasterers, masons, painters gardeners, £1,860.

a coat, until it was stretched as tight as the cloth on a billiard-table, moved towards the stove and tested the heat of the irons with his wet fingers, the hot metal hissing as he touched it like a cat spitting. The new, stiff uniforms, with the metal buttons shining like a row of large, brass-headed tacks on a double door, are hung up against the walls. The men bend over their work, silent as mussulmen at their devotions, so that the first impression on seeing the hands moving about is, that they are the gesticulations of so many dumb men.

The other side of the room is, however, not so quiet; for the eighty prison cobblers, seated on rows of forms, are hammering on their lapstones or knocking in the sprigs. The men wear big leathern aprons, like smiths', and some of them, with the last between their knees, are covering it with the dead black skin, pulling it out with nippers until you expect to see it split, and then tacking it down into its place. Others are bending forward, and screwing up their mouths with the exertion of making the awl-holes round the tough brown soles. Others, again, are throwing their arms wide open as they draw out the waxed threads. Two or three lads, working near the wall, are rubbing some newly-finished boots up and down with a piece of wood, as though they were burnishing the well-tightened calf and foot.

*_** *The Printing-office and Needle-room.*—To see the printing-office, where the prison lesson-books are set up in type and worked off, we had to leave the main prison and cross over to that for misdemeanants. We found the prison printers sharing the same room with the "needle-men," for as there is not more typographical work required than will keep three "hands" employed, a separate workshop cannot be spared, so valuable is every bit of space at Coldbath Fields.

When female prisoners were sent to this jail, all the needle-work was performed by them; but since their removal to Tothill Fields the men have had to do the labour. The apartment, scarcely larger than a back parlour, was filled with the black-chinned needle-workers, who sat on forms, some darning old flannel-jackets, others making up bed-ticks. One, with a pair of spectacles almost as clumsily made as if they belonged to a diver's helmet, was "taking up" some rents in a mulberry-coloured counterpane, but *he* used his needle and thread somewhat after the manner of a cobbler making boots.

Against the wall of this needle-room stood a small printing-press, made so clumsily out of thick pieces of wood and unpolished iron, that there was no difficulty in telling that it had been manufactured in the prison. A good-looking lad, with a face smiling as if he had never known vice, stood by the side of the press, with his coat off and shirt sleeves tucked up, busy placing paper, half transparent with dampness, upon the little form of type that he was printing off. He was engaged in pulling a slip entitled, "A FEW TEXTS FROM THE BIBLE"— the same as we had seen suspended on the walls of all the cells.

Close by was the frame on which was placed the case of types, with its square divisions for each letter, like the luggage-label trays at railways. Another lad, with a compositor's "stick" in his hand, was picking up the metal types as quickly as a pigeon does peas, and placing them in their printing order, stopping every now and then to look at the written paper before him. In a side-room, we found the head printer busily folding up sheets of letter paper, with a newly-printed heading, on which the prisoners write whenever they send to their friends.

The tickets for extra provisions from the kitchen, as well as those certifying the number of men locked up at night and again unlocked in the morning, and indeed all the small printing of the prison, is done in this office by criminals.

We cannot too highly commend the introduction of printing among the forms of prison labour, and we believe that to the House of Correction belongs the honour of being the only jail where it is at present pursued. It is at once a thoughtful, refining, and pleasant

MAT-ROOM AT COLDBATH FIELDS PRISON.

occupation, which, in its higher forms, forces the workman to meditate upon not only the proprieties of speech, but the elegancies of thought and sentiment, and which, even when applied to nothing more than the prison forms and lessons, is at one and the same time of great service to the economy of a jail, as well as *being*, from the nicety of the art, of an elevating tendency to the workmen employed.

*** *Mat-room.*—Mat-making appears to be a favourite occupation with prison authorities; doubtlessly owing to the facility with which a man can be taught the occupation, and because such kinds of manufacture afford considerable occupation to others in preparing the different materials, "hands" being required, not only to pick the coir, but also to make the rough cordage for the mat; and in a jail labour is so plentiful, that the difficulty is to find sufficient employment for *all* the prisoners.

All the mats made at Coldbath Fields are contracted for by a wholesale dealer, who is allowed to place foremen over the prisoners, both to instruct the new, and superintend the old hands. There are thirty-three prisoners employed in the mat-room; but including those who dress the flax and coir, and spin the rope, occupation is afforded for about sixty hands.

It is a very peculiar sight to enter the large workshop set apart for the mat-makers, especially after leaving the adjacent oakum-room, where the silence of the junk-pickers is only broken by the sound of the moving arms; for the mat-room is alive with the clatter of tools and looms, and all the tumult of a busy workshop, so that the absence of all sound of the human voice appears to be the result of a close application to labour, rather than a prison punishment.

The big room, with its stone-paved floor, and iron-work roof, is as large as if a spacious yard had been covered in, and what with windows and sky-lights, it is almost as light as a photographer's studio.

The air smells of tan, like a ship-builder's yard; but what first strikes the attention is the long row of looms ranged against the side of the "shop" fitted with windows, and which, at first, give one the notion that they are the frames of so many turned-up press bedsteads, placed out of the way, as on a cleaning day. In a recess, on another side, there are more of these looms; so that the building reminds one of a furniture broker's store. Moreover, mats lie about in every direction; some piled up on the table, and others hanging to the walls, or strewn on the floor; and large square baskets filled with coir form reservoirs of rough material to keep the hands at work.

The looms are used for manufacturing cocoa-nut fibre matting, and cheap hearth-rugs—a form of manufacture, which, compared with silk-weaving, is as different as house-carpenters' work is to cabinet-makers'. The gauze-like threads of the Spitalfields machine are replaced by coarse brown string; and the silk-weaver's shuttle, not so big as the hull of an ivory frigate, which darts with a whiz through the brilliant fibre of the Jacquard loom, is laid aside for one as big as a dressing-case boot-jack; and this had to be pushed and coaxed along the cordage that stretches across the beams like the strings of some coarse musical instrument. The battens come thumping down with a dead, heavy sound, while the muscles, swelling and moving in the bare arms of the weaver, show the exertion required to form the stiff coir into the required position.

The young men prisoners, seated at spinning-wheels, are rocking to and fro as they twirl round the humming disc that winds off the balls of coarse rope. The older hands are occupied with the harder work of making the rope door-mats; some plying a needle like a skewer, and others hammering with a wooden mallet to make the rows of the design lie evenly.

"This man is manufacturing what we call a diamond sennit mat," said the officer, lifting up the stiff brown article, and showing to us its back, with the cords crossing each other in a lozenge pattern. "This," he continued, "is a close mat with a sennit centre," pointing to one with an open-work pattern in the middle of it. Indeed, in the different patterns around, we could recognize all the various kinds of mats which ornament the halls and passages of the Metropolis.

One of the boys was working at a stand fitted up with immense reels of crimson worsted, pulling off the threads so rapidly that the frayed edges threw out a bright-coloured smoke, which powdered his shoulders and the ground around as if the reflection of a painted window had fallen there. With this showy worsted the edges of the better kinds of mats are ornamented. The rug manufactory constitutes the fine arts department of the prison mat-room. The overseer, anxious that we should see specimens of the work, called to a man who was clipping down the rough crop of a newly-made door-mat into a smooth lawn of fibre, and desired him to spread out some of the rolled-up rugs before us. "This one," explained the overseer, as we were looking at the rude design of a rose as large as a red cabbage, "is a cheap article, made mostly out of yarn; but here is the best style of goods we make," and another rug was spread out, with a full length tiger worked upon it.

₊ *Artisan Prisoners.*—Printing, tailoring, shoemaking, and mat-making are not the only crafts which the prisoners are permitted to follow in Coldbath Fields. The whitewash on the walls has been laid on by prison plasterers; many parts of the prison have been erected by prison bricklayers and masons; the wood and iron work receives its annual coat of colour from prison painters; and even the tin mugs, out of which the men take their gruel, are manufactured by prison tinmen. This is as it ought to be; and the only pity is, that there are less degrading occupations pursued among men who need *elevating* influences more than any

other class of persons.   We print a list of the handicrafts pursued in the prison, and append the price at which the labour is estimated in the prison books, where it is reckoned as so much profit to the jail, from its saving the necessity of employing and paying for out-door labour.

TRADE.	TRADE.	TRADE.	TRADE.
Bricklayers.	Plumbers.	Tinmen.	Bookbinders.
Plasterers.	Glaziers.	Blacksmiths.	Basket-makers.
Masons.	Sawyers.	Upholsterers.	Carpenters.
Painters.	Coopers.		

All men, employed at the above trades, are charged for at the rate of 5s. per diem.

Gardeners, working in the garden, are reckoned at the rate of 2s. per diem; and labourers, employed in the works, at the rate of 1s. per diem.

Number of Artificers (other than tailors, shoemakers, and mat-makers)		
employed throughout the prison 25		
,, Gardeners ,, ,, . . . 5		
,, Labourers ,, ,, . . . 18		
Total 48		

Some of the valuations of the prison labour appear to us to be somewhat high—for instance, we doubt whether many working basket-makers or sawyers ever receive, when free, as much as 5s. for their day's work.

Now, the estimate for the labour of the prisoners at the Hulks (see p. 203) amounts in the aggregate to only about one-third of the price charged at Coldbath Fields.   For instance, the labour of carpenters, blacksmiths, painters, plumbers, and coopers, among the convicts at Woolwich, is valued at 2s. 6d., or exactly one-half of that set down at the House of Correction; whilst that of shoemakers, tailors, washers, and cooks is reckoned at 1s. 6d. instead of 5s.   Hence, either the Hulks are too low, or the House of Correction is too high, in its appraisement, for between them is a difference of 50 and 75 per cent. in the amount charged.   Besides, it should be remembered that the greater proportion of the artisans employed in jails are unskilled men; and it is most unfair that one, who is but learning his trade, should be charged for at prices equivalent to that demanded by the quickest and most experienced hands.

Therefore, calculating the labour at Coldbath Fields at the same value as the Hulks (and, from its being a "short-term" prison, the labour at the House of Correction cannot be even of the *same* value), the "estimated profit of work or labour done by the prisoners for the benefit of the county, city, or borough," which, in the return of the House of Correction, is valued at £4,320 12s. 8d., ought, *at the very least*, to be reduced one-half, or to £2,160 6s. 4d., and so the cost of the management of the prison should be raised from £16,466 2s. 5d., to the more formidable sum of £18,626 8s. 9d.

We were told that it was very rarely that working bookbinders came to the prison. This, probably, may be owing to the fact that a large proportion of that kind of labour is now performed by women; and as the House of Correction at Coldbath Fields no longer receives female prisoners, such operatives seldom come within the walls.   We congratulate the male portion of the working bookbinders, however, upon this high testimony to their honour and principle.

¶ i—δ.

Education and Religious Instruction of the Prisoners.

*** *The School-room.*—As we were standing at the entrance of the felons' prison, a gentleman passed us dressed in black, and carrying under his arm a roll of what, from the marbled-paper coverings, were evidently copy-books. We instinctively asked if he **were** not the schoolmaster, and learnt that he was then on his rounds to collect together his class. The school hours commence at half-past seven in the morning, and end at half-past five in the evening. Each class consists of twenty-four scholars, and these are changed every hour. All the prisoners who are unable to read and write are forced to submit to instruction.

We directed our steps to the westward portion of the main prison, where, in a kind of outbuilding, the classes are held.

The prison school-room is about the size of an artist's studio, being large enough to admit of twelve desks, arranged in four rows in front of the open space where the master's rostrum is placed. Each desk is sufficient for three scholars, but, to prevent talking, only two are allowed, one at each end, the middle place being kept vacant.

In ordinary schools the desks are notched and carved with names and initials, or covered all over with writings and drawings; but in this felon academy they were as white and free from ink or incisions as the top of a butterman's counter. Even the circle of little black dots around the ink holes were of that morning's sprinkling.

Against the whitewashed walls were hung maps as big as the sheets of plate-glass in a linen-draper's window, and the varnish of these had turned yellow as an old blanket, so that although we knew the two circles, joined in the centre like an hour-glass, to be the chart of the World, and the triangular-shaped one to be England and Wales, yet we were obliged to go up close to another before we could read through the discoloured glazing that it was the Holy Land. Over the master's raised chair was an immense black board, with the letters of the alphabet painted in white upon it; whilst, to impress upon the "scholars" the necessity to be tidy, a printed maxim is hung between the windows, to the following effect :—" A PLACE FOR EVERYTHING AND EVERYTHING IN ITS PLACE."

Presently the pupils entered, in a long line, headed by the master. Each prisoner seemed to know his seat, for he went there as readily as a horse to his stall. All was silent as in a dumb asylum, the only sound being the rustling of the copy-books on their being distributed. A few minutes afterwards all the "pupils" were leaning over the desks, squaring out their elbows in every variety of position—some with their tongues poked out at the corner of the mouth, and others frowning with their endeavours to write well.

It was a curious sight to see these men with big whiskers, learning the simple instruction of a village school. Some of them with their large fingers cramped up in the awkwardness of first lessons; others wabbling their heavy heads about as they laboured over the huge half-inch letters in their clumsy scrawl.

The schoolmaster is assisted in his duties by two prisoners, who, by their proficiency and good conduct, have been raised to the position of hearers—and to them the scholars repeat their lessons. A big sailor-looking man, with red whiskers growing under his chin, advanced to the hearer's desk. Not a word was spoken as the copy-book was handed in. The prison-tutor pointed in silence to a mistake, the pupil nodded, and, on another signal, began to read aloud what he had written, " *Give to every man that asketh, and of him that taketh away thy goods ask him not again.*"

Another—a lad with a bandage round his face, and heavy, dingy-coloured eyes—was sent back for having too many blots and erasures. This man, when repeating his lessons, stumbled over the sentence, " There shall be wailing and gnashing of teeth," calling it " genashing " instead.

Once the head master had occasion to speak. A lad with ruddy skin, and light hair, had a defect in his speech, and could not pronounce his " r's," so that he read out, " Whatsoever is wight that shall ye weceive." "*Do* try and pronounce your ' r's' better," said the master, kindly; and thereupon there was a shuffling of feet from the other pupils, as if the only method of laughing under the silent system was with the shoes.

The books—of which there are three—from which the prisoners are taught are all printed and bound by prisoner workmen in the jail. In the first book the lessons are of the simplest form, beginning with the letters of the alphabet, then gradually comprising letters and words mixed up together, and concluding with short sentences. In the second lesson book one of the objects of the instruction is to make the pupils, by means of nonsense sentences, pay attention to the copy before them, for they are apt to read, we were told, only the commencement of a sentence, and jump at the meaning of the remaining portion. Accordingly these lessons are made into kinds of puzzles, like the following :—" train save thirst ring train thou shall soap save train pick thou." The third book contains lessons from the gospels ; and by the time the scholar is able to copy out and read those correctly, his education, as far as the prison limit of reading and writing is concerned, is supposed to be completed.*

*** *Chapel.*—The chapel is situate immediately over the entrance hall of the main or felons' prison. It is a kite-shaped, triangular building, seeming as if it were some spare corner of the prison that had been devoted to the purpose; the clergyman's place—for you can hardly call the little desk and arm-chair set apart for the minister a pulpit—being in a kind of small gallery at the apex of the triangle, and the seats for the prisoners below towards the base. Reckoning the seats in the gallery and on the ground, there is room for about 500 men.

The chapel is certainly a primitive and curious building. There are three compartments

* TABLE SHOWING THE STATE OF INSTRUCTION OF THE PRISONERS IN COLDBATH FIELDS PRISON, FOR THE YEAR ENDING MICHAELMAS, 1855.

Can neither read nor write . . .	2,172	Can read and write well	—
Can read only	395	Superior education	—
Can read or write, or both, imperfectly .	3,556	Total	6,123

" An average of 144 prisoners," says the last annual report of the chaplains, " are daily under instruction ;" and of 309 who passed through the school during the year, the state of instruction on admission and discharge, respectively, is represented in the following table :—

	On Admission.	On Discharge.					
STATE OF EDUCATION OF PRISONERS.	Total.	Neither read nor write.	Read imperfectly.	Read and write imperfectly.	Read and write tolerably.	Read and write well.	Total.
Number that could neither read nor write . .	52	12	18	17	5	..	52
„ „ read imperfectly . .	138	..	22	54	42	20	138
„ „ read and write imperfectly .	111	..	..	16	42	51	111
„ „ read and write tolerably .	8	..	..	..	2	6	8
Total	309	12	40	87	91	77	309

TABLE SHOWING THE AGES OF THE PRISONERS IN COLDBATH FIELDS PRISON, FOR THE YEAR ENDING MICHAELMAS, 1855.

Under 17 years of age	—	45 years and under 60 . . .	631
17 years and under 21	1,682	60 years and upwards . . .	156
21 „ „ 30	2,155	Total	6,123
30 „ „ 45	1,499		

Proportion under 30 years of age . . . 62·6 per cent.
Proportion 30 years and upwards . . 37·3 „

DORMITORY AT COLDBATH FIELDS PRISON.

on the ground-floor, and three in the gallery, separated from each other by a tall, strong, wooden partition, so that each storey presents somewhat the appearance of a huge three-stalled stable. Instead of panelling in front of the men, as in other chapels, stout iron bars rise up, close set together, such as would be placed before an elephant's cage.

The governor, in lieu of a pew, has a comfortable arm-chair placed in the gallery, on one side of the chaplain's desk, and another row of arm-chairs is arranged as tidily as against a drawing-room wall, to receive visitors and the principal warders. Immediately under the gallery, on the ground-floor, is the communion-table, and on one side of it hangs a notice-board, stating that "COMMUNICANTS DESIROUS OF PARTAKING OF THE SACRAMENT" must give due notice to the clergyman.

On entering the chapel, in company with the governor, we found the felon congregation already assembled, each cage being as closely packed with men as the gallery of a cheap theatre. On one side of the dirty-gray mass of prisoners, stood up the dark-uniformed warder. All the men had their caps off, showing every variety of coloured hair. There was one man, a big square-shouldered negro, whose white eyes, as he rolled them about, seemed like specks of light shining through holes in his dark skin ; and we also observed a Malay, with his slanting eyes and dried mummy skin, whose long, straight hair hung from his pointed skull like the tassel on a fez. Nearly all the congregation appeared to be youths, for we could only here and there distinguish a bald or white head. Some of these elderly sinners had spectacles on, and were busily hunting out in their Bible the lessons to be read that day. The building was silent as a criminal court when sentence is being passed.

When the prayer was ended, a sudden shout of "Amen" filled the building, so loud and instantaneous, that it made us turn round in our chair with surprise; the 500 tongues had been for a moment released from their captivity of silence, and the enjoyment of the privilege was evinced by its noisiness. It was wonderful to watch the men as they made their responses. No opera chorus could have kept better time. The chaplain's voice, as it read the next line, appeared like a weak whisper, so deadened was the ear; but in a little while we began to grow accustomed to the discharges of sound. We could see, too, that the men took pleasure in their prayers. Whether they understood the true meaning of the words they uttered we cannot tell, but they knew the drill of the service as perfectly as a parish clerk, and appeared to be aware that the only time when they might raise their voices and break through the dumbness man had imposed upon them, was when they were addressing their God, so that to them the consolation of prayer must be especially great.

One of the lessons of the day was the 7th chapter of St. Luke, and to it the prisoners listened with the earnestness of children hearing a story. As soon as the chapter was given out, some of the men opened their Bibles, and, wetting their thumbs, turned the leaves over rapidly as they sought for the page ; others at first sat still, but as the clergyman progressed, their interest became aroused, and they leant their bodies forward, some resting their heads on their hands, others with their ears turned towards the make-shift pulpit as if to catch every sentence of the sacred history.

The first passage that appeared to fix their attention was that describing how the widow's only son was restored to life. Probably, many of them had never before heard of the miracle, for as the words were spoken, "Young man, I say unto thee, arise!" a kind of wondering fear seemed to agitate the felons, as of old it did the men of Nain. The congregation was greatly interested as it listened to how a woman in the city, "which was a sinner," brought an alabaster box of ointment and anointed the Saviour's feet, as he sat at meat in the Pharisee's house. It seemed to us that they could hardly comprehend the motive which prompted her "to wash his feet with tears," and wipe them with the hair of her head and kiss them, and they appeared to be expecting to hear of some great reward having been given to her.

When the morning service had ended, the erring flock, under the guidance of the warders, left their pews in the chapel, and in a few moments afterwards were occupied with their different prison duties.

On Sunday *all* the men are taken to divine service once a day, part in the morning and the remainder in the afternoon; for the chapel in the felons' prison contains only 507 sittings, and that in the misdemeanants' prison but 274; and as the usual number of prisoners in the entire building is seldom below 1,300, of course only half of that number can attend service at one time. Those who are left behind are not, however, allowed to remain without religious instruction. Three men in each yard have been appointed by the chaplain to read aloud to their fellow-prisoners, and each relieves the other every half-hour. The book for the Sunday's reading is issued by the chaplain. It is of a purely religious character, and is usually "The Penny Sunday Reader," containing short sermons. Tracts are also distributed in the different yards, so that those who prefer reading to themselves, instead of listening to what is being read aloud, may do so.

The governor informed us that this reading aloud is so much liked by the prisoners, that it is not an unfrequent occurrence for boys who, for some breach of the prison discipline, have been placed in solitary confinement, to send him a request to be allowed to be present in their yards whilst the reading is going on. Surely this excellent principle of reading aloud to the prisoners might be applied on a week-day, in the oakum-picking room at least, and the silent system be thereby made productive of some positive good.*

¶ i—ε.

The Prison Accommodation, Cells, and Dormitories.

The extent of accommodation at Coldbath Fields prison has already been mentioned (at page 281). The prison is capable of holding, altogether, 1,453 persons, and 919 (or, as at Tothill Fields, not quite two-thirds of the whole) of these can be accommodated with separate sleeping cells. The daily average number of prisoners in the year ending Michaelmas, 1855, was 1,388, while the greatest number at any one time during that year was 1,495; so that occasionally the prison contains three per cent. more than it has *proper accommodation* for. The gross prison population, *i.e.*, the number of different individuals who were confined within the walls in the same year, amounted to 9,180; of these, 1,437 were remaining in custody at the end of the previous year, and the other 7,743 "passed through" the prison in the course of that ending Michaelmas, 1855.

₊ *Cells.*—As regards the "separate sleeping cells," of which we have seen there are 919 altogether, they differ in size in each of the three different prisons, which make up the entire House of Correction. The largest are to be found in the old building, erected

---

* The greater proportion of the books given out to the prisoners are those published by the "Christian Knowledge Society." The following is a list of some of the other volumes circulated in the prison :—

Chambers's Miscellaneous Tracts, in volumes.	History of Ireland.
The Home Friend, in volumes.	,, Scotland.
The Leisure Hour, ,,	,, France.
Knight's Shilling Volumes.	Histories of various other countries.
Travels by Land and Sea.	Lives of the Reformers.
A number of small Biographical Works.	Works of the Reformers.
History of England.	A variety of Tracts and purely Religious Books.

The Library consists of—Bibles 1,290
Prayer Books . . . 1,290
Other volumes . . 1,330

in 1794, and now set apart for felons; next in space come those appropriated to the vagrants, built in 1830; and the smallest ones are those situate in the misdemeanant's prison, constructed in 1832. We shall describe the cells we visited in the felons' prison, for these may be considered as the best form of the separate sleeping apartments in the entire establishment.

The cells are situate in the wings and corridors, on the first and second floors of the building, as well as on one side of all the eight exercising yards. The entrance to each cell is guarded by a narrow door, solid as that of a fire-proof deed-box, and just wide enough to allow a man to enter, whilst heavy bars and bolts make the fastenings secure. Every one of them is eight feet two inches long by six feet two inches broad, and has an arched groined roof springing from the sides, at an elevation of six feet, until it attains its highest pitch of ten feet. If it were not for the height of the apartment, the chamber would be about the size of an ordinary coal-cellar.

The walls and roof are brilliant with whitewash, so that one could almost imagine the cell to have been dug out of some chalk cliff, and the stone flooring has been holy-stoned until it is as clean as the door-step of a " servants' home." Fastened up to hooks set in the stone-work, and stretching across at the farthest end, is the hammock of cocoa-nut fibre, brown and bending as a strip of mahogany veneer, with the bed-clothes folded up in the counterpane rug, tightly as a carpet-bag. Hanging up against the wall are boards, on which are pasted printed forms of the morning and evening prayer, as well as "A FEW TEXTS FROM THE BIBLE," which latter paper has been compiled, we believe, by the governor himself—ever earnest in his efforts to effect the religious reformation of the criminals under his charge. A wooden stool completes the furniture of the cell.

Over the door is a fanlight window, glazed inside, and protected without by heavy cross-bars. In some of the cells another grated opening is let into the back wall.

As we entered the cell it felt chilly as a dairy, so we asked the warder if it were not cold. "Not at all," was the answer. "In summer the men like being in the cells, in winter they prefer the dormitories." This desire on the part of the prisoners to quit the cells in winter, induced us to inquire whether, during the cold weather, the building were not heated by hot air or hot water-pipes. We were much startled to find that no such attention had been shown to the necessities of the wretched inmates. Again, seeing that no arrangements had been made for lighting the apartment with gas, we asked how the men managed for light in winter when, long before the locking-up time, the night has set in, and it is perfectly dark at the time of their entering the cells. We were informed that the men in the separate cells went to bed, although in the dormitories, where gas exists, they are allowed to remain reading until ten o'clock. Again, we found that no provision had been made to enable a prisoner to call for assistance in case he was taken ill during the night, and that his only chance of help under such circumstances, depended upon his ability to make sufficient noise to attract attention. Further, the ventilation of the chamber was most imperfect.

Now, it does not require many lines to point out the defective condition of such places. It was not the object of the law which condemned these criminals to lose their liberty, that they should be deprived likewise of warmth, light, assistance in sickness, and pure air. If their sins against society require that they should be shut out from the fellowship of the world, it forms no part of their sentence that they should suffer also the colds of winter—that if suddenly afflicted or attacked by a fit (such as we have detailed as occurring in the oakum-room, accidents, we were told, that are in no way of *rare* occurrence), they should have no means of invoking immediate assistance, or that, in order to obtain air fit to breathe, they should be forced to run the risk of an open window afflicting them with influenza or catarrh. Why should books be given out and yet gas-light denied to those in separate cells, especially when, in the dormitories, their no less culpable, but more fortunate, companions in guilt are passing their time in perusing some volume?

By the 2nd and 3rd Victoria, cap. 56, it is enacted that no cell shall be used for separate confinement which is not of such a size, and lighted, warmed, ventilated, and fitted up in such a manner, as may be required by a *due regard to health*, and furnished with the means of enabling the prisoner to communicate at any time with an officer of the prison. Yet, because at Coldbath Fields the prison is conducted on the silent system, and the inmate is separately confined for only twelve instead of twenty-four hours of the day, the Act does not affect the matter; and a cell which belonged to the barbarous prison times of the past century, which affords a shelter scarcely superior to that of a coal-cellar, is appointed as the sleeping-place of a man who may have to pass three years of his existence within it. Either the cells at Pentonville are wantonly luxurious, or those at Coldbath Fields disgracefully defective.

But if the cells in the old prison, built in 1794, are bad, what excuse can be made for the negligent humanity which permitted those in the more modern buildings erected in 1830, and set apart for the vagrants and misdemeanants, not only to be planned after the old model, but also to be made smaller by several inches in length as well as breadth. In the more primitive felons' jail one might expect to meet with defective arrangements; but in a comparatively modern building it is shocking to find that even a less enlightened scale of accommodation has been adopted.*

The prison authorities assert that the ventilation of the cells is sufficient and healthy. They point triumphantly to the extremely sanitary condition of the prison—the healthiest in London they say. In answer to this we urge that the House of Correction is a short-sentence prison, where offenders are sent for terms averaging from three days to three years, and the returns do not admit of its being compared as to its *daily average amount of sickness* with that of other prisons. From the prison returns for the year 1855, we learn that out of the 7,743 prisoners committed to Coldbath Fields during the twelve months, 1,796 were for terms under fourteen days—1,424 for terms under one month—2,342 for terms under three months, and 974 for less than six months. These form a total of 6,536 prisoners for terms ranging from seven days to less than six months, and there remain only 1,207 for the longer sentences.†

The prisoners are locked up for twelve hours out of the twenty-four. We will, for the

---

* The following table contains the number of cubic feet of air contained in the different sized cells of the House of Correction :—

In the old or Felons' prison	502
In the Misdemeanants' prison	337
In the Vagrants' prison	375

Whilst the amount of air contained in a cell of the Model Prison at Pentonville amounts to 911 cubic feet.

† TABLE SHOWING THE TERMS OF IMPRISONMENT OF THE PRISONERS CONFINED IN COLDBATH FIELDS PRISON IN THE COURSE OF THE YEAR ENDING MICHAELMAS, 1855.

SENTENCES.	Under Summary Conviction	After Trial.	Total.	Per Centage
Under 14 days	1,786	10	1,796	23
14 days, and under 1 month . . .	1,414	10	1,424	21
1 month, and under 2 months . . .	1,630	14	1,644	19
2 months, and under 3 months . .	660	38	698	9
3 months, and under 6 months . .	538	436	974	12
6 months, and under 1 year . . .	95	633	728	9
1 year, and under 2 years . . .	—	282	282	4
2 years, and under 3 years . . .	—	20	20	0·2
3 years, and upwards	—	—	—	—
Unlimited terms of imprisonment .	—	—	—	—
Transferred to other governors . .	—	177	177	2
Whipped, fined, or discharged on sureties .	—	—	—	—
Sentence deferred	—	—	—	—
Total	6,123	1,620	7,743	99·2

sake of the argument, suppose it to be winter time, when the windows are all closed to increase the warmth. The closely-shut cell in the felon prison contains 502 cubic feet of air. A man breathes about twenty times in a minute, inhaling about eighteen pints of air in that time; or, reducing the calculation to cubic feet, we may say he consumes about sixty cubic feet of air in the twelve hours, evolving in the same period twelve cubic feet of carbonic acid gas. Now, carbonic acid gas is an extremely noxious poison—indeed, one measure of it mixed with *five* of the atmosphere, is fatal to life. Even when present in very minute quantities, it is highly injurious to health. Professor Brande tells us that, " when so far diluted with air as to admit of being received into the lungs, it operates as a narcotic poison, producing drowsiness and insensibility." And further on he adds—" When the gas is inspired in the lowest poisonous proportion, the symptoms come on very gradually, and the transition from life to death is *usually tranquil;* this is what we learn from the history of suicides."

The scientific gentlemen appointed to report upon what should be the size of the separate cells at Pentonville prison decided that the health of the inmate required at least 911 cubic feet of air, and, even with this capacity, it was found necessary to alter the ventilation, so that perfect health might be maintained. Now, is it not unjust that men ordered to perform " hard labour" should be doomed to pass twelve hours of the day in an atmosphere which produces " drowsiness and insensibility," and so unfits them for their work?

We were likewise assured that even the cold of a winter's night, passed in a stone-walled and paved cell, so far from being injurious to the inmates, is, on the contrary, invigorating and healthy. A man leaving a warmed apartment, we were reminded, is very liable to catch cold, and the warders themselves say that they never suffer so much from the cold as after leaving a fire.

That the prisoners themselves feel the chilliness of the cells acutely is proved by their stopping up with their clothes the cracks and openings of the doors. Some time since, during a severe winter, a man perished in his cell—it was thought, from cold. Cold forms no portion of the prisoner's sentence; and until it does, the air in the stone cells of Coldbath Fields prison should be raised above freezing point. Moreover, the surgeon's printed report tells us that seventeen deaths out of the twenty-nine, or more than 58 per cent. of those which occurred in the course of last year, are recorded to have been " labouring under various affections of the substance of the lungs and bronchial passages;" in plain English, to have died from the effects of cold.*

The prison authorities themselves do not offer a word of excuse for not lighting up the cells. In winter it is dark when the men are locked up in them, and it is dark when they rise, so that twelve hours are passed in total obscurity. Even some of the cells in the galleries are in summer so obscure that it is impossible to distinguish anything in them beyond the whitewashed walls. Again we say, why give the men books, if the only time when it is possible to read them is to be passed in darkness? We should see the absurdity of presenting a

---

* TABLE SHOWING THE NUMBER OF CASES OF SICKNESS, LUNACY, AND DEATH, IN THE COURSE OF THE YEAR ENDING MICHAELMAS, 1855.

Slight indisposition	.	.	.	. 1,916	Lunatics	.	.	4
Infirmary Cases	.	.	.	. 131	Pardons on medical grounds .	.	.	15
				——	Deaths	.	.	29
Total	.	.	.	. 2,047	Greatest number of sick at any time	.	.	62
				——	Daily average number of sick	.	*not given*	

Of the twenty-nine who died, seventeen are recorded, says the surgeon's report, as having laboured under the various affections of the substance of the lungs and the bronchial passages. " Amongst the great variety of complaints," it is added, " boils of a carbuncular form have been very prevalent, and numerous abscesses have occurred. The number of these cases has been singularly great this year, amounting to 209, some of a very formidable character, and one proving fatal. Of feigned complaints the number has been considerable— 3,972."—*Mr. Wakefield's Report to the Justices for the County.*

library to a blind school; and yet is not this instance somewhat parallel? Confining a rebellious prisoner in a dark cell forms the greatest punishment the governor has power to inflict, and yet to lock up *unoffending* prisoners in an unlighted chamber for twelve hours daily is the ordinary routine of this prison.*

As regards the defective arrangements for enabling the prisoners to call for assistance, if attacked by sickness in the night, we were told that a watchman patrols each prison, visiting every yard once in the half hour. Nevertheless, the fact of several sudden deaths having occurred in the cells demands, in our opinion, some such arrangements as exist at Pentonville.

It appears, however, that there is every probability of the prison being pulled down, a railway company, whose line is to pass through the building, having undertaken to erect another prison in lieu of the existing one.

In conclusion, however, we should remind the reader that the defects here pointed out are defects of the *old* school of prison economy, and evidence rather as to the slight regard that was paid even to the physical necessities of prisoners only a few years ago, than as to any dereliction of duty on the part of the present authorities. It is easy to rebuild jails after the very best model—*upon paper;* but not quite so easy for visiting justices to make improvements in them out of a limited county-rate; and let us in fairness add, that every exertion is used by the present governor to render the House of Correction at Coldbath Fields as commodious and salutary as possible under the circumstances.

** *Dormitories.*—By the aid of spacious sleeping-rooms the felons' prison, which contains only 356 cells, is made to accommodate 889 prisoners. There are altogether five such apartments at Coldbath Fields, all situate in the old portion of the building, and built on the same plan, the smallest capable of making up 82 beds, the largest 101.

The dormitories are eighty-three feet in length, and twenty-five feet broad; and if the pointed roofs, with their grained tie-beams, were more lofty, they would do very well for rude chapels. At one end are the lavatories, made out of slate, with a porcelain basin let into each of the ten divisions, the bright brass button showing that water is continually laid on.

The manner in which the hammocks are arranged is ingenious enough, for every inch of space is taken advantage of. Four stout iron bars, resting on supports a foot from the floor, run along the entire length of the building, the first next the passage, like a long thick curtain-rod just above the ground, and the others ranged at a distance of six feet from each other. To these bars the hammocks are suspended, so that three rows are obtained, while a passage of some five feet wide along one side of the room is still left for the warders to patrol up and down during the night.

During the day-time, when the bed-clothes are folded up into a close bundle, and the brown cocoa-nut fibre of the hammocks is visible, the rows of tightly-stretched beds attached at either end to the long iron bars seem interminable. They form a kind of raised platform, gradually slanting upwards to the wall, as if they were so many sacks that had been carelessly laid across the rails.

Here, hanging against the wall, is a line of printed forms of the morning and evening prayers, ranged like the slates in a school-room.

The men lie with their heads to each other's feet, and, being near the ground, the warders, on their raised stools, can command a bird's-eye view of all the sleepers. The

---

* In the year 1850 the Committee on Prison Discipline reported as follows:—" That in regard to some of the details of discipline which have been brought before them, this Committee recommends that the means of lighting every cell (except cells for an infraction of prison rules) should be provided in every prison, and that *no prisoner should be left in darkness for more than a maximum time, which can be required for rest, viz., eight hours.*

sides of the hammocks curl round the prisoners' forms, so that they look like so many mummies ranged along three deep.

We paid a night visit to these dormitories, and the sight was most curious. When we reached the prison it was past eight o'clock, and all the prisoners were locked up in their cells, so that the building appeared deserted. The only warder we met was in the crypt-like corridor, and he wore over his boots slippers of flannel, gliding in and out of the columns noiselessly as a spectre. Though it was yet day-light, we could hear, as we passed the different cells, the heavy snoring or the restless tossing of the inmates.

When we reached the dormitory, the appearance of the place had curiously changed since the morning. The men were nearly all lying down, some asleep, others stretched out on their backs, staring up at the timber roof, and all were covered over with their brown-red rugs. So silent was the room, it seemed like an immense dead-house—as if we had entered some huge "morgue," where some hundred corpses were laid out on the floor before us.

Some of the men were sleeping with their clothes on, and as if they had thrown themselves down tired with the day's "hard labour;" others, with their forms curled up till the knees nearly touched the chest, had stowed themselves away for the night, for under the head was the pillow of rolled-up clothes.

We had expected to find some of the prisoners sitting up in their hammocks reading; but, although it was broad day-light, not one had a book in his hand—the men being, probably, too tired with their day's work to care for anything but rest.

As the evening progressed, some of the prisoners, who had been dozing with their clothes on, seemed to wake up and become aware that they had better prepare for the night's rest. So they got up slowly, like persons half-asleep, and began to undress themselves. It was a relief to see a human being stirring, for it proved that life existed in the prostrate crowd before us.

Close to where the warders sat were two rings of gas burning beneath tin pots, from which issued the curling steam of the coffee allowed for the officers' refreshment through the night.

It has been asserted that a great deal of conversation is carried on between the prisoners in these dormitories as the men lie huddled there together. We certainly did not *hear* any talking, and the place was as still as a church in the night; the heads of the prisoners, however, are within a foot of each other, and the ear is hardly to be relied on in such a case; for it may be easily deluded by the lowness of the whisper, so that the matter resolves itself into a trial of skill between the quickness of the warder, and the cunning of the prisoner.

As we peeped, at a later hour, through the little inspection-hole in the closed door of the dormitory, we could see those who were conversing together. One of the men was lying flat on his back, with his handkerchief raised to his mouth, and though the eye on the side towards the warder was shut as if in sleep, the other one was wide open, and kept on winking at his apparently slumbering neighbour, in a manner which showed that the two men were having a nice quiet chat together. The two warders, however, were not near enough to hear this infringement of the rule, and had we ourselves not advanced very silently to the inspection-hole, we probably should also have been deprived of the chance of witnessing it. There can, indeed, be no doubt that it is utterly absurd in a prison conducted on the silent system, with the special view of avoiding intercourse among the criminals, to herd together a hundred such men, and place them in exactly that position which is the most favourable for intercommunion.

The ventilation of these immense buildings is of that primitive kind which consists of a hole made in the wall near the top of the roof. When the gas is lighted, and the place becomes heated, a current of air is doubtlessly established; but that the foul atmosphere is not entirely removed is proved by the discretionary power vested in the night-warders, to open one of the windows whenever they perceive, by the "closeness" of the room, that the air, despite the openings near the ceiling, has become offensive with the exhalations of the hundred sleepers.

¶ i—ζ.

Of the Silent System.

The discipline followed at Coldbath Fields becomes an interesting study, from the fact that it is considered as the type of that form of prison government which is distinguished by the name of the " silent associated system."

We have purposely avoided offering any remarks upon the efficiency of this mode of discipline at other institutions—as, for instance, at Millbank and Brixton prisons—because we were desirous, before hazarding our opinion, of noting its operation at that establishment where all allow it is to be seen in its greatest force.*

We have before said, it is almost self-evident that every system of prison discipline, so far as it affects the liberty of communication among prisoners, must be either (1) associative, (2) separative, or (3) mixed.

1. Of the *associative* form of discipline there are two widely distinct varieties—
    a. Prisoners may be allowed to associate indiscriminately, and to indulge in *unrestrained intercourse* one with the other.
    b. Prisoners, though allowed to associate, may be made to labour as well as to exercise, and take their meals *in perfect silence.*

2. The *separative* form has likewise two subdivisions—
    a. *The partially separate,* which consists in dividing the body of prisoners into *classes,* or groups, according to their crimes, ages, or characters, and so keeping the more desperate and hardened offenders apart from the more inexperienced and hopeful.
    b. *The entirely separate,* which consists in secluding every prisoner *individually* from the others, and so putting an end to all intercourse among them, by the positive isolation of each from the rest.

3. As regards the *mixed* form, there is but one order—
    Prisoners may be placed in *separation* for a certain term, by way of "probation" (as it is called), and then put to work in *association* under the silent system.

The two great experiments, which have of late years been tried in this country, with a view to prevent the further corruption of the inmates of our prisons, are the separate system practised at Pentonville, and the silent associated system pursued at Coldbath Fields.

The separate system was introduced at the former institution in the year 1842. The silent associated system at the latter in 1834.

That these two systems are each an eminent improvement upon the old classified system of our prisons, and more particularly upon that more ancient system of indiscriminate intercourse among criminals, and both instituted with the kindest possible intentions towards the criminals themselves, none that are open to reason can for a moment doubt.

The two systems, however, differ essentially, even in their objects. The silent system

* "The best example of the silent system," said Colonel Jebb, in his evidence before the Committee on Prison Discipline, "would, I think, be found in Coldbath Fields or Westminster Bridewell."

seeks to put an end to the contamination of prisoners by stopping all *inter*-communion among them. The separate system seeks not only to do this, but at the same time to bring about the reformation of the prisoners by inducing *self*-communion. The one endeavours to attain a *negative* good by checking a capital evil, and the other to work a *positive* good, in addition to the negative one.

The two systems again differ in their requirements. That which seeks to compass its end by the individual separation of the prisoners demands, of course, a peculiarly built and specially commodious institution (since it is one of the essential conditions of that system that each prisoner shall be provided with a cell to himself, and such cell must necessarily be of far greater capacity than an ordinary sleeping chamber, as it is required to form at once the work-shop of the man by day and his bed-room by night). The silent system, however (though, in its integrity, it exacts a separate sleeping cell for each prisoner*), may—by the aid of large dormitories, tended with the most active supervision during the night, as well as by the addition of spacious work-rooms, wherein the men can labour in association during the day—be applied to old prisons, even where the cells are not only too few in number, but too small in size for the requirements of the separate system.

Hence we find that new prisons are generally constructed on the separate plan, whilst in old ones the silent associated form of discipline is usually adopted, the latter circumstance being due partly to that widely-prevailing disposition to cobble and patch up some old worn-out thing, so that it may serve as a make-shift for an office it never was fitted for, rather than be at the expense and trouble of providing a new one, specially adapted to the object in view.

That the separate system attains the same end as, and far more effectually than, the silent system, there can be no doubt, since the *surest* mode of preventing intercommunion in jails is to prevent the association of the prisoners. To construct a building, however, with a separate cell for each inmate that it is intended to accommodate is likely to be considerably more expensive than the erection of one with large dormitories and associated work-rooms. (Each cell at Pentonville, by-the-bye, cost upon an average £150, whereas the expense of building the old prison at Coldbath Fields averaged not less than £283 per cell.) Nevertheless, in a prison conducted upon the silent associated system, the extra sum required to be paid annually in salaries to warders, so as to ensure that thorough supervision of the prisoners, which is so necessary for the due carrying out of this form of prison government, increases the continual cost of management so far beyond that of one maintained on the "separate" plan, as to render the latter much more desirable even in an *economical* point of view. For instance, we have before shown that, according to the returns, there is 1 warder at Pentonville to superintend every 17 prisoners, whereas, at Coldbath Fields, 1 warder is required to superintend every 13 prisoners; so that at the former establishment each warder can watch over upwards of 30 per cent. more persons than he can at the latter one.

It would hardly require a moment's deliberation, therefore, in order to decide as to which is the preferable of these two modes of prison government,† were it not that the

---

* "Under the silent system, properly worked out," said the Inspector-General of Prisons, before the Parliamentary Committee on Prison Discipline, "the prisoner would have a separate sleeping-cell, though the classification of the 4th of George IV. might in some degree be put aside. The prisoners can be assembled together in large numbers under that system, but, whilst they are so assembled, they are under the strictest supervision and control, and are employed in various industrial occupations or at hard labour on the tread-mill."

† Mr. Chesterton, in his book upon "Prison Life," while arguing against the effects of the separate system, cites, with peculiar paralogical aptness, the following case, as evidence of the evils arising from the physical depression induced by that system; but as the example strikes us as being a strong instance of the benefits

separate system is found to be so dangerous to the mental health of those subject to it, that the authorities have deemed it necessary, not only to shorten the term of confinement under it, but also greatly to relax and modify the severity of the original discipline. We have before shown that, whilst the average ratio of insanity from 1842 to 1850 was 58 lunatics per annum, to every 10,000 of the gross prison population throughout England and Wales, still, at Pentonville, the average yearly proportion of lunacy from 1843 to 1851, was 62·0 per 10,000 prisoners; so that had the inmates of all the prisons throughout the country been submitted to the same stringent discipline as at the "Model Prison," the gross number of criminal lunatics, between 1842 and 1850, would, so far as we can judge, have been increased more than tenfold, or have risen from 680 to 7,173. (See GREAT WORLD, pp. 103-5, 115, 143-4, 168). Now, as the driving of a man mad forms no part of his original sentence, it is clear that prison authorities have no earthly right to submit a prisoner to a course of discipline, which, if long protracted, would have the effect of depriving

---

resulting from *temporary* isolation from the world, we quote it here as evidence of the deep impression that can be made by separation upon the hearts of even the most hardened criminals :—

"John Bishop, the monster who was executed for the cruel murder of the Italian boy, whom he burked in order to secure the price of the body in the school of anatomy, was," he says, "without exception, the most finished ruffian within my memory. He was a man of powerful frame, of repulsive countenance, and of brutal address and manners. Consigned to my charge on remand, and with the direction to be kept apart (an occasional instance in those days), he entered the prison uttering oaths and execrations, and indulging in the grossest language, while he assailed the subordinates, and even myself, with menace and defiance. He had received no provocation, but gave vent to the irrepressible brutality of his nature. Fourteen days of exclusive self-communing incarceration," continues the late governor, "produced in this abandoned criminal a change so marked and depressing, as to constitute an instructive commentary upon the wear and tear which unrelieved reflection will produce upon a guilty mind. Bishop was, by law, entitled to supply himself with a generous diet, and he was permitted to take daily exercise in the open air, and to have an ample supply of books, so that feebleness could not have been induced by diminished sustenance, nor be referable to anything else than the terror resulting from solitary ruminations. Certain it is, that iron-souled miscreant became so meek and subdued, so prone to tears, so tremulous, and agitated, that at the end of fourteen days, when he was again sent up to the police-office, he could hardly be recognized as the same coarse and blustering bully who had so recently entered the prison. *It was impossible to see the effects of solitude upon a conscience stricken by crime more signally exemplified.* When committed to Newgate, I found, on inquiry," he adds, "that renewed association with lawless men had revived the brutality so inseparable from his nature."

That this softening of a criminal's nature is by no means an extraordinary effect of separate confinement, Messrs. De Beaumont and De Tocqueville also bear witness, in their Report upon the system as administered in Philadelphia. "Do you find it difficult to endure solitude?" was a question put by them to one of the prisoners. "Ah, sir," the man answered, "it is the most horrid punishment that can be imagined." "Does your health suffer from it?" was the next inquiry. "No!" he replied, "but my soul is very sick." Of another it was said, "he cannot speak long without shedding tears." The same remark, they add, may be made "of *all* whom we have seen." Some, again, confessed that the Bible, and others that religion was "their greatest consolation."

Mr. Chesterton argues, that the state of mental depression which separate confinement induces, is *sympathetically* derived from the physical prostration to which solitude gives rise, and that unreasoning observers are apt to hail that which is merely the effect of bodily weakness as the sign of spiritual conversion and promise of amendment. "In vain," he says, "may the prisoners become imbued with a shallow devotion, and pronounce the study of the Bible a pleasure. They most probably seize upon those resources," he tells us, "because none other are available, and such ebullitions of piety proceed, in most cases," the late governor adds, "from morbid sensibility, which vanishes on the first serious trial of their reality." But though it may be true that the ratio of the annual re-commitments to the separate prison at Glasgow amounted to 50 per cent., or, in other words, that one-half of the prisoners annually committed to the jail have been found to return to it ; still this in no way affects the truth of the contrition and religious fervour induced by the separation for the *time being;* but it merely proves what all admit, that criminals are persons of weak, impulsive natures, incapable of *lasting* impressions. Nor is it of any weight to assert that the mental depression, induced by separation, arises from physical prostration ; for such mental depression is the feeling that all who desire the criminal's reformation must seek to produce, as it is impossible for any one to repent his past life, and yet exist in a state of bodily and spiritual liveliness. (See p. 168 of GREAT WORLD OF LONDON.)

him of his reason. We cannot but concur, therefore, in the opinion of Sir B. Brodie and Dr. Ferguson, that "the utmost watchfulness and discretion on the part of the governor, chaplain, and medical officers are requisite, in order to administer with safety the discipline enforced at Pentonville."

Now it must in candour be admitted, that the silent associated system as practised at Coldbath Fields is open to no such objections. In the year ending Michaelmas, 1855, there were only four lunatics out of a gross prison population of 9,180, which is at the rate of only 4·3 per 10,000, and even less than the normal proportion for all England (5·8). Let us, however, dismiss all prejudice from our minds, and calmly weigh the advantages and disadvantages of this form of discipline, with the view to discovering whether its defects may not be, in a measure, remedied and its benefits improved.

"The silent system," writes Mr. Chesterton, who being, as it were, the metropolitan father of that form of penal discipline, may be regarded as its chief advocate, "has never yet been attempted in this country with the space necessary for its perfect development."* Notwithstanding this he proceeds to tell us that, though professional thieves *may* communicate under it, to a very limited extent, by significant signs—comprehensible to themselves only—and though even unlimited communication (were it possible) among them could not further corrupt *their* natures, it is still a comforting reflection that, by means of that form of discipline, the uninitiated, who are ignorant of the import of such signs, are safe from the contaminating influence of their more hardened associates. "Moreover," he says, in another part of the same work, "the silent system inflicts no injury upon the health, however protracted the sentence, the bodily and mental sanity being sustained under it to the last, in the ordinary ratio of mankind. The legitimate opportunities it affords," he adds (vol. ii., p. 27), "nay, the demands it makes for the use of speech are numerous. The daily responses in chapel by the prisoners, as well as their communications with the governor, the chaplain, the schoolmaster, and various officers, all tend healthfully to employ the tongue. It is only communication between prisoner and prisoner that is interdicted." "We do all we can in the prison to prevent contamination," the same gentleman observed, in his evidence before the Parliamentary Committee in 1850; "and in my opinion the associated silent system, properly carried out, is as effectual for all purposes of prison discipline as any that can be devised. The prisoners *do* communicate, but I find that all the communications are of a very trifling description, and that nothing like contamination takes place generally among them."

Here, then, it will be remarked, that the special merit (and it assuredly commends itself as no slight one to those who know what was the state of our prisons in the olden time) claimed for this form of prison government, even by its chief supporter, is, as we have said, of a purely negative character, viz., it does *not* allow the contamination of one prisoner by another, it does *not* injure the health of those who are subjected to its regimen.

Let us, then, endeavour to discover at what expense these eminent advantages are gained. We will in fairness continue to quote from Mr. Chesterton himself. In the course of his examination before the House of Commons, he was asked, "Have you compared the number of punishments in the jail under your system with any other jail upon the separate system?" "Yes, I have," was the answer; "and I know that our punishments are *very great*." "You punish for anything like a sign being passed from one prisoner to another?" he was then asked. "Yes," he replied. "Or any attempt to communicate?" "Yes." "Your punishments in 1848 were as many as 11,624." "Yes, they were." Mr. Chesterton, it should be added, defends this excess of punishments by saying he considers that punishments in general tend to soften, and have a beneficial effect upon prisoners' natures.

We will, however, for the sake of putting this important point clearly before the mind,

* "Revelations of Prison Life," vol. ii., p. 23

proceed to compare the number of punishments, as well as the number of prisoners punished, at Coldbath Fields and at Pentonville prisons, in the course of the year 1854-1855.

TABLE SHOWING THE ABSOLUTE AND RELATIVE NUMBER OF PUNISHMENTS, AND NUMBER OF PRISONERS PUNISHED, AT COLDBATH FIELDS AND PENTONVILLE PRISONS, DURING THE YEAR 1854—55.

PUNISHMENTS AT COLDBATH FIELDS PRISON.		PUNISHMENTS AT PENTONVILLE PRISON.	
Number of punishments.	*Number of prisoners punished.*	*Number of punishments.*	*Number of prisoners punished.*
For neglect of work . 1,255 For *noise, talking, insolence, and bad language* . . 5,421 For various acts of disobedience and disorder 2,347 Total number of punishments in the course of 1854—55 . . 9,023 Gross prison population 9,180 Proportion of punishments to gross prison population . 98 per cent.	Reported once . 1,208 „ twice . 607 „ thrice . 355 „ four times 138 „ more than four times, "some few" Total punished . ——2,308 Discharged *without* having been reported once . . . 4,984 Others unreported . 1,888 Total unpunished . 6,872 Gross prison population . . 9,180 Proportion of prisoners punished to gross prison population, 25 per cent. Proportion of prisoners unpunished . 75 per cent.	For disobedience and disturbing prison . 232 For misconduct in school and chapel, and making obscene communications . . 169 For communicating with fellow-prisoners 171 For trying to send letters out of prison . 2 For wilfully destroying prison property . 89 For insubordination and false charges against officers . . . 3 For fighting and wrangling . . . . 30 For attempting and proposing to others to escape . . . 12 Feigning and threatening to commit suicide, and impositions on surgeon . . . 9 For having dirty cells . 4 For purloining bread . 22 For having tobacco in possession . . 14 —— 757 Number of cases punished . . . 601 Gross prison population 925 Proportion of punishments to gross prison population . 65 per cent.	Reported once . . 158 „ twice . . 43 „ thrice . . 24 „ four times . 13 „ more than four times 25 Total number punished 263 Number unpunished . 662 Gross prison population 925 Proportion of prisoners punished to gross prison population, 28 per cent. Proportion of prisoners unpunished to gross prison population, 72 per cent.

Now let us collate these data, as regards the number of punishments as well as the number punished in the year at Coldbath Fields prison, with the same facts at Pentonville.

By the above comparative table, it will be seen at a glance that, though the proportion of prisoners refusing to submit to discipline, and consequently those upon whom punishment had to be inflicted, was very nearly the same at both Coldbath Fields and Pentonville prisons—or 25 per cent. in the former case, and 28 per cent. in the latter—nevertheless, the *proportionate amount of punishment* required to be inflicted was by no means similar; for, whilst at Pentonville the ratio of the punishments to the gross prison population was only 65 per cent., at Coldbath Fields the ratio was as high as 98 per cent.! or, in plain language, it was found necessary to inflict 33 per cent. more punishments upon the refractory prisoners at the Middlesex House of Correction than upon those at the Model Prison.

That this excess of punishments is to be ascribed to the exactions of the silent system, rather than to any undue severity on the part of the present excellent governor, we are happy to be able to bear witness; and the returns themselves are proof positive upon the point; for, whereas the daily average proportion of the prisoners punished amounted to 3 per cent. of the daily population in Mr. Chesterton's time, it was only 1¾ per cent. in the course of last year.

Now the excess of punishment required for the enforcement of the silent system, it should be borne in mind, is not only an excess over and above that which is found necessary for the maintenance of the discipline at other prisons; but the *whole* of such punishments are inflictions which were *never contemplated by the law,* and which formed no part of the legal penalty imposed upon the prisoner.* They are punishments merely for *arbitrary* offences, or, in other words, offences against an *arbitrary* form of discipline, known only within the prison walls, and to which the prisoner is sentenced without either jury to try him, or counsel to protect him, and for which, therefore, nothing but the most cogent necessity, as well as the highest moral advantages, can be received as justification with all righteous minds.

One other stringent objection against the silent associated system of prison discipline is, that speech proceeds from a natural impulse among men to give articulate utterance to the thoughts, and feelings passing within them, and that the silent form of prison discipline not only imposes a wilful restraint upon this innate propensity, but it likewise places prisoners in those very circumstances in which there is the greatest temptation for the continual exercise of it; so that a man is thrown by the authorities into precisely those conditions which are most likely to lead to a breach of the discipline (that is to say, he is put among several hundreds of others, a large number of whom were probably his former companions, and all of whom are at least his fellow-sufferers "in trouble"), and yet he is punished for the least infraction of the arbitrary prison rules.

The prisoner under the silent *associated* system is allowed to mingle with his fellows. He forms one of the five hundred who pick oakum side by side, or one of the twenty-four who tread the wheel, or of the eighty who work as tailors together. But what is strictly denied to him is the right to talk with those who are working at his elbow. If he requires anything, he may address an officer, but he must not utter a word to the prisoner next him. He has, as it were, his tongue taken from him at the same time that his own clothes are changed for the suit of prison gray.

He has been sentenced, for a certain offence, to lose his liberty for a time; still, on arriving at the prison, he finds that, in addition to his freedom, he must part, also, with his right of speech. He is then placed amidst hundreds similarly circumstanced to himself, all of them suffering from the same cause, and feeling, therefore, towards each other, a sympathy which longs to vent itself in speech; but, though surrounded with temptations to speak on every side, he is denied the right to condole with his neighbours; for there is a retinue of warders continually watching over them all, and ready to have any one punished even for " a significant look or a sign."

Who can wonder, then, that the punishments under such a system should be found— even though they have been considerably reduced by the present management—to range as high as 33 per cent. over and above what is necessary for the maintenance of order at other prisons !

The silent system of prison discipline, it is evident, can be carried out only by means of operating in two different ways upon the natures of the various prisoners. The more timid and less sensitive may, by dread of the punishment under it, be cowed into rapid submission to its requirements; whilst the more irritable and wayward may, after a long course of suffering, be ultimately worried into subjection to the discipline. But neither of these states of mind appears to us to be in any way connected with that reformation of character which every form of prison government should, at least, aspire to induce. Mere slavish obedience to arbitrary forms cannot possibly give rise to that elevation of soul without which the criminal must for ever remain sunk in moral and spiritual turpitude;

---

* The nature of the punishments inflicted at Coldbath Fields in the course of 1854—55, was as follows :—

Placed in handcuffs and other irons	. . 2	Confined in dark and solitary cells	. . 470
Whipped 5		Put upon short diet, and other punishments	8,546

9,023

whilst a continual sense of irritation under the most galling control, so far from being connected with either a state of contrition for the past or virtuous resolves for the future, must give rise, rather, to an infinity of deceits and falsities with the view of tricking the warders; so that the mind, instead of being calm and sedate with its weight of sorrow for past misdeeds, will be busy in planning all kinds of low artifices and dissimulations whereby to hold secret converse with those around; or else being made sullen, as well as taciturn, the men will pass their time in moody moroseness.*

But the silent system, as we have before said, springs from that love of extremes that belongs to the extravagant rather than the rational form of mind. Because the liberty of speech has been found to be productive of evil among criminals, wiseacres have thought fit to declare that henceforth prisoners shall not speak at all, even though it be only by intercommunion that the wisest and best of us have become a whit wiser and better than brutes. Such an injunction is about upon a par in wisdom with that of the old lady who asserted that, because there was danger in bathing, her son should not enter the water until he could swim. But are there no other faculties that prisoners apply to a bad purpose *besides speech?* Is not sight as much an instrument of evil among them as even the voice itself? Yet, who would be bold enough to propose—as Eugène Sue has with the murderer—that because the faculty of seeing renders criminals more expert and dangerous to society, therefore they should be deprived of sight altogether? Surely, dumbness is not calculated to have a more moral effect upon men's hearts than blindness; and if the object be to decrease the power of doing evil among criminals, we must all feel satisfied that a blind bad man is more impotent for harm than a dumb one. But the main object of all forms of prison discipline should be not merely to prevent men becoming more corrupt in jail, but to render them more righteous; not merely to check bad thoughts, but to implant good ones. Yet what can mere silence teach?—especially silence in the midst of a multitude that is calculated to distract self-communion rather than induce it.

---

* "It is impossible," it has been truly said, "to maintain perfect silence, and yet allow of *association;*" for the year ending Michaelmas, 1855, the number of punishments, as we have shown, amounted to no less than 9,023, and of these nearly two-thirds, or as many as 5,421 were for *noise, talking, insolence,* and *bad language.* The prison authorities themselves confess that it is utterly impossible to stop all intercommunication among the prisoners. "They certainly *do* communicate," confessed Mr. Chesterton, before the Select Committee on Prison Discipline. A large amount of communication is carried on by signs. "They ask one another,' we are told, "how long they are sentenced for, and when they are going out, and the answers are given by laying two or three fingers on the wheel to signify so many months, or else they turn their hands to express the number of days before unlocking." Again, the Rev. Mr. Kingsmill, in his chapter on "Prison and Prisoners," informs us, that "The position of stooping, in which the prisoners work at picking oakum, gives ample opportunity of carrying on a lengthened conversation without much chance of discovery; so that the rule of silence is a dead letter to many. At meals, also, in spite of the strictness with which the prisoners are watched, the order is constantly infringed. The time of exercise, again, affords an almost unlimited power of communicating with each other; for the closeness of the prisoners' position, and the noise of their feet, render intercommunication at such times a very easy matter. . . . Farther, the prisoners attend chapel daily, and this may be termed the golden period of the day to most of them; for it is here, by holding their books up to their faces and pretending to read with the chaplain, that they can carry on the most uninterrupted conversation."

The principal mode of communication, however, is by talking without moving the lips, and in this practice many of the old prisoners are very expert. One person, lately discharged from the prison, has often exhibited to us his adroitness in that respect, and proved to us that it is quite possible for prisoners to talk even while the warder's eye is fixed intently upon them, without the least signs of utterance being discoverable by sight. Moreover, at Tothill Fields, a series of benches, with high backs, have recently been constructed, and arranged on a slant, in order to put a stop to the talking that, despite the vigilance of the matrons, goes on among the female prisoners. This arrangement, however, has been found to facilitate communication, by acting as a conductor to the sound rather than impeding it; and the matron at that prison informed us, that though she could hear the voice proceeding from a certain quarter, still it was impossible by her eye to detect the actual person speaking.

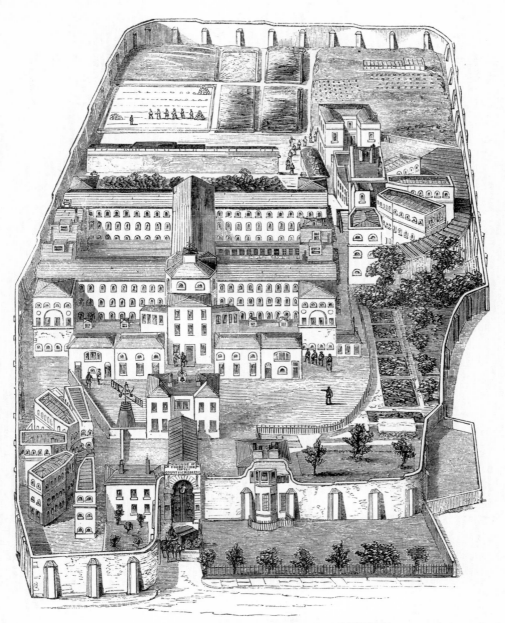

BIRD'S-EYE VIEW OF COLDBATH FIELDS PRISON.

How much time that might be profitably employed is utterly wasted every day in sheer moody taciturnity under the silent system. At Coldbath Fields, we see assembled together some 500 of the most ignorant and depraved portion of our population—a class of people requiring instruction, not so much in mere reading and writing, as in the first principles of religion and morality, of worldly honour, and even common worldly prudence, more than any other body of men, and *yet who are allowed to remain, for upwards of eight hours out of the twelve composing the prison day, in a state of utter mental idleness.* Surely such stark waste of intellect as goes on under this silent associated system is absolutely wicked, as well as disgraceful to the time in which we live. If there be an age which owes more than any other to the advantages of intercommunication it is the present—distinguished as it is for its railroads, its steam-vessels, its penny postage, its electric telegraphs, cheap literature, and steam printing-presses; so that it becomes a positive marvel of inconsistency, as to how, at such a period, the leading minds of the country could ever have been induced to tolerate a system of prison-government that assumes to make men better by putting a stop to all intercommunication whatever. It is only by intercommunion that the faculties of the human mind become in the least developed. A human being, when left to himself, grows up—like Peter, the wild boy of Bohemia—an unreflective, and indeed hopeless brute; whilst a man of education, by mere intercommunication with the most profound and righteous thinkers, both living and dead, contains stored in his own mind the wisest and best thoughts—the accumulated experience of the principal sages and worthies that have lived almost from the commencement of the world. Those who know and feel this, and know, moreover, what a wondrous faculty is that of speech, and how much of a man's boasted reason is due to the expression of thoughts and feelings by articulate sounds, cannot but see in the silent system a wilful rejection of God's greatest gift, perhaps, to man.

Surely all that is necessary in order to check unrestricted intercourse among criminals, is to stop all communion on *depraved* subjects. To go farther than this, and put an end to the communication of even good thoughts among them, by enjoining absolute silence, is not only absurd as over-reaching the end in view, but positively wicked, from the utter waste of intellectual power which results from such a course. In the best regulated tailors' work-shops at the west end of the Metropolis, it is not uncommon for the journeymen to pay one of their own body to read to them while they are engaged at their labour. Under the silent system, however, no such educational process is permitted during the work, and the men are condemned to remain two-thirds of the day with their mental faculties utterly in abeyance, or else engaged, from the mere want of better occupation, in planning tricks by which to indulge in some secret communication, in the very face of the warders themselves.

We would have the terrible and wasteful silence of the oakum-room turned to some good account, rather than allow the men to be left, as now, to brood moodily over their own degraded thoughts, or else to be continually chafing under the irritation of excessive and arbitrary control. We would have the stillness enjoined by that system taken advantage of, and some one put to read to the prisoners from a book that was at once of an elevating and interesting

---

* The distribution of time followed in the daily routine of discipline at the House of Correction, is as follows :—

6h. 25m.	The gun fires, and the prisoners rise. The officers for the day enter, are mustered, and examined in the outer yard. Cells are unlocked, and the prisoners counted in their yards.	9h. 15m.	Prepare for chapel.
		9h. 30m.	Service commences.
		10h.	Go to work.
		2h.	Dinner, and exercise in the yards.
7h.	Work commences.	3h.	Go to work.
8h. 20m.	Breakfast and exercise in the yards.	5h. 30m.	Supper.
		6h.	Commence locking up.

Time employed at labour . . . . 8h. 8m.
Time for meals . . . . 1h. 30m.
Exercise for those not employed at tread-wheel labour . . 1h. 30m.

character, and we would condemn only those who interrupted the reading to a term of the same painful and unbroken silence as is now enforced.

Such a plan has, as we have shown, already been put in practice, at this prison on the Sundays, and we have chronicled, in our account of it, that it is not uncommon even for refractory prisoners to request permission to be present at these readings. We feel assured were this *instructive form* of the silent associated system judiciously carried out, not only might the eight hours that are now spent in absolutely unprofitable silence—in silence that is barren of all good as well to the criminal himself as to society in general—be turned to the best possible account by being made the means, not only of implanting some few honourable and righteous principles in the hearts of the prisoners, but likewise, by occupying their minds for the time being, of diverting them from the low tricks and cunning now carried on, and so putting an end to the necessity of such an inordinate proportion of punishments as is at present required to enforce silence from the listless men.

** Stars.—To induce the prisoners to conduct themselves with propriety during their stay in Coldbath Fields prison, the system of stars, as badges of good conduct, has been adopted; one of these is given for every three months during which a man has not been reported for misbehaviour. These badges are in the shape of a red star, which is stitched to the prisoner's sleeve. We were told that at one time there was a man in the jail who had gained eleven such stars. Half-a-crown is given for each of the good-conduct badges on the day the prisoner is liberated.

We inquired of one of the warders whether he considered that these rewards had any influence over the prisoners' reformation. He replied that he thought not, and indeed, that he considered the half-crowns given for them as so much money thrown away. "The best-behaved men," he continued, "are the old offenders—those who have been imprisoned before; they know the prison rules and observe them. Do you see that man with four stars on his sleeve?" he added, pointing to a prisoner in the exercising yard; "you observe he has a greater number of badges than any here, and yet it is the third time he has been in jail, as you can tell by the white figure on his other sleeve." Indeed, the prison authorities, examined before the Parliamentary Committee in 1850, one and all admitted that the worst class of offenders outside the prison is invariably the best conducted within the prison walls.

We may add, by way of conclusion to this account of the regulations at Coldbath Fields prison, that if any of the men should die during the term of incarceration, they are buried at the expense of the county. An undertaker contracts with the prison to do all the funerals at 28s. each; and, for this, he supplies a one-horse hearse, fetches the body away, and pays for a grave in the Victoria Cemetery, Bethnal Green. All the friends of the deceased receive notice, and, if they choose to attend, a time is fixed for the procession to leave the gates.

** Report Office.—Whenever a warder discovers a man in his yard speaking, laughing, or otherwise breaking the rules of the prison discipline, he enters the prisoner's number in the report-book, and the next morning all those who have thus offended are led into the hall at the entrance of the felons' building, and arranged in rows, to await their turn to be taken in before the governor, and receive his sentence of punishment.

The day we were at Coldbath Fields prison was a Monday, and consequently there was a considerable number of unruly prisoners to be reported, for the list included the offenders of Saturday and Sunday. We found about fifty prisoners, spaced out at equal distances like so many chess-men, whilst the different warders stood by, carrying under their arms what we at first mistook for tea-trays, but subsequently discovered to be the report-books, which are covered with japanned tin sides. We picked our way through the gathering of offenders, passing in and out of them, whilst they remained silent and still as so many statues, and as soon as the governor had entered the "justice hall," we pushed back the spring-door and followed him.

The apartment was about the size, and had much the look, of a lawyer's back-office. A long mahogany desk ran along one side of the wall; a couple of oak-grained cup-boards flanked each side of the fireplace, over which, as an ornament, hung a model of the new building for oakum-picking. The governor took his seat at a small desk before the window at the end, the chief warder perched himself upon a high stool, and then the court was declared to be sitting.

"Bring in the first case," was the order, and the spring-door creaked as it opened to admit a sub-warder and a youth, whose coarse features were pale with excitement, whilst his firmly-closed lip showed that he was determined on making a vigorous defence.

Caps were taken off, and the pleadings began.

"I report this man for insolence," commenced the sub-warder, and, despite the prisoner's nervous ejaculations of "No, sir! Please, sir! No, sir!" the officer related how the man had moved a table, and when reprimanded moved it still more loudly and laughed.

Then the prisoner entered on his defence. "Guv'ner, I did no such thing. He's been down on me ever since I've been in prison. He said to me, says he, 'Don't move that table'—which was by accident—and I never touched it, guv'ner, s'elp me."

"Did he laugh?" asked the governor of the warder, and on the officer replying in the affirmative, sentence was delivered. "You should attend to what the officers say, and then you wouldn't get into trouble." Turning over the leaves of a report-book, Captain Colvill added, "You have been reported three times this month—you must lose half your dinner;" and the prisoner, with a shrug of the shoulders, as much as to say, "he didn't care," was led from the room.

The next case was one of a man having given away to another prisoner a portion of his bread. The case was fully proved, despite the culprit's denials, by the evidence of another man in the same yard; whereupon the reported felon meanly "split" upon two others, who, he declared, had often exchanged their gruel and cocoa. This was an important case, and the parties concerned were ordered to be brought forward. They both denied the charge, assuring the "guv'ner," with oaths, that it was "no such thing."

"If you tell me a lie, I'll punish you worse than for the offence," threatened the governor. But, in spite of the warning, the men vociferated their innocence. A short investigation proved that they were guilty, and the judgment was a heavy one, for the next three days' dinner was docked one-half.

"You'll find that all the prisoners are innocent," remarked the governor, satirically, whilst the next case was being brought in.

One, a handsome lad, with a large, bright eye, was accused of having a paper containing some pepper in his possession. He had been employed in the kitchen, and had taken it for no perceptible object beyond the desire to thieve something. He had two red stars on his arm, and as a punishment one was taken off and half a dinner docked.

Another lad, with a clean, respectable-looking face, that betokened education and gentle birth, was brought up for tearing his rug or counterpane. He never spoke, but kept his eyes down; when the governor addressed him he blushed. We were afterwards told that he was very respectably connected, and in prison for the first time. We were glad the case was not fully proved against him, and almost felt personally grateful to the governor for the kind tone and feeling with which he spoke to the boy.

More than half the complaints were for talking. In each case the warder had scarcely commenced saying "I have to report this man for speaking," when the excited prisoner would exclaim, "It isn't true, guv'ner; may I die, if I said a word." But the evidence in nearly every instance was of a most conclusive nature. One offender—a very bad case—was condemned to three days' confinement on bread and water, the others lost half their dinners, thus causing a considerable saving to the kitchen supplies for the day.

The prisoner who behaved the worst of all those reported was the youngest, a mere boy of fifteen or sixteen, of short stature, with a narrow forehead and full broad jaw. He had been caught talking, and when detected laughed, and on being reprimanded had commenced dancing. Such a glaring defiance of authority from one so young interested even the chief warder, who, from the top of his tall stool, denounced the stripling criminal as the worst behaved boy in the prison. The lad began crying the moment he entered the office, and the moment he found the case going against him, his little arms and legs went stiff with passion, and he grew abusive. He, too, was condemned to three days' solitary confinement on bread and water, "And," added the governor, "if you don't behave better for the future, I shall have to report you to the magistrates and have you whipped again."

"I don't care for that!" answered the lad as he was led out.

After the prisoners, two sub-warders were brought in, accused by their superior officers with breaking the prison rules by sleeping in church during the sermon. Both were fined.

The punishments over, those who had applications to make to the governor personally were admitted to his presence. One wished to write a letter to a friend to become bail for him; and as the prison regulations only allow the prisoners one letter in three months, a special permission was required. On condition that nothing but the subject of bailing should be touched upon, the request was granted.

Two applications were for stars for good conduct; and as no report had been made against either of the men for three months, they, too, were successful.

Another, who seemed so delighted with the opportunity of talking, that he continued doing so until his breath was exhausted, wished to make some inquiries about three postage stamps which his wife had sent him in a letter, and which he had never received. He insisted upon repeating nearly the whole of his wife's epistle, gave a short outline of why he was in prison, and only quitted the room when he had, for the tenth time, been told that the missing property would be searched for and taken care of.

The most curious application was from a short, bilious-looking man, who entered blubbering to beg of the governor to let him be confined in a dark cell. Before he came in, the chief warder had prefaced his entry with a hint that "he was not all right in his head." The poor fellow commenced a long tale of his having been in the Crimea, in the land transport service, and said he objected to being stared at as he was. We believe he was subsequently handed over to the doctor.

An elderly man with large, swollen, watery eyes, and thick lips that worked violently as he spoke, was the last applicant. He bowed with obsequious politeness, and said that since his heavy misfortune had placed him in his present unhappy condition, he was most desirous of sending word to a highly-respectable gentleman, whose friendship he had in more prosperous times been proud to own, to tell him that he wished to give up the lodgings he had taken at his house.

Never was man so thankful as this polite prisoner for so trifling a favour granted. He repeated, "Thank you, sir, I am indebted to you," three times; his voice, at each exclamation, growing more expressively grateful. He was in prison for swindling.

When the business was over, the report-books, with their japanned tin bindings (about twenty in number), were placed in a rack, and the governor declared the court broken up. When we left we found the hall cleared of its crowd, the only prisoners to be seen being the three or four lads who, down on their hands and knees, like the pictures of sportsmen deer-stalking, were holy-stoning the pavement of the corridor.

¶ i—η.

Of the Different Kinds of Prisons and Prisoners, and Diet allowed to each.

*** *Vagrants' Prison.*—At Coldbath Fields prison the old and silly classification enjoined by the 4th of George IV. still continues in force, for here are to be found, to this day, special places for vagrants, misdemeanants, and felons—though such a system of separation cannot possibly be of the least avail, since it is well known that the late inmate of the felons' prison not only often gets re-committed as the reputed thief, or rogue and vagabond, and so has a place assigned him among the vagrants, but is afterwards (not unfrequently) sent back to the same prison for assault or fraud, whereupon he is ranked among the misdemeanants, and accordingly located in *that* part of the jail. If the several branches of the criminal profession were as widely distinct as that of law, divinity, and medicine, and if the utterer of base coin, who legally belongs to the class of misdemeanants, never indulged in thimble-rigging, and thus never rendered himself liable to be committed under the vagrant act for "gaming," nor ever did a bit of simple larceny, nor ever, therefore, came to be indicted and convicted as a felon—then might such a division of prisoners be about as scientific and instructive with regard to the subject of crime and criminals in general, as an alphabetic arrangement of the various members of the animal kingdom might be for the purposes of natural history. As it is, however, the classification enjoined by the 4th George IV. is about as idle for the purpose of preventing the contamination of one class of prisoners by another, as it would be to group together all those who were committed under like aliases; since the John Smith of one session becomes the William Brown of another, even as the felon of to-day is the vagrant or reputed thief of to-morrow.

The Coldbath Fields House of Correction consists, as we have before said, of three distinct prisons—one for felons, another for misdemeanants, and a third for vagrants. The latter building is situated at the south-western corner, on the Gray's-Inn-Lane side, and occupies the point of ground enclosed by the bending of the outer wall, as it turns down from Baynes Row into Phœnix Place.

On entering the principal gates, there is seen to the left, through the strong iron railings which enclose the paved court like a cage—towards the quarter where the fan for regulating the tread-wheel is revolving—a broad tower, built in the mixed styles of a chapel and a granary; for it has a half-ecclesiastic appearance, the windows being tall and arched; whilst the walls have become so weather-beaten, that the yellow plastering with which they are covered has turned white in places, seeming as if covered with flour. That tower is the central "argus"-like portion of the vagrants' prison.

This prison, which was built in 1830, is designed in the half-wheel form, with four wings radiating like spokes from the central building. Though at first only calculated to accommodate 150 prisoners, it has since been enlarged, so that it now contains 177 cells. The second and third yards each contain a tread-wheel.

The plan of this prison is of the ancient kind. On each side of the yards are ranged the cells, those in the ground-floor opening into the exercising ground, whilst in the galleries, on the first and second floor, the cells are ranged on either side of the passage. The cell furniture here is similar to that allowed to the felons, and consists simply of bedding and a stool, whilst hanging to the walls are boards, on which are pasted forms of morning and evening prayer; the cells, themselves, however, are inferior to those of the felons' prison in respect to size, being one foot less in width and breadth; though in all other respects they are similar in style, and, like them, neither warmed, ventilated, nor lighted.

Attached to the vagrants' prison is a strong room or cell, for either unruly or lunatic criminals. It is larger than the usual cells, and instead of a door has a strong iron grating before it, through which the incarcerated man can look out into a kind of passage before him, and which also enables the warder to watch him without the necessity of unlocking the door. The day on which, accompanied by the governor, we visited this portion of the jail, a man had been placed here for attempting the life of one of the warders. Hearing Captain Colvill's voice, he rose up from the dark corner in which he had been seated, and, advancing to the grating, requested that he might be permitted to have a bath. This prisoner had stabbed one of the officers in the back with a knife stolen from a warder's locker. Had the Millbank tin knives, however, been in use at this prison, such an act could not have been perpetrated.

The offences which, according to law, fall under the denomination of vagrancy, are principally as follows :—

Begging or sleeping in the open air.	Indecent exposure of person.	Obtaining money by false pretences.
Disorderly prostitution.	Leaving families chargeable.	Reputed thieves, rogues and vagabonds, suspected.
Fortune telling.	Incorrigible rogues convicted at sessions.	
Gaming.		

We have already spoken of vagrancy in London (see p. 43, GREAT WORLD OF LONDON), and shown that, judging by the returns from the Metropolitan unions and the mendicants' lodging-houses, as well as the asylums for the houseless, there is good reason to believe that there are 4,000 habitual vagabonds distributed throughout the Metropolis, and that the cost of their support annually amounts to very nearly £50,000. That vagrancy is the great nursery of crime we have said, and that the habitual tramps are often first beggars and then thieves, and, finally, the convicts of the country—the evidence of all the authorities on the subject goes to prove. Out of a return of 16,901 criminals in London that were known to the police in 1837, no less than 10,752, or very nearly two-thirds of the whole were returned as being of "migratory habits." Moreover, throughout England and Wales there was, between the years of 1840 and 1850, an average of 21,197 vagrants committed to prison every year, so that the gross vagabond population of the entire country may probably be taken, at the very least, at that number; whilst in every 100 summary convictions by the magistrates, throughout England and Wales, the number of persons committed as vagrants was no less than 28·9, and those as reputed thieves 23·4, or, together, more than 50 per cent. of the whole. (*Seventeenth Report of the Inspectors of Prisons of Great Britain*, p. xvii.)

"I have never been able to comprehend," says Mr. Chesterton, the late governor of Coldbath Fields, while treating of the peculiarities of vagrants in his work upon "Prison Life," "the preference given by hale, able-bodied men, who, rather than face creditable industry, will stand shivering in the cold, with garments barely sufficient to cloak their nakedness—purposely rent and tattered—in order to provoke a sympathy but rarely excited. Their vocation entails upon them endless imprisonments, and the entire life seems to me to be one of so much privation and discomfort, that it is marvelous how any rational being can voluntarily embrace it.

"The tramps or ubiquitary wanderers," adds the late governor, "display a taste far superior to that of the London 'cadgers.'"

One such tramp assured Mr. Chesterton, that the life he led suited him; he enjoyed the country, he said, realized a pleasing variety, and managed, in one way or another, to get his wants adequately supplied.

⁎ *Misdemeanants' Prison.*—Facing the kitchen, at the Bagnigge Wells corner of the felons' prison lies that for the misdemeanants, so that the three distinct prisons are built on a kind of diagonal line, which stretches from the north-eastern to the south-western corner of the boundary wall, across the ground enclosed within it.

The misdemeanants' prison is decidedly the handsomest of the three buildings. It is built of brick, with white stone copings to the windows, which give a liveliness to the brown tint of the front. As seen from the grounds, the structure reminds one of some barracks. In the centre is a handsome, comfortable-looking dwelling-house (the abode of the deputy-governor), with muslin curtains hanging before the windows, and the parlour looking out on to the little terrace, surrounded by a handsome stone balustrade; on each side extends the two-storeyed wings, with the plain brick-work pierced by strongly-bound, half-circular openings, whilst the entrance to the prison itself is through a kind of cellar-door, placed like an arch under the bridge formed by the double flight of stone steps which lead up to the deputy-governor's house.

The half-wheel style of architecture has likewise been adopted in the erection of this prison, the spokes forming four distinct wings. By excavating the ground, the architect has managed to make the building, which outside appears to have but two storeys, have, in the interior, three; and thus 386 cells have been obtained. All the wings converge to the centre building, with which they communicate by means of covered-in bridges, whose sides of rough unpolished glass give them a light and pleasing look.

In the first yard there is an extensive oakum-picking shed, capable of holding nearly 200 men; and close to it are the laundry and the washhouse.

The cells in the misdemeanants' prison are the smallest of all those in the House of Correction, for not only are they less by a foot, both in breadth and length, than those in the felons' building, but they are also one foot less in height. They, too, are neither warmed, well-ventilated, nor lighted.

Three of the yards have each at their base a wooden shed in which the men take their meals; whilst in the fourth yard the oakum-room occupies the same position. There are also slate lavatories for the men to wash at, on rising in the morning. The other sides of all the yards alike are occupied by cells which open into the paved court.

Out of one hundred consecutive cases taken at random from the prison books, we found that forty belonged to the misdemeanant class, and that the men had been convicted of the following offences in the following proportions :—

Assault	. . . 2	Fraud	. . . 3	Perjury . . . 1
Attempt at Rape	. 2	Obtaining goods under		Uttering . . . 26
Cutting and wounding	3	false pretences. . 3		

** *Fines.*—Nearly one-half (48 per cent.) of the prisoners sent to Coldbath Fields are sent there owing to their not possessing sufficient money to pay the fine for which the police magistrate has commuted their particular breach of the law. Had the offender been in a position to hand over to the clerk of the court the sum of money demanded, he would have been permitted to go at large; but his purse being empty, he is committed to prison. Hence, it is clear that the offender is no longer sent to jail because he has broken the laws of the land, but because he has not sufficient means to discharge the amount of the pecuniary penalty in which he has been mulct; and, consequently, it is equally clear, that the man has changed his position of a criminal into that of a debtor to the State, so that his imprisonment does not in reality differ much from that of a defaulter at the county court, both men being confined in a jail for a small debt that they are unable to discharge.

It is not our intention at present to discuss the question as to whether it be politic for a State to compound crimes by the payment of so much money in the shape of fines. We are merely talking of the law as it exists, and say that since it is deemed expedient, in certain cases, to change a penal offence into a debt to the State, it is not *just* that the State-debtor should, after the commutation of the sentence, be dealt with as a criminal.

The question, therefore, becomes, whether it be right to treat a State-debtor with similar rigour to that with which we would punish a felon. That the offenders who are committed to jail by the police magistrates, from inability to pay the fines imposed upon them, are not of a *very* terrible character, is proven by the fact that a sum of money is considered as an equivalent for their infraction of the law. That they are incarcerated for their poverty, rather than their transgression, is shown by the fact that they may regain their liberty during any period of their sentence, immediately the sum in which they have been mulct is paid to the governor of the prison; for the moment afterwards, the prison uniform of dirty gray is cast off, and the gates opened for the egress of the offender—a mode of obtaining freedom which is precisely similar to the process gone through at all debtors' prisons.

Let us put the following case :—A workman, "out upon the spree," takes too much to drink, and being found in a helpless state by the police, is carried off to the station-house, and, the next morning, fined 5s. by the presiding magistrate. Now, it is most probable that this fool either spent or lost all his wages in his dissipation, so that he is unable, at that particular moment, to pay the fine; consequently, although this man may, in all other respects, be a well-conducted and industrious citizen, yet, for the lack of sixty pence, he must be sent to jail to suffer seven days' imprisonment—even though his labour, and therefore his liberty, be really worth 5s. per diem to him. If he have a wife and family, and the chandler's shop-keeper, hearing of the man's imprisonment, refuse them credit during his absence, the mother and children must go to "the union;" and the frequent attendance of the parish-officers at the prison gates in such cases, when the day of liberation comes round, proves that this is far from being an uncommon occurrence.

Viewing this matter in a moral light, nothing can be more disastrous than such proceedings. A person who has been in prison is a marked man in the world. It matters not though he plead that he was only guilty of not having 5s. in his pocket, the answer is, and will continue to be, "you have been in jail." He will find masters turn from him, and refuse him work; decent landlords will deny him lodgings, and he will, consequently, have to seek shelter in less particular quarters, his children being thus brought into association with the young vagabonds infesting such places; and if he ever appear again at a police-court, no matter how frivolous the charge, he will be recognized as a jail-bird, and classed among the "*known*" offenders—until at length, deprived of all character, he will probably enlist himself among the regular criminals, and prefer to live without labouring at all.

Talking this subject over with one of the head officers at the House of Correction, the official advanced the following case in proof of what we urged :—

"A mechanic," he said, "goes out, perhaps, for a spree on the Wednesday night, takes a drop too much, becomes riotous, and is fined five shillings. The man has done three days' work (it often happens so), but as he is not paid until the Saturday, he cannot draw his money, consequently, he is sent here, and has to remain with us as a criminal until the pay-day arrives, when his wife obtains the wages, and liberates him."

The object of wise legislation should be to keep men out of prison as long as possible; for not only is an impending punishment much more efficacious as a deterrent to men than a punishment which has been already inflicted on them, but the wholesome dread of prison—that dread which acts upon all with any regard for character, even stronger than any abstract sense of rectitude—this feeling once removed, and the man is almost lost to society. The aim of recent legislation, however, seems to be, to multiply rather than decrease the number of imprisonable offences—as the Ordinary of Newgate, has well shown; so that, now-a-days, it is almost impossible for a poor man to escape jail. A slip of the foot as he walks the streets may cause him to break a pane of glass, and so, if he cannot pay for the damage, gain for him admission within the prison walls. Let a cabman murmur at his fare—a street trader, in his desire to obtain an honest living, obstruct the thoroughfare—a sweep shout out his calling in the streets—a dustman ring his bell—or others commit a host of such like petty offences—and to prison they must go, to wear a prison dress, and do the work of felons. What do these persons learn in jail? To dread the place, think you? No, indeed. They find the reality of prison far less terrible than their fancy had imagined it. The place is a palace compared with many of their homes. The cares of life—the struggle for bread that goes on outside—all cease within the prison gates. They are well fed, well housed, well clothed—better, perhaps, than ever they were in their lives before, and without a fear, too, for the morrow.*

"Thirty-three per cent. of *re*-commitments to Coldbath Fields was the steady ratio for years," writes Mr. Chesterton, the late governor; and the prison returns for the last year inform us that out of a total of 7,743 prisoners, who were sent there during the twelve months, 2,517 had been previously confined in the same prison—being at the rate of 32½ per cent.† Does this exhibit any very lively dread of returning to the place.

Now, the principle of punishment by fines appears to us to be an admirable mode of keeping men out of prison and yet of punishing them sufficiently for slight offences. But in order to keep men out of prison as long as possible, every facility should be given to the poor (and they are the principal class fined) for the payment of the penalty. A fine is simply a debt due to the State, and why should the State be a harsher creditor than it permits its subjects to be. Are there no other ways of recovering a debt than by criminal imprisonment. Society, by the establishment of the county courts, where debts are permitted to be paid by small instalments, recognises the great principle of making imprisonment a last resort, and giving the poor every chance of avoiding it. Nor does the legislature hold it just that debtors should be associated with felons and criminals, for it has ordered a special place to be appropriated to the confinement of debtors, apart from thieves and vagabonds.

* The following table will give the reader some notion as to the relative proportion of the several offences for which the prisoners are committed to Coldbath Fields; for we find, from calculations based on the returns made to the Justices for the last July quarter, that the per centage of the various crimes for which the prisoners are incarcerated is as under :—

	Per Cent.		Per Cent.		Per Cent.
Felonies, with imprisonment and hard labour	43·83	Begging or Sleeping in open air	·77	Leaving Families Chargeable	·15
Common Assaults	13·82	Unlawful Collection of Dust	·61	Assaults Unnatural	·08
Simple Larceny	10·19	Wilful Damage	·61	Bastardy	·08
Reputed Thieves	8·25	Drunk and Disorderly	·55	Cruelty to Animals	·08
Unlawful Possession	3·99	Conspiracies to Defraud	·55	False Characters	·08
Uttering or Possessing Base Coin	3·69	Cutting and Maiming	·47	Keeping Brothels	·08
Soldiers by Court Martial	2·62	Attempt at Burglary	·38	Stealing Fruit, Plants, Trees, &c.	·08
Frauds tried at Sessions	2·39	Illegally Pawning	·38	Trespassing, Fishing, Poaching, &c.	·08
Assaults on Police Constables	1·94	Excise Offences	·30	Wilful and Corrupt Perjury	·08
Assaults on Women and Children, with Intent	1·16	Indecent Exposure of Person	·30	Obtaining Money by False Pretences	·08
Misdemeanour	·93	Dog Stealing	·24		
Misbehaviour in Workhouse	·93	Furious Driving and Insolence to Fares	·15		100·0
		Abduction	·08		

† TABLE SHOWING THE NUMBER OF RE-COMMITMENTS TO COLDBATH FIELDS PRISON DURING THE YEAR ENDING MICHAELMAS, 1855.

The number of prisoners (except debtors) confined in this prison in the course of the year who have been previously committed to this prison.	Prisoners of 17 years of age and upwards.
Committed once before	1,579
Ditto twice before	584
Ditto thrice before	153
Ditto four times or more	201
Total number of re-commitments in the course of the year	2,517
Total number of commitments	7,743

The government has thus shown that it regards the commingling of debtors and criminals as both iniquitous and impolitic; then why, we ask, should it persist in sending the very poorest form of debtor—the one who cannot pay even five shillings—to eat and mix with the dregs of society, to pick oakum beside the burglar, and drink from the same tin with the felon? Could not the county court system be applied to the recovery of fines as well as of small debts, and the penalty be liquidated by instalments? To the honest, but imprudent, man—and this is the class of persons whom we are bound chiefly to consider—such a step would be the greatest of all blessings; a leniency which, while it punished the offender, would do so without sending his wife and family to the workhouse, and which, by the continued smarting of small weekly payments, would be far more likely than imprisonment to teach him to shun wrong-doing for the future.

Some may object to this scheme on the ground that it would be difficult to obtain the instalments from the State-debtors, so that a large proportion would escape punishment altogether. Our answer is based upon information obtained from one of the county court judges, who assured us that, out of several thousand cases tried by him in the course of the year, the imprisonments for non-payment of the instalments amounted to less than ten per thousand.

Further, in illustration of the iniquity of the present principle of summary imprisonment for inability to pay a certain fine, we subjoin an extract from Mr. Chesterton's (the late governor's) book, in which an instance is given of a man who, made desperate by the disgrace of being sent to prison, put an end to his existence there. There can be no doubt that this poor creature would have paid the amount if only a few days' grace had been granted him; for, as the governor tells us, the money was brought to the gate within an hour or two after his death. "Within a short period of my retirement, a man effected suicide by hanging, who had simply been committed for seven days in default of the payment of a very trifling fine. He was discovered in the morning suspended in his cell, the body being perfectly cold. To render this sad event still more afflicting, the paltry fine *of a few shillings* was tendered on the forenoon of the discovery, and but a few hours of patient endurance would have seen the deceased relieved from a confinement which had so evidently unsettled his intellect."

But while proposing that the principle of fines in lieu of imprisonments should be extended, and, in conjunction with the principle of payment by instalments, be applied to those minor infractions of social rules, which, assuredly, do not belong to the criminal class of offences (such as crying "sweep," ringing bells by dustmen, obstructing the thoroughfare by street traders, sleeping in the open air, being drunk and disorderly, accidental breaking of windows, hawking without a license, fortune-telling, and a variety of such like peccadilloes), and proposing this change mainly because we hold it to be most politic in a State to keep a man out of prison as long as possible, rather than be too eager to disgrace and corrupt him by thrusting him into it on every paltry pretence—we are, at the same time, well aware that this old Saxon principle of "mulcts" is far from being a just punishment, when the same pecuniary penalty is alike inflicted upon the affluent and the needy. Assuredly the well-to-do and, therefore, the well-educated, have not one tithe of the excuse for their transgressions that can be fairly pleaded by those who have seldom been schooled by any kinder master than want and ignorance. Moreover, the wealthier classes have not only less excuse for their offences, but also greater means of paying whatever penalty may be imposed upon them; so that to attach a *definite* fine, or so many days' imprisonment, to a breach of the law, is to enable the very class of people who deserve the severest punishment to get off with the lightest infliction; whilst it is also to treat with the greatest rigour of the law, those towards whom every principle of humanity, and even equity, commands us to be lenient.

We would, therefore, while proposing such a change as that here suggested, propose also that such fines, instead of being fixed as now at *definite* sums, to be inflicted alike upon *all* classes, should be made to bear something like a just proportion to the means of the offenders. For this purpose, it seems to us that the amount of the fine should be based on a per centage of the annual rental paid by the person in custody, the magistrate having a discretion allowed to him to vary the ratio, according to the enormity of the outrage—from say $2\frac{1}{2}$ to 10 per cent. Further, in case of inability to pay, we would have no man's liberty valued at less than an ordinary labourer's wage of 2s. 6d. a-day, and so put an end to the barbarism of some men being committed to prison by magistrates on account of non-payment of fines, for a term which estimates their freedom at $4\frac{1}{2}d$. per diem, while others value the luxury of being at large as high as 3s. $1\frac{1}{2}d$. a-day. On the 29th September, 1855, the official returns tell us that—

The total number of prisoners in Coldbath Fields was 1,301
        Of these—
The number convicted at assizes and sessions was 823
    ,,   ,,   summarily 478
                             ——1,301

Hence, it appears that more than 36 per cent. of the prisoners there are committed by the magistrates.

It will be seen, by the facts cited below, that some regular scale requires to be laid down as to the proportion that the term of the imprisonment should bear to the amount of the fine imposed by their worships; so that, henceforth, summary decisions may be rendered less incongruous, and less like mere caprices of the moment. The magistrates all obviously entertain different notions as to the imprisonment that should be attached to the non-payment of each fine—one awarding fourteen days for a *5s.* offence, another considering seven days to be a just period in lieu of a fine of 22s.* That our magistrates are honourable

---

* In proof of the above assertion we subjoin an analysis of forty-eight cases of fines, taken from 100 consecutive offences, selected at random from the prison books.

Thirteen of these were for *common assaults*, one of which got seven days, or 10s. fine; another, seven days, or 20s. fine; another, twelve days, or 32s. fine; two others, fourteen days, or 20s. fine; another, fourteen days, or only 10s. fine; one other, twenty-one days, or 60s. fine; another, thirty days, or 20s. fine; two others, thirty days, or 40s. fine; and two, thirty days, or 60s. fine.

Further, ten more of the offences consisted of *assaults on the police*, and for these the punishments were as follows :—One had five days, or 10s. fine; another, seven days, or 5s. fine; a third, the same number of days, and yet 10s. fine; a fourth, eight days, or 20s. fine; a fifth, ten days, or 30s. fine; a sixth, fourteen days, or only 10s. fine; and two others, the same number of days, and yet 20s. fine; another, twenty-one days, or 60s. fine; and the last, thirty days, or 20s. fine.

Nine of the cases, on the other hand, were for *assaults on females*. Of these, one had fourteen days, or 20s. fine; two, thirty days, or 40s. fine; one other, forty-two days, or 60s. fine; and the remaining five, sixty days, or 100s. fine.

Besides the above, there were seven cases of being *drunk and riotous*, and three of these were sentenced to seven days, or 5s. fine; three to seven days, or 10s. fine; and one to fourteen days, or 20s. fine.

Against the Cab Act there were two offences; the one was sentenced to seven days, or 22s. fine, and the other to fourteen days, or 20s. fine.

For *illegally pawning*, one case got fourteen days, or 8s. fine, and the other as much as sixty days, or 140s. fine.

Then, for *damage done to a window*, of which there were two instances; one of the offenders had seven days, or 6s. 6d. fine, and the other *fourteen days, or 5s. fine.*

For *stealing fruit*, the punishment was seven days, or 5s. 2d. fine; and, in a bastardy case, thirty days was given in lieu of 22s. fine.

Nor did the London magistrates seem to have any more settled notion as to the daily *value* of a man's liberty than they had concerning the punishments which they adjudged it necessary to inflict for the same offence; for, whilst some justices appraised the luxury of being at large at the rate of $4\frac{1}{2}d$. *per diem*, others estimated it at no less than 3s. $1\frac{1}{2}d$. a-day, *e.g.* :—

On analysing these same forty-eight cases in which fines had been inflicted, we found that in one of them

men, stern and upright in their judgments, neither allowing themselves to be influenced by wealth or poverty, not even the most suspicious can do other than believe. Still they are afflicted with human constitutions and human ailments, and their minds, like those of other men, are influenced by the derangements of their bodily systems. A disordered stomach may make even the most righteous nature see that act as a heinous offence, and worthy of the severest punishment, which the same person, in a state of perfect health, would regard as but a trivial error.

₊ *Of the Prison Kitchen and Diet.*—The kitchen, where the daily food of the 1,300 inhabitants of Coldbath Fields prison is cooked, is as large and lofty as a barn, so that despite the heat required for the culinary purposes, the air is cool, and even the panes in the

a British subject's liberty was valued at $4\frac{1}{2}d.$ a-day; this consisted of damage done to glass, for which the sentence was fourteen days, or $5s.$ fine.

In the next case the freedom was estimated at $6\frac{3}{4}d.$ a-day, and this was for illegally pawning—the sentence being fourteen days, or $8s.$ fine.

Then came three cases where the liberty was considered to be worth $8d.$ per diem. These were—one common assault, one assault on police, and one bastardy case, in all of which the sentence was thirty days' imprisonment, or $20s.$ fine.

After this we have six cases, valuing the liberty at $8\frac{1}{2}d.$ per diem. Three of these were for being drunk and riotous, and one for an assault on the police, each of which was sentenced to seven days' imprisonment, or $5s.$ fine; whereas the other two cases, which consisted of a common assault and an assault on the police, were respectively sentenced to fourteen days, or $10s.$ fine.

Then followed one case in which the liberty was appraised at $8\frac{3}{4}d.$ a-day. This was for stealing fruit, the sentence being seven days, or $5s.$ $2d.$ fine; and another (breaking a window) valuing the liberty at $11d.$ per diem, the punishment being seven days, or $6s.$ $6d.$ fine; and a common assault, in which the magistrate thought the liberty was worth $1s.$ $1\frac{3}{4}d.$ a-day, and adjudged the offender either to forty-five days' imprisonment, or $50s.$ fine.

In the next four cases, the worth of the liberty was estimated at $1s.$ $4d.$ per diem; two of these were for common assault, and two for assaults on females, all being alike sentenced to thirty days' imprisonment, or $40s.$ fine.

Next we find the liberty rise, in the magistrate's opinion, to $1s.$ $5d.$ a-day; for two cases of common assault, and assault on the police, and three cases of being drunk and riotous, were alike condemned to seven days, or $10s.$ fine; and there were several other cases at the same rate, of which seven were adjudged to fourteen days' imprisonment, or $20s.$ fine; and the last to forty-two days' imprisonment, or $60s.$ fine—consisting of such different acts as two common assaults, two assaults on police, two assaults on females, and one against the Cab Act.

In five other cases the value of the liberty was increased to $1s.$ $8d.$ the day. These were all assaults on females, and the punishment, in every case, was sixty days' imprisonment, or $100s.$ fine.

On the other hand, $2s.$ a-day was the price affixed to the men's freedom; in five cases the sentence being thirty days' imprisonment, or $60s.$ fine, for two common assaults, and five days, or $10s.$ fine, for an assault on the police.

Moreover, in a case of illegally pawning, the value of the liberty was set down at $2s.$ $4d.$ the day, the sentence being sixty days, or $140s.$ fine.

Again, in an assault on the police, the estimate of the value of the liberty was not less than $2s.$ $6d.$ the day, for in that case the decision was eight days, or $20s.$ fine.

Then, by another gentleman on the bench, the price of the liberty was raised to $2s.$ $8d.$ the day, for a common assault, which was punished with twelve days, or $32s.$ fine; whilst, in another assault case, in which the adjudication was seven days, or $20s.$ fine, the average value of the liberty was taken at $2s.$ $10d.$ per diem; whereas, in another common assault, as well as one on the police, the amount of the appraisement leaped up to $2s.$ $10\frac{1}{4}d.$ a-day; for the sentence, in both of these cases, was twenty-one days, or $60s.$ fine.

In another assault on the police, however, $3s.$ was reckoned to be the worth of a man's freedom, as the penal infliction was ten days, or $30s.$ fine; and lastly, in an offence against the Cab Act, which got seven days, or $22s.$ fine, it was found that the valuation for the liberty, in this instance, was taken at an average of $3s.$ $1\frac{3}{4}d.$ per diem.

Nor did these vague ideas and fluctuations in the liberty market, at the London police-offices, arise from any specific difference in the offences themselves, but simply from the different sense of justice in the magisterial mind.

sky-lights let into the slanting wood roof, are free from condensed vapour. Everything is cooked by steam, and the whole place seems to be conducted on the gigantic scale of an American boarding-house; for there is but one pot to be seen, and that holds at least ten gallons. In a kind of recess, surrounded by an iron railing, are the two boilers for generating the steam, the black round tops arching up from the crimson brick-work, and each with a small white plume of steam hissing out of the safety valves. The different articles of food are being prepared for the prisoners' dinners in the immense square iron tank—for they are more like cisterns than boilers—ranged against the wall. In one, with the bright copper-lid, which is so heavy that it has to be raised by means of an equipoise, are 100 gallons of cocoa, the red-brown scum on the top heaving and sinking with the heat; in another are suspended hampers of potatoes; whilst other compartments contain 150 gallons of what, from the "eyes" of grease glittering on the surface, you guess to be soup, or which, from its viscid, pasty appearance, you know to be the prison gruel.

It takes two cooks three hours and a half merely to weigh out the rations required for this enormous establishment. One of these stands beside a mass—high as a truss of hay—of slices of boiled meat, and, with extraordinary rapidity, places pieces of the pale lean and the yellow fat in the scales, until the six-ounce weight moves. The other is occupied with the potatoes, dividing the hamper filled with the steaming, brown-skinned vegetables into portions of eight ounces each. The sight of such immense quantities of provisions, and the peculiar smell given off from the cooling of boiled meats, has rather a sickening effect upon any one, like ourselves, not hungry at the time. All the soup is made out of bullocks' heads; and in the larder, hanging to hooks against the slate-covered wall, we beheld several of these suspended by the lips, and looking fearfully horrible, with the white bones showing through the crimson flesh, so that the sight called up in our mind our youthful fancies of what we had imagined to be the character of Bluebeard's closet.

A curious use is, by the by, made of the jaw-bones of these bullocks' heads. After the flesh and all its "goodness" has been boiled from it, the "*maxilla* inferior," as doctors call it, is used to form ornamental borders to the gravel walks in the grounds, in the same way as oyster-shells are sometimes turned to account in the nine-feet-by-six gardens in the suburbs.

The dinner hour for the prisoners is two o'clock; and as 1 pint of gruel and $6\frac{2}{3}$ ounces of bread do not coincide with an Englishman's notion of that meal, we were desirous of seeing whether the prisoners ate their rations with any appearance of relish after their labour.

In the yard which we visited, the men were being exercised until the repast was ready; marching up and down in a long chain, as smartly as if the object was to put a finishing edge upon their appetites. Big tubs, filled with thick gruel, had been carried into the dining-sheds, and a pint measure of the limpid paste had been poured into the tin mugs, and this, together with a spoon and the $6\frac{2}{3}$ ounces of bread, were ranged down the narrow strips of tables, that extend in three rows the whole length of the place. As the clock struck two, the file of prisoners in the yard received an order to "Halt," and, after a moment's rest, the word of command was given to take their places at the table. Then the chain moved to the door; and, as each human link entered, he took off his old stocking-like cap, and passing down between the forms reached his seat. The men sat still for a second or two, with the smoking gruel before them, until the order was given to "Draw up tables!" and instantly the long light "dressers" were, with a sudden rattle, pulled close to the men. Then the warder, taking off his cap, cried out, "Pay attention to grace!" and every head was bent down as one of the prisoners repeated these words:—

"Sanctify, we beseech thee, O Lord, these thy good things to our use, and us to thy service, through the grace of Jesus Christ." A shout of "Amen!" followed, and directly afterwards the tinkling of the spoons against the tin cans was heard, accompanied by the peculiar sound resembling "sniffing," that is made by persons eating half-liquid messes

LIBERATION OF PRISONERS FROM COLDBATH FIELDS HOUSE OF CORRECTION.

with a spoon. Two prisoners, carrying boxes of salt, passed along in front of the tables, from man to man, while each in his turn dipped his spoon in and helped himself. The "good things," as the water-gruel and bit of bread are ironically termed in the grace, were soon despatched, and then the men, reaching each little sack of books which had been suspended above their heads from the ceiling, like so many fly-catchers, passed the remainder of their dinner-hour reading.

There is one point in the prison dietary for which we can see no sufficing reason. All prisoners committed to jail for fourteen days and under (and whose crimes are therefore the lightest) are made to live on gruel and bread, whilst those whose term of imprisonment exceeds fourteen days and does not extend to two months, obtain a somewhat improved diet; and all sentenced to any term *above* two months (and who have therefore been guilty of the heaviest offences) are allowed meat or soup every day, and, indeed, partake of the best kind of food permitted by law in a prison.

The dietary adopted at Coldbath Fields is based upon that recommended by the prison inspectors, and ordered by Her Majesty's Secretary of State for the Home Department. It differs, however, slightly in the weight of food. Thus, the daily allowance of bread recommended by the government for prisoners confined for terms under fourteen days is 24 oz., whilst that served out at the House of Correction is limited to 20 oz. Again, the House of Correction prisoners, who are sentenced to more than fourteen days and less than two months, have their breakfast and dinner bread docked of a slight weight; but, on the other hand, the meat served twice a-week is doubled. Therefore, the criminals who suffer the *most*, owing to this difference between the government and county allowances of food, are those who have been guilty of the *slightest* offences, *i.e.*, the class whose term of imprisonment does not exceed fourteen days.

In framing the prison dietaries, the length of the term to which the prisoner is condemned has been taken into consideration, and for the following reasons:—" Imprisonment," say the authorities, "has naturally a depressing influence over the mind, which greatly diminishes the powers of nutrition in the body, and the longer the term the more marked will be the effect." To counteract this evil, recourse is had to the stimulus afforded by an increase of food—the loss of health and strength being, as Sir James Graham has humanely expressed it, "a punishment not contemplated by law, and which it is unjust and cruel to inflict."

Days.	First Class—*i.e.*, all Prisoners whose terms of Imprisonment exceed two Months.								Second Class—*i.e.*, all Prisoners whose terms of Imprisonment do not exceed two months, and do exceed fourteen days.									Third Class—*i e.*, all Prisoners whose terms of Imprisonment are 14 days and under.					
	Breakfast.		Dinner.				Supper.		Breakfast.		Dinner.					Supper.		Breakfast.		Dinner.		Supper.	
	Bread.	Cocoa.	Bread.	Meat.	Potatoes.	Soup.	Bread.	Gruel.	Bread.	Gruel.	Bread.	Meat.	Potatoes.	Soup.	Gruel.	Bread.	Gruel.	Bread.	Gruel.	Bread.	Gruel.	Bread.	Gruel.
	Oz.	Pint	Oz.	Oz.	Oz.	Pint	Oz.	Pint	Oz.	Pint	Oz.	Oz.	Oz.	Pint	Pint	Oz.	Pint	Oz.	Pint	Oz.	Pint	Oz.	Pint
Monday .	6⅔	1	6⅔	6	8	...	6⅔	1	6⅔	1	6⅔	...	...	...	1	6⅔	½	6⅔	1	6⅔	1	6⅔	½
Tuesday .	6⅔	1	6⅔	6	8	...	6⅔	1	6⅔	1	6⅔	6	8	...	...	6⅔	½	6⅔	1	6⅔	1	6⅔	½
Wednesday .	6⅔	1	6⅔	...	...	1½	6⅔	1	6⅔	1	6⅔	...	...	1	...	6⅔	½	6⅔	1	6⅔	1	6⅔	½
Thursday .	6⅔	1	6⅔	6	8	...	6⅔	1	6⅔	1	6⅔	...	...	...	1	6⅔	½	6⅔	1	6⅔	1	6⅔	½
Friday . .	6⅔	1	6⅔	...	...	1½	6⅔	1	6⅔	1	6⅔	...	...	...	1	6⅔	½	6⅔	1	6⅔	1	6⅔	½
Saturday .	6⅔	1	6⅔	6	8	...	6⅔	1	6⅔	1	6⅔	6	8	...	...	6⅔	½	6⅔	1	6⅔	1	6⅔	½
Sunday . .	6⅔	1	6⅔	...	...	1½	6⅔	1	6⅔	1	6⅔	...	...	1	...	6⅔	½	6⅔	1	6⅔	1	6⅔	½
	46⅔	7	46⅔	24	32	4½	46⅔	7	46⅔	7	46⅔	12	16	2	3	46⅔	3½	46⅔	7	46⅔	7	46⅔	3½

Hence, the greater allowance of diet granted to the longer sentence men rests upon the fact that the minds of such prisoners are more depressed than those committed for a shorter period. The meat and soup for dinner are given as a species of medicine, which the short-term men, who carry to jail a body healthy with recent liberty and a mind supported by the knowledge of a speedy liberation, are not supposed to require.

But is this really so? Which of these two classes of men, the one who enters a prison for the first time, or the one who has been recommitted again and again, is the more likely to be affected by his degraded position? First offenders are seldom severely punished, whereas the old jail-birds, after many recommitments, get heavy sentences. The man, therefore, who is sent to prison for a few days, is likely to be more depressed than he who is committed for two years.

That the greatest mental depression is experienced on first entering a prison, there are numerous and convincing proofs. The cases of suicide in a jail are those committed by newly-arrived criminals. Whenever a prisoner has attempted to starve himself to death, it has generally been at the commencement of his incarceration, and it is only after he has in a measure become reconciled, by a few days' sojourn, to the scenes around him, that he has relented of his purpose, and taken food.

Again, is not this rule of giving better diet to long-term prisoners productive of evil, as offering a premium, as it were, for heavy offences. The professed thieves, many of whom pass a good part of their lives in a jail, are well acquainted with the discipline and dietary of every prison in the Metropolis. They are aware that gruel and bread await them if they attempt and fail in some petty undertaking; and therefore manage so that by a three months' committal they can enjoy the luxury of the highest class of diet, or that which provides meat or soup for their dinner every day out of the seven. We must bear in mind that, with this class of society, food forms one of the greatest enjoyments; indeed, all the gains of their robberies are disposed of in eating and drinking, and other animal propensities; so strongly, indeed are they influenced by the quantity of their meals, that very lately a prisoner at Coldbath Fields, on the mere supposition that the bread served to him at dinner was smaller than that of his neighbour, was so angered, that, breaking open one of the warder's boxes, he obtained possession of a knife, and, two days after the imaginary wrong had been committed, stabbed the officer whom he taxed as the author of it.*

* TABLE OF EXPENDITURE AND RECEIPTS OF COLDBATH FIELDS PRISON IN THE YEAR 1854, COMPARED WITH THE AVERAGE FOR ALL OTHER PRISONS IN 1853.

COST OF PRISON PER ANNUM.		Average Cost per Prisoner per Ann.		RECEIPTS OF PRISON PER ANNUM.		
	Gross Cost per Annum.	Coldbath Fields.	All other Prisons in England and Wales.		£ s. d.	£ s. d.
	£ s. d.	£ s. d.	£ s. d.	Net Profit received for manufacturing or other Work done by the Prisoners .	2,056 7 7	
Total cost of Prison Diet and Extra Allowances, by order of the Surgeon, and Wine, Beer, &c.	12,617 11 2	9 1 9½	5 4 11	Estimated Profit of Work or Labour done by the Prisoners for the benefit of the County, City, or Borough .	4,320 12 8	
,, Male Clothing, Bedding, and Straw .	1,665 11 4	1 4 0	1 7 2	Gross Earnings of Prisoners .		6,377 0 3
,, Officers' Salaries and Rations, and Pensions to Retired Officers .	11,014 2 8	7 18 8½	10 7 6	Amount received for Subsistence of Military and Naval Prisoners .		52 13 0
,, Fuel, Soap, and other cleansing materials, Oil and Gas .	1,475 14 8	1 1 3	1 19 6	Amount received for the Support of Vagrants.* .		9 17 1
,, Stationery, Printing, and Books, Furniture and Utensils, &c., Rent, Rates, and Taxes .	630 15 0	0 9 1	0 13 9¾	Amount received from Treasury for Removal of Transports .		81 10 9
,, Support of Prisoners removed under Contract to be confined in other Jurisdictions, and removal of Convicts and Prisoners to and from Trial, and to other Prisons for punishment, &c. .	955 5 0	0 13 9	0 12 9¾	Amount received for the Subsistence of Revenue Prisoners .		176 11 6
,, Sundry Contingencies not enumerated .	1,708 18 3	1 4 7½	1 1 9¼	Amount charged to Treasury for Maintenance of Prisoners convicted at Assizes and Sessions, and Weekly Rate per head .		9,509 2 0
				Other Receipts .		259 7 10
Total expenses for the Prison for the year, not including Repairs, Alterations, and Additions .	30,067 18 1	21 13 2½	21 7 5¾	Total .		£16,466 2 5
,, Repairs, Alterations, and Additions in and about the Prison in the course of the year .	928 14 2	0 13 4½	2 9 5			
Repayment of Principal or Interest of Money Borrowed .	—	—	2 12 9¾	Average Earnings of each Prisoner per annum .		4 11 10½
Grand Total .	30,996 12 3	22 6 7	26 9 8½	Ditto on all Prisons of England and Wales .		2 1 5
Daily average number of Prisoners .		1,388	16,691			
Gross cost of Prison, per head, per annum, exclusive of repairs . £21 13 2½				* This is money found in possession of vagrants while begging, and ordered by the committing magistrate to go towards their support in prison.		

NETT COST OF THE PRISON TO THE COUNTY FOR THE YEAR, ETC.   £ s. d.

Total Expenses of the Prison for the year, not including Repairs, Alterations, and Additions . 30,067 18 1
Total Receipts of Ditto . 16,466 2 5

Cost to the County, City, or Borough, not including Repairs, Alterations, or Additions . 13,601 15 8
Repairs, Alterations, and Additions during the year . 928 14 2

Total Expenses of the Prison for the year, including Repairs, Alterations, and Additions, and excluding Receipts . 14,530 9 10

Nett cost of each Prisoner, at Coldbath Fields, per annum . £10 9 4¼
,, ,, in all Prisons of England and Wales, per annum . . 18 8 0¾
,, ,, at Coldbath Fields, per diem . . 0 0 6¾
,, ,, in all Prisons of England and Wales, per diem . 0 1 0

Now, by the above comparative table, we perceive that the average *gross* cost of Coldbath Fields prison is

We can see no sure remedy for these dietary evils, but by the introduction into prison management of the principle we have before spoken of—that of making the increased comfort of the prisoner dependent upon his own labour. Let "punishment diet" be the only eleemosynary allowance; but, at the same time, give each class of criminals alike the opportunity of adding meat to their meal, by making the luxury contingent upon a certain quantity of work done.* Let such a task be the price of so much food, and not only will it be found to act as a premium and incentive to the industrious, but it will have the still more beneficial effect of proving to those who least understand the value and object of labour, that it has its rewards and consolations; and that the same strength which was employed and failed in breaking open a door or forcing a lock would, if devoted to more honourable pursuits, be

a fraction less than the average for all the other prisons of England and Wales; for, though the average expense of the diet for each prisoner is nearly as much as 75 per cent. *more* than the average cost per prisoner for all England and Wales, the average cost of management (notwithstanding the exigencies of the silent system) is upwards of 30 per cent. *less*, whilst the cost of bedding, as well as of lighting, washing, and cooking, are also considerably below the mean. On the other hand, the average *nett* annual cost of each prisoner at Coldbath Fields is as much as 75 per cent. less than the average nett cost for all other prisons. This is owing partly to the earnings of the prisoners at Coldbath Fields being over-estimated (see *ante*, p. 318), so that, whilst the average sum annually earned by each prisoner throughout England and Wales is £2 1s. 5d., the individual earnings at Coldbath Fields are made to appear as high as £4 11s. 10½d. per annum; but it is principally due to the fact, that the sum charged to the Treasury for the maintenance of prisoners convicted at assizes and sessions amounts (at 4s. per head per week) to no less than £9,500; and, as this is very nearly one-third of the gross cost of Coldbath Fields prison, it is manifest that the nett cost of that establishment to the country must fall considerably under the mean.

* Since writing the preceding article, the Nineteenth Report of the Inspectors of Prisons has been published; and as this furnishes us with the means of comparing the proportion of punishments at the Middlesex House of Correction with that of all other prisons throughout England and Wales, we append the following table:—

TABLE COMPARING THE NUMBER OF PUNISHMENTS, AS WELL AS THEIR PER CENTAGE TO THE GROSS PRISON POPULATION, AT COLDBATH FIELDS HOUSE OF CORRECTION, WITH THE NUMBER AND PER CENTAGE AT ALL OTHER PRISONS IN ENGLAND AND WALES.

PUNISHMENTS.	COLDBATH FIELDS, 1854-55. Gross Prison Population, 9,180.		PRISONS OF ALL ENGLAND AND WALES, 1853. Gross Prison Population, Adult Males . . . . } 96,891.		Excess or deficiency per cent.
	No. of punishments.	Per centage of punishments to gross prison population.	No. of Punishments.	Per centage of punishments to gross prison population.	
Placed in handcuffs and other irons . .	2	·02	70	·07	— ·05
Whipped	5	·05	115	·11	— ·06
Confined in dark and solitary cells . .	470	5·11	9,743	10·05	— 4·93
Stoppage of diet and other punishments	8,546	93·09	32,928	33·98	+59·20
TOTAL	9,023	98·27	42,856	44·11	+54·16

Hence, we perceive that whilst at Coldbath Fields the heavier punishments, such as handcuffs, whipping, and confinement in dark or solitary cells, are, in round numbers, 5 per cent. *less* than at other prisons, the slighter punishments there, such as stoppage of diet, are, within a fraction, as much as 60 per cent. *more*.

It is but just to add, before closing this article, that the governor of Coldbath Fields prison remonstrates against the opinion given (at p. 336) as to the effects of the "star system;" and it would certainly appear, from the subjoined return, that that gentleman is right and ourselves wrong. It is due to our own judgment, however, to say, that our ideas on the subject were derived from communications with the warders of the prison, and that they seem to have formed their opinions somewhat too hastily. The governor says, "I deny that the worst men are the best-conducted prisoners;" and in proof of the statement, he furnishes us with the

sure to succeed in gaining an honest and reputable existence; so that, when they quit prison, they may leave it intent on earning their own living for the future.*

annexed table, showing that the *smallest* proportion of stars (viz., 2½ per cent.) is obtained by the old "jail-birds," and the *greatest* proportion (58 per cent.) gained by those who have never been in prison before:—

TABLE SHOWING THE SENTENCES AND NUMBER OF RE-COMMITTALS OF THE PRISONERS OBTAINING "STARS" AT COLDBATH FIELDS PRISON:—

	Sentences.	Men.	Stars.	Per centage.		Sentences.	Men.	Stars.	Per centage.
Not in prison before.	Under 6 months	7	7		In prison twice before.	Under 6 months	..	..	
	6 and under 12	70	81			6 and under 12	7	8	
	12 and upwards	103	185			12 and upwards	17	36	
	TOTAL	180	273	58		TOTAL	24	44	9½
In prison once before.	Under 6 months	2	2		In prison more than twice before.	Under 6 months	1	1	
	6 and under 12	26	28			6 and under 12	1	1	
	12 and upwards	54	101			12 and upwards	5	9	
	TOTAL	82	131	30		TOTAL	7	11	2½

	Men.	Stars.
Total number of stars worn on 2nd August, 1856	293	459

NUMBER OF STARS PAID FOR ON DISCHARGE, FROM 18TH JUNE TO 18TH AUGUST, 1856:—

To prisoners sentenced to less than six months.		To prisoners sentenced to 6 months and under 12.		To prisoners sentenced to 12 months and upwards.	
Men.	Stars.	Men.	Stars.	Men.	Stars.
69	69	80	122	37	110

No account as to former imprisonments.

N.B.—Several men sentenced to three months are paid for stars on discharge, if they have not been reported; but these never wear the stars, as they are discharged when entitled to them.

Against such arguments it is impossible to say a word, except to acknowledge ourselves in fault, which we do most readily. The governor adds, with exemplary consideration for those under his care, " In many cases I think it advisable to reward men for good conduct, and to give prisoners, on discharge, some chance of looking for honest employment, if so disposed."

The star system appears, also, to be beneficial as *inducing* conformity to discipline by means of rewards, rather than *enforcing* it by means of punishments. The only *external* motives to human conduct are some such rewards and punishments; both lead to the same end, but the one attains the object by attraction and the other by repulsion. As in a magnet, these attractions and repulsions (of rewards and punishments) are the *two* forces that induce motion, in human beings, in a given direction. Some men, it must be admitted, require deterrents or repellents to cause them to act as we wish; such characters seem to be comparatively deficient in the *attractive* qualities of human nature, or, in other words, almost incapable of being moved by some prospective good. Nevertheless, *all* persons are assuredly not of this kind, and therefore stars and good-conduct badges strike us as being excellent methods of *leading* men to comply with discipline, and those prison rules and regulations which are necessary for the orderly government of a jail. Hence the star system, judiciously applied, is likely to prove an admirable mode of reducing the amount of punishments at Coldbath Fields prison; and no one would rejoice at such a result more than the writer of this article—unless, indeed, it were the governor himself.

* It gives us, likewise, great pleasure to be able to record the fact here, that since writing the preceding remarks on the silent system, the governor of Coldbath Fields, ever ready to avail himself of any suggestion as to the improvement of the characters of those under his charge, has tried the plan of reading aloud, as proposed (at p. 335) in this work, and we are happy to add, in the words of the governor himself, "it answers very well." With commendable prudence, Captain Colvill made the experiment first in the smaller work-rooms, saying that he feared " it would lead to irregularity where many were together." In a later communication to us, however, he writes, " the reading aloud seems to answer very well, and I am trying it with greater numbers. It was proposed by one of our visiting justices some time back." All honour, then, to the justice for the proposal of such a plan, and to the governor for the execution of it!

ENTRANCE TO TOTHILL FIELDS PRISON.

¶ ii.

THE MIDDLESEX HOUSE OF CORRECTION, TOTHILL FIELDS.

(FOR FEMALE AND JUVENILE OFFENDERS.)

There is no quarter of the Metropolis impressed with such strongly-marked features as the episcopal city of Westminster. We do not speak of that vague and straggling electoral Westminster, which stretches as far as Kensington and Chelsea to the west, and even Temple Bar to the east; but of that Westminster proper—that triangular snip of the Metropolis which is bounded by the Vauxhall Road on one side, St. James's Park on another, and by the Thames on the third—that Westminster which can boast of some of the noblest and some of the meanest buildings to be found throughout London (the grand and picturesque old Abbey, and the filthy and squalid Duck Lane—the bran-new and ornate Houses of Parliament, and the half-dilapidated and dingy old Almonry)—which is the seat at once of the great mass of law-makers and law-breakers—where there are more almshouses, and more prisons, and more schools (the "Gray-coat," the "Blue-coat," the "Green-coat," and the more modern "Ragged," or No-coat, for instance, as well as the ancient and honourable one bearing the name of the city itself)—more old noblemen's mansions and more costermongers' hovels—more narrow lanes, and courts, and more broad unfinished highways—whose Hall is frequented by more lawyers, and whose purlieus are infested by more thieves—whose public-houses are resorted to by more paviors—whose streets are thronged by more soldiers—on whose door-steps sit more bare-headed wantons—and whose dry arches shelter more vagabond urchins than are to be noted in any other part of the Metropolis—ay, and perhaps in any other part of the world.

₊ *Of the old " Spitals," Sanctuaries, and " Lokes," and the modern " Rookeries."*— Yet much of the incongruous character of modern Westminster may be traced back to the peculiarities of the ancient city. Parent Du Chatelet, the celebrated French statist, has shown that the *Quartier de la Cité* in Paris, which is now the headquarters of the French thieves, was formerly the site of a well-known sanctuary; and so it was with the City of Westminster itself.

"The church at Westminster hath had," says Stow, "great privilege of sanctuary within the precinct thereof; from whence it hath not been lawful for any prince or other to take any person that fled thither for any cause." Edward the Confessor, according to the old London historian, granted it a charter, in which were these words:—"I order and establish for ever, that what person, of what condition or estate soever he be, from whence soever he come, or for what offence or cause it be, whether for his refuge unto the said holy church (of the blessed Apostle of St. Peter, at Westminster), he be assured of his life, liberty, and limbs, * * * * and whosoever presumes or doth contrary to this my grant, I will hee lose his name, worship, dignity, and power, and that with the great traytor, Judas, that betraied our Saviour, he be in the everlasting fire of hell."

This sanctuary, Stow tells us, extended to the church, churchyard, and close. " At the entrance of the close," he says, in another part, "there is a lane that leadeth towards the west, called ' Thieving Lane,'" (this is now styled Princes Street, and runs from Storey's Gate to the open space which is in front of the Abbey, and still bears the name of the Sanctuary); "for that thieves," he adds, "were led that way to the gate-house while the Sanctuary continued in force."*

* Under the dominion of the Normans there appear to have existed two kinds of sanctuary, or places of protection to criminals and debtors from arrest—one *general*, which belongs to every church—the other *peculiar*, which originated in a grant, by charter, from the king.

The *general* sanctuary afforded a refuge to those only who had been guilty of *capital* felonies. On reaching it, the felon was bound to declare that he had committed felony, and came to save his life. By the common law of England, if a person, guilty of felony (excepting sacrilege), fled to a parish church or churchyard for sanctuary, he might, within forty days afterwards, go clothed in sackcloth before the coroner, confess the full particulars of his guilt, and take an oath to abjure the kingdom for ever—swearing not to return unless the king's license were granted him to do so. Upon making his confession and taking his oath, he became attainted of the felony; he had forty days, from the day of his appearance before the coroner, allowed him to prepare for his departure, and the coroner assigned him such port as he chose for his embarkation, whither the felon was bound to repair immediately, with a cross in his hand, and to embark with all convenient speed. If he did not go directly out of the kingdom, or if he afterwards returned into England, without license, he was condemned to be hanged, unless he happened to be a clerk, in which case he was allowed the benefit of clergy.

A *peculiar* sanctuary might (if such privilege were granted by the king's charter) afford a place of refuge even to those who had committed high or petty treason; and a person escaping thither might, if he chose, remain undisturbed for life. He still, however, had the option of taking the oath of abjuration, and quitting the realm for ever.

Sanctuary, however, seems in neither case to have been allowed as a protection to those who escaped from the sheriff after having been delivered to him for execution.

"The right of sanctuary," says Mr. Timbs, "was retained by Westminster after the dissolution of the monasteries, &c., in 1540. Sanctuary men were allowed to use a whittle only at their meals, and compelled to wear a badge. They could not leave the precinct, without the Dean's license, between sunset and sunrise." In the Westminster Sanctuary were two cruciform churches, built one above the other, and the lower one in the form of a double cross; the upper one is supposed, by Dr. Walcott, to have been for debtors and the inhabitants of the Broad and Little Sanctuaries, whilst the lower one is said to have been appropriated to criminals. The privilege of sanctuary caused the houses within the precinct to let for high rents; but this privilege was totally abolished in 1623, by James I., though the bulk of the houses which composed the precinct was not taken down till 1750. To the Westminster Sanctuary, Judge Tresilian (*temp.*

It is well known that there were formerly many other such sanctuaries, or "privileged places," throughout London. From Edward the Confessor's time to the Reformation (a period of about five hundred years), any place or building that was consecrated by the clergy for religious uses, served to screen offenders from the justice of the law and the sentence passed upon them for their crimes. There were likewise several privileged places, in which persons were secure from arrest. These were principally the old Mint, in Southwark; the Minories, and St. Katharine's Hospital, about the Docks; Fulwood's Rents, and Baldwin's Gardens, in Gray's Inn Lane; and Whitefriars (vulgarly called *Alsatia*), between Fleet Street and the Thames.*

Now, with the exception of Whitefriars, the old sanctuaries and privileged places continue to this day to be the principal nests of the London beggars, prostitutes, and thieves. True there are other quarters, such as St. Giles and the purlieus of Brick Lane, Spitalfields, that are infested by a like ragged, wretched, and reckless population; but these will be found to have been originally the sites of hospitals, either for the poor or the diseased.†

The two largest of the old leper hospitals in London, for instance, were those of St. James, Westminster, and St. Giles-in-the-Fields. There was also a celebrated "*Loke,*" or leper hospital, in Kent Street, in the Borough, and this is now one of the worst districts in the Metropolis; whilst Spitalfields was the site of an ancient almshouse.‡

Richard II.) fled for refuge; but was dragged thence to Tyburn, and there hanged. In 1460, Lord Scales, as he was seeking sanctuary at Westminster, was murdered on the Thames. Elizabeth Woodville, queen of Edward IV., escaped from the Tower, and registered herself and her family "Sanctuary women," and here "in great penury, forsaken of all friends," she gave birth to Edward V., "born in sorrow, and baptized like a poor man's child." She is described by More, as sitting "alow on the rushes" in her grief. Here, too, Skelton, the satirist, found shelter from the revengeful hand of Cardinal Wolsey. One Robert Hawley, Esquire, moreover, escaped from the Tower, and took Sanctuary at Westminster; whereupon the Tower Constable, Sir Alan Boxhull, followed him to the church, and killed him in the choir, at the time of high mass (11th August, 1378). After this the church was closed for four months, and Boxhull and his followers excommunicated.

* The Southwark Mint was, perhaps, the most notorious of all the London places of refuge. It became, we are told, early an asylum for debtors, coiners, and vagabonds, as well as for "traitors, felons, fugitives, outlaws, &c., together with such as refused the law of the land." It was one of the haunts of Jack Sheppard, and Jonathan Wild kept his horses at the Duke's Head, in Red Cross Street. Indeed, the Mint at length got to be such a pest, that special statutes (8th and 9th of William III., and 9th and 11th George I.) were passed, ordering the abolition of its privileges; and one of these acts relieved all debtors who had taken sanctuary in the Mint from their creditors, provided the claims against them were under £50. The exodus of the refugee-felons and debtors, in July, 1723, after the passing of the 9th of George I., is described as having been like one of the Jewish tribes going out of Egypt, for the train of "Minters" is said to have included some thousands in its ranks, and the road towards Guildford (whither they were journeying to be cleared at the Quarter Sessions, of their debts and penalties) to have been positively covered with the cavalcade of caravans, carts, horsemen, and foot-travellers. —*Weekly Journal, Saturday, July 20, 1723.*

In 1442, the district of the hospital of "St. Katharine's, at the Tower," was made a royal precinct, and no one could be arrested there for debt, except by an order from the Board of Green Cloth.—*Timbs' London.*

Mr. Cunningham also tells us, "that the privileges of sanctuary, which continued to the precinct of Whitefriars after the dissolution, were confirmed and enlarged, in 1608, by Royal Charter. Fraudulent debtors, prostitutes, and other outcasts of society, made it a favourite retreat. Here they formed a community of their own, adopted the language of pickpockets, openly resisted the execution of any legal process, and, extending their cant terms to the place they lived in, new-named their precinct by the well-known appellation of *Alsatia.*"

† "A hospital, or '*spital,*' signified a charitable institution for the advantage of poor, infirm, and aged persons—an almshouse in short; while '*spittles*' were mere lazar-houses, receptacles for wretches in the leprosy and other diseases—the consequence of debauchery and vice."—*Gifford: Note to Massinger's Works.*

‡ St. Giles, we are told, was so named after an hospital for lepers that was dedicated to the saint, and built on the site of a small church upon the ground occupied by the present edifice—the gardens and precincts extending between High Street and Crown Street and west of Meux's brewery. This was founded

It would appear, then, that the several "rookeries," or vagabond colonies distributed throughout the Metropolis, were originally the sites either of some sanctuary, or refuge for felons and debtors, or else of some "spital" or "loke" for the reception of the poor, the impotent, or the leprous; and that the districts in which such asylums were situate thus came to be each the *nucleus* or *nidus* of a dense criminal and pauper population. For as the felon of the present day is at times found among the partakers of the eleemosynary hospitality of the "casual ward," and the vagrant often numbered among the in-door patients of our hospitals for the sick, so is it probable that the ancient "sanctuary-men" occasionally mixed with the diseased congregation crowded around some old metropolitan "loke," or else formed one of the horde of beggars that swarmed about the precincts of the obsolete religious houses and spitals. Hence around each such sacred spot a heterogeneous outcast tribe got to be gathered, and these doubtlessly were left to dwell and intercommune alone, shunned, as they must have been, by all decent people, either for their crimes, their maladies, or their filth and squalor.

But not only must such a refuse race have intercommuned apart from the rest of London society, and each individual thus have tended to render his neighbours worse than they were by nature or habit, but they would have *interbred* with the lowest class of women,* and so have served to render every one of the old "religious" haunts positive nests of vice, misery, and disease—hatching felons, lepers, and mendicants, like vipers in a muck-heap.

Surely, if it be possible to procreate gout, consumption, and insanity—if these subtle derangements of the human constitution are capable of being spawned from father to child, it is far from improbable that an outcast race, such as that which must have been

at the beginning of the twelfth century, by Matilda, queen of Henry I.; and Henry VIII., soon after the dissolution of religious houses, converted the chapel of the hospital into a parish church, of the name of St. Giles'-in-the-Fields. "Edward III.," says a document quoted by Stow, "sent commandement that all leprous persons within the saide citie and suburbes should avoid, within fifteen daies, and no man suffer any such leprose person to abide within his house, upon paine to forfeit his saide house, and to incurre the kinge's further displeasure. And that the sheriffs should cause the said lepers to be removed into some *out places of the fieldes*, from the haunt and company of all sound people; whereupon it followed that the citizens required of the guardian of St. Giles' Hospital, to take from them, and to keep continually the number of fourteene persons, according to the foundation of Mathilde the queen."

About the year 1413 the gallows was removed from the Elms in Smithfield to the north end of the garden wall of St. Giles' Hospital; and, when the gallows was again removed to Tyburn, "St. Giles' became," says Mr. Timbs, "a sort of half-way house for condemned criminals," owing to the custom of giving a bowl of ale, at the hospital gate, to every malefactor on his way to execution—a practice which was afterwards continued, we are told, at an "hostel" built upon the site of the monastic house, and which served to give a moral taint to the neighbourhood. In the time of the Puritans, St. Giles' was a refuge for the persecuted tipplers and ragamuffins of London and Westminster. St. Giles' was first colonized by the Irish immigrants in the reign of Queen Elizabeth.

Spitalfields, on the other hand, was named from its having been the site and property of the priory and hospital of St. Mary Spittle, Without Bishopgate, and founded, 1197, by Walter Brune, citizen of London, and Rosia his wife, for Augustine canons. At the dissolution of religious houses, in 1534, it had 130 beds for the receipt of the poor of this charity.

* Such women had generally a special district set apart for them in the olden times, and this was mostly near some "privileged place." "Next on this bank," says Stow, speaking of Bankside at Southwark, "was some time the *Bordello*, or Stewes, a place so called of certain stew-houses, privileged there for the repair of incontinent men to the like incontinent women. I find," he adds, "that, in the 4th of Richard II., these stew-houses belonged to William Walworth, then Lord Mayor of London, and were farmed by *froes* (*fraus*) of Flanders; but were spoiled by Wat Tyler and other rebels of Kent. * * * These allowed stew-houses," he further tells us, "had signs on their fronts towards the Thames—not hanged out, but painted on the walls—as 'the Boar's Head,' 'the Cross Keys,' 'the Gun,' 'the Castle,' 'the Crane,' 'the Cardinal's Hat!' 'the Bell,' 'the Swan,' &c. I have heard ancient men of good credit report, that these single women were forbidden the rites of the Church so long as they continued their sinful life, and were excluded from Christian burial, if they were not reconciled before their death. Therefore there was a plot of ground, called 'the single women's churchyard,' appointed for them, far from the parish church."

GIRLS' SCHOOL AT TOTHILL FIELDS PRISON.

BOYS EXERCISING AT TOTHILL FIELDS PRISON.

huddled round the sites of the ancient London sanctuaries and hospitals, should beget natures like their own—deficient alike in moral and physical energy, and therefore not only averse to the drudgery of regular labour, but incapable of that continued tension of the will which men call moral purpose or principle. If Jews engender Jews, with minds and characters almost as Hebraic as their noses—if gipsy blood have a tendency to induce a propensity for gipsy habits—if, in fine, there be the least truth in ethnology, or, indeed, in the principles which regulate improvements in the breeding merely of "stock," then assuredly must there be a greater chance of habitual thieves and beggars begetting kindred natures to their own, rather than the opposite. Accordingly, ethnic crime and pauperism would appear, not only to be consistent with the ordinary laws of human life, but to be as natural as hereditary insanity, to which, indeed, it seems to bear a faint similitude; for, as in cases of mental disease, the faculty of attention is well known to be the first to exhibit symptoms of derangement, so the temperament of the habitual criminal is invariably marked by a comparative incapability of continuous application to any one subject or pursuit, whilst the same bodily restlessness as characterises the lunatic, is also the distinctive type of the vagrant.*

The old sanctuaries and spitals, or places of refuge and shelter, continued in full force until the dissolution of the religious houses, which took place principally between 1534—9, and at the same period several statutes (26th, 27th, and 37th Henry VIII.) were passed, regulating, limiting, and partially abolishing the privilege of refuge.† This change, history tells us, was followed by what has been termed the "age of beggars and thieves;" for, though we have no definite account as to the numbers of outcasts and mendicants harboured by the religious houses in the olden time, nevertheless the statements as to the proportion of beggars and priests, to the rest of the population, in the foreign episcopal cities, at the period of their dissolution by the French army under the Revolution, will give us some notion as to the hordes of paupers and criminals that must have formerly been maintained among us under such a system.‡

When, therefore, the parasitical multitudes infesting the neighbourhood of the old abbeys and monasteries, &c., came to be deprived of their ordinary means of subsistence, by the stoppage of the alms, in consequence of the dissolution of the institutions upon which they

---

* These criminal or mendicant *races* are by no means peculiar to our own country. According to Dr. Andrew Smith's observations in South Africa, almost every tribe of people there who have submitted themselves to social laws, and recognised the rights of property and the reciprocal moral duties of a civilized caste, are surrounded by hordes of vagabonds and outcasts from their own community. Such are the Bushmen and the "Sonquas" of the Hottentot race—the term *Sonqua* meaning, literally, *pauper*. The Kafirs, again, have their Bushmen as well as the Hottentots, and these are called "*Fingoes*"—a word signifying beggars, wanderers, or outcasts. The Lappes, moreover, seem to have borne a somewhat similar relation to the Finns; that is to say, they appear to have been a wild and predatory tribe, who sought the desert, like the Arabian Bedouins, whilst the Finns cultivated the soil like the more industrious Fellahs. Further, such outcast parasitical tribes are distinguished by certain characteristics, which not only belong to them generally, but also agree with the propensities of our own vagrant and thievish population; viz., a repugnance to regular and continuous labour—a want of providence in laying up stores for their future sustenance—the adoption of a secret language as a means of disguising their designs—a love of gambling and delight in all kinds of perilous adventures—a high admiration of brute courage, or "pluck," as it is called, and tricks of low cunning— as well as a special delight in "sports" which consist principally in watching the sufferings of sentient creatures.

† It was not until the 21st of James I. that such places were wholly forbidden. The 28th cap. and 7th sect. of that Act ordains, that no sanctuary or privilege of sanctuary shall thereafter be admitted or allowed in any case.

‡ Cologne, at the time of the occupation of the "holy city" by the French, at the end of the last century, contained no less than 1,200 beggars, and 2,500 ecclesiastics, out of a population of 90,000 and odd inhabitants; so that about one-twenty-fifth part of the entire people consisted of priests and mendicants, or not less than one-twentieth if children be excluded from the calculation.

depended, it is evident that society must have had to deal with a moral pestilence, such as we in these days can hardly conceive. The statutes that were framed at this period, however, against vagrants and persons "whole and mighty in body," who refused to work "for such reasonable wage as was commonly given," may be cited as instances of the state of the country after the abolition of the old religious houses and privileges. The 27th Henry VIII., cap. 25 (A. D. 1536), orders, that a "sturdy beggar is to be whipped the first time he is detected in begging; that he is to have his right ear cropped for the second offence; and, if again found guilty of begging, he is to be indicted for wandering, loitering, and idleness, and, when convicted, to suffer execution of death as a felon and an enemy to the commonwealth." This Act, however, being found ineffectual from over-severity, another, which was considered more lenient, was passed in 1547 (1st Edward VI., cap. 3); and, according to that, every able-bodied person who did not apply himself to some honest labour was to be taken for a vagabond, branded on the shoulder, and adjudged as a slave for two years to any one who should demand him; and, if not demanded by any one as a slave, he was to be kept to hard labour on the highway in chains. During this time he was to be fed on bread and water and refuse meat, and made to work by being beaten. If he ran away in the course of his two years' slavery, he was to be branded on the cheek, and adjudged a slave for life; and if he ran away a second time, he was to suffer death as a felon. Still, this statute seems to have been almost as useless as the one it repealed, and accordingly, twenty-five years afterwards, another Act was passed (14th Elizabeth, cap. 5, A. D. 1572), wherein it was declared, that all persons able to labour, and "not having any land or master, nor using any lawful craft or mystery," and who should refuse to work, should, "for the first offence, be grievously whipped and burned through the gristle of the right ear, with a hot iron of the compass of an inch about;" for the second, such parties should be deemed felons; and for the third, they should suffer death as felons, without the benefit of clergy. Twenty odd years again elapsed, and then the 39th of Elizabeth, caps. 3 and 4, was enacted, ordaining that every able-bodied person that refused to work for ordinary wages, was to be "openly whipped until his body was bloody, and forthwith sent, from parish to parish, the most straight way to the parish where he was born, there to put himself to work as a true subject ought to do." Three years subsequent to this again these *terrible* laws were changed for the kindlier 43rd Elizabeth, cap. 2, which instituted, for the first time, workhouses for the poor, and ordered the overseers to raise sums for providing materials "to set the poor on work," and also for the relief of lame, blind, old, and impotent persons.

It is manifest, however, that such asylums could have given shelter and employment only to the *honest* poor, and that the habitual mendicant and thief, who loved to "shake a free leg," as it is called by the fraternity, and who preferred cadging and pilfering to industry, would have looked upon such institutions as little better than prisons, and doubtlessly have confounded them with the houses of correction that were originally associated with every workhouse throughout the kingdom.

It was but natural, therefore, that the sites of the old sanctuaries, and spitals, and lokes should have remained—long after the dissolution of the institutions which originally caused the crowd of thieves, lepers, and beggars to locate themselves in such quarters—as the principal abiding places of the "pariah" population throughout the metropolis, and, indeed, the country in general; for not only would habit induce such people to continue in the same place (and the well-to-do are mostly unaware how difficult it is to dislodge the poor from their old dwellings, even though they be filthy and tumble-down to the last degree), but, owing to the old "privileged" localities being shunned by all honest and decent people, they would there be sure at once of meeting with their "old pals," and of getting quit of the company of all uncongenial characters.

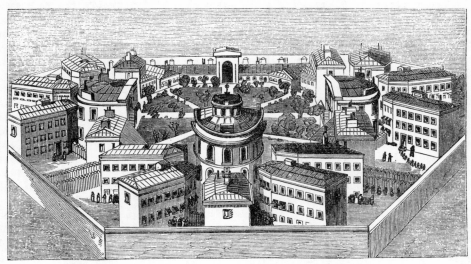

BIRD'S-EYE VIEW OF TOTHILL FIELDS PRISON (SEEN FROM THE BACK).

¶ ii—a.

The History, Character, and Discipline of the Prison.

Tothill Fields Prison (or Bridewell, as it was originally called) stands on one of those Cockney champagne districts—like Moor*fields*, Spital*fields*, Spa*fields*, Goodman's-*fields*, Lock's-*fields*, Lincoln's Inn *Fields*, St. Giles'-in-the-*Fields*, &c.—which have long since become a dense mass of bricks and mortar, veined with streets and alleys, and of which every patch of green sward has been for so many years covered over by the spreading red walls and paving-stones of the Metropolis, that even "the oldest inhabitant," or the most ancient chronicle, cannot tell us where originally stood the celebrated *hills* and *plains* whose double existence is, in the present case, recorded in the name of the Westminster prison.   Who can point out to us now the famous hill that once rejoiced in the proud name of "*Tot*"—now, that no acclivity, with so heavy a "gradient" (to use a term that sprang up with the introduction of railways) even as that of the far-famed steep of Ludgate, is to be found for many parishes round—not even from the united "seas," as a magisterial friend calls them, of "Chel-" and "Batter-," down to the combined "friars," "White" as well as "Black."

"If a place could exist," wrote Jeremy Bentham, in 1798, "of which it could be said that it was in *no* neighbourhood, that place would be Tothill Fields."

Mr. Peter Cunningham, however, tells us that "Tothill Fields, particularly so called, comprised that (triangular) portion of land between Tothill Street, Pimlico, and the river Thames—an uncertain boundary," he adds, "but the best that can be given."*

---

* "Tothill Fields," says Wykeham Archer, the artist and antiquarian, in his "Vestiges of Old London," 'were, within three centuries, part of a marshy tract of land lying between Millbank and Westminster Abbey, and on which stood a few scattered buildings, some of them being the residences of noble personages." ("Millbank was so called," he adds in a note, "from a mill which occupied the site of the old Peterborough House." Peterborough House was pulled down in 1809. It stood at the end of the present College Street, where was formerly the Abbey Water Mill, built by one Nicholas Littlington.) "From the west gate"—(of the old palace at Westminster, and which gate formerly stood at the entrance to Dean's Yard)—"runneth along Tothill Street," says Stow. "Herein is a house of the Lord Gray of Wilton, and on the other side, *at the entry into Tothill Field*, Stourton House, which Gyles, the last Lord Dacre of the South, purchased and

The origin of "*Tothill*," according to the same author, is "the Toot-hill, or the Beacon Field;" (Welsh *twt*, a spring or rising), for not only does an ancient lease, he assures us, so style a "close" in this neighbourhood, but "there is a place of the same name near Caernarvon Castle also called "The Beacon Hill;" so that, it is suggested, the metropolitan district now bearing that title was probably, in former times, the highest level in Westminster suitable for a beacon.*

These fields, in the reign of Henry III. (1216—1272) formed part of a manor in Westminster, belonging to John Mansell, "the king's councillor and priest," says Stow, "who did invite to a stately dinner (at his house at Totehill) the kings and queens of England and Scotland, with divers courtiers and citizens, and whereof there was such a multitude that seven hundred messes of meat did not serve for the first dinner." By an act passed in the same reign, 34 Henry III., the Abbot of Westminster was given "leave to keepe a markett in the Tuthill every Munday, and a faire every yeare, for three days." Two centuries afterwards, the fields in the neighbourhood were used for appeals by combat; and Stow describes "a combate that was appointed to have been fought," the 18th of June, "in Trinity Tearme, 1571," for a "certain manour or demaine lands," in the Isle of Harty, "adjoining to the Isle of Sheppey, in Kent," and for which "it was thought good," says the historian, that "the court should sit in Tuthill Fields, where was prepared one plot of ground, one and twenty yardes square, double railed for the combate, without the West Square." In the time of Nich. Culpepper, the author of the well-known "*Herbal*," these fields were famous for their parsley. In 1651 (25th August) "the Trained Bands of London, Westminster," &c., to the number of 14,000, we are told, "drew out into Tuttle Fields." Here, too, were built the "Five Houses," or "Seven Chimneys," as pest-houses for victims to the plague, and in 1665 the dead were buried "in the open Tuttle Fields;" and here, some short while

built new"—(this house is still standing in what is now called Dacre Street—a small lane leading out of the Broadway—and its garden formerly occupied the site that is now styled Strutton Ground)—"whose lady and wife, Anne, left money to build an hospital for twenty poor women and so many children, which hospital," adds the old historian, "her executors have new begun *in the field adjoining*." This institution is now known as Dacre's Almshouses, or Emanuel Hospital, and stands in Hopkins' Row, at the back of York Street.

"*From the entry into Tothill Field*," Stow proceeds to say, "*the street is called Petty France*"—(this, again, is the modern York Street)—"in which, upon St. Hermit's Hill"—(now merely a court, and the name corrupted into Herman's Hill)—"*on the south side thereof*, Cornelius Van Dun, a Brabander born, built twenty houses for poor women to dwell rent free." These were styled the Red Lion Almshouses, and stood, till six years ago, at the extreme end of York Street, on the tongue of land formed by the junction of that street with Hopkins' Row at the back, and the site of which is now occupied by St. Margaret's new workhouse. It would seem, therefore, that "Totehill Field," as Stow calls it, was but *one* large plain at the beginning of the seventeenth century, and that the entrance to it was at the part now styled "the Broadway," Westminster—the ancient Petty France, or modern York Street, being the locality which stretches "*from it, or at the end of Tothill Street*." In York Street, the site of Van Dun's Almshouses is, as we have said, occupied by the new workhouse, and at the Broadway the house of Gyles Lord Dacre assuredly stood, since the almshouses, which we are told were erected by his lady and wife, Anne, "on the *field adjoining*," are still standing in the *next street* (Hopkins' Row). How far the Totehill Field extended back from the Broadway it is difficult to state, but it is clear it could not lie "*between* Millbank and Westminster," as Mr. Archer suggests, and yet have its *entry* at the Broadway. Mr. Cunningham's definition, viz., that it comprised the portion of lands bounded by Tothill Street, Pimlico, and the Thames, is probably more correct.

* Mr. Archer derives Tothill from "*Teut*," the chief divinity of the Druids, and the equivalent of "*Thoth*," the Egyptian Mercury, saying that the "*Tot*," or "*Thoth*" hill, was the place whence proclamations were made. An ancient manuscript spells the name "*Tuttle*," and the Normans, it is well known, called the whole of the abbey and palace precinct, south of Pall Mall, "Thorney Island and *tout le champ*." This, it is thought, has been clipped first into "*tout-le*," and then corrupted into "*tuttle*." "Toot-hills," says Mr. Cunningham, however, "occur in many parts of England, under the several forms of 'Toot,' 'Tut,' 'Tot,' 'Tote,' &c. The same topographical radicle is found in the local titles of *Totness*, *Tutbury*, and also *Tooting* and *Totten*-ham." In Rocque's map (1746), *Toote Hill* is marked just at a bend in the Horseferry Road.

afterwards, "1200 Scotch prisoners, taken at the battle of Worcester," were interred; for the accounts of the churchwardens of St. Margaret's, Westminster, says the author of *The Hand-book of London*, exhibit a payment of "thirty shillings for 67 loads of soil laid on the graves of Tothill Fields, wherein," it is added, "the Scotch prisoners are buried." Some of the Scotch were "driven like a herd of swine," says Heath's Chronicle, "through Westminster to Tuthill Fields," and there sold to several merchants and sent to the Barbadoes.

About the same period the people used to resort to a maze in these same fields, that, according to an old writer, was "much frequented in the summer-time, in fair afternoons," the fields being described as "of great use, pleasure, and recreation" to the king's scholars and neighbours. And Sir Richard Steele, writing in *The Tatler*, in 1709, says, "here was a military garden, *a bridewell,* and, as I have heard tell, a race-course." A bear-garden, kept by one William Wells, stood upon the site of Vincent Square.

Tothill Fields was also, in the seventeenth century, a celebrated duelling-ground; the last "affair of honour" fought there, of which we have any account, took place, it is said, in 1711, when Sir Chomley Dering was killed by a Mr. Thornhill—the tom-fools fighting with pistols so near that the muzzles touched.

The "Bridewell" of which Steele spoke as existing in Tothill Fields at the beginning of the eighteenth century, was erected nearly a hundred years before—viz., in 1618; for in the garden of the present House of Correction at Westminster, let into the wall that stretches from the gate between B and C prisons, is a small square stone, about the size of a draught-board, with the following inscription nearly erased :—

A Portion of the old
Tothill Fields Prison,
in
1618
taken down Anno Domini
1836.

This ancient prison, say the London chronicles, was altered and enlarged in the year 1655; and verily, in corroboration of the statement, we find, in the garden surrounding the present building, and at some little distance from the before-mentioned tablet, the stone frame, or skeleton as it were, of the old prison gateway, in shape like the Greek letter Π, standing by itself as a memorial, at the back of B prison, between what are now the female work-rooms, but which a few years ago formed the site of the then prevalent tread-wheels. This cromlech-like relic is covered with ivy, and looks at first more like some piece of imitation ruin-work than the remains of a prison portal; for the doorway is so primitive in character (being not more than 5 feet 10 inches high and 3 feet wide), that it seems hardly bigger than the entrance to a cottage; nevertheless, an inscription, painted on the lintel, assures us that it was the

GATEWAY OR PRINCIPAL ENTRANCE TO TOTHILL FIELDS PRISON, 1665.
Taken down and removed to this site Anno Domini 1836.

Moreover, in the wall of what is termed 4 and 5 prison, B side—and just under the small, covered bridge that leads from the upper part of the jail here to the chapel over the governor's house—there is another memorial-stone built into the brickwork, after the fashion of the tablet first described, and in this is cut the following inscription, setting forth the class of offenders for which the ancient prison was originally designed :—

> Here are several Sorts of Work
> For the *Poor* of this *Parish* of St.
> *Margaret, Westminster,*
> As also the *County* according to
> LAW, and for such as will Beg and
> Live Idle in this City and Liberty
> of *Westminster,*
> ANNO 1655.

Thus, then, we perceive that Tothill Fields prison was originally intended as a " bridewell," or house of correction, in connection with the parish of St. Margaret, Westminster, *i.e.,* a place for the " penitentiary amendment " of such "sturdy beggars " and "valiant rogues" as objected to work, as well as others falling under the legal description of vagrant.

Hence it would appear that the Tothill Fields Bridewell* (a name that it bore till almost within the last few years), was, in the first instance, designed as a penal establishment in connection with the poor-house, and, like that establishment, originally maintained at the expense of the county or city, and governed by the justices of the locality.

This old prison, we learn from the chief warder of the present establishment, occupied the plot of ground which adjoins the north side of the " Green Coat School," and which is now covered by the line of newly-built shops on the west side of Artillery Row, giving into Victoria Street, and situate at the north-eastern corner of the new prison itself ; so that— as this same Green Coat School, or " St. Margaret's Hospital," as it was formerly styled, was dedicated, as far back as 1633, to the relief of the poor fatherless children of St. Margaret's parish—it is probable that "the hospital or abiding house" for the poor, and its next-door neighbour, the "bridewell," or " house of correction," for the compulsory employment of such paupers as were "mighty in body" and objected to work, were originally conjoint parish institutions—the one for granting relief to the industrious poor, and the other for punishing the idle ; for the 43rd of Elizabeth, c. 2 (which was passed in the year 1601), directed the overseers of the poor in every parish " to take order for setting to work the *children* of all indigent parents," as well as all such persons having no means of maintaining themselves ; and also gave power to the justices to send to the house of correction all able-bodied persons who would not work.   Hence these twin establishments of the pauper prison (or bridewell) and the pauper school—the one erected in 1618, and enlarged in 1655, and the other established in 1633—were most probably among the first institutions raised for carrying out the injunctions of the original poor law enacted in 1601.

The fellow house of correction for Middlesex seems to have been originally set up at Coldbath Fields at about the same period—" in the reign of the first James" (A.D. 1603—25), says Mr. Dixon.

---

* " A bridewell," says one of the Middlesex justices, in a letter to us, " is another name for a house of correction."   The City Bridewell, however (Bridge Street, Blackfriars), was, when open (it has been closed for the last two years now), restricted to the reception of unruly apprentices and vagrants, committed to jail *for three months and less ;* whereas a house of correction is understood to be a place of safe custody and punishment, to which offenders are sent when *committed* either summarily or at sessions, for, generally speaking *two years and less.*

FEMALE PRISONERS' OWN CLOTHES STORE AT TOTHILL FIELDS PRISON.

BOYS' SCHOOL-ROOM AT TOTHILL FIELDS PRISON.

But though originally designed as a bridewell for *vagrants*, Tothill Fields was converted, we are told, at the beginning of the eighteenth century (in the reign of Queen Anne, A.D. 1702—14), into a jail for the confinement of *criminals* also; and Howard, writing towards the end of the same century (1777), " describes it," says Mr. Hepworth Dixon, " as being remarkably well managed at that period, holding up its enlightened and careful keeper, one George Smith, as a model to other governors.

Some thirty odd years ago, however, the erection of a new prison was decided upon, and an Act for that purpose obtained in 1826. Then a different site was chosen, and a piece of land on the western side of the Green Coat School, and near the Vauxhall Bridge Road, having been selected, £16,000 was paid for a plot that was 8 acres 2 roods and 17 poles in extent, and the foundations commenced.* The designs were furnished by Mr. Robert Abraham, and the building, which cost £186,178 19s. 4d. (says our precise informant), was finished and opened for the reception of prisoners in the year 1834; after which the old prison was pulled down, and the relics already described transferred to the new one, as we have said, in 1836.

The new prison at Tothill Fields is situate on the southern side of Victoria Street, and has its front in Francis Street—a small thoroughfare giving into the Vauxhall Bridge Road. According to the guide-books, it is a solid and even handsome structure, and one of great extent as well as strength. " Seen from Victoria Street," says one London topographer— though, by the bye, it is in no way visible in that direction—" it resembles a substantial fortress." The main entrance is on the Vauxhall side of the building in Francis Street, and the doorway here is formed of massive granite blocks, and immense iron gates, ornamented above with portcullis work. " Viewed from this point," the author of " London Prisons " describes the exterior (though there is nothing but a huge dead wall and the prison gateway to be seen) " as being the very ideal of a national prison—vast, airy, light, and yet inexorably safe."†

The building is said to be one of the finest specimens of brickwork in the Metropolis, and consists of three distinct prisons, each constructed alike, on Bentham's " panopticon " plan, in the form of a half-wheel, *i. e.*, with a series of detached wings, radiating, spoke-fashion, from a central lodge or " argus " (as such places were formerly styled)—one of such lodges being situate, midway, in each of the three sides of a spacious turfed and planted court-yard; so that the outline of the ground-plan of these three distinct, half-wheel-like prisons resembles the ace of clubs, with the court-yard forming an open square in the centre.

" For a house of correction," Mr. Hepworth Dixon considers " it is one of the very worst erections in London " (nevertheless, it is infinitely superior to Coldbath Fields); and, he adds, " seeing that it was built only a few years ago, it is astonishing that it should have been so ill arranged. It is," he proceeds to say, " very badly designed, the *radical* principle, as illustrated at Pentonville, and other prisons, being utterly neglected, and the detached buildings (or wings) which radiate from each of the central lodges being, for all practical purposes of control, really so many separate prisons." " There is no concealing the fact," subjoins the author, in another part of his book, " that this building is a huge and costly blunder."

* For this, and much more information in connection with the above prison, we are indebted to Mr. Antrobus, one of the visiting justices, and a gentleman who is well known to all social philosophers and jurists for his efforts concerning the reformation of juvenile offenders, as well as his admirable work entitled, " The Prison and the School."

† " Indeed it *is* 'inexorably safe,' " the authority above quoted tells us—there never having been but one escape from it, and that was owing to the carelessness of the door-keeper, who laid down his key, when a prisoner picked it up, unlocked the door, and walked away.—*Dixon's " London Prisons."*

The Westminster new prison, as rebuilt in 1834, contained (1) a "jail"* for untried male prisoners as well as debtors, (2) a house of correction for males *after* conviction (when sentenced to a shorter term than that of transportation), and (3) a prison for women.

This tripartite arrangement of the new Tothill Fields prison appears to have been adopted in conformity with the requirements of the 4th of George IV., cap. 64—shortly after the passing of which Act the erection of a new prison at Westminster appears to have been decided upon. But the notions that prevailed, at the period of its erection, concerning prison

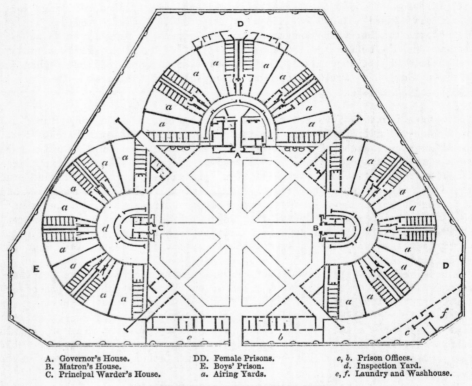

A. Governor's House.	DD. Female Prisons.	c, b. Prison Offices.
B. Matron's House.	E. Boys' Prison.	d. Inspection Yard.
C. Principal Warder's House.	a. Airing Yards.	e, f. Laundry and Washhouse.

GROUND-PLAN OF TOTHILL FIELDS PRISON.

requirements and discipline, were far from being sufficiently settled to warrant the construction of an institution based upon vague and inefficient ideas of classification; and accordingly, when it was found expedient to establish houses of detention *expressly* for the con-

* A common jail is said to have been defined by the 4th of George IV., cap. 64, s. 5. But this statute, which refers principally to the classification of prisoners, enjoins merely, in the section alluded to, that when any house of correction shall be annexed to the common jail, it shall be lawful for the magistrates to divide the house of correction *and* its adjoining common jail into such number of compartments as would be required for carrying into effect the classification of prisoners directed by that Act—the same as if the two prisons had been distinct and separate establishments. The magistrates, however, are to declare what part of the united building shall be considered as the *jail* and what other part be regarded as the *house of correction*, and to direct what classes of prisoners shall be confined in each part—"*provided*," says the Act, "*that prisoners for debt shall always be confined in the part appropriated as and for the jail.*" One of the Middlesex magistrates, in a letter addressed to us, defines a common jail as a place of safe custody for prisoners before trial and debtors, so that, according to this definition, a "common jail" = a "house of detention" + a "debtors' prison."

finement of prisoners *before* trial, and to have special places for the safe custody of debtors, the Westminster prison came to be restricted to the confinement of criminals (other than transports or convicts) *after* conviction only. This change occurred in 1845.

In the year 1850 a still more important alteration ensued in the character of the Westminster prison; up to that period Tothill Fields bridewell had been appropriated to the reception of *all* classes of convicted prisoners, not being transports or convicts; but, at the April Quarter Sessions in that year, one of the Middlesex magistrates (Mr. Thomas Turner) moved to the effect, that a committee be appointed to consider and report upon the practicability and expediency of appropriating each of the houses of correction for the county of Middlesex to the reception of distinct classes of offenders.*

In accordance with the recommendations of that report, it was determined, in July, 1850, that the House of Correction at Westminster should be henceforth restricted to the reception of convicted *female* prisoners and males *below* the age of seventeen years, and that all convicted male prisoners of the age of *seventeen years and upwards* (and those *only*) should, for the future, be sent to the House of Correction at Coldbath Fields; whilst persons *committed for want of sureties*, or *safe custody merely*, were to be conveyed to the House of Detention at Clerkenwell.

This change, which effected the best possible classification of prisoners (a classification which, while it was really the only one rationally required, was also that one alone which the several Acts of Parliament concerning the separation of criminals—of felons from misdemeanants, and misdemeanants, again, from vagrants—had *not* enjoined) produced at once, not only an immense saving in the number of officers necessary for the government of each of the prisons, but also brought the prisoners into precisely such groups as are essential as well to the preservation of order and decency, as to the due comprehension of the subject of crime in general.

---

* The words of the motion were, "That a Committee be appointed to consider and report upon the practicability and expediency of classifying prisoners committed to the houses of correction for the county of Middlesex, and appropriating each prison to the reception of distinct classes of offenders, and to submit to the Court such scheme as they may consider best adapted for carrying out this arrangement, if the principle be approved by them."

The Committee appointed by the Court consisted of the following justices :—

Thos. Turner, Esq.	B. Rotch, Esq.	B. J. Armstrong, Esq.	Edmd. E. Antrobus, Esq.
J. Wilks, Esq.	C. Devon, Esq.	C. Woodward, Esq.	J. T. Brooking, Esq.
P. Laurie, Esq.	W. Buchanan, Esq.	Henry Warner, Esq.	

And the Report made by them was as follows :—"That your Committee have procured returns to be made to them of the number of prisoners of different classes confined in the houses of correction for this county, at various periods, ending 29th June last; they have also had plans submitted to them of the same buildings respectively, and have inquired particularly into their respective accommodations. The Committee have, moreover, examined the governors of each of the houses of correction upon the subject referred to them, and they have unanimously agreed upon the following resolutions, which they recommend to the adoption of the Court—the arrangements therein comprised not only affording, in the opinion of your Committee, facilities for the better description and management of prisoners, but also being calculated to effect an important saving in the prison expenditure. Resolved :—

"1. That all persons *committed for want of sureties*, or *safe custody* merely, be sent to the *House of Detention* at *Clerkenwell*.

"2. That all male prisoners *below the age of* 17 years, not included in the foregoing resolution, be sent to the *House of Correction, Westminster*.

"3. That all *female prisoners*, except such as are included in the first resolution, be sent to the *House of Correction, Westminster*.

"4. That all *male* prisoners *of the age of* 17 *years and upwards*, except such as are included in the first resolution, be sent to the *House of Correction, Coldbath Fields*."

These resolutions were adopted by the Court of Quarter Sessions, July 18, 1850.

PLANTED COURT-YARD AND GOVERNOR'S HOUSE, AT TOTHILL FIELDS PRISON.
(From a Photograph by Herbert Watkins, 179, Regent Street.)

By the table given below, showing the number of male and female officers employed, as well as the gross amount of salaries paid at each of the Middlesex houses of correction for the year *before*, and the year *after*, the above-mentioned change was introduced, it will be seen that the justices were enabled, by the adoption of this most wise and efficient measure, to manage the two prisons with twenty officers less, and thus to reduce the sum paid annually in salaries to the extent of £1,719 ; or, in other words, to decrease the conjoint staff of officers, as well as the cost of management, very nearly ten per cent. respectively ;* for,

* TABLE SHOWING THE NUMBER OF MALE AND FEMALE OFFICERS, AS WELL AS THE GROSS AMOUNT PAID IN
SALARIES TO SUCH OFFICERS IN THE HOUSE OF CORRECTION, COLDBATH FIELDS, AND IN THE HOUSE OF
CORRECTION AT WESTMINSTER, DURING THE YEARS ENDING MICHAELMAS, 1850-51.

	COLDBATH FIELDS.			TOTHILL FIELDS.			BOTH ESTABLISHMENTS.		
	1850.	1851.	Differ-ence.	1850.	1851.	Differ-ence.	1850.	1851.	Differ-ence.
Number of Male Officers employed	89	103	+ 14	60	40	— 20	149	143	— 6
Ditto Female	29	....	— 29	23	38	+ 15	52	38	— 14
Total number of Officers employed	118	103	— 15	83	78	— 5	201	181	— 20
Sum paid annually in Sala-ries to such Officers . .	£10,902	£9,990	— £912	£7,548	£6,741	— £807	£18,450	£16,731	—£1719

though the staff of *male* officers at Coldbath Fields, after the change, had to be increased fourteen, on account of *all* the adult *male* prisoners for Middlesex being then sent to that prison only, nevertheless, it was found that the staff of *female* officers there admitted of being reduced not less than twenty-nine, owing to the *female* prisoners being *all* removed from it, and that a saving of fifteen officers altogether might thus be effected at this one establishment; whilst at Tothill Fields, though the staff of *female* officers required to be increased fifteen on account of its becoming the *sole* receptacle for the *female* prisoners of the county, still, by the removal of *all* the adult *male* prisoners, the staff of *male* officers was, on the other hand, capable of being decreased to the extent of twenty, and, consequently, a saving of five officers altogether became possible at *that* particular establishment.

To the Middlesex magistrates, therefore, belongs the high honour of having not only erected a special place of safe custody for the confinement of prisoners *before* trial, or, in other words, of having been the originators of "houses of detention" for secluding the probable innocent man from the convicted criminal, but also of having voluntarily—for no Act of Parliament has yet ordered such a proceeding—determined upon the removal of the young and thoughtless out of the contact, and therefore the contagion, of the old and hardened offender—the one measure being as distinguished for its justice as the other is for its benevolence and wisdom.

The Westminster prison has thus, in the course of years, passed from the old bridewell, originally designed for the "compulsory setting to work" of such stalwart paupers as objected to labour for the bread they ate—into, first, a prison for vagrants and others charged with trivial offences, or, in other words, into a prison for petty criminals also; then into a place of confinement for *all* classes of prisoners, both before and after trial; afterwards into an institution for the imprisonment of *all* classes of offenders *after* trial *only*, when sentenced to terms less than that of transportation; and, finally, into a receptacle for merely *female* prisoners and *juveniles*.

The Westminster prison, as at present constituted, consists of three distinct prisons, arranged, as we have said, one at each of the three sides of the planted quadrangle which forms the court-yard, and called respectively A prison, B prison, and C prison—the latter, or B and C prisons, being appropriated to the reception of females, and the former, or prison A, set apart for boys.

The total amount of accommodation afforded by the prison is returned officially as follows:—

	Boys.	Females.	Total.
The (gross) number of prisoners the prison is capable of containing when more than one prisoner sleeps in one cell	300	600	900
The number of prisoners (out of the above) the prison is capable of containing in separate sleeping cells	198	351	549

The prison, therefore, has *separate* sleeping accommodation for not quite two-thirds of the number it is capable of containing. The numbers that it really *does* contain in the course of the year are as under:—

	Boys.	Females.	Total.
The greatest number of prisoners at any time in the course of the year ending Michaelmas, 1855	280	676	956
The daily average number of prisoners throughout the year ending Michaelmas, 1855	270	600	870

Hence, we perceive that though the entire prison has accommodation only for 900 prisoners of both sexes, even when more than one prisoner sleeps in one cell, it sometimes contains as much as 7 per cent. beyond that amount.

Of the gross prison population for the year, the returns are here given :—

	Boys.	Females.	Total.
The number of prisoners remaining in custody at the close of the year ending Michaelmas, 1854	243	623	866
The number of prisoners committed in the course of the year ending Michaelmas, 1855	1,909	5,359	7,268
The gross prison population for the year ending Michaelmas, 1855	2,152	5,982	8,134

The official staff consists of 1 governor, 2 chaplains, 1 surgeon, 3 clerks, 1 storekeeper, 1 principal warder, and 31 male warders; 1 principal matron, and 47 matrons or female warders.

Hence, we find that as there are altogether 31 male warders to a daily average of 270 boys throughout the year, the proportion is 1 officer to less than every 9 boys, which is nearly as high as Millbank, and considerably higher than Coldbath Fields, where the proportion is 1 officer to every 13 prisoners. Again, as there are 47 female warders to a daily average of 600 female prisoners, the porportion here is 1 officer to not quite 13 prisoners; whilst, for the whole prison, the proportion of officers to prisoners is 1 to 11. At Pentonville the officers are to the prisoners as 1 to 17.*

At Tothill Fields, however, the ratio of officers to prisoners is far from being excessive; for we find, by the Nineteenth Report of the Inspectors of Prisons (p. 161), that, throughout the prisons of England and Wales, the proportion of officers to prisoners is as follows :—

	Males.	Females.	Total both sexes.
Daily average number of prisoners in the whole of the prisons in the course of the year 1853	13,609	3,082	16,691
Number of officers employed in all the prisons collectively	1,504	420	1,924
Number of prisoners to each officer throughout the prisons of England and Wales	9·0	7·1	8·6
Number of prisoners to each officer at Tothill Fields prison	8·7	12·7	11·0
Number of prisoners to each officer at Coldbath Fields prison	13·8	—	13·0

* The subjoined table, copied from the "Special Report of the Visiting Justices" for 1856, shows the number of prisoners and officers for the last quinquenniad :—

TABLE SHOWING THE AVERAGE NUMBER, AS WELL AS THE GREATEST NUMBER OF PRISONERS AND OFFICERS, TOGETHER WITH THE AMOUNT PAID IN SALARIES FOR EACH YEAR, FROM 1851-55.

	1851.			1852.			1853.			1854.			1855.		
	Males.	Females.	Total.	Males.	Females.	Total.	Males.	Females.	Total.	Males.	Females.	Total.	Males.	Females.	Total.
Average number of prisoners throughout the year ending Michaelmas	220	430	650	248	472	720	236	523	759	276	631	907	270	600	870
Greatest number of prisoners at any one time in the course of the year	251	517	768	257	541	798	257	631	888	325	731	1056	289	676	965
Number of officers	40	38	78	40	39	79	40	41	81	40	44	84	40	48	88
Amount paid in salaries, &c.	—		£6733 10s.	—		£6750 12s.	—		£6961 16s.	—		£7161 16s.	—		£7203 6s.

It is with the juvenile, or A, prison, that we purpose dealing first. This comprises four distinct radiating wings, diverging from the lodge in the centre, which constitutes the principal warder's house. These wings though radiating, are still detached from the central lodge, and therefore supervision is virtually prevented. The octant space between each of the wings is devoted to an airing-yard, of which there are four. There are altogether 193 separate sleeping cells distributed throughout the boys' division of the Westminster prison, as well as a large dormitory at the upper part of one of the wings, capable of containing some 80 odd lads.

On the day of our second visit to this prison, there were altogether 271 boys, under seventeen years of age, confined in it; 87 of these had slept in the dormitory on the previous night, 7 in the reception cells, and the remaining 177 in the separate cells throughout the several wings.*

The separate cells are 8 feet long by 6 broad and 9 high, and have a capacity of 432 cubic feet, which, it will be seen, is less than one-half that of the model cells at Pentonville; neither is there any special apparatus here for ensuring the ventilation of the building, mere holes in the wall being resorted to as a means of removing the foul air and supplying fresh; nor are the cells fitted with gas, or supplied with water, or indeed closets, or any appliance for summoning the warder in case of emergency during the night. In fact, the construction of the cells is about as defective, in a sanitary point of view, as can well be imagined, the prison being unprovided with any apparatus, not only for ensuring perfect ventilation, as we have said, but even for warming and lighting the cells in the long winter nights. Some of the windows are what are called "*l'ouvre*" ones, that is to say, they are unglazed, and fitted with a venetian-blind-like screen, with shutters inside, to be closed at night; other windows are "hoppered," having a kind of wedge-like screen fastened before them.

The furniture of the cells consists of an iron bed, a straw mattress in sacking or tick, a rug, and one blanket during summer and three in winter, but they contain neither table nor chair, a small stool only being provided, and a zinc pan added as a night utensil.

Mr. Frederick Hill (late inspector of prisons), in his admirable book upon "CRIME; *its Amount, Causes, and Remedies*," says, while treating of the construction of prisons, "that if *the ventilation be vigorous* (for which purpose he recommends a slow fire, in a common flue

---

* A more particular account of the distribution is subjoined :—

STATEMENT OF THE DISTRIBUTION OF PRISONERS THROUGHOUT THE BOYS' PRISON OF THE MIDDLESEX HOUSE OF CORRECTION AT WESTMINSTER, JULY 7TH, 1856.

Prison.	No. of cells.	No. of inmates.	Prison.	No. of cells.	No. of inmates.	Prison.	No. of cells.	No. of inmates.		No. of inmates.
1 A . . .	21	21	4 A . . .	28	28	8 A . . .	10	8	Dormitory over 2 and	
2 „ . . .	18	18	5 „ . . .	28	28	Recep. cells	14	7	3 portion of prison	
3 „ . . .	18	18	6 „ . . .	28	28		—	—	A	87
			7 „ . . .	28	28	Total in sep. cells	193	184	Total in prison A .	271

The work-rooms here consist of—

1. The large oakum-room, 83 feet long by 36 feet wide, at end of 7 and 8 airing-yard, and holding . . . . } 220 boys
2. Shoemaking-room, 18 feet by 21 feet, in prison 8 A, containing . . . } 13 boys
3. The tailoring-room, 18 feet by 21 feet, in prison 8 A, containing . . . . } 26 boys
4. The carpenter's shop, 18 feet by 21 feet, in prison 8 A, containing . . } 2 boys
5. The oakum-store, 18 feet by 21 feet, at side of court-yard, containing . } 6 boys

The garden ground surrounding the building within the walls measures about . . . . } 2 acres.

The garden ground attached to the prison outside the walls measures about . . . . } 3 acres.

In garden work there are employed upon an average . . . . } 8 boys.

or shaft, or else a rude kind of air-pump, to be worked by the prisoners), a cell that is about 10 feet long, 7 feet wide, and 8 feet high" (or, in other words, having a capacity equal to 560 cubic feet) will, for ordinary purposes, be *sufficiently large*." The cells at Tothill Fields, where no special ventilating apparatus is employed, however, contain, as we said, only 432 cubic feet, and are thus within a fraction of 23 per cent. smaller than that which Mr. Hill declares to be just large enough for health, *provided the ventilation be vigorous*. Again, the same author, while speaking of the various modes of warming cells, recommends either hot air or hot water, but in no case does he advise that the cells shall be unheated throughout the severest winters; indeed, he objects to stone floors as being "great abstracters of heat," and withdrawing it from that part of the body which, he tells us, it is most important should be warm. Nor does he in any case recommend that prisoners should be locked up in their cells for twelve and a half hours out of the twenty-four, in utter darkness during the winter—a waste of time and opportunity for mental improvement that appears to us to be positively wicked. Indeed, it is astonishing that a body of gentlemen like the Middlesex magistrates, to whom the public is indebted for most important prison improvements, should allow such a glaring defect as an unventilated, unlighted, and unheated jail to remain for a single day.

The discipline enforced at this prison is the "silent associated" form, though a large number of the prisoners have not separate sleeping cells at night—a measure which is considered to be absolutely necessary for the beneficial working of the system. Mr. Dixon, some years back, spoke of this defect, and it is even worse now than at the time he wrote. "This crowding of prisoners together in the night is an unpardonable fault," he said; "under whatever system of discipline the culprit is placed during the hours of work or study, he should be compelled to sleep alone. A body of eighty felons lying in a common room (although an officer stay all night in the apartment) will suffer more corruption and contamination in ten hours, than they would in ten months of silent fellowship in the school or workroom."

The *sanitary condition* of Tothill Fields prison is, notwithstanding the defective construction of the cells, better than might have been anticipated. "The statistical information afforded by the annexed table," says the Special Report of the Visiting Justices for the July Quarter Sessions, 1856, "cannot but be considered eminently satisfactory.*

Nevertheless, compared with the prisons throughout the country, it will be found far from healthy. Thus, in 1853, the per centage of sickness (including cases of "slight indisposition" as well as "infirmary cases"), for all classes of prisoners in the prisons throughout England and Wales, was 27·2; whilst the per centage for the females only was 30·4, and for the boys no more than 16·9. At Tothill Fields, however, in the same year, the per centage for all classes of prisoners was 49·0 (or nearly double that of all England), whilst that

* TABLE SHOWING THE NUMBER OF CASES OF SICKNESS, LUNACY, AND DEATH, IN THE COURSE OF THE YEARS ENDING MICHAELMAS, 1851—55.

	1851.			1852.			1853.			1854.			1855.		
	Males.	Females.	Total.	Males.	Females.	Total.	Males.	Females.	Total.	Males.	Females.	Total.	Males.	Females.	Total.
Cases of slight indisposition -	884	2,966	3,850	833	2,469	3,302	759	2,694	3,453	851	2,620	4,471	594	3,669	4,263
Infirmary cases - - -	11	86	97	4	109	113	4	80	84	4	147	151	5	120	125
Total cases of sickness - -	895	3,052	3,947	837	2,578	3,475	763	2,774	3,537	855	3,767	4,622	599	3,789	4,388
Lunatics - - - -	—	2	2	—	3	3	—	3	3	—	3	3	—	—	—
Pardons on medical grounds -	—	1	1	—	1	1	—	—	—	—	—	—	—	—	—
Deaths - - - -	1	4	5	2	6	8	1	8	9	2	16	18	1	6	7
Greatest number of sick at any one time	2	13	15	1	13	14	2	14	16	1	16	17	1	14	15

for the females was 50·4, and for the boys 45·3—both considerably higher than the ratio throughout the country.*

But it may be hardly fair to contrast a metropolitan prison with country ones; still, even when compared with Coldbath Fields, it will be seen, by the table given on the next page, that the sanitary condition of Tothill Fields is certainly not super-eminent; since the proportionate quantity of sickness at the latter institution is more than double what it is at the former. The ratio of the mortality, as well as that of the pardons on medical grounds, at the Coldbath Fields House of Correction is, however, much higher than at the Westminster one.

"It is indeed remarkable," adds the Special Report for Tothill Fields Prison, "that though no less than 7,753 boys and 23,392 females (or 31,145 persons altogether) have been committed to the Westminster prison during the five years (1851—55, both inclusive), only seven boys and forty females have died."

* TABLE SHOWING THE GROSS NUMBER AND CENTESIMAL PROPORTION OF CASES OF SICKNESS, PARDONS ON MEDICAL GROUNDS, LUNACY, AND DEATH, OCCURRING THROUGHOUT THE PRISONS OF ENGLAND AND WALES, IN THE COURSE OF THE YEAR 1853 :—

	Total Adult.	Total Juvenile.	Total Adult and Juvenile.		Total Adult.	Total Juvenile.	Total Adult and Juvenile.
I. SICKNESS.				**III. CRIMINAL LUNATICS.**			
Cases of Slight Indisposition.				Males	105	....	105
Males	23,346	1,998	25,344	Females	27	....	27
Females	8,355	328	8,683				
				Both Sexes	132	....	132
Both Sexes	31,701	2,326	34,027	*Proportion per cent. of Lunatics to Daily Average Prison Population.*			
Infirmary Cases.							
Males	3,345	221	3,566	Males	0·7	....	0·7
Females	1,049	64	1,113	Females	0·8	....	0·8
Both sexes	4,394	285	4,679	Both Sexes	0·79	....	0·79
All Cases of Sickness.							
Males	26,691	2,219	28,910				
Females	9,404	392	9,796				
				IV. DEATHS.			
Both Sexes	36,095	2,611	38,706	Males	178	10	188
				Females	26	2	28
Proportion per Cent. of Sickness to gross Prison Population.							
Males	27·5	16·9	26·2	Both Sexes	204	12	216
Females	34·5	16·4	30·4	*Proportion per Cent. of Deaths to Daily Average Prison Population.*			
Both Sexes	28·4	16·8	27·2				
				Males	....	....	1·3
II. PARDONS ON MEDICAL GROUNDS.				Females	....	....	0·7
Males	63	...	63	Both Sexes	....	....	1·29
Females	14	....	14				
Both Sexes	77	....	77				
Proportion per Cent. of Pardons on Medical Grounds to Daily Average Prison Population.							
Males	0·4	....	0·4				
Females	0·4	....	0·4				
Both Sexes	0·4	....	0·4				

Now, this gives a gross mortality of 47; and as the average number of prisoners for the same period has been 250 boys and 531 females, or 781 altogether, we find that the ratio of mortality among the boys was 2·8 per cent. for the whole period, or 0·56 per annum, and among the females 7·5 for the whole period, or 1·5 per annum, whilst for the prison generally the ratio was 6·0 throughout the above-mentioned quinquenniad, and 1·2 for each year of it respectively—a proportion which is certainly 0·1 lower than that at Coldbath Fields, and considerably less than at Millbank (where the annual rate of mortality is as high as 6·91 per 100 of the average number of prisoners) or the Hulks (where it is 2·4 per cent.), though hardly so low as at Pentonville or Brixton—the yearly ratio being 1·1 at the former institution, and 1·0 at the latter.

"The small number of deaths which have taken place," adds the Report, with high Christian consideration, "is the more surprising, when it is considered that thousands who enter the prison are persons leading an abandoned life, or in a comparative state of destitution, dwelling in localities where the houses or tenements are, in numerous instances, unfit for human habitation, subject to every kind of deprivation and ill treatment, and to whom *acts of care and words of kindness are almost unknown.*" Still the deaths at Tothill Fields, in comparison with the average population, are not only lower than at any metropolitan prison with which we have yet dealt, but, it will be seen below, they are even less than they are throughout the prisons of England and Wales;* and it should be added, that though the Asiatic cholera visited the Metropolis in 1854, only five died at this prison from its effects,

* TABLE SHOWING THE NUMBER OF CASES OF LUNACY AND DEATH IN THE PRISONS OF ALL ENGLAND AND WALES, IN EACH YEAR, FROM 1841—53, BOTH INCLUSIVE :—

Years.		Total Prison Population in England & Wales.	Daily Average No. of Prisoners in England & Wales.	Number of Criminal Lunatics.*	Proportion per cent. of Lunatics to Daily Average Number of Prisoners.	Number of Deaths.*	Proportion per Cent. of Deaths to Daily Average Number of Prisoners.
	1841	140,764	15,445	79	·51	231	1·50
	1842	153,136	16,718	76	·46	214	1·28
	1843	152,445	17,218	64	·39	227	1·32
	1844	143,979	16,062	96	·60	140	·87
	1845	124,110	13,165	99	·75	143	1·09
ENGLAND	1846	123,236	12,979	92	·71	107	·82
AND	1847	131,949	14,021	96	·69	201	1·43
WALES.	1848	160,369	16,627	89	·54	267	1·60
	1849	166,942	18,288	68	·37	341	1·86
	1850	150,995	17,025	119	·69	200	1·17
	1851	156,794	19,249	101	·53	161	·84
	1852	149,326	17,579	108	·61	184	1·05
	1853	142,167	16,691	132	·79	216	1·29
Annual Mean . .		145,862	16,236	94	·59	202	1·24

* The Criminal Lunatics and Deaths exhibited in this table do not include those that have occurred in the prisons of Parkhurst, Pentonville, and Millbank, which were enumerated in the tables previous to 1843.—(*Note to the Nineteenth Report of Inspectors of Prisons,* p. xxvii.)

TABLE SHOWING THE CENTESIMAL PROPORTION OF SICKNESS, LUNACY, DEATHS, &C., TO THE PRISON POPULATION OF TOTHILL FIELDS AND COLDBATH FIELDS, FOR THE YEAR 1854-55, AND ALL ENGLAND AND WALES, FOR 1853, &C.

| | TOTHILL FIELDS. | | | Adult Males. | |
				COLDBATH FIELDS.	ALL ENGLAND AND WALES.
	Boys.	Females.	Total.		
Number of cases of sickness to every 100 of the gross prison population, for the year ending Michaelmas, 1855	27·8	63·3	53·9	22·3	26·5
Number of lunatics to every 100 of the daily average population for the same year	0·0	0·0	0·0	0·6	·59
Number of pardons on medical grounds to every 100 of daily average population for the same year	0·0	0·0	0·0	1·0	0·0
Number of deaths to every 100 of daily average population for the same year.	0·37	1·0	0·80	1·3	1·24

and that these deaths are included in the forty-seven, before given, as having occurred between 1851—55.

The Special Report further tells us, that " only eleven cases of insanity have occurred in the five years. Five of these," it is said, " came into the prison under circumstances which induced the visiting justices to suspect the mind to be in some degree affected; thus proving that the system pursued, and the discipline observed, is prejudicial neither to the mind nor to the body." Now this amount of insanity, compared with the annual average number of female prisoners, will be found to be at the rate of only 0·41 per cent. per annum, whilst the annual average proportion of lunacy for *all* the prisons of England and Wales is not less than 0·59 in every 100 prisoners.

It now only remains for us to contrast the ratio of *punishments* at this prison, with that of the several prisons throughout the country. The following table exhibits the number and per centage of the different kinds of punishments inflicted in all other penal institutions:—

TABLE SHOWING THE TOTAL NUMBER AND PER CENTAGE OF PUNISHMENTS, FOR OFFENCES IN ALL THE PRISONS OF ENGLAND AND WALES, IN THE COURSE OF THE YEAR 1853.

PUNISHMENTS.	ADULT PRISONERS. Males . . . . 96,891 Females . . . 29,765 Both sexes . . 126,656		JUVENILE PRISONERS. Males . . . . 13,115 Females . . . 2,395 Both sexes . . . 15,510		ADULT AND JUVENILE PRISONERS. Males . . . . 110,006 Females . . . 32,160 Both sexes . . 142,166	
	Number punished.	Proportion per 100 adult prisoners.	Number punished.	Proportion per 100 juvenile prisoners.	Number punished.	Proportion per 100 of all prisoners.
1. *Handcuffs and other irons.*						
Males . . .	70	0·07	5	0·03	75	0·06
Females . . .	14	0·04	1	0·04	15	0·04
Both sexes . . .	84	0·06	6	0·03	90	0·06
2. *Whipping.*						
Males . . .	115	0·1	58	0·4	173	0·1
Females . . .	—	—	—	—	—	—
Both sexes . . .	115	0·1	58	0·4	173	0·1
3. *Dark cells.*						
Males . . .	5,305	5·3	1,610	12·2	6,915	6·2
Females . . .	759	2·5	101	4·2	860	2·6
Both sexes . . .	6,064	4·7	1,711	11·0	7,775	5·4
4. *Solitary cells.*						
Males . . .	4,438	4·5	1,146	8·7	5,584	5·0
Females . . .	981	3·3	104	4·3	1,085	3·3
Both sexes . . .	5,419	4·2	1,250	8·0	6,669	4·6
5. *Stoppage of diet.*						
Males . . .	19,773	20·4	11,616	88·5	31,389	28·5
Females . . .	4,630	15·5	647	27·0	5,277	16·4
Both sexes . . .	24,403	19·2	12,263	79·0	36,666	25·7
6. *Other punishments.*						
Males . . .	13,155	13·5	336	2·5	13,491	12·2
Females . . .	331	1·1	43	1·8	374	1·1
Both sexes . . .	13,486	10·6	379	2·4	13,865	9·7
7. *Total.*						
Males . . .	42,856	42·2	14,771	111·8	57,627	52·3
Females . . .	6,715	22·5	896	37·4	7,611	23·6
Both sexes . . .	49,571	39·4	15,667	101·1	65,238	46·1

A glance down the columns of the above table will show us that the young prisoners are far more frequently punished than the old ones; for, whilst only 19 in every 100 of the *adult* prison population had their diet stopped in 1853, as many as 79 in every 100 of the *juveniles* suffered that form of punishment. The stoppage of diet, too, will be seen to constitute the most frequent of all the penal inflictions to which recourse is had in the various prisons throughout the country; for it will be observed, that out of 65,000 punishments in the course of the year, rather more than one-half of the number, or 36,000, consisted of a reduction of the ordinary supply of food. Again, it will be found that though there were only 4 adult prisoners in every 100 placed in dark cells, there were as many as 11 juveniles similarly treated; and that, whilst 8 in every 100 young prisoners were confined in solitary cells, not more than 4 adults underwent the same correction. Further, the number of adults whipped was only 1 in the 1,000, whilst of the juveniles subjected to the same castigation the proportion was four times as great. Indeed, a comparison of the total number of punishments inflicted on the old and young teaches us, either that the juvenile prisoners are much more difficult to manage than the adults, or else that they are more tyrannically treated by their jailers; for, whereas there are altogether only 39 punishments inflicted on each century of adult prisoners, there are upwards of 100 punishments to every century of juvenile ones.

As regards the difference in the coercive treatment to which male and female prisoners are subject, it will be perceived that the women and girls are, in *all* cases, less severely dealt with than are the men and boys; for instance, the gross total of punishments in the foregoing table shows that 52 per cent. of the male prisoners are punished, and only 23 per cent. of the females.

Having, then, arrived at the fact that the average proportion of punishments throughout the prisons of England and Wales is 42 per cent. for the *adult male* prisoners, and but $22\frac{1}{2}$ per cent. for the *adult females*, whilst it is nearly 112 per cent. for the *juvenile male* prisoners, and $37\frac{1}{2}$ for the *juvenile female* ones, let us proceed to apply this knowledge to the ratio of punishments prevalent at the Westminster House of Correction, with a view to discover whether the treatment at that prison be mild or severe. The subjoined tables, taken from the last Special Report of the Visiting Justices, will enable us to make the requisite comparison :—

TABLE SHOWING THE NUMBER AND PER CENTAGE OF PUNISHMENTS AT TOTHILL FIELDS PRISON, AND ALSO THEIR EXCESS OR DEFICIENCY IN COMPARISON WITH THE PRISONS OF ENGLAND AND WALES.

	BOYS.									
PUNISHMENTS.	Number Punished in Each Year.					Total for five years, 1851—55.	Average No. punished every year.	No. punished in every 100 boy prisoners.	No. punished in all other prisons to every 100 boy prisoners.	Excess or deficiency at Tothill Fields prison.
	1851.	1852.	1853.	1854.	1855.					
1. Handcuffs & other irons . . .	..	1	2	..	..	3	0·6	0·03	0·03	0·0
2. Whippings . . .	..	..	2	..	..	2	0·4	0·02	0·40	— 0·38
3. Dark cells . . .	..	1	..	..	..	1	0·2	0·01	12·20	— 12·19
4. Solitary ditto . .	5	3	7	4	1	20	4·0	0·22	8·70	— 8·48
5. Stoppage of diet .	4,755	6,817	7,303	6,750	5,769	31,394	6278·8	3·45	88·50	— 85·05
6. Other punishments	..	..	..	..	..	...	..	..	2·50	— 2·50
TOTAL . . .	4,760	6,822	7,314	6,754	5,770	31,420	6284·0	3·45	111·80	— 108·35
Committals during the Year . . .	1,772	1,841	1,683	1,882	1,909	9,087	1817·4	..	..	..

	FEMALES.										
PUNISHMENTS.	Number Punished in Each Year.					Total for five years, 1851—1855.	Average No. punished every year.	No. punished in every 100 boy prisoners.	No. punished in all other prisons to every 100 boy prisoners.	Excess or deficiency at Tothill Fields prison.	
	1851.	1852.	1853.	1854.	1855.						
1. Handcuffs & other irons	5	3	6	18	..	32	6·4	0·12	0·04	+	0·08
2. Dark cells . . .	15	28	40	51	55	189	37·8	0·69	2·60	—	1·91
3. Solitary ditto . .	108	133	239	76	90	646	129·2	2·38	3·30	—	0·92
4. Stoppage of diet .	1,700	1,523	1,948	2,358	2,041	9,570	1914·0	35·38	16·40	+	18·98
5. Other punishments	..	..	..	..	..	..	..	..	1·10	—	1·10
Total . . .	1,828	1,687	2,233	2,503	2,186	10,437	2087·4	38·57	23·60		14·97
Committals during the Year . . .	5,082	5,343	5,506	5,753	5,359	27,043	5408·6	..	..		..

Here, then, it may be noted that the punishments inflicted on the boy prisoners are strikingly *below* the average of all other prisons, whilst those to which the females are subject are considerably *above* the mean. Indeed, so extremely small is the per centage of punishments for the boys at this prison, when compared with the high ratio for the same class of prisoners throughout England and Wales, that we must own it appears to us, if the necessary discipline of a jail can be maintained among boys at the low rate of 3·45 punishments per hundred prisoners (as at Tothill Fields), there must be something like wanton severity exercised upon the younger male prisoners throughout the country generally, in order to raise the proportion of punishments as high as 112 per cent.

For our part, we do not hesitate to confess that we consider the low rate of punishment, prevalent in the juvenile male part of Tothill Fields prison, to be a high honour to all the authorities in connection with that establishment; for we believe that that prison government is the best which maintains order and discipline among the prisoners with a *minimum* amount of penal inflictions. Some people there are, who are of opinion that our prisons are being rendered so near akin to schools, as to hold out to the poor, by means of the comforts attainable within them, almost a premium to be criminal. We incline partly to the same opinion, and have assuredly no desire to strip the prison of its character as a place of *"penitentiary* amendment." It is our impression that there is a strong and injurious disposition abroad, now-a-days, to convert our jails into institutions for inducing mere moral reformation rather than penance; that is to say, there is a wish current through a large part of the community to give our prisons an educational instead of a penal character, and to endeavour to make our criminals better men by means of scholastic and industrial training, rather than by sorrow and contrition, as though it were thought better to inform the head than to soften the heart and chasten the spirit.

This appears to us to be the great criminal mistake of the day; but while we believe that it is necessary, not only for the due regulation of society, but also for the well-being even of the criminals themselves, that a prison should be made something else than a place of mere intellectual improvement (or "reformation" as it is called), as well as "incapacitation" for the criminal, nevertheless we are no advocates for the exercise of *unnecessary* and *irresponsible* power on the part of the authorities within the prison walls. The punishment that every man has to suffer for an infraction of the laws should be made a matter of public judgment, and the offender left as little as possible to the *private* sense of justice of any individual afterwards, so that only such penalties should be enforced in a prison as are absolutely requisite for ensuring the prisoner's conformity to the discipline of the establishment. It is for these reasons that we consider all concerned in the management of the juvenile male portion of the Westminster House of Correction, to be entitled to the highest praise—magistrates, governor, warders, and all; for, so far as our experience goes, it is the prison in which strict discipline is maintained at the expense of the lowest amount of physical coercion.

We wish the returns would allow us to say as much for the *female* portion of the same establishment. The statistics, however, show us, strange to say, that the punishments in connection with this portion of the Westminster House of Correction are almost double as much, proportionally, as they are throughout the prisons of England and Wales; for it will be seen, on reference to the tables above given, that whilst there are only 4 in every 10,000 female prisoners placed in handcuffs in all other jails, the ratio is three times as high at Tothill Fields, viz., 12 in the 10,000. Again, at this prison, 35 females in every 100 have their diet stopped in the course of the year, whilst only 16 in the 100 are so treated at other penal institutions; so that whilst the ratio of punishments to the number of female prisoners amounts to but little more than 23 per cent., as an average for all the prisons of England and Wales, it is upwards of half as much again, or 38½ per cent. at the Westminster House of Correction.

Still, metropolitan female prisoners may be more difficult to control than provincial ones, and certainly the punishments at this prison are but slight in comparison with those inflicted at Brixton, for *there* the ratio is nearly five times as high as at Tothill Fields, as may be seen by the subjoined comparative statement:—

			Tothill Fields Prison.	Brixton Prison.
Per centage of Female Prisoners placed in handcuffs			0·12	4·83
Ditto	ditto	in dark cells . .	0·69	43·55
Ditto	ditto	in solitary cells .	2·38	5·13
Ditto	ditto	stoppage of diet .	35·38	50·90
Ditto	ditto	other punishments .		77·86
Per centage of all kinds of punishment to the gross prison population . . . . }			38·57	182·27

It should, however, in fairness, be remembered that Brixton is a "long-term prison," being appropriated solely to those females who have been sentenced either to transportation or penal servitude.

¶ ii—β.

Of the Boy Prison at Tothill Fields and Boy Prisoners generally.

Before dealing with the convict prisons of the Metropolis, we proceeded to sum up the gross convict population of the country generally, and to compare it with that of the Capital in particular. The separation of the male prisoners in the Middlesex Houses of Correction into *adult* and *juvenile*, and the appropriation of a special prison to the boy criminals of the metropolitan county, renders it expedient, for the due comprehension of the subject at present in hand, that we should set before the reader some statement as to the extent of the boy prison population throughout England and Wales.

Those who have never looked into the matter will, doubtlessly, be startled to learn that the average number of juvenile prisoners annually "passing through" the jails of the entire country amounts to no less than 11,749; so that if our gross prison population, under seventeen years of age, were to be collected together into one town, they would be sufficient to fill a city as large as that of Bedford, Stafford, Preston, Salisbury, or Ramsgate, and be found very nearly equal to half the population of the entire county of Rutland.

The following table shows the number of juvenile prisoners for a series of years, as well as the centesimal proportion of such offenders to the rest of the prison population throughout

SERVING OF DINNER IN THE OAKUM-ROOM OF THE BOYS' PRISON AT TOTHILL FIELDS.

England and Wales; and it will be seen thereby that the *juvenile* prisoners are about **10 per cent.**, and the *adult* about 90 per cent., of the gross prison population.* The proportion, however, of the juvenile to the adult members of the entire community is as 40 to 60

* TABLE SHOWING THE NUMBERS AND CENTESIMAL PROPORTION OF JUVENILE OFFENDERS AND ADULTS SUMMARILY CONVICTED AND TRIED AT SESSIONS AND ASSIZES, THROUGHOUT ENGLAND AND WALES, FOR EACH YEAR FROM 1841—1853.

| | Juvenile prisoners, or those under 17 years of age. | | | | | | | | | Adult prisoners. | | | Grand total adult and juvenile prisoners of both sexes in England and Wales. |
| | Under 12 years. | | 12 years and under 14. | | 14 years and under 17. | | Total. | | Total both sexes. | 17 years and upwards. | | Total both sexes. | |
	Males.	Females.	Males.	Females.	Males.	Females.	Males.	Females.		Males.	Females.		
1841—Numbers	916	178	1989	321	5932	1169	8837	1668	10,505	60,665	19,211	79,876	90,381
Per centage to gross prison population	1·32	·85	2·86	1·54	8·53	5·60	12·71	7·99	10·35	87·29	92·01	89·65	100·00
1842—Numbers	1013	218	2233	305	6636	1195	9884	1718	11,602	70,423	19,642	90,065	101,667
Per centage	1·26	1·02	2·78	1·43	8·26	5·59	12·30	8·04	10·17	87·70	91·96	89·83	100·00
1843—Numbers	995	186	2152	271	6818	1289	9967	1746	11,713	71,910	19,444	91,354	103,067
Per centage	1·21	·88	2·63	1·28	8·33	6·08	12·17	8·24	10·21	87·83	91·76	89·79	100·00
1844—Numbers	984	148	2156	302	6892	1294	10,032	1744	11,776	67,283	18,921	86,204	97,980
Per centage	1·27	·72	2·79	1·46	8·91	6·26	12·97	8·44	10·71	87·03	91·56	89·29	100·00
1845—Numbers	820	145	1780	182	6436	1290	9036	1537	10,573	61,769	18,783	80,552	91,125
Per centage	1·16	·71	2·51	·90	9·09	5·95	12·76	7·56	10·16	87·24	92·44	89·84	100·00
1846—Numbers	946	126	1826	229	6467	1247	9239	1602	10,841	58,723	20,368	79,091	89,932
Per centage	1·39	·5,	2·69	1·04	9·52	5·68	13·60	7·29	10·45	86·40	92·71	89·55	100·00
1847—Numbers	1107	167	2067	304	7202	1227	10,380	1698	12,078	62,413	21,129	83,542	95,620
Per centage	1·52	·73	2·84	1·33	9·89	5·37	14·25	7·43	10·84	85·75	92·57	89·16	100·00
1848—Numbers	1332	215	2633	401	7899	1317	11,866	1933	13,799	76,907	23,651	100,558	114,357
Per centage	1·50	·84	2·97	1·57	8·90	5·15	13·37	7·56	10·47	86·63	92·44	89·53	100·00
1849—Numbers	1255	176	2547	365	7244	1366	11,048	1907	12,955	81,745	25,015	106,760	119,715
Per centage	1·35	·62	2·75	1·36	7·81	5·08	11·91	7·06	9·49	88·09	92·94	90·51	100·00
1850—Numbers	1107	166	2296	313	6288	1106	9728	1598	11,326	73,081	22,664	95,745	107,071
Per centage	1·34	·68	2·77	1·29	7·59	4·56	11·72	6·53	9·13	88·28	93·47	90·87	100·00
1851—Numbers	1181	206	2393	329	6888	1295	10,462	1830	12,292	75,946	22,728	98,674	110,966
Per centage	1·37	·84	2·77	1·34	7·97	5·27	12·11	7·41	9·76	87·89	92·59	90·24	100·00
1852—Numbers	1121	193	2294	395	6604	1214	10,019	1802	11,821	69,997	22,079	92,076	103,897
Per centage	1·40	·81	2·87	1·65	8·25	5·08	12·52	7·54	10·03	87·48	92·46	89·97	100·00
1853—Numbers	1253	243	2115	386	6291	1165	9659	1794	11,453	64,239	22,692	86,931	98,384
Per centage	1·69	·99	2·86	1·58	8·51	4·76	13·06	7·33	10·20	86·94	92·67	89·80	100·00
Annual mean of all classes of prisoners—both summarily convicted and tried at sessions—Numbers	1079	182	2191	316	6738	1244	10,012	1737	11,749	68,854	21,256	90,110	101,859
Per centage to the total number of the same age in prison	1·37	·79	2·78	1·36	8·58	5·42	12·73	7·57	10·15	87·27	92·43	89·85	100·00
Annual mean of those summarily convicted—Numbers	892	149	1737	233	4944	864	7577	1248	8825	49,055	16,255	65,310	74,134
Per centage	82·66	81·86	79·27	73·73	73·37	69·55	75·67	71·84	75·11	71·24	76·47	72·47	72·78
Annual mean of those tried at assizes and sessions—Numbers	187	33	454	88	1793	374	2435	489	2924	19,800	5000	24,800	27,725
Per centage	17·34	18·14	20·73	26·27	26·63	30·45	24·33	28·16	24·89	28·76	23·53	23·53	27·22

in every 100 persons, or, in the aggregate, as seven millions to eleven millions of individuals.

Now, a careful study of the above statistical data will lead us to the following facts :—

1st. That the *juvenile female* prisoners bear a less proportion to the *adult female* ones (the one being $7\frac{1}{2}$ per cent., and the other $92\frac{1}{2}$ per cent., of the whole of the female prison population) than do the *juvenile male* criminals to the *adult males* of the same class; for, with the latter, the mean centesimal proportion is as $12\frac{3}{4}$ to $87\frac{1}{4}$.

2nd. That, under 12 years, the *young male* criminals are not quite $1\frac{1}{3}$ per cent., and the *young females* of the same age only a fraction more than $\frac{3}{4}$ per cent., of the gross number of males or females throughout the prisons; whilst, between 12 and 14 years of age, the *young males* are about $2\frac{3}{4}$ per cent., and the *young females* about $1\frac{1}{2}$ per cent., of the entire number of prisoners belonging to either sex; whereas, between 14 and 17 years of age, the *young male* prisoners are about $8\frac{1}{2}$ per cent., and the *young females* $5\frac{1}{2}$ per cent., of the whole.

3rd. That about three-fourths of the entire number of prisoners confined within the prisons are *summarily convicted;* and whilst 72 in every 100 *adult* prisoners are committed by the magistrates, there are rather more, or 75 in every 100, of the aggregate *juvenile* offenders so dealt with, and upwards of 80 in every 100 similarly treated, when the offenders are of very *tender* years.

The juvenile criminal population passing through the correctional prisons of London, in the course of the year, would appear to be close upon 2,500 in number; for from the Nineteenth Report of the Prison Inspectors we gather the following figures :—

	Males.	Females.	Both sexes.
Number of juvenile prisoners in the Westminster House of Correction, Tothill Fields	1,448	227	1,675
Number of juvenile prisoners in the Surrey House of Correction, Wandsworth	544	81	625
Number of juvenile prisoners in the City House of Correction, Holloway	111	28	139
Number of juvenile prisoners in the City Bridewell, Bridge Street, Blackfriars	162	13	175
Total juvenile offenders passing through the correctional prisons of London	2,265	349	2,614

In addition to these, there are the juvenile offenders passing through the detentional prisons of the Metropolis, and these, according to the same returns, may be quoted as follows :—

	Males.	Females.	Both sexes.
Number of juvenile offenders passing through the House of Detention, Clerkenwell	272	55	327
Number of juvenile offenders passing through Horsemonger Lane prison	93	14	107
Number of juvenile offenders passing through Newgate	61	13	74
Total juvenile offenders passing through the detentional prisons of London	426	82	508

To these, again, must be subjoined the number of juvenile criminals in the convict prisons; and, according to the Government returns, they would appear to be as follows :—

	Males.	Females.	Both sexes.
Number of juvenile prisoners passing through Pentonville prison . . . . . }	14	0	14
Number of juvenile prisoners passing through Millbank . . . . . . }	188	14	202
Number of juvenile prisoners passing through Brixton . . . . . . }	—	8	8
Number of juvenile prisoners passing through the Hulks, Woolwich . . . . }	150*	0	150
Total number of juvenile prisoners passing through the convict prisons of London . }	352	22	374

The metropolitan account, therefore, as to the number of juvenile offenders, stands thus :—

Passing through the London convict prisons	374
,, ,, London correctional prisons	2,614
,, ,, London detentional prisons	508
Total	3,496

Hence we perceive that there are, in round numbers, 3,500 juvenile criminals annually entering the metropolitan prisons; and of these 3,043, or a fraction more than 87 per cent., are males, and the remainder females; so that the gross number of juvenile prisoners in the Metropolis would appear to be very nearly 29 per cent., or between one-third and one-fourth, of the entire number throughout the country; whilst, if we assume the total number of prisoners (of all ages) passing through the metropolitan jails in the course of the year, to be upwards of 40,000 (see *ante*, p. 83), we shall find that the proportion of juveniles to adults is about $8\frac{1}{2}$ to $91\frac{1}{2}$ in every hundred : consequently, it would appear that the juvenile criminals of the Metropolis bear a smaller proportion to the adults than do those of the entire country.

This conclusion is contrary to what would have naturally been expected, for we should have reasoned, *à priori*, that where there was greater density of population, as in the Capital, *there* would probably have been greater chance of contamination, owing to the association of children in the streets, and therefore a greater tendency to juvenile delinquency. We are, however, still inclined to believe—despite the returns—that such is the fact, and that the proportion of juvenile criminals in London *appears to be less* than in the country, simply because the proportion of adult prisoners there is *more*. That such is the bare truth may be proven in the following conclusive manner:—The number of persons in England and Wales who are under seventeen years of age amounts, as we have said, to 7,056,699 individuals, so that, as there are altogether 11,749 criminals under that age passing through the prisons of the country, this gives a proportion of 16·6 criminals in every 10,000 of the gross juvenile population. In London, however, the number of persons under seventeen years of age is 839,057, whilst the number of criminals of the same age, passing through the prisons in the course of the year, is, as we have seen, 3,496, and that gives a proportion of 41·6 criminals in every 10,000 of the juvenile population of London; so that thus it is demonstrated that, instead of the ratio of juvenile criminals in the Capital being *less* than in the country generally, it is really more than as much again.†

* There are no returns in the Government reports as to the ages of prisoners at Woolwich; we have, therefore, assumed the number to be one-tenth of the gross prison population there.

† It is necessary to warn the reader, that the numbers here given as the amounts of the juvenile criminal population of the country generally, represent not the number of *distinct* juvenile prisoners, but merely the totals "passing through" the prisons of England and Wales as well as the Metropolis in the course of the year. What may be the annual average number of *individual* young offenders appearing in the metropolitan

We land then, statistically, at the melancholy and degrading conclusion, that there are altogether between 11,000 and 12,000 juvenile criminals annually passing through the prisons of England and Wales, and that between 3,000 and 4,000 of that number appear in the jails of the Metropolis; so that even if we reduce these amounts one-half, in order to allow for those who enter the jails more than once in the course of the twelvemonth (and the recommittals during the year often amount to one-third of the whole prisoners), as well as for those who are passed after trial from the detentional to either the correctional or convict prisons throughout the country—and if we admit, too, that there are only as many young thieves and vagrants without the walls of our prisons as within them—we shall still make the army of our boy and girl criminals amount to the same prodigious number. We ourselves, however, are disposed to believe that, calculating those at large as well as those in prison, the numbers may be more correctly stated at between 15,000 and 20,000 habitual juvenile delinquents for the country generally, and between 5,000 and 7,000 for London alone.

The question consequently becomes, how is it that so large a body of young offenders are continually associated with our people—for we are speaking of no extraordinary occasion, the data for the above conclusions having been drawn from the mean of several years (see Table, p. 377). Nor can we help asking ourselves what fate eventually befalls these young graduates in crime—how many are expatriated for their iniquities—how many die and rest unrecorded among the gravestoneless mounds of the convict and prison burial-grounds—how many settle down among the "respectable" rate-paying "fences" of the country—how many become the proprietors of thieves' lodging-houses and "padding-kens," and how many, think you, good simple reader, are really reclaimed?

To men who puzzle their brains with the subtle riddles of social philosophy, these are matters pregnant with the highest interest, and the mere flash of them across the mind lights many a long train of thought in the eagerness of the imagination to compass the magnitude of the subject. One of the most difficult problems in physiology is the principle of waste and supply. How are those minute destructions of tissue, that are now known to accompany every movement of the muscles and mind, continually repaired and renovated, so that our frame remains ostensibly the same, as well in its material fabric as in size and weight. So, in the science of social economics, it is an inquiry of the highest moment as to how the great body of outcasts is annually thinned and repaired; and even as the social philosopher desires to know in what manner the ranks of the street-walkers are maintained at the same number almost as regularly as the army of the State, and strives to learn what fate attends

prisons, it is difficult even to conjecture; for the "Reports" afford us but few data for the calculation. By a return, however, given in the Report of the Committee of Justices on juvenile delinquencies in the county of Surrey, we find that, out of an annual average of 707 juvenile prisoners passing through the Surrey House of Correction, no less than 257, or upwards of one-third of the whole, had been re-committed during the year. We must, therefore, in order to arrive even proximately at the number of individual juveniles passing through the London correctional prisons in the course of each twelvemonth, reduce the amount above given by at least one-third, and this will leave 1,743 for the gross number of juvenile criminals passing through the London correctional prisons throughout the twelvemonths. Again, by a return in the same Report, we find that out of an annual average of 486 juvenile prisoners passing through the Surrey County Jail at Horsemonger Lane, no less than 238, or nearly 50 per cent. of the whole, were sent thence to the Surrey House of Correction at Wandsworth; so that, if we reduce the number of juvenile prisoners passing through the detentional prisons to the same extent, we shall have only 254 left for those who do not afterwards appear in the returns of the houses of correction. Again, as regards the convict prisons, Millbank is the *depôt* for all sentenced to transportation or penal servitude, and the juvenile prisoners appearing within its walls are ultimately transferred to some other Government jail. The same occurs at Pentonville, many being removed thence to the Hulks. For these reasons, the number of distinct juvenile convicts annually appearing in the Government prisons of the Metropolis may be safely reduced from 374 to 300; hence we come to the conclusion that there are about 2,300, or, to err on the safe side, 2,000, individual juvenile prisoners passing through the London jails, and this out of a gross prison population of between 20,000 and 25,000 persons.

the old "*unfortunates*" (it is strange how all castes of criminals would make out their lot in life to be a matter of ill luck), and whence come the young creatures who serve to recruit annually the great mass of wantons; for the fresh supplies are so regularly added, that the mind is almost led to believe that some similar *organic* arrangement exists in society for the repair of the used-up members, the same as in the human frame itself. Thus it is, too, with the great horde of thieves and vagabonds, that, like a train of camp-followers, ever attend the vast army of our people on their march towards "the good time," and who, taking no part in the great battle of life, stand by only to plunder those who have fought the fight.

The subject of juvenile crime, however, helps to strip the matter of a considerable portion of its difficulty. It is no longer hard to tell how the predatory maggot got within the social nut, for here we detect the criminal ovum lying in the very blossom of the plant; and as in certain processes of the body we can discover, microscopically, the new tissue in the course of being secreted from the blood, and see little spiculæ of bone thrown down, one after another, from the same mysterious fluid, in the wondrous and beautiful efforts of nature to repair a limb—in like manner can we behold, with the enlarged vision of experience, how the young criminal tends to renovate the wasted ranks of the old offenders.

All allow that the juvenile delinquent ripens, in due course of criminal fruition, into the confirmed old convict, or the more wily "fence;" and the mind, therefore, is pushed in its reasonings a step further back, and led to ask itself, if the vagrant child be father to the felon man, what is the parentage of the young vagabond himself—out of what social vices is he begotten—to what defects in our system should he be affiliated?

Let us see!

Men have assigned almost as many different causes for crime as they have for the cholera. The pestilence is due to noxious gases, say the Board of Health; drunkenness is the parent of all crime, cry the Total-abstinence League. The epidemic rages, one declares, because there is a deficiency of electricity in the atmosphere; knowledge is power, another exclaims, and ignorance the mother of all evil. Again, the modern plague has been attributed by physicians to sporules of fungi floating in the atmosphere—to particles of excrementitious matter imbibed in the water—to a deficiency of "ozone" and an excess of "zymosis"—as well as to our national iniquities, it being regarded by many as a scourge from the Almighty. And so, in like manner, the moral plague of crime has been referred to density of population—to poverty—to vagrancy—to the temptation of large masses of property in towns—to the non-observance of the Sabbath—and, lastly, to the fall of man and the consequent innate proneness of all to evil.

Some years back, however, we took the trouble of testing the greater number of the popular reasons for crime, by collating the statistics in connection with each theory, and thus found that none of the *received* explanations would bear the searching test of figures. Crime could not be referred to ignorance, for we discovered that in many parts of the country (as, for instance, North and South Wales, Cornwall, Shropshire, York, Nottingham, Rutland, Northampton, Bedford, Huntingdon, Cambridge, Suffolk, and Berks), where the ignorance was *above* the average, the criminality of the people was *below* it; and so, again, where the criminality of the people was *higher* than the mean rate, as in Middlesex, Oxford, Warwick, Gloucester, Hants, &c., the amount of ignorance was *lower* than ordinary.*

* Gloucester, for instance, which is the most criminal of all counties, has 26 criminals to every 10,000 of the population; Middlesex, 24½; Warwick, 21; Oxford, 17; whilst the average for all England is 16½; but these counties, though the *most criminal*, tested according to the ratio of their ignorance (as proven by the number who signed the marriage register with marks), are among the *most highly educated;* that is to say, in Middlesex only 18 people usually sign with marks out of every 100 married; in Gloucester, 35 people in 100 do so; in Warwick, 38; and in Oxford, 39; whereas the average for all England and Wales is 40. On the other hand, in North Wales, which is one of the *least criminal* districts, there are only 7 criminals in every 10,000 of the people; in Cornwall there are 8; South Wales, 8½; York, 11½; Notting-

Nor can crime, on the other hand, be said to be due to the density of population and the consequent greater facility for inter-contamination among the people; for, whilst the population is *more* than ordinarily crowded in Surrey, Kent, Durham, and Nottingham, in these counties the ratio of criminals to the population is *less* than the average. So, again, in Essex, Hereford, Buckinghamshire, Oxford, Wilts, Hants, Somerset, Leicester, and Norfolk, the number of persons to the hundred square acres is *below* the mean, and the number of criminals to every 10,000 of the population *above* it.*

We proved, moreover, that crime is *not* referable to poverty, ascertaining, by the same unerring means, that in those counties where the proportion of paupers is above the average, the proportion of criminals falls often below it, and *vice versâ*. Nor could it be ascribed to vagrancy, for where the poor-law returns show that there are the greatest number of persons relieved in the "casual wards" of the several unions, the criminal returns do not, on the other hand, indicate a like excessive proportion of offenders convicted. Further, the theory that crime is due to the temptation of large masses of property, does not hold good; for it does *not* follow, according to the returns for the property and income-tax, that in those districts where the greatest wealth abounds there also do thieves, rogues, and vagabonds flourish to an inordinate degree. Neither can it justly be said that where there is the greatest drunkenness there is the greatest crime likewise, for this theory, like the rest, will not bear being tried by statistical records; besides, it is a well-known fact, that there is a less proportionate number of criminals in Prussia than in England, nevertheless, Mr. M'Culloch tells us, "that the consumption of spirits throughout that kingdom is equal to between forty and forty-five millions of our imperial gallons in the course of the year;" and he adds, "that it may be worth while observing, as illustrative of the habits of the people of that country and our own, that the entire quantity of British and foreign spirits, entered for home consumption in the United Kingdom in 1840, amounted to only twenty-five and a half million gallons, notwithstanding our population is double that of Prussia. Indeed," he continues, "the annual consumption of spirits in Prussia amounts to about three gallons to each individual, whilst the consumption of Great Britain and Ireland is only about three-quarters of a gallon per head. The consumption of beer, too, in Prussia," he says, "also exceeds its consumption in the United Kingdom in a corresponding proportion."

---

ham, 11¾; Berks, nearly 13; and Rutland, nearly 14; Northampton, 14¼; Cambridge, 14¾; Shropshire, nearly 15; Bedford, 15¼; and Suffolk, 15¾; all being *below* the average, which is very nearly 16½ for all England. Still, these counties, though the *least criminal*, are among the *most ignorant;* for though out of every 100 married, only 40, upon an average, sign the register with marks, throughout England and Wales, there are in South Wales, 57 in 100 who do so; in Bedford, 56; North Wales, 55; Huntingdon, 49; Rutland, 49; Shropshire, 48; Suffolk, 48; Cambridge, 45; Cornwall, 45; York, 44; Northampton, 43; Berks, 42; and Nottingham, 42.

* The numbers for these counties were as follows :—The average number of persons to every 100 acres throughout England and Wales is 49·7. In Surrey, however, there are 44 people to every 100 acres; in Kent, 63; in Durham, 62; and in Nottingham, 55. On the other hand, the average number of criminals for all England and Wales is, as we have said, 16·4 to every 10,000 of the population; in Durham, however, there are only 7·8 criminals to every 10,000 people; in Nottingham, 11·8; in Surrey, 16·3; and in Kent, 16·4; so that it cannot be asserted that the *most crowded* are the *most criminal* places. Nor, on the contrary, are the *least crowded* places the *least criminal* ones, for in Wiltshire there are only 27·7 persons to every 100 acres; in Buckinghamshire, 31·3; in Norfolk, 33·3; in Essex, 34·5; in Oxford, 37·0; in Hants, 38·4; Somerset, 43·5; Hertford, 43·5; and Leicester, 45·4—all of which are *below* the average density of 49·7 for the whole country, and yet these counties are *above* the average in criminality; for whilst there are only 16·4 criminals in every 10,000 throughout England, there are 17·1 in the same number of people in Norfolk; in Leicester, 17·1 also; in Hertford, 17·5; in Hants, 17·7; in Oxford, 17·8; in Wiltshire, 18·9; in Essex, 19·1; in Somerset, 19·9; and in Buckinghamshire, 20·4. These calculations were made, as we have said, some years ago, and before the appearance of the census of 1851; the averages were, in all cases, deduced from a series of ten years.

Again, the theory which refers crime to a breach of the Sabbath would, we feel assured, if tried by the returns of the last census, as to the numbers of people attending service in the various chapels and churches throughout the country on a given day, be found to bear no relation to the number of criminals in the same districts. And, lastly, that religious conjecture which dates all criminal offences as far back as the fall of man, appears to us to err in confounding crime with sin, and in believing the breach of a human law to belong to the same category as the infraction of a divine one. Sin appears to us to be a human defect, and crime a social one. To the one all men are liable, since it is impossible for any to be perfect; to the other but few are subject, and those chiefly who are born to the hardships rather than the comforts of life; and, according to Christianity, it is the wealthy who are the most sinful, since we are told that it is as impossible for a rich man to enter the kingdom of heaven as it is for a camel to pass through the eye of a needle; whereas, according to Mr. Redgrave's returns, it is mainly the poor and the unlettered who belong to the criminal classes.

If, then, the various popular conjectures as to the causes of crime in this kingdom have no truth in them, it behoves us sedulously to search for some other principle to which the existence of those swarms of thieves and vagabonds, which infest the country as well as the town, may be referred. Now, the first thing that strikes the mind accustomed to take broad and comprehensive views of such matters is, that our nation is by no means *singular* in having a race of social outcasts surrounding and preying upon the industry of the community. Even the Hottentots, we have before said, have their "sonquas" and bushmen, and the Kafirs their "fingoes," to trouble their peace and make free with their property—the same as we have our vagrants, pickpockets, and burglars. But if to these people went one of our social philosophers, primed with the fashionable conjectures as to the causes of crime in a community, and told them that rogues and vagabonds were due either to a non-observance of the Sabbath, or to the density of the population, or to an ignorance of reading and writing, or to the fall of man, or to the love of intoxicating liquors—how heartily would these same simple Kafirs and Hottentots laugh at the narrow view such an one took of human nature? Surely, even the weakest-minded must see that our theories of crime, to be other than mere visionary hypotheses, must explain roguery and vagabondage *all over the world*, and not merely be framed with reference to that little clique among human society which we happen to call our own State.

We have elsewhere said that the whole human race is divisible into wanderers and settlers—that is to say, into those who are in the habit of *seeking* and *taking* what they require for their sustenance or their pleasure, and those who are in the habit of *producing* and *growing* what they want. The main difference between an animal and a plant is, that the vegetable has its living brought to it, while the other has either to go forth and seek it, or else to work for it. No sentient creature can stick its feet in the ground and draw nutriment from the soil, without any exertion of its own. In a primitive state of society, before the world came to be too thickly peopled for the spontaneous productions of the soil to yield man a sufficiency of fruits and roots to satisfy his cravings, the earth, in those generous climates where the human family seems to have sprung into existence, would appear to have been one vast garden filled with enough natural food for all. Hence *appropriation* would no more have existed at such times, than men would think now-a-days of appropriating the waters of the ocean or the sands of the desert, in the midst of the sea or the Great Sahara itself. It is only when scarcity begins that property comes into existence, and then men begin to fight and quarrel for that which others have taken to themselves. When, however, the scarcity increases to such an extent that the earth has to be forced and stimulated to unusual productiveness, and men by their labour get to rear crops and cattle that would not otherwise have existed, it is but natural that they who have called things into existence by their industry and care, should come to regard such things as their own individual right, and to believe that a wrong was done to them by any who attempted to deprive them of their possessions.

This forcing of the earth to inordinate fertility would have constituted the dawn of civilization, and it is evident that the earliest efforts would have been made by the *more sedate and prudent* of the human race, whilst the more reckless and restless would have wandered on, content to seek a precarious existence in either the spoils of the chase or the plundering of their more industrious neighbours. It is within the records of European history, as to how the so-called nobles of the olden time not only despised the dwellers in cities, but looked upon all industrial occupations—arts as well as commerce—as fit only for beasts, regarding every one who pursued any business or craft, as well as those engaged in commerce, as "*res non personæ*"—creatures but little better than beasts of burden; while the barons themselves felt pride only in hunting and warfare, and lived buried in vast forests with a multitude of slaves and knights about them, ready to sally forth and plunder the industrious citizens. The Bedouin Arab is the *modern* type of the mediæval baron; as with the old European nobles, robbery is regarded by the Sheikh to this day as an honourable occupation; he considers the country in which he pitches his tent as sacred ground, and looks upon the plunder of the pilgrim caravan as the mere levying of tribute or payment for permission to pass through his territory (see *Burckhardt's Notes on Bedouins*, pp. 84—89). The Teutonic nobles, between the 11th and 12th centuries, were but the older European forms of the modern Arabian Sheikh; and "tolls," like our own "black mail," were exacted by them from the passing merchants, even as the Bedouin demands his tribute-money at the present day.

Those who forget how, in olden times, industry was regarded as base and slavish, and plunder and warfare as the only honourable occupations worthy of freemen, cannot understand why it is that the still uncivilized gipsy mother says to her child, "And now, having said your prayers, go out and steal;" or why the equally uncivilized professional thieves of the present day should divide all society into "flats" and "sharps," and, classing themselves among the wiser portion of humanity, should, like the ancient barons, look with scorn upon all who labour for their living as either mean or witless.

Our criminal tribes, therefore, may be regarded as that portion of our society who have not yet conformed to civilized habits. What the Bedouins are to the Fellahs, the Lappes to the Finns, the Fingoes to the Kafirs, and the Sonquas to the Hottentots, the Gipsies to the Europeans generally, and, indeed, the old baron to the ancient citizen, our modern thieves and beggars are to the more prudent and striving portion of our race.

Still the question becomes—why do these folk not settle down to industrial pursuits like the rest of the community? Why do they not adapt themselves to the more comfortable practices of civilized society? In the first place, then, it is evident that some men are naturally of more erratic natures than others; even gentlefolks know the pleasure of travelling, of continually passing through fresh scenes, and meeting with fresh excitements, countries, characters, and adventures; but a delight in going upon foreign tours is simply a delight in vagabondage, with the power of putting up at more comfortable abiding-places than the casual ward. And it is a strange ethnological fact that, though many have passed from the steady and regular habits of civilized life, few of those who have once adopted the savage and nomadic form of existence abandon it, notwithstanding its privations, its dangers, and its hardships. This appears to be due mainly to that love of liberty, and that impatience under control, that is more or less common to all minds. Some are more self-willed than others, and, therefore, more irritable under restraint; and these generally rebel at the least opposition to their desires. It is curiously illustrative of the truth of this point, that the greater number of criminals are found between the ages of 15 and 25; that is to say, at that time of life when the will is newly developed, and has not yet come to be guided and controlled by the dictates of reason. The period, indeed, when human beings begin to assert themselves is the most trying time for every form of government—whether it be parental, political, or social; and those indomitable natures who cannot or will not brook ruling, then become heedless of all authority, and respect no law but their own.

Another circumstance which tends to make men prefer a wandering and predatory, to a settled and industrious life, is, that though all have an instinctive aversion to labour, some find the drudgery of it more irksome than others. We have before spoken (p. 301) of this innate repugnance to continued physical exertion, and shown how wages are paid to "labourers" as a bribe for the performance of the more arduous forms of it, and sums given to be allowed to indulge in those more agreeable kinds of muscular exercise which are termed sports or amusements. Whenever the muscles are made to move by the mere force of the will, we are invariably conscious of an *effort*, and this effort becomes more or less fatiguing according as the muscular action is protracted. Dr. Marshall Hall has shown that the brain is the organ of fatigue, and that those operations which are performed instinctively, such as the play of the lungs, and the contraction and expansion of the heart, are unattended with any sense of weariness from long-continued motion. Flies, again, he tells us, remain for days on the wing, without showing any symptoms of being tired; and so those physical exercises which we delight in—such as dancing, skating, riding—produce little or no weariness in the limbs; whilst labour, which is performed simply for the sake of the food it brings, rather than from any taste for the work, soon grows irksome, not only from the continued effort necessary for the performance of it, but also from that prolonged constraint of the mental faculties which is required in order to keep the attention fixed upon one subject. The mind, at such times, is indeed working against itself. The craving for *immediate* pleasure makes it long to be away in the fields, indulging in some more congenial sport, whilst a sense of the *prospective* good to be derived from the reward attached to the task in hand, forces the workman to continue toiling against his own impulses and instincts. It is this labour that all men are striving to avoid; some, by frugality, are hoping to amass, through small regular savings, a sufficiency to allow them to live at length a life of ease; others seek the more easy forms of trade and speculation; while others, again, who have little or no fear of the law, nor any sense of independence and honesty, endeavour rather to gain an easy subsistence by begging or by theft.

Crime, said the Constabulary Commissioners, in their First Report, arises from a desire to acquire property by a less degree of labour than ordinary industry; and habitual criminals, therefore, are those persons who feel labour to be more irksome than others, owing to their being not only less capable of continued application to one subject or object, but more fond of immediate pleasure, and, consequently, less willing to devote themselves to those pursuits which yield only prospective ones. This explanation agrees thoroughly with the criminal character, for it is well known that such persons are distinguished by a comparative incapability of protracted attention, as well as by an inordinate love of amusement, and an indomitable repugnance to regular labour.

"I have never been able to comprehend," says Mr. Chesterton, the late governor of Coldbath Fields, in a passage of his work on "Prison Life," before quoted, "the preference given by hale able-bodied men, who, rather than face creditable industry, will stand shivering in the cold, with garments barely sufficient to clothe their nakedness, and purposely rent and tattered in order to provoke sympathy. The tramps or ubiquitary wanderers display a taste," he adds, "far superior to that of the London cadgers. One such assured me that the life he led suited him; he enjoyed the country, he said, realized a pleasing variety, and managed, in one way or other, to get his wants adequately supplied."

Crime, then, it may be safely asserted, is *not* due, as some say, to an inordinate density of the population, nor to a love of intoxicating liquors, nor to an inability to read and write, nor to unwholesome dwellings, nor to a non-observance of the Sabbath; but simply to that innate love of a life of ease, and aversion to hard work, which is common to *all* natures, and which, when accompanied with a lawlessness of disposition as well as a disregard for the rights of our fellow-creatures, and a want of self-dignity, can but end either in begging or stealing the earnings and possessions of others.

Labour is a necessity of civilized life, and he, therefore, who refuses to work or trade must, perforce, prey upon the labours or gains of his neighbours; and if it be possible to win large sums of money with little or no toil, by dishonest means, and but small sums with heavy and long toiling, by honest industry, who can wonder that so many of our poor prefer the lucrativeness of crime, even with all its perils, to the slender reward of more honourable courses? One of the warders at Millbank assured us, that many of the youths imprisoned there kept some five or six persons when at large, and gained often £50 in the week by picking pockets (*ante*, p. 257). We, ourselves, knew a coiner who could get his £5 a week by passing bad money; and one housebreaker of our acquaintance assured us that he had once made £100 a week for fourteen weeks, by a series of burglaries. Indeed, from calculations we have entered into upon the subject, we find that a professional pickpocket commits, upon an average, 1,000 robberies to one detection. The ordinary career of the "light-fingered gentry," for example, is, as the men say, "six months out (of prison) and four months in." A pickpocket, in regular work, reckons to take his six purses a day, Sundays included; and as there is generally some public entertainment, fête, or assembly going on one day in every week—either a race, or a flower show, a fancy bazaar, a review, a confirmation, a regatta, or a May meeting— we are assured that the average number of purses obtained by a London swell-mobsman amounts to not less than fifty every week during the time he is at large, and this, for twenty-five weeks, would give as many as 1,250 robberies committed before being detected; and yet the men who reap these large gains by dishonest means, would not be able to earn their guinea a week by honest labour.

To reduce crime, therefore, we must do all we can to make theft less lucrative and more certain of detection, on the one hand, as well as to increase the rewards of industry, on the other, and to render it a more honourable vocation in the State.

Such, then, would appear to be the cause of habitual crime in the abstract. But we have before said, a considerable number of our criminals are bred to the profession as regularly as the children of the Chinese are born to particular crafts. A large proportion of the London thieves are "Irish Cockneys," having been born in London of Irish parents. This shows, we believe, not that the Irish are naturally more criminal than our own race, but simply that they are poorer, and that their children are, consequently, left to shift for themselves, and sent out to beg more frequently than with our people. Indeed, juvenile crime will be found to be due, like prostitution, mainly to a want of proper parental control. Some have wondered why the daughters of the poorer classes principally serve to swell the number of our street-walkers. Are poor girls naturally more unchaste than rich ones? Assuredly not. But they are simply worse guarded, and therefore more liable to temptation. The daughters of even middle-class people are seldom or never trusted out of the mother's sight, so that they have no opportunity allowed them for doing wrong. With the poorer classes, however, the case is very different. Mothers in that sphere of life have either to labour for their living, or else to do the household duties for themselves, so that the girl is employed to run errands alone from the tenderest years, and, when her limbs are strong enough to work, she is put out in the world to toil for herself. *She* has no maids to accompany *her* when she walks abroad, and often her only play-ground is the common court in which her parents reside.

The same circumstances as cause the ranks of our "unfortunates" to be continually recruited from the poorer classes, serve also to keep up the numbers of our juvenile delinquents, and to draft fresh supplies from the same class of people. In a natural state of things, it has clearly been intended by the Great Architect of the universe that the labour of the man should be sufficient for the maintenance of the family—the frame of the woman being in itself evidence that she was never meant to do the hard work of society, whilst the fountains of life that she carries in her bosom, as well as the kindlier and more affectionate qualities of her nature, all show that her duty was designed to be that of a mother and a nurse to the children, rather than a fellow-labourer with the man. Our artificial state of society, however, and the scanty remuneration given to many of our forms of labour, as well as the high price of rent and provisions among us, render it now almost impossible for a family to be supported by the man alone, and hence most of the wives of the unskilled portion of our work-people have, now-a-days, to forego their maternal duties, and to devote themselves to some kind of drudgery by which they can add to the petty income of the house. Either the mother has to do slop-work, or to go out "charing," or washing—or harvesting, and hop-picking, in the season—or to sit all day at some fruit-stall in the streets—or, indeed, to do a variety of things other than mind the little ones that God Almighty has entrusted to her care.

If, then, the mother be away from home the greater part of her time, and the children, consequently, left to gambol in the gutter with others as neglected as themselves, what reward, think you, can society look for from such a state of moral anarchy and destitution? Either a mother's love and care was a useless piece of luxury in the great scheme of human nature; or, if it were a necessity conceived by the highest wisdom, for the due rearing and fostering of the future race—if it were essential for the proper working out of the organization of society, that the early part of every man's existence should be entrusted to a creature distinguished from the sterner sex by the extreme lovingkindness and gentleness, as well as the timidity of her character, surely that society which tolerates the subversion of such a natural state must expect to reap a bitter harvest. Let every man among us look back and remember where he learnt his first lessons of goodness. Surely all can answer, that the kindly teachings of their mother have made them better men than ever the lessons of the schoolmaster or the sermons of the clergyman could have effected; and if those who have been mercifully placed in a different sphere all know and feel this, is it not easy to understand what must be the consequence when the mother has no time left to watch over and fondle her little ones, and when the cares of life are of so all-absorbing a nature that her very heart is hardened by them, and she gets to wreak upon her children the miseries and spleen that are forced upon her.

That this constitutes the real explanation of juvenile delinquency, is proven by the fact that a large proportion of young criminals have either been left orphans in their early childhood, or else they have been subject to the tender mercies of some step-parent. Anything which serves to deprive the young of their natural protector, or to render home unlike what a home should really be—or any unnatural treatment of the younger members of a family, such as over-strictness, or even over-laxity of discipline—must all tend to swell the ranks of our young criminals, and, eventually, of our old ones; and thus it is that juvenile delinquency may be, either directly or indirectly, traced to orphanage—or ill-treatment, or neglect of children by their parents—or else to drunkenness and vicious habits on the part of the father or mother, or to defective dwellings, and the promiscuous association of children in the streets—or to the want of proper schooling, and industrial as well as religious training—all of which, however, are more or less necessarily included in the larger condition of the want of due maternal and paternal care.

Few, indeed, are aware of the really destitute state of the young thieves who swarm in our prisons, and how many of them are deprived of the good counsel and training of parents, either by being orphans, absolutely or morally—that is to say, either by having been deprived of either father, or mother, or both, or else, worse still, by having one or both of their parents drunkards or beggars, or old jail-birds of some kind or other. Mr. Antrobus tells us that, on reference to the school-register at Westminster for 1852, it appears that out of 1,490 boys who were received there, 65, or 4·3 per cent. of the whole, were totally destitute, whilst 390, or as many as 26·7 per cent., had one or both parents drunkards, whilst the relations of many others either were then, or had been, imprisoned or transported. At another time the same gentleman found that, out of 175 boys, 99 or 56⅓ per cent., had relatives who might strictly be classed under the denomination of old jail-birds. For instance, 10 had fathers in prison, 1 had a father who was transported, 6 had mothers in prison, 53 had brothers in prison, 9 had brothers transported, 4 had sisters in prison, 6 had cousins in prison, 5 had cousins transported, 3 had uncles in prison, 1 had an uncle transported, and 1 an aunt in prison. Again, out of 192 young girls, the following were the statistics concerning their parentage:—47 had neither father nor mother, 3 had a stepmother only, 2 a stepfather only, 53 had no father, 14 had no mother, 11 had a father and stepmother, 7 a mother and stepfather, and 4 were not able to say whether their parents were living or not. Again, out of 12 others, 6 had parents who had separated and were living with other persons, 2 were illegitimate children, 3 had parents who were insane, and only 1 was of a respectable family.

One prolific cause, too, of the increase of juvenile offenders is the fact, that children are sent to prison for the most trivial offences. "The great object," says Mr. Antrobus, "in separating an offender from society, must ever be to make him or her a better member of it. In sending a child of 8, 10, 12, or 14 years of age, to prison, and often only for a few days, is this object," he asks, "likely to be accomplished?"

"Send a child to prison for taking an apple, an orange, a few walnuts!" exclaims this most kind-hearted and right-minded magistrate, "or even for snatching some trifling article, imprudently or culpably exposed for sale in the streets, or, indeed, for having a vagrant parent—the act is monstrous, and can only tend to increase the moral pestilence which reigns, and which all deplore."

The same gentleman then cites a table of the number of children under 14 years of age who were committed to Tothill Fields for various petty thefts during the years 1851-52, and by this he shows that no less than 55 children, under 14 years of age, were committed to prison for stealing fruit, or some article *under* the value of sixpence; 48 for stealing something of the value of sixpence and under one shilling; 48, again, for taking something worth between one and two shillings; and 40 for appropriating something that was estimated at between two and four shillings—the whole having been sentenced to terms under two months; and thus evidently proving that they were not old offenders. "Now, a boy or girl," says Mr. Antrobus, "sent to prison for a few days or weeks, cannot, if uneducated, be either reformed or morally trained; and very few are otherwise. It is almost impossible to conceive," he adds, "any other effect to be produced on the juvenile offender by imprisonment, except that of imparting to him or her a recklessness of character, which will lead to the committal of greater crimes."

For the due elucidation of this part of the subject we have compiled the following table from the last Special Report of the Visiting Justices of Tothill Fields Prison :—

WORK-ROOM, ON THE SILENT-SYSTEM, AT THE HOUSE OF CORRECTION, TOTHILL FIELDS.

TABLE SHOWING THE NUMBER OF BOYS AND GIRLS, UNDER FOURTEEN YEARS OF AGE, WHO HAVE BEEN COMMITTED TO TOTHILL FIELDS PRISON, DURING THE FIVE YEARS 1851—55, FOR STEALING MONEY OR GOODS, AND SETTING FORTH THE SUPPOSED VALUE OF THE SAME, TOGETHER WITH THE TERMS OF IMPRISONMENT FOR SUCH OFFENCES.

	Amount or Supposed Value of Goods Stolen.											Terms of Imprisonment.
	Under 6d.	6d. and under 1s.	1s. and under 2s.	2s. and under 4s.	4s. and under 6s.	6s. and under 8s.	8s. and under 10s.	10s. and under 15s.	15s. and under 20s.	20s. and upwards.	Total.	
Boys	88	40	41	42	11	9	6	5	1	7	260	Under 7 days.
Girls	—	—	—	2	—	—	—	—	—	—	2	
Boys	70	27	24	13	6	6	—	2	—	1	150	7 and under 14 days.
Girls	1	—	—	—	2	—	—	—	—	—	3	
Boys	40	42	35	23	9	4	3	1	2	5	180	14 and under 21 days.
Girls	—	2	1	2	—	—	—	1	—	—	6	
Boys	8	6	14	9	—	—	—	—	—	1	38	21 days and under 1 month.
Girls	—	3	—	—	—	—	—	—	—	1	4	
Boys	66	74	65	74	30	16	9	6	2	24	366	1 month and under 2 months.
Girls	1	1	7	3	5	—	1	2	—	3	23	
Boys	7	10	14	35	16	9	4	9	2	13	119	2 and under 3 months.
Girls	—	—	—	6	2	—	1	1	—	4	14	
Boys	28	32	36	39	27	18	4	7	8	22	221	3 and under 6 months.
Girls	1	2	1	5	3	3	2	5	2	5	29	
Boys	6	1	21	27	28	21	10	14	8	23	159	6 and under 9 months.
Girls	—	—	3	3	—	—	2	1	—	3	12	
Boys	—	—	1	2	—	1	1	2	—	—	7	9 and under 12 months.
Girls	—	—	—	—	—	—	1	—	—	—	1	
Boys	—	—	1	—	2	4	1	2	—	7	17	12 months and under 2 years.
Girls	—	—	—	—	—	—	—	—	—	1	1	
Boys	—	2	5	15	9	3	3	2	—	17	56	2 years and upwards.
Girls	—	—	—	—	—	—	—	—	—	1	1	
Boys	299	234	257	280	148	90	42	50	23	121	1,564	Total for 5 years.
Girls	3	8	12	21	12	3	7	10	2	18	96	
Boys	—	—	—	—	—	—	—	—	—	—	1,471	Other Offences.
Girls	—	—	—	—	—	—	—	—	—	—	271	
Boys	—	—	—	—	—	—	—	—	—	—	3,035	Grand Total.
Girls	—	—	—	—	—	—	—	—	—	—	367	

Boys . . 48 } Committed for robbing parents. | Boys . . 42 } Committed for robbing employers.
Girls . . 6 }   Girls . . 12 }

Hence we find, that out of an average of 313 boys under fourteen years of age, annually committed for stealing goods or money, not less than 60 in number, or 20 per cent. of the whole are, on an average, sent to prison every year for purloining articles of less value than 6d.; 47 for stealing goods worth between 6d. and 1s.; 51 the amount of whose theft was estimated at between 1s. and 2s.; 56 at between 2s. and 4s.; 29 at between 4s. and 6s.; 18 at between 6s. and 8s.; 8 at between 8s. and 10s.; 10 at between 10s. and 15s.; 4 at between 15s. and 20s.; and 40 at 20s. and upwards.

Now, that mere schooling—the teaching of reading, writing, and arithmetic—can ever hope to abate the sad evil of juvenile crime, is, in our opinion, a fallacy of the most dangerous nature, because it is one of the popular notions of the day. "Reading and writing," said the late Dr. Cooke Taylor, "is no more knowledge than a knife and fork is a good dinner;" and even if it *were* knowledge, we do not believe that mere secular education—the develop·

ment of pure intellect—is a certain remedy against infractions of the law. "The heart," said Coleridge, "has its logic as well as the head;" and if it be deaf to reason, how shall we reach it by addressing our arguments to the brain alone? Surely Palmer knew well enough how to read and write, and was deeply versed in science too, and yet *he* was criminal by means of this very science itself. The cultivation of the feelings, however—the education of the moral sentiments—the development of the conscience—the teaching of duties and rights —the inculcation of a love of the beautiful, the true, and the just—are matters that every criminal nature needs to be informed upon; and yet people fancy that Dillworth, and Guy, and Mangnall's Questions, and the Tutor's Assistant and Catechisms, can supply the defect. Years ago, we pointed out to the heads of the Ragged Schools, that though they had instituted a vast educational machinery for the prevention of juvenile crime, they had made not the least impression upon the statistical records of the country; for that our prisons swarmed with even a greater number of young offenders, in proportion to the population, than when they began their labours; and no sooner were the articles published in the *Morning Chronicle*, than we were pelted with dirt from every evangelical assembly throughout the Metropolis; and even my Lord Ashley, with high Christian charity and telling platform rhetoric, did us the honour to say (though we had merely quoted figures from the criminal returns of the country), that "we had asserted things which we dare not repeat at the bar of our God."

A few weeks ago, however, we spoke with a gentleman who has assuredly had the largest experience of any in connection with the young criminals of this country; and he told us, that people were now beginning to see that the Ragged Schools had *not* been attended with that amount of benefit which persons originally had been led to expect from them!

Indeed, it is demonstrable, by our criminal records, that with all our educational endeavours to improve and instruct the prisoners, we are in no way reducing the crime of the country (for still the same ratio of 15 criminals to every 10,000 of our population continues from year to year); but rather we are *decreasing* only the proportion that are wholly unable to read and write, and *increasing* the per centage of those who are able to read and write imperfectly; or, in the words of an intelligent policeman, "we are teaching our thieves to prig the articles marked at the highest figures."

In the criminal returns of 1848, the following significant table was given:—

TABLE SHOWING THE CENTESIMAL OF INSTRUCTION OF PERSONS OF ALL AGES COMMITTED FOR TRIAL, FROM 1839 TO 1848 INCLUSIVE.

Years.	Unable to read or write.	Able to read and write imperfectly.	Able to read and write well.	Superior instruction.	Instruction could not be ascertained.
1839	33·53	53·48	10·07	0·32	2·60
1840	33·32	55·57	8·29	0·37	2·45
1841	33·21	56·67	7·40	0·45	2·27
1842	32·35	58·32	6·77	0·22	2·34
1843	31·00	57·60	8·02	0·47	2·91
1844	29·77	59·28	8·42	0·42	2·41
1845	30·61	58·34	8·38	0·37	2·30
1846	30·66	59·51	7·71	0·34	1·78
1847	31·39	58·89	7·79	0·28	1·65
1848	31·93	56·38	9·83	0·27	1·59

"The instruction of the offenders," added Mr. Redgrave, of the Home Office, "has been without much variation, exhibiting, on a comparison of the last ten years, a *decreased* proportion of those entirely uninstructed;" and, it might be added, a corresponding *increase* of those who are able to read and write imperfectly.

The subjoined table, however, which has been compiled from the Nineteenth Report of the Inspectors of Prisons, gives the latest returns upon the subject, and for all classes of prisoners in England and Wales:—

TABLE SHOWING THE PROPORTION PER CENT. AS TO THE EDUCATIONAL KNOWLEDGE OF THE SEVERAL PRISONERS THROUGHOUT ENGLAND AND WALES, IN THE COURSE OF THE YEARS 1842—53, BOTH INCLUSIVE.

Years.	Can neither read nor write.	Can read only.	Can read or write, or both imperfectly.	Can read and write well.	Of superior education.	State of instruction not ascertained.	Total.	Years.	Can neither read nor write.	Can read only.	Can read or write or both imperfectly.	Can read and write well.	Of superior education.	State of instruction not ascertained.	Total.
1842.								**1848.**							
Assizes and sessions	39·79	27·21	28·93	4·07	—	—	100·00	Assizes and sessions	37·05	26·43	32·56	3·96	—	—	100·00
Summary convictions	39·90	21·65	33·43	4·18	·16	·68	100·00	Summary convictions	35·30	22·49	37·35	4·18	·16	·52	100·00
Total	39·84	24·43	31·18	4·13	·08	·34	100·00	Total	36·18	24·46	34·95	4·07	·08	0·26	100·00
1843.								**1849.**							
Assizes and sessions	38·50	25·85	31·94	3·71	—	—	100 00	Assizes and sessions	38·57	25·26	33·14	3·03	—	—	100·00
Summary convictions	40·16	21·20	33·95	3·84	·17	·68	100·00	Summary convictions	37·79	21·12	36·86	3·60	·16	·47	100·00
Total	39·33	23·53	32·94	3·78	·08	·34	100 00	Total	38·18	23·19	35·00	3·31	·08	·24	100·00
1844.								**1850.**							
Assizes and sessions	39·72	26·95	30·11	3·22	—	—	100·00	Assizes and sessions	39·17	25·11	31·66	4·06	—	—	100·00
Summary convictions	36 87	22·82	35·49	4·14	·16	·52	100·00	Summary convictions	37·31	21·00	37·66	3·52	·16	·35	100·00
Total	38·29	24·89	32·80	3·68	·08	·26	100·00	Total	38·24	23·06	34·66	3·79	·08	·17	100·00
1845.								**1851.**							
Assizes and sessions	35·67	28·98	31·79	3·56	—	—	100·00	Assizes and sessions	39·37	22·93	34·73	2·93	·04	—	100·00
Summary convictions	34·68	21·51	38·61	4·61	·16	·43	100·00	Summary convictions	37·34	20·11	38·73	3·38	·13	·31	100·00
Total	35·18	25 24	35·20	4·09	·08	·21	100·00	Total	38·36	21·52	36·73	3·15	·09	·15	100·00
1846.								**1852.**							
Assizes and sessions	37·73	28·85	30·26	3·10	—	—	100·00	Assizes and sessions	39·74	25·69	30·82	3·66	·09	—	100·00
Summary convictions	33·81	20·88	40·94	3·81	·16	·40	100·00	Summary convictions	38·09	20·89	37·54	3·39	·09	—	100·00
Total	35·77	24·86	35·60	3·49	·08	·20	100·00	Total	38·92	23·29	34·18	3·52	·09	—	100·00
1847.								**1853.**							
Assizes and sessions	36·63	28·92	30·86	3·59	—	—	100·00	Assizes and sessions	36·63	27·53	32·87	2·95	—	—	100·00
Summary convictions	34·50	21·33	39·39	4·11	·16	·51	100·00	Summary convictions	36·85	20·35	39·44	2·98	·08	·30	100·00
Total	35 57	25·12	35·13	3·85	·08	·25	100·00	Total	36·74	23·94	36·16	2·97	·04	·15	100·00

ANNUAL MEAN.

For all Classes.	Can neither read nor write.	Can read only.	Can read or write, or both imperfectly.	Can read and write well.	Of superior education.	State of instruction not ascertained.	Total.
Assizes and sessions	38·21	26·65	31·64	3·49	·01	—	100·00
Summary convictions	37·23	21·24	37·14	3·81	·15	·43	100·00
Juveniles	42·52	24·42	30·21	2·68	·02	·15	100·00
Adults	33·50	21·82	37·62	6·49	·31	·26	100·00

DIFFERENCE PER CENT. BETWEEN THE EDUCATIONAL KNOWLEDGE OF PRISONERS IN 1842 AND 1853.

	Can neither read nor write.	Can read only.	Can read or write, or both imperfectly.	Can read and write well.	Of superior education.	State of instruction not ascertained.	Total.
All classes in 1842	36·96	22·34	33·67	6·50	·19	·34	100·00
„ 1853	33·83	21·88	38·49	5·27	·24	·29	100·00
Difference	— 3·13	— ·46	+ 3·82	— 1·33	+ ·05	— ·05	
Adults in 1842	35·89	21·96	34·59	6·97	·22	·37	100·00
„ 1853	32·86	21·66	39·32	5·59	·27	·30	100·00
Difference	— 3·03	— ·33	+ 4·73	— 1·42	+ ·05	— ·07	
Juveniles in 1842	45·21	25·37	26·49	2·78	·01	·14	100·00
„ 1853	41·54	24·22	31·87	2·19	·01	·17	100·00
Difference	— 3·67	— 1·15	+ 5·38	— ·59	—	+ ·03	

Thus, then, we perceive that the sole result of all our educational attempts in connection with juvenile prisoners has been, *not* to make any marked impression upon their numerical amount (for in the year 1842, 11,602 passed through the prisons of all England and Wales, whereas in 1852 the number that did so was 11,821, whilst in 1853 it was 11,453), but rather to decrease the number of those who can neither read nor write, or who can read only; for it will be seen, on reference to the above returns, that in 1842 there was 45·21 per cent. of juvenile prisoners who were wholly uneducated, whereas in 1853 there was only 41·54 per cent. belonging to the same class. Again, of those who could read only there was 25·37 per cent. in 1842, and only 24·22 per cent. in 1853, so that, with these two *uneducated* classes, there had been a *reduction* of very nearly 5 per cent. in the twelve years. During the same period, however, it will be found, on reference to the above table, that the proportion of young prisoners who could read and write imperfectly had been *increased* in an equal ratio; for whilst in 1842 the *imperfectly educated* class of juvenile prisoners was only 26·49 per cent., in 1853 it was no less than 31·87 per cent., or upwards of 5 per cent. more than it had been twelve years before.

Now, surely, the unprejudiced will admit that there is no gainsaying such facts as these, for they must be allowed to be overpowering evidence that this same educational panacea for crime has proved comparatively fruitless. Do people in the nineteenth century still require to be told that reading and writing are but the instruments of acquiring knowledge, rather than knowledge itself; and that the faculty which, with righteous persons, may be applied to the study of the Bible or other good works, may, on the other hand, be used by unrighteous ones for the perusal of Jack Sheppard and such like degrading literature? It should be remembered that it is only within a few centuries that even gentlefolks have been able to read or write at all—and yet in the olden time such people were not utterly criminal because they were utterly unlettered; and the reason why the thieves of the present day belong principally to the ignorant classes, is because they come mostly from the poorer portion of our community, and a want of education is indicative of the want of means to obtain it. Accordingly, if any other test was to be taken, which should be, like the want of education, a sign as to the want of means in the class—such, for instance, as the use of different kinds of pocket-handkerchiefs—tables might be drawn up showing that the *smaller number* of criminals indulged in white cambric ones, and that a considerable proportion carried red cotton bandannas, whilst by far the *larger number* used none at all; and thence theories might be framed, that the blowing of the nose with the fingers was productive of crime.

Now, it must not be imagined, from what is here written, that we are adverse to the spread of education among the people—far from it. We readily admit, that the sole test of high wisdom is leading a virtuous and happy life, and that the profoundest knowledge can but tend to the profoundest goodness, because virtue alone yields the greatest happiness both here and hereafter; and we grant, therefore, that crime, which, sooner or later, ends in misery, can but be dictated by folly, and produced by ignorance. Nevertheless, mere reading and writing are but the means of obtaining either *good* or *bad* knowledge, according to the cultivation and tendencies of the mind which uses them, and so may become an instrument of evil in the hands of a viciously-disposed person, even as they are of good to the virtuous-minded.

What our young criminals stand far more in need of than reading and writing, is industrial training. They require to be taught, not only the habit of industry, but also the use and the dignity of it. The majority of the young, and, indeed, even the old, criminals are utterly ignorant of all means of getting their own living; for, according to the account given by Mr. Antrobus, one of the visiting justices at the Westminster House of Correction, "out of 1,481 boys committed to the Westminster prison during the year ending Michaelmas, 1852, only 129, or 8¾ per cent., had received any industrial education;

and, on investigation, it appeared that very few even of those had more than a slight knowledge of the trade to which they said they belonged."[*]

It is manifest, therefore, that if youths be educated to no trade or business, and be reared in habits of idleness rather than industry, they can hardly be expected, when they come to man's estate, to delight in labouring for their living, or to have much faith in their own powers, or any sense of self-respect—or, indeed, any of those virtues which tend to give a man a consciousness of his own dignity and position in the great scheme of human nature.

Nor are these mere day-dreams on our part, for the most successful experiments that have been made of late years, concerning the reformation of the young, are those in connection with industrial schools. At the Philanthropic Farm School, at Redhill, it is said that some 75 per cent. of the juvenile offenders who are sent there are led to adopt an honest life; and the industrial ragged schools of Sheriff Watson, in Aberdeen, as well as the shoe-

---

[*] We extract the following table from Mr. Antrobus's instructive and benevolent work, "*The Prison and the School:*"—

RETURN OF THE TRADES OF BOYS COMMITTED TO THE HOUSE OF CORRECTION AT WESTMINSTER, DURING THE YEAR ENDING MICHAELMAS, 1852.

Shoemakers 25	Painters 4	Blacksmith . . . 1
Tailors 11	Rope-makers 3	Cabinet-maker . . . 1
Paper-stainers . . . 8	Chair-makers . . . 3	Baker 1
Whitesmiths, Gunsmiths, Locksmiths, and Copper-	Butchers 3	Other trades . . . 32
smiths 6	Glass-blowers . . . 3	
	Carvers and Gilders . . 2	Total . . . 129
Plasterers 5	Bookbinders . . . 2	Clerks 2
Carpenters 5	Basket-makers . . . 2	No trade or occupation . 1,350
French Polishers . . 5	Hatters 2	
Printers 4	Bricklayer 1	Grand Total 1,481

As regards the industrial knowledge of the females in the same prison, Mr. Antrobus supplies us with the subjoined table concerning the attainments of 646 females :—

RETURN AS TO THE STATE OF INDUSTRIAL EDUCATION OF THE FEMALES COMMITTED TO THE WESTMINSTER HOUSE OF CORRECTION, JUNE, 1853.

	Ability to Sew or having a slight Knowledge of Needlework.				Ability to Knit.			
	None.	Some.	Learned in prison.	Total.	None.	Some.	Learned in prison.	Total.
Number	58	469	119	646	161	367	158	686
Per cent.	8·9	72·6	18·5	·100	23·5	53·5	23·5	·100

Of the 469 females who are here stated to be able to sew, or have some slight knowledge of needlework, "one-half," the author tells us, "were able to accomplish merely the most simple work in the crudest manner. It is, however, not from any lack of ability," adds Mr. Antrobus, "that this extreme ignorance arises, for it is surprising how very soon the great majority of the younger women (under 25 years of age) learn the various works taught in the prison—the average time taken by them in learning to make a straw bonnet, complete from first to last, being only six weeks, *i. e.*, fourteen days to learn the plait, and twenty-eight days to accomplish the cleaning, blocking, and making-up."

Again, the same authority publishes a table of the trades of the prisoners committed to Coldbath Fields, which proves, as he says, "that it is not the mechanic or artisan that encumbers a prison, for out of 6,643 prisoners committed in the year ending Michaelmas, 1852, only 667 (or 10 per cent.) had any knowledge of a trade."

black brigade, in connection with the ragged schools of the Metropolis, have been of more service towards reclaiming boys from evil courses, than all the spelling-books, and gram- mars, and catechisms in Europe.

We now come to the second consideration, which we proposed at the beginning of this article, viz., what fate eventually befalls the young criminals of our country?

That the juvenile offender ultimately ripens into the old felon and transport is admitted by all; still, it cannot be said that the whole of the 15,000 or 20,000 boy thieves and vagrants infesting the country grow up to be the future convicts. Many of our young criminals are transferred to that admirable institution, the Philanthropic Farm School, at Reigate,* and are there trained to agricultural pursuits, with a view to their ultimate settlement in the colonies; for the reverend gentleman at the head of that establishment has ably shown that it is almost idle to expect to reclaim the youthful delinquent in this country, surrounded, as he generally is, by a crowd of felon relatives and friends. It is asserted that this institution reclaims some three-fourths of those who come under its care. God speed it! we say.

How many other young criminals are won to honest courses by similar institutions and reformatories throughout the country we are not, at present, able even to conjecture. Suffice it, many are applying themselves, heart and soul, to the good work of the redemption of those poor wretches who seem to have been born with a handcuff about their wrist, the same as the more lucky members of society are said to come into the world with a silver spoon in their mouth; for, surely, even the sternest-minded amongst us must admit, that he who enters upon life *viâ* some convict nursery has a very different career before him to the one whose birth is hailed by the firing of cannon, and whose mother's couch is surrounded by all the ministers of state.

A small proportion of the gross number of juvenile offenders, however, die in the prisons of the country—but only about 1 per 1,000; for in the year 1853 there were merely 12 deaths out of a gross prison population of 11,749 boys and girls under 17 years of age. How many of the same class are summoned to their last account outside the prison walls it is impossible to say; still, the mortality among them can hardly tend to thin the ranks of our infant vagabonds to any considerable extent.

Admitting, however, that the reformatories, and farm schools, and industrial institutions, as well as the boy convict prisons, are attended with the best possible success, it certainly cannot be said that, even with the deaths among the class, 25 per cent. of the entire number of our young criminal population are snatched from their wretched life. It will be found, on consulting the prison returns, that no less than 33 per cent. of the young thieves and vagrants are re-committed to each of our jails in the course of the year, so that, as this large per centage refers only to the boys who are known to the authorities of the prison in which they may happen to be incarcerated for the time being, it is highly probable (if the returns upon the subject could possibly be obtained) that the per centage of those who had been previously committed to some jail or other throughout the country would be found to amount, at the very least, to two-thirds of the whole. We incline, then, to the belief that the proportion of juvenile offenders annually removed from the 15,000 to 20,000 at which we have estimated the gross numbers of the young criminal popu- lation of the country, by reformatories and other institutions, amounts barely to one- third of the whole. Consequently, there would remain some 10,000 or 12,000 unaffected by our many efforts towards the reformation of the class, and who must, ultimately,

---

* There are also usually some 600 young prisoners at the Boy Convict Prison, at Parkhurst (the average daily number in confinement there was 593, in the year 1853), and of these about 100 appear to be received annually.

pass into the body of the adult professional thieves that are continually preying on our community.

The next point to be settled is—how many are required to be added every year to the number of our old habitual offenders, in order to maintain the criminal population at the ratio of 15 to every 10,000 of our people, at which it has stood for several years? But this problem there is a simple method of solving. We have before shown that, under the old system of transportation, some 2,000 convicts were, for a series of years, annually shipped off to the penal colonies, so that if we could learn, by any means, the proportion that the old habitual criminals among these bore to the "first-offence men," we should be enabled to state, with some little certainty, how many fresh hands must yearly join our criminal bands in order to keep up the stock.

Now, by a series of compilations and deductions made from the criminal returns of the country,* we have attempted to classify the offences, not only according to their causes,

* TABLE SHOWING THE ANNUAL AVERAGE RATIO OF THE SEVERAL CLASSES OF CRIMINALS TO THE GENERAL POPULATION OF THE COUNTRY, FROM THE YEAR 1844 TO 1853.

CLASS I.—CRIMES OF FEROCITY AND MALICE.

ORDER A—Casual.

	No. of criminals in every 1,000,000 of population.
Murder cases	20·16
Homicidal and assault cases . .	58·46
Arson cases	9·73
Destruction cases . . .	1·89
Total of all casual cases of ferocity and malice . . .	90·20

ORDER B—Habitual.

Burglary cases	79·03
Highway robbery cases . . .	25·84
Smuggling (armed) cases . .	0·09
Poaching (armed) cases . .	7·35
Escape cases	1·45
Total all habitual cases of ferocity and malice	113·99
Total all cases of ferocity and malice	204·19

CLASS II.—CRIMES OF CUPIDITY AND TEMPTATION.

ORDER A—Casual.

Breach of trust cases . . .	142·64

ORDER B—Habitual.

Cattle stealing, &c., cases . .	24·17
Larceny cases	984·79
Petty offence cases . . .	9·73
Receiving cases	77·65
Forgery cases	0·49
Coining cases	28·02
Other felony cases . . .	6·69
Total all habitual cases of cupidity and temptation . . .	1134·19
Total all cases of cupidity and temptation	1276·83

CLASS III.—CRIMES OF LUST, INDECENCY, PERVERTED APPETITES, &C.

ORDER A—Casual.

	No. of criminals in every 1,000,000 of population.
Lust cases	15·57
Shame cases (as concealing births, &c.) .	4·58
Indecency cases . . .	0·23
Cases against marriage laws . .	4·62
Unnatural offence cases . .	6·31
Total all casual cases of lust, &c. :	31·38

ORDER B—Habitual.

Brothel cases	5·82
Total all habitual cases of lust, &c.	37·20

CLASS IV.—EVIL SPEAKING.

Threatening cases	1·44
Perjury cases	3·83
Total all cases of evil speaking .	5·27

CLASS V.—POLITICAL CASES.

Political cases	1·54

Total all cases of casual crimes : .	264·22
,, ,, habitual crimes . .	1254·00
Total mixed crimes (as evil speaking, &c.)	6·81
Total	1525·03

Total all cases of ferocity and malice .	204·19
,, ,, cupidity and temptation	1276·83
,, ,, lust, indecency, &c. .	37·20
,, ,, evil speaking . .	5·27
,, ,, political offences . .	1·54
	1525·03

but also according as they are pursued as a matter of trade or living; and thus, by sub-dividing each of the five classes of offences, into which we have arranged all crimes, into two orders—the casual and habitual—according as they are the acts of either regular or, so to speak, accidental offenders, we have been enabled to arrive at something like the proximate truth as to the proportions of the casual and habitual offenders.

By means of this statistical analysis, we have demonstrated (see Table at p. 395) that there are altogether 15·25 criminals in every 10,000 of our population; and that of these 2·64 (or $17\frac{1}{3}$ per cent. of the whole) belong to the *casual* class, whilst 12·54 (or $82\frac{1}{3}$ per cent.) appertain to the *habitual* class, and 0·06 hardly admit of being arranged under either head. At this ratio, then, of the habitual to the casual criminals, the 2,000 convicts that were annually sent out of the country, until within the last few years, without producing the least diminution of the stock of old offenders at home, must have required some 1,650 professional thieves to have been annually added to the felon ranks.

Further, some few of the more successful and lucky criminals occasionally pass into a half honest form of life. Some, for instance, take to cab-driving, others to costermongering, others to dealing in "marine stores," as it is called, and others to keeping low lodging-houses, whilst others, again, die in the convict prisons, or the hospital, or workhouse; so that, altogether, we are led to believe that some 2,000 criminals, at least, are required to be added every year to the general stock, in order to maintain that steady ratio of offenders to the population, which has continued in this country for nearly the whole of the present century.

Hence it would appear that, of the great body of our juvenile criminals, about one-fifth (or 2,000 out of the 10,000 that we have calculated to remain after all our efforts at reformation) may be said to pass annually into the ranks of the adult habitual offenders, and thus to serve to keep up that unvarying army of British Arabs, or Sonquas, or Fingoes, that continually prey upon the industry of our people.

In conclusion, it must not be presumed that the above statistical details are here given with any desire that the reader should put *implicit* faith in them. Such recorded facts as *could* be collected in connection with the matter have been cited from the best authorities, and conjectures have been made with all that caution which is so necessary in reasoning upon subjects concerning which we cannot arrive at any certainty. But the writer was anxious of opening the question concerning the amount of waste and supply among the criminal body of this country; and it is believed that the matter, once started, will originate in the mind of all those interested in the great social problem of crime, a desire to obtain more reliable information concerning the number that annually disappear from, and are drafted into, the criminal ranks. Moreover, when the subject of juvenile delinquency comes to be regarded in its relation to the crimes committed by the adult and habitual offenders of the country, the writer is assured that more earnest and philosophic experiments will be tried in connection with the reformation of our young outcasts.

The following significant table will form an apt appendix to the above article, showing, as it does, that out of some 9,000 and odd young offenders, committed to the Westminster House of Correction between the years 1851—55, for thirty different infractions of the law, there were no less than 6,000, or about 70 per cent., committed for four offences alone, and these were mostly of a dishonest character; whilst the remaining 3,000, it will be seen, were sent to prison for such trivial offences as throwing stones, obstructing highways, unlawful ringing and knocking at doors, &c., &c.; matters surely for which it is unwise, if not unjust, to subject a child to the lasting disgrace, if not contamination, of a jail :—

TABLE SHOWING THE AVERAGE NUMBER AND PROPORTION PER CENT. OF JUVENILE MALE PRISONERS ANNUALLY COMMITTED TO TOTHILL FIELDS PRISON, FOR THE SEVERAL OFFENCES ENUMERATED BELOW :—

	Total from 1851—55, both inclusive.	Annual Mean.	Proportion per cent.
Simple larceny	1,835	367·0	19·97
Reputed thieves, rogues, and vagabonds	1,674	334·8	18·22
Unlawful possession of property	1,668	333·6	18·15
Felonies, with imprisonment and hard labour	1,435	287·0	15·62
Begging, or sleeping in the open air	848	169·6	9·23
Stealing fruit, plants, trees, &c.	369	73·8	4·02
Assaults, common	286	57·2	3·11
Misdemeanours, throwing stones, &c.	247	49·4	2·69
Wilful damage	198	39·6	2·15
Assaults on police	180	36·0	1·95
Gaming	110	22·0	1·25
Misbehaviour in workhouses	96	19·2	1·04
Obstructing highways	91	18·2	0·99
Disorderly apprentices	48	9·6	0·52
Drunk and disorderly	21	4·2	0·23
Illegally pawning	18	3·6	0·19
Cruelty to animals	15	3·0	0·16
Unlawful ringing and knocking at doors	10	2·0	0·11
Frauds (summarily convicted)	6	1·2	0·07
Obtaining money by false pretences	6	1·2	0·07
Furious driving, insolence to fares, &c.	5	1·0	0·05
Dog stealing	5	1·0	0·05
Frauds tried at Sessions	4	0·8	0·04
Indecent exposure of the person	2	0·4	0·02
Unlawful collection of dust	2	0·4	0·02
Excise offences	2	0·4	0·02
Trespass, fishing, poaching, &c.	2	0·4	0·02
Receiving embezzled property	2	0·4	0·02
Attempts at burglary	1	0·2	0·01
Assaults, unnatural	1	0·2	0·01
Total	9,187	1837·4	100·00

¶ ii.—γ.

Of the Interior of Tothill Fields Prison.

Assuredly, if it were not for the massive iron gates, weighing no less than three tons, and the sternly-handsome stone gateway, with the dwarf wall skirting the carriage-way that leads to the prison portal, we should hardly, on being ushered across the planted court-yard that leads to the governor's house, be led to imagine that we were entering a house of correction. True, there is the same military-looking warder, habited in the undress surtout indulged in by officers of the army, and the same little office next the gateway, with the row of cutlasses strung together on a chain, like herrings on a rush, and the same sloping desks and ugly ledgers as you see at other prisons; nevertheless, the turfed quadrangle, fringed by lines of drooping ash-trees, with their leafy branches bending down to the earth, as if they were so many arborescent fountains springing from the ground, and the pale-green tufts of feathery-like acacias—all skirting the triangular patches of bright grass into which the court-yard is divided, and where a little pyramid of black shot is seen arranged at each point of the verdant turf—with here and there, too, a white pet rabbit grazing on the lawn, or a corpulent cat basking in the sun—and the stately-looking governor's house showing at the end of the avenue, with the gold letters of the black clock under the pediment twinkling in the light, and the steps slanting down from either side of the doorway, that seems to have been lifted up to the first floor—all these things, as we walked down the prison pathway, gave us a notion of being in the precinct of some trim academy, rather than a jail. Nor did the sight of the black maid-servant, who came to the door while we waited for the governor, with her bright-coloured, turbaned head-dress, and long jetty tresses hanging about her shoulders, like skeins of the softest floss-silk, serve to remove the impression.

In a few moments, however, we were ushered through a tall, open-barred gate, and then the dismal-looking, embrazure-like windows, that remind one of lunatic asylums and union workhouses, and, indeed, everything that has ugly associations in the mind, rapidly dispelled the agreeable impressions that the first sight of the place had produced upon us.

Here were the same radiating blocks of buildings that we had been accustomed to see for the last six months of our life, and the same smell of oakum in the air, the same diamond gates at each of the doors, and the same warders, with bunches of keys in the shiny cartouche-box at their hip, and with the brass coat of arms on their stand-up collar, and the same train of prisoners in sad-coloured dresses, branded on the arms with letters and figures and marks, either indicative of the number of times they have been re-committed, or the class to which they belong, or the badges they have obtained for good conduct while in prison.

On the day of our second visit to Tothill Fields prison, we had arrived some few minutes after the firing of the gun that summoned the warders to their duties—for it is our custom, when studying the routine of a prison, to begin the day with the officials and to end with the closing of the institution for the night; and accordingly, when we entered the boys' prison, we found a detachment of young prisoners drawn up at the extremity of one of the triangular paved airing-yards in rows of five, and each with his satchel of books lying on the stones at his feet, and with a couple of warders standing by in attendance upon them.

These boys were waiting to enter the lavatory at the end of the yard, whilst hanging against the walls were long jack-towels, at which some jacketless young criminals, with their check shirts wide open at the neck, and their hair matted into pencils with the wet, were busy drying their skin.

MOTHERS, WITH THEIR CHILDREN, EXERCISING AT TOTHILL FIELDS PRISON.

Some, again, were busy combing their hair, standing with their head down, as if "**giving a back**" at leap-frog, and with their wet locks hanging, like a fringe of camel's-hair **brushes**, straight down from their forehead, whilst the attendant warders cried to one of the **young** prisoners, "Your brace over your shoulder, do you hear, there?" and to another, "**Dry yourself well, boy.**"

Of the lads that remained drawn up in the yard, one-half were rosy-cheeked, **their** skin shiny with the recent scrubbing, and their hair ribbed like corduroy with the teeth of the comb; the other half stood with their gray prison jackets thrown loosely over their shoulders, after the fashion of a hussar, and the flat sleeves dangling **limp** and empty as a Greenwich pensioner's by their sides; whilst from inside of the adjoining lavatory—where the soapy water in the troughs round the walls was of the same semi-opaque colour as the celebrated "sky-blue" of the Turnham Green and Wandsworth academies—there issued a spluttering and hissing sound from the batch of prisoners washing themselves, that reminded one of the noise made by the steam eternally escaping from the knot of locomotives at the Chalk Farm Railway Station.

"The boys take a warm bath once a month, besides the usual one on reception," said the chief warder, who stood at our elbow; "and they likewise have a foot-bath twice every week."

It was soon time for the young prisoners to fall in, previous to entering the oakum-room; and accordingly the newly-washed troop, who appeared cleaner and fresher than they probably had ever looked before in all their lives, were marched across the airing-yard and drawn up behind the bars of the tall iron gate at the other end.

This gate serves to separate the triangular, flagged space between the prison wings from the arc-shaped inspection-yard surrounding the chief warder's house; and when we had passed through it, we beheld a number of similar gangs of urchin-prisoners drawn up at the gates of the other airing-yards, and all with their faces glistening with the morning's soaping.

As we turned round to take a general view of the boys' prison, the various openings between the blocks of buildings, diverging from the central space in which we stood, reminded us somewhat of the many thoroughfares radiating from the Seven Dials; and the reader has but to imagine the several streets of that classic district to be replaced by the exercising-yards of the prison, and the monster-lamped public-houses and penny-ice shops that now form the termini of the various lines of houses converging to the St. Giles's centre, to stand for the gable ends of the different prison wings, and the numberless bird-fanciers' shops and halfpenny shaving ditto, to be changed into long fortress-looking walls, pierced at intervals with embrasure-like windows—the reader has but to fancy thus much, we say, to have as good an ideal sketch as we can give him of the boys' prison at Tothill Fields. To complete the picture, however, he must imagine the buildings to be all new and the colour of nankeen with their unsullied yellow bricks, and the spaces between them to look as clean and desolate as the streets of the Metropolis during a heavy shower, and the entrance to each airing-yard to be railed off by a high iron gate, after the fashion of some deserted inn of court.

Accompanied by the chief warder, we now passed to what is called "airing-yard 7 and 8," that is to say, to the paved triangular space between the prison wings bearing those numbers respectively; for we should here state that the boys' prison at Tothill Fields consists (like each of the two divisions devoted to the females) of five distinct wings or radii, with a triangular court-yard between every two of them—the first and last of such wings being single prisons, and the three others double ones, and the so-called double prisons having each an entrance from the airing-yard on either side of them.* Thus,

* In each double prison there are fifty-six separate cells, excepting in prison 2 and 3, which has only thirty-six, on account of the large dormitory occupying the upper floor. No. 1 (single) prison has twenty-one cells, and No. 8 (also a single prison) but ten cells; for the school-room, tailors' and shoemakers' shops, are situate in this part of the building.

prison 1 is a "single prison," and next to it comes airing-yard 1 and 2; then follows "prison 2 and 3," and then airing-yard 3 and 4; after this we have "prison 4 and 5," and after that airing-yard 5 and 6; the latter adjoins "prison 6 and 7," which, in its turn, forms one side of airing-yard 7 and 8; whilst at the other side of the airing-yard stands the remaining single "prison 8." Across the further end or base of the triangular airing-yard, termed "7 and 8," there is built a large shed, and this forms the oakum-room of the boys' prison; thither the young prisoners who, as we have said, stood drawn up in gangs at the gates of the various yards after their morning wash, were now about to pass, in order to begin their day's labour at "teasing" the old junk.

As we entered this yard, we found it littered with tubs, having each a board across the top, on which stood a tin can and holystone ready for scouring the flags, whilst a prisoner was busy washing a pile of metal panikins, in the centre of the open space.

"You can pass them in now," said the warder; and the order was no sooner given than the keys rattled in the locks of the nearest exercising-yard, and the gates groaned as they turned heavily on their hinges. "Pass on," said one of the warders; and then the boys from "6 and 7" came filing along, one after another, in a continuous stream, each with his small canvas satchel of books dangling from his hand; these were immediately followed by the urchins from "3 and 4," and when this yard was emptied, those from "1 and 2" kept up the apparently endless line.

We now entered the oakum-room at the end, as we said, of yard 7 and 8, and found the interior of the shed somewhat like a large barn, with the whitewashed tie-beams and rafters showing overhead. The shed was filled with seats, that ranged from one end of the long room to the other, and stood on a slightly-inclined plane, so as to have the appearance of a large booth at a fair or stand at a race-ground—with the exception that the side which is usually open at such places was, in the prison, fitted with the peculiar lengthy windows that, in the district of Spitalfields, are termed "long-lights." Here was the same tarry smell of oakum as is peculiar to all such places.

At the time of our entry, the serving out of the oakum for the day's labour was going on. At one end of the room was a warder, sitting beside a small box of hooks and a pair of large, buttermonger-like scales. Near these stood three boy-prisoners, with baskets of brown, tarry, old junk, and bits of rope close beside them. One of the boys placed a bundle of the junk into the scale-pan, whilst another stood by with the weights in his hand —two pounds in one and one and a half in the other—and placed either the heavier or the lighter one in the scale, according as the lad to whom the bundle of strands was served out was older or younger.

"Boys of sixteen," said the chief warder to us, "have two pounds of junk given out to them; those under sixteen, one and a half pound; and those under nine years of age, only one pound. Some of the young ones, however, who have been in the prison many times before, have one and a half pound to do; and they manage it better even than the older lads."

The oakum is ready weighed into parcels of the various quantities before it comes to the work-room, and being sorted into different baskets, it has, in the morning, only to be served out. The weights, however, are placed in the scale at the same time, so that the prisoner may see that he gets no more than his fair allowance.

As we stood beside the warder at the end, the boys came filing past the scales, the balance clicking the while, as the several bundles were thrown from the baskets into the pan, and the hooks rattling in the box as each of the prisoners dipped into it.

In a few minutes the lads were all busy at their day's work, with the hooks tied just above the knee; some "fiddling away," as the prison phrase goes, at the unravelled yarn passed across the hook, and others rolling the loosened strands backwards along the other thigh, which seemed to be coated with glue, from the tar with which it had got to be covered, while the atmosphere of the place grew gradually hazed with the dust of the abraded tow flying in the air.

A death-like silence prevailed throughout the place, and round the room the warders sat on high, lawyer's-clerk-like stools, with their eyes intently fixed on the young urchins, and ready to put a stop to the least attempt at communication among them.

"They are kept at the oakum-work for nearly five hours altogether in the day," the chief warder informed us; "and they are expected," he added, "each to do the quantity served out to them in that time. They begin at a quarter past seven, and continue working till half-past four, with the intervals of an hour and three-quarters for their meals during the day, as well as an hour for exercising, and another hour and three-quarters for schooling and Divine service."*

We afterwards learnt, on visiting the oakum-store, that there is, altogether, about from 24 to 26 cwt. of oakum picked, on an average, every week, in Tothill Fields prison. Of this quantity, the boys do nearly one-half, or between 11 and 12 cwt.†

* The following is a list of the routine in the boys' prison at Tothill Fields :—

h. m.
6 25. Gun fired for admission of warders.
6 30. Unlocking of prisoners' cells and washing of boys.
7 0. Work begins.
8 30. Breakfast.
9 15. Chapel.
10 15. Exercise, work, and school; the boys being thus occupied, in different detachments, at the same time.
2 0. Dinner.
3 0. Work, exercise, and school.
4 30. Work ends.
5 0. Work given in.
5 30. Supper.
6 0. Lock up for the night.
6 15. Warders go off duty.

Time occupied in meals, 2¼ hours.
    "   "   in exercising, chapel, and schooling, 2¾ hours.
    "   "   in labour, 6 hours.

† We were furnished with the following official account of the quantity of oakum picked at this prison :—

A STATEMENT OF THE QUANTITY OF JUNK ISSUED TO EACH PRISONER, MALE AND FEMALE, DAILY.

Boys.			Females.		
At the age of 16.	Under the age of 16.	Under the age of 9.	16 years of age and upwards.	Under the age of 16.	Females with their children.
2 lbs.	1½ lb.	1 lb.	1½ lb.	1 lb.	1 lb.

A SEPARATE ACCOUNT OF OAKUM PICKED DAILY BY THE MALE AND FEMALE PRISONERS.

Boys.					Females.				
Date—1856.	Number employed.	Quantities.			Date—1856.	Number employed.	Quantities.		
		cwt.	qrs.	lbs			wt.	qrs.	lbs.
June 29—Saturday . .	164	2	0	0	June 29—Saturday . .	189	2	2	0
July 1—Monday . .	153	1	3	9	July 1—Monday . .	182	2	0	8
" 2—Tuesday . .	162	2	0	0	" 2—Tuesday . .	186	2	0	17½
" 3—Wednesday . .	152	1	2	24	" 3—Wednesday . .	183	2	0	14
" 4—Thursday . .	157	2	0	24	" 4—Thursday . .	190	2	0	11
" 5—Friday . . .	154	2	0	2	" 5—Friday . . .	194	2	0	13
Total	942	11	3	3	Total	1,124	13	0	7½

                                           cwt. qrs. lbs.
Total picked by the boys in the week . . 11   3   3
Average per diem 1   3 23 14 oz.
Average by each boy, per diem . . . 1 6$\frac{4}{15}$
Gross quantity of oakum picked by boys, per annum, about 31 tons.

This, at £4 10s. per ton, which is the price paid for the picking, gives, as the yearly earnings of the

In the oakum-room, at the period of our visit, there were altogether about some 150 of mere children congregated together. Some of the boys, seated on the lower forms, were dressed in a suit of prison-blue, marking that they were imprisoned for misdemeanours, and *not* sentenced to hard labour. Others were habited in suits of iron-gray, to note that they have been sentenced to be kept at hard labour, being known technically as "summary boys," *i. e.*, they had been committed by the magistrates, rather than after trial. Others, again, had yellow collars to the waistcoats of their gray suits, and this was to mark them as "sessions'" prisoners, or, in other words, as those who had been tried and found guilty of larceny or felony. All the boys wore striped tricolour woollen night-caps, which were arranged, by tucking down the peak, into the form of an ordinary day-cap. Besides these vestiary distinctions, there were others, which consisted of letters and marks attached to the left arm—such as either a large figure 1 or 2, in yellow cloth, to denote the class of prisoners to which they belonged—the third-class prisoners being unmarked, and consisting of such as had been sentenced to be imprisoned for fourteen days, or under. The second-class prisoners, however, on the other hand, were under imprisonment for three months; whilst the first were those who had more than three months' incarceration to undergo. Moreover, some of the boys had red marks, besides the yellow ones, to indicate the number of times they had been previously committed; others, again, had badges, showing that they were imprisoned for two years, whilst others had a yellow ring on the left arm, to denote that their sentence was penal servitude.

Once conversant with these distinctions, it was indeed a melancholy sight to look at that century and a-half of mere children in their prison clothes. Some were so young, that they seemed to need a nurse, rather than a jailer, to watch over them; others, again, had such frank and innocent-looking faces, that we could not help fancying they had no business there; whilst others had such shamelessness and cunning painted in their features, that the mind was led insensibly towards fatalism, and to believe in criminal races as thoroughly as in cretin ones. Many, again, were remarkable for those peculiar Irish gray eyes, which seem, with their long black lashes—as Lady Morgan said—"to have been put in with dirty fingers."

We have before remarked, that the greater number of the professional thieves of London belong to what is called the Irish-Cockney tribe; and at the boys' prison at Tothill Fields we can see the little Hibernian juvenile offender being duly educated for the experienced thief. Some bigots seek to make out that the excess of crime in connection with the Irish race is due directly or indirectly to the influence of the prevailing religion of that country; and small handbills are industriously circulated among the fanatic frequenters of Exeter Hall, informing one how, in Papal countries, the ratio of criminals to the population is enormously beyond that of Protestant kingdoms. From such documents, however, the returns of Belgium are usually omitted, for these would prove that there is really no truth in the theory sought to be established; since it is shown, by the tables printed by Mr. M'Culloch in his "Geographical Dictionary," that whereas the ratio of criminals to the gross population of the country is in Papal Belgium 1·9, and in Romanist France 2·3, to every 10,000 individuals, it is in Protestant England as many as 12·5 to the same definite number of people, and in Sweden as high as 87·7; so that it is plain that mere differences of religious creeds cannot possibly explain the different criminal tendencies among different races of people.*

gross number of the boys employed in oakum-picking, £132. Therefore, each boy-prisoner employed at oakum-picking may be said to earn about 17*s.* per annum by their labour.

Now, by the official returns, we find that the average cost per head of the prisoners at Tothill Fields is within a fraction of £8, so that it follows that there is a loss of very nearly £7 a-year upon each of the boys so employed.

* "In Belgium," says Mr. M'Culloch, "the amount of crime, with regard to the population, and to the criminal records of France and England, is comparatively small. M. Ducpetiaux, in a work published in

As to what may be the cause of crime in Ireland we are not in a position to speak, not having given any special attention to the matter; but the reason why there appears a greater proportion of Irish among the thieves and vagrants of our own country, admits of a very ready explanation. The Irish constitute the poorest portion of our people, and the children, therefore, are virtually orphans in this country, left to gambol in the streets and courts, without parental control, from their very earliest years; the mothers, as well as the fathers, being generally engaged throughout the day in some of the ruder forms of labour or street trade. The consequence is, that the child grows up not only unacquainted with any industrial occupation, but untrained to habits of daily work; and long before he has learned to control the desire to appropriate the articles which he either wants or likes, by a sense of the rights of property in others, he has acquired furtive propensities from association with the young thieves located in his neighbourhood.

He has learnt, too, what is much worse, thieves' morals—morals which, once in the heart, it is almost hopeless to attempt to root out. He has learnt to look upon "pluck," or daring, as the greatest virtue of life; he has learnt to regard all those who labour for an honest living as "flats," or, in plain English, fools; he has learnt to consider trickery, or "artful dodges," as he calls them, as the highest possible exercise of the intellect, and to believe that the main object in life is amusement rather than labour. His attention has never been trained to occupy itself with any one subject for five minutes together, nor have his impulses been placed under the least restraint. What wonder, then, that he grows up a mere savage amongst civilized men!

But whatever be the cause, the fact is incontestible, that a very large proportion of the juvenile prisoners are the children of Irish parents. Indeed, as one looks up and down the

1835, entitled, '*Statisque Comparée de la Criminalité en France, en Belgique, en Angleterre et en Allemagne*,' gives the following results of the several official returns:—Of England, from 1827 to 1833, taking the population at 13,500,000 ; of France, from 1825 to 1832, population 32,500,000 ; and of Belgium, from 1826 to 1832, population 4,000,000."

Countries.	Annual Average.			Number Accused to every 10,000 of Population.
	Total Accused.	Acquitted.	Condemned.	
England	16,924	3,556	13,368	12·5
France	7,340	2,954	4,386	2·3
Belgium	766	142	624	1·9

Mr. Clarke, the Local Inspector and Chaplain of the jail in the county Donegal, Ireland, furnishes the following comparative statistics of crime in England, Scotland, and Ireland in 1852 :—

TABLE SHOWING THE PROPORTION OF, OR PERSONS CHARGED WITH, CRIMINAL OFFENCES TO THE POPULATION (EXCLUSIVE OF CASES OF SUMMARY JURISDICTION) IN EACH OF THE THREE DIVISIONS OF THE UNITED KINGDOM.

Division.	Population in 1851.	Number of Accused in 1852.	Number of Accused in every 10,000 of the Population.
England and Wales .	17,922,768	27,510	15·3
Ireland	6,515,794	17,678	27·2
Scotland.	2,870,784	4,027	14·0
United Kingdom . .	27,309,346	49,215	18·0

different forms in the boys' oakum-room at Tothill Fields, the unmistakable gray eyes are found to prevail among the little felons assembled there.*

* We have been at considerable pains to ascertain, from the Government Returns, the districts furnishing the greatest number of juvenile offenders. For this purpose, we have collated the records furnished in the Reports of the Inspectors of Prisons for five years consecutively, and ascertained the annual average number of prisoners of all ages, as well as the annual average number of those under 17 years of age—or, in other words, the juvenile offenders for each county in England and Wales. We have then estimated the proportion per cent. that the juvenile offenders bear to those of all ages. The result is given in the following table :—

TABLE SHOWING THE ANNUAL AVERAGE PER CENTAGE OF JUVENILE PRISONERS TO THE GROSS PRISON POPULATION, OF ALL AGES, FOR EACH COUNTY IN ENGLAND AND WALES, FROM 1849-53 (BOTH INCLUSIVE).

COUNTIES.	Annual average number of prisoners of all ages.	Annual average number of juvenile prisoners.	Annual average per centage of juvenile prisoners.	COUNTIES.	Annual average number of prisoners of all ages.	Annual average number of juvenile prisoners.	Annual average per centage of juvenile prisoners.
Bedford . .	813·6	45·2	5·5	Norfolk . . .	2406·8	313·6	14·0
Berks . . .	1408·2	146·8	10·4	Northampton . .	1196·0	87·0	7·2
Bucks . .	913·8	83·8	9·1	Northumberland.	2338·2	383·2	16·3
Cambridge . .	1436·2	122·0	8·5	Nottingham . .	1420·0	145·8	10·2
Chester . .	3472·4	375·8	10·8	Oxford	1251·6	98·0	7·9
Cornwall . .	865·0	86·4	9·9	Rutland . . .	104·6	11·0	10·5
Cumberland . .	703·0	80·0	11·3	Salop	1297·4	112·8	8·5
Derby . . .	1218·2	117·6	9·6	Somerset . . .	4413·8	670·8	15·2
Devon . . .	3047·8	306·0	10·0	Southampton . .	2776·6	298·2	10·7
Dorset . . .	986·4	107·2	10·8	Stafford . . .	3970·4	328·2	8·2
Durham . .	2058·0	126·2	6·1	Suffolk . . .	1958·6	175·0	8·4
Essex . . .	2345·6	266·6	11·3	Surrey	8403·0	1231·8	14·6
Gloucester . .	2652·8	317·2	11·9	Sussex . . .	1872·6	215·4	11·5
Hereford . .	617·8	41·2	6·6	Warwick . . .	3479·2	481·2	13·8
Hertford . .	1117·6	91·2	8·1	Westmoreland .	319·2	20·0	6·2
Huntingdon .	384·4	24·6	6·4	Wilts	1509·6	118·8	7·8
Kent	4663·6	432·8	9·3	Worcester. . .	1611·2	160·6	9·9
Lancaster . .	2114·0	2438·2	11·0	York	11368·8	1041·0	9·1
Leicester . .	1588·2	153·4	9·6	North Wales . .	970·8	51·2	5·2
Lincoln . .	2489·0	203·0	8·1	South Wales . .	2363·2	126·4	5·3
Middlesex . .	2556·2	4275·4	13·1	Total for England and Wales .	143769·8	16008·2	11·1
Monmouth .	1085·0	82·4	7·6				

Arranging, then, the counties in their order, according as the per centage of juvenile offenders is either above or below the general average for the whole country, we have the subjoined result :—

Counties in which the Proportion of Juvenile Prisoners is Above the Average.

Northumberland .	16·3	Norfolk	14·0	Gloucester . . .	11·9	Essex	11·3
Somerset . . .	15·2	Warwick . . .	13·8	Sussex	11·5	Cumberland . ..	11·3
Surrey	14·6	Middlesex . . .	13·1				

Counties in which the Proportion of Juvenile Prisoners is Below the Average.

Lancaster . . .	11·0	Cornwall . . .	9·9	Shropshire . . .	8·5	Northampton . .	7·2
Chester . . .	10·8	Worcester . . .	9·9	Suffolk	8·4	Hereford . . .	6·6
Dorset . . .	10·8	Leicester . . .	9·6	Stafford	8·2	Huntingdon . .	6·4
Southampton . .	10·7	Derby	9·6	Hertford . . .	8·1	Westmoreland . .	6·2
Rutland . . .	10·5	Kent	9·3	Lincoln	8·1	Durham . . .	6·1
Berks	10·4	Bucks	9·1	Oxford	7·9	Bedford . . .	5·5
Notts	10·2	York	9·1	Wilts	7·8	South Wales . .	5·3
Devon	10·0	Cambridge . . .	8·5	Monmouth . . .	7·6	North Wales . .	5·2

Average for all England and Wales . . . . . 11·1

Hence we perceive that those counties in which the large towns are situate furnish the greater proportion of young criminals; for, whereas there is upon an average but 11 juvenile offenders in every 100 prisoners throughout England and Wales, Northumberland (in which the town of Newcastle is situate) has

We know of no sight in London so terribly pathetic—if not tragic—as this same oakum-room, at the boys' prison at Westminster. We envy not the man who can enter a jail with the same light heart as he goes to a theatre. To behold large numbers of men-, or even women-, felons—dense masses of wild passions, as it were, gathered together under one roof, such as one sees either working, like so many spectres, in the large rooms at Coldbath Fields, or praying with one voice in the chapels of the convict prisons, or sleeping in their hammocks between the decks at the Hulks—is a scene that always stirs the heart and brain with thoughts too deep for utterance. The ordinary citizen knows crime only as an ex-

no less than 16 in the 100; while Somerset, of which Bristol is the chief town, yields 15 in the 100. Again, Surrey, from its connection with the Metropolis, Norfolk (of which Norwich is an integrant part), and Warwick (to which Birmingham belongs), and Middlesex (London), and Gloucester (the city of Gloucester), all return from 14½ to 12 young "jail birds" to each century of prisoners. So, too, Lancaster (the seat of Liverpool and Manchester) and Chester show so large a per centage, as to be only just *below* the average; whilst the more primitive districts of Westmoreland and Durham, and the various parts of North and South Wales, give only between 5 and 6 per cent. of youthful delinquents.

As regards the Metropolis itself, the annexed table (which has been kindly furnished to us by one of the Middlesex magistrates) shows that 41 per cent. of the boys confined in Tothill Fields prison, are sent from the Great Marlborough Street police-office, and 24 per cent. from Bow Street ditto; whilst the districts of Clerkenwell and Marylebone supply only 8 per cent. respectively, and Westminster and the Thames police-office each nearly 5½ per cent.; making altogether about 94½ in every 100 young criminals sent by the metropolitan districts, and leaving only about 5½ for those coming from the rural districts of the county of Middlesex. Of the latter, again, it will be seen that Hammersmith furnishes by far the greater proportion. Then follows Uxbridge, then Brentford, Barnet, and Twickenham; whilst Hounslow, Highgate, Tottenham, Enfield, and Southall, contribute none to the returns, which, it should be remembered, have in all instances been made to comprise a series of years.

TABLE SHOWING THE PLACES FROM WHICH THE BOY-PRISONERS AT TOTHILL FIELDS WERE COMMITTED DURING THE YEARS ENDING 1852-54.

	1852.		1853.		1854.		Total.	Mean.	Per centage.
	Under 12 years of age.	12 and under 14.	Under 12.	12 and under 14.	Under 12.	12 and under 14.			
Metropolitan Districts—									
Great Marlborough Street .	5	13	22	22	14	19	95	31	41·9
Bow Street	4	27	8	9	3	5	56	18	24·3
Clerkenwell	2	3	2	3	—	7	17	6	8·1
Marylebone	—	—	2	5	5	5	17	6	8·1
Westminster	1	6	1	2	2	1	13	4	5·4
Thames Police-court	—	—	1	7	1	2	11	4	5·4
Worship Street	—	—	—	1	1	—	2	1	1·3
Total Metropolitan	12	49	36	49	26	39	211	70	94·6
Rural Districts—									
Hammersmith	—	1	—	—	3	3	7	2	2·7
Uxbridge	—	—	—	1	—	1	2	1	1·3
Brentford	—	—	—	—	—	1	1	—	—
Barnet	—	—	—	—	1	—	1	—	—
Twickenham	—	—	—	—	—	1	1	—	—
Hounslow	—	—	—	—	—	—	—	—	—
Highgate	—	—	—	—	—	—	—	—	—
Tottenham	—	—	—	—	—	—	—	—	—
Enfield	—	—	—	—	—	—	—	—	—
Southall	—	—	—	—	—	—	—	—	—
Total Rural	—	1	—	1	4	6	12	4	5·4
Grand Total Metropolitan and Rural.	12	50	36	50	30	45	223	74	100

ceptional thing—he hears or reads of merely *individual* instances, and has never been accustomed to think of it, much more to look upon it *in the mass;* so that the first sight of a large concourse of thieves, and murderers, and cheats, fills him with entirely new impressions. Crime seems then to be as much a part of the organization of society as even religion itself; and soon there follows the inquiry—Must such things always be? Though we get rid of some two thousand old criminals every year, will there ever be some two thousand young ones ready to spring into their place?*

The answer to the question is to be found only in such places as we are now describing. We have before spoken of convict-nurseries—of baby-felons, born and suckled in prison; and now we have to speak of felon-academies, where the young offender is duly trained and educated for the Hulks. True, the place is called a house of correction; but, rightly viewed, it is simply a criminal preparatory school, where students are qualified for matriculating at Millbank or Pentonville. Here we find little creatures of six years of age branded with a felon's badge—boys, not even in their teens, clad in the prison dress, for the heinous offence of throwing stones, or obstructing highways, or unlawfully knocking at doors—crimes which the very magistrates themselves, who committed the youths, must have assuredly perpetrated in their boyhood, and which, if equally visited, would consign almost every child in the kingdom to a jail.

A table of the ages of the wretched little beings confined in Tothill Fields prison affords a wondrous insight into the criminal history of the country. Between the years 1851 and 1855 there were upwards of 9,000 boys, under seventeen years of age, committed to the House of Correction at Westminster. This gives an annual average of 1,800 and odd, and of these, upwards of 1,500, or about 85½ per cent., were committed by the magistrates; whilst, of the number so committed, 945 were between fourteen and seventeen years of age,

* THE ANNEXED TABLE SHOWS THE NUMBER OF TRANSPORTS FOR A SERIES OF YEARS:—

	Years.	Total number convicted at Assizes and Sessions.	Total number of Transports.	Proportion per cent. of Transports to total number Convicted.	Proportion of Transports per 10,000 gross population of England and Wales.
ENGLAND AND WALES	1841	19,548	3,788	19·38	23·80
	1842	22,513	4,229	18·79	26·26
	1843	21,425	4,166	19·44	25·57
	1844	19,054	3,437	18·04	20·84
	1845	17,932	3,092	17·25	18·53
	1846	18,071	2,894	16·02	17·13
	1847	28,121	2,726	13·10	15·95
	1848	22,856	3,207	14·04	18·55
	1849	21,715	3,099	14·27	17·71
	1850	20,308	2,514	12·38	14·20
	1851	21,663	2,943	13·58	16·40
	1852	21,160	3,860	18·24	21·25
	1853	20,642	2,526	12·24	13·72
Annual mean		20,593	3,268	15·91	19·22

Hence it would appear that the average number of transports is, in round numbers, about 3,250 per annum, and this out of a total of 20,500 convicted, which is an average of about 16 per cent. of the gross number found guilty, or very nearly 2 in every 10,000 of the whole population of the country. By a table before given (see *ante*, p. 97), it was shown that the number actually transported during the twenty years from 1830 to 1850, yielded an average of 2,477 per annum. Of the transports, one-half, or 50·9 in every 100, are, upon the average, sentenced to 7 and under 10 years' term; 31·7 to 10 and under 14 years; 3·5 to 14 and under 15 years; 8·8 to 15 years and under 21; 0·9 to 21 years and upwards; and 4·3 for life.

398 between twelve and fourteen, and 209 less than twelve; so that, out of every 100 boys sent to this prison, it would appear that no less than 13½ are mere children. The details are given as under:—

TABLE SHOWING THE AGES OF THE BOY-PRISONERS CONFINED IN THE WESTMINSTER HOUSE OF CORRECTION, DURING THE YEARS ENDING MICHAELMAS, 1851—55, AS WELL AS THE AVERAGE NUMBER FOR ALL ENGLAND AND WALES.

	Summarily convicted.				Convicted at Sessions.	Total.
	Under 12 years of age.	12 and under 14.	14 and under 17.	Total.		
1851	184	391	906	1,481	291	1,772
1852	168	424	941	1,533	308	1,841
1853	204	314	930	1,448	235	1,683
1854	268	414	973	1,655	227	1,882
1855	222	446	978	1,646	263	1,909
Total . .	1,046	1,989	4,728	7,763	1,324	9,087
Annual mean . .	209	398	945	1,552	265	1,817
Per centage . .	13·5	25·6	60·9	85·4	14·6	100
Annual mean of all England and Wales for 1841-51	856	1,697	4,926	7,479	2,560	10,039
Per centage . .	11·4	22·7	63·9	74·5	25·5	100·0

Here we perceive that there are 10 per cent. more boys committed to prison by the Middlesex magistrates than by those of the country generally; and of those so committed, the proportion of young offenders, under 14 years, is considerably beyond that of all England and Wales.

Now, it is a principle of justice that all persons who are not of *sane* mind are legally irresponsible for their acts; and, surely, if the law itself allow that none are fit to be trusted with the care of property, or the exercise of any political privilege, until they are 21 years of age—all below that term being legal "infants"—and if religion itself assert that the young are incapable of sin until they have reached the years of discretion, it can be neither just nor righteous to condemn, as felons, little things that are as unable to appreciate the principle of the rights of property, as they are to comprehend the Divine Nature itself.

The time is assuredly not far distant when our treatment of what are termed juvenile offenders, will be ranked in the same barbarous category with the manner in which we formerly dealt with the insane and idiotic. If any doubt the truth of such a statement, let them pay a visit to Tothill Fields prison, and see there young creatures, whose years even a savage could reckon up, with half-military officers to watch over them, and immured in a building whose walls are as thick as those of a fortress, and the gates as solid as the door to an iron safe.

If it were not for the pathos of the place, we really believe this boys' prison would rank as the great laughing-stock of the age; for here one finds all the pompous paraphernalia of Visiting Justices, and Governors. and Warders, with bunches of keys dangling from thick chains, and strings of cutlasses hanging over the mantelpiece of the entrance-office—and all to take care of the little desperate malefactors, not one of whom has cut his "wisdom teeth;" whilst many are so young that they seem better fitted to be conveyed to the place in a perambulator, than in the lumbering and formidable prison van.

Still, the consequences of our wicked treatment of these poor children are too serious for jesting. Suppose you or I, reader, had been consigned to such a place in our school-boy days, for those acts of thoughtlessness which none but fanatics would think of regarding as *crime*. Suppose *we* had had to spend fourteen days at picking oakum, in a prison, for every runaway knock we had given, or every stone we had thrown, or even for every act of petty dishonesty we had committed—what think you would have been the effect of such treatment on our after-lives? Had we been herded with young thieves in our youth, is it likely we should ever have grown to be gentlemen? Had the prison been stripped of its terror and its shame in our childhood, do you think we should have lived to dread entering it after we arrived at man's estate?

Puritans should remember, moreover, that theft is a *natural* propensity of the human constitution, and honesty an *artificial* and *educated* sentiment. We do not come into the world with an instinctive sense of the rights of property implanted in our bosom, to teach us to respect the possessions of others, but rather with an innate desire to appropriate whatever we may fancy. It is only *by long training and schooling* that we are made to see it is but just, that every one should enjoy that which he himself creates or earns, and it is this *developed* idea of justice that serves, in after years, to keep our hands from picking and stealing. On our return from Tothill Fields, we consulted with some of our friends as to the various peccadilloes of their youth, and though each we asked had grown to be a man of some little mark in the world, both for intellect and honour, they, one and all, confessed to having committed in their younger days many of the very "*crimes*" for which the boys at Tothill Fields were incarcerated. For ourselves, we will frankly confess that at Westminster School, where we passed some seven years of our boyhood, such acts were daily perpetrated; and yet if the scholars had been sent to the House of Correction, instead of Cambridge or Oxford, to complete their education, the country would now have seen many of our playmates working among the convicts in the dock-yards, rather than lending dignity to the senate or honour to the bench.

At the time of our visit to Tothill Fields, two incidents occurred which may serve to give the reader some slight notion as to the evils of such places as the Westminster House of Correction. Standing within the prison gateway was a man whose heavy boots were yellow with dry clay, and whose plush waistcoat gave signs of his being either some "navvy" or brickmaker. The man touched his fur-cap as we passed, and hoped we would help him with a trifle to carry him and his boy (who was about to be liberated) towards Enfield. The child was eight years old, we learnt; his offence had been stealing some half-dozen plums from an orchard—his sentence fourteen days' imprisonment and a flogging!

On another occasion, we requested permission of the Chairman of the Visiting Justices to be allowed to have a sketch made of the serving of the breakfast in the large room of the boys' prison. The answer was, that the magistrates thought it inexpedient to allow us to do so, for that in the other engravings we had already published, the prison appeared by far too comfortable to please their minds, and that if we could select any object of a *deterrent* character we should be at liberty to engrave *that*.

The latter anecdote affords a striking instance of the defects of the present system, especially when coupled with the former, for the two are as intimately conjoined as cause and effect. In the one we see an over-disposition to make children, of almost tender years, acquainted with the economy of a prison, and that even for faults of a comparatively trivial character—or faults, at least, that need a teacher rather than a jailer to correct; whereas, in the other instance, we find the very magistrates themselves afraid of making known the internal regulations of the jail over which they preside. That there is nothing especially terrible in the arrangements at Tothill Fields surely is no fault of ours; and yet, though the place is almost a paradise in comparison with the hovels to which the poor little inmates have been generally accustomed, and the food positive luxury to their ordinary fare when at liberty, still these same justices continue to consign little creatures to the prison, and that often for offences which they know their own children commit day after day.

Our prisons (and more especially the correctional ones) are getting to be regarded as refuges by a large proportion of our outcasts. We have before shown that at Coldbath Fields the proportion *recommitted* is no less than 33 per cent. of the whole number of prisoners. At Tothill Fields, however, the ratio is even higher, as will be seen by the following:—

TABLE SHOWING THE NUMBER OF BOY-PRISONERS WHO HAVE BEEN PREVIOUSLY COMMITTED TO THE WESTMINSTER HOUSE OF CORRECTION DURING THE YEARS ENDING MICHAELMAS, 1851-55.

Years, &c.	Previously Committed.					Total No. of committals.
	Once.	Twice.	Thrice.	Four times and more.	Total No. recommitted.	
1851	364	128	54	152	698	1,772
1852	361	184	80	257	882	1,841
1853	330	183	97	253	863	1,683
1854	316	154	97	341	908	1,882
1855	342	208	82	266	898	1,909
Total	1,713	857	410	1,269	4,249	9,087
Annual mean .	342	171	82	254	849	1,817
Per centage .	18·8	9·4	4·5	14·0	46·7	100·

Here, then, we find, according to the returns of the last five years, that not one-third, as at Coldbath Fields, nor one-fourth, as is the average for all the prisons of England and Wales, but *very nearly one-half of the boys at Tothill Fields are recommitted each year*, so that the jail there, instead of being a place of terror and aversion to the young criminals, is really made an asylum and a home by many of them. No wonder, then, that the magistrates wished us to find out and depict some "deterrent" about the place. Justices, however, have still to learn the great penal lesson, viz., to keep a person out of prison as long as possible—to use the jail as the very last resource of all, and to understand that if it were made a thousand times as terrible as it is, it would be even then far less awful in reality than in imagination. The rule with the Middlesex magistrates, though, appears to be the very reverse, viz., to thrust a lad into prison on the most trifling occasion, and to familiarize him, even in his childhood, with scenes that he should be made acquainted with the very last of all in his manhood. That government is the best, says the English axiom, which governs the least—consistently with order and decency; and so we say again, that penal discipline is the most efficacious which punishes as little as possible—consistently with justice and propriety.

The subjoined table shows the proportion of recommittals throughout England and Wales, and it will be seen that the average ratio of prisoners recommitted barely exceeds 25 per cent., whereas it has been before shown that the proportion at Tothill Fields amounts very nearly to 50 per cent.

At Tothill Fields, it will be observed, the proportion of prisoners once recommitted to that prison is upwards of 7 per cent. in excess of that for the country generally; whilst of those who are *four times and more* recommitted, there is the same excessive proportion likewise.

TABLE SHOWING THE TOTAL NUMBER OF PRISONERS, IN THE PRISONS OF ENGLAND AND WALES, WHO HAVE BEEN ASCERTAINED TO HAVE BEEN RECOMMITTED, AS WELL AS THE PROPORTIONS PER CENT. OF EACH CLASS OF RECOMMITTALS TO THE GROSS PRISON POPULATION, FOR EACH YEAR FROM 1841 TO 1853, BOTH INCLUSIVE.

YEARS.	Once recommitted.	Twice recommitted.	Thrice recommitted.	Four times or more recommitted.	Total of recommittals.	Total of criminal population.
1841. Number of prisoners	15,356	6,398	4,508	6,565	32,827	128,190
Proportion per cent.	12·5	5·0	3·0	5·1	25·6	100·0
1842. Number of prisoners	16,792	6,826	3,491	6,753	33,862	139,388
Proportion per cent.	12·1	4·9	2·5	4·8	24·3	100·0
1843. Number of prisoners	16,367	7,064	3,541	7,411	34,383	140.218
Proportion per cent.	11·7	5·0	2·5	5·3	24·5	100·0
1844. Number of prisoners	15,781	6.849	3,661	8,440	34,731	136,558
Proportion per cent.	11·5	5·0	2·7	6·2	25·4	100·0
1845. Number of prisoners	14,324	6,496	3,729	8,564	33,113	126,794
Proportion per cent.	11·3	5·1	2·9	6·8	26·1	100·0
1846. Number of prisoners	13,585	6,245	3,568	9,060	32,458	124,452
Proportion per cent.	10·9	5·0	2·9	7·3	26·1	100·0
1847. Number of prisoners	14,417	6,419	3,347	8,742	32,925	131,191
Proportion per cent.	10·9	4·9	2·5	6·6	24·9	100·0
1848. Number of prisoners	16,759	7,204	3,749	9,513	37,225	150,611
Proportion per cent.	11·1	4·8	2·5	6·3	24·7	100·0
1849. Number of prisoners	1,857	7,792	3,945	9,932	39,826	157,273
Proportion per cent.	11·6	4·9	2·5	6·3	26·3	100·0
1850. Number of prisoners	16,463	7,319	4,003	9,639	37,424	142.094
Proportion per cent.	11·6	5·1	2·8	6·8	26·3	100·0
1851. Number of prisoners	16.827	7,226	3,793	8,924	36,820	147,725
Proportion per cent.	11·4	5·0	2·5	6·0	24·9	100·0
1852. Number of prisoners	15,427	6,596	3,620	8,953	34,596	139.688
Proportion per cent.	11·0	4·7	2·6	6·4	24·7	100·0
1853. Number of prisoners	14,421	6,695	3,536	8,886	33,565	132,069
Proportion per cent.	10·9	5·1	2·7	6·7	25·4	100·0
Annual mean number of prisoners	15,744	6,860	3,732	8,668	34,904	138,250
Proportion per cent.	11·4	5·0	2·7	6·2	25·3	100·0
Proportion per cent. at Tothill Fields	18·8	9·4	4·5	14·0	46 7	100·0

But the reader may desire facts rather than strictures upon such matters.

Let us deal, then, first with the class of Misdemeanants. Well, as we said, these are clad in blue, and seated on one of the lower forms in the oakum-room. We questioned the boys severally as to the offences for which they were imprisoned, and subjoin a list of the answers, taken down in the presence of the chief warder.

"What are you here for, boy?" said we.

"Heaving a highster-shell through a street-lamp, please, sir," was the reply.

"He's been in here before three times," said the warder; "and very probably committed the offence merely to get another month's shelter in the place."

"And you?" we asked, passing on to another.

"A woman said I hit her babby."

"And you?"

"Heaving clay." This one had been fourteen times in the same prison—"Mostly for cadging, sir," interrupted the urchin; "and only twice of them times for prigging." "He's a young crossing-sweeper," said the warder, "and is generally to be seen about the West End when he's out."

"Heaving stones," exclaimed another, as we moved towards him.

"Threatening to stab another boy, sir." "Four times in prison before," the officer added.

"Stealing a bell in a garden, please, sir."

"Heaving stones, sir."

"Heaving stones." In four times before.

"Heaving stones."

"Heaving stones."

Here, then, out of ten cases, there was only one of a malicious and two of a criminal character; whilst the majority were imprisoned for such offences as all boys commit, and for which imprisonment among thieves is surely the worst possible remedy.

At a later part of the day we accompanied the warder to the airing-yard, to see the boys exercising. This was done much after the fashion of other prisons, the lads circling round and round, and each walking some six or seven feet apart from those next him. There were about forty boys altogether in the yard. "They exercise," said the warder, "in detachments, for about an hour each; we keep them walking briskly, and in cold mornings we make them move along in double quick time."

As the little troop paced over the flag-stones, their heavy prison boots sounded very differently from what their naked feet are wont to do when outside the prison gates; and we could tell, by their shuffling noise and limping gait, how little used many of them had been to such a luxury as shoe leather. Then each boy had a small red cotton pocket-handkerchief tied to the button-hole of his jacket (for no pockets are allowed in the prison garb), and we could not help wondering how many of the forty young "offenders" there, had ever before known the use of such an article.

While the lads kept on filing past us, the chief warder, at our request, called over the number of times that those who had been recommitted had been previously in prison. This he did merely by quoting to us the red figures stitched to the arm of the "known" delinquents.

The following cyphers indicate the number of recommittals among the band:—4, 3, 2, 4, 2, 10, 3, 3, 10, 7, 6, 3, 4, 3, 4, 4, 2, 4, 6, 4, 3, 9, 2, 4, 2. Thus we see that, out of the 40 exercising in the yard, there were no less than 25 who had paid many previous visits to the prison.

After this, one of the lads, who had been ten times recommitted, was called from out of the ranks, and questioned as to his age and antecedents.

"How old are you, boy?"

" Thirteen years, please, sir."

" What are you in for?"

" Coat and umbereller, sir. This makes seven times here and three times at Coldbath Fields, please, sir."

" How long have you got now?"

" Three calendar months. This makes four times, please, sir, that I've had three calendar months, and I've had two two-monthses as well—one of the two monthses here, and one at Coldbath Fields; and I've done one six weeks, and one two days besides, sir. It's mostly been for prigging," added the young urchin.

" What did you take?"

" I took a watch and chain once, sir, and a pair of goold bracelets another time. I did a till twice, and this time it's for the coat and umbereller, as I told you on afore. The two days I had was for a bottle of pickles, but that there was three or four year ago."

" Oh, father's in a consumptive hospital down in the country," he went on, in answer to our queries. " Mother's at home, and she lives in S—— Street, in the Gray's Inn Road."

" Why, I began thieving about four year ago, please, sir," he said, in answer to us. " I went out with a butcher-boy. He's got four year penal servitude now."

" Did I ever go out to work? Oh, yes, sir. I was at work at a brush-maker's for about five months, and I've worked at Mr. Cubitt's in the Gray's Inn Road. I go out with one boy when I go prigging. I went into the shop with a bit of a old seal to sell, when I took the watch; and I tried on the same dodge when I took the pair of goold bracelets. Mother mends china and glass, please, sir. I don't mean to go out prigging no more. Not if I can get any work, I won't."

This boy was a sharp-featured cunning-looking young vagabond, with a pucker at the corners of his mouth, that showed (though his eyes were cast down in affected penitence) that he was ready to break into laughter at the least breach of gravity. Indeed, he needed but the man's body-coat with the tails dragging on the ground, and the trousers tied up with string instead of braces, and bare muddy feet, to mark him as one of the confirmed young London thieves. Whether this was the result of innate vice, or owing to the want of proper paternal care (his father, be it remembered, was in a consumption hospital, whilst his mother went out mending china), we leave it for others to say. Assuredly, had he been sent to a school for some few years, instead of to a prison for two days, when he stole the bottle of pickles, there might have been some chance of reclaiming him; but now the task seemed almost hopeless. In a few years more he will, probably, be at one of the convict prisons, swelling the numbers of the old experienced offenders.

But do not let us judge by isolated instances.

Here is the case of another of the boys, whose red mark on the sleeve of his jacket showed that he, too, had been ten times in prison before.

" Sixteen years of age, please, sir," said the lad, " and in for stealing a coat. I've been at prigging about four year. I had one calendar month here for a pair of boots. Then I stole a box of silver pencil-cases from a jeweller's shop. I bought an old aypenny ring, and broke it up, and while the gennelman was looking at it to see whether it was goold or not, I slipped the pencil-cases under my coat. I got four calendar months for that there, sir. Then I was took for two bundles of cigars, and had one month here. After that I was took for some meerschaum pipes, and had another month. I was took for a coat besides, and got three calendar months in Coldbath Fields. I guv my age seventeen that time, so as to get sent there. I guv it seventeen this time, too, but they was fly to it."

" Why would you rather go to Coldbath Fields?" we inquired.

" Oh, I'd choose anything for a change, sir," was the characteristic and candid reply.

" Then I was sent to Holloway for tossing," went on the boy, " and had fourteen days of it there. I don't know what I was took for the other time. Father's a hingineer, and I aint got no mother, please, sir. I've been to work with father when I've come out from my 'prisonments, but I've soon cut it and gone thieving again. I've been in a national school and a philanthropic over by Bedlam—it's called the House of Occupation."

We next inquired as to what he intended to do when he regained his liberty once more.

" Do ?" he answered, without the least fear, though the warder stood at his side, "Why, when I gets out here I shall go thieving again."

" But why ?" we asked.

" Why I shall go thieving, cos I aint got no other way of gettin' a living."

" But won't your father keep you ?" said we.

"Oh! father," echoed the boy in a tone of disrespect ; "he'll think he's got enough to do to keep his-self."

"Would he turn you from his door then?" was our next question.

" Oh no, he wouldn't turn me out. He'd give me a lodging and ' vittles,' and if I got any work he'd do all he could to help me ; but, you see, I don't like work, and I don't like being at home neither. I seem to like thieving. Still if I got work this time, though I mightn't like it at first, I'd try to keep to it."

This boy, unlike the other, had a frank and open countenance, and bore none of the signs of London roguery impressed upon his features. Nevertheless, our experience among this peculiar class of characters has taught us to place little or no reliance upon either physiognomical or phrenological traits. Indeed we have often speculated in company with the warders on such matters, and generally found that the prisoners whom we picked out as the better class of characters were far from being so in the estimation of their jailers. There is a natural disposition to believe that physical and moral beauty are some way connected— though really they are conjoined only in the association of ideas, and there is no rational cause why the best-looking should not be ill-natured, and even the deformed possessed of the highest virtue. It must be admitted, however, that dwarves generally are not remarkable for their kindness of heart, and that handsome people, on the other hand, are likely to grow vicious from their personal vanity and craving for admiration.

But crime, we repeat, is an effect with which the shape of the head and the form of the features appear (so far as our observation goes) to have no connection whatever—indeed it seems to us, in the majority of instances, to be the accident of parentage and organization. Granted that a being of intense energy of character may be able to overcome the taint of birth in a prison nursery, and that indomitable will may rise superior even to convict extraction. But with the general run of human beings the rule would seem to be, that a felon father or mother generally begets a felon child, and that orphanage, either actual or virtual, is usually attended with the same result among the very poor—being bereft of parents seeming to be equivalent in its moral effects to being born of bad or too indulgent ones. " Of the children," says Mr. Antrobus, in the Special Report of the Visiting Justices, " a large proportion have either nominal stepfathers or stepmothers, fathers or mothers, brothers or sisters, who have become criminal—parents, who are constantly in a state of intoxication, or living surrounded by destitution and misery ; whilst very many are without even a relation or a friend." Again, we say the great mass of crime in this country is committed by those who have been bred and born to the business, and who make a regular trade of it—living as systematically by robbery or cheating as others do by commerce or the exercise of intellectual or manual labour ; and the records of the country show, when duly analysed and systematised, that in every 10,000 of our population there are 15 criminals annually accused of some offence or other, whilst of these 15 not less than $12\frac{1}{2}$ are charged with acts that those only could perform who had been regularly reared and educated to the " profession."

Here, for example, is a short conversation that we entered into with another lad, while visiting this prison. The boy had a badge on his arm, that showed he had been as many as fourteen times in prison, though he was certainly not that number of years old.

"Where do you live, lad?" said we to him.

"No. 21, S—— Street, Gray's Inn Lane," returned the youngster, as he looked with a half-impudent leer up into our face.

"But that's where your father and mother live, isn't it?" said the warder.

"Yes, father lives in S—— Street, and I lives in a lodging-house, in Charles Street, Drury Lane," was the urchin's answer.

"Why don't you live with your father and mother?"

"Cos father won't keep me unless I'm at work."

"But won't he let you stay with him till you get work?"

"No, that he won't—not even when I go out here; and that's why I go to the lodging-house."

"Do you go thieving from that place?" we asked.

"Yes; I goes out thieving with other boys," was the unabashed reply of the young vagabond. "Been fourteen times in prison," he added, smiling, as if proud of the fact, when he saw us looking at the figures on his arm, in order to assure ourselves of the truth of his numerous recommitments. "I have had three calender months four times," he ran on, "and one fourteen days, and I don't know how many two monthses and monthses besides."

"And when you leave this prison, you'll go out with the other boys thieving again, I suppose?" asked we.

"No, I aint a-going this time; for I means to hook it, and go to sea."

At another part of the day we saw some eighteen more prisoners exercising in one of the airing-yards, and again, as the boys filed past us, we copied down in our note-book the red figures on their sleeves, indicating the number of times they had, respectively, been recommitted to prison.

Here is the result :—10, 2, 4, 7, 7, 3, 6, 2, 14, 7, 12, 10, 2, 4.

Who, then, can doubt that our prisons are really becoming refuges, or who can wonder at the fact, when the late Chairman of the Visiting Justices tells us that the parents of numbers of the young prisoners live "surrounded by destitution and misery, and very many without even a relation or a friend. Under these circumstances," add the Justices themselves, in their last Special Report, "it cannot be a matter of surprise that so many commit offences which consign them to the prison;" especially, it should be said, when the prison is so much more comfortable than their own homes. Now, it must not be imagined, from the latter remark, that we believe our jails can be emptied by rendering them of a more deterrent character—the experiment has been tried long ago, and found to be a disgraceful failure. It is impossible, in the present age, with the advanced notions of society as to its duties even to the criminal, to reduce the prison food, or the prison clothing, or the prison accommodation, to any sterner standard; for the diet has been nicely calculated, and pared down to the precise quantity sufficient to support life, and health, and strength, on the most economical principles; the clothing, on the other hand, is merely such as is required to retain the warmth of the body, and the accommodation that only which is necessary for the prevention of disease, by the too close crowding of the inmates; nor can we ever again indulge in the thumb-screws, or other barbarous tortures, by which our forefathers thought to goad men into fancied rectitude. All such things, thank God, have passed away for ever, and those who still uphold them are as much unfitted for the age in which they live, as Zadkiel, the astrologer, or the "table-turners," or "spirit-rappers," and the like.

There is but one way to empty our prisons, and that is by paying attention to the outcast children of the land. So long as the State forgets its paternal duty, just so long must it expect its offspring to grow up vicious and dishonest; and it is simply for our wicked neglect of the poor desolate and destitute little creatures about us, that our country swarms with what are termed "the dangerous classes," and our people, tested by the national records, appear to be more than sevenfold as criminal as our Catholic neighbours in France and Belgium. For it is plain that if the State would but become the foster-father of the wretched little orphans that now it leaves magistrates to thrust into jail, and if it would but train them to habits of industry and rectitude, instead of allowing them to grow up utterly unskilled in any form of honest labour, and, moreover, thoroughly ignorant of all rights and duties, as well as being not only insensible to the dignities and virtues of life, but positively taught to believe that the admirable lies in all that is base and hideous.*

We still considered it necessary, for the thorough elucidation of our subject to interrogate each of the prisoners in the large work-room as to their age, the number of times they had been in prison, and the offences for which they had been sentenced. The particulars of our investigation are here subjoined:—

1st Prisoner,	14 years of age,	10 times in prison,	for	picking pockets.
2nd	,,	16	,,	4	,,	stealing copper nails.
3rd	,,	16	,,	4	,,	picking pockets.
4th	,,	15	,,	2	,,	,, ,,
5th	,,	14	,,	16	,,	area sneaking.
6th	,,	13	,,	2	,,	picking pockets.
7th	,,	15	,,	4	,,	stealing lead.
8th	,,	13	,,	2	,,	stealing 4s. 6d. out of a till.
9th	,,	13	,,	2	,,	stealing lead.
10th	,,	14	,,	17	,,	picking pockets.
11th	,,	11	,,	5	,,	stealing silver tea-kettle.
12th	,,	13	,,	3	,,	picking pockets.
13th	,,	12	,,	3	,,	,, ,,
14th	,,	14	,,	5	,,	stealing chickens.
15th	,,	14	,,	6	,,	stealing a copper boiler.

* We are, however, still of opinion, that a great change for the better might be made in our prisons, by ordering that the amount of food supplied should be made to depend upon the amount of work done. This, we repeat, would serve, not only to make the rule of life within a prison conform to that without the walls, but to do away with the present refuge and asylum character of our jails, for surely a refuge is merely a place that people fly to in order to obtain food, clothing, and shelter, without trouble or labour on their part; and this is precisely what obtains in our prisons of the present day. To do away with this anomaly, it is necessary to make the provisions supplied to prisoners purchasable as they are in the world, by different quantities of industry, and to supply *gratuitously* only the present punishment diet of bread and water. Such, we hold, should be the rule in every jail throughout the kingdom; but most especially in those institutions which are set apart for the reception of young offenders. The most dangerous lesson that a boy-criminal can possibly learn is, that food, shelter, and raiment are to be had within a prison for nothing. Upon such a nature, more particularly, we should take especial pains to impress the high truth, that the necessities and luxuries of life are procurable only by industry; and by showing him how he, by his labour, can contribute to his own enjoyment, teach him at once the use and value of work. As it is, however, the first lesson he learns inside a prison is, that industry brings no reward, and that labour is at once a punishment and a disgrace. To put an end to this absurd perversion of natural laws, all that is required is that prisoners, on their entry into a jail (after conviction), should be placed in a punishment cell, on punishment diet, and made to *earn* such creature comforts as the present regulations allow, by different amounts of work for each article—a bed being purchasable by a certain quantity of labour, and a cup of cocoa, or a dish of soup, by other quantities, according as the authorities might appraise them. As it is, however, the natural order of things is precisely reversed—the food and bedding, and even better kind of cell, are given to each prisoner *as a right*, and he is put to labour merely as an arbitrary punishment, and that simply because it is a thing to which he has an inveterate aversion; whilst the punishment diet, and the punishment cell are resorted to merely as the means of intimidating him into conformity to the prison rules. That which is now the *last* resource, therefore, should be made the *first* expedient; and if this were the case, the refuge character of our prisons would no longer exist.

16th Prisoner, 10 years of age, 2 times in prison, for stealing 4d.

17th	,,	11	,,	10	,,	stealing pigeons.
18th	,,	12	,,	3	,,	stealing a coat.
19th	,,	13	,,	5	,,	stealing lead.
20th	,,	13	,,	2	,,	picking pockets.
21st	,,	12	,,	5	,,	pawning a jacket.
22nd	,,	15	,,	5	,,	stealing a jacket.
23rd	,,	14	,,	4	,,	stealing 9s. from till.
24th	,,	10	,,	1	,,	*spinning a top!*
25th	,,	12	,,	1	,,	stealing lead.
26th	,,	13	,,	3	,,	stealing ten bottles of wine.
27th	,,	14	,,	2	,,	stealing canvas.
28th	,,	11	,,	6	,,	*spinning a top!*
29th	,,	13	,,	3	,,	stealing brass. [tences.
30th	,,	13	,,	1	,,	obtaining money under false pre-
31st	,,	14	,,	3	,,	stealing brass and lead.
32nd	,,	5	,,	2	,,	stealing 5s. 9d. from till.
33rd	,,	13	,,	1	,,	stealing jewelry and pencil-cases.
34th	,,	16	,,	1	,,	going into Kensington Gardens to
35th	,,	14	,,	6	,,	stealing a guinea-pig. [sleep.*
36th	,,	12	,,	2	,,	picking pockets.
37th	,,	13	,,	1	,,	suspicion.
38th	,,	15	,,	5	,,	stealing silver plate.
39th	,,	14	,,	3	,,	picking pockets.
40th	,,	13	,,	3	,,	stealing a watch and timepiece.
41st	,,	15	,,	8	,,	stealing brass.
42nd	,,	15	,,	4	,,	stealing meat.
43rd	,,	14	,,	11	,,	stealing some calico.
44th	,,	14	,,	2	,,	stealing carpet.
45th	,,	13	,,	6	,,	picking pockets.
46th	,,	14	,,	6	,,	,, ,,
47th	,,	14	,,	2	,,	,, ,,
48th	,,	14	,,	9	,,	pulling down palings.
49th	,,	12	,,	3	,,	stealing meat.
50th	,,	13	,,	8	,,	stealing lead.
51st	,,	13	,,	2	,,	,, ,,
52nd	,,	15	,,	1	,,	,, ,,
53rd	,,	12	,,	1	,,	stealing gold watch and chain.
54th	,,	13	,,	7	,,	stealing money from till.
55th	,,	18	,,	4	,,	picking pockets.
56th	,,	16	,,	1	,,	stealing beef.
57th	,,	16	,,	3	,,	stealing bacon.
58th	,,	14	,,	4	,,	picking pockets.
59th	,,	16	,,	10	,,	stealing ladies' mantles.
60th	,,	13	,,	3	,,	picking pockets.
61st	,,	13	,,	1	,,	,, ,,
62nd	,,	14	,,	7	,,	,, ,,
63rd	,,	15	,,	2	,,	stealing a silk gown.
64th	,,	16	,,	2	,,	stealing watch.
65th	,,	12	,,	4	,,	stealing bread.

* This boy said his father wouldn't keep him. His sentence for the above *heinous* offence was one month.

66th Prisoner,	13	years of age,	6	times in prison,	for housebreaking.
67th ,,	15	,,	4	,,	picking pockets.
68th ,,	11	,,	1	,,	begging.
69th ,,	13	,,	3	,,	stealing 2s. 6d.
70th ,,	11	,,	1	,,	killing a dog.
71st ,,	16	,,	1	,,	highway-robbery of watch.
72nd ,,	13	,,	1	,,	picking pockets.
73rd ,,	15	,,	1	,,	stealing a watch.
74th ,,	16	,,	7	,,	picking pockets.
75th ,,	14	,,	6	,,	,, ,,
76th ,,	13	,,	3	,,	stealing two caps.
77th ,,	14	,,	2	,,	highway-robbery of a watch.
78th ,,	14	,,	2	,,	stealing coals.
79th ,,	14	,,	1	,,	picking pockets.
80th ,,	10	,,	2	,,	,, ,,
81st ,,	10	,,	2	,,	stealing brass.
82nd ,,	11	,,	1	,,	picking pockets.
83rd ,,	15	,,	2	,,	stealing boots.
84th ,,	16	,,	1	,,	picking pockets.
85th ,,	14	,,	3	,,	,, ,,
86th ,,	12	,,	6	,,	,, ,,
87th ,,	16	,,	3	,,	stealing a coat.
88th ,,	15	,,	11	,,	picking pockets.
89th ,,	15	,,	3	,,	,, ,,
90th ,,	16	,,	1	,,	stealing 1s. from till.
91st ,,	13	,,	2	,,	stealing sack of white rags.
92nd ,,	15	,,	4	,,	stealing candied lemon-peel.
93rd ,,	16	,,	1	,,	stealing lead.
94th ,,	10	,,	1	,,	stealing seven razors.
95th ,,	15	,,	7	,,	picking pockets.
96th ,,	14	,,	1	,,	stealing a coat.
97th ,,	14	,,	2	,,	stealing lead.
98th ,,	15	,,	2	,,	,, ,,
99th ,,	15	,,	2	,,	stealing 9s. 6d. from employer.
100th ,,	16	,,	4	,,	stealing 4 pigeons.
101st ,,	16	,,	2	,,	stealing lead.
102nd ,,	14	,,	7	,,	picking pockets.
103rd ,,	16	,,	5	,,	stealing cigars.
104th ,,	14	,,	2	,,	stealing bread.*
105th ,,	15	,,	5	,,	stealing copper.
106th ,,	14	,,	5	,,	stealing cigars and pipes.
107th ,,	16	,,	1	,,	stealing £2 16s. from employer.
108th ,,	16	,,	9	,,	picking pockets.
109th ,,	14	,,	4	,,	,, ,,
110th ,,	14	,,	2	,,	,, ,,
111th ,,	15	,,	1	,,	stealing sack of oats and beans.
112th ,,	14	,,	10	,,	stealing lead.
113th ,,	16	,,	4	,,	picking pockets.
114th ,,	16	,,	1	,,	,, ,,
115th ,,	15	,,	2	,,	suspicion.

* This, the boy confessed, was not from want; he intended to sell it.

116th Prisoner,	13 years of age,	5 times in prison, for	picking pockets.
117th	,,	13	,,	2	,,	suspicion.
118th	,,	16	,,	1	,,	stealing £2 from employer.
119th	,,	16	,,	2	,,	stealing four silk handkerchiefs.
120th	,,	14	,,	2	,,	*getting over a wall !*
121st	,,	16	,,	2	,,	picking pockets.
122nd	,,	14	,,	1	,,	stealing brass.
123rd	,,	15	,,	8	,,	stealing 9s. 6d. from a till.
124th	,,	16	,,	2	,,	taking sweepings of a barge of coals.
125th	,,	15	,,	9	,,	picking pockets.
126th	,,	16	,,	3	,,	,, ,,
127th	,,	16	,,	4	,,	stealing £2 8s. from a till.
128th	,,	14	,,	9	,,	picking pockets.
129th	,,	16	,,	13	,,	stealing lead.
130th	,,	16	,,	1	,,	,, ,,
131st	,,	16	,,	1	,,	stealing some cotton print.
132nd	,,	13	,,	1	,,	stealing 3s. from employer.
133rd	,,	16	,,	4	,,	stealing cigars.
134th	,,	15	,,	2	,,	stealing candied lemon-peel.
135th	,,	14	,,	3	,,	stealing cigars.
136th	,,	14	,,	5	,,	pieking pockets.
137th	,,	14	,,	3	,,	,, ,,
138th	,,	16	,,	2	,,	,, ,,
139th	,,	15	,,	5	,,	,, ,,
140th	,,	15	,,	7	,,	,, ,,
141st	,,	14	,,	3	,,	,, ,,
142nd	,,	16	,,	5	,,	,, ,,
143rd	,,	16	,,	3	,,	,, ,,
144th	,,	15	,,	5	,,	stealing coat.
145th	,,	12	,,	2	,,	stealing brass.
146th	,,	13	,,	1	,,	stealing books.
147th	,,	16	,,	1	,,	stealing chair.
148th	,,	14	,,	6	,,	picking pockets
149th	,,	17	,,	1	,,	leaving his ship.
150th	,,	16	,,	4	,,	stealing from a till.
151st	,,	16	,,	2	,,	stealing quarter of a sheep.
152nd	,,	15	,,	3	,,	picking pockets.
153rd	,,	13	,,	4	,,	,, ,,
154th	,,	16	,,	3	,,	stealing meat.
155th	,,	16	,,	7	,,	picking pockets.
156th	,,	14	,,	3	,,	stealing cigars. [employer.
157th	,,	16	,,	1	,,	stealing two felt hats and a cap from
158th	,,	16	,,	1	,,	stealing 4s. 1d. from master.
159th	,,	15	,,	6	,,	stealing lead.
160th	,,	16	,,	1	,,	stealing some corn.
161st	,,	16	,,	9	,,	stealing some cotton print.
162nd	,,	16	,,	3	,,	stealing cigars.
163rd	,,	16	,,	2	,,	burglary, with two other boys.
164th	,,	14	,,	2	,,	stealing some jackets.
165th	,,	16	,,	11	,,	picking pockets.
166th	,,	16	,,	1	,,	stealing from a till.

167th Prisoner, 15 years of age, 1 times in prison, for stealing 10 bottles of wine.

168th	,,	14	,,	4	,,	picking pockets. [in it.*
169th	,,	16	,,	1	,,	taking a lady's reticule, with £2 15s.
170th	,,	16	,,	4	,,	picking pockets.
171st	,,	14	,,	3	,,	stealing 18s. 6d. from a till.
172nd	,,	16	,,	4	,,	stealing a coat.
173rd	,,	16	,,	1	,,	robbing master of £4.
174th	,,	15	,,	3	,,	picking pockets.
175th	,,	18†	,,	1	,,	stealing tools.
176th	,,	13	,,	3	,,	stealing some oil-cloth.
177th	,,	11	,,	1	,,	stealing gold rings.
178th	,,	14	,,	5	,,	stealing some walnuts from market.
179th	,,	16	,,	1	,,	picking pockets.
180th	,,	15	,,	2	,,	,, ,,
181st	,,	16	,,	1	,,	stealing shoe-brushes.
182nd	,,	16	,,	6	,,	stealing a watch.
183rd	,,	14	,,	3	,,	picking pockets.
184th	,,	13	,,	1	,,	stealing £1 7s. from employer.
185th	,,	15	,,	9	,,	picking pockets.
186th	,,	16	,,	1	,,	,, ,,
187th	,,	15	,,	3	,,	,, ,,
188th	,,	16	,,	7	,,	stealing a pair of boots.
189th	,,	13	,,	10	,,	stealing coat and umbrella.
190th	,,	15	,,	5	,,	stealing £2 15s. from a till.
191st	,,	16	,,	1	,,	robbing master of 10¾d.
192nd	,,	14	,,	1	,,	picking pockets.
193rd	,,	16	,,	2	,,	stealing a watch.
194th	,,	15	,,	2	,,	picking pockets.

Besides these, there were others in the long-room, whose ages and number of times of imprisonment we omitted to take down, and who were confined for the following offences:—

Stealing 2d., stealing a watch, ditto some lead, ditto bread, ditto some cloth, picking pockets, stealing 4s. from a till, stealing some carpet, picking pockets, *breaking a window!* stealing a bit of soap, ditto a scrubbing-brush, going into offices with his mother's keys, picking pockets, taking some stone-mason's tools, stealing some gratings, picking pockets, stealing some lead, ditto ditto, taking a waistcoat, ditto a pair of boots, ditto £1 from his father.

Of the misdemeanants, the fines for the non-payment of which they had been sent to prison, were as under:—

One had been sentenced to pay 10s., or suffer 14 days' imprisonment, for "heaving stones."

Another, to pay £1, or undergo the same imprisonment, for the same offence.

Another had had the same penalty imposed, or the same term of imprisonment, for a like his breach of the law.

Whereas a fourth had been fined £2, or one month for a similar "*crime.*"

A fifth had had 5s. or seven days imposed upon him for "heaving clay about," as he called it.

Whilst a sixth had been fined £2 or one month's imprisonment for breaking a street lamp.

* Boy said he pulled it forcibly from the lady's arm.
† This prisoner had given his age at `7, so as to be sent to Tothill Fields.

Now the conclusions to be drawn from the above list appear to us to be—

1. That the greater proportion of the boys confined in Tothill Fields prison are there for picking pockets—indeed as many as 66 in 194 (or rather more than one-third of the whole) are in prison for this offence; and that most of these, young as they are, are old "jail birds," some of them having been a greater number of times in prison than they are years old. One, for instance, whose age was but 14, confessed to having been committed no less than 17 times. Whilst others, though but 10 years of age, had already been more than once recommitted for the same crime.

2. Next to the picking of pockets, the purloining of metal constitutes the largest proportion of the offences committed by the young, there being about 12 in every 100 of the boy-prisoners sentenced for this crime; and these again are mostly all habitual offenders, the majority having been several times recommitted.

3. Some few of the boys are imprisoned for serious crimes. Some for burglary, for instance, others for housebreaking, and others for highway robbery of watches; whilst others, again, though less daring, have been concerned in the purloining of silver tea-kettles, of jewelry, and pencil-cases, and silver plate, and watches, and timepieces, and gold chains, and rings, and ladies' reticules, &c.

4. Many of the other offences belong to the class perpetrated by those who are expressively termed "sneaks." These consist of what is styled the "frisking of tills," the pilfering of meat, bread, wine, coats, umbrellas, boots, cigars, chickens, pigeons, guinea-pigs, sacks of rags, oats, beans, coals from barges, and indeed anything that the urchins can lay their hands upon.

5. In addition to these there is still a small class of boys confined for the robbery of their employers, the amounts taken ranging from 10¾d. up to £2 odd; but these, on the other hand, are mostly inexperienced offenders, and belong to a class who at least have been engaged in some industrial occupation, and who should be in no way confounded with the young habitual thieves.

6. Further, there is a considerable number who are confined for offences that not even the sternest-minded can rank as crime, and for which the committal to a felon's prison can but be regarded by every righteous mind, not only as an infamy to the magistrate concerned, but even as a scandal to the nation which permits the law-officers of the country so far to outrage justice and decency. To this class of offences belong the spinning of tops, the breaking of windows, the "heaving" of stones, the sleeping in Kensington Gardens, getting over walls, and such like misdemeanours, for many of which we see, by the above list, that the lads were suffering their first imprisonment.

Now, the latter conclusion serves to show that juvenile crime is not *always* begotten by bad, or no parental care, but springs frequently from a savage love of consigning people to prison for faults that cannot even be classed as immoral, much less criminal.

¶ ii—δ.

Of the Boys' Work at Tothill Fields.

The labour performed at this prison consists of almost the same forms as those we have already described at Coldbath Fields, and the convict institutions of the Metropolis. Oakum-picking constitutes, as usual, the greater proportion of the work, though the amount earned by the prisoners at such an occupation yields barely £1 per head per annum, whilst the cost of maintenance, clothing, &c., is more than seven times as much. There are also certain gangs put to tailoring and shoemaking, and some two or three individuals to carpentry, whilst a few are employed in gardening.

In all the forms of work, however, the vital defect is, that the labour is enforced as a matter of punishment rather than as the means of educating the young prisoners in some handicraft, or, indeed, inculcating in them the love of honest exertions. Of industrial training there is not a shadow, nor, to do the authorities justice, the *least pretence*. In fact, we much question if any of the worthies who are entrusted with the care of these wretched little outcasts, ever puzzled their brains as to how habits are formed at any time, or speculated on that wondrous function of the human machinery which, after a time, transforms those acts of volition which require a special effort, and are consequently more or less irksome to perform *at first*, into acts of an automatic character, which become at length, rather than being irksome to do, irksome to leave undone—and that merely by being repeated at *regular and frequent intervals*.

Again, all persons affecting the least philosophy, know that the highest worldly lesson, perhaps, a being can be taught, is that of self-reliance—to have faith in his own powers to contribute to his own happiness, and to know and feel that he exists in an atmosphere of circumstances which are fraught with the keenest misery to the indolent, but which the Almighty has given us, one and all, more or less, the faculty to mould to our own enjoyment and comfort, if we have but the will and the determination to do so. The wretched children, however, at Tothill Fields are still allowed to grow up with the notion deep-rooted in their brain, that the best and easiest means of obtaining the objects of their desires is either to appropriate, or beg for, the property of others, and to regard labour as a scourge and a punishment, rather than the safest and readiest means of contributing to their pleasures. True, the children are duly taught to spell and to write, and to chatter catechisms and creeds that they cannot understand. The State, however, we hold, has more to do with the formation of good citizens than good Christians. The office of an enlightened and liberal Government is to see that each man does his duty to his neighbour; nor has it any right to meddle with the duty individuals owe to God, for grant the contrary, and it is possible to justify all those religious tyrannies and persecutions from which every true Protestant thinks it the great glory of the age to have escaped.

Now, we do not hesitate to confess that there is in *all* prisons a great deal too much care for the happiness of a being in the future world, and too little for his happiness in the present; in a word, we believe there is too much faith placed in the influence of the chaplain, and too little in the knowledge of the physician (using the word in its comprehensive German sense). No man desires more devoutly to see the world Christianized than ourselves —none wishes more ardently to behold the day when religion shall become a deep abiding presence in the soul, and the perfection of the Divine Nature be the true standard of excellence to which all men shall endeavour to shape their actions. But none, at the same time, can have a deeper loathing and contempt for those *outward* shows of godliness—those continued " lip-services"—the everlasting " praying in public places," which the revelation of our every-day's commercial and prison history teaches us to believe, constitute the flagrant " shams" of the age. The same social vice that leads would-be saintly and really fraudulent bankers to ride to their counting-houses in public omnibuses with the Bible on their knees, leads even thieves, both old and young, to affect puritanical forms of godliness, viz., with the view of obtaining credit with man rather than their Maker; and though some little good, certainly, has been done towards abating the amount of hypocrisy in prisons, by the abandonment of the " penitentiary system," as it was called, nevertheless, till men have the courage to speak honestly upon these matters, we fear there is little hope of doing much good with our criminals.

What is wanted (and the defect is nowhere so apparent as at this same Tothill Fields prison), is really good, sound, wholesome, labour training—the education of decent and industrious habits, and the practical inculcation, above all things, of the value and dignity of work. At the Westminster House of Correction, however, industry brings no reward; the 1 or 2 lbs. of oakum are picked, the prison shoes are mended, the clothes made, or the ground tilled, by the boys, without any positive good accruing from the work. And yet these poor lads require more than any in the land to be taught the very opposite lesson. Suppose, now, the governor, the warders, and even the chaplain himself, were to be expected to do their prison offices for nothing. How long, think you, would *they* remain at their post, or how long would they continue even honest, when they found their labours unrequited?

Nevertheless, it is not quite so easy to practice any regular system of industrial education in our prisons at the present time. The magistrates still delight to send lads to jail merely for a few days, just to let them see, as it were, how different a place it is from their own home; for it will be found, from the subjoined table, that one-fourth, or 24·8 per cent. of the entire number of prisoners passing through the Westminster House of Correction are committed for less than 14 days! whilst the average sentence for the whole of the 1,800 and odd boys sent there is not more than three months. The particulars will be found below.*

Of course it is idle to expect that any impression can be made upon a young offender in so short a period, other than the teaching him that there is a comfortable house and good food always ready for him at Westminster, and for which the terms of admission are merely throwing an oyster-shell through one of the street lamps.

But let us proceed to describe what we saw and learnt in the shoemakers' and tailors' room at this prison.

These workshops are both situate on the first floor of the wing styled No. 8 prison, and each consists of a room, hardly larger than a suburban parlour, and which has been formed by knocking three of the ordinary cells into one. The walls are whitewashed, the roof vaulted, and the floor paved with bricks.

Around the shoemakers' shop shelves are ranged; and upon these we found bundles of new shoes in quires, as it were, with the heel of one thrust into the other, and crowds of heavy, lumpish-looking lasts; whilst in one corner were bags of women's old shoes waiting to be

---

* TABLE SHOWING THE TERMS OF IMPRISONMENT OF THE BOYS CONFINED IN TOTHILL FIELDS PRISON DURING THE YEARS ENDING 1851-55.

Terms of Imprisonment.	1851.	1852.	1853.	1854.	1855.	Annual Mean.	Per centage to total Committals.
Under 14 days	523	463	423	483	360	451	24·8
14 days and under 1 month . .	382	327	302	329	272	322	17·7
1 month and under 2 months .	424	429	375	417	494	428	23·6
2 months and under 3 . . .	137	155	155	204	241	178	9·8
3 months and under 6 . .	220	251	258	309	337	275	15·1
6 months and under 1 year . .	175	145	98	49	128	119	6·6
1 year and above	32	26	47	53	64	44	2·4
Total Committals	1,893	1,796	1,658	1,844	1,896	1,817	100·0

By the above table it will be seen, that the magistrates of late years have shown a commendable tendency to *decrease* the imprisonments under 1 month, and to *increase* those above it. Thus, in the year 1851, the number of imprisonments for the former term amounted to 905, whilst in 1855 they were only 632, though the gross number of committals was nearly the same in both years. The number of longer imprisonments, however, was 986 in 1851, and 1,264 in 1855; so that, as the Special Report states, though the prison seemed to be fuller in the latter year, the increased number of inmates arose from "the lengthened term for which they were committed."

repaired, and baskets full of pieces and rolls of leather. At a desk stood the presiding warder, surrounded with tools that reminded one of small cheese-cutters; whilst the air was as redolent of cobbler's-wax as the oakum-room we had just left was of tar. Across the shop the boys were ranged on small benches, and each with a "kit," or open tray, at his side; whilst a gas-pipe, that burnt dimly in the daylight, rose straight up out of the bricken floor, and stood close at the elbow of the workers, each of whom was half-encased in a leather apron, like so many young draymen.

"Take off your caps, boys, and cease that hammering," cries the warder, as we enter. "This is our monthly book of the work done," continues the officer, pointing to a long, thin volume that lies open on the desk. "We do mostly repairs, and those figures you see here represent the quantity mended in the course of the month. There's 507 pairs, you see, mended in January last, 385 in February, 367 in March, 490 in April, 426 in May, 497 in June; and, besides this, we made 5 new pairs of shoes in January, 8 in February, 12 in March, 13 in April, 3 in May, and the same number in June; and that with 13 boys employed in the shop." (This gives an average of about $7\frac{1}{3}$ pairs made in the course of each month, and upwards of 445 pairs mended in the same time, which is at the rate of not quite 9 pairs mended by each hand during the week.) "We can't estimate their labour at much, sir," the man went on, "because they are all young hands. Here's the account, you see, for the week ending the 7th of June. The earnings of the 13 boys for that week are valued at £2 4s."

We then proceeded to inquire as to the mode in which the labour was estimated.

"Now, a job like that," said the warder, "which is what we call half-soling, we reckon at 5d. the pair; it's only done in a rough way, you see, and the time it will take a boy depends upon the time he has been learning. A new hand, with even my assistance, will be a couple of days over it; but if he has been a bit at the work, he'll do it in a day. We have the lads, however, for such short terms, that we cannot get them to be ready at the business. I estimate the work by the job or piece. Half-heeling, like that, I should put down 1d. for. In the week ending the 14th of June, the boys earned £2 1s. 4d.; in the week ending the 21st, £2 4s., and in that ending the 28th, £2 3s. 4d." (This makes the month's earnings amount to £8 12s. 8d., which is at the rate of rather more than 3s. 3d. a-week, or £8 12s. per annum for each hand; so that, at this rate, each of the young prisoners would be more than self-supporting.)

In the book of the work done, there were remarks attached to the name of each boy; and here seven were entered as having "improved," three as "not improved," two were said to be "learning," and against the name of the other was written, "can close a little." In the next week nine were entered as having "improved," and only two as having "not improved," whilst the remaining two were said to be "learning to repair."

The next point of inquiry was, how long the lads continued under the instruction of the officer. The warder referred to his book and said, as he came to the names of the different boys, as follows:—

"Now, there's that boy, C——, I had him about six months. Then John B——, there, he's gone to the school at Redhill, I had him for about two months. Here's a boy named R——, I had him only for about three weeks; and this boy, L——, I had for about five weeks, as near as I can tell. Sometimes I don't keep them for more than a week, they get into trouble, are put into the cells, and so are constantly on the change."

We now proceeded to interrogate the lads employed as to their ages. Nine of them said they were 16, one was 15, another 14, and the other two 13 years old.

The first boy we questioned said, "that he had never done any work before he came to the prison. He had been at shoemaking three months." He confessed he was really 18 years of age, but had said he was 16 in order to get sent to this prison. He had stolen some tools, and was never in prison before. His sentence was eight calendar months. He had never been put to any trade. Had no father—only a stepfather. Had been at shoemaking in the prison about three months.

The second boy had been learning the business for only a week. He had never been in any prison before, and was there for stealing £4 from his master. Had been an errand-boy at a green-grocer's shop. His sentence was nine calendar months.

The third boy appeared pale and sickly. He had stolen a piece of oil-cloth, and was sentenced to two calendar months; he had been in prison thrice before; had both father and mother, and had worked as a shoemaker outside.

A fourth boy had been twice in Tothill Fields and once in Maidstone; he had taken 18s. 6d., with two other boys, out of a shop-till. Had got three calendar months. Used to work at shoemaking, along with his father. His mother was living, too.

The father of the fifth was also a shoemaker; "but," said the lad, "he never taught me." This lad was in prison for stealing a half-quartern loaf. "Me and two more took it," were his words; "we didn't want it, we meant to sell it." He had been three times in this prison, and once in Wandsworth.

The sixth boy had a stepmother, who treated him badly. He had stolen £2 8s. from a man at a public-house where he lodged, and had got four years' penal servitude. Had been in prison five times before. Was waiting for an order to go to Redhill. Was a stone-mason by trade.

The next prisoner had a stepmother also, but she treated him well. He was a coster-monger by trade, and was in for two pairs of boots, which he had taken from a shop door. He had got eight months' sentence, and had been recommitted half a dozen times.

The lad next the last-mentioned looked ill; he was a bootmaker by trade, and had both father and mother living. He was in for stealing some shoe-brushes; there were three more boys in with him. He had got three calendar months, and had been twice recommitted.

Another lad confessed himself a pickpocket. He said he went out regularly with a "school" of boys. "He used to get hankychers, and purses sometimes." Had been in twice before, and had got three months. Was a "hawk-boy," he said, at the plasterers' trade. His mother was alive, but he had no father.

Another stated that he "thieved a gold watch;" he had "screwed it," he said; and one other boy was with him. He'd got three months for it. Was never in Tothill Fields before, but was twice at the House of Detention. Had both father and mother living.

The next was in for stealing four silk handkerchiefs out of a window, and had got six calendar months. He was of no trade, and had both father and mother.

One of the two remaining lads was a shoemaker outside. He was in for stealing 3s. from his master's till. Was never in prison before, and had got four calendar months. Father and mother both alive.

The other, and the last boy, was no trade. He had been sentenced to two years' imprison-ment for picking a woman's pocket of 10s. "He went out regularly with a gang of other boys," he said. Had been six times in Tothill Fields, twice in Wandsworth, and once in Chelmsford. His father was a bricklayer's labourer, and had been a soldier. He had never sent him to school, or put him to any trade.

This completed the history of the several lads employed; but, before leaving, we were further informed, that the shoemaking work was done only for the prison. New shoes are valued at 2s. 4d. the pair for making, closing and all.

We also learnt here, that it is not usual to keep "two years' boys" at Tothill Fields. "There's an order now," said our informant, "that all boys sentenced for twelve months and upwards, shall be reported to the Home Office, with the view to their being sent to Redhill. There's farm labour there for the lads," said the warder; "and when I was down at the place three weeks ago, the crops were beautiful, I assure you, sir."*

---

* The subjoined is the form issued to boys previous to their being sent to the Philanthropic Farm School, and the appended certificate has to be signed by them, though how the Government authorities can expect a mere child to understand the wording of an Act of Parliament, and how they can ask an "infant,'

The tailors' shop, at this prison, is the same in size and style as the shoemakers', with the exception that the bricken pavement is partly covered with a raised floor, that serves for a shop-board for the boys at work. At the time of our visit, there were some 20 lads sitting cross-legged here like so many veritable young Turks. The usual complement of juvenile tailors is 26, we were told, but when we were there, some few were at the school-room. In one corner of the apartment was a kind of counter for cutting out, fitted with drawers, and littered with blue cloth, and in the opposite corner sat the presiding warder on a stool. Against the wall stood a small press, and there was a new pair of trousers hanging by the window.

"Some of those that are at work here," said the warder, in answer to our inquiries, "have been three months on the board; that is the longest time any of the boys you see have been working in the shop, though I *do* sometimes get a hand or two that remains with me for six months. Many of these lads, however, have been only ten days at the work at present; but some have been at the trade before, and if we know they are of use, we employ them. We have them, however, for so short a time, that it's impossible to learn them much."

to affix his name to a document, when, in law, he has no power to commit any act of his own, is beyond us to appreciate :—

"CONDITIONAL PARDON TO YOUNG OFFENDERS.

"*1st & 2nd Victoria, Cap. 82, Sect.* 11.

"Whereas Her Majesty has lately exercised Her Royal Prerogative of Mercy in granting Pardon to Young Offenders who have been sentenced to Transportation or Imprisonment, upon the condition of placing himself or herself under the care of some Charitable Institution for the Reception and Reformation of Young Offenders named in such Pardon, and conforming to and abiding by the Orders and Rules thereof: And whereas the same has been found beneficial : And whereas it is expedient that some Provision should be made for carrying the same more fully into effect; Be it therefore enacted, That from and after the passing of this Act, in case any Young Offender who has been or shall be hereafter sentenced to Transportation or Imprisonment has been or shall be pardoned by Her Majesty for such Offence upon such condition as aforesaid, and has or shall accept such conditional Pardon, and shall afterwards abscond from such Institution, or wilfully neglect or refuse to abide by and conform to the Rules thereof, it shall and may be lawful to and for any Justice of the Peace acting in and for the County, City, Riding, or Division, wherein the said Offender shall actually be at the Time he shall so abscond or neglect or refuse as aforesaid, upon due Proof thereof made before him, upon the Oath of One credible Witness, by Warrant under his Hand and Seal, to commit the Party so offending for every such Offence to any Gaol or House of Correction for the said County, City, Riding, or Division, with or without hard Labour, for any period not exceeding Three Calendar Months for the First Offence, and not exceeding Six Calendar Months for the Second or any subsequent Offence, in case the Managers or Directors of any such Charitable Institution shall be willing to receive any such Young Offender after his or her being convicted of absconding, neglecting, or refusing as aforesaid; and in every Case such Imprisonment shall be in addition to the original Sentence of such Young Offender; and after the Expiration of the Time of such additional Punishment, if the Managers or Directors of any such Charitable Institution shall refuse to receive such Offender, or if Her Majesty shall not be pleased to exercise Her Royal Prerogative in pardoning the Breach of the condition on which the former Pardon was granted, the said Party shall forfeit all Benefit of the said Pardon, and shall be remitted to the original Sentence, and shall undergo the Residue thereof, as if no such Pardon had been granted."

"CERTIFICATE.

"I do hereby acknowledge that the Clause in the above-recited Act of Parliament has been read over and explained to me, and that I   of my own free will and accord do promise that I will conform to and abide by the Rules and Orders of the Philanthropic Farm School, at Redhill, in the county of Surrey, and will go abroad whenever I may be found sufficiently instructed or otherwise suitable for emigration by the Governors of that Institution, and that I receive my Pardon upon such Conditions.

"Dated this   day of
"*Witness.*"

"The total number of boys under 17 years of age," says the Special Report of the Visiting Justices of 1856, "who have been committed to this prison, during the five years ending Michaelmas, 1851, amounted

" They're working now at the prisoners' clothing, and part of the officers' **uniform.** **We** do all the repairs of the prison, and don't do any work for out of doors."

" The earnings of last week," the officer went on, as we interrogated him on the subject, " were £1 16s.; the week before they were £1 6s. 4d.; before that, £1 12s. 6d.; and £1 8s. 6d. for the previous one; that's for 26 boys." (This gives an average of £1 10s. 10d. per week, earned by the entire shop, which is at the rate of 1s. 2½d. per week for each boy, or £3 1s. 9d. per annum.*)

" The greater number of the lads are of very little use except at repairing clothing." continued the officer. " There are only about eight or nine of all those now on the board that I can put on the new work. One here," he said, pointing to a lad, " has been at tailoring work outside. Most all of them have been taught in this prison. That boy, P——, yonder, is one of the best hands I have; he's been taught here, and is in very frequently. He's been in—let me see!—How many times have you been in, P——?"

" Four times," replied the lad.

" Ah! and I should think he has been about nine months on the board altogether," added the warder. " And there's D——, too, he's been recommitted about the same number of times, and been about as long at the trade. The boys prefer this work to the oakum-picking. They express a wish to improve themselves, so as to be able to get a living outside, though very few take advantage of it."

to no less than 7,763, while only 263 (not 3½ per cent.) were received into reformatory asylums from it." The distribution of these is shown in the following table :—

TABLE SHOWING THE NUMBER OF BOYS RECEIVED INTO PHILANTHROPIC INSTITUTIONS DURING THE YEARS ENDING MICHAELMAS, 1851—55.

Philanthropic Institutions.	1851.	1852.	1853.	1854.	1855.	Total.
Philanthropic Farm School . .	4	3	11	3	2	23
The London Colonial Dormitory .	30	34	11	9	10	94
The Ragged School Dormitory .	20	—	—	—	—	20
The House of Occupation . . .	3	5	—	2	2	12
Juvenile Refuge	—	9	—	—	—	9
The House in the East	—	1	23	3	16	43
Kentish Town School	—	1	14	—	—	15
Pear Street Refuge	—	4	—	—	—	4
Boys' Home, Wandsworth . . .	—	—	—	13	12	25
St. Giles' Industrial School . .	—	—	—	6	1	7
Metropolitan Reformatory, Brixton	—	—	—	—	5	5
Grotto Passage Industrial School	—	—	—	—	5	5
Boys' Refuge, Whitechapel . .	—	—	—	—	1	1
Total	57	57	59	36	54	263

Average received into reformatory asylums from 1851—55 . . . . 52.

* It is difficult to understand why the earnings in the tailors' shop, where double the number of hands are employed, are but little more than half those of the shoemakers'. Out of doors a tailor earns as much money as a shoemaker, so that, according to Cocker, if the labour of 13 boys employed at shoemaking is estimated at £2 3s. 2d., that of 26 boys, working at an equally profitable calling, should be worth £4 6s. 4d. We have seen, however, that the earnings of the entire 26 boy-tailors, are computed at only £1 10s. 10d., so that it is evident that the value of boy-shoemaker's work must be considerably overrated, as we showed to be the case at Coldbath Fields. Indeed, the estimates formed at the correctional prisons as to the earnings of the prisoners are comparatively worthless, being generally left to the mere caprice of the trade-warder; so that at those prisons where special pains are taken—as, for instance, at Wandsworth—to arrive at more accurate results, the prisoners seem, by the returns, to have been comparatively idling, whilst at other institutions, like Coldbath Fields, the prison is made to appear several thousand pounds less expensive to the country than it really is. Surely the Government should not allow such a state of statistical confusion to continue.

One lad we spoke to said, " Yes, I like tailoring better than oakum work. I want to learn a trade."

The boy P—— said, " He didn't do any tailoring outside, but it was better and easier work than the oakum. He did, though, one week's work at it last time he was out. I went," he added, " for a week on trial to a shop, and I was going back on the Monday, but got took on the Sunday while I was out thieving with some other boys."

We asked him whether he made or repaired his own clothes when he was at liberty, and his answer was, " that he liked to be able to do something for his-self." The officer informed us, moreover, that the lads generally preferred tailoring, because they were not so liable to get reported for not doing the precise quantity of work.

We then conferred with the warder as to his mode of valuing the labour done by the prisoners.

" We estimate the work on these boys' jackets," he said, taking up one of the ordinary prison garments, " at 9d. each, the trousers at the same, and the waistcoats at 6d.—that is, for making; and for repairing we put the work down at 1d. a garment, taking one with the other. Making officers' uniform trousers we value at 4s.; the waistcoats at the same price; the coats are made at Coldbath Fields."

In the carpenters' shop we found only one boy-prisoner, who was busy making a deal boot-jack for one of the officers. This shop was about the same size as that of the tailors' and shoemakers'. We now lost the tarry smell pervading the oakum-room, and the waxy and leathery odour of the shoemakers' shop, as well as the singed-blanket perfume of the tailors', for here the nostrils were regaled by a strong turpentiney smell of deal; and shears, and tape measures, and cutting boards, and kits, and lasts, and small cheese-cutters, as well as hooks, and heaps of fuzzy oakum, reminding of a pile of ladies' " *frisettes*," now gave way to benches, and tool-boxes, and planks, and curly shavings littering the floor.

In the carpenters' shop, two boys are generally kept employed. The carpenter himself was away at the period of our visit, at work in the females' prison, and the other lad had been sent to the oakum-room until his return.

The boy at work was an intelligent-looking youth, and sixteen years of age. He was in prison for stealing two felt hats and a cap from his employer. It was his first offence. His father and mother were both alive. On his coming up to London, from the country, he had a situation in a lawyer's office, he told us, and afterwards was employed at a hatter's. It was from the shop at which he worked that he stole the articles for which he was imprisoned.

" I was very foolish," he said to us, with apparent earnestness, " and hope to do better for the future. My time expires on Wednesday-week," he added, with a twinkle of the eye, and a slight quiver of the lip, " and father is going to try and apprentice me, or get me work. I've had four calendar months. No, sir, I never was at the carpentry trade before I came here, and I like it well enough. I once lived with Mr. F——, in Regent Street, and he would give me a good character. I am sure I don't know whether I shall go on at carpentry, until I've seen father."

This boy's work, the chief warder informed us, was not returned as labour of any value. " One of the carpenter boys," he added, " who had lately gone out, was worth, he should say, about 10s. or 12s. a-week. He had been employed at the trade outside with his uncle, who was a carpenter. Boys, generally, are found to like carpentering, and some are very quick at the craft."

In the oakum-store—which is one of the small offices ranged round the planted court-yard—we found nine more prisoners engaged, and here were large coils of old rope, and huge scales dangling from the beam overhead, and canvas bags and baskets filled with pieces of junk, ready cut up, besides a large screw-press, on which was painted—

"PRISONERS ARE NOT ALLOWED TO SPEAK TO EACH OTHER."

Some of the boys employed here were seated on small stools, and one, on an inverted basket, was busily unpicking the "strands" of the junk, whilst others were repicking the oakum that had been badly done.

One boy, too, was laying strings of spun-yarn in a large tub, ready for packing the picked oakum into "cheeses," or bundles of half cwts. "The spun yarn," said the officer in attendance, "is laid in the tub, and the oakum 'treaded' in, and then pressed down by the screw-press there." In this store the junk is weighed, and tied into bundles of 1 lb. and 1½ lb. and 2 lbs. The price paid by the contractor who supplies the prison with junk for picking into oakum, is £4 10s. the ton.

"That boy there," continued the officer, pointing to a lad at work in one corner of the apartment, "is making a mat. We estimate the value of such work at 4d. the square foot, and that one is about 6 feet, and the labour upon it worth 2s. He will make about 1½ of such mats in the course of the week. He never did anything of the kind before he came here. He's got 12 months' imprisonment, and has been about three months with us; he can make a mat very well now."*

The garden work only remains to be described, to complete our account of the prison labour at Tothill Fields.

The garden at this prison consists of about two acres within the walls, and three acres outside of them. Around the prison runs a small strip, barely more than fifty feet wide, and part of this is devoted to the governor's flower-beds and vegetables. Here, too, is a small lawn to be seen, and a puny fountain playing like an inverted watering-pot, with bits of slag and flint piled about its base. The high and yellow boundary wall of the prison is seen behind this, and, immediately overlooking it, the eye rests upon the back of the newly-built houses in Victoria Street. As we pass along, we hear the cry of the babies shut up with their mothers in prison C 4 and 5, and afterwards we come to the spot where the old tread-wheels formerly existed; and on our requesting to know the chief warder's opinion as to the effect of that form of labour upon prisoners' minds, he says, as we journey along towards the garden without the walls, "I think the old tread-wheel here, sir, did no good; that kind of useless labour, to my fancy, never made a man better—it never reformed a prisoner, of course, for it's only intended as a punishment. The wheels have been taken down about ten years—long before the transfer of women took place; it was in 1846, if my memory serves me right. The place was wanted for work-rooms, and that was one reason for their being removed, but some of the magistrates were against that kind of work. Mr. Welsby was, for one. He said it was useless labour; and he, I think, was the principal cause of its being done away with. We never had more than two tread-wheels here, and each used to be worked by 30 hands at a time; boys were generally put on with the men, but women never. Before the wheels were divided, each hand used to do between 10,000 and 12,000 feet of ascent daily; but latterly, after the division into boxes, 7,000 used to be the number." The outer garden is enclosed by a low wall, and is on the side of the prison towards Pimlico. It consists of an oblong piece of ground, planted with potatoes, cabbages, turnips, beans, peas, carrots, parsnips, and onions—all for prison use. This piece of land has only been enclosed four years. It was given to the prison for as much more land on the northern side of the building where Victoria Street now stands. There was a garden

* During the week previous to our inspection of this prison, two mats had been made, and 19¾ lbs. of coir used in the manufacture of them, the cost of which was estimated to amount to 4s. 6¼d. at 2¾d. per lb. The mats were 6 feet long and 4 feet wide, and the nett earnings of the boy employed were computed at 4s.

there of the same kind as the present. About eight boys, on an average, keep this in order throughout the year, though perhaps there are a few more employed upon it in the spring.

"I think the garden labour," said the warder, "very good for the prisoners; but, of course, we should require a larger tract of land than we could get here, in the heart of West-minster, to keep all our prisoners employed at such work. Some of the boys like the field labour, and some do not—they object to the heavy work, such as wheeling and digging." Here we found five boys at work, in company, with an officer, three digging-in manure, a fourth hoeing, and another carrying water. The value of the whole of the crops, last year, was £25, we were told; though in other years they had yielded £30.* Hence, assuming the gross earnings of the eight boys to be £20, exclusive of the rent, we have about £2 10s. per annum for the value of the labour of each.

"It's very very bad ground here," said the warder, "very poor; for three foot down we get sand itself; and that's one reason why we can't have better crops. Another reason is, we can take only the short-sentence boys, for we are afraid of employing the two years' lads out here; so as soon as we have got one gang, they go, and we have to look about for another. Besides, town lads prefer oakum-picking; for digging, they say, galls their hands. That boy you observe working alone yonder, goes out in a day or two, or I shouldn't leave him by himself. The wall is low you see."

This completes our account of the work done at Tothill Fields prison.

We have seen that there are, upon an average, 157 boys employed in the oakum-room, and that these earn about 18s. each per annum.

In the shoemakers' shop, there are generally 13 employed; and these gain, according to the apparently over-rated estimates, upwards of £8 a-year each.

In the tailors' shop there are 26 boys at work, each calculated to earn about £3 per annum.

In the carpenters', there are 2 boys, whose labour is not returned as of any value at all.

In the oakum-store, 9 prisoners are employed, earning about the same as those in the large work-room, besides one engaged at matmaking, whose gains are estimated at 4s. a-week, or about £10 a-year.

And in the garden, 8 lads are employed, whose average earnings seem to be of the value of about £2 10s. annually.

Now the expense of maintaining and clothing, &c., each prisoner, at Tothill Fields, is about £8 per annum; so that there is a heavy loss upon all these forms of labour, excepting that of shoemaking and matmaking; the former of which, at least, there is good reason for supposing to be grossly over-estimated.† This makes the gross value of 216 boys' labour amount to £374 17s. 6d. per annum, or, as nearly as possible, £1 14s. 8d. per head. The average value of the labour of the prisoners throughout England and Wales is £2 1s. 3d. (see *ante*, p. 350).

¶ ii.—ε.

Of the Boy-Prisoners' School-room and Library.

The school-room we found to be situate opposite to the tailors' shop, and it had the true academical fittings. There were the ordinary long, narrow desks, with the sloping ledge,

---

* The potatoes, estimated at £4 per ton, were worth about £10; the cabbages, about £7 10s., at 4d. per dozen; the tares yielded about £2 10s.; and the onions, at 3s. the bushel, were valued at 18s.

† To the above list should be added, 4 boys employed in the planted court-yard, while the mowing is going on, and one of whom is kept continually at work in the same place.

hardly wider than that of a pew, and pierced at intervals with holes, for ink-stands, that reminded one of the miniature flower-pots for dwarf plants.   Then the walls were stuck all over with black boards covered with Scripture texts, as, for instance:—

> "I WILL ARISE, AND GO TO MY FATHER,
> AND SAY UNTO HIM, FATHER, I HAVE SINNED
> AGAINST HEAVEN, AND BEFORE THEE."

> "BOAST NOT THYSELF OF TO-MORROW,
> FOR THOU KNOWEST NOT WHAT A DAY
> MAY BRING FORTH."

On the opposite wall hung some long strips of boards, with Roman numerals upon them, and the alphabet in different characters, as well as the Multiplication Table, and sheets of lessons in large type; whilst against the end of the room, near the door, were large maps, and a book-case, with the warder's high desk just in front of it.

At the time of our entry, the warder schoolmaster was hearing the boys read from the Bible, the class standing in a line near the wall, each with a book in his hand. At the opposite end of the school-room was another detachment of lads, stammering over one of the large printed sheets, which a second warder held in his hand.   Some of the lads read quickly, and others boggled sadly over the words, as, for instance—"And into whatsoever 'ouse ye enter,"—("Look at it, boy! don't you see there's an h to the word?" cries the warder.) "And into whatsoever house ye enter fust,"—("How often am I to tell you that there's no such word as fust?   Spell it.")—"f-i-r-s-t," proceeds the lad, " say ye, peace be unto this 'ouse,"—("What! 'ouse again?")—-" house," quickly adds the youngster.

The next verse was read off rapidly and glibly enough, by one who seemed but half the age of the other.

"I don't think you can manage it—can you, R——?" said the warder, addressing a heavy-looking Irish lad, whose turn it was to proceed with the reading.

"Go on next boy," he adds.

"But—I—say—unto—you—that—in—that—day—it—shall—be—more—tol-de-rol"— ("What!" cries the warder, "tolerable, you mean.")—"tol'ble—for—Sodom—and— Tomorrer."—(" Gomorrah, boy—can't you see?")

At the other end of the room the lads were making even greater havoc with the words; and though the lesson consisted of simple monosyllables, such as " The old man must be led by the hand, or he may fall into the deep pit," one-half of the big boys, even those of sixteen, were unable to accomplish the task.

The warder schoolmaster informed us that there were five classes every day, and of those who attended the school there were only 30 who could read and write well, whereas there were as many as 92 who could read and write imperfectly, and 94 who could hardly read at all.

"They are just like those boys at the other end of the room, who are spelling words of one syllable.   Fifty in every one hundred we get here," he went on, " don't know their letters when they come in, even though they are some of the oldest boys that can be sent to us. Each prisoner has one hour's schooling every day.   Some we have very great difficulty in teaching.   Now here's one.   Come here, L——.   He's thirteen years old, and has been in the prison not less than a year altogether, and yet he doesn't know more than his letters now. He used to be sent to us for begging, but latterly he has come in for thieving.   He's taken to picking pockets within this last year or so."

"But it is only here and there," the warder went on, "that we meet with a boy who is very difficult to teach; they're generally like other boys.   I have been managing the school here for the last thirteen years, and about 2,200 come under my care in the course of the twelvemonth."

The schoolmaster then produced some of the boys' copy-books, and pointed to them with no little pride as he said, " That's learnt in the prison. It's not bad, is it, considering he's only been at it for three months?"

The prison library, the warder further informed us, consists of travels and voyages; of periodicals, such as the " Leisure hour;" of the " History of England;" of narratives, such as " The Loss of the Kent;" of small works on Natural History, like the " Book of Birds;" and some few works of fiction, such as " Robinson Crusoe." The volumes are supplied, he told us, by the chapel clerk, who takes down the boys' names and gives out the books the next day. Prisoners are allowed to keep the books they have to read as long as they please; but if they misconduct themselves, the privilege of reading is stopped. They are allowed to amuse themselves with their books during meal times, and after supper for about half an hour before being locked up for the night, at six o'clock. In the summer, they can read in their cells, as well as in the dormitory; but in winter they cannot do so, as no lights are allowed them, nor is the prison heated, and, consequently, they have to remain from six in the evening until half-past six in the morning in utter darkness and idleness.

This appears to us so gross a defect, as to be a positive scandal to the country in which it is allowed to continue.

Concerning the system of education, we have nothing further to urge. Those who believe that boys of criminal propensities are to be made a thought better by such schooling, as we have here given the reader a sense of, must be as deficient in their knowledge of human nature as zealots usually are.

Of course, the teaching of reading and writing is a negative good; but it becomes almost an evil when people get to believe that it has any positive moral or religious effects, *per se,* and so to forgo, as is invariably the case in our prisons of the present day, all education of the feelings, and principles, and even the tastes, of those confined within them. The most valuable of all schooling is surely that of the heart, and the next that of the hands, especially for the poorer classes, who are mostly the inmates of our jails; and to educate either of these there is hardly any attempt made in our prisons of the present day.

¶ ii—ζ.

Of the Reception and Discharge of Prisoners at Tothill Fields.

Of the appearance and demeanour of the boys at chapel there is little demanding special notice; and we have already fully described the service at Pentonville, as well as that at Coldbath Fields.

Of the serving of the breakfast and dinner, again, the illustration printed in this work will afford a better idea of the process than words can give. We may say, however, that at the end of the oakum-room, where the serving takes place, a warder stands, with a large white apron half covering his uniform, and with a ladle in his hand. Before him, raised on a bench, are two large tubs, such as are used for washing; one of these is white within with the thick gruel, and the other brown with the cocoa it contains. On another bench by his side is a large basket full of small loaves, like puny half-quarterns. Near him is a boy, stationed by a large basket of tins, and close at hand, on a mat, is a heap of metal spoons.

" Come on, front row," cries the warder; and immediately the prisoners on the foremost bench come filing past the " long lights," each lad picking a spoon from the mat as he goes by. Then the lad stationed by the tin basket hands them, one by one, a pannikin, and, each boy carrying this to the tubs, gets it filled either with a pint, or half a pint of gruel, according as he be merely a vagrant, and belong to the second or third class; or a pint of cocoa, if he be a felon, and lucky enough to rank as a first-class criminal. The prisoner receives, at the same time, a loaf of bread, which is only 5⅓ oz. in weight, if his offence be of the the lightest character; but one of 6⅔ oz., if of a graver nature.

The dinner is served in the same manner, with the exception that the tubs then are filled not only with gruel for the more innocent, though less favoured, third-class prisoners, but sometimes with soup, of which the first and second class get a pint, whilst the soup is occasionally displaced for tins of meat and potatoes for the more profligate and better-treated portion of the prisoners.*

On one of the days of our inspection of this prison, we were informed that three fresh prisoners had just arrived, and we accordingly hastened to the reception-room, to be present at the process of admission. The reception-wards at Tothill Fields are situate in that part of the building which faces Francis Street, forming part of the offices that are ranged round the planted court-yard.

Here we found two wretched shoeless and ragged creatures, and one more decently clad youth, his darned clothes telling that, at least, *he* had a mother who took some little care of him. The latter boy, we were told, had just been sent from the Sessions; he was thirteen years of age, and had got two years' imprisonment for stealing brass. This heavy sentence had been passed upon the lad with the view of getting him sent to some reformatory institution. His father was dead, we were told, and his mother had a large family of eight children, said our informant. The warder, who had seen her, added that she appeared a very decent sort of woman, and gave her boy excellent instruction and advice. She was an India-rubber weaver, and earned but little, though she had many mouths to feed—her youngest child being only four years of age.

The other boys were of a very different stamp. One of these, who was but thirteen years old, and was habited in an old coat and plaid waistcoat, with a red cotton handkerchief about his neck, had been in the prison three times before—indeed, it was only eight weeks since he had quitted it, and he had had three weeks' imprisonment then. His present sentence

* We append the scale of the provisions furnished to the different classes of boy-prisoners :—

DIET TABLE—HOUSE OF CORRECTION AT WESTMINSTER—1856.

DAYS.	FIRST CLASS.—All Prisoners under 17 years of age, whose terms of Imprisonment exceed 3 months.									SECOND CLASS.—All Prisoners under 17 years of age, whose terms of Imprisonment are more than 14 days and not exceeding 3 months.									THIRD CLASS.—All Prisoners under 17 years of age, whose terms of Imprison do not exceed 14 days.					
	Breakfast.		Dinner.					Supper.		Breakfast.		Dinner.					Supper.		Breakfast.		Dinner.		Supper.	
	Bread.	Cocoa.	Bread.	Meat.	Potatoes.	Soup.	Gruel.	Bread.	Gruel.	Bread.	Gruel.	Bread.	Meat.	Potatoes.	Soup.	Gruel.	Bread.	Gruel.	Bread.	Gruel.	Bread.	Gruel.	Bread.	Gruel.
	Oz.	Pint	Oz.	Oz.	Oz.	Pint	Pint	Oz.	Pint	Oz.	Pint	Oz.	Oz.	Oz.	Pint	Pint	Oz.	Pint	Oz.	Pint	Oz.	Pint	Oz.	Pint
Monday .	6⅔	1	6⅔	...	...	1	...	6⅔	1	6⅔	1	6⅔	...	...	1	...	6⅔	½	5⅓	½	5⅓	1	5⅓	½
Tuesday .	6⅔	1	6⅔	6	8	...	...	6⅔	1	6⅔	1	6⅔	...	...	...	1	6⅔	½	5⅓	½	5⅓	1	5⅓	½
Wednesday .	6⅔	1	6⅔	...	...	1	...	6⅔	1	6⅔	1	6⅔	...	...	...	1	6⅔	½	5⅓	½	5⅓	1	5⅓	½
Thursday .	6⅔	1	6⅔	6	8	...	...	6⅔	1	6⅔	1	6⅔	6	8	...	...	6⅔	½	5⅓	½	5⅓	1	5⅓	½
Friday .	6⅔	1	6⅔	...	...	1	...	6⅔	1	6⅔	1	6⅔	...	...	1	...	6⅔	½	5⅓	½	5⅓	1	5⅓	½
Saturday .	6⅔	1	6⅔	...	...	...	1	6⅔	1	6⅔	1	6⅔	...	...	...	1	6⅔	½	5⅓	½	5⅓	1	5⅓	½
Sunday . .	6⅔	1	6⅔	6	8	...	...	6⅔	1	6⅔	1	6⅔	6	8	...	...	6⅔	½	5⅓	½	5⅓	1	5⅓	½
Total .	46⅔	7	46⅔	18	24	3	1	46⅔	7	46⅔	7	46⅔	12	16	2	3	46⅔	3½	37⅓	3½	37⅓	7	37⅓	3½

The ingredients forming the above dietary to be in the following proportions :—For every hundred pints, 3 lbs. 2 oz. of Cocoa, 8 lbs. of molasses, or 4 lbs. of raw sugar, and 12½ pints of milk; Gruel, 9 lbs. of oatmeal, and 1 lb. of salt; Soup, for every hundred pints, 2 ox-heads, 3 lbs. of barley, 6 lbs. of peas, 3 lbs. of rice, 1 lb. of salt, and 2 oz. of pepper, with a due proportion of vegetables; beef and mutton alternate fortnights in the winter months, viz., from October to March, and beef only from April to September, inclusive. The meat diets are issued cold.

was six weeks, for picking ladies' pockets. He stood unabashed, half shivering, without shoes. "There, stand on the mat, boy," said the officer, kindly, to him.

The other, who was dressed in a buttonless Oxonian coat, pinned close up to the neck, and with a crimson silk handkerchief about his throat, had the peculiar side-locks indicative of the London thief. He, too, was an old frequenter of the prison, and had been there about a year ago. "I've been thieving ever since I was here before," he said, in answer to our questions. "Mother sells things in the street. I aint got no father—never had one, that I know on. I've done often two pockets a-day since I've been out. It wouldn't have lasted as long as it has, if I'd ha' done that number all the year round. Sometimes I do odd jobs for mother, do you see; and when I'm not at work for her, I goes pickpocketing on my own hook."

The conversation was stopped by the warder crying, "Come this way, boys!" and straightway the two shoeless, experienced, and shameless young thieves, passed on grinning into the examination-room, whilst the more decent boy, caught in his first offence, followed sobbing in their wake.

"Have you got anything in your pockets?" inquires the officer. "You'd better say; for you will be punished if any article is found upon you afterwards."

"I've got a loaf, please, sir," says the least depraved of the lads, as he takes a piece of bread from his pocket.

"That's a House of Detention loaf, aint it?" asked the warder, as his experienced eye recognizes the shape and make. "Well, you can keep that," he adds. "Now, go in there and take off your clothes, and mind you wash yourself thoroughly with the soap. Do you hear?" he says, as he leads the boys to a kind of box-lobby, and opening the doors to the baths, which seem like small cisterns sunk in the floor, he bids them go in, and be as quick about washing themselves as they can.

Outside here is a boy-prisoner sorting suits of prison clothes on the ground, from a basket, and as soon as one suit is complete, he thrusts it into one of the bath-rooms, for the use of the new-comer within.

"They sleep in the reception-room the first night," says the warder, "and have their supper and breakfast in the examination-room;" and, as he says the words, we can hear the boys breathing hard and spluttering, while they splash the water about in the adjacent baths.

In an adjoining room, hanging up against the wall, are several handcuffs on pegs, and instruments that appear like leathern bottles, but which, we are informed, are muffles, which were sent from Hanwell some years ago, when some lunatic prisoners were given to tearing up their clothes. These muffles are attached to a strap, which goes round the waist; sometimes they are applied to women who destroy their garments.

In a few minutes the boys made their appearance again in the prison dress, and those who were shoeless before came out now comfortably shod. They had all the look of old jail-birds; for, in the suit of gray, it was almost impossible to distinguish the more decent boy from the others.

One of the habitual young thieves said, with a smile, as he pointed to the less experienced lad, "He's got on his own boots, please, sir; and his own hankycher, too, instead of the stock."

The warder locks the boys up in the bath-rooms, and telling the lads he's going to get them some soup or gruel from the kitchen, walks off in that direction, informing us, by the way, that the new-comers will have to remain till the surgeon sees them on the morrow, and passes them up to their room. "The boys mostly prefer being in the dormitory," he adds. "Very few, indeed, will volunteer for the cells."

These dormitories are not only at variance with the principles of the silent associated system, upon which the Westminster House of Correction is said to be conducted, and which requires, in its integrity, that the prisoners, though working in company by day, should be provided each with a separate sleeping apartment by night, but they reduce the discipline of the prison to that state of promiscuous herding of the prisoners which was the great vice of the prison arrangements of former times, and that at the very period when there is less supervision on the part of the officers than at any hour of the day. Indeed those prisons, where the inmates are congregated in considerable numbers in large dormitories by night, possess all the objectionable features of the Hulks. And the boys' prison at Tothill Fields, with its common sleeping-rooms, where some 80 odd lads are crowded together, with their beds lying on the ground as close as the hammocks swing between the decks of the convict ships at Woolwich, is a place that is about upon a par with the prison regulations in the beginning of the present century, and a state of things that should not be allowed to exist for a single day in this country, with our present knowledge of the evils of such association. In this establishment, there is only one such dormitory, and this is situate on the upper floor of the prison 3 and 4, being one large room that stretches the entire length and width of the building. In this place, at the time of our visit, no less than 87 boys had slept the night before. The room contains 50 iron bedsteads, 25 of which are ranged on either side of it, whilst the remaining beds are formed by strewing the requisite number of mattresses along the boards. The dormitory is 80 feet long, and 32 feet wide, so that, allowing each of the 25 bedsteads to be 3 feet wide, it is evident that there would not be even one inch of space between it and the beds on either side of it; while, if we reckon the mattresses at 5 feet long, it is equally plain that, from the width of the apartment, again, there can be a gangway of only 12 feet in breadth between the rows, even if we suppose the double line on either side to be immediately head to foot. Moreover, we have before stated, scientific authorities have agreed that, even where perfect ventilation exists, a cell having a capacity of upwards of 900 cubic feet is necessary for the maintenance of the perfect health of each prisoner confined in it. But the dormitory to which we refer is only 12 feet high, and therefore contains not quite 40,000 cubic feet, thus allowing but little more than 350 cubic feet of air for each prisoner to breathe during the night. It is true there is a skylight of pierced glass in the roof, but it must be also remembered that these apertures can only remove the upper stratum of the atmosphere within the apartment, and that therefore the prisoners must remain immersed for many hours in a noxious medium of their own exhalations; and if a small aperture in the upper part of the room be sufficient to ensure perfect ventilation, it is obvious that such large and expensive apparatus as ventilating shafts and flues would not be applied to every new building.

In this dormitory there are two officers keeping watch during the night. Nevertheless, as the boys are locked up in it as early as six o'clock in the evening, and not liberated till half-past six in the morning, and left there, too, without any occupation to divert their minds from intercourse, it is manifest that, even with tenfold the supervision, all kinds of moral pollution must go on with the prisoners. Indeed, the mind is naturally led to ask, what can be the use of keeping lads silent throughout the day, and with warders all around them, placed in elevated situations, so as to detect and prevent the slightest communication either by look or by gesture, and yet to place the very same young urchins at night in the best possible position for intercommunication, and with not one tithe of the supervision of the day-time.

We now come to the last subject we have to touch upon in connection with the boys' prison at Tothill Fields. We have already spoken of the number of punishments, and shown that they are far below the average number of all England and Wales—a fact which, we repeat, greatly redounds to the honour of all connected with this prison. We ourselves can bear witness to the order and regularity maintained, at the period of our visit, by the young profligates confined here. And those prison authorities are assuredly the best who can attain this end with the infliction of the least possible physical suffering. Nor should we forget, in our appreciation of this part of the economy of the Westminster House of Correction, the many inducements that there are to apply a greater amount of coercion to boys rather than to men, so that the government of this prison appears to be carried on upon as mild and considerate a plan as any in the kingdom.   The reports seemed certainly far from being heavy on any of the days that we were at the prison, and the majority were for the boyish tricks of laughing, talking, and being disorderly, whilst two were for talking and shouting in their cells—an offence which is due mainly to the circumstance of the boys being locked up as early as six, and not allowed any light even to read by in the winter evenings, so that as there is only one warder patrolling the prison throughout the night, it is obvious that the lads, being aware of the opportunities that they have for intercourse, naturally resort to that as the means of whiling away the terrible tedium of solitude and darkness.   Indeed, one of the authorities assured us, that it was impossible to stop the communication among the youngsters, owing to this absurd and wicked regulation.

"Now the man's calling the discharges out," said our official guide, directing our attention to one of the warders, who had entered the oakum-room with a slate in his hand, and from which he was reading off the names of certain prisoners.

"James C——," said the officer; "William W——, Thomas D——, John D——," &c.; and as the warder repeated the names, the boys made answer, and coming out from their places, arranged themselves in a row beside the man.   Then the warder asked each boy what was his name, and how long he had been in the prison, whilst, as the lad replied, he looked at the slate to see if the answer agreed with the particulars set against the name. After this, the officer led the boys towards the store-room, where they were furnished with their own clothes, and soon conducted down to the gate, where they were drawn up within the porch, immediately outside the governor's office.

To this part of the building we directed our steps, when we heard that all was ready for carrying out the process.   Here we found some half-dozen lads, who had shed the prison garb, and were habited in their own rags and tatters.   But half an hour before, they were warmly and comfortably clad, and now many of them stood shivering in their scanty and rent apparel.   One was without a jacket, and another with his coat pinned up, so as to hide the want of a waistcoat.

"William C——" was called out within, and the warder outside the office door, echoing the name, told the boy who answered to it to step inside.   He was placed in a small passage in front of a window looking into the office, where stood the clerk close against a desk on the other side.

"Have you ever been here before?" said the clerk.   "No," was the answer.

"Belongs to Millbank," said one of the warders; "and some friend is here for him."

"Let him step in," replied the clerk.   The friend had no sooner made his appearance, than the clerk inquired, "Who are you?"

"His brother," was the answer.

"The magistrates have given this boy a shilling, and they hope they'll never see him here again, so do you take care of him."   And with this admonition, and the money, the couple withdrew.

"James H——" was next shouted out, whereupon a little boy made his appearance outside the office window, his head scarcely reaching above the sill.

"You've been in for robbing your mother, eh?   What a horrible fellow you must be to do that!   Why must you go plundering her, of all persons in the world?   The next boy to you has been flogged, and that will be your fate if ever you come here again, I can tell you."

"Anybody for this boy?" the clerk inquired of the attendant warder.

"Nobody for him, sir," was the reply.

"Where does your mother live?" demanded the clerk.

"In G—— Street, St. Luke's," said the boy, with a smile on his lip, and utterly unaffected by what had been said to him.

"He's been here often before," the governor observed to us. "He's a bad boy, indeed."

"Henry N——" was the next boy called for.

"How long have you been here?" the clerk began with this one.

"Six weeks, sir."

"And how often before?"

"Three times here, and twice in the House of Detention."

"Ay, we're getting a little of it out. Nobody for this boy, I suppose," he added.

"No, sir," was the answer.

"Thomas W——" was then called.

"What time have you been here?"

"Ten days, please, sir," said a small boy, in a whining voice, while the clerk stretched his head forward out of the window to get a peep at him.

"And how often before?"

"Six times, please, sir," was the answer given, in the same whining tone.

"Now, that's very pretty for a boy of your age—isn't it? And how came you to break sixty panes of glass? for that's the offence you were charged with."

"I did it along with other boys, sir—heaving stones."

"A set of mischievous young urchins!" the clerk exclaimed. "Was it an empty house?" he asked.

"No, please, sir—it was an old factory; and there was about a hundred panes broken before, so the boys was trying to smash the rest on them."

"Anybody there for this boy, of the name of Thomas W——?"

"No, sir, nobody," the warder replied.*

* Previous to the discharge of any prisoner, the following blank form of letter is filled up and sent to the parents or friends of the lad, in order that they may be at the gate, at the appointed time, to take charge of him:—

"HOUSE OF CORRECTION, TOTHILL FIELDS, WESTMINSTER.

"_____day of _____185_____is acquainted that_____

will be discharged from the above prison on _____next, at_____o'clock in the_____

when it is requested that_____ friends will attend to receive_____"

It would not be fair to close this article without printing a copy of the rules of the prison, the same as we have done with others:—

"RULES RELATING TO THE TREATMENT AND CONDUCT OF THE PRISONERS, AS CERTIFIED BY HER MAJESTY'S SECRETARY OF STATE, AS PROPER TO BE ENFORCED.

"1. All prisoners are on admission to be placed in a reception-cell. To be strictly searched. All knives, sharp instruments, dangerous weapons, or articles calculated to facilitate escape, to be taken from them; all money and other effects brought in with them, or subsequently sent in for their use and benefit, to be taken care of. Such money and effects to be entered in the prisoners' property book.

"2. Every prisoner is to be examined by the surgeon before he be passed into the proper ward. And to be cleansed in a warm or cold bath, and have his hair cut, as the surgeon may direct; he is not to be stripped and bathed in the presence of any other prisoner.

"3. The wearing apparel of every prisoner to be fumigated and purified, if requisite; and, if necessary, may be burned. If the wearing apparel of prisoners before trial be insufficient, or necessary to be preserved for the trial, such prisoners may be furnished with a plain suit of coarse cloth. In the case of convicted prisoners, their wearing apparel to be taken charge of, and they provided with a prison dress. No prisoner, unless under conviction for felony, to be clothed in a party-coloured dress.

"4. Male prisoners to be shaved at least once a-week; and convicted prisoners to have their hair cut at least once a-month.

"5. Convenient places to be provided with water, soap, towels, and combs. And every prisoner to be required to wash daily; all prisoners, if the surgeon so advises, to be placed in a bath at least once a month.

"6. Every prisoner to be provided with a separate bed or hammock, either in a separate cell, or in a cell

"Very well, let them all go."

The moment afterwards, the officer in charge of the outer gate opened the door, and the liberated boys were once more at large in the world.

with not less than two other male prisoners. To be provided with a hair, flock, or straw mattress, two blankets, and a coverlid.

" 7. Every prisoner to be allowed as much air and exercise as shall be recommended by the surgeon.

" 8. Every prisoner who does not maintain himself to be allowed a sufficient quantity of plain and wholesome food, according to the dietaries provided for each class of prisoners. A prisoner may require his food to be weighed or measured, and shall not thereby be subjected to any privation or inconvenience.

" 9. No spirits, wine, beer, cider, or other fermented liquor, shall be admitted for the use of any prisoner without a written order of the surgeon.

" 10. No tobacco to be admitted for the use of any prisoner, except by written order of the surgeon.

" 11. No prisoner to be permitted to see any visitor out of the place appropriated for that purpose, except in special cases under a written order signed by a visiting justice; and, in the case of prisoners seriously ill, by a written order of the governor and surgeon. Male prisoners to be visited in the presence of the governor or subordinate officer. This rule is not to extend to prisoners when they see their legal advisers.

" 12. No person shall be admitted to visit a prisoner on a Sunday, except in special cases by a written order of a visiting justice; and in no case shall a prisoner under punishment for offences committed within the prison, or in solitary confinement under sentence of any court, be permitted to receive any visits from friends without an express order in writing from a visiting justice, stating the grounds on which such order is given.

" 13. Persons may be permitted by order of a visiting justice, or by the governor, to visit at any reasonable hour prisoners confined for non-payment of penalties or for want of sureties, for the purpose of making arrangements for the payment of the penalty or the finding of sureties.

" 14. Any near relation or friend may be allowed to see a prisoner dangerously ill, under an order in writing signed by the governor and surgeon.

" 15. Any prisoner of a religious persuasion differing from that of the Established Church may, on request to the governor, be visited by a minister of his persuasion on Sundays, or any other days, at such reasonable hours as may not interfere with the good order of the prison. Any books which such ministers may wish to supply to the prisoners of their persuasion must be first submitted to a visiting justice for approval.

" 16. No prisoner who is a Jew or Mahometan to be compelled to labour on his sabbath.

" 17. No prisoner to be allowed to receive or send any letter except from or to a visiting justice, without previous inspection by the governor.

" 18. No prisoner to receive or send any parcel, or receive any food, clothing, bedding, or other articles, without previous inspection.

" 19. Officers on duty to attend to complaints of prisoners, and report the same to the governor.

" 20. A prisoner complaining of illness, to be reported without delay to the surgeon; and not to be compelled to labour until after the surgeon has seen him.

" 21. No prisoner not sentenced to hard labour to be employed on the tread-wheel, either with or without his consent.

" 22. No prisoner to be employed as warder, assistant-warder, wardsman, yardsman, overseer, monitor, schoolmaster, or in the discipline of the prison, or in the service of any officer thereof, or in the service or instruction of any other prisoner.

" 23. All prisoners to attend Divine service, unless prevented by illness, or permitted to be absent.

" 24. Provision to be made for the instruction of prisoners in reading and writing, under the direction of the visiting justices.

" 25. Prisoners of the Established Church shall be provided with books and tracts of religious, moral, and useful instruction, under the direction of the chaplain; and prisoners of persuasions differing from the Established Church, under the direction of the visiting justices. Each prisoner who can read shall be furnished with a Bible and Common Prayer Book during Divine service; and a Bible and Common Prayer Book placed in each day-room, and (during the summer months) in each sleeping cell.

" 26. Prisoners going to work, to chapel, to the airing-yards, or to any other part of the prison, to be attended by one or more officers; and silence maintained.

" 27. Prisoners to obey the rules of the prison, and the lawful orders of the governor and other officers, and not to treat with disrespect any of the officers or servants of the prison or any person therein. They are not to be idle or negligent in their work; they are not to be guilty of swearing, or of indecent or disorderly conduct; nor to commit any kind of nuisance, nor wilfully damage any bedding, any part of the prison, or any article of property therein.

" 28. Silence, night and day, must be observed, any breach of it to be punished by the stoppage of a

The lad whose brother had come to meet him had two others outside, dressed in fustian jackets and of no very respectable appearance, waiting to welcome him.

The other boys looked round about to see if they could spy any friend of theirs loitering in the neighbourhood.   None was to be seen.

Of all the young creatures discharged that morning, not a father, nor a mother, nor even a grown and decent friend, was there to receive them!

We stood at the prison door, watching the wretched, friendless outcasts turn the corner, and saw the whole of them go off in a gang, in company with the suspicious-looking youths in fustian jackets, who had come to welcome the one whose brother alone had thought him worth the fetching.

We could not help speculating upon the impending fate of these discharged children, and of the shocking heartlessness of the State which can forget its duties as a father to them.

Where were they to go ?   Who was there to counsel and protect them ?   The only home that was open to receive them was the thieves' lodging-house, and the only friends and advisers they could find in the world, the old and experienced inmates of such places.

meal, or part thereof, and a repetition of offence by increased stoppages, or by solitary confinement on bread and water only, or by such other punishment as the law has provided. Singing or whistling in the cells, work-rooms, or yards, is strictly prohibited, and the following are also declared to be acts of disorder and to be punishable as such, viz :—any attempt to barter or exchange provisions, any marking, defacing or injuring the doors, walls, tread-wheels, forms, tables, clothes, bedding, books, or utensils whatsoever of the prison, any attempt at communication by signs, writing, or stratagem of any sort ; any unnecessary looking round or about, each prisoner being required to look before him either at Divine service or at work, meals, exercise, or passage from one part of the prison to the other, any secreting of money, tobacco or forbidden articles, either on first admission into the prison or afterwards ; any purloining or contriving to purloin provisions, books, combs, or any other article, or, when employed in the grounds, purloining vegetables or fruit, &c., growing therein ; or any wilful disobedience of such orders of the governor or officers of the prison as shall be in accordance with law and the rules of the prison.

" 29. Any convicted prisoner who shall neglect or refuse to perform the labour allotted to him, or who, shall make or attempt to make any wound, sore, or " fox " on his person, or counterfeit fits, or any ailment, for the purpose of obtaining the sanction of the surgeon to be excused labour, or an increased allowance of diet, or any indulgence either in or out of the infirmary, or shall be guilty of a breach of the prison rules, shall be liable to be punished by being kept in solitary confinement on bread and water only, for such time not exceeding one month as the visiting justices shall think fit.

" 30. The governor may examine any persons touching offences committed by prisoners, and determine thereupon ; and order any prisoner so offending to be punished for not more than three days, as the case may deserve. The several punishments for prisoners are—close confinement in their own cells, or in refractory cells, allowance of bread and water only for food, or reduction of the ordinary allowance of food ; or, in case of necessity, offenders may be placed in irons (but not for more than twenty-four hours at one time without a written order by a visiting justice). In cases of greater or repeated offence, a visiting or other justice may order close confinement for a month, or personal correction in the case of prisoners convicted of felony or sentenced to hard labour.

" 31. A prisoner's earnings, or money in the hands of the governor, shall be liable and may be applied towards the repair of any injury done by him wilfully to the prison, or to county property, or other property therein.

" 32. Any prisoner whose term of imprisonment would expire on a Sunday, shall be discharged on the Saturday next preceding."

The subjoined is the official notice concerning the " star system," as it is called .—

" REWARDS TO PRISONERS FOR GOOD CONDUCT.

" A Red Star on the left arm shall be worn as a mark of good conduct by prisoners, for every three months they may have been in the prison without any complaint or report being made against them.   They may, however, be deprived thereof in case of misconduct.

" A prisoner in possession, at the time of his or her discharge, of one or more Stars may receive a reward to be determined by the visiting justices.

" By order of the visiting justices,

" CHARLES CHEETHAM, Governor."

¶ ii.—η.

Of Juvenile Offenders, in Connection with the Increase of Crime in this Country.

From what has been already shown in connection with the details of the boys' prison at Tothill Fields, as well as concerning the number of boy-prisoners, or juvenile offenders, as they are called, in the prisons of the country generally, we believe no thinking person can come to any other conclusion, than that it is from such classes as these the old and habitual criminals among us are originally derived, and annually recruited, so as to keep on supplying, year after year, with but slight fluctuations, the same number for trial at our sessions and assizes, and the same number of convicts, without any apparent decrease of the criminal stock of the country. Nevertheless, persons who are unused to the study of such matters, are inclined to adopt hasty theories concerning the origin of crime among us, and to refer it to circumstances which, though they may tend to swell the number of *casual* criminals, cannot strictly be said to have any influence on the formation of *habitual* ones.

It is manifest that, in order to obtain a regular living by criminal courses, it is necessary that the same apprenticeship should be served to the different forms of that business, as to any other trade. A novice, who tried to pick a pocket, or break into a house, or coin a piece of false money, would be detected in the very first attempt, and a stop probably be put to his career even in the outset. Those who are acquainted with the intricate machinery necessary for carrying on a successful course of crime, even for a short period—how, for instance, with burglars, it is necessary to be in connection with "putters-up" to plan the robberies, companions wherewith to execute them, and "fences" to receive the property when stolen—how, with coiners, it is essential to know where to obtain the apparatus and materials, and the "smashers" by whom to pass the "shoful" pieces off upon the public—and how, with pickpockets too, it is necessary to go out with "stalls" to cover the actual offender, and others to whom to pass the handkerchief, or the purse, immediately it is taken; so that one might as well think of starting as an attorney, without being acquainted with the legal offices and practice of the courts, as well as the proper counsel and pleaders to employ.

A moment's reflection, however, will teach the keen-witted, that crime is as much a business among us, as manufacturing or trading in any article of wealth. Hence, it is clear that the professional criminals of this country must be regularly bred and educated to the craft—for such it really is.

That the juvenile offenders are the principal class from whom the old habitual ones are derived becomes positively indisputable, when the facts are brought clearly before the mind. Among the boy-prisoners, a large proportion of Irish lads are always to be found; and we have before said, that a considerable number of the regular thieves are declared, even by the class themselves, to be Irish-Cockneys. Further, we have proved that the majority of the convicts of the country are between the ages of 17 and 25; and when this is coupled with the fact, that the average duration of a thief's career is, according to the best authorities, somewhere about six years, it is plain that the juvenile offender must, in the course of time, pass into the full-grown thief.

A thief's life, the men themselves say, consists generally of four months in prison and six months out; and, during this period, the mobsmen calculate that they commit some six robberies a day, or, on an average, fifty per week; for there is generally something going on, they say, one day in the seven—either a race, or a fair, or a review, or a flower-show, or a confirmation, or a popular preacher to draw large crowds together. Hence, it would appear, that not less than 1,000 robberies must be committed by each regular hand to one detection. It is obvious, therefore, that to perpetrate such an amount of depredations without discovery must require not only long practice, but great knowledge of the movements of the police, as well as considerable cunning and sleight of hand, all of which are utterly incompatible with any sudden additions of untrained persons to the class.

Notwithstanding these plain facts, however, learned professors *will* occasionally read papers before meetings of scientific gentlemen, in order to prove that the fluctuations in the number of our criminals are due to the greater or less prosperity of the nation, and that years of distress are years in which malefactors abound, and years of plenty those in which our murderers, and burglars, and pickpockets cease to indulge in their natural propensities.

Now, surely it can be no offence to these sages to insinuate, that they are as unacquainted with the characters of the people concerning whom they are speculating, as geologists are with the habits of the megatherium and iguanodon. They forget that crime is made up of many elements—that a large proportion of it consists of acts of ferocity and malice—such as assaults, and attempts to kill, and of actual manslaughter; though such propensities surely cannot be referred to a scarcity of food amongst the people, since an increase in the number of assaults is known to be connected with a greater consumption of spirituous liquors. Again, another form of crime consists of acts of lust, indecency, shame, &c.; and these, also, have assuredly nothing to do with any deterioration in the comforts of the community.

A third division of the same subject is made up of the crimes of evil-speaking, such as perjury, &c.; but these, too, cannot possibly be said to be influenced by years of prosperity or the reverse.

The only kind of crimes, indeed, that would appear, at first sight, to be attributable to the increased poverty of the people, are those offences which consist of the appropriation of the property of others, such as acts of felony, larceny, sheep-stealing, embezzlement, illegally pawning, forgery, and the like. But even these will be found, when duly analysed, to consist mainly, as we have said, of such acts as it is impossible for any one to commit without an almost certainty of being detected at the very outset, and of practices which persons certainly do not adopt on the spur of the moment, but to which they are regularly bred and trained. By far the greater proportion even of this class of crimes consists of those of which a large proportion of our population make a regular trade; and as well might it be said that the numbers of clergymen, or merchants, or the engineers of the country, vary with the varying wealth of our people, as that our habitual criminals do so.

Moreover, those who desire to be convinced upon the subject, can put the matter to the test of figures, and see whether the fluctuations in the number committed for trial agree with the variations in the number of the able-bodied paupers through a long series of years. The amount of pauperism in the land is the true test as to the prosperity or distress of the country; and if it can be shown, which assuredly it cannot (for years ago we put the matter to the ordeal of statistics), that in those counties and in those years in which there is a greater number of able-bodied poor relieved, there is also a greater number of persons tried at the assizes or sessions throughout the country—then, but not *till* then, it may be truly asserted, that the greater or less number of criminals is governed by a greater or less amount of misery in the land.

Now, the mistake which is usually made in all such theories lies in fancying not only that there is but *one* kind of crime, viz., theft of some form or other, but also in confounding *habitual* with *casual* criminals. The number of habitual criminals, however, is influenced only by the number of convicts annually drafted from the criminal ranks into our prisons, or transported to our colonies, as well as by the number of those *quondam* young offenders who yearly arrive at man's estate. There may be a few others occasionally added to the body from association with some of the tribe; but these are merely exceptional cases, and serve to increase the bulk of the professionals to a very small degree. With the casual crimes the case is entirely different, and these being accidental offences, arising generally either from the cupidity or temptation of the culprits, they are often brought about by an increased pressure of circumstances, and therefore it is but natural that the number of them should vary with the varying prosperity of the nation.*

Further, we have before shown that whereas the number of criminals, in relation to the population of the country (exclusively of those summarily convicted), yields an average during the last 20 years of 15½ to every 10,000 of the population, the habitual criminals make up about 12½ of the ratio, whilst the casual ones constitute merely the small remainder. And it will be found, by studying the criminal records of the country, that the casual ones increase and decrease with different years; whilst the habitual ones remain more or less stationary, altered only by the numbers who are regularly added to or removed from the ranks.

For the sake of putting the criminal question into something like a scientific form, we have drawn up the following series of tables, wherein the crimes are regularly classified according to the causes, or rather the impulses dictating them; whilst each class is separated into two main divisions, according as the crimes included under them are, or are not, capable of being made a means of living or matter of trade by those who practice them. Moreover, the numbers accused of each of the several offences have been calculated, with relation to a definite number of the population, for each quinquennial period during the last twenty years; and thus the reader is placed in a position to observe the various increments and decrements of the different crimes, as well as among the widely-different classes of criminals.

By these tables, which, it should be added, include every crime given in the Government Returns, it will be seen that there are, according to the average for the last twenty years, 12·8 habitual criminals, and 2·8 casual ones to every 10,000 of our people; and that whereas the ratio of the habitual criminals was 13·1 during the decenniad ending 1843, it was 12·5 to the same number of the population in the one ending 1853, so that there was a slight decrease (0·6 per 10,000 of the population) in the course of that period; whilst, with the casual criminals, the average ratio was 3·0 in the same number from 1834 to 1843, and 2·7 between 1844 and 1853; thus showing a decrease of 0·3 per 10,000. These are facts which teach us how slight an impression has really been made upon the great body of criminals by all our late endeavours.

As regards the different kinds of crimes committed by these two distinct classes of criminals, it will be found, that whilst the records show a ratio of 15·7 criminals of both classes per 10,000 of the population, not less than 12·8 of these belong to the class who commit crimes of dishonesty of some kind or other, and that as many as 11½ of this proportion appertain to the habitual order of offenders. Of the remainder, 2·3 of the 15·7 criminals indulge in acts of ferocity and malice, and only 0·3 in offences of a lustful or indecent character.

---

* The above remarks refer principally to a paper that was read before the last meeting of the British Association, and entitled, " A Deduction from the Statistics of Crime for the last Ten Years," and in which it was stated that " the returns of the committals for trial at assize and quarter sessions in England and Wales from 1844 to 1854 (the last year for which they have been published) show clearly that crime increases when the physical condition of the people deteriorates, and *vice versâ*. In 1844 the number of committals," it was said, "was 26,542; in 1845, 24,303; 1846, 25,107; 1847, 28,833; 1848, 30,349; 1849, 27,816; 1850, 26,813; 1851, 27,960; 1852, 27,510; 1853, 27,057; and in 1854, 29,359. The first year," argues the professor, " in which the committals increased is 1847—a year of distress—the rise then being nearly 4,000. This rise was maintained, with an addition of nearly 1,500 in 1848, likewise a year of distress, partly owing to the same causes as in 1847, and partly on account of political disturbances and apprehensions. In 1849, the causes which before had depressed the condition of the labourer died away. Food was cheap and employment abundant. Emigration had removed many of the working-classes, and those who remained at home found the demand for their services increased; and in that year we find the committals decline by nearly 2,500. The succeeding years were likewise seasons of prosperity, and during these the criminal returns exhibit no marked fluctuation. In the last year of the series the number of committals rose by a little over 2,000, but at the same time the condition of the people was impaired, owing to the enhanced price of food and other necessaries of life, and also to the waste of the national resources and partial derangement of trade occasioned by the war."

TABLE SHOWING THE RATIOS OF THE ACCUSED TO EVERY 10,000,000 OF POPULATION THROUGHOUT ENGLAND AND WALES, AND ALSO THE INCREASE OR DECREASE FOR EACH CRIME, ARRANGED IN CLASSES AND ORDERS, DURING THE SEVERAL QUINQUENNIAL AND DECENNIAL PERIODS FROM 1834-1853.

CRIMES.	Quinquennial Ratios from 1834-43.			Quinquennial Ratios from 1844-53.			Decennial Ratios from 1834-53.			Average Ratio for 20 years.
	1834-38.	1839-43.	Increase or Decrease.	1844-48.	1849-53.	Increase or Decrease.	1834-43.	1844-53.	Increase or Decrease.	
Class I. CRIMES OF FEROCITY AND MALICE. ORDER A.—CASUAL CRIMES. 1. MURDEROUS CASES.										
Murder	47·6	39·9	— 7·7	41·9	41·1	— 0·8	43·6	41·5	— 2·1	42·5
Attempts to murder, attended with dangerous bodily harm . . . . Ditto, unattended with do. Shooting at, stabbing, wounding, &c., with intent to maim . . .	92·2	139·4	+ 47·2	136·4	148·3	+ 11·9	116·6	142·5	+ 25·9	129·5
Killing and maiming cattle .	23·6	19·8	— 3·8	19·1	16·1	— 3·0	21·7	17·6	— 4·1	19·6
Total Murderous Cases .	163·4	199·1	+ 36·7	197·4	205·5	+ 8·1	181·9	201·6	+ 29·7	191·6
2. HOMICIDAL AND ASSAULT CASES.										
Manslaughter	148·8	131·5	— 17·3	118·9	121·3	+ 2·4	139·8	120·1	— 19·7	129·9
Assaults and inflicting bodily harm . . . Ditto (common) . . .	507·4	433·7	— 73·7	452·7	380·3	— 72·4	469·3	195·5	— 273·8	332·4
Ditto on peace officers in the execution of their duty .	302·9	300·9	— 2·0	200·2	145·1	— 55·1	301·9	171·8	— 130·1	236·9
Rescue and refusing to aid peace officers	18·1	14·3	— 3·8	5·8	3·1	— 2·7	16·1	4·4	— 11·7	10·2
Riot, breach of peace, &c. .	407·9	338·9	— 69·0	234·4	153·6	— 80·8	372·3	192·8	— 179·5	282·6
Total Homicidal and other Assaults	1,385·1	1,219·3	— 165·8	1,012·0	803·4	— 208·6	1,299·4	684·6	— 614·8	992·0
3. ARSON CASES.										
Setting fire to dwelling-house, shop, &c., persons being within . . Ditto horse, warehouse, corn-stack, &c. . . .	35·8	32·9	— 2·9	76·3	97·1	+ 20·8	34·3	87·0	+ 52·7	60·6
Ditto crops, plantations, heaths, &c.	4·7	4·8	+ 0·1	6·6	8·7	+ 2·1	4·7	7·6	+ 2·9	6·2
Attempts to commit arson, set fire to crops, &c. . .	3·1	2·4	— 0·7	3·4	2·0	— 1·4	2·7	2·7	0·0	2·7
Total Arson Cases . .	43·6	40·3	— 3·3	86·3	107·8	— 21·5	41·7	97·3	— 55·6	69·5
4. DESTRUCTIVE CASES.										
Riot, and feloniously destroying buildings, machinery, &c. .	5·1	18·5	+ 13·4	2·8	2·2	— 0·6	12·0	2·5	— 9·5	7·2
Destroying textile goods in course of manufacture .	1·2	1·7	+ 0·5	0·8	·01	— 0·79	1·4	·04	— 1·3	60·9
Ditto hop-binds, trees, shrubs, &c.	7·1	6·4	— 0·7	2·6	3·6	+ 1·0	6·9	3·0	— 3·9	4·8
Other malicious offences .	6·6	13·5	+ 6·9	11·5	15·2	+ 3·7	10·1	13·4	+ 3·3	11·7
Total Destructive Cases .	20·0	40·3	+ 20·3	17·7	21·1	+ 3·4	30·4	18·9	— 21·5	24·6
All Casual Crimes of Ferocity and Malice . .	1,612·1	1,499·0	— 113·1	1,313·4	1,137·8	— 175·6	1,553·7	1002·4	— 551·3	1,207·7

CRIMES.	Quinquennial Ratios from 1834-43.			Quinquennial Ratios from 1844-53.			Decennial Ratios from 1834-53.			Average Ratio for 20 years.
	1834-38.	1839-43.	Increase or Decrease.	44-48.	1849-53.	Increase or Decrease.	1834-43.	1844-53.	Increase or Decrease.	
CLASS I.—*Continued.*										
ORDER B.—HABITUAL CRIMES.										
1. BURGLARIOUS CASES.										
Burglary . . . . . .)	202·5	357·9	+ 155·4	275·4	·2	+ 31·8	282·7	292·7	+ 10·0	287·7
Do. attended with violence)										
Housebreaking	313·4	398·4	+ 85·0	330·9	333·5	+ 2·6	357·3	332·7	— 24·6	345·0
Breaking within curtilage .	55·1	51·3	— 4·8	36·0	38·1	+ 2·1	53·1	37·1	— 16·0	45·1
Do. into shops, warehouses, counting-houses—stealing	91·0	134·5	+ 43·5	118·2	96·9	— 21·3	113·5	105·8	— 7·7	109·6
Misdemeanours with intent to commit, &c.	13·9	15·5	+ 1·6	14·2	19·9	+ 4·7	14·8	17·1	+ 2·3	15·9
Sacrilege	7·2	9·7	+ 2·5	4·0	5·7	+ 1·7	8·6	4·9	+ 3·7	6·8
Total Burglarious Cases .	683·1	967·3	+ 284·2	778·7	801·3	+ 22·6	830·0	790·3	+ 39·7	810·1
2. HIGHWAY ROBBERY CASES.										
Robbery . . . . . .)										
Do. and attempt to rob with armed company .	219·3	243·9	+ 24·6	211·4	264·3	+ 52·9	231·9	238·8	+ 6·9	235·3
Do. attended with cutting and wounding . . .)										
Assaults with intent to rob, and with menaces . . .	41·7	27·8	— 13·9	18·6	19·8	+ 1·2	34·6	18·7	+ 15·9	26·7
Stealing in dwelling-houses and persons put in fear .	2·1	2·7	+ 0·6	0·6	1·2	+ 0·6	2·5	0·9	+ 1·6	1·7
Total Highway Robbery Cases	263·1	274·4	+ 11·3	230·6	285·3	+ 54·7	269·0	258·4	+ 11·6	263·7
3. PIRACY CASES.										
Piracy.	0·2	2·9	+ 2·7	4·0	·02	— 3·98	1·6	2·0	+ 0·4	1·8
Total Piracy Cases . .	0·2	2·9	+ 2·7	4·0	·02	— 3·98	1·6	2·0	+ 0·4	1·8
4. SMUGGLING CASES.										
Assembling armed to aid smugglers	3·8	..	— 3·8	..	..	..	1·8	0·0	— 1·8	0·9
Assaulting and obstructing officers	2·1	3·6	+ 1·5	·04	1·6	+ 1·66	2·9	0·9	— 2·0	1·9
Total Smuggling Cases .	5·9	3·6	— 2·3	·04	1·6	+ 1·66	4·7	0·9	— 3·8	2·8
5. POACHING CASES.										
Poaching, being out armed taking game	77·7	79·6	+ 1·9	66·6	80·0	+ 13·4	78·6	73·5	— 5·1	71·0
Total Poaching Cases . .	77·7	79·6	+ 1·9	66·6	80·0	+ 13·4	78·6	73·5	— 5·1	71·0
6. ESCAPE FROM CUSTODY CASES.										
Prison-breaking, harbouring and aiding the escape of felons	11·0	14·4	+ 3·4	12·8	10·3	— 2·5	12·8	11·5	— 1·3	12·2
Being at large under sentence of transportation .	2·1	2·5	+ 0·4	2·0	4·0	+ 2·0	2·3	3·0	+ 0·7	2·6
Total Escapes from Custody	13·1	16·9	+ 3·8	14·8	14·3	— 0·5	15·1	14·5	— 0·6	14·8
All Habitual Crimes of Ferocity and Malice .	1,043·1	1,344·7	+ 301·6	1,094·74	1,182·52	+ 87·78	1,199·0	1,139·6	— 59·4	1,155·2

CRIMES.	Quinquennial Ratios from 1834-43.			Quinquennial Ratios from 1844-53.			Decennial Ratios from 1834-53.			Average Ratio for 20 years.
	1834-38.	1839-43.	Increase or Decrease.	1844-48.	1849-53.	Increase or Decrease.	1834-43.	1844-53.	Increase or Decrease.	
Class II. CRIMES OF CUPIDITY AND TEMPTATION. ORDER A.—CASUAL CRIMES. BREACH OF TRUST CASES.										
Larceny by servants . .	620·1	920·3	+ 300·2	928·2	959·0	+ 30·8	785·3	944·0	+ 158·7	864·6
Stealing goods in process of manufacture . .	2·5	2·5	+ 0·0	0·6	1·2	+ 0·6	2·5	0·9	— 1·6	1·7
Ditto fixtures, trees, &c. .	[109·5	195·4	+ 85·9	183·2	156·0	— 27·2	153·9	169·6	+ 5·7	161·8
Ditto and receiving post letters	4·0	12·2	+ 8·2	10·0	14·0	+ 4·0	8·2	12·2	+ 4·0	10·2
Embezzlement	176·0	223·7	+ 47·7	217·5	208·1	— 9·4	200·7	212·7	+ 12·0	206·7
Forging of other forged instruments (such as cheques, bills of exchange, &c.)	45·8	83·8	+ 38·0	87·7	86·8	— 0·9	65·4	87·0	+ 21·6	76·2
All Casual Crimes of Cupidity and Temptation .	957·9	1437·9	+ 480·0	1,427·2	1,425·1	— 2·1	1,216·1	1,426·4	+ 210·3	1,321·2
ORDER B.—HABITUAL CRIMES. 1. AGRICULTURAL CASES.										
Cattle stealing	24·3	30·4	+ 6·1	22·0	19·2	— 2·8	27·4	20·3	— 7·1	23·9
Horse stealing	104·3	107·5	+ 3·2	78·1	60·8	— 17·3	106·0	69·2	— 36·8	87·6
Sheep stealing	195·9	234·5	+ 38·6	154·3	134·5	— 19·8	215·9	144·5	— 71·4	180·2
Deer stealing	3·9	4·1	+ 0·2	5·0	2·5	— 2·5	4·0	3·7	— 0·3	3·8
Fish stealing	4·7	4·9	+ 0·2	5·5	2·7	— 2·8	4·8	4·0	— 0·8	4·4
Total Cattle Stealing, and similar Cases . . .	333·1	381·4	+ 48·3	264·9	219·7	— 45·2	358·1	241·7	— 116·4	299·9
2. LARCENY CASES (chiefly civic).										
Larceny, to the value of £5, in a dwelling-house . .	111·8	120·4	+ 8·6	116·4	134·9	+ 18·5	116·3	125·9	+ 9·6	121·1
Ditto from the person . .	1,033·1	1,018·6	— 15·5	1,094·3	1,168·2	+ 73·9	1,025·6	1,132·4	+ 106·8	1,079·0
Ditto (simple) . . , ,	8,256·0	9,835·4	+ 1,579·4	8,938·7	8,265·2	— 673·5	9,072·2	8,616·6	— 455·6	8,844·4
Total Larceny Cases . .	9,400·9	10,974·4	+ 1,573·5	10,199·4	9,548·3	— 581·1	10,214·1	9,874·9	— 339·2	10,044·5
3. PETTY CASES.										
Stealing from vessels in port	42·0	79·8	+ 37·8	84·0	55·9	— 28·1	61·6	69·6	+ 8·0	65·6
Child stealing	2·7	1·8	— 0·9	2·0	2·0	0·0	2·2	2·0	— 0·2	2·1
Misdemeanours, with intent to steal	11·9	12·5	+ 0·6	20·0	31·1	+ 11·1	12·3	25·7	+ 13·4	19·0
Total Petty Cases . .	56·6	94·1	+ 37·5	106·0	89·0	— 17·0	76·1	97·3	+ 21·2	86·7
4. RECEIVING CASES (chiefly by fences and cheats).										
Receivers of stolen goods .	458·2	524·9	+ 66·7	407·3	443·5	+ 36·2	492·7	425·9	— 66·8	459·3
Frauds and attempts to defraud (cheats)	284·5	364·5	+ 80·0	337·9	362·4	+ 24·5	325·9	350·6	+ 24·7	338·2
Total Receiving Cases .	742·7	889·4	+ 146·7	745·2	805·9	+ 60·7	818·6	776·5	— 42·1	797·5
5. FORGERY CASES.										
Forging Bank of England notes ("shoful" thieves)	2·2	7·3	+ 5·1	1·6	7·2	+ 5·6	6·8	4·5	— 2·3	5·6
Possessing ditto	0·2	0·7	+ 0·5	0·1	0·7	+ 0·6	0·5	·04	— 0·1	0·3
Total Forgery Cases .	2·4	8·0	+ 5·6	1·7	7·9	+ 6·2	7·3	4·54	— 2·77	5·9

CRIMES.	Quinquennial Ratios from 1834-43.			Quinquennial Ratios from 1844-53.			Decennial Ratios from 1834-53.			Average Ratio for 20 Years.
	1834-38.	1839-43.	Increase or Decrease.	1844-48.	1849-53.	Increase or Decrease.	1834-43.	1844-53.	Increase or Decrease.	
CLASS II.—*Continued.*										
6. COINING CASES.										
Counterfeiting the current coin	12·3	11·6	— 0·7	5·9	5·0	— 0·9	11·9	5·4	— 6·5	8·7
Possessing, &c., implements for coining . . .	9·8	16·4	+ 6·6	9·4	8·6	— 0·8	13·2	9·1	— 4·0	11·1
Buying and putting off counterfeit coin . . .	4·5	0·9	— 3·6	0·7	0·0	— 0·7	2·7	0·3	— 2·4	1·5
Uttering and possessing do.	209·3	220·0	+ 10·7	200·6	326·7	+ 126·1	214·9	265·4	+ 50·5	240·1
Total Coining Cases . .	235·9	248·9	+ 14·7	216·6	340·3	+ 123·7	242·7	280·2	+ 37·5	261·4
7. OTHER FELONY AND MIS-DEMEANOUR CASES.										
Felonies not included in the above	6·4	6·9	+ 0·5	5·5	7·5	+ 2·0	6·7	6·5	— 0·2	6·6
Misdemeanours, ditto . .	58·1	100·5	42·4	77 3	44·5	— 32·8	80·0	60·4	— 19·6	70·2
Total other Felony and Misdemeanour Cases .	64·5	107·4	+ 42·9	82·8	52·0	— 30·8	86·7	66·9	— 19 8	76·8
All Habitual Crimes of Cupidity and Temptation	10,834·1	12,703·6	+1,869·5	11,616·6	11,083·1	— 533·5	11,803·6	11,342·0	— 461·6	11,572·7
Class III.										
CRIMES OF LUST, SHAME, INDECENCY, PERVERTED APPETITES, ETC.										
ORDER A.—CASUAL CRIMES.										
1. LUSTFUL CASES.										
Rape and carnally abusing girls under 10 years of age	38·4	56·7	+ 18·3	67·4	75·6	+ 8·2	48·0	71·6	+ 23·6	59·8
Assaults with intent to ravish and carnally abuse.	84·4	82·9	— 1·5	84·5	77·2	— 7·3	83·5	80·8	— 2·7	82·2
Carnally abusing girls between 10 and 12 years of age	3·6	2·8	— 0·8	3·9	2·8	— 1·1	3·2	3·3	+ 0·1	3·2
Total Lustful Cases . .	126·4	142·4	+ 16·0	155·8	155·6	— 0·2	134·7	155·7	+ 21·0	145·2
2. SHAME CASES.										
Concealing the births of infants	29·1	33·9	+ 4·8	40·3	45·0	+ 4·7	31·5	42·7	+ 11·2	37·1
Total Shame Cases . . .	29·1	33·9	+ 4·8	40·3	45·0	+ 4·7	31·5	42·7	+ 11·2	37·1
3. INDECENT CASES.										
Indecently exposing the person	13·6	5·9	— 7·7	4·5	1·4	— 3·1	9·6	2·3	— 7·3	5·9
Total Indecent Cases .	13·6	5·9	— 7·7	4·5	1·4	— 3·1	9·6	2·3	— 7·3	5·9
4. CASES AGAINST THE MARRIAGE LAWS.										
Abduction	1·0	2·3	+ 1·3	1·0	1·2	+ 0·2	1·7	1·1	— 0·6	1·4
Bigamy	27·0	41·9	+ 14·9	45·4	44·9	— 0·5	34·7	45·1	+ 10·4	39·9
Total Cases against Marriage Laws	28·0	44·2	+ 16·2	46·4	46·1	— 0·3	36·4	46·2	+ 9·8	41·3

CRIMES.	Quinquennial Ratios from 1834-43.			Quinquennial Ratios from 1844-53.			Decennial Ratios from 1834-53.			Average Ratio for 20 years.
	1834-38.	1839-43.	Increase or Decrease.	1844-48.	1849-53.	Increase or Decrease.	1834-43.	1844-53.	Increase or Decrease.	
CLASS III.—*Continued.*										
5. UNNATURAL CASES.										
Sodomy	16·2	22·9	+ 6·7	33·5	34·9	+ 1·4	19·7	32·7	+ 13·0	26·2
Assaults with intent to commit	45·8	34·8	— 11·0	38·2	20·8	— 17·4	40·1	30·4	— 9·7	35·2
Total Unnatural Cases .	62·0	57·7	— 4·3	71·7	55·7	— 16·0	59·8	63·1	+ 3·3	61·4
All Casual Crimes of Lust, Shame, Indecency, and Perverted Appetite . .	259·1	284·1	+ 24·0	318·6	303·8	— 14·8	272·0	310·0	+ 38·0	290·9
ORDER B.—HABITUAL CRIMES.										
1. BROTHEL CASES.										
Keeping disorderly houses .	97·4	106·6	+ 9·2	66·4	50·3	— 16·1	102·2	58·2	— 44·0	84·0
2. ABORTION CASES.										
Attempts to procure the miscarriage of women	3·6	3·3	— 0·3	2·0	4·0	+ 2·0	3·5	4·1	+ 0·6	3·8
All Habitual Crimes of Lust, Shame, Indecency, &c.	101·0	109·9	+ 8·9	68·4	54·3	— 14·1	105·7	62·3	— 43·4	80·2
Class IV. CRIMES OF EVIL SPEAKING. ORDER MIXED. 1. THREATENING CASES.										
Obtaining property by threats to accuse of unnatural crimes . . .	..	1·4	+ 1·4	2·0	2·7	+ 0·7	0·7	2·4	+ 1·7	1·6
Sending menacing letters to extort money . . .	1·1	2·1	+ 1·0	2·0	2·4	+ 0·4	1·6	2·2	+ 0·6	1·9
Ditto letters threatening to burn houses, &c.	5·2	3·5	— 1·7	4·1	15·2	+ 11·1	4·3	9·8	+ 5·5	7·0
Total Threatening Cases .	6·3	7·0	+ 0·7	8·1	20·3	+ 12·2	6·6	14·4	+ 7·8	10·5
2. PERJURY CASES.										
Perjury and subornation of perjury	17·2	32·1	+ 14·9	21·8	54·0	+ 32·2	24·9	38·3	+ 13·4	31·6
Total Perjury Cases . .	17·2	32·1	+ 14·9	21·8	54·0	+ 32·2	24·9	38·3	+ 13·4	31·6
All Crimes of Evil Speaking	23·5	39·1	+ 15·6	29·9	74·3	+ 44·4	31·5	52·7	+ 21·2	42·1
Class V. CRIMES OF POLITICAL PREJUDICE. 1. POLITICAL CASES.										
High treason and compassing to levy war . . .	0·0	1·9	+ 1·9	1·4	0·0	— 1·4	1·0	0·6	— 0·4	0·8
Riot, sedition, &c. . . .	0·0	184·5	+ 184·5	30·0	0·3	— 29·7	95·3	14·8	— 80·5	55·0
Total Political Cases .	0·0	186·4	+ 186·4	31·4	0·3	— 31·1	96·3	15·4	— 80·9	55·8
All Crimes of Political Prejudice	0·0	186·4	+ 186·4	31·4	0·3	— 31·1	96·3	15·4	— 80·9	55·8

SUMMARY OF THE PRECEDING TABLES.

A.—CASUAL CRIMES.

CRIMES.	Quinquennial Ratios from 1834-43.			Quinquennial Ratios from 1844-53.			Decennial Ratios from 1834-53.			Average Ratio for 20 years.
	1834-38.	1839-43.	Increase or Decrease.	1844-48.	1849-53.	Increase or Decrease.	1834-43.	1844-53.	Increase or Decrease.	
CLASS I.—CASUAL CRIMES OF FEROCITY AND MALICE.										
1. Murderous cases . . .	163·4	199·1	+ 35·7	197·4	205·5	+ 8·1	181·9	201·6	+ 19·7	191·6
2. Homicidal and Assault cases	1,385·1	1,219·3	− 165·8	1,012·0	803·4	− 208·6	1,299·4	684·6	− 614·8	992·0
3. Arson cases	43·6	40·3	− 3·3	86·3	107·8	+ 21·5	41·7	97·3	+ 55·6	69·5
4. Destructive cases . . .	20·0	40·3	+ 20·3	17·7	21·1	+ 3·4	30·4	18·9	− 11·5	24·6
All Casual Crimes of Ferocity and Malice	1,612·1	1,499·0	− 113·1	1,313·4	1,137·8	− 175·6	1,553·7	1,002·4	− 551·3	1,207·7
CLASS II.—CASUAL CRIMES OF CUPIDITY AND TEMPTATION.										
1. Breach of trust cases .	957·9	1,437·9	+ 480·0	1,427·2	1,425·1	− 2·1	1,216·1	1,426·4	+ 210·3	1,321·2
All Casual Crimes of Cupidity and Temptation .	957·9	1,437·9	+ 480·0	1,427·2	1,425·1	− 2·1	1,216·1	1,426·4	+ 210·3	1,321·2
CLASS III.—CASUAL CRIMES OF LUST, SHAME, INDECENCY, &c.										
1. Lustful cases	126·4	142·4	+ 16·0	155·8	155·6	− 0·2	134·7	155·7	+ 21·0	145·2
2. Shame cases	29·1	33·9	+ 4·8	40·3	45·0	+ 4·7	31·5	42·7	+ 11·2	37·1
3. Indecent cases . . .	13·6	5·9	− 7·7	4·5	1·4	− 3·1	9·6	2·3	− 7·3	5·9
4. Cases against Marriage Laws	28·0	44·2	+ 16·2	46·4	46·1	− 0·3	36·4	46·2	+ 9·8	41·3
5. Unnatural cases . . .	62·0	57·7	− 4·3	71·7	55·1	− 16·6	59·8	63·1	+ 3·3	61·4
All Casual Crimes of Lust, Shame, Indecency, and Perverted Appetite . . .	259·1	284·1	+ 25·0	318·7	303·2	− 15·5	272·0	310·0	+ 38·2	290·9
Total of all Casual Crimes .	2,829·1	3,221·0	+ 391·9	3,059·2	2,856·6	− 192·2	3,041·5	2,738·8	− 302·7	2,819·8

B.—HABITUAL CRIMES.

CRIMES.	Quinquennial Ratios from 1834-43.			Quinquennial Ratios from 1844-53.			Decennial Ratios from 1834-53.			Average Ratio for 20 years.
	1834-38.	1839-43.	Increase or Decrease.	1844-48.	1849-53.	Increase or Decrease.	1834-43.	1844-53.	Increase or Decrease.	
CLASS I.—HABITUAL CRIMES OF FEROCITY AND MALICE.										
1. Burglary cases . . .	683·1	967·3	+ 284·2	778·7	801·3	+ 22·6	830·0	790·3	− 39·7	801·1
2. Highway-robbery cases	263·1	274·4	+ 11·3	230·6	285·3	+ 54·7	269·0	258·4	− 10·6	263·7
3. Piracy cases . . .	0·2	2·9	+ 2·7	4·0	·02	− 3·98	1·6	2·0	+ 0·4	1·8
4. Smuggling cases . . .	5·9	3·6	− 1·3	·04	1·6	+ 1·64	4·7	0·9	− 3·8	2·8
5. Poaching cases . . .	77·7	79·6	+ 1·9	66·6	80·0	+ 11·4	78·6	73·5	− 5·1	71·0
6. Escapes from custody cases	13·1	16·9	+ 3·8	14·8	14·3	− 0·5	15·1	14·5	− 0·6	14·8
All Habitual Crimes of Ferocity and Malice . . .	1,043·1	1,344·7	+ 301·6	1,094·74	1,182·52	+ 87·78	1,199·0	1,139·6	− 59·4	1,155·2

SUMMARY OF THE PRECEDING TABLES.
B.—HABITUAL CRIMES—*Continued.*

CRIMES.	Quinquennial Ratios from 1834-43.			Quinquennial Ratios from 1844-53.			Decennial Ratios from 1834-53.			Average Ratio for 20 years.
	1834-38.	1839-43.	Increase or Decrease.	1844-48.	1849-53.	Increase or Decrease.	1834-43.	1844-53.	Increase or Decrease.	
CLASS II.—HABITUAL CRIMES OF CUPIDITY & TEMPTATION.										
1. Cattle stealing and similar cases	333·1	381·4	+ 48·3	264·9	219·7	— 45·2	358·1	241·7	— 116·4	299·9
2. Larceny cases	9,400·9	10,974·4	+ 15,73·5	10,199·4	9,568·3	— 631·1	10,214·1	9,874·9	— 339·2	10,044·5
3. Petty cases	56·6	94·1	+ 37·5	106·0	89·0	— 17·0	76·1	97·3	+ 21·2	86·7
4. Receiving cases . . .	742·7	889·4	+ 146·7	745·2	805·9	+ 59·7	818·6	776·5	— 42·1	797·5
5. Forgery cases	2·4	8·0	+ 5·6	1·7	7·9	+ 6·2	7·3	4·5	— 2·7	5·9
6. Coining cases	235·9	248·9	+ 14·7	216·6	340·3	+ 123·7	242·7	280·2	+ 37·5	261·4
7. Other felony and misdemeanour cases . .	64·5	107·4	+ 41·9	82·8	52·0	— 30·8	86·7	66·9	— 19·8	76·8
All Habitual Crimes of Cupidity and Temptation .	10,834·1	12,703·6	+ 1,869·5	11,616·6	11,083·1	— 533·5	11,803·6	11,342·0	— 461·6	11,572·7
CLASS III.—HABITUAL CRIMES OF LUST, SHAME, INDECENCY &c.										
1. Keeping disorderly houses	97·4	106·6	+ 9·2	66·4	50·3	— 16·1	102·2	58·2	— 44·0	80·2
2. Abortion cases	3·6	3·3	— 0·3	2·0	4·0	+ 2·0	3·5	4·1	+ 0·6	3·8
All Habitual Crimes of Lust, Shame, Indecency, and Perverted Appetites .	101·0	109·9	+ 8·9	68·4	54·3	— 14·1	105·7	62·3	— 43·4	84·0
Total of all Habitual Crimes	11,978·2	14,158·2	+ 2,180·0	12,779·7	12,319·9	— 459·8	13,108·3	12,543·9	— 564·4	12,811·9

SUMMARY OF MIXED CRIMES.

CRIMES.	Quinquennial Ratios from 1834-43.			Quinquennial Ratios from 1844-53.			Decennial Ratios from 1834-53.			Average Ratio for 20 years.
	1834-38.	1839-43.	Increase or Decrease.	1844-48.	1849-53.	Increase or Decrease.	1834-43.	1844-53.	Increase or Decrease.	
CLASS IV.—CRIMES OF EVIL SPEAKING.										
1. Threatening cases . .	6·3	7·0	+ 0·7	8·1	20·3	+ 12·2	6·6	14·4	+ 7·8	10·5
2. Perjury cases	17·2	32·1	+ 14·9	21·8	54·0	+ 32·2	24·9	38·3	+ 13·4	31·6
All Cases of Evil Speaking	23·5	39·1	+ 15·6	29·9	74·3	+ 44·4	31·5	52·7	+ 21·2	42·1
CLASS V.—CRIMES OF POLITICAL PREJUDICE.										
Political cases	0·0	186·4	+ 186·4	31·4	0·3	— 31·1	96·3	15·4	— 80·9	55·8
All Cases of Political Prejudice	0·0	186·	+ 186·4	31·4	0·3	— 31·1	96·3	15·4	— 80·9	55·8
Total of all Mixed Crimes	23·5	225·5	+ 202·0	61·3	74·6	+ 13·3	127·8	68·1	— 59·7	97·9
Gross Total of all Crimes	14,832·8	17,604·7	+ 2,771·9	15,850·3	15,261·2	— 649·7	16,277·6	15,350·8	— 926·8	729·6

GENERAL SUMMARY.

CRIMES.	Quinquennial Ratios from 1834-43.			Quinquennial Ratios from 1844-53.			Decennial Ratios from 1834-53.			Average Ratio for 20 years.
	1834-38.	1839-43.	Increase or Decrease.	1844-48.	1849-53.	Increase or Decrease.	1834-43.	1844-53.	Increase or Decrease.	
CLASS I. **CRIMES OF FEROCITY AND MALICE.**										
Casual	1,612·1	1,499·0	— 113·1	1,313·4	1,137·8	— 175·6	1,553·7	1,002·4	— 551·3	1,207·7
Habitual	1,043·1	1,344·7	+ 301·6	1,094·74	1,182·52	+ 87·78	1,199·0	1,139·6	— 59·4	1,155·2
Total	2,655·2	2,843·7	+ 188·5	2,408·14	2,320·32	— 87·82	2,752·7	2,142·0	— 610·7	2,362·9
CLASS II. **CRIMES OF CUPIDITY AND TEMPTATION.**										
Casual	957·9	1,437·9	+ 480·0	1,427·2	1,425·1	— 2·1	1,216·1	1,426·4	+ 210·3	1,321·2
Habitual	10,834·1	12,703·6	+ 1,869·5	11,616·6	11,083·1	— 533·5	11,803·6	11,342·0	— 461·6	11,572·7
Total	11,792·0	14,141·5	+ 2,349·5	13,043·8	12,508·2	— 535·6	13,019·7	12,768·4	— 251·3	12,893·9
CLASS III. **CRIMES OF LUST, SHAME, INDECENCY, &C.**										
Casual	259·1	284·1	+ 25·0	318·7	303·2	— 15·5	272·0	310·0	+ 38·2	290·9
Habitual	101·0	109·9	+ 8·9	68·4	54·3	— 14·1	105·7	62·3	— 43·4	84·0
Total	360·1	393·0	+ 33·9	387·1	357·5	— 29·6	377·7	372·3	— 5·6	374·9
CLASS IV. **CRIMES OF EVIL-SPEAKING.** }	23·5	39·1	+ 15·6	29·9	74·3	+ 44·4	31·5	52·7	+ 21·2	42·1
CLASS V. **CRIMES OF POLITICAL PREJUDICE.** }	0·0	186·4	+ 186·4	31·4	0·3	— 31·1	96·3	15·4	— 80·9	55·8
ALL CLASSES OF CRIMES.										
Casual	2,829·1	3,221·0	+ 391·9	3,059·3	2,856·1	— 193·2	3,041·5	2,738·8	— 302·8	2,819·8
Habitual	11,978·2	14,158·2	+ 2,180·0	12,779·7	12,319·9	— 459·8	13,108·3	12,543·9	— 564·4	12,811·9
Mixed	23·5	225·5	+ 202·0	61·3	74·6	+ 13·3	127·8	68·1	— 59·7	97·9
All Crimes . . .	14,830·8	17,604·7	+ 2,773·9	15,900·3	15,250·6	— 666·3	16,277·6	15,350·8	— 926·9	15,729·6

Now, the preceding table shows the following general results (drawn from an average of the last twenty years) as regards the number of offenders annually committed for trial throughout England and Wales:—

First, with respect to the different classes of criminals, we find—

1. There are 15·7 criminals, of all kinds, to every 10,000 of our population.

2. Not less than 12·8 of these 15·7 individuals belong to the *habitual class* of offenders, or those who make a regular trade of crime, whilst 2·8 appertain to the *casual class*, and barely 1 to the *mixed class*.

Secondly, with respect to the increase or decrease of the different classes of criminals, we perceive—

1. There has been a slight decrease of the whole during the last decenniad, though this decrease amounts to a reduction of only 0·9 in the ratio, so that little or no impression appears to have been made upon the criminal tendencies of the people by all our late educational and reformatory movements.

2. The habitual class of criminals has decreased 0·5 in the course of the last ten years, the casual criminals 0·3, and the mixed 0·05.

Thirdly, concerning the several kinds of crime of which the various classes of criminals are accused, it will be seen—

1. Out of the before-mentioned ratio of 15·7 criminals to every 10,000 of our people, no less than 12·89 are committed for crimes of "cupidity and temptation" (such as theft, fraud, forgery, coining, &c.); whilst as many as 11·57 of these belong to the habitual class of thieves, and only 1·32 to the casual ditto.

2. There are 2·36 in every 10,000 of the population who are annually charged with crimes of "ferocity and malice;" and of these one-half belong to the casual, and the other half to the habitual class of offenders.

3. There are, on the other hand, only 0·37 individuals per 10,000 of the people charged every year with crimes of lust, shame, indecency, &c., of whom 0·29 belong to the casual class, and only 0·08 to the habitual.

4. The remaining 0·09 (out of the 15·7 criminals of all classes) are annually accused of crimes of evil-speaking (such as threatening, or false swearing), or of political prejudice (as high treason, riot, &c.)

Fourthly, as regards the increase or decrease of the several kinds of crime, we may observe—

1. Whilst all classes of criminals have decreased 0·9 in each 10,000 of the people, those annually accused of the *casual* crimes of "ferocity and malice" have decreased, during the last ten years, to the extent of 0·5; the main reduction having taken place in the homicidal and assault cases, whereas a slight increase has ensued in the more serious, murderous, and arson cases. Those, however, indulging in the *habitual* crimes of ferocity and malice (such as burglary, highway robbery, &c.) have also experienced a slight diminution—equal to 0·06 in each 10,000 of the population.

2. Those accused of the *casual* crimes of "cupidity and temptation" (such as larceny by servants, embezzlement, forging of cheques or bills, stealing post letters, or goods in the process of manufacture) have increased to altogether 2 in every 10,000 of the people—the greater proportion of this increase having occurred among servants accused of larceny. Those committed, however, for the *habitual* crimes of the same class have experienced a small decrease among their numbers, including, more particularly, the crimes of cattle, horse, and sheep stealing, as well as that of simple larceny; whilst the crimes of larceny from the person, and in a dwelling-house, as well as misdemeanours, and frauds, and uttering base coin, have, more or less, increased—the greatest augmentation being among the perpetrations of the professional pickpockets.

3. Those accused of the *casual* crimes of "lust, shame, and indecency," have likewise increased to a small amount, viz., 0·03 in each 10,000 of the population—the largest addition having occurred among those annually charged with rape, sodomy, &c.; whilst the crimes of concealment of birth and bigamy have all suffered a trifling extension of the ratio. With the *habitual* crimes of the same class, such as brothel-keeping and procuring abortion, there has been a trifling diminution.

4. The crimes of "evil-speaking" show no decrease whatever; indeed, the numbers charged with using threats, in order to extort money, have more than doubled themselves within the last ten years; and those accused of perjury have likewise increased considerably—more than 50 per cent.

5. Crimes of "political prejudice" (such as high treason and sedition), on the other hand, have diminished as much as those of evil-speaking have augmented among us.

After the above exposition of the several kinds of crime and classes of criminals, it is, perhaps, needless to recur to the fallacy that crime fluctuates with the varying prosperity of our people. To place the matter, however, beyond the possibility of doubt, we have drawn up the following diagram, in which the annual alterations in the ratio of criminals to the population admit of being readily compared with the variations in the average price of corn for a series of years, which is sufficiently long to enable us to see whether there be any truth or not in the principle :—

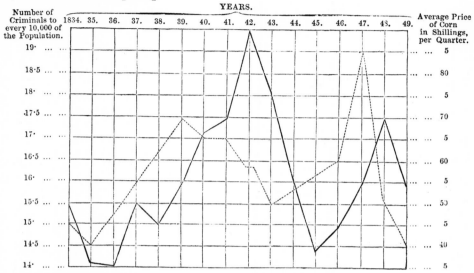

DIAGRAM SHOWING THE RELATIVE FLUCTUATIONS IN THE PRICE OF CORN AND THE RATIO OF CRIMINALS TO THE POPULATION, FROM THE YEAR 1834 TO 1849.

(The dotted line indicates the price of corn, and the black line the ratio of criminality.)

Here it will be seen that in the year 1842, when the ratio of criminals was as high as $19\frac{1}{3}$ to every 10,000 of the people, corn was comparatively low in price; for though it had been nearly 70s. the quarter in 1839, it had gradually fallen to less than 60s. in 1842. During the same period, however, crime had been as gradually rising, having been only $15\frac{3}{4}$ in 1839, and, as we said, $19\frac{1}{3}$ in 1842.

Again, in the year 1845, when the ratio of criminals had sunk to less than $14\frac{1}{3}$ in every 10,000 of the population, corn had been gradually rising from 1843, and had again reached the same price as it was in 1842. Further, in 1847 corn had risen to the very high price of 85s. the quarter, and yet crime in the same year was comparatively low—the ratio being then but 15·8 per 10,000 people.

Thus, then, we find that when in 1842 crime was very high, the price of corn was moderately low; whilst in 1847, when corn was dear, crime was comparatively rare among us.*

* We subjoin the ratio of criminals throughout England and Wales to every 10,000 people during the last twenty years :—

YEARS.	No. of Criminals per 10,000 People.	YEARS.	No. of Criminals per 10,000 People.
1834	15·5	1844	16·0
1835	14·1	1845	14·4
1836	14·0	1846	14·7
1837	15·6	1847	15·8
1838	15·1	1848	17·4
1839	15·7	1849	15·8
1840	17·2	1850	15·1
1841	17·4	1851	15·5
1842	19·3	1852	15·1
1843	18·1	1853	14·7
Annual mean	16·1	Annual mean	31·3

The number of able-bodied paupers relieved throughout England and Wales for a series of years would show the same results. Indeed, the only rational conclusion to be arrived at—and it is the one to which we have come after testing statistically, we repeat, almost every theory on the subject that has been propounded—is, that the great mass of crime is a trade and profession among us, and that those forms of dishonesty which make up nearly four-fifths of the delinquencies of the country are practised as a means of living by certain classes, as regularly as honesty is pursued for the same purpose by others.*

Nor can we explain the continual existence of so large an amount of iniquity in the land, other than by the fact of the offenders being regularly born and bred to the business. Not only in our juvenile prisons do we see the future bandits and ultimate convicts of the country, but we see also the bitter results of the State's gross neglect of its parental duties to the outcast and destitute children among us. Twist and turn the question as we may, we shall find at length—if we come to the matter really willing to fathom and eager to embrace the truth of this most vital problem—that *habitual* crime is purely the consequence of want of proper fatherly care to the young; and this is demonstrated to us by the fact, that in those countries where the education of all children is enforced by law, and the young are thus made to pass the principal part of their time under the eyes of a teacher and adviser—if not a guardian and a friend—the national records show a less comparative amount of crime than in those nations where the youthful poor, as with us, are allowed to remain gambolling as well as gambling all the day in the gutter with fellow-idlers and profligates, if not thieves. This is the sole reason to be cited why in Holland and Prussia, and even Catholic Belgium, there are less criminals, in proportion to the population, than with us; for though the teaching of reading and writing in our prisons is shown by figures to be almost unavailing as a means of reformation—and even reformation itself to be extremely difficult, unless accompanied with expatriation and the consequent removal of the young offender from the intercourse and temptations of his former associates—nevertheless, by a large system of national education, the destitute and outcast children of the land would be rescued from idleness and the pollution of the streets, and would pass the greater part of their time in connection with those whose express duty it would be to counsel and train them to industry and virtue.

Again, therefore, we say we have little faith in prison teaching, or even national reformatories, as a means of decreasing the offenders of the country. Crime, in its habitual form, seems to us as radically incurable as lock-jaw or confirmed consumption, or the kindred disease known as *noli-me-tangere*. The only hope is to *prevent* juvenile delinquency; and as even the cholera itself can be warded off by due ventilation and cleanliness—being but a physical scourge from the Almighty, in punishment for the national neglect of the dwellings and comforts of the poor—so is crime but a moral pestilence, ordained by God to rouse us to our duty to those wretched little actual or virtual orphans, whom, for some inscrutable reason, He has willed to begin life as outcasts among us.†

* This is further proved by the large proportion of "*known*" offenders who are re-committed to our prisons in the course of the year. We have before shown (see table, p. 410) that these constitute, at least, one-quarter of the gross prison population; so that, supposing the "not *known*" habitual offenders confined in our prisons to be only as numerous as the "known" ones, it is obvious that one-half of our criminals are regular jail-birds, to whom theft is a business, and the prison a refuge.

† We cannot conclude this account of the juvenile prison and juvenile prisoners at Tothill Fields without drawing attention once more to the fact, that the criminal period of life appears to be between fifteen and twenty-five years of age—the time, as we have said, when the will comes to be developed, and has not yet learnt to be guided and controlled by the reason. At page 117, while treating of Pentonville prison, we pointed out the circumstance that 55·7 prisoners in every 100 were between seventeen and twenty-five years of age. And again, at page 377, in the table showing the per centage of juvenile offenders throughout England and Wales, we showed that only 10·15 in every 100 persons were (according to the average of the last thirteen years) under seventeen, and as many as 89·85 per cent. above that age; whereas the last census returns

¶ ii.—θ.

Of the Female Prison at Tothill Fields, and Female Prisoners generally.

From the juvenile prison at Westminster, and the consideration of juvenile crime in the abstract, we pass to the female portion of the same institution, as well as to the more general subject of crime among women.

prove that the centesimal proportion of all classes of persons of the same ages is as 39·2 to 60·8; so that whilst the juvenile offenders are nearly 30 per cent. below the ratio of the entire population, the adult prisoners are nearly the same amount above it.

This fact had long ago been noticed by Mr. Redgrave in the Government returns. "The comparison of the ages of offenders, with the population of the same age," said that gentleman in the year 1842, "shows the great proportion of offenders between the age of fifteen and twenty-five years, and how rapidly that proportion declines after the age of thirty, becoming less than the proportion in the general population after forty, and falling suddenly off at each period, on passing that age." "It has been shown," he added in the next year's report, "by the calculations prefixed to former tables, that the centesimal proportion of the ages of offenders in the seven years ending with 1841, had not varied above 1 per cent. in any one of the periods under which the ages had been classed. In 1842 this classification was altered to assimilate it to the quinquennial classification adopted in the general census; but by this change the comparison with the previous years was lost." Hence the tables of the ages of those committed for trial do not extend very far back, nor have they been continued of late years; nevertheless, those already printed furnish us with a sufficiently large series of years to establish the law, that the great mass of crime in this country is committed by *young men*—those, in fact, who, having passed their apprenticeship as juvenile offenders, have entered upon their habitual career—"the duration of which," says Mr. Redgrave, "may be inferred from the rapidly-decreasing proportions which those above forty years of age bear to the population at the same period of life."

In the tables of 1848 we have the last returns as to the ages of those committed for trial, and here we find it stated that "the ages of criminals had for several years progressively shown an increased proportion of the younger criminals. The apparent sudden decrease, last year, of offenders under the ages of fifteen, must be attributed to the operation of the statute 10 and 11 Vic., c. 82, passed in July, 1847, which empowers justices to punish summarily for simple larceny offenders whose ages do not exceed fourteen years, thus removing many of such cases from the criminal tables, in which they had previously appeared as indictable offences"—but correspondingly increasing the summary convictions. "The relative state of the commitments, with respect to the ages of the criminals, is clearly exhibited in the subjoined table, which gives the relative proportion of accused per 100 committed, and is not disturbed by the fluctuations in the absolute numbers sent for trial. From this table it appears that nearly one-half the commitments in 1848 were of persons between the ages of fifteen and twenty-five.

Ages.	Centesimal Proportion in the Years.							
	1842.	1843.	1844.	1845.	1846.	1847.	1848.	Census of 1841.
Aged under 15 years	5·3	5·7	6·0	6·4	6·5	6·1	3·6	36·0
„ 15 and under 20 years	22·0	22·7	23·3	24·1	24·5	24·2	23·8	9·9
„ 20 „ 25 „	24·7	24·3	24·1	24·2	23·3	23·0	25·2	9·7
„ 25 „ 30 „	15·3	14·9	14·9	14·3	14·6	14·7	15·4	8·0
„ 30 „ 40 „	16·8	16·4	15·3	15·6	15·8	16·7	16·8	12·9
„ 40 „ 50 „	8·3	8·1	8·3	8·2	8·4	8·5	8·6	9·6
„ 50 „ 60 „	3·8	3·5	3·9	3·6	3·4	3·6	3·4	6·4
„ 60 years and above	1·8	1·9	2·0	1·7	1·8	1·8	1·7	7·2
Ages not ascertained	2·0	2·5	2·2	1·9	1·7	1·4	1·5	0·3

Thus, then, we perceive that whilst the proportion of offenders *under* fifteen years and *over* forty is far below those of the ratio for the entire population of the country, the proportion, on the other hand, of the offenders *above* fifteen and *under* forty is considerably above it. In the year 1848, for instance, those between fifteen and twenty-five years of age who were sent for trial made up exactly 49 per cent. of the whole commitments; whereas, according to the census returns, there are only 19·6 per cent. of persons of that age throughout the country, whilst those between twenty-five and forty years old constituted 32·2 per cent. of the gross committals, and only 20·9 per cent. of the entire population. Above forty, however, the proportions

As a body, women are considerably less criminal than men. We know not whether this be due to the fact of the female nature being more kindly or less daring than that of the male; but so it is—the returns of the country, for a long series of years, showing that in every 100 prisoners there are but some 20 odd women; so that males would appear to be, at least, four times more vicious than females; for, according to the tables in the census, there is a greater proportion of the latter than the former in the country; and therefore, if the criminal tendencies were equal in either sex, our criminal records should exhibit a greater number of women than men annually accused of crime.

Moreover, if it could be possible to obtain accurate returns as to the number of "public women" throughout the country, it would be found that by far the greater proportion of the female offenders is derived from that class; and thus it would be proven, that among the chaste portion of the female sex crime is comparatively unknown.

There would appear, then, to be, generally speaking, but one great vice appertaining to the gentler sex, viz., prostitution; and the reason of this would seem to be two-fold. The great mass of crime in the country we have shown, by an analysis of the Government returns, to be pursued regularly as a means of subsistence by criminals. Hence, what theft is to the evil-disposed among men, street-walking is to the same class among women—an easy mode of living; so that those females, among the poorer classes of society, who are born to labour for their bread, but who find work inordinately irksome to their natures, and pleasure as inordinately agreeable to them, have no necessity to resort to the more daring career of theft to supply their wants, but have only to trade upon their personal charms in order to secure the apparent luxury of an idle life.

The truth of this is proven by M. Parent du Chatelet, in his work upon the "*Femmes*

were reversed, there being but 15·2 per cent. of persons committed at a more advanced age, and as many as 23·5 per cent. of the entire population at the same period of life.

As regards the districts contributing the greater proportion of young criminals, we have the following information in the Government tables of 1843 :—

" The comparative ages in the ten most agricultural and the ten most manufacturing and mixed counties show the earlier commencement of crime in the manufacturing than in the agricultural counties, and—as proved by the diminished proportion of criminals between the age of twenty and twenty-five years—its shorter career.

	Manufacturing Districts.	Agricultural Districts.
Aged under 15 years	6·6	4·8
,, 15 and under 20 years . . .	24·6	21·
,, 20 ,, 25 ,, . . .	24·2	26·9
,, 25 ,, 30 ,, . . .	15·1	15·6
,, 30 ,, 40 ,, . . .	16·3	17·6
,, 40 ,, 50 ,, . . .	8·2	8·5
,, 50 ,, 60 ,, . . .	3·5	3·3
,, 60 years and above	1·5	2·3."

Here, then, we find that the proportion of offenders under twenty years of age is nearly 5½ per cent. less in the agricultural districts than in the manufacturing; whereas, between the ages of twenty and forty, the proportion is reversed, being 4½ per cent. less in the manufacturing than in the agricultural parts.

"This variation," says Mr. Redgrave, "may be affected by the early employment of children in manufactures, or even by the occupations and consequent habits of their parents." We are, however, inclined to believe that the cause of the difference may, with greater probability, be traced to the prevalence of large towns in the manufacturing districts and the early street-association among the children of the poor, as well as the greater facilities in cities for disposing of the metal and the other produce of petty robberies at the marine-store shops. This view, indeed, appears to be borne out by the table printed at p. 404, in which it is shown, by an average of five years, that the greater number of juvenile offenders come from Northumberland (in which Newcastle is situate), Somerset (of which Bristol is the chief town), Surrey (with which the Metropolis is connected), Norfolk (of which Norwich is the capital, as it were), Warwick (to which Birmingham belongs), Middlesex (the great metropolitan county), and Gloucester (the county for the city of that name), in all of which the proportion of young criminals is found to be above the average.

Publiques" of Paris, wherein he shows not only that the large majority of the street-walkers come from the working-classes, but that the greater proportion are derived from the class pursuing the most irksome form of all labour, as well as subject to the greatest temptations—domestic servants. Again, those engaged in the ill-paid business of needlework, as well as with the vanities of dress-making, or theatrical employment, alike serve to swell the ranks of the " unfortunates;" for in each and all of these classes the payment is not only small, but the allurements are great—from the servant, who daily contrasts the comparative luxury and ease of her mistress's life with the hardships of her own, to the milliner, who longs to be able to wear the fine things she is ever engaged in making for others, and the actress, who has learnt to crave for admiration as part of the very business of life.

The other reason why prostitution constitutes the chief delinquency of the female sex, is because the indulgence in it demands the same insensibility to shame on the part of woman as dishonesty in man. Mandeville, long ago, showed that society was held together chiefly by the love of approbation and dread of disapprobation among mankind; and, though the philosopher endeavoured to prove, what is obviously absurd, that there is no right nor wrong, except such matters as have come, by general consent, to be universally praised or blamed, nevertheless, all must admit, that the desire to be admired, and the disinclination to be despised, which exists in the breast of all people, is one of the most important instruments in the machinery of human society.

Indeed, it is this continual fear of what the world will say—this ever-active sensibility as regards public opinion—the perpetual craving for credit and reputation and standing among the various classes of people—that prompts and keeps the great mass of mankind to righteous courses, far more than any moral sense or any aspiration to fashion their actions according to the standard of the Great Exemplar and Teacher; for the eye, which men fancy to be ever watching and weighing their conduct, is that of this same public opinion rather than of All-perfection and Justice. An external standard of admiration, instead of an internal principle of righteousness, rules the world—a dread of shame among men, rather than an innate hatred of what is iniquitous—whilst what is termed civilization consists principally in the development of human vanity to an inordinate degree; and hence the *polite* and artificial form of society, though apparently more moral, is assuredly more false and dishonest than the natural and barbaric mode of life. Nevertheless, what is lost in truthfulness and spontaneous rectitude is gained in the general welfare by the common conformity to those principles of decency and virtue which moral fashion prescribes for the guidance of such as have little internal principle to dictate and govern their own conduct.

Shame, therefore, in such a condition of social existence, becomes one of the great means of moral government in a State; so that to exhibit a callousness to the feeling, is to lapse, as it were, into the savage form of life, and to proclaim that our actions are no longer controlled by a consideration for the thoughts and feelings of our neighbours; and hence it is that other men feel naturally disinclined to place trust in such as have rendered themselves, by some base or mean act, subject to the opprobrium of their fellows; whilst they who have done so, having once lost caste in the world and broken the ice of shame, get to be as desperate and reckless as sinking drowning men, and to be ultimately absorbed in the whirlpool of infamy and crime.

If, however, such be the result with men, the effect of the violation of this great social principle must be even more strongly marked in women—owing to the sense of shame being naturally more acute in the gentler than in the sterner sex. Some philosophers have classed the love of approbation as an elementary propensity of human nature. It seems to us, however, that human beings like praise, simply because the admiration of others serves to increase their self-esteem, or, in other words, to exalt the admiration of themselves—for this self-esteem is essential not only to our happiness, but to our existence itself. It is of the highest importance for our welfare, for instance, that we should have faith in our own powers, since none can be of such use to us as we can to ourselves. But those whose powers are the weakest, and who are, therefore, the most diffident as to their own endowments, not only require to have their faith continually sustained, but naturally find the greatest delight in approbation. Hence it is that the weakest people are the vainest, or most open to flattery, as well as alive to shame; whilst those who have the greatest confidence in themselves are ever the proudest, and but little affected even by the contempt of others.

Thus, then, it is that women, being the weaker portion of humanity, are naturally not only more fond of being admired, but more bashful or morally timid than men; so that shame is the great ruling principle of their lives; whilst those who become callous to it, as well as reckless as to how their acts are regarded by others, are viewed by the rest of the world as creatures in whom the brightest feminine qualities have been effaced, and whose natures and passions are subject to none of the ordinary principles of restraint. The reason, therefore, why prostitution is the one chief delinquency of the female sex is because it is the one capital act of shamelessness, and that which consequently fits the creature for the performance of any other iniquity. Hence we can readily understand how it is that the great mass of female criminals are drawn from the ranks of the street-walkers of the country; for, as juvenile delinquency constitutes the apprenticeship of the habitual male offender, so prostitution is the initiatory stage of criminality among women.

The criminal records of the country, in a measure, corroborate the above remarks.

The gross prison population of the country for 1853, including those summarily convicted, as well as those tried at assizes and sessions, amounted to nearly 100,000 individuals of both sexes. Of these the numbers for the adult and juvenile prisoners of either sex were as follows :*—

	Males.	Females.	Total.
Adults	64,239	22,692	86,931
Juvenile	9,659	1,794	11,453
Total both sexes	73,898	24,486	98,384

* The annual mean for a series of years is given below, to avoid depending on *particular* results :—

	Males.	Females.	Total.
ADULTS.			
Summarily convicted	49,054	16,256	65,310
Tried at assizes and sessions	19,800	5,000	24,800
Total	68,854	21,256	90,110
JUVENILES.			
Summarily convicted	7,577	1,248	8,825
Tried at assizes and sessions	2,435	489	2,924
Total	10,012	1,737	11,749
ALL AGES.			
Summarily convicted	56,631	17,504	74,135
Tried at assizes and sessions	22,235	5,489	27,724
Total	78,866	22,993	101,859

The annual mean per centage for the same numbers being :—

	Males.	Females.	Total.
ADULTS.			
Summarily convicted	71·24	76·47	72·47
Tried at assizes and sessions	28·76	23·53	27·53
Total	100·00	100·00	100·00
JUVENILES.			
Summarily convicted	75·67	71·84	75·11
Tried at assizes and sessions	24·33	28·16	24·89
Total	100·00	100·00	100·00
ALL CLASSES.			
Summarily convicted	73·45	74·15	73·78
Tried at assizes and sessions	26·55	25·85	26·21
Total	100·00	100·00	100·00

And the centesimal proportions, as regards the adults and juveniles, as under :—

	Males.	Females.	Total.
Adults	86·94	92·67	89·80
Juveniles	13·06	7·33	10·20
	100·00	100·00	100·00

Whilst those with respect to the males and females were :—

	Males.	Females.	Total.
Adults	71·43	28·57	100·00
Juveniles	84·33	15·67	100·00
Total	72·06	27·94	100·00

But not to rely upon fallacious criteria of any one year, the following decennial table has been prepared, showing at once the relative numbers and proportions of males and females of all ages summarily convicted, as well as tried at assizes and sessions throughout England and Wales :—

TABLE SHOWING THE NUMBERS AND PER CENTAGES OF MALE AND FEMALE OFFENDERS SUMMARILY CONVICTED AND TRIED AT SESSIONS AND ASSIZES, FROM 1841 TO 1850, BOTH INCLUSIVE.

Years.	Summarily Convicted.				Tried at Assizes and Sessions.				All Classes.			
	Numbers.		Per Centage.		Numbers.		Per Centage.		Numbers.		Per Centage.	
	Males.	Fem.	Males.	Fem.	Males.	Fem.	Males.	Fem.	Males.	Fem.	Males.	Fem.
1841	47,629	15,667	75·3	24·7	21,873	5,212	80·8	19·2	69,502	24,879	76·9	23·1
1842	54,784	15,723	77·7	22·3	25,523	5,637	81·9	18·1	80,307	21,360	79·0	21·0
1843	57,361	15,835	78·4	21·6	24,516	5,355	82·1	17·9	81,877	21,190	79·5	20·5
1844	55,605	15,693	78·0	22·0	21,710	4,972	81·4	18·6	77,315	20,665	78·9	21·1
1845	50,688	15,354	76·8	23·2	20,117	4,966	80·2	19·8	70,805	20,320	77·7	22·3
1846	48,261	16,638	74·4	25·6	19,701	5,332	78·7	21·3	67,962	21,970	74·5	25·5
1847	50,481	17,000	74·8	25·2	22,312	5,827	79·3	20·7	72,793	22,827	76·2	23·8
1848	64,574	19,697	76·6	23·4	24,199	5,887	80·5	19·5	88,773	25,584	77·6	22·4
1849	69,522	21,441	76·5	23·5	23,271	5,481	80·9	19·1	92,793	26,922	77·5	22·5
1850	61,645	18,963	76·5	23·5	21,164	5,299	80·0	20·0	82,809	24,262	77·3	22·7
Annual Mean	56,055	17,201	76·5	23·5	22,439	5,397	80·6	19·4	78,494	22,598	77·7	22·3

By this it will be seen that the annual average for the last decenniad has been upwards of 100,000 offenders; of whom 78,500, or 77¾ per cent., have been males, and 22,500, or 22⅓ per cent., females. Of this number, it will be further observed, 73,000, or nearly three-fourths, are, upon the average, summarily convicted; of whom 56,000, or 76½ per cent., are males, and 17,000, or 23½ per cent., females; whilst the remaining 27,800 are generally committed for trial, and of these about 22,400, or 80½ per cent., are males, and 5,400, or 19½ per cent., females.

Hence it would appear that the female offenders are, upon the average, between one-fourth and one-fifth of the male offenders in number; and that whilst the number of females summarily convicted is not quite equal to one-fourth of the males, the number of women committed for trial is not quite one-fifth of the men sent to the sessions. The proportion of males to females, however, throughout England and Wales, according to the last census, is as 100 to 105. Now, as there are upon an average 15·7 persons annually committed for trial out of every 10,000 of the population, it would appear, from the above returns, that 12·7 of the 15·7 are males, and the remaining 3 females.

But though this would appear to speak highly in favour of the honour and virtue of the female portion of our race, nevertheless, according to the returns of Mr. Redgrave, the criminality of women has been annually increasing among us at a considerable rate for many years past. In the returns of 1839 that gentleman said, "with respect to the sexes of criminals, it is worthy of remark that for several years the proportion of females has been increasing. Comparing the number of males and females, the centesimal proportion of the latter was, in 1834, 18·8; in 1835, 20·0; in 1836 and 1837 it was 21·6 (though the fraction, if carried further, still shows a small increase in 1837); in 1838, 22·1; and in 1839, 23·2."

Again, in 1844, he drew attention to the fact—"It has been stated in former tables, that from 1835 to 1840 there had been a gradual increase in the proportion of females. In 1841 this increase was slightly checked, and in the following year the decrease in the proportion was considerable. But in 1843 an increase again commenced, and was succeeded by a further increase in 1844. These fluctuations will be best shown by the following figures :—

	No. of Females.	Proportion to 100 Males.			No. of Females.	Proportion to 100 Males.
1834	3,571	18·8		1840	5,212	23·7
1835	3,456	20·0		1841	5,200	23·0
1836	3,736	21·6		1842	5,569	21·6
1837	4,205	21·6		1843	5,340	22·0
1838	4,189	22·1		1844	4,993	23·1."
1839	4,612	23·2				

Whilst in 1852, he added, "the numbers still prove a continuance of the proportional increase of females which has been uninterrupted since 1848," when, as stated above, there was a slight decrease.

	No. of Females.	Proportion to 100 Males.			No. of Females.	Proportion to 100 Males.
1845	4,962	25·6		1849	5,401	24·1
1846	5,257	26·5		1850	5,265	24·4
1847	5,930	25·9		1851	55,69	24·8
1848	5,763	23·4		1852	5,625	25·7

The same eminent authority concluded, in 1853, by remarking that "the increase has been unusually large this year, the proportion having risen from 25·7 to 29·5 females in 100 males; while twenty years since it was only 18·8 females to the 100 males.*

Next, as regards the offences with which the females sent for trial are mostly charged, we find that these generally consist of what are termed, in the Government returns, "Offences against property committed without violence"—particularly simple larceny, larceny by servants, and receiving stolen goods (the offences of this class including, in the year 1846, 88 per cent. of the females committed, and only 77 per cent. of the males). In indictments for perjury, and for keeping disorderly houses, the females also form a large proportion. In murder, and attempts to murder, they constitute above one-fourth the commitments; in arson, above one-sixth; but for robbery, burglary, and housebreaking, one-twelfth only.

Some two or three years ago the following proportions were given by Mr. Redgrave as regards the per centage of females included in the different classes of crime :—

* It will be observed that there is a slight difference between the numbers last quoted and those given in the previous table, concerning the females committed for trial. The numbers in the former instance are cited from Captain Williams' report, bearing date, 1856; whilst those in the latter case are after Mr. Redgrave's returns. Moreover, the proportions of females to males differ slightly, the female ratios having been calculated to 100 prisoners of both sexes; whilst in Mr. Redgrave's returns they are calculated to 100 males.

In offences against the person, such as murder, and attempts
at murder, manslaughter, concealing birth, bigamy,
assaults, &c., the proportion of females was, in 1851, 13·4 to 100 males.

In offences against property, committed with violence, such
as burglary, housebreaking, and highway robbery,
the proportion was .... 7·7 „

In the same class of crimes, however, committed without
violence, including the offences of simple larceny,
embezzlement, and receiving stolen goods, &c., the
proportion was as high as .... 28·6 „

In the malicious offences against property, such as arson,
incendiarism, destruction of machinery, &c., and
maiming cattle, the proportion was at its lowest ebb, or 5·1 „

In forgery, and offences against the currency, such as
attempting to pass bad money, or forged notes, it rose
again to .... 23·1 „

Whilst in the miscellaneous offences of high treason,
smuggling, poaching, prison-breaking, perjury, riot,
and keeping disorderly houses, it was not quite .... 20·* „

But the most remarkable feature in the recent history of female crime is the large and
increasing proportion of females annually charged with murder. During the last fifteen
years the numbers and proportions of females accused of this crime have been as follows :—

In the Five Years.	Males.		Females.	
1835-39	.	.	223	.	92 or 42 females to 100 males.
1840-44	.	.	221	.	126 „ 57 „ „
1845-49	.	.	205	.	160 „ 78 „ „

In the subjoined table, however, we have a still clearer view of the enormous increase of the grave crime of murder among women, and by which it will be seen that
though the proportion of female murderers was, in 1835-39, only 42 in every 100 male
murderers, in 1847 the per centage was not less than 89·4; and, in 1851, it had risen to
124·2; so that whilst the crime of murder among men has been comparatively decreasing,
among women it has been proportionably on the increase :—

	Males accused of murder.		Females accused of murder.		
1842	. . 39	.	28 or 71·8 females to 100 males.
1843	. . 52	. .	33 „ 63·4	„	„
1844	. . 46	. .	29 „ 63·0	„	„
1845	. . 41	. .	24 „ 58·5	„	„
1846	. . 42	. .	26 „ 61·9	„	„
1847	. . 38	. .	34 „ 89·4	„	„
1848	. . 42	. .	34 „ 80·9	„	„
1849	. . 42	. .	42 „ 100·0	„	„
1850	. . 28	. .	24 „ 85·7	„	„
1851	. . 33	. .	41 „ 124·2	„	„

* In the year 1841 the following was the proportion of females in the different classes of offences :—

1st class (offences against the person) .... 10·9 per 100 males.
2nd „ (ditto against property, with violence) .... 6·3 „ „
3rd „ (ditto ditto, without violence) .... 26·4 „ „
4th „ (malicious offences against property) .... 8·0 „ „
5th „ (offences against the currency) .... 23·1 „ „
6th „ (miscellaneous offences) .... 19·5 „ „

The next step in our exposition of the phenomena of female crime, is to set forth the localities in which the criminality among women appears to be greater or less. With this view we have drawn up the following table, in which the average has been calculated from the Government returns for the last ten years:—

TABLE SHOWING THE ANNUAL AVERAGE PER CENTAGE OF FEMALES TO MALES COMMITTED FOR
TRIAL IN EACH COUNTY THROUGHOUT ENGLAND, FROM 1844 TO 53, BOTH INCLUSIVE.

COUNTIES.	Average annual number committed for trial.			Average annual per centage.	
	Males.	Females.	Total.	Males.	Females.
Bedford	159·6	21·0	180·0	88·37	11·63
Berks	277·1	46·0	323·1	85·76	14·24
Bucks	253·6	22·4	276·0	91·88	8·12
Cambridge	249·1	38·3	287·4	86·67	13·33
Chester	711·1	198·5	909·6	78·18	21·82
Cornwall	199·2	60·4	2596·1	76·73	23·27
Cumberland	101·1	39·3	1404·1	72·01	27·99
Derby	215·4	30·0	245·4	87·77	12·23
Devon	600·3	194·4	794·7	75·54	24·46
Dorset	204·6	43·9	248·5	82·33	17·67
Durham	250·4	65·9	316·3	79·17	20·83
Essex	536·2	69·2	605·4	88·17	11·43
Gloucester	804·4	182·4	986·8	81·52	18·48
Hereford	188·6	43·6	232·2	81·22	18·71
Hertford	265·0	27·8	292·8	90·51	9·49
Huntingdon	78·8	13·3	92·1	85·55	14·45
Kent	761·4	176·7	938·1	81·17	18·83
Lancaster	2408·5	864·9	3273·4	73·58	26·42
Leicester	286·0	44·7	330·7	86·48	13·52
Lincoln	407·1	87·8	494·9	82·26	17·74
Middlesex	3179·9	1022·3	4202·2	75·67	24·33
Monmouth	238·4	78·8	317·2	73·16	24·84
Norfolk	597·6	111·1	708·7	84·33	15·67
Northampton	243·4	38·2	281·6	86·43	13·57
Northumberland	182·1	59·9	242·0	75·25	24·70
Nottingham	282·5	44·7	327·2	86·34	13·66
Oxford	250·8	39·0	289·8	86·54	13·46
Rutland	28·8	4·4	33·2	86·74	13·26
Salop	256·1	6·55	321·6	79·63	20·37
Somerset	658·8	143·4	802·2	82·12	17·88
Southampton	562·3	119·1	681·4	82·52	17·48
Stafford	795·7	189·3	985·0	80·79	19·21
Suffolk	451·5	76·1	527·6	85·58	14·42
Surrey	849·0	246·5	1095·5	77·49	22·51
Sussex	392·7	90·9	483·6	81·21	18·79
Warwick	750·7	155·7	906·4	82·82	17·18
Westmoreland	43·5	8·2	51·7	84·14	15·86
Wilts	361·8	59·6	421·4	85·85	14·16
Worcester	485·8	109·9	595·7	81·56	18·44
York	1518·9	357·1	1876·0	80·96	19·04
North Wales	240·7	61·7	302·4	79·59	20·41
South Wales	408·2	142·4	550·6	74·14	25·86
Total for England and Wales	21734·7	5494·3	27229·0	79·82	20·18

Arranging the counties in their order, according as the per centage of female offenders is either above or below the general average, we have the subjoined result :—

Counties in which the Per Centage of Female Prisoners is Above the Average.

Cumberland	. 27·99	Devon	. 24·46	Chester	. 21·82
Lancaster	. 26·42	Middlesex	. 24·33	Durham	. 20·83
South Wales	. 25·86	Cornwall	. 23·27	North Wales	. 20·41
Monmouth	. 24·84	Surrey	. 22·51	Shropshire	. 20·37
Northumberland	. 24·70				

Average for all England and Wales . . . . . 20·18

Counties in which the Per Centage of Female Prisoners is Below the Average.

Stafford	. 19·21	Southampton	. 17·48	Leicester	. 13·52
York	. 19·04	Warwick	. 17·18	Oxford	. 13·46
Kent	. 18·83	Westmoreland	. 15·86	Cambridge	. 13·33
Sussex	. 18·79	Norfolk	. 15·67	Rutland	. 13·26
Hereford	. 18·71	Huntingdon	. 14·45	Derby	. 12·23
Gloucester	. 18·48	Suffolk	. 14·42	Beds	. 11·63
Worcester	. 18·44	Berks	. 14·24	Essex	. 11·43
Somerset	. 17·88	Wilts	. 14·16	Hertford	. 9·49
Lincoln	. 17·74	Nottingham	. 13·66	Bucks	. 8·12
Dorset	. 17·67	Northampton	. 13·57		

Here, then, we perceive that in the majority of those counties in which the per centage of female offenders is inordinately great, that peculiar form of courtship which is termed "bundling," or some equally loose modification of it, is known to prevail—as in Cumberland, Northumberland, and Durham, South Wales, North Wales, and Monmouth, Cornwall, and Devon, as well as Lancashire, Cheshire, and Shropshire—the metropolitan county being also that in which there is the greatest number of prostitutes; whilst the midland counties, as Bucks, Herts, Beds, Cambridge, &c., are those in which the females appear to be the least criminal.

In the Government returns, Mr. Redgrave makes an attempt to connect the difference in the proportion of female crime throughout the different parts of the country, with the difference of employment among women.

"As this difference," he says, in the report for 1847, "arises apparently from the occupations of the population, the following comparison has been made of the commitments in the chief industrial and agricultural districts; and it will be seen that, except in the metropolitan county, the greatest proportion of female commitments has taken place in those counties where females are employed in the rudest and most unfeminine labours :—

	1843.	1847.
"*Southern Welsh Mining District.*—Wales, South . . .	29·4	36·9
Northern Mining District.—Cumberland, Northumberland, Durham	29·1	33·6
District of the Woollen and Cotton Manufactures.—Yorkshire, Lancashire . . . . }	28·0	30·6
Metropolitan County.—Middlesex	30·8	29·4
Northern Welsh Mining District.—Wales, North . .	18·8	28·4
Hardware, Pottery, and Glass.—Stafford, Warwick, Worcester .	19·0	24·9
Smaller Cotton, Woollen, Silk, and Lace Fabrics.—Chester, Derby, Notts, Leicester . . . . }	18·0	23·3

South and South-Western Agricultural District.—Sussex, Hants, Wilts, Dorset, Somerset . . . . } 19·4   21·2

North-Eastern and Eastern Agricultural District.—Lincoln, Norfolk, Suffolk, Essex . . . . } 18·5   20·6

Midland Agricultural Counties.—Cambridge, Northampton, Hertford, Bedford, Bucks, Oxford, Berks . . . . } 13·1   14·5."

We are, however, rather inclined to connect female criminality with unchastity, rather than "rude" employment among women; and it will, we believe, be found to be generally true that those counties in which the standard of female propriety is the lowest, or where the number of prostitutes is the greatest, there the criminality of the women is the greatest.

We have now but to set forth the ages at which the career of female vice is found to predominate.

We have before shown (p. 357) that there is, proportionally, less juvenile delinquency among females than among males; the average per centage of young girls imprisoned throughout England and Wales being only $7\frac{1}{2}$ of the whole of the female prisoners, whilst the mean proportion of boys is as much as $12\frac{3}{4}$ per cent. of the gross number of male prisoners. We showed, moreover, that, under twelve years, the young female criminals were only a fraction more than $\frac{3}{4}$ per cent. of the female prisoners; whilst the young male criminals of the same age are very nearly $1\frac{1}{2}$ per cent. of the male prisoners; then, between twelve and fourteen years of age, the young females are about $1\frac{1}{2}$ per cent., and the young males about $2\frac{3}{4}$ per cent., of the entire number of prisoners belonging to either sex; whereas, between fourteen and seventeen years of age, the female prisoners are about $5\frac{1}{2}$ per cent., and the males $8\frac{1}{2}$ per cent., of the whole.

"The returns prove, as might be anticipated," says Mr. Redgrave, "that females are not led into the commission of crime so early as males; this probably arises from the greater parental restraint they are subjected to in early life, as well as from the numbers who commence an evil course by prostitution—an assumption which would account for the increased proportion that, after the age of twenty-five, the females bear to the males. The calculation which follows is made upon the commitments of 1846 * :—

Concerning the comparative degree of instruction between the female and the male

Ages of Prisoners.	Males.		Females.	
	Numbers.	Centesimal proportion.	Numbers.	Centesimal proportion.
Aged under 15 years	1,426	7·18	214	4·07
,, 15 years and under 20	4,893	24·65	1,243	23·64
,, 20 ,, ,, 25	4,674	23·55	1,182	22·49
,, 25 ,, ,, 30	2,810	14·16	845	16·07
,, 30 ,, ·, 40	3,046	15·35	926	17·61
,, 40 ,, ,, 50	1,632	8·22	488	9·28
,, 50 ,, ,, 60	652	3·28	207	3·94
,, 60 years and above	371	1·87	85	1·62
Ages not ascertained	346	1·74	67	1·28
	19,850		5,257	

* In the "Sixteenth Report of the Inspectors of Prisons," there is a decennial table upon the same subject, and including the gross number of prisoners, both summarily convicted as well as tried at assizes and sessions. Not to depend upon the returns for any one year, we have copied from this table the propor-

prisoners of all ages, we find, by the decennial tables, that the annual mean from 1841 to 1850 was as follows :—

TABLE SHOWING THE ANNUAL MEAN AS TO THE RELATIVE STATE OF INSTRUCTION BETWEEN MALE AND FEMALE PRISONERS FOR THE DECENNIAD ENDING 1850.

State of Instruction.	Numbers.		Per Centage.	
	Males.	Females.	Males.	Females.
Can neither read nor write .	26,339	9,822	35·5	43·5
Can read only	15,752	6,384	20·1	28·2
Can either read or write, or both imperfectly . .	31,053	5,847	39·6	26·0
Can read and write well .	4,835	467	6·1	2·0
Superior education . . .	211	7	0·3	0·0
State of instruction not ascertained	303	71	0·4	0·4
Total . . .	78,494	22,598	100·0	100·0

Thus, then, we discover that the female criminals belong to a more ignorant class even than the males, for we see that upwards of 70 per cent. of the former are unable to write, whilst but little more than 50 per cent. of the latter are in the same degraded condition.

The results, therefore, that we arrive at from the above elaborate data are—

1. That females, taken in the aggregate, are considerably less criminal than males ; the entire female prisoners of the country constituting but little more than 20 per cent., and the males as much as 80 per cent., of the gross prison population of England and Wales.

2. That female crime—and especially that of murder—has increased among us within the last twenty years, rising from 18 per cent. in 1835, to 25 per cent. in 1853.

tions as to the ages of the male and female prisoners for 1841 and 1850, as well as the annual mean for the entire ten years :—

TABLE SHOWING THE RELATIVE AGES OF PRISONERS OF BOTH SEXES SUMMARILY CONVICTED, AS WELL AS COMMITTED FOR TRIAL, IN THE YEARS 1841 AND 1850, TOGETHER WITH THE ANNUAL MEAN FOR TEN YEARS.

Ages of Prisoners.	1841.		1850.		Annual mean for ten years.	
	Males.	Females.	Males.	Females.	Males.	Females.
Aged under 12 years	1·32	·85	1·34	·68	1·33	·76
,, 12 years and under 14 .	2·86	1·54	2·77	1·29	2·77	1·32
,, 14 ,, ,, 17 . .	8·53	5·60	7·59	4·56	8·68	5·53
,, 17 ,, ,, 21 . .	23·74	24·88	22·99	22·97	24·06	24·50
,, 21 ,, ,, 30 . .	33·78	35·45	33·97	35·88	32·21	35·73
,, 30 ,, ,, 45 . .	19·55	21·61	21·44	24·04	20·78	20·94
,, 45 ,, ,, 60 . .	7·88	8·37	7·46	7·97	7·99	8·93
,, 60 years and upwards . .	1·75	1·64	2·06	2·26	1·95	2·24
Ages not ascertained	·59	·60	·38	·35	·23	·05
Total	100·00	100·00	100·00	100·00	100·00	100·00

Here we perceive that under the age of seventeen the male offenders, according to the decennial average, are 5 per cent. more than the females ; that from seventeen to twenty-one the ratio between the two sexes is very nearly equal ; whilst from twenty-one to thirty the female prisoners are some 3 per cent. in excess. We also perceive that there has been a tendency for the number of female prisoners under twenty-one to decrease—the per centage of those under twenty-one, in the year 1841, having been 32·87, whilst in 1850 the per centage of females below the same age had fallen to 29·50. Between the ages of twenty-one and thirty scarcely any alteration occurred ; whilst above the age of thirty, the proportion of female committals has increased nearly 3 per cent. within the last ten years.

3. That the counties in which there is an inordinate proportion of female criminals to males, are those in which there is a low standard of female virtue, or in which the number of prostitutes is excessive.

4. The crimes to which the female prisoners are mostly prone are those of simple larceny, larceny by servants, as well as uttering base coin, perjury, and keeping disorderly houses; the latter class of crimes being those generally committed by the prostitute class, as the passing of bad money for the coiners with whom they cohabit, and false swearing in order to procure the acquittal of their associate thieves.

5. That the female criminals begin their career of crime at a later period of life than the males, there being a smaller per centage of female prisoners than males below the age of puberty, and a correspondingly greater proportion after the age of 21 years.

Lastly. That the female criminals belong to a far more ignorant and degraded class than the males, there being only one-half of the male prisoners who are unable to read or write, whilst nearly three-fourths of the females are incapable of doing so.

We have now only to show the number of female criminals in the Metropolis, as well as to set forth the proportion they bear to the males, in order to ascertain how much greater is the criminality of the London women than that of the country generally.

The number of females "passing through" the London detentional prisons in the course of the year would appear to be near upon 3,500 in 9,000 and odd prisoners of both sexes, as may be gathered from the following returns for 1853, as given in the Nineteenth Report of the Prison Inspectors:—

	Males.	Females.	Total both Sexes.	Proportion of Females to 100 of gross Prison Population.
Number of prisoners passing through the House of Detention, Clerkenwell . .	5,672	2,291	7,963	
Number of prisoners passing through Horsemonger Lane prison	2,042	761	2,803	
Number of prisoners passing through Newgate	1,575	380	1,955	
Total passing through the London detentional prisons	9,289	3,432	12,721	26·9

In addition to these, there are the prisoners "passing through" the London houses of correction, and the number of females among these would appear to amount to rather better than 8,000, out of a gross total of very nearly 25,000 prisoners of both sexes.

	Males.	Females.	Total both Sexes.	Proportion of Females to 100 of gross Prison Population.
Number of prisoners passing through the Middlesex House of Correction, Coldbath Fields	9,665	—	9,665	
Number of prisoners passing through the Westminster House of Correction, Tothill Fields	1,923	6,010	7,933	
Number of prisoners passing through the City House of Correction, Holloway .	975	365	1,340	
Number of prisoners passing through the Surrey House of Correction, Wandsworth	3,558	1,474	5,032	
Number of prisoners passing through the City Bridewell, Bridge Street, Blackfriars	723	256	979	
Total passing through the London correctional prisons	16,844	8,105	24,949	32·5

To these, again, must be subjoined the numbers in the metropolitan convict prisons; and, according to the Government returns for the year 1854-55, the female convicts would appear to amount to 860 odd in 5,760 prisoners of both sexes :—

	Males.	Females.	Total both Sexes.	Proportion of Females to 100 of gross Prison Population.
Number of prisoners passing through Pentonville prison	925	—	925	
Number of prisoners passing through Millbank prison	2,461	198	2,659	
Number of prisoners passing through Brixton prison	—	664	664	
Number of prisoners passing through Hulks (Woolwich)	1,513	—	1,513	
Total passing through the London convict prisons	4,899	862	5,761	14·9

The metropolitan account, therefore, as to the number and per centage of the female criminals stands thus :—

Number and per centage of females passing through the London convict prisons	862 or 14·9 per cent. of gross prison population.	
Number and per centage of females passing through the correctional prisons	8,105 ,, 32·5 ,, ,, ,,	
Number and per centage of females passing through the detentional prisons	3,432 ,, 26·9 ,, ,, ,,	
Total	12,399 28·5 ,, ,, ,,	

Thus, then, we perceive that there are upwards of 12,000 female criminals "passing through" the London prisons in the course of the year, and this out of a gross prison population of 43,000 and odd individuals of both sexes;* and this gives a proportion of 28·5 females to every 100 prisoners of both sexes, which, it will be seen, by referring to the table at page 460, exceeds by more than 5 per cent. the proportion of female prisoners for the whole country. Of the 12,399 females passing through the London prisons, 752, or 6 per cent. of the whole, are juveniles under the age of 17 years; whilst the 31,000 and odd males passing through the same establishments include no less than 19 juveniles in every 100 —a fact which thoroughly agrees with what has been before shown, that the females do not, generally, commence their criminal career until after the age of puberty. It is, however, a somewhat startling fact that the London women make up more than one-tenth of the gross prison population of the whole country, viz., 12,000 and odd in a gross total of rather more than 100,000 prisoners.

It now remains for us to state, generally, the characteristics of the London female criminals, and then to pass on to the exposition of the economy of the female prison at Westminster.

The most striking peculiarity of the women located in the London prisons is that of utter and imperturbable shamelessness. Those who are accustomed to the company of

* The reader should be warned that many of these appear more than once in the above accounts those, for instance, at Millbank are transferred to Brixton, and the majority of those at Horsemonger Lane to Wandsworth. The same occurs with the females from Newgate and the House of Detention. Again, many are recommitted, and so are counted more than once in the correctional and detentional returns for the year. The total number of distinct or individual female criminals may, perhaps, be 6,000, or half that above stated.

modest women, and have learnt at once to know and respect the extreme sensitiveness of the female character to praise or blame, as well as its acute dread of being detected in the slightest impropriety of conduct, or in circumstances the least unbecoming the sex, and have occasionally seen the blood leap in an instant into the cheeks, till the whole countenance has come to be suffused with a deep crimson flush of modest misgiving, and lighted up with all the glowing grace of innocence itself, and have noted, too, how in such states it seems to be positive pain to the abashed creature to meet the gaze of any rougher nature than her own—such persons can hardly comprehend how so violent a change as that which strikes us first of all in the brazen and callous things we see congregated within the female prisons, can possibly have been wrought in the feminine character.

Two questions at such times divide the mind : Is shame not *natural* to woman—an artificial and educated sentiment, rather than an innate and spontaneous one ? Or were the bold-faced women and girls that one beholds, as we pass along the prison work-rooms, tittering rather than blushing at their infamy, and staring full in the face of the stranger, instead of averting their head in order to avoid his glance—were these ever modest and gentle-natured, as those with whom we are in daily intercourse ? Is this the *true* female nature, and that which we know merely the *disguised* and *polite* form of it ?

There is but one answer to such queries.

Shame is *as* unnatural to woman as it is for mankind to love their enemies, and to bless those that persecute them. It is *as much* an educated sentiment as is the appreciation of the beautiful and the good, and *as thoroughly* the result of training as is a sense of decency and even virtue ; for in the same manner as the conscience itself remains dormant in our bosoms till developed, like the judgment, or indeed any other faculty, by long teaching and schooling ; so shame itself, though the main characteristic of civilized woman, may continue utterly unawakened in the ruder forms of female nature.

Many of the wretched girls seen in our jails have, we verily believe, never had the sentiment educated in them, living almost the same barbarous life as they would, had they been born in the interior of Africa ; whilst in others, though the great governing principle has been partially developed, the poor wretches, by a long course of misconduct, have become so hardened to the scorn and reproofs of their fellow-creatures as to be utterly barbarized, and left without the faintest twinge of moral sense to restrain their wild animal passions and impulses ; so that in them one sees the most hideous picture of all human weakness and depravity—a picture the more striking because exhibiting the coarsest and rudest moral features in connection with a being whom we are apt to regard as the most graceful and gentle form of humanity.

And yet they who have studied the idiosyncrasy of these degraded women know that they are capable, even in their degradation, of the very highest sacrifices for those they love. The majority of the *habitual* female criminals are connected with some low brute of a man who is either a prize-fighter, or cab-driver, or private soldier, or pickpocket, or coiner, or costermonger, or, indeed, some such character. And for this lazy and ruffian fellow, there is no indignity nor cruelty they will not suffer, no atrocity that they are not ready to commit, and no infamy that they will hesitate to perform, in order that he may continue to live half-luxuriously with them in their shame. A virtuous woman's love is never of the same intensely passionate and self-denying character as marks the affection of her most abject sister. To comprehend this, we must conceive the wretched woman shunned by almost all the world for her vice—we must remember that, in many instances, she has lost every relative and friend, and that even her parents (whose love and care is the last of all to cease) have cast her from them, and that she is *alone* in the great wilderness of life and care—friendless at the very time when she needs and longs most for a friend to protect and console her. We must endeavour, too, to conceive what must be the feelings of such a woman for the *one* person, amid all mankind, who seems to sympathize with her, and who is ready to shield her from the taunts and cuffs of the world; for most strange indeed it is, that those who seem to be the least like women of all, and appear to be the least loving and self-denying in their natures, should be characterized even in their debasement by the tenderest attribute of the female constitution, and remarkable for a love that is more generous, more devoted, more patient, and more indomitable than any other.

We once troubled our head with endeavouring to discover what qualities in man partake of the admirable in the eyes of such women as these. Do they love the half brutes with whom they cohabit, and from whose hands they bear blow after blow without a murmur, giving indeed only kisses in return; and for whose gross comforts they are daily ready to pollute both their body and soul?—do they love these fellows, we asked ourselves, for any personal beauty they fancy them to possess; or what strange quality is it that makes them prize them beyond any other being in the world?

We soon, however, discovered that they care little about the looks of their paramours, for not only are the majority of such men coarse and satyr-like in feature, but these women, generally speaking, have even a latent contempt for the class of public performers who are wont to trick their persons out to the best possible advantage. Again, it is not honour, nor dignity of character, nor chivalry of nature, nor energy of disposition, nor generosity of temperament that they think the highest attributes of man; for the fellows with whom they cohabit are mean and base to the last degree, selfish as swine, idle as lazzaroni, and ruffianly even as savages in their treatment of females.

In a word, it is *power* and *courage* that make up the admirable with woman in her shame; and hence the great proportion of what are termed "fancy men" are either, as we have said, prize-fighters, or private soldiers, or cab-drivers, or thieves, or coiners, or indeed fellows who are distinguished either for their strength, or "pluck," or their adventurous form of life.

Another marked peculiarity of the character of the female criminals is the periodical indulgence of many of them in violent outbursts of temper, if not fury, and that, too, without any apparent cause.

We have already drawn attention to this striking characteristic while treating of the female prisons at Brixton and Millbank, and shown that special canvas dresses, and indeed strait waistcoats, have to be resorted to, in order to prevent the women, when subject to these wild fits of passion, from tearing to ribbons every article of dress about them, and that occasionally they destroy the tables, windows, and bedding in their cells, so that the casements have to be covered with sheets of perforated iron, and even the shelves to be made of the same material, set into the walls; whilst not only are the female prisoners more violent and passionate than the males, but their language, at such times, is declared by all to be far more gross and disgusting than that of men in similar circumstances.

Nor is it less remarkable that some of the women, who are liable to such outbreaks, will occasionally, when they feel the fit of fury coming on, ask of their own accord to be shut up in a separate cell.

There would appear to be two causes for such wildness of conduct—the one physical, and perhaps referable to the same derangement of functions as Esquirol, in his work upon madness, has shown to be intimately connected with insanity among women; and the other moral, in the want of that feeling of shame which, as we have said, is the great controlling principle with women, so that the female criminal being left without any moral sense, as it were, to govern and restrain the animal propensities of her nature, is really reduced to the same condition as a brute, without the power to check her evil propensities.

¶ ii.—ι.

Of the Interior of the Female Prison at Westminster.

It has been before stated that, at the April Quarter Sessions of the year 1850, Mr. Thomas Turner, one of the Middlesex magistrates, moved to the effect, "that a committee be appointed to consider the expediency of appropriating each of the Middlesex Houses of Correction to distinct classes of offenders," and that, in accordance with the recommendation of the committee then appointed, it was determined, in July 1850, "that the Westminster House of Correction should be thenceforth restricted to the reception of convicted female prisoners, as well as males below the age of seventeen."

This change enabled the Middlesex magistrates to manage their two houses of correction with twenty officers less, and at an annual saving of £1,719 in salaries to officials.

That portion of the Westminster House of Correction which now constitutes the female prison there consists of two distinct semicircular blocks of buildings, situate at what are termed the B and C sides of the prison; the former being at the back of the governor's house, adjoining Victoria Street, and the latter at the side of it towards the river, and facing the boys' prison A, which stands on the side next the Vauxhall Road.

At the time of our visit, there were some 611 female prisoners located within the B and C portions of the building—337 in the cells and dormitories of "B side," and 274 in those of "C side"—the particular distribution being as follows :—

B side.			Female Prisoners.	C side.			Female Prisoners.
In the cells of No. 1 prison there were		.	21	In the cells of No. 1 prison there were		.	12
„	2	„	27	„	2	„	27
„	3	„	28	„	3	„	27
„	4	„	21	„	6	„	28
„	5	„	23	„	7	„	26
„	6	„	28	„	8	„	8
„	7	„	28	Total sleeping in separate cells		. —	128
Total sleeping in separate cells		—	176	In Dormitory, C 4	„	.	102
In Dormitory B 1 .	.	. .	47	In Nursery	„	.	44
„ B 2 .	.	. .	55	Total sleeping in association		. —	146
„ B 3 .	.	. .	44				
In Infirmary	.	. .	15	Total in C side	.	. .	274
Total sleeping in association	.	. —	161	„ B side	.	. .	337
				Grand total locked up in the female prison the night previous to our visit		}	611
Total on B side	.	. . .	337				

In the official returns to the Home Secretary, however, it is stated that the female portion of the prison is capable of containing only 600 prisoners, even when more than one prisoner sleeps in a cell; and that it has *separate* sleeping accommodation for but 351 women; and yet here we find the maximum accommodation exceeded, and no less than 248, or more than 40 per cent., of the female prisoners huddled together in dormitories by night —an arrangement which partakes of all the worst features of the Hulks, without the excuse of ship-board to palliate the infamy.

And yet, even though the female prison, at the time of our visit, contained more women than it was fitted to accommodate, we find, by the official returns, that it is occasionally made to hold some three score more; for, according to the last report, the greatest number of female prisoners located within it at one time during the year ending Michaelmas, 1855, was not less than 676, whilst the daily average of female prisoners throughout the whole of the same year was 600—the very point of its maximum accommodation.

The gross population of the female prison at Westminster, for the same year, was as follows :—

Number of female prisoners remaining in custody at the close of the year ending Michaelmas, 1854 . . . . } 623

Number of prisoners committed in the course of the year ending Michaelmas, 1855 . . . . } 5,359

Gross population of the female prison for 1855 . . . 5,982

Of this number, 279, or 4·6 per cent. of the whole, were under the age of seventeen years. Of the 279 juveniles, 241 had been summarily convicted, and 38 convicted at sessions; whilst of the 5,703 adult women, 4,655 were imprisoned upon summary convictions and 1,048 after trial.

We have before drawn attention to the fact, that the amount of sickness among the females at Tothill Fields is unusually high, when compared with that of the female prisons of all England and Wales. In 1853, the per centage of indisposition among the females at the Westminster House of Correction was 50·4, whereas that for the female prisoners throughout the country for the same year was 20 per cent. less, or 30·4 (see pp. 370, 371). We should also here repeat, that the punishments at the female prison at Westminster appear to be excessive, when contrasted with those inflicted upon the same class of prisoners throughout England and Wales; for whilst the average ratio of punishments to the number of female prisoners amounts to but little more than 23 per cent. for the whole country, it is upwards of half as much again, or 38½ per cent., at Tothill Fields prison.

The cells, again, in the female branch of the same establishment are as disgracefully defective, both as regards capacity and ventilation, as those in which the boys are located, whilst they are also as utterly deficient of all means of heating or lighting during the long winter evenings, the women being then locked up in the dark and cold for more than 12 hours out of the 24—a practice which renders it impossible to prevent them talking with the inmates of the neighbouring cells, as we were assured they did immediately the night patrol had passed.

It is but just, however, while repeating these strictures, that we should append the counter-statement of one of the Middlesex magistrates, who says, in a letter addressed to us after the publication of our previous remarks upon the economy of this prison :—

"Many thanks for the proofs, which I have carefully read, and which appear very correct.

"You will, I am sure, permit me to add a few words in explanation respecting the cells, punishment of the women, &c.

"The Westminster prison was the first erected on an improved plan, and was considered at the period a model prison. Experience has, however, proved that it is far from perfect, neither could it be warmed and ventilated in an efficient manner but at an enormous cost. The question has been often under the consideration of the visiting justices, but from this cause has been abandoned.

"Another and far superior course has been adopted, that of building a new wing on the principle of Pentonville, the House of Detention, &c., with certified cells, at an expense of £11,000. The works will be commenced in a few days. Should this wing be approved of, the entire prison can be altered, the plan having been so arranged.

"*Punishments of the Women.*—These arise from the violation of the prison rules under the 'silent associated system' (rules which are not required under the 'separate system'), as well as from the violent conduct of the prisoners sent for short terms, and from the great number who are frequent—I may add, constant—inmates of our prison, and who are almost always under punishment, although every effort has been made to reform them.

"*Sanitary Condition of the Prison.*—The number of cases of slight indisposition among the women arise—firstly, from women being subject to complaints from which men are free; and, secondly, from the large number who are more or less suffering, on entering the prison, from the effects of intoxication, dissipation, and starvation."

In reply, we have merely to urge that the relative amount of sickness among the females at this prison was tested by that of *other females at all the other prisons of England and Wales*, so that the plea which attributes the excessive proportion of indisposition among the female prisoners at Tothill Fields to the fact that women are subject to complaints from which men are free cannot be of any logical avail.

Again, it is no rational justification of the excessive amount of punishment inflicted upon the females at this same prison, to assert that it is necessary to enforce the regulations of the silent associated system of prison discipline; for as this same system is in force in the majority of prisons throughout England and Wales, and the ratio of punishments at Tothill Fields was *compared with that of the average for all the female prisons of England and Wales*, it follows, either that the discipline of other prisons must be most lax, or else that the government of this one is unnecessarily harsh and tyrannical.

¶ ii.—κ.

Of the School-room, Work-rooms, and Nursery, and "Own Clothes'" Store at Tothill Fields Prison.

The are two school-rooms in the females' prison at Westminster, one in C 8 for women, and the other in B 8 for girls.

The former has little peculiar about it to warrant special description. We found it fitted with rows of sloping desks, pierced with inkstands similar to those in the boys' prison before noticed, and the walls hung with the same didactic illustrations.

Here the women learn reading, writing, spelling, catechism, &c., the classes being five in number, and including altogether 122 scholars, all of whom are under twenty-four years of age, "though," said the teacher to us, "we take any above that age that the chaplain may please to send." Each class attends the school for an hour every day. There is likewise a Bible-class which receives prisoners up to any age—the oldest prisoner in it now being 46. "And," added the teacher, "there's 36 women in the class at present."

Any female prisoner can go to school if she expresses a wish to do so; and the women, we were told, often ask to be allowed to attend the classes. "For it's a great relief to the prison life, and they know they're learning something," continued our informant.

At the time of our visit there were nineteen in the school-room, and, as we entered it, the women, at the bidding of the teacher, rose and curtseyed.

"Some of the women here have learnt from the alphabet," said the warder, pointing to one or two who were duller-looking than the rest.

As we glanced along the three rows of white caps, there was not one abashed face or averted tearful eye to be seen, whilst many grinned impudently on meeting our gaze.

The warder, to let us see the acquirements of her scholars, bade one of them read a passage from the Bible, that each held in her hand. The woman, however, made such a sad bungle of the verse, that the teacher had again to assure us that the reader had learned her letters in the jail.

The other school at Tothill Fields, is, as we said, devoted to the education of the young girls imprisoned there, and this is a far more touching scene than the one for the elder women, for here the pupils are, some of them, of such tender years that the heart positively aches again to see little female creatures of only eight years of age habited in the prison clothes, and their faces utterly unfeminine in the boldness of their looks, the premature leer in their eye, and wanton-like smile upon their lip.

This was a half cosy little room fitted with forms, on which some sixteen mere children were seated. Over the mantelpiece hung a black board, on which was painted the following notice :—

> PRISONERS ARE NOT TO SPEAK
> TO EACH OTHER.

And beside this dangled the official placard concerning " THE REWARDS TO PRISONERS FOR GOOD CONDUCT." (See foot note, p. 438). Against the fire-place stood a table, on which were spread samplers and round patch-work d'oyleys, bordered with fringe and other small mosaic-like articles of needlework; while the floor, though bricken, was covered with a warm rug.

As usual, the room resounded with the noise of the pupils rising like a detachment of little soldiers, as our attendant matron ushered us into the place.

The girl prisoners were clad in blue and white-spotted cotton frocks, and caps with deep frilled borders, and most of them had long strips of shiny straw plait dangling from their hands, which they kept working at instinctively with their little fingers, while they looked with wonder up into our face. Some, as usual, were pretty-looking creatures, that enlisted all one's sympathies, almost to tears, in their favour, whilst others had so prematurely brazen a look, that the heart shrunk back as we inwardly shuddered at the thought that our own little girl—half angel though she seem now—born in the same circumstances, and reared among the same associates, would assuredly have been the same young fiend as they.

Here, strange to say, we found a flaxen-haired, fair-faced little boy, who held fast hold of the matron's hand, and clung closer to her skirts at the sight of a strange man in the school.

"He's the son of one of the prisoners, sir," said the matron, as we rested our palm on the little fellow's head, to assure him that we meant no harm to him. "His mother has got four years' penal servitude, and was sent away to Millbank; but they wouldn't receive her there on account of the child, since they had no nursery at that place. The mother and the boy have been here two years now, sir, and he comes to us every day to learn his prayers and letters. His name is Tommy."

"Poor little man! In a few more years," we could not help inwardly exclaiming, "you will most probably make your appearance in this same prison—year after year—by legal right, rather than by Government sufferance; and a few years after that, again, you will doubtlessly be found among the masked convict troop at Pentonville, and then seen labouring, almost under the muzzle of a warder's musket, in the neighbourhood of the public dock-yards or Government quarries; and, finally, all trace of you will be lost in the gravestoneless burial-ground of some one or other of the convict prisons, with nothing but the little blue stunted convict-flower lifting its head above your grave.

Poor little felon child! how like are you to this same little, stunted, convict-flower—

dwarfed in your moral and intellectual growth, and yet here, blooming with the very hue of heaven in your eyes, amid all kinds of human corruption !

"Our number of scholars," proceeded the teacher, in answer to our question, "varies generally from 20 to 23 or 24; but the school is rather low, and we have but 16 at present."

They learn writing, ciphering, and catechism, as well as the collect for the next Sunday.

"Stand up, those girls who are going to say the collect in chapel to-morrow," cried the matron, who seemed to think, naturally enough (for it is the great fallacy of all our educational systems), that to convert these little creatures into religious parrots is really to make them religious agents.

In an instant, some half-dozen mere children started up from their seats, in acknowledgment of the fact that they had got the collect by rote, though it was clear, from their years, that one might as well have thought to have made Christians of them by teaching them to jabber the Sermon on the Mount in the original Greek.

"That little girl, there," continued the teacher, "is the youngest we have here at present; she is eight years old, and didn't know her letters when she came in."

The little felon-babe stood up, in obedience to the command of the officer, while we stooped down to question her as to the reason why a tiny thing like her, that could hardly articulate distinctly, had been adjudged a felon.

"What are you here for?" we asked.

"Stealing a pair of boots," was the reply.

"Your father is a bricklayer, is he not?" inquired the matron, on our turning round to interrogate her concerning the parents of the child.

The little prisoner nodded assent, and told us that she had gone out with her brother to steal the boots. She didn't know, however, how old he was, but was sure that he had never been in prison, and that he did not go out thieving regularly.

We then asked her why she had taken the boots, and her answer was, "'Cause I hadn't got none of my own."

"She has three months' imprisonment," the warder added.

Now surely for magistrates to put the brand of thief upon a mere infant like this, is about upon a par, both in intellect and humanity, with those wiseacre justices of the olden time who sat in judgment upon corpses for the heresy of their souls when alive, and who condemned dogs to be burnt as witches. When will society be made to understand that the real criminals, in cases of infantine "delinquency" like this, are the parents who allow their offspring to run wild in the streets, and not the little children that Christ himself likened in their innocence to the kingdom of God, and whom even the law considers to be morally incapable of performing any act of their own? And when will our legislators comprehend the iniquity as well as absurdity of sending mere babies to associate with older thieves as a means of teaching them right from wrong ?

"The next in age is ten," continued the matron. "Which is the one who is ten?" she inquired. "Oh! you, B——; you are, eh?"

Then another little creature stood up, and she was but an inch or two higher than the last. After this those of twelve years old rose from their seats, and the first of these to whom we spoke had three red stars on her arm, as badges of good conduct during her imprisonment, whilst she drooped her eyelids, as we questioned her, with a shame that was as beautiful as it was rare to behold in such a place.

"Bad money, sir," she answered, in a half whisper, to our inquiries as to the nature of her offence. "Aunt gave it me, please, sir; I was along with her when I was took."

The next prisoner, a chubby-cheeked thing of the same age, said, with a half-suppressed grin, in reply to our interrogatory as to what she was in prison for, "Pickpocketing, please, sir."

" There's another one in the prison on the same charge with her, but she was taken out of this room for bad behaviour," interpsoed the matron at our elbow. " The other one done it, sir, and gave it to me," said the child.

" This girl didn't know her letters when she came here," the warder interposed.

Another child—a red-headed and freckled-faced girl—whom we questioned, though but a mere baby in years, had been twice in the same prison—the first time for six months, and on this occasion for twelve months, having stolen some things from a reformatory school to which she had been sent on obtaining her liberty. The cause of her " delinquency" was soon explained; it was the old story.

" She has a stepmother that isn't over kind to her," said the matron.

" But why did you steal the things from the school ?" we asked.

" I did it because they didn't give me enough to eat," was the reply. " I ran away from the place, for I didn't want to stop there. It was a—Refuge, I think they call it—in St. Giles's."

The warder then informed us, that that school-room was for girls up to the age of sixteen ; and, before we left, she exhibited to us several of the copy-books belonging to her scholars— pointing out the while, with no slight pride, the progress that the wretched little creatures had made under her care. It should be added, that the gradual improvement in the penmanship was as marked as it was creditable to her zeal.

" That girl," exclaimed the matron, as she spread open a book, one entire page of which was covered with repetitions of the line—

" Have peace with all men,"

" had never handled a pen until she came here, and that's only a few weeks ago."

*** *The Nursery at Tothill Fields Prison.*—The next most interesting portion of the female prison at Westminster is the part set aside for the mothers and their infants, and situate in No. 4 prison, C side, immediately under what is termed the straw-plait or needle-room.

At the time of our visit there was some half-score iron bedsteads ranged along either side of the room, which was about the size of an ordinary barn. Some of the bedding was turned back, while in others the beds were ready made for the night. At the corners of the bed-steads sat the mothers with their children in their arms, some dancing them in the air— others teaching them, as they leant back, to walk up their bodies—and others tickling the little things as they rolled them on the counterpane; whilst the entire room resounded with the kissing and prattling of the mothers, and the gurgling, and crying, and laughing of the babes.

There were altogether 33 children, we were told, then in the prison, and 3 of these were under 6 months old, 12 from 6 to 12 months, and the remainder between 1 and 2 years, " beyond which age," said our informant, " we seldom receive them here, though I have never heard of any limit as to age; and there is one child now in the prison who is four years old, but that is because his mother has already been two years imprisoned here."

" Sometimes," the officer went on, " the mothers wish to send their children out again, still that is but rare. As a rule, I really don't think they are different from other people in their feelings for their little ones, and some of them are very fond of them; though one woman we have got in now (she is just behind us) treated her child very badly—so bad, indeed, that we were obliged to take it from her." The prisoner referred to was a gloomy, morose-looking creature, and scarcely seemed to notice the infant lying in her lap, even though it was smiling up into her face.

" The mothers," proceeded the warder, as we continued to question her, " have all a pound and a-half of oakum to pick in the course of the day, and they go into the work-room if their children are upwards of eight months old, while their little ones are taken care of by the women remaining in the nursery.

"There, you see, is a woman with two infants yonder, sitting by the bed near the door," said the officer, "she's minding another prisoner's child. Oh, yes, they're very good and patient to one another's children, and we seldom have cases of ill-treatment here to punish."

We had heard that the nursery at Tothill Fields was conducted upon the silent system, and though we had seen enough of disciplinarian folly in the course of our tour round the London prisons, nevertheless we could hardly believe that prison regulations could be carried to so wicked and unfeeling an extreme.

True, at the female prison at Brixton, we had found the women in the associated wings allowed to converse the greater part of the day, but nevertheless forced to break off all communication one with the other, and to observe strict silence at stated intervals—though for what earthly reason, or for what fancied good, further than the mere tyrannical display of authority, it was difficult to divine; for the stranger naturally said to himself, if intercourse among prisoners be bad, why allow them to speak to one another at all? and if it be found to be fraught with no ill effect, why this arbitrary imposition of silence for a mere hour at a time, during the fore and after part of the day?

Again, we had found the prisoners unmasked at the convict depot at Millbank, and free to recognize their former associates and friends; whilst at Pentonville, whither they were consigned after the first few months of their conviction, their faces were studiously screened one from the other, and even the chapel parted off into separate bins, as it were, so that each should be kept *religiously* aloof from the rest; whereas, at the Hulks, whither they were sent after some nine months of this wretched penal masquerade, their faces were again bare, and they were brought into closer communion than they could even enjoy in the low lodging-houses of London.

Further, we had noted that the work to which the convicts were put at one prison was discarded immediately they had become in any way skilled at it, and they were removed to another. The prisoner who had served a short time perhaps at gardening at Millbank, being employed at tailoring or shoemaking at Pentonville, and then, after three-quarters of a year's labour at such work, transferred to scraping shot, or breaking stones, or stacking wood at Woolwich.

Hence we were fully prepared to find the silent system at the Westminster House of Correction carried out even to the absurd extreme of forbidding mothers to prattle to their children, and infants to talk and gambol with one another.

Nevertheless, we are happy to be able to confess that we were in error upon this point, and that our informant, hearing that the nursery at Tothill Fields was conducted on the silent system, had impressed us with false notions as to the regulations in force, and led us erroneously to imagine that the little prison infants were reared in positive silence— denied even the privilege of listening to the tones of their mothers' voice. We found, however, upon investigation, that the silence enjoined extended merely to communication among the women themselves, the mothers being not only allowed to speak freely to their babes, but the children having full liberty to talk and play one with the other; and, indeed, that the most captious could not fairly quarrel with the regulations of this portion of the prison, which seemed to be conducted rather with all kindly consideration for the wretched women and children confined within it.

Sad as it is to see so many little cherub things entering life in such a place, still it is due to the prison authorities to say that no inhumanity of theirs renders the wretched lot of the inmates more wretched than it necessarily is.

Indeed, a moment's reflection amid such scenes as these is sufficient to melt even the stoniest natures; for if the innocent babbling and baby pranks of the little felon infants themselves do not thrill the heart with a positive spasm of sympathy, at least the eyes even of the sternest stranger must tingle with compassion to note the wretched mothers caressing and fondling the little things, as if they were the only bit of all the black, blank world without that made life bearable to them.

For ourselves, we do not mind confessing that the sight moved us more than even the highest wrought drama we had ever witnessed. For if a sense of the miserable start in life which these poor little things have made touched *us* to the very core—stranger as we were, with nothing but our common humanity to make the after fate of the babes worth a moment's thought to us—"How," we inwardly exclaimed, "must it wound and bruise the hearts of those wretched mothers to find the very being in the world whose life they wished to be happier and brighter than any other in creation, beginning its young days with a gloom and seeming fate about it that was almost appalling to contemplate.

Nor is it any sentimentality on our part that leads us to believe that the women located in this portion of the prison are of a superior caste to those seen in the other wards of the same institution. Not only do we miss here the brazen looks and the apparent glorying in their shame that prevails among the more debased of the female prisoners, but there is a greater gravity, as well as a seeming sadness, impressed upon the countenances of the mothers in the nursery that makes the visitor at once respect the misery, and pity rather than loathe the degraded situation of the poor creatures.

Again, the very fact of their being mothers is sufficient to prove that these prisoners do not belong to the class of "public women," since it is a wondrous ordination of Benevolence that such creatures as are absolutely shameless and affectionless should be childless as well; so that the sight of these baby prisoners was at once a proof to us that the hearts of the women that bore them were not utterly withered and corrupt, and that they still had sufficient humanity left to feel at once the degradation of their own position, and to almost hate themselves for the atmosphere of misery which their crimes had wrapt about the lives of their little ones.

Such thoughts as these, flitting fitfully through the brain, render the prison nursery perhaps the most deeply pathetic of all the scenes in the world. The maternal fondling here is no longer lovely to see, but positively sad and solemn to behold.

That woman yonder who keeps dabbing her hand over her little one's mouth, in order to make it babble again, how gravely and almost mournfully does she seem to *play* with the child!

This one, again, suckling her infant, has her eyes fixed intently on the babe, as it digs its head, like a young lamb, against its mother's side, and we can almost guess the wild conflict of emotion that is raging in her heart the while.

Yonder woman, too, who has placed her infant to kick and roll on the bed, and is leaning over it now, as with her apron-strings she tickles it in the folds of its fat little neck, seems barely to rejoice in its smiles, for she is probably speculating at one moment as to what wretched fate awaits it in the world; the next minute praying to have it dead in her lap; and then, as she snatches it up, and hugs it half frantically to her bosom, wishing she were as innocent as it, and prizing it as the only thing that still loves and clings to her in all the world.

As we stood noting these things in our book, the little flaxen-haired boy, whom we had seen in the school-room at the earlier part of our visit, came and looked up in our face, wondering at what we were doing there.

The bright blue eyes of the little creature gazing intently at us, set us thinking again of the stunted convict-flower, shining like a faint spark of heaven's light amid the withering hearts of the unheeded felons.

*** *The Female Work and Work-rooms at Tothill Fields Prison.*—There is little in connection with this part of our subject demanding special mention. Neither crank-work nor treadwheel-work, nor pump-work, nor, indeed, any of those repulsive and unfeminine forms of hard labour to which women were put only a few years ago in our prisons, any longer prevail at the Westminster House of Correction.

The forms of labour pursued in this establishment have assuredly nothing harsh nor unwomanly about them, and nothing, we should add, to which it is possible, even for the most fastidious, to raise an objection. For though, if the prison itself were situate in the suburbs, and the more profitable employment of market-gardening resorted to, it might be possible to render the prisoners self-supporting (and Mr. Charles Pearson has proved, before a Parliamentary Committee, that 1,000 prisoners occupied on 1,000 acres would be sufficient to reduce the cost of maintenance, and even superintendence, to *nil;* whereas at Tothill Fields prison the average earnings of the inmates are but £1 15s. 9½d. per head per annum; whilst the annual cost of their food and clothing amounts to £9 7s. 10¼d., and that of superintendence to £9 15s. more—each individual confined there thus costing the county nearly £20, and earning less than £2 in the course of the year); nevertheless, so long as our jails are allowed to remain in our towns—where they are no more fit to be than grave-yards—we must acknowledge that, at the Westminster House of Correction, the women are employed in the fittest as well as most prudent manner possible under the circumstances.

Though we hold that a heavy wrong is done to the community by every individual that is not self-supporting within it, and that it should be one of the main objects of those placed in authority over the people to render each person in the State capable of self-maintenance; still it appears to us to be most inconsiderate, if not wicked, on the part of prison officials to set criminals to work at those occupations for which the markets are already overstocked, and by which the honest poor out of doors find it difficult to eke out their lives. For since it is obvious that criminal labour can be sold cheaper than any other, which requires the minimum price paid for it to be sufficient to cover the cost of the maintenance of the labourer, honest folk can only compete with such work by becoming criminal in return, and adding to their wages either by prostitution or theft.

We have, in another place, shown this to be the rule, more particularly among the badly-paid slop-workers of the Metropolis; and yet we find, at Brixton and Millbank, the prisoners engaged in executing large contracts for the Houndsditch Jews, and thus rendering honesty and virtue more and more hard to be carried on in connection with industry at the east end of the Metropolis.

It is but just, however, to the Middlesex magistrates to make known, that at Tothill Fields we do not find the women engaged, as we noted them at Brixton, in making up shirts for Moses, or employed, as at Millbank, in "sank" work for the more competitive of the army clothiers—the work done by the females at Westminster being merely such as is required and used at the other county establishments, and none, so far as we could ascertain, going into the market to beat down the wages of independent and honest workpeople.

The several forms of labour pursued at this prison are oakum-picking, straw-plaiting, knitting, and laundry-work; whilst the majority of the work done goes to the county lunatic asylum at Hanwell.

In these work-rooms one sees almost the same large assemblages of criminals as at Cold-bath Fields, and the sight of the dense mass of female infamy, clad in the one monotonous prison dress, and all as silent as death, produces an intensely powerful effect upon the mind; whilst the contemplation of such an immense variety of feature, impresses the beholder with a sense that every form of physical as well as moral ugliness is here presented to his view; for there is scarcely one well-formed, and certainly not one innocent-looking, face to be detected among the wretched crowd, and in the countenances of many the marks of prema-ture disease, or of long-continued ill-treatment, or confirmed dissipation may be noted—the lingering bronzy traces of the blackened eye—the blotched and crimson cheeks, and the cancerous nose—together with the callous and brazen smile on every lip, and startling shamelessness in every glance—of the young as well as old—all serve to make up a picture and a scene that has not its parallel for hideousness in the civilized world.*

The oakum-room is a large shed similar to that in the boys' prison, and situate at the end of C 8 yard. Here we found some 200 and odd women ranged upon several long benches, and with the warders stationed round the room—the work differing in no way from that already described in connection with the boys; while the most ghost-like silence reigned throughout the place—there being no attempt made either to instruct or occupy the minds of the prisoners during the operation.

The females under the age of 16, as well as those staying in the nursery, have 1 lb. of oakum to pick per diem, whereas the boys under the same age have to do 1½ lbs.; and the females of 16 years and upwards, 1½ lbs., whilst the elder boys have 2 lbs.

In the course of the week preceding our visit, there had been, on an average, 187 women and girls employed at oakum-work daily (see p. 401), and these had picked altogether a few pounds more than 13 cwt. during that time, which is at the rate of 2 cwt. and 20 lbs. for the whole of the females, and not quite 1 lb. 5 oz. for each daily—the average for the boys being a fraction more than 1 lb. 6 oz. each per diem. Accordingly, it will be found that there is rather more than 33 cwt. of oakum picked by the female prisoners collectively in the course of the year, and this, at the price of £4 10s. the cwt. paid by the contractor for the picking, would make the aggregate earnings of the women and girls employed at this work amount to very nearly £150, or a fraction more than 15s. each per annum, whilst the boys, severally, earn about 17s. per annum.

The women are all clad in close white caps with deep frills, and a loose blue and white spotted dress, so that, from the colours being more marked than those in the boys' prison, the sight of the assembly has a far more peculiar effect. Some of the prisoners have a number stitched upon their arm, to indicate that they are there for three months and

* The ratio of recommittals among the women of Tothill Fields shows the female prisoners there to belong, generally speaking, to the most hardened class of offenders—27·0 per cent. of them having been imprisoned four times and more.

TABLE SHOWING THE NUMBER OF FEMALES IMPRISONED IN THE WESTMINSTER HOUSE OF CORRECTION IN THE COURSE OF THE YEARS ENDING MICHAELMAS, 1851-55.

Years, &c.	Previously Committed.				Total No. recommitted.	Total No. of committals.
	Once.	Twice.	Thrice.	Four times and more.		
1851	834	358	149	1,228	2,569	5,082
1852	852	441	220	1,397	2,910	5,343
1853	855	455	254	1,622	3,186	5,506
1854	856	469	241	1,671	3,237	5,753
1855	893	494	251	1,508	3,146	5,359
Total	4,290	2,217	1,115	7,426	15,048	27,043
Annual mean .	858	443	223	1,485	3,009	5,408
Per centage .	15·9	8·3	4·2	27·0	55·5	100·0

By the above data, then, we see that more than one-half (55·5 per cent.) of the females committed to Tothill Fields are old habitual offenders—not less than 27·0 per cent. of the entire number of persons committed to the prison having been there *four times and more!* previously. Of the boys at the same prison, however, only 46·7 per cent. have been before committed (see p. 409), whilst the ratio of recommitted prisoners of all ages and both sexes, throughout England and Wales, is only 25·3 per cent.; so that it would appear that the females return to the Westminster House of Correction in *more than double* the average proportion for all other prisons!

over, and entitled to the first-class diet; whilst the arms of others are marked with a cloth figure of 2, as a sign that their term of imprisonment is less than three months and more than twenty-one days. A large proportion of the women, on the other hand, have no such marks upon their sleeves, and these are what are technically termed "days' women," being there merely for a week or two, and mostly in default of payment of some small fine.*

* The following table shows the terms of imprisonment undergone by the females at Tothill Fields for a series of years :—

TABLE SHOWING THE TERMS OF IMPRISONMENT OF THE WOMEN IN TOTHILL FIELDS PRISON FROM 1851 TO 1855.

Terms of imprisonment.	1851.	1852.	1853.	1854.	1855.	Annual mean.	Per centage to total committals.
Under 14 days.							
Girls under seventeen . . .	93	91	105	74	80	88	1·6
Women above seventeen . . .	2,119	2,251	2,134	2,172	1,974	2,130	39·3
Total	2,212	2,342	2,239	2,246	2,054	2,218	40·9
14 days and under 1 month.							
Girls	63	51	61	61	60	59	1·1
Women	1,312	1,251	1,336	1,224	1,257	1,276	23·5
Total	1,375	1,302	1,397	1,285	1,317	1,335	24·6
1 month and under 2 months.							
Girls	25	33	43	65	53	44	0·8
Women	741	797	898	914	824	835	15·4
Total	766	830	941	979	877	879	16·2
2 months and under 3 months.							
Girls	8	6	13	18	29	15	0·3
Women	184	154	166	248	256	201	3·7
Total	192	160	179	266	285	216	4·0
3 months and under 6 months.							
Girls	25	32	21	39	25	28	0·5
Women	328	277	256	345	318	305	5·7
Total	353	309	277	384	343	333	6·2
6 months and under 1 year.							
Girls	14	9	22	14	14	15	0·3
Women	308	280	305	431	323	329	6·1
Total	322	289	327	445	337	344	6·4
1 year and above.							
Girls	1	0	4	3	1	2	0·0
Women	88	76	98	104	102	93	1·7
Total	89	76	102	107	103	95	1·7
Total committals.							
Girls	229	222	269	274	262	251	4·6
Women	5,080	5,086	5,193	5,438	5,054	5,170	95·4
Grand total	5,309	5,308	5,462	5,712	5,316	5,421	100·0

Here, then, we perceive that nearly one-half, or 40·9 per cent., of the females confined in this prison are sent there for less than fourteen days, so that a large number of the prisoners keep returning periodically

On the occasion of our visit, we sought to ascertain what proportion of the whole of the women present in the oakum-room was imprisoned for their inability to pay the few shillings penalty to which they had been adjudged; and no sooner had the matron requested all those who were there for fines to stand up, than almost every third woman started from her seat, and, upon counting up the number that had risen, we found there were some 60 out of 180 odd; whilst one wretched woman, fancying we were some one in authority, began raving away from the back of the room, saying, that she "ought to have gone out that morning as her three weeks were up."

Thus, then, it would appear that were the principle of payment by instalment established for fines as well as small debts, the female prison at Tothill Fields would most probably be considerably thinned of its inmates, and those who, in the eyes of justice, can only be regarded as "Crown debtors," no longer ranked as felons. For admitting that many either would not or could not pay a few pence per week in liquidation of the penalty imposed, and assuming that only one-half did so (though the experience of the county courts would make us believe that there would not be a tithe of the number defaulters), it is manifest that not only would the Government be acting up to the very first principle of enlightened penology, viz., to endeavour to keep people out of prison as long as possible, rather than thrust them into it for the most trivial offences—but the country would be saved some hundred thousands per annum in prison expenses. Thus, according to the latest returns, the grand total of the gross cost of all the prisons of England and Wales (exclusive of the Government establishments for convicts) amounts to upwards of £450,000 per annum, or nearly £27 per head, for a daily average of 16,691 prisoners, so that as the mean annual earnings of each prisoner are only a fraction more than £2, there is a clear loss of just upon £25 upon every one imprisoned throughout the year. Hence, supposing there to be only one-fourth of the average number of prisoners confined for non-payment of their fines (and out of the gross number of committals, 75 per cent. are summary convictions, under which the fines are generally imposed), it is obvious that, even if we admit only half the penalties to be paid up under such an arrangement, the country would be an immense gainer by the change—receiving not only the fines which it now loses, but saving the expense of keeping 25 per cent. of the daily average number of prisoners throughout the year, which, at the nett cost of £25 per head, would leave a clear profit of not less than £100,000 a-year.

to the place; whilst as much as 65·5 per cent. of the whole are imprisoned for less than one month, and as many as four-fifths of the gross number of committals for less than two months. The same rule holds good even with the girls, more than one-half being committed for terms that render it impossible to make the least impression upon their natures, and which serve to convert the prison into a temporary "refuge for the destitute" rather than a place of penance and reformation. By reference to the table given at p. 422, showing the length of the imprisonments for the boys at the same prison, it will be found that upwards of 65 per cent. of the young male prisoners are committed for short terms likewise. The present table, however, shows—like that for the boys before given—that there has been a tendency of late on the part of the magistrates to lengthen the terms of imprisonment; for it will be seen that the number of committals for *less* than one month, both for the girls as well as women, have been considerably reduced in number since 1851, whilst those for *more* than one month have been correspondingly increased.

"After the age of seventeen, a lamentable increase," say the visiting justices in their last special report, "occurs in the number of girls committed to the prison at Westminster." A fact, by-the-by, which perfectly agrees with the statistics of female crime before cited. "It is probable," the justices add, "that before this age the girls are kept more at home than boys, and have less opportunity of becoming corrupted by vicious association; whereas, after it, they are, on the other hand, thrown on their own resources, without having received either moral or religious instruction, and get engaged as servants in situations where their morals are neglected, and where neither their comforts nor happiness are cared for, so that, exposed to evil examples and to the artifices of the depraved, it is not singular that they should fall; and having fallen, having lost friends and character, they should in despair resign themselves to an abandoned life, and become frequent inmates of the prison."

The straw-plait room is situate on the first floor of prison 4, C side; it extends the whole length of the wing, and the engraving which we have given will afford a far better idea of the scene there presented to the view, than any string of words can possibly convey to the mind.

Here, again, there are some two hundred prisoners working in the most oppressive silence, and seeming as they twiddle the straws in and out their fingers, without uttering a word, as if they were all wrapt in a profound dream, and mechanically performing some every-day work with their eyes wide open, as somnambulists are wont to do.

The loquacity of women has grown into a proverb among us, so that all can readily understand how hard female prisoners must find it to have to remain for six hours every day working in stark silence, close beside those who are suffering in common with themselves.

We, however, who have heard the positive outburst of talking that occurs among the women at Brixton the very instant that the striking of the clock announces the silent hour to be at an end, can frame some slight notion as to the galling irritation of the restraint imposed upon the women's tongues at Tothill Fields. Indeed the reader has but to turn to the table at p. 375, showing the number of punishments annually inflicted upon the females at this prison, in order to discover how, to reduce the poor wretches to dumbness, the food itself has to be continually cut off, and even handcuffs and "other irons" resorted to, and that to a degree far beyond what is found necessary to enforce the discipline at any other female prison in the kingdom.

Still, it seems never to have occurred to the minds of any of the visiting justices, that the time thus absolutely and wilfully wasted in silence might easily be turned to profitable account, as well as the excessive amount of punishment decreased by placing some one to read to the women, during their work, from some interesting and good book; and the poor wretches thus be no longer left, from sheer want of some slight mental occupation, to brood hour after hour over their own thoughts until they irritate themselves almost to madness under the galling and petty tyranny of the "system."

"The women like the straw-plaiting at first," said the matron to us, "but they soon get tired of it; and they dislike it in winter especially, because it's cold to the fingers. They generally wish to get away to some new pursuit after a short time, for they cannot bear to sit long at the same thing. I don't know," the warder went on, "that they are different in this respect to other people, but out of doors they have many things to employ their mind which they don't find here. Besides, it's a long time to be over the same work, and that, too, without speaking a single word. The long-term women," added the officer, "we send to the work-room, and some go to the oakum-room, though they are mostly for seven, fourteen, or twenty-one days who are set to oakum-picking. All prisoners pass through the C prison first. Some may be there for a fortnight, and some only for a few days; the length of time depends upon the number going out, but all the women are placed in the oakum-room immediately on their entering the prison.

"There's a great number of bonnets and hats made here," proceeded the matron, "for the lunatics at the Hanwell Asylum; none of the things we make are sold to the shops. Sometimes ladies order bonnets of us, which they wish to give away to some institution; but no work is done here for the trade. We've been doing straw-work since the last four years. That basket there is very nicely made. We've not long begun that style of work; indeed, that's only the second we've finished. One of the magistrates had the first."

The basket to which our attention was drawn was a small hand-basket, somewhat of the shape of a portable writing-desk, and the straw worked into a series of small pyramids, after the fashion of a pine-apple. This stood on a large counter at the end of the room, upon

which were arranged small sheaves of new straw, and one or two planter-like round hats for
ladies, of the open pastry-work class of "fancy" manufacture; and near this was a prisoner
scrubbing away at a new straw bonnet on a block, whilst one or two of the warders were
examining a lady's hat that stood ready trimmed on the dresser.

"This is rather a dull pink, ain't it, Mrs. ———?" inquired one of the matrons of
the female superintendent, as she raised one of the strings of the ready-trimmed round
hats. "Yes, it is rather dull," was the reply; "but you know gay colours, Miss ———,
won't do here."

The knitting-room is situate in prison 1, B side, and is remarkable only for its slanting,
pew-like arrangement—an elaborate piece of absurdity, designed by some wiseacre with a
view to prevent the female prisoners talking, but which, owing to the high wooden partition
at the back of each row of prisoners acting as a sounding-board, has served as the best possible contrivance for allowing them to communicate in secret.

This place is about the size of a village school-room, and contained, at the time of our
visit, some 35 women, all ranged on the slant, as it were, in long narrow pews, stretching
diagonally across the room. Just peeping above the tops of the partitions, the white caps of
the prisoners could be seen, while ranged along the wall upon a raised gallery, stood a
couple of warders looking down into the sloping troughs, as it were, and crying occasionally,
"I can hear some one talking there," though, by the ingenious arrangement, it was now
almost impossible to detect the offender—an arrangement which, if the justices had been
acquainted with the commonest rules of acoustics, would assuredly never have been executed; and one which, had they the least knowledge of human nature, and been aware that
it is better and safer at all times to lead than to drive people towards any end in view, they
would never have listened to for a moment, but have preferred to have afforded the women
some mental occupation over their work, as a means of winning them into silence, rather
than seeking to force them into it by pure carpentry.

The laundry-work calls for no particular notice, further than saying that on the occasion
of our visit there were some fifteen women employed in it, and that it was conducted on the
silent system, the women, though working in association, having two warders placed over
them, in order to prevent communication among them.

Nor would our account be complete did we omit to state, that at half-past four the
women cease working—after which time they are permitted to read if they like, books being
supplied to them for the purpose—and that at six o'clock they are locked up in their cells or
dormitories for the night, the older females being placed in the latter and the younger ones
in the former.

In the dormitories warders are stationed through the night, to see that no talking goes
on among the prisoners, two officers remaining on duty from six in the evening till ten,
and two others from ten at night till six in the morning. Nevertheless, we were assured
it was impossible to put a stop to the secret communication that nightly went on in spite
of them. Moreover, there are two female warders stationed at B and C lodges, whose duty it
is to go round and inspect the prisons during the night. There is, too, a chief warder on
duty besides.

As a rule, we were told that the officers consider the "long-terms," that is to say, the
long-sentence women, to behave the best, though latterly they have found these rather
refractory.

At the time of our last visit there was only one prisoner in a dark cell, and, on the
occasion of a previous one, we were witness to the kindness and good sense with which one
of the visiting justices spoke to a woman in one of the refractory cells—a half-maniac kind

of creature who was then disturbing the whole prison, first with her shouts, then with her songs, and finally with her screams.*

* We append a statement of the expenses and receipts of this prison:—

TABLE OF THE EXPENDITURE AND RECEIPTS OF TOTHILL FIELDS PRISON FOR THE YEAR 1854, COMPARED WITH THAT OF COLDBATH FIELDS, AND THE AVERAGE OF ALL OTHER PRISONS IN ENGLAND AND WALES.

COST OF PRISON PER ANNUM.

Items of Expenditure.	Gross Cost per Annum.			Average Cost per Prisoner per Annum. Tothill Fields. 1854.			Coldbath Fields. 1854.			All other Prisons in England and Wales. 1853.		
	£	s.	d.	£	s.	d.	£	s.	d.	£	s.	d.
Total cost of Prison Diet and Extra Allowances, by order of the Surgeon, and Wine, Beer, &c. . .	6,889	5	3	7	18	4½	9	1	9½	5	4	11
" Male Clothing, Bedding, and Straw . .	1,282	12	3	1	9	5¾	1	4	0	1	7	2
" Officers' Salaries and Rations, and Pensions to Retired Officers .	8,489	12	6	9	15	2	7	18	8½	10	7	6
" Fuel, Soap, and other cleansing materials, Oil and Gas . . .	974	10	9	1	2	5	1	1	3	1	19	6
" Stationery, Printing, and Books, Furniture and Utensils, &c., Rent, Rates, and Taxes . .	92	6	2	0	2	1¼	0	9	1	0	13	9¾
" Support of Prisoners removed under Contract to be confined in other Jurisdictions, and removal of Convicts and Prisoners to and from Trial, and to other Prisons for punishment, &c. .	98	18	6	0	2	3¼	0	13	9	0	12	9¾
" Sundry Contingencies not enumerated . .	720	8	6	0	16	6¾	1	4	7½	1	1	9¼
Total expenses for the Prison for the year, not including Repairs, Alterations, and Additions . .	18,547	13	11	21	6	4½	21	13	2½	21	7	5¾
" Repairs, Alterations, and Additions in and about the Prison in the course of the year . .	579	6	7	0	13	3¾	0	13	4½	2	9	5
Repayment of Principal or Interest of Money Borrowed .	—			—			—			2	12	9¾
Grand Total .	19,127	0	6	21	19	8¼	22	6	7	26	9	8½
Daily average number of Prisoners .				870			1,388			16,691		
Gross cost of Prison, per head, per annum, exclusive of repairs				£21	6	4½	£21	13	2½	£21	7	5¾

RECEIPTS OF PRISON PER ANNUM.

	£	s.	d.	£	s.	d.
Nett Profit received for manufacturing or other Work done by the Prisoners	460	14	8			
Estimated Profit of Work or Labour done by the Prisoners for the benefit of the County, City, or Borough . .	1,096	11	4			
Gross Earnings of Prisoners .				1,557	6	0
Amount received for the Support of Vagrants				2	3	5
Amount received for the Subsistence of Revenue Prisoners .				46	7	6
Amount charged to Treasury for Maintenance of Prisoners convicted at Assizes and Sessions .				5,308	16	0
Other Receipts . . .				117	9	8
Total . .				£7,032	2	7
Average Earnings of each Prisoner at Tothill Fields per annum .				1	15	9½
Ditto at Coldbath Fields . .				4	11	10½
Ditto of all Prisoners of England and Wales				2	1	5

NETT COST OF THE PRISON.

	£	s.	d.
Total Expenses of the Prison for the year, not including Repairs, Alterations, and Additions .	£18,547	13	11
Total Receipts of ditto	7,032	2	7
Cost to the County, City, or Borough, not including Repairs, Alterations, and Additions .	11,515	11	4
Repairs, Alterations, and Additions during the year	579	6	7
Total Expenses of the Prison for the year, including Repairs, Alterations, and Additions, and excluding Receipts	12,094	17	11
Nett cost of each Prisoner, at Tothill Fields, per annum	£13	18	0½
" " at Coldbath Fields, per annum . . .	10	9	4¼
" " in all Prisons of England and Wales, per annum .	18	8	0¾
" " at Tothill Fields, per diem	0	0	9¼
" " at Coldbath Fields, per diem	0	0	6¾
" " in all Prisons of England and Wales, per diem .	0	1	0

By the above comparative table, we find that the annual gross cost of each prisoner at Tothill Fields is some half-dozen shillings less than at Coldbath Fields, and about 1*s.* 1*d.* less than the mean for all the prisons

*** *The Female Prisoners' Own Clothes' Store, Tothill Fields.*—In civilized communities dress enters so fully into our notions of individuals, that a particular kind of garment has as much human character about it as even a definite form of countenance.

Sam Weller's well-known description of the inmates of the White Hart Inn, in the Borough, by the boots and shoes he had to clean, affords us as graphic a picture of the persons staying at the tavern as would the figures of even the people themselves:—"There's a pair of Hessians in 13," said he, in answer to the inquiry as to who there was in the house; "there's two pair of halves in the commercial; there's these here painted tops in the snuggery inside the bar; and five more tops in the coffee-room, besides a shoe as belongs to the wooden leg in No. 6; and a pair of Wellingtons, a good deal worn, together with a pair of lady's shoes in No. 5."

At Tothill Fields prison the warders in charge of the prisoners' own clothing are wont to indicate the female characters incarcerated there by the style of bonnet entrusted to their care, and to speak of the "hat and feathers they had in a few days ago for being drunk and riotous," the same as if the article of millinery had been the chief offender, and the female herself but a mere *particeps criminis* in the affair.

"We haven't many smart bonnets in now, sir," said the warder, as she conducted us round the store for the "long-terms," and pointed out to us the peculiarities of the different kinds of head-gear stowed away in the large square compartments that were fitted round the room.

"This silk and blond," she said, "trimmed with '*ruches*' and with roses, and geraniums inside, is in for 'pickpocketing;' and this purple velvet one, with feath.. s at the side, has got twelve months for shoplifting. Here, too, is a fancy Tuscan, with : bon '*ruches*,' quite fashionable, but dirty enough, you see, sir, inside—that's got six months for the same offence.

"Yes, sir, it *is*, as you say," went on the officer, "the grandest ones that come here are mostly for stealing in shops.

"Here's another, though, sir," said the matron, as she seemed suddenly to recollect herself, and started off to a compartment on the opposite side—"a grand Leghorn, with a fall of bugles, you see, in front. This is a play-actress, and has four calendar months for stabbing her husband.

"The next one, too, sir, *was* a very pretty thing once," she remarked, as she took the bonnet from the round squabby bundle of clothes on which it stood. "It's horsehair, with green trimming, and has eight calendar months for passing bad money.

"Now here's one of those common willow-bonnets, trimmed with flowers—that's for illegally pawning, I think; and that flattened, old faded plush, for I cannot exactly say what.

"Oh, yes! we've a good many shabby ones," proceeded the warder, in answer to our question. "Here's a common-looking thing, an old cotton velvet, trimmed with faded pink ribbon; that's a misdemeanour in for three calendar months."

throughout the country. The average cost of the diet, per head, however, is upwards of 50 per cent. more than that of all England and Wales. The expense of the clothing, again, is slightly in excess, though the cost of superintendence is somewhat less per prisoner. Again, the average amount for soap, fuel, as well as stationery, printing, &c., and the support of prisoners removed to other jails, are all greatly below the annual expense per head, both at Coldbath Fields and the country prisons generally; so that the comparatively *high* cost of the diet, clothing, &c., for each individual prisoner, is reduced, by the comparatively *low* cost of the superintendence and other subordinate items, to a fraction below the standard for the whole kingdom. But if the gross cost of each prisoner at Tothill Fields be only a fraction less than the general average of all our prisons, the nett cost is some 25 per cent. below it. This is mainly owing to the fact of there being at Tothill Fields neither principal nor interest to repay, and the cost of the repairs being proportionally small; and the average earnings of the prisoners individually, it will be seen, are somewhat below the general average, rather than considerably above it, as at Coldbath Fields, where the value of the work done is most unfairly estimated

We were then conducted into the short-term room, where were kept the clothing, &c., of those females whose sentence was *less* than three months. The clothes here were stowed away in the same manner as in the other store—a round bundle, with a bonnet on the top, being placed in each of the square compartments which covered the walls of the room.

"This grand pink and white silk, with cherry-coloured figured ribbons and blond curtain and flowers, is in for fourteen days," said the matron.

"What for?" we asked, as we wrote down the particulars in our note-book.

"Streets," was the laconic and significant reply. "Just see how greasy and dirty it is at the back, sir; that's from its having been worn half on the shoulders. Here is another grand-looking, yellow silk affair, that's all grubby inside; it has got a piece of net, too, for the crown, with the ribbon passed over it to save the silk, you see. There's deception for you! The same as in everything now a-days. That's the streets again, sir; and for the same term as the last.

"This is an old faded straw thing, you see," said the warder, as she held up a colourless and shapeless article that was half in shreds. "It's got the plait of the crown all loose and hanging down like an apple-paring. That's for begging or sleeping in the open air—I can't say which. And this ragged and rusty old black crape affair is a regular visitor of ours; it's for breaking a lamp, I think, this time, though it's generally in for being drunk and disorderly. I do believe I've known it these last five years.

"Oh, yes, sir! they are all fumigated before they are put away here; if they were not we should be swarming, notwithstanding the finery. The sulphur often takes the colour out," went on the officer, "so that the women don't know their own things. But we are as careful over them as we can be for the poor creatures, for it would be hard, indeed, if we spoilt their clothes when they came here, as very few that we see in this place have more than they stand up in."

The caption-papers that accompany a prisoner from one jail to another are a peculiar class of document, which, for the sake of completeness, should not be omitted from our account of the London prisons.

A boy or woman, for instance, who is convicted at the Middlesex or Westminster Sessions, on being transferred from the detentional prison in which he or she has been confined before trial, to the House of Correction at Westminster, will have such a caption-paper forwarded with either of them, as the case may be, to the governor of the latter institution. In this paper the nature of the offence of which the individual has been convicted, as well as the sentence adjudged, will be duly set forth; and if the prisoner were afterwards to be removed to any convict prison, a copy of this caption-paper would be furnished to the authorities of the future place of custody, together with a return setting forth all particulars in connection with the identity and antecedents of the offender, as well as the circumstances of his case.

A copy of such a caption-paper, together with the return sent to the governor of one of the London convict prisons, is here subjoined:—

CAPTION.

West=Riding OF THE County of York. } At the General Quarter Sessions of the Peace, holden *by adjournment* at *Sheffield* in and for the West-Riding of the County of York, on *Friday* the *Fourth* day of *January* in the *Nineteenth* Year of the Reign of our Sovereign Lady Victoria, by the Grace of God, of the United Kingdom of Great Britain and Ireland, Queen, Defender of the Faith, and in the Year of our Lord, One Thousand Eight Hundred and Fifty *Six;* Before certain Justices of our said Lady the Queen, assigned to preserve the peace in the said Riding; and also to hear and determine divers Felonies, Trespasses, and other Misdemeanours done and committed therein.

Whereas at this present Quarter Sessions of the Peace, *J——— R———, late of Wakefield, in the West-Riding of the County of York, Labourer,* is and stands convicted of *Larceny, committed after a previous conviction for Felony.*

𝔈𝔱 𝔦𝔰 𝔱𝔥𝔢𝔯𝔢𝔲𝔭𝔬𝔫 𝔬𝔯𝔡𝔢𝔯𝔢𝔡 𝔞𝔫𝔡 𝔞𝔡𝔧𝔲𝔡𝔤𝔢𝔡 𝔟𝔶 𝔱𝔥𝔦𝔰 𝔠𝔬𝔲𝔯𝔱, That the above-named Convict be kept in **Penal** Servitude for the term of *Four years.*

BY THE COURT,

B——— D———,

𝔇𝔢𝔭𝔲𝔱𝔶 𝔒𝔩𝔢𝔯𝔨 𝔬𝔣 𝔱𝔥𝔢 𝔓𝔢𝔞𝔠𝔢.

To Mr. E——— S ———, }
Keeper of the House of
Correction at Wakefield. }

    I hereby certify that the above is a true copy of the Original Caption and Order of Court, containing the sentence by virtue of which the above-named Convict is in my custody.

E——— S———,

𝔊𝔬𝔳𝔢𝔯𝔫𝔬𝔯 𝔬𝔣 𝔱𝔥𝔢 𝔥𝔬𝔲𝔰𝔢 𝔬𝔣 𝔒𝔬𝔯𝔯𝔢𝔠𝔱𝔦𝔬𝔫 𝔞𝔱 𝔚𝔞𝔨𝔢𝔣𝔦𝔢𝔩𝔡,
𝔦𝔫 𝔱𝔥𝔢 𝔚𝔢𝔰𝔱=𝔕𝔦𝔡𝔦𝔫𝔤 𝔬𝔣 𝔜𝔬𝔯𝔨𝔰𝔥𝔦𝔯𝔢.

RETURN to accompany the caption of a convict on his removal to a convict prison, and subsequent transfers :—

Name and Aliases	*J——— R———.*
Age	*30.*
Single or Married, and Number of Children	*Single.*
Read and Write	*Imperfectly.*
Trade or Occupation . . .	*Saw-handle maker.*
Crime, stating Particulars . . .	*Stealing from a Dwelling-house at Shef-field 12lbs. of Beef, and pre. con.*
Date and Place of Committal . .	*8 December, 1855. Sheffield.*
Date and Place of Conviction . .	*4 January, 1856. Sheffield Sessions.*
Sentence	*4 years' Penal Servitude.*
Name and Residence of Family or next of kin .	*Mother, H——— R———, G——— St. Park, Sheffield.*
Religion	*Church.* Health . . . *(Bronchitis).*

Information relative to former Convictions.

County or Borough Prisons.

Whether Previously Transported	*None.*
Previous Convictions, stating Particulars.	*York Assizes, December, 1846, Assault upon, an indictment for Burglary and Wounding, 3 cal. mon.* *Pontefract Sess., 1848, Stg. Trousers, 6 months.*
Summary or Otherwise, stating Particulars.	*16 July, 1847, Rogue and Vagabond, 3 months.* *25 July, 1853, Rogue and Vagabond, 14 days.*

Periods and Places of Confinement, from Date of *Committal* to Removal to a Convict Prison, stating whether in Separation or Association.

Name of Jail.	Description of Confinement.	Months.	Days.	Character and Conduct.
Wakefield.	*Separate.*	3	21	*Good.*

E——— S———, *Governor of Wakefield House of Correction.*
Date, 29 *March,* 1856.

The subjoined is the indorsement :—

Name, J——R——.

DATES OF COMMITTAL, CONVICTION, RECEPTION,
AND REMOVAL.

Committal......8 *December,* 1855.

Conviction ....4 *January,* 1856.

Removed from } *Wakefield Prison.*
Date ......} 29 *March,* 1856.

Received in .. } *Millbank Prison,*
Date ......} 29 *March,* 1856.

Removed from } *Died 8h. 35m. P.M.*
Date ......} 11 *April,* 1856.

Description.

Complexion . . .	*Light.*
Hair	*Brown.*
Eyes	*Blue.*
Height	*5 feet 4 inches.*
Description of Person .	*Rather slender.*

Scars, Cuts, Moles, Marks, &c., on Body and Limbs.

*Scar centre of forehead, scar on right jaw, mole near left
shoulder-blade, mole right arm-pit.*

E—— S——,
Governor of Wakefield House of Correction.

Date, 29 *March,* 1856.

The following, on the other hand, is the form of "summary conviction" sent from the
police office with the prisoner to the place of commitment :—

SOUTHWARK POLICE COURT.

*Metropolitan
Police District,
to wit.* }
To all and every the Constables of the Metropolitan Police Force, and to the Keeper of the
House of Correction at Wandsworth, in the County of Surrey, and within the Metro-
politan Police District :

Whereas R—— R—— was on this day duly convicted before the undersigned, one of the Magistrates
of the Police Courts of the Metropolis, sitting at the Southwark Police Courts in the County of Surrey, and
within the Metropolitan Police District, upon the oath of W—— H——, taken before me in the presence
and hearing of the said R—— R—— ; for that he, on the Fifteenth day of September, in the Year of Our
Lord, One Thousand Eight Hundred and Fifty-six, in the Parish of Saint George the Martyr, in the County
of Surrey, and within the said District, did unlawfully assault and beat the said W—— H——, contrary to the Statute in such case made and provided.

And it was thereby adjudged, that the said R—— R——, for the said offence, should forfeit and pay
the sum of Ten Shillings, and it was thereby further adjudged, that if the said sum should not be paid forthwith, the said R—— R—— should be imprisoned in the House of Correction at Wandsworth, in the
County of Surrey, and within the said District, for the space of Fourteen days from the date hereof, unless
the said sum should be sooner paid, which said sum he hath neglected to pay.

These are therefore to command you, aud every of you, the Constables of the Metropolitan Police Force,
to take the said R—— R——, and him safely to convey to the House of Correction aforesaid, and there
to deliver him to the Keeper thereof, together with this precept; and I do hereby command you, the said
Keeper of the said House of Correction, to receive the said R—— R—— into your custody, in the
said House of Correction, there to imprison him for the space of Fourteen days from the date hereof, unless
the said sum shall be sooner paid.

Given under my Hand and Seal this Sixteenth day of September, in the year of Our Lord, One
Thousand Eight Hundred and Fifty-six, at the Police Court aforesaid.

B—— C——

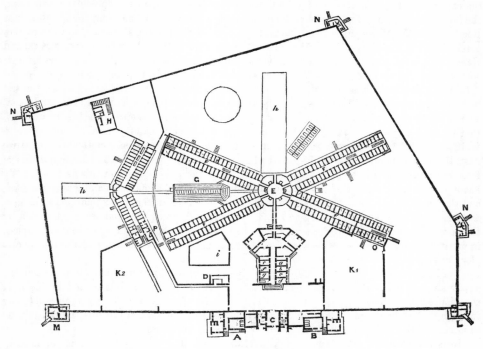

GROUND-PLAN OF WANDSWORTH PRISON.

A. Governor's House.	F. Corridors, with separate cells on either side.	K. Male Infirmary Yard.
B. Chaplain's ditto.		K 2. Female ditto ditto.
C. Outer Gate.	G. Kitchen.	L. Surgeon's Residence.
D. Chapel.	H. Laundry.	M. Assistant Chaplain's ditto.
E. Central Hall.	I. Drying Ground.	N, N, N. Warder's ditto.

O. Male Infirmary.
P. Female ditto.
a, b, c, d, e, f, g. Clerks', Governor's and Chaplain's offices, &c.
h. Site for additional wing.
i. Coal Yard.

¶ iii.

THE SURREY HOUSE OF CORRECTION, WANDSWORTH.

(FOR ALL CLASSES OF CONVICTED CRIMINAL OFFENDERS.)

The ascent of a mountain in the tropics, and gradual passage through the several atmospheric layers of different climates, reveals, as we rise above the plains, the mountain sides prismatically belted, as it were, with the rainbow hues of various zones of fruits and flowers—the same as if we had passed *along* rather than *above* the surface of the globe—from the brilliant and glowing tints of vegetable nature at the tropics, to the sombre shades of the hardier plants and trees peculiar to the colder regions, even till we ultimately reach, at the peak, the colourless desolation of the poles themselves.

But this journeying upwards through the various botanical strata, as it were, of the earth is hardly more peculiar and marked than is the rapid transition now-a-days, while travelling on some London railway, from town to the country; for as we fly along the house-tops through the various surburban zones encircling the giant Metropolis, we can see the bricken city gradually melt away into the green fields, and the streets glide, like solid rivers, into the roads, and cabs and busses merge into wagons and ploughs, while factories give place to market-gardens, and parks and squares fade gradually into woods and corn-fields.

Perhaps this change, from civic to rustic scenery—this dissolving view, as it were, of the capital melting into the country, is nowhere better seen than in a half-hour's trip along the Southampton rail; for no sooner have we crossed the viaduct spanning the Westminster Road, and looked down upon the drivers at the back of the passing Hansoms, and the carters perched on the high box-seats of the railway-carriers' vans, as well as the passengers ranged along the roof of the Kennington omnibuses; and had a glimpse, moreover, at the bright-coloured rolls of carpets standing in the first-floor windows of the great linendrapery styled " LAMBETH HOUSE," than we are whisked into the region of innumerable factories—the tall black chimneys piercing the air as thickly as the minarets of some Turkish city; and then, even with the eyes shut, the nose can tell, by the succession of chemical stenches assailing it, that we are being wafted through the several zones of Lambeth manufactures. Now we get a whiff of the gutta-percha works; then comes a faint gust from some floor-cloth shed; next we dash through an odoriferous belt of bone-boiling atmosphere; and after that through a film of fetor rank with the fumes from the glazing of the potteries; whereupon this is followed by bands of nauseous vapours from decomposing hides and horses' hoofs, resin and whiting works; and the next instant these give place to layer after layer of sickening exhalations from gas-factories, and soap-boiling establishments, and candle-companies; so that we are thus led by the nose along a chromatic scale, as it were, of the strong surburban stenches that encompass, in positive rings of nausea, the great cathedral dome of the Metropolis, like the phosphoric glory environing the head of some renowned catholic saint.

Nor is the visional diorama that then glides past us less striking and characteristic than the nasal one. What a dense huddle and confused bricken crowd of houses and hovels does the city seem to be composed of; the very train itself appears to be ploughing its way through the walls of the houses, while each gable end that is turned towards the rail is used as a means to advertise the wares of some enterprising tradesman.

Now the cathedral-like dome of Bedlam flits before the eye, and now a huge announce-ment tells us that we are flying past the famed concert-tavern called Canterbury Hall. Then we catch just a glimpse of the green gardens and old ruby towers of Lambeth Palace; and no sooner has this whizzed by, and we have seen the river twinkle for a moment in the light, like a steel-plate flashing in the sun, than we are in the regions of the potteries, with their huge kilns, like enormous bricken skittles, and rows of yellow-looking pipes and pans ranged along the walls. The moment afterwards the gas-works, with their monster black iron drums, dart by the window of the carriage; and the next instant the old, gloomy, and desolate-looking Vauxhall Gardens, with its white rotunda, like a dingy twelfth-cake ornament, glides swiftly by. Then we have another momentary peep down into the road, and have hardly noted the monster railway taverns, and seen the small forest of factory chimneys here grouped about the bridge, with Price's gigantic candle-works hard by, than we are flying past the old Nine Elms station. No sooner has this flitted by than the scene is immediately shifted, and a small, muddy canal is beheld, skirted with willows; and then the tall metal syphon of the water-works, like a monster hair-pin stuck in the earth, shoots rapidly into sight; whereupon the view begins to open a bit, revealing Chelsea Hospital, with its green copper roof and red and white front, on the other side of the river; while the crowd of dwellings grows suddenly less dense, and the houses and factories dwindle into cottages with small patches of garden. Here, too, the London streets end, and the highroads, the lanes, and hedges make their appearance; while large, flat fields of the suburban market-garden rush by, each scored with line after line of plants. Nor is it many minutes more before these vast plains of cabbage and tracts of potatoes are succeeded by a glance of sloping lawns and pleasant-looking country villas, ranged alongside the raised roadway; immediately after which we are in the land of railway cuttings, with the line sunk in a trough of deep green shelving banks, instead of being buried, as it was only a few minutes before, among the sloping roofs and chimney-pots of the smoky London houses.

Another instant, and the train rattles through a little tunnel, and then is heard the sharp, shrill scream of the whistle; whereupon porters dart by the carriage windows, crying, "Clapham Common! Clapham Common!" and the instant afterwards are landed at the little rustic station there.

The House of Correction at Wandsworth has, externally, little to recommend it to the eye, having none of the fine, gloomy character and solemnity of Newgate, nor any of the castellated grandeur of the City Prison at Holloway; neither can it be said to partake of the massive simplicity of the exterior of Tothill Fields, nor to possess any feature about it that will bear comparison with the noble portcullis gateway at Pentonville.

To speak plainly, the exterior of the Surrey House of Correction is mean and ill-proportioned to the last degree, while the architecture of the outbuildings exhibits all the bad taste of Cockney-Italian villas, and none of the austere impressiveness that should belong to a building of a penal character. Again, the central mass rising behind the stunted gateway is heavy even to clumsiness, and the whole aspect of the structure uncommanding as a Methodist college.

Nevertheless, the situation is admirably chosen for the health of the inmates. Built upon a gravelly soil, upon a large open tract of country, it seems to preclude the possibility of an epidemic ever raging among the prisoners. Nor do we know a more pleasant and countrified spot than the furze-tufted Common on which it stands, the view embracing a panorama for many miles round; in the distance the Crystal Palace may be seen shining like a golden bubble in the sun, whilst, looking towards the Metropolis, the Victoria Tower looms with exquisite grace from out the gray background of the London smoke; though, were it not for this glimpse of the great city, the stranger might fancy himself miles away from the Metropolis, so thoroughly primitive and half-desolate a look has the Common itself. Indeed, the only buildings near are the Freemasons' Female School, with its high red brick central tower, and the little roadside public-house, with its adjoining tea-gardens, beside the Tooting Road. Nor is there any sign of the bustle or hurry of London life about the place, unless, indeed, it be the occasional passing of the trains along the neighbouring lines of rail; but even then the white steam merely is seen issuing in jets at different parts of the earth as it travels along, while the ground rumbles almost with a subterranean noise—for the rail runs far below the level of the Common, and the passage of the trains can only be heard and felt rather than seen.

¶ iii—a.

The History and Construction of the Prison.

In the final report of the Committee of Justices appointed to superintend the erection of the House of Correction at Wandsworth, there is so lucid a history of the circumstances which led not only to the construction of the new prison for the county of Surrey, but likewise to the institution of houses of correction in general, that we cannot do better than avail ourselves of this excellent narrative.

⁎ *History of Houses of Correction in General.*—"The chief of the earlier statutes against vagrancy," say the Justices, "were :—

"The 7th Richard II. c. 5, passed in 1383.
"The 11th Henry VII. c. 2, passed in 1426.
"The 19th Henry VII. c. 2, passed in 1504.

"By the first, justices and sheriffs, and the mayors, bailiffs, constables, and other governors of towns, are required to examine diligently all 'faitors' (*i.e.*, idlers) and vagabonds, and compel them to find surety for their good behaviour. If they commit a second offence, or cannot find surety, they are to be sent to the next jail, to remain there until the coming of the justices assigned for the delivery of the jails, who 'shall have power to do upon such that which there to them best shall seem to be done by law.'

"By the second statute, which was passed for the purpose of mitigating the severity of the former, the power to commit to the jail is taken away, and vagabonds and beggars are directed, for a first offence, to be kept in the stocks three days and three nights, on bread and water, and then sent out of the town. For a second offence, they are to be kept six days and six nights in the stocks, on like fare.

"By the last of these statutes, such offenders are to be placed in the stocks for only one day and one night for a first offence, and three days and three nights for a second; and impotent or aged offenders are not to be placed in the stocks at all.

"Such was the moderation of the law for the suppression of vagrancy," we are told, "when Henry VIII. commenced his reign. Shortly afterwards, however, it was considered necessary to provide other means for 'the punishment of sturdy vagrants and beggars.' The statute passed for this purpose was the 22nd Hen. VIII. c. 12 (A.D. 1531), by which justices are required to cause all persons, 'whole and mighty in body,' who shall beg, or be vagrants, and not able to account how they get their living, to be whipped, and then to have them sworn to return to the place where they were born, or where they last dwelt three years, and there put themselves to labour.

"The severity of this statute was greatly increased by the 27th Hen. VIII. c. 25 (A.D. 1536), which enacted, that 'a valiant beggar, or sturdy vagabond,' shall at the first time be whipped and sent to the place where he was born, or has been living for the last three years; and that if he continue his roguish life, he shall have the upper part of the gristle of his right ear cut off; and if, after that, he be taken wandering in idleness, or doth not apply to his labour, or is not in the service of a master, he shall be adjudged and *executed* as a felon.

"By the 1st Edw. VI. c. 3 (A.D. 1548), all former statutes on this subject are repealed; and it is enacted, that every person, not impotent, aged, or sick, found loitering or wandering, and not seeking work, or leaving it when engaged, shall be a vagabond; and every such person, on being apprehended by his master, and convicted before two justices, shall be marked, by means of a hot iron, with the letter V, and be compelled to serve his master two years. If he leave before the expiration of such service, he shall be again marked, in like manner, with the letter S, and be his master's *slave for ever*. A third offence was to be punished with death.

"This statute was repealed by the 3rd and 4th Edw. VI. c. 16 (A.D. 1550-51), by which the 22nd Hen. VIII. c. 12, was revived.

"In the 14th Eliz. c. 5 (A.D. 1572), which is little less severe than the 27th Hen. VIII. above recited, we find a long list of persons declared to be 'rogues, vagabonds, and sturdy beggars.' Justices are required to commit them to the common jail, *or such other place as shall be appointed by the bench of justices, or not less than three of them, at any of their general sessions.*

"*This is the first recognition of any place of confinement apart from the common jail*, and the reason given for it is, that 'the common jails, in every shire within this realm, are like to be greatly pestered with a more number of prisoners than heretofore'—*summary jurisdiction* by this statute being abolished.

"By the 18th Eliz. c. 3 (A.D. 1576), which was passed to amend the last recited Act, one, two, or more abiding houses or places, convenient in some market or corporate town, or other place or places, are directed to be provided by the justices of every county, and to be called '*Houses of Correction*'—*and this is the first appearance of that title.*

"For this purpose, the justices are directed to tax the districts under their respective jurisdictions, and to appoint collectors of such taxes. They are also required to appoint governors of these houses of correction, which are to be erected or provided in one year, or before the end of the second year, ' or else the money levied to be repaid.'

"By the same statute, amended by the 39th Eliz. c. 5 (A.D. 1597), every person may, during 20 years, by deed enrolled in the High Court of Chancery, erect, found, and establish any hospitals, maisons dieu, abiding-places, or houses of correction, as well for the finding, sustentation and relief of the maimed, poor, needy, or impotent people, as to set the poor to work; such hospitals or houses to be incorporated, and have power to hold freeholds, not exceeding the annual value of £200; but no such hospital is to be founded without being endowed to the extent of £10 per annum.

"In the year 1597 two statutes were passed, the 39th Eliz., chapters 3 and 4, the former entitled ' An Act for the Relief of the Poor;' the latter, ' An Act for the Punishment of Rogues, Vagabonds, and Sturdy Beggars.' Until this period, provision was made for both these classes by the same statutes; *but they then became, and have ever since been, the subjects of separate legislation.* By the latter of these Acts it was lawful (not compulsory) for the justices to erect one or more houses of correction within their several counties, and to appoint a governor and provide all things necessary for governing the same, and for the punishment of offenders. Herein *summary jurisdiction* is not only revived, but it is extended to constables, headboroughs, and tithingmen, as well as to justices of the peace, who, for the punishment of first offences in vagrancy, are empowered to inflict a whipping on the offender 'until his or her body be bloody.' Headboroughs and tithingmen are, however, ' to be assisted by the advice of the minister and one other of the parish.'

"By the 7th James I. c. 4, passed in 1609, it is declared that the laws for the erection of houses of correction, and for the suppressing and punishing rogues, vagabonds, &c., ' have not wrought so good effect as was expected, as well for that the said houses of correction have not been built as was intended, as also for that the said statutes have not been duly and severely put in execution;'—and it is enacted, that before Michaelmas day, 1611, there shall be erected, or provided, by the justices in every county where there is not already a house of correction, one or more house or houses of correction, together with mills, turns, cards, and such like necessary implements, to set the said rogues to work; and if a house of correction be not provided in any county by Michaelmas day, 1611, ' then every justice within such county shall forfeit for his neglect £5, one moiety thereof to be unto him or them that shall sue for the same.' A governor is also to be appointed, who is to employ the rogues, vagabonds, &c., committed to the house of correction, and to punish them by putting fetters upon them and moderately whipping them. The prisoners to be in no sort chargeable to the county, but to have such allowance as they shall deserve by their labour.

"This statute was continued by two others in the reign of Charles I., after which the times became unfavourable for the amelioration of the prisoners' condition. During a period of considerably more than a century, little was done in this respect beyond the passing of a few statutes, having for their object the repairing, enlarging, erecting, and providing houses of correction, and rendering somewhat less severe the punishment of vagrants. The effective superintendence and discipline of all prisons, however, appear to have been greatly neglected.

"Some attempts were made in the year 1701, by the Society for Promoting Christian Knowledge, to obtain the introduction of a system of discipline in the prisons of London, but their efforts do not appear to have been successful; neither can it be ascertained that any benefit resulted from the 32nd Geo. II. c. 28 (A.D. 1759), by which justices are required to prepare rules for the good government of all prisons, which rules, after being approved by the judges, are to have the full force of law.

"Howard speaks of our prisons, both jails and houses of correction, or 'bridewells,' as he calls them, as being, at the time of his first inspection, the scenes of filth and contagion, of idleness and intemperance, of extortion and cruelty, of debauchery and immorality, of profaneness and blasphemy; and also as being places in which all sorts of prisoners—debtors, and felons—men and women—the young beginner and the old offender—were confined together. His attention was directed to the state of our prisons in the spring of 1773, when he became sheriff for the county of Bedford; and we find that during this very year the statute the 13th Geo. III. c. 58, providing clergymen to officiate in every jail in England, was passed. In the following year he obtained the passing of the 14th Geo. III. c. 20, 'relieving acquitted prisoners from the payment of fees to jailers,' as well as the 14th Geo. III. c. 59, 'for the preservation of the health of prisoners in jails,' requiring that jails should be kept clean and well ventilated, that infirmaries and baths therein should be provided, that an experienced surgeon or apothecary should be appointed, that the prisoners should be furnished with needful clothing, and that they should be prevented being kept under ground, *when it could be done conveniently.*

"Howard intended this last statute to have effect in all prisons, but was surprised to learn that it was applicable only to county jails, and did not, in any respect, affect houses of correction. This circumstance led to the passing of the 22nd Geo. III. c. 64 (A.D. 1782), explained and amended by the 24th Geo. III. c. 55 (A.D. 1784), by which justices of the peace are required to cause all houses of correction to be inspected, with a view to their being made 'more convenient and useful, having regard to the classes of the several persons who shall be kept there, according to the nature of their crimes and punishments; and to the keeping every part of such prison clean and wholesome.' And they are required to provide separate apartments for all persons committed upon charges of felony, or convicted of any theft or larceny, and committed for punishment by hard labour, in order to prevent any communication between them and the other prisoners. They are also to provide separate apartments for the women, who shall be committed thither. By this statute various rules, orders, and regulations, given for the better government of prisoners, are to be duly observed and enforced, and power is given to the justices to appoint, if they see fit, a minister of the Church of England to perform divine service every Sunday.

"*These last-mentioned statutes may be considered as the commencement of a new era in the management of houses of correction.* Ever since they were passed, legislators and magistrates have been alike anxious that prisons of this kind should be, as far as possible, effective in the suppression of crime, and new laws have been from time to time made, and new regulations adopted for the accomplishment of this great object; tread-wheel labour was introduced into most of the houses of correction in the kingdom, prisoners were subdivided into more numerous classes, and the silent system was enforced; but the result of these several changes was not satisfactory."

₊ *History of Surrey House of Correction at Wandsworth.*—The Building Committee of the Surrey Magistrates having given the above concise history as to houses of correction in general, now proceed to speak of those for their own county in particular. "The magistrates for the county of Surrey," they add, "have not been remiss in the care of the prisoners under their charge. Under the provisions of the 31st Geo. III. c. 22 (a private Act obtained by themselves—A.D. 1791), they caused the county jail, in Horsemonger Lane, to be erected, and immediately after the invention of tread-wheel labour, in 1822, the houses of correction at Brixton and Guildford were built. These prisons were constructed after the best examples of prison architecture known at that time; and as extensive a system of

classification and discipline was at all times maintained in each as the nature of the buildings and the number of the prisoners would admit.

"Moreover, at the General Quarter Sessions, held at Reigate, in April, 1845, when the attention of the public had become directed to the system of discipline on trial at Pentonville, a large Committee of Magistrates was appointed 'for the purpose of inquiring generally into the present system of prison discipline and management in the county; and into the propriety of adopting the separate system in the county prisons,' &c.

"This Committee presented, at the Easter Sessions, 1846, its report, which was printed and circulated amongst the magistrates. In it they stated it as their opinion, that the separate system could not be introduced into any of the prisons of the county without their entire reconstruction. They further stated, that these prisons were by no means in a satisfactory state, being neither in accordance with the recommendations of the prison inspectors, nor, in some instances, with the strict letter of the law.

"This report was approved by the Sessions, but shortly afterwards the number of prisoners in each of the several houses of correction in the county became so great, as to render imperative the adoption of immediate measures for their proper custody.

"It happened, however, shortly afterwards, that the surgeon of Brixton prison presented a report at the Kingston Sessions (October, 1846), in which it was stated that 'during the winter months in the past year, fever of a severe form was very general throughout the prison, which was increased in consequence of the overcrowded state of the cells, in many of which four persons are often obliged to sleep, three of whom occupy a space of only three feet nine inches in width, so that when epidemic or contagious diseases arise they are much augmented.'

"This led to a Committee of twenty-two Magistrates being appointed, for the purpose of ascertaining the best means by which adequate accommodation might be provided for the prisoners of the county.

"This Committee presented, at the following Epiphany Sessions, a lengthened report, of which the following is a summary :—

"That the deficiency of cells in the county could not be estimated at less than *four hundred and forty*; and if the Sessions should direct the discontinuance of the use of the prison at Kingston (which the Committee recommended), a further deficiency of about sixty cells would be thereby occasioned, making a total deficiency of five hundred cells.

"That in consequence of this great deficiency, there were at the House of Correction at Brixton no less than seventy cells, in each of which three prisoners ordinarily slept, the dimensions of these cells being only eight feet by six feet, and eight feet high.

"That such prisoners slept on the floor of the cell, on two mattresses, placed together, and under the same covering.

"That this was the case with males as well as females.

"That this deficiency led to similar results at the House of Correction at Guildford, where the cells were only four inches wider, and a little higher.

"That the then existing prisons of the county were not capable of sufficient extension to meet the deficiency, and that, consequently, a new prison must of necessity be erected on some other site.

"That it was expedient that a new prison, capable of containing 750 prisoners, and susceptible of further extension, should be erected on some convenient site, hereafter to be determined on; and that the Houses of Correction at Kingston, Brixton, and Guildford should be abandoned and disposed of.

"That the permanent annual expenditure for the staff and repairs in one large prison would be so much less than in three or four smaller ones, as not only to justify the increased outlay, but to render it desirable as a measure of economy.

"This report, having been printed and circulated amongst the magistrates of the county, was taken into consideration at the General Quarter Sessions, held by adjournment at Newington, on the 22nd day of March, 1847, prior to which the number of prisoners in the House of Correction at Brixton had so greatly increased that not only were three and sometimes four prisoners placed in a cell to sleep, but from twenty to forty for some time had been placed together to sleep on straw with blankets on the floor of the school-room; and the visiting justices of the prison, with the view of obtaining some relief, had solicited and obtained from the Secretary of State pardons for twenty prisoners,* who were discharged without undergoing the whole of their sentences. An inquest also having been held near this time at Brixton—as is required by law in the case of the death of every prisoner—the jury added to their verdict, 'And we, the jury, request the coroner to forward a representation of the great number of prisoners confined in this house of correction beyond the calculated accommodation, for the consideration of the visiting justices, lest a contagious fever should break out, to the great alarm and danger of the inhabitants of the locality.'

"A state of things so extensively interfering with the due administration of justice—so completely at variance with the enactment, requiring, as a general rule, that every prisoner should have a separate sleeping-cell, and that every male prisoner, without exception, should have a separate bed—so dangerous to health—so subversive of morality and discipline—and so repugnant to every feeling of delicacy, could not be continued. The Sessions, therefore, resolved that a new house of correction for 700 prisoners should be erected, arranged as recommended; and the Committee was re-appointed to carry the same into effect.

"The Committee immediately commenced their labours. They resolved that the site of the new prison should be within a mile of a railway station, and not further from London than six or eight miles."

₊ *Capacity and Cost of the Wandsworth Prison.*—"At the Sessions held in Midsummer, 1847, the Committee recommended the purchase of the site on which the prison has since been erected, at the cost of £300 per acre, exclusive of buildings, trees, and crops, that were to be taken at a valuation. It was stated to contain about 24 acres, but was afterwards found to contain 26a. 2r. 30p.

"A less expensive site could, no doubt, have been obtained at a greater distance from London, but such a purchase would so have increased the cost of conveying prisoners, and would have so interfered with the supplies of the prison by public competition, as to render it one of obvious impropriety.

"The Committee also purchased about eight acres more land, in front of the prison, for £350, subject to the condition that no building should be erected upon it except a lodge—the prison being thus effectually protected from annoyance on three sides, whilst there is little probability of any arising on the fourth.

"At the following Sessions (Michaelmas, 1847), the Committee, after much careful consideration, recommended that the separate system of prison discipline should be adopted in the new prison, in which the Court concurred.

"The Committee ultimately appointed Mr. D. R. Hill, of Birmingham, a gentleman of considerable experience in erections of this kind, to prepare the plans required, and to act generally as architect during the progress of the work.

"These plans are uniform and complete for a prison containing 708 prisoners, on the separate system, and are yet so arranged as to admit of the buildings being enlarged to such an extent as to be suitable for 1,000 prisoners, without interfering with the original buildings, or destroying their uniformity.

---

* The pardons of fifteen more were obtained shortly afterwards, for the same reason.

"The area enclosed within the boundary wall, including the wall and the residences of the officers, &c., is 12A. 0R. 11P.; and including the gardens in front and the road on either side, &c., 16A. 1R. 29P.

"The prison contains 708 cells, suitable for the separate confinement of prisoners, together with 24 reception cells, 22 punishment cells, and 14 large rooms erected for misdemeanants of the first class, but generally used for prisoners subject to fits, or in other respects improper objects for separate confinement. As there are at all times some prisoners in these large rooms, as well as in the reception cells and infirmaries, it is believed there is ample accommodation in the prison for 750 prisoners.

"The contract for the main buildings having been executed, the works were commenced early in the spring of the year 1849."

The gross cost of the prison, according to the statement of accounts appended to the final report of the Building Committee, was as follows:—

	£	s.	d.	£	s.	d.	£	s.	d.
Land, Mr. Potter				8,006	5	0			
Ditto, Lord Spencer				350	0	0			
Buildings, trees, and crops				1,110	0	0			
Valuations, wages, taxes, tithes, &c.				374	0	3			
Total cost of land, &c.							9,840	5	3
Main-buildings, amount of contract				101,000	0	0			
Additional ditto	3,867	6	7						
Less works not executed £ 81 15 3									
Less brick duty 337 1 8									
	418	16	11						
				3,448	9	8			
Total cost of buildings							104,448	9	8
Ventilation and warming							4,401	12	6
Distribution of water							4,655	10	3
The well							988	10	0
Pumps							648	3	0
Furniture, fittings, &c.							2,546	5	3
Gas							1,015	17	0
Locks, bolts, bells, &c.							1,772	8	11
Commission							3,663	18	0
Secretary							289	5	2
Clerk of the works							586	17	7
Roads							662	8	3
Printing, books, stationery, &c.							195	17	7
Insurance							30	0	0
Materials							552	9	6
Miscellaneous							11	1	8
							136,308	19	7
Balance in hand							4,010	11	9
							140,319	11	4

" In considering the cost of the building, the prison must be regarded as one for 1,000 prisoners—sufficient land having been enclosed within the boundary walls, and the central halls, the chapel, the kitchen, the infirmaries, the reception and punishment cells, the offices, the pumps, the drains, and indeed all parts of the building, having been erected for this large number of prisoners—although the extra 250 cells have not yet been provided."

*** *Reasons for Building the Chapel on the Separate System.*—" During the erection of the prison, the Committee ascertained that some of the inspectors of prisons objected to prisoners being placed in enclosed pews, or stalls, in prison chapels, that all the fittings of this kind in the large prison at Wakefield had been removed, and also that in some prisons, recently erected, the prisoners, whilst in chapel, are not in any respect separated, but are seated on forms placed across the chapel floor, the back seats being slightly elevated. Under these circumstances, all further proceedings in the preparation of fittings for the chapel were suspended until the subject could be again considered.

" The chapel arrangements, as contracted for, corresponded exactly with those in use at Pentonville, and the objections raised to them were found to be :—

" *First*.—The possibility of the prisoners in adjoining stalls communicating with each other, if not most vigilantly watched, by thrusting slips of paper under the doors separating the stalls.

" *Secondly*.—The annoyance and confusion that might be, and sometimes was, occasioned by prisoners becoming ill, or pretending to be so, whilst placed in those stalls, to which access could only be obtained by the removal of a considerable number of other prisoners from their places.

" *Thirdly*.—The difficulty of getting the female prisoners and their officers in and out of the chapel without being observed by the male prisoners.

" And *Lastly*.—That some chaplains prefer social worship on principle, and consider that their ministration is more effective when the service is so conducted.

" On the other hand, the removal of all partitions," adds the report, " must be regarded as an abandonment of the principle of the separate system, and of the advantages presumed to result from prisoners not knowing each other ; also as involving considerable risk, owing to the number of officers being always small in comparison with the number of prisoners, and as being scarcely in accordance with those statutory regulations required to be observed in prisons respecting classification.

" The Committee moreover ascertained that by the adoption of a different mode of fittings, involving the abandonment of some of the seats in the chapel, the prisoners in a large number of the seats could be approached without interfering with any of the other prisoners, and the means of communicating with each other above mentioned effectually prevented. They also ascertained, that by the erection of a screen along one side of the chapel the females could come in and go out without being observed by the males.

" These arrangements have been introduced, and an effective means of inspection provided, consequently three of the objections have been in a great measure removed. With regard to the fourth, whilst the Committee would treat with great deference the opinions of those clergymen who would have *social* worship in prisons, they are aware that this is a subject on which there is much difference of opinion, and they feel it would not be prudent to give up this part of the separate system without greater experience of its ill effects.

" The prison was opened for the admission of male prisoners in November, 1851, and for female prisoners in the April following."

*** *Form of Hard Labour Adopted at the Surrey Prison.*—" With respect to the best means by which sentences to hard labour might be effectively carried out in the prison, the Committee were of opinion, that tread-wheel labour is not only inexpedient on account of its great cost, but also of its inapplicability to a prison conducted on the separate system; and they recommended that tread-wheel labour should not be adopted in the new prison, because they considered that in a prison under the separate system, means for the individual occupation of prisoners at efficient hard labour, in compliance with the sentences of the Courts, should be provided in the cells.

"The best method by which this may be effected is by means of labour-machines, provided that such machines, unexceptionable in their construction, can be procured.

"Accordingly, 100 of the best labour-machines were bought, and they have been found to answer the purpose for which they were intended.

"The only means of enforcing *hard labour* properly so-called, in contradistinction to the ordinary occupations of life, are the 100 labour-machines already mentioned, and the pumps. All prisoners sentenced to hard labour, and passed by the surgeon as 'fit,' are put to the machines when they first come into the prison, and are kept at them (making 15,000 revolutions per day) for terms varying from one month to three, if their sentences last so long. The length of time during which a prisoner is kept at the machine varies according to the length of his sentence and the necessity for transferring him, in order to make room for fresh comers. When the admissions are small, the prisoners are kept three months at the least at the machines, if sentenced to so long periods; but when the admissions are numerous, this cannot always be effected. From the machines they are transferred to the pumping classes, where they remain for a limited period; after which they are employed in the garden, or at trades, or at work about the prison, or in picking oakum.

"The employments for male prisoners, *not being hard labour*, are gardening, carpentering, tailoring, shoemaking, matmaking, bricklayer's and smith's work, netting, painting, and cleaning.

"The whole employment for female prisoners consists of work in the wash-house and laundry, picking coir, needlework, and cleaning.

"It is obvious, therefore, that a sufficient provision has not yet been made for the effectual enforcing of all hard-labour sentences; and, indeed, for the female prisoners there is no hard labour whatever except washing."

*** *Of the System of Prison Discipline at Wandsworth.*—"It cannot, perhaps, be expected that any proceedings in prisons will produce much permanent impression on the minds of prisoners born and reared in crime, and who have not only become fascinated with the excitement of criminal life, but have no course open to them on their discharge from prison, except that of returning to their former haunts of vice. Fortunately, however, *all* prisoners are not of this hopeless class. Many of them have friends anxious for their welfare, and ready to assist them in their efforts to obtain an honest livelihood. They have, probably, fallen in an unguarded moment, under the influence of some strong temptation, or have been led into crime by bad companions, into whose society they had fallen, not being sufficiently aware of the evil consequences certain to result from such an association.

"On prisoners of this kind the discipline of the prison may reasonably be expected to have a beneficial effect. The deterring character of the imprisonment, the opportunities for reflection, the solemn warnings, the judicious advice, and the kind entreaties to which every prisoner is subjected, cannot always be unavailing, and it is believed they have a satisfactory result in a large proportion of such cases as have just been mentioned.

"Whilst, therefore, the discipline of this prison may be fairly expected to do good, it is obvious that no prisoner there can receive any moral injury from it. The charge so frequently made against the associated system of discipline, that prisoners under it are generally corrupted rather than improved, is here no longer applicable.

" It appears to the Committee, that it cannot be too deeply impressed on the mind of the Court and the public at large, that the principle of the 'separate system' is not *entire solitude* or *silence*, but the *complete separation* of prisoners from each other. It is, indeed, an important feature of the system, that prisoners under it should have frequent intercourse with the governor, chaplain, surgeon, schoolmaster, taskmaster, and other officers; and it is satisfactory to report that no circumstances have occurred in the prison to induce the Committee to think less favourably of the system than when it was determined on by the county, and they look forward with confidence to its entire success.

" For the juvenile offenders, no distinct provision has been made in the prison at Wandsworth, in the anticipation that some comprehensive measure for their treatment will shortly be adopted. The consideration of this subject cannot prudently be much longer neglected, since there is reason to believe, that whilst the aggregate number of prisoners has considerably diminished, the number of juvenile delinquents has increased. A separate school-room has been provided for them, and much time and attention is devoted to their instruction, at the same time it must be confessed these alone are not sufficient to remedy this serious evil; it is, therefore, trusted that Parliament will provide at no distant period some effective scheme for the reformation of this class of offenders, and thereby cut off from the ranks of maturer criminals those dangerous recruits, who are now but too ready to unite with them in the performance of the most daring crimes."

The Committee conclude by stating that " they cannot terminate their proceedings more agreeably to themselves, than in congratulating the county on having secured the services of a gentleman as governor so eminently qualified to superintend this great prison with effect; and who, by his abilities and assiduity, conducted it through all the difficulties attendant upon the introduction of a new system of discipline, in a new and scarcely completed building, and who has now reduced it to a state of order which has elicited the admiration of those who are most competent to form a just opinion of its merits."*

---

* RULES AND REGULATIONS RELATING TO THE CONDUCT AND TREATMENT OF PRISONERS IN THE HOUSE OF CORRECTION, AT WANDSWORTH, IN THE COUNTY OF SURREY.

" The governor shall exercise his authority with firmness, temper, and humanity; abstain from all irritating language, and not strike a prisoner. He shall bear in mind that the object of his duties, and of those of all officers and servants under his direction, is not only to give full effect to the sentences awarded to the prisoners during their confinement, but also to instil into their minds sound moral and religious principles, and induce in them practical habits of industry, regularity, and good conduct. With this view, while enforcing strict observance of the rules regarding labour and discipline, the governor shall be careful to encourage any effort at amendment on the part of the prisoner, and shall require all officers and servants of the prison, in their several capacities, to do the same.

" He shall direct that all prisoners on admission be placed in a reception cell, that they be strictly searched, and that all knives and other sharp instruments or dangerous weapons, or articles calculated to facilitate escape, be taken from them; except as hereinafter provided with respect to debtors and misdemeanants of the first division; but in no case shall any prisoner of any class whatever be searched in the presence of any other prisoner.

" He, or some other officer, shall, as soon as possible after the admission of a prisoner, note down in the prison register, the prisoner's name, age, height, features, &c.; he shall take charge of, and enter, or cause to be entered, in the Prisoner's Property Book, an inventory of all money, clothes, and other effects which the prisoner may have on his admission, or which, from time to time, may be sent to the prison for his use; he shall take charge of them for safe custody only, and for the purpose of being restored as directed by one or more of the visiting justices; or (in the case of misdemeanants of the first division) as directed by the rules for that class.

" He shall cause copies of such of the rules as relate to the treatment and conduct of prisoners (printed in legible characters) to be fixed up in each cell, and he shall read, or cause to be read, such rules to such prisoners as cannot read; and once in every three months he shall repeat the same.

" He shall enforce a high degree of cleanliness in the prison, as well as respects every part of the building and yards, as the persons of the prisoners, their clothing and bedding, and everything in use.

" He shall direct that every prisoner wash himself thoroughly, at least once every day, and his feet at

VENTILATING SHAFT, WANDSWORTH.

On the day of our last visit there were altogether 830 male and female prisoners located in the prison, and these were distributed in the following manner:—

PRISONERS IN CUSTODY AT THE SURREY HOUSE OF CORRECTION, WANDSWORTH, 17TH SEPTEMBER, 1860.

MALES.		FEMALES.	
Ward A	155	Ward F & G	71
„ B	149	„ H	106
„ C	13	„ Infirmary—sick	2
„ D	172	„ „ nurses	1
„ E	122	„ „ itch	2
„ Infirmary—sick	17	„ Punishment	3
„ „ nurses	2	„ Reception	5
„ „ itch	1		
„ Punishment	4	Total	190
„ Reception	5		
Total	640		

General total 830

least once each week: and he shall see that each prisoner has a towel, a comb, and a sufficient supply of soap.

"He shall direct that all prisoners, except misdemeanants of the first division, or unless they are excepted by the medical officer, on their admission into the prison, be washed in a bath before they shall be passed into their proper wards; but no prisoner shall be stripped or bathed in the presence of any other prisoner.

"He shall direct that in no case the hair of any female prisoner be cut, except when he thinks it necessary on account of vermin or dirt, or when the medical officer deems it requisite on the ground of health; and that the hair of male prisoners be not cut except for the purpose of health and cleanliness. He shall see that male prisoners be shaved at least once a week.

"He shall direct that all convicted prisoners, except misdemeanants of the first division, be supplied with a complete prison dress, and that all such prisoners be required to wear it; and he shall see that misdemeanants of the first division be allowed to have the prison dress, if they desire it, and be required to wear it, if their own clothes be insufficient or unfit for use, or necessary to be preserved for the purposes of justice.

"He shall direct that every prisoner be supplied with clean linen, including shirt (whether of linen, cotton, or flannel), stockings, and handkerchief, at least once in every week.

"He shall direct that every prisoner be supplied with sufficient bedding for warmth and health.

"He shall direct that the prisoners have three meals each day; and that at least two of these be hot.

"He shall direct that no prisoner be set to work immediately after any meal.

"He shall, under the direction of the visiting justices, make due provision for the enforcement of hard labour in the case of such prisoners as are sentenced thereto. He shall also, under the direction of the visiting justices, provide employment, with the requisite materials and instructions, for all other prisoners (except misdemeanants of the first division, and prisoners for bail on sureties), and shall see that misdemeanants of the first division have the option of employment.

"He shall direct that strict silence be at all times observed by the convicted prisoners: and the prisoners shall be confined to their cells on Sundays, except when attending Divine Service or school.

"He shall see that no prisoner who is a Jew be compelled to labour on his Sabbath; but such prisoner shall be confined to his cell in the same manner as all prisoners on Sundays.

"He shall see that all prisoners, including those sentenced to hard labour, have such an amount of time allowed to them for instruction as the visiting justices may appoint.

"He shall allow prisoners to see their legal advisers on an order from a visiting justice. Every person, however, claiming admission as a legal adviser must be a certificated attorney or solicitor, or his authorized clerk.

"He shall not allow convicted prisoners to see their relations and friends until after the expiration of the first three months of their imprisonment; but subsequently to that period he shall allow them to receive visits once in the course of each successive three months. In case of sickness or other special circumstances, however, he shall allow convicted prisoners to see their relations and friends at other times; such special circumstances to be entered in his journal.

"Upon the special application of a prisoner of a religious persuasion differing from that of the Established Church, he shall allow such prisoner to absent himself from chapel; and in accordance with the spirit of the law, with respect to prisoners of a religious persuasion differing from that of the Established Church, he shall allow a minister of such persuasion, at the special request of any such prisoner, to visit him, in

¶ iv.—β.

The Interior of the Prison.

On our summons at the bell and presenting our order from the visiting justices of the prison, we were admitted by the warder, a tall silver-headed man, within the porter's-lodge. He was attired in the uniform of the officers of the establishment, white trowsers, blue sirtout coat, and cap with peak. The porter's-lodge is a neat little apartment on our right hand, as we enter the prison gate, and suitably furnished. Its furniture consists of a desk and stool for the warder, and several chairs, on which visitors can be seated, along with

order to give him the instruction and counsel which he would otherwise receive in his class or private cell from the chaplain, under such restrictions imposed by the visiting justices as shall guard against the introduction of improper persons, and as shall prevent improper communications. (See NOTE.)

"He shall not permit the admission of visitors to prisoners on a Sunday, except in special cases by a written order of a committing or visiting justice, and except in the case of a minister visiting any prisoner of a religious persuasion differing from that of the Established Church.

"He shall allow prisoners to send and receive one letter in the course of each quarter of a year, unless a visiting or committing magistrate shall have issued an order to the contrary, or unless he shall know a sufficient cause why any such letter should not be sent or received; in which latter case he shall record the fact in his journal.

"He shall inspect every letter to or from a prisoner, except such letters as are addressed to a visiting justice or other proper authority; and in every case where he shall deem it necessary to withhold a letter either to or from a prisoner, he shall record the fact in his journal, and shall without delay lay such letter before a visiting justice for his decision.

"The chaplain may inspect every letter to and from a prisoner, except those of misdemeanants of the first division, and except such as are addressed to a visiting justice, or other authority.

"The matron, or some other female officer, shall search every female prisoner on admission; and the same course shall be pursued by her with reference to female prisoners on admission as that prescribed for the governor with reference to male prisoners. All money or other effects brought into the prison by any female prisoner, or from time to time sent in for her use and benefit, shall be transferred to the governor.

"Every prisoner, as a general rule, and as far as may be practicable, shall be kept in separate confinement.

"Such arrangements shall be made in the prison as the visiting justices, from time to time, shall consider as best calculated to prevent the mutual recognition of prisoners.

"No prisoner shall be allowed to remain in bed more than eight hours during one night, except by the direction of the surgeon of the prison.

"The visiting justices shall direct such books as they think proper to be distributed for the use of the prisoners who do not belong to the Established Church; and should examine books sent in for the use of such prisoners, and reject such as they deem improper.

"They may, under special circumstances (by an order in writing by two or more of them), allow to prisoners food, clothing, or other necessaries, besides the gaol allowance.

"They may, in special cases (by an order in writing, by two or more of them), suspend any of the rules for misdemeanants of the first division, reporting the same to the Secretary of State for his direction thereon.

"They may authorize any prisoner to be employed within the prison in the service of the prison, but not in its discipline, or in the service of any officer, or in the service or instruction of any other prisoner.

"They may, if they shall at any time observe, or be satisfactorily informed, of any extraordinary diligence or merit in any prisoner under their inspection, report the same to the justices in general or quarter session assembled, in order that such justices may, if they thnk proper, recommend any such offender to the royal mercy, in such degree, and upon such terms as to them shall seem meet; and if her Majesty shall thereupon be graciously pleased to shorten the duration of such prisoner's confinement, such prisoner shall, upon his or her discharge, together with necessary clothing, receive such sum of money for his or her subsistence as the visiting justices for the time being shall think proper, so as such sum shall not exceed twenty shillings,

---

"NOTE. Roman Catholic prisoners, and Dissenters of every denomination, are desired to take notice, that the clergyman of their religion will be sent for, when they ask for him, as he cannot come unless each prisoner who wishes to see him makes a request to the governor of the prison. This notice is given in order that all may have an opportunity of sending for a clergyman of their own religion, if they desire his presence."

a fire-screen. On the wall hangs a list of the visiting justices in a dark frame, together with a list of the justices in the Central Criminal Court. Alongside the desk is a small letter-box containing the letters sent to post by the officers of the prison as well as the prisoners.

We were introduced by the governor to the chief warder, a noble specimen of a prison officer. Though in mature life and his hair silvered, he is a man of great energy and intelligence, with enlarged experience of prison discipline, and has been connected with the prison for the last ten years. His dress was distinguished from the inferior officers of the prison by having the neck and wrist of his sirtout and also the back embroidered with lace. By the kindness of the governor, this active and accomplished superior officer accompanied us in our visit of inspection over the prison.

nor be less than five shillings, in case such offender shall have been confined for the space of one year, and so in proportion for any shorter term of confinement.

"There shall be in each division a sufficient number of dark and other cells, adapted to solitary confinement, for the punishment of refractory prisoners, and for the reception of such prisoners as may by law be confined therein.

"In case any criminal prisoner shall be guilty of any repeated offence against the rules of the prison, or shall be guilty of any greater offence than the gaoler or keeper is by 4 Geo. IV., c. 64, empowered to punish, the said gaoler or keeper shall forthwith report the same to the visiting justices, or one of them, for the time being; and any one such justice, or any other justice acting in and for the county, or riding, or division of a county, or for the district, city, town, or place to which such prison belongs, shall have power to inquire, upon oath, and to determine concerning any such matter so reported to him or them, and to order the offender to be punished by close confinement for any term not exceeding one month, or by personal correction, in the case of prisoners convicted of felony, or sentenced to hard labour.

"In cases of urgent and absolute necessity, a visiting justice may, by an order in writing, direct any prisoner to be kept in irons; such order to specify the cause thereof, and the time during which the prisoner is to be kept in irons, such time in no case to extend beyond the next meeting of visiting justices.

"Every person who shall assault, or violently resist any officer of a prison in the execution of his duty, or who shall aid or incite any person so to assault or resist any such officer, shall for every such offence, on conviction thereof by the oath of one or more witnesses, or upon his or her own confession, before two justices of the peace, be liable to a penalty, not more than £5, to be levied, if not forthwith paid, by distress and sale of the goods and chattels of the offender; or in the discretion of the justices before whom he or she shall be convicted, may be imprisoned, with or without hard labour, for any time not more than one calendar month, or if the offender be already under sentence of imprisonment, then such offender, for every such offence, shall be imprisoned, with or without hard labour, for any time not more than six calendar months, in addition to so much of the time for which he or she was originally sentenced, as may then be unexpired.

"The governor shall have power to hear all complaints touching any of the following offences; that is to say, disobedience to the rules of the prison; common assaults by one prisoner upon another; profane cursing and swearing; indecent behaviour, or any irreverent behaviour at chapel; all of which are declared to be offences, if committed by any description of prisoners; absence from chapel without leave; idleness or negligence in work, or wilful damage or mismanagement of it; which are also declared to be offences if committed by any prisoner under charge or conviction of any crime. He may examine any persons touching such offences, and may determine thereupon; and may punish all such offences by ordering any offender to close confinement in a refractory or solitary cell, and by keeping such offender upon bread and water only for any term not exceeding three days; but he shall not determine any of these cases without previous examination; neither shall he delegate his authority in these matters to any other person.

"No punishments or privations of any kind shall be awarded except by the governor, or by a visiting or other justice.

"He shall not, under any pretence, continue close confinement in any cell with bread and water for prison offences for a longer period than three days; but in the event of continued or renewed misconduct, he shall submit the case to a visiting or other justice, under the provisions of the 42nd section of the Gaol Act.

"He shall not put handcuffs or any other description of irons on a prisoner, except in cases of absolute necessity; and he shall enter in his journal full particulars of every such case, and give notice thereof forthwith to a visiting justice. He shall not continue handcuffs or any other irons on a prisoner longer than twenty-four hours without an order in writing from a visiting justice, specifying the cause thereof, and the time during which the prisoner is to be ironed."

On a table in the side of the porter's-lodge we observed several folio volumes of the "Prisoners' Letter and Visit Book," with "Indices."

The chief warder stated, that on the friends of the prisoners applying to visit, it is the

THE FOLLOWING ARE THE PRESCRIBED RATES OF DIET:—

CLASS 1.

Convicted prisoners confined for any term not exceeding seven days.

	Males.	Females.
DAILY.	*Breakfast.*—1 pint of oatmeal gruel. *Dinner.*—1 lb. of bread. *Supper.*—1 pint of oatmeal.	1 pint of oatmeal gruel. 1 lb. of bread. 1 pint of oatmeal gruel.

CLASS 2.

Convicted prisoners for any term exceeding seven days, and not exceeding twenty-one days.

	Males.	Females.
DAILY.	*Breakfast.*—1 pint of oatmeal gruel; 6 oz. of bread. *Dinner.*—12 oz. of bread. *Supper.*—1 pint of oatmeal gruel; 6 oz. of bread.	1 pint of oatmeal gruel; 6 oz. of bread. 6 oz. of bread. 1 pint of oatmeal gruel; 6 oz. of bread.

CLASS 3.

Convicted prisoners employed at hard labour for terms exceeding twenty-one days, but not more than six weeks; and convicted prisoners not employed at hard labour for terms not exceeding twenty-one days, but not more than four months.

	Males.	Females.
DAILY.	*Breakfast*—1 pint of oatmeal gruel; 6 oz. of bread.	1 pint of oatmeal gruel; 6 oz. of bread.
SUNDAY, THURSDAY.	*Dinner.*—1 pint of soup; 8 oz. of bread.	1 pint of soup; 6 oz. of bread.
TUESDAY, SATURDAY.	*Dinner.*—3 oz. of cooked meat, without bone; 8 oz. of bread; ½ lb. of potatoes.	3 oz. of cooked meat, without bone; 6 oz. of bread; ½ lb. of potatoes.
MONDAY, WEDN'SDAY FRIDAY.	*Dinner.*—8 oz. of bread; 1 lb. of potatoes.	6 oz. of bread; 1 lb. of potatoes.
DAILY.	*Supper.*—Same as breakfast.	Same as breakfast.

Prisoners of this class employed at hard labour to have, in addition, one pint of soup per week.

CLASS 4.

Convicted prisoners employed at hard labour for terms exceeding six weeks, but not more than four months; and convicted prisoners not employed at hard labour, for terms exceeding four months.

	Males.	Females.
DAILY.	*Breakfast.*—1 pint of oatmeal gruel; 8 oz. of bread.	1 pint of oatmeal gruel; 6 oz. of bread.
SUNDAY, TUESDAY, THURSDAY, SATURDAY, MONDAY, WEDN'SDAY FRIDAY,	*Dinner*—3 oz. of cooked meat, without bone; ½ lb. of potatoes; 8 oz. of bread.	3 oz. of cooked meat, without bone; ½ lb. of potatoes; 6 oz. of bread.
	Dinner.—1 pint of soup; 8 oz. of bread.	1 pint of soup; 6 oz. of bread.
DAILY.	*Supper.*—Same as breakfast.	Same as breakfast.

CLASS 5.

Convicted prisoners employed at hard labour for terms exceeding four months.

	Males.	Females.
SUNDAY, TUESDAY, THURSDAY, SATURDAY.	*Breakfast.*—1 pint of oatmeal gruel; 8 oz. of bread. *Dinner.*—4 oz. of cooked meat, without bone; 1 lb. of potatoes; 6 oz. of bread.	1 pint of oatmeal gruel; 6 oz. of bread. 3 oz. of cooked meat, without bone; ½ lb. of potatoes; 6 oz. of bread.
MONDAY, WEDN'SDAY FRIDAY.	*Breakfast.*—1 pint of cocoa, made of ¾ oz. of flaked cocoa or cocoa-nibs, sweetened with ¾ oz. of molasses or sugar; 8 oz. of bread. *Dinner.*—1 pint of soup; 1 lb. of potatoes; 6 oz. of bread.	1 pint of cocoa, made of ¾ oz. of flaked cocoa or cocoa nibs, sweetened with ¾ oz. of molasses or sugar; 6 oz. of bread. 1 pint of soup; ½ lb. of potatoes; 6 oz. of bread.
DAILY.	*Supper.*—1 pint of oatmeal; 8 oz. of bread.	1 pint of oatmeal gruel; 6 oz. of bread.

CLASS 6.

Prisoners sentenced by court to solitary confinement.

	Males.	Females.
DAILY.	The ordinary diet of their respective Classes.	The ordinary diet of their respective Classes.

CLASS 7.

Prisoners under punishment for prison offences, for terms not exceeding three days:—1 lb. of bread per diem.

Prisoners in close confinement for prison offences, under the provisions of the 42nd section of the Jail Act.

	Males.	Females.
DAILY.	*Breakfast.*—1 pint of gruel; 8 oz. of bread. *Dinner.*—8 oz. of bread. *Supper.*—1 pint of gruel; 8 oz. of bread.	1 pint of gruel; 6 oz. of bread. 6 oz. of bread. 1 pint of gruel; 6 oz. of bread.

Ingredients of Soup and Gruel.—The soup to contain, per pint, 3 ounces of cooked meat, without bone, 3 ounces of potatoes, 1 ounce of barley, rice, or oatmeal, and 1 ounce of onions or leeks, with pepper and salt. The gruel to contain 2 ounces of oatmeal per pint. The gruel on alternate days to be sweetened with ¾ ounce of molasses or sugar, and seasoned with salt. In seasons when the potato crop has failed, 4 ounces of split peas made into a pudding may be occasionally substituted; but the change must not be made more than *twice* in each week. Boys under fourteen years of age to be placed on the same diet as females.

duty of the porter to examine the visit book and learn if the visit is due; as relatives or friends of the prisoners, by the regulations of the establishment, are only admitted within the prison walls at stated times.   If the visit is due, notice is sent to the governor's clerk for the purpose of the necessary visiting papers being made out, which are forwarded to the chief warder, who sends the prisoner to the visiting room to meet with his friends.   These papers are returned to the governor's office in the course of the evening.

On the prisoners' letters being received, the porter looks into the letter-book to see whether they are due, and should he find them so, writes the word "*due*" on the cover.   If otherwise, he writes "not due."   They are forwarded to the governor's office for his examination, or in his absence, to the chief warder, who officiates as deputy governor, and are subsequently sent to the chaplain or assistant chaplain for their inspection; after which they are delivered to the prisoners.   This is done in the event of the letters being due.   When "not due" they are reserved to be given to the prisoner on a future occasion.   All letters are delivered up to him on his discharge from prison.

Money is occasionally enclosed in letters to the prisoner, which is placed to his account. Such sums are sometimes sent to enable those incarcerated to return to their friends.   When they are under twenty-one years of age, their friends are informed by circular of the date of the discharge, and requested to attend to receive them.

Having asked the porter in reference to the letters written by prisoners to their friends, he stated, "I enter them in a book, close them, and put them in the letter-box."

The chief warder called our attention to the non-resident officers' attendance book; that is, those officers who do not reside within the prison walls.   We found their names were all carefully entered; their time of coming on duty as well as of leaving duty.   In the event of their not attending at the proper time in the morning, it is the duty of the porter to report the same to the chief warder for the information of the governor.

On the mantelpiece of the porter's-lodge lies a Bible, a beautiful symbol of the character of this excellent establishment.

In the company of the deputy governor, we leave the porter's-lodge, and pass through the courtyard, which is gravelled and carefully drained.   We enter the prison by a flight of steps, where one of the long corridors of the interior opens to our view.   When near the entry door the chief warder conducted us into the inner porter's-lodge, where a Crimean soldier, one of the light cavalry brigade, who took a part in the daring charge at Balaclava under Lord Cardigan, officiates as warder.   He is a strong-built powerful man, in the prime of life, more like a heavy dragoon than a light-armed hussar.   In the lodge of the inner warder, is a large yellow oaken cupboard.   Here are contained the keys of the prison, all systematically arranged and suspended along its interior during the night.   The governor then keeps the key of the cupboard, and at six o'clock in the morning it is delivered to the chief warder, and given by him to the inner porter, when the keys of the prison are distributed among the different officers.

We noticed a dark painted tin box in the cupboard.   The inner porter informed us, "It is for the purpose of keeping the master keys belonging to the governor, surgeon, chaplain, and chief warder."

The chief warder remarked, with reference to these master keys, "They are for the external doors, cell doors, and mortice locks of the offices and lodges."

The inner warder, pointing to a deal table in the apartment, stated it is used for the purpose of the governor or chief warder signing the receipts of prisoners delivered by the prison vans for incarceration in the prison.   In this apartment the male prisoners are discharged by the governor.   Here they are ranged before him, seated at this table, before they leave the walls of the establishment.

The inner porter called our attention to a book kept for inserting the names of visitors to the prison, along with their address and the name of the officer who attends them.   There is a column for any observations they may make as to the arrangements of the prison. This book generally rests on another small table in a corner of the lodge.

The inner lodge is on our right hand as we enter the prison. Alongside of it is the clerk's room, and on our left is the prisoners' friends' waiting room, and the apartment occupied by the assistant chaplain.

As we proceed into the interior beyond these offices, the passage widens. It is paved with York slab, and the roof is arched and supported with iron girders and metal pillars. There is an entry from the passage on each side—one leading to the courtyard in the direction of the female prison on our left, and the other on the right, conducting us to the dead-house and officers' water-closet.

Further along, we come to the governor's office and the office of his clerk, the visiting justices' committee-room, a waiting-room for the prisoners' friends, and a water-closet.

We pass through a wooden door, iron grated and glazed, in the upper part, which is generally kept locked. The circular range of apartments, last referred to, leads to a continuation of the passage about the same width as the other corridors.

On each side, is a room for the prisoners receiving the visits of their friends, about the size of two cells. A portion of the interior is enclosed within strong iron bars like the cage of a menagerie, having a small gate to admit the prisoner, which is kept locked.

On the opposite side of the apartment is a corresponding space for the friends, fenced with similar iron bars, where they enter by a door from the passage. An officer of the prison remains in the intervening space between these strong iron gratings during their interview, to prevent any improper communication passing between them. The roof is arched as in the other prison cells. The walls of the visiting rooms are painted of a yellow stone colour tastefully pencilled, and the flooring is of Dutch tile.

There is a large room on the left-hand side of the passage leading to the central hall, used for the purpose of assorting clean linen when received from the laundry. It is roofed and paved in a similar manner to the prisoners' visiting-room, and has a fireplace and three glazed windows, the partitions between the panes—as in the cells—being made of iron.

We now come into the wide central hall, which is lofty and well lighted from the roof where we have a magnificent picture, in the fine, lofty, far-extending corridors radiating around us, the passage along which we passed forming, as it were, a sixth corridor to complete the unity of the circular wings. Here we found several of the officers of the prison in their uniforms lingering in the hall, engaged in their various duties, or actively flitting along from corridor to corridor and from apartment to apartment. Several of the prisoners, with masks, in their dark gray prison dress, consisting of jacket, vest, and trousers, and dark cap, are engaged in cleaning the corridors. They have a curious and sinister appearance as they look at us with hasty stolen glance through the eyelet openings of their mask, which screen their features, as at Pentonville. As we stood in the central hall, with the deputy-governor by our side, we saw a file of prisoners, in their prison attire and masks, pass along to the chapel from the galleries in the corridors. Some of them were young boys, who tripped along with an active, light tread, their hands crossed behind their backs; others were young lads of 17, with vigorous, active step; while others were more advanced in life. Some were thin and lank; while one or two were of corpulent appearance. They walked along with measured step, generally with their head stooping and hands crossed behind, several feet distant from each other, under the supervision of two or three warders. In the centre of this large prison the air was as clear and salubrious as in the meadows around the prison walls; the well-lighted cheerful-looking corridors were admirably clean; and everything around us in this prison, conducted on the separate system, wore a cheerful and business-like aspect.

In the centre of this spacious hall is a large stone of about nine feet in diameter, cut in the form of a hexagon. It is surrounded by a strong perforated iron flooring about six feet in width, giving light and ventilation to the storerooms below. The lofty and ample roof rises in a dome of the form of a hexagon, supported by strong iron girders, and lighted by sash windows along the side.

Each corridor has long ranges of cells along the two light and elegant galleries, in addition to the cells on the area beneath, level with the central hall; and are lighted at the extremities by large windows like those of a cathedral, nearly equal in dimensions to the length and breadth of the end of the corridor.

The following are the number of cells in each corridor, and the number of prisoners in them at the time of our visit:—

CORRIDORS.

	Cells.	Occupied at the time of our visit by			Cells.	Occupied at the time of our visit by
A. 1	48	46		D. 3	48	5
2	48	47		E. 1	38	38
3	47	44		2	39	37
B. 1	47	45		3	38	37
2	48	50				———
3	48	47				527
C. 1	65	40		In infirmary		7
2	67			„ itch ward		4
3	67			„ reception ward		16
D. 1	45	46				———
2	48	45		In all		554

The corridors are respectively named A, B, C, D, and E. The basement cells are termed No. 1, the first gallery No. 2, and the second gallery No. 3.

The infirmary is situated in the E wing ward, the itch ward in the basement of E, and the reception cells are in the area below the central hall, where the stores are kept.

These five wings and the apartments and offices connected therewith are the Male prison. The Female prison is a smaller compact building, of three wings radiating around a centre, and is situated on our left hand as we enter the prison. Since the time when the description of Wandsworth Prison appeared in an earlier portion of this work, about four years ago, a new wing has been erected in a line with the passage leading into the main prison, and another wing has been built to the female prison, both of which were embraced in the original plan of the buildings, and give unity and completeness to the male and female branches; so that it is now, in an architectural point of view, so far as regards the completeness of its arrangements, one of the best correctional prisons, if not the best, in the United Kingdom.

As we enter the central hall by the passage from the entry gate, we see on the left-hand side a bell handle, which communicates with the governor's house. Alongside are two other bells—one communicating with the reception ward, and the other with the female prison.

In a portion of the wall between the entrance passage and corridor A there is a square cavity extending from the lowest range of cells to the top of the corridor, where there is machinery to hoist the provisions from the kitchen in the area below to the various cells above.

Before leaving the central hall we remarked there were two galleries around it communicating with the different corridors, A, B, C, D, and E, and also with the chapel, which is above the entrance-passage. There is a staircase on each side of the corridors leading to the different galleries—one between A and B, and another between D and E. There is also a staircase in the C wing, communicating with the galleries above and the chapel.

⁎ *Reception Cells.*—On entering the prison opposite to the lodge of the inner porter is a

stair leading down to the reception ward in the area below. There are 16 reception cells, all of uniform dimensions. On measuring one of them we found it at top of the arched roof 9 feet high, and at bottom of arch 8 feet 6 inches, and to be 5 feet 2 inches wide and 15 feet 10 inches in length. Each of those cells has an iron-grated window covered with glass, 2 feet 4 inches long and 2 feet 8 inches wide. In each window there are three ventilating panes. Over the door of the reception cells there is an opening for ventilation, and underneath the flooring there is another air passage.

Here the chief warder referred us to the engineer of the establishment for a fuller explanation of the sanatory arrangements of these cells. The engineer stated—"The chief warder showed you the air-flue in the outside of the prison. This air-flue communicates with an apparatus for heating the air. The air is heated by means of hot water in pipes passing through the building, and is distributed from a patented apparatus by 'Haden' over the passage, from whence it passes into the cells through apertures above the doors."

The chief warder having directed the attention of the engineer to the extraction of the confined air, the latter explained—"The air passes into the extraction flue, of which there is one in every cell, connected with a trunk shaft on the top of the building."

In each reception cell there is a stone-coloured night utensil, the top of which is covered with a wooden lid, and serves the prisoner as a seat; and a metal water box painted black, fixed into the corner of the wall, along with a copper wash-basin beneath it, as shown in the engraving. The cell is whitewashed, tidy, and comfortable in appearance. The door has a circular inspection-plate, through which the officers of the prison are able to observe the movements of the prisoner from the passage, without entering the cell; and under this inspection-plate is a trap 10 inches long by 11 inches broad, for the purpose of conveying the food and utensils to and from the cell. The flooring is of asphalte. On the outside of the cell door is a small metal plate, with the number of the cell painted on it. On the prisoner's ringing the bell this plate is thrown out, and does not return till put back by the officer.

We then passed into the receiving room, and were introduced to the reception warder. This apartment is 21 feet square, and is fitted round with wooden shelves, for the purpose of keeping the prison clothing to be given to the criminal while undergoing his sentence. We noticed a large deal desk in the room, for taking down the prisoner's description. This is invariably done on his entering the reception ward. Within the desk are contained articles from the pockets of the prisoners, kept here for safe custody, and carefully returned to them on their discharge, consisting of tobacco boxes, pocket knives, pocket books, purses, watches, pawn tickets, breast pins, &c., &c.

The warder brought forward the "prisoners' property book," in which all these articles are carefully registered.

He also showed us the blank duplicates to be filled up on the prisoner's admission, treating on his age, education, religion, trade, place of birth, residence, whether he has parents or not, single or married, &c.; also giving his personal description, together with an inventory of his clothing and other personal property.

₊ *Prisoner's Own Clothing Room.*—This apartment is alongside of the receiving room, and is about 20 feet long and 18 feet broad. The walls around are lined with wooden racks, on which bundles of the prisoners' clothing are deposited. There are other two oblong racks in the centre of the apartment, which also contains a charcoal stove. It has three windows, 3 feet 2 inches long and 2 feet 2 inches wide, two of them provided with flaps for ventilation. In the centre of this room there is a gas bracket, and over the door is a ventilating aperture with a light iron screen on the inner side. This apartment is about the same height as the reception cells.

As we looked around us on the bundles of tattered and half-worn clothing of various hues and textures, we could almost fancy we were in a broker's shop or old clothes store in Rosemary

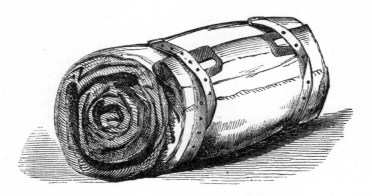

PRISONER'S MATTRASS, WANDSWORTH.

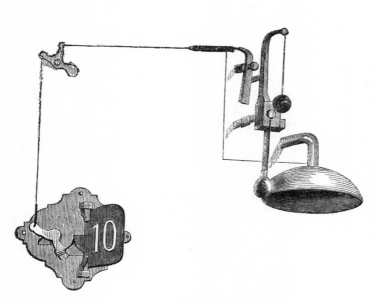

CELL INDICATOR, WANDSWORTH.

Lane; only, the storeroom before us was more salubrious, and the material around more carefully arranged. In some bundles we could detect the red coat of an unfortunate soldier who had been guilty of some theft or assault; in another we saw the good dark coat and light fancy vest of a civilian, who had possibly lived a "fast" life beyond his income, and was now incarcerated in the prison for embezzlement of his employer's property. There was the rough working dress of a day labourer, which we could trace from the heavy hob-nailed shoes and blue smock frock; and on another rack we observed the tattered clothes of a wretched vagrant.

The chief warder, our most intelligent guide, remarked—"You will observe, sir, the bundles are all numbered and arranged numerically."

The reception warder, pointing to bundle 63, observed—"These belong to an Italian who states he is an interpreter. He is an educated man, and of better class than the generality of the prisoners. The bundle consists of a good black surtout coat, a light fancy vest, a clean white ironed shirt, and a pair of drab trousers in good condition. He is middle-aged, rather good looking, and of middle stature, and is imprisoned here for being guilty of indecent conduct.

"This other bundle," said the reception warder, "belongs to a cripple with a wooden leg, a tailor by trade, and of middle age. He was charged with wilful damage to a pane of glass, and has been sentenced to twenty-one days' imprisonment." The bundle, on being opened, contained a light jean coat, a shepherd's plaid vest, invisible green trousers, with a dark braid stripe along the side, a clean white shirt, and dark silk neck-tie.

"No. 695," the official continued, "belongs to a prisoner brought here for wilful damage to a pane of glass. He is a very strange little man, a dwarf, of 4 feet 5 inches high, and about thirty-five years of age." The chief warder here stated—"He has been very frequently in this and other prisons connected with the metropolis." On opening the bundle the clothes appeared to be a tissue of rags, unfit to be worn by any human being, and could scarcely cover the nakedness of the wretched little man. "You will observe," said the chief warder, "his clothes are of the very worst description, all hanging in rags and tatters. He has no hat, and his shoes are without soles."

"Bundle 615," said the reception warder, "belongs to a deaf and dumb man, who is middle-aged. Has been sentenced to prison for seven days, under the vagrant act. The clothes consist of corduroy trousers, light-brown coat, and wide-awake hat. All of them," said the chief warder, "are in a filthy and disgusting condition."

₊ *Reception Store Room.*—Leaving the apartment in which the prisoners' own clothing is deposited, we again returned to the reception room, where, as we have said, a supply of the prison dress is kept. Along the wooden shelves around the room are piles of apparently new clothing for the criminals, of the usual dark gray colour. There we saw large quantities of jackets, vests, trousers, and caps with masks. We also found stores of blue striped cotton shirts, flannels, and drawers, blue worsted stockings with white rings, and shoes.

The warder informed us—"This is a small stock kept in hand to furnish the prisoners on being admitted to the prison. You will remark," he added, "the clothing is arranged on the shelves according to the various sizes, and numbered 1, 2, 3, 4, 5, and 6, and that the articles are all marked with the prison type. The shoes," he stated, "are strong, and are made by the prisoners. The clothes are made by them also."

On a large table in the reception room is displayed an assortment of braces, shoes, stocks, register numbers, class numbers, and caps. There are scales and weights for weighing the prisoners when they enter and leave the prison, with a standard measure for ascertaining their height. This room has two windows of the same description as in the prisoners' own clothing store, with a flap, for ventilation in one of them.

We proceeded to the *Bath Room* attached to the reception cells. Here are four slate baths. The bath cells are 11 feet 3 inches long and 4 feet wide, containing slate baths 6 feet long, 2 feet 1 inch wide, and 2 feet 1 inch deep. They are supplied with hot and cold water by means of pipes, and have a waste pipe communicating with the main drain. These bath cells are floored with asphalte.

The passage between the reception cells is floored with Dutch tile.

Before leaving the reception ward we visited the apartment where the prisoners' clothing is fumigated and cleansed from vermin and offensive smell. It is about 16 feet long, 10 feet wide, and 9 feet high, and has a window with a flap for ventilation. There is a large iron furnace here, with a great oven, provided with iron racks to contain bundles in the interior, which are exposed to the action of the heat and the fumes of brimstone. On a large shelf in the room we saw piled a considerable number of bundles of prisoners' clothing which had been cleansed. "We keep them in," said the reception warder, "for twelve or fourteen hours, when they are taken to the prisoners' own clothing room, where they are laid, in bundles systematically arranged, on the shelves in the manner already described."

The reception ward is situated under the long passage entering into the interior of the prison.

. *Cells.*—Leaving the basement of the prison for the present, we returned to the corridors to inspect the cells. There are no dormitories and no associated rooms here, as in several of the other metropolitan prisons. The prisoners are all confined in separate cells. On proceeding with the chief warder into a cell in one of the corridors, we found its dimensions to be 13 feet long, by 7 feet wide, and 9 feet high. In size and arrangements it is exactly similar to the others along the various corridors, and is very nearly as large as the model cells at Pentonville, also on the separate system, the latter being 13⅓ feet long by 7½ feet broad, and 9 feet high.

The furniture consists of a small deal table, an earthenware night-utensil or water-closet, covered with a wooden lid, which serves, as we have already said, as a seat to the prisoner, and a small metal water box fitted into one of the corners of the cell. "By a water box," said the chief warder, "I do not mean that it contains water, but is a shield for the water-tap, to prevent the prisoners tampering with it." The water pipe communicates with the night utensil and washing bowl. There is a gas jet in each cell. In a corner beside the door there are three small shelves. On the upper one generally rests the bedding, rolled up like a lady's muff, as seen in the engraving. On the other shelves are a tin plate, a shining tin pannikin, a wooden spoon, a wooden salt cellar, two combs, a brush, and soap box, with a Bible and prayer book, and one or more library books. The bedding consists of a canvas hammock, a coverlet, two blankets, and one pair of sheets. There are two iron hooks on each side of the cell, on which the hammock is suspended. The bed clothes are all marked with the prison mark.

A copy of the rules of the prison is suspended on the wall, and a list of the dietary prescribed to prisoners by the order of Government. We also see suspended a card containing the prisoner's name, offence, sentence, date of admission, expiration of sentence, his trade, and previous committals (if any).

In each cell is a bell-handle, by which the prisoner is able to communicate his wants to the officer. This bell-handle communicates with the metal plate outside the wall of the cell in the passage, on which is printed the number of the cell.

There is an inspection opening in the door of the cell, covered with glass and protected with a light wire screen, and also an aperture for receiving the food, &c., as in the reception cells.

Here we took particular notice of the dress worn by the prisoners. The clothing in this correctional prison consists of a dark-gray jacket, vest, and trousers, a blue striped cotton shirt, a pair of worsted stockings, a pair of shoes, a stock made of the same materials as the jacket, a pocket handkerchief, flannel shirt and drawers, and a gray cap of the same description as the clothes, with a mask covering the face, having eyelet-holes. A piece of alpaca is inserted over the mouth for freer respiration. At first the mask was made of the same materials as the cap.

On the left arm of the jacket is the register number, *i. e.*, the number the prisoner bears on the register book. The white number in the jacket shown us is "2820." "This," said the chief warder, "is the number of his register when admitted into the prison."

"Every second year the registered number commences afresh. The '5' placed above this number on the same arm indicates the class diet the prisoner is entitled to, which is seen by referring to the prison dietary. Upon the back of the dark-gray jacket is painted in white letters two inches long H.C.W.S., *i. e.*, House of Correction, Wandsworth, Surrey."

On the left breast is a brass hook, with cell number also painted in white, referring to corridor, division, and number of the cell.

Here we asked the chief warder to explain to us in a few words the preliminary process before the criminal is brought to the cell.

He continued :—" When a prisoner is brought to the prison by warrant of commitment signed by one or more of the magistrates belonging to the county of Surrey, or by an order from Sessions or the Central Criminal Court, he is taken to the reception ward, undressed, and a warm bath given him. He is then equipped in prison dress, and brought up into the interior of the prison for the night. In the morning he is examined by the surgeon, who pronounces him fit or otherwise for hard labour. The prisoners not sentenced to hard labour are also examined by the surgeon at the same time. The rules of the prison are read over to them, after which they are sent, with their cards, by the chief warder to their respective cells. We insert a copy of one of those cards which, as we have said, is suspended on the walls of the cell :—" Registered No. 4781. Name, J. F. Religion (in red ink), Roman Catholic. Age, 42. Trade, a labourer. Previous committals, 2, Wandsworth. Offence, misdemeanour, unlawful possession of a pair of boots. Sentence, two calendar months' hard labour. By whom committed, B. C., Esq. Received 27th June, 1861. Expiration of sentence, 26th August."

On the back of this same card is written as follows :—" E, 1-38, June 28, unfit at present. E, 1-8, 2nd August, 10,000. Infirmary, August 6. E, 1-38, August 23."

"From this card you will see," said the chief warder, "that the prisoner was examined by the surgeon on the 28th of June last, and pronounced 'unfit at present.' He was afterwards examined by the surgeon on 2nd August, and considered fit to perform 10,000 revolutions. On 6th August he was taken to the infirmary, and discharged from thence on the 23rd, and finally liberated from prison on the 26th August, on the expiry of his sentence."

*** *Oakum Picking.*—In company with the chief warder we visited several of the cells where the prisoners were engaged picking oakum. This process has been fully and repeatedly described in earlier portions of this work.

A great number of the prisoners of different ages were thus occupied, some of them taking it easy, others labouring with energy to finish their allotted task.

*** *Mat-making.*—Passing along the various corridors, we inspected several of the cells in corridor C, where the prisoners were engaged at mat-making. The chief warder informed us twenty-eight persons were busy at this occupation. We were introduced to the trade instructor, who showed us over his ward and gave us the necessary explanations. The mat frame, as shown in the engraving, consists of two strong upright beams fixed under the arched cell by wooden wedges, with a heavy cross-beam slung by two short ropes to the beams. A cross-bar at the bottom of the frame is fastened down with ropes to pull the warp tight, so

EXTERIOR OF THE SURREY HOUSE OF CORRECTION AT WANDSWORTH.
(From a Photograph by Herbert Watkins, 179, Regent Street.)

CELL, WITH PRISONER AT "CRANK-LABOUR," IN THE SURREY HOUSE OF CORRECTION.

as to make the mats properly. Above the lower cross-beam a flat moveable board 8 inches wide, and 5 feet long, and 1 inch thick, is inserted, with a narrow stick above about $4\frac{1}{2}$ feet long, to reverse the warp. Sometimes they are longer when the mat requires it. There is also another stick projected backward and forward by the hand. A common shoemaker's knife is used to trim the mat in the course of manufacture. There is also a beater with five blunt iron teeth and a short handle, for the purpose of binding the fabric properly together.

These are the implements for making a common diamond cocoa-nut fibred mat. Each mat-maker is furnished with a yard measure for taking its dimensions. The mats are made of cocoa-nut fibre spun into yarn, and the workman in weaving stands in front of his work.

There are other mats made of cocoa-nut fibre yarn plaited, having as many as twenty strands in the plait. After being plaited by some of the prisoners, it is given to others to be made into sennit mats.

We went to another cell, where we were shown a sennit mat. In the course of being made it is fixed on a board with four iron pins, and worked with a sailor's palm, needle, and pincers, a shoemaker's knife, and a hammer.

In another cell we were shown the binding of the mats. On coming from the frame they are brought to a prisoner, who binds them with a needle, palm, and pincers. The deputy-governor informed us that on the day of our visit six prisoners were plaiting sennit for mats.

We visited a different cell, and saw the mats finished by being trimmed with a pair of large garden shears, after which they are ready for sale.

Before leaving the ward for mat-making, we looked into several other cells, to see the prisoners engaged at their work.

In one we saw a boy of about fourteen years of age plaiting coir yarn and cutting the strands with a shoemaker's knife. His mask was up. He had an interesting good-looking countenance, and in his solitary cell appeared to be comfortable and cheerful.

In another cell we found an elderly middle-aged and quiet-looking man similarly engaged. His head was bent down at his work as he busily proceeded with his toil. The cell was well lighted, and the bright sunbeams shone cheerfully on his deal table.

In another cell we saw a young man of about twenty-six years of age busy at mat-making in the frame. He appeared to belong to the lower orders, from his countenance and manner. The sun shone on the frame and mat, and he was active and business-like.

In a different cell we saw another young man, about twenty-one years of age, engaged in a like occupation. He stood by the mat frame with his shirt sleeves rolled up and his arms bare. His white braces were tied in front of his dark-gray prison trousers. Like the other prisoners, his mask was laid aside in his cell. He had a white band tied round his dark-gray cap. When we left he was hammering at the mat with the iron-headed beater.

In another cell we saw a lad of about seventeen, pale-faced and good-looking, sitting before his frame on a board laid across the small table, which was turned up. He was putting the yarn into the frame, and cutting it to the proper length.

In another cell the trade instructor stood beside a prisoner, a boy of fifteen, taking the dimensions of one of the mats suspended on the frame. The lad had a dark string tied round his forehead, to bind up his straggling locks. The chief warder observed—"that in this prison the hair is not cut except for the purpose of cleanliness."

Having finished our inspection of the mat-making ward, we passed with the chief warder by the large window in one of the galleries in corridor C, where a beautiful and extensive prospect stretched around us, beaming under the smile of an unclouded sky. We looked around on a fair spreading vale, finely embroidered with hedgerows and trees, and dotted with straggling cottages, hamlets, and villas, while beyond rose the graceful range of the Surrey hills in the neighbourhood, crowned with woods waving in luxuriant foliage.

The landscape was beginning to assume the fading hues of autumn. We saw the train sweeping along the lovely vale, with its wreath of steam and smoke.

₊ *Shoemaking.*—We also visited the shoemakers' ward, and were introduced to the trade instructor. He told us—"We have twelve shoemakers at work, mostly young men. Three of them are experienced tradesmen; the others are employed as cobblers mending the prisoners' shoes. The chief warder informed us that all the prison shoes are made and repaired by felons in the establishment.

Two prisoners were then engaged in making harness, who were said by the trade instructor to be good workmen. They are making a set of new chaise harness, with German-silver fittings. "We can show you," continued the trade instructor, "some fine specimens of shoemaking, both in the closing and making departments." Taking up a pair of shoes, he said—"There is a pair of fancy shoes made by a prisoner that was liberated a few days ago, who was with us for nine months. And here," he added, "is a pair of gentlemen's boots, with side springs. The closing and making, in regard to workmanship, are fit for the best shop in London."

₊ *Chapel.*—Meantime the bell rang for chapel service, which required the attendance of the chief warder. We left the corridor where we were inspecting the cells, and followed the files of masked prisoners into the chapel, a cheerful-looking commodious building, situated above the long passage leading into the prison. It is capable of containing 422 prisoners in separate stalls, 389 of which are enclosed. There were 12 open stalls in the front seat facing us as we sat alongside the pulpit. When the stalls are full 12 other prisoners can be accommodated on the staircases in the centre and sides of the gallery. The engraving of the chapel presented in an earlier part of this work only gives one-half of the gallery, with the inspection warders overlooking them.

The minister and clerk sit on elevated seats erected in the centre of the chapel somewhat resembling the pulpit in an ordinary chapel, entering by a staircase behind. They sit alongside of each other, with a higher seat for the governor or deputy-governor erected between them, and overlooking them, the governor's seat having a most commanding position, suitable to his superior office. In front of the elevated seats occupied by the governor, chaplain, and clerk, are inscribed the apostles' creed, Lord's prayer, and ten commandments. In an enclosure beneath the pulpit are the communion table, and two chairs covered with puce cloth. Round the altar are cushions made of blue serge. Between this enclosure and the bottom of the gallery is an open space paved with Dutch tile, about 26 feet long and 12 broad, in the form of a crescent.

The first block of seats on each side is similar in construction to those described in Pentonville prison. The rest of the seats behind these and above are opened by doors in the back and front. They are kept locked during service, and are unlocked after it is over, for the prisoners to return to their cells.

There are galleries for the male and female officers ranged around the back and sides of the pulpit, with two seats on each side of the area beneath. A high wooden partition screens the females from the view of the male prisoners on the opposite side of the gallery.

In the centre of the gallery facing the pulpit a clock has been placed for the convenience of the chaplain.

There are places of inspection for the officers, generally two on each side of the gallery, in front of the criminals, as at Pentonville.

The chapel is well lighted by numerous iron-framed windows in the sides and roof, and is ventilated in the roof. In the winter season it is heated by Haden's patent heating apparatus.

Off the chapel is a small vestry.

'The prisoners enter the chapel by means of two staircases communicating with the central hall, and by a covered bridge leading from the upper part of the A and E wings.

As we looked around us, the scene was a novel and peculiar one. When the prisoners were seated in their stalls, while the assistant chaplain was conducting the service, and the assistant teacher officiating as clerk in the responses, from our seat we could not see any of the prisoners in the galleries with the exception of one little boy in the front seat, next to the pulpit, on the one side, and a middle-aged woman and several young girls on the other. The whole of the prisoners were fully under the inspection of the deputy-governor above us, and of the warders over the galleries, but were hid from our view. The middle-aged woman listened with very becoming demeanour, read her prayer-book, and attended carefully to the service. A little girl about twelve years of age sat by her side, with a well-formed, pale, interesting countenance, and fair hair, very unlike a felon. She noticed us to be a stranger, and eyed us with evident curiosity. The little boy in the front seat was clad in the dark prison dress. He was a sharp little fellow, with a keen dark eye, and had been newly brought into prison. Though young in years, he had the callous manner of an old offender. He sat part of the time during service looking up to the chaplain with his hands clasped in each other, with the greatest coolness and unconcern, as though the prison to him was a familiar scene.

The prisoners stood up occasionally during the service, when we saw their heads peering over the edges of the stalls. Most of them were from seventeen to thirty years of age. Some of them had a pleasing countenance, and not a few had a full intellectual brow. We only saw one bald-headed man among them. From our position we did not have so good a view of the female prisoners in their blue prison dress, but from the slight glance we had of them, they appeared to have generally a more degraded appearance than the males.

We observed the registered numbers on the separate stalls, corresponding with the number of the prisoner's cell, which enables the warders to detect any impropriety during service, such as scratching on the panels of the stalls. On one of the occasions when we were present at service, a complaint was brought before the deputy-governor that one of the prisoners had scribbled in his stall.

In consequence of the large number of prisoners in Wandsworth prison, and the limited number of seats in the chapel, there are four services held on Sundays, so that each prisoner goes to chapel twice. The first service in the morning contains as many males as the chapel can conveniently hold, about 400. At the second the rest of the males are present, and the whole of the females. The third is attended by the whole of the females, and the portion of the males who were at the second service; and the prisoners who were at the morning service are present at the fourth and last.

The first service begins at nine o'clock, the second at a quarter to eleven, the third at a quarter to two, and the fourth at three o'clock.

By this arrangement both parties, male and female, attend chapel twice on Sunday, and hear a sermon once.

The prisoners are unmasked while at divine service in the chapel, as well as while in their separate cells.

₊ *Exercising Grounds.*—We passed on to the exercising ground, situated on the north-eastern corner of the boundary walls at the end of E wing. There are three circles in each exercising ground. A warder patrols in the second or centre one, while in the other two on each side of him the prisoners are walking at stated distances from each other. The outer-most and largest circle is for the stronger and more athletic men, and the inner for weak persons and boys. At the time of our visit there were upwards of 50 prisoners exercising on this ground. Between the outer and second circles a crop of parsnips was planted, and within the other circles potatoes had been recently dug up. The neighbouring ground in

sight between the D and E wings was planted with potatoes, onions, and cabbages. The prisoners walked with their faces masked, and their hands behind their back, in quiet and apparently thoughtful attitude. They were very orderly during our visit, and scarcely a word was uttered by the officers. The day was bright and sunny, which gave a more cheerful tone to the scene. Each prisoner kept steadily about four yards apart. Sometimes they came too close to each other for the purpose of talking, and were recalled by the manly voice of the warders—" No. 44, not so close there," or "Not so quick, 48." The only sound we heard within the grounds was the pattering of their feet as they steadily went round the circles, and the occasional calls of the officers. Another warder walked near to the outer circle, to keep a sharp scrutiny over the prisoners. Both officers were attired in white trousers, blue surtout coats, and caps with peaks, with a dark shining leather pouch, like a cartouch box, slung behind.

They generally continue out for an hour each day in the exercising grounds, when another detachment of prisoners take their places. Their movements are in a great measure similar to those at Pentonville, so that it is unnecessary to give a fuller recital.

The chief warder pointed out to us, among the masked men exercising in dark gray dress, the little dwarf whose tattered clothes we saw in the prisoners' own clothes store-room. He had a very diminutive appearance alongside of the other criminals, and sauntered very carelessly in a stooping posture. The prison dress was a comfortable change to him, as to many others on the ground, whose clothes when at large are in a squalid and wretched condition.

We noticed a tall athletic man, evidently of a superior order to the generality of the prisoners, who had been guilty of embezzling the property of his master, a draper in the metropolis.

Although the prisoners are masked to conceal their features, yet from the outlines of their form as seen through the prison dress, and from their gait, they are generally recognizable by their 'pals' and acquaintances in the prison.

₊ *The Pump House.*—We afterwards proceeded to visit the wards where the prisoners are subjected to hard labour. Leaving the exercising ground, and passing the end of D wing, the pump-house presented itself to our view, about twenty yards from the junction of the C and D wings. The greater part of the surrounding ground is cultivated and filled up with leeks and cabbages. The pump-house is an oblong building about 54 feet long and 32 feet broad. The machinery runs along the centre of the building. There are twelve stalls on each side, each of them furnished with a handle connected with the central machinery, which, when set in motion, conveys the water into cisterns on the roof of the prison. The prisoners are employed on these machines an hour at a time, and during that period rest three times for five minutes, so that they are kept working forty-five minutes. They are in charge of two officers. One is stationed outside the building, and the other on the floor above the men at the pumps, overlooking them. On each side of the pump-house is a urinal and water closet for the use of the prisoners.

The warder outside walks round the pump-house, and attends to the wants of the prisoners. It is also his duty to look after the changing of the prisoners, and to intimate the same to the officer inside the prison, who prepares a fresh gang of men.

The duty of the officer inside the pump-house is to see that the prisoners do their work steadily, and to intimate any irregularity or idleness in his report book to the deputy governor. The number of revolutions performed at the pumps the day before our visit was 4703, which is about the average number.

The prison and the other houses connected with the establishment adjoining the boundary wall are supplied by water drawn from an artesian well, 480 feet deep, immediately beneath the pump-house.

The water is first conveyed into the main cistern, from which it is conducted through all parts of the male and female prisons. Between 5000 and 6000 gallons of water are pumped daily during working days.

We observed a wooden indicator, about 4 feet 6 inches in length, on the D wing, showing the depth of water in the main cistern.

₊ *Mill House.*—We next visited the grinding mills on the basement of A wing. In this ward of the prison, wheat is ground by the prisoners in separate cells by hand-mills, patented by Dean & Sons, Birmingham. They are turned by hand labour similar to a grindstone, and are considered hard labour. The prisoners are kept three hours a-day on these hand-mills, and grind on an average half a bushel during that time, when they are relieved by other prisoners, who execute the same amount of work. There are twenty of these mills. Nineteen of them are in steady work, and one is generally kept unused for the miller to dress the stones. The prisoners engaged at this hard labour fill up the rest of their time picking oakum.

The mills on an average grind a bushel a-day. They grind the wheat and dress the flour. The passage between these cells is supported by iron girders and pillars, and paved with York slab. There is a large bin at one end for the purpose of mixing the flour, and scales and weights for measuring it. In the passage we observed two rows of sacks filled with flour, bran, and wheat, besides a considerable number of empty sacks.

Each cell in this ward has an inspection plate, through which the officer can overlook the prisoner at his toil; and there is a signal plate outside the cell, by which the prisoner can apprise the officer in case of necessity.

₊ *Hard Labour Machines.*—We also inspected the hard-labour machines in corridor E 1, patented by Botten. They move by a crank hand, and perform on an average 12,000 revolutions a-day. The prisoner in the first cell we visited had to perform 12,000 revolutions; some have only 10,000. There is an indicator on the machine to tell the amount of work performed.

The hard-labour machine consists of an iron instrument in a square wooden box, supported on a wooden cylinder, resting on a broad wooden base.

The chief warder, pointing to the hard-labour machine in the cell, said to the warder in attendance :—" Open this, Mr. Hooper, and explain shortly the nature of the machinery."

" These weights here," said the officer, pointing to the weights enclosed in the wooden box, " are for regulating the pressure. This drum works within these two caps, one beneath and one at the top. There is a tongue underneath here that acts on a roller, which also regulates the pressure, and prevents the machine from being turned in any other way than one. There is also a dial seen from the exterior of the wooden box, which is marked for 16,000 revolutions, and the hand signifies the number performed."

The pressure can be altered, and the hard labour consequently lightened or increased, by removing the weights, or adding to them. The machine without the weights is 7 lbs. pressure. Two weights added to it, increase the pressure to 10 lbs., and the whole of the weights introduced brings it to 12 lbs.

The pressure of the machine is prescribed by the medical officer. There are 100 machines, all in E 1, some have wood and others have iron covers.

We went with the deputy governor over several of the cells to see the prisoners engaged at this labour.

In one cell in E 2, we saw a lad of seventeen years of age, with reddish hair, and amiable countenance, resting beside the machine, as if exhausted with the work. He soon after resumed, and appeared to be good-humoured at his toil, working slowly and steadily; occasionally tossing his head back to throw the hair from over his brow.

A young man sat in the corner of another cell with his cheek leaning on his hand, and his elbow resting on the table. He appeared to be absorbed reading. The labour machine stood beside him, with the handle pointing upwards, as if he were exhausted, and was recruiting his strength, by taking a glance at some book which interested him.

In another cell, a young man, under the middle size, was stripped to his shirt and trousers at the labour machine, bending over it with his temples bound with a handkerchief. His movement was rather stiff, as though he were exhausted with the work.

In a different cell, a man stood by the machine with his one hand resting on it, tired with the work, and was wiping his face with a towel. He was a heavy-browed young man, apparently belonging to the lower orders.

⁎ *School.*—We accompanied the chief warder into the juvenile school-room, where we were introduced to the teacher, Mr. Ellis, a silver-headed, kind, and intelligent officer. He was then engaged with his class. The pupils were ranged in stalls along the back of a large well-lighted airy room under the chapel. There were nineteen scholars present, ranging from seven to thirteen years of age. They had on the dark gray prison dress; their hair uncut, and many of them of an interesting appearance, very unlike criminals. Many of them had a clear and ingenuous expression.

One little pale-faced boy was reading his lesson to his kind-hearted teacher. "Three of them," said Mr. Ellis, "don't know the alphabet, nor even the Lord's Prayer. Ten of the class are able to read the Testament. The other six are in the primer." Some of the boys in their separate stalls in the class-room were busy writing copies on their slate. One boy had copied from a Bible, which lay before him, a verse of the 26th chapter of Proverbs: "As snow in summer, as rain in harvest, so honour is not seemly for a fool!" He was a sharp-eyed lad of fourteen, with a finely formed countenance.

Another boy, with a clear, gentle, deep eye, was busy writing on his slate, "In all labour there is profit." His fingers were dark with picking oakum.

One lad, with a dark eye and broad face, was writing over and over upon his slate the word "property," in very neat penmanship. On the other side of his slate he had a question in simple proportion.

Many of these boys had a well formed countenance, and most of them looked very intelligent, more so than the generality we meet in the street. Some of them had a fine full forehead. Their demeanour towards their officer was respectful yet cheerful. The school-room was well-lighted, better than many of the public schools over the metropolis.

On the walls were suspended a map of the World, a map of England and Wales, and another showing the travels of Saint Paul. There was a large black board in the apartment. The teacher sat beside a large table in front of his pupils.

There is a stove for heating the school in winter, and two presses with shelves for school books, with pigeon-holes to contain tracts. There were a number of Bibles and Prayer-books in the two presses.

From the juvenile class-room we went with the chief warder to the adult class, which is taught in the chapel, and in that portion of it seen in the engraving. The assistant-teacher, whom we saw officiating as clerk in the chapel, was here busy with his class. He stood in front of it, in the elevated station usually occupied by one of the inspection warders, with the Bible in his hand, and a large black board before him. On this board were written the words, "The Lord is gracious, his mercy is everlasting, and his truth endureth to all generations."

He was engaged at the Bible lesson. The prisoners, who were of the same general appearance as those we saw in the chapel, were very respectful. We heard the teacher chide one of the men for frivolity, and threaten to send him out of the class-room. Others he commended in a kind spirit for the manner in which they read their lesson. They generally read in a quiet tone; some with great stumbling and hesitation, and others very fluently. Some of them had an engaging appearance, and had nothing in their countenance to indicate their criminal character. There were forty-three in the class. While the others were reading, the rest were writing on their slates, as in the juvenile class-room.

The senior teacher, Mr. Ellis, informed us they had three classes a-day—two for adults, and one for juveniles. The first adult class met four times, and the second and third three times a-week. The chapel is generally occupied the whole day with the school and chapel services. "Some of the juveniles" the teacher stated, "learn their letters in the prison, and improve very much. Others are very hardened and careless, though their mind is in other respects very acute. Some of them will not give attention to learning. Their behaviour is in general good, though I sometimes have to bring a few refractory pupils before the governor."

"Many of the adults," said Mr. Ellis, "display considerable acquaintance with Bible knowledge, and all of them have a Bible in their cells. I have had long experience in prisons under different systems of prison discipline—the separate system as well as the others, and have 130 scholars at present under my care. I go round and invite them, or they apply to come. Boys under fourteen are compelled to attend the class. In the case of those more advanced it is voluntary."

"In reference to the juvenile criminals, strange to say, some of them are able to write who cannot read, and six of them cannot write." On turning to his note-book Mr. Ellis continued, "Two of the juveniles have been three times in prison; one has been five times; two of them twice; and one four times. My decided opinion is that the chief fault in many cases lies with the parents. The boys are either the children of drunkards, or have lost their parents and are without proper guardians. They are generally neglected or mistrained, and have not had a proper opportunity of learning to do their duty."

₊ *The Bakery.*—We also inspected the bakery, which is situated near the kitchen, and were introduced to the baker. "I have to call your attention," said Mr. Claridge, "to the two nine-bushel ovens made by 'Thomas Powell,' Lisle Street, Leicester Square, London. They are registered, and are peculiar in their construction. The fire enters them by a furnace heated with coals, and passes into a descending flue in connection with the boiler-house shaft. These ovens are now coming into general use. The time they take to heat is about three quarters of an hour."

Having inquired as to the work done at the bakery, Mr. Claridge continued, "I have four men assisting me in the bakehouse. We commence to work at six o'clock in the morning, when we put in the sponge with one of Stevens' patent dough-making machines. This machine is superior to hand labour in preparing the dough. At seven o'clock the assistant bakers (prisoners) leave the bakehouse to attend chapel. On their return they clean and prepare the bread. After breakfast, the bread prepared on the previous day is put into a basket ready for delivery to the storekeeper at ten o'clock, and carefully weighed."

In reference to the preparation of the bread, the baker informed us, "The dough after lying an hour is thrown out by the machine and weighed off to be made into the several loaves. The loaves are baked three-quarters of an hour. We generally have about four batches. The ovens hold about 1200 of the six ounce, and about 1000 of the eight ounce loaves. We finish work about half-past five, when the prisoners who officiate as assistant bakers are taken back to their different cells.

"The bread remains in the bakehouse for the night, and is delivered to the storekeeper in the morning, as before stated. The bread is brown, of a coarse but wholesome quality. In addition to this we prepare some of finer flour for the infirmary."

The bakehouse is situated at the end of the kitchen, and is separated from the scullery by a passage leading to the female prison, and entered by a door always kept locked, the key of which is kept by the baker. There is another door opposite leading into the courtyard, communicating with the stores. The bakery is about forty feet long and thirteen feet broad. The two ovens occupy the inner end of the building, and there are three tables for "scaling" off the dough. The dough machine is close to the ovens. There is a sink supplied with hot and cold water by means of pipes from the cisterns above, and a bread-rack on which to place the bread when taken from the ovens.

There is an extra trough in addition to the dough machine, which is seldom required.

The floor is paved with York slabs, and partly with Dutch tile. The apartment is high and airy, lighted from a glass roof extending along the whole length of the bakehouse. During the summer season an awning is suspended underneath the glass to screen the sunlight.

** Kitchen.—During our visit to Wandsworth Prison, we several times visited the spacious kitchen, which is a long airy apartment forty-five feet long and thirty-nine feet wide, somewhat similar to the bakery. There are three long dressers with shelves underneath.

Having asked Mr. Mumford, the cook, as to the persons employed in the kitchen, he stated, "I have an officer assisting me, and four prisoners. There are four seventy gallon steam coppers for cooking soup, gruel, etc., along with four steamers for cooking potatoes. As to the work," he added, "we commence our duties in the kitchen at half-past five, by getting the morning's cocoa and gruel prepared. Before this the night watchman comes down to the boiler-house to get up the steam. At six o'clock the men come down to assist. At a quarter before seven the cocoa and gruel are taken from the coppers, and at half-past seven breakfast is sent to the female prisoners, and at the same time breakfast is served out to the prisoners in the male prison. The bread is carried away in baskets, and the gruel in tin pannikins, as described in the other prisons. At this time the cook draws stores for the day's issue. Dinner, consisting of meat and potatoes, is prepared by one o'clock, and sent up to the various corridors. And at seven o'clock in the evening supper is made ready, when oatmeal, gruel, and bread are served out, which closes the culinary labours of the day.

The butcher meat served out to the prisoners, as well as potatoes, are of good quality and carefully prepared; superior to what is generally sold in many respectable eating-houses in the metropolis.

** Punishment Cells.—We visited the punishment cells, which are fourteen in number; seven of them being lighted with a small iron-framed window, and seven of them being completely dark.

They have double doors, which are kept locked, to prevent effectually any communication from without. We entered one of those dark cells which did not admit a single beam of light when the doors were closed upon us, and all around us was as silent as the grave. The furniture of these cells consists of an iron bedstead, securely fixed in the floor, and a water-closet. There is also a bell to communicate with the officers of the prison in case of sickness, and a trap in the door to convey food as in the other cells. When under confinement here, the prisoners are kept on bread and water. There is no difference between the fourteen punishment cells except that seven of them have an iron-framed window, and the other seven have not. They are of the same dimensions as the ordinary cells in the corridors above. The bedding at night consists of a straw mattress, two blankets, and a rug handed in at nine o'clock in the evening, and taken away in the morning; when a tub of water is given to the prisoners for the purpose of performing their ablutions.

At the time of our second visit there were eight criminals in the punishment cells of the male prison, for the following offences :—For shouting in cell; for exposing their features;

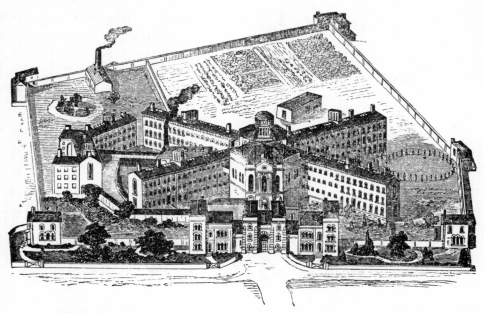

BIRD'S-EYE VIEW OF THE SURREY HOUSE OF CORRECTION AT WANDSWORTH.

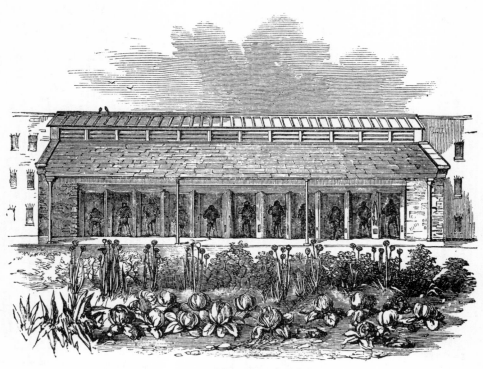

PUMP-ROOM AT WANDSWORTH PRISON.

(From a Photograph by Herbert Watkins, 179, Regent Street.)

for refusing to work, and insolence to officer; for taking a library book out of another prisoner's cell when unlocked for chapel; for spitting on the leaves of his Bible; for idleness at hard-labour machine, and talking at exercise. We may add, that two females were then in the punishment cells of the female prison, one for eating soap, which is sometimes done to get upon the sick-list, and have better diet, or to be relieved from labour; and the other was punished for disobedience to her officer.

In another cell, under basement D, we saw a whipping-post, where juvenile criminals are occasionally flogged by order of the magistrates. This is done by means of a birch-rod, both of which are seen in the engravings.

Near to this cell is a padded-room, used in extreme cases for refractory prisoners. It is similar to those in lunatic asylums.

At the time of our second visit to Wandsworth Prison, the following was a classification of the prisoners according to their respective employments:—

Mat-making	32	Cooper		1
Plaiting sennit	3	Upholsterer		1
Tailoring	17	Bakers		4
Shoemakers	14	Tinman, 1; bookbinder 1		2
Mechanics—3 carpenters	3	At pumps		24
Smiths	1	On the flour-mills		43
Labourers (53), including cooks	53	Unfit for labour in cell, on surgeon's		
Stokers, 2; gardeners, 8	10	list, yet not sufficiently indisposed		
Cleaners and others employed about		for infirmary		3
prison	24	Punishments		8
Whitewashers	8	In infirmary		10
Central hall cleaner	1	Oakum pickers		170
Chapel cleaners	2	Hard-labour machines		95
Sundry trades	11	Woodcutter		1
Painters	3			

Total of males 544

*** *Store-rooms.*—We were introduced by the deputy governor to Mr. Goddard, the store-keeper, who led us through an extensive range of store-rooms in the area of the prison, beneath the corridors. In one apartment we found carefully assorted piles of prisoners' clothing, of all sizes; vests, jackets, trousers, caps, stockings, striped cotton shirts, flannel shirts, drawers, and shoes.

There was a large store of raw materials to be made up into prison clothes, as required. Calico, for drawers; canvas, for hammocks; flannel, for shirts and drawers; sheeting, for shirts; huckaback, for towels; with other furnishings. In these general stores are arranged articles for female clothing, such as striped shifting; blue serge, for petticoats; alpaca, for veils, worn in the place of masks, etc.

There are, also, tastefully arranged stores of tapes, threads, cottons, buttons, needles, pins, etc. "In addition to these," said the storekeeper, "we have materials for making officers' uniforms; superfine blue cloth, pilot and doeskin, and chamois leather. The prisoners' clothing," he informed us, "is also made by the prisoners. The officers' clothes," he also added, "are made and issued once a-year, consisting of a uniform surtout coat, trousers, vest, cap, belt, and pouch. Also a great-coat once in three years, together with a pair of shoes."

In the stores we found wools, for making fancy mats; silk-twists, for uniforms; silk-thread, braid, needles, and here are also racks filled with 500 or 600 new blankets, ready for issue, with a number of yellowish-brown rugs, similar to those previously described.

There are huge bales of gray army cloth for prisoners' clothing.

WHIP, OR ROD, WANDSWORTH.

WHIPPING-POST, WANDSWORTH.

We visited an apartment containing quantities of ironmongery for the use of the carpenters and other tradesmen in prison; nails, screws, brass nails, etc. We also saw racks piled with shoes, male and female, neatly arranged in sizes.

From this we passed into a general store-room containing numerous articles of prison manufacture, such as clothes-baskets, bushel-baskets, bread-baskets, brushes, coir and fancy mats; also brushes of all descriptions, cell-brushes, scrubbing, blacklead, whitewash, and paint brushes, mops, shaving bowls, boxes for collecting dust in the cells, and mattresses of cocoa-nut fibre, for the sick in the infirmary.

The store-keeper stated, " that the infirmary mattresses made by prisoners, from coir fibre, were found superior to flock or horse-hair, and are preferred by the medical men in this institution."

There we were shown a table covered with all sorts of tools required in the establishment; bakers' dough knives, and knives for shoemakers, bookbinders, and painters; also hammers, pincers, and gimlets, and other iron implements.

We accompanied the storekeeper and chief warder to the provision store, and saw the bread received from the bake-house. The shelves around the room were full of large baskets loaded with small loaves of two different sizes. There is bread of a finer quality made for the infirmary of pure white flour. The common bread is of a coarser quality, but very sound and nutritious. There are about fifty pounds of infirmary bread baked daily." The baker stated, " these huge piles of loaves were baked the preceding day for the use of the prisoners."

In this store was a large quantity of oatmeal, which we also inspected, with large bins of rice, barley, sugar, yellow split pease, and chocolate-coloured cocoa-nuts. There are also quantities of sago, arrowroot, mustard, pepper, and coffee.

We observed a windmill for grinding the small brown cocoa-nuts, like beans, for the prisoners' breakfast. This cocoa is much superior in quality to what is generally sold in the shops; and, being ground and prepared in the prison, is perfectly free from adulteration. There is also a weighing machine to weigh all the bread and provisions received in the store.

In another part of the store-room was a large puncheon of treacle for dietary purposes, and a large block of salt, white as newly fallen snow.

In a corner of this store-room was a large heap of potatoes, which the chief warder informed us were grown in the prison-ground. They are of the kind termed " Shaws " and " Regents," of superior quality.

The stores, which are very extensive, farther contain a large quantity of whiting, bath-bricks, jute, birch-brooms, oils of various kinds, sperm, sweet, and lamp; the lamp oils being used by the engineers in the machinery, etc., and the sweet oils for the hand-labour machines.

We were shown into another store, where we saw stacks of the best pale yellow soap, several barrels of beer, bottles of stout, bottled wines, port and sherry, also brandy and gin. The latter articles are supplied for the infirmary, and are at the discretion of the surgeon.

These stores are all well ventilated, and kept by Mr. R. H. Goddard in a very careful and systematic way.

We were next shown into the wheat and flour store, which contains a large quantity of wheat ready for grinding, besides a considerable quantity of flour in sacks, and the offal from the wheat termed bran. The wheat is of superior quality, weighing 62 lbs. a bushel.

In this store is a " smutting " machine for cleaning the grain before it is sent to the mills for grinding. On inspecting it, we were surprised to find the quantity of dust and dirt which was extracted. It is worked by hand-labour, and secures greater cleanliness.

We were next shown a large two stone bran-mill, erected for the purpose of regrinding the bran made from the wheat, to extract the flour more effectually. This mill is wrought by hand-labour. There are three compartments in the interior for fine flour, pollard, and offal. From the peculiar way in which the stones are cut, the mill thoroughly cleanses the flour from the bran.

On the following day we resumed our visit to Wandsworth Prison, when Mr. Goddard showed us over the remainder of his stores.

On entering a large store-room in the B basement, we found a huge pile of materials for making mats. In one compartment we saw a stack of yellowish cocoa fibred yarns for mat-making. They are technically termed "coir dolls." We observed bales of Bombay yarn for the same purpose, also large bags containing cuttings of the coir, commonly called "ends," which are issued to female prisoners, and picked into fibre.

In the same store-room we saw bundles of picked coir of one quarter cwt. each. This fibre is sold for many purposes. For example, it is disposed of to manufacturers for mattress or chair stuffing, in the place of horse-hair.

We also found large quantities of sacks made by the prisoners, and sold to farmers and millers. The storekeeper stated, "He had about 1000 yards of sacking on hand." In this apartment were stacks of diamond and sennit mats made from coir. "Here," said the storekeeper, "we have fancy mats, rope and sennit mats, and there are always a large quantity on hand. The sale of these articles," he said, "was very extensive." On looking to various specimens they were evidently of good quality.

We were shown into a store of old rope or junk, where we saw a prisoner engaged chopping it in pieces with a broad axe, for the purpose of being picked into oakum.

In an adjoining gloomy store-room were huge heaps of junk, and in another apartment were bundles of picked oakum of half a hundred weight each, ready for sale. Also a large pile of sacks filled with tailors' cuttings, and oakum waste sold for the benefit of the county.

We were afterwards introduced into a lighter and more cheerful store-room, containing tubs, pails, and buckets, made by the prisoners, which closed our inspection of the vast stores of this admirably managed prison.

We ascertained that the mats, rugs, etc., manufactured here, are not contracted for by mercantile establishments, as in Holloway and several other Metropolitan prisons, where tradesmen are introduced to superintend this department. They are made entirely under the inspection of the warders of the prison, and are afterwards disposed of by the prison officials; hence they generally have a great quantity of raw material and a large stock of manufactured goods on hand. The discipline of Wandsworth House of Correction is carried on with military precision, but the arrangements at Holloway prison, in reference to *productive labour*, are certainly far superior, and are well worthy the serious consideration of the authorities of the former prison, in many respects so excellently managed. At Holloway there are no hand labour machines, as at Wandsworth, used for no earthly purpose but for "grinding the wind." Every description of prison-work there has a useful tendency, and even the hard labour on the treadwheel is ingeniously economized to pump water for the use of the prison.

¶ iii.—Δ.

The Female Prison.

On entering the female prison, we were introduced by the governor to the matron, who kindly allowed her chief warder to guide us over the interior.

We retraced our steps to a small apartment on the left hand side of the gravelled court-yard, in front of the male prison, where the female prisoners are received by the governor on leaving the prison vans, prior to being admitted by the gatekeeper, a lady-like experienced officer, within the female branch of the establishment. They are conducted along a covered walk, paved with Dutch tile, leading by a grass-plot and through the matron's garden, to a flight of steps in front of the F wing. The garden is beautifully adorned with parterres of flowers, roses, dahlias, and geraniums, and rare plants, while a row of young evergreen laurels festoon the outer side of the entry to the female prison.

There is a small entrance hall in front of the prison, on the right hand side of which is a door leading to the infirmary, and on the left to the matron's private apartments, of which the female chief warder alone possesses a key, by which she can visit her at any hour of the day or night.

*** *The Reception Ward.*—We descend by a staircase on our left hand to the reception ward, on the basement of F wing, which is about fifty-seven feet long and fifteen feet broad. The roof is arched in the centre, spanned by iron girders, and supported from beneath on metal pillars. It is floored with Dutch tile, and lighted by the glass panelled entrance door as well as from the cells on each side, while the walls around are beautifully whitewashed. There is a small desk in this ward where the reception warder takes down a minute description of the various prisoners as they enter; and also a large press where a supply of clean linen is kept for the use of the prisoners, with a number of shining tins piled over it. At the extremity of the ward, is a small recess, with a water-tap and sink for cleansing purposes, as well as for the use of the prisoners.

On the right hand as we enter, there are two slate baths supplied with hot and cold water, similar to those in the male prison, with footboards attached to them for the convenience of the prisoners. There are eight reception cells in this ward of about the same dimensions as those in the male prison, furnished with an iron bedstead, straw mattress, blankets and coverlet, and also a water-tap, etc., as in the other cells. They are floored with asphalt, and well-lighted and ventilated. In dimensions they are twelve feet seven inches long, six feet seven inches wide, and seven feet ten inches at the bottom, and nine feet at the top of the arch.

We accompanied the reception warder to the *prisoners' own clothing-room*, which consists of two cells, with a framework of racks in the centre, and others along the walls copiously supplied with bundles of apparel of different hues and textures, carefully assorted.

"There," said the reception warder, pointing to the top of the centre racks, "are the clothes of the prisoners confined for two years' for misdemeanors and felonies. For example, here are the clothes of a schoolmistress, sentenced to three years' imprisonment for maltreating a child who had been placed under her care, consisting, as you see, of a black dress, gray shawl, black bonnet, and under-clothing; and here is a bundle belonging to a woman to be confined two years for robbing a man with violence in the Waterloo Road."

Turning to a series of racks in another side of the room, "Here are the clothes of women confined for twelve months—being chiefly pickpockets, shoplifters, etc."

We found the most of the clothing in this room was in tolerably good condition, though much of it was of a plainer sort, belonging to persons of the lower orders. The chief warder informed us, "there is only one fashionably-dressed prisoner at present in custody."

On proceeding to *another store-room* of nearly similar dimensions, situated in the dressing-room ward, where the prisoners are equipped in their own clothing before they are discharged, we found it to be of similar dimensions to the one described. We noticed the bundles here were of an inferior description, some of them ragged and dirty, and without a bonnet. The chief warder informed us, "These belong to prisoners mostly confined for short terms of imprisonment—under two months;" and continued that, "they chiefly belong to females guilty of assault, and drunken and disorderly conduct—some of them paupers." The reception warder conducted us into an adjoining cell, and showed us the clothes of a prisoner which had been spread out to dry. The smell was very disagreeable. They consisted of an old ragged cotton skirt, the colours being almost obliterated, another drab merino skirt, hanging in tatters; an old dark jacket and cap; the shoes were old and rent, and covered with mud. "The clothes are in such a pitiable condition," observed the chief warder, "no rag-shop would receive them, yet they belong to a stout, good-looking woman about twenty-six years of age, to be confined seven days for drunkenness."

The reception warder stated, "The generality of our prisoners consists of persons guilty of petty felonies, drunken and riotous conduct, picking pockets and shoplifting, coining and uttering base coin."

There is a large cupboard in the reception ward containing shelves stored with various articles of prison dress, consisting of blue woollen and brown serge petticoats, calico under-clothing, blue cotton jackets and neckerchiefs, gray jean stays, blue worsted stockings, white calico caps, and small black alpaca veils, used as masks, along with stout pairs of shoes. The prisoners who wear flannel on their admission to the prison, are allowed the same while under confinement.

The dressing ward is about fifty-one feet long and eighteen feet wide, paved and roofed similar to the reception ward, and consists of six cells, each of them furnished with an iron bedstead. The prisoners are dressed and get their breakfast here prior to their being taken to the governor to be discharged.

When the prisoners arrive, they are examined either by the matron or chief warder, in the small lobby at the entrance to the prison. They are then passed down to the reception warder, when they are stripped of their clothing, bathed, and equipped in prison dress, and after being inspected by the surgeon are taken to their respective wards.

In answer to our inquiry, the reception warder stated, "I enter all the prisoners in the register, and affix the register number to the sleeve of their blue jacket, as well as the number of their cells."

₊ *Central Hall.*—We proceeded up a staircase leading through a strong iron-grating on the right hand side of corridor F to the central hall adjoining, with three corridors radiating around it. In the centre are two large well-chiselled stones of a sexagonal form, surrounded with a massive perforated iron-grating of like form, about six feet in diameter, which gives light to the store-rooms on the basement. The central hall is about twenty-four feet in diameter, having a lofty roof rising in the form of a sexagon, with sash windows near the top. Each of the corridors is about 144 feet long, with a circular arched massive roof, lighted by ample sky-lights, and with a long window at the extremity nearly the size of the corridor. There are two galleries in each corridor similar to the male prison, with iron bridges at each extremity, and on the top of the rails is a truck to convey the prisoners' food. The corridors are paved with York slab, and are furnished with food carriages to convey the trays with provisions along the lower cells. A circular staircase leads down to the store-rooms below, between corridors G and H.

In the central hall, between corridors F and G, there is a brass bell-pull, connected with a gong over the second landing. It is used in conducting the various duties of the day, and is sounded by understood signals. There are three smaller bells, one communicating with the front door, another with the matron's private apartment, and another with the chief warder's sitting-room.

As we entered the inner hall, a long file of female prisoners in their dark gray cloaks and alpaca veils, were returning from the chapel service. They entered by the door in front of the prison, and moved along with slow and measured step at stated distances, under the inspection of several female warders, and dispersed to their respective cells in the various corridors, presenting a very animated scene. The numbers of their cells and divisions are attached to their cloaks in white letters, by which their officers are able to distinguish them. As we passed, one of the prisoners had overstepped her place, and was recalled to order by the voice of the chief warder, "Fall back, G 3.18." Several female warders were stationed in different galleries as they passed to overlook their movements, many of them

ADULT SCHOOL IN THE CHAPEL, ON THE SEPARATE SYSTEM, AT THE SURREY
HOUSE OF CORRECTION, WANDSWORTH.

elegantly attired in mourning dresses on account of the recent death of Prince Albert. As the prisoners marched along with military order and precision, the matron glanced along the corridors to see that her officers were all in their proper place, when she returned to her office. Soon after we observed her step into a cell opposite, where one of the prisoners—an old woman, a cripple—had been absent from chapel.

We heard the slamming of the doors of the various cells. The chief warder informed us, " It is the imperative duty of the warders of the different divisions to see that the cells are properly shut."

Soon after we saw a number of male prisoners pass along one of the galleries of corridor F under the care of a warder of the male prison, who had been engaged repairing and painting an empty ward in corridor H. Meantime the gong sounded for dinner, when the storekeeper, attended by three prisoners, went down-stairs to the basement to receive the trays of provisions from the kitchen, which were forthwith served up in the various corridors, as in the male prison.

*** *Matron's Clerk.*—We were introduced by the chief warder to the matron's clerk, who furnished us with the following list of the cells, and the manner in which they are at present occupied :—

		No. of Cells.	No. of Prisoners.
Corridor F	1	14	8
,,	2	21	20
,,	3	23	22
,, G	1	28	23
,,	2	29	18
,,	3	29	21
,, H	1	24	19
,,	2	29 not occupied, as it is under repair.	
,,	3	29	25
Infirmary			10
Reception ward			0
Punishment cells			0
Total			166

The greatest number of prisoners in one day during the last year . 210
The smallest number ,, ,, ,, . 134
The average number ,, ,, ,, . 170

The official staff consists of the matron, chief warder, store-keeper, matron's clerk, reception warder, infirmary warder, laundry warder, and assistant-laundry warder, eight common warders, the schoolmistress and the portress, who also discharges duties as a warder in corridor F.

We were shown a number of books in reference to the treatment of the prisoners, etc., carefully kept. Our attention was particularly called to one of them relating to Roman Catholics. The following judicious regulation was prefixed to it :—

"The matron's clerk will from henceforth undertake, independent of the rules laid down for the warders' guidance, to look to every prisoner of the Roman Catholic religion. She will visit each after they are in their cell; she will ascertain if they desire to remain from chapel; if they do, put a black distinguishing mark on their door "—(here the matron's clerk produced from a small drawer in her desk, a circular dark badge)—" report them to the governor for leave of absence; enter the same in her book, which she will keep for the express purpose.

" In order to keep this very important rule in exact order, the clerk will lay her book on the matron's office table every morning, taking particular care to call the matron's attention to the same.

"In this book are entered the names of the prisoners who are Roman Catholics, with memoranda as to when they were seen by the priest, their wish to stay from or go to the ordinary chapel service, with their desire for books," etc.

*** *The Laundry.*—We followed a number of prisoners after dinner to the laundry, a detached building, situated at the extremity of the H wing. We passed through the adjacent drying ground. The chief warder remarked to us—"That in this ground the atmosphere is particularly salubrious and pure."

The laundry is a large lofty building about fifty feet high, and forty-eight feet wide. We found a number of prisoners busily engaged; some were bending down washing, and others stoning the floor. There were two girls among them—one a young pickpocket, a fair-haired girl, with a very interesting countenance. An elderly woman with spectacles was sitting by one of the large windows, knitting stockings, while a plain-looking, robust prisoner, of about thirty-five years of age, was cleaning a mangle. On looking around us, we found the laundry was supplied with two mangles, and with a long deal table, for folding the clothes, extending nearly the whole length of the apartment. On our left hand is another table, also used for folding the clothes. In a corner of the room are six drying horses, heated from a furnace flue, and near to it is a large stove for heating the irons. There are several flower-pots in the window with Australian onions—very rare plants—which are kept here on account of the heat of the laundry.

The warder stated to us—"There are twenty-eight prisoners at present employed in the laundry; some of them very young, others of more advanced years. This is about the average number. Nineteen are engaged washing, four of them are wringing the clothes, and the others are employed in other operations. One woman is constantly employed here mending the men's stockings."

In answer to our interrogatories, the laundry warder informed us—"We begin our work at six o'clock in the morning, and finish at five o'clock in the afternoon. Excepting the time spent at chapel and dinner, etc., we are employed in washing clothes for the male and female prison."

We passed through folding doors at the extremity of the laundry to the washing cells, which are nineteen in number. Each of them is nine feet long, and three and a-half feet wide, with stone flooring, the walls being whitewashed. Each is furnished with a washing-trough, supplied with taps of hot and cold water, and also with a foot-board. The prisoners were busy at their work in the various cells, endeavouring to finish the task allotted them. A heap of clothing lay on the floor beside each of them, ready to be washed. There is a circular opening, about an inch in diameter, in the door of each cell, in which the prisoner inserts a portion of one of the garments to be washed, as a signal to the officer when she requires her attention.

On going into another apartment with lofty roof, paved with Dutch tile, we found two prisoners busy at the wringing-machine: one of them, a young dark-complexioned girl of about eighteen years of age, with a modest and interesting appearance, who had been imprisoned for some petty felony—her first offence; and another good-looking young prisoner of about twenty-two years of age. The machine was manufactured by Seyrig, Alliott, and Manlowes, Lenton Works, Nottingham. While we were present they filled it with shirts soaked with water, and on turning the two handles it whirred and clattered, and by the rapid circular motion of twirling round, the wet was extracted from the clothes, and fell to the bottom, and was discharged through an opening in the machine into a drain beneath the floor. On the garments being taken out, they were thoroughly wrung, and ready to be taken to the drying-machines.

On looking around us we found a large number of bundles of prison clothes piled against the wall, consisting of towels, shirts, petticoats, etc.; at the extremity of the room two large rinsing tubs were supported on an iron bar, over a large sink. A prisoner was engaged taking a quantity of shirts, caps, etc., from a large basket, and placing them in one of the rinsing troughs, amid a cloud of steam. On our right hand was a pump for conveying water from a large reservoir below into a cistern in this apartment.

We went into the adjoining furnace-room, and saw a large copper built in with brick, and a furnace underneath it. There is another one alongside to heat the drying-horses, as well as the water in a cistern for the use of the prisoners.

As we passed along corridor H, we observed a considerable number of the female prisoners in their dark gray cloaks and alpaca veils on the exercising ground, and several warders moving in a reverse order, overlooking them. Some infirm prisoners, and mothers with young children, sauntered about the grounds.

As we proceeded along this corridor, we entered a cell set apart for the use of the Roman Catholic priest. It is furnished with a small table covered with dark blue cloth, and a chair, and hassocks for kneeling. The chief warder informed us that he brings a list of the prisoners the priest wishes to see, these are brought down by the matron's clerk, placed in the corridor, and sent to him separately, so that he sees them quite alone. The matron's clerk attends to him. There is a pane of glass in the door of this cell, where the trap would be in an ordinary one.

₊ *The Teacher.*—On being introduced to the teacher, she stated to us that there are no classes taught in the female branch of the prison. "My duties," she added, "consist in visiting the prisoners separately in their cells. I call on each prisoner on her entrance into the prison, although she be only confined for a few days.

"When I enter the cell, I ascertain if the prisoner is a Catholic or a Protestant. If a Catholic, I say no more. But if a Protestant, I learn if she can read and write. Very few, as a general rule, are able to do so. A great number of the young do not know their letters, and are very ignorant. Many of the young women, from seventeen to twenty-two years of age, cannot read, and very few of the old are able to do so.

"I find," said the teacher, "that the young felons are often better educated than those of riper years. At present I am engaged teaching twenty-eight prisoners the alphabet and monosyllables in their separate cells, and to write on their slates. They advance to the second class book after being proficient in the primer, should their time allow. It consists of simple stories from sacred history. After this they are introduced to the New Testament."

The chief warder observed—"After they can read the New Testament, we consider they are able to read in the cell by themselves, and are then supplied with library books, moral and religious, and on general information."

"Most of the females in this prison," continued the teacher, "belong to the lowest order. We seldom have a well-educated prisoner here. In such a case, I generally supply them with library books. I usually go round the cells at a quarter-past nine, and continue my labours till six o'clock in the evening, with the exception of an hour for dinner. I find my pupils, in general, to be tractable, but not very quick, in their learning. With few exceptions, they are very dull scholars. The young women are more attentive than the younger girls, and make better progress. I often read to them in their cells, and many of them are deeply interested in the narratives. They are not so fond of religious reading. The elderly women are in general very obtuse.

"Sometimes I visit as many as forty in their cells in one day. At other times I have only about fifteen pupils. The general average is about thirty-eight. I seldom remain longer than five or ten minutes in the cell. I believe they learn better separately than if formed into classes.

"I lately had a little girl under my care for three months. She did not know her letters when she came to the prison; but before she was discharged she could read the Testament tolerably well. I could adduce a number of illustrations of this kind.

"I don't think that those prisoners who have made good progress in their education come so frequently back as the others. Much depends on home associations. Many of them are worse than homeless, as they have unprincipled parents. I refer to young women from sixteen to twenty years of age, belonging to the unfortunate class.

"The female prisoners are in general very grateful for the use of the library books, and I have no doubt these greatly cheer and benefit them in their cells. I seldom have to report a prisoner for misbehaviour, perhaps not above twice in a twelvemonth, and these instances have been for destroying their books, and not for insolence."

*** *Punishment Cells.*—We visited these cells at the basement of corridor H, which are very similar in their general appearance to those in the male prison. They are eight in number, four of them being dark. There was a little girl of twelve years of age confined in one of them at the time of our visit, who had been singing in her cell, against the prison rules. We saw her taken to the punishment cell by the chief warder, about an hour before. She was drumming in passionate mood at the door of her cell. On our looking in through the eyelet opening, we saw her sitting crouching in a corner of the cell, with only one garment wrapt around her, and her blue prison clothes torn into a heap of rags by her side. After we left, she continued to beat the door in a violent manner. The reception warder told us "she was a very perverse, stubborn girl, and had been shown great forbearance." She added, "that few of the prisoners are confined in the punishment cells, and never until other means have been had recourse to."

On going into an adjoining light punishment cell, we found the furniture to consist of an iron bedstead, water-tap, and water-closet, and a bell communicating with the main body on the prison. One of the light cells is partially lighted through boarding firmly fixed on the outside. It is generally considered to be a greater punishment than the dark cells. The prisoners often beg hard to be taken out of this cell.

The dark cells have an iron bedstead with wooden centre.

The chief warder afterwards showed us a book in which reports of the prisoners' misconduct are entered, and the punishments awarded by the governor. "For the past fortnight," she stated, "there have been four punishments inflicted for misconduct; one for idleness, one for the prisoner taking needles from another cell, when the occupant was in the exercising ground; one for singing in her cell, and another for disorderly conduct on the exercising ground. I have not seen any of the prisoners tear her clothes into shreds for the past eighteen months, as the little girl has done."

The chief warder continued, "Talking is a very common offence, and also marking the painted stalls in chapel, but the latter has been considerably checked of late."

*** *The Storekeeper.*—We were introduced to the storekeeper, and descended a staircase leading from the central hall to the store-rooms beneath. On being ushered into a neat store-room, about the size of two cells, set around with racks, she observed to us, "This is a store containing the new prison clothing; there is a deal table in the centre of the room used in cutting out the prison clothes. The racks are filled with a goodly assortment of garments, consisting of grogram and blue petticoats, blue cotton jackets with small white spots, flannel shifts and drawers, striped calico shifts, and blue neckerchiefs, packed in small bundles of ten each, coloured cotton pocket handkerchiefs, calico day-caps, striped calico night-caps, linen towels with a red stripe, drab jean stays, blue checked frocks for girls of various ages, and neat little flannel shoes for children, made by an old infirm prisoner."

On shelves beneath were deposited a quantity of the prisoners' gray cloaks. Alongside

INTERIOR OF THE SURREY HOUSE OF CORRECTION, WANDSWORTH,
WITH THE PRISONERS TURNING OUT AFTER DINNER.

were webs of blue serge, grogram, and jean, and a stock of prisoners' shoes—all most carefully arranged.

The storekeeper showed us the books of the store, "There," she said, "is a book which contains an account of prison clothing for the male prison. For example, on 25th May I received 707½ yards of shirting, and between the 5th and 27th June, at various dates, I returned 28⅗ shirts all made by the female prisoners. This gives you an illustration of the manner in which these stores are kept. I take," she added, "a particular account of all clothing made for the female prisoners, in addition to the cotton and flannel shirts, sheets, towels, etc., for the male prison. I have twenty-eight prisoners employed at needlework. The generality are employed picking coir, which I serve out to them at six in the morning. Each prisoner gets 2 lbs. of coir a-day. The youngest of the girls have the same quantity served out to them, and generally manage to pick it, but it is not binding on them to do so. I also keep the property of the prisoners, which is carefully returned to them on their being liberated."

The storekeeper showed us another book, in which an account is kept of the articles used in cleaning, such as soap, soda, etc., and of the articles broken or otherwise destroyed, which are replaced once a-week; also a book stating the number of shoes sent to be repaired, When returned to her, they are entered on the opposite page. There was another book in which the articles of clothing condemned by the governor are inserted; and likewise another volume containing the monthly returns of the condemned clothing. We were shown the prisoners' work book, in which is set down all the work done in the prison—picking coir, needle-work and laundry-work. There is a book for keeping a daily record of this; another for a week, another for a month, and a different one for the quarterly statements.

We visited an apartment very similar to the last, containing a store of the clothing in use. On each side of the room is deposited, on racks and shelves, a smaller assortment of clothing for daily use, together with a large quantity of blankets, rugs, and hammocks.

On our left hand is the kitchen, consisting of three cells, generally used as the warders' mess-room.

Opposite to the kitchen is the scullery, about the dimensions of three cells. It contains a large rack copiously supplied with plates, as well as a series of shelves with cooking utensils, along with a sink supplied with hot and cold water. Two prisoners were here employed, one of them was scrubbing with all her might, and the other washing some utensils at the sink.

There is a large mess-room off the kitchen, with a series of cupboards for the use of the warders.

Meantime a bell rang, and the storekeeper admitted a truck from the main store of the male prison with a quantity of towelling and calico for drawers, to be placed under her care.

We accompanied the storekeeper to a smaller store-room on the right hand side of the basement under the central hall. There we saw a large rack containing pieces of the best yellow soap, cut into various sizes, and placed in piles of ten. The larger pieces were for the use of the laundry, and the smaller for the prisoners' use in their cells. They are so carefully arranged, that the matron by a glance of her eye can tell the quantity on hand. On a side table we saw a small machine for cutting the soap, which is executed with great despatch. We particularly admired the exceedingly careful manner in which these stores were arranged.

In answer to our interrogatories, the storekeeper stated, "My duties commence at six o'clock in the morning, when I go to the chief warder to get the keys of the stores. I have the assistance of one prisoner to serve out the coir, and about this time I return the property of the prisoners who are to be discharged.

"I receive the breakfast from the kitchen, consisting of bread and gruel, at a quarter-past seven o'clock. It is sent to me in trays, when I get it conveyed by the hoisting machine to the different divisions, each basket being marked with its own letter and number. I also attend to serve up the dinner at a quarter to one o'clock.

"In the course of the afternoon, I go round the cells and inspect the prisoners who are employed at needle-work, and am busy the remainder of the day cutting out the clothes and arranging for the next day's duties. The supper is served up at six o'clock." The store-keeper added, "Every quarter I take a particular inventory of the stock in my store, and render a minute account of it."

₊ *Visiting the Cells.*—We learned that the prisoners are not classified over the various corridors. Before leaving the female branch of the prison, we looked into several of the cells, and found persons of various ages busy sewing, knitting, or picking coir. We jotted down a few pictures as we passed along.

On looking into a cell we saw a woman of about forty-five years of age, seated in a corner of her cell by a small table, picking coir. A brown heap of twisted material lay on the floor at her feet. She wrought very actively with a modest, thoughtful countenance.

In another cell we saw a smart woman of about thirty years of age. A quantity of un-twisted coir lay on the table before her. She was less expert in her work than the other prisoner, although she appeared to be a person of more energy of character.

On the door of a cell, as we passed, we saw a dark badge indicating that the inmate was a Roman Catholic, and did not attend chapel.

We entered a cell occupied by a woman and child, which was considerably larger than the ordinary cells. The chief warder stated to us, "When a prisoner is received who has an infant, we give her one of the large cells adjoining the central hall, with an iron bedstead instead of a hammock, a straw bed and bedding, similar to the other prisoners."

In another cell we saw a fair-complexioned young girl of seventeen years of age, con-fined for uttering base coin. She looked much older. We found her engaged sewing; on our retiring, she bent on the table and wept.

Before leaving, on the third day of our visit, we visited the cell where the little girl was confined, whom we had seen in the punishment cell. She was clad in another prison dress, and was reading a book, and appeared to be quiet and subdued in her manner. She had been subjected to a punishment of bread and water for two days. From her card we found she was under confinement for picking pockets; there was nothing remarkable in her appearance.

The storekeeper informed us, "The great mass of the prisoners of various ages are inferior needlewomen. Many come here who cannot sew, but who become tolerably proficient before they leave the prison. At first," she observed, "we give them towels and handker-chiefs to hem. As they progress, they get better work, such as shirts and day-caps. We have no fine work for them. Some are very awkward, and others are tolerably good sewers. I teach them to sew, and find them very grateful for my instruction. Some of them are able to sew their own dress by the time their sentence expires; they are not instructed in shaping."

In reference to those who pick coir, she added, "Some are as expert the first day as when their punishment expires."

VEILED FEMALE PRISONER AT THE SURREY HOUSE OF CORRECTION, WANDSWORTH.

(From a Photograph by Herbert Watkins, 179, Regent Street.)

A RETURN OF THE TERMS OF IMPRISONMENT, AND SENTENCES OF CRIMINAL PRISONERS CONFINED IN THE HOUSE OF CORRECTION, AT WANDSWORTH, DURING THE YEAR ENDING THE 29TH SEPTEMBER, 1861.

Prisoners of Seventeen Years of Age, and upwards.

Terms of Imprisonment	Sex	Terms of Imprisonment of Session, Central Criminal Court, and Assize Prisoners	Terms of Imprisonment under Summary Convictions	Total
Under Fourteen Days.	M.	...	339	339
	F.	...	319	319
Fourteen Days and under One Month.	M.	2	486	488
	F.	1	337	338
One Month and under Two Months.	M.	8	330	338
	F.	6	171	177
Two Months and under Three Months.	M.	12	226	238
	F.	4	70	74
Three Months and under Six Months.	M.	49	337	386
	F.	21	128	149
Six Months and under One Year.	M.	86	104	190
	F.	37	63	100
One Year and under Two Years.	M.	115	...	115
	F.	25	...	25
Two Years and Upwards.	M.	5	...	5
	F.	1	...	1
Unlimited Term of Imprisonment.	M.	...	...	...
	F.	...	...	...
Whipped.	M.	...	...	...
Paid Fine or found Sureties.	M.	...	117	117
	F.	...	63	63
Total Adults.	M.	277	1822	2099
	F.	95	1088	1183
Grand Total of both Sexes.		372	2910	3282

Prisoners under Seventeen Years of Age.

Terms of Imprisonment	Sex	Terms of Imprisonment of Session, Central Criminal Court, and Assize Prisoners	Terms of Imprisonment under Summary Convictions	Total
Under Fourteen Days.	M.	...	92	92
	F.	...	10	10
Fourteen Days and under One Month.	M.	2	188	190
	F.	...	18	18
One Month and under Two Months.	M.	2	145	147
	F.	1	17	18
Two Months and under Three Months.	M.	6	83	89
	F.	...	14	14
Three Months and under Six Months.	M.	4	116	120
	F.	...	13	13
Six Months and under One Year.	M.	4	9	13
	F.	1	4	5
One Year and under Two Years.	M.	14	...	14
	F.	...	...	...
Two Years and Upwards.	M.	...	...	...
	F.	...	...	...
Unlimited Term of Imprisonment.	M.	...	...	...
	F.	...	...	...
Whipped.	M.	...	54	54
Paid Fine or found Sureties.	M.	...	...	...
	F.	...	...	...
Total Juveniles.	M.	32	633	665
	F.	2	76	78
Grand Total of both Sexes.		34	709	743

A Return of the Number of Prisoners received at the House of Correction, Wandsworth Common, during the Year ending 29th September, 1861.

Offence	Prisoners of 17 Years of Age and Upwards — Sessions M.	F.	Central Criminal Court M.	F.	Assize M.	F.	Prisoners under 17 Years of Age — Sessions M.	F.	Central Criminal Court M.	F.	Assize M.	F.	Prisoners of 17 Years and Upwards, Summarily Convicted — Metropolitan Police District M.	F.	Surrey Constabulary District M.	F.	Borough of Guildford M.	F.	Kent Prisoners M.	F.	Prisoners under 17 Years, Summarily Convicted — Metropolitan Police District M.	F.	Surrey Constabulary District M.	F.	Borough of Guildford M.	F.	Kent Prisoners M.	F.	Courts Martial — Foot Guards and Militia M.	Total Adult and Juvenile M.	F.	General Total of both Forces.
Felony	167	71	39	9	8	1	22	1	3	1	4		409	323	49	6	7	2			89	21	5	2						803	436	1239
Misdemeanor	33	3	30	11			2		1				639	330	61	7	8	1	35	83	364	35	21	2			46	3		1240	476	1716
Vagrants													284	279	33	13	1	2			14	8	2							334	302	636
Poachers													2		4															6		6
Excise													9	3																9	3	12
Customs													4																	4		4
Rogue and Vagabond													248	34	28	5	1				90	4	1	1	1	1				368	44	412
Insubordination (Adults)																																
Total	200	74	69	20	8	1	24	1	4	1	4		1595	969	175	31	17	5	35	83	557	68	29	5	1	1	46	3		2764	1261	4025

SURREY.—HOUSE OF CORRECTION, WANDSWORTH.

A Return of Prisoners, Male and Female, received during the Year ending the 29th September, 1861.

	Ages. — Juveniles — Under Ten Years.	Under Twelve Years.	Under Fourteen Years.	Under Sixteen Years.	Under Seventeen Years.	Total.	Adults — Under Twenty-one Years.	Twenty-one Years and Upwards.	Total.	Totals — Received.	Previous Committal.
Males	18	82	122	263	180	665	540	1559	2099	2764	746
Females	..	3	10	28	37	78	255	928	1183	1261	516
Totals	18	85	132	291	217	743	795	2487	3282	4025	1262

	Previous Committals to Wandsworth — Juvenile — First Offence.	One before.	Two before.	Three before.	Four before.	Five or more.	Adults — First Offence.	One before.	Two before.	Three before.	Four before.	Five or more.	Other Prisons — County Jail.	Brixton, Kingston, or Guildford.
Males	468	94	46	24	18	15	1550	280	104	52	49	64	66	149
Females	67	6	3	1	..	1	678	214	101	50	24	116	17	6
Totals	535	100	49	25	18	16	2228	494	205	102	73	180	83	155

(Signed) RICHARD ONSLOW, *Governor.*

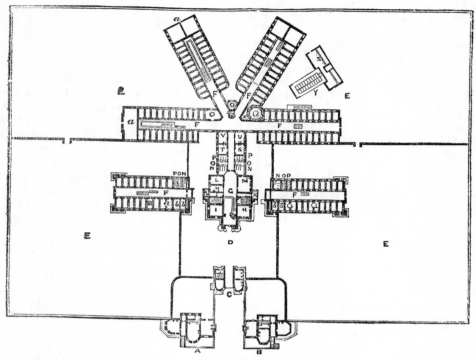

GROUND PLAN OF HOLLOWAY PRISON.

A. Governor's House.	F, F, F, F, F, F. Corridors.	M. Magistrates' Committee Room.	T. An Anteroom.
B. Chaplain's ditto.	G. Main Passage.	N, N, N, N. } Prisoners' Visiting	U. Deputy Governor's Office.
C. Outer Gate.	H. Governor's and Clerks' Offices.	O, O, O, O. } Room, with diffe-	V. Surgeon's Room.
D. Inner Gate.	I. Reception Warder's Office.	P, P, P, P. } rent compartments.	W. Treadwheel and Pumps.
E, E, E, E. Courtyard and Exer-cising Grounds.	K. Lobby.	Q. Storeroom.	a, a. Associated Rooms.
	L. An Anteroom.	S. Waiting Room	

¶ iv.

THE CITY HOUSE OF CORRECTION, HOLLOWAY.

(FOR ALL CLASSES OF CONVICTED CRIMINALS.)

On a cold morning in December, while the great Metropolis around us was enveloped in gloom, we sallied along Tottenham Court Road on our first visit to Holloway Prison. There had been a slight frost during the preceding night, which had not however been sufficient to indurate the wet streets saturated by recent rains. The stars were shining serenely from a cloudless sky, as yet unsullied by the smoke of ten thousand chimneys. The lamps were still lit along the far-extending street, and beamed like other stars in the distance. This thoroughfare, although resounding during the day with the incessant din of vehicles and traffickers, was now almost silent and deserted. One solitary cab was loitering on the stand, the cabman being seated in front of the vehicle, equipped in his drab greatcoat and warm muffler, on the look-out for an early fare. As we strode along Tottenham Court Road, we met several workmen, variously attired, proceeding along to their customary toil; some with their basket of tools slung over their shoulder, and others carrying a small bundle in their hand. We observed lights in several places of business as we passed at this early hour of the day. In some upholsterers' shops, the shopmen and others were busily engaged cleaning their large ware-rooms, or dusting their furniture, and assorting a portion of it carefully in their large windows, with a view to attract the public eye. Through the fanlight over the door of an occasional gin palace, the gas was burning low, and we could learn the inmates were already astir, although scarcely a light was seen in any of the adjacent dwellings.

We passed several lofty commercial buildings, and entered the Euston Road. At the angle of the two streets we found a young costermonger stationed by his barrow, with an ample supply of yellow oranges in beautiful fresh condition, and green heaps of faded-looking apples. The centre of the road was effectually barricaded by the operations carried on in connection with the underground railway from Paddington to the City. Here a very lively and interesting scene presented itself to our notice. The works in this locality extended over a considerable space. Part of the street was in the process of excavation, and the subsoil was drawn up in small waggons, by means of a windlass wrought with a snorting steam-engine, which emitted a white column of steam into the dark sky. A portion of the street had been already excavated, and the workmen were variously employed by the glare of torches; some wheeling barrowfuls of bricks and stones along wooden planks placed across strong wooden beams, which spanned the chasm beneath; others mixing the mortar to build the subterranean arch; some were preparing the asphalt over blazing furnaces, to overlay it, and others were busy underground, covering the arch with loose soil or gravel, to consummate the work.

As we proceeded along the Euston Road, we passed St. Pancras Church and spire on our right—an elegant stone building of a peculiar style of architecture, beautifully chiselled, and in some places finely carved. The strip of ground around it is tastefully laid out, the grass being smoothly shaven, and the walks carefully laid with gravel; several milk vans, laden with their white cans, whirled smartly along, and some empty coal waggons, with their heavy rumbling wheels, and jingling harness. A short distance beyond, on our left hand, we reach the church of St. Luke's, King's Cross, a small, fanciful, and grotesque building, with a strange contracted roof, resembling a Chinaman's hat. We observed a few coffee stalls, with a dim light gleaming beside them, some in an open lane, others in a small wooden shed at the inner side of the pavement, where a man or woman was retailing coffee and bread to the workmen and others who proceeded along. A few paces farther, and we reach King's Cross, as the day began to break. Near to it is the station of the Great Northern Railway, a large building of yellowish brown brick, with two large iron-framed windows of a semi-circular form fronting us, overlooking six arches on the ground floor. The Great Northern Hotel, a lofty and extensive building, has been recently erected in the vicinity. The wooden inclosures around King's Cross, as well as along the Euston Road, and even the gables of many of the houses in the vicinity, were covered with large flaming placards of various colours, some of them printed in letters two feet in dimension, inviting the public to Christmas pantomimes, music saloons, casinos, and other entertainments.

King's Cross, in general a bustling thoroughfare, was at this early hour of the morning comparatively deserted, except by a few large railway vans, heavily loaded, which lumbered lazily along, and by a few workmen hastening to their daily labour. We proceeded up the slope of the Pentonville Road, on our way to Islington, passing the policeman attired in his warm great coat, dark shining belt and cape, sauntering along with slow and measured step. Many of the houses on our right hand, as in the Euston Read, had a grass or garden plot in front, in some cases planted with shrubs or trees, stripped of their foliage.

On the top of the hill we met one of the warders of the Middlesex Detentional Prison, a tall military-looking man in uniform, hastening down towards Clerkenwell to enter on his duties for the day. As we reached the Angel Tavern, Islington, a dense mist loomed over the sky. There was no omnibus in the vicinity, nor a single group of people near the corner of the street.   We bent our steps along High Street, Islington, one of the busiest promenades in the north of the Metropolis, and a gay shopping street, occupied by drapers, milliners, dressmakers, and others, very similar in its character to Newington Causeway, on the Surrey side.   In some of the drapers' shops we found smart young shopmen standing by the counter ready for business, but there was scarcely a single customer within.   We passed the triangular patch of meadow, styled Islington Green, and directed our way by the Upper Street, to Highbury Park, where we had a sweet rural glimpse as we turned the angle leading to Holloway.   There we took a seat in the omnibus, which whirled us along to a beautiful cluster of suburban villas, with rural prospect and salubrious air, in the vicinity of the City Prison.

The House of Correction at Holloway is a noble building of the castellated Gothic style. The wide extended front adjacent to the Camden Road is of Kentish rag-stone, with Caen stone dressings.   The sides of the chapel and the back wings are of brick, the windows of the cells having Parkspring stone sills, with splayed brick reveals.

About sixty feet in front of the inner gate is a neat porter's-lodge, and on each side of it, without the prison walls, are two elegant residences for the governor and chaplain, with large gardens attached to them.

The prison is built on a rising ground, on the west of the Holloway Road, originally purchased by the City Corporation to be used as a cemetery at the time of the cholera in 1832.   The ground, consisting of ten acres, is surrounded by a brick wall about eighteen feet high.

At the back of the prison lie some beautiful green meadows, and fields of arable land, a portion of which belongs to the City; in the distance rise the green Muswell and Hornsey hills, and the commanding slope of Highgate, together with Hampstead Heath, where the redoubtable Dick Turpin occasionally roamed; while away to the south extend the immense piles of architecture of the huge Metropolis, with its hundred spires, by this time wreathed in a dense cloud of smoke and mist.

¶ iv.—a.

The History and Construction of the Prison..

In a report presented by the Prison Committee to the Court of Common Council, on 20th January, 1843, we have a condensed statement of the reasons respectfully submitted to the Court of Aldermen by the Committee of the Court of Common Council, why a new prison should not be erected in the City, but rather at Holloway :—

"It is assumed that Giltspur-street Prison, as well from its construction as from its confined space, is totally inadequate for the purposes of a house of correction. It is also assumed, that all parties are agreed that a new house of correction has become necessary. The question then to be decided is, whether such prison should be erected within the walls of the City, or in some open space at a distance from it.

"The Committee, with a view to determine this point, have carefully examined ten plans, and the proposed sites selected, which are marked upon the plan prepared by the architect.

"No 1 is an enlargement of Giltspur-street Prison, the total area of which, even when enlarged, would be only two roods and thirty-seven perches. It is submitted that this space is insufficient for the contemplated purpose; that plan is therefore rejected.

"Nos. 2 and 3 being an enlargement of Newgate, the total area of which would only be two acres and two perches; this also was considered insufficient.

"No. 4 involved the destruction of the Debtors' Prison in Whitecross Street, which would have given a site of four acres and nineteen perches. It was rejected because of the destruction of the Debtors' Prison, and the necessity of providing a new prison for them, it being foreseen that by the enactment of new laws that prison would be fully occupied, and therefore it would require as large a space in some other situation to have erected a new prison for them; in addition to which, in order to make up the four acres and nineteen perches, a large plot of ground to the north must have been purchased at a cost of at least £133,000.

"Nos. 5 and 9 were plans for building a new prison upon ground adjoining the Debtors' Prison; the largest of the two plans would have given a site of only two acres, three roods, and fifteen perches, and would have cost, exclusive of the building of the prison, £141,800; these were therefore rejected.

"No. 8 is a plot of ground in Goswell Street, beyond the boundary of the City, where a site of four acres might have been obtained, but at a cost of £214,000.

"No. 10 embraces an area of three acres and two perches, and embraces the site of the late Fleet Prison, with additional land proposed to be taken, running up from Farringdon Street to the Old Bailey. This, with the cost of the site of the Fleet Prison, deducting the value of the materials sold, amounted to £154,800.

"In all these estimates the cost of the site only is put down; the cost of erecting the prison, it is assumed, would be nearly the same whether built in or out of the City."

The committee rejected all these plans.

"The reasons which induce the committee to select a spot out of the City, are, first, that as much space as may now, or at any future time, be required, can be obtained to erect a prison upon any plan to accommodate four hundred prisoners, with ample airing grounds, spaces for workshops, etc., annexed, for a sum not exceeding £5000, thereby effecting a saving to the City of at least one hundred and thirty thousand pounds. Secondly, that upon the space so to be obtained, a prison, with all modern improvements, both as regards the discipline and the reformation of the prisoners, might be erected, which could not be so well accomplished within a narrow space. Thirdly, because the health of the prisoners would be better preserved; for although persons living within the City find it very healthy, yet it must be remembered that they are constantly moving about, and great numbers residing out of the City for a part of the year; and even the poorest take excursions occasionally, by which means their health is renovated, whereas prisoners are confined to the spot, and it may be for a long time; it is therefore desirable, upon the score of humanity, that they should be placed in the healthiest locality; and as the Government have restrained transportation, except for very serious offences, it is probable that the terms of imprisonment may be extended for three, four, or five years. On every ground, therefore, it seems desirable that the prison or house of correction should be placed out of the City, and that it should be built within the county of Middlesex. First, because the City of London holds the county in fee. Secondly, because the sheriffs of London are always the sheriffs of Middlesex; and Newgate, although within the City, is the common jail of the county. Thirdly, because many of the aldermen are magistrates of Middlesex, and have therefore co-ordinate jurisdiction in that county with the justices thereof. And lastly, because the county mainly surrounds the City, and all parts of it where a prison could be built are more accessible and more within the daily walks of the City authorities than other counties.

"For these reasons, the committee examined a plot of ground belonging to the corporation, situate at Holloway, and came to the conclusion that it was desirable to erect a new prison there. First, because of its easy access from all parts of the City and the

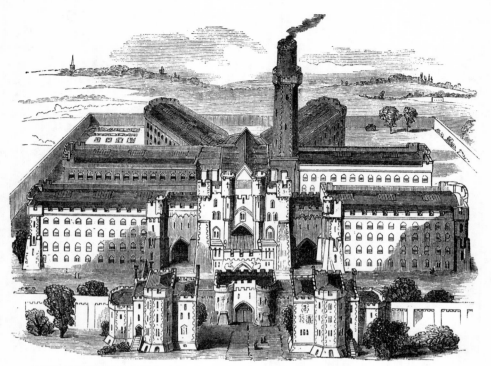

BIRD'S-EYE VIEW OF THE HOUSE OF CORRECTION FOR THE CITY OF LONDON, HOLLOWAY.

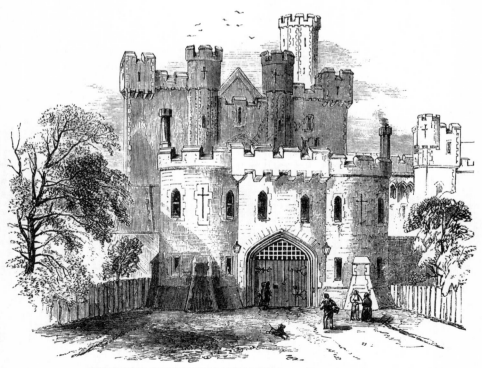

OUTER GATE AT THE CITY HOUSE OF CORRECTION, HOLLOWAY.

metropolis. Secondly, because of the great saving of expense in the purchase of a site. Thirdly, on the ground of its salubrity, its soil, its being capable of being well-drained, and of the ample space which may be obtained for all the purposes which may be required.

" Other reasons entered into the consideration of these questions, which it is unnecessary to detail. The committee had only one object, to select the best site, to get the largest space, to save the most money, to erect the most suitable prison, to preserve the City's rights and privileges, to uphold the character of the magistracy, and to have a prison which should indeed be a model.

" On the 11th March, 1847," continue the prison committee in their report, " the Lord Mayor laid before the Court of Common Council a report of the Jail Committee to the Court of Aldermen, on having received several offers of sites for a new house of correction, and drawing the attention of the court to the land belonging to this city at Holloway, which was referred to your committee to consider, with power to confer with the Court of Aldermen thereon ; and, before carrying the same into execution, to report to this court.

" On the 23rd of the same month, the Court of Aldermen appointed the Lord Mayor and seven Aldermen to be a special committee, to act with us in relation to prisons ; and on the 31st, we appointed a sub committee, consisting of ten members, including the chairman, to confer with the committee of Aldermen upon the several matters referred respecting the erection of a new prison, and to report to us.

" On the 14th of April, 1847, the special committee of the Court of Aldermen and subcommittee appointed by us met as a joint committee, and it was resolved unanimously that it should be recommended that the intended new prison be erected on the land belonging to this city at Holloway. And on the 13th May, the joint committee resolved that it was inexpedient that any portion of the land at Holloway should be permanently appropriated to any other purpose till it was ascertained what quantity would be required for the prison. That the construction of the prison should be such as to admit of its future adaptation to any mode of discipline which might afterwards be adopted. These resolutions were subsequently adopted by us, and submitted (*inter alia*) to your honourable court, in a report presented and agreed to on the 1st July, 1847.

" On the 29th day of July, 1847, the prisons committee presented to the Court of Common Council the following report, which was agreed to ; viz. :—

" ' We, of your special committee, appointed on the 20th day of March, 1846, to cooperate with the Court of Aldermen, and to view and examine the prisons belonging to this city, and report our opinion as to the accommodation afforded to prisoners, the opportunity for classification and separate confinement, and whether there exists any necessity for building a new prison, or enlarging or altering the existing prisons, with a view to carry into effect the improvements in prison discipline which modern experience has suggested on the subject, and to report thereon, DO CERTIFY that, in addition to our report presented to this honourable court on the 1st day of July instant, in which we stated the several proceedings in the conferences which had taken place between your committee and the special committee of jails of the Court of Aldermen in relation to the proposed new house of correction, with a recommendation that the same should be built on the City's ground at Holloway, we have now to report that, at a further conference, it was mutually agreed that the construction of the new prison should be such as to admit of its future adaptation to any mode of discipline that might hereafter be determined upon, and that the same should be constructed for not less than four hundred prisoners, and that separate sleeping cells should be constructed. We jointly referred it to the City Architect (Mr. Bunning) to prepare a plan upon this principle, and to submit the same to us for consideration.

" ' That we have since received from him a plan accordingly, classed and arranged as under :—

　　" ' For adult male prisoners :

" ' Four wings, containing 72 each, each wing consisting of three stories to accommodate 24 prisoners 288

　　" ' For female prisoners :

" ' One wing containing three stories, to accommodate 56

　　" ' And for juvenile prisoners :

" ' A further wing of three stories, to accommodate 56

" ' Total 400

" ' The prison to occupy a site of eight acres, and the small triangular piece of ground on the north thereof to be retained for any purposes which may hereafter be determined upon.

" ' That both committees, having duly considered that plan, and heard the architect in explanation thereof, unanimously approve the same; and we recommend it to this honourable court for adoption, subject to such modifications, if any, as may, upon further consideration, be deemed expedient, provided that no steps be taken until the estimate of the expense of such new house of correction is reported to this honourable court, and their sanction had thereto.'

" On the 10th of February, 1848, the prison committee presented to the Court of Common Council another report, viz. :—

" ' We, of your special committee in relation to prisons, to whom on the 29th day of July last it was referred, in accordance with the terms of our report on that day presented, to prepare an estimate of the expense of carrying into execution the plans which accompanied our report, and which were agreed to by this honourable court, DO CERTIFY that we have duly proceeded therein and referred it to the sub-committee appointed to confer and act in conjunction with the jail committee of the Court of Aldermen, to consider of and prepare the necessary estimate as required.

" ' That the sub-committee have reported to us, That on the 4th day of December last, Mr. Bunning was directed to prepare the plans on the enlarged scale required by the Act of Parliament, in order that they might be transmitted to the Secretary of State for approval.

" ' That Mr. Bunning was also directed to prepare and submit an estimate of the expense of erecting the building, that the same might be reported to the Courts of Aldermen and Common Council.

" ' That the sub-committee had since received such estimate, amounting to about the sum of £80,000.

" ' That Mr. Bunning having submitted the large plans to the Secretary of State, agreeably to the instructions given to him, had since laid before the sub-committee a letter from Mr. Phillipps, returning the same with the approval of Sir George Grey certified thereon, together with certain suggestions contained in a memorandum drawn up by Colonel Jebb, the Inspector-General of Prisons (as to certain details of the prison arrangements).

" ' That the sub-committee had considered and approved of the suggestions Nos. 1, 2, 3, and 4, in the memorandum.' "

On the 26th September, 1849, the first stone of the new prison was laid by the Right Honourable Sir James Duke, Lord Mayor, assisted by David Williams Wire, Esq., Chairman of the Prison Committee of the Court of Common Council, and Alderman Challis, Chairman of the Jail Committee of the Court of Aldermen, and the building was finished in 1852.

The daily average number of prisoners for the past year . . 343

The greatest number at any one time during the year . . 389

STATE OF EXPENDITURE IN RELATION TO THE ERECTION OF A NEW HOUSE OF CORRECTION FOR THE
CITY OF LONDON, AT HOLLOWAY.

	£.	s.	d.
By contract for Building	77,890	7	2
,, formation of Sewer	975	0	0
,, sinking Artesian Well	1,300	0	0
,, Iron Tanks, Water-closets, Baths, etc.	3,245	12	1
,, Warming and Ventilation	3,541	3	0
,, Tarpaulins	84	4	7
,, Pumps and Apparatus	565	0	0
,, Gas Fittings	899	9	10
,, Stoves	117	16	0
,, Locks, Latches, Bolts, Bells, etc.	504	5	0
,, Clerk of the Works	1,615	11	1
,, Trees, Shrubs, Plants	64	14	0
,, Interest on Temporary Loans	61	4	0
,, Law Expenses	143	1	7
,, Books, Stationery, and Printing	19	19	0
,, Miscellaneous Expenditure	520	3	4
	91,547	10	8
Balance	1,152	9	4
	92,700	0	0

¶ iv.—β.

The Interior of Holloway Prison.

As we approached the outer gate of the prison by the enclosed entry flanked on our right hand by the chaplain's house, and on our left by that of the governor, both uniform in appearance and of elegant construction, as represented in the engraving, the battlements and lofty tower of the prison rose conspicuously before us, reminding us of some noble castle of the olden feudal times. On our knocking at the outer iron bolted gate, an elderly modest-looking officer appeared at the grating, and admitted us within the walls of the prison. He was attired in the prison uniform, consisting of a surtout and trousers of dark blue cloth and cap with peak, with a dark shining leathern belt, from which was suspended an iron chain with the keys of the prison attached.

We were ushered into the presence of the governor, who, on our presenting our order from the visiting magistrates, introduced us to Mr. Clark, chief warder, to conduct us through the interior of the prison. The latter had a gold-lace band round his cap, and his uniform handsomely embroidered with lace to distinguish him from the other officers.

⁎⁎ The Outer Gate and Courtyard.—We first inspected the lodge occupied by the gate warder, consisting of a small room on each side of the gateway.

The one on the right hand is furnished with an oaken table, and a large oaken case set beside the wall as we enter, containing an assortment of rifles, pistols, cutlasses, and bayonets, tastefully arranged. Alongside is a cupboard, in the interior of which is a series of hooks to contain the keys of the prison.

Over the mantel-piece is a letter-box, where letters are deposited to be sent to the Post-office and for delivery at the prison; opposite to it is a time-indicator, surmounted by a dial-plate. On the wall are suspended a City Almanack, giving a list of all the different Courts, and a list of the magistrates at the Central Criminal Court, Guildhall, and the Mansion-house.

The chief warder called our attention to a book deposited on a desk, where the visitors to the prison are required to sign their names, and requested us to enter our name in it.

The desk contained a visiting-book for the prisoners' friends; also a book for visitors who have received orders from the magistrates to visit the prisoners; another for solicitors who visit the prison; and a fourth records the attendance of ladies who aid female prisoners on their liberation, by getting them into institutions or providing them with situations in the metropolis.

The gate warder handed us several other books; and added, "There is a book to record the visits of the chaplain and surgeon to the prison; also a book to note the labourers and tradesmen employed within the establishment."

He farther showed us a volume in which the vehicles entering the prison gate are recorded, with the numbers of the cabs, carriages, etc.; and the non-resident officers attendance book, specifying the precise time they are occupied in duty; and one containing the names of the male and female prisoners, alphabetically arranged, with the date of their discharge.

At the time of our visit a cheerful fire was burning in the grate, with a comfortable rug on the hearth, and a neat cocoa-nut mat at the door, made by the prisoners. There are several bells here; one communicating with the reception ward, another with the chaplain's house, and a third with that of the governor.

We proceeded to the small room on the opposite side of the archway, where the warder at the gate generally sits and takes his meals, while the one we left is generally occupied as his office. This small apartment in construction and dimensions is exactly similar to the other we have already described, and is neatly furnished with an oaken table and several oaken chairs. There is here a comfortable fireplace, and gas jet, and also a bell communicating with the governor's house. On the wall is affixed a copy of the Rules relating to the treatment and conduct of the prisoners.

Leaving the porter's lodge we enter the pointed arch, which is thirteen feet in breadth, and twenty-nine in length, and at the upper extremity sixteen feet high. The chief warder called our attention to the outer folding-gate of the prison, about eleven feet square. It is composed of solid oak four inches thick, riveted with strong bolts of iron, with a small iron grating about eight inches square, occasionally closed with a wooden trap.

There is also a narrow wicket gate in one of the folds of the large gate for the ingress and egress of the visitors, which is fastened, as in the case of the large gate, with a patent lock. The top of the arch over the prison gate is fenced with strong massive iron bars.

The chief warder has a suite of apartments over the porter's lodge; consisting of a kitchen, pantry, parlour, two bed-rooms, with scullery, sink, and water-closet attached.

Leaving the porter's lodge we enter the courtyard, where the prison has a very imposing appearance, with its castellated front, and the lofty wide extended range of buildings forming the female wing on our right, and the juvenile wing on our left hand, each consisting of three floors.

The porch of the prison with the inner gate projects a considerable way from the main building in front as seen in one of the engravings, and the pillar on each side is surmounted by a large winged griffin rampant facing the doorway. One of them has a key in one of his talons, and a large dark leg-iron in the other. And the other has one of his talons extended as though he were aiming to seize hold of his prey, while the other clasps a set of massive leg-irons.

EXTERIOR OF THE CITY HOUSE OF CORRECTION AT HOLLOWAY.

The court-yard in front of the prison is neatly gravelled and carefully drained, and bordered with flowers and shrubs, such as wallflower, hollyhock, and evergreens of different kinds. At the back of the lodge, on each side of the arch, is a small grotto, ingeniously erected by the gate-warder, with a miniature fortification beside one of them.

** *Office, cells, etc. of the Reception-ward.*—We were admitted by the inner warder, an intelligent Scotchman, into the main prison. On entering by the wicket-gate, similar to the one in the outer lodge, already described, we found ourselves in a spacious hall, beneath the glazed roof of the porch, which sloped upward towards the lofty turrets in front of the prison. The reception ward is situated on the basement; and an ample stone staircase, on the right hand of the reception ward, leads to the central hall and the corridors of the adult prison. The staircase is enclosed by a massive chiselled stone balustrade, which extends across the hall above, on the first floor, in the direction of the office of the clerk and storekeeper, and elegantly fences the extremity of the wide passage entering into the main prison.

The hall of the reception ward on the basement is about forty-eight feet in length and twenty-one in breadth, with cocoa-nut matting, leading to the reception warder's office on the left hand, and to the reception cells in front.

We accompanied the reception warder into his office, about eighteen feet by fifteen: a comfortable apartment, well lighted and ventilated, provided with several writing-desks, like a lawyer's office, suited for four clerks, surmounted with brass fittings, on which the books of the prison are conveniently deposited, with a gas-jet over it. On a side-table several books were laid. "Here," said the reception warder, opening a large book, "is the register in which we enter the descriptions of the male prisoners, and there is a similar one for female prisoners. There is another book, termed the clothing and trinket book, in which a record is kept of the various articles belonging to the prisoners; and here is an index to them."

Pointing to standard measures, which stood near to the window, "There," said the warder, "we take the height of the various prisoners, and also their weight."

The office of the reception warder is floored with wood, and arched with brick, supported by iron girders. The walls are painted of a light colour and tastefully pencilled to resemble large carefully hewn blocks of stone, as in the outer walls of the reception ward.

There are two bells here; one of them communicating with the front gate, and the other with the reception or inner gate. The windows are secured, on the exterior, with strong iron bars.

We then proceeded along the hall of the reception ward. At the farther extremity, before we reached the cells, we observed a narrow metal grating extending across from the one side of the floor to the other, which contained hot-air pipes. "This hot-air flue," said the chief warder, "extends along the centre of the reception ward, and gives warmth to the various cells. It extends to the female wing on the right hand, and to the juvenile wing on the left."

There is a board over the door leading to the reception ward, intimating that "Silence is to be strictly observed" by the prisoners.

The reception warder told us that the dark passage on the left led to the juvenile, and that on the right to the female branch of the prison, passing through an archway between them on each side; over which was another communication from the main passage on the floor above. At the farther end of the reception hall there is a tap to draw water for the use of the ward, and a water-closet adjoining.

We entered the apartment containing the *prisoners' own clothing*, on the right side of the reception ward. There we found a large quantity of prisoners' garments carefully packed in bundles and deposited in racks around the walls, arranged according to their sentences, each of them labelled with the name, register, number, and sentence of each. There is a stove for the airing of the clothes in the centre of the room.

Many of the bundles contained ragged and soiled clothing, with a large proportion of respectable and fashionable garments. " Some bundles," said the warder, " belong to rogues and vagabonds, pickpockets and burglars, others to sailors and soldiers. We have several returned convicts imprisoned for picking pockets, and for receiving stolen property. A good number of the prisoners have been clerks in lawyers' offices, and travellers and warehousemen in commercial houses, brought here for embezzling their masters' property; and some have been in good position in society, and are now under sentence for fraudulent bankruptcy. In addition to these, we have many tradesmen and mechanics for various offences. Some of the prisoners have been convicted for uttering base coin, others for lead-stealing, some for swindling, and many for petty felonies."

"At present," said the reception warder, "a good deal of the prisoners' clothing requires to be fumigated. I attribute this to the fact that a great mass of people are at present out of employment, and many are driven to the low lodging-houses of the metropolis for shelter. Many of our prisoners are covered with vermin, and in a most deplorable condition. A great number of them have very respectable clothing, which does not require to be fumigated. We generally find the most expert thieves are respectably attired, and cleanly in their persons."

There is a small apartment adjoining this store-room, where the prisoners' clothes are fumigated.

We passed on through a door at the extremity of the reception hall, fronting the inner gate of the prison, to the reception cells. This door has plate-glass inserted into the upper panels, which gives the interior a more cheerful appearance. The passage between the cells is sixty-nine feet in length, and a portion of it twenty-one feet in breadth and about ten feet in height; the remainder being as narrow as ten feet.

The Bath-room of this ward is on our left hand. It is about twenty feet long, nine feet wide, and ten feet in height, at the top, and nine feet at the bottom of the arch. There are two baths in this room, separated from each other by a wooden partition. They are comfortable and commodious, and are supplied with hot water from a cistern in the furnace-room, and with cold water from a tank at the roof of the prison.

Adjoining the bath-room is *a small store of prison-made clothing*, carefully arranged on the shelves, consisting of dark gray jackets, vests, and trousers, with braces, stocks, and shoes. There is also a large chest-of-drawers containing linen, stockings, flannel-shirts, and drawers, etc. for the use of the prisoners. The walls of the bath-room are tastefully pencilled, similar to the office of the reception warder. It is provided with a fireplace to air the garments, and a cocoa-nut matting in the centre of the floor, for the comfort of the prisoners when undressed.

We followed the chief warder into one of the *reception cells*, which was thirteen feet long and seven feet wide, and nine feet at the bottom, and nine feet six inches at the top of the arch. It is ventilated by a grating over the door, connected with hot-air flues, extended throughout the building, and also by a trap in the window. The window of the cell is three feet six inches wide, and eighteen inches high, slightly rounded at the top, as seen in the engraving.

"The furniture of the cell," said the reception warder, "consists of a small deal table, attached to the right-hand side of the cell," which he folded down, like the leaf of a table; "also a water-closet, fixed into one of the farther corners of the cell, which has a wooden lid, and serves as a seat to the prisoner; a wash-hand basin and a tub for washing the feet."

Above the table is a gas-jet, over which the prisoner has no control. The chief warder observed, "It is lit at dusk, and extinguished at nine o'clock at night, when the prisoners retire to rest."

A copy of the rules and regulations of the prison, and of the dietary, are suspended in each cell, so that the prisoners may know how to conduct themselves.

On the right-hand corner, beside the door, are three small triangular shelves. The bedding, rolled firmly up and fastened with two leathern straps, is generally laid on the upper one; containing a pair of blankets, a rug, a pair of sheets, a horse-hair mattress, and a pillow, which, at night, are put into a hammock, suspended on two strong iron hooks on each side of the cell. "On the second shelf," added the governor, who had just entered the cell, "is a plate, together with a tin jug for gruel, a wooden salt-cellar, and a wooden spoon. On the lower shelf are deposited a Bible, prayer-book, and hymn-book; two combs and a brush, a cocoa-nut fibre rubber for polishing the floor, and underneath the lower shelf is a small drawer, containing the materials for cleaning the window of the cell.

"On the right-hand side of the door," continued the governor, "there is a small handle, of easy access to the prisoner, by which he is able to ring at any moment when he requires the attendance of an officer." This handle communicates with a bell outside, which is in hearing of the officer in charge. On the officer coming to the door of the cell he opens this wooden trap, which is about nine inches by seven.

"Above the trap is, you observe," said the governor, "a small circular inspection opening, covered with glass on the exterior and fine wire in the interior, by which the officer can inspect the cell from the outside, without the knowledge of the prisoner. After six o'clock in the evening the officers put on list shoes, so that they are able to patrol the corridors in silence, and the prisoner is not aware when he is visited."

The walls of the reception cells, like those in the corridors above, are whitewashed. There are six altogether, ranged on both sides of the ward. In the wide passage between these cells we saw a number of ladders, placed along the wall on our right hand, which are used in cleaning the windows and repairing the prison. On a stand in the centre, is a long ladder, set on wheels, resembling a fire-escape. We were informed it is used for cleaning the windows in the upper galleries of the prison.

There is a wooden machine in the same ward, to which boys are fastened when whipped by order of the magistrates. The governor observed to us, "I am happy to record that no prisoner has been flogged in this prison for prison offences for the last ten years, since its opening. None have been punished except those ordered by the magistrates at the police courts."

₊ *Discharge of Prisoners.*—We accompanied the governor to the office of the reception warder, as a party of prisoners were about to be liberated on the expiry of their sentence. They stood ranked up in single file in the reception hall. They were conducted separately into the presence of the governor, chief warder, and Mr. Keene, the clerk and keeper of the stores. The first prisoner brought in was a little Irish lad, with strongly marked Hibernian features, who was accosted thus :—

Governor. Boy, have you any friends to receive you when you leave the prison?

Boy. My mother lives in town, and my sisters are feather-strippers.

Gov. Were you ever in prison before?

Boy. No.

Gov. What was it which induced you to commit this felony?

Boy. I got into bad company, who enticed me away from my mother's house.

Gov. Where did you go after this?

Boy. I lived in a lodging-house, in Flower and Dean Street.

Gov. How old are you, boy?

Boy. I am eleven years old, and was never in prison before.

Gov. Had you any shoes when you came to prison?

Boy. I had a pair of old shoes, without soles.

The governor thereupon ordered one of the officers to provide him with a pair of shoes and stockings, on being discharged from custody.

The lad was conducted back to the reception hall, and another prisoner, a plain-looking lad, about twelve years of age, was introduced into the presence of the governor. He was dressed in shabby fustian trousers, a dark jacket, and light coloured neckerchief. He was charged with intent to steal.

Gov. Have you learned any business?

Boy. I was for a time working in a painter's shop.

Gov. Are you to keep out of bad company for the future?

Boy. Yes. I should like to go to sea.

The governor inquired of the chief warder the particular nature of the charge brought against him, when the latter stated it was for attempting to steal a handkerchief.

Gov. (addressing the boy). Did you steal any on former occasions?

Boy. I took twelve before, and sold them in Petticoat Lane.

Gov. What did you get for them?

Boy. Sometimes I have got as high as 1*s.* 6*d.* for some, and at other times only 2*d.*

Gov. How did you spend your money?

Boy. I paid 3*d.* a night for my lodging when I was able, and sometimes lived with my mother. I spent money gambling with other boys, and was often chastised by my mother for sleeping out.

A young man, about nineteen years of age, of a pale thin countenance, with a blue vacant eye, evidently of imbecile mind, was led into the reception warder's office. He stated he had been occasionally employed to drive cattle, that his father was dead, and his mother was married again to a soldier. He said that he was not right in his head when he came into the prison, and had slept several nights in sheds before he was arrested, and that he frequently had no bed to sleep in.

He was brought to the prison in a disgusting condition, covered with rags and vermin. The governor told the warder to give him some clothes, and desired him to keep himself clean. He advised him to go to the union to sleep when he had no money to pay for a night's lodging. The prisoner replied, " he would rather stay out at night than go to the union." The poor lad stated he had no friend in the world to take an interest in him, and thanked the governor for his kindness. He had been imprisoned for a petty felony, no doubt caused by his utter destitution.

A smart young man, of about nineteen years, beneath the middle size, a costermonger, who had been tried for having a squabble with the police, and who contrasted favourably with the lad that had just retired, was led before the governor. He stated, in answer to the interrogatories, that he was of Irish descent—his parents having belonged to the county of Kerry—that his mother was dead, and his father was an invalid. He keeps house with his sister, a young girl of about fourteen years of age.

We were present on another occasion, when a number of prisoners were discharged. One of them was a young man, of about thirty years of age, of dark, sallow complexion, with a long sharp face, and Irish features, charged with intent to steal.

Gov. Have you any friends in London?

The prisoner sighed, held down his head mournfully, and said nothing.

Gov. What are you to do to-day?

The prisoner stood with tears in his eyes, and made no reply.

The governor, turning to the clerk and storekeeper, told him to give the prisoner a shilling.

Gov. (looking to the prisoner). Are you willing to work in future for an honest livelihood?

TREAD-WHEEL AND OAKUM-SHED AT THE CITY PRISON, HOLLOWAY,

(WITH A DETACHMENT OF PRISONERS AT WORK ON THE WHEEL, AND THOSE WHO HAVE BEEN RELIEVED EMPLOYED PICKING OAKUM.)

Pris. I work here, and do not see how I should not work outside.

Another prisoner was introduced, a thin, tall young man, with a finely formed broad brow, an open intelligent countenance, and curly hair, attired in a decent dark dress, with a velvet neck to his coat.

Gov. (addressing the prisoner). You are a smart young man, and might enlist in the army.

Pris. I cannot be admitted into the army, as I am ruptured.

Gov. Have you learned to read ?

Pris. Yes.

Gov. You work well here, and might be industrious outside.

Pris. (smiling). I HAVE to work here.   (After a pause he added), But who will give me work when I am out of prison ?

Gov. You'll get work if you earnestly try to find it.   Will you promise that you will do what you can to lead an honest, industrious life ?

Pris. I'll try.

Gov. Have you any money ?

Pris. No, sir.   I do not know what to do.   I have no money, and have no friends to assist me.

Gov. I shall give you something to assist you for the present ; but remember (eyeing the prisoner keenly), do not come back to me again.

The prisoner gave him a military salute and retired.

A middle-aged man, a bricklayer, in light working dress, was ushered in.   He was a robust man, with high narrow forehead, clear gentle eye, carroty whiskers, and intelligent countenance, and was charged with stealing 26 lbs. of lead.

In answer to the interrogatories of the governor, he stated that he had a wife and six children—had never been in prison before—was not constantly in work out of doors, and had stolen the lead, to prevent his family from starving.   He had the appearance of an honest man ; and the expression of his countenance was clear and ingenuous.   The governor gave him 2s. 6d., and warned him not to be guilty of crime in future.

Another prisoner, introduced into the office of the reception warder, was a tall, middle-aged man, with a grey wig, long thin face, high narrow forehead, and clear callous-looking eye—very like an old offender.   He was neatly dressed in a dark tweed suit, and stood erect, with his great-coat on his arm.

Gov. (turning his eye on him). Were you ever here before ?

Pris. I never saw you in my life before.

After a pause, the prisoner turned round and gave an angry glance at the chief warder.

Chief Warder (addressing him). You look very hard at me.

As he left the office, the governor remarked to us, " That man is one of the most expert thieves in London, and a trainer of thieves."

A dark-complexioned, decent-looking man was then brought in.   He was attired in corduroy trousers, brown vest and silk stock, and had a blue great-coat on his arm, and had been convicted of having deserted his wife and five children.

Gov. I am sorry to see a man like you here.   Have you learned any trade ?

Pris. I am a labourer, and have no trade.   I was working at a pin-manufactory before I was brought here, and have often been out of work during this year, and my goods have been seized for arrears of rent.

Gov. You had a moustache when you came here ; and from your general appearance, I fear you are addicted to keeping company with other females besides your wife.   I hope you will not desert your wife any more.

Another prisoner was brought in.   He was a good-looking smart young man, of about twenty-three years of age, with blooming complexion, and fashionably attired : a pickpocket, charged with intent to steal a watch.

Gov. Young man, what are you to do when you are liberated?

Pris. I don't know.

Gov. Have you a home?

Pris. Yes.

Gov. What trade or calling does your father pursue?

Pris. He is a painter.

Gov. What is your occupation?

Pris. I have not learned any trade. I am troubled with a weak chest.

Gov. Have you no means of honest livelihood?

Pris. I learned mat-making here four years ago; but have no character to get employment.

Gov. Is your father a respectable man?

Pris. Yes. I must lead a different life than I have been doing for some time past.

Gov. How were you led into crime?

Pris. Bad company enticed me away.

Gov. Does your father know where you are?

Pris. Yes.

Gov. Have any of your friends visited you since you were here?

Pris. Yes.

After being examined separately by the governor, in presence of the chief warder and the clerk of the prison, the prisoners were conducted by the reception warder to the porter at the outer gate (who was furnished with a list of their names by the clerk), when they were liberated from prison.

We watched the last company discharged leave the gate of the prison. They proceeded a short distance with the measured tread and regular order of prison discipline, when they began to disperse—some of them going in the direction of the City, and the others bending their steps to the public-house opposite.

₊ *Mode of Receiving the Prisoners.*—In answer to our inquiries, the reception warder stated, the prisoners are always conveyed to the prison in a van, escorted by officers. This is generally done in the afternoon, after the sittings of the police-courts. They are forthwith admitted into the reception ward, where they are received by the governor or the chief warder, who ascertains if the warrants and the prisoners correspond. They are then committed to the custody of the reception warder, and placed in the reception cells, in their own clothing. They are afterwards taken from the cells separately and examined by the reception warder in his office.

A minute description of their person is taken, giving their name, age, height, weight, complexion, colour of hair, the colour of their eyes, whether of stout or slender make, their religion, state of instruction, whether married or single, whether they have any children, and if so, how many, the parish and country where born, the place of their last residence, trade or occupation, the magistrate who committed them, whether from the Central Criminal Court, the Mansion House, or Guildhall, their offence, their sentence, the expiration of their sentence, and other remarks.

In this description of the prisoner, particular notice is taken of the marks on his body, such as if he has wounds, or scars, or inkmarks, or is pitted with small-pox, etc.

After having passed this examination, the prisoners are separately removed to their respective cells. They are then taken by the reception warder into the bath and dressing-room, where their hair is cut according to sentence. They are here stripped of their own garments. A particular account of each separate article is taken in the clothing and property book, kept for the purpose, where the prisoner sees it carefully entered, and signs his name to attest its being correct.

This book is signed by the officer who receives the articles, and by the prisoner on his discharge, when the property received is returned to him.

These articles are carefully arranged and examined by the reception warder, and made up into bundles, with the names of the prisoners, their numbers, and sentences attached, and are carefully deposited on the rack in the storeroom.

When, upon examination, any of the clothing taken from the prisoners is found to be unclean, it is placed in a fumigating-stove, and thoroughly cleansed from vermin and infection.

The prisoners are taken from thence into the bath-room, where they are thoroughly cleansed in a warm bath, and then removed into the dressing-room adjoining, where they are supplied with an entire suit of prison clothing. They are afterwards removed to the reception cells, where they remain till the following morning, when they are taken by the reception warder into his office, and the prison rules are read and explained to them.

They are examined by the medical officer in the office of the reception warder, who certifies as to their state of health, and notice is taken of any ailment under which they may be labouring, which is duly entered. The medical officer decides as to their ability to perform the labour enjoined in their sentence.

The prisoners are again placed in the reception cells, where they are carefully visited by the governor in his daily inspection of the prisoners, after which they are removed into the body of the prison, to undergo their sentence. They are then committed to the care of the principal warder in charge at the central hall, when they are again examined by the chief warder, and appointed to their respective cells in the various corridors.

"At the expiry of their sentence," continued the reception warder, "they are placed in the reception cells, where they are stripped of the prison clothing and their own garments are returned to them. They are weighed in the weighing-machine, and their weight duly entered, to ascertain if they have gained or lost during their imprisonment."

They are afterwards examined by the governor in the reception office in the manner we have recorded in the presence of the chief warder and the clerk of the prison, when their case is carefully considered, and clothing and money given to them, as the case may require. They are sometimes sent to a home in the metropolis, or employment is found for them, and an outfit supplied at the expense of the City.

*** *Stores.*—We were introduced to Mr. C. A. Keene, the clerk and steward, who wished us to inspect his stores before proceeding to the main prison.

He first conducted us to the Clothing Department, situated at the basement, on the left of the female prison, in close proximity to the kitchen. This apartment is twenty-four feet long and twenty-one feet broad, lighted with two windows, four feet ten by three feet six, the panes of glass being set in iron frames, similar to those in the other cells. It is floored with wood, and roofed with brick and iron girders, the walls being painted of a light colour, and tastefully pencilled like the Reception Hall.

On the right hand as we enter is a number of presses or cupboards, containing male and female prison-clothing, officers' uniforms, and bedding, systematically arranged. On the top of these presses is a large number of shining tins for the use of the prisoners. There is also a chest of drawers, with small goods, such as needles, thread, and ironmongery ware, and over it is a rack covered with tins, different in size and shape, to prevent their being mixed together in the various branches of the prison.

On a table in the centre of the room is ranged an assortment of clothing for the children of the Emmanuel Hospital, all of which is made in Holloway Prison. Their dress consists of corduroy trowsers and brown jackets and vests.

The clothing of the male prisoners consists of jackets, vests, and trowsers, of gray army cloth, and stocks, braces, and caps. The caps are made of blue indigo-dyed worsted, and the stockings of a gray worsted, knitted by the female prisoners. Shirts of red striped calico, flannel shirts and drawers of blue striped serge, are also made by the female prisoners. These are systematically arranged, and neatly tied up in separate bundles of a dozen each. There is also a considerable store of shoes of the same quality, sizes from two to ten—No. 2 being very small, and No. 10 very large.

The clothing is arranged in like manner, having the number of the size wrought in. The clothes are from two to seven sizes.

The female clothing consists of a blue gown with a red stripe; petticoats made of linsey-woolsey; shifts of red striped calico, the same material as the men's shirts; and neckerchiefs of blue check of a large pattern; the linen caps are similar to those worn in workhouses; the stockings are made of a dark blue indigo-dyed worsted, similar to the male prisoners' caps; the cloaks, furnished with hoods, are made of linsey-woolsey, similar to the petticoats.

The bedding is of two different kinds, for the infirmary and the ordinary cells. The infirmary bedding consists of blue and white check coverlets or counterpanes, such as are used in hospitals in the metropolis; the sheets and pillow-cases are made of blue striped calico; the blankets are of substantial quality, white and clear in appearance, bordered with red stripes. The ordinary bedding for the cells consists of a hammock made of strong canvas, a rug, and a blanket, the latter being similar to that used in the infirmary, with sheets and pillow-case made of a coarse brown material, termed "Forfar sheeting." The bed is made of canvas stuffed with coir fibre.

On the left side of the room is exposed a large quantity of shoes made for the boys and girls of the Emmanuel Hospital.

On the mantel-piece is a large number of wooden salt-cellars, turned in the prison, for the use of the prisoners.

Leaving this storeroom, we pass through a courtyard situated on the left of the female wing leading from the larger courtyard in front of the prison, behind the archway, to the kitchen. Part of this courtyard adjoining the kitchen is covered with a roof of fluted glass, for the purpose of receiving stores that require to be weighed. Here we found a large patent weighing-machine of a lever description, made by Short and Fanner, of St. Martin's-le-Grand. It is considered to be a very exact and valuable instrument, and weighs from half a-pound to twenty-four cwt.

We were shown into the Hardware Store, consisting of two divisions. One of these contains a large number of iron bedsteads that were removed from the old prison at Giltspur Street, in the City (the Compter), to be used in Holloway Prison when necessary. There are several old chests of drawers, and sundry iron fittings, also removed from the old prison, which are brought into use here as occasion may require.

On entering the other division, we found a large drawing of one of the huge griffins at the entrance of the prison. This storeroom is of a very peculiar shape, and is situated at the basement of the B wing. It is floored partly with asphalte and partly with York slab. There are five windows in this storeroom, precisely similar to those in the cells; the panes are of fluted glass set in an iron framework.

On the left hand of the stair there are racks in which large quantities of brown leather are deposited for the manufacture of boots and shoes, with a considerable stock of brushes of various kinds carefully arranged. The scrubbing-brushes and cell-brushes are made by the prisoners.

There is a large pile of bars of soap to be used in the laundry, and in cleaning the prison, and large wicker baskets lined with tin, for the purpose of carrying away the dust and rubbish from the corridors and offices of the prison. Along the walls are placed bread-baskets, clothes-baskets, and other articles made by the prisoners.

Facing the doorway are two large chests of drawers with cupboards, containing locks and general fittings of cell-doors, also the iron tools used by the smiths and carpenters, wooden spoons, and cocoa-nut rubbers, the latter being used for polishing the asphalte floors. These rubbers are made by the prisoners from the cocoa-nut husk, and are found to be very useful in cleaning the floors. They are composed of the husk pegged and glued together, nearly in the form of a cone, of a convenient size for the hand. Samples of these have been got by many governors of prisons, with the view of adopting them in their own establishments.

In the centre of this storeroom is a table with a pair of scales for weighing blacklead, starch, and other small goods, and at the farther end are arranged quantities of soda, whiting, and lampblack. We observed a considerable number of water closets, such as those used in the prison cells, and pieces of stone-pipe used in the draining of the prison. There are also large cans of oils used for various purposes, such as for the machinery in the engine-room, the treadwheel, and the pumps, and for painting the walls of the prison, together with a large number of bundles of firewood.

Mr. Keene particularly called our attention to a pile of white bricks used for cleaning hearthstones, which are considered to be very economical. Various parties have taken specimens of them for the use of public buildings.

We then accompanied him to the Provision Store, situated at the farther end of the kitchen, on the right hand. It is thirty-three feet long and fifteen feet broad, being the basement of four cells. This apartment contains six large bins of oatmeal, barley, and cocoa. At the end of the storeroom is a rack for the reception of bread when received from the contractor, previously to its being issued to the cook. On the right hand side are four dressers built in a recess, and on one of them are deposited several large blocks of salt.

Under the centre arch is a mill for grinding cocoa for the use of the prison. The cocoa, made from the nuts is considered much superior to that generally purchased in the shops. There is here a weighing-machine, used for distributing the provisions daily to the cook, and a puncheon of molasses, for sweetening the cocoa and gruel served out to the prisoners.

This apartment has a wooden tank, lined with lead, for supplying water to the kitchen. It is well lighted and ventilated, and paved with York slab.

In close proximity there are cellars for the reception of potatoes, for the use of the prison.

We afterwards went with Mr. Keene to the cook's store, a small room adjoining the kitchen, about twenty-six feet long and fourteen wide, extending over the space of three cells, with windows similar.

It is floored with asphalte, and roofed with brick.

We observed two large trays of bread on one of the dressers—being part of the day's allowance, received from Mr. Keene on the previous evening. On another dresser there was a number of knives, used by the prisoners. In the centre of the storeroom was a large block of ash, where the butcher-meat is chopped by the cook. There is here an iron-bar, to which hooks are attached, on which the meat is suspended.

₂ *Newly-arrived Prisoners.*—Leaving the storerooms, we returned to the Reception Ward, to be present when the governor inspected the prisoners who were brought in the prison-van last evening.

We accompanied him over the different cells. In one of them we saw a clever little boy, of fourteen years of age, with engaging countenance, and soft Irish tongue. Though young in years he was an old offender, and an adroit pickpocket. On the present occasion he was brought to Holloway Prison on a charge of felony, and was sentenced to fourteen days' imprisonment, and four years in a reformatory. He had previously been three years in a reformatory on the Surrey side, and had the reputation of being a very bad boy.

In answer to the interrogatories of the governor, he stated that his parents came from Manchester, and his father was a bricklayer, and addicted to intoxicating drink; that he himself lived by thieving, and chiefly frequented London Bridge and Whitechapel. He confessed he had been seven times imprisoned—three times in Wandsworth, twice at Maidstone, once in Westminster Bridewell, and once in Holloway.

He was very restless in his manner while examined by the governor, and often arched his eyebrows and protruded his tongue in an artful manner, and appeared to be proud of what he had done, rather than ashamed of it.

He farther added, that he lodged in Kent Street, at the east end of the metropolis, along with a number of other boys, young felons, like himself, where a great many girls also lodged. He paid 3d. a night for his bed, and as soon as he got his breakfast he went regularly out to thieve, with other two boys. He dipped the pockets, and gave the articles stolen to his companions. He sometimes also stole money from shop-tills.

In another cell we saw a young man, about nineteen years of age, the son of an Irishman, an old Indian soldier, who was charged with stealing a coat. He was a smart little lad, with a keen eye and firm lip. He was carefully examined by the governor; the details being of a sorrowful character. He was a painful instance, among many which are ever and anon occurring, where the children of respectable parents are led into crime by bad company through the insidious temptations which abound in our great metropolis.

The next prisoner was a young man, of seventeen years of age, with a very low forehead and thin, pale, earnest-looking countenance. While being examined he stood with his hands behind his back. He had been imprisoned for a petty felony at a gentleman's house.

He told the governor he had neither father or mother—that his mother died two years and a half ago, after which he resided in lodging-houses, and got his livelihood by thieving. He said he was willing to work, if he could get honest employment. He did not like to be a thief, and would gladly abandon it, if he could. He had no one to care for him, and was entirely destitute.

Gov. Would you like to go to sea?

Pris. I would gladly go, if I could get an opportunity.

Gov. If you behave well I shall take you by the hand; but remember, boy, and do not deceive me.

Pris. I promise to do so.

The reception warder observed, he was to be six weeks here, so that he would have time to observe his conduct.

On going into another cell, the governor, after looking intently on another Irish lad, about seventeen years of age, with small head and large eyes, turned to us and said, "Here is a man I have done as much for as though he were my own son."

Then, addressing the prisoner, he added, "You told me, when last in custody, you were to go over to Ireland to your uncle, a shoemaker there; having partly learned shoemaking in prison, under my care. I paid your passage and sent you over, and you promised to learn a trade and become a decent man." Turning to us and the reception warder, the governor added, "To my astonishment, he has come here again, to be imprisoned for two months, for going over premises at the wharf, about one o'clock at midnight."

Pris. I was seven weeks with my uncle.

Gov. Why did you not stay?

Pris. Because he kept jawing me.

Gov. You came back to get into company with your old companions.

Reception Warder. This is a very bad case.

Gov. You know, boy, you have a very bad temper. I tried to help you, and you have come back to me again.

On going into the next cell, where there was a quiet, decent-looking man, the governor observed, "Here is a very unfortunate man, who is repeatedly getting drunk, and is thereby brought into trouble. He never was charged with stealing in his life, but squabbles on the streets."

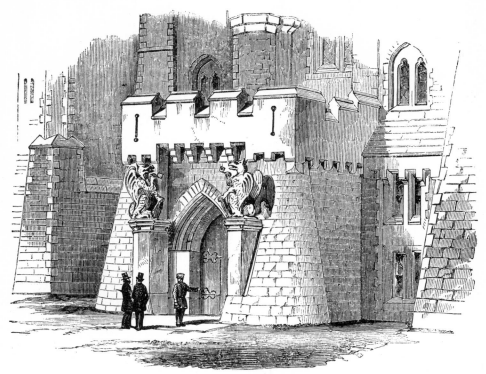

INNER GATE OF THE CITY PRISON, HOLLOWAY.

INTERIOR OF THE KITCHEN AT THE CITY PRISON, HOLLOWAY.

Pris. I am here for other people's faults this time.

Gov. You know the magistrates of the City would not send you here for other people's faults.

Pris. The others quarrelled, and drove me right through a pane of glass.

Gov. How often have you been in prison before?

Pris. Thirty-two times.

Reception Warder (addressing the governor). Thirty-three times, sir.

Gov. Your chief misfortune is drink. This sends you frequently to prison.

The inmate of the adjoining cell was a young man, beneath the middle size, with a well-formed countenance. On the governor entering the prisoner appeared lazy and indifferent, for which he was rebuked.

Gov. This man is sentenced to three months' imprisonment, for attempting to pick pockets, in company of a young woman.

Gov. How long have you been out of prison?

Pris. Eighteen months. I have tried to get honest employment, and could not succeed.

Gov. Be candid with me, and do not deceive me. You know you formerly pretended you were subject to fits. Why did you say so?

Pris. To get quit of the hard labour.

Gov. This is very wrong. It is not only the value of the labour—you insult your Maker by pretending you are afflicted with diseases you don't have.

The other prisoner in the male reception-cells was a smart youth, of upwards of twenty years of age, with a heavy under-face, red hair, and wrinkled brow, having the appearance of a fast young man.

On entering the cell, the governor remarked, "A more intelligent lad I never had in prison."

Pris. I had good prospects before me.

Gov. Are these all gone now?

Pris. Yes.

Gov. Through drink?

Pris. Yes.

Gov. For yourself, or for other people.

Pris. Other people too. I had a good situation in one of the boats of the Navigation Company, and have cooked in the Prince of Wales steamer. I was a time-keeper at the Exhibition of 1851, and have received a good education.

⁎⁎ *Main Passage.*—Leaving the reception ward, we proceeded with the chief warder up the staircase, which is elegantly matted, and leads to the main passage, communicating with the central hall, seen through the glass-panelled doors, directly in front of us. The hall, at this extremity, is about twenty feet wide.

On our right hand is the governor's office, and alongside is a handsome cheerful apartment, for the convenience of the board of magistrates, who inspect the prison. The latter is tastefully furnished, with a Turkey carpet and a long mahogany table, with a writing-desk at one end, and an ample supply of mahogany chairs. On the left is the clerk's office, with an anteroom also attached. On each side is a staircase, leading to a suite of upper rooms in the two floors above.

There are two doors, with panes of glass in the upper panels, between the governor's office and the central hall, which are generally kept locked. The one is situated about thirty-five feet in the interior, and the other at the farther end, opening into the various corridors. On the outside of the first door referred to, the walls are tastefully pencilled, the passage is paved with York slab, and the roof is arched, with seven immense iron girders. At the extremity of the outer hall, bounded by the latter door, is a door leading, on the right hand, to a small room, with several stalls, erected alongside of each other, for relatives and friends communicating with the prisoners. They are roofed with wire, to prevent anything being thrown over, or conveyed to the latter, who are stationed in similar stalls on the other side. The wire-screen also extends on the side of the visiting-boxes facing the prisoners. A copy of the prison rules, relating to the conduct and treatment of the prisoners, certified by the Secretary of State, on the 6th of June, 1860, is hung up on the walls.

On the left of the outer hall is the record office and the solicitor's room, and also a room for persons visiting the prisoners, exactly similar to the one already described.

The outer hall is furnished with a bell communicating with the offices of the clerk, chief warder, chaplain, and other surrounding apartments.

We passed onwards through one of the folding-doors into the inner passage. On the right hand, as we enter, are two doors, communicating with the prisoners' visiting-room, one of them leading into a narrow passage, between the stalls, of about five feet wide, where an officer is stationed during the interview between the prisoners and their friends, and the other into the stalls, where the prisoners are admitted, which are covered with a wire-screen, similar to the other stalls alluded to. On the same side of the inner passage is the office of the deputy-governor, with a waiting-room attached to it.

On the opposite side of the passage are two similar doors, leading into the other apartment, where the prisoners meet with those relatives and friends who visit them; another door leads to the surgeon's room, with an anteroom attached. The inner hall is floored with asphalte, shining black as ebony.

We accompanied the chief warder into his office, and was shown the general receipt book of male prisoners incarcerated in the prison; the general report book, and the prisoners' misconduct book; the latter of which, by the way, had unusually few entries inserted, there not having been lodged a single complaint against any prisoner for four days previously. We also saw the thermometer journal, in which the temperature of sixteen portions of the prison is recorded three times a day.

Having inquired of the chief warder as to the manner in which the prisoners are disposed over the various corridors, and in reference to the work allotted them, he gave us the following information:—

"After the prisoners are bathed in the reception ward, they are inspected by the surgeon on the following morning, who certifies as to their fitness for labour, independent of what their sentence may be. I then receive them from the reception warder. I find if the register number put on their arm corresponds with the number in the receipt-book for male prisoners, together with their name, age, occupation, previous conviction (if any), name of the committing magistrate, and their excuse from labour (if any), with the date of their discharge. I insert the whole of this on a card, which is given to the prisoner, and is hung up in his cell, together with a copy of the prison rules and dietary."

The prisoners are allotted to their respective wards according to their criminal character, sentence, and occupation.

The following is a list of the cells in the various corridors:—

Corridors.	Floors in each.	No. of cells.	No. of cells in each corridor.
A	1	20	
	2	19	
	3	21	71
	4	11	
B	1	21	
	2	20	
	3	22	77
	4	14	

Corridors.	Floors in each.	No. of cells.	No. of cells in each corridor.
....		21	
	2	20	
	3	22	67
	Refractory cells *	4	
D	1	24	
	2	25	
	3	25	80
	Refractory cells	6	
Juvenile wing E	1	17	
	2	20	
	3	24	70
	Refractory cells	6	
	Reception cells	3	
Female wing F	1	16	
	2	20	
	3	24	65
	Refractory cells	2	
	Reception cells	3	
Reception ward for male adults at entry hall of prison.		8	

Total   438

We were furnished with the following classification of prisoners shewing the manner in which they are distributed over the Prison :—

Corridor A 1 }
          2 } Felons not known.
          3 }
          4   Summary felons.

" B 1 } Mixed long fines and tradesmen.
    2 }
    3 } Summary felons.
    4 }

" C 1   Convicted misdemeanours.
    2   Do   and summary misdemeanours.
    3   Known, convicted, and summary misdemeanours.

" D 1 }
    2 } All known felons, frequently in prison.
    3 }

Juvenile wing E 1   Convicted felons and long fine--known.
              2   Summary felons—known.
              3   Unknown felons, and summary convictions.

Female wing F 1   Felons known.
            2   Do. unknown.
            3   Unknown felons and misdemeanours.

∗ Central Hall.—We went forward with the chief warder to the central hall, a semi-circular space about forty feet in length, with four handsome corridors radiating around it, as seen in the engraving of the ground-plan of the prison. The floor of the central hall and of the extensive corridors consists of asphalte, finely polished daily with blacklead

* In consequence of the good behaviour of the prisoners the present governor has converted these four refractory cells into a workshop.

and brush; the walls are of a light colour, resembling the entry hall, and similarly pencilled in a tasteful manner. The central hall rises in the form of a lofty dome, surmounted by a glass roof, in the form of a sexagon, set in a massive iron frame, several tons in weight, with a large grating for ventilation.

Here we found two principal warders in attendance, in their uniforms, with keys suspended from their dark shining belts, and three gold laced stripes on their right arm. On the right, as we enter the central hall, is a neat writing-office set in a glass framework, where one of the principal warders is frequently on duty, and supervises the various corridors.

There are two skylights in the flooring of the central hall, 4 ft. 6 in. wide, by 6 feet long, consisting of very thick glass, supported on iron bars, giving light to the kitchen beneath. There is also a trap with a lifting machine on either side of the hall, between corridors A and B, and corridors C and D, communicating with the kitchen, by which trays of provisions are hoisted up on cradles to the different cells, along conducting-rods of bright steel, about 40 feet in height; the details of which process is fully given in the description of Pentonville Prison.

In the central hall is a corkscrew metal staircase, leading from the basement to the different galleries, which is surmounted with a dial; and also a large bell which summons the prisoners to their labour, and calls them to chapel.

While we lingered in the central hall with the chief warder, we saw several of the prisoners, in their dark gray prison dress, engaged in cleaning the various corridors around us. They had a more cheerful appearance than the masked men at Wandsworth and Pentonville, and proceeded about their work with great alacrity; some were sweeping the dark floors with long brooms, and others were kneeling down and scrubbing them with energy, until the asphalte shone with a bright polish. Several of the officers in their dark blue uniforms were stationed in the different galleries, attending to their wards. We noticed a detachment of prisoners walk in single file through the central hall, with their hands behind their back, giving a military salute to the chief warder as they passed on from the exercising ground and treadmill to their different cells.

We also saw the schoolmaster moving from cell to cell in one of the galleries, attended by a prisoner, who carried a basket of library books, to be deposited for the use of the prisoners.

We inspected several of the corridors, which are about 133 feet in length from the central hall, and are lighted from the roof by two large skylights, which have openings at the sides for ventilation. A and B wings in addition to those are lighted by large windows at the extremities, provided with fluted glass. At dusk, each of the corridors is lighted with gas.

There is a staircase at the extremity of corridors B and C, leading to the galleries above; with one nearer to the centre in A and D wings. There is also a staircase leading to the basement of each.

Having taken a general survey of the main prison, we now proceeded to a more careful inspection of the arrangements of the interior.

In passing from the central hall on the right of corridor A is a small storeroom, about the size of two cells, for the convenience of the various corridors of the adult male pris n. We noticed on a rack a large pile of prisoners' clothing of various sizes, consisting of trousers, jackets, vests, caps, handkerchiefs, flannel shirts, and drawers. Above this was placed an assortment of brooms and brushes for cleansing the prison, while beneath, there was a row of drawers, in which were deposited sundry other articles used in the cells. A prisoner— an active young man—who has been warehouseman to a firm in the city, was in attendance at the time we entered.

₊ Cells.—We entered one of the adjoining cells, which is 7 feet wide, and 13 feet long at the top, and 9 feet at the bottom of the arch. It is floored with asphalte, as all the other

cells are, and kept carefully polished and whitewashed. The furniture, consists of a small folding table, attached to one of the sides of the cell, a copper basin, and water-closet, and a water tap covered, resembling those in Wandsworth Prison, with pipes inside, communicating with the water-closet and wash-basin, a soap-box, with soap, a nail brush, and small piece of flannel for cleansing.

In a corner beside the door is a small triangular cupboard with three shelves, on the top of which is the hammock rolled up, and bound firmly together by two strong leather straps. The furniture here is exactly the same as in the cells in the reception ward, except that here there are several library books for the use of the prisoners. In the cell we entered, we saw two or three volumes—one of them titled "Summer in the Antarctic Regions," and another containing the "Narrative of the Loss of the 'Amazon,'" and "Life in New Zealand."

There is a hot-air flue over the door. At the opposite side of the cell, nearly on a level with the asphalte flooring, there is an extraction flue; while under the window is a ventilator, admitting pure air at the pleasure of the prisoner. The deputy-governor opened the ventilator, when a current of fresh air was admitted into the cell.

We were introduced to the engineer of the prison, who gave us a fuller explanation of this ventilating apparatus. He stated, in front of the cell doors, under the asphalte flooring, is a flue enclosing four pipes on each side. It is connected with the main flue, and conveys the warm air through the iron grating over the cell door. The iron grating at the back of the cell, near to the floor, conveys the air into an extraction flue, leading to the roof of the building, discharging it into a ventilating shaft, situated at the angle of the C and D wing and a portion of the kitchen.

"You observe," said the engineer, "that on the right side of the door there is a small, dark iron handle. When turned round by the prisoner in his cell, it communicates with a gong in the centre of the corridor, which gives notice to the warder in charge, and at the same time a small metal plate is thrown out at the exterior of the cell, by which he is able to learn which of the prisoners in his ward has struck the gong."

The window of the cell is 3 ft. 6 in. by 18 in., similar to those in the reception ward.

On the wall is suspended a card, containing the prisoner's registered number, his age, etc., as already referred to; and alongside is a copy of the prison regulations as to the disposal of his time, from 5·45 A.M., to 9 P.M., specifying how he is to be occupied in his cell, as well as out of it, in chapel, at school, on the exercise ground, etc.

Corridor A is divided into four wards. Nos. 1, 2, 3, consist of felons guilty of their first offence, and No. 4 of parties tried summarily.

. *Mat-rooms.*—As many of the prisoners in corridor A were absent from their cells at their other exercises and employments, we meantime visited the basement, where we saw a number of mats, rugs, and matting, of various kinds, and of different colours and designs, carefully packed up ready for removal. At the further end of the basement is a deal table, where a prisoner was stationed binding the mats; and in the right-hand corner was a pile of worsted of different colours, pink, yellow, black, roan, green, puce, and brown, ready to be woven into fancy rugs and mats.

We were introduced by the chief warder to Mr. Davies, an active and most intelligent man, who holds the office of mat and rug instructor. He is not an officer of the prison, but is employed by contractors over this large department of prison labour. We entered a mat-room, where twenty-two prisoners were engaged at their looms, weaving different descriptions of mats and rugs. This apartment is spacious and well lighted, with a lofty roof, about 27 feet high. It is ventilated by flues on each side, connected with the main shaft. There is a staircase on the left, leading to a mat-room above of a similar size, about the dimensions of twelve ordinary cells. The prisoners were of various ages, varying from twenty to forty-five. We observed an elderly man of sixty years of age, of superior appearance, employed in winding coloured worsted for the use of the looms, while a younger man beside him was working at a spindle; several of them had their jackets off as they plied the shuttle on the loom. Four men were engaged in the centre of the room, putting a chain on a beam; one man was guiding the chain, other two were stationed by it, one of them with his arms crossed, resting on an iron bar, by the assistance of which this operation is done; and another lad, of about nineteen years of age, was busy holding up the chain to guide it properly.

The trade instructor called our attention to another description of mat-making from cocoa-nut fibre, of a heavier description, used in halls, at front doors, and in private houses and public offices.

Pointing to one of the looms beside us, he explained—It is formed of a square wooden frame with internal fittings, consisting of iron buttons, and a reed and harness, through which is drawn each thread of the chain used in the construction of the mats. The rug chain forms the back of the mat or rug. The face of the mat consists of coloured worsted, and the best description of cocoa-nut fibre.

The prisoners had generally a quiet, industrious demeanour as they were engaged at their toil, under the supervision of one of the warders of the prison.

The floor was littered with mats newly cut from the looms, with bundles of coir, termed "dolls," and with coloured fibre, the latter being used in introducing the initials of the names of parties by whom the mats were ordered.

On our leaving this mat-room, the deputy-governor conducted us into another associated room up-stairs, containing looms similar to the one described. There were tables here, where several prisoners were employed finishing the mats, by sewing borders upon them made of plaited sennit, and a large shearing machine, used in cutting the face of the mats and rugs. This room is well lighted and ventilated, and presented a very lively appearance of industry.

Mr. Davies informed us, that the mats and rugs, of various kinds, made in Holloway Prison, are contracted for by his employers. "I believe," he added, "that they have done so for the past seven years; and this work is executed under my supervision. The discipline is maintained by the presence of a warder in each mat-room. The cheapest description of mats we make here are of a common description, used for ordinary household purposes, as well as for carriages, chaises, dog-carts, etc. They are made with red, green, and blue borders.

"The next quality consists of a superior description of mats, with fancy borders. These are more coloured, and fetch a better price in the market. They are much superior in quality to the others just alluded to, and are chiefly used among the higher circles—the price being commensurate with their quality. This comprises the two kinds of rug-mats. Some door-mats are made with a fibre face, without the aid of colouring. These are used for the interior of houses, and are very durable and remarkably fine in appearance, when well finished."

With reference to the heavier description of cocoa-nut fibre bass-mat, Mr. Davies observed, "These are made from the fibre, spun into strands of a moderate size. They are used for doors of public offices, and occasionally in private houses, and are in almost universal demand. The material is so tenacious, that water has comparatively no power to rot or injure it, consequently they are of great durability. In fact," said Mr. Davies, "we have some in the prison that have been in daily use for several years, and are apparently as substantial as ever. If I may be allowed to suggest, they would be very useful for dog-kennels, belonging to parties in the sporting world. No ordure of the dogs would rot them. They have a brushlike face, favourable to cleanliness. They could be easily made to fit the kennels, and I believe, if they were changed daily, they would be the means of preventing much distemper among valuable dogs."

Mr. Davies showed us some mats made for the South Western Railway Company, with the initials of the company inscribed in the body of the mats. They were evidently of superior workmanship, and reflect credit on the firm under whose superintendence they have been manufactured in the prison.

There is another description of mat made in the prison, which has a fancy border, with various devices. They are extremely strong, as well as elegant in appearance.

We were next shown a large stock of hearth-rugs, many of them very beautiful in design, after choice patterns, and the various colours being carefully blended in unison, produced a most harmonious effect. "These rugs," said Mr. Davies, "are made with the fingers, in contradistinction to many of the so-called velvet-pile rugs, that are made by the warp passing through what we technically call the 'harness,' and thus forming the body of the rug, making them very light and thin. The latter are not by any means to be compared with the substantial rugs made by the fingers. The velvet-pile rugs have a beautiful appearance, but are devoid of warmth, and are not lasting.

"Here we also manufacture cocoa-nut matting, which is in universal demand, and is used in churches, public offices, and dwelling-houses, being often substituted for oilcloth. It is not made with a fibre face, like the mats, but is wrought in the looms, similar to the texture of canvas. It has great durability, and is of a lighter description, and capable of being applied to more general use.

"The prisoners commence their operations in the mat-room at the ordinary description of mat-making, and are generally about a month in becoming proficient in making common mats. Some have a quicker aptitude than others. There is a young man in the mat-room, in Corridor B," continued Mr. Davies, "who has only been occupied at this labour about fourteen days, and has made proficiency from the lowest to the highest description of mats in this short time, being a man of uncommon ability. I never had such an instance before."

While we were engaged with Mr. Davies, in his office, obtaining information, a prisoner, a modest-looking, pale-faced young man, of about twenty-five years of age, called in, asking directions regarding the manufacture of his mat. Mr. Davies remarked to us and the chief warder, "This is a particularly clever young man. He makes first-class work, and a large quantity of it—considerably more than most of the others. I believe he has been a carman outside. He does not seem to work hard; yet he accomplishes a great amount of labour. Several of his companions waste their strength, and would appear, to a superficial eye, to be doing more work than he.

"Some of the men become proficient in a short time; others are more obtuse, and are never proficient at it.

"The prisoners work seven hours a-day, beginning their labour at seven in the morning, and finishing at a quarter to seven o'clock in the evening. They are occupied several hours in the interval at their meals, at chapel and school, and in the exercising ground.

Many of the prisoners learn mat-making in the prison, and are able to earn a livelihood on their being discharged, if they were disposed to work, and could find employment. Some of them are carpenters, smiths, and belong to other trades, who, on their liberation, pursue their ordinary avocations; others are habitual felons, who, on their being released from prison, generally return to their old criminal courses.

Meantime a young man, with a dull stolid look, came into the office of the trade-instructor and wanted one of the implements used in mat-making to be exchanged. Mr. Davies remarked, "This is a specimen of the troublesome class I have to deal with. They do little work, and give me an infinite deal of trouble. On the other hand, I am happy to say I have not a few who do their duty in apparently a conscientious manner.

"The persons employed in dressing the mats," he continued, "are taken from the looms in rotation, and work the machine which is employed in shearing them. Four prisoners are employed on this machine. The elderly men are generally employed in the lighter occupation of sewing the mats.

"Mats and rugs, etc., are generally made in looms in this prison. We have also frames for manufacturing them. The latter are not required at present, but were lately in use.

" I have the supervision of five associated rooms in corridors A and B, containing sixty-one weavers; fourteen persons engaged in sewing the mats, and three winding and preparing the material for the use of the workmen."

The chief warder introduced us to the warder in charge, a tall, athletic man in officers' uniform. The latter stated that in each mat-room every loom is numbered. Each prisoner's cell number and register number are marked against the loom they work in; and the mats as they are brought in from day to day, are regularly entered. A weekly return is made showing the amount of the prisoner's work, as well as of his earnings.

The prisoners are not allowed to speak to each other, but to the trade instructor and warder in charge.

Leaving the upper mat-room we found ourselves in the first gallery of Corridor A. The chief warder called our attention to several gongs in the centre of the galleries which are connected with the prisoners' cells as already mentioned; and to a slate suspended beside each ward on which are entered the prisoners' diet and labour.

Before leaving Corridor A, we went into several of the cells, where prisoners are confined for their first offence. We found an old man seated in a corner of his cell, with a quantity of junk lying by his side. He had a disabled hand, and was not able to separate the strands of the rope which looked as hard as a carved bar of oak. The chief warder kindly showed him the mode of untwisting the rope which was to be teased into oakum. The old man told us a very pitiable tale. He had been engaged as a messenger to a gentleman at Gravesend to collect the pilot dues from the shipping masters there, and had, unfortunately, on one occasion, when the worse of intoxicating liquor, been arrested with an ox-tail unlawfully in his possession. He was sentenced to fourteen days' imprisonment with hard labour, but was exempted, the surgeon having certified his unfitness for it; which was signified by the red cross on one of the arms of his jacket.

The chief warder conducted us into another cell, where we found a robust, dark-complexioned man of about forty years of age. He informed us he had been a porter to a wine merchant in the city, and had taken several sample bottles of brandy to the amount of £5, and was sentenced to six calendar months' imprisonment. He told us he had a wife and family, and that this was also his first offence.

In another cell we found a smart, fair-complexioned young man, who had at one time been in business as a draper, and had spent large sums in fast life in London. He had wasted his means among thoughtless and dissipated young men and girls, and was now in prison for stealing a counterpane and sheet, of the value of a few shillings, having been reduced to desperate shifts from poverty. He had been sentenced to six calendar months' imprisonment.

In an adjoining cell we saw a good-looking young man, of about nineteen years of age, picking oakum. He had been a clerk in a lawyer's office in the City, and had forged an order for two law books from a library, to be disposed of for a small sum of money to spend in pleasure. He was in the habit of frequenting theatres and dancing saloons. He now undergoes a sentence of twelve months' imprisonment with hard labour. He observed to the chief warder it was his first offence.

After inspecting the cells and associated rooms of Corridor A, we went with the chief warder to Corridor B. On looking over the gallery into the basement of this wing we saw four prisoners engaged winding in the vicinity of the other mat-room.

At the extremity of Corridor B are two large, airy rooms, about 24 feet square, and upwards of 20 feet high. One of them is occupied as a school-room for the adult males, and the other as an associated room for tailors and shoemakers.

₊ *Schools of the Male Prison.*—We entered the adult school-room, which is an airy, well-lighted apartment, situated on the second gallery. There is a table in the room, beside which the teacher is seated, and several forms are ranged in front and on each side ; the seats being raised toward the back.

There is also a black board beside the table in front of the seats. On the left hand, near the fireplace, is a book-case containing library books, maps, music books, etc., and on the walls are suspended maps of the British Empire, Palestine, and the World, with plates of the Theory of the Seasons and the Holy Tabernacle.

The class was not assembled at the time of our visit.

We accompanied the reception warder to the juvenile school-room, at the juvenile wing of the prison, and found Mr. Barre, the teacher, busy with a class of boys, who were reading their primers. The lessons consisted of monosyllables, such as " They walk by faith and not by sight;" " Their steps are known of the Lord, and he has joy in their way." The teacher was seated in his uniform by a table, with a class of half a dozen boys ranged on a form before him. Some were writing on their slates, while others were reading. Sometimes they read together, and at other times one boy read by himself.

On the mantel-piece was a black board, and a map of England and Wales was suspended on the wall. The boys apparently belonged to the lowest order of society. Some of them appeared to be very intelligent, and were very attentive. A very interesting lad sat beside us, with light blue eyes, fair complexion, and well-formed countenance. Alongside was a robust, heavy-browed Irish boy, with a large head, and his face marked by smallpox. He had a small gray eye, and spoke in soft, Irish accents.

A pale-faced lad in the centre of the class appeared to be a better scholar than some of the others, and had a very engaging, thoughtful appearance.

After hearing them read for some time, the teacher exercised them in simple questions of mental arithmetic, which aroused their attention considerably. A fair-haired Irish boy showed little interest in his reading, but his face beamed with pleasure, and his eye sparkled while his teacher proposed to the class repeated questions such as the following :—" Suppose a man to be 64 years old, and to have a son 25 years of age, how much older is the father than the son ?" And, again, " What is the value of 24 pence ?"

The teacher concluded with a few judicious, moral remarks. In showing the value of arithmetic, he impressed upon them the importance of thinking for themselves, and observed " that the boy who cleans knives would do this better if he thought for himself." On the other hand, he pointed out the danger of their not being considerate ; that they were more easily seduced into bad company, and led into crime. He showed them the necessity of care in little things ; that it illustrates a man's character, and leads to fortune in after life. He exhorted them not to be a burden to others, but to labour cheerfully for themselves, and closed with an interesting and impressive illustration : A little boy saw a gentleman drop his handkerchief, and smartly picked it up and ran with it to him. The gentleman offered him a piece of money, but the boy declined to accept it. Struck with the noble spirit of the poor boy, he went to see his parents who lived in the next street, and also called on his schoolmaster, who highly recommended him. He got the boy a humble situation in his commercial establishment, where by industry and perseverance he afterwards became a partner of the firm.

The teacher told his pupils there was work in London for the steady and industrious.

Mr. Barre informed us :—" I teach four classes daily, which consist of boys and adults. There are two classes of adults in the morning, and two consisting of juveniles in the afternoon. The first class of adults are those who are learning their letters and monosyllables. They are also exercised in mental arithmetic, and are taught to write letters on their slates ; none of them write in copy-books. There are, on an average, 20 persons attending this class ; their age averaging from 18 to 30, some of them as old as 60. A considerable number do not know the letters, and in the majority of cases these belong to the ordinary felon class. As a rule, the pupils are very obtuse in learning, particularly when they exceed the age of 25.

"I find," said Mr. Barre, "the best means of stimulating them to think is by simple questions in mental arithmetic and other questions of a general character. By this means, numbers get very interested in the class. When I succeed in getting their attention, they make satisfactory progress; in some cases they make great proficiency. As a rule, I find that in these cases they seldom come back to the prison. It has often gratified me when I found the trouble I had taken with them was not thrown away. Those prisoners who have learned to read and write are full of gratitude.

"The class I have referred to meets three times a-week, and the pupils have also work to do in their cells in writing and cyphering. When I see them bring their slates well filled and done satisfactorily, I frequently go to them privately in their cells, and urge them on, and congratulate them upon their progress.

"The second adult class consists of pupils further advanced in their education; some of whom have been transferred from the lower class. Their instruction consists of reading, writing, arithmetic, the elements of geography, and subjects of a general character.

"I can always tell," continued Mr. Barre, "when they are interested, and if I see their attention flag on one subject I immediately change to another.

"The grand secret is to interest them in what they are doing. I try to instil into their minds that if they do not learn something every day it is a day wasted; and I am in the habit of reviewing the lessons of the preceding day, to impress them more fully into their memory, and to build them up in solid improvement.

"I have about 20 adults attending this class, which meets three times a-week, their age averaging from 16 to 30. The younger prisoners are generally the most proficient. The minds of the young are keener and more elastic than those of more advanced years, and more susceptible of retaining their acquirements.

"I have other two classes of adults whose attainments nearly resemble each other. Their education consists, in addition to the instruction imparted to the others, of a more advanced knowledge of geography, the outlines of history, and some of the higher rules of arithmetic as far as Practice and Vulgar and Decimal Fractions. These classes meet twice a-week, and are attended by 45 prisoners, their ages averaging from 16 to 30.

"We have also a singing class held on Friday afternoon, for practice in Psalmody and the Outlines of Hullah's System of Music, in which the prisoners take great delight. I learn them tunes and anthems for the chapel. This class is attended by about 40 persons, generally of the best educated, and the best behaved men in the prison.

There are two juvenile classes, consisting of boys from 8 to 16 years of age. The branches of education taught are, in a good measure, similar to those in the adult classes. One of them consists of boys who do not know their letters, or are learning monosyllables. A large number of the boys in the juvenile prison are of this order. They are taught reading, writing on the slate, and the elements of general knowledge, such as the outlines of the History of England, and the elementary principles of arithmetic, by questions and answers. This class is instructed every day in the juvenile wing, as we have already noticed.

"The boys in general feel interested in the school and its exercises. One of the severest punishments which can be inflicted on them is to prevent them from attending the class. I am particularly interested in the juvenile classes. In many cases I am gratified in finding that the pupils make decided progress. I often find that in the course of six months many of these who have commenced to learn the letters with me are able to read the Testament, and have made considerable progress in other branches of education.

"There is a higher juvenile class consisting of boys who are able to read tolerably. They are taught reading, writing, and arithmetic, and the outlines of general subjects. Many of these pupils, from the influences which are brought to bear upon them, are considerably advanced in their acquirements before they leave prison, when their sentence is of any duration. Their behaviour in school is very correct. I have been teacher in the prison for eight years, and never had occasion to report a single prisoner for bad conduct while under my care. I believe the chief reason of this is, that they are led to take an interest in the classes. "I find," says Mr. Barre, "that boys are like men. If they feel that people are really interested in them there is less likelihood of their misconducting themselves; on the contrary, there is every inducement for them to act in a commendable way.

"Sometimes I have a lot of raw recruits in my class. They seem at first a little fidgetty, but a few stern or kind remarks has a beneficial effect on them, I never jar their feelings by making any personal remark, but allude to their misbehaviour in a general way, which I find to be preferable. I want them to feel at home with me, and wish them to forget, if they will let me, that they are criminals, and to fancy themselves to be my guests at home in my parlour; that they have come to learn as much from me as they possibly can, and that the boy who makes the greatest progress is the one I shall take the greatest interest in. It is always a painful duty to me to be supposed watching any one. I wish them to behave as well when my eye is taken off them, as when I am looking to them, and then they will be sure to be benefited by their contact with me.

"This is the spirit in which I conduct the operations in my school, and it has the effect of attaching them to me in almost every case. I have seen some of the greatest felons blush deeply when my eye has caught them in some slight misconduct. My chief aim is always to gain a good moral impression, and then the influence is lasting.

"I select the pupils for the various classes in this way. I visit all the prisoners when received into prison, and take a note of their state of education, and report to the chaplain in reference to those who are deficient, and obtain his sanction to their attendance in the school. Those whose sentence is less than six weeks are not eligible to attend school. Some felons have acquired a fair education in the prison; but of this class," said Mr. Barre, "we have no adults who were not with us when boys.

"There is a circulating library in the prison, which is under my control. The books, which are on general information, and moral and religious in their character, are distributed throughout the cells, and changed every week. There are two books—a secular and a religious volume—left in each. The majority of the prisoners take great interest in them, and read them attentively at meal hours and in the evening. The library is one of our most useful auxiliaries in promoting the mental and moral improvement of the prisoners, and is of great advantage to us.

"I always endeavour," continued Mr. Barre, "to keep the mind well employed, and frequently change the books of many of the prisoners that have a thirst for reading, who also have an opportunity of applying for additional books from the officer. The better educated prisoners, such as clerks and commercial travellers, take great advantage of the library. In going my rounds over the male prison, I know pretty well the parties who are fond of reading, and always take care to provide them with books to entertain and improve them.

"The highest class of adults write outlines of the chaplain's sermons, and some of them do it exceedingly well.

"The more respectable and better educated men do not come to the classes, but read in their cells, and are supplied with slates on which they write English composition exercises— sometimes of a poetical character—some of them, from specimens furnished us, not devoid of literary ability."

STATE OF EDUCATION FOR THE YEAR ENDING SEPTEMBER, 1861.

SUMMARY CONVICTIONS. CENTRAL CRIMINAL COURT CONVICTIONS.

Males.

	Not read nor write.	Read only.	Imp.	Well.	Total.		Not read nor write.	Read only.	Imp.	Well.	Total.
October.........	10	13	26	9	58	October.........	6	...	2	11	19
November......	26	15	46	12	99	November......	2	1	9	8	20
December	20	8	42	10	80	December.....	1	...	2	2	5
January	22	12	49	10	93	January	1	...	7	2	10
February	24	16	57	8	105	February	2	...	4	6	12
March	22	12	58	9	106	March..........	...	...	...	...	...
April..........	26	7	32	12	77	April..........	2	1	16	11	30
May	16	16	37	11	80	May	2	1	2	4	9
June	26	4	46	11	87	June	5	...	6	1	12
July	20	8	55	12	95	July	1	...	6	1	8
August	17	13	48	10	88	August	1	1	12	3	17
September	20	17	59	10	101	September	3	...	9	12	24
Totals...	249	141	555	124	1069	Totals...	26	4	75	61	166

NUMBER OF PREVIOUS COMMITTALS.

Males.

SUMMARIES.				CENTRAL CRIMINAL COURT.				Total.
Once.	Twice.	Thrice.	4 times and over.	Once.	Twice.	Thrice.	4 times and over.	
164	81	38	139	18	5	5	12	462

Females.

	Not read nor write.	Read only.	Imp.	Well.	Total.		Not read nor write.	Read only.	Imp.	Well.	Total.
October.........	9	2	11	...	22	October	1	...	...	...	1
November......	27	15	14	2	58	November	2	1	2	...	5
December	7	8	10	3	28	December	...	...	...	...	...
January	10	9	13	1	33	January	...	...	3	...	3
February	12	11	14	...	37	February......	...	...	...	...	...
March	14	13	14	3	44	March	1	...	...	...	1
April...........	11	7	14	3	35	April	1	1	3	...	5
May	13	11	10	...	34	May	1	...	...	...	1
June	6	7	8	...	21	June	...	...	1	...	1
July	14	0	13	3	40	July	1	3	3	1	8
August	15	19	11	1	36	August........	1	...	2	1	4
September ...	15	7	13	5	40	September	1	...	...	...	1
Totals...	153	109	145	21	428	Totals...	9	5	14	2	30

NUMBER OF PREVIOUS COMMITTALS.

Females.

SUMMARIES.				CENTRAL CRIMINAL COURT.				Total.
Once.	Twice.	Thrice.	4 times and over.	Once.	Twice.	Thrice.	4 times and over.	
61	33	14	70	2	2	2	...	184

*** *Tailors' and Shoemakers' Room.*—We went into the associated room adjoining the adult schoolroom, in corridor B, where a number of the felon tailors and shoemakers are employed. It is of similar dimensions to the latter, and on the day of our visit was occupied by eleven shoemakers and fifteen tailors.

The tailors were seated cross-legged on a large board, in an elevated position, on one side of the room, with gas fittings in the centre, and the shoemakers were ranged in rows on the other side.

The *tailors* were employed making different articles of dress, such as coats, vests, trousers, etc., for the children of the Emmanuel Hospital, and dark gray clothing for prison use. Most of them were young men, several of a very interesting appearance, some were middle-aged. A smart, fair complexioned youth in the centre, was busy pressing the seam of a brown cloth jacket, another was busy repairing a pair of prison trousers, sewing the white lining on the dark gray cloth, with his shirt sleeves rolled up, and the brass register number suspended on his breast. A middle-aged man, with an intellectual appearance, was bending down sewing the padding into the breast of a coat. A younger man, of genteel appearance, was actively pressing the seam of a pair of trousers, while his companion, a young lad of about seventeen, was stitching at the sleeve of a brown jacket. Many of them sat with their jackets off; several of them regarded us with an open, frank, good-humoured countenance. Others looked with thoughtful curiosity, wondering what could be the object of our visit, and some stole occasional glances at us, as they sat with drooping head over their work. Mr. Taylor, the warder in attendance, informed us, that some of them had been convicted of embezzlement; others of unlawful possession of goods; some for attempting to pick pockets, and one for deserting his wife and family.

"We make here," he added, "all the prison clothing for the male juveniles and adults, the uniforms for the officers of the prison, as well as of Newgate, and for the officers at the Guildhall and the Mansion House. In addition to this, we make clothing for the boys of the Emmanuel Hospital, Westminster, numbering about thirty. We also do slop-work for different mercantile firms in the Metropolis, consisting of jackets, vests, trousers, and overcoats, and execute the necessary repairs on the prison clothing.

"There are some of the prisoners here," said Mr. Taylor, "who have never used the needle until they came into the prison. After being with us for about six months, they are able to make vests and trousers, and assist in making coats. These could scarcely get a livelihood by their work out of doors; but others, who have been here for about eighteen months, are capable of making a comfortable livelihood. There are others who had learned to sew before they entered the prison, who have become more expert during their imprisonment, and by the time their sentence expires, will be tolerable workmen. There are some employed here who are fair workmen, and have entirely got the knowledge of their business while in prison.

"Some of these," said Mr. Taylor, "for example, that fair-complexioned, genteel young man, who sits opposite to us, are first-rate tradesmen, able to take their place in the most fashionable establishments in London. Here is a handsome overcoat made by two of the prisoners, which is a good specimen of their workmanlike ability."

Each prisoner is expected to make one pair of trousers a-day, and very few of them make more than this. They are engaged at work about eight hours a day, exclusive of the time spent in chapel, at school, and on the exercising ground.

The *shoemakers* were sitting by their stalls, some of them making boots and shoes, and others were busy repairing the prison shoes. One man was engaged hammering a welt, another was scraping the heel of a boot with a knife. A young, fair-complexioned lad, appeared to be absorbed in closing an upper leather; a middle-aged, pale-faced man, with a very flat chest, was busy sewing the welt of a female boot. The boot was fastened on his knee by a leathern strap, held tight by his left foot.

There is a counter on the other side of the room for the warder, with drawers underneath, to contain materials required in his department. At the back of the counter is a rack with lasts of different sizes, a heap of old brown and mouldy shoes condemned by the governor, lay on one side of the room, which are occasionally cut up, and used to repair the prison shoes.

We observed a fire-place and stove with an oven, to heat the tailors' irons. A prison warder generally stands by, overlooking the various workmen.

"Most of the young men here," remarked the warder to us, "have learned what they know of shoemaking with me."

In answer to our inquiries, he informed us—"We make all the shoes worn in the prison by males, as well as females, and likewise for the officers of the prison, and the pupils of the Emmanuel Hospital, and execute the necessary repairs. These fully engage all our hands. I generally get the new beginners to work at closing the uppers, which is a very simple process. From closing the uppers they advance to sewing the bottoms to the uppers, and are very soon able to finish an ordinary shoe.

"We make fine work occasionally, such as the officers' shoes, which are tastefully done. There are prison tailors with us at present who would do credit to the first establishments in London." Here the warder showed us a Balmoral boot made for a boy, a very handsome article, the bottoms being of superior work, and also the stitching of the upper.

"The workmen generally finish one boot a-day ; some of them do more. We begin our work at seven in the morning in winter, and continue till eight in the evening, with the exception of the hours at chapel, school, meals, and exercise.

"Some of the workmen who have been entirely trained with me, will be able to get a decent livelihood at their trade by the time they leave us. There are several here that have had some training previously, who will become more proficient by the time their imprisonment expires. In the course of repeated imprisonments, some ultimately become tolerable workmen.

"You see that boy there," said the warder, "in the centre of the group. He has learned shoemaking with me, and is now able to make a pair of shoes in tolerably good condition. That middle aged man, with his head bending beside his knee, is a first-rate workman."

On leaving the associated room by the door which opens into the gallery, we saw one of the prisoners laving the face of another with soap, preparatory to being shaved.

Adjoining this room is a store, into which we were conducted by the chief warder, and shown a stock of garments consisting of jackets, trousers, and vests, prepared for the boys of the Emmanuel Hospital, with a variety of other clothes and materials.

Retracing our steps along the gallery towards the central hall, we saw on the floor beneath a file of prisoners in dark gray prison dress, and blue caps, with the register number on the arms of their jackets, and the brass circular plate, containing the number of their cell, suspended on their breast. A warder in uniform stood in attendance. We noticed that the flooring of the galleries is composed of blue slate, fenced on the outer side by an iron railing of a tasteful design, painted of a stone colour, the top, along which the food carriages are rolled, being painted of a mahogany tint to give it the appearance of wood.

Before leaving the B wing we visited several of the cells. In one of them we found a smart young man with a very interesting appearance. When brought to the prison he was very genteelly dressed in a dark suit of clothes, cap with peak, gloves, and Inverness cape. To use his own words, he thinks it must have been a thief who invented the latter article of dress. He was about twenty-one years of age, beneath the middle size, with a broad brow and finely-formed countenance, and rich dark eyes, and is reported to be a very expert pick-pocket, and has been several times previously convicted. He told us his parents were respectable people, and his mother died when he was about four years of age. After this his father married another woman, and became a drunkard. His stepmother was unkind to him, and turned him out of doors to get his livelihood in the best way he could. At this time he became acquainted with several thieves and learned picking pockets, at which he was considered to be expert.

In answer to our interrogatories, he states that for about three years he had cohabited with a female who sincerely loved him, and assumed his name. On one occasion, while he was in Holloway Prison, she was there along with him, and used to write his name on the dinner covers, which was detected by the officers of the prison. On his release, after twelve months' confinement, he had resolved to live an honest life; parted from this young woman so deeply attached to him, and wrought as a labourer in St. Katherine's Docks at 2s. 6d. per day, when he again became unfortunate, and was driven to steal.

The young man further stated with an earnest, ingenuous countenance, "After I leave prison what am I to do?" My father is a poor drunkard. My stepmother would take money from me, rather than assist me, and would not inquire where I got it? I have a younger sister employed at a match manufactory, who only earns from 6s. to 7s. per week. She would gladly assist me with 2s. 6d., and consider it a treasure, but I feel within myself I could not take it from her. I would gladly accept any honest employment, however menial, and most willingly enter Her Majesty's royal navy for any period to get away from my old companions, and criminal life."

We entered another cell, where we saw a tall gentlemanly-looking youth with a particularly high forehead, and clear gentle hazel eye. He had recently been indisposed. In answer to the inquiries of the chief warder, he stated he was much better. We looked to his card, and found he was charged with felony. We asked him the particular nature of his offence. He stated he had been a waiter at a private boarding-house in the metropolis, and that an old gentleman, recently returned from Tasmania, had taken a great fancy to him. As the old gentleman was going to York, he intrusted him with the keys of his apartments, and in an unguarded moment he pledged some silver plate belonging to him, to raise funds to enable him to proceed on a jaunt into the country. On the chief warder asking him if there was not a female connected with the matter, he admitted, with a smile, there was, but added that she had no connection with the felony. It appears he loved a young woman in a tradesman's family, and intended to take a trip with her into the country, and with this motive he robbed the old gentleman of his plate.

In another cell we saw a fair-complexioned, good-looking man, of about thirty years of age, about five feet six inches in height, with an uncommonly smart appearance. The chief warder knew him to be a most accomplished pickpocket and burglar of the highest class, and has observed his career for the past nineteen years. Strange to say, he happened to be the very person we had scared for picking a lady's pocket in Cheapside about three months ago, as recorded in the fourth volume of the "London Labour and the London Poor." He is at present undergoing three calendar months' hard labour, for picking a lady's pocket of a watch in the City two days subsequent to this occurrence, and was arrested chiefly by the treachery of a female with whom he had cohabited. He was very conversant on the burglaries and robberies of various descriptions he had committed in the course of his career. Many of them were perpetrated in the City as well as over the United Kingdom. He had lately returned from Flanders. He is a returned convict, and one of the most adroit thieves in London.

In another cell we saw a plain-looking youth of twenty-three years of age, who had been fourteen times in prison. The first occasion was when he was seven years of age. He was formerly at St. Patrick's Roman Catholic School, Lambeth, and remarked to us few of the pupils who attend this school turn out well.

In an adjoining cell we saw an elderly man, almost bald in front, with a long thin face. and blue, earnest eyes. He was a shoemaker by trade, and charged with stealing a door-mat. He had been eight times previously convicted. His infirmity, according to his own confession, was strong drink. He is very inoffensive when sober, and was at one time in a good situation in the Duke of York's Military School, Chelsea. He gave us a profound military salute on leaving his cell.

In the next cell was a painful spectacle. There we saw a silver-headed old man of between sixty and seventy years of age, who had been guilty of stealing books from a shop-door in Bishopsgate Street. He said he committed the felony to keep him from starving, and that this was his first offence. He generally worked as a labourer at the docks. He had an open frank appearance very different from the majority of the criminals around him.

The following is an inventory of the work done for the past year:—

Shoemaking.

	Made.	Repaired.
Shoes for prisoners	218	2177
Prisoners' own shoes repaired before discharge	—	150
Hammock straps	180	908
Uniform belts and straps for officers	20	
Pouches	20	
For Emmanuel Hospital :—		
Boys' boots	64	206
Girls' do.	75	115
Officers' own, and families boots and shoes	76	150

The following is a state of the work done in this department during the last year :—

Mat-making.

	Made.
Rug and diamond mats	14,781
Board mats	798
Imitation board mats	831
Double boarded mats	2818
Outsizes	2073
	21,301

The following is a list of the articles of clothing made and repaired during the last year :—

Tailoring.

		Made.	Repaired.
Jackets for prisoners		146	2339
Vests for prisoners		268	1218
Pairs of trousers for prisoners		267	3169
Braces for prisoners		164	233
Stocks for prisoners		60	86
Hammocks for prisoners		—	520
Uniform great-coats for officers		32	28
,, frock-coat ,,		43	48
,, trousers ,,		51	72
Drawers ,,		20	
Caps ,,		37	
Jackets ,,		1	
Vests ,,		1	

Clothing for the Emmanuel Hospital, consisting of—

	Made.
Suits of boys clothes	33
Outfits for boys to send to sea	36

₊ *Infirmary.*—We entered the C ward, at the farther extremity, and saw two large rooms, exactly similar in dimensions to those we visited in the B wing, which are here used as an infirmary. We found several prisoners confined by slight indisposition. There is a dispensary adjoining, which is furnished with medicines for the use of the prisoners. It is under

HEATING APPARATUS AT THE CITY PRISON, HOLLOWAY.

LIFTING APPARATUS FOR SERVING THE DINNER AT THE CITY PRISON, HOLLOWAY.

the immediate care of a warder, and has the appearance of a druggist's shop with the phials carefully labelled and arranged on shelves erected around the walls. One of those large rooms made use of for infirmary purposes was empty. It is furnished with a table in the centre, and a form on either side, with a copious supply of bedsteads and chairs. It is well ventilated by flues, and one of the large windows can be drawn down from the top to admit a current of fresh air. There is a comfortable fireplace in the room.

We proceeded to the other room with the infirmary warder. There we found nine beds in the apartment. There was only one patient in bed, an old man, who was suffering from rheumatism. There were six other invalids in the room afflicted with rheumatism and cold, while a seventh acted as nurse. There happened to be no serious case of illness at the time of our visit. Some were reading by the comfortable fire, or seated on the bedsteads.

The bedding consisted of a straw palliasse, a blue striped mattress stuffed with wool, a pair of blankets, a pair of sheets, a pillow containing horse-hair, and a blue striped coverlet of a neat appearance. At the side of each bed there is a portable cupboard where the prisoners can deposit their utensils and food. There are also several shelves in the room, which is lighted by gas jets.

A pale-faced young man sat on a seat by the fire in apparently a very infirm condition, suffering from a pulmonary complaint. He breathed with great difficulty, his breast heaving convulsively at each respiration.

Another smart young man was confined, who was occasionally subject to fits.

₊ *Chapel.*—The chapel is a large and elegant building, fitted to accommodate the whole of the prisoners at one service. It is much larger than the one at Wandsworth. The adults are ranged in two divisions along the far extending galleries in front. The juveniles meet in an inclosure on the left hand, and the females in another on the right, and are not seen by each other. The chaplain occupies a pulpit in the centre of a pew, erected adjoining the wall, in front of the adults, about the same height as in other chapels. The governor and his family sit on the right hand, and the chaplain's family on the left. There is besides accommodation for the chief warder, and any of the magistrates or other visitors. On the wall, beneath the pulpit, is tastefully inscribed a copy of the Lord's Prayer, the Ten Commandments, and the Apostles' Creed. Underneath this is the Communion table fenced within an oaken railing, raised two steps above the level of the floor.

A lofty strong iron railing separates the adults in the gallery from the area below. The lower part of the gallery is divided by a low wooden railing, with a stair on each side leading to the second landing, and extending upwards on each side of this passage to an entry on the third landing above, which is on a level with the highest galleries in the corridors. The interior of the chapel is lighted at dusk with a circlet of gas lights suspended from the lofty roof as well as by a series of gas jets on each side of the galleries.

So soon as the bell rang, we entered the chapel along with the governor, and sat in the elevated pew before referred to, entered by a door from behind, and had a commanding view of the adults ranged along in the ample galleries, attired in their dark prison dress. It was a more cheerful scene than the chapel service at Wandsworth and Pentonville, where the heads of the prisoners could only be seen occasionally peering over the iron clasped boxes in which they were confined. Most of the adults were from eighteen to thirty years of age, yet we noticed several bald-headed men amongst them, some of them with a very respectable appearance. One elderly gentleman in particular, imprisoned for fraudulent bankruptcy, had a superior air to the mass of the felons around him. We could single out a few good-looking young men, clerks and others, with an engaging manner. The mass of the prisoners belong to the ordinary felon class of the metropolis; some with a dull dark beetling brow, and others with a sharp clear aspect, indicating a more acute and lively mind. Many of them we conjectured, from their arched eyebrows and peculiar features, were of Hibernian extraction. Two warders, with their backs to each other, were stationed in the centre of the gallery. One of the principal warders sat at the back of the gallery facing the chaplain.

Many of the female prisoners were of a degraded appearance, though we could single out a number of good-looking felons among them, some of them very expert shoplifters and pickpockets.

The religious services were listened to with the greatest propriety. Many showed a devout frame of mind in the devotional exercises, and apparently joined with great fervour in the Psalmody, which was most decorously conducted. The chaplain delivered an admirable discourse, which was listened to with marked attention.

At the close of the services, the governor informed us that fifteen of the adults had not read their books during worship, and remarked that thirty-five of the seventy females present, were unable to read.

He further added, "That some of the prisoners present had lately rode in their carriages to their place of business in the City, and were here incarcerated for fraudulent bankruptcy."

In answer to our inquiries regarding the chapel service, the reception warder gave us the following information :—"At a quarter-past eight o'clock the principal warder in charge rings the bell for the prisoners to proceed to the chapel. The warders then unlock the cells in the various corridors. The prisoners pass in files along the galleries, about three yards apart from each other. At the chapel door, a principal warder and an ordinary warder, count the prisoners of each corridor passing into the chapel, as a check on the number of prisoners in the reception wards. They enter the chapel from the second and third landings adjoining the central hall, and after service are again conducted back to their cells in a similar manner."

We were introduced by the governor to the chaplain, when we learned that prisoners of all sects of religion attend the chapel with the exception of one Roman Catholic, a very eccentric man. All controversial subjects are excluded from the services.

Every morning, immediately on leaving chapel, those prisoners who were admitted into the prison on the previous day, are brought before the chaplain, who takes a note of their register number, and the number of their cell, whether married or not, number of children, the parish and county to which they belong, their trade or occupation, whether in work or not, their previous commitments, their offence, the cause of their offence, their sentence, the date of their discharge, their education and religious training, and whether they have attended Divine worship during the last six months.

The chaplain generally gives them something to learn, such as Scripture texts, suitable to their position and state of mind, which they commit to memory, and repeat to him about a fortnight or a month after. When they are in difficulty as to the meaning of any passage of Scripture in their Bible readings in the cells, they are urged to come to him for an explanation immediately after service.

The Rev. Mr. Owen, the chaplain, "considers it a very interesting sphere of labour. Leaving out the professional thief, who rarely reforms;" he states, "there are many, who date their first serious impressions from the time of their imprisonment. He has in his possession several letters written to him by prisoners on the eve of their discharge, and after some months' absence, in which, while they deplore the sin that brought them to prison, they thank God that it pleased Him, while there, to open their eyes to their position in his sight; and here, it must be remembered, that they have no motive for hypocrisy, as, unlike a convict prison, they gain no remission of sentences by good behaviour. The solitude of the cell has a beneficial effect on most characters, not hardened in vice. The prisoners are all very fond of the singing-class which assembles every Friday to practise the psalms and hymns for the Sunday. Occasionally the chaplain's wife, with the help of the schoolmaster and the harmonium, teaches them a new tune, which seems to give them much pleasure. Many a prisoner who is unimpressed by anything else, is moved to tears while singing a hymn. There are many educated men amongst the prisoners, but the chaplain has not had one educated female under his charge. There are eight lady visitors, who meet the chaplain every Thursday in the committee-room. After engaging in prayer, they call on the female prisoners in their various cells. Those who wish to reform have the offer of admission into a reformatory."

₊ *Hearing Reports.*—Leaving the chapel, we accompanied the governor down the back staircase leading to his office, to hear the applications made by the prisoners, as well as the reports (if any), brought before him for misconduct. This is a handsome apartment, and elegantly furnished. We here observed a table of calculations or ready reckoner of provisions, according to the Government scale. Opposite the number of prisoners, ranging from 10 up to 500, it shows the exact weight in pounds and ounces, thereby saving much time in making out the calculation for the issue of provisions. There is a corresponding table in the steward's office.

A good-looking man, of about thirty years of age, was introduced into the office. He modestly stated to the governor, "I wish to write a letter to my wife. She asks me to write to her. My sentence expires on the 19th of February. I would also feel obliged if you would permit my hair and whiskers to grow." His request was granted.

An elderly man, with silver hair, and genial countenance, wished to have a sheet of foolscap paper to write to his friends.

Gov. I shall send it you to-day.

A young man, of short stature—a German Jew—was then ushered in. He was about twenty-two years of age, dark-complexioned, with low forehead; and had an air of petulance. He complained, in an irritable tone, that a prisoner in the tailors' associated room, had taken away his thread. The governor told him to be quiet, and to keep his temper.

A tall, good-looking, dark-complexioned man came in, and requested, in Irish accents, if the governor would allow his hair and whiskers to grow, as his sentence would expire in six weeks. He was imprisoned for a brawl with the police, when in a state of intoxication. His request was acceded to.

A cripple, of about forty years of age, was then ushered in. He had lost one of his legs in the late Crimean war, and was charged with obtaining money on false pretences. He asked permission to allow his beard, whiskers, and moustache to grow. The governor stated he would not permit the moustache, but he would allow his beard and whiskers to grow.

A tall young man, of about eighteen years of age, with a long face, and frank countenance, stepped up towards the governor. He was an Irishman, with a narrow brow, and full underface. He was charged with wrangling with the German Jew above referred to, in the tailors' associated room. He complained that the Jew unreasonably wished to appropriate all the thread to himself, and acted just as he pleased.

Gov. Don't pay any attention to him. You see he has an irritable disposition. If I hear any more complaints against him, I shall shift him from the shop.

Upon this the German Jew was called in as the other retired. The governor told him he saw through his artful design; and thought there was something wrong. He had brought an application to see him (the governor), because there was a report against himself. He warned him to take care of his conduct, and not to quarrel about such trifling matters.

The other young man was then called in.

Gov. Is this thread yours?

Young man. The other prisoners, besides us, know it is mine. It was lying on the board, and was free to all. This man (the Jew) keeps it to himself, and kicks up a row about it.

Gov. In future, I shall give you your thread separately, so that there shall be no occasion to quarrel.

The Jew. (Contorting his countenance). I have been in a hundred tailors' shops, and never was meddled with in this way.

Gov. If you are brought up to me again for squabbling in the tailors' shop, I shall put you in a dark cell.

The Jew. What is squabbling?

Gov. Quarrelling.

The German Jew looked very cross, and left the apartment with his hands behind his back.

A little, sharp, fair-complexioned lad was charged by a warder with changing places on the exercising ground.

Gov. Why did you do it, boy?

Warder. He wanted to go alongside of some one he knew.

(The lad stood mute, with his hands behind his back.)

Gov. Will you do it again?

Pris. No, sir.

Gov. If you are brought before me another time, I will remember. How often have you been reported since you came to the prison?

Pris. Twice, sir.

The governor remarked to us. "For the past eight days there have only been two punishments inflicted, which was done by stopping the bread at supper. This was for the offence of giving and receiving bread.

*** *The Tread-wheel.*—We visited the tread-wheel, which is worked to pump water for the whole prison, and situated between the C and D wings. The apartment in which it is contained is about 24 feet 6 inches in breadth, and 54 feet 6 inches in length, having a small inclosure penned off opposite the wheel, containing machinery, connecting the wheel with the pumps, which are adjoining. The tread-wheel consists of two divisions or compartments, the larger one being intended for the adults, and the smaller for juveniles. There are sixteen boxes in the larger compartment and eight in the other.

In front of the wheel there are eighteen inclosed seats erected alongside of each other in the larger compartment, where the prisoners are engaged in picking oakum in the intervals of labour. There are ten boxes in the smaller compartments where the juveniles work; two of them being generally occupied by the prisoners engaged on the handles of the pumps in the inclosure already referred to.

There are two warders in charge of the tread-wheel, one on the one side, and another on the other; all of which arrangements have been admirably sketched in an engraving given in a former part of the work.

Between these two divisions, and on the right hand side as we enter, there is an inclosed space, in which a portion of the machinery is situated, and a well has been sunk to the depth of 370 feet, from which the water is pumped by the treadmill, and conveyed to large tanks on the top of the building, from which the whole of the prison is supplied.

At the time of our visit there were ten prisoners engaged in the larger division of the wheel and eight on the smaller, and two of them were bending and straining at the pump handles. As the wheel turned steadily round, each man took an upward step, keeping time with the velocity of the wheel. Some had stripped off their jackets to work with greater freedom; several were toiling lazily at the work, and others were active and elastic, particularly some of the younger lads, who took it remarkably easy. Most of them were young men, varying from sixteen to thirty-five years of age, many of them being short and active, and evidently felons of the metropolis. One or two of them appeared to be clerks or shopmen, from their superior look and manner even in the prison dress. One man, advanced in life, sat on one of the seats near us, with a heavy, stupid countenance; many

SEPARATE WASHING CELL,
IN THE FEMALE PRISON AT THE CITY HOUSE OF CORRECTION, HOLLOWAY.

of the others had the keen sharp eye and roguish look, characteristic of many of our London felons.

Those sitting in the seats in front were busy picking oakum, in the interval of tread-wheel labour, as they were occasionally relieved from the wheel, and others took their places. They did not appear to be so fatigued with the hard labour as we expected—not nearly so much as those toiling at the hand-mills in the separate cells in Wandsworth prison.

One of the prisoners, a young man who had been slightly indisposed, was offered some medicine by one of the warders, but refused to take it, and was chided for his disobedience by the reception warder who accompanied us.

There is a bell attached to the wheel, which rings every two minutes and a half, marking a certain number of revolutions. At certain intervals, three prisoners come down from the wheel, and other three leave the seats in the area, and take their places.

Each man, on going to the wheel, steps up on a form in front, and thence plants one foot on the wheel, at the same time laying hold with his hand on an iron handle to keep himself in an upright position. In the event of his not keeping pace with the wheel, he is brought down, and liable to be injured. From the motive of self-preservation, he is compelled to keep pace with it. At the top of each box or inclosure there is a ventilator for the admission of fresh air, and it is numbered in the inside, by which number the prisoner is called when there is occasion. There is a corresponding number on the outside, for the use of the officer on duty.

At the extremity of the shed on the left hand, there is a water-closet, and upon the walls on either side is a notice that silence is to be strictly observed. The building is well lighted and ventilated.

Each prisoner remains on the wheel for twenty minutes at a time, and alternately picks oakum in the seats in front for other twenty minutes. The wheel is five feet in diameter, and makes three revolutions in two minutes and a half.

The tread-wheel labour generally lasts from seven o'clock in the morning till four o'clock in the afternoon, with the exception of the hours spent in chapel, at meals, etc. The prisoners are employed on the wheel on an average of four hours and a half per day. The labour is not very oppressive to a considerable number of them. Some, however, appear to be very fatigued at the close of the day. We observed a long file of prisoners from the tread-mill passing through one of the corridors on their way to their cells, who were, apparently, in no way exhausted with their day's task.

The average amount of distance travelled by the prisoners on the wheel is about 6500 feet in winter, and about 8700 feet in summer—much below the maximum height allowed by law, which is 11,000 feet. When sufficient water is obtained the prisoners are taken off and placed at more remunerative labour.

The greatest regularity and good order prevail here.

Adjoining the treadwheel and attached to it is a shed covered with zinc, containing twenty-two separate stalls, with a pump-handle in each, to give additional assistance to the wheel if necessary, as both can be employed to pump water for the use of the prison.

⁎ *Exercising Grounds.*—There are five exercising grounds attached to Holloway Prison—one close to the female wing on one side of the courtyard leading into the prison, and another to the juvenile wing on the opposite side, and three at the back of the main prison, one of them near the end of B wing, another near to the C wing, and a third between the B and C wings, as seen in the bird's-eye view of the prison.

Leaving the tread-wheel, we visited the adult exercising grounds: The prisoners were then actively engaged in exercise in the various concentric circles, all within sight of each other, attended by several warders, and under the inspection of one of the principal warders.

The spaces between the two extreme exercising concentric circles were planted with kitchen vegetables, while the central one was a hard beaten portion of ground between the B and C wings, which had not been planted, but is used as a drying ground. There are four iron posts in the latter, to which drying lines are attached, with a lamp in the centre lighted with gas at dusk.

The day of our visit was bitterly cold, and the prisoners were walking smartly along to keep themselves in heat, particularly in the central ground, where they hurried round in double quick time. Many of them were pale and shivering from the keen biting air; others were of a bluish tint, and some of their cheeks were of a dull red. They generally kept about three yards apart from each other. The generality of them were of the ordinary felon stock. In the prison-dress it would, in many cases, be difficult to distinguish the casual from the habitual offender. There was less military precision in their movements on this occasion than in the case of the gloomy masked men at Wandsworth and Pentonville, but this we believe, was owing to the inclemency of the weather.

There is a carriage-drive around the back of the prison. The surrounding grounds are planted with kitchen vegetables of various descriptions, for the use of the prisoners, and with a large quantity of mangold-wurzel, which is sold to dairies.

There is a pavement extending around the exterior of the wings, about six feet in breadth, close to the prison.

While we stood in the garden along with the reception warder, overlooking this lively scene, we saw another gang of prisoners taken out to replace this detachment which was removed to the different corridors.

The adult exercising grounds are fenced by a lofty wall stretching across from the extremity of the D wing to the boundary wall separating it from the grounds attached to the female wing, and from the extremity of the A wing to the opposite boundary wall, dividing it from the garden attached to the juvenile prison. The exercising circles are overlooked by the range of houses on the left hand.

We were conducted into the garden attached to the female prison, where we found the warder in charge, perched on a ladder placed against the wall, overlooking five of the prisoners, mostly young lads, engaged in removing earth from a mound to fill up a cesspool at the corner of the garden. On being introduced to him, he stated, " It is my duty to superintend the gardening operations. At present I have twelve men assisting me over the grounds. In general I have from ten to twenty. We sow and plant a large quantity of potatoes, leeks, cabbage, and other vegetables, for the supply of the prison.

⁎ *The Kitchen.*—We visited the kitchen, situated in the basement of D wing, and were introduced to the cook. It was then about mid-day. He was busily engaged preparing dinner, which was about to be served up.

There are six large boilers in the kitchen with copper lids—each of them having a steam pipe communicating with a large boiler in an adjoining recess. One boiler contained a large quantity of broth, with huge pieces of beef. The cook uplifted several of them on a large fork; they appeared to be of excellent quality. They were carried away by one of the prisoners in attendance, to be cut up into small portions to be put into the dining tins, and distributed to the various prisoners in the different cells. We had a small quantity of soup served up to us, which was very wholesome and palatable.

Another boiler contained a large quantity of potatoes which had just been cooked. They were York Regents of an excellent quality.

A different boiler contained an enormous quantity of gruel, made of the best Scotch oatmeal, to be served out for supper in the evening. It was filled to the brim, with a white creamy paste mantling on the surface. Cocoa is given on alternate days, and is prepared in the other coppers we saw alongside.

Our readers have been furnished with an excellent engraving of the interior of the kitchen in a foregoing part of the work.

There are three doors leading through to a large central apartment, which contains a long table on the side next the scullery, used for cutting up the bread and weighing it out, and another table at the extremity on the left hand, used for cutting up the meat on those days when soup is prepared. We observed a large fireplace here used for cooking such articles as are ordered by the surgeon for the use of the infirmary, with an oven attached to it.

The kitchen is paved with York slab, and neatly pencilled. There is a gas bracket suspended from the roof in the centre, and over the door leading into the cutting-up room is a dial for the convenience of the cook.

We passed on to the scullery, which contains two sinks for the purpose of washing the tins and other dishes. They are supplied with a tap at each end, one supplying hot, and the other cold water. The bread trays are deposited on a table at the side of the room when not in use, and the bright tins are carefully set in rows on a rack on another side. Here we found a prisoner with some broth and mutton, which had been prepared for the use of the infirmary.

We proceeded into the cutting-up room, where we found several prisoners, assistants of the cook, cutting up the meat for dinner, on a large table, while others were engaged in filling the pannikins with potatoes and meat for dinner. Each pannikin is divided into two compartments, one containing potatoes, and the other meat, each pannikin being furnished with a knife.

The cook generally has four assistants in his work. An additional hand is occasionally employed in the kitchen, who helps the engineer in attending to the furnace and other duties.

The greater part of the long table in the cutting-up room was covered with trays fitted with dinner tins, and the floor was also littered with them.

On the wall is suspended a long dark board for the cook's guidance, with a note of the provisions to be served out to the different wards. It is corrected every morning by one of the principal warders, who gives the necessary instructions.

We passed on to a large apartment nearly of a semi-circular form, situated under the central hall. At each end is a windlass for hoisting up provisions to the various corridors, and in the centre is a spiral staircase leading up through the central hall to the galleries of the prison.

We ascended to the central hall, and saw the principal warder in charge superintending the serving up of the dinner. The trays were conveyed along to the extremity of the different galleries on food carriages, similar to the mode pursued in Pentonville and other prisons. This operation was executed with great order and despatch.

In answer to our interrogatories, the cook informed us:—"The fire is generally lit about three o'clock in the morning by one of the night watchmen, when the steam is got up to prepare the gruel or cocoa, served up for breakfast on alternate days.

"I begin my duties," said the cook, "at seven o'clock in the morning, when the gruel and cocoa is served up with bread to the different corridors; sometimes cocoa and bread, at other times gruel and bread. These are the breakfast operations. The butcher in general arrives about ten o'clock, when we prepare for dinner, consisting of meat and potatoes, or soup and potatoes, which are served up at one o'clock to all the branches of the prison.

"The gruel for supper is prepared at an early period of the day, generally at dinner-time, and stands in the copper for several hours. By this means it becomes thicker, and its qualities are improved, and besides it economizes our fuel. The bread is cut and weighed out, to be served up with the gruel for the prisoners' supper, which ends the culinary operations of the day."

We were informed there is no baker in the prison. The bread is contracted for by a tradesman in the Metropolis, who supplies the prison every day. It is made of second flour, and we found it to be of excellent quality.

We proceeded to the D wing in company with the chief warder. On visiting the cells we found a number of prisoners engaged picking oakum. As we passed along, we found it was an imperative duty in this prison for the prisoners to shut the doors of their cells, and at the same time for the officer to test their being closed.

We visited the basement of corridor D, where there are eight large commodious baths, similar to those we found in the reception ward. We passed through a door into a passage, where there were several punishment cells, all of them then empty. We learned there are very few punishments inflicted in this prison.

The doors resemble those of ordinary cells : about five feet distant is another door, which deadens the noise created by any refractory prisoner. At present there are six dark cells, but originally there were sixteen. Ten of them have been made into a workshop, "and it is contemplated," said the governor to us, "to convert three of the present number into light cells."

₊ *The Engineer's Department.*—We were introduced to the engineer of the prison, who conducted us to the heating apparatus, or furnace-room, situated in the basement under the surgeon's room, beneath the wide passage or hall conducting to the main prison, of which our artist has furnished an engraving.

"These," said the engineer, pointing to the other side of the apartment, "are the boilers where we heat our water to warm all the cells in the prison, as well as the chapel and other offices. You observe four square boilers ranged in a row in this apartment, heated by means of furnaces underground, and there are the pipes conducting from them into the main prison.

"The boiler on the left-hand side heats the A and B wing; the one next to it heats the juvenile wing, and a portion of the chapel and the reception cells. The adjoining one warms the female wing and the other portion of the chapel. The boiler on the right-hand warms the C and D wings.

The engineer called our attention to several flow-pipes, which run along each wing in flues, connected with the cells in the corridors, and then flow into the basement cells. From thence the return-pipes flow into a boiler supplied by the expansion cistern, six feet above the level of the flow-pipe. "You observe," said he, "that cluster of four pipes connected with the female and juvenile wings, chapel, and reception cells.

"We keep the fires burning night and day when the weather is cold, keeping the temperature up in the winter, which renders the cells very healthy, with a sufficient quantity of warm air passing into them continually from the flues, where the hot-water pipes are.

"Each of the cells has an extraction flue that conveys the impure air into a large flue on the roof of each wing, and these large flues are connected with, and discharge themselves into, the ventilating shaft."

The heating apparatus room is of considerable size, with a deep sunk passage in the centre, where the stokers trim the fire, as seen in the engraving. It is lighted by two iron grated windows on each side, and has a stone staircase leading down to the furnaces.

In the corner on the left-hand there is a large cistern containing hot water, to supply the baths in the reception ward, and likewise for the baths given to the prisoners in the various corridors, in winter once a month, in summer once a fortnight. It generally contains about 500 gallons, and is heated by means of steam conveyed from the steam boiler in the ventilating shaft.

We thereupon went to the central hall, where we entered a small apartment at the end of D wing, containing two large cisterns connected with the boilers in the furnace-room. They answer two purposes—one of them fills the pipes with cold water, and the other allows the water as it heats to expand. Two large flow-pipes are extended along the centre of the apartment connected with the expansion cistern, and in addition to this, there is a supply pipe to fill the cistern with water.

We proceeded with the engineer to the base of the lofty ventilating shaft of the prison, which adjoins the kitchen, and is situated at the angle of the C and D wings. " You see," said the engineer, " this large mass of iron work, which is an iron funnel extending to the top of the central tower. I shall tell you the use of this. In the summer time, when the weather is hot, we are obliged to keep a large fire in the centre of the shaft to assist our ventilation, as the air must be kept warmer in the shaft than the atmosphere passing through the cells, as otherwise they would not be satisfactorily ventilated, and the air would not pass properly through." Within the iron funnel in the shaft, there are three large square iron flues connected with the horizontal flues underground, for conveying the smoke from different fireplaces, such as in the steward's office, laundry, etc.

In this room we also observed two large steam boilers on a level with the floor, used for cooking the prisoners' food, and likewise for heating the water in the cistern in the furnace room to bathe the prisoners.

The engineer then conducted us to his workshop, situated in the basement of C wing adjoining the carpenter's shop. The walls were decorated with a large assortment of iron tools of various descriptions, used in operations over the prison, all carefully arranged. At one end of the shop was an iron turning-lathe, and a bench with two iron vices attached to it.

We passed on to the pumps worked by the tread-wheel. In a small recess connected with the tread-wheel shed, we found two prisoners busy at work on a cross handle, assisting the tread-wheel in pumping water, and likewise a large fly-wheel close to the wall, a shaft being connected with it at one end, and an eccentric wheel at the other, with which the rods of the pumps are connected. From the eccentric wheel are two iron arms connected with the shaft, and by this means the water is pumped and conveyed to cisterns on the top of the entrance of the building, at an elevation of eighty-five feet from the ground.

" We usually pump," said the engineer, " 1300 gallons per hour, with one single strong pump, taking an eighteen inch stroke. The pumps are situated in the well, 150 feet from the surface of the ground. The well is 370 feet deep, but the water rises up within five feet of the pump.

We were then introduced to the carpenter. He stated to us, " We have very seldom good carpenters here; I have at present two prisoners engaged with me in my shop. They have been trained to this kind of work, but are not good workmen, and I employ them in the general repairs of the prison, and in the houses of the chaplain and governor. We only engage those men to work here who have been accustomed to this employment out of doors. I and my assistants execute all the carpenter's work required in the prison.

₊ *Visiting the Prisoners in their Cells.*—We accompanied the chief warder to corridor C, to visit several of the more remarkable of the various classes of prisoners confined there; so that we might have a more just and discriminating acquaintance with the special character of Holloway Prison.

On entering one of the cells we saw a dark complexioned man of short stature, a Dutch Jew. He had a broad face, and a brow of a peculiar form, sloping suddenly back, with full dark eyes. He had been guilty of using threats, and did not find the necessary security for his future good conduct. He told us he was born in Amsterdam, and was a cigar-maker by trade. By his own confession, " he took drink—dat vas de reason he got into trouble."

We went into another cell along with the governor, who was going his stated rounds over the prison. We found here a robust, well-formed youth, of twenty-one years of age, about five feet six in height, with a particularly finely formed countenance. On looking at his card, we learned he was under confinement for picking pockets.

Gov. "This is one of the cleverest lads I have got in the prison." Turning to the prisoner, he added, "I am willing to take you by the hand and assist you, if you will co-operate with me. Are you willing to go home to your friends?"

Pris. (His rich dark eye glistening with interest). Yes, sir, I shall go home to Newcastle, and leave London.

Gov. I will write to your friends, and tell them to take back their prodigal son. Perhaps you will write yourself. Will you do so now?

Pris. Yes, I will.

Gov. (Turning to us and the chief warder). This young man will learn any trade with the greatest expertness.

When the governor had retired, the prisoner informed us, in answer to our inquiries, that he had been a thief for the past twelve years—had chiefly been engaged in picking pockets, and belonged to the cleverest class except those who frequent the banks. He is remarkably expert in stealing from ladies' pockets. He was over in Paris twice, and had made excursions to the leading towns in Scotland, where he had been very successful in picking pockets. In Paris he found double trouble in stealing from ladies, as they have two pockets, one on each side. He was in the habit of going to public assemblies in London, of various kinds, as well as to churches, and committing depredations. He had once been arrested at Calais, in company with two known pickpockets, and was sent over the English channel as a suspicious character—his fare having been paid out of the money he had on his person at the time of his arrest.

In another cell we found a modest-looking man, with reddish hair. He was rather under the middle height, about thirty-five years of age, and confined for picking pockets. He told us he had entered into crime when twelve or thirteen years of age. He chiefly lived by picking pockets, and generally frequented Newington Causeway or the Borough, and went to all the fairs, and to the west-end theatres.

In a cell adjoining we found a plain-looking man, about thirty years of age, who had been imprisoned for stealing pewter pint-pots in the City, and was detected by the police when endeavouring to sell them to a marine-store dealer. He told the chief warder it was done to support his wife and family, who were in extreme want.

In another cell we saw a quiet-looking man, of forty years of age, sentenced to two calendar months for the unlawful possession of two doormats. He had formerly been a bricklayer's labourer, and was employed in building the very prison in which he was confined. Since that time he had fought as a soldier in the Crimea during the Russian war. He was an Irishman, and belonged to Dublin.

We next visited several of the cells in corridor D, the only wing of the main prison which remained to be visited.

In one of them we saw a stout-made young man, of short stature and dark complexion, about twenty-one years of age, with nothing very striking in his appearance. He stood with a piece of junk he had been picking in his hand. He had been stealing for the past five years. Of late, he has chiefly rifled gentlemen's pockets of watches, etc. He had sometimes succeeded in getting £50 at a time, and was most successful at fairs. He was a hawker, and his father travels the country, selling hardware. He said he would willingly work in any honest way if he had any one to assist him, but was not inclined to go into a reformatory.

He further added, in answer to the interrogatories of the chief warder, that he generally went to work with a man, and sometimes a woman, who acted as a stall. He considered that to take six watches, was a good day's work.

In one of the cells we saw a young man, of about twenty-one years of age, with a strange conical-shaped head, broad at the underface, and very narrow towards the top of the head. The chief warder remarked to us that the prisoner was suffering from disease in his legs, owing to a family complaint, and also by fast life. He is confined six calendar months for stealing a handkerchief, and has been no less than fourteen times in Holloway Prison, and in several other prisons besides.

On going into the next cell, we found another prisoner, aged about forty-five years, a cabman, who told us a very doleful story. He had been intrusted with a chest of tea by some party unknown to convey in his cab to a particular place in the metropolis. He supposes the police were after the man who had hired him, as he made his escape immediately after he had given the property into his custody. For the unlawful possession of this chest of tea, he had received a sentence of twelve months' imprisonment with hard labour. He has a wife and family, for whom he appeared to be much concerned.

In one of the cells we saw a remarkably good-looking, fresh-complexioned boy, of about seventeen years of age, very handsome, and apparently very intelligent. The governor remarked that, when genteelly dressed, he might pass for a nobleman's son. The chief warder stated he had been several times in prison. On this occasion he was imprisoned eighteen calendar months for picking pockets. He had at one time been confined in Westminster Bridewell for two months, and was afterwards removed to a reformatory at Reigate for two years. He served his time there, and got a situation in one of the telegraph offices in the metropolis, where he remained for two months. He said that he had left of his own accord, as he was about to be punished for making a mistake in a message. He got another situation, and remained there two or three weeks, when he rejoined his old companions in Keate Street, Spitalfields. Since then he has been six times in prison. The governor informed us that the authorities of the prison had taken the greatest interest in this boy, but he was afraid it was all in vain. The governor asked him if he would go to a reformatory on being released from prison, but he did not relish this proposal.

Gov. If I had a house adjoining the prison where I could learn this boy a trade, and have him under my eye for five years, he would become a useful member of society; but leave him to his old companions, and he will one day be transported.

The boy was meantime smiling in his usual light-hearted, thoughtless manner.

Gov. Have you any friends to take an interest in you?

Pris. I don't know, sir. I have got no father. My mother lives at Bethnal Green, and is a nurse. I have not seen her for two years.

This poor lad is a remarkably fair specimen of many others who have a good disposition, but are led thoughtlessly astray by those bad associates and pernicious influences which abound in our great metropolis.

Before leaving corridor D, we were very desirous to see two other prisoners, remarkably expert thieves, the one a lobby-sneak, and the other a burglar; but they were not then in their cells. We accompanied the chief warder to his office, where they were shortly afterwards introduced to us.

The first was a middle-sized man, of about thirty-five years of age, with pale face, small gray eyes, and gentle manner. In answer to the interrogatories of the chief warder, he stated that his parents were respectable people, residing in the Borough. He began his criminal career by stealing from his mother's till, and had ran away from school, and left his home at about ten years of age. In the course of his life he had been engaged in two burglaries, and had slipped into houses and committed felonies innumerable times—he could not tell how many. He had also been a good pickpocket in his day, but had now lost the nerve. He was once transported, and had been confined in prison about seventeen years altogether.

He told us he had never been rogue and fool enough to get married. To use his own words, "I should have considered myself a fool if I had married one of my own class of people, because I knew very well in my own mind, or by experience, that when I got into trouble, she would be playing the harlot with some one else, and I was never rogue enough to take an inoffensive female from her home and deceive her with professing what I never was or intended to be."

He added, "I often committed my felonies by means of false keys, and by entering fanlights and by the windows at the back of the house. I have taken a great quantity of plate by sneaking in the areas."

When he got into prison on this occasion he was out begging. The steel had been taken out of him, and he was hard up.

The other prisoner brought into the chief warder's office was a smart, vigorous, intelligent young man, of about five feet seven inches in height, with a fine broad brow and well-formed countenance. He had a keen, penetrating eye, which twinkled with humour and was very frank and communicative.

He informed us he was born in Scotland, the son of Scotch parents. He had engaged in almost every kind of felony, and had committed many housebreakings and burglaries. He did not use the mask in his burglaries, and considered they were only apprentice boys at their work who did so. He was exceedingly nimble, and could climb to a housetop by the spout as quickly as a person could go up a stair.

On one occasion he went out at midnight, with other four companions, to plunder a jeweller's shop in the metropolis. They were detected by a policeman, who sprung his rattle, when other officers came up. Two of his pals struggled with the former and nearly killed him; he and another burglar ran away in the direction of the Thames. On that winter evening, being hotly pursued, he swam across the river with his clothes on. He stated that he had been a thief for the past nine years, being mostly engaged in burglary, and generally worked in the interior of the house. He "put up" the burglaries he committed, and sometimes cried with vexation till he cleared his way through obstacles. He had been a sad rake among the girls, and before his arrest had kept two females. He has frequently seen large advertisements over the metropolis offering a reward for the detection of burglaries he had committed, but which could not be traced to him.

He said he had been very lucky for a considerable time, and had made the City ring with his exploits. He believed that during the past eighteen months he had got about £1500 by his burglaries, but had gambled it away and wasted it.

*** *The Juvenile Wing of the Prison* is situated to the left of the reception ward, and is reserved exclusively for young male offenders from seventeen years of age and downwards.

On entering the corridor, we were introduced to Mr. White, one of the warders, who stated:—"At present we have nineteen juveniles under seventeen years of age. Our prisoners here are under the same routine of prison discipline as in the other corridors. The boys under fourteen years of age are exempted from hard labour by Act of Parliament. From the nature of their offence, they are sometimes sentenced to it, as, for example, in picking pockets, but with prisoners of those tender years it is not carried into effect. Instead of working at the treadwheel, they are employed picking oakum, or some other occupation.

In the juvenile wing there are three reception cells and a bath-room, with one bath of smaller dimensions than those in the adult reception ward, and also a store of prison clothing for juveniles, carefully arranged, along with a store-room containing the prisoners' own clothing.

There is a staircase leading from the reception ward to a small lobby entering into the corridor. On the right side of it are four small wooden compartments, where the friends and relatives of the juveniles visit them. These are covered over on the top with a wire-screen, similar to what we found in the adult branch of the prison. There is a door in the corridor by which the prisoners are introduced to similar compartments on the other side of the visiting-room, with another door in the centre, where a warder usually patrols during the time of the interview.

There are six refractory cells in this wing of the prison, but at the time of our visit there were no prisoners confined in them. "It rarely happens," said Mr. White, "we have any delinquents in custody." There are few punishments inflicted in this prison, yet the discipline is strictly maintained.

Adjoining these dark cells there is a bath-room, containing two other baths for the use of the juvenile prisoners.

While we visited this corridor, which is similar in form and dimensions to the others, several boys were engaged sweeping and cleaning the asphalt floors. Some of the older lads were at treadwheel labour, and others were picking oakum and plaiting bass in their cells. The utmost silence prevailed over all the wards, broken only by the occasional tread of a warder proceeding along one of the galleries, and the noise of the cleaners in the basement of the corridor as they plied their brushes and cocoa-nut husk rubbers on the floor.

We visited several of the cells along with the governor, who was then going his usual rounds over the prison, and found several boys picking oakum. We inspected them on a subsequent occasion with Mr. Grant, the reception warder of the adult prison, and found them similarly occupied. The most of them appeared to be Irish Cockneys—many of them of the ordinary felon character. Some of them were smart and intelligent; others appeared to be dull and very ignorant.

Two of these juveniles were afterwards ushered into the governor's office, the one a clever sneak, and the other an exceedingly adroit pickpocket.

The former was a little fair-complexioned Irish lad of about sixteen years of age, with good features. He stood before the governor with his hands behind his back, and his head leaning to one side in a timid manner. In answer to various interrogatories, he stated that his mother was dead, and his mother-in-law, who is addicted to dissipated habits, ill-treated him. He confessed he had commenced to steal when he was eleven years of age, and had been six times in prison. He did not pick pockets, but stole from shops along with a companion. He generally went in and the other boy remained without. He thought it was safer for him to go in, and hand the article stolen to the boy at the door, who ran off with it. If he was caught there would be nothing found upon him, and he had a better chance of escaping. He lived in Keate Street, Spitalfields. On one occasion he stole a pair of boots, on another he took a ham, then a bundle of cigars, after this a box of revolvers, etc., and was sentenced to various terms of imprisonment.

The other boy was also of Irish extraction. He was a firm-made little fellow of dark complexion, with a fine dark eye, which occasionally shone with brilliancy. He is reputed to be one of the cleverest young pickpockets in London. He informed us he was fifteen years of age, and had one brother and two sisters in Australia, and three sisters living at home, who are all well behaved. He stated he had been led into crime by bad boys, and had now been thieving for four years and a-half. He lived at Keate Street, with a number of other lads like himself. In particular, he mentioned one of the name of Malony, a very expert thief, who could pick pockets very dexterously on the fly, *i. e.* when the parties were walking along the street.

He had often been arrested for attempts at picking pockets, but had only been once convicted, and was sent to Wandsworth. When at large he chiefly worked at picking-pockets in the City, but did not consider it to be so easy as in Middlesex. Before he came to prison, he sometimes went to Oxford Street, where many ladies call with carriages at the shops.

He informed us he had sometimes been so successful as to take nine or ten purses in one day. Many fashionably dressed ladies do not carry any money in their pocket, while plain country people have often a well filled purse.

During his recital, the little felon knit his brow and firmed his lip, and occasionally spoke with his eyes shut. Sometimes his countenance shone with animation, and in other moods he looked like a simple country boy. He appeared to be a lad of superior ability.

ORDINARY DISTRIBUTION OF A PRISONER'S TIME.

Summer, from	to		Winter, from	to		
5 45	—	...	6 45	—	A.M.	Rise; open ventilator, and spread bedding, and wash.
6 0	7 20	...	7 0	7 30	„	Employment.
7 20	8 10	...	7 30	8 10	„	Breakfast, and prepare school lessons, clean cell, and make-up bed.
8 10	9 0	...	8 10	9 0	„	Chapel.
9 0	12 45	...	9 0	12 45	P.M.	Exercise, employment, school, etc.
12 45	2 0	...	12 45	2 0	„	Dinner, and prepare school lessons.
2 0	5 45	...	2 0	6 45	„	Employment and school.
5 45	6 30	...	6 45	7 30	„	Supper, and work in cell.
6 30	8 0	...	7 30	8 0	„	Employment in cell.
8 0	8 45	...	8 0	8 45	„	Sweep cell, wash, read or write, and prepare school lessons.
8 45	9 0	...	8 45	9 0	„	Sling hammock; go to bed.

On SUNDAYS.

6 45 ... ... A.M.	Rise.	2 0 ... to 3 0 ... ... P.M.	Exercise.
8 0 ... ... „	Breakfast.	3 0 ... ... „	Chapel.
9 0 ... ... „	Exercise.	5 30 ... ... „	Supper.
10 45 ... ... „	Chapel.	8 0 ... ... „	Bed.
1 0 ... ... P.M.	Dinner.		

¶ iv. γ.

The Female House of Correction, Holloway.

WE accompanied the governor to the female prison, which is situated opposite to the juvenile wing, and were introduced to the matron, and entered a small lobby on the ground floor beneath the archway connected with the main prison. On our right hand is a small room neatly furnished for the use of the laundry warder, with a bedroom adjoining. In the lobby are two bells, one communicating with the door on the exterior, and the other being a night-bell connected with the rooms of the female officers of the prison.

At this time several female prisoners came downstairs from the corridor above, with the shining tins for dinner to be conveyed to the kitchen.

₌ *Reception Ward.*—Leaving the lobby, we descend four stone steps into the reception ward on the basement. The central floor is laid with asphalt, with a narrow stripe of pavement on each side, adjoining the cells.

On the right are the matron's apartments, consisting of a kitchen and bedroom. On the left is a bath-room containing two baths and a sink, also a dressing-room, somewhat similar to those in the adult prison. There are three reception cells in this ward.

At the extremity of the reception ward are two dark cells, but no prisoners were confined in them at the time of our visit. They are similar to those in the main prison, and are furnished in a similar manner.

We then passed into the store-room containing *the prisoners' own clothing*, together with an *assortment of prison dress*. The prisoners' own clothing was laid in racks along the wall in the interior of the apartment, and the prison garments were assorted on shelves.

The female prison clothing in Holloway Prison consists of three wincey petticoats in winter, and two in summer; a blue gown, a checked apron, a blue checked neckerchief, a small printed pocket handkerchief, and a white linen cap. Likewise a pair of blue worsted stockings, and a thick substantial shawl, both knitted by the female prisoners. The bedding is the same as in the other corridors.

The matron informed us, " There is only a small portion of the bundles of clothes fumigated; belonging chiefly to the lowest class, such as vagrants and prostitutes, many of them of Irish extraction."

We saw a considerable number of bundles of more elegant appearance on the shelves. The matron stated that, at present there is a larger number of fashionable pickpockets and shoplifters in the female prison than she has ever previously known. " We generally have some showy pickpockets," she added, " but never so large a number. Their ages vary from twenty to thirty-five years of age—seldom above thirty-five.

As we passed along the ward, from the window of the matron's room we saw a large company of the female prisoners in the exercising ground, their heads being covered with their hooded shawls. They moved along with active step, under the charge of a female officer.

Leaving the reception ward, we went to the corridor above, where a very animated scene presented itself to our view. A large number of the female prisoners were exercising around the galleries under the inspection of the female chief warder, who was stationed on a bridge across the first gallery, while a female warder was stationed on a bridge in the higher gallery. After exercising for some time they returned to their various cells.

The female warders were attired in a brown dress, with a dark head-dress.

The chief warder informed us the first gallery contains the prisoners tried at the Central Criminal Court, convicted of the most heinous offences, and in the second gallery are disorderly prisoners and others tried at the Summary Courts.

On the first day of our visit the prisoners were occupied in the following employments :— Picking oakum, 12; at needle-work, 14; in the laundry, 8; engaged in general cleaning, 6; nursing, 2; sick in cells, 2; in infirmary, 4; in reception ward, 3; knitting caps and stockings, 15; in all 66 prisoners.

** Laundry.—This is a large, well-aired, commodious apartment. At a large table in the centre of the room, several female prisoners were actively engaged in folding up a quantity of female underclothing, while some bundles were piled on the table beside them. There was another table at the left side of the room, on which a portion of the clothes lay folded, others of the prisoners were busy mangling. There is a large copper at the extremity of the laundry, in which the clothes are boiled. It is supplied with steam by a large cistern above it. There is also a screen in which the linen is laid out to dry.

We noticed several large bundles containing male prisoners' clean clothing ready for use.

Adjoining the laundry is a drying-room, furnished with six clothes horses, which can be drawn out and into a recess, where the wet clothes are exposed to the action of heated air. Two of the prisoners were ironing white linen.

We observed here a pretty young woman—an expert and fashionable pickpocket. She had a very fine face and figure, and her bright eyes were fringed with long black eyelashes. We learned from the chief warder that she cohabits with a low fellow in the City, and has been frequently in confinement charged with picking pockets. She was handsomely dressed when brought to the prison.

" You see that prisoner," said the chief warder, referring to a plain-looking, middle-aged woman, who was sitting beside the mangle, " she is also an expert pickpocket, and an old offender."

The prisoners employed in the laundry are allowed a pint of beer every day, of which they were partaking at the time we entered.

In the proximity of the laundry are eight washing boxes, supplied with hot and cold water by means of taps, where some of the female prisoners were busy washing.

Meantime several male prisoners came in escorted by a warder (while the females had for a short time retired), and carried off several large bundles of white linen to the male prison.

The female prisoners in the laundry wash the clothing for all the branches of the prison.

*** *The School.*—The female classes are convened in a large comfortable apartment at the extremity of the corridor on the first gallery. On the walls are suspended a map of the two hemispheres, and another of England, along with a number of pictorial illustrations of Scripture subjects. A black-board is set on a stand. The teacher, an active intelligent lady, stood in front of the class, which was ranged on a deal form in front of her. There were from twelve to fifteen females present in the adult class at the time we visited them, consisting chiefly of fashionable pickpockets and shop-lifters. Their ages averaged from seventeen to thirty-five. Some of them were good-looking, and apparently modest— one or two had a superior air about them. One prisoner in particular, a tall, fair complexioned, handsome woman—a fashionable pickpocket—had a striking and commanding appearance, even in her felon garb. She was brought to the prison in a rich black dress with three flounces, and a handsome cloth cloak, an elegant bonnet beautifully trimmed, and boots with military heels. Her petticoats were also of the best materials. " She was dressed and garnished with jewellery," said the teacher, " like one of the finest ladies in the land, and from her appearance and manner no one would have suspected her real character." She resided at Kensington with a worthless character, and hired an old woman to keep her child at the rate of £1 a week." A young woman of about twenty-two years of age, with a fresh, blooming complexion, also a pickpocket, sat by her side ; while her eye drooped on her book, her countenance was lit up by a beautiful expression, but on looking up, as she did occasionally, she appeared less interesting. Another young woman, a pickpocket, of about nineteen years, sat beside them, with a very ingenuous appearance. On the matron interrogating her as to the particular nature of her offence, she burst into tears. A good-looking young woman of about twenty-four years of age, who had been detected picking pockets sat opposite to us. She had formerly been a barmaid in the city and had been led astray by bad company. A plain-looking, dissipated woman sat next her, who had led a very wild and romantic career in the Metropolis, as the paramour of a daring burglar. She still cohabits with him, and now picks up a base livelihood by roaming the west end at midnight, and plundering drunken men. Another woman, respectable-looking, of about thirty years of age, who had been guilty of forging a bank cheque, sat at the farther end of the class. Some of them were reading attentively, others with their slates on their knee, and a few knitting stockings.

The teacher was busy when we entered with the reception warder, explaining the three Kingdoms of Nature to the class. We did not remain long on this occasion.

On a subsequent day we visited the class with the matron, which was then engaged with the Bible lesson. Most of the prisoners read very fluently and correctly, and conducted themselves with great propriety of demeanour. They afterwards clustered around the map of England, alongside of their amiable teacher, and appeared to take great interest in their geography lesson.

After the class had been dismissed, and the prisoners had retired to their several cells, the teacher gave us the following information :—

" There are two classes here. One of them is attended by those learning the elements of reading and writing. There are about twelve pupils attending this class, their ages averaging from fifteen to forty. Some of them learn very rapidly, but others are very obtuse. There are several with me at present who have learned to read with tolerable ease in the course of six months, and are able to write a letter to their friends. The younger prisoners are the most proficient scholars. This class is held four times a-week.

" The other class consists of adults, who are taught reading, writing, and arithmetic, geography, and general information. In age they vary from twenty to forty-five. These often make great progress. This class is also held four times a week.

"On Saturday we have a class for the women attending the laundry. The school is generally appreciated by the prisoners.

"There is also a circulating library belonging to the prison. The books are distributed once a-week in the various cells, and oftener if it is considered proper.

"Some well educated female prisoners read out of the library who do not attend the classes. There are seldom so many of this superior order in the prison that I could muster a class. They generally avail themselves of the use of the circulating library, and write exercises on their slate in English composition."

*** *The Outer Watchman.*—One morning we visited the prison about half-past six o'clock. It was then dusk, and the crescent moon was nearly obscured by a cloudy sky, and scarcely a star was visible. As we approached Holloway Prison we saw the long windows at the extremities of the adjacent corridors dimly lighted, while the tapering dark tower stood out in dark profile against the dull gray sky. The great Metropolis stretched around to the south, wrapt in mist, and the noise of its busy traffic which used to break on our ear like the roar of the restless ocean, had not yet been awakened from the gloom of night. We only heard the occasional roll of a vehicle passing in the distance, the shrill call of a railway whistle summoning the lieges to an early train, and the solemn chime of the clocks in the neighbouring church steeples as they announced in the quiet sombre air the flight of winged time.

On knocking at the outer gate we were admitted by the warder within the walls of the prison. Shortly after we heard the bell in the interior of the prison summoning the prisoners to their daily labour.

As we wandered about the courtyard, the outer watchman hove in sight with lighted lantern in hand, as he was proceeding on duty around the inner walls. We accompanied him in one of his rounds, until we reached the back of the prison, when he flashed his bull's eye on our note-book, and gave us the following information:—

"I commence duty," he said, "at nine o'clock in the evening. It is my duty to inspect all external doors, etc., and to see that articles are not thrown over the walls by persons from without. I go round with my lighted lantern in hand to see that all is right, and to ascertain that no prisoner has a light in his cell, and that there is no communication from without.

"I not only keep watch without, but enter the interior of the prison, and have a master-key which opens the external doors. I frequently go into the interior and communicate with the watchman within, and inform him if all is right. Should I observe a light in any of the cells, I proceed at once to the interior to find out the cause. It may be that the chief warder has visited some of them. He is called up by the inner watchmen when any of the men are sick.

"I light the kitchen fire between one and two o'clock, and get the steam up, and attend to it afterwards. I remain till the gruel is cooked, when I proceed to my work outside. I leave duty about a quarter past seven o'clock in the morning, when the warders assemble to enter on their various duties for the day.

*** *Employment of Prisoners.*—The following is a state of the various employments in which the prisoners were engaged on one of the days we visited the prison:—

Employments.	Men.	Boys.	Females.	Total.
Mat-making	70	...	...	70
Balling, plaiting, etc.	7	5	...	12
Treadwheel	47	5	...	52
Carry forward	124	10	...	134

	Men.	Boys.	Females.	Total.
Brought up	124	10	...	134
Picking oakum	2	1	9	35
Cleaning	4	1	8	13
Extra ditto, oakum, etc.	15	4	...	19
Window cleaning	2	2	...	4
Whitewashing	4	...	...	4
Wood chopping	...	...	...	...
Cutting junk, and packing	4	...	...	4
Gardeners	20	1	...	21
Smiths and Stokers	7	...	...	7
Cooks	5	...	...	5
Carpenters	2	...	...	2
Coopers	1	...	...	1
Brushmakers	1	1	...	2
Basketmakers	1	...	...	1
Bookbinders	2	...	...	2
Painters and Glaziers	2	...	...	2
Bricklayers	2	...	...	2
Tailors	19	1	...	20
Shoemakers	11	...	...	11
Barbers	2	...	...	2
Needlework	...	...	16	16
Knitting	...	...	14	14
Washing	...	...	8	8
Excused and Sick	4	2	6	12
Infirmary	6	...	3	9
Nurses	1	...	2	3
Dark punishment cells	...	...	...	0
Light cell	...	...	...	0
Clerks, etc.	2	...	...	2
Picking hair, etc.	2	...	...	2
Total	268	23	66	357

LIST OF THE DIETARY FOR PRISONERS AT HOLLOWAY PRISON.

Approved by the Secretary of State, 24th April, 1850.

CLASS I.

Convicted prisoners confined for any term not exceeding seven days :—

	MALES.			FEMALES.	
Breakfast	Oatmeal gruel	1 pint.	Breakfast	Oatmeal gruel	1 pint.
Dinner	Bread	1 lb.	Dinner	Bread	1 lb.
Supper	Oatmeal gruel	1 pint.	Supper	Oatmeal gruel	1 pint.

CLASS II.

Convicted prisoners for any term exceeding seven days, and not exceeding twenty one days :—

	MALES.			FEMALES.	
Breakfast	Oatmeal gruel	1 pint.	Breakfast	Oatmeal gruel	1 pint.
"	Bread	6 oz.	"	Bread	6 oz.
Dinner	Bread	12 oz.	Dinner	Bread	6 oz.
Supper	Oatmeal gruel	1 pint.	Supper	Oatmeal gruel	1 pint.
"	Bread	6 oz.	"	Bread	6 oz.

Prisoners of this class, employed at hard labour, to have in addition 1 pint of soup per week.

CLASS III.

Convicted prisoners employed at hard labour, for terms exceeding twenty-one days, but not more than six weeks; and convicted prisoners not employed at hard labour, for terms exceeding twenty-one days, but not more than four months :—

MALES.			FEMALES.		
Breakfast .	Oatmeal gruel	1 pint.	Breakfast .	Oatmeal gruel .	1 pint.
„	Bread . . .	6 oz.	„	Bread . . .	6 oz.

Wednesday and Friday.

Dinner .	Soup . . .	1 pint.	Dinner .	Soup . . .	1 pint.
„	Bread . . .	1 oz.	„	Bread . . .	6 oz.

Tuesday and Sunday.

Dinner .	Cooked meat, without bone . .	3 oz.	Dinner .	Cooked meat, without bone . .	3 oz.
„	Bread . . .	8 oz.	„	Bread . . .	6 oz.
„	Potatoes . .	½ lb.	„ .	Potatoes . .	½ lb.

Monday, Thursday, and Saturday.

Dinner .	Bread . . .	8 oz.	Dinner .	Bread . . .	6 oz.
„	Potatoes . .	1 lb.	„	Potatoes . .	1 lb.

(or 1 pint of gruel when potatoes cannot be obtained.)

Supper, same as breakfast.

CLASS IV.

Convicted prisoners employed at hard labour for terms exceeding six weeks, but not more than four months; and convicted prisoners not employed at hard labour, for terms exceeding four months :—

MALES.			FEMALES.		
Breakfast .	Oatmeal gruel	1 pint.	Breakfast .	Oatmeal gruel .	1 pint.
„	Bread . .	8 oz.	„	Bread . . .	6 oz.

Sunday, Tuesday, Thursday, and Saturday.

Dinner .	Cooked meat without bone . .	3 oz.	Dinner .	Cooked meat, without bone . .	3 oz.
„	Potatoes . .	½ lb.	„	Potatoes . .	½ lb.
„	Bread . .	8 oz.	„	Bread . . .	6 oz.

Monday, Wednesday, and Friday.

Dinner .	Soup . . .	1 pint.	Dinner .	Soup . . .	1 pint.
„	Bread . .	8 oz.	„	Bread . . .	6 oz.

Supper, same as breakfast.

CLASS V.

Convicted prisoners employed at hard labour for terms exceeding four months :—

MALES.			FEMALES.		

Sunday, Tuesday, Thursday, and Saturday.

Breakfast .	Oatmeal gruel .	1 pint.	Breakfast .	Oatmeal gruel .	1 pint.
„	Bread . . .	8 oz.	„	Bread . . .	6 oz.
Dinner .	Cooked meat, without bone . .	4 oz.	Dinner .	Cooked meat without bone . .	3 oz.
„	Potatoes . .	1 lb.	„	Potatoes . .	½ lb.
„	Bread . . .	8 oz.	„ .	Bread . .	6 oz.

Monday, Wednesday, and Friday.

Breakfast .	Cocoa . . .	1 pint.	Breakfast .	Cocoa . . .	1 pint.

made of ¾ oz. of flaked cocoa, or cocoa nibs, sweetened with ¾ oz of molasses or sugar.

„	Bread . . .	8 oz.	„	Bread . .	6 oz.
Dinner	Soup . . .	1 pint.	Dinner .	Soup . . .	1 pint.
„	Potatoes . .	1 lb.	„	Potatoes . .	½ lb.
„	Bread . .	8 oz.	„	Bread . .	6 oz.
Supper .	Oatmeal gruel .	1 pint.	Supper .	Oatmeal gruel .	1 pint.
„	Bread . . .	8 oz.	„	Bread . . .	6 oz.

CLASS VI.

Prisoners sentenced by court to solitary confinement:—

MALES.	FEMALES.
The ordinary diet of their respective classes.	The ordinary diet of their respective classes.

CLASS VII.

Prisoners for examination before trial, and misdemeanants of the first division, who do not maintain themselves:—

MALES.	FEMALES.
The same as Class IV.	The same as Class IV.

CLASS VIII.

Destitute debtors:—

MALES.	FEMALES.
The same as Class IV.	The same as Class IV.

CLASS IX.

Prisoners under punishment for Prison offences for terms not exceeding three days:—
1 lb. Bread per diem.

Prisoners in close confinement for prison offences, under the provision of the 42nd Section of the Jail Act:—

MALES.			FEMALES.		
Breakfast	Gruel	1 pint.	Breakfast	Gruel	1 pint.
"	Bread	8 oz.	"	Bread	6 oz.
Dinner	Bread	8 oz.	Dinner	Bread	6 oz.
Supper	Gruel	1 pint.	Supper	Gruel	1 pint.
"	Bread	8 oz.	"	Bread	6 oz.

Note—The soup to contain, per pint, 3 oz. of cooked meat, without bone, 3 oz. of potatoes, 1 oz. of barley, rice, or oatmeal, and 1 oz. of onions or leeks, with pepper and salt.

The gruel to contain 1½ oz. of oatmeal per pint, when made in quantities exceeding fifty pints; and 2 oz. of oatmeal per pint when made in less quantities.

The gruel on alternate days to be sweetened with ¾ oz. of molasses or sugar to each pint, or seasoned with salt.

Boys under fourteen years of age to be placed on the same diet as females.

RETURN SHOWING THE AVERAGE EXPENSES OF HOLLOWAY PRISON FOR SEVEN YEARS, AND FOR THE LAST TWO YEARS.

	Average for the last Seven Years, and Daily Average for Seven Years.			Average for the last Two Years, and Daily Average for Two Years.		
Daily average number of prisoners	338			332		
	£	s.	d.	£	s	d.
Total cost of ordinary and extra diet, clothing, and bedding ...	2625	6	3	2133	1	8
Ditto per head, per annum	7	15	4	7	6	7¾
Ditto ditto for a week	0	2	11¾	0	2	9¾
Ditto fuel, gas, cleaning materials, furniture, books, stationery, prisoners on discharge, and other sundries ...	1305	6	0	1082	8	2
Ditto per head, per annum	3	17	2¾	3	5	2
Ditto ditto for a week	0	1	5¾	0	1	3
Ditto officers salary and uniforms	3476	14	2	3676	19	7
Ditto ditto per head, per annum	10	5	8½	11	1	6
Ditto ditto per week	0	3	11¼	0	4	3
Ditto for new buildings, additions, alterations, etc.	319	8	11	175	11	4
Ditto ditto per head, per annum	0	18	10¾	0	10	6¾
Ditto ditto per week	0	0	4¼	0	0	2¼
Total expenditure for seven years	£7750	1	3	7390	13	1¾
Ditto ditto of prisoners per head per annum for seven years..	22	18	7	22	5	2¼
Expenditure of prisoner per head, per week	0	8	9¾	0	8	6½

RETURN SHOWING THE TIME AND VALUE OF MALE PRISONERS' LABOUR.

No. of days.			Trade.				Rate. s. d.				Value. £ s. d.		
2792	...	...	Tailors	...	...	...	2 0	...	...	279	4	0
1532	...	...	Shoemakers	...	...		2 0	...	...	153	4	0
866	...	...	Carpenters		...	...	2 0	...	...	86	12	2
2517	...	...	Smiths	...	...	...	2 0	...	...	251	14	10
448	...	...	Stokers	...	...	...	1 0	...	...	22	8	0
17	...	...	Turners	...	...	...	2 0	...	...	1	14	0
56	...	...	Painters	...	...	...	2 0	...	...	5	12	0
84	...	...	Bricklayers		...	...	———	...	...	8	8	0
1036	...	...	Washers	...	...	...	1 3	...	...	64	7	0
30	...	...	Brushmakers		...	...	2 0	...	...	3	0	0
84	...	...	Basketmakers		...	...	2 0	...	...	8	8	0
179	...	...	Bookbinders		...	...	2 0	...	...	17	18	0
58	...	...	Tinmen	...	...	...	1 3	...	...	3	12	6
70	...	...	Coopers	...	...	...	2 0	...	...	7	0	0
252	...	...	Woodchoppers		...	...	1 0	...	...	12	12	0
1815	...	...	Gardeners	...	...	...	1 3	...	...	113	9	0
1820	...	...	Cooks	...	...	...	1 3	...	...	113	15	0

Total £1152 18 6

The average daily consumption of water is one tank of 3500 gallons, which is the price charged by the New River Company 7s. 6d. per tank would amount to   136 17 6

£1289 16 0

NOTE.—There has been £69 received since. It is a return for mangold-wurzel, grown on the ground, paid since into the Chamber.

RETURN SHOWING THE VALUE OF THE WORK PERFORMED BY FEMALE PRISONERS.

				£ s. d.
Articles of clothing made for the use of the prisoners				£37 17 5
„ „ repaired „				73 2 4
Washing 112,345 garments, or 5617 score, at 1s. per score				230 17 3
Total				£391 17 0

	£ s. d.
Total amount of male prisoners' labour	£1289 16 0
„ female „	391 17 0
Total	£1681 13 0

	£ s. d.
Total expenses of prison	£8092 19 2
„ receipts of moneys for prison labour, etc.	3085 16 9
Cost to City	£5007 2 5
Deduct estimated value of Prisoners' labour	1681 13 0
Net total cost	£3325 9 5

CHAMBERLAIN'S GATE—A MOST MISERABLE DUNGEON REBUILT BY RICHARD WHITTINGTON,
AND CALLED BY HIM NEW GATE.
[From an old engraving.]

DETENTIONAL PRISONS.

¶ i.

NEWGATE JAIL.

Mr. Hepworth Dixon, in his excellent work on the prisons of London, observes, with regard to Newgate, " that it is massive, dark, and solemn, arrests the eye and holds it." He farther adds, " a stranger in the capital would fix on it at a glance, for it is one of the half dozen buildings, in this wilderness of bricks and mortar, which have a character; of all the London prisons, except the Tower, it alone has an imposing aspect."

In its strong and impressive architecture, as well as in its own eventful history, it rises in stern grandeur above all the other prisons in England. Our readers will pardon us in these circumstances, taking a glance into the chronicles of London, not only to learn the past reminiscences connected with Newgate, but also to become acquainted with the prisons of London in bygone times.

Maitland states that the original Old Bailey Prison got the name of Newgate, as it was erected in the reign of Henry the First, several hundred years after the four original gates of the city.

It is an interesting circumstance that it should have been erected by the famous Richard Whittington, Lord Mayor of London. Stow records " it was built by an Act of Parliament granted by Henry the Sixth to John Coventre, Jenken Carpenter, and William Grove, executors to Richard Whittington, to re-edify the jail of Newgate, which they did with his goods."

It was the common jail for the county of Middlesex, but was not so large and commodious as the present building. It was situated on the north side of Newgate Street, with its front looking down the Old Bailey instead of being in a line with it as now. The edifice was of an ornamental style, similar to a triumphal entrance to a capital, crowned with battlements and towers, and adorned with statues, having a wide arch in the centre for carriages, similar to Temple Bar, with a postern in the north side for foot passengers, as seen in the engraving.

This old jail was gutted by the great fire of London in 1666, which extended from Billingsgate to St. Dunstan's Church, near Temple Bar, and destroyed above 12,000 houses, the damage being estimated at ten millions. As most of those houses were built of wood, they were burned down to the ground; but the walls of Old Newgate being of solid granite survived that catastrophe. The building was afterwards repaired in the year 1672.

In early times Newgate, as well as the other jails in England and the Continent, was in a deplorable condition. In the words of John Howard, " the prisoners were kept in close rooms, cells, and clammy dungeons 14 or 15 hours out of the 24. The floors of some of those caverns were very damp—in some of them there was an inch or two of water, and straw, or miserable bedding, was laid on the floors. There were seldom any bedsteads in them, and the air was offensive beyond expression." Howard farther observes, " my readers will judge of the malignity of the air when I assure them that my clothes were, in my first journeys, so offensive, that, when in a post-chaise, I could not bear the windows drawn up, and was therefore obliged to travel commonly on horseback. The leaves of my memorandum book were so tainted that I could not use it till after spreading it an hour or two before the fire. I did not wonder that in these journeys my jailers made excuses, and did not go with me into the felons' wards."

Jail fever was then very prevalent, in consequence of cleanliness and ventilation being generally neglected. Howard observes: " From my own observations in 1773, 1774, and 1775, I was fully convinced that more prisoners were destroyed by it than were put to death by all the public executions in the kingdom." He farther observes, "A cruel custom obtains in most of the jails, which is that of the prisoner demanding of the new comer, garnish, footing, or, as it is called in some London gaols, ' chummage.' ' Pay or strip,' are the fatal words. I say fatal, for they are so to some who, having no money, are obliged to give up part of their scanty apparel. If they have no bedding or straw to lie on, they contract diseases which often prove mortal."

At this time criminals were treated with far greater severity than in our day; and desperate crimes were much more frequent. Many of the prisoners before trial, as well as after sentence, were loaded with heavy irons by night and day, against which Howard protested. Townsend says: " In the early part of my time, such as from 1781 to 1787, where one prisoner is convicted now, I am positively convinced there were five then. We never had an execution wherein we did not grace that unfortunate gibbet with ten, twelve, or more persons; and on one occasion I saw forty at once. But this unfortunate slaughter did no good at all. The more hangings there were, the more hardened and desperate the criminals became."

Highway robberies were then rife on Hounslow Heath, Blackheath, Finchley Common, Wimbledon Common, and on the Romford Road. Townsend states: " I have been in Bow Street in the morning, and while I was leaning over the desk heard three or four people come in and say, ' I was robbed by two highwaymen in such a place: I was plundered by a single highwayman in such a place.' By means of the horse patrol which Sir Richard Ford planned, people now travel safely."

The rookeries of thieves in Saint Giles, Westminster, and in the Old Mint, in the Borough, were in their glory about the beginning of the 18th century, when Jack Sheppard and Jonathan Wild performed their notable exploits. Toward the end of that century, at the time Howard lived, robberies had been considerably checked, yet numerous executions took place at Tyburn, at the angle of Oxford Street and the Edgeware Road, near to where the Marble Arch, Hyde Park, now stands.

The low scum of the citizens, in those days, were regaled with those gloomy exhibitions; and at the peal of the bell of St. Sepulchre's Church, assembled around Newgate, from the slums and disreputable localities of the city, and accompanied the cart conveying the criminals to Tyburn on its dismal procession along the Tyburn Road, now transformed into Oxford Street. On certain occasions when a noted highwayman, or burglar, or other criminal, was to be executed, crowds of most respectable citizens might be seen wending their way from all parts of the city toward the fatal tree.

The last execution at Tyburn took place on the 7th of November, 1783. In the same month the first criminal was hanged in front of Newgate, which henceforth became the place of execution. This change appears to have been made at the suggestion of Howard, from philanthropic motives, to do away with the unseemly processions to Tyburn.

In connection with this melancholy subject we extract a piece of curious information from the chronicler Stow, which we give in his own words: " Only let it be added that Mr. Robert Dow, merchant-tailor, that deceased 1612, appointed the sexton, or bellman, of St. Sepulchre's to pronounce solemnly two exhortations to the persons condemned, for which, and for ringing the passing bell for them as they were carried to the cart by the said church, be left to him 26s. 8d. yearly, for ever.

" The exhortation to be pronounced to the condemned prisoners in Newgate the night before their execution—

> " You prisoners that are within,
> Who, for wickedness and sin,

" after many mercies shown, you are now appointed to die to-morrow, in the forenoon; give ear and understand that to-morrow morning the great bell of St. Sepulchre's shall toll for you, in form and manner of the passing bell as used to be tolled for those that are at the point of death. To the end that all goodly people hearing that bell, and knowing it is for you going to your deaths, may be stirred up heartily to pray to God to bestow his grace and mercy upon you whilst you live. I beseech you, for Jesus Christ his sake, to keep this night in watching and prayer for the salvation of your own souls, while there is yet time and place for mercy, as knowing to-morrow you must appear before the judgment-seat of your Creator, there to give an account of all things done in this life, and to suffer eternal torments for your sins committed against Him, unless upon your hearty repentance you find mercy through the merits, death, and passion of your only mediator and advocate, Jesus Christ, who now sits at the right hand of God to make intercession for as many of you as penitentially return to him."

The admonition to be pronounced to the convicted criminals as they are passing by Saint Sepulchre's Church to execution—

" All good people, pray heartily to God for these poor sinners who are now going to their death, for whom this great bell doth toll."

" You that are condemned to die, repent with lamentable tears. Ask mercy of the Lord for the salvation of your own souls, through the merits, death, and passion, of Jesus Christ, who now sits at the right hand of God to make intercession for as many of you as penitentially return unto him.

> " Lord have mercy upon you!
> Christ have mercy upon you!
> Lord have mercy upon you!
> Christ have mercy upon you!"

EXTERIOR OF NEWGATE.

Writing in 1777, Howard states, that "the total number of executions for the previous twenty-three years had been 678, and the annual average was 29 or 30." He remarks: "I could wish that no persons suffered capitally but for murder, for setting houses on fire, and for house-breaking, attended with acts of cruelty. The highwayman, the footpad, the habitual thief, and people of this class, should end their days in a penitentiary-house rather than on a gallows. That many cartloads of our fellow-creatures are, once in six weeks, carried to slaughter is a dreadful consideration. And this is greatly heightened by reflection, that with proper care and proper regulation, much the greater part of these wretches might have been made into useful members of society, which they now so greatly dishonour in the sight of all Christendom."

We have reason to believe that the original Newgate Jail, in the general arrangements of its cells and wards was similar to the building erected in its place, but less commodious. It was seldom visited by the sheriffs and magistrates, who did not like to venture within the wards, "least they should soon be in their graves," and no government inspector was appointed till the year 1777. Howard informs us: "In many jails, and in most bridewells (Newgate included) there is no allowance of bedding or straw to lie in, and if by any means they (the prisoners) get a little, it is not changed for months together, and is almost worn to dust. Some lie on rags and others on the bare floor. The keepers told him "the County allows no straw, and the prisoners have none but at their cost."

Stimulated by the noble philanthropy of Howard, a large new prison was erected by the magistrates of the City, from designs furnished by George Dance, the City architect. It was set on fire during the Protestant Riots of 1780, by an infuriated mob, led by the fanatic Lord George Gordon, but afterwards repaired. The interiors of the side wings have also been recently changed, yet the outer walls still stand as massive as ever, and will possibly do so for many centuries to come.

In 1783, John Howard, when referring to the old Prison of Newgate, writes thus:— "The builders seemed to have regarded nothing in their plan but the single article of keeping prisoners in safe custody. The rooms and cells were so close as almost always to be the constant seats of disease and sources of infection. The City had, therefore, very good resolution to build a new jail (which he did not consider as a model to be followed). I am of opinion that without more than ordinary care the prisoners in it will be in great danger of the jail fever."

In a later volume of his works, when writing an account of the present venerable Prison of Newgate, then nearly erected, he observes that "there was *no alteration* since his former publication. In three or four rooms there were nearly one hundred and fifty women crowded together, many young creatures with the old and hardened, some of whom had been confined upwards of two years. On the men's side there were many boys of twelve or fourteen years of age, some almost naked. In the men's infirmary there were only seven iron bedsteads; and at my last visit, there being twenty sick, some of them naked and with sores in a miserable condition lay on the floor with only a rug. There were four sick in the infirmary for women, which is only fifteen feet and a half by twelve, has but one window and no bedsteads, the sewers being offensive, and the prison not whitewashed. Unless room be given for the separation of the prisoners, and a reform be made in the prisons, an audacious spirit of profaneness and wickedness will continue to prevail in the lower class of the people of London."

In 1787 there were in Newgate 140 debtors and 350 criminals—490. In 1788 there were 114 debtors and 499 criminals—613. From which time to 1810, a space of twenty-three years, Newgate continued in a wretched misguided condition. The number of prisoners was increasing, and there was no proper classification of them.

In 1808, Sir Richard Philips, one of the sheriffs of the City, in his letter to the Livery of London, after complaining of want of room, air, food, etc., adds :—"that he has been shocked to see boys of thirteen, fourteen, and fifteen confined for months in the same yard with hardened, incorrigible offenders. Among the women, all the ordinary feelings of the sex are outraged by their indiscriminate association. The shameless victims of lust and profligacy are placed in the same chamber with others who, however they may have offended the laws in particular points, still preserve their respect for decency and decorum. In immediate contact with such abandoned women, other young persons are compelled to pass their time between their commitment and the Sessions, when of course it often happens that the bill is not found against them by the Grand Jury, or they are acquitted by the Petty Jury. When the female prisoners lie down on their floors at night, there must necessarily, at least in the women's wards, be the same bodily contact and the same arrangement of heads and legs as in the deck of a slave-ship. The wards being only forty-three feet wide, admit by night of two rows to lie down at once in a length of thirty-seven feet; that is to say, twenty-five or thirty women, as it may be, in a row, having each a breadth of eighteen inches by her length."

This stifling confinement of the women in 1808, when Newgate was crowded with female prisoners, still continued in 1817. In 1818, the Honourable Mr. Bennet, M.P., wrote a letter to the Common Council and Livery of the City of London, in reference to the abuses existing in Newgate, and urging the necessity of an immediate reform in the management of that prison.

The Prison of Newgate was calculated to hold only 427 prisoners; but on one occasion about this time 822 prisoners, debtors and criminals, were huddled together, and sometimes even as many as 1200; which overcrowding created infectious jail fever. The prisoners were not provided with bedding, and the food allowed them was hardly sufficient to sustain life.

Mr. Bennet writes:—"The keeper of Newgate never attended Divine service, and the ordinary did not consider the morals of even the children who were in the prison as being under his care and attention. *No care was taken to inform him of the sick till he got a warning to perform a funeral.* There was no separation of the young from the old, the children of either sex from the most hardened criminal. Boys of the tenderest years, and girls of the ages of ten, twelve, and thirteen were exposed to the vicious contagion that predominated in all parts of the prison; and drunkenness prevailed to such an extent, and was so common, that unaccompanied with riot it attracted no notice."

In 1815 some good arrangements were made as to a better allowance of food, clothing, and coals, and several other matters, but the classification of persons was still neglected. They still continued to herd together in the associated rooms and yards, and through the facility of intercourse which subsisted between the prisoners and their friends and acquaintances who visited them, extensive burglaries and robberies were plotted in Newgate, and notes were forged and coining was carried on within its gloomy walls. By bribing the turnkeys intoxicating liquors were often introduced into the prison, and profligate women were permitted to visit the prisoners, under the pretext they were their wives, and by paying the small fee of one shilling were allowed to remain during the night in wards containing several beds, not separated from each other by a single curtain. There were then fifteen condemned cells, which inconveniently contained forty-five persons, three in each cell. In his evidence before the Police Committee, Mr. Bennet states:—"On the 19th of February, 1817, there were eighty-eight persons condemned to death in Newgate, of which five had been sentenced in the July preceding, four in September, and twenty-nine in October. The evil of this assemblage of persons is the entire absence of all moral or religious feeling. The greater part of the criminals know that on them the sentence of the law will not be executed; while those whose fate is certain, or who doubt what the event may be, are compelled to associate and live with the rest; lessening the *ennui* and despair of the situation by unbecoming merriment, or seeking relief in the constant application of intoxicating stimulants. I saw

Cashman a few hours before his execution smoking and drinking, with the utmost unconcern and indifference. Nor indeed is this all. Supposing the prisoners of two Sessions are under sentence, one reported and the other not; there is no separation between those who are to be executed and those who are unreported; the latter are gay, and even joyous, while the former pass the few hours to remain to them in a feverish dream.

"The new keeper, Mr. Brown, has commenced a system of reform in all the departments of the prison, which, if persevered in, will produce the most salutary results. He is endeavouring to check the abuses which have prevailed in the management of the prison; amongst these abuses the sale of offices have been the most serious, and I have been informed that the place of wardsman to the different wards has been often purchased of the turnkeys. I knew an individual who told me that he offered fifty guineas for one of these situations, and was refused; no doubt because a better price was got. The introduction of spirits still continues, and till the admission of strangers is better regulated, will never be wholly prevented."

With reference to the female prisoners, the Honourable Mr. Bennet observes in his letter to the Common Council and Livery of the City of London:—" The humane and excellent management of Mrs. Fry and the Society of Friends, has placed this part of the prison in a state of comparative excellence. No praise of mine can add weight to the tribute of general applause which Mrs. Fry and her Committee of Friends have received from all who have witnessed their efforts."

Mr. Bennet concludes his judicious and admirable letter in these words:—" I cannot refrain from expressing my astonishment at a Report which the Grand Jury of Middlesex, who, in the discharge of their duty, inspected Newgate last session, have thought to make of the state of that prison. They could not have noticed the want of proper classification, nor the state of the condemned cells, nor the manner in which the prisoners sleep, nor the promiscuous assemblage of all kinds of misdemeanants in the five yards, nor the want of separation of old and young offenders in all parts of the prison; for if they had noticed these deficiencies, I am sure twenty-four Englishmen could not have passed a vote of high admiration. The slight want of matting and covering is, in fact, a want of proper rugs and bedding; and the nudity or the deficiency of shirts, shoes, and stockings, cannot but be taken as trifling exceptions to those excellent arrangements which are the theme of this extraordinary panegyric."

Since the year 1817, when these words were penned by Mr. Bennet, the arrangements of Newgate have at various intervals been greatly reformed. In 1858, the associated rooms and offices of the wings adjoining Newgate Street were removed, and a corridor erected with interior arrangements similar to those of the Model Prison at Pentonville, and in 1860 the old buildings of the female wing were taken down and a corridor built in their place after the same style. Yet the massive exterior remains the same as in the time of John Howard.

¶ i.—a.

Interior of Newgate Jail.

*** *The Lodge.*—We enter the Lodge of Newgate Jail by a door, elevated a few steps above the level of the street, in a line with the Old Bailey, flanked by dark huge masses of stone, forming part of the wall, which is about four feet thick. This outer door is only about four feet and a half high, and is covered on the top with formidable iron spikes—the open space above being farther fenced with two strong iron bars with transverse iron rods. There is another massive oaken inner door alongside, faced with iron, of enormous strength, which is only shut at night. It reminds us of the terrible prisons in the old barbaric times, when criminals were more desperate than in our day, before Howard commenced his angelic mission over the dungeons of England and the Continent. This door has a very strong Bramah lock with a big brazen bolt, which gives a peculiarly loud rumbling sound when the key is turned; and at night it is secured with strong iron bolts and padlocks, and by an iron chain. The great bolts penetrate a considerable way into the massive stone wall.

The lodge is a small sombre-looking high-roofed apartment, with a semicircular iron-grated window over the doorway, and a grated window on each side, and is floored with wood. On our left hand is a small room, occupied by a female warder who searches the female visitors to the prison, lighted by an iron-grated window; and on our right is an ante-room leading to the governor's office. Another heavy oaken door, faced with iron, leads into the interior of the prison; and alongside, is an iron-grated window communicating with the interior.

The warder in attendance, a genial-looking officer with robust frame, introduced us to the governor, when we produced our order from the visiting justices of the prison. He kindly allowed the deputy-governor to attend us over the various wards. Before leaving the lodge we inspected the prison books, which were similar to those we found in several of the prisons already described.

On the walls are suspended different notices by the Court of Aldermen in accordance with Act of Parliament. One of them forbids liquors to be introduced into the prison, another refers to visiting the prisoners, and a third, to the attorneys and clerks who should visit them respecting their defences.

The deputy-governor opened the ponderous iron-bolted door leading into a gloomy passage with arched roof, conducting along the back of the porter's lodge towards the male corridor and kitchen. On our right hand is a strong door of the same description, leading to the female prison, secured by ponderous lock and bolts.

We meantime turned to the left, and came to another strong oaken door faced with iron. In this sombre passage the gas is kept burning, even at mid-day. As we passed along we saw the sunbeams falling on a stone flooring through an iron grating, opening into the interior of the old prison yard.

On passing through this heavy door, which is kept locked, the passage widens. Here we saw a long wooden seat for the accommodation of the prisoners who are to appear before the governor to have their descriptions taken. This passage leads, on the right-hand side, into a room called the bread-room, where we observed a warder in the blue prison uniform, who is detained here on duty.

₊ *The Bread-room.*—We went with the chief warder into the bread-room, which is also used to take descriptions of the prisoners, being well-lighted and very suitable for this purpose. It has a wooden flooring, and is whitewashed. In this apartment is an old leaden water-cistern, very massive, and painted of a stone colour, curiously carved, with the city coat of arms inscribed on it, and dated 1781. There is here also a cupboard containing a curious assortment of irons used in the olden time, as well as a number of those used in the present day, of less formidable appearance. There are here deposited the leg-irons worn by the celebrated burglar and prison-breaker, Jack Sheppard, consisting of an iron bar about an inch and a half thick, and fifteen inches long. At each end are connected heavy irons for the legs, about an inch in diameter, which were clasped with strong iron rivets. In the middle of the cross-bar is an iron chain, consisting of three large links to fasten round the body. We found these irons to weigh about twenty pounds.

There is also in this cupboard a "fac simile" of the heavy leg-irons of the celebrated

GATEWAY AT NEWGATE,

WITH GROUP OF PRISONERS' FRIENDS WAITING TO BE ADMITTED.

Dick Turpin, the mounted highwayman. These consist of two iron hoops about an inch thick, to clasp the ankle, and about five inches in diameter. A ring goes through and connects with the iron clasp which secures the ankle with a long link on each side, about ten inches in length and above an inch in thickness. These long links are connected with another circular link by a chain passing through to fasten round the body. They are about thirty-seven pounds in weight.

We also observed some of the old irons which were formerly put on the prisoners capitally convicted, and kept upon them, during day and night, till the morning of execution. There is also an axe which was made to behead Thistlewood and the other Cato Street conspirators, guilty of high treason, which was not, however, used. This axe is large and heavy, about nine inches wide at its broad edge, and an inch and a half thick at the back, and must have required to be wielded by a strong-armed executioner. It weighs about eleven pounds. There is also a leathern belt about two and a half inches wide for pinioning the persons to be executed. It goes round the body and fastens behind with straps to secure the wrist, and clasp the arms close to the body. There is likewise another, used by the executioner on the drop in securing the legs. A number of these straps had been used in pinioning notorious murderers executed at Newgate, whose tragic histories are recorded in the "Newgate Calendar;" and many of these leg-irons had fettered the limbs of daring highwaymen in the olden time, who used to frequent Blackheath and Hounslow Heath. The massive and gloomy architecture of Newgate and its strong iron keeps, and these terrible relics, give us a glimpse into the stern prison discipline of London of a bygone day.

There are manacles of a more recent date, for the wrist and leg, used in the removal of convicts to the various prisons.

In another cupboard in this room is contained the bread provided for the prisoners. There is also a machine for weighing it out. An officer generally sleeps here at night to ring the alarm bell in case any of the prisoners should be sick, or should attempt to escape from the prison.

There is here a door leading to vaults under the prison, where you descend by a flight of stone steps.

Before leaving this room the deputy-governor informed us :—" The leg irons referred to were attached to an iron belt, which went round the body, and were generally so short the prisoners could not walk with freedom while encumbered with them." Then he showed us one of these iron belts, which had three joints, one end of it lapped over upon the other, and a staple was inserted through one of the openings, of which there were five in number about an inch distant, similar to a leather strap; so that by this means the belt could be securely put on prisoners of different size. Through the staple which fastened the belt a padlock was generally inserted and was kept locked. There was a ring on each side of the belt, to which the handcuffs could be easily attached in case of necessity.

₊ *Murderers' Busts.*—We meantime returned to an anteroom leading into the governor's office, on the left hand side of the lodge, lighted by an iron grated window looking into the Old Bailey. There is a cupboard here containing arms for the officers in the event of any outbreak in the prison; consisting of pistols, guns, bayonets, and cutlasses. On the wall hung two very old paintings of Botany Bay, when convicts were first sent to that penal colony, and also a painting of Davies who was executed many years ago for the murder of his wife at Islington. It is roughly executed, and was done by himself before he was apprehended. His brow is lofty and full. His underface is rather sensual, but is by no means characteristic of a murderer. Judging by his countenance, he does not appear to be a desperate character, but to have been casually led into crime.

Along two shelves over the door, and on the top of an adjoining cupboard are arranged three rows of the busts of murderers who have been executed at Newgate.

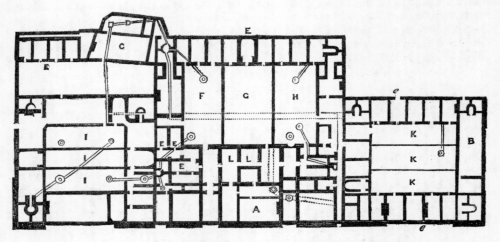

GROUND PLAN OF NEWGATE JAIL BEFORE THE RECENT ALTERATIONS.

A. Governor's Office.
B. Matron's Apartments.
C. An Associated Room.
D. An Airing Yard.

E. Day and Sleeping Rooms.
F. Chapel Yard.
G. Middle Exercising Yard for untried Prisoners.

H. Another ditto
I. Yards for Convicts and Boys.

K. Female Exercising Yards.
L. Passage along the interior of the Jail.

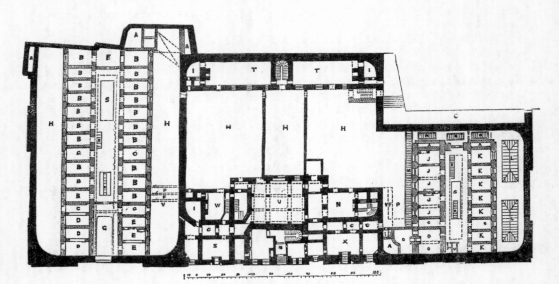

PRESENT GROUND PLAN OF NEWGATE.

A. Fresh Air Shaft.
B. Ordinary Cells in Male Corridor.
C. Passages along the interior.
D. Murderers' Cells.
E. Reception Cells, etc.
F. Male Officers' Rooms.
G. Van entrance.

H. Exercising Yards for Male and Female Prisoners.
I. Matron's Apartments.
K. Cells for Female Prisoners.
L. Washhouse and Laundry.
M. Flat Light to Basement Cells of Female Wing.

N. Male Officer's Room.
O. Sub-matron's Apartments.
P, F, V. Places where Prisoners are Visited by their Friends.
R. Stairs leading to Upper Galleries of Corridors.

S. Opening for Light to Basement of Male Corridor.
T. Infirmary.
U. Solicitors' Room.
W. Chaplain's Room.
X. Porter's Lodge.
Z. Kitchen.

The deputy-governor pointed out to us the bust of the miscreant Greenacre, who had a very sinister appearance. The brow is narrow and low, and the underface sensual, strongly indicative of a man of low passionate character. Another bust was pointed out to us as that of Daniel Good, for murdering a female, a paramour of his, and burning the body in his stable. The countenance was better moulded than that of Greenacre. The mouth had a peculiar expression, yet the face did not indicate the daring nature of his crime. "There," said the deputy-governor, looking to a full, large bust, "is Courvoisier, who was executed for the murder of Lord William Russell. The brow is low, the lower part of the face sensual, and the neck full and protruding under the ears. "You will remark," said the deputy-governor, "the upper lip of most of the group is thick, which might be caused by the process of hanging." Some of them had their eyes open, and others had them shut. We saw the bust of Lani, executed for the murder of a prostitute in the vicinity of the Haymarket, a heavy, brutal-looking countenance; and that of Mullins, lately executed for the murder of an old lady at Stepney, who was so base as to charge an innocent man with the offence. He had a heartless, politic, hypocritical expression of face, and we could believe him to have been guilty of the most atrocious crimes.

₊ *The Kitchen.*—On leaving the anteroom we pass through the lodge along the gloomy passage to the back above referred to, and retrace our steps through the heavy iron bolted door on the left. On our way to the kitchen we pass along the side of a room enclosed with glass panelling, in the centre of a large apartment with groined roof. It is used for the solicitors conversing with the prisoners respecting their defence. There we observed the son of a French baron committed to Newgate for a month for not giving evidence against his father in reference to an assault committed upon him. He was conversing with a lady who occasionally visited him during his confinement.

We proceeded along a narrow, gloomy passage lighted with gas, and went into the kitchen, which was very similar in dimensions and general appearance to the lodge, entering by a large door of massive structure furnished with similar locks and bolts. Opposite to it, fronting the Old Bailey, are two other ponderous doors, through which the culprit passes to the drop on the morning of the execution. On such occasions over the door leading from the passage are two irons fixed, on which two long rods are suspended with black curtains attached to them.

In the kitchen are two large coppers, sufficient to cook food for 300 prisoners. The steam is conveyed away from the coppers by means of copper pipes, that lead through a grated window into the open air. On shelves were ranged bright tins for the use of the prisoners, and wooden trays to carry the food from the kitchen to the various prison cells.*

₊ *Corridor of Male Prison.*—Leaving the kitchen, and bending our steps to the left, we go along another sombre passage of the same character as the one described.

---

* THE FOLLOWING IS THE DIETARY OF NEWGATE JAIL.

Breakfast for Male Prisoners :—
    8 oz. of bread.
    1 pint of oatmeal gruel, alternately seasoned with salt and molasses.
  Ditto for Female Prisoners :—
    Same diet as the males, with the exception that they have 6 oz. instead of 8 oz. of bread.
Dinner. On Sunday, Tuesday, Thursday, and Saturday the males and females have 3 oz. of cooked meat
    without bone, 8 oz. of bread, and half a pound of potatoes.
    On Monday, Wednesday, and Friday they have a pint of soup and 8 oz. of bread.
    The soup contains 3 oz. of meat with vegetables.
    The females have 6 oz. of bread instead of 8 oz.
Supper. The same as the breakfast.

Passing through a door at the extremity, we enter a covered bridge leading across a court into the corridor of the male prison. It has four galleries, numbered respectively together with the cells, on the ground floor A, B, C, D, and E, and is surmounted with a glass roof, which presents a very cheerful appearance very unlike the remaining portion of the old prison. We observed a stair on the outside communicating with each gallery, which is girdled with an iron balustrade. There is also a hoisting machine, by which provisions can be conveyed to each gallery in the short space of a minute and a half. There is a machine for weighing the provisions, in the centre of the corridor, and a dial over the second gallery. The following is a note of the cells, and the manner in which they are occupied, together with the classification of the prisoners :—

	No. of cells.		List of prisoners.	Classification.
Basement	11	Reception ward.	0	
Basement A	17	. . .	15	Remanded prisoners.
Gallery B	27	. . . .	22	Transports and penal servitude men.
— C	26	. . .	16	Felons.
— D	26	. . .	13	Misdemeanours.
— E	26	. . .	Empty.	

In answer to our interrogatories, the deputy-governor gave us the following statement :— "The prisoners are brought here in prison vans from the various police courts over the metropolis, being committed for trial by the magistrates. The City magistrates commit to Newgate, and send prisoners for remand as well as for trial. The metropolitan police courts only send those who have been committed for trial. Those sentenced by the justices of the metropolitan police courts are sent to the House of Correction at Coldbath Fields, whereas those in the City are sent to Holloway Prison. Prisoners convicted of a capital offence remain in Newgate until they are executed or reprieved. Some are incarcerated in Newgate for short terms by the judges of the Old Bailey, such as for contempt of court, and others are sent by the House of Commons for a similar offence."

"Newgate," continued the chief-governor, "is a house of detention for prisoners before trial, as well as for those sentenced to penal servitude, kept here for a short time awaiting an order from the Secretary of State to remove them to the Government depôts for the reception of convicts. In all cases of murder tried at the Old Bailey, the prisoners are sent here. When convicted they are given over to the sheriff of the county where the offences have been committed. If done in Essex, the murderer is removed to Chelmsford; if in Kent he is removed to the county gaol at Maidstone, and if in Surrey he is taken to Horsemonger Lane Gaol."

On the basement of this wing are the reception cells, and bath rooms, and the punishment cells.

** *Cells.*—The deputy-governor showed us into one of the cells in the corridor, which we found to be 7 feet wide, 13 feet long, and 8 feet 10 inches high, at the top of the arch. It has a window with an iron frame protected by three strong iron bars outside. The furniture consists of a small table which folds against the wall, under which is a small wooden shelf containing brushes, etc., for cleaning the cell, a small three legged stool, and a copper basin well supplied with water from a water-tap. On turning the handle of the tap in one direction the water is discharged into the water-closet, and on turning it the reverse way it is turned into the copper basin for washing. Each cell is lighted with gas, with a bright tin shade over it. On the wall is suspended the prisoner's card.

There are three triangular shelves in a corner of the cell, supplied with bedding, etc., as in other prisons we visited. The floor is laid with asphalt; over the door is a grating admitting heated air, with an opening under the window opposite to admit fresh air at the pleasure of the prisoner. Under the latter, and near the basement of the cell is a grating similar to the one over the door, leading to the extraction shaft carrying off the foul air, and causing a clear ventilation.

Each cell is furnished with a handle communicating with the gong in the corridor, by which the prisoner can intimate his wants to the warder in charge; and the door is provided with trap and inspection plate.

All the cells in the corridor are of the same dimensions, and similarly furnished.

Before leaving the corridor, about three o'clock in the afternoon, we visited several of the cells. We first went to Gallery B, occupied by penal servitude men. In one cell we saw a pleasant-looking, dark-complexioned man of about 30 years of age, sitting with one knee crossed over the other reading a book.

In another we saw a man of the same age, apparently of Hibernian stock, sitting with his feet on a three-legged stool. He had finished picking his quantity of oakuum, which lay in a treacle coloured heap on the floor. The deputy-governor informed us he was an old hand, and more expert at his work than the others.

We found a tall, good looking man of the same age, walking to and fro in his cell, who had also finished picking his oakum. The deputy-governor informed us he was a notorious housebreaker, who had already been transported for four years, and was now sentenced to another longer term of fifteen years for housebreaking. He stated he was an interpreter, and was able to speak several languages. When brought to the prison he was elegantly dressed in the first of fashion. He was the finest looking fellow we ever saw in a prison, and had a noble and commanding presence.

In one of the cells we saw a dark-complexioned young man of about 30 years of age with his back to us teazing oakum. He had a pile of oakum lying before him, but his work was not nearly done. He was a postman sentenced to penal servitude for appropriating the contents of some of the letters committed to his care. The deputy-governor observed, "They work steadily, but do not have the knack of the old hands, who do their work more expeditiously."

In an adjoining cell was another postman charged with a like offence.

While in the corridor we saw a well dressed, gentlemanly man of mature years, pass up a stair into a cell in Gallery C. He had just come from having an interview with his legal adviser, on a very serious charge of embezzlement.

On looking into one of the cells, we saw a prisoner with his vest and coat taken off, sitting at a table writing with manuscripts spread before him. He appeared to be a smart, business man, and had been a cashier to an extensive wholesale commercial house in the City, along with the person just referred to, and had also embezzled a heavy sum. He had been a fast young man, and frequented different dancing rooms, which led to his ruin.

In another cell we saw a respectable looking man in middle life, seated at his table with his head leaning on his hand, and copious manuscripts spread before him. On seeing us approach he appeared to be a little sensitive. He was dressed in a fine black coat and vest, and light trousers. He was charged with obtaining goods to the enormous amount of £12,000, and represented himself to be a merchant. He resided in Belgravia, an aristocratic locality of London. The deputy-governor remarked, "it rarely happens criminals of this kind are caught in the meshes of law, though no doubt such transactions are carried on by swindlers of that description to a great amount."

In another cell we saw a foreigner, an artist, who had gained an ignoble celebrity by attempting to extort money from a lady, his lover. He was apparently about 35 years of age, and was handsomely equipped in a dark fashionable suit. While we were present he was occupied writing, possibly preparing for his trial.

₊ *Reception Cells, Baths, and Punishment Cells.*—On proceeding to the basement we visited the reception cells, which are eleven in number, of the same dimensions as those in the corridor above, and fitted up in the same manner.

There are three slate baths, about six feet long, two feet broad, and two feet and a half deep, provided with footboards. They are heated by means of pipes communicating with the boiler in the engine-room. Two of them are fitted up in one cell, with a dressing-room adjoining. The other bath is in a long room, where there is a fireplace and a large metal vessel, heated by steam, to cleanse the prisoners' clothes from vermin and infection. This resembles a large copper, and is about two and a half feet in diameter and three feet deep, with an ample lid screwed down so firmly that no steam can escape. The clothes are put into it and subjected to the action of the steam for about a quarter of an hour, when the vermin is destroyed. The clothes are not in the slightest degree injured. This vessel is heated by means of a steam-pipe connected with the boiler in the engine room. The bath is similar to the others already noticed.

The dark cells are situated at the extremity of the new wing on the basement. They are six in number, and are of the same dimensions as the other cells. No light is admitted into them, but they are well ventilated. The furniture of each consists of a wooden bench, to serve as a bed—though it is a hard one—and a night utensil; and the flooring is of stone. There are two doors on each cell. When shut, they not only exclude a single beam of light, but do not admit the slightest sound.

The deputy-governor remarked, "There are very few ₊punishments inflicted in this prison. Sometimes the prisoners infringe the prison rules, by insolence to their officers or making away with their oakum instead of picking it. We have only had two persons in the dark cells for the past two years."

Opposite the bath room is an engine room, fitted up with two immense boilers for heating the whole of the prison and keeping the baths supplied with hot water. The engineer informed us that, during the winter, nearly a ton of coals is consumed per day. The pipes are conveyed into the different cells for the purpose of heating them. Along the walls are arranged a copious supply of iron tools for the purpose of repairing the different locks, etc.

₊ *The Visiting of Prisoners by their Friends.*—Leaving the corridor of the male prison we returned to the passage across the court, covered with thick glass, where relatives and friends are permitted occasionally to visit the prisoners. On each side of it is a double grating, fenced with close wirework, of about four feet wide, occupied by the prisoners. The relatives take their station on each side of the passage during the interviews, and a warder is stationed by their side to overlook them. On one occasion we were present when several of the prisoners were visited by their friends. One of them was a man of about fifty years of age—a Jew—charged with having been concerned in the forgery of Russian bank notes. He was an intellectual-looking fair-complexioned man, with a long flowing beard and a very wrinkled brow, and his head bald in front. He was very decently dressed, and appeared deeply interested while he conversed in broken English through the wire-screen with an elderly woman, who appeared to be warmly attached to him, and who was profoundly affected with his situation. He appeared to be a shrewd man of the world. Alongside was a genteel-looking young man, with sallow complexion and fine dark eye, who was visited by a tall young woman, decently dressed, who stood with a white bundle in her hand. It appeared this prisoner was under remand for stealing clothes from his employers. He looked sullen, and though apparently attached to the young woman, was very taciturn, and looked around him with a very suspicious air. A modest-looking elderly man, with silver hair, genteely attired in dark coat and vest and grey trousers, stood with a bundle in his hand, and was busily engaged conversing with a little smart woman of advanced years, dressed in a grey dress and dark shawl. We learned he was charged with embezzlement.

PRISONERS' CONSULTING ROOM, NEWGATE.

On the other side of the passage two young lads, dressed as costermongers, were visited by two plain-looking young girls, apparently belonging to their own order, who did not look by any means very concerned. Meantime a middle-aged woman was introduced into the passage, dressed like the wife of a mechanic, and her eyes red with weeping. She held a white handkerchief in one of her hands, and was under great excitement. Soon after, a plain-looking boy, of about twelve years of age, was brought out of the corridor adjoining, and came up to her. On seeing him, she gave an outcry, and burst into tears. Soon after, she changed her mood and looked angry, while her son began to make protestations of his innocence. She cautioned him not to be refractory, as, she said, "that would break her heart more than anything." She told him she would come again and see him. The bell rang, which was the signal that the time allowed for visiting was expired, when she reluctantly followed the steps of the other visitors who were proceeding back towards the lodge of the prison. The boy wept aloud as she was leaving him, and was removed back to his cell. It appeared he was charged with passing bad money.

*** *The Murderers' Cells.*—Leaving the male corridor we pass through an iron gate on the left into a small passage, paved with slate, beside an exercising-ground bordering on Newgate Street, which extends along the farther side of the new wing. On turning to the left, towards the front of the prison, we came to two rooms reserved for murderers. Each of these is about the size of two common cells, and has an arched brick roof supported on iron girders. The wretched men confined in these are watched day and night by a warder. The furniture consists of a wooden bedstead about nine inches in height from the floor, supplied with the following bedding : a mattress, three blankets, a pair of sheets, and a pillow, a table larger than in the ordinary cells, and a settle about six feet in length. It is lighted by an iron-grated window with fluted glass. The floor is laid with asphalt. There is also an alarm bell, which communicates with the adjoining corridor, where a warder is constantly on duty night and day. There are three triangular shelves in a corner of the room, furnished pretty similar to the ordinary cells. A knife is not allowed them—the food being cut up into small pieces in the kitchen before it is brought to the prisoner; this is to prevent his laying violent hands on himself. Every precaution is taken in such an extreme case. As this wing of the prison has been recently erected, there has only been one murderer confined in one of them—the miscreant Mullins—for murdering Mrs. Emsley of Stepney, whose conviction was chiefly owing to the ingenious and admirable management of the late Inspector Thornton of Scotland Yard. Mullins was a middle-aged man of a wretched appearance. He was a returned convict, and had been at one time in the constabulary force in Ireland. "During the time he was in custody, before his execution," said the deputy-governor, "he conducted himself very well, and was quiet and orderly as most in his situation are." The cell alongside is of a similar character.

*** *Burying Ground of the Murderers.*—On leaving the murderers' cells we followed the deputy-governor through the midst of the convicts clad in dark-grey prison dress, consisting of jacket, vest, and trowsers, and Scotch cap. At the farther end of the exercising ground we proceeded through the corridor, and went under the covered arch leading into an exercising-yard of the same description as the opposite side of the new wing. We continued our course until we reached the airing-yard attached to the female prison, which, like the others, is covered with pavement, where we entered a long passage about eight feet wide, extending from the extremity of the associated rooms of the old prison, now to be used as an infirmary, to the nearest corner of the female wing, where it turns off in a right angle along the back of the female prison to the Sessions House adjoining. This portion contiguous to the female wing is the graveyard of the murderer; so that when conducted to and from the dock of the Old Bailey he passes over the ground which is to be his own grave. It is bounded on the one side by the lofty walls of the female prison, and on the other by a very high wall flanking it from the adjacent outlying dwellings. It is laid with pavement, portions of which have been displaced by the sinking of the ground, perhaps caused by the mouldering of the bodies beneath. Along the walls, on each side, are the initials of the surnames of the assassins, such as G for Greenacre, G for Good, M for Mullins, L for Lani. This plain-looking passage is invested with tragic interest, when we think of the mouldering bones of the murderers rotting beneath, and carry our imagination back to the deeds of horror they transacted, the recital of which have brought paleness to many a cheek.

₊ *Exercising Grounds.*—There are four exercising grounds, all of them paved, connected with the male wing, in addition to a fifth belonging to the female branch of the prison. Two of them consist of a long narrow strip of ground on each side of the male wing. The other two are situated between the old associated rooms at the back of the prison and the rooms set apart for the chaplain and the solicitors.

In proceeding from the new wing of the male prison we go through a strong iron door into a large square exercising ground, about fifty feet long and forty-eight feet broad. In a corner of it is another grated enclosure for visiting the prisoners. It extends on each side of the door through which the criminal passes to the drop to be executed. There is here a pump connected with an artesian well in the ground below. On looking around us we are surrounded with the dark lofty walls of the old prison, about forty feet high, together with the red brick walls of the new wings, which are in some places armed with iron spikes, to prevent the escape of the prisoners. On one occasion we saw a detachment of prisoners in this exercising ground. They were clad in their own apparel, and were marching actively round the square, about three yards apart from each other. Some of them appeared to be felons of the lower order, in miserable, poverty-stricken attire; others were dressed as labouring men. A remarkable group of five persons was pointed out to us by one of the warders as being charged with the forgery of the Russian bank notes. They were of Jewish extraction, but of different style of countenance. An active good-looking man, of about thirty-five years of age, with fine features, attired as a well-dressed mechanic, is charged with forging the plate, and the others are implicated, more or less, in the transaction. One of them, a thin-faced, slim, smart, fair-complexioned youth, of about twenty-five years of age, was dressed in a drab greatcoat and hat. Other two had strongly-marked Jewish features, and were of dark complexion, and apparently of about forty years of age. The other was the intelligent-looking man we saw in the visiting ground, as already noticed. He appeared to us, although not the forger of the plate, to be the chief of the gang.

Adjoining this square exercising ground, and behind the solicitor's room, is a yard of narrower dimensions, divided from the other by a wall about fourteen feet high, formidably crowned with strong iron spikes. There is also a pump in this yard, communicating with another artesian spring, and an iron grating about three feet from the wall adjoining the grated windows of the solicitor's room. There were no prisoners exercising here at the time of our visit.

On a subsequent visit we saw several boys exercising in the narrow court adjoining the murderers' cells. A pale-faced, knock-kneed lad of about fourteen years of age, with a very sinister look, was charged with getting money by a forged order. He was dressed in dark clothes. A little schoolboy, of ten years of age, with a very innocent-looking face, was charged with stealing a glazier's diamond, and is now under remand. He was dressed in ordinary trowsers and dark grey jacket. Another genteel lad, of about fifteen years of age, is charged with stealing money from his employer, a hosier, in Regent Street. Another boy, dressed in shabby black dress, is charged with attempting to hang himself. He was under-waiter in an eating-house in the City, and had formed an attachment for a girl who preferred another. In chagrin and despair, the poor lad attempted to take his own life by hanging himself in the kitchen where he was employed. As we looked on his gentle quiet countenance we could scarcely believe he was capable of such a desperate deed.

Soon after, the boys were removed from the exercising ground, and were replaced by a gang of men clad in the grey prison dress. They were mostly from 18 to 35 years of age, and were all under sentence of penal servitude for different periods. " They are detained here but a limited time," said the deputy-governor, " awaiting an order from the Secretary of State to be removed to one of the government prisons. Meantime they are employed picking about three pounds of oakum a day." They consisted of pickpockets, burglars, forgers, and others, along with two murderers; and did not by any means appear to be so dejected as we would have expected. A bright-eyed tall English youth was pointed out to us as a convicted burglar. A quiet middle-aged man, of about thirty years of age, with a dejected mien, had been guilty of forgery to a serious amount. He had been a solicitor in the metropolis, with an extensive business and bright prospects, but he had lived a gay life, beyond his means, which led to his crime and ruin. A young man of colour was charged with passing bad money. He had lately returned from penal servitude for four years. We particularly observed the young lad, Reeves, charged with murdering his sister in Drury Lane. He is of robust frame, about sixteen years of age, fair-complexioned, with a full intelligent countenance, and modest demeanour. He walked actively around the exercising ground, smiling occasionally to an Irish youth, a prisoner. The deputy-governor observed he was a very quiet well-behaved lad, and must have been exasperated by ill-treatment to the commission of his bloody deed.

The other murderer, Maloney, charged with murdering a woman in Westminster, is a strong athletic man, of about forty-five years of age, and is apparently a quick-tempered, determined man. He was evidently in good spirits.

₊ *Old Associated Rooms.*—Before treating of the old associated rooms, which are now about to be transformed into an infirmary, we may advert to the alterations which have been lately made in Newgate Prison. The old sombre prison of our day was a new building in the time of the redoubtable prisonbreaker, Jack Sheppard. The whole of his daring exploits were achieved in an older building of smaller dimensions, the site of which extended in the direction of Giltspur Street. The present gaol of Newgate was erected in 1784, under the direction of George Dance, junior, architect and clerk of the city works. Only a small portion of the old gaol was left till lately, at the farther extremity fronting Newgate Street. The whole of the erections within the wing contiguous to Newgate Street were cleared away in 1858, consisting of associated rooms, cells, small exercising yards, etc., and a new wing was erected in the form of a large lofty corridor, extending from the one extremity of the building to the other.

In 1861 the female prison was taken down and a new wing erected, consisting of a corridor and laundry, after the more approved modern plan of prison architecture. The central portion of Newgate, consisting of the governor's residence, lodge, kitchen, chaplain's room and solicitor's room, together with the associated rooms at the back, were left untouched. They are built in more massive and gloomy style, and leave a more solemn impression on the mind than the light airy corridors of our modern model prisons. There are six of those asssociated rooms ; two of them adjoining the female exercising ground are to be fenced off and appropriated to the females, and the other four to be attached to the male branch of the prison, and to be used as an infirmary.

On ascending the massive stone staircase which leads to one of those large associated rooms, we saw strong iron rods fixed into the wall. By this means the warder could climb up to look through the inspection openings made into the solid wall. The doors leading into these rooms are fenced with iron, and secured with strong lock and bolts. On entering one of them we found it to be about thirty-seven feet long, sixteen feet wide, and fourteen feet high. A long deal table, about sixteen inches in breadth, extends along the centre of the room, with forms on each side. Between this table and the back wall are eighteen wooden bunks, built over each other in three tiers, as on board ship, in which the prisoners sleep. There are four windows in the room with panes of glass in iron frames, protected from without by strong iron bars. The flooring consists of oak caulked with oakum, and with strong iron framework between the ceiling and the flooring. There is a fireplace with a narrow chimney, fenced at intervals with cross-bars of iron let into the solid wall, and a coal cellar and water-closet attached. In such places as these the criminals of the olden times—common thieves, pickpockets, burglars, and others—used to herd together indiscriminately; and no doubt many of them, in their own way, had a jolly time of it. They were supplied with provisions by their pals and relatives, and were not compelled to live on the prison fare as now. The deputy-governor informed us that as many as twenty would sometimes be found in one of these rooms, which were nurseries of crime—the old hardened felon contaminating the young and inexperienced. At the time he came to the prison, about twenty-five years ago, the prisoners slept on the floor upon rope mats with woollen coverlets, which were afterwards replaced by wooden bedsteads, similar to the berths as on board ship. Then, as now, the prisoners did not do any labour before trial; but after trial were sent to correctional prisons.

"In those days," continued the deputy-governor, "the doors of these rooms were left open from morning to night, and the prisoners had access to each other's rooms, as well as to the exercising yards, until the time of locking up at night. A bell rang at dusk all the year round, for them to come in to their respective wards, when the officers visited them and ascertained if the proper number was present. There was no picking oakum then and no labour; but the food supplied them is better now. Before trial, the prisoners had it in their choice to take the gaol allowance or to procure food of their own."

Before the recent alterations of the prison commenced in 1858, an old cell was said to be seen where Jack Sheppard had been confined. It was an associated room, about eighteen feet square, with lofty ceiling, and was situated on the second storey, over the ground now occupied as the central square exercising ground of the male prison. The door was of massive strength, and the windows were double-barred. The roof consisted of lath and plaster, behind which were solid bars of iron and an oaken roof, and sheets of copper. There were ring-bolts attached to the oaken floors, to which the prisoners' heavy chains were attached. We visited a cell of similar dimensions on the second storey, contiguous to the solicitor's room, which is at present used as an infirmary. There we found one solitary prisoner extended on a bed, seriously indisposed, and apparently in a critical condition.

₊ *The Chapel.*—We visited the chapel, which is of moderate size. It has two galleries, one for females with a black screen before it, and the other for the men under sentence of penal servitude. In front of the female gallery is painted the royal arms—the lion and the unicorn; and in front of the male gallery is the city arms, with the motto, "Domine dirige nos"—(O Lord, direct us.)

There is a pulpit and reading-desk similar to those in an ordinary chapel, which are wainscoted and covered with dark cloth. On each side, in the area below, there are seats for the prisoners detained for trial, enclosed within iron stanchions. Alongside of the cells in the gallery, on the male side, is a pew for the magistrate, and another seat for the sheriffs when attending service on the morning the prisoner is to be executed. The condemned sits on a chair in the area below, by the side of the pulpit, beside the governor's pew, with a warder by his side. There are a few seats in the area of the chapel for the officers of the prison. Several long windows, looking into the interior of the courts, are protected by iron stanchions. The chapel has a wooden flooring, and is lighted by a dark-painted gas chandelier.

There is an altar enclosed in an iron railing, covered with dark cloth and cushion; over it is inscribed a copy of the Ten Commandments, and over against it a copy of the Lord's Prayer and the Creed.

We were not present at any of the services.

The deputy-governor stated—" We have prayers every morning from half-past 9 to 10 o'clock, and have two services on Sundays, in the morning and afternoon."

¶ i.—β.

The Female Prison.

On advancing through the lodge into the interior of the prison, and turning along the passage to the right we pass through a heavy door, faced with iron, leading through the female exercising ground to the female wing of the prison. The yard is of an irregular form, being narrower at this end, and having a portion fenced off with strong iron railing for female prisoners receiving the visits of their friends. The visitors stand in a narrow passage 3 feet wide and 15 feet long, and converse with the prisoners, who take their station on the exercising ground. An officer patrols in an intervening space, a few feet wide, between them. This visiting ground is covered with thick glass, so that the friends of the prisoners are sheltered during the inclemency of the weather.

Crossing the exercising ground we pass beneath an iron and slate bridge leading from the new female wing to the chapel. We then enter a wide passage, eight feet wide, and go through an iron gate leading into the corridor of the female wing, which is very similar in its general construction to that of the male, only it is not so large, and has three galleries instead of four. As we enter the female corridor we observe two boxes fitted up with glass windows and doors, for the use of the solicitors meeting the prisoners, with the view of conducting their cases, having a wooden partition between them. There is a seat in front for the prisoner when advising with her agent. Each of these boxes is furnished with a table, an inkstand, and a chair.

In the centre of the corridor we find a staircase leading down to the basement, and near the farther end is a stair connected with the first gallery. The corridor is lighted by a cheerful glass roof, similar to that in the male wing, and the galleries are encircled with railings. On the right of this passage, as we enter, two small rooms have been furnished for the sub-matron, a young active warder; and on our left hand are three apartments fitted up for the matron—the other side of the corridor consisting of a series of cells for the prisoners, and termed A, while the three galleries above are respectively named B, C, and D.

*** *Reception Cells, Punishment Cells, and Bath Rooms.*—We descended with the matron to the basement, and visited the *Reception Ward*, consisting of nine cells about the same size as those in the male branch of the prison.

These are much darker than those in the corridor above. There was not a single prisoner confined in them at the time of our visit, nor had there been so for several days previous. They were furnished very similar to those in the male reception ward already described.

There are two bath rooms in the reception ward, each containing two baths, which are dimly lighted during the day, being situated on the basement, under the gloomy shadows of the surrounding walls. The baths are 3 feet 6 inches deep, 5 feet 6 inches long, and 2 feet wide, and are set in a wooden framework. They are supplied with hot and cold water by means of pipes connected with the male prison.

The matron informed us there are 58 cells in the female prison, which are generally occupied by about 25 prisoners. At the time of our visit there were fewer than usual.

There is another bath room of a larger size, and more cheerfully lighted, at the extremity of the reception ward, containing a bath similar to the others we have mentioned, with a footboard as in the other bath rooms. In this bath room is a fumigating apparatus, resembling a large copper, painted black, and resting on a brick pediment. There is a steam-pipe let in to the bottom of this vessel, through the flooring, to cleanse the dirty linen and clothing.

There are two dark cells contiguous to those we have mentioned in the reception ward. Each of them is furnished with a wooden bedstead having a board raised 2½ inches, on which the prisoner reclines her head. The bedstead is about 6 feet in length, and 2 feet 3 inches in breadth. These cells are floored with slate, and roofed with brick.

*** *The Laundry.*—On entering the laundry, which is about thirty-six feet long and eighteen feet broad, we observed two large coppers built into brickwork, and supplied with steam by means of pipes. There is also a water-pipe which supplies them with water. On the outside of the brickwork, connected with the bottom of the coppers, there is a tap which carries off the water, when soiled, through an iron grating into a drain under the flooring. Adjoining are two new wooden rinsing troughs, with two pipes, to supply them with hot water, and a wringing machine with two crank handles, patented by " Manlove, Alliott, and Company, engineers, Nottingham." There are six washing-boxes, each of them provided with two washing-troughs having a wooden partition between them. The larger of the troughs is supplied with hot and cold water, and the smaller one with cold water only. We found several female prisoners busy washing. They wash the clothes in the larger one, and use the other for rinsing. The doors of these boxes have no wooden panels, but are faced with iron gratings, by which the warder on duty can see the prisoners at their work.

We passed into the ironing-room, which is supplied with six wooden horses, where the clothes are hung up to dry and exposed to the action of steam. They are drawn out and in upon iron slides about twelve feet long. In this apartment is contained a store of the female prison clothing, consisting of blue wincey gowns with dark stripe, a blue checked apron, a petticoat, a blue checked neckerchief and white cap, along with underclothing. It is also furnished with a large table for folding and ironing the clothes, a mangling machine, and a stove for heating the irons. At the time of our visit there was a large table in the centre of the room, containing a great heap of male prison clothing, along with a pile of sheets for the use of the male and female prison, the prisoners were about to wash.

This apartment is nearly forty feet in length and eighteen feet in breadth, and is lighted by a large oblong skylight, similar to the other apartment—the roofs of both being lofty and airy. The apartment is floored with wood, with the exception of the part opposite to the drying horses.

The laundry warder informed us—"There are at present four female prisoners employed in washing the clothes belonging to the male and female prison. They commence their work at 7 o'clock in the morning, and finish at 5 in the afternoon. As a general rule, they are engaged from Monday to Friday afternoon.

On leaving the laundry we visited several of the cells in the corridor above, which were more gloomy and lonely in appearance than in any other prison we had visited—partly caused by the overhanging clouds of smoke which loom over the city, and partly by the sombre lofty surrounding walls of the prison.

Most of the prisoners were ordinary-looking persons, charged with common offences. In one of the rooms used as an infirmary we saw an elderly woman, of about fifty years of age, her countenance very haggard, walking to and fro in her cell with her head covered. She is charged with throwing vitriol on a child, and had been confined with bronchitis, but is now in a convalescent state. The matron informed us she has been in a better position in life than most of the other prisoners. After a time she sat down beside a woman of about thirty-five years of age—a miserable, distressed-looking creature—charged with strangling her child, who was then employed knitting. A very coarse-looking young woman was confined along with them, charged as an accomplice in a burglary, who had been placed beside them to attend to their wants. This was one of the most dismal pictures we had seen in the course of our visits to the London prisons.

₊ *The Engineer.*—We were introduced to the engineer of the prison, who informed us that he superintended the warming and ventilating of the prison, and likewise executed repairs of various kinds, such as locks, bells, gas fittings, etc.

He conducted us into the boiler-room, which contains two steam boilers used for warming the main prison by means of pipes extending through both wings. These boilers also supply steam to the hot water tanks for the baths in both prisons. The steam is also conducted by means of pipes into two coppers in the laundry for boiling the clothes, and also into the drying closet, where the clothes are spread out on the six wooden horses. Sometimes it is used for the ventilation of the prison in summer, by rarefying the air in the extraction shaft, which rises 60 or 70 feet high.

The vitiated air is extracted from the cells by smaller flues connected with the main flue, and thence passes into the extraction shaft. By the powerful extraction consequent on the height of the shaft about 30 cubic feet of fresh air is drawn through each cell in a minute. This prison is ventilated on the same principle as the model prisons, from designs invented by Haden and Son, Trowbridge.

The engineer conducted us to the shaft, and showed us the various pipes used in the ventilation. Passing from the extraction shaft we saw the machine for destroying vermin in the prisoners' clothing by means of steam being admitted into it, which is much superior to fumigating with brimstone, adopted in many other prisons.

In answer to our queries, the engineer stated, "I generally have one of the prisoners to assist me as a stoker, and sometimes I have a smith or carpenter in the repairs required in the prison. I commence my duties in the morning at a quarter to six o'clock in the summer, and a quarter to seven in the winter, and finish at half-past five o'clock in the afternoon, excepting Sundays. I leave every Sunday morning at ten o'clock.

₊ *The Sessions House* is situated adjoining to Newgate. The older wing is uniform with it in external appearance, and was the ancient Sessions House. In former times there was only one High Criminal Court held there, but the business is now divided among three; and sometimes a fourth is held in the Grand Jury room, all within the same building in the Old Bailey. The heavier offences are tried here, such as forgery, arson, coining, manslaughter, murder, etc. At one or other the Recorder and the Common Serjeant are seated on the bench and other judges of the State.

The old Court-room, which is represented in the engraving, is only about 50 feet square. There are six small moveable desks, on which the judges take their notes, and write their communications, comfortably seated on cushioned seats of a crimson colour. The panelling behind them is covered with crimson cloth sadly faded. Over the centre of the bench there is a tasteful wooden canopy, surmounted with the Royal arms beautifully carved. A sword of Justice, with a gold handle and ornamental scabbard is usually suspended under the canopy during the sittings of the Court. Opposite to the bench, on the other side of the Court-room is the dock, a small enclosure, 13 feet by 19, where the criminals stand to take their trial. The jury-box, consisting of two long seats, is situated on the right hand of the judges. The Clerk of the Arraigns occupies a desk beneath the bench, and fronting the dock. The attorneys are seated around a table, in the area of the Court, covered with green cloth, and the counsel in wig and gown, their official costume, occupy three seats alongside. **Behind** the latter there are several seats for the reporters, with others for the friends of the judges, and for a portion of the jury in waiting. The prisoners enter the dock by a staircase behind communicating with the cells beneath. The governor of Newgate occupies a seat at the corner of the dock, by the side of the prisoners and their attendants. Behind and above the dock there is a small gallery for the public, where heads are seen peering over as in the engraving, and there are usually a number of solicitors, barristers, witnesses, and policemen clustered around the area, and to be seen in the various passages.

There are seven doors entering into the old Court-room; two of them on the side next to Newgate, one of them in the area being for witnesses, and another more elevated being a private entrance for the judges. On the opposite side there are two doors, one for the jury and counsel, and the other a private entrance for the judges and magistrates who take their seats on the bench. There is another door behind the bench, by which any of the judges are able to retire when disposed; and on each side of the dock there is a door for the entrance of the witnesses, solicitors, and jury.

This Court-room is lighted by three large windows towards Newgate, and by three smaller sombre windows on the opposite side.

The deputy-governor of Newgate informed us, that all classes of heavy offences are tried at the Old Bailey Criminal Court, which is the highest in England. The prisoners are brought from the prison of Newgate and placed in cells under the courts, until they are called to the bar to be tried. They are then brought into the dock to answer to the criminal charges brought against them. The indictments are read over to each of them, and they are asked by the Clerk of the Arraigns if they are guilty or not guilty. If they plead guilty, they are ordered in the meantime to stand back. If they plead not guilty, they remain at the bar until all the pleas are taken of the other prisoners at the dock. After this is done the jury are called into the jury box, to proceed to investigate the different cases. The prisoners can object to the jurymen before being sworn. If the prisoner at the bar is found guilty, he is sentenced by the judge, and removed to the prison. If he is declared not guilty, a discharge is written out by the governor, and he retires from the bar.

In the case of a murderer, he is taken to the Court in custody of an officer. He is arraigned at the bar in the same way as the other classes of prisoners. If found guilty he is taken back to the condemned cell, where he is watched day and night until he is executed, which generally takes place within three weeks thereafter.

The deputy-governor stated:—" I find the murderers to be of very different characters. Some are callous and ruffian-like in demeanour, but others are of more gentle and peaceable disposition, whom you heartily pity, as you are convinced from all you see about them, that they had been incited to the commission of their crime through intemperance or other incidental causes, foreign to their general character. We find those to be worst who premeditated their crimes for gain. There have been few murderers here who assassinated from revenge. I have seen 29 criminals executed in front of Newgate, and was present in the Court at the trial of most of them. Palmer was one of the most diabolical characters among penal offenders I ever saw in Newgate, and Mrs. Manning the most callous of females. Palmer was a gentlemanlike man, educated for a surgeon. By giving himself up too much to gambling and field sports he was led to the murder of J. P. Cooke to repay his losses. He was executed at Stafford, and was only temporarily under our custody here. In person he was strong built, about the ordinary height, and had very strong nerves. Mrs. Manning was a very resolute woman, but her husband was a very imbecile character, and had been dragged into crime through the strong mind of his wife, who had formerly been lady's maid to the Duchess of Sutherland.

" I was in charge of Greenacre," added the deputy-governor, " the night previous to his

CONDEMNED CELL, NEWGATE.

execution. He was a coarse-looking man of about fifty years of age, and was a hardened miscreant. He murdered a female who cohabited with him in 1837, and cut up her body and distributed it over different parts of the metropolis. This case made a very great sensation at the time, and there were upwards of 16,000 spectators at his execution. The houses fronting Newgate charged three guineas for a station at their windows to witness the execution. Two sovereigns were given for a seat on the roofs of some of the houses. There were numbers of persons of distinction on the house-tops and in the windows opposite.

"I have seen some of the murderers very unnerved when on the eve of their execution; as, for example, Hocker, a schoolmaster, tried in April 1845, for the murder of Mr. Delarue in the fields at Hampstead. He was a young man, and assumed the greatest bravado up to the moment of his execution. The officers in Newgate knew very well it was only pretended. After he was pinioned on the morning of his execution, it was evident to all present that he was unnerved, and had lost his former effrontery. On the first stroke of the prison bell, which gave the signal to the culprit to move forward to the place of execution, his face changed to different colours, and he fell backwards, overcome, into the arms of his attendants. He was obliged to be carried out and placed under the fatal beam, and was held up by the officers till the executioner drew the bolt."

The deputy-governor informed us he has taken notes of the executions in Newgate since 1816, when criminals were hanged for cutting and wounding, burglary, forgery, uttering base coin, etc. The law was changed in 1836 in reference to capital punishments, and the sentence of death is now restricted to murder and high treason. In 1785 nineteen persons, and in 1787 no less than eighteen were executed at one time.

When females are convicted of murder, they are asked by the Clerk of Arraigns if they have anything to urge why sentence of death should not be passed on them. The matron who sits in the dock beside a female culprit, asks if she is in the family way. A curious case took place in 1847. Mary Ann Hunt, being convicted of murder, was asked by the Clerk of the Arraigns if she had anything to urge why sentence of death should not be passed upon her. She replied through the matron in the dock that she was with child. An unusual step was here taken. A jury of twelve married women were summoned to Court, who on being sworn, examined her. After they were absent for some time, they returned into the Court, and stated she was not with child. She was afterwards examined by the medical officer in Newgate, and found to be pregnant. She gave birth to a son on the 28th of December following. When before the Court she must have been eight months gone with child.

"During the time I have been in Newgate," said the deputy-governor, "I have only seen two women executed. The murderers generally sleep well on the night before their execution.

"The scaffold is erected immediately before the execution. The workmen commence about one o'clock in the morning, and finish about six o'clock. Executions generally take place on the Monday morning. The wooden fences around the scaffold to keep back the spectators, are generally put up on the Monday. The scaffold is about the size of a large caravan, the sides being let down, and a beam erected over it. The floor is composed of two parts, constructed so as to fall down to each side. The executioner touches a handle similar to a common pump handle, which detaches the bolt underneath, and the murderer is suspended by the neck in presence of the vast confluence of people. He generally hangs for one hour, when a coffin is brought and placed under the body. The executioner in presence of the sheriffs, or some of the authorities, takes hold of the body and puts it into the coffin, after having cut the rope. The coffin is then brought into one of the wards of the prison, and is afterwards buried in the interior of Newgate in the afternoon of the same day, in presence of the governor or the under-sheriffs.

The deputy-governor stated that before being interred the body is inspected by the medical officer of Newgate in the presence of the sheriffs, and ascertained to be lifeless; and a cast is generally taken of the head and face. "The greatest confluence of people," he added, "1 ever saw assembled at an execution here was in the case of Greenacre in 1837, and Mullins in November 1860. There were about 16,000 people present on each of these occasions. The crowd generally musters on the Sabbath evening at eight o'clock, and increases during the night, consisting, to a great extent, of boys and girls. The greater portion of the spectators assemble between six and seven o'clock.

GENERAL STATISTICS OF NEWGATE JAIL FOR THE YEAR ENDING SEPT. 1860.

NUMBER OF PRISONERS.

	Males.	Females.
For trial at Assizes and Sessions...	907	208
Summary Convictions	—	—
Want of sureties	—	—
Remanded and discharged	148	69
Debtors and civil process............	3	—
Mutiny Act	1	—
Tota commitments 1059		277

PREVIOUSLY COMMITTED TO ANY PRISON.

	Males.	Females.
Once	177	57
Twice................................	71	12
Thrice	24	2
Four times	10	4
Five times	2	—
Seven times, and above five........	3	—
Ten times, and above seven........	2	—
Above ten times	—	...
Total 289		75

AGE AND SEX.

	Males.	Females.
Under twelve years	9	6
Twelve to sixteen years	43	5
Sixteen to twenty-one years	206	59
Twenty-one to thirty ,,	434	101
Thirty to forty ...... ,, ...	193	65
Forty to fifty......... ,, ...	113	33
Fifty to sixty......... ,, ...	34	5
Sixty and above	23	3
Age not mentioned	—	—
Total 1055		277

CASES OF SICKNESS.

	Males.	Females.
Greatest number at one time	18	5
Deaths	1	—
Infirmary cases......................	19	10
Slight indisposition	690	70
Insanity...............................	—	—
Total 725		85

DEGREE OF INSTRUCTION.

	Males.	Females.
Neither read nor write	146	62
Read, or read and write imperfectly	607	185
Read and write well..................	293	30
Superior instruction..................	9	—
Instruction not ascertained	—	—
Total 1055		277

CAPACITY AND STATE OF THE PRISON.

	Males.	Females.
Constructed to contain..............	192	—
Greatest number at any one time .	123	43
Daily average number in the year, male and female		92
Total 315		135

PUNISHMENTS FOR OFFENCES IN PRISON.

	Males.	Females.
Whipping	—	—
Irons or handcuffs	—	—
Solitary or dark cells	1	1
Stoppage of Diet	77	6
Other punishments	4	—
Total 82		7

ESTABLISHMENT OF OFFICERS.

	Males.	Females.
Governor and Deputy	2	—
Chaplain	1	—
Surgeon	1	—
Clerk and Schoolmaster	2	—
Schoolmistress	—	1
Upper warders' matron	2	1
Under warders	9	1
Other sub-officers	4	—
Total 21		3

STATE OF EDUCATION OF FEMALE PRISONERS COMMITTED TO NEWGATE FOR TRIAL.

	Neither read nor write.	Read only.	Imperfect.	Well.	Superior.	Total.	No. of previous convictions.			
							1	2	3	4 and over.
October............	7	1	8	2	...	18	2	...	...	1
November.........	5	7	7	1	...	20	2	2	...	3
December	5	1	2	...	...	8	...	...	...	...
January............	1	2	10	...	...	13	2	...	...	1
February	6	1	2	3	...	12	...	1	...	1
March	6	3	6	1	...	16	1	...	...	1
April	4	...	4	3	...	11	...	...	...	...
May	1	1	5	2	...	9	...	...	...	...
June	4	3	5	1	...	13	3	...	...	...
July	6	6	11	...	...	23	2	...	...	...
August	3	2	3	1	...	9	1	...	...	...
September	5	1	4	1	...	11	...	...	...	...
Totals......	53	28	67	15		163	13	4		7

¶ ii.—α

COUNTY HOUSE OF DETENTION, CLERKENWELL.

WE were admitted within the prison walls by a door near to the large front gate, and were shown the books of the gate warder, a smart and energetic officer, which were most carefully kept. Crossing the courtyard, we entered the pillared portal of the prison, and were led into the presence of the governor, who requested the deputy-governor to conduct us over the establishment.

As we enter the prison, on our right hand is the office of the clerk, and opposite to it a door leading to the reception ward of the female prison. Beyond this is a flight of steps on our right hand, leading down to the stores on the basement, and on the other side of the passage is a winding staircase leading up to the committee room for the visiting justices. Farther into the interior is the waiting-room for visitors, and adjoining is the governor's office.

On our left hand is the warders' mess-room, along with three waiting-rooms for the attorneys who visit the prisoners, with a view to conduct their defence.

₊ *Reception Ward.*—There are eight reception cells here, four on each side of the passage, beyond the offices already mentioned. As seen by a reference to the ground plan, the outer cells are widest, and gradually contract towards the innermost one, which is near to the central hall. We found the dimensions of the outermost cell to be nineteen feet two inches in length, five feet eight inches in width, and nine feet at the bottom, and ten feet at the top of the arch. It is floored with asphalt, like the others, and beautifully white-washed. The innermost cell is eight feet four inches long, and five feet eight inches wide, and of the same height as the one referred to. Each of them is lighted by a window three feet six inches long, and one foot four inches wide, and is ventilated by a flap in the centre of the window, and from a shaft near the top of the window for cold air, and a grating in the corner of the cell near the door, which admits warm air through a flue.

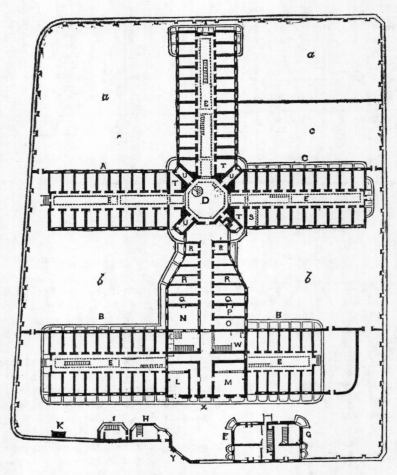

GROUND PLAN OF COUNTY HOUSE OF DETENTION, CLERKENWELL.

A. & C. Male Wings.
B. Female Wings.
D. Central Hall.
E. Passages in the Interior.
F. Governor's House.

G. Garden attached to the same.
H. Porter's Lodge.
I. K. Offices attached to it.
L. Entry to Female Corridors.
M. Clerk's Office.

N. Warder's Mess-room.
O. P. Waiting-rooms.
Q. Attorney's Rooms.
R. Reception Cells.
S. T. Cells for the Refractory.

W. Governor's Office
X. Entry to Main Building.
Y. Large Prison Gate.
a, b, c. Exercising Yadrs

While visiting these reception cells, a number of warders, in their blue uniforms, were bustling in the long hall preparing to conduct two files of prisoners to the prison vans for trial at the Sessions. One or two of these were respectably dressed, and had been charged with embezzlement. They did not appear to feel very comfortable when ranked up in line with a band of felons. Among the group we discerned one or two sturdy labourers, in their white smock-frocks, and could trace the quick clear eye and roguish look of the habitual felon. As one band was conducted into the prison van, and whirled off, a policeman being seated in front, another detachment was brought from the interior of the prison, and took its place in another van, which also drove off.

We descended to the basement, and found eleven other reception cells, each about half the size of an ordinary cell. They had no furniture except a seat, fixed into the wall. Alongside were seven baths for the prisoners, about the same dimensions as the latter reception cells, in addition to a bath for the warders, and one for the governor.

The reception warder informed us: " The prisoners are received here from the county of Middlesex and the metropolitan police courts on this side of the river, with the exception of those in the city. They consist of prisoners on remand, or for trial at the Middlesex Sessions; person in default of bail, deserters from the army, and cabmen for infringing the Hackney Carriage Act. They are generally brought here in vans from the police-courts referred to, or from the county, being occasionally escorted hither by the police. Each constable brings a commitment along with the prisoner, which is handed over to me.

" The prisoners are brought from the van to the outer hall of the prison. The serjeant in charge states the number he has in custody, and from what courts they have come, which is duly entered, after which they are lodged meanwhile in the reception cells above. So soon as the vans have all arrived from the different courts, the prisoners are taken down to the basement, when they are thoroughly searched, their property taken from them, and their names and ages carefully set down. They are then taken to the bath-rooms and cleansed, after which they are formed in line, and the rules of the prison read to them.* After this routine they are brought up into the centre of the prison, and distributed to their several wards.

---

* RULES RELATING TO THE CONDUCT AND TREATMENT OF PRISONERS, CERTIFIED AS PROPER TO BE ENFORCED PURSUANT TO THE 5TH AND 6TH WM. IV., CAP. 38, AND THE 2ND AND 3RD VIC., CAP. 56.

Prisoners Committed for Trial—for Examination—or want of Sureties, and those Committed as Deserters, or under the Hackney Carriage Act.

1. All prisoners shall, on admission, be placed in a separate cell. They shall be strictly searched by the governor, or by an officer appointed by him for that purpose, or by the matron and a female officer, or by two female officers appointed as aforesaid, if a female prisoner. All knives, sharp instruments, dangerous weapons, or articles calculated to facilitate escape, or otherwise desirable in the discretion of the governor to be removed, shall be taken from them; all money and other effects brought in with them, or subsequently sent in for their use and benefit, shall be taken care of for them. The governor shall take charge of such money and effects, and make an inventory of them, to be entered in the prisoners' property book.

2. Every prisoner shall be examined by the surgeon before being passed into his or her proper cell; having been examined, they shall be cleansed in a warm or cold bath, as the surgeon may direct. The hair of female prisoners shall only be cut in cases when necessary for the removal of dirt, or the extirpation of vermin, or when the medical officer deems it requisite on the ground of health; male prisoners shall be shaved at least once a week, and their hair cut when necessary for the preservation of health and cleanliness. No prisoner shall be stripped or bathed in the presence of any other prisoner.

3. The wearing apparel of every prisoner shall be fumigated and purified; and if the surgeon thinks it necessary, wearing apparel may be burned. Prisoners before trial may wear their own clothes, if sufficient and proper; but if the wearing apparel of prisoners before trial be insufficient, improper, or necessary to be preserved for the purposes of justice, such prisoners may be furnished with a plain suit of coarse cloth.

4. As convenient places for the prisoners to wash themselves are provided, with a sufficient allowance of water, soap, towels, and combs, every prisoner shall be required to wash thoroughly once a day, and his feet at least once in every week.

5. Every prisoner shall be provided with a separate hammock, in a separate cell. Every prisoner shall

"In the event of any of their garments being in a bad condition, a suit of prison clothing is furnished them, consisting of a dark blue jacket, vest, and trowsers, and good under clothing. Their own clothes being restored to them on their liberation.

be provided with sufficient bedding for warmth and health ; and, when ordered by the surgeon, with two sheets and a pillow in addition. The whole shall be kept properly clean.

6. No tobacco shall be admitted for the use of any prisoner, except by written order of the surgeon.

7. No prisoner shall be permitted to see any visitor out of the place appropriated for that purpose, except in special cases under a written order, signed by a visiting justice ; and in the case of prisoners seriously ill, by a written order of the governor and surgeon. Male prisoners are to be visited in the presence of the governor or subordinate officer ; female prisoners in the presence of the matron or other female officer. This rule is not to extend to prisoners when they see their legal advisers. The governor may require the name and address of persons presenting themselves as visitors, and when he has any grounds for suspicion, may search, or cause to be searched, male visitors ; and may direct the matron, or some other female officer, to search female visitors ; such search, whether of male or female visitors, not to be in the presence of any prisoner ; and in case of any visitor refusing to be searched, the governor may deny him or her admission to the prison.

8. Any near relation or friend may be allowed to see a prisoner dangerously ill, under an order in writing, signed by the governor and surgeon.

9. Any prisoner of a religious persuasion differing from that of the Established Church, may, on request to the governor, be visited by a minister of his persuasion on Sundays, or on any other days, at such reasonable hours as may not interfere with the good order of the prison ; the name and address of such minister to be left in the governor's office, and to be communicated by him to the visiting justices. Any books which such minister may wish to supply to the prisoners of their persuasion, must be first submitted to a visiting justice for approval.

10. No prisoner shall receive or send any parcel, or receive any food, clothing, or other articles, without previous inspection by the governor, or by an officer appointed by him.

11. Officers on duty shall attend to complaints of prisoners, and report the same forthwith to the governor.

12. If a prisoner complain of illness, the case shall be reported without delay to the governor and surgeon.

13. All prisoners shall regularly attend Divine Service, unless prevented by illness, or permitted to be absent by the governor or a visiting justice.

14. Prisoners of the Established Church shall be provided with books and tracts of religious, moral, and useful instruction, under the directions of the chaplain ; and prisoners of persuasions differing from the Established Church, under the direction of the visiting justices. Each prisoner who can read shall be furnished with a Bible and Common Prayer Book in his cell.

15. All prisoners are bound to obey the rules of the prison, and the lawful orders of the governor and other officers, and not to treat with disrespect any of the officers ; nor to be absent from Divine Service, unless prevented by illness, or excused ; they are to behave properly during its performance ; they are not to be guilty of swearing, or of indecent or disorderly conduct ; nor to commit any kind of nuisances, nor wilfully damage any bedding, any part of the prison, or any article or property therein.

16. Singing, whistling, or shouting in the cells, rooms, or yards, is strictly prohibited ; and the following are declared to be acts of disorder, and to be punishable as such, viz. :—Any attempt to barter or exchange provisions ; any marking, defacing, or injuring the doors, walls, or chairs, tables, clothes, bedding, books, or utensils whatsoever, of the prison ; any secreting of money, tobacco, or forbidden articles ; any purloining, or contriving to purloin, provisions, books, combs, or any other article ; or any wilful disobedience of such orders of the governor or officers of the prison as shall be in accordance with law and the rules of the prison. The governor may examine any persons touching such offences, and may determine thereupon, and may punish all such offences by ordering any offender to close confinement in a refractory or solitary cell, and by keeping such offender on bread and water only, for any term not exceeding three days ; but he shall not determine any of these cases without previous examination ; neither shall he delegate his authority in these matters to any other person. No punishments or privations of any kind shall be awarded, except by the governor.

17. Prisoners going to chapel, to the airing yards, or to any other part of the prison, shall be attended by one or more officers, and silence maintained.

18. Prisoners shall make their own beds, and clean their own cells. Prisoners shall not be compelled to work or labour, but may have the option of employment. But nothing in this rule shall prevent the governor from requiring prisoners of these classes to make their own beds; and clean the cells, wards, yards, and passages of the division of the prison to which they belong.

19. Prisoners shall be permitted to maintain themselves, and to procure and to receive at proper hours, a

BIRD'S-EYE VIEW OF THE HOUSE OF DETENTION, CLERKENWELL.

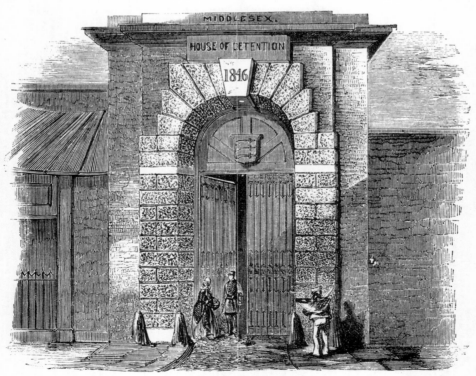

GATE OF THE HOUSE OF DETENTION.

" With reference to their discharge," he added, " the warders of the different divisions copy from the commitments the date of release of each prisoner. There are some discharged every morning. At a quarter-past nine o'clock in the morning, each warder brings out such prisoners, who are ranged in line. A list is furnished to the reception warder, from which

reasonable quantity of cooked provisions, and malt liquor not exceeding one pint in any one day of twenty-four hours; and any linen, clothing, or other necessaries (subject to a strict search, and under such regulations as may be deemed expedient, in order to prevent extravagance and luxury in a prison), and such articles so procured, may be paid for out of the monies belonging to such prisoners in the hands of the governor. No part of such food, malt liquor, or other articles, shall be given, sold to, or exchanged with any other prisoner ; and any prisoner transgressing this rule shall be prohibited from procuring any food, other than the prison allowance, or other articles, for such a period as a visiting justice may direct.

20. Prisoners shall not receive the prison allowance of food on the days whereon they procure or receive food from their friends under the foregoing rule.

21. Prisoners who do not maintain themselves shall receive the regular prison allowance of food.

22. Prisoners shall be permitted to see their relations or friends on any week day, without any order between the hours of twelve and two in the afternoon; and at any other time on a week day, by an order in writing from a visiting or committing justice, unless a visiting or committing magistrate shall have issued an order to the contrary, or unless the governor shall know sufficient cause why any person should not be admitted, in which case the name of the applicant, together with the name of the prisoner whom he applied to visit, and the date of the refusal, shall be entered by him in his journal. But no prisoner shall be allowed to see more than two visitors on any one day, nor shall any visitor be allowed to remain longer than twenty minutes with a prisoner, without the especial permission of the governor, in which case the extended visit shall be considered as a second visit to the prisoner. The names and addresses of all such visitors, with the relationship to the prisoner, if any, shall be inserted in a book to be kept for that purpose; and the prisoners shall be permitted to see their legal adviser (by which is to be understood a certificated attorney or his authorized clerk) on any day at any reasonable hour, and in private if required. Prisoners may write or receive letters, to be inspected by the governor, except any confidential written communication prepared as instructions for their legal adviser; such paper to be delivered personally to the legal adviser or his authorized clerk, without being previously examined by any officer of the prison : but all such written communications, not personally delivered to the legal adviser or his clerk, are to be considered as letters, and are not to be sent out of the prison without being previously inspected by the governor. Any person presenting himself for admission as the clerk of an admitted attorney, shall in the absence of his principal, produce to the governor, in such case, evidence (satisfactory to such governor) of his being such an accredited agent; and the legal adviser or his clerk shall name the prisoner whom he wishes to visit.

23. Any person bringing or attempting to bring into the prison, contrary to the rules, any spirituous or fermented liquor, may be apprehended and taken before a police magistrate, and upon conviction, committed to prison for three months, unless such offender shall immediately pay down such sum of money, not exceeding twenty pounds, nor less than ten pounds, as the magistrate shall impose.

24. Every prisoner in separate confinement shall be supplied with the means of enabling him to communicate at any time with an officer of the prison.

25. Every prisoner shall be supplied with, and have the option of employment.

26. Every prisoner shall be furnished with the means of moral and religious instruction, and with suitable books.

27. Every prisoner shall have the means of daily taking as much exercise in the open air as the medical officer shall deem necessary.

28. The governor shall cause copies of such of the rules as relate to the treatment and conduct of the prisoners (printed in legible characters) to be fixed up in each cell, and the same shall be read to each prisoner within twenty-four hours after admission.

29. Prisoners committed for want of sureties, on summary orders, and deserters, shall be allowed to associate in the exercise yard for three hours daily, should the weather or other circumstances permit ; in other respects they shall be treated as prisoners for trial or for examination.

30. If the governor shall at any time deem it improper or inexpedient for a prisoner to associate with the other prisoners of the class to which he or she may belong, it shall be lawful for him to confine such prisoner with any other class or description of prisoners, or in any other part of the prison, until he can receive the directions of a visiting justice thereon, to whom he shall apply with as little delay as possible, and who, in every such instance, shall ascertain whether the reasons assigned by the governor warrant such deviation from the established rules, and shall give such orders in writing as he shall think fit, under the circumstances of the particular case.

he calls out the different names, and ascertains if he has the right prisoners, and the courts to which they are to be forwarded. They are then passed by the clerk in the office, and the commitments handed to the police serjeant in the van."

** *Central Hall.*—There is a bright iron gate, in addition to a wooden door, leading from the main building in front into the inner hall. We observe on our right hand a brass tablet recording that the foundation stone of this prison was laid by the most noble the Marquis of Salisbury, on the 4th May, 1846. The central hall has a lofty octagonal roof, lighted from a series of skylights, and by long narrow windows at the extremities of the corridors. There is a spiral staircase communicating with the corridor in front, termed the second division, consisting of three stories with two galleries, named respectively D, E, F. On our right hand is the corridor of the first division, termed A, B, C, and directly opposite is the corridor of the third division, styled G, H, I, the first and second divisions being parallel with the two wings of the female prison in front. The general arrangements of the corridors are so similar to those at Pentonville and other prisons we have already sketched, that a farther description is unnecessary. The central hall and corridors are floored with stone and not with asphalt as at Holloway.

As we looked around us, several of the warders in their blue uniforms, with their stand-up collars, ornamented with three sabres on a brass shield, as at Coldbath Fields, were lingering in the central hall, or busy over the galleries, while a number of prisoners were kneeling down beside their pails washing, or stoning the floor. Everything around us had the active, vigorous air of military discipline.

** *Chapel.*—Meanwhile the bell rang for chapel service, and we went up a staircase leading to the governor's seat, alongside the pulpit, as at Holloway Prison. There was only a solitary warder then present, and not a single prisoner could be seen in any of the pews, which sloped upwards along the extensive gallery beneath us. Soon after, a file of prisoners, some of them considerably advanced in life, entered the pews at the back of the gallery, and at the same time a troop of boys occupied those in front. While the male prisoners were assembling, the female portion was coming into the chapel and occupying another gallery behind and above, quite out of sight of the male prisoners; and shortly after the seats were well filled with a numerous audience. Two female warders sat behind the female prisoners, and two male warders took their station on each side of the males. The congregation was of a very motley character. Most of the females were very plainly dressed, and from their appearance and manners, we could easily discern they belonged to the lower order of society. Many of them had coarse masculine features, and were Englishwomen, and not Irish cockneys. We did not see a single pretty girl among them, like some of those we found in Holloway Prison. The generality of the boys were poor and ragged, some of them were very keen eyed and restless in their manner; others were apparently the children of decent parents. The men were very different in their character, one man had the appearance of a swell, with his auburn whiskers stylishly cut, and his locks nicely adjusted over his fine forehead. Another man, in middle life, with a very corpulent paunch, sat before him, dressed in a suit of corduroy. We noticed a silver-headed man in a brown overcoat, who had evidently seen better days.

While we were penning these notes, a neighbouring steeple clock struck the hour in deep solemn tone, which was followed by the sharp tinkling sound of the bell within the prison. A flush of interest broke over the countenances of the prisoners as they heard the hour announced. Soon after the chaplain entered in his white gown, followed by an elderly warder, who officiated as clerk. During the devotional exercises, most of the prisoners leaned forward on the seat in front of them. The corpulent man, in corduroy, bent his head almost to his knees. Some of the little boys beneath us bent forward, with their hands over their face, while others sat erect with a composed look, or were looking restlessly about them. A little fair-haired boy, of about twelve years of age, particularly caught our attention. As we looked on his open, frank, winning face, we were sorry to find him among the little felons around him. One lad sat leering to another beside him, in great indifference. Another boy sat beside him dressed in a dark pinafore, with a very firm yet haggard countenance, who looked as if he had been sadly wronged by the home influences which had surrounded him. A young man of colour sat at the end of the seat beside them, with a very meek expression of countenance, alongside of a little pert urchin of seven years of age, with a peculiarly restless manner.

As we glanced at the grown-up male prisoners, a particularly good-looking young man caught our attention, with a finely formed thoughtful countenance. In the middle of the throng we saw a Pole, a sallow-looking man with a very grim aspect. A gentle looking young man, a pickpocket, was seated by the side of a calm, determined burglar, evidently an Irish cockney. While a few prisoners of more respectable appearance were to be seen in a range of stalls at the back of the gallery, reserved for the better order.

During the service, the prisoners appeared to become more absorbed and thoughtful. Many of them leaned over on the seats in front, and some looked at their service books.

This was a very interesting sight, and of a peculiar character, as here we did not see them masked in prison dress, but in their own clothing and marked individuality, as they are to be seen in the public streets.

⁎ *The Kitchen.*—We visited the apartments on the basement, where several prisoners are employed as carpenters, blacksmiths, and painters, connected with the establishment, and having nothing of special interest to record, we passed on to the kitchen, which is about thirty-six feet by twenty-seven. The flooring is of stone, and the roof is built with brick, supported on iron girders and pillars. There are two tables in the centre, for trays and shining tins, along with two dressers. The kitchen is provided with a steam apparatus, and several coppers, one for soup, another for gruel, in addition to a large steamer for preparing meat. There are three small coppers—one for cocoa, a second for potatoes, and one for making beef-tea for the infirmary.*

Behind the kitchen is a scullery for washing the tins and trays; it is about twenty-one feet square, and contains several dressers, a sink for washing, and a copper to provide hot water. It is paved with stone, the roof being also supported on pillars.

* DAILY DIET LIST.

	Prisoners committed for 3 months and upwards. Male and Female Adults.						Under 3 Months. Male Adults.				Under 3 Months. Female Adults.				Males and Females under 17 Years of Age.			
	Bread.	Cocoa.	Meat when cooked.	Potatoes.	Soup.	Gruel.	Bread.	Meat when cooked.	Soup.	Gruel.	Bread.	Meat when cooked.	Soup.	Gruel.	Bread.	Meat when cooked.	Soup.	Gruel.
	oz.	pints	oz.	oz.	pints	pints	oz.	oz.	pints	pints	oz.	oz.	pints	pints	oz.	oz.	pints	pints
Sunday ...	20	1	6	8	...	1	20	6	...	2	16	6	...	2	16	4	...	2
Monday ...	20	1	...	...	1½	1	20	...	1	2	16	...	1	2	16	...	1	2
Tuesday ...	20	1	6	8	...	1	20	6	...	2	16	6	...	2	16	4	...	2
Wednesday	20	1	...	...	1½	1	20	...	1	2	16	...	1	2	16	...	1	2
Thursday ..	20	1	6	8	...	1	20	6	...	2	16	6	...	2	16	4	...	2
Friday	20	1	...	...	1½	1	20	...	1	2	16	...	1	2	16	...	1	2
Saturday ...	20	1	6	8	...	1	20	...	...	3	16	...	...	3	16	...	...	3

N.B.—Prisoners not receiving such allowance, are allowed to provide for themselves; and all Prisoners are allowed to be visited by their friends, from 12 till 2 daily, Sundays excepted.

The cook and his assistants commence duty at 7.30 in the morning; breakfast is sent up at 8.30, dinner at 2, and supper at 5.30, ending the operations for the day at 6 o'clock. The cook in his turn, along with the warders, officiates on night duty.

₊ *Visiting the Cells.*—We accompanied the chief warder to one of the cells in the first division, and found it to be 11 feet long, 7 feet wide, and 8 feet 8 inches high. It is ventilated near the top of the window, and through another iron grating near the floor, at the side of the door, and has a brick roof, and flooring of asphalt. Each of these cells is furnished with a small table, a three-legged stool, a stone night utensil, an iron wash basin, and a coir hammock, kept strapped during the day on two hooks in the wall, and has three triangular shelves for food, utensils, &c. A copy of the rules of the prison is suspended on the wall, with prayers for morning and evening. The door has a trap by which the food is transmitted, in the interior of which is a light iron screen, through which the prisoners are permitted on certain occasions to have communication with their friends. There is also a small circular inspection plate. On the exterior of the door is suspended a small tin case, like an envelope, containing the prisoner's card, with his name, offence, &c. The ordinary cells over the various corridors are of the same dimensions, and similarly furnished.

The chief warder informed us " that in the first and second division—A, B, C, D, E, F, were confined parties on remand and for trial at the Middlesex Sessions, while in the third division—G, H, I, were deserters, persons in default of sureties, and cabmen incarcerated under the Hackney Carriage Act.

He stated the A division contained fifty-seven cells, exclusive of a padded one, and three special cells fitted up differently.

We entered one of those special cells. The chief warder remarked, " You see the gas pipe is removed, and a wire-screen is inserted into one of the panes of the window for ventilation, in addition to the apparatus in the ordinary cells. The light is admitted through a glass pane over the door, out of the prisoner's reach. These cells are used for persons who are committed for having attempted to commit suicide.

We went into a padded cell, where a prisoner had been recently confined, who had been suffering under delirium tremens when admitted into the prison. In his frenzy he had torn the wire-screen over the door of his cell, broke the pane of glass, and wrenched off the gas-pipes, in an insane attempt to get out of his cell. This cell is of the ordinary size, and is fitted up with coir, packed into the strongest canvas, attached to the walls like panelling. There is a wire-screen over the window, and the flooring is of wood, covered with a thick stuffed coir mattress, for the safety of the prisoner, when in his violent paroxysms. On proceeding into one of the special cells referred to, we saw the wretched inmate, a man of about fifty years of age, who appeared to be a strong-built labouring man. He was now in a convalescent condition, and stated to us " he had recovered his spirits, and was beginning to feel in a more hopeful and bright condition of mind."

As we ascended the staircase leading up into one of the galleries of this corridor, we found a stout lad of about fourteen years of age, dressed in a blue guernsey, and corduroy trowsers, engaged in cleaning. He was confined for threatening his mother-in-law, and appeared to be robust and resolute. The chief warder remarked to us, " Some of the prisoners volunteer to assist in cleaning the prison ; some repair shoes, others work as smiths, carpenters, or painters. We cannot compel any of them to labour, farther than to clean their cells."

On going into another cell, we saw the poor coloured man we had noticed in the chapel. He is charged with a petty felony, to which he had been driven by extreme want. He stated he had been a cook on board a vessel, the "Ann," of London, which had been sold off, and he was thereby cast out of employment, and was here a stranger in a foreign land. He belonged to Halifax, North America. His clothes were in a wretched state, and his shoes were hanging in shreds.

INTERIOR OF THE HOUSE OF DETENTION, CLERKENWELL,
(AS IT APPEARS AT THE TIME OF THE VISITS OF THE PRISONERS' FRIENDS).

In an adjoining cell we found a sharp-featured, pale-faced boy, about fourteen years of age, attired in a drab over-coat, who had been committed the previous day for secreting himself in a railway train. The chief warder, on entering, remarked, "You will hear his story; it is worth the while." The lad stated—"He was an apprentice at a spoon and fork manufactory at Sheffield. His master was cruel to him, and he ran away from his employment. His father and mother wished to compel him to stay, but he went into a second class carriage on the Midland Railway, and proceeded to London. On being asked for his ticket by the guard, he pretended he had lost it, and was allowed to proceed to the metropolis, whereupon he was taken into custody. He was to be permitted to write home to his relations to acquaint them with his misfortune."

On visiting another cell we saw a profoundly-affecting scene, not uncommon in our detentional prisons. We found a fine-looking genteel boy, with beautiful English features. He had an oval face, blue eye, rosy cheek, and curly hair. He was about twelve years of age, dressed in a dark faded overcoat, and had been charged with stealing from a till. He was very poorly clad, and his shoes were in a wretched condition. He had been urged to steal by two young convicted thieves, who had made him their tool in the business, while they had adroitly managed to escape. Soon after, his mother, a careworn, poverty-stricken woman of about thirty-five years of age, came in, and was in extreme anguish when she saw her little boy. He burst into tears at the sight of his broken-hearted mother, but soon appeared to forget his own distress in her presence. The poor woman was convulsed with agony too deep for tears, and looked as if her heart would break. She pressed her hands to her throbbing temples, and seized hold of our arm to prevent herself from falling. She was led away to a seat outside the door of the cell, and was sitting there in silent anguish as we passed along the gallery.

We proceeded with the chief warder to the central corridor, termed the second division of the male prison, containing about seventy cells. He observed, "We have six strong cells for prisoners who have attempted to escape from prison, or are otherwise desperate characters." On being shown into one of them, we found that in addition to the ordinary iron-framed window there were iron bars on the exterior, and the door was plated in the interior with iron. On looking into several of the cells as we passed along, we did not see anything worthy of special notice.

On visiting the corridor of the third division we got a farther glimpse into the romance of our London prisons, where fact frequently transcends the singular and startling recitals of fiction. We went into a cell where we found an old bald-headed man, with silver hair, bending on his seat, apparently absorbed in some deep and consuming sorrow. He was wrinkled and careworn, and had a long thin face, with a dreamy imbecility in his eye, occasionally kindling into sudden flashes of energy. He was dressed in a shabby worn greatcoat with a velvet collar, a dark spotted vest, and corduroy trowsers. He told us he was a native of Colchester, in Essex, and had loved a woman about forty years ago, but the correspondence between them had been broken off. It seems some wags in Colchester, who knew the weakness of the frail old man, told him, by way of a practical joke, that his Dulcinea resided in London, in a certain locality. He came to London with £17 in his pocket, on a sentimental journey to see her. He endeavoured to force himself into a house to see the object of his affections, against the wish of the inmates, and was given into the hands of the police. He stated he was a farmer in comfortable circumstances, and that his brother was also a large farmer residing near Colchester.

As we passed along one of the galleries we saw a remarkably fine-looking old man, who had been a soldier in the Grenadier Guards, confined for assaulting his wife. He is in custody for six months, as he could not find security for his better behaviour. He was assisting one of the warders.

In another cell we observed a young Irish lad, of about nineteen years of age, in a very shabby tattered dress, like a wretched beggar.   He told us he was a gunner in the Artillery, but had for a time deserted, and been labouring as a cooper in the metropolis.   At last he got wearied of it and gave himself up as a deserter to return to his former military service.   How a man could exchange the comfortable dress of an artilleryman and his cleanly habits, for a life of squalor and rags, is one of those enigmas which cannot be easily explained even by those who know the wild freedom of low life in London !   On a subsequent day we saw two fine-looking young artillerymen come to the prison to escort their prodigal companion back to his old quarters.

In an adjoining cell we found a Polish refugee, a stern-looking man, beneath the middle size, whom we had particularly observed in the chapel.   He was a soldier in the Polish service up to the year 1830, and had come to Portsmouth with a large detachment of exiles. He now works as a shoemaker.   He is in custody for trying to force his way into the presence of the secretary of the Polish Refugee Association.

In another cell, through the inspection plate, we saw rather a notable character, in his way.   We had, in our boyhood, heard him address a Scotch constituency, as a candidate for representation of the Montrose Burghs.   He was then a handsome young man, who had just written a book (little known) on the French Revolution ; and no doubt aspired to great future eminence.   Even then he appeared to be rather a crochetty individual, and to be wanting in solid judgment.   But how is the picture changed now ?   See him here in his cell, a blighted being, attired in a shabby dark dress, his countenance the picture of morbid melancholy ! The chief warder observed—" He was detained here twelve months for threatening a Scotch Member of Parliament.   At the expiry of that time, being unable to find bail for his future conduct, he has been subjected to other twelve months' imprisonment."

₊ *Exercising Grounds.*—Before leaving the male prison we visited the various exercising grounds.   Two of them are situated at the back of the prison, on each side of the central wing, which is at right angles to the other two wings of the male branch of the establishment.   The prisoners we saw here consisted of persons committed for examination and for trial ; but as we gave a description of their general appearance during the chapel service, we need not enter into any further detail here.   They marched around their circles, similar to the other prisons, under the supervision of several warders.   A smart young man, dressed as a sailor, was pointed out to us as a beggar.   The chief warder informed us he had burned his arm with caustic, or other chemical ingredient, to create a sore in order to excite the compassion of the public, and had thereby effectually disabled himself in a more serious manner than he had intended.   We observed the corpulent man in corduroy going round an inner circle with the little boys.   He was an hostler at a public house, and had inflated himself with large potations of porter.   He was very unwieldy in his movements.

We went into the smaller exercising ground for prisoners for want of sureties, committed as deserters, or confined under the Hackney Carriage Act.   We found a cluster of cabmen of a poorer set walking in company in the square enclosure ; and three young deserters generally kept together.   We saw the old romantic lover in the brown overcoat, walking quietly, and with melancholy air, apparently engrossed with his own thoughts.   The Polish refugee, equipped in a cap and dark coat, walked solitary, looking keenly around him at his companions in tribulation ; and the would-be M.P., already referred to, promenaded with his hands in his trowsers pockets.   He was attired in a dark frockcoat and warm muffler, and was having a quiet interview with the tall old Grenadier guardsman.

To look on the plain exterior of this motley group, who could dream of the romantic events, and eventful changes of their lives, so little apparent to the superficial eye !

PRISON VAN TAKING UP PRISONERS AT THE HOUSE OF DETENTION.

¶ ii.—β.

The Female Prison.

The female prison extends on each side of the front of the prison as seen in the engraving given in an earlier part of this work, the two wings being connected together, and forming a continuous line in the upper galleries, over the entrance hall of the central main building. We entered the female prison by a door on the left hand, opposite to the clerk's office, and were introduced to the matron of the establishment, who desired an experienced female officer to conduct us over the interior.

** *Reception Ward.*—We passed down to the basement by a staircase, leading to the reception hall. There are ten reception cells, five on one side of the ward, and five on the other, alongside of each other. They are about the same dimensions as those on the basement of the male prison, and are furnished with a water-closet in one corner, and a seat in another. There is a handle inside communicating with a signal plate outside the cell. A current of fresh air is admitted through a ventilating apparatus near the top of the cell beside the window.

On the other side of this ward there are four bath-rooms, each containing a composition bath about five feet nine inches long, two feet three inches wide, and two feet four inches deep, with a footboard. Those rooms in the interior of the ward are about the size of an ordinary cell, but those towards the exterior are only three feet wide, and about the size of the reception cells. There is an additional zinc bath. Each bath is supplied with hot and cold water by a cistern heated by a furnace at the outer extremity of the reception ward. Adjoining the latter bath is a room with an asphalt floor, where prisoners are searched.

Contiguous to these there are two dark punishment cells furnished simply with an iron bedstead. The female warder observed to us, "We seldom have any female prisoners confined here."

On the basement there is a small store. We observed two large presses on one side of the room, one of them containing the winter, and the other the summer clothing of the prisoners, which is of a lighter description. The female prisoners' clothing consists of a woollen linsey jacket and skirt, a flannel petticoat, and chemise, blue worsted stockings, a checked cotton handkerchief for the neck, worn underneath the jacket, and a pair of leather shoes. "In summer," added the warder, "the outer dress is of cotton instead of woollen."

** *The Laundry.*—It is situated on the basement in front of the governor's house, in the eastern wing of the female prison. It contains a large copper with taps to admit cold water, and discharge hot water. There are five boxes with two washing troughs in each, supplying hot and cold water, with a footboard in front, and in the farther extremity of this apartment are seven drying-horses similar to those we found in Newgate female prison. The laundry is about thirty-three feet long and thirteen feet wide. In an adjoining room there is a mangle, with a dresser for folding the clothes. Bundles of garments and bedding were piled on the floor.

There is also a wringing machine, as in the laundries at Wandsworth and Newgate. Another apartment is contiguous, in which the clothes are ironed and folded, containing a stove for heating the irons. The warder informed us, "There are generally six prisoners employed here daily." At the time of our visit the laundry was deserted, and not a single prisoner was to be seen.

** *The Corridor, etc.*—The two wings of the female prison, although apparently divided by the main building on the exterior, form one long corridor in the interior. There is a slate

platform, about sixty feet wide, stretching across the first gallery of the corridor from the female warders' dressing-room to two doors leading up by two staircases to the gallery in the chapel, where the female prisoners are congregated. Another slate platform across the gallery above is only nine feet wide. On the lower gallery there is a large hall thirty feet long and twenty-one feet wide, where the bail prisoners exercise, and where the other prisoners occasionally walk in wet weather. It has a lofty ceiling, and the floor is covered with coir matting.

The female warder informed us, "The female branch of the prison is divided into six wards, A, B, C, D, E, F, in addition to ten reception cells. Amounting in all to 112 cells."

On entering one of the cells in the corridor, we found it to be eleven feet five inches long, six feet eleven inches wide, eight feet at the bottom, and eight feet ten inches at the top of the arch. It is furnished similar to those in the male prison.

On going round several of the cells, we did not find any case of particular interest. The most of the prisoners were confined for common offences.

We visited the exercising ground at the back of the left wing, and adjoining the exercising ground for male prisoners in default of sureties, cabmen and deserters. It is ninety-three feet long and thirty-nine feet wide, and is laid with pavement.

We were furnished, on one of the days of our visit, with the following statement of the prisoners then confined in the male and female branches of the prison:

Males	.	.	.	.	.	166	Children	.	.	.	.	.	4
Females	.	.	.	.	.	70							
	Total	.	.	.	236			Total	.	.	4

For Sessions—					*Males.*						*Females.*
Trial	.	.	.	.	39	Trials	.	.	.	.	21
Remands	.	.	.	.	99	Remands	.	.	.	.	32
Bails	.	.	.	.	19	Bails	.	.	.	.	17
Cabmen	.	.	.	.	6						
Deserters	.	.	.	.	3						
	Total	.	.	.	166			Total	.	.	70

DISCHARGED.

In Sessions—					*Males.*							*Females.*
Remands	.	.	.	.	24	.	.	.	.	.	.	4
Bails	.	.	.	.	17	.	.	.	.	.	.	1
Cabmen	.	.	.	.	2							
Deserters	.	.	.	.	—							
	Total	.	.	.	43			Total	.	.		5

REMAINING.

| Males | . | . | . | . | . | 123 | Females | . | . | . | . | 65 |

GENERAL STATISTICS OF CLERKENWELL DETENTIONAL PRISON
FOR THE YEAR ENDING SEPTEMBER 1860.

NUMBER OF PRISONERS.	Males.	Females.	DEGREE OF INSTRUCTION.	Males.	Females.
For trial at Assizes or Sessions	1170	439	Neither read nor write	1281	697
Summary convictions	—	—	Read, or read and write imperfectly	3414	1301
Want of sureties	577	168	Read and write well	557	113
Remanded and discharged	3595	1534	Superior instruction	90	30
Mutiny Act	303	—	Instruction not ascertained	—	—
Total commitments	5645	2141	Total	5342	2141

PREVIOUSLY COMMITTED TO ANY PRISON.

	Males.	Females.
Once	719	294
Twice	252	105
Thrice	104	72
Four times	55	65
Five times	94	50
Seven times, and above five	97	45
Ten times, and above seven	—	—
Above ten times	—	—
	1321	631

AGE AND SEX.

	Males.	Females.
Under twelve years	185	27
Twelve to sixteen	736	156
Sixteen to twenty-one	1210	450
Twenty-one to thirty	1558	684
Thirty to forty	849	439
Forty to fifty	547	269
Fifty to sixty	184	91
Sixty and above	73	25
Age not ascertained	—	—
Total	5342	2141

CAPACITY AND STATE OE THE PRISON.

	Males.	Females.
Constructed to contain	224	100
Greatest number at one time	207	99
Daily average in the year	208	

CASES OF SICKNESS.

	Males.	Females.
Greatest number at one time	4	5
Deaths	1	—
Infirmary cases	128	48
Slight indisposition	—	—
Insanity	—	2
Total	133	55

PUNISHMENTS OF OFFENCES IN PRISON.

	Males.	Females.
Whipping	—	—
Irons or handcuffs	—	—
Solitary or dark cells	5	1
Stoppage of diet	55	8
Other punishments	—	—
Total	60	9

ESTABLISHMENT OF OFFICERS.

	Males.	Females.
Governor or deputy	2	—
Chaplain	1	—
Surgeon	1	—
Clerk or schoolmaster	1	—
Schoolmistress	—	—
Upper warders matron	11	6
Under warders	7	6
Other sub-offibers	—	—
Total	23	12

¶ iii.—a

HORSEMONGER LANE JAIL.*

We approach the Surrey Detentional Prison by a narrow lane, leading from the bustling thoroughfare of Stone's-end. It is inclosed within a dingy brick wall, which almost screens it from the public eye. We enter the gateway of the flat-roofed building at the entrance of the prison, on one side of which is the governor's office, and an apartment occupied by the gate-warder, and on the other is a staircase leading up to a gloomy chamber, containing the scaffold on which many a wretched criminal has been consigned to public execution. Emerging from the gateway, the governor's house, a three-storied building, stands right in front of us, on the other side of the courtyard, having a wing of the debtors' prison on each side, all of them built of brick. We observed several officers of the prison in their blue uniforms, with keys depending from their dark polished belts. The right wing of the prison contains sheriffs' debtors, who maintain themselves, or are supported by their relatives and friends;

* The Surrey County Jail, commonly called Horsemonger Lane Jail, is situate in the Parish of St Mary's, Newington, in the Parliamentary Borough of Lambeth, and in the East Half Hundred of Brixton, in the said County.

the left wing is set apart for county court debtors and those sheriffs' debtors who are unable to do so. In front of each there is a portion of ground, seventy-four feet by fourteen, laid with pavement, and covered with a low, flat, iron roof, where the debtors are frequently seen promenading or loitering beside the lofty iron railings which fence it, surmounted by formidable iron spikes. In the covered walk, before the right wing, the debtors had been evidently in better pecuniary circumstances, to judge from their exterior. Some of them looked like tradesmen, who had become embarrassed in their means. Others were like gay men about town, with moustache and fashionable dress, who also had once seen better days.

On the other side, the debtors appeared to belong generally to a poorer class of society, such as labourers, poor tradesmen, and others. Many of the debtors, particularly on the wing to the right, seemed to have the easy air of strangers loitering at a watering-place.

The court-yard is flanked on the left hand by the infirmary, a detached building, containing wards for debtors and criminals; and is bounded on the right by the sessions' house, the front of which faces Newington Causeway.

There is a carriage drive round the right wing of the debtors' prison to the criminal prison, the wings of which are nearly in the form of a hollow square behind it. There is a similar drive on the left side, leading past the infirmary to the female wards.

We enter an archway, opposite the sessions-house, leading to the male criminal prison, a large massive gate, fenced on the top with iron bars. On our left hand is a small room, occupied as an office by the chief warder, and on our right is a door leading into the reception ward.

⁎ *Reception Ward.*—We were introduced to the reception warder, who showed us over his department. The reception cells are situated behind the right wing of the debtors' prison, and are parallel to it, being separated by a narrow court. On entering one of them we found it to be eleven feet by seven feet four inches, and nine feet two inches at the bottom, and ten feet at the top of the arch. It is lighted by a square window, four feet long and two feet high. There are two shelves in an inner corner, containing a tin can, a salt-cellar, a spoon, towel, comb, and brush. The furniture further consists of a small deal table and a small stool. In the corner opposite there is a basin, supplied with plenty of water, at the pleasure of the prisoner, together with a piece of soap. The hammock is rolled up and attached to a hook on the side of the cell. The gas-jet has an iron cover to protect it. Each cell is floored with wood, and the walls are carefully whitewashed. A copy of the rules and regulations of the prison is suspended for the use of the prisoner, with a prayer for morning and another for evening, together with the Lord's Prayer. Notice is also given that complaints relative to the conduct of any of the officers may be made by the prisoner to the governor, or to any magistrate visiting the gaol. There is a handle in the cell communicating with the gong in the corridor, as in other prisons.

The cell is ventilated by an iron grating, near the floor, beside the door, through which a current of heated air is admitted. It ascends through another iron grating at the roof of the cell, communicating with the air-shaft on the top of the building. There is also a flap in the window for the admission of fresh air.

There are eight reception cells, all of them roofed with brick. The doors are, each of them, provided with a circular inspection plate, and a trap for introducing food, and also a smaller trap, with wire screen, through which the prisoner may have an interview with his friends. The corridor in the reception ward has not a groined roof, like the other corridors, but is spanned with a round arch. It is situated on our left hand, as we enter the prison.

We enter the *Bath-room*, which is about eighteen feet by eighteen. This apartment is on our right hand as we enter the male prison, and has a groined roof, supported in the centre by strong stone pillars, three feet square. There is an iron grating over hot-air pipes, extending across the room, beside the door, for the purpose of warmth and ventilation. Here

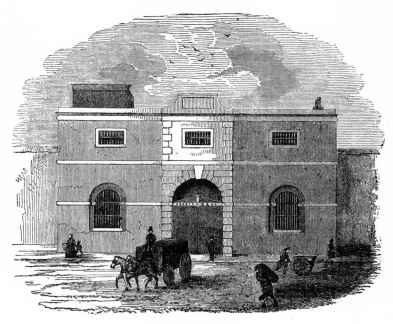

EXTERIOR OF HORSEMONGER LANE JAIL.

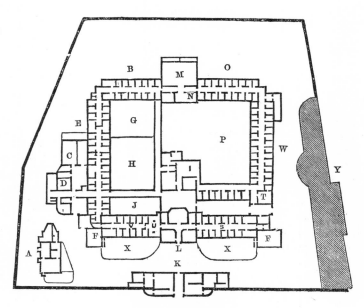

GROUND PLAN OF HORSEMONGER LANE JAIL.

A. Infirmary.	G. Boys' Airing Yard.	M. Chapel.	T. Men's Baths.
B. Boys' Cells.	H. Women's Airing Yard.	N. School-room.	U. Female Debtors.
C. Laundry.	I. Kitchen, etc.	O. Cells.	V. Common Debtors.
D. Women's Baths.	J. Female Debtors' Yard.	P. Men's Airing Yard.	W. Men's Side.
E. Women's Side.	K. Offices.	Q. Court.	X. Airing Courts.
F. Visitors' Room.	L. Governor's House.	S. Master Debtors.	Y. Sessions House.

we found two baths, five feet two inches long, two feet wide, and two feet deep, with separate doors. They are supplied with hot and cold water. There are standard measures here for ascertaining the height and weight of the prisoners, with a supply of prison clothing for their use. The reception warder stated, " When a prisoner is admitted here, and has not a proper suit of clothes, he is supplied with prison clothing, consisting of a blue vest, jacket, and trowsers, with shirt and stockings, in addition, should he require them. He is also furnished with two blankets, a pair of sheets, and a rug, as bedding."

There is a cistern here to supply the baths with hot water, with a furnace beneath. An assortment of leg irons is suspended on the wall. The reception warder conducted us into a small apartment on the basement, to which we descend by a flight of steps. Here there is a machine, patented by Jeakes, Great Russell Street, Bloomsbury, to destroy vermin. We saw several bundles of clothes in process of fumigation.

₊ *The Kitchen, etc.*—We went to the kitchen, which is about twenty-seven feet square, and is provided with four boilers and a large dresser. There is a large table in the centre, for cutting up the meat, etc., and to contain the trays. The kitchen is floored with stone, and lighted by a skylight. We noticed a food carriage, laden with trays of soup, meat, and potatoes, ready to be served up for the prisoners' dinner. The soup was of excellent quality. In one of the large boilers the soup had been made ready. In another the butchermeat was prepared, and in a third the gruel was cooked for supper.

A small room off the kitchen is used as the warder's mess-room and scullery. It is furnished with a dresser, washing-trough, table, and forms, and is well lighted and ventilated.

On proceeding into the bread-room we found a great quantity of small loaves arranged on shelves around the room, six ounces and eight ounces in weight—the one for male and the other for female prisoners.

While we were present, a large quantity was brought into the prison by a baker, sent by the tradesman who contracts to supply the prison. A quantity of fresh butchermeat was hung on hooks around the wall.

The food trays are conveyed to the different corridors of the male prison by means of a hoisting machine.

The Engineer.—We accompanied the engineer into a small apparatus-room at the extreme corner of the A division, on the right hand, provided with Haden and Son's ventilating apparatus. There is a large boiler above the furnace, where water is heated and conveyed to a tank at the top of the prison. It descends through pipes, and travels along the corridors beneath the flagstones, and afterwards returns to the boiler to be re-heated. Above the furnace there are two iron cases, about six feet by four, alongside of each other. The fire, after operating in the furnace, passes into the first case, then into the second, and from thence ascends up the chimney. This generates an amount of heated air, which would be lost if the cases were not applied, as otherwise it would go directly up the chimney. The air condensed by these cases passes out into corridor A through a square grating over the door of the furnace-room, and through two other gratings about two feet square.

There is another apparatus-room of the same kind at the opposite side of corridor A.

The engineer showed us into a cell in corridor A, and pointed out to us an iron grating for ventilation near the door. He observed " this is for warming the cell during winter, and for ventilation in summer." The cells are warmed by hot-water pipes that pass round the basement, and are connected with the cistern already referred to at the roof of the prison. He pointed out to us another grating on the groined roof of the cell, by which the vitiated air is extracted. We accompanied him to the roof of the prison, and saw the cistern where the heated water ascends from the boiler below, and descends into the basement as before stated. He showed us the ventilating shaft, adjoining which two horizontal extraction flues of triangular shape are connected. These horizontal flues are connected with the ventilating flues of the prison. They are about four feet in diameter at the base, and two feet six inches at the apex. In this shaft is a ventilating apparatus, five feet six inches by two feet six inches. The shaft is about seven feet square, covered with a slate roof supported on iron ribs. It is situated at the extreme corner on the left hand, and over-tops the rest of the building. There is a similar one at the right hand corner.

We followed the engineer through a small square opening, and mounted on the roof of the prison, where we had a commanding view of the various exercising grounds in the interior, as well as of the widely extended buildings of the great metropolis, with its beetling domes and spires. The engineer called our attention to four tanks on the roof of the prison into which the water is pumped.

On descending from the roof of the prison, and passing along corridor A, we observed fifteen circular iron gratings, about fifteen inches in diameter, for the purpose of admitting heated air into the corridors from the pipes below.

₊ *Chapel.*—We proceeded to the chapel, which is situated at the back of the prison, as seen in the ground plan. It is about thirty-nine feet wide, and thirty-four feet long. The pulpit is in an elevated position to the right, covered with red cloth, and beneath is a seat for the clerk. On the left is a lofty seat for the Governor, which gives him a commanding view of the auditory. Between the pulpit and the Governor's pew there is a communion-table, also covered with red cloth, the space within the inclosure around it being carpeted. On the wall over against it are inscribed the Ten Commandments, the Lord's Prayer, and the Creed.

There are four long seats in front of the pulpit, separated by a wooden partition six feet in height, occupied by the debtors during the service. A number of seats in the area behind are set apart for misdemeanants and felons committed for re-examination or for trial, while the convicted prisoners sit in elevated separate boxes behind. The female prisoners occupy the gallery above, out of sight of the males in the area beneath.

The debtors generally enter the chapel first, and proceed to their seats in the interior. The prisoners under remand, etc., then advance to their seats in the centre, and the convicts enter last. Meantime the females are assembling in the gallery above.

The chapel service commences at half-past nine o'clock. On Sundays there are two services, one in the morning at half-past nine, and the other in the afternoon at two o'clock.

₊ *Exercising Grounds.*—There are three paved exercising grounds within the hollow square of Horsemonger Lane Criminal Gaol. The larger one for the adult males is about one hundred and fourteen feet square, that of the juveniles is sixty feet by forty-two, and the female exercising ground is seventy-five feet by sixty, all situated, as seen in the ground plan. We observed a considerable number of prisoners airing in the adult yard, consisting of common felons and ragged mendicants and others, with three soldiers, charged with burglary, belonging to cavalry and infantry regiments. The general appearance of the greater number was very similar to those we saw in Clerkenwell Prison. They were for the most part in their own garb; some of them walked with the haughty air of men who had been wronged by being unjustly suspected of crime; others had a more modest demeanour, while some of the poor cadgers in their rags sneaked along with downcast eye. One of the warders observed to us, " These prisoners were mostly charged with felonies, and common offences."

In the Juvenile Exercising Yard we found a small party of boys exercising, some of them charged with petty felonies, others with picking pockets, and one poor fair-haired lad with begging. He was dressed in a blue-prison misdemeanant's garb.

₊ *Visiting the Cells.*—We found the corridors in Horsemonger Lane Jail to be very different from those in the other prisons. Here we had no lofty roof, and no airy galleries,

but dingy low-set corridors, of about twelve feet high, and seven feet wide, around each of the three stories, spanning a row of cells on each side, a warder being often seated at the extreme angles by a small table, beside cheerfully-lighted windows overlooking his ward. These corridors had groined roofs, which gave them a more interesting appearance. The interior arrangements of the prison, and the general appearance of the exterior, as well as the manners of the officials, presented to us a more homely and provincial aspect than any of the other London prisons, and were very different from the Surrey House of Correction at Wandsworth.

The chief warder informed us that basement A contained prisoners under remand, and for trial at the Sessions and Central Criminal Court; corridor B, on the floor above, was occupied by prisoners incarcerated for want of sureties, and those who are summarily convicted of assaults, but not sentenced to hard labour. Penal servitude men are also detained here for a time after conviction, as at Newgate. Corridor C contains persons summarily convicted, or otherwise, when the cells beneath are full.

We entered a cell in corridor A, which is 9 feet 1 inch long, and 7 feet 6 inches wide, and 11 feet 1 inch at the top of the groined arch. It is furnished very similar to the reception cells, provided with wooden flooring, and ventilated in like manner. There are fifty-one cells in this corridor, forty-three of them being occupied; but there was no one confined in the dark cell.

The warder observed to us, "that detentional prisoners are allowed by the county to maintain themselves before their trial." The chief warder, then passing along the corridor, stated "that they are permitted to get a pint of beer if they choose." He particularly called our attention to this: "that it is an imperative condition that they must be maintained entirely at their own expense, or that of their friends, or they must be contented with the prison diet."

As we passed along the corridor, we observed several females, some respectable in appearance, others of a more questionable aspect, visiting several of the criminals and conversing with them through the wire screen, in the doors of their cells. We proceeded with the warder to one of the cells, and saw a quantity of provisions introduced along with some clean linen. The wife and mother of the prisoner stood alongside. The former was a quiet, modest-looking woman in middle life, and the latter an elderly-looking person who appeared to be very distressed for the misfortune of her son. The prisoner was a robust, decent-looking man, a carman, and was charged with stealing several firkins of butter.

We went up-stairs to corridor B, on the second story, and were introduced to the warder on duty. He informed us there were thirty-two cells here, three associated rooms, a padded room for lunatics, and a condemned cell for prisoners under sentence of death. We were shown into one of the associated rooms which is about the size of two cells, and is furnished similar to two of them. At present it is used as a dormitory. On going into another we found an old sharp-featured man confined for using threatening language. Having failed to produce a surety for his better conduct in future, he was imprisoned for three months. Another shabbily-dressed elderly man was committed for trial at the sessions for embezzling from his employer. A young good-looking man, a deserter, was also confined here beside them, who was waiting for a military escort. The first-named sharp-featured man had recently attempted to commit suicide by cutting his throat, but was fortunately prevented. As we stood beside him, and looked into his quiet-looking countenance, we could not have dreamed he would have dared to do such a desperate deed.

The warder stated to us that, about a year ago, a man of about forty-five years of age, formerly an employé at a blind school in the metropolis, was imprisoned there for setting fire to a hay-rick and was committed for trial. On the day previous to trial, he hung himself up to a hook of the window by a handkerchief. One of the prisoners who slept in the room with him awoke and saw him suspended, and gave an outcry. The warder, who slept in the room adjoining, and the watchman on duty both ran to the cell. The watchman instantly cut him down. The medical officer was sent for, and arrived about ten minutes after; he was occupied from three o'clock in the morning to eleven o'clock in the forenoon, using means to restore animation. He was successful, and the wretched man was removed to the hospital, and taken, a day afterwards, to the assizes. He was acquitted on the ground of insanity, and sent to a lunatic asylum.

In answer to our interrogatories, the warder observed, " The prisoners in general spend their time reading books from the prison library. Those who cannot read, walk up and down their cell, and sometimes lie down and sleep. There is a shoemaker in an adjoining workshop who is generally busy mending shoes in the prison. He does it, instead of sitting idle, to pass his time more pleasantly."

In one of the cells we saw a man of colour lying on his bed, charged with stealing two pigs' flays, while in a state of destitution. The poor fellow lay covered with a chocolate-coloured counterpane, with a blue handkerchief bound around his temples. He told us he belonged to Kingstown, Jamaica. He spoke English tolerably well, and was lately an able seaman on board a man-of-war, and had never been in prison before.

Meantime, a genteel, well-dressed young woman passed along the corridor for the purpose of visiting a young man of about nineteen, a clerk, charged with ravishing a girl between ten and twelve years of age. He had been paying his addresses to a sister of this girl, who lived at Brixton. The clerk was rather a smart-looking youth. He told us his mother resides at Gravesend, and protested his innocence of the infamous crime laid to his charge. He has since been convicted at the sessions, and sent to Wandsworth prison for twelve months.

On looking into another cell, we saw a prisoner sentenced to penal servitude, engaged reading by his table, having just finished his dinner. He was born in Canada, and came to this country with his father in early life, to secure certain property left by an uncle. He was a good-looking man, a costermonger, and complained he had been hunted by the police from pillar to post, and driven into misfortune. He had been fined four times in one week for selling his fruit in the Borough, and had been pointed out and marked by the officers as a convicted thief. He thought there were good men in the police which he had learned by experience; but there were others of different character, who acted a cruel and unjust part. This prisoner had tried to strangle himself in Wandsworth prison some time ago. He appeared now more resigned to his fate.

We went to the padded room, which was an ordinary cell with coir-packed canvas around the walls. It is floored with wood, and lighted from the passage.

We visited the condemned cell, which is about the size of four cells, supported in the centre with two pillars, and has a stone floor. It is furnished with two iron bedsteads and a washstand in one corner and a water-closet in another. An officer is constantly in attendance night and day when a murderer is confined.

" I have been eight years in this jail," said the warder, " and have only known one man incarcerated here who was executed. Dr. Smethurst was for a time confined in this cell, charged with poisoning Miss Banks. Youngman was also imprisoned here, who assassinated his mother, sweetheart, and brother, at Walworth, and was executed on 5th September, 1860. He was a sullen, resolute fellow, of about twenty-four years of age."

There are thirty-five cells in corridor C on the floor above, one of them being a condemned cell, similar in dimensions to that we visited. There was not a single prisoner incarcerated there at the time of our visit.

The chief warder observed to us—" The number of our prisoners varies very much from time to time. Last Saturday, for example, we had 152 in the jail, and to-day we have 138. On the 22nd of December last, we had only ninety, while in October they amounted to 206."

Each of the three corridors extending round the two sides, and a portion of the third side, forming the male branch of the square-shaped criminal prison, is about 427 feet in length.

*** *The Infirmary.*—We visited the Infirmary, a detached building on the left side of the court-yard, with iron-grated windows, and were introduced to the warder in charge.

It consists of two wards; one for debtors, and another for criminals. There was no patient then in the debtor's ward, and there were only three persons in the criminal ward, one of whom is suffering from an abscess, and another, a fine-looking young man, from the amputation of one of his legs.

The portion of the Infirmary allotted to the criminals consists of four, and that to the debtors of two rooms. There is also a bath-room and a surgery in the building. Two of those occupied by criminals are large, and the other two are of smaller dimensions. "Each large room," said the warder "accommodates ten or twelve prisoners conveniently, and the small rooms contain four each." The large rooms are each of them furnished with iron bedsteads, a large dining-table, and forms which serve as seats. The rooms are all well ventilated, and the windows are protected without by strong iron bars.

¶ iii.—β.

The Female Prison

We enter the Female Prison by a small court-yard behind the right wing of the debtor's prison, proceeding through a gateway leading to the office of the chief warder and the reception cells.

*** *Female Reception Ward.*—There are nine reception cells here of the same dimensions as those in the male prison, and similarly furnished. They were then empty. In the passage there are two bells, one communicating with the wards for female debtors, and the other with the wards for female criminals.

On entering the *matron's store-room* we found it contained an ample assortment of clothing and bedding of various kinds, consisting of striped cotton shirts, grey calico chemises, flannel and linsey petticoats, bluechecked neckerchiefs, blue cotton gowns, chocolate-coloured worsted rugs, and sheets and blankets, etc., all carefully arranged.

We were shown into a bath-room, 18 feet by 15, where there were two zinc baths similar to those in the male branch of the prison, with slate partitions between them. Here we also saw a standard measure for taking the prisoners' height, and a cupboard containing the prisoners' own clothing, chiefly belonging to an inferior class charged with assault, stealing from the person, shoplifting, etc.

These reception cells are situated right and left of the long passage entering into the female prison.

*** *The Laundry* is about 21 feet square, and lighted by a large skylight. There are six drying horses here heated by a stove underground used likewise for heating the irons. A large ironing board extends along one of the sides of the apartment. There is also a mangle here and a cupboard containing clean clothing.

We passed from the laundry to the washing cells through a small room in which there is a steam boiler to heat the water for washing. There are five washing cells. In one of them two prisoners were engaged at the wooden troughs, one with a child by her side. These cells are 7 feet 2 inches wide, and 9 feet 9 inches long. The troughs are supplied with hot and cold water.

In another room there are two coppers for boiling the clothing, and a wringing machine similar to the one we saw in Holloway Prison. Opposite to this is another apartment where the unwashed clothing is contained. The matron stated, "We wash for the whole of the prisoners who require it, debtors as well as criminals. We have at present eight persons employed in the laundry, which is the general number. Sometimes we have more; we commence our work here at ten o'clock in the morning, and end at six in the evening."

₊ *The Teacher.*—We were introduced to Miss Moseley, the teacher, who replied, in answer to our queries—"I teach the various females separately in the prison. Sometimes me have a considerable number able to read. The prisoners are seldom longer than three months under my care. I often find that some who did not know their letters when they entered the prison, are able to read the Testament by the time they leave, and learn to write besides. As a general rule, I find the young are the most docile scholars. I teach all the prisoners who are unable to read, however short their stay, and visit them in their cells for that purpose."

₊ *Visiting the Cells.*—The matron informed us that "the female prison consists of four divisions—E, F, G, and H—the latter being the reception ward. The E division is appropriated for convicts only. Sometimes, however, I place prisoners for want of sureties and remanded prisoners in them. The F division is reserved for prisoners under remand, committed for trial, and confined for want of sureties; and E is set apart for prisoners summarily convicted of assaults and other misdemeanours."

The cells in the female prison are of the same dimensions as those in the male branch, and are similarly furnished. There is one dark cell for punishment floored with wood, which is seldom occupied.

At the time of our visit the five cells in division E were all occupied. We accompanied the matron to the F division, consisting of twenty-two cells, with three larger associated cells. There are three rooms here used as an infirmary. We entered one of them 14 feet 10 inches by 8 feet 4 inches, similar in dimensions to the other two. It has a wooden flooring, is lighted by two windows, and contains a fireplace. It is furnished with two iron bedsteads, a larger table than in the other cells, and is lighted by two windows.

The lying-in ward consists of three cells furnished with bedsteads, tables, chairs, etc. There is a cell used for persons in a foul condition, suffering under the itch and covered with vermin. "Some prisoners are in such a disgusting condition," said the matron, "that we have to cut their hair off, and others are covered with dreadful eruptions of the skin. Such parties are of different ages, from 13 to 60, but most of them are young. Many of the young girls are afflicted with horrid disease, and in a sad condition. We have such frequently remanded for a few days or weeks. There is a bath attached to the infirmary."

We were shown into an associated cell about the size of two ordinary cells. There are three of them in this division which are used for persons who require to be watched, such as prisoners suspected of attempting suicide, subject to fits, etc. We observed four hammocks rolled up and suspended on hooks against the wall, with a large strong beam of wood lying alongside, which is placed at night across the centre of the cell, and serves as a support to one of the sides of the hammocks. The flooring is of stone.

We visited several of the cells, but did not find any of the cases particularly deserving of notice.

The staff of the female prison consists of the matron, the schoolmistress, the laundry warder, infirmary warder, female debtors' warder, a general warder, and an assistant warder.

STATISTICS OF HORSEMONGER LANE JAIL.

FOR YEAR ENDING SEPTEMBER 1860, FROM THE GOVERNMENT RETURNS.

NUMBER OF PRISONERS.

	Males.	Females.
For trial and tried at Assizes and Sessions	485	131
Summary convictions	437	223
Want of sureties	73	71
Remanded and discharged	819	416
Debtors and civil process	451	33
Mutiny Act	190	—
Total of commitments	2455	874

PREVIOUSLY COMMITTED TO ANY PRISON.

	Males.	Females.
Once	313	140
Twice	93	78
Thrice	48	35
Four times	31	22
Five times	24	18
Seven times, and above five	20	18
Ten times, and above seven	16	11
Above ten times	8	6
Total	553	328

AGE AND SEX.

	Males.	Females.
Under twelve years	43	5
Twelve to sixteen	172	31
Sixteen to twenty-one	442	215
Twenty-one to thirty	573	262
Thirty to forty	312	158
Forty to fifty	172	121
Fifty to sixty	66	31
Sixty and above	32	15
Age not ascertained	2	3
Total	1814	841

BIRTHPLACE.

	Males.	Females.
England	1577	695
Wales	11	6
Scotland	19	10
Ireland	157	111
Colonies, and East Indies	8	4
Foreign countries	33	7
Not ascertained	9	8

CAPACITY AND STATE OF THE PRISON.

	Males.	Females.
Numbers constructed to contain	213	62
Greatest number at any one time	144	47

	Males and Females.
Daily average number in the year	148

STATE OF INSTRUCTION.

	Males.	Females.
Neither read nor write	492	286
Read, or read and write imperfectly	1221	545
Read and write well	93	7
Superior instruction	3	—
Instruction not ascertained	5	1
Total	1814	843

DISPOSAL OF THE PRISONERS CONFINED ON COMMITMENT, REMAND, OR REMOVAL.

	Males.	Females.
Number in prison at the commencement of the year	100	43
Committed during the year	2455	874
Removed to the prison during the year	4	1
Total	2559	918

CASES OF SICKNESS.

	Males.	Females.
Greatest number at any one time	16	12
Deaths	2	—
Infirmary cases	5	5
Slight indisposition	423	192
Insanity	2	—
Total	448	209

PUNISHMENTS FOR OFFENCES IN PRISON.

	Males.	Females.
Whipping	—	—
Irons or handcuffs	—	—
Solitary or dark cells	2	4
Stoppage of diet	57	8
Other punishments	—	—
Total punishments	59	12

ESTABLISHMENT OF OFFICERS.

	Males.	Females.
Governor and deputy	1	—
Chaplain	1	—
Surgeon	1	—
Clerk and schoolmaster	2	—
Schoolmistress	—	1
Upper warders' matron	1	1
Under warders	12	4
Other sub-officers	4	—
	22	6

TABLES OF DIETARIES.

CLASS 1.

Convicted prisoners sentenced to any term not exceeding seven days :—

Males.				*Females.*		
Breakfast	Oatmeal gruel	1 pint.	Breakfast	Oatmeal gruel	1 pint.
Dinner	Bread	1 lb.	Dinner	Bread	1 lb.
Supper	Oatmeal gruel	1 pint.	Supper	Oatmeal gruel	1 pint.

CLASS 2.

Convicted prisoners sentenced to any term exceeding seven days, and not exceeding twenty-one days :—

Males.				*Females.*		
Breakfast	Oatmeal gruel	1 pint.	Breakfast	Oatmeal gruel	1 pint.
„	Bread	6 oz.	„	Bread	6 oz.
Dinner	Bread	12 oz.	Dinner	Bread	6 oz.
Supper	Bread	6 oz.	Supper	Bread	6 oz.
„	Oatmeal gruel	1 pint.	„	Oatmeal gruel	1 pint.

Prisoners of this class employed at hard labour, to have, in addition, one pint of soup per week.

CLASS 3.

Convicted prisoners employed at hard labour for terms exceeding twenty-one days, but not more than six weeks ; and convicted prisoners not employed at hard labour for terms exceeding twenty-one days, but not more than four months :—

Daily.

Males.				*Females.*		
Breakfast	Oatmeal gruel	1 pint.	Breakfast	Oatmeal gruel	1 pint.
„	Bread	6 oz.	„	Bread	6 oz.

Sunday and Thursday.

Dinner	Soup	1 pint.	Dinner	Soup	1 pint.
„	Bread	8 oz.	„	Bread	6 oz.

Tuesday and Saturday.

Dinner	Cooked meat, without bone	3 oz.	Dinner	Cooked meat, without bone	3 oz.
„	Bread	8 oz.	„	Bread	6 oz.
„	Potatoes	½ lb.	„	Potatoes	½ lb.

Monday, Wednesday, and Friday.

Dinner	Bread	8 oz.	Dinner	Bread	6 oz.
„	Potatoes	1 lb.	„	Potatoes	1 lb.

Daily.

Supper	Same as breakfast.	Supper	Same as breakfast.

CLASS 4.

Convicted prisoners employed at hard labour for terms exceeding six weeks, but not more than four months ; and convicted prisoners not employed at hard labour for terms exceeding four months :—

Daily.

Males.				*Females.*		
Breakfast	Oatmeal gruel	1 pint.	Breakfast	Oatmeal gruel	1 pint.
„	Bread	8 oz.	„	Bread	6 oz.

Sunday, Tuesday, Thursday, and Saturday.

Dinner	Cooked meat, without bone	3 oz.	Dinner	Cooked meat, without bone	3 oz.
„	Potatoes	½ lb.	„	Potatoes	½ lb.
„	Bread	8 oz.	„	Bread	6 oz.

Monday, Wednesday, and Friday.

Dinner	Soup	1 pint.	Dinner	Soup	1 pint.
	Bread	8 oz.	„	Bread	6 oz.

Daily.

| Supper | Same as breakfast. | Supper . | Same as breakfast. |

CLASS 5.

Convicted prisoners employed at hard labour for terms exceeding four months :—

Sunday, Tuesday, Thursday, and Saturday.

	Males.				Females.	
Breakfast	Oatmeal gruel	. . 1 pint.	Breakfast	Oatmeal gruel	. .	1 pint.
„	Bread	8 oz.	„	Bread . . .	.	6 oz.
Dinner	Cooked meat, without bone	4 oz.	Dinner	Cooked meat, without bone		3 oz.
„	Potatoes	1 lb.	„	Potatoes . . .	.	½ lb.
„	Bread	6 oz.	„	Bread . . .	.	6 oz.

Monday, Wednesday, and Friday.

Breakfast	One pint of cocoa, made of ¾ oz. of flaked cocoa or cocoa-nibs, sweetened with ¾ oz. of molasses or sugar.		Breakfast	One pint of cocoa, made of ¾ oz. of flaked cocoa or cocoa-nibs, sweetened with ¾ oz. of molasses or sugar.		
„	Bread	8 oz.	„	Bread . . .	.	6 oz.
Dinner	Soup	1 pint.	Dinner	Soup . . .	.	1 pint.
„	Potatoes	1 lb.	„	Potatoes . . .	.	½ lb.
„	Bread	6 oz.	„	Bread . . .	.	6 oz.

Daily.

Supper	Oatmeal gruel	. . 1 pint.	Supper	Oatmeal gruel	. .	1 pint.
„	Bread	8 oz.	„	Bread . . .	.	6 oz.

CLASS 6.

Prisoners sentenced by Court to solitary confinement :—

Males.	Females.
The ordinary diet of their respective classes.	The ordinary diet of their respective classes.

CLASS 7.

Prisoners for trial and examination, misdemeanants of the first division, who do not maintain themselves, and destitute debtors :—

Males.	Females.
The same as Class 4.	The same as Class 4.

CLASS 8.

Debtors committed under the 8th and 9th Vict., cap. 127, and 9th and 10th Vict., cap. 95 ; fraudulent debtors committed by Commissioners of Bankrupts under the Bankruptcy Laws ; and debtors remanded for fraud from Insolvent Debtors' Courts :—

Males.	Females.
The same as Class 3.	The same as Class 3.

CLASS 9.

Prisoners in close confinement for prison offences for terms not exceeding three days :—

1 lb. of Bread per diem.

Prisoners in close confinement for prison offences under the provisions of the 42nd Section of the Jail Act :—

Daily.

	Males.				Females.	
Breakfast	Bread	8 oz.	Breakfast	Bread . .	.	6 oz.
„	Gruel	1 pint.	„	Gruel . .	.	1 pint.
Dinner	Bread	8 oz.	Dinner	Bread . .	.	6 oz.
Supper	Bread	8 oz.	Supper	Bread . .	.	6 oz.
„	Gruel	1 pint.	„	Gruel . .	.	1 pint.

Ingredients of Soup and Gruel.—The soup to contain, per pint, three ounces of cooked meat, without bone ; three ounces of potatoes ; one ounce of barley, rice, or oatmeal ; and one ounce of onions or leeks, with pepper and salt. The gruel to contain two ounces of oatmeal per pint. The gruel, on alternate days, to be sweetened with three-quarter ounce of molasses, or sugar, and seasoned with salt. In seasons when the potato crop has failed, four ounces of split peas made into a pudding may be occasionally substituted ; but the change must not be made more than *twice* in each week. Boys under fourteen years of age to be placed on the same diet as females.